FOUNDATIONS OF
ARTIFICIAL INTELLIGENCE
VOLUME 1

Foundations of Artificial Intelligence

VOLUME 1

Series Editors

J. Hendler
H. Kitano
B. Nebel

ELSEVIER
AMSTERDAM–BOSTON–HEIDELBERG–LONDON–NEW YORK–OXFORD
PARIS–SAN DIEGO–SAN FRANCISCO–SINGAPORE–SYDNEY–TOKYO

Handbook of Temporal Reasoning in Artificial Intelligence

Edited by

M. Fisher
Department of Computer Science
University of Liverpool
Liverpool, UK

D. Gabbay
Department of Computer Science
King's College London
London, UK

L. Vila
Department of Software
Technical University of Catalonia
Barcelona, Catalonia, Spain

2005
ELSEVIER
AMSTERDAM–BOSTON–HEIDELBERG–LONDON–NEW YORK–OXFORD
PARIS–SAN DIEGO–SAN FRANCISCO–SINGAPORE–SYDNEY–TOKYO

ELSEVIER B.V.
Radarweg 29
P.O. Box 211, 1000 AE Amsterdam
The Netherlands

ELSEVIER Inc.
525 B Street, Suite 1900
San Diego, CA 92101-4495
USA

ELSEVIER Ltd
The Boulevard, Langford Lane
Kidlington, Oxford OX5 1GB
UK

ELSEVIER Ltd
84 Theobalds Road
London WC1X 8RR
UK

First edition 2005

Library of Congress Cataloging in Publication Data
A catalog record is available from the Library of Congress.

British Library Cataloguing in Publication Data
A catalogue record is available from the British Library.

ISBN: 0-444-51493-7
ISSN (Series): 1574-6526

♾ The paper used in this publication meets the requirements of ANSI/NISO Z39.48-1992 (Permanence of Paper).
Printed in The Netherlands.

Contents

REASONING TECHNIQUES

APPLICATIONS

Preface

This collection represents the primary reference work for researchers and students working in the area of Temporal Reasoning in Artificial Intelligence. As can be seen from the content, temporal reasoning has a vital role to play in many areas of Artificial Intelligence. Yet, until now, there has been no single volume collecting together the breadth of work in this area. This collection brings together the leading researchers in a range of relevant areas and provides an coherent description of the variety of activity concerning temporal reasoning within the field of Artificial Intelligence.

To give readers an indication of what is to come, we provide an initial, simple example. By examining what options are available for modelling time in such an example, we can get a picture of the variety of topics related to temporal reasoning in Artificial Intelligence. Since many of these topics are covered within chapters in this Handbook, this also serves to give an introduction to the subsequent chapters.

Consider the labelled graph represented in Figure 1:

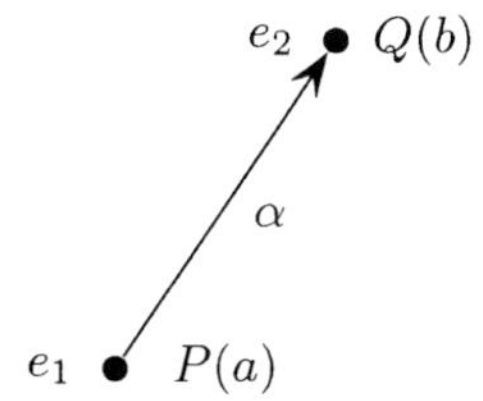

Figure 1: Simple graph structure.

This is a simple directed graph with nodes e_1 and e_2. The edge is labelled by α and $P(a)$ and $Q(b)$ represent some contents associated with the nodes. We can think of P and Q as predicates and a and b as individual elements. This can represent many things. The two nodes might represent physical positions, with the 'α' representing movement. Alternatively, e_1 and e_2 might represent alternate views of a systems, or mental states of an agent, or relationships. Thus this simple graph might characterise a wide range of situations. In general such a situation is a small part of a bigger structure described by a bigger graph. However, we have simply identified some typical components.

Now add a temporal dimension to this, i.e., assume our graph varies over time. One can think of the graph as, for example, representing web pages, agent actions, or database updates. Thus, the notion of change over time is natural. The arrow simply represents an accessibility relation with a parameter α and with $P(a)$ and $Q(b)$ relating to node contents. As time proceeds, the contents may change, the accessibility relation may change; in fact, everything may change.

Now, if we are to model the dynamic evolution of our graph structure, then there are a number of questions that must be answered. Answers to these will define our formal model and, as we will see below, the possible options available relate closely to the chapters within this collection.

Question 1: *What properties of time do we need for our application?*
Formally, we might use $(T, <, 0)$ to represent our flow of time, where T represents the temporal structure, $0 \in T$ represents 'now' and '$<$' characterises the earlier–later relation within T. The choice of T thus significantly affects the formalisation and properties of the theory, and some options are as follows.

Option 1.1 Take the flow of time as the Natural Numbers.

Option 1.2 Take the flow of time as points and intervals and various relations between them, including varying additional granularity, and the question of whether time is discrete or continuous continues.

Option 1.3 Any other kind of reasonable structure.

Question 2: *How do we connect the model of time with the changes in our graph structure?*

Option 2.1 For each time t (point, interval, etc.) let G_t be a graph for that time.

Option 2.2 Make each component in a general graph G time dependent. So, in Figure 2, we parameterise the elements in Figure 1 with a temporal component:

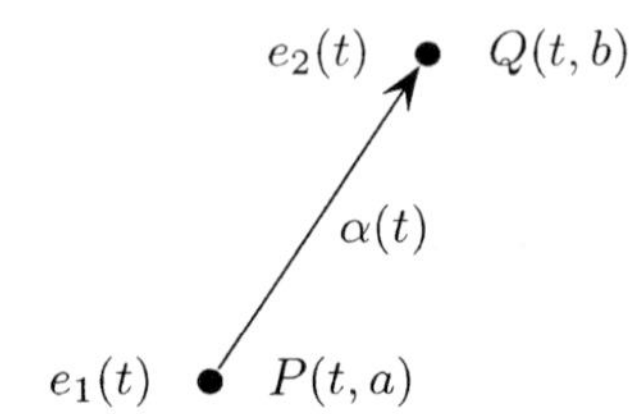

Figure 2: Simple graph with a temporal parameter.

Option 2.3 We ask how is time created? Is it given to us as in Question 1 or is it generated by our actions on the graph? Is the future open or do we create it by executing actions? If we opt for the action view we need a language of actions on the graphs so that we can generate the temporal movements. This approach will immediately connect time with the graph.

Question 3: *How do we talk about the temporal graph?*

Typically, we need a mixed language to talk about the change. There are, again, several options:

Option 3.1 Use Option *2.1* and devise a special language to talk about time and special connectives to connect the graph with time. In technical terms we are forming the product $T \times G$.

Option 3.2 Use Option *2.2* and use classical logic or logic programming (or any other language tailored for our application) to represent change directly.

Option 3.3 Use Option *2.3* and use a state langauge to talk about the graph, an action language to generate time and a metalevel connecting language. Of course, all this can sometimes be embedded in the same language (e.g. Prolog).

Question 4: *Can we identify sublanguages that can do all relevant tasks, while ensuring both naturalness of expression and computational tractability?*

We can again consider a number of possibilities.

Option 4.1 Computational fragments of classical logic: logic programming, description logics, etc.

Option 4.2 Modal/dynamic logics.

Option 4.3 Temporal logics.

Question 5: *What are the various problems arising from the choice of representation?*

Option 5.1 Theorem proving requirements.

Option 5.2 Nonmonotonic problem of representation (persistence, frame problem, etc).

Option 5.3 Updates, deletions, change, etc.

Option 5.4 Planning problems.

Question 6: *What are the synchronisation aspects?*
Consider Figure 1 again. We may wish to traverse the graph from e_1 to e_2. If the graph changes during traversal, we may need to synchronise in order to ensure the graph we have is up-to-date. And there are yet more questions concerning this.

- How long does it take to move from e_1 to e_2?
- How long does it take to execute an action?
- How long does it take to update the graph?

Note that synchronisation questions are only now being studied logically!

Question 7: *What metalevel questions are relevant?*
Suppose we wish to describe how the graph changes. We may receive instructions describing it, or its updates, or its states, in some specific language. How do we implement that? How do we synchronise the time involved in the input and the time in the graph?

Question 8: *Are there additional features?*
These can be imposed on top of the previous questions.

Option 8.1 Probabilistic features. To deal with change computationally we need to have some knowledge of how things change. We can either supply algorithms or supply probabilites controlling the change.

Option 8.2 Fuzzy features. We can make everything fuzzy.

Option 8.3 Partiality: lack of complete infomation; partial models, mechanisms to overcome our lack of information, etc.

Option 8.4 Inconsistency and its problems.

Question 9: *Can we identify special features relevant to major application areas?*

Option 9.1 Databases.

Option 9.2 Law and legal domains.

Option 9.3 Medicine.

Option 9.4 Dynamics, space and time.

Option 9.6 Natural language analysis.

Option 9.7 Agent-based systems.

Thus, we can see that, even for such a simple initial scenario, there is a very wide range of questions and applications. Looking at the above classifications and at the detailed table of contents, it is not difficult to see the role each chapter plays in this Handbook. Note that each chapter has to address several of these options together in an integrated way with emphasis on the main subject matter of the chapter.

We hope that you, the reader, will find this Handbook both interesting and useful, as the chapters have been contributed by many of the world's leading researchers in temporal reasoning. We would like to thank all these authors for their patience, and for their excellent expositions. We also thank them, together with a number of other experts, for helping us review versions of chapters in this Handbook. Finally, we would like to thank those at Elsevier Publishers who have worked so hard to ensure that this Handbook came into existence.

Michael Fisher, **Dov Gabbay** and **Lluis Vila** [Liverpool, London and Barcelona 2004]

Contributors

Alessandro Artale email: artale@inf.unibz.it

Faculty of Computer Science, Free University of Bozen-Bolzano I-39100 Bozen-Bolzano BZ, Italy

Chitta Baral email: chitta@asu.edu

Department of Computer Science and Engineering, Arizona State University, Tempe, Arizona 85287, USA

– The authors would like to acknowledge the help of Marc Denecker in explaining abductive logic programming system.

Howard Barringer email: howard@cs.man.ac.uk

Department of Computer Science, University of Manchester, Manchester M13, UK

Jan Chomicki email: chomicki@cse.buffalo.edu

Department of Computer Science and Engineering, University at Buffalo, New York 14260-2000, USA

Dan Clancy email: clancy@ptolemy.arc.nasa.gov

NASA Ames Research Center, California 94035, USA

Marc Denecker email: marcd@cs.kuleuven.ac.be

Department of Computer Science, Katholieke Universiteit Leuven, B-3001 Heverlee, Belgium

Clare Dixon email: C.Dixon@csc.liv.ac.uk

Department of Computer Science, University of Liverpool, Liverpool L69, UK

Thomas Drakengren email: thomas.drakengren@cainetech.com

Caine Technologies, c/o Drakengren, Varpmossevagen 55A, SE-436 39, Askim, Sweden

– The authors wish to thank the anonymous reviewer and Charlotte Drakengren for their useful comments.

Jérôme Euzenat email: Jerome.Euzenat@inrialpes.fr

INRIA Rhône-Alpes, Montbonnot Saint Martin, 38334 Saint-Ismier, France

Michael Fisher email: M.Fisher@csc.liv.ac.uk

Department of Computer Science, University of Liverpool, Liverpool L69, UK

Maria Fox email: Maria.Fox@cis.strath.ac.uk

Department of Computer and Information Sciences, University of Strathclyde, Glasgow G1 1XQ, UK

Enrico Franconi email: franconi@inf.unibz.it

Faculty of Computer Science, Free University of Bozen-Bolzano I-39100 Bozen-Bolzano BZ, Italy

Dov Gabbay email: dg@dcs.kcl.ac.uk

Department of Computer Science, King's College, London WC2R, UK

Antony Galton email: A.P.Galton@exeter.ac.uk

School of Engineering, Computer Science and Mathematics, University of Exeter, Exeter EX4, UK

Michael Gelfond email: mgelfond@cs.ttu.edu

Department of Computer Science, Texas Tech University, Lubbock, Texas 79409, USA

Alfonso Gerevini email: gerevini@ing.unibs.it

Dipartimento di Elettronica per l'Automazione, Università di Brescia, 25123 Brescia, Italy

– Figure 8.15 was kindly provided by Bernhard Nebel. The description of the time-graph approach is based on material contained in some papers the author wrote with Len Schubert. The author would like to thank the anonymous reviewer and Alessandro Saetti for useful comments on a preliminary version on this chapter.

Steve Hanks email: hanks@u.washington.edu

Department of Computing and Software Systems, University of Washington Tacoma, Washington, USA

– This work was supported, in part, by ARPA / Rome Labs Grant F30602–95–1–0024 and in part by NSF grant IRI–9523649.

Peter Jonsson email: `petej@ida.liu.se`

Department of Computer and Information Science, Linköping University, SE-581 83 Linköping, Sweden

Elpida Keravnou email: `elpida@ucy.ac.cy`

Department of Computer Science, University of Cyprus, CY-1678 Nicosia, Cyprus

Manolis Koubarakis email: `manolis@intelligence.tuc.gr`

Department of Electronic and Computer Engineering, Technical University of Crete, Chania, Crete, Greece

– This work was partially supported by the CHOROCHRONOS project funded by the EU's 4th Framework Programme (1996-2000) and by a grant from the Greek General Secretariat for Research and Technology (1998-1999). The author would also like to thank Spiros Skiadopoulos, Peter Jeavons and David Cohen for their collaboration on various topics related to this work.

Benjamin Kuipers email: `kuipers@cs.utexas.edu`

Computer Science Department, University of Texas at Austin, Texas, USA

– This work took place in the Intelligent Robotics Lab at the Artificial Intelligence Laboratory, The University of Texas at Austin. Research of the Intelligent Robotics lab is supported in part by NSF grants IRI-9504138 and CDA 9617327, and by funding from Tivoli Corporation.

Derek Long email: `Derek.Long@cis.strath.ac.uk`

Department of Computer and Information Sciences, University of Strathclyde, Glasgow G1, UK

David Madigan email: `madigan@stat.rutgers.edu`

Department of Statistics, Rutgers University, New Jersey, USA

– This work was supported, in part, by NSF grant DMS–97–04–573.

Alice ter Meulen email: `atm@let.rug.nl`

Center for Language and Cognition, University of Groningen, The Netherlands

Angelo Montanari email: `montana@dimi.uniud.it`

Dipartimento di Matematica e Informatica, Università di Udine, Udine, Italy

Han Reichgelt email: han@georgiasouthern.edu

Department of Information Technology, Georgia Southern University, Statesboro, Georgia, USA

Mark Reynolds email: mark@csse.uwa.edu.au

School of Computer Science and Software Engineering, The University of Western Australia, Australia

Yuval Shahar email: yshahar@bgumail.bgu.ac.il

Department of Information Systems Engineering, Ben-Gurion University of the Negev, Israel

David Toman email: david@uwaterloo.ca

School of Computer Science, University of Waterloo, Waterloo, Ontario, Canada.

– This chapter is an extended and updated version of [Chomicki and Toman, 1998]. The authors gratefully acknowledge the United States National Science Foundation (grants IIS-9110581 and IIS-9632870) and the Natural Sciences and Engineering Research Council of Canada for their support of this research.

Kristof Van Belleghem email: kristof@cs.kuleuven.ac.be

Department of Computer Science, Katholieke Universiteit Leuven, B-3001 Heverlee, Belgium.
(Currently at: PharmaDM, Kapeldreef 60, B-3001 Leuven, Belgium)

Lluis Vila email: vila@lsi.upc.es

Department of Software, Technical University of Catalonia, Barcelona, Spain

– The author's contributions to this collection were supported by the Spanish CICYT under grant TIC2002-04470-C03-01 and under "Web-I(2)" grant TIC2003-08763-C02-01.

Michael Wooldridge email: M.Wooldridge@csc.liv.ac.uk

Department of Computer Science, University of Liverpool, Liverpool L69, UK

Hajime Yoshino

Meiji Gakuin University, Tokyo, Japan

Foundations

Handbook of Temporal Reasoning in Artificial Intelligence
Edited by M. Fisher, D. Gabbay and L. Vila

Chapter 1

Formal Theories of Time and Temporal Incidence

Lluis Vila

The design of intelligent agents acting in a changing environment must be based on some form of temporal reasoning system. Such a system should, in turn, be founded on a formal theory of time. Theories of time are based on some primitive time units (instants, intervals, etc.) and determine both the expressiveness of the language and the completeness of the reasoning system.

The time theory of a temporal reasoning system is closely connected with the so-called theory of *temporal incidence*, meaning the set of domain-independent properties for the truth-value of temporal propositions throughout time. Classically, for a given domain, we distinguish between two classes of temporal propositions: changing domain properties (or *fluents*) and events whose occurrence may cause change on fluents.

Formal theories of time and temporal incidence involve some controversial issues such as (i) the expression of *instantaneous events* and *fluents* that hold instantaneously, (ii) the *dividing instant problem* and (iii) the formalization of the properties for *non-instantaneous holding of fluents*.

This chapter surveys the most relevant theories of time proposed in Artificial Intelligence according to various representational issues including the ones above. Also, the chapter presents a brief overview of *temporal incidence theories* and proposes a theory of temporal incidence defined upon a theory of instants and periods whose key insight is the distinction between continuous and discrete fluents.

1.1 Introduction

An intelligent agent interacting in a changing environment must be able to reason about these changes as well as the events and actions causing them, the effects it may have in the rest of the environment and the time when all these things happen or cease happening. Therefore, the design of intelligent agents acting in a changing environment must be based, among other components, on some form of temporal reasoning system. If we want this system to be well-founded and its properties formally studied it must be based upon a formal theory of time. Time theories are based in some time primitive unit (instants, intervals, etc.) and determine both the expressiveness of the language as well as the completeness of the reasoning system.

As a matter of fact, time has been recognized as a fundamental notion in reasoning about changing domains and many frameworks for reasoning about change and action are built upon a temporal representation [McDermott, 1982; Allen, 1984; Kowalski and Sergot, 1986; Dean and McDermott, 1987; Williams, 1986; Shoham, 1987; Kuipers, 1988; Forbus, 1989; Galton, 1990; Schwalb *et al.*, 1994; Pinto, 1994; Miller and Shanahan, 1994; Koubarakis, 1994a; Iwasaki *et al.*, 1995; Fusaoka, 1996; Bacchus and Kabanza, 1996; Vila and Reichgelt, 1996]. In these frameworks, the domain at hand is formalized by expressing how propositions are true or false throughout time. Commonly there is a distinction between propositions describing the state of the world (*fluents*) and those representing occurrences that happen in the world and may change its state (*events*). Examples of fluents are "the light is on", "the ball is moving at speed v", and "the battery charge is increasing", and examples of events are "turn the light off", "kick the ball" and "the controller sent a signal to the relay".

A temporal representation has two basic components: (i) a theory of time, and (ii) a theory of temporal incidence. The *theory of time* defines the structure of the primitive time units (e.g. *transitivity* of the ordering relation over instants). The *theory of temporal incidence* defines the domain-independent properties for the truth-value of fluents and events throughout time (e.g. if a fluent is true during a period it must be true during the instants within that period).

Time and temporal incidence are issues that traditionally attracted the interest of areas such as philosophy [Whitehead, 1919; Russell, 1956; Hamblin, 1972; Kamp, 1979; Newton-Smith, 1980], *physics* and *linguistics* [Kenny, 1963; Vendler, 1967; Davidson, 1967; Jackendoff, 1976; Mourelatos, 1978; Dowty, 1979; Allen, 1984; Bach, 1986]. But, why are time and temporal incidence theories important for *automated temporal reasoning* ? They have impact on major properties of the system for answering queries with some temporal component such as "Was the light open when the controller sent the signal to the relay ? "At what times has been the light on and the door open simultaneously ?". Consider, for instance, *Constraint Logic Programming* [Jaffar and Maher, 1994] with temporal constraints [Hrycej, 1993; Brzoska, 1993; Früehwirth, 1996; Schwalb *et al.*, 1996]: the theory of time characterizes the *constraint domain* which determines the properties for the constraint solving procedure; the theory of temporal incidence has impact on the completeness of the overall proof procedure.

From an efficiency point of view, these theories enable inferring implicit, redundant or inconsistent temporal information that can be used to expedite the query answering search. For example, consider two tasks competing on a single resource. The theory of temporal incidence allows us to infer that the time periods during which these tasks utilize the common resource do not overlap. In turn it enables some temporal constraint propagation.

A lot of research in *Artificial Intelligence* has focussed on formalizing time and temporal incidence [van Benthem, 1983; Allen and Hayes, 1985; Ladkin, 1987; Shoham, 1987; Tsang, 1987a; Allen and Hayes, 1989; Galton, 1990; Lin, 1991; Vila, 1994]; however it turns out not to be a simple task. First because a theory of time must naturally reflect commonsense intuitions about time, and sometime these intuitions have to do with instantaneous phenomena while others more naturally concern durative phenomena. Second because they must be adequate to describe events that happen and change the values of fluents without contradicting those intuitions. For instance, determining the value of a fluent at the time it changes has been a controversial issue (the so-called *dividing instant problem*). Moreover, we may face different types of change: discrete, continuous, etc. Real world domains usually involve parameters whose change is modelled as continuous and others whose change is viewed as discrete. A system with both types of change is called a *hybrid system*, and its model a *hybrid model* [Iwasaki *et al.*, 1995]. For example, consider an electro-mechanical battery charger: re-charging a battery can be viewed as a continuous change whereas closing a relay would be better regarded as discrete*. When both types of change happen concurrently, describing what is true and false becomes more difficult.

This chapter presents these challenges more precisely, presents the most relevant theories of time proposed in Artificial Intelligence and discusses the successes and failures with respect to these representational issues. Also, the chapter presents a brief overview of temporal incidence theories and proposes a theory of *temporal incidence* defined upon a theory of instants and periods whose key insight is the distinction between continuous and discrete fluents.

1.2 Requirements and Problems

In this section we identify some problematic issues that must be addressed when formalizing time and temporal incidence:

Instantaneous Events A dynamic system often involves events that are naturally modelled as instantaneous. Some prototypical examples are "turn off the light", "shoot the gun", "start moving", "sign a contract". Representing such events can cause some problems, especially when *sequences* of them occur in presence of continuous change (Section 1.11 discusses this in detail).

Fluents that Hold at an Instant We often talk about the value of fluents at certain instants (e.g. "the temperature of patient X at 9:00 was high", "Was the light red when the car hit John?"). Also, modelling *continuous change* requires having fluents that may hold at isolated instants. A simple, representative example is the parameter *speed* (v) of a ball tossed upwards in what we call the *Tossed Ball Scenario* (TBS) (see Figure 1.1). The ball moves up during

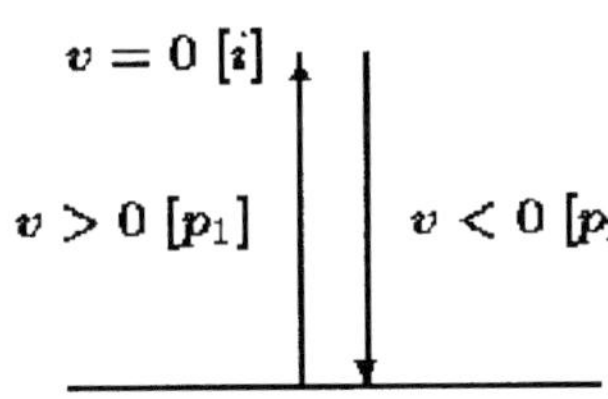

Figure 1.1: The Tossed Ball Scenario (TBS).

p_1 and down during p_2. By continuity of v, there must be a time piece "in between" p_1 and p_2 where the $v = 0$. Since the ball cannot be stopped in the air for a while, such a time piece can only be durationless. However, being able to talk about the truth value of fluents at durationless times may lead to the problem described next.

*Hybrid models are important because many daily used electro-mechanical devices are suitably modelled as such.

The Dividing Instant Problem (DIP) Let us assume that time is composed of both instants and periods, and we need to determine the truth-value of a fluent f (e.g. "the light is on") at an instant i, given that f is true on a period p_1 ending at i and is false at a period p_2 beginning at i (see Figure 1.2) [Hamblin, 1972; van Benthem, 1983; Allen, 1984; Galton, 1990]. The problem is a matter of logical consistency: if periods are closed then f

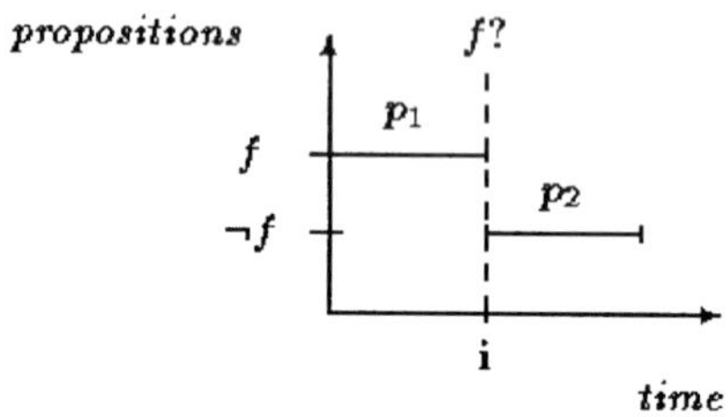

Figure 1.2: The Dividing Instant Problem.

and $\neg f$ are both true at i which is inconsistent; if they are open we might have a "truth gap" at i; finally, the choices open/closed and closed/open are judged to be artificial [Allen, 1984; Galton, 1990].

Non-Instantaneous Holding of Fluents Formalizing the properties of temporal incidence for non-instantaneous fluents can be problematic. There are two major classes of them. The first class are properties about the holding of a fluent at related times. Instances of this class are:

- *Homogeneity*: If a fluent is true on a piece of time it must hold on any sub-time [Allen, 1984; Galton, 1990].
- *Concatenability**: If a fluent is true on two consecutive pieces of time it must be true on the piece of time obtained by concatenating them. Notice that there may be different views for the meaning of *consecutive*.

The second class are properties relating the holding of contradictory fluents at related times. It includes:

- *Non-holding*: If a fluent is not true on a piece of time, there must be a sub-time where its negation holds [Allen, 1984; Galton, 1990].
- *Disjointness*: Any two periods such that a fluent is true on one and its negation is true on the other, must be disjoint. There may be different views for the meaning of *disjoint* too.

*As opposed to homogeneity, very little attention has been paid to concatenability. Nevertheless, it is a semantical issue that also may have some computational benefits since it allows for a compact representation of a fluent holding on numerous, overlapping periods.

Non-Atomic Fluents The holding of negation, conjunction and disjunction of atomic fluents can be a non-trivial issue [Shoham, 1987; Galton, 1990].

After presenting our theories of time and temporal incidence we shall revisit all these issues. Next, we'll discuss theories of time. Starting from different intuitions, several theories of time have been proposed*. They can be classified into three classes according to whether the primitive time units are instants, periods or events†.

1.3 Instant-based Theories

Instants are defined as a durationless pieces of time. An alternative, more precise definition identifies instants to pieces of time whose begin and end are not distinct. In *physics* it has been standard practice to model time as an unbounded continuum of instants [Newton, 1936] structured as the real numbers set. Instant-based theories have been used in several AI systems [McCarthy and Hayes, 1969; Bruce, 1972; Kahn and Gorry, 1977; McDermott, 1982; Shoham, 1987].

An instant-based theory is defined on a structure $\langle \mathcal{I}, \prec \rangle$ with a number of properties:

- *Ordering.* The *minimum* properties for instants ordering are those of a *partially ordered set* (POSET):

  $$\begin{array}{ll} \textbf{IRREF} & \neg(i \prec i) \\ \textbf{ASYM} & i \prec i' \Rightarrow \neg(i' \prec i) \\ \textbf{TRANS} & i \prec i' \wedge i' \prec i'' \Rightarrow i \prec i'' \end{array}$$

  Additionally, one may want to impose some *"linearity"* of time. If it is imposed only towards the past

  $$\textbf{Left-LIN} \quad i' \prec i \wedge i'' \prec i \Rightarrow i' \prec i'' \vee i' = i'' \vee i'' \prec i'$$

  we obtain a branching time structure towards the future [McDermott, 1982] that might be appropriate to model various possible futures. Otherwise, we can impose linearity on both directions

  $$\textbf{LIN} \quad i \prec i' \vee i = i' \vee i' \prec i$$

  forcing instants to be arranged in a single line.

- *Boundedness.* The instants ordered structure may have beginning and end or, conversely, have no end towards past and future. The later is caputured by the following axiom:

  $$\textbf{SUCC} \quad \forall i \exists i' \; (i' \prec i') \quad \forall i \exists i' \; (i \prec i)$$

  The idea of unbounded time corresponds to a more general view whereas bounded time can be more appropriate in some particular contexts.

- *Dense/Discrete.* Denseness forces to have an instant between any two instants

  $$\textbf{DENS} \quad \forall i, i' \; (i \prec i' \Rightarrow \exists i'' \; (i \prec i'' \prec i'))$$

---

*Some intuitions as well as pointers to some relevant works are from [Lin, 1991].

†Note that the word event is overloaded: in the context of time theories, *event* denotes any temporal proposition, thus it includes both events and fluents as defined in the introduction section.

This property may be important to model continuous change. A consequence is that any stretch of time can be decomposed into sub-times which can have interest in planning where tasks are usually decomposed into subtasks. Another consequence is that one cannot refer to the previous and next instants. Discreteness is enforced by the following axiom:

$$\textbf{DISC} \quad \forall i, i' \, (i < i' \Rightarrow \exists i'' \, (i \prec i'' \wedge \neg \exists i''' \; i \prec i''' \prec i''))$$
$$\forall i, i' \, (i < i' \Rightarrow \exists i'' \, (i'' \prec i' \wedge \neg \exists i''' \; i'' \prec i''' \prec i'))$$

As it happens, each finite strict partial order is also discrete.

The above principles are sufficient to achieve a certain level of completeness. Two theories are known to be *syntactically complete* [van Benthem, 1983]: the *unbounded dense linear* theory axiomatized by

IRREF, TRANS, LIN, SUCC, DENS

and the *unbounded discrete linear* theory axiomatized by

IRREF, TRANS, LIN, SUCC, DENS

The alternatives to instant-based theories are theories built upon primitive units more related to our experience than instants. One alternative are period-based theories since "periods are usually associated with events that take time". A further step in that direction is directly developing theories based on events.

1.4 Period-based Theories

Period-based theories interested researchers in philosophy, linguistics and AI [Walker, 1948; Hamblin, 1972; Newton-Smith, 1980; Dowty, 1979; Allen, 1984; Allen and Hayes, 1989]. For instance, Allen proposes a theory exclusively based on periods and the 13 relations between pairs of them shown in Figure 1.3. This theory has been analysed and reformulated

A `Before` B	B `After` A
A `Meets` B	B `Met_by` A
A `Overlaps` B	B `Overlapped_by` A
A `Starts` B	B `Started_by` A
A `During` B	B `Contains` A
A `Finishes` B	B `Finished_by` A
A `Equal` B	B `Equal` A

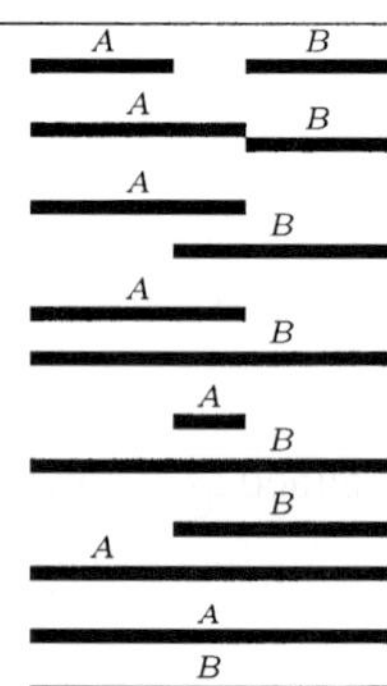

Figure 1.3: The 13 relations between temporal intervals.

in terms of the sole relation `Meets` by Allen & Hayes and Ladkin.

1.4.1 Allen's Period Theory

Allen [Allen, 1983] takes an initial structure $\langle \mathcal{P}, \mathbf{AR} \rangle$ where $\mathbf{AR}$ denotes the set of the 13 primitive period relations that correspond to every possible simple qualitative relationship that may exist between two intervals (see Figure 1.3). The behaviour or $\mathbf{AR}$ is informally specified by the following axiom schemas [Allen, 1984]:

1. Given any period, there exists another period related to it by each relationship in $\mathbf{AR}$.
2. The relationships in $\mathbf{AR}$ are mutually exclusive.
3. The relationships have a transitive behaviour, e.g. if p_1 `Before` p_2 and p_2 `Meets` p_3 then p_1 `Before` p_3.

We shall henceforth refer to this theory as $\mathcal{A}$. We propose the following formalization:

$\mathbf{A_1}$ $\forall P \in \mathcal{P}, R \in \mathbf{AR}\, \exists P'(R(P, P'))$
$\mathbf{A_2}$ $\forall P, P' \in \mathcal{P}, R \in \mathbf{AR}\, \forall R' \in \mathbf{AR} - R\, (R(P, P') \Rightarrow \neg R'(P, P'))$
$\mathbf{A_3}$ Allen's transitive table [Allen, 1983]

1.4.2 Allen & Hayes's Period Theory

Allen's theory is re-defined in terms of the `Meets` relation in [Allen and Hayes, 1985]* ($\|$ denotes `Meets` and $\oplus$ the or-exclusive logical connective):

$\mathbf{AH_1}$ $\forall p, q, r, s\, (p\|q \wedge p\|s \wedge r\|q \Rightarrow r\|s)$
$\mathbf{AH_2}$ $\forall p, q, r, s\, (p\|q \wedge r\|s \Rightarrow \exists t\, (p\|t\|s) \oplus p\|s \oplus \exists t\, (r\|t\|q))$
$\mathbf{AH_3}$ $\forall p\, \exists q, r\; q\|p\|r$
$\mathbf{AH_4}$ $\forall p, q, r, s\, (p\|q\|s \wedge p\|r\|s \Rightarrow q = r)$
$\mathbf{AH_5}$ $\forall p, q\, (p\|q \Rightarrow \exists r, s, t\, (r\|p\|q\|s \wedge r\|t\|s))$

We call it $\mathcal{AH}$. It has been also by Ladkin [Ladkin, 1987] who (i) claims that axiom $\mathbf{AH_5}$ is redundant (it is, in fact, not true [Galton, 1996a]), (ii) relates $\mathcal{AH}$ to other period-based theories of time, (iii) completely characterizes its models, and (iv) proposes a completion to obtain an axiomatization of the theory of rational intervals which is proved to be *countably categorical* [van Benthem, 1983] and, therefore, complete. The completion is obtained by adding the following *denseness* axiom $\mathbf{N_1}$:

$\mathbf{N_1}$ $\forall p, q, r, s\, \exists x, y\, \text{Pointless}(p, q, x, y) \wedge \text{Pointless}(x, y, r, s)$

where pointless is defined as follows:

Definition 1.4.1. ("pointless") *Given the intervals p, q, r, s, Pointless(p, q, r, s) iff*

$$\exists u, v, w\; [p, q] \sim_{\mathcal{I}} [u, v] \wedge [r, s] \sim_{\mathcal{I}} [v, w]$$

and $\sim_{\mathcal{I}}$ denotes the period relation of "having the same meeting point".

*Notice that this re-definition is not equivalent to Allen's initial axiomatics. Both are analyzed below in deeper detail.

1.4.3 Relation between $\mathcal{A}$ and $\mathcal{AH}$

Surprisingly, $\mathcal{A}$ and $\mathcal{AH}$ are not that similar. On the one hand $\mathcal{A}$ accepts models which do not fit in $\mathcal{AH}$.

Lemma 1.4.1. $\mathcal{A} \not\subset \mathcal{AH}$

Proof. We may find several counter-examples of models of $\mathcal{A}$ which are not models of $\mathcal{AH}$.

- Counter-example 1 (axiom $\mathbf{AH_4}$): Let us take M as the set of non-empty open intervals on Q plus a second "copy" of an arbitrary interval, let us take for instance (1,2)', which happens to be different from its "original" (1,2) though it keeps every relation that (1,2) has with any other interval. Thus, M is a model of $\mathcal{A}$ but it is not a model of $\mathcal{AH}$ since it does not satisfy $\mathbf{AH_4}$.
- Counter-example 2 (axiom $\mathbf{AH_2}$): Let us take M as two copies of the set of non-empty open intervals on Q, being the intervals in one copy not related by any relationship the intervals of the other copy. M is a model of $\mathcal{A}$ but linear ordering is not satisfied since any interval in one copy is not ordered with respect to any interval of the other one.

□

On the other hand, $\mathcal{A}$ is stronger than $\mathcal{AH}$ since it imposes *denseness* Axiom $\mathbf{A_1}$ in $\mathcal{A}$ guarantees decomposability which in period-based theories corresponds to denseness. Contrarily, $\mathcal{AH}$ has been designed to be weak enough to embrace both discrete and dense models.

Lemma 1.4.2. $\mathcal{AH} \not\subset \mathcal{A}$

Proof. As a counter-example take any discrete model –for instance the intervals formed over the set of integer numbers. It is a model of $\mathcal{AH}$ [Allen and Hayes, 1985] but is ruled out by $\mathbf{A_1}$. For instance, there is no period which `Overlaps` the period [1,2]. □

1.4.4 Revised $\mathcal{A}$

A more accurate look at $\mathcal{A}$ reveals that nothing accounts for the intuition that "periods are all contained in a single time dimension"*. Our refinement of $\mathcal{A}$ is based on adding an axiom schema with such a role:

Definition 1.4.2. ($\mathcal{A}'$) *$\mathcal{A}'$'axiomatization is $\mathcal{A}$'s plus the following additional axiom schema:*

$$\mathbf{A'_1} \quad \forall P, P' \, \exists R \in \mathbf{AR} \; R(P, P')$$

This refinement produces a rather remarkable change in the accepted models. We demonstrate it by analyzing how this theory relates to Allen & Hayes's theory. We use the definitions of period relations in terms of the single relation `Meets` given in [Allen and Hayes, 1985].

Lemma 1.4.3. $\mathcal{A}' \subseteq \mathcal{AH}$

*This is an idea which Allen seems to be in sympathy with since he explicitly refuses alternative structures like McDermott's *branching time* construction.

Proof.

AH$_1$. Suppose $\neg r \| s$.

Then, by $\mathbf{A'_1}$, there must be a period relation R such that $R \neq \|$ and rRs. It is easy to check that whatever relation we take, it stands in contradiction with the period transitivity table and/or with axiom A_2. For example let us assume that (r `Before` s), which is equivalent to (s `After` r). Using the period constraints in the premise and our assumption, we have (p `Meets` s `After` r `Meets` q). By successively applying Allen's transition table we get

(p `After Met_by Overlaps Overlapped_by During Contains Start Started_by Finishes Finished_by Equal` q)

which is inconsistent with $p \| q$ in the premise.

AH$_2$. From the hypothesis (a) $p \| q \wedge r \| s$ we want to show that one of the following alternatives exclusively hold: (b) $p \| s$, (c) p `Before` s, (d) r `Before` q –according to the definition of `Before`. By A'_1 we know that one of the 13 period relations must hold between p and s. Since (b) and (c) are mutually exclusive (by A_2) we only need to prove the following three statements:

1. (a) $\wedge \neg(p \| s) \wedge \neg(p$ `Before` $s) \Rightarrow r$ `Before` q
2. (a) $\wedge\, p \| s \Rightarrow \neg(r$ `Before` $q)$
3. (a) $\wedge\, p$ `Before` $s \Rightarrow \neg(r$ `Before` $q)$

1. Let us assume $\neg(p \| s)$, $\neg(p$ `Before` $s)$ and $\neg(r$ `Before` $q)$. By $\mathbf{A'_1}$ and $\mathbf{A_2}$ one of the other 12 period relations holds. If $r \| q$ then from $r \| q \wedge r \| s$ it follows –by applying the transitivity table– that $q(= \vee$ `Starts` $\vee$ `Started_by`$)s)$, which combined with $p \| q$ by transitivity and conjunction gives $p \| s$ which stands in contradiction with our starting assumption. For any other case it holds that $\exists t' \ (p \| t' \| s)$ (this can be checked by revising the definition of the remaining 12 relations in terms of $\|$) that is equivalent to p `Before` s which is contradictory with the hypothesis $\neg(p$ `Before` $s)$. **2** and **3** are shown by assuming r `Before` q and standing in contradiction by consecutively applying the transitivity table a number of times.

AH$_3$. is trivially derived from $\mathbf{A_1}$.

AH$_4$. (By $\mathbf{A_1}$) q and r must be related by some period relation, namely R. Suppose that R is not $=$. Then using the definitions of each period relation one stands in contradiction with one from $\{p \| q, q \| s, p \| r, r \| s\}$.

□

Lemma 1.4.4. $\mathcal{AH} \vdash \mathbf{A'_1}, \mathbf{A_2}, \mathbf{A_3}$

Proof. $\mathbf{A'_1}$ and $\mathbf{A_2}$. For any two periods I, J we have (by $\mathbf{AH_3}$) that $\exists a, b, a', b' \ a \| I \| b$ and $a' \| J \| b'$. By $\mathbf{AH_2}$ we have

1. $\exists t_1 \ a \| t_1 \| J \oplus a \| J \oplus \exists t'_1 \ a' \| t'_1 \| I$
2. $\exists t_2 \ a \| t_2 \| b' \oplus a \| b' \oplus \exists t'_1 \ J \| t'_2 \| I$

3. $\exists t_3\ I \| t_3 \| J \oplus I \| J \oplus \exists t'_3\ a' \| t'_3 \| b$
4. $\exists t_4\ I \| t_4 \| b' \oplus I \| b' \oplus \exists t'_4\ J \| t'_4 \| b$

We may combine these different mutually exclusive choices. We obtain 3^4 *a priori* possible alternatives, but not every combination is feasible. We must use the remaining $\mathcal{AH}$ axioms to discard disallowed possibilities. For instance, let us take the first choice in (1): $\exists t_1\ a \| t_1 \| J$. (By $\mathbf{AH_5}$) there exists t_2 and b such that $t_2 = t_1 + J$ and $a \| t_2 \| b'$ which is the first choice in (2) and, due to the $\oplus$, the sole one allowed. Thus, we have (1.2) $a \| t_1 \| J \| b'$. This is compatible with every choice in (3) each of which in turn is compatible with some in (4). Finally we get (1.2) with each of the following relations:

$$
\begin{array}{l}
I \| t_3 \| J \\
I \| J \\
a' \| t'_3 \| b \wedge I \| t_4 \| b' \\
a' \| t'_3 \| b \wedge I \| b' \\
a' \| t'_3 \| b \wedge J \| t'_4 \| b
\end{array}
$$

By exhaustively applying this process we obtain an exclusive disjunctive formula where each disjunctive element exactly matches the definition in terms of the single relation `Meets` of one of the 13 period relations. Thus, we prove the mutual exclusivity of period relations ($\mathbf{A_2}$). Their existence ($\mathbf{A'_1}$) is also guaranteed since every auxiliary period has been introduced either through $\mathbf{AH_3}$ or $\mathbf{AH_2}$ and period addition used at some stages is supported by $\mathbf{AH_5}$.

$\mathbf{A_3}$ is easy though a bit tedious to prove by using the transitivity table [Allen and Hayes, 1985]. □

Regarding $\mathbf{A_1}$, the relationships `Meets` and `Before` (and their inverses) can be easily derived from one and two applications respectively of axiom $\mathbf{AH_3}$ towards the future (towards the past), but this is not the case for the remaining ones. To derive them we would require the *denseness* axiom $\mathbf{N_1}$:

Lemma 1.4.5. $\mathcal{AH}$, $\mathbf{N_1} \vdash \mathbf{A_1}$

Proof. By using the denseness axiom one may always find the appropriate endpoints which define the period P' that satisfies $R(P, P')$. □

Theorem 1.4.1. $Th(\mathcal{AH}, \mathbf{N_1}) \equiv \mathcal{A}'$

Proof. Given lemmas 1.4.3, 1.4.4 and 1.4.5, it suffices to prove that $\mathcal{A}' \vdash \mathbf{N_1}$ which is straight forward by applying $\mathbf{A_1}$ with the relationship `Started_by` on the period bounded by the initial points. □

1.4.5 Extending $\mathcal{A}$ with Instants

Allen's theory can be properly extended with instants by implementing the idea of instants as period the meeting points. Now the ontology is made of non-empty sets of instants and periods in a structure such as $\langle \mathcal{I}, \mathcal{P}, \texttt{Limits}, \mathbf{AR} \rangle$. where `Limits` is a instant-period relation. $\mathcal{A}'$ axioms are extended with the following:

$$
\begin{array}{ll}
\mathbf{IM_1} & \forall P, P'\ (P \| P' \Rightarrow \exists i\ (\texttt{Limits}(i, P) \wedge \texttt{Limits}(i, P'))) \\
\mathbf{IM_2} & \forall i \exists P, P'\ (P \| P' \wedge \texttt{Limits}(i, P) \wedge \texttt{Limits}(i, P'))
\end{array}
$$

1.5 Events

Event-based theories are motivated by the following intuition:

> "time is no more than the totality of temporal relations between the events and processes which constitute the history of our world. Then defining time is a question about the actual relations between these events and processes."

This approach mostly interested philosophers such as [Russell, 1956; Whitehead, 1919; Kamp, 1979] and a few AI people [Tsang, 1987a].

Time is defined as the structure $\langle E, \prec, O\rangle$ where E is a non-empty set of events, $\prec$ is a precedence relation and O is a overlapping relation. The axioms of the theory, called $\mathcal{E}$, are as follows [Kamp, 1979]:

$\mathbf{E_1}$	$e \prec e' \Rightarrow \neg(e' \prec e)$	**NO SYM($\prec$)**
$\mathbf{E_2}$	$e \prec e' \wedge e' \prec e'' \Rightarrow e \prec e''$	**TRANS($\prec$)**
$\mathbf{E_3}$	$eOe' \Rightarrow e'Oe$	**SYM(O)**
$\mathbf{E_4}$	eOe	**REFL(O)**
$\mathbf{E_5}$	$e \prec e' \Rightarrow \neg(eOe')$	**SEP**
$\mathbf{E_6}$	$e \prec e' \wedge e'Oe'' \wedge e'' \prec e''' \Rightarrow e \prec e'''$	**TRANS($\prec, O$)**
$\mathbf{E_7}$	$e \prec e' \vee eOe' \vee e' \prec e$	**LIN**

$\mathbf{E_1}$ and $\mathbf{E_2}$ state partial order for $\prec$. O is reflexive and symmetric ($\mathbf{E_1}$ and $\mathbf{E_2}$) but not transitive. $\mathbf{E_5}$ to $\mathbf{E_7}$ state relations between $\prec$ and O: they are mutually exclusive, exhibit a sort of transitivity and establish a linear ordering over events. The properties of $\mathcal{E}$ have extensively studied in [Kamp, 1979] and later in [Tsang, 1987a; Lin, 1991].

Since period-based theories are based on the intuition that periods are the stretches of time occupied by events, the properties of periods and events are very similar. However, event-based theories are conceptually different in the sense that events are not "pure time entities" but the occurrences themselves. In other words, a clear dissociation between occurrences and their times of occurrence is not established.

1.5.1 Relation between $\mathcal{E}$ and $\mathcal{AH}$

Since events happen on periods, period-based theories and event-based are very similar. The main distinction is that two events that happen at the same are not necessarily the same events. If we take Allen's relations as the reference, $e \prec e'$ is equivalent to e `Before` $\vee$ `Meets` e' and O is equivalent to $\neg(e \prec e') \wedge \neg(e' \prec e)$. According to Tsang [Tsang, 1987b], $\mathcal{E}$ can be extended to obtain a theory equivalent to $\mathcal{AH}$ by adding the following axioms (where ! and $\cap$ denote period intersection and union respectively):

$\mathbf{E_8}$	$\exists e'\ e' \prec e \wedge \neg(\exists x\ (e' \prec x \wedge x \prec e)$
$\mathbf{E_9}$	$e \prec e' \wedge e' \prec e'' \Rightarrow e \prec e''$
$\mathbf{E_{10}}$	$eOe' \Rightarrow e!e'$
$\mathbf{E_{11}}$	$\exists e''\ e'' = e \cup e$

$\mathbf{E_8}$ and $\mathbf{E_9}$ are needed to guarantee period meeting unboundedness ($\mathbf{AH_e}$ axiom), $\mathbf{E_{10}}$ is needed to derive axiom $\mathbf{AH_1}$, and $\mathbf{E_{11}}$ is needed to derive $\mathbf{AH_2}$ and $\mathbf{AH_5}$. Given the theory $\mathbf{E_1} \div \mathbf{E_{11}}$, called $\mathcal{E}^*$ by Tsang, we have:

Theorem 1.5.1. $\mathcal{E} \equiv \mathcal{AH}$

1.6 Analysing the Time Theories

Let us now analyze these alternatives from the philosophical, notational, computational technical viewpoints:

Philosophical Event-based theories clearly are the most attractive from a philosophical point of view as they are directly based on perceived phenomena. However, as noticed by [Lin, 1991], are instant and period -based theories that have gained wide acceptance in AI:

> "The reason for this seems to be that people are accustomed to think that time is an "independent" entity where events take place."

Period-based theories are appealing since they make this distinction while they preserve the starting intuition that our direct experience is with events that take time. In fact, period-based theories capture the most relevant relations between events.

Several philosophical arguments have been put forward against instants such as "Our direct experience is with phenomena that take time", "It takes to many instants to make up a durable experience ?" [Hamblin, 1972; Kamp, 1979], "the point-based, continuous model ...they start with is too rich" [Allen and Hayes, 1989], "...(instant-based models) permit the description of phenomenally impossible states of affairs" [Hamblin, 1972]. One argument in favor of instants must be mentioned though. As with durative events, we seem to have mental experience with instantaneous phenomena as well. It is reflected by many references in natural language expressions (see the examples given in Section 1.2 such as "the time I started moving" or "the temperature of the patient at 9:00"). The claim is not about the existence of instantaneous phenomena but about the fact that we are accustomed to think about the notion of instantaneous.

Notational vs. Computational Two types of expressions must be considered: *temporal assertions* and *temporal relations*. We next discuss both, being the second the one that has some computational consequences.

Expressing temporal assertions: If our ontology is provided with instants, expressing instantaneous events and instantaneous holding of fluents is straight forward. This becomes a difficult issue in period-based theories because instants cannot be represented as very short periods (as proposed in [Allen, 1984]) because a short period does not *divide* a period into two meeting periods. For example, if i in Figure 1.2 is modelled as a short period then p_1 does not meet p_2. The same applies to expressing instantaneous fluents (like in the TBS). The proposal of modelling instants as *indivisible* periods, called *moments* [Allen and Hayes, 1985], does not work either for the same reason. The option of representing instants as zero duration periods is problematic too because Allen's transitive table needs to be transformed into a much weaker table, otherwise the distinction between the period relations that are not `Before`, `Equal` and `After` becomes meaningless [Schwalb, 1996].

A sounder, more sophisticated technique is defining instants as sets of periods. Mathematicians proposed a number of set-theoretic constructions of points from intervals such as (i) an instant is identified with the maximal set of intervals that have a non-empty intersection [Whitehead, 1919] (called *nests*), or (ii) an instant is defined as the equivalence class of pairs of meeting intervals that meet "at the same place"*. Now, the points are (i) whether

* Attributed to Bolzano.

there is any simpler, more natural alternative to this class of instants, and (ii) whether these instants can be used to talk about the occurrence of events and holding of fluents. We discuss both in forthcoming sections.

Expressing temporal relations: Any temporal relation between two periods can be specified in terms of instant relations between the endpoints of the periods. In particular, every basic period relation in Figure 1.3 can be specified by a conjunction of binary instant relations. Furthermore, some temporal relations are more efficiently expressed in terms of relations between instant than between periods. For example

$$p_1 \texttt{Before Meets Overlaps Finished\_by Contains}\, p_2 \equiv \texttt{begin}(p_1) \prec \texttt{begin}(p_2)$$

However, the instant-based notation may be less efficient because of several reasons. First, a binary relation may become higher arity relation ($n \geq 2$) when stated in terms of instants. For example, given the periods p_1 and p_2,

$$p_1 \texttt{ Before After } p_2 \equiv \texttt{end}(p_1) \prec \texttt{begin}(p_2) \;\vee\; \texttt{end}(p_2) \prec \texttt{begin}(p_1)$$

Second, instant-based expressions are sometimes more cumbersome. Third, as the number of events grows, the number of conjunctive combinations grows exponentially (as noticed by Tsang [Tsang, 1987a]). For example,

$$p_1 \texttt{ Overlaps Finishes } p_2 \quad \wedge \quad p_2 \texttt{ Meets Overlaps } p_3$$

is represented as the disjunction of each element of the cartesian set expressed in terms of instant relations, namely

$$
\begin{array}{lcl}
\texttt{begin}(p_1) \prec \texttt{begin}(p_2) \wedge \texttt{end}(p_1) \prec \texttt{end}(p_2) & \wedge & \texttt{end}(p_2) = \texttt{begin}(p_3) \\
\vee & & \\
\texttt{begin}(p_1) \prec \texttt{begin}(p_2) \wedge \texttt{end}(p_1) \prec \texttt{end}(p_2) & \wedge & \texttt{begin}(p_2) \prec \texttt{begin}(p_3) \wedge \texttt{end}(p_2) \prec \texttt{end}(p_3) \\
\vee & & \\
\texttt{begin}(p_2) \prec \texttt{begin}(p_1) \wedge \texttt{end}(p_1) = \texttt{end}(p_2) & \wedge & \texttt{end}(p_2) = \texttt{begin}(p_3) \\
\vee & & \\
\texttt{begin}(p_2) \prec \texttt{begin}(p_1) \wedge \texttt{end}(p_1) = \texttt{end}(p_2) & \wedge & \texttt{begin}(p_2) \prec \texttt{begin}(p_3) \wedge \texttt{end}(p_2) \prec \texttt{end}(p_3)
\end{array}
$$

expressed in terms of instant relations.

Having a compact, low order expression of temporal relations is not only a notational issue but it also has some impact on the computational cost of reasoning with them.

Technical Instant-based axiomatizations apparently allow for a better understanding and control of the properties we want for time. There is no general agreement on this point. The interested reader may compare the theories provided in the appendices.

1.7 Instants and Periods

According to the above analysis, it seems that an interesting approach would be a theory of time based on both instants and periods. It would enjoy the following advantages:

- *Natural expression*: Instants are used to express instantaneous events and fluents, and periods to express the durable ones.

- *Efficient notation and computation*: Either instant or period relations, according to what is more efficient, can be used to express the temporal relations at hand.

To define such a theory two alternatives have been explored: (i) starting with a concerted instant-period ontology, or (ii) defining instants from periods. Semantical arguments, such as the DIP, led a number of researchers to follow the second alternative. In Section 1.6 we have seen that simple techniques of representing an instant as a period do not work, and only more complex mathematical constructions do. The interest of deriving instants from periods is unclear since (as noted by Allen & Hayes [Allen and Hayes, 1989]) "we may end up in the same place" as if we start with an instants structure, whereas both the axioms and the instants construction are clearly less intuitive. Indeed we show (Section 1.7.2) that Allen & Hayes's theory [Allen and Hayes, 1985; Allen and Hayes, 1989] together with "derived instants" admits the same models than our instant-period theory of time.

Therefore, if we want both instants and periods its preferable to take the route of starting with both as ontological primitives of our time model. To our knowledge, the only proposal in this direction is Galton's theory of time which we discuss below and elsewhere in this collection.

1.7.1 Galton's Instants and Periods Theory

In Galton's theory [Galton, 1990] neither periods are a set-theoretic construction from instants nor vice versa. Both have the same ontological status as a primitive. The underlying intuition is

> "...there being an instant at the point where two periods meet".

Time is defined as the structure $\langle\, I, P, \texttt{Within}, \texttt{Limits}, \text{Allen's relations}\,\rangle$ where I and P are non-empty sets of instants and periods respectively, `Within` and `Limits` are instant-period relations with the obvious meaning. In addition to the 13 Allen's period relations, the period relation `In` is defined as the disjunction of `During`, `Starts` and `Finishes`. The set of axioms (we call it $\mathcal{G}$) is as follows (i denotes an instant and p, q, r periods):

$$\begin{array}{ll}\mathbf{G_1} & \forall p \exists i\ \texttt{Within}(i,p)\\ \mathbf{G_2} & \texttt{Within}(i,p) \wedge \texttt{In}(p,q) \Rightarrow \texttt{Within}(i,q)\\ \mathbf{G_3} & \texttt{Within}(i,p) \wedge \texttt{Within}(i,q) \Rightarrow \exists r\ (\texttt{In}(r,p) \wedge \texttt{In}(r,q))\\ \mathbf{G_4} & \texttt{Within}(i,p) \wedge \texttt{Limits}(i,q) \Rightarrow \exists r\ (\texttt{In}(r,p) \wedge \texttt{In}(r,q))\end{array}$$

We assume that by "...together with the various relations between intervals ..." ([Galton, 1990], p166) Galton means that $\mathcal{A}$ axioms are also included. Neither that nor a characterization of the models of the theory is formally given by Galton. $\mathcal{G}$ avoids DIP-like arguments and turns out to be useful for Galton to prove the relations between his temporal occurrence predicates (such as HOLDS_{on}, HOLDS_{in}, HOLDS_{at}), however they exhibit two major shortcomings. The first regards the relations between instants. They are not sufficient for the needs of a practical reasoner. For instance, the relation `Limits` is not sufficient for distinguishing between the begin and the end of a period. Notice that there is no account for any ordering over instants. Although it is a very basic notion, it is neither explicitly stated nor induced by the period axioms as we discuss next. The second shortcoming regards the connection between instants and periods. Although it is not easy to figure out what are the intended models of $\mathcal{G}$, a careful analysis reveals that the theory is not strong enough to properly connect instants and periods. It is easy to identify examples of counter-intuitive, accepted models:

Example 1.7.1. *Let us take a basic model M composed of an infinite set of periods and Allen's relations satisfying $\mathcal{I}_{\mathcal{A}}$ axioms plus an infinite set of instants which make M satisfy I_1 -for example INT($\mathcal{Q}$) as periods and Q as instants:*

- *Example model 1: M plus a single instant $i \notin Q$ which limits a certain period P in M and only that one. In particular it does not limit any of those periods that meet or are met by P.*
- *Example model 2: M plus a single instant $i \notin Q$ which limits a certain period P in M and is not within any period. In particular it is not within any of those periods that overlap P.*
- *Example model 3: M plus a single instant $i \notin Q$ which limits a certain period P in M and also is within P.*

The obvious undesirable consequence of $\mathcal{G}$ weakness is that some queries will not receive the expected intuitive answers. In the first example, given the assertions $\texttt{Within}(i,p)$ and $\texttt{Meets}(p,p')$, it is not possible to derive an answer for the query $\texttt{Limits}(i,p')$.

1.7.2 $\mathcal{IP}$

$\mathcal{IP}$ [Vila and Schwalb, 1996] has two sorts of symbols, instants ($\mathcal{I}$) and periods ($\mathcal{P}$) which are formed by two infinite disjoint sets of symbols, and three primitive binary relation symbols $\prec : \mathcal{I} \times \mathcal{I}$ and $\texttt{begin}, \texttt{end} : \mathcal{I} \times \mathcal{P}$.

The first-order axiomatization of $\mathcal{IP}$ theory is as follows:

$\mathbf{IP_1}$	$\neg(i \prec i)$
$\mathbf{IP_2}$	$i \prec i' \Rightarrow \neg(i' \prec i)$
$\mathbf{IP_3}$	$i \prec i' \wedge i' \prec i'' \Rightarrow i \prec i''$
$\mathbf{IP_4}$	$i \prec i' \vee i \prec i' \vee i = i'$
$\mathbf{IP_{5.1}}$	$\exists i' \, (i' \prec i)$
$\mathbf{IP_{5.2}}$	$\exists i' \, (i \prec i')$
$\mathbf{IP_6}$	$\texttt{begin}(i,p) \wedge \texttt{end}(i',p) \Rightarrow i \prec i'$
$\mathbf{IP_{7.1}}$	$\exists i \, \texttt{begin}(i,p)$
$\mathbf{IP_{7.2}}$	$\exists i \, \texttt{end}(i,p)$
$\mathbf{IP_{8.1}}$	$\texttt{begin}(i,p) \wedge \texttt{begin}(i',p) \Rightarrow i = i'$
$\mathbf{IP_{8.2}}$	$\texttt{end}(i,p) \wedge \texttt{end}(i',p) \Rightarrow i = i'$
$\mathbf{IP_9}$	$i \prec i' \Rightarrow \exists p \, (\texttt{begin}(i,p) \wedge \texttt{end}(i',p))$
$\mathbf{IP_{10}}$	$\texttt{begin}(i,p) \wedge \texttt{end}(i',p) \wedge$ $\wedge \texttt{begin}(i,p') \wedge \texttt{end}(i',p') \Rightarrow p = p'$

$\mathbf{IP_1}$ – $-\mathbf{IP_4}$ are the conditions for $\prec$ to be a *strict linear order* — namely irreflexive, asymmetric, transitive and linear– relation over the instants*. $\mathbf{IP_5}$ imposes unboundedness on this ordered set. $\mathbf{IP_6}$ orders the extremes of a period. This axiom rules out durationless

*Notice that $\mathbf{IP_1}$ is actually redundant since it can be derived from $\mathbf{IP_2}$. We include it for clarity.

periods which are not necessary since we have instants as a primitive. The pairs of axioms $\mathbf{IP}_{7..}$ and $\mathbf{IP}_{8..}$ formalize the intuition that the beginning and end instants of a period always *exist* and are *unique* respectively. Conversely, axioms $\mathbf{IP}_9$ and $\mathbf{IP}_{10}$ close the connection between instants and periods by ensuring the *existence* and *uniqueness* of a period for a given ordered pair of instants.

Next we characterize the models of $\mathcal{IP}$ and determine its relationships with other theories.

The Models

The models are defined over $\mathcal{IP}$-structures.

Definition 1.7.1. **($\mathcal{IP}$-structure)** *An $\mathcal{IP}$-structure is a tuple $\langle \mathcal{I}_d, \mathcal{P}_d, <_d, \texttt{begin}_d, \texttt{end}_d \rangle$ where $\mathcal{I}_d$ and $\mathcal{P}_d$ are sets of instants and periods respectively, $<_d$ is a binary relation on $\mathcal{I}_d$ and $\texttt{begin}_d, \texttt{end}_d$ are binary relations on $\mathcal{I}_d, \mathcal{P}_d$.*

Periods are merely viewed as ordered pairs of instants.

Definition 1.7.2. **($\texttt{pairs}$)** *Given a set $\mathcal{S}$ over which an ordering relation $<$ is defined, we note by $\texttt{pairs}(\mathcal{S})$ the set of $<$-ordered pairs of distinct elements of $\mathcal{S}$: $\texttt{pairs}(\mathcal{S}) = \{(x, y) \mid x, y \in \mathcal{S} \wedge x < y\}$. Over a set of pairs we define the following relations: (i) $first(x, (y, z)) \stackrel{def}{=} x = y$ and (ii) $second(x, (y, z)) \stackrel{def}{=} x = z$.*

Now we show — similar to Ladkin [Ladkin, 1987] — that the elements and the pairs of an unbounded linear order $\mathcal{S}$ form a model for $\mathcal{IP}$.

Theorem 1.7.1. **(a model)** *Given an infinite set $\mathcal{S}$ and an unbounded strict linear order $<$ on it, the $\mathcal{IP}$-structure $\langle \mathcal{S}, \texttt{pairs}(\mathcal{S}), <, first, second \rangle$ forms a model of $\mathcal{IP}$.*

Proof. (sketch) It is easy to prove that every axiom of $\mathcal{IP}$ is satisfied if we interpret the instants on the set $\mathcal{S}$, the periods on the set $\texttt{pairs}(\mathcal{S})$, the ordering as $<$, and $\texttt{begin}$ and $\texttt{end}$ relations as first and second respectively. □

Indeed these are the only models of $\mathcal{IP}$.

Theorem 1.7.2. **(the models)** *Any model $M = \langle \mathcal{I}_d, \mathcal{P}_d, <_d, \texttt{begin}_d, \texttt{end}_d \rangle$ of $\mathcal{IP}$ is isomorphic to the structure $\langle \mathcal{I}_d, \texttt{pairs}(\mathcal{I}_d), <_d, first, second \rangle$ where $\texttt{pairs}$, first and second are defined as above.*

Corollary 1. *Every model of $\mathcal{IP}$ is completely characterized by an infinite set $\mathcal{S}$ and an unbounded strict linear order $<$ on it (not necessarily dense).*

Note that $\mathcal{IP}$ accepts both dense and discrete models of time.

Dense $\mathcal{IP}$

The sub-theory that embraces dense models only, we call it $\mathcal{IP}_{dense}$, is axiomatized by adding the *denseness* axiom over instants:

$$\mathbf{IP}_{11} \quad i \prec i' \Rightarrow \exists i'' \, (i \prec i'' \prec i')$$

Theorem 1.7.3. (dense models) *The models of* $\mathcal{IP}_{dense}$ *are characterized by the set of elements and the set of ordered pairs of distinct elements of an unbounded,* dense, *strict linearly ordered set. Moreover* $\mathcal{IP}_{dense}$ *is a* complete *axiomatization for the theory of rationals and rational intervals, namely* $Th(\mathcal{Q}, INT(\mathcal{Q}))$.

Relation between $\mathcal{IP}$ and $\mathcal{AH}$

To compare our theory with Allen & Hayes theory (called $\mathcal{AH}$) we use the same technique as Ladkin [Ladkin, 1987]. Instants are derived from periods by first defining the notion of pair of meeting periods, second applying the equivalence relation "having the same meeting point" and, finally, associating an instant to each class. Let us call the resulting theory $\mathcal{I}_{\mathcal{AH}_{\sim\mathcal{I}}}$. Its class of models is the same as $\mathcal{IP}$.

Theorem 1.7.4. $\mathcal{IP} \equiv \mathcal{I}_{\mathcal{AH}_{\sim\mathcal{I}}}$

Theorem 1.7.5. $\mathcal{IP}_{dense} \equiv Th(\mathcal{AH}, N_1)$

Relation between $\mathcal{IP}$ and $\mathcal{G}$

As we discuss in Section 1.6, the instants in $\mathcal{G}$ do not correspond with the places where periods meet. For instance, nothing forces the instant that exists within a period by axiom $\mathbf{G_1}$ to be a place where two periods meet. They do not correspond to the idea of period endpoints either, which is our approach. As a matter of fact, $\mathcal{G}$ is weaker than $\mathcal{IP}_{dense}$.

Theorem 1.7.6. $\mathcal{IP}_{dense} \subset \mathcal{G}$

Proof. (sketch) $\mathcal{G}$ axioms are derived from $\mathbf{IP_{10}}$, linearity, extremes ordering, existence of both instants and periods and density. □

The reason of $\mathcal{G}$ weakness is the loose connection between instants and periods. There is no direct relation between $\mathcal{IP}$ and $\mathcal{G}$: $\mathcal{IP}$ accepts discrete models, whereas $\mathcal{G}$ imposes a sort of denseness by axiom $\mathbf{G_1}$. Characterize the models of $\mathcal{G}$ and its relation with $\mathcal{IP}$ is an open issue.

1.8 Temporal Incidence

For the sake of showing how a time theory is put at work, we complement this survey of theories of time with a section on temporal incidence, we propose a specific temporal incidence theory that works very well with an instant-period time theory, and, finally, we show on an example how the representational issues above a outlined th a classical example from naive physics.

Classical temporal logics in AI [McCarthy and Hayes, 1969; McDermott, 1982; Allen, 1984; Shoham, 1987; Haugh, 1987; Galton, 1991] mostly agree upon the temporal incidence properties that distinguish *fluents* from *events*. Fluents hold homogeneously whereas events event occurrences are anti-homogeneous. Instant-based approaches allow (i) a direct expression of instantaneous events and fluents, and (ii) an easy specification of temporal incidence properties. In McDermott's framework, for example, homogeneity of fluents is specified by

$$\text{Throughout}(T_1, T_2, F) \Leftrightarrow \forall\, T_1 \leq T \leq T_2\ \text{True}(T, F)$$

These advantages are more obvious in Shoham's work where a much richer categorization of proposition types is defined.

In period-based theories temporal incidence specification is more difficult. For example, Allen's axiom for fluent homogeneity is as follows:

$$\textbf{H.2} \quad \textsc{Holds}(F, I) \Leftrightarrow \forall\, I' \in I\, \exists I'' \in I'\ \textsc{Holds}(F, I'')$$

It is not only a cumbersome axiom, but in fact allows some non-intended models*. Moreover Galton [Galton, 1990] proves that axiom **H.2** conflicts with axiom **H.4** which specifies the *holding of negated fluents*. It is not clear how it can be avoided.

Also, period-based theories have problems to express the holding of a fluent at an instant, either because instants cannot be directly referred or because of the DIP. Allen & Hayes's reply to this issue as follows ([Allen and Hayes, 1989], Section 4):

> "We avoid it by resolutely refusing to allow fluents to hold at points".

They propose the following alternative: "One could define a notion of a fluent X being true at a point p by saying that X is true at p just when there is some interval I containing p during which X is true". It is easy to see that it does not work for modelling continuous fluents (consider the $v = 0$ fluent in the TBS). In Section 1.10 we determine the conditions for the DIP to be a problem and we propose a simple approach that satisfies them.

Let us now address the issue of modelling continuous change. There is a general agreement upon the importance of this issue for common-sense reasoning. In spite of it, no previous work formally accounts for the essential temporal incidence differences between holding of discrete and continuous fluents. Galton's work [Galton, 1990] is the only attempt in that direction, up to our knowledge. Fluents are diversified into instantaneous/durable and states of position/states of motion:

> "A *state of position* can hold at isolated instants; if it holds during a period it holds at its limits (e.g. a quantity taking a particular value). ... A *state of motion* cannot hold at isolated instants (e.g. a body being at rest)."

Galton's approach presents two problems:

1. The utility of Galton's new classes of fluents is not clear since more than one class is needed to model a single continuously changing parameter. Let us illustrate it with the TBS. Consider the fluent $f = (v \neq 0)$. It cannot be modelled as a state of position because f holds on both p_1 and p_2 which must contain the limiting instant i where $\neg f$ holds ($v = 0$). A state of motion cannot be used either because it cannot hold at isolated instants: we are not allowed to say that $\neg f$ is true at i.

2. While states of position are *concatenable*, states of motion are not always. It is rather counter-intuitive: it seems that states of position should not be concatenable since the parameter they represent may have a different value at the meeting point. Since it is not the case for states of motion it seems that they should be concatenable. Next we follow this intuition.

*An instance, due to Shoham, is a model in which time has the structure of real numbers and a property holds only over all its subintervals whose endpoints are rational.

1.9 $\mathcal{CD}$

$\mathcal{CD}$ the theory of temporal incidence initially proposed in [Vila and Schwalb, 1996], is based on the following ideas:

1. *We allow fluents to hold at points.* It allows modelling continuously changing fluents and makes the resulting theory much simpler to define. We discuss why it in fact does not originate any problem.

2. *We distinguish between continuous and discrete fluents.* We diversify fluents according to whether the change on the parameter they model is *continuous* or *discrete*.

To present our approach we assume the standard temporal reified first-order language with equality (as in [McDermott, 1982; Allen, 1984; Galton, 1990]) as underlying language. We propose a temporal representation with the following features:

- *Time theory*: We take $\mathcal{IP}_{dense}$. We define the instant-to-period relations (such as `Within`) and period-to-period relations (such as `Meets`) upon $\prec$, `begin` and `end`.

- *Reified propositions*: Reified propositions are classified into *continuous fluents*, *discrete fluents** and *events*.

- *Temporal Incidence Predicates (TIPs).* We introduce a different TIP for each combination of temporal proposition and temporal primitive (similar to [Kowalski and Sergot, 1986; Galton, 1990]):

$\text{HOLDS}^{\sim}_{on}(f,p)$	$\stackrel{def}{=}$	The continuous fluent f holds throughout the period p
$\text{HOLDS}^{\neg}_{on}(f,p)$	$\stackrel{def}{=}$	The discrete fluent f holds throughout the period p
$\text{HOLDS}^{\sim}_{at}(f,i)$	$\stackrel{def}{=}$	The continuous fluent f holds at the instant i
$\text{HOLDS}^{\neg}_{at}(f,i)$	$\stackrel{def}{=}$	The discrete fluent f holds at the instant i
$\text{OCCURS}_{on}(e,p)$	$\stackrel{def}{=}$	The event e occurs on the period p
$\text{OCCURS}_{at}(e,i)$	$\stackrel{def}{=}$	The event e occurs at the instant i

Terminology. Henceforth we use the following notational shorthands. We use `begin` and `end` in functional form (e.g. $i = \texttt{begin}(p)$). HOLDS_{on} stands for both $\text{HOLDS}^{\sim}_{on}$ and $\text{HOLDS}^{\neg}_{on}$, and HOLDS_{at} for $\text{HOLDS}^{\sim}_{at}$ and $\text{HOLDS}^{\neg}_{at}$.

$\mathcal{CD}$ axioms are as follows. Since instants and periods are both primitives, we are not forced to accept any assumption on the relation between the holding of a fluent on a period and its holding at the period endpoints. A fluent holds during a period iff it holds at its *inner* instants:

$$\textbf{CD}_1 \quad \text{HOLDS}_{on}(f,p) \Leftrightarrow (\texttt{Within}(i,p) \Rightarrow \text{HOLDS}_{at}(f,i))$$

From it, nothing can be derived about the holding of f at $\texttt{begin}(p)$ and $\texttt{end}(p)$.

Continuous Fluents A continuous fluent may hold both during a period and at a particular instant without any restriction. This is not the case for discrete ones.

*We use the equality relation to express a fluent representing a parameter taking a certain value. E.g. the speed of a ball being positive on p is expressed as $\text{HOLDS}(\text{speed} = +, p)$. We omit necessary axioms imposing the exclusivity among the different values of a parameter.

Discrete Fluents The genuine property of discrete fluents is that *they cannot hold at an isolated instant*:

$$\textbf{CD}_2 \quad \textsc{Holds}_{\overset{\neg}{at}}(f,i) \Rightarrow \exists p\,(\textsc{Holds}_{\overset{\neg}{on}}(f,p) \wedge (\texttt{Within}(i,p) \vee \texttt{begin}(i,p) \vee \texttt{end}(i,p)))$$

Our distinction between continuous and discrete events is different from Galton's distinction between states of position and states of motion. Identifying it as a key property in modelling changing domains is a contribution of this chapter.

Non-Instantaneous Events The intuition behind events (both instantaneous and durable) is that of an *accomplishment* that may have relevant consequences over the state of the world. Unlike preceding approaches, *our theory does not include any axiom governing the occurrence of events that take time*. It reflects the intuition that whether two *accomplishments* may happen concurrently depends on the abstraction degree of the analysis. For example, the event "I programmed the program p1" can not occur over two periods that are not disjoint. It is not the case, however, if the event under consideration is merely "programming a program". Therefore, no domain-independent axiom can be stated as part of a general theory of temporal incidence.

Non-Atomic Fluents Our theory directly addresses the issue of the holding of non-atomic fluents with the following axioms:

Negation:	$\textbf{CD}_3$	$\textsc{Holds}_{at}(\neg f, i) \Leftrightarrow \neg\textsc{Holds}_{at}(f,i)$
Conjunction:	$\textbf{CD}_4$	$\textsc{Holds}_{at}(f \wedge f', i) \Leftrightarrow \textsc{Holds}_{at}(f,i) \wedge \textsc{Holds}_{at}(f',i)$
Disjunction:	$\textbf{CD}_5$	$\textsc{Holds}_{at}(f \vee f', i) \Leftrightarrow \textsc{Holds}_{at}(f,i) \vee \textsc{Holds}_{at}(f',i)$

Deriving the properties of non-instantaneous holding of non-atomic fluents from these axioms is straight forward.

1.10 Revisiting the Issues

Let us see now how the problems presented in Section 1.2 are addressed using $\mathcal{IP}$ together with $\mathcal{CD}$.

Instantaneous Events Since we take instants as primitive, we can directly express instantaneous events using the predicate $\textsc{Occurs}_{at}$. In the DIP scenario, for instance, we can write $\textsc{Occurs}_{at}(\text{switchoff}, i)$. In Section 1.11 we discuss how to handle *sequences of instantaneous events*.

Instantaneous Holding We allow talking about a instantaneous holding of fluents by using $\textsc{Holds}_{at}$ predicates. Axiom $\textbf{CD}_1$ ensures that we are able to express the holding of contradictory fluents ending or beginning at a certain instant without conflict. Furthermore, we can express the holding of a continuous fluent at an isolated instant. The TBS scenario, for example, is merely represented as follows:

$$\begin{array}{ll} \textsc{Holds}_{\overset{\sim}{on}}(\text{speed} = +, p_1) & \\ \textsc{Holds}_{\overset{\sim}{at}}(\text{speed} = 0, i) & \texttt{end}(p_1) = i = \texttt{begin}(p_2) \\ \textsc{Holds}_{\overset{\sim}{on}}(\text{speed} = -, p_2) & \end{array}$$

The Dividing Instant Problem The DIP is not a problem for temporal incidence theories where the following two conditions hold:

1. The holding of a fluent over a period does not constrain its holding at the period's endpoints.

2. One can express that a fluent holds at an instant.

These conditions avoid logical contradiction and a truth gap at the dividing instant, respectively. In Figure 1.2 fluent f can be regarded as discrete and the DIP scenario can be formalized as follows:

$$\text{HOLDS}_{on}^{\neg}(\text{light} = \text{on}, p_1) \wedge \texttt{Meets}(p_1, p_2) \wedge \text{HOLDS}_{on}^{\neg}(\text{light} = \text{off}, p_2)$$

Given this information only, the query $\text{HOLDS}_{on}^{\neg}(\text{light} = \text{on}, \texttt{end}(p_1))$ merely gets no answer. The additional information required to answer it is domain-dependent. Some fluents hold on and at the end of a period (e.g. the fluent "being in contact with the floor" for a ball being lifted up), other fluents hold at the beginning and throughout the period (e.g. "not being in contact with the floor" for a ball that falls on the floor). In the light example, the most appropriate might be having three fluents light=on, light=off and light=changing, where the first and the second hold over open periods and the third holds at the dividing instant. Our approach avoids making any commitment about the holding at period's endpoints, whereas provides the means to safely specify what happens *at* the dividing instant. It requires an adequate theory of concatenability that we present below.

Non-Instantaneous Fluent Holding A nice feature of our proposal is that the above few axioms are enough to easily derive the fundamental properties of temporal incidence of fluents. For instance, *Allen's Homogeneity* $\text{HOLDS}_{on}^{\sim}(f, p) \Leftrightarrow \texttt{In}(p', p) \Rightarrow \text{HOLDS}_{on}^{\sim}(f, p')$ is easily derived from $\mathbf{CD_1}$. Before presenting the concatenability properties we define few basic notions. Given any two periods p, p' such that $\texttt{Meets}(p, p')$, $\texttt{meetpoint}(p, p') \stackrel{def}{=} \texttt{end}(p)$ and $\texttt{concat}(p, p') \stackrel{def}{=} p''$ s.t. $\texttt{begin}(p'') = \texttt{begin}(p) \wedge \texttt{end}(p'') = \texttt{end}(p')$. Also $\texttt{In} : \mathcal{P} \times \mathcal{P} \stackrel{def}{=} \texttt{Starts} \vee \texttt{During} \vee \texttt{Finishes}$, $\texttt{Disjoint}_{on}^{\neg} : \mathcal{P} \times \mathcal{P} \stackrel{def}{=} \texttt{Before} \vee \texttt{After}$ and $\texttt{Disjoint}_{on}^{\sim} : \mathcal{P} \times \mathcal{P} \stackrel{def}{=} \texttt{Before} \vee \texttt{Meets} \vee \texttt{Met\_by} \vee \texttt{After}$. The properties for concatenability are as follows:

Theorem 1.10.1. (Concatenability of discrete fluents)
If $\texttt{Meets}(p, p')$ *then*

$$\text{HOLDS}_{on}^{\neg}(f, p) \wedge \text{HOLDS}_{on}^{\neg}(f, p') \Leftrightarrow \text{HOLDS}_{on}^{\neg}(f, \texttt{concat}(p, p'))$$

Theorem 1.10.2. (Concatenability of continuous fluents)
If $\texttt{Meets}(p, p')$ *then*

$$\text{HOLDS}_{on}^{\sim}(f, p) \wedge \text{HOLDS}_{on}^{\sim}(f, p') \wedge \text{HOLDS}_{at}^{\sim}(f, \texttt{meetpoint}(p, p')) \Leftrightarrow$$
$$\Leftrightarrow \text{HOLDS}_{on}^{\sim}(f, \texttt{concat}(p, p'))$$

Concatenability can be regarded as a special case of *joinability*. Given two periods p and p', $\texttt{join}(p, p')$ is defined as a period p'' such that $\texttt{begin}(p'') = \texttt{min}(\texttt{begin}(p), \texttt{begin}(p'))$ and $\texttt{end}(p'') = \texttt{max}(\texttt{end}(p), \texttt{end}(p'))$, where $\texttt{min}$ and $\texttt{max}$ are defined according to $\prec$.

Theorem 1.10.3. (Joinability of discrete fluents)
If $\neg\texttt{Disjoint}^{\neg}_{on}(p,p')$ *then*

$$\text{HOLDS}^{\neg}_{on}(f,p) \wedge \text{HOLDS}^{\neg}_{on}(f,p') \Leftrightarrow \text{HOLDS}^{\neg}_{on}(f,\texttt{join}(p,p'))$$

Theorem 1.10.4. (Joinability of continuous fluents)
If $\neg\texttt{Disjoint}^{\sim}_{on}(p,p')$, *or*
$\texttt{Meets}(p,p') \wedge \text{HOLDS}_{at}(f,\texttt{meetpoint}(p,p'))$, *or*
$\texttt{Met\_by}(p,p') \wedge \text{HOLDS}_{at}(f,\texttt{meetpoint}(p',p))$
then

$$\text{HOLDS}^{\sim}_{on}(f,p) \wedge \text{HOLDS}^{\sim}_{on}(f,p') \Leftrightarrow \text{HOLDS}^{\sim}_{on}(f,\texttt{join}(p,p'))$$

There are also a number properties relating the holding of contradictory fluents at distinct, related times.

Theorem 1.10.5. (non-holding of discrete fluents)

$$\neg\text{HOLDS}^{\neg}_{on}(f,p) \Leftrightarrow \exists p'\ \texttt{In}(p',p) \wedge \text{HOLDS}^{\neg}_{on}(\neg f,p')$$

Theorem 1.10.6. (non-holding of continuous fluents)

$$\neg\text{HOLDS}^{\sim}_{on}(f,p) \Leftrightarrow \exists i\ \texttt{Within}(i,p) \wedge \text{HOLDS}^{\sim}_{at}(f,i)$$

Theorem 1.10.7. (disjointness)

$$\text{HOLDS}_{on}(f,p) \wedge \text{HOLDS}_{on}(\neg f,p') \Rightarrow \texttt{Disjoint}^{\sim}_{on}(p,p')$$

At this point one may ask for how long can we go enumerating properties of temporal incidence. To answer this question, let us analyze the issue from a more general perspective. The above properties are particular cases of the following scheme (f is a fluent and $\overline{p}$ denotes the collection of periods $p_1,\ldots,p_n$) :

If $\text{HOLDS}(f,\overline{p})$ and $f \models f'$ then $\text{HOLDS}(f',\overline{p}')$
If $\text{HOLDS}(f,\overline{p})$ and $f \models \neg f'$ then $\text{HOLDS}(\neg f',\overline{p}')$

The scope of this chapter goes as far as showing that the most basic properties of this scheme are theorems of our theory.

1.11 Example: Modelling Hybrid Systems

In this section we illustrate the application of the proposed theory in qualitative modelling of physical systems. A (qualitative) model that includes both discrete and continuously changing parameters is called a *hybrid model*. Many physical systems, such as most electromechanical devices like photocopiers, cars, stereos, are suitably modelled as a hybrid model. Several approaches have been proposed to represent "qualitative" hybrid models [Nishida and Doshita, 1987; Forbus, 1989; Iwasaki and Low, 1992; Iwasaki *et al.*, 1995], however some semantical problems arise because of the different nature of discrete and continuous change. We shall see that an adequate theory of time and temporal incidence is fundamental to overcome them.

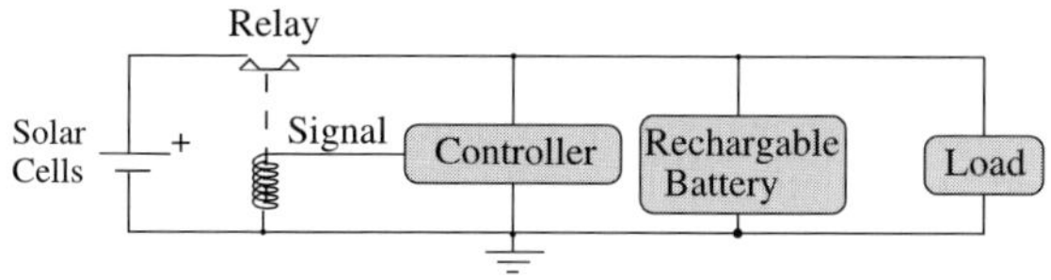

Figure 1.4: The hybrid circuit example.

Let us consider a particular example from [Iwasaki *et al.*, 1995] (we borrow the example, the qualitative model, the intended environment and a tentative solution). Figure 1.4 shows a simple circuit in which electric power is provided to a *load* either by a *solar cells* array or by a *re-chargeable battery*.
A part of the continuous behavior of this system is described as follows:

C0: "If the sun is shining and the relay is closed then the solar array acts as a constant current source and the battery accumulates charge."

The discrete events are specified as follows:

D1: "If the relay is closed, when the signal from the controller goes high, then the relay opens."

D2: "If the relay is open, when the signal from the controller goes low, then the relay closes."

D3: "If the signal is low, when the controller detects that the charge level in the battery has reached the threshold q_2, then the controller turns on the signal to the relay."

Now, let us consider a particular predicted qualitative behavior. A qualitative behaviour is described as a sequence of states that hold alternatively at an instant and throughout a period. The transition from one state to another is produced either by a continuous or by a discrete change. Quoting Iwasaki *et al* [Iwasaki *et al.*, 1995]: "...we would like to model discrete events as being instantaneous". Problems arise when sequences of them occur. For instance "the signal goes high and *immediately after* the relay closes". The following predicted behavior and the explanation about why sequences of discrete events are problematic are borrowed from [Iwasaki *et al.*, 1995]. Given the initial state of our example where the *signal* is *low*, the *relay* is *closed* and the sun is shining, the intended environment would be as follows:

s_1	(t_1, t_2)	$Q_{BA} < q_2$	*signal* = *low*	*relay* = *closed*
s_2	t_2	$Q_{BA} = q_2$	*signal* = *low*	*relay* = *closed*
$s_{2.1}$	$t_{2.1}$	$Q_{BA} = ?$	*signal* = *high*	*relay* = *closed*
$s_{2.2}$	$t_{2.2}$	$Q_{BA} = ?$	*signal* = *high*	*relay* = *open*
s_3	$(t_{2.2}, \text{-})$	$Q_{BA} < q_2$	*signal* = *high*	*relay* = *open*

The state $s_{2.1}$ is produced by the signal going high, and $s_{2.2}$ by the relay closing.

It is not clear how to model neither the times of s_2, $s_{2.1}$ and $s_{2.2}$ nor the time spans and the discrete events between them. If we assume that discrete events take no time, we encounter the following logical problem: "The antecedent for rules specifying discrete events often includes the negation of the consequence; this leads to a contradiction when events are treated as implications." An alternative is assuming that discrete changes take a very little period. It is problematic too since the value of every continuous variable that changes concurrently becomes unknown after a sequence of actions. In the example, the charge of the battery would keep continuously increasing for a short period. After a number of discrete events these small variations accumulate and complicate the computation of parameter values.

Several solutions have been proposed to solve this quandary. They are based on complicating the model of time by either introducing *mythical* time ([Nishida and Doshita, 1987], *direct method*), extending the real numbers with infinitessimals ([Nishida and Doshita, 1987], *approximation method*)[Alur *et al.*, 1993], or using non-standard analysis [Iwasaki *et al.*, 1995]. Next we show that none of these is necessary. We use our theory of instants/periods and continuous fluents/discrete fluents/events as follows:

- Discrete events are modelled as instantaneous events.
- Continuous/discrete quantities are modelled as continuous/discrete fluents.

Since HOLDS_{on} is defined as holding at the inner points only, the value of a fluent that changes because of an instantaneous event is not defined at the time that the event's time unless there is some specific knowledge about it. The sequence of states representing the intended environment becomes simpler:

s_1	(t_1, t_2)	$Q_{BA} < q_2$	$signal = low$	$relay = closed$
s_2	t_2	$Q_{BA} = q_2$	$signal = ?$	$relay = ?$
s_3	$(t_2, \text{-})$	$Q_{BA} < q_2$	$signal = high$	$relay = open$

Indeed, this solution is much simpler than the previously proposed techniques. The formalization of the environment is as follows:

$\text{HOLDS}^{\sim}_{on}(Q_{BA} < q_2, p_1)$	
$\text{HOLDS}^{\neg}_{on}(signal = low, p_2)$	
$\text{HOLDS}^{\neg}_{on}(relay = closed, p_3)$	
$\text{HOLDS}^{\sim}_{at}(Q_{BA} = q_2, \text{end}(p_1))$	
$\text{OCCURS}_{at}(turn\_on(signal), \text{end}(p_1))$	$\text{end}(p_1) = \text{end}(p_2)$
$\text{HOLDS}^{\neg}_{on}(signal = high, p_4)$	$\texttt{Meets}(p_2, p_4)$
$\text{OCCURS}_{at}(open(relay)), \text{end}(p_3))$	$\text{end}(p_2) = \text{end}(p_3)$
$\text{HOLDS}^{\neg}_{on}(relay = open, p_5)$	$\texttt{Meets}(p_3, p_5)$

1.12 Concluding Remarks

A theory of time and temporal incidence is the foundation for a proper temporal representation, independently of both the temporal qualification method and the underlying representation language. In this chapter we identified the problematic issues that need to be addressed, namely the expression of *instantaneous events* and *fluents*, the *dividing instant problem* (DIP) and the formalization of the properties *for non-instantaneous holding of fluents*.

In this chapter we have surveyed the most relevant theories of time in Artificial Intelligence and we have discussed the pros and cons of each of them. Also, we presented a brief overview of temporal incidence theories and proposes a theory of *temporal incidence* called $\mathcal{CD}$ defined upon a theory of instants and periods (such as $\mathcal{IP}$) whose key insight is the distinction between continuous and discrete fluents.

Handbook of Temporal Reasoning in Artificial Intelligence
Edited by M. Fisher, D. Gabbay and L. Vila

Chapter 2

Eventualities

Antony Galton

The previous chapter has discussed the many different ways in which we can construct formal models of time. These models provide temporal frameworks within which it is possible to represent many of things which can go on in time, but they do not on their own provide a means for representing those things themselves. Such a model of time is like a new diary or calendar which provides the dates in their correct temporal relationships but has nothing written into it yet. This chapter is concerned with the kinds of things that can be written into such a temporal framework.

2.1 Introduction

What are these "things"? There are many general words to describe various classes of things which we might want to write into our calendar. Suppose I mark over a week in August the words "On holiday all week". This indicates a *state* which obtains throughout that week. On the other hand, I might mark, on a particular day, "Heathrow depart 10.25 a.m.". This refers to an *event* which happens at a particular point in time. This distinction between states and events is one of the most fundamental, but there are many other distinctions that have been made between many subtly or not-so-subtly different kinds of things that can go on in time. Some words that have been used for this purpose are *situation*, *state of affairs*, *process*, *act*, *action*, *activity*, *accomplishment*, *achievement*, *happening*, *occurrence*, and *eventuality*.

Most of these words are used in everyday language with more or less precise non-technical meanings, but they have also all been used as technical terms, sometimes in different ways by different authors. A need has often been felt for a single most general term to cover the whole range of meanings presented by these terms. Working in a linguistic context, Comrie [Comrie, 1976, p. 13] suggested *situation* for this purpose, but in an Artificial Intelligence context this term has a rather more specific meaning and is therefore inappropriate. The term *eventuality* was suggested by Bach [Bach, 1986] as a catch-all to cover events, states, processes, and the like, and as it has not, as far as I know, been used for any more specific purpose I shall use it in this chapter as the general term to cover all the categories mentioned above.

Two terms that I shall not be using in this context are *fact* and *property*, both of which have been used for what is better referred to as a *state*. The former was used by McDermott [McDermott, 1982] to contrast with *event*; you could have a fact holding at a time or an event happening at a time. Unfortunately this does not fit in with our normal use of the term 'fact':

we might say that it is a fact that I was in London on 24th March, but equally that it is a fact that I went to London on 24th of March. The former is a fact about a state, the latter a fact about an event. I take it that the correct way to talk about facts is as expounded by Jonathan Bennett [Bennett, 1988]. Similarly, it seems odd to call my being in London a *property*, as James Allen did in [Allen, 1984]. It seems more natural to say that being in London was a property that I temporarily possessed on 24th of March, and one might just say that *my* being in London was a property of that *time* (though this sounds a little odd); again, though, this does not establish the desired contrast with events, since one could equally say that my going to London (an event) was a property of the time at which it occurred.

The plan of this chapter is to survey systematically the range of different eventualities that can be described in a series of systems of increasing complexity. We begin with the simplest of all possible systems, a system with just one primitive two-valued state undergoing variation in discrete time. We shall see that even with such a simple system it is already possible to describe an astonishing range of temporal phenomena, which correspond at least roughly with many of the concepts we use in describing temporal phenomena in the real world. We next complicate matters somewhat by introducing more than one state—or equivalently, allowing our single state to become many-valued, i.e., a fluent. The next complication we introduce is to model time as continuous rather than discrete, but still insisting that our primitive fluents undergo only discrete variation. The final stage in the development is to look at the case of continuous change, where the variation in value of a fluent needs to be represented by means of a continuous function of time. We shall close our survey with an examination of a single real-world system, which, by viewing it at different levels of granularity, we can model in any of the ways we have described.

2.2 One state in discrete time

2.2.1 The simplest possible temporal system

The simplest possible system in which temporal phenomena occur has one state, which may be either "on" or "off". Assuming a discrete time series, the evolution of such a system can be portrayed as a bit-string of indefinite length, the 1s denoting the "on" state, the 0s the "off" state:

$$\cdots 0001101101\ 0010100101\ 0001010000\ 1111101000 \cdots$$

Such a sequence is sometimes known as a *history*. For convenience we shall always group the bits in a history into blocks of ten. We shall call the "on" state of this system S; the "off" state is its negation which we shall denote $-S$. Assigning an integer designation to each time in the discrete series, with the usual order, we shall write $Holds(S, n)$ to mean that the "on" state holds at the time denoted n, and likewise $Holds(-S, n)$ to indicate that the "off" state holds then. We shall write things like $t = n$ to indicate that a time t that we are interested in is assigned the integer value n.

We shall write $[m, n]$ to denote the interval composed of all the atomic intervals k such that $m \leq k \leq n$. Note that in this notation $[m, m]$ is just another way of denoting the atomic interval m. We shall extend our use of the predicate $Holds$ to apply to non-atomic (or *extended*) intervals as follows:

$$Holds(S, [m, n]) \leftrightarrow \forall k(m \leq k \leq n \rightarrow Holds(S, k)).$$

Thus state S holds on the interval $[m, n]$ if and only if it holds on each of the atomic intervals of which $[m, n]$ is composed. A simple consequence of this definition is the rule **HOM** which will be introduced in Section 2.2.4.

2.2.2 Instantaneous transitions

Even a system as simple as this can furnish us with examples of a wide range of temporal phenomena. The simplest case is that of an **instantaneous transition**. This occurs when the state S changes either from "on" to "off" or from "off' to "on". In the history

(**S1**) 0000000000 1111111111 0000000000

we see one example of each. If the series shown here begins at $t = 1$ then the transition from "off" to "on" occurs between times $t = 10$ and $t = 11$, and the transition from "on" to "off" occurs between times $t = 20$ and $t = 21$. This leads to a little difficulty in describing exactly *when* the transitions occur; if the times in the model are $t = 1, t = 2, t = 3, \ldots$, then neither transition occurs *at* any time, but rather each of them occurs *between* two times. This incidentally provides a compelling reason why we have to distinguish between two types of time, intervals and instants. The times $t = 1, t = 2, t = 3, \ldots$ are **atomic intervals**; we may assign to each of them a notional duration of 1 (indivisible) unit. They may be concatenated together to form longer (non-atomic) intervals, e.g., the interval [11,20] on which the state S is "on" in example **S1**. An instantaneous transition such as the change from "off" to "on" does not occur on any interval, atomic or otherwise, although there are many non-atomic intervals *within* which it occurs: in our example the transition from "off" to "on" occurs within the interval [10,11] and also within any interval containing this, e.g., [8,12] or [7,20]. But the single unique "time" *at* which the transition occurs isn't an interval at all, but rather the point at which two intervals meet. This is an **instant**. We shall denote it 10][11.

We now have two different kinds of eventuality, sharply distinct from one another yet intimately related. On the one hand we have a **state**, our S, which on each atomic interval is either "on" or "off" (one might say "true" or "false" if S were regarded as a statement). When S is "on" we say that it **holds**. If S (or $-S$) holds over a sequence of consecutive atomic intervals, we can say that it holds over the longer interval comprising those atomic intervals; in example **S1**, we have $Holds(S, [10, 15])$ and $Holds(-S, [3, 6])$, for example. On the other hand we have **instantaneous events**, the transitions from $-S$ to S and vice versa. We shall denote the former event $Ingr(S)$, and the latter $Ingr(-S)$. Events do not hold, they **occur**. An instantaneous event occurs not on an interval but at the interface between two neighbouring intervals, an instant. We can write, for example **S1**, $Occurs(Ingr(S), 10][11)$ and $Occurs(Ingr(-S), 20][21)$.

2.2.3 Can a state hold at an instant?

Does it make sense, in this system, to speak of a state holding *at an instant*, as opposed to over an interval? If it does, it does so only derivatively: states primarily hold on intervals. But there is a sense in which we could say that if S holds on interval n and also on interval $n + 1$ then it holds at the instant $n][n + 1$ which marks their meeting point. If we say this then there will be some instants, such as 10][11 and 20][21 in example **S1**, at which neither S nor $-S$ holds; these are precisely the instants at which there occur the transition events associated with S. Note that there are also *intervals* over which, in another sense, neither S nor $-S$ holds: for example, it is not the case either that S holds over the interval [7,13] or that $-S$ holds over that interval. This is because S holds over some parts of the interval, and $-S$ holds over other parts. The holding of a state like S, whether over intervals or at instants, completely reduces to the question of which atomic intervals it holds on. Clearly, in this discrete system we can very well manage without ascribing states to instants at all.

We can also, as a matter of fact, manage without ascribing instantaneous events to instants either, but only by establishing an essentially arbitrary convention. If $Ingr(S)$ occurs at the instant $n][n+1$, then we could decide that we shall eliminate reference to instants by saying that it occurs at the atomic interval n; or alternatively we could choose the opposite convention and say that $Ingr(S)$ occurs at $n+1$.* Although this is possible, it can lead to confusion (see the end of Section 2.2.4); it is certainly conceptually quite wrong, since it seems to ascribe the duration of an atomic interval to an event which is durationless.

2.2.4 A state holding for a while: the operator Po

We may wish to refer to an event which consists of S starting to hold, holding for a while, and then ceasing to hold. This happens with S over the interval [11,20] in example **S1**. We shall write $Po(S)$ to denote this event.† The event $Po(S)$ consists of the state S holding for a while. The reader will naturally wonder in what way this is any different from the state S itself. The answer is that for the event to occur it is essential that the interval over which S holds is bounded by times at which S does not hold. Thus in example **S1**, $Po(S)$ occurs *only* on the interval [11,20], whereas S holds over any subinterval of this, e.g., [12,15], [11,16], [16,17], as well as atomic subintervals such as 13 and 14. Thus we can write

$$\begin{array}{ll} Holds(S,[11,20]) & Occurs(Po(S),[11,20]) \\ Holds(S,[12,15]) & \neg Occurs(Po(S),[12,15]) \\ Holds(S,12) & \neg Occurs(Po(S),12) \end{array}$$

We can formulate two general rules as follows:

(**HOM**) $$Holds(S,i) \wedge i' \sqsubset i \rightarrow Holds(S,i')$$

(**UNI**-Po) $$Occurs(Po(S),i) \wedge i' \sqsubset i \rightarrow \neg Occurs(Po(S),i')$$

The notation $i' \sqsubset i$ means that i' is a *proper subinterval* of i, that is, the atomic subintervals which make up i' form a proper subset of the set of atomic subintervals which make up i. The designation **HOM** is short for *homogeneous*, the point being that states occupy time in a uniform way so that any part of an interval over which a state holds is also an interval over which that state holds.‡ This contrasts with the designation **UNI**-Po, for *unitary*, the point here being that an occurrence of an event like $Po(S)$ is a single indivisible unit; no proper

*The former alternative recalls Von Wright's [von Wright, 1965] binary proposition-forming operator T such that the proposition pTq (read "p and next q") is true at time t if and only if p is true at t and q is true at $t+1$. Using this operator, if p represents the proposition that the state S holds, then the proposition $(\neg p)Tp$ effectively records the occurrence of $Ingr(S)$.

†The designation Po was introduced in [Galton, 1984].

‡The axiom here designated **HOM** was proposed by Hamblin [Hamblin, 1971], and independently by Allen [Allen, 1984]; it has been used by many authors since.

part of the time of such an occurrence is also the time of such an occurrence. More generally we shall say that an event-type E is **unitary** if it satisfies the formula*

(**UNI**) $$Occurs(E, i) \wedge i' \sqsubset i \rightarrow \neg Occurs(E, i')$$

In the sequence

0000000000 1000000000

we see an occurrence of $Po(S)$ having the shortest possible duration. This is not an instantaneous event, since it does have duration, albeit minimal; a truly instantaneous event such as $Ingr(S)$ has no duration at all, occurring as it does at a durationless instant. We could describe the occurrence of $Po(S)$ here as *momentary*. We have, in this example,

$$Occurs(Ingr(S), 10][11),\ Occurs(Po(S), 11),\ Occurs(Ingr(-S), 11][12).$$

Here the event $Ingr(S)$ occurs immediately before the event $Po(S)$, marking its beginning, and the event $Ingr(-S)$ occurs immediately after $Po(S)$ marking its end. That is one reason why it would be confusing to adopt a convention whereby one or other of the events $Ingr(S)$ and $Ingr(-S)$ was said to occur on the atomic interval 11.

We can classify events as **instantaneous** or **durative** depending on whether they occur at instants or on intervals. Amongst durative events we can distinguish **momentary** and **extended** occurrences depending on whether they occupy atomic or non-atomic intervals.

2.2.5 Events and their occurrences

We have referred to both **events** and **occurrences**. We do not use these terms interchangeably. An event such as $Po(S)$ or $Ingr(S)$ is an **event type**: it can manifest itself as many different occurrences. For example, in the sequence

(**S2**) 0000001111 1110000011 1000000000 0001111111 0000000000

there are three occurrence of each of these event types. Occurrences are sometimes called **event tokens**. Events and their occurrences have very different ontological status. The event $Po(S)$ exists, in an abstract sense, so long as the state S exists; whether or not any occurrences of this event exist depends on the particular incidence of state S in the history we are considering. In the history

0000000000 0000000000 0000000000 0000000000 0000000000

there is no occurrence of $Po(S)$, although the event type still exists in the sense that although there are in fact no occurrences of it, there could have been some.

An event-type such as $Po(S)$ or $Ingr(S)$ is defined in terms of the state S by giving a necessary and sufficient condition for there to be an occurrence of the event at a given time. We shall call this the **occurrence condition** for the event. The occurrence conditions for $Ingr(S)$ and $Po(S)$ are:

Ingr $Ingr(S)$ occurs at $n][n+1$ iff $-S$ holds on n and S holds on $n+1$.

Po $Po(S)$ occurs on $[m, n]$ iff S holds throughout $[m, n]$ and $-S$ holds on both $m-1$ and $n+1$.

*Note that for Allen [Allen, 1984], and many subsequent authors, *all* event-types are unitary, **UNI** being postulated as an axiom.

2.2.6 A state holding for a certain duration

We can restrict $Po(S)$ to a certain duration as follows. For an integer d, let $For(S,d)$ be the event which consists of S holding for exactly d consecutive atomic intervals. Here d is the *duration* of the event. For example, in the sequence **S2** there are two occurrences of $For(S,7)$ (on the intervals [7,13] and [34,40]) and one occurrence of $For(S,3)$ (on [19,21]). The occurrence condition for $For(S,d)$ is:

For $For(S,d)$ occurs on $[m,n]$ iff $n-m=d-1$, S holds throughout $[m,n]$ and $-S$ holds on both $m-1$ and $n+1$.

The occurrences of the event $For(S,1)$ are just the *momentary* occurrences of $Po(S)$. In general, the occurrences of $For(S,k)$ form a subset of the occurrences of $Po(S)$. We shall say that $For(S,k)$ is a **subtype** of $Po(S)$, where the exact definition of subtype is as follows:

> Event type E' is a subtype of event type E if any occurrence of E' is necessarily also an occurrence of type E.

The word "necessarily" in this definition means that we have to consider all possible sequences in determining whether one event is a sub-event of another.

2.2.7 Repetition events

For an event, E, let $Consec(E,k)$ be the event which consists of exactly k consecutive non-overlapping occurrences of E. In example **S2** there is an occurrence of $Consec(Po(S),3)$, and an occurrence of $Consec(For(S,7),2)$, both occurring on the interval [7,40], and two occurrences of $Consec(Po(S),2)$, on the intervals [7,21] and [19,40]. There are also occurrences of $Consec(Ingr(S),2)$ on [7,18] and [19,33].

The definition of consecutive events is complicated by the possibility of overlapping occurrences of an event type. Here we take the view that in order for two occurrences of E, say e_1 and e_2, to count as consecutive, there must be no occurrences of E either beginning or ending in the interval between the end of e_1 and the beginning of e_2. Thus e_2 is the first occurrence of E to begin after the end of e_1, and e_1 is the last occurrence of E to end before the beginning of e_2. This requirement is formalised in the definitions given below.

Separate occurrence conditions for $Consec(E,k)$ have to be given depending on whether E is instantaneous or durative:

Consec-D If E is a durative event, then

- $Consec(E,1)$ occurs on $[m,n]$ iff E occurs on $[m,n]$;
- For $k>1$, $Consec(E,k)$ occurs on $[m,n]$ iff there are integers p,q, where $m\leq p<q\leq n$, such that E occurs on $[m,p]$ but not on any interval ending in $[p+1,q-1]$, and $Consec(E,k-1)$ occurs on $[q,n]$ but not on any interval beginning in $[p+1,q-1]$.

Consec-I If E is an instantaneous event, then

- $Consec(E,2)$ occurs on $[m,n]$ iff E occurs on both $m-1][m$ and $n][n+1$;

- For $k > 2$, $Consec(E, k)$ occurs on $[m, n]$ iff there is an integer p, where $m < p \leq n$, such that E occurs at $m - 1][m$ but not at any instant between m and p, and $Consec(E, k - 1)$ occurs on $[p, n]$.*

If E is durative, $Consec(E, 1)$ is the same event as E itself; for instantaneous E the definition does not apply to the case $k = 1$, but we could if we wish supplement the definition by stipulating that $Consec(E, 1) = E$ in this case also.

Note the effect of iterating the operator $Consec$. In the sequence

(**S3**) 0001110001 1100011100 0111000111 0001110001 11000

the event $Consec(Po(S), 3)$ occurs on the intervals [4,18], [10,24], [16,30], [22,36], and [28,42], i.e., five times; but we do not have an occurrence of $Consec(Consec(Po(S), 3), 5)$ here since these occurrences are not all consecutive.

On the other hand, $Consec(Consec(Po(S), 3), 2)$ has two overlapping occurrences, on the intervals [4,36] and [10,42].

An alternative type of repetition event, which we shall denote $Times(E, k)$, *does* allow overlapping occurrences. The occurrence conditions are

Times-D If E is durative, then

- $Times(E, 1)$ occurs on $[m, n]$ iff E occurs on $[m, n]$;
- For $k > 1$, $Times(E, k)$ occurs on $[m, n]$ iff there are integers p, q, where $m \leq p \leq n$ and $m < q \leq n$, such that E occurs on $[m, p]$ but not on any other subinterval of $[m, n]$ beginning before q, and $Times(E, k - 1)$ occurs on $[q, n]$.

Times-I If E is instantaneous, then $Times(E, k)$ occurs on $[m, n]$ iff $Consec(E, k)$ does.

In example **S3**, both

$$Times(Consec(Po(S), 3), 5)$$

and

$$Times(Consec(Consec(Po(S), 3), 2), 2)$$

occur on [4,42]. For instantaneous events, $Times$ is the same as $Consec$. This is because these two operators only behave differently from one another when applied to event-types which can have overlapping occurrences. Here we are assuming that distinct occurrences of the same instantaneous event-type must occupy distinct instants, and hence cannot overlap.

The operator $Times$, as we have defined it, has one inevitable shortcoming. It does not cover the case where there are two distinct but strictly simultaneous occurrences of an event type. It is not possible to handle this case in the present framework: this can only be done by introducing a separate category of terms to refer to individual occurrences.

Although a number of authors have discussed repetitions of events, little systematic work has been done on this. Allen [Allen, 1984] suggests a definition of an event TWICE(E) which roughly corresponds to our Consec(E,2), although Allen's definition is faulty because the event thereby defined does not satisfy the principle **UNI** which he lays down as an axiom

*Note that it is not necessary to include a further condition that $Consec(E, k - 1)$ does not occur on any interval beginning in $[m + 1, p - 1]$ since this is implied by the non-occurrence of E in this interval.

to be satisfied by all events. To explore this area further, it would be interesting to devise an algorithm for detecting occurrences of events of the form

$$Op_1(Op_2(Op_3(\ldots Op_n(Po(S), k_n), \ldots k_3), k_2), k_1)$$

where each Op_i is either $Consec$ or $Times$.

A related issue is *periodic* events, where we are not concerned with some definite number of repetitions of a basic event, but rather with an ongoing state of affairs consisting of regularly or irregularly repeated occurrences of a given event type. We discuss this below in Section 2.2.11. For a fuller treatment of repetitive and periodic events, see other chapters.

2.2.8 Sequential composition of events

Related to these repetition events are *sequence* events. Given two event-types E_1 and E_2, an occurrence of their **sequential composition** consists of an occurrence of E_1 followed by an occurrence of E_2. We can distinguish two varieties of sequential composition, according to whether or not the second event is required to follow the first immediately. We shall use the notation $E_1; E_2$ for the **immediate sequential composition**, which requires the occurrence of E_2 to follow immediately on from the occurrence of E_1, and $E_1;; E_2$ for the **general sequential composition**, which does not require this (but allows it). The occurrence conditions are complicated by the fact that one or (in the case of general composition) both of the component events might be instantaneous.

There are many ways in which we might choose to define the composition operators. Possible occurrence conditions for immediate sequential composition (**ISC**) and general sequential composition (**GSC**), which might be modified to suit particular special purposes, are:

ISC If E_1 and E_2 are both durative, then $E_1; E_2$ occurs on the interval $[m, n]$ iff there is an integer k, where $m \leq k < n$, such that E_1 occurs on $[m, k]$ and E_2 occurs on $[k+1, n]$.

If E_1 is durative and E_2 is instantaneous, then $E_1; E_2$ occurs on $[m, n]$ iff E_1 occurs on $[m, n]$ and E_2 occurs at $n][n+1$.

If E_1 is instantaneous and E_2 is durative, then $E_1; E_2$ occurs on $[m, n]$ iff E_1 occurs at $m-1][m$ and E_2 occurs on $[m, n]$.

GSC If E_1 and E_2 are both durative, then $E_1;; E_2$ occurs on the interval $[m, n]$ iff there are integers k and l, where $m \leq k < l \leq n$, such that E_1 occurs on $[m, k]$ but not on any interval $[p, q]$ such that $k < q < l$, and E_2 occurs on $[l, n]$ but not on any interval $[r, s]$ such that $k < r < l$.

If E_1 is durative and E_2 is instantaneous, then $E_1;; E_2$ occurs on $[m, n]$ iff there is an integer k, where $m \leq k \leq n$, such that E_1 occurs on $[m, k]$ but not on any interval $[p, q]$ such that $k < q < n$, and E_2 occurs at $n][n+1$ but at no instant $l][l+1$ where $k \leq l < n$.

If E_1 is instantaneous and E_2 is durative, then $E_1;; E_2$ occurs on $[m, n]$ iff there is an integer k, where $m \leq k \leq n$, such that E_1 occurs at $m-1][m$ but at no instant $l-1][l$ where $m < l < k$ and E_2 occurs on $[k, n]$ but not on any interval $[p, q]$ where $m \leq p < k$.

If E_1 and E_2 are both instantaneous, then $E_1;;E_2$ occurs on $[m,n]$ iff E_1 occurs at $m-1][m$ and E_2 occurs at $n][n+1$, and neither event occurs on any instant $l-1][l$ where $m < l < n+1$.

In example **S2** there is an occurrence of the event-type $For(S,7);;For(S,3)$ on [7,21], and hence an occurrence of $(For(S,7);;For(S,3));;For(S,7)$ on [7,40]. From the definitions one can prove that the event-types $(E_1;;E_2);;E_3$ and $E_1;;(E_2;;E_3)$ are always identical in the sense of having the same occurrences as each other in every possible history; hence we may drop the brackets and write $E_1;;E_2;;E_3$. The same goes for the operator ";".

For a durative event E we can define a *repetition* operator *Rep* such that an occurrence of $Rep(E,n)$ comprises n consecutive occurrences of E in immediate succession. It can be defined recursively in terms of ";" as follows:

Rep $Rep(E,1) = E$
$Rep(E,n+1) = Rep(E,n);E$

$Rep(E,n)$ is a subtype of $Consec(E,n)$, covering just those occurrences of the latter in which the component occurrences of E follow on from one another without delay. Similarly, we can define *Consec* itself in terms of ";;" as follows:

$$\begin{aligned} Consec(E,1) &= E \\ Consec(E,n+1) &= E;;Consec(E,n) \end{aligned}$$

and this definition can be shown to be equivalent to the one given earlier.

2.2.9 An event in progress: the operator *Prog*

In addition to defining classes of events by laying down their occurrence conditions, our present framework allows us to define new classes of *states* by laying down appropriate **holding conditions**. An example of this is the *progressive* state which obtains at those times when some event is in the process of occurring, i.e., when it is in progress. In the sequence

0000000000 1111000111 0000000000

the event $Consec(Po(S),2)$ occurs on the interval [11,20], so at any time during this interval that event is in progress. We shall say that the state $Prog(Consec(Po(S),2))$ holds throughout this interval.

The holding condition for states of the form $Prog(E)$ is

Prog For a durative event E, the state $Prog(E)$ holds on the atomic interval k iff E occurs on an interval $[m,n]$ such that $m \leq k \leq n$.

The operator *Prog*, which maps events onto states, is closely related to the operator *Po* which maps states onto events; they stand to one another approximately as inverses.

Thus, given a state S, the state $Prog(Po(S))$ holds at a time k iff $Po(S)$ occurs on an interval $[m,n]$ such that $m \leq k \leq n$. But if $Po(S)$ occurs on $[m,n]$ and $m \leq k \leq n$, then S must hold at k. Thus $Prog(Po(S))$ entails S (meaning that the latter must hold whenever the former holds). The converse entailment does not hold however, since e.g., in the sequence

0000000000 1111111111 1111111111 $\cdots$

where S holds at *all* times from $t = 11$ onwards, $Po(S)$ does not occur at all, and hence $Prog(Po(S))$ does not hold.

The two states S and $Prog(Po(S))$, although intimately related, are nonetheless distinct, and in fact represent two different levels of description of what is going on. The state S is *basic* in the sense that the holding or not holding of S over an atomic interval is simply a given fact, specifiable independently of its holding or not holding at any other time. We could say that S is a description at Level 0. The event $Po(S)$ is defined in terms of S, so its occurrence or non-occurrence at different times is dependent on the pattern of holding and not holding of S. It is one level further up on the dependence hierarchy, Level 1. The state $Prog(Po(S))$ is at a higher level still, since its holding depends on the occurrence of $Po(S)$ which in turn depends on the pattern of holding and not holding of S. Thus to say that $Prog(Po(S))$ holds at time k has implications not just for the state of the world at $t = k$ but also for the state of the world at earlier and later times. In fact we can easily prove, from the conditions **Po** and **Prog**, that

$$\begin{aligned}&Holds(Prog(Po(S)), k) \equiv \\ &\quad Holds(S, k) \wedge \exists m, n(m < k < n \wedge Holds(-S, m) \wedge Holds(-S, n)).\end{aligned}$$

The other respect in which Po and $Prog$ are approximately inverse to one another concerns the relationship between the events E and $Po(Prog(E))$. (Here E has to be durative.) If $Po(Prog(E))$ occurs on $[m, n]$ then $Prog(E)$ holds throughout $[m, n]$ but does not hold at $m - 1$ or $n + 1$. This means that if $m \leq k \leq n$ then E occurs on some interval $[m_k, n_k]$, where $m \leq m_k \leq k \leq n_k \leq n$. It may be that all the ks are associated with the same occurrence of E; if so, that occurrence must occupy exactly the interval $[m, n]$ and therefore corresponds exactly to the occurrence of $Po(Prog(E))$. This will always be the case if $E = Po(S)$, so we can identify $Po(S)$ and $Po(Prog(Po(S)))$.

More generally, though, there may be overlapping or immediately consecutive occurrences of E spanning the interval $[m, n]$. An example of overlapping occurrences is furnished by the sequence

0000000111 0001110001 1100000000.

Here there are two occurrences of $Consec(Po(S), 2)$, on the intervals [8,16] and [14,22]. This means that $Prog(Consec(Po(S), 2))$ holds throughout [8,22], and since it does not hold at 7 or 23, the event $Po(Prog(Consec(Po(S), 2)))$ occurs on [8,22].

The same sequence gives us an example of immediately consecutive occurrences. The event $For(S, 3); For(-S, 3)$ occurs on [8,13] and [14,19]. Hence we can see that this event holds over [8,19]. On the other hand it does not hold at 7 or 20,* and hence

$$Po(Prog(For(S, 3); For(-S, 3)))$$

occurs on [8,19]. These examples show that in general $Po(Prog(E))$ is not the same as E: it is only for events E of a type that does not admit overlapping or immediately consecutive occurrences that this identity holds. Examples of such events are $Po(S)$ and $For(S, n)$.

* $For(S, 3); For(-S, 3)$ does not occur on [20,25], since $For(-S, 3)$ doesn't hold on [23,25]: in order for this to be the case we would need $-(-S))$, i.e., S, to hold at 26.

2.2.10 Completed events: the operator $Perf$

$Prog$ gives us one way of deriving states from events, enabling us to describe the state of the world at a time in terms of the events that are in progress then. Another way is to describe the world in terms of events that are completed. For this we use the operator $Perf$ which has the following holding condition:

Perf For a durative event E, the state $Perf(E)$ holds at k iff E occurs on some interval $[m, n]$ such that $n < k$.

For an instantaneous event E, the state $Perf(E)$ holds at k iff E occurs at some instant $n][n + 1$ such that $n < k$.

The operator $Perf$ roughly corresponds to the perfect tense in English, so that, for example, if E is the event "John flies across the Atlantic", $Perf(E)$ is the state "John has flown across the Atlantic".

The relationship between Po and $Prog$ is roughly paralleled by that between $Ingr$ and $Perf$. The facts, easily verified, are as follows:

1. If E is an instantaneous event, then the first occurrence of this event is also the only occurrence of $Ingr(Perf(E))$.
2. If E is a durative event, then the event $Ingr(Perf(E))$ marks the completion of the first occurrence of E.
3. If state S holds, but has not always held, then so does the state $Perf(Ingr(S))$.

One can also define a temporal mirror-image of $Perf$, which we denote $Pros$, with holding condition

Pros For a durative event E, the state $Pros(E)$ holds at k iff E occurs on some interval $[m, n]$ such that $k < m$.

For an instantaneous event E, the state $Pros(E)$ holds at k iff E occurs at some instant $n - 1][n$ such that $k < n$.

2.2.11 Frequency of occurrence

Our final state-forming operator is the *Frequentative* operator $Freq$. Given an event E, the state $Freq(E)$ holds if E is occurring repeatedly. In English this is the natural interpretation of the Continuous Tense when used with a verb denoting an event with no or very short duration, as in "John is knocking at the door", which says there is a sequence of knocks rather than a single knock in progress. It is impossible to give a precise formal definition of this notion, but the following definition, for all its crudeness, enables us to express roughly what we want. We shall use $Freq(E, p/q)$ to mean that E is occurring with a frequency of at least p occurrences in q atomic intervals:

Freq For an event E, the state $Freq(E, p/q)$ holds at k iff k is in an interval $[m, n]$ on which occurs $Times(E, r)$ for some r such that $r/(n - m + 1) \geq p/q$.

This construction is related to, but not the same, as the notion of a *periodic* event type, which occurs at regular intervals, or else in correlation with other specified event types. Such events have been the focus of considerable research in the temporal representation and reasoning community, e.g., by [Terenziani, 1996]. For further discussion, see Chapter 5.

2.2.12 Processes and activities

Progressives and frequentatives are examples of *processes*. Here we treat a process as a kind of state, but one which has a texture on larger timescales than the atomic. A very simple process is illustrated by the sequence

0101010101 0101010101 0101010101 0101010101

which simply consists of our basic state alternating between "on" and "off" on consecutive atomic intervals. We can treat this as a state at a higher level of description. Suppose we label it as $Alt(S)$. Then $Alt(S)$ holds throughout the above sequence, and hence on every atomic interval making up the sequence. Its holding on any one such interval is not determined by what is the case at that interval considered in isolation, but by what is the case over a larger context in which that interval occurs. This can lend a somewhat indeterminate character to the process, which becomes particularly apparent if we consider a situation in which the process starts or stops, e.g., the sequence

0000000000 1010101010 1010101010 1111111111

Here $Alt(S)$ clearly holds over the interval [11,30], and clearly does not hold at any time during either [1,9] and [32,40]. But does it hold on the atomic intervals 10 and 31? There is no principled way of choosing whether to regard the holding of $-S$ at 10 as a continuation of the unbroken holding of $-S$ over [1,9], or as the first state in the process $Alt(S)$ which continues over [11,30]; and likewise at the other end.

The process $Alt(S)$ can be regarded as *uniform* in that it looks the same throughout the time that it holds. Some processes are *progressive* in that they involve a systematic change during the time that they hold. An example would be a processes by which state S comes to hold for an ever greater proportion of time. This is illustrated in the sequence

$\cdots$ 0000000010 0000010000 0100001000 1001011011 1011110111 1101111111 $\cdots$

in which determination of the onset and termination of the process is even more problematic.

2.3 Systems with finitely-many states in discrete time

In the previous section we saw that even with a single binary state in discrete time an astonishing range of different kinds of eventuality can be described. There are several ways in which we could make the system we are studying more complicated. Two obvious choices are (i) to consider a state having more than two values, and (ii) to consider more than one state. These are in fact equivalent, as we shall show.

2.3.1 One many-valued state *vs* many binary states

The first option is to generalise from a state which can assume only the two values "on" and "off" to a state which can assume a range of values, which for the present we shall assume to be finite. A state of this kind is known, following McCarthy and Hayes [McCarthy and Hayes, 1969], as a **fluent**. Indeed, an ordinary two-valued state can be regarded as the limiting case of a fluent in which the range of values is reduced to two—a so-called **boolean fluent**. A general finite-valued fluent f can take values from some pre-assigned set $V_f =$

$\{f_1, f_2, \ldots, f_n\}$. To say that at time k the fluent f takes value f_i we write $Holds(f = f_i, k)$. A history can then be portrayed as a sequence of values from V_f, e.g.,

$$\cdots f_3 f_3 f_3 f_4 f_5 f_6 f_6 f_6 f_6 f_2 f_3 f_3 f_1 f_1 f_1 f_1 \cdots$$

The second option is to consider a finite set of binary states $\mathbf{S} = \{S_1, S_2, \ldots, S_n\}$. Each of these states behaves like the single state S considered in the Section 2.2. A history must be presented as a correlated set of sequences, one for each state in $\mathbf{S}$:

S_1 :	⋯	0	0	0	0	0	0	1	1	1	0	0	0	0	0	0	1	1	1	1	1	⋯
S_2 :	⋯	0	0	0	1	1	1	1	1	1	1	1	1	1	0	0	0	0	0	0	0	⋯
S_3 :	⋯	1	1	1	1	1	1	1	1	0	1	1	1	1	1	1	1	0	0	0	1	⋯

The states are not necessarily independent of one another. In the example above, S_1 and S_3 are never "off" together. This might be a coincidence, or it might be that we are using S_1 and S_3 to model states in the world which necessarily have this property.

We can replace the three states S_1, S_2, and S_3 by a single fluent f which takes eight values according to the rule

$$f = v(S_1) + 2v(S_2) + 4v(S_3),$$

where $v(S_i)$ is 1 or 0 according as S_i is "on" or "off". The triple sequence shown above can then be represented by a single sequence for f:

$$\cdots 44466677366664451115 \cdots$$

Since S_1 and S_3 are never off together, the values $f = 0$ and $f = 2$ do not occur. We can build in this dependency between S_1 and S_2 by making f six-valued rather than eight-valued.

This shows us how we can take an arbitrary finite-valued fluent f and replace it by means of a finite set of binary states. Suppose we have a fluent f which takes values from the set $\{a, b, c, d, e\}$. Since $2^2 < 5 \leq 2^3$, we shall need three binary states to model this. But three independent states give rise to eight values; to reduce these to five we must introduce appropriate dependencies. There are many ways of doing this. A simple solution is to have states S_1, S_2, S_3 such that whenever S_1 is "on", S_2 and S_3 must both be "off". Then a suitable mapping between values of f and values of the S_i is:

f	S_1	S_2	S_3
a	off	off	off
b	off	off	on
c	off	on	off
d	off	on	on
e	on	off	off

On this scheme we can explain the "meaning" of the three states as follows:

S_1 is the state $f = e$.
S_2 is the state $(f = c) \vee (f = d)$.
S_3 is the state $(f = b) \vee (f = d)$.

Of course, a simpler, but much less economical, way of representing the fluent f by means of a set of binary states is to have one such state for each possible value of f, thus $f = a$, $f = b, \ldots$, and $f = e$, and constrain these states to be pairwise incompatible.

We have shown that the two suggested extensions to a one-state system, namely a many-state system and a system with a many-valued fluent, are interconvertible, and therefore in a formal sense equivalent. This means that we can choose whichever system most suits us for any particular purpose and be assured that any results we derive are transferable, *mutandis mutatis*, to the other system. Not only that, but we can also, if we wish, use a "mixed" system in which there are several many-valued fluents instead of, or in addition to, a number of binary states.

All the phenomena we saw in the previous section in connection with a single binary state also exist in the more complicated systems we are now considering. But in addition, there are further interesting phenomena which are worth exploring here.

2.3.2 State-spaces, adjacency, and quasi-continuity

The set V_f of values that can be assumed by a fluent f can be thought of as a kind of "space", and change in the value of f as a kind of "motion" through this space. One interesting possibility is that such "motion" resembles ordinary motion in being continuous. Of course, in a discrete space, continuity as we ordinarily understand it is not possible; but if we endow the space with an *adjacency* relation defining the "next-door neighbours" of each of the values of f making up the space, then we can describe a motion through the space as "quasi-continuous" so long as any instantaneous change in the value of f is between next-door neighbours.

As an example, suppose we have a 9-valued fluent, taking integer values in the range 0, …, 8. Many different adjacency relations can be defined on this space, of which three are illustrated in Figure 2.1.

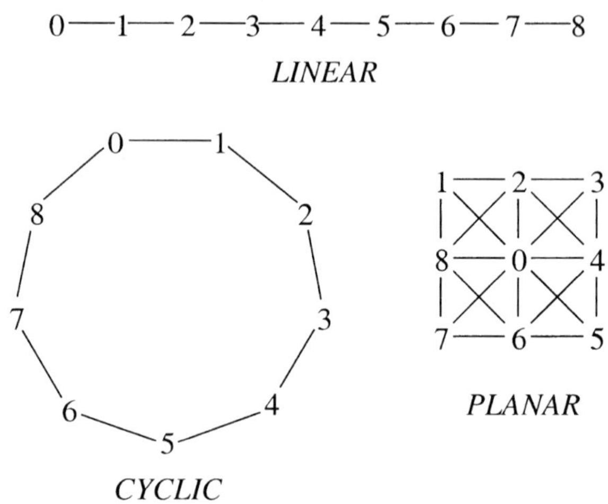

Figure 2.1: *Three adjacency relations on* $\{0,1,2,3,4,5,6,7,8\}$.

If change of value of f is constrained to be quasi-continuous in the sense defined above, then each of the three adjacency relations portrayed here defines certain sequences as possible and others as impossible. For example, the sequence

$$\cdots 88888880000000 \cdots \tag{S4}$$

is possible in the cyclic and planar spaces, but not in the linear one, whereas the sequence

$$\cdots 22222224444444 \cdots$$

is only possible in the planar space. The sequence

$$\cdots 2222222255555555 \cdots \tag{S5}$$

is ruled out in all three spaces.

2.3.3 Instantaneous and Durative Transitions

Example **S4** above illustrates a phenomenon we have already seen in connection with a single state: an instantaneous transition. Now instead of being a transition from "on" to "off", as in the previous section, it is a transition from one value of the fluent, $f = 8$, to another value, $f = 0$. We therefore cannot represent it by means of the operator $Ingr$. Instead we shall introduce a new operator for this.

Example **S5**, if it could occur, would also represent an instantaneous transition. However, in all three of the value-spaces illustrated, it is only possible to get from $f = 2$ to $f = 5$ by passing through some intermediate values. In the linear model, we might have

$$\cdots 22222223334445555555 \cdots$$

and this sequence is also possible in the other two models. The other models have other possibilities as well, e.g.,

$$\cdots 22222222108765555555 \cdots$$

which is possible in both the cyclic and planar models, and

$$\cdots 222222222888666655555555 \cdots$$

which is only possible in the planar model. In all these cases, what we have is a **durative transition** between the states $f = 2$ and $f = 5$.

We shall use the same operator $Trans$ to construct both instantaneous and durative transitions, but give separate occurrence conditions for the two cases, as follows:

Trans If S_1 and S_2 are two mutually incompatible states, then the event $Trans(S_1, S_2)$ has

- an instantaneous occurrence at $m][n$ iff S_1 holds at m and S_2 holds at n, and
- a durative occurrence on $[m, n]$ iff S_1 holds at $m - 1$ and S_2 holds at $n + 1$ and both $-S_1$ and $-S_2$ hold on $[m, n]$.

The reason for the third conjunct in the condition for a durative occurrence is that it ensures that $Trans(S_1, S_2)$ satisfies the condition **UNI**.

2.3.4 Formal and material progressive operators

In everyday language, we might describe the event $Trans(f = f_1, f = f_2)$ in the terms "The value of f changes from f_1 to f_2", and many kinds of change we observe in the world can be described in this way. Now suppose we want to say instead that "The value of f is changing from f_1 to f_2". This says that a certain state obtains that can be characterised in terms of an event which is in progress. The obvious way to represent this is using the progressive operator to form the state

$$Prog(Trans(f = f_1, f = f_2)),$$

but this is in some respects problematic. The holding conditions of this complex state can be derived from **Prog** and **Trans** as follows:

$Prog(Trans(f = f_1, f = f_2))$ holds at m iff there are times l and n such that $l < m < n$ and

- $f = f_1$ holds at l,
- $f = f_2$ holds at n,
- neither $f = f_1$ nor $f = f_2$ holds on any subinterval of $[l + 1, n - 1]$.

In the planar model illustrated in Figure 2.1, consider the sequence

$$\cdots 1112186600\ 0111000445\ 433 \cdots$$

Note that $f = 2$ holds at time $t = 4$, that $f = 5$ holds at $t = 20$, and neither of these states holds at any time during the interval [5,19]. It follows that $Trans(f = 2, f = 5)$ occurs on this interval, and therefore that $Prog(Trans(f = 2, f = 5))$ holds on all of its subintervals. At $t = 10$, f has the value 0. If at this time we ask what is happening, is it a satisfactory answer to say that the value of f is changing from 2 to 5? There are two possible objections to this: first, that at $t = 10$, the value of f is not actually changing at all, since it remains 0 over the interval [9,11]; and second, even if one grants that, on a longer perspective, the value is indeed changing, the immediate change is between 6 and 1 (there being an occurrence of $Trans(f = 6, f = 1)$ on the interval [9,11]), i.e., a movement further from 5 and nearer to 2, so it would be perverse to describe this as part of a transition from 2 to 5.

The problem here arises from trying to use abstract models to explain the meanings of linguistic phenomena which are normally only encountered in concrete contexts. In some concrete exemplifications of the abstract pattern presented above, it would indeed be appropriate to say that the change here represented by $Trans(f = 2, f = 5)$ is in progress at $t = 10$, whereas in others it would not. As an example of the first kind, consider the following. On a certain day, I drive from Bristol to Northampton. I stop for lunch in Swindon and drive on. When I get to Oxford, I realise that I have left my wallet in Swindon. I rush back to where I had lunch and to my relief find that the wallet is safe. I then drive on through Oxford to Northampton. The journey is portrayed in Figure 2.2. Suppose that while I am driving back between Oxford and Swindon someone asks me what I am doing. I reply "I'm driving from Bristol to Northampton", and this is surely a perfectly correct and reasonable reply, even though I am just then travelling in exactly the opposite direction to the way I should be going in order to drive from Bristol to Northampton. It is very much a matter of the perspective one adopts. I am indeed simultaneously driving from Bristol to Northampton and from Oxford to Swindon; the former description is appropriate when taking a broader perspective, involving not just a longer time-scale but also more ulterior purposes than the narrower perspective within which the latter description is more appropriate.

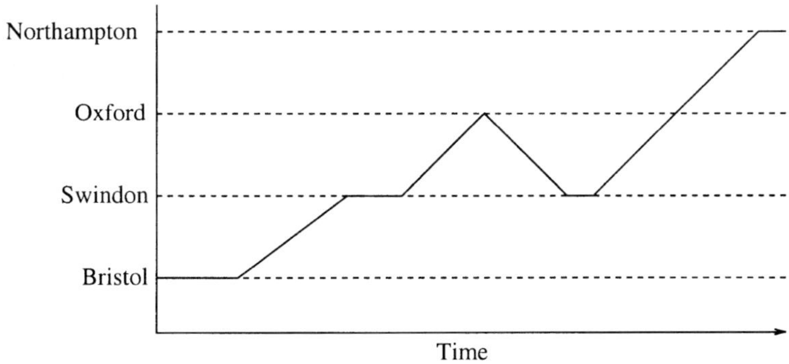

Figure 2.2: *A journey from Bristol to Northampton.*

Now consider a more extreme case. Suppose someone who lives in Bristol moves house to Oxford, and then several years later moves again to Northampton. Suppose further that they never revisit Bristol after having left it, and never visit Northampton before moving house there. Both journeys—from Bristol to Oxford, and from Oxford to Northampton, are undertaken by car. It would surely be stretching things to say, during this person's years-long sojourn in Oxford, that they were in the process of driving from Bristol to Northampton. The only circumstance that could render this in the least plausible is that the person set off from Bristol with the intention of eventually settling in Northampton, always regarding the stay in Oxford as only temporary.

We can define two extremes. On the one hand there is the **formal progressive** represented by our operator $Prog$. The state $Prog(E)$ is true at any time between the start of an occurrence of the event E and its end. It takes no account of whether or not the states or activities obtaining at these times contribute in any way to the final completion of E. This represents the broadest perspective, a perspective that is able to overlook all temporary deviations from, or interruptions to, the progress of the event. At the other extreme is what might be called the **material progressive**, which does take into account only those states or activities which make a material contribution to the progress of the event E. In our example, "I am driving from Bristol to Northampton", when interpreted in this narrow, material sense, is only true at those times when I am actually driving, and when the driving I am doing is indeed taking me forward along the route from Bristol to Northampton—in other words to the times in Figure 2.2 where the graph of my journey has positive gradient, thus excluding both the time I spend in Swindon having lunch and the time I spend driving back to retrieve my wallet. We frequently use both the material and the formal senses of the progressive.* The

*Nor should one forget that we frequently—perhaps most frequently of all—use the progressive in a "modalised" sense that does not commit us to the eventual completion of the event in question. This leads to the so-called "imperfective paradox" [Dowty, 1979] by which, while on the one hand it cannot be true that I have been driving without it also being true that I have driven, on the other hand it *can* be true that I have been driving from Bristol to Northampton, without it ever being true that I have driven from Bristol to Northampton.

difficulty with the material sense is that it seems to be impossible to give a formal holding condition for it.

2.3.5 Formal and material perfect-tense operators

A similar difficulty affects the operator $Perf$, which corresponds to some, but not all, uses of the English perfect tense. At 1.30 p.m. on Monday I truthfully say "I have had lunch". At the same time on Tuesday I truthfully say "I have not had lunch yet". We cannot represent these two statements as $Perf(E)$ and $-Perf(E)$for the same event E, since the holding condition for $Perf(E)$ implies that if it holds at a certain time then it must also hold at *any* later time: in short, $Perf(E)$ is *irrevocable*. There are two ways we might avoid this difficulty.

One way is to claim that when I say "I have had lunch" on Monday, what I mean is "I have had Monday's lunch", and this remains true ever after, whereas when I say "I have not had lunch" on Tuesday, what I mean is "I have not had Tuesday's lunch". Formally, we would have to represent these two statements as $Perf(E_1)$ and $-Perf(E_2)$, using different event-types to avoid the incompatibility.

The alternative solution is to say that as with the progressive, we use the perfect in a range of different senses, with at one extreme the **formal perfect** represented by $Perf$, with the property of irrevocability built into that operator, and at the other extreme a **material perfective** which takes account of the material state resulting from the occurrence of an event and only continues to affirm that the event has happened so long as that state persists. In linguistics these two senses of the perfect are recognised as just two amongst a larger number, commonly given as four [Comrie, 1976]. As with the material sense of the progressive, it is impossible to give formal holding conditions for the material perfect.

2.3.6 Logical operations on states

We now turn to consider various logical operations on states, fluents and events. Regarding states, we have already met $-S$, the negation of state S, which holds on just those atomic intervals on which S does not hold. We have just given, in effect, the holding condition for $-S$, which we here state formally as

State-Neg The state $-S$ holds on the atomic interval n iff S does not hold on n.

From this condition we can readily derive the condition for $-S$ to hold over an arbitrary interval, as follows:

> The state $-S$ holds on the interval $[m, n]$ iff there is no atomic interval k, where $m \leq k \leq n$, on which S holds.

Note in particular that we *cannot* say, for an arbitrary interval, that $-S$ holds over it iff S does not hold over it, the reason being, of course, that S may hold on some of its subintervals, and $-S$ on others.

In Section 2.3.1 we identified a state S_3 with a disjunction $(f = b) \vee (f = d)$ of fluent-values. We must be a little more precise about this. Given a fluent f and a possible value for it, say b, the expression $f = b$ denotes that state which is "on" on precisely those atomic intervals when f has the value b, and "off" on all other atomic intervals. Thus $(f = b) \vee (f = d)$ is a disjunction of states, and we need to define its occurrence condition. In general, for states S_1 and S_2, we can define their disjunction $S_1 \vee S_2$ by the rule

State-disj The state $S_1 \vee S_2$ holds on the atomic interval n iff either S_1 or S_2 (or both) holds on n.

As with negation, we *cannot* say that $S_1 \vee S_2$ holds over an arbitrary interval if and only if either S_1 holds over it or S_2 holds over it (the "if" part is correct, but not the "only if" part).

State-disjunction enables us to bundle a set of states together in order to refer to states of affairs in more general terms. For example, in the planar adjacency model of Figure 2.1, we could introduce some bundled states as follows:

$$\begin{aligned} Top &= f = 1 \vee f = 2 \vee f = 3 \\ Right &= f = 3 \vee f = 4 \vee f = 5 \\ Bottom &= f = 5 \vee f = 6 \vee f = 7 \\ Left &= f = 7 \vee f = 8 \vee f = 1 \end{aligned}$$

We can then use these states as arguments for our operators, for example $Trans(Left, Right)$. This is a genuinely higher-level event-description than $Trans(f = 1, f = 3)$ and the like: while it is true that any occurrence of $Trans(Left, Right)$ must also be an occurrence of some more primitive event of the form $Trans(f = a, f = b)$, where $f = a$ is one of the disjuncts defining $Left$ and $f = b$ is one of the disjuncts defining $Right$, the converse does not hold. For example, in the sequence

1111111880 0443333333

there is an occurrence of $Trans(f = 1, f = 3)$ on the interval [8,13], but there is not an occurrence of $Trans(Left, Right)$ on that interval, even though $f = 1$ implies $Left$ and $f = 3$ implies $Right$. There *is* an occurrence of $Trans(Left, Right)$ in this sequence, but it occurs on the interval [10,11], being also an occurrence of $Trans(f = 8, f = 4)$.

In general we can say that for an interval i, $Occurs(Trans(S_1 \vee S_2, S_3 \vee S_4), i)$ implies

$$Occurs(Trans(S_1, S_3), i) \vee Occurs(Trans(S_1, S_4), i) \vee \\ Occurs(Trans(S_2, S_3), i) \vee Occurs(Trans(S_2, S_4), i),$$

but the converse implication does not hold. With other operators, we may not even have such a simple implication as that. For example, in the sequence

0000000000 1111188888 0000000000

there is an occurrence of $Po(Left)$ on [11,20], but no occurrence of the form $Po(f = x)$ on that interval; while on the other hand there is an occurrence of $Po(f = 1)$ on [11,15], and an occurrence of $Po(f = 8)$ on [16,20], but $Po(Left)$ does not occur on either of these intervals.

Turning now to *conjunction*, we define the state $S_1 \wedge S_2$ by the occurrence condition

State-conj The state $S_1 \wedge S_2$ holds over the atomic interval n if both S_1 and S_2 hold over n.

This rule generalises straightforwardly to arbitrary intervals:

The state $S_1 \wedge S_2$ holds over the interval $[m, n]$ iff S_1 and S_2 both hold over $[m, n]$.

As with state-disjunction, the behaviour of state-conjunction in interaction with operators like $Trans$ and Po is complex. We shall not labour the details here; the reader should have no difficulty in constructing appropriate examples to illustrate the various relationships.

2.3.7 Logical operations on events

Given two events E_1 and E_2, there seem to be two ways to form a third event that might reasonably be called their conjunction. These are perhaps best illustrated by means of concrete examples:

- Suppose that Mary and John both take the cross-channel ferry from Dover to Calais. There is an occurrence of the event "Mary travels from Dover to Calais" and also an occurrence of the event "John travels from Dover to Calais", and the two occurrences occupy exactly the same interval of time. We can say that over that interval Mary travelled from Dover to Calais *and* John travelled from Dover to Calais. This gives us one kind of conjunction of two events.

- Consider an occurrence of the event "Mary travels from Dover to Calais". The very same occurrence is also an occurrence of the events "Mary travels from England to France" and of "Mary has a boat trip". Thus we can say that Mary travelled from England to France *and* Mary had a boat trip. If we think of all the possible occurrences of the former event-type as forming one set, and all the possible occurrences of the latter as forming another, then the event we are talking about is in the intersection of the two sets, and it seems natural to construct an event-type whose possible occurrence are precisely all the elements of that intersection. This event would be another kind of conjunction of two events, and would be a subtype of both of them (in fact their maximal common subtype).

At first sight these two kinds of conjunction seem to be sharply distinct, but it proves to be quite hard to characterise the distinction unambiguously. Let us use the notations $E_1 \wedge E_2$ and $E_1 \cap E_2$ for the two kinds of conjunction. What we should like to say is something like the following:

- The event $E_1 \wedge E_2$ occurs on the interval $[m, n]$ iff both the events E_1 and E_2 occur on $[m, n]$.

- X is an occurrence of $E_1 \cap E_2$ iff X is an occurrence both of E_1 and of E_2.

Unfortunately, these two definitions provide us with no ground for distinguishing between $E_1 \wedge E_2$ and $E_1 \cap E_2$. This is because the first definition characterises an event-type, as usual, in terms of its occurrence condition, i.e., the condition for there to be an occurrence of the event at a given time, whereas the second definition refers instead to the occurrences of an event as individuals with implicit criteria of identity. We need to know what it means to say that an occurrence described in one way is the very same occurrence as an occurrence described in another way. Intuitively it seems that an occurrence of "Mary travels from Dover to Calais" cannot be identical to an occurrence of "John travels from Dover to Calais", since one of them involves Mary and the other involves John. Implicitly, we are appealing to some criterion of identity for occurrences which entails that occurrences involving different participants cannot be identical. An obvious criterion to use would be that occurrences are identical if they involve the same participants undergoing the same changes. Davidson [Davidson, 1969] has a clever example to show that this can lead to counterintuitive results. Consider a metal ball which rotates through 35 degrees while getting warmer. Is the rotation of the ball the same occurrence as the warming of the ball? Davidson points out that in both cases we are referring to the same movements of the same molecules; it is impossible, even in principle, to separate out movements which contribute to the rotation from movements which contribute to the warming. By the suggested criterion of identity, they are the same occurrence, whereas intuitively we might have good grounds for regarding them as different.

We here touch on an issue that has been the subject of much philosophical discussion: the characterisation of events generally, of which the matter of event identity is one important aspect. To pursue this further here would take us too far from our main theme; a useful reference is [Casati and Varzi, 1996].

2.4 Finite-state systems in continuous time

Up to now we have assumed that the flow of time can be represented by means of a discrete series of indivisible intervals. For many purposes this is a satisfactory model of time, and as we have seen, it certainly allows us to define many temporal phenomena of interest. In many contexts, however, it is more usual to model the flow of time as a continuum, ordered like the real numbers rather than the integers.* "Ordering time like the real numbers" represents a radical departure from the discrete model we have been assuming up to now, since whereas in the discrete model we have atomic intervals to provide the elementary building blocks out of which all other intervals are built, and in terms of which instants (the meeting-points of adjacent atomic intervals) can be defined, in the continuous model there are no such building blocks, since every interval can be endlessly subdivided into smaller ones. In the discrete model, all temporal phenomena can be defined in terms of the holding of states on atomic intervals; in the continuous model there is no similar set of intervals such that all temporal phenomena can be defined in terms of the holding of states on intervals of the set. There are two approaches we might take here: either to take the elementary facts to be the holdings of states over arbitrary intervals (with appropriate dependencies amongst such facts), or to shift the burden of supporting the elementary facts from intervals onto instants. We shall examine the former approach in this section, and the latter in the next.

Since we no longer have atomic intervals, we cannot use designations like $[m, n]$, where m and n are integers, to denote arbitrary intervals in this system. Nor, since at this stage we do not wish to rely on instants to provide the conceptual underpinning of our temporal model, will we use designations like (x, y), where x and y are real numbers. Instead, we shall simply use notations like i and j to represent intervals, these forming a set on which the standard Interval Calculus relations ('meets', 'overlaps', etc; see previous chapter, Fig. 1.3) are defined, and we shall continue to use the predicate $Holds$ for assigning states to *these* intervals, e.g., $Holds(S, i)$. Lacking atomic intervals, we are no longer in a position to derive the rule **HOM** as a simple consequence of any more basic principles. Instead we have to postulate it as an axiom of our system. As before, we shall find no reason to say that a state holds on an instant, although we can still define instants as the meeting points of intervals; that is, whenever interval i meets interval j (i.e., $i\texttt{Meets}j$), we can define an instant $i][j$ at which they meet, the criterion of identity for instants being given by the rule

$$i][j = i'][j' \text{ iff } i \text{ meets } j'.$$

*There is also, of course, an intermediate possibility, which is to order time like the rational numbers. It is not always appreciated what a bizarre model of time is implied by this option: in particular, rational time is unable to provide an intuitively reasonable model of continuous change.

(We could equally put 'i' meets j' instead of 'i meets j'': the axiom $\mathbf{AH}_1$ given in Chapter 1, §1.4.2, ensures that these two conditions stand or fall together.) An ordering relation $\prec$ on instants can be defined by the rule

$i][j \prec k][l$ iff there is an interval r such that i meets r and r meets l.

If interval i meets interval j, we shall use the notation $i + j$ to denote the interval which begins when i begins and ends when j ends; $i + j$ therefore represents the "sum" of the two intervals in an intuitively natural sense.*

Almost all the phenomena discussed in the previous section can be described in the current setting also, although the definitions have to be modified in order to take account of the non-existence of atomic intervals. In some of the following definitions we refer to the "beginning" and "end" of an interval i, denoted $beg(i)$ and $end(i)$ respectively; these refer to the instants which mark the meeting points of i with intervals which respectively meet or are met by i.

Ingr$_{\text{CONT}}$ $Ingr(S)$ occurs at $i][j$ iff $-S$ holds on some interval which meets j, and S holds on some interval which i meets.

Po$_{\text{CONT}}$ $Po(S)$ occurs on i iff S holds on i and $-S$ holds both on an interval which meets i and an interval which i meets.

Consec-D$_{\text{CONT}}$ If E is a durative event, then

- $Consec(E, 1)$ occurs on i iff E occurs on i;
- For $n > 1$, $Consec(E, n)$ occurs on i iff there is an initial subinterval j and a final subinterval k of i such that $end(j) \preceq beg(k)$, E occurs on j but not on any interval l such that $end(j) \prec end(l) \prec beg(k)$, and $Consec(E, n-1)$ occurs on k but not on any interval l such that $end(j) \prec beg(l) \prec beg(k)$.

Consec-I$_{\text{CONT}}$ If E is an instantaneous event, then

- $Consec(E, 2)$ occurs on i iff E occurs at both $beg(i)$ and $end(i)$.
- $Consec(E, n)$ occurs on i iff E occurs at $beg(i)$, and there is a proper final subinterval j of i such that $Consec(E, n-1)$ occurs on j and E does not occur between $beg(i)$ and $beg(j)$.

Times-D$_{\text{CONT}}$ If E is a durative event, then

- $Times(E, 1)$ occurs on i iff E occurs on i;
- For $n > 1$, $Times(E, n)$ occurs on i iff i has a proper initial subinterval j and a proper final subinterval k such that E occurs on j but not on any other subinterval of i beginning earlier than k, and $Times(E, n-1)$ occurs on k.

Times-I$_{\text{CONT}}$ If E is an instantaneous event, then $Times(E, n)$ occurs on i iff $Consec(E, n)$ occurs on i.

*The existence of such an interval is ensured by axiom $\mathbf{AH}_5$ of Allen and Hayes; see Chapter 1, Section 1.4.2.

ISC$_{\text{CONT}}$ If E_1 and E_2 are both durative, then $E_1; E_2$ occurs on the interval i iff there are intervals j, k such that $i = j + k$, E_1 occurs on j, and E_2 occurs on k.

If E_1 is durative and E_2 is instantaneous, then $E_1; E_2$ occurs on i iff E_1 occurs on i and E_2 occurs at $end(i)$.

If E_1 is instantaneous and E_2 is durative, then $E_1; E_2$ occurs on i iff E_1 occurs at $beg(i)$ and E_2 occurs on i.

GSC$_{\text{CONT}}$ If E_1 and E_2 are both durative, then $E_1;; E_2$ occurs on the interval i iff i contains an initial subinterval j and a final subinterval k such that $end(j) \preceq beg(k)$, E_1 occurs on j but not on any interval l such that $end(j) \prec end(l) \prec beg(k)$, and E_2 occurs on k but not on any interval l such that $end(j) \prec beg(l) \prec beg(k)$.

If E_1 is durative and E_2 is instantaneous, then $E_1;; E_2$ occurs on i iff there is an initial subinterval j of i such that E_1 occurs on j but not on any interval k such that $end(j) \prec end(k) \prec end(i)$, and E_2 occurs at $end(i)$ but at no instant t such that $end(j) \preceq t \prec end(i)$.

If E_1 is instantaneous and E_2 is durative, then $E_1;; E_2$ occurs on i iff there is a final subinterval j of i such that E_2 occurs on j but not on any interval k such that $beg(i) \prec beg(k) \prec beg(j)$, and E_1 occurs at $beg(i)$ but at no instant t such that $beg(i) \prec t \preceq beg(j)$.

If E_1 and E_2 are both instantaneous, then $E_1;; E_2$ occurs on i iff E_1 occurs at $beg(i)$, E_2 occurs at $end(i)$, and neither event occurs on any instant dividing i.

Trans$_{\text{CONT}}$ If S_1 and S_2 are two mutually incompatible states, then the event $Trans(S_1, S_2)$ has

- an instantaneous occurrence at $i][j$ iff S_1 holds over some interval which meets j and S_2 holds over some interval which i meets; and
- a durative occurrence on i iff S_1 holds over some interval which meets i and S_2 holds over some interval which i meets, and both $-S_1$ and $-S_2$ hold on i.

We can similarly modify the holding conditions of states, as follows:

Prog$_{\text{CONT}}$ For a durative event E, the state $Prog(E)$ holds on the interval i iff E occurs on an interval j such that i is a subinterval of j.

Perf$_{\text{CONT}}$ For a durative event E, the state $Perf(E)$ holds on the interval i iff E occurs on some interval which is before or meets i.

For an instantaneous event E, the state $Perf(E)$ holds on the interval i iff E occurs on some instant no later than the beginning of i.

Pros$_{\text{CONT}}$ For a durative event E, the state $Pros(E)$ holds on i iff E occurs on some interval which i is before or meets.

For an instantaneous event E, the state $Pros(E)$ holds on i iff E occurs at some instant no earlier than the end of i.

The one operator we defined over discrete time which does not straightforwardly carry over into continuous time is For. The event-type $For(S, n)$ cannot be defined in continuous time unless we stipulate how durations are to be measured. Discrete time comes with its own inherent measure of duration, obtained by counting atomic intervals, but for continuous time we have to define duration separately, over and above the definition of qualitative ordering relation on intervals.

We have changed the notation and the language we use for talking about intervals, but how much has really changed in the transition from discrete to continuous time? This depends on how much we allow ourselves to exploit the infinitely dissectible nature of the time line. A common procedure is actually to negate the potential dissectibility by insisting that the pattern of holding of every state behaves in a way that can, in effect be simulated in discrete time. This is done by introducing a "non-intermingling" principle [Galton, 1996b]. The most satisfactory form of this principle is that of Davis [Davis, 1992], which we may formulate as the following "finite dissection" rule:

FD Every interval i can be partitioned into finitely many non-overlapping intervals $i = i_1 + i_2 + \cdots + i_n$ such that for $1 \leq m \leq n$, either S or $-S$ holds on i_m.

Suppose now that **FD** holds for every state, and that we have only finitely many primitive states $S_1, \ldots, S_k$. Take an arbitrary interval i. For each state S_k, there is a partition $i = i_{k,1} + i_{k,2} + \cdots + i_{k,n_k}$ into subintervals over which S_k has constant value. From this partition we can derive a set of instants

$$\mathcal{I}_k = \{i_{k,1}][i_{k,2}, i_{k,2}][i_{k,3}, \ldots, i_{k,n_k-1}][i_{k,n_k}\}.$$

Let

$$\mathcal{I} = \{t_0, t_s\} \cup \bigcup_{k=1}^{n} \mathcal{I}_k,$$

where t_0 and t_s are the beginning and end of i respectively. Relabel the elements of $\mathcal{I}$ in ascending order as $t_0 < t_1 < t_2 < \ldots < t_{s-1} < t_s$. Now for $0 < r \leq s$, consider the interval $j_r = (t_{r-1}, t_r)$ which begins at t_{r-1} and ends at t_r. Then each of the states $S_1, \ldots, S_k$ has constant value over this interval, since for each of the states it is a subinterval of one of the elements of the partition of i determined by that state. Hence *the world does not change over the interval* j_r.

Since we can partition any interval into non-overlapping subintervals over which no change occurs, our temporal model is isomorphic to a discrete time model in which each of these "non change" intervals is an atomic interval (or, if we prefer, is composed of some *finite* sequence of atomic intervals). We conclude, then, that in the presence of *finitely many* primitive states and the *finite dissection* principle, a continuous-time model does not yield any phenomena over and above what is already afforded by discrete-time models.

This does not mean that finite-state, finite-dissection continuous-time (FFC) models are of no value. Suppose, for example, we have a FFC model $\mathcal{M}$. Corresponding to this there will be a discrete model $\mathcal{M}_\mathrm{D}$ constructed as described above. Now suppose we wish to add an extra primitive state to the model. We can do this to the FFC model without in any way disturbing what we already have in place: we still have the same intervals with the same relations between them, and all temporal phenomena definable in terms of our initial set of primitive states remain unchanged. All that happens is that we are *adding* some new information. Call the new FFC model $\mathcal{M}'$. We can construct a discrete model $\mathcal{M}'_{\mathrm{D}}$ from this model also. Now consider the relationship between $\mathcal{M}_{\mathrm{D}}$ and $\mathcal{M}'_{\mathrm{D}}$. Whereas $\mathcal{M}$ and $\mathcal{M}'$ have exactly the same instants and intervals, in general we will expect $\mathcal{M}'_{\mathrm{D}}$ to have *more* atomic intervals than $\mathcal{M}'_{\mathrm{D}}$. An atomic interval n in $\mathcal{M}_{\mathrm{D}}$ might be divided into a sequence $n', n'+1, n'+2, \ldots, n'+m$ in $\mathcal{M}'_{\mathrm{D}}$, since although the primitive states in the former model all remain unchanged over the interval n, the new state which has been added to produce the latter model might change its value m times over that interval.

It follows that unless we know in advance some discrete sequence of intervals such that none of the states we will ever need to consider in our model changes value within any of the intervals in the sequence, we would be well advised to opt for a continuous model of time. This allows us much more flexibility when it comes to updating our model by the addition of new states (or even change of information regarding the pattern of incidence of existing states). And of course, if we want to relax either the finite-state constraint, or the finite-dissection rule, then continuous time immediately affords phenomena that prevent the simple transformation to a discrete model.

2.5 Continuous state-spaces

Up to now we have considered models in which the number of distinct primitive states or fluents is finite, and in which each fluent can take on only finitely many distinct values. As soon as we relax these constraints, new phenomena appear.

We shall consider a single fluent f which is capable of taking arbitrary real-number values. (We could restrict this to real numbers in a given range, e.g. $(0,1)$, but this will not make any difference to what we consider below.) Suppose we have intervals i, j, and k such that i meets j and j meets k, that the state $f=0$ holds over i, that $f=1$ holds over k, and that neither $f=0$ nor $f=1$ holds over any subinterval of j. By $\mathbf{Trans}_{\mathrm{CONT}}$, it follows that $Trans(f=0, f=1)$ occurs over the interval j. But what exactly happens over the interval j?

In the previous sections we have adhered to the principle that the only sense in which a state can be said to hold at an instant is that it holds over an interval within which that instant falls. In the finite-state setting of those sections this is indeed a perfectly reasonable principle. If we apply it to the present case, what do we obtain?

We consider two possibilities. The first is that the finite dissection principle **FD** holds. In that case, we can divide j up into a sequence of contiguous subintervals $j_1, j_2, \ldots, j_n$ over each of which the value of f is constant. For $r = 1, \ldots, n$, let f take the value v_r over interval j_r. We have the situation pictured in Figure 2.3(a). This transition comprises a sequence of *discontinuous* steps, since for each r the value of f changes from v_r to v_{r+1} without passing through any intermediate values.

Can we get f to change continuously by relaxing the condition **FD**, while maintaining the requirement that whenever any state holds, it holds over an interval? Only by means of a highly artificial construction! To illustrate, we shall construct a continuous function $f:(0,1)\rightarrow(0,1)$. The construction proceeds in a sequence of stages as follows:

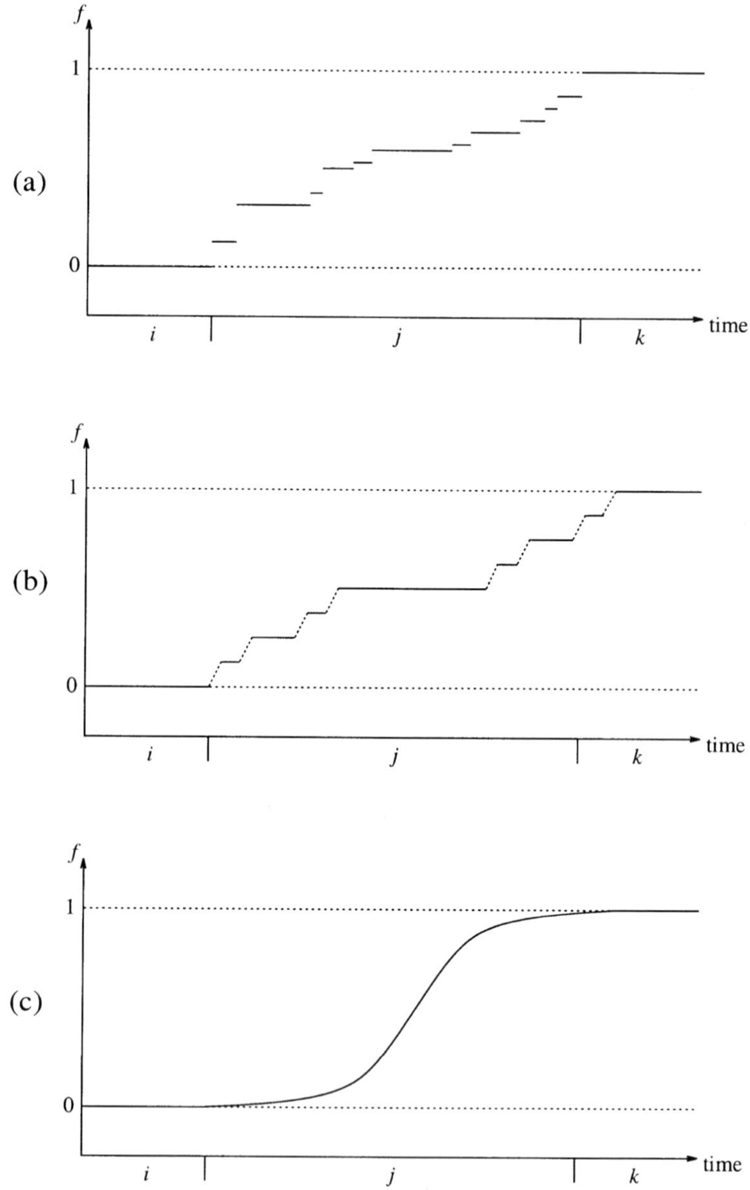

Figure 2.3: *Transitions from* $f = 0$ *to* $f = 1$.

Stage 1	For $x \in [1/3, 2/3]$, let $f(x) = 1/2$
Stage 2	For $x \in [1/9, 2/9]$, let $f(x) = 1/4$
	For $x \in [7/9, 8/9]$ let $f(x) = 3/4$
Stage 3	For $x \in [1/27, 2/27]$ let $f(x) = 1/8$
	For $x \in [7/27, 8/27]$ let $f(x) = 3/8$
	For $x \in [19/27, 20/27]$ let $f(x) = 5/8$
	For $x \in [25/27, 26/27]$ let $f(x) = 7/8$
$\vdots$	$\vdots$
Stage n	For $x \in [1/3^n, 2/3^n]$ let $f(x) = 1/2^n$
	For $x \in [7/3^n, 8/3^n]$ let $f(x) = 3/2^n$
	$\vdots$
	For $x \in [\frac{3^n-2}{3^n}, \frac{3^n-1}{3^n}]$ let $f(x) = \frac{2^n-1}{2^n}$
$\vdots$	$\vdots$

If we identify j with the temporal interval $(0, 1)$, this gives us the graph shown schematically in Figure 2.3(b). The change represented here is continuous, in the sense that the total change over an interval around any instant can be made as small as we like by choosing the interval to be short enough; note, however, that the set of values actually taken by the fluent is the set of rational numbers in [0,1] of the form $2^q p$ (where p and q are integers). Moreover, for every value of the form $2^q p$, there is some interval (of length 3^{-q}) over which the fluent takes that value. If all change were of this kind, then just as in the case of FFC systems, we would never need to say that a state holds at an instant.

As we have noted, the example just described is highly artificial. Nobody really believes that change in the real world occurs in this way! A much more natural model for change is illustrated in Figure 2.3(c). Here the fluent f is represented as a *smooth* continuous function. Often such functions will be expressible analytically by means of a formula such as $f(t) = 3x^2 - 2x^3$, which more or less fits the graph in our illustration over the interval $j = (0, 1)$. With this kind of change, we can no longer insist that it makes no sense to say that a state holds at an instant. During the course of a continuous change such as the one illustrated, no state of the form $f = v$ holds over an interval, yet for each v in the range $(0, 1)$, this state holds at some instant during the interval j. For example, the state $f = \frac{1}{9}$ holds at an instant exactly one third of the way through the interval—the instant to which it is natural, in this context, to assign the number $\frac{1}{3}$.

For this kind of description to be possible, we need to break away from our previous assumption and take seriously the idea of a state holding at an instant. The obvious possibility is to embrace the standard mathematical account of continuous change, by which the time line is represented by the real numbers, with each real number corresponding to exactly one instant, and a continuously-varying fluent represented by a continuous function on the real numbers. In this model, fluents are *primarily* evaluated at instants rather than over intervals, and hence conceptual priority is given to instants over intervals.

On this basis we define what it is for a state to hold over an interval by means of the equivalence

$$Holds(S, i) \Leftrightarrow \forall t \in iHolds(S, t).$$

Here we use the conventional set-theoretic notation $t \in i$ to express the relation between an instant and an interval within which it falls, without necessarily thereby embracing the idea that an interval *is* a set of instants. All the definitions in Section 2.4 can now be carried over unchanged into the present setting.

The mathematical language that is used in this kind of model is far removed from the everyday, qualitative terms we use for describing and reasoning about change in the world of experience. The mathematical language is necessary for the precise quantitative work required in many technical and scientific contexts, but it cannot be necessary for *all* our reasoning about change, since otherwise we would be unable to perform such reasoning without it: yet manifestly in our everyday lives we are frequently able to obtain an understanding of situations involving change that is at least adequate to enable us to achieve the more mundane of our everyday goals, without ever broaching on the complexities of a mathematical analysis. An important goal for AI is precisely to provide a model of the world which is capable of supporting this kind of everyday, rough-and-ready, qualitative reasoning.

It seems that a number of points of view are possible here. The most uncompromising would be to insist that we make full use of the available mathematical machinery, translating *all* everyday qualitative descriptions into the language of such machinery. To many this seems like overkill, and in any case the computational complexities involved may be prohibitively expensive. An alternative route is to embrace the conceptual clarity afforded by the finite-state interval-based models we have been looking at in previous sections, acknowledging that such models are unable to capture continuous phenomena, but using them to construct approximations to such phenomena that are adequate for whatever our immediate purposes are. This is very much in the *satisficing* spirit of AI, which prefers an imperfect solution that *works* to a theoretically perfect solution that is unmanageable in practice.

Aside from practicality, there are also philosophical reasons for questioning the viability of the standard mathematical model as a true account of time and change. For on the one hand, an instant is nothing: that is, it has no duration, and exists only as a point of potential division of an interval. As such, instants cannot provide the "substance" from which the extended temporal continuum is constructed. On the other hand, the standard mathematical account of continuity suggests that everything that happens is reducible to the holding of states at instants. It begins to seem paradoxical that anything can ever happen at all!

In order to escape from this paradox, while retaining the full power of the mathematical analysis of continuity, we must look for a way to achieve the same effect in a system in which intervals still play the leading role. One way of doing this might be as follows. Take the primitive notion of temporal incidence to be the holding of a state over an interval. Remember, though, that we have a wide range of states to choose from, and in particular, the state which holds over an interval may be specified as a disjunction of more primitive states. To achieve the effect we require, we must generalise the notion of disjunction to allow infinitely many disjuncts, in effect introducing existential quantification over states. Thus if f is a real-valued fluent, we shall want to introduce a state such as $0 < f < 1$, which can be regarded as the disjunction of an infinite set of states $\bigvee\{f = x \mid 0 < x < 1\}$, or as a quantified state of the form $\exists x(0 < x < 1 \wedge f = x)$. In a similar way, we can form infinite conjunctions, in effect introducing universal quantification over states.

We can now define what it means to say that state S holds at instant t as follows. First, consider the set of all intervals within which t falls, which can be defined as $\mathcal{I}_t = \{i+j \mid t = i][j\}$. For each such interval, we can find states which hold over that interval; if need be, we form a disjunction to make sure we cover the whole interval. Now let

$$S_t = \bigwedge_{i \in \mathcal{I}_t} \{S \mid Holds(S, i)\}.$$

This is the conjunction of all the states holding over any interval within which t falls. We can then stipulate that a state S holds at t if and only if it is entailed by S_t. To illustrate, we look at a case of continuous change and a case of discontinuous change.

1. *Continuous change.* Let the fluent f take the value 0 over the interval (0,1) and 1 over the interval (3,4), with intermediate values over the interval (1,3). Thus the event $Trans(f = 0, f = 1)$ occurs on (1,3). Assume that the value of f changes at a uniform rate over that interval. What is the value of the fluent at $t = 2$? We note that on the interval $(2 - \epsilon, 2 + \epsilon)$, where $\epsilon > 0$, the state $1.5 - \frac{1}{2}\epsilon < f < 1.5 + \frac{1}{2}\epsilon$ holds. Thus

   $$S_2 = \bigwedge_{\epsilon > 0} \{1.5 - \tfrac{1}{2}\epsilon < f < 1.5 + \tfrac{1}{2}\epsilon\} = (f = 1.5).$$

   We conclude that the value of f at $t = 2$ is 1.5.

   This example has an air of circularity: the point is to show how we can derive the state holding at an instant from a knowledge of states holding over intervals. But how do we know that f takes values in the range $(1.5 - \frac{1}{2}\epsilon, 1.5 + \frac{1}{2}\epsilon)$ over the interval $(2 - \epsilon, 2 + \epsilon)$? The simplest way of determining this is to calculate that f has the value $1.5 - \frac{1}{2}\epsilon$ at $t = 2 - \epsilon$, and similarly at the other end of the interval (noting also that f is increasing monotonically throughout the interval). Thus although it is possible, *given* a knowledge of what states hold over what intervals, to derive the states holding at instants, it is not at all clear where the knowledge, supposed given, could have come from, other than a prior knowledge of what states hold at what instants, the very information we were trying to derive!

2. *Discontinuous change.* Suppose $f = 0$ over the interval (0,1), and $f = 1$ over the interval $(1, 2)$. What can we say about the value of f at $t = 1$? This is the classic Dividing Instant Problem. We note that on the interval $(2 - \epsilon, 2 + \epsilon)$, where $\epsilon > 0$, the state $f = 0 \vee f = 1$ holds. Hence

   $$S_2 = \bigwedge_{\epsilon > 0} \{f = 0 \vee f = 1\} = (f = 0 \vee f = 1).$$

   This corresponds to the solution to the Dividing Instant Problem according to which the value of f at the instant of transition is indeterminate; and this certainly seems the most appropriate answer to give in the case of discontinuous change envisaged here.

It is possible that some such approach as this might work, despite the appearance of circularity noted above, but it does not appear to have been investigated in any detail. For the present, we must leave it as an open question; the main lesson to be learnt from this section is that continuity—a subject which received much attention from ancient and medieval philosophers as well as modern mathematicians—is difficult, and that the modern mathematical approach is surely not the last word on the subject.

2.6 Case study: A game of tennis

In this section we shall illustrate the systems described in the previous section by showing how they can be used to describe a single objective situation at different levels of detail.* The situation we shall consider is a tennis match. A tennis match between two players consists of a certain number of *sets* each consisting of a certain number of *games*. Each game consists of a certain number of *points*. Thus we have a hierarchical structure which lends itself well to a description at different levels. We shall by-pass a consideration of the upper levels, and concentrate on a single game in the match.

As already mentioned, the game consists of a sequence of points. Physically, a point consists in the players attempting to hit the ball from one end of the court to the other until one of a number of termination conditions obtains—e.g., the ball hits the net or lands outside a certain designated area of the court, or it lands inside the area but the player whose turn it is to hit it fails to do so. Each such condition determines which player wins the point. The game is won by the first player to have at least two more points than his opponent *and* at least four points altogether. The bizarre conventions regarding the naming of scores are shown in Figure 2.4, in which the possible courses of the game are shown as paths through a finite-state automaton. In this figure S represents a point won by the server, who is the first to hit the ball after each point, and R represents a point won by his opponent, who returns the serve.

Figure 2.4 most naturally lends itself to a description of the game as a finite-state system operating in discrete time. All possible games are covered by the diagram. An example of a particular game might be presented as

(0–0)(15–0)(15–15)(15–30)(15–40)(30–40)(deuce)(advantage R)(deuce)(advantage S)(game to S)

The individual "times" here are, essentially, points, in the sense of covering all the play following one point and leading up to the next.

The example of the tennis game differs from the finite-state systems we considered earlier in one important respect, which is that whereas in the earlier systems it was assumed that the primitive facts defining the system were states, with all events defined in terms of them, in the tennis example it is more natural to take certain events as the primitive elements, and define states in terms of them. At the level of detail shown in Figure 2.4, there are two primitive events, namely "S wins a point" and "R wins a point". The state represented by the score 15–30 is defined as, essentially "Since the start of the game, S has won one point and R has won two points". The sequence of states illustrated above can also be represented as a sequence of events:

SRRRSRRSSS

and representations of this kind are interchangeable, in the present example, with the state-based representations we had earlier. This interchangeability relies on the finite-state system being deterministic; with a non-deterministic system it is not possible to recover the state sequence from the event sequence. And if there is more than one primitive event type that can effect the transition between a particular pair of states, then it is also impossible to

*A detailed technical account of levels of detail in temporal representation can be found in Chapter 3; here we handle the issue in an informal way only.

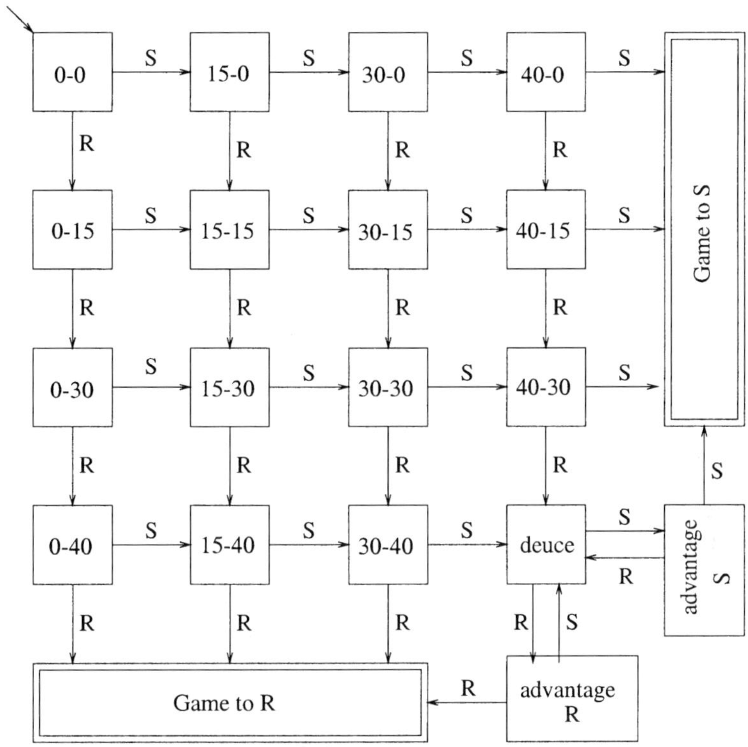

Figure 2.4: *How a game is won in tennis.*

recover the event sequence from the state sequence. In such cases the full history would have to be given by a mixed state and event sequence such as

$$(0\text{–}0)\xrightarrow{S}(15\text{–}0)\xrightarrow{R}(15\text{–}15)\xrightarrow{R}(15\text{–}30)\xrightarrow{R}(15\text{–}40)\xrightarrow{S}(30\text{–}40)\xrightarrow{S}(\text{deuce})\xrightarrow{R}$$
$$(\text{advantage R})\xrightarrow{S}(\text{deuce})\xrightarrow{S}(\text{advantage S})\xrightarrow{S}(\text{game to S})$$

We can define higher-level states on this system by forming disjunctions of the primitive states shown in the diagram. An example is "R is winning", which is the disjunction

$$(0\text{–}15) \vee (0\text{–}30) \vee (0\text{–}40) \vee (15\text{–}30) \vee (15\text{–}40) \vee (30\text{–}40) \vee (\text{advantage R}).$$

In the sequence above, this state holds at times 4, 5, 6, and 8. Thus there is an occurrence of the event Po(R is winning) (i.e., "R was winning for a while") on the interval [4,6]. One might say "after the third point, R started winning", i.e., $Occurs(Ingr(\text{R is winning}), 3][4)$. Another high-level state is "Break point", used by tennis commentators to describe the situation in which R only needs to win the next point in order to win:

$$(0\text{–}40) \vee (15\text{–}40) \vee (30\text{–}40) \vee (\text{advantage R}).$$

In the automaton, the arcs representing transitions from state to state are labelled "S" or "R" according to whether the server or his opponent wins the next point. These transitions can be regarded as instantaneous event-types. More exactly, the event-type "R wins the point" can be given a disjunctive occurrence condition of the form

$$\begin{aligned} Occurs(\text{R's point}, n][n+1) \quad \Leftrightarrow \quad & (Holds(\text{0–0}, n) \wedge Holds(\text{0-15}, n+1)) \vee \\ & (Holds(\text{15–0}, n) \wedge Holds(\text{15–15}, n+1)) \vee \\ & \vdots \\ & (Holds(\text{deuce}, n) \wedge Holds(\text{advantage R}, n+1)) \vee \\ & (Holds(\text{advantage R}, n) \wedge Holds(\text{game to R}, n+1)) \end{aligned}$$

Note that we are defining the occurrence condition for R to score a point in terms of transitions between particular scores—which is of course the reverse of the real logical dependence, in which the current score is determined by the previous score together with who won the last point. This order of dependence could be captured by a set of holding conditions such as

$$\begin{aligned} Holds(\text{15–30}, n) \quad \Leftrightarrow \quad & (Holds(\text{0–30}, n-1) \wedge Occurs(\text{S's point}, n-1][n)) \vee \\ & (Holds(\text{15–15}, n-1) \wedge Occurs(\text{R's point}, n-1][n)) \end{aligned}$$

At this level of granularity, it is in the nature of the game that none of the primitive states can hold over two or more consecutive atomic intervals. In fact, apart from "deuce" and the two advantage states, none of them can occur more than once in the entire game. We can move to a finer granularity, while still operating with a finite-state system in discrete time, by tracking the events within a point. Each point consists of a sequence of *shots*; a shot is an event in which a player hits, or attempts to hit, the ball. A shot may be considered "good" or "bad". To win the point a player needs to deliver a "good" shot which the opponent responds to with a "bad" shot. The different ways in which a point may be won by a succession of shots are shown in the finite-state automaton in Figure 2.5.

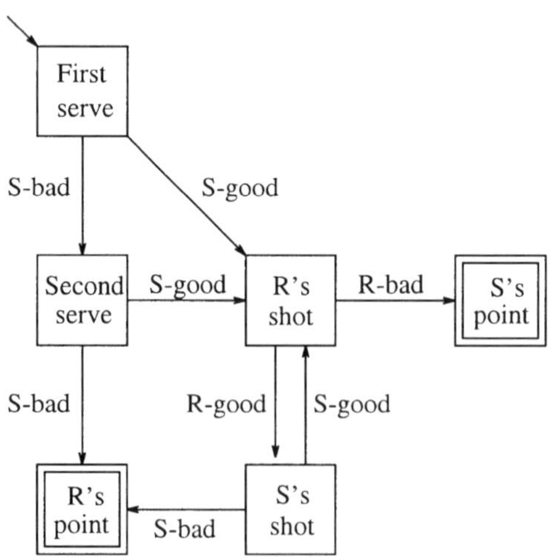

Figure 2.5: *How a point is won in tennis.*

Writing X^+ and X^- to represent good and bad points for player X, we can represent the history of a particular point in the form

$$S^- S^+ R^+ S^+ R^+ S^+ R^+ S^-$$

and of course each point in a game can be analysed in this form also, giving us a two-level representation as follows:

$$\underbrace{S^+R^-}_{S} \quad \underbrace{S^+R^+S^+R^-}_{S} \quad \underbrace{S^-S^+R^-}_{S} \quad \underbrace{S^+R^+S^+R^+S^-}_{R} \quad \underbrace{S^-S^-}_{R} \quad \underbrace{S^+R^+S^+R^+S^+R^-}_{S}$$

0–0	15–0	30–0	40–0	40–15	40–30	Game to S

At the next level of detail, we do not introduce any new states or events, but we do take into account how long each shot takes. For this purpose we move to a continuous model of time. The game shown above can now be represented as shown in Figure 2.6. As is to be expected from our earlier remarks, we do not see any new qualitative phenomena in this representation; the extra information conveyed is all quantitative, concerning the relative durations of what previously were treated as atomic intervals.

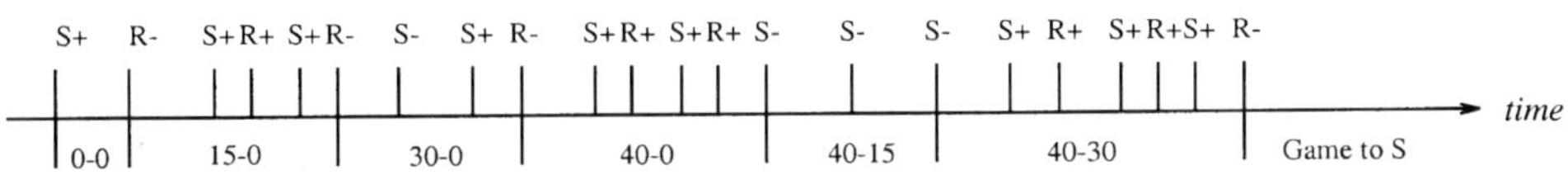

Figure 2.6: *A game of tennis in continuous time.*

At the final level of detail, not only time itself, but also the fluents defined over time, take values from continuous ranges. In the tennis example, this is the point at which we turn from the rather abstract, conventionalised point of view characterised in terms of scores, advantages, and so on, to a lower-level, physicalistic point of view from which the game is characterised in terms of the motions of bodies—the players and the ball—about the court.

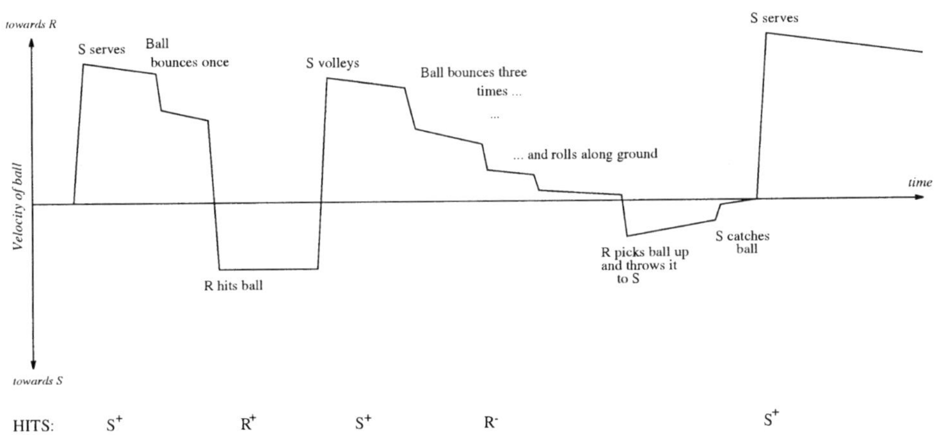

Figure 2.7: *Speed of ball along court plotted as a function of time.*

There are innumerable different fluents we could consider here, of varying relevance to the higher-level descriptions of the game. For the sake of illustration, we shall take just one fluent, which generates a good deal of interest in tennis circles, namely the speed of the ball. What is of particular interest is the speed at which the ball is served at the start of each point, but of course the ball *has* a speed at every instant of the game.

In Figure 2.7 we present a history of one point in terms of ball-speed; more precisely, what is plotted (on the vertical axis) is the component of velocity parallel to the long axis of the court, with the direction from server to opponent taken as positive. The correlation with the previous level of description is shown by the inclusion of terms like S^+ to indicate the type of hit as characterised at that level. It has to be admitted that the graph shown here is entirely imaginary, no real data of this kind being available to the author, but I hope it is not too implausible!

The main lesson to be learnt from this case study is that there is no question of there being one correct way to describe what goes on in time. In the preceding sections we looked at a number of different frameworks within which such descriptions can be given, which are incompatible in the sense that if there is one "correct" model then only one of the frameworks can merit that title. But as we have seen in this section, each of the frameworks can provide a valid way of representing a particular piece of (possible or actual) history, depending on what aspects one wants to focus on.

Handbook of Temporal Reasoning in Artificial Intelligence
Edited by M. Fisher, D. Gabbay and L. Vila

Chapter 3

Time Granularity

Jérôme Euzenat & Angelo Montanari

A temporal situation can be described at different levels of abstraction depending on the accuracy required or the available knowledge. Time granularity can be defined as the resolution power of the temporal qualification of a statement. Providing a formalism with the concept of time granularity makes it possible to model time information with respect to differently grained temporal domains. This does not merely mean that one can use different time units, e.g., months and days, to represent time quantities in a unique flat temporal model, but it involves more difficult semantic issues related to the problem of assigning a proper meaning to the association of statements with the different temporal domains of a layered temporal model and of switching from one domain to a coarser/finer one. Such an ability of providing and relating temporal representations at different "grain levels" of the same reality is both an active research theme and a major requirement for many applications (e.g., integration of layered specifications and agent communication).

After a presentation of the general requirements of a multi-granular temporal formalism, we discuss the various issues and approaches to time granularity proposed in the literature. We focus our attention on the main existing formalisms for representing and reasoning about quantitative and qualitative time granularity: the set-theoretic framework developed by Bettini et al. [Bettini *et al.*, 2000] and the logical approach systematically investigated by Montanari et al. [Montanari, 1996; Franceschet, 2002] for quantitative time granularity, and Euzenat's relational algebra granularity conversion operators [Euzenat, 2001] for qualitative time granularity. We present in detail the achieved results, we outline the open issues, and we point out the links that connect the different approaches. In the last part of the chapter, we describe some applications exploiting time granularity, and we briefly discuss related work in the areas of formal methods, temporal databases, and data mining.

3.1 Introduction

The usefulness of the addition of a notion of time granularity to representation languages is widely recognized. As an example, let us consider the problem of providing a logical specification of a wide-ranging class of real-time reactive systems whose components have dynamic behaviors regulated by very different — even by orders of magnitude — time constants (*granular systems* for short) [Montanari, 1996]. This is the case, for instance, of a pondage power station that consists of a reservoir, with filling and emptying times of days or weeks, generator units, possibly changing state in a few seconds, and electronic control devices, evolving in milliseconds or even less [Corsetti *et al.*, 1991a]. A complete specification of the power station must include the description of these components and of their interactions. A natural description of the temporal evolution of the reservoir state will probably use days: "During rainy weeks, the level of the reservoir increases 1 meter a day". The description of the control devices behavior may use microseconds: "When an alarm comes from the level sensors, send an acknowledge signal in 50 microseconds". We say that systems of such a type have *different time granularities*. It is not only somewhat unnatural, but also sometimes impossible, to compel the specifier of these systems to use a unique time granularity, microseconds in the previous example, to describe the behavior of all the components. For instance, the requirement that "the filling of the reservoir must be completed within m days" can be hardly assumed to be equivalent to the requirement that "the filling of the reservoir must be completed within n microseconds", for a suitable n (we shall discuss in detail the problems involved in such a rewriting in the next section). Since a good language must allow the specifier to easily and precisely describe all system requirements, different time granularities must be a feature of a specification language for granular systems.

A complementary point of view on time granularity is also possible: besides an important feature of a representation language, time granularity can be viewed as a formal tool to investigate the definability of meaningful timing properties, such as density and exponential grow/decay, as well as the expressiveness and decidability of temporal theories [Montanari *et al.*, 1999]. In this respect, the number and organization of layers (single vs. multiple, finite vs. infinite, upward unbounded vs. downward unbounded) of the underlying temporal structure plays a major role: certain timing properties can be expressed using a single layer; others using a finite number of layers; others only exploiting an infinite number of layers. In particular, finitely-layered metric temporal logics can be used to specify timing properties of granular systems composed by a finite number of differently-grained temporal components, which have been fixed once and for all (n-layered temporal structures). Furthermore, if provided with a rich enough layered structure, they suffice to deal with conditions like "p holds at all even times of a given temporal domain" that cannot be expressed using flat propositional temporal logics [Emerson, 1990] (as a matter of fact, a 2-layered structure suffices to capture the above condition). ω-layered metric temporal logics allow one to express relevant properties of infinite sequences of states over a single temporal domain that cannot be captured by using flat or finitely-layered temporal logics. This is the case, for instance, of conditions like "p holds at all times 2^i, for all natural numbers i, of a given temporal domain".

The chapter is organized as follows. In Section 3.2, we introduce the general requirements of a multi-granular temporal formalism, and then we discuss the different issues and approaches to time granularity proposed in the literature. In Sections 3.3 and 3.4, we illustrate in detail the two main existing formal systems for representing and reasoning about quantitative time granularity: the set-theoretic framework for time granularity developed by Bettini et al. [Bettini *et al.*, 2000] and the logical approach systematically explored by Montanari et al. [Montanari, 1996; Franceschet, 2002]. In Section 3.5, we present the relational algebra granularity conversion operators proposed by [Euzenat, 2001] to deal with qualitative time granularity and we briefly describe the approximation framework outlined by Bittner [Bittner, 2002]. In Section 3.6, we describe some applications exploiting time granularity, while in Section 3.7 we briefly discuss related work. The concluding remarks provide an assessment of the work done in the field of time granularity and give an indication of possible research directions.

3.2 General setting for time granularity

In order to give a formal meaning to the use of different time granularities in a representation language, two main problems have to be solved: the qualification of statements with respect to time granularity and the definition of the links between statements associated with a given time granularity, e.g., *days*, and statements associated with another granularity, e.g., *microseconds* [Montanari, 1996]. Sometimes, these problems have an obvious solution that consists in using *different time units* — say, months and minutes — to measure time quantities in a *unique model*. In most cases, however, the treatment of different time granularities involves more difficult semantic problems. Let consider, for instance, the sentence: "every month, if an employee works, then he gets his salary". It could be formalized, in a first-order language, by the following formula:

$$\forall t_m, emp(work(emp, t_m) \rightarrow get\_salary(emp, t_m)),$$

with an obvious meaning of the used symbols, once it is stated that the subscript m denotes the fact that t is measured by the time unit of *months*.
Another requirement can be expressed by the sentence: "an employee must complete every received job within 3 days". It can be formalized by the formula:

$$\forall t_d, emp, job(get\_job(emp, job, t_d) \rightarrow job\_done(emp, job, t_d + 3)),$$

where the subscript d denotes that t is measured by the time unit of *days*.
Assume now that the two formulas are part of the specification of the same office system. We need a *common model* for both formulas. As done before, we could choose the finest temporal domain, i.e., the set of (times measured by) *days*, as the common domain. Then, a term labeled by m would be translated into a term labeled d by multiplying its value by 30. However, the statement "every month, if an employee works, then he gets his salary" is clearly different from the statement "every day, if an employee works, then he gets his salary". In fact, working for a month means that one works for 22 days in the month, whereas getting a monthly salary means that there is one day when one gets the salary for the month. Similarly, stating that "every day of a given month it rains" does not mean, in general, that "it rains for all seconds of all days of the month". On the contrary, if one states that "a car has been moving for three hours at a speed greater than 30 km per hour", he usually means that for all seconds included in the considered three hours the car has been moving at the specified speed. The above examples show that the interpretations of temporal statements are likely to change when switching from one time granularity to another one. The addition of the concept of time granularity is thus necessary to allow one to build granular temporal models by referring to the natural scale in any component of the model and by properly constraining the interactions between differently-grained components.

Further difficulties arise from the *synchronization problem* of temporal domains [Corsetti *et al.*, 1991a]. Such a problem can be illustrated by the following examples. Consider the sentence "tomorrow I will eat". If one interprets it in the domain of hours, its meaning is that there will be several hours, starting from the next midnight until the following one, when it will be true that I eat, *no matter in which hour of the present day this sentence is claimed.*

Thus, if the sentence is claimed at 1 a.m., it will be true that "I eat" at some hours t whose distance d from the current hour is such that $23 \leq d < 47$. Instead, if the same sentence is claimed at 10 p.m. of the same day, d will be such that $2 \leq d < 26$. Consider now the sentence "dinner will be ready in one hour". If it is interpreted in the domain of minutes, its meaning is that dinner will be ready in 60 minutes *starting from the minute when it is claimed*. Therefore, if the sentence is claimed at minute, say, 10, or 55, of a given hour, it will be always true that "dinner is ready" at a minute t whose distance d from the current minute is *exactly* 60 minutes. Clearly, the two examples require two different semantics.

Thus, when the granularity concept is applied to time, we generally assume a set of differently-grained domains (or layers) with respect to which the situations are described and some operators relating the components of the multi-level description. The resulting system will depend on the language in which situations are modeled, the properties of the layers, and the operators. Although these elements are not fully independent, we first take into consideration each of them separately.

3.2.1 Languages, layers, operators

The distinctive features of a formal system for time granularity depend on some basic decisions about the way in which one models the relationships between the representations of a given situation with respect to different granularity layers.

Languages. The first choice concerns the language. One possibility is to use the same language to describe a situation with respect to different granularity layers. As an example, the representations associated with the different layers can use the same temporal logic or the same algebra of relations. In such a way, the representations of the same situation at different abstraction levels turn out to be *homogeneous*. Another possibility is to use different languages at different levels of abstraction, thus providing a set of *hybrid* representations of the same situation. As an example, one can adopt a metric representation at the finer layers and a qualitative one at the coarser ones.

Layers. Any formal system for time granularity must feature a number of different (granularity) layers. They can be either explicitly introduced by means of suitable linguistic primitives or implicitly associated with the different representations of a given situation.

Operators. Another choice concerns the operators that the formal system must encompass to deal with the layered structure. In this respect, one must make provision for at least two basic operators:

contextualization to select a layer;

projection to move across layers.

These operators are independent of the specific formalism one can adopt to represent and to reason about time granularity, that is, each formalism must somehow support such operators. They are sufficient for expressing fundamental questions one would like to ask to a granular representation:

- converting a representation from a given granularity to another one (how would a particular representation appear under a finer or coarser granularity?);
- testing the compatibility of two representations (is it possible that they represent the same situation under different granularities?);
- comparing the relative granularities of two representations (which is the coarser/finer representation of a given situation?).

Internal vs. external layers. Once the relevance of these operators is established, it must be decided if the granularity applies within a formalism or across formalisms. In other terms, it must be decided if an existing formalism will be extended with these new operators or if these operators will be defined and applied from the outside to representations using existing formalisms. Both these alternatives have been explored in the literature:

- Some solutions propose an internal extension of existing formalisms to explicitly introduce the notion of granularity layer in the representations (see Sections 3.4.1 and 3.4.2 [Ciapessoni *et al.*, 1993; Montanari, 1996; Montanari *et al.*, 1999]), thus allowing one to express complex statements combining granularity with other notions. The representations of a situation with respect to different granularity layers in the resulting formalism are clearly homogeneous.
- Other solutions propose an external apprehension which allows one to relate two descriptions expressed in the same formalism or in different formalisms (see Sections 3.3, 3.4.3, and 3.5 [Euzenat, 1995b; Fiadeiro and Maibaum, 1994; Franceschet, 2002; Franceschet and Montanari, 2004]). This solution has the advantage of preserving the usual complexity of the underlying formalism, as far as no additional complexity is introduced by granularity.

3.2.2 Properties of languages

The whole spectrum of languages for representing time presented in this book is available for expressing the sentences subject to granularity. Here we briefly point out some alternatives that can affect the management of granularity.

Qualitative and quantitative languages. There can be many structures on which a temporal representation language is grounded. These structures can be compared with that of mathematical spaces:

set-theory when the language takes into account containment (i.e. set-membership);

topology when the language accounts for connexity and convexity;

metric spaces when the language takes advantage of a metric in order to quantify the relationship (distance) between temporal entities.

vector spaces when the language considers alignment and precedence (with regard to an alignment). As far as time is considered as totally ordered, the order comes naturally.

A quantitative representation language is generally a language which embodies properties of metric and vector spaces. Such a language allows one to precisely define a displacement operator (of a particular distance along an axis). A qualitative representation language does not use a metric and thus one cannot precisely state the position of objects. For instance, Allen's Interval Algebra (see Chapter 1) considers notions from vector (before) and topological (meets) spaces.

Expressive power. The expressive power of the languages can vary a lot (this is true in general for classical temporal representation languages, see Chapter 6). It can roughly be:

exact and conjunctive when each temporal entity is localized at a particular known position (a is ten minutes after b) and a situation is described by a conjunction of such sentences;

propositional when the language allows one to express conjunction and disjunction of propositional statements (a is before or after b); this also applies to constrained positions of entities (a is between ten minutes and one hour after b);

first-order when the language contains variables which allow one to quantify over the entities (there exists time lap x in between a and b);

"second-order" when the language contains variables which allow one to quantify over layers (there exists a layer g under which a is after b).

3.2.3 Properties of layers

As it always happens when time information has to be managed by a system, the properties of the adopted model of time influence the representation. The distinctive feature of the models of time that incorporate time granularity is the coexistence of a set $\mathcal{T}$ of temporal domains. Such a set is called *temporal universe* and the temporal domains belonging to it are called (temporal) *layers*. Layers can be either overlapping, as in the case of `Days` and `Working Days`, since every working day is a day (cf. Section 3.3), or disjoint, as in the case of `Days` and `Weeks` (cf. Section 3.4).

Structure of time. It is apparent that the temporal structure of the layers influences the semantics of the operators. Different structures can obviously be used. Moreover, one can either constrain the layers to share the same structure or to allow different layers to have different structures.
For each layer $T \in \mathcal{T}$, let $<$ be a linear order over the set of time points in T. We confine our attention to the following temporal structures:

continuous T is isomorphic to the set of real numbers (this is the usual interpretation of time);

dense between every two different points there is a point

$$\forall x, y \in T\ \exists z \in T(x < y \rightarrow x < z < y);$$

discrete every point having a successor (respectively, a predecessor) has an immediate one

$$\forall x \in T((\exists y \in T(x < y) \rightarrow \exists z \in T(x < z \wedge \forall w \in T \neg(x < w < z))) \wedge (\exists y \in T(y < x) \rightarrow \exists z \in T(z < x \wedge \forall w \in T \neg(z < w < x)))).$$

Most formal systems for time granularity assume layers to be discrete, with the possible exception of the most detailed layer, if any, whose temporal structure can be dense, or even continuous (an exception is [Endriss, 2003]). The reason of this choice is that each dense layer is already at the finest level of granularity, and it allows any degree of precision in measuring time. As a consequence, for dense layers one must distinguish granularity from metric, while, for discrete layers, one can define granularity in terms of set cardinality and assimilate it to a natural notion of metric. Mapping, say, a set of rational numbers into another set of rational numbers would only mean changing the unit of measure with no semantic effect, just in the same way one can decide to describe geometric facts by using, say, kilometers or centimeters. If kilometers are measured by rational numbers, indeed, the same level of precision as with centimeters can be achieved. On the contrary, the key point in time granularity is that saying that something holds for all days in a given interval does not imply that it holds at every second belonging to the interval [Corsetti *et al.*, 1991a]. For the sake of simplicity, in the following we assume each layer to be discrete.

Global organization of layers. Further conditions can be added to constrain the global organization of the set of layers. So far, layers have been considered as independent representation spaces. However, we are actually interested in comparing their grains, that is, we want to be able to establish whether the grain of a given layer is finer or coarser than the grain of another one. It is thus natural to define an order relation $\prec$, called *granularity* relation, on the set of layers of $\mathcal{T}$ based on their grains: we say that a layer T is finer (resp. coarser) than a layer T', denoted by $T \prec T'$ (resp. $T' \prec T$), if the grain of T is finer (resp. coarser) than that of T'. There exist at least three meaningful cases:

partial order $\prec$ is a reflexive, transitive, and anti-symmetric relation over layers;

(semi-)lattice $\prec$ is a partial order such that, given any two layers $T, T' \in \mathcal{T}$, there exists a layer $T \wedge T' \in \mathcal{T}$ such that $T \wedge T' \prec T$ and $T \wedge T' \prec T'$, and any other layer T" with the same property is such that T" $\prec T \wedge T'$;

total order $\prec$ is a partial order such that, for all $T, T' \in \mathcal{T}$, either $T = T'$ or $T \prec T'$ or $T' \prec T$.

We shall see that the set of admissible operations on layers depends on the structure of $\prec$.

Beside the order relation $\prec$, one must consider the cardinality of the set $\mathcal{T}$. Even though a finite number of layers suffices for many applications, there exist significant properties that can be expressed only using an infinite number of layers (cf. Section 3.4.2). As an example, an infinite number of arbitrarily fine (discrete) layers makes it possible to express properties related to temporal density, e.g., the fact that two states are distinct, but arbitrarily close.

Pairwise organization of layers. Even in the case in which layers are totally ordered, their organization can be made more precise. For instance, consider the case of a situation described with respect to the totally ordered set of granularities including `years`, `months`, `weeks`, and `days`. The relationships between these layers differ a lot. Such differences can be described through the following notions:

homogeneity when the (temporal) entities of the coarser layer consist of the same number of entities of the finer one;

alignment when the entities of the finer layer are mapped in only one entity of the coarser one.

These two notions allow us to distinguish four different cases:

year-month the situation is very neat between years and months since each year contains the same number of months (homogeneity) and each month is mapped onto only one year (alignment);

year-week a year contains a various number of weeks (non homogeneity) and a week can be mapped into more than one year (non alignment);

month-day while every day is mapped into exactly one month (alignment), the number of days in a month is variable (non homogeneity);

working week-day one can easily imagine working weeks beginning at 5 o'clock on Mondays (this kind of weeks exists in industrial plants): while every week is made of the same duration or amount of days (homogeneity), some days are mapped into two weeks (non alignment).

How the objects behave. There are several options with regard to the behavior of the objects considered by the theories. The objects can

persist when they remain the same across layers (in the logical setting, this is modeled by the Barcan formula);

change category when, moving from one layer to another one, they are transformed into objects of different size (e.g., transforming intervals into points, or vice versa, or changing an object into another of a bigger/lower dimension, see Section 3.6.4);

vanish when an object associated with a fine layer disappears in a coarser one.

3.2.4 Properties of operators

The operator that models the change of granularity is the *projection* operator. It relates the temporal entities of a given layer to the corresponding entities of a finer/coarser layer. In some formal systems, it also models the change of the interpretation context from one layer to another. The projection operator is characterized by a number of distinctive properties, including:

reflexivity (see Section 3.5.2 self-conservation p. 105 and Section 3.4.1 p. 85) constrains an entity to be able to be converted into itself;

symmetry (see Section 3.5.2 inverse compatibility p. 106 and Section 3.4.1 p. 85) states that if an entity can be converted into another one, then this latter entity can be converted back into the original one;

order-preservation (for vectorial systems, see Section 3.3 p. 69, Section 3.5.2 p. 105, and Section 3.4.1 p. 86) constrains the projection operators to preserve the order of entities among layers;

transitivity (see below) constrains consecutive applications of projection operators in any "direction" to yield the same result as a direct projection;

oriented transitivity (see Section 3.5.2 p. 106 and Section 3.4.1 downward transitivity p. 85 and upward transitivity p. 86) constrains successive applications of projection operators in the same "direction" to yield the same result as a direct projection;

downward/upward transitivity (see Section 3.4.1 pp. 85-86 and [Euzenat, 1993]) constrains two consecutive applications of the projection operators (first downward, then upward) to yield the same result as a direct downward or upward projection;

Some properties of projection operators are related to pairwise properties of layers:

contiguity (see Section 3.4.1 p. 86), or "contiguity-preservation", constrains the projections of two contiguous entities to be either two contiguous (sets of) entities or the same entity (set of entities);

total covering (see Section 3.3 p. 69 and Section 3.4.1 p. 86) constrains each layer to be totally accessible from any other layer by projection;

convexity (see Section 3.4.1 p. 86) constrains the coarse equivalent of an entity belonging to a given layer to cover a convex set of entities of such a layer;

synchronization (see Sections 3.3 and 3.4.1), or "origin alignment", constrains the origin of a layer to be projected on the origin of the other layers. It is called synchronization because it is related to "synchronicity" which binds all the layers to the same clock;

homogeneity (see Section 3.4.1 p. 86) constrains the temporal entities of a given layer to be projected on the same number of entities of a finer layer;

Such properties are satisfied when they are satisfied by all pairs of layers.

3.2.5 Quantitative and qualitative models

In the following we present in detail the main formal systems for time granularity proposed in the literature. We found it useful to make a distinction between quantitative and qualitative models of time granularity. Quantitative models are able to position temporal entities (or occurrences) within a metric frame. They have been obtained following either a set-theoretic approach or a logical one. In contrast, qualitative models characterize the position of temporal entities with respect to each other. This characterization is often topological or vectorial. The main qualitative approach to granularity is of algebraic nature.

The set-theoretic approach is based upon naive set theory and algebra. According to it, the single temporal domain of flat temporal models is replaced by a temporal universe, which is defined as a set of inter-related temporal layers, which is built upon its finest layer. The finest layer is a totally ordered set, whose elements are the smallest temporal units relevant to the considered application (*chronons*, according to the database terminology [Dyreson and

Snodgrass, 1994; Jensen *et al.*, 1994]); any coarser layer is defined as a suitable partition of this basic layer. To operate on elements belonging to the same layer, the familiar Boolean algebra of subsets suffices. Operations between elements belonging to different layers require a preliminary mapping to a common layer. Such an approach, originally proposed by Clifford and Rao in [Clifford and Rao, 1988], has been successively refined and generalized by Bettini et al. in a number of papers [Bettini *et al.*, 2000]. In Section 3.3, we shall describe the evolution of the set-theoretic approach to time granularity from its original formulation up to its more recent developments.

According to the logical approach, the single temporal domain of (metric) temporal logic is replaced by a temporal universe consisting of a possibly *infinite* set of inter-related differently-grained layers and logical tools are provided to qualify temporal statements with respect to the temporal universe and to switch temporal statements across layers. Logics for time granularities have been given both non-classical and classical formalizations. In the non-classical setting, they have been obtained by extending metric temporal logics with operators for temporal contextualization and projection [Ciapessoni *et al.*, 1993; Montanari, 1996; Montanari and de Rijke, 1997], as well as by combining linear and branching temporal logics in a suitable way [Franceschet, 2002; Franceschet and Montanari, 2003; Franceschet and Montanari, 2004]. In the classical one, they have been characterized in terms of (extensions of) the well-known monadic second-order theories of k successors and of their fragments [Montanari and Policriti, 1996; Montanari *et al.*, 1999; Franceschet *et al.*, 2003]. In Section 3.4, we shall present in detail both approaches.

The study of granularity in a qualitative context is presented in Section 3.5. It amounts to characterize the variation of relations between temporal entities that are induced by granularity changes. A number of axioms for characterizing granularity conversion operators have been provided in [Euzenat, 1993; Euzenat, 1995a], which have been later shown to be consistent and independent [Euzenat, 2001]. Granularity operators for the usual algebras of temporal relations have been derived from these axioms. Another approach to characterizing granularity in qualitative relations, associated with a new way of generating systems of relations, has recently come to light [Bittner, 2002]. The relations between two entities are characterized by the relation (in a simpler relation set) between the intersection of the two entities and each of them. Temporal locations of entities are then approximated by subsets of a partition of the temporal domain, so that the relation between the two entities can itself be approximated by the relation holding between their approximated locations. This relation (that corresponds to the original relation under the coarser granularity) is obtained directly by maximizing and minimizing the set of possible relations.

3.3 The set-theoretic approach

In this section, we present several contributions to the development of a general framework for time granularity coming from both the area of knowledge-based systems and that of database systems. We qualify their common approach as set-theoretic because it relies on a temporal domain defined as an ordered set, it builds granularities by grouping subsets of this domain, and it expresses their properties through set relations and operations over sets. In the area of knowledge representation and reasoning, the addition of a notion of time granularity to knowledge-based systems has been one of the most effective attempts at dealing with the widely recognized problem of managing periodic phenomena. Two relevant set-theoretic approaches to time granularity are the formalism of collection expressions proposed by Leban et al. [Leban *et al.*, 1986] and the formalism of slice expressions developed by Niezette and Stevenne [Niézette and Stevenne, 1992]. In the database area, time granularity emerged as a formal tool to deal with the intrinsic characteristics of calendars in a principled way. The set-theoretic approach to time granularity was originally proposed by Clifford and Rao [Clifford and Rao, 1988] as a suitable way of structuring information with a temporal dimension, independently of any particular calendric system, and, later, it has been systematically explored by Bettini et al. in a series of papers [Bettini *et al.*, 1998a; Bettini *et al.*, 1998b; Bettini *et al.*, 1996; Bettini *et al.*, 1998c; Bettini *et al.*, 1998d; Bettini *et al.*, 2000]. As a matter of fact, the set-theoretic framework developed by Bettini et al. subsumes all the other ones. In the following, we shall briefly describe its distinctive features. A comprehensive presentation of it is given in [Bettini *et al.*, 2000]

3.3.1 Granularities

The basic ingredients of the set-theoretic approach to time granularity have been outlined in Clifford and Rao's work. Even though the point of view of the authors has been largely revised and extended by subsequent work, most of their original intuitions have been preserved.

The temporal structure they propose is a temporal universe consisting of a finite, totally ordered set of temporal domains built upon some base discrete, totally ordered, infinite set which represents the smallest observable/interesting time units.

Let T^0 be the chosen base temporal domain. A temporal universe $\mathcal{T}$ is a finite sequence $\langle T^0, T^1, \ldots, T^n \rangle$ such that, for $i, j = 0, 1, \ldots, n$, if $i \neq j$, then $T^i \cap T^j = \emptyset$, and, for $i = 0, 1, \ldots, n-1$, T^{i+1} is a constructed intervallic partition of T^i. We say that T^{i+1} is a constructed intervallic partition of T^i if there exists a mapping $\psi_i^{i+1} : T^{i+1} \rightarrow 2^{T^i}$ which satisfies the following two properties: (i) $\psi_i^{i+1}(x)$ is a (finite) convex subset of T^i (convexity) , and (ii) $\bigcup_{x \in T^{i+1}} \psi_i^{i+1}(x) = T^i$ (total covering). If we add the conditions that, for each $x \in T^{i+1}$, $\psi_i^{i+1}(x) \neq \emptyset$ and, for every pair $x, y \in T^{i+1}$, with $x \neq y$,$\psi_i^{i+1}(x) \cap \psi_i^{i+1}(y) = \emptyset$, the temporal domain T^{i+1}, under the mapping ψ_i^{i+1}, can be viewed as a partition of T^i. Furthermore, the resulting mapping ψ_i^{i+1} allows us to inherit a total order of T^{i+1} from the total order of T^i as follows (order-preservation). Given a finite closed interval S of T^i, let $first(S)$ and $last(S)$ be respectively the first and the last element of S with respect to the total order of T^i. A total order of T^{i+1} can be obtained by stating that, for all $x, y \in T^{i+1}$, $x < y$ if and only if $last(\psi_i^{i+1}(x)) < first(\psi_i^{i+1}(y))$.

In [Bettini *et al.*, 1998c; Bettini *et al.*, 1998d; Bettini *et al.*, 2000], Bettini et al. have generalized that simple temporal structure for time granularity. The framework they propose is based on a *time domain* $\langle T, \leq \rangle$, that is, a totally ordered set, which can be dense or discrete. A *granularity* g is a function from an index set I_g to the powerset of T such that:

$$\forall i, j, k \in I_g (i < k < j \wedge g(i) \neq \emptyset \wedge g(j) \neq \emptyset \Rightarrow g(k) \neq \emptyset) \qquad \text{(conservation)}$$

$$\forall i, j \in I_g (i < j \Rightarrow \forall x \in g(i) \, \forall y \in g(j) \, x < y) \qquad \text{(order preservation)}$$

Typical examples of granularities are the business weeks which map week numbers to sets of five days (from Monday to Friday) and ignore completely Saturday and Sunday. I_g can be any discrete ordered set. However, for practical reasons, and without loss of generality, we shall consider below that it is either $\mathbb{N}$ or an interval of $\mathbb{N}$.

The *origin* of a granularity is $g_0 = g(min_<(I_g))$ and its *anchor* is $a \in g_0$ such that $\forall x \in g_0(a \leq x)$. The *image* of a granularity g is $Im(g) = \cup_{i \in I_g} g(i)$ and its *extent* is $Ext(g) = \{x \in T : \exists a, b \in Im(g)(a \leq x \leq b)\}$. Two granules $g(i)$ and $g(j)$ are said to be *contiguous* if and only if $\nexists x \in T(g(i) \leq x \leq g(j))$.

3.3.2 Relations between granularities

One of the important aspects of the work by Bettini et al. is the definition of many different relationships between granularities:

$$g \trianglelefteq h \equiv \forall j \in I_h, \exists S \subseteq I_g(h(j) = \cup_{i \in S} g(i)) \qquad (g \text{ groups into } h)$$

$$g \preceq h \equiv \forall i \in I_g, \exists j \in I_h(g(i) \subseteq h(j)) \qquad (g \text{ is finer than } h)$$

$$g \sqsubseteq h \equiv \forall i \in I_g, \exists j \in I_h(g(i) = h(j)) \qquad (g \text{ is a subgranularity of } h)$$

$$g \leftrightarrow h \equiv \exists k \in \mathbb{N}\, \forall i \in I_g(g(i) = h(i+k)) \qquad (g \text{ is shift-equivalent to } h)$$

$$g \trianglelefteq h \text{ and } g \preceq h \qquad (g \text{ partitions } h)$$

$$g \widehat{\subseteq} h \equiv Im(g) \subseteq Im(h) \qquad (g \text{ is covered by } h)$$

$$g \trianglelefteq h \text{ and } \exists r, p \in \mathbb{Z}^+(r \leq |I_h| \wedge \forall i \in I_h(h(i) = \cup_{x=0}^{k} g(j_x)) \wedge h(i+r) \neq \emptyset \Rightarrow h(i+r) = \cup_{x=0}^{k} g(j_x + p))) \qquad (g \text{ groups periodically into } h)$$

Apart from the case of shift-equivalence, all these definitions state, in different ways, that g is a more precise granularity than h. As an example, the groups into relation groups together intervals of g. In fact, it can groups a subset of the elements within the interval, but in such a case the excluded elements cannot belong to any other granule of the less precise granularity. Finer than requires that all the granules of g are covered by a granule of h. So h can group granules of g, but never forget one. However, it can introduce granules that were not taken into account by g (between two g-granules). Sub-granularity can only do exactly that (i.e., it cannot group g-granules). Shift-equivalence is, in spirit, the relation holding between two granularities that are equivalent up to index renaming. It is here restricted to integer increment. Partition, as we shall see below, is the easy-behaving relationship in which the less precise granularity is just a partition of the granules of the more precise one.

It is noteworthy that all these relationships consider only aligned granularities, that is, the granules of the more precise granularity are either preserved of forgotten, but never broken, in the less precise one.

These relations are ordered by strength as below.

Proposition 3.3.1. $\forall h, g(g \sqsubseteq h \Rightarrow g \preceq h \Rightarrow g \widehat{\subseteq} h)$

It also appears that the shift-equivalence is indeed the congruence relation induced by the subgranularity relation.

Proposition 3.3.2. $\forall h, g(g \leftrightarrow h \textit{ iff } g \sqsubseteq h \textit{ and } h \sqsubseteq g)$

It is an equivalence relation and if we consider the quotient set of granularity modulo shift-equivalence, then $\sqsubseteq$ but also $\preceq$ and $\trianglelefteq$ define partial orders (and thus partition as well) and $\widehat{\subseteq}$ is still a pre-order.

3.3.3 Granularity systems and calendars

For the purpose of using the granularities, it is more convenient to study granularity systems, i.e., sets of granularities related by different constraints.

A *calendar* is a set S of granularities over the same time domain that includes a granularity g such that $\forall h \in S(g \trianglelefteq h)$. Considering sets of granularities in which items can be converted, there are four important design choices:

The choice of the absolute time set $\mathcal{A}$ dense, discrete or continuous.

Restriction on the use of the index set if it is common to all granularities, otherwise, the restriction hold between them; the authors offer the choice between $\mathbb{N}$ or $\mathbb{N}^+$. More generally, the choice can be done among index sets isomorphic to these.

Constraints on the granularities no gaps within a granule, no gaps between granules, no gaps on left/right (i.e., the granularity covers the whole domain), with uniform extent.

Constraints between granularities which can be expressed through the above-defined relationships.

They define, as their reference granularity frame, the *General Granularity on Reals* by:

- Absolute time is the set $\mathbb{R}$;
- index set is $\mathbb{N}^+$;
- no restrictions on granules;
- no two granularities are in shift-equivalent.

Two particular units $g_\top$ and $g_\bot$ can be defined such that:

$$\forall i \in \mathbb{N}^+, g_\bot(i) = \emptyset \text{ and } g_\top(i) = \begin{cases} T & \text{if } i = 1; \\ \emptyset & \text{otherwise.} \end{cases}$$

It is shown [Bettini *et al.*, 1996] that under sensible assumptions (namely, order-preservation or convexity-contiguity-totality), the set of units is a lattice with respect to $\preceq$ in which $g_\top$ (resp. $g_\bot$) is the greatest (resp. lowest) element. In [Bettini *et al.*, 2000], it is proved that this applies to any granularity system having no two granularity shift-equivalence (i.e., $\leftrightarrow = \emptyset$). This is important because any granularity system can be quotiented by shift-equivalence.

Finally, two conversion operators on the set of granularities are defined. The *upward conversion* between granularities is defined as:

$$\forall i \in I_g, \uparrow_g^h i = \begin{cases} j & \text{if } \exists j \in I_h(g(i) \subseteq h(j)); \\ undefined & \text{otherwise.} \end{cases}$$

Notice that the upward operator is thus only defined in the aligned case expressed by the "finer than" relationship.

Proposition 3.3.3. *if $g \preceq h$, then $\uparrow_g^h$ is always defined.*

The *downward conversion* between granularities is defined as:

$$\forall j \in I_h, \downarrow_g^h j = \begin{cases} \langle i, k \rangle & \text{if } h(j) = \cup_{x=i}^{i+k-1} g(x); \\ undefined & \text{otherwise.} \end{cases}$$

The result is thus the set of elements covered by $h(j)$. Obviously, here the "groups into" relation between the granularities ensures the totality of the downward conversion.

Proposition 3.3.4. *if $g \trianglelefteq h$, then $\downarrow_g^h$ is always defined.*

3.3.4 Algebra for generating granularities

As it is usual in the database tradition, the authors investigate the many ways in which granularities can be freely generated by applying operations to other granularities. This can be used for defining the free generated system from a set of base granularities over the same temporal domain and a set of operations. With these operations will naturally come corresponding conversion operators.

Two set of operations are identified: grouping (or group-oriented) operations, which create a granularity by grouping granules of another granularity, and selection (or granule-oriented) operations, which create a granularity by selecting granules of another granularity.

These operations are informally described below. Interested readers must refer to [Bettini *et al.*, 2000] which adds new notions (label-aligned subgranularities) for facilitating their introduction.

Grouping operations are the following:

$group_m(g)$ groups m granules of a granularity g into one granule of granularity $group_m(g)$;

$alter_{l,k}^m(g, g')$ modifies granularity g such that any l^{th} granule having k additional granules of g' (g' must partition g, k can be negative);

$shift_m(g)$ creates a granularity shift-equivalent to g modulo m;

$combine(g, h)$ creates a new granularity whose granules group granules of h belonging to the same granule of g;

$anchor - group(g, h)$ creates a new granularity by adding to each granule of h all following granules of g before the next granule of h.

Selection operations are the following:

$subset_m^n(g)$ selects the granules of g whose index are between m and n;

$select - up(g, h)$ selects the granules of g that contain at least one granule of h;

$select - down_k^l(g, h)$ selects the l granules of g starting with the kth in each granule of h;

$select - by - intersect_k^l(g, h)$ selects the k granules of g starting with the lth in each ordered set of granules intersecting any granule of h;

$union(g, h)$, $intersection(g, h)$, $difference(g, h)$ are defined as the corresponding operations on the set of granules of two subgranularities of the same reference granularity.

A consequence of the choice of these operations is that the operators never create finer granularities from coarser ones (they either group granules for a coarser granularity or select a subset of the granules of one existing granularity). This can be applied, for instance, generating many granularities starting with the `second` granularity (directly inspired from [Bettini *et al.*, 2000]):

$$
\begin{aligned}
\texttt{minute} &= group_{60}(\texttt{second})\\
\texttt{hour} &= group_{60}(\texttt{minute})\\
\texttt{USEasthour} &= shift_{-5}(\texttt{hour})\\
\texttt{day} &= group_{24}(\texttt{hour})\\
\texttt{week} &= group_{7}(\texttt{day})\\
\texttt{busi-day} &= select-down_{1}^{5}(\texttt{day}, \texttt{week})\\
\texttt{month} &= alter^{12*400}_{2+12*399,1}(\texttt{day}, alter^{12*100}_{2+12*99,-1}(\texttt{day}, alter^{12*4}_{2+12*3,1}(\texttt{day},\\
&\quad alter^{12}_{11,-1}(\texttt{day}, alter^{12}_{9,-1}(\texttt{day}, alter^{12}_{6,-1}(\texttt{day}, alter^{12}_{4,-1}(\texttt{day},\\
&\quad alter^{12}_{2,-3}(\texttt{day}, group_{31}(\texttt{day}))))))\\
\texttt{year} &= group_{12}(\texttt{month})\\
\texttt{academicyear} &= anchor-group(\texttt{day},\\
&\quad select-by-intersect_{1}^{1}(\texttt{busi-day}, select-down_{9}^{1}(\texttt{month})
\end{aligned}
$$

As a matter of fact, these granularities can be generated in a more controlled way. Indeed, the authors distinguish three layers of granularities:

L_1 containing the bottom granularity and all the granularities obtained by applying $group$, $alter$, and $shift$ on granularities of this layer;

L_2 including L_1 and containing all the granularities obtained by applying $subset$, $union$, $intersection$, and $difference$ on granularities of this layer and selections with first operand belonging to this layer;

L_3 including L_2 and containing all the granularities obtained by applying $combine$ on granularities of this layer and $anchor - group$ with the second operand on granularities of this layer.

Granularities of L_1 are full-integer labelled granularities, those of L_2 may not be labelled by all integers, but they contain no gaps within granules. These aspects, as well as the expressiveness of the generated granularities, are investigated in depth in [Bettini *et al.*, 2000].

3.3.5 Constraint solving and query answering

Wang et al. [Wang *et al.*, 1995] have proposed an extension of the relational data model which is able to handle granularity. The goal of this work is to take into account possible granularity mismatch in the context of federated databases.

An extended temporal model is a relational database in which each tuple is timestamped under some granularity. Formally, it is a set of tables such that each table is a quadruple

$\langle R, \phi, \tau, g \rangle$ such that R is a set of tuples (a relational table), g is a granularity, $\phi : \mathbb{N} \longrightarrow 2^R$ maps granules to tuples, $\tau : R \longrightarrow 2^{\mathbb{N}}$ maps tuples to granules such that $\forall t \in R, t \in \phi(i) \Rightarrow i \in \tau(t)$ and $\forall i \in \mathbb{N}, i \in \tau(t) \Rightarrow t \in \phi(i)$.

In [Bettini *et al.*, 2000], the authors develop methods for answering queries in database with granularities. The answers are computed with regard to hypotheses tied to the databases. These hypotheses allow the computation of values between two successive timestamps. The missing values can, for instance, be considered constant (persistence) or interpolated with a particular interpolation function. These hypotheses also apply to the computation of values between granularity.

The hypotheses (H) provide the way to compute the closure ($\overline{D}^H$) of a particular database (D). Answering a query q against a database with granularities D and hypotheses H consists in answering the query against the closure of the database ($\overline{D}^H \models q$). Instead of computing this costly closure, the authors proposes to $reduce$ the database with regard to the hypotheses (i.e., to find the minimal database equivalent to the initial one modulo closure) and to add to the query formulas allowing the computation of the hypotheses.

The authors also define quantitative temporal constraint satisfaction problems under granularity whose variables correspond to points and arcs are labelled by an integer interval and a granularity. A pair of points $\langle t, t' \rangle$ satisfies a constraint $[m, n]g$ (with $m, n \in \mathbb{Z}$ and g a granularity) if and only if $\uparrow^g t$ and $\uparrow^g t'$ are defined and $m \leq | \uparrow^g t - \uparrow^g t'| \leq n$. These constraints cannot be expressed as a classical TCSP (see Chapter 7). As a matter of fact, if the constraint $[0\ 0]$ is set on two entities under the hour granularity, two points satisfy it if they are in the same hour. In terms of seconds, the positions should differ from 0 to 3600. However, $[0\ 3600]$ under the second granularity does not corresponds to the original constraint since it can be satisfied by two points in different hours.

The satisfaction problem for granular constraint satisfaction is NP-hard (while STP is polynomial) [Bettini *et al.*, 1996]. Indeed the modulo operation involved in the conversions can introduce disjunctive constraints (or non convexity). For instance, next business day is the convex constraint ($[1\ 1]$), which converted in hours can yield the constraint $[1\ 24] \vee [49\ 72]$ which is dependent on the exact day of the week.

The authors propose an arc-consistency algorithm complete for consistency checking when the granularities are periodical with regard to some common finer granularity. They also propose an approximate (i.e., incomplete) algorithm by iterating the saturation of the networks of constraints expressed under the same granularity and then converting the new values into the other granularities.

The work described above mainly concerns aligned systems of granularity (i.e., systems in which the upward conversion is always defined). This is not always the case, as the week/month example illustrates it. Non-aligned granularity has been considered by several authors. Dyreson and collaborators [Dyreson and Snodgrass, 1994] define comparison operators across granularities and their semantics (this covers the extended comparators of [Wang *et al.*, 1995]): comparison between entities of different granularities can be considered under the coarser granularity (here coarser is the same as "groups into" above and thus requires alignment) or the finer one. They define upward and downward conversion operators across comparable granularities and the conversion across non-comparable granularities is carried out by first converting down to the greatest lower bound and then up (assuming the greatest lower bound exists and thus that the structure is a lower semi-lattice): $\downarrow^g_{g \wedge g'} \uparrow^{g'}_{g \wedge g'} x$. Comparisons across granularities (with both semantics) are implemented in terms of the conversion operators.

3.3.6 Alternative accounts of time granularity

The set-theoretic approach has been recently revisited and extended in several directions. In the following, we briefly summarize the most promising ones.

An alternative string-based model for time granularities has been proposed by Wijsen [Wijsen, 2000]. It models (infinite) granularities as (infinite) words over an alphabet consisting of three symbols, namely, ■ (filler), □ (gap), and ≀ (separator), which are respectively used to denote time points covered by some granule, to denote time points not covered by any granule, and to delimit granules. Wijsen focuses his attention on (infinite) periodical granularities, that is, granularities which are left bounded and, ultimately, periodically groups time points of the underlying temporal domain. Periodical granularities can be identified with ultimately periodic strings, and they can be finitely represented by specifying a (possibly empty) finite prefix and a finite repeating pattern. As an example, the granularity `BusinessWeek` ■■■■■□□ ≀ ■■■■■□□ ≀ ... can be encoded by the empty prefix ε and the repeating pattern ■■■■■□□≀. Wijsen shows how to use the string-based model to solve some fundamental problems about granularities, such as the equivalence problem (to establish whether or not two given representations define the same granularity) and the minimization problem (to compute the most compact representation of a granularity). In particular, he provides a straightforward solution to the equivalence problem that takes advantage of a suitable *aligned form* of strings. Such a form forces separators to occur immediately after an occurrence of ■, thus guaranteeing a one-to-one correspondence between granularities and strings.

The idea of viewing time granularities as ultimately periodic strings establishes a natural connection with the field of formal languages and automata. An automaton-based approach to time granularity has been proposed by Dal Lago and Montanari in [Dal Lago and Montanari, 2001], and later revisited by Bresolin et al. in [Bresolin *et al.*, 2004; Dal Lago *et al.*, 2003a; Dal Lago *et al.*, 2003b]. The basic idea underlying such an approach is simple: we take an automaton $\mathcal{A}$ recognizing a *single* ultimately periodic word $u \in \{\square, \blacksquare, \blacktriangleleft\}^{\omega}$ and we say that $\mathcal{A}$ represents the granularity G if and only if u represents G. The resulting framework views granularities as strings generated by a specific class of automata, called Single-String Automata (SSA), thus making it possible to (re)use well-known results from automata theory. In order to compactly encode the redundancies of the temporal structures, SSA are endowed with counters ranging over discrete finite domains (Extended SSA, ESSA for short). Properties of ESSA have been exploited to efficiently solve the equivalence and the granule conversion problems for single time granularities [Dal Lago *et al.*, 2003b]. The relationships between ESSA and Calendar Algebra have been systematically investigated by Dal Lago et al. in [Dal Lago *et al.*, 2003a], where a number of algorithms that map Calendar Algebra expressions into automaton-based representations of time granularities are given. Such an encoding allows one to reduce problems about Calendar Algebra expressions to equivalent problems for ESSA. More generally, the operational flavor of ESSA suggests an alternative point of view on the role of automaton-based representations: besides a formalism for the direct specification of time granularities, automata can be viewed as a low-level formalism into which high-level time granularity specifications, such as those of Calendar Algebra, can be mapped. This allows one to exploit the benefits of both formalisms, using a high level language to define granularities and their properties in a natural and flexible way, and the automaton-based one to efficiently reason about them. Finally, a generalization of the automaton-based approach from single periodical granularities to (possibly infinite) sets of granularities has been proposed by Bresolin et al. in [Bresolin *et al.*, 2004]. To this end, they identify a proper subclass of Büchi automata, called Ultimately Periodic Automata (UPA), that captures regular sets consisting of only ultimately periodic words. UPA allow one to encode single granularities, (possibly infinite) sets of granularities which have the same repeating pattern and different prefixes, and sets of granularities characterized by a finite set of non-equivalent patterns, as well as any possible combination of them.

The choice of Propositional Linear Temporal Logic (Propositional LTL) as a logical tool for granularity management has been recently advocated by Combi et al. in [Combi *et al.*, 2004]. Time granularities are defined as models of Propositional LTL formulas, where suitable propositional symbols are used to mark the endpoints of granules. In this way, a large set of regular granularities, such as, for instance, repeating patterns that can start at an arbitrary time point, can be captured. Moreover, problems like checking the consistency of a granularity specification or the equivalence of two granularity expressions can be solved in a uniform way by reducing them to the validity problem for Propositional LTL, which is known to be in PSPACE. An extension of Propositional LTL that replaces propositional variables by first-order formulas defining integer constraints, e.g., $x \equiv_k y$, has been proposed by Demri in [Demri, 2004]. The resulting logic, denoted by PLTL^{mod}(Past LTL with integer periodicity constraints), generalizes both the logical framework proposed by Combi et al. and the automaton-based approach of Dal Lago and Montanari, and it allows one to compactly define granularities as periodicity constraints. In particular, the author shows how to reduce the equivalence problem for ESSA to the model checking problem for PLTL^{mod}(-automata), which turns out to be in PSPACE, as in the case of Propositional LTL. The logical approach to time granularity is systematically analyzed in the next section, where various temporal logics for time granularity are presented.

3.4 The logical approach

A first attempt at incorporating time granularity into a logical formalism is outlined in [Corsetti *et al.*, 1991a; Corsetti *et al.*, 1991b]. The proposed logical system for time granularity has two distinctive features. On the one hand, it extends the syntax of temporal logic to allow one to associate different granularities (temporal domains) with different subformulas of a given formula; on the other hand, it provides a set of translation rules to rewrite a subformula associated with a given granularity into a corresponding subformula associated with a finer granularity. In such a way, a model of a formula involving different granularities can be built by first translating everything to the finest granularity and then by interpreting the resulting (flat) formula in the standard way.

A major problem with such a method is that there exists no a standard way to define the meaning of a formula when moving from a time granularity to another one. Thus, more information is needed from the user to drive the translation of the (sub)formulas. The main idea is that when we state that a predicate p holds at a given time point x belonging to the temporal domain T, we mean that p holds in a subset of the interval corresponding to x in the finer domain T'. Such a subset can be the whole interval, a scattered sequence of smaller intervals, or even a single time point. For instance, saying that "the light has been switched on at time x_{min}", where x_{min} belong to the domain of minutes, may correspond to state that a predicate *switching_on* is true at the minute x_{min} and exactly at one second of x_{min}. Instead, saying that an employee works at the day x_d generally means that there are several minutes, during the day x_d, where the predicate *work* holds for the employee. These minutes are not necessarily contiguous. Thus, the logical system must provide the user with suitable tools that allow him to qualify the subset of time intervals of the finer temporal domain that correspond to the given time point of the coarser domain.

A substantially different approach is proposed in [Ciapessoni *et al.*, 1993; Montanari, 1994; Montanari, 1996], where Montanari et al. show how to extend syntax and semantics of temporal logic to cope with metric temporal properties possibly expressed at different time granularities. The resulting metric and layered temporal logic is described in detail in Subsection 3.4.1. Its distinctive feature is the coexistence of three different operators: a contextual operator, to associate different granularities with different (sub)formulas, a displacement operator, to move within a given granularity, and a projection operator, to move across granularities.

An alternative logical framework for time granularity has been developed in the classical logic setting [Montanari, 1996; Montanari and Policriti, 1996; Montanari *et al.*, 1999]. It imposes suitable restrictions to languages and structures for time granularity to get decidability. From a technical point of view, it defines various theories of time granularity as suitable extensions of monadic second-order theories of k successors, with $k \geq 1$. Monadic theories of time granularity are the subject of Subsection 3.4.2.

The temporal logic counterparts of the monadic theories of time granularity, called temporalized logics, are briefly presented in Subsection 3.4.3. This way back from the classical logic setting to the temporal logic one passes through an original class of automata, called temporalized automata.

A coda about the relationships between logics for time granularity and interval temporal logics concludes the section.

3.4.1 A metric and layered temporal logic for time granularity

Original metric and layered temporal logics for time granularity have been proposed by Montanari et al. in [Ciapessoni *et al.*, 1993; Montanari, 1994; Montanari, 1996]. We introduce these logics in two steps. First, we take into consideration their purely metric fragments in isolation. To do that, we adopt the general two-sorted framework proposed in [Montanari, 1996; Montanari and de Rijke, 1997], where a number of metric temporal logics, having a different expressive power, are defined as suitable combinations of a temporal component and an algebraic one. Successively, we show how flat metric temporal logic can be generalized to a many-layer metric temporal logic, embedding the notion of time granularity [Montanari, 1994; Montanari, 1996]. We first identify the main functionalities a logic for time granularity must support and the constraints it must satisfy; then, we axiomatically define metric and layered temporal logic, viewed as the combination of a number of differently-grained (single-layer) metric temporal logics, and we briefly discuss its logical properties.

The basic metric component

The idea of a logic of positions (topological, or metric, logic) was originally formulated by Rescher and Garson [Rescher and Garson, 1968; Rescher and Urquhart, 1971]. In [Rescher and Garson, 1968], the authors define the basic features of the logic and they show how to give it a temporal interpretation. Roughly speaking, metric (temporal) logic extends propositional logic with a parameterized operator Δ_α of positional realization that allows one to constrain the truth value of a proposition at position α. If we interpret the parameter α as a displacement with respect to the current position, which is left implicit, we have that $\Delta_\alpha q$ is true at a position x if and only if q is true at a position y at distance α from x. Metric temporal logics can thus be viewed as two-sorted logics having both formulas and parameters; formulas are evaluated at time points while parameters take values in a suitable algebraic structure of temporal displacements. In [Montanari and de Rijke, 1997], Montanari and de Rijke start with a very basic system of metric temporal logic, and they build on it by adding axioms and/or by enriching the underlying structures. In the following, we describe the metric temporal logic of two-sorted frames with a linear temporal order (*MTL*); we also briefly consider general metric temporal logics allowing quantification over algebraic and temporal variables and free mixing of algebraic and temporal formulas (*Q-MTL*).

The *two-sorted temporal language* for *MTL* has two components: the algebraic component and the temporal one. Given a non-empty set A of constants, let $T(A)$ be the set of terms over A, that is, the smallest set such that $A \subseteq T(A)$, and if $\alpha, \beta \in T(A)$ then $\alpha + \beta, -\alpha, 0 \in T(A)$. The first-order (algebraic) component is built up from $T(A)$ and the predicate symbols $=$ and $<$. The temporal component of the language is built up from a non-empty set $\mathcal{P}$ of proposition letters. The set of formulas over $\mathcal{P}$ and A, $F(\mathcal{P}, A)$, is the smallest set such that $\mathcal{P} \subseteq F(\mathcal{P}, A)$, and if $\phi, \psi \in F(\mathcal{P}, A)$ and $\alpha \in T(A)$, then $\neg\phi$, $\phi \wedge \psi$, $\top$ (true), $\bot$ (false), and $\Delta_\alpha\phi$ (and its dual $\nabla_\alpha\phi := \neg\Delta_\alpha\neg\phi$) belong to $F(\mathcal{P}, A)$. Δ_α is called the (parameterized) *displacement operator*.

A *two-sorted frame* is a triple $\mathbf{F} = (T, \mathbf{D}; \text{DIS})$, where T is the set of (time) points over which temporal formulas are evaluated, $\mathbf{D}$ is the algebra of metric displacements in whose domain D terms take their values, and $\text{DIS} \subseteq T \times D \times T$ is an accessibility relation, called displacement relation, relating pairs of points and displacements. The components of two-sorted frames satisfy the following properties. First, $\mathbf{D}$ is an ordered Abelian group, that is, a structure $\mathbf{D} = (D, +, -, 0, <)$, where $+$ is a binary function of displacement composition, $-$ is a unary function of inverse displacement, and 0 is the zero displacement constant, such that:

(i)	$\alpha + \beta = \beta + \alpha$	(commutativity of $+$);
(ii)	$\alpha + (\beta + \gamma) = (\alpha + \beta) + \gamma$	(associativity of $+$);
(iii)	$\alpha + 0 = \alpha$	(zero element of $+$);
(iv)	$\alpha + (-\alpha) = 0$	(inverse),

and $<$ is an irreflexive, asymmetric, transitive, and linear relation that satisfies the comparability property (*viii*) below:

(v) $\neg(\alpha < \alpha)$;
(vi) $\neg(\alpha < \beta \wedge \beta < \alpha)$;
(vii) $\alpha < \beta \wedge \beta < \gamma \rightarrow \alpha < \gamma$;
$(viii)$ $\alpha < \beta \vee \alpha = \beta \vee \beta < \alpha$.

Furthermore, there are two conditions expressing the relations between $+$ and $-$, and $<$:

(ix) $\alpha < \beta \rightarrow \alpha + \gamma < \beta + \gamma$;
(x) $\alpha < \beta \rightarrow -\beta < -\alpha$.

As for the displacement relation, we first require DIS to respect the converse operation of the Abelian group in the following sense:

Symmetry: $\forall i, j, \alpha\, (\text{DIS}(i, \alpha, j) \rightarrow \text{DIS}(j, -\alpha, i))$.

Furthermore, we require DIS to be reflexive, transitive, quasi-functional (q-functional for short) with respect to both its third and second argument, and totally connected:

Reflexivity: $\forall i\, \text{DIS}(i, 0, i)$;
Transitivity: $\forall i, j, k, \alpha, \beta\, (\text{DIS}(i, \alpha, j) \wedge \text{DIS}(j, \beta, k) \rightarrow \text{DIS}(i, \alpha + \beta, k))$;
Q-functionality - 1: $\forall i, j, j', \alpha\, (\text{DIS}(i, \alpha, j) \wedge \text{DIS}(i, \alpha, j') \rightarrow j = j')$;
Q-functionality - 2: $\forall i, j, \alpha, \beta\, (\text{DIS}(i, \alpha, j) \wedge \text{DIS}(i, \beta, j) \rightarrow \alpha = \beta)$;
Total connectedness: $\forall i, j \exists \alpha\, \text{DIS}(i, \alpha, j)$.

From the ordering $<$ on the algebraic component of the frames, an ordering $\ll$ on the temporal component can be defined as follows:

$$i \ll j \text{ iff for some } \alpha > 0, \text{DIS}(i, \alpha, j). \tag{3.1}$$

According to Definition 3.1, we have that i and j are $\ll$-related if there exists a positive displacement between them. It is possible to show that $\ll$ is a strict linear order [Montanari and de Rijke, 1997] (it is worth noting that, without the properties of quasi-functionality with respect to the second argument and total connectedness, Definition 3.1 does not produce a strict linear order).

The interpretation of the language for *MTL* on two-sorted frames based on an ordered Abelian group is fairly straightforward: the first-order (algebraic) component is interpreted on the ordered Abelian group, and the temporal component on the temporal domain. Basically, a two-sorted frame $\mathbf{F}$ can be turned into a *two-sorted model* by adding an interpretation for the algebraic terms and a valuation for proposition letters. An interpretation for algebraic terms is given by a function $g : A \rightarrow D$ that is automatically extended to all terms from $T(A)$. A valuation is simply a function $V : \mathcal{P} \rightarrow 2^T$. We say that $\alpha = \beta$ (resp. $\alpha < \beta$) is *true* in a model $\mathbf{M} = (T, \mathbf{D}; \text{DIS}; V, g)$ whenever $g(\alpha) = g(\beta)$ (resp. $g(\alpha) < g(\beta)$). *Truth* of temporal formulas is defined by means of the standard semantic clauses for proposition letters and Boolean connectives, plus the following clause for the displacement operator:

$$\mathbf{M}, i \Vdash \Delta_\alpha \phi \quad \text{iff} \quad \text{there exists } j \text{ such that DIS}(i, g(\alpha), j) \text{ and } \mathbf{M}, j \Vdash \phi.$$

Let Γ denote a set of formulas. To avoid messy complications we only consider one-sorted consequences $\Gamma \models \phi$; for algebraic formulas '$\Gamma \models \phi$' means 'for all models $\mathbf{M}$, if $\mathbf{M} \models \Gamma$, then $\mathbf{M} \models \phi$'; for temporal formulas it means 'for all models $\mathbf{M}$, and time points i, if $\mathbf{M}, i \Vdash \Gamma$, then $\mathbf{M}, i \Vdash \phi$'.

The following example shows that the language of *MTL* allows one to express meaningful temporal conditions.

Example 3.4.1. *Let us consider a communication channel C that collects messages from n different sources $S_1, \ldots, S_n$ and outputs them with delay δ. To exclude that two input events can occur simultaneously, we add the constraint (notice that preventing input events from occurring simultaneously also guarantees that output events do not occur simultaneously):*

$$\forall i, j\, \neg(\mathtt{in}(i) \wedge \mathtt{in}(j) \wedge i \neq j),$$

which is shorthand for:

$$\neg(\mathtt{in}(1) \wedge \mathtt{in}(2)) \wedge \ldots \wedge \neg(\mathtt{in}(n-1) \wedge \mathtt{in}(n)).$$

The behavior of C is specified by the formula:

$$\forall i\,(\mathtt{out}(i) \leftrightarrow \Delta_{-\delta}\mathtt{in}(i)),$$

which is shorthand for a finite conjunction.

Validity in *MTL* can be axiomatized as follows. For the displacement component, one takes the axioms and rules of identity, ordered Abelian groups, and strict linear order, together with any complete calculus for first-order logic. For the temporal component, one takes the usual axioms of propositional logic plus the axioms:

(AxND)	$\nabla_\alpha(p \to q) \to (\nabla_\alpha p \to \nabla_\alpha q)$	(normality);
(AxSD)	$p \to \nabla_\alpha \Delta_{-\alpha} p,$	(symmetry);
(AxRD)	$\nabla_0 p \to p$	(reflexivity);
(AxTD)	$\nabla_{\alpha+\beta} p \to \nabla_\alpha \nabla_\beta p$	(transitivity);
(AxQD)	$\Delta_\alpha p \to \nabla_\alpha p$	(q-functionality - 1).

Its rules are modus ponens and

(D-NEC)	$\vdash \phi \Longrightarrow \vdash \nabla_\alpha \phi$	(necessitation rule for ∇_α);
(REP)	$\vdash \phi \leftrightarrow \psi \Longrightarrow \vdash \chi(\phi/p) \leftrightarrow \chi(\psi/p)$	(replacement),
	where (ϕ/p) denotes substitution of ϕ for the variable p;	
(LIFT)	$\vdash \alpha = \beta \Longrightarrow \vdash \nabla_\alpha \phi \leftrightarrow \nabla_\beta \phi$	(transfer of identities).

Axiom (AxN) is the usual distribution axiom; axiom (AxS) expresses that a displacement α is the converse of a displacement $-\alpha$; axioms (AxR), (AxT), and (AxQ) capture reflexivity, transitivity, and quasi-functionality with respect to the third argument, respectively. A suitable adaptation of two truth preserving constructions from standard modal logic to the *MTL* setting allows one to show there are no *MTL* formulas that express total connectedness and quasi-functionality with respect to the second argument of the displacement relation [Montanari and de Rijke, 1997]. The rules (D-NEC) and (REP) are familiar from modal logic. Finally, the rule (LIFT) allows one to transfer provable algebraic identities from the displacement domain to the temporal one.

A *derivation in MTL* is a sequence of formulas $\sigma_1, \ldots, \sigma_n$ such that each σ_i, with $1 \le i \le n$, is either an axiom or obtained from $\sigma_1, \ldots, \sigma_{n-1}$ by applying one of the derivation rules of *MTL*. We write $\vdash_{MTL} \sigma$ to denote that there is a derivation in *MTL* that ends in σ. It immediately follows that $\vdash_{MTL} \alpha = \beta$ iff $\alpha = \beta$ is provable from the axioms of the algebraic component only: whereas we can lift algebraic information from the displacement domain to the temporal domain using the (LIFT) rule, there is no way in which we can import temporal information into the displacement domain. As with consequences, we only consider one-sorted inferences '$\Gamma \vdash \phi$'.

Theorem 3.4.1. *MTL is sound and complete for the class of all transitive, reflexive, totally-connected, and quasi-functional (in both the second and third argument of their displacement relation) frames.*

The proof of soundness is trivial. The completeness proof is much more involved [Montanari and de Rijke, 1997]. It is accomplished in two steps: first, one proves completeness with respect to totally connected frames via same sort of generated submodel construction; then, a second construction is needed to guarantee quasi-functionality with respect to the second argument.

Propositional variants of *MTL* are studied in [Montanari and de Rijke, 1997]. As an example, one natural specialization of *MTL* is obtained by adding discreteness. As in the case of the ordering, the discreteness of the temporal domain necessarily follows from that of the domain of temporal displacements, which is expressed by the following formula:

$$\begin{array}{l}\forall\alpha\,\exists\beta,\beta'(\alpha<\beta\wedge\forall\gamma(\alpha<\gamma\rightarrow(\beta=\gamma\vee\beta<\gamma))\wedge\\ \beta'<\alpha\wedge\forall\delta(\delta<\alpha\rightarrow(\beta'=\delta\vee\beta'<\delta)))\end{array}$$

Proposition 3.4.1. *Let* $\mathbf{F}=(T,\mathbf{D};\mathrm{DIS})$ *be a two-sorted frame based on a discrete ordered Abelian group* $\mathbf{D}$. *For all* $i,j\in T$, *there exist only finitely many* k *such that* $i\ll k\ll j$.

For some applications, both *MTL* and its propositional variants are not expressive enough, and thus they must be extended. In particular, they lack quantification and constrain displacements to occur as parameters of the displacement operator only. The following example shows how the ability of freely mixing temporal and displacement formulas enables one to exploit more complex ways of interaction between the two domains, rather than to only lift information from the algebraic domain to the temporal one.

Example 3.4.2. *Let us consider the operation of a traffic light controller* C *[Henzinger* et al., *1994]. When the request button is pushed, the controller makes a pedestrian light turn green within a given time bound after which the light remains green for a certain amount of time. Moreover, assume that* C *takes a unit of time to switch the light and that the time needed for its internal operations is negligible.*

We require that C *satisfies the following conditions:*

(i) whenever a pedestrian pushes the request button ('request is true'), then the light is green within 5 time units and remains green for at least 10 time units (this condition guarantees that no pedestrian waits for more than 5 time units, and that he or she is given at least 10 time units to cross the road);

(ii) whenever request is true, then it is false within 20 time units (this condition ensures that the request button is reset);

(iii) whenever request has been false for 20 time units, the light is red (this condition should prevent the light from always being green).

By taking advantage of the possibility of quantifying displacement variables and of using displacement formulas, the behavior of C *can be specified by the conjunction of the following formulas:*

$$\begin{array}{lcl}\text{request} & \rightarrow & \exists x(0<x\leq 5\wedge\forall y(x\leq y<x+10\rightarrow\nabla_y\text{lightIsGreen}));\\ \text{request} & \rightarrow & \exists z(0\leq z\leq 20\wedge\Delta_z\neg\,\text{request});\\ \multicolumn{3}{l}{\forall x(0\leq x<20\rightarrow\nabla_x\neg\text{request})\rightarrow\nabla_{20}\text{lightIsRed},}\end{array}$$

together with a formula stating that at each time point the traffic light is either red or green:

$$\text{lightIsGreen} \leftrightarrow \neg\, \text{lightIsRed}.$$

Different implementations of C, all satisfying the given specification, can be obtained by making different assumptions about the value of temporal parameters, e.g., by varying the delay between requests and resets. It is worth noting that, even if there are no restrictions on the frequency of requests, the above specification is appropriate only if that frequency is low; otherwise, it may happen that switching the light to red is delayed indefinitely. A solution to this problem is discussed in [Montanari, 1996].

Systems of quantified metric temporal logic (*Q-MTL* for short) are developed in [Montanari and de Rijke, 1997]. The language of *Q-MTL* extends that of *MTL* by adding algebraic variables (and, possibly, temporal variables) and by allowing quantification over algebraic (and temporal) variables and free mixing of algebraic formulas and temporal propositional symbols. *Q-MTL* models can be obtained from ordered two-sorted frames $\mathbf{F} = (T, \mathbf{D}; \text{DIS})$ by adding an interpretation function g for the algebraic terms and a valuation V for proposition letters, and by specifying the way one evaluates mixed formulas at time points. An axiomatic system for *Q-MTL* (we refer to the simplest system of quantified metric temporal logic; other cases are considered in [Montanari and de Rijke, 1997]) is obtained from that for *MTL* by adding a number of axiom schemata governing the behavior of quantifiers and substitutions:

(AxF) $\forall x\, (\phi \rightarrow \psi) \leftrightarrow (\forall x\, \phi \rightarrow \forall x\, \psi)$ (functionality);
(AxEVQ) $\phi \rightarrow \forall x\, \phi$, for x not in ϕ
(elimination of vacuous quantifiers);
(AxUI) $\forall x\, \phi \rightarrow \phi(\alpha/x)$, with α free for x in ϕ
(universal instantiation),

the Barcan formula for the displacement operator:

(AxBFD) $\forall x\, \nabla_\alpha \phi \rightarrow \nabla_\alpha \forall x\, \phi$, with $x \notin \alpha$ (Barcan formula for ∇_α),
where $x \notin \alpha$ stands for $x \neq \alpha$ and x does not occur in α,

the axioms relating the algebraic terms and the displacement operator (axiom (AxAD4) can actually be derived from the other axioms):

(AxAD1) $\alpha = \beta \rightarrow \forall x \nabla_x \alpha = \beta$; (AxAD2) $\alpha \neq \beta \rightarrow \forall x \nabla_x \alpha \neq \beta$;
(AxAD3) $\alpha < \beta \rightarrow \forall x \nabla_x \alpha < \beta$; (AxAD4) $\alpha \not< \beta \rightarrow \forall x \nabla_x \alpha \not< \beta$,

and the rule:

(UG) $\vdash \phi \Longrightarrow \vdash \forall x\, \phi$ (universal generalization).

The completeness of *Q-MTL* can be proved by following the general pattern of the completeness proof for *MTL*, but the presence of mixed formulas complicates some of the details. Basically, it makes use of a variant of Hughes and Cresswell's method for proving axiomatic completeness in the presence of the Barcan formula [Hughes and Cresswell, 1968].

The addition of time granularity

Metric and Layered Temporal Logic (*MLTL* for short) is obtained from *MTL* by adding a notion of time granularity [Ciapessoni *et al.*, 1993; Montanari, 1994; Montanari, 1996]. In the following, we first show how to extend two-sorted frames to incorporate granularity; then, we present syntax, semantics, and axiomatization of *MLTL*; finally, we briefly describe the way in which the synchronization problem (cf. Section 3.2) can be dealt with in *MLTL*.

The main change to make to the model of time when moving from *MTL* to *MLTL* is the replacement of the temporal domain T by a temporal universe $\mathcal{T}$ consisting of a set of *disjoint* linear temporal domains/layers, that share the same displacement domain D. Formally, $\mathcal{T} = \{T^i : i \in M\}$, where M is an initial segment of $\mathbb{N}$, possibly equal to $\mathbb{N}$. The set $\bigcup_{i \in M} T^i$ collects all time points belonging to the different layers of $\mathcal{T}$. $\mathcal{T}$ is assumed to be *totally ordered* by the granularity relation $\prec$. As an example, if $\mathcal{T} = \{\texttt{years}, \texttt{months}, \texttt{weeks}, \texttt{days}\}$, we have that $\texttt{days} \prec \texttt{weeks} \prec \texttt{months} \prec \texttt{years}$. A finer characterization of the relations among the layers of a temporal universe is provided by the *disjointedness* relation, denoted by $\sqsubset$, which is quite similar to the *groups-into* relation defined in Section 3.3. It defines a partial order over $\mathcal{T}$ that rules out pairs of layers like `weeks` and `months` for which a point of a finer layer (`weeks`) can be astride two points of the coarser one (`months`). As an example, given $\mathcal{T} = \{\texttt{years}, \texttt{months}, \texttt{weeks}, \texttt{days}\}$, we have that $\texttt{months} \sqsubset \texttt{years}$, $\texttt{days} \sqsubset \texttt{months}$, and $\texttt{days} \sqsubset \texttt{weeks}$. This means that `years` are pairwise disjoint when viewed as sets of `months`; the same holds for `months` when viewed as sets of `days`.

The links between points belonging to the same layer are expressed by means of (a number of instances of) the *displacement* relation, while those between points belonging to different layers are given by means of a *decomposition* relation that, for every pair $T^i, T^j \in \mathcal{T}$, with $T^j \prec T^i$, associates each point of T^i with the set of points of T^j that compose it. We assume that the decomposition relation turns every point $x \in T^i$ into a set of contiguous points (decomposition interval) of T^j (*convexity*). This condition excludes the presence of 'temporal gaps' within the set of components of a given point, as it happens, for instance, when `business months` are mapped on `days`. In general, the cardinalities of the sets of components of two distinct points $x, y \in T^i$ with respect to T^j may be different (*non homogeneity*). This is the case, for instance, with pairs of layers like `real months` and `days`: different months can be mapped on a different number of days (28, 29, 30, or 31). In some particular contexts, however, it is convenient to work with temporal universes where, for every pair of layers T^i, T_j, with $T^j \prec T^i$, the decomposition intervals have the same cardinality (*homogeneity*). For instance, this is the case of temporal universes that replace `real months` by `legal months`, which, conventionally, are 30-days long. We constrain the decomposition relation to respect the ordering of points within layers (*order preservation*). If $T^j \sqsubset T^i$, e.g., `seconds` and `minutes`, then the intervals are disjoint; otherwise, the intervals can possibly meet at their endpoints, e.g., `weeks` and `months`. We further require that the union of the intervals of T^j associated with the points of T^i covers the whole T^j (*total covering*). From order preservation and total covering, it follows that, for all pairs of layers T^i, T^j, with $T^j \prec T^i$, the decomposition relation associates contiguous points of T^i with contiguous sets of points of T_j (*contiguity*). This excludes the presence of 'temporal gaps' between the decomposition intervals of consecutive points of the coarser layer, as it happens, for instance, when `business weeks` are mapped on `days`. Finally, we require that, for every i, j, k, if $T^j \sqsubset T^k \sqsubset T^i$, then the decomposition of T^i into T^j can be obtained from the decomposition of T^i into T^k and that of T^k into T^j (*downward transitivity*). The same holds for $T^k \sqsubset T^j \sqsubset T^i$ (*downward/upward transitivity*). In the following, we shall also consider the inverse relation of *abstraction*, that, for every pair $T^i, T^j \in \mathcal{T}$, with

$T^j \prec T^i$, associates a point $x \in T^j$ with a point $y \in T^i$ if x belongs to the the decomposition of y with respect to T^j. Every point $x \in T^j$ can be abstracted into either one or two adjacent points of T^i. If $T^j \subset T^i$, x is abstracted into a unique point y, which is called the *coarse grain equivalent* of x with respect to T^i.

Besides the algebraic and temporal components, the *temporal language* for *MLTL* includes a *context sort*. Moreover, the displacement operator is paired with a contextual operator and a projection operator. Formally, given a non-empty set C of context constants, denoting the layers of the temporal universe, and a set Y of context variables, the set $T(C \cup Y)$ of context terms is equal to $C \cup Y$. The set $T(A \cup X)$ of algebraic terms denoting temporal displacements is built up as follows. Let A be a set of algebraic constants and X be a set of algebraic variables. $T(A \cup X)$ is the smallest set such that $A \subseteq T(A \cup X)$, $X \subseteq T(A \cup X)$, and if $\alpha, \beta \in T(A \cup X)$ then $\alpha + \beta, -\alpha, 0 \in T(A \cup X)$. Finally, given a non-empty set of proposition letters $\mathcal{P}$, the set of formulas $F(\mathcal{P}, A, X, C, Y)$ is the smallest set such that $\mathcal{P} \in F(\mathcal{P}, A, X, C, Y)$, if $\phi, \psi \in F(\mathcal{P}, A, X, C, Y)$, $x \in X$, $y \in Y$, $c, c', c'' \in T(C \cup Y)$, and $\alpha, \beta \in T(X \cup A)$, then $\alpha = \beta, \alpha < \beta, c' \prec c'', c' \subset c'', \neg\phi, \phi \wedge \phi, \Delta_\alpha \phi$ (and $\nabla_\alpha \phi$), $\Delta^c \phi$ (and its dual $\nabla^c \phi := \neg\Delta^c \neg\phi$), $\Diamond\phi$ (and its dual $\Box\phi := \neg\Diamond\neg\phi$), $\forall x\phi$, and $\forall y \phi$ belong to $F(\mathcal{P}, A, X, C, Y)$. Δ^c is called the (parameterized) *contextual operator*. When applied to a formula ϕ, it restricts the evaluation of ϕ to the time points of the layer denoted by c. The combined use of Δ_α and Δ^c makes it possible to define a derived operator Δ^c_α of *contextualized* (or *local*) *displacement*: $\Delta^c_\alpha \phi := \Delta^c \Delta_\alpha \phi$ (and its dual $\nabla^c_\alpha \phi := \nabla^c \nabla_\alpha \phi$). In such a case, the context term c can be viewed as the sort of the algebraic term α (*multi-sorted algebraic terms*). $\Diamond$ is called the *projection operator*. When applied to a formula ϕ, it allows one to evaluate ϕ at time points which are descendants (decomposition) or ancestors (abstraction) of the current one. Restrictions to specific sets of descendants or ancestors can be obtained by pairing the projection operator with the contextual one.

The *two-sorted frame* for time granularity is a tuple

$$\mathbf{F} = ((\mathcal{T}, \prec, \subset), \mathbf{D};\ \mathrm{DIS}, \mathrm{CONT}, \updownarrow)$$

where $\mathcal{T}$ is the temporal universe, $\prec$ and $\subset$ are the granularity and disjointedness relations, respectively, $\mathbf{D}$ is the algebra of metric displacements, $\mathrm{DIS} = \bigcup_{i \in M} \mathrm{DIS}_i$ is the displacement relation, $\mathrm{CONT} \subseteq \bigcup_{i \in M} T^i \times \mathcal{T}$ is the relation of contextualization, and $\updownarrow \subseteq \bigcup_{i \in M} T^i \times \bigcup_{i \in M} T^i$ is the projection relation. $\mathcal{T}$ is totally (resp. partially) ordered by $\prec$ (resp. $\subset$). For every layer T^i, the ternary relation $\mathrm{DIS}_i \subseteq T^i \times D \times T^i$ relates pairs of time points in T^i to a displacement in D. We assume that all DIS_i satisfy the same properties. The relation CONT associates each time point with the layer it belongs to. In its full generality, such a relation allows one point to belong to more than one layer (overlapping layers). However, since we restricted ourselves to the case in which $\mathcal{T}$ is totally ordered by "$\prec$', we assume that $\mathcal{T}$ defines a partition of $\bigcup_{i \in M} T^i$. This amounts to constrain CONT to be a total function with range equal to $\mathcal{T}$. The projection relation $\updownarrow$ associates each point with its direct or indirect descendants (downward projection) and ancestors (upward projection). More precisely, for any pair of points x, y, $\updownarrow (x, y)$ means that either x downward projects on y or x upward projection on y. Different temporal structures for time granularity can be obtained by imposing different conditions on the projection relation. Here is the list of the basic properties of the projection relation, where we assume variables x, y, z to take value over (subsets of) $\bigcup_{i \in M} T^i$ and variables α, β to take value over D:

reflexivity every point x projects on itself

$$\forall x \ \updownarrow(x, x)$$

uniqueness the projection relation does not link distinct points belonging to the same layer

$$\forall x, y, T^i((x \in T^i \wedge y \in T^i \wedge x \neq y) \rightarrow \neg \updownarrow(x, y))$$

refinement - case 1 for any pair of layers T^i, T^j, with $T^j \prec T^i$, any point of T^i projects on at least two points of T^j

$$\forall T^i, T^j, x \ \exists y, z((T^j \prec T^i \wedge x \in T^i) \rightarrow (y \in T^j \wedge z \in T^j \wedge y \neq z \wedge \updownarrow(x, y) \wedge \updownarrow(x, z)))$$

refinement - case 2 for any pair of layers T^i, T^j, with $T^j \prec T^i$, and every point $x \in T^i$, there exists at least one point $y \in T^j$ such that x projects on y and no other point $z \in T^i$ projects on it

$$\forall T^i, T^j, x \ \exists y((T^j \prec T^i \wedge x \in T^i) \rightarrow (y \in T^j \wedge \updownarrow(x, y) \wedge \forall z((z \in T^i \wedge z \neq x) \rightarrow \neg \updownarrow(z, y))))$$

separation for any pair of layers T^i, T^j, with $T^j \subset T^i$, the decomposition intervals of distinct points of T^i are disjoint

$$\forall T^i, T^j, x, y, x', y'((T^j \subset T^i \wedge x \in T^i \wedge y \in T^i \wedge x \neq y \wedge x' \in T^j \wedge y' \in T^j \wedge \updownarrow(x, x') \wedge \updownarrow(y, y')) \rightarrow x' \neq y')$$

symmetry if x downward (resp. upward) projects on y, then y upward (resp. downward) projects on x

$$\forall x, y(\updownarrow(x, y) \rightarrow \updownarrow(y, x))$$

By pairing symmetry and separation, it easily follows that, whenever $T^j \subset T^i$, each point of the finer layer is projected on a unique point of the coarser one (*alignment*).

downward transitivity if $T^k \subset T^j \subset T^i$, $x \in T^i$ projects on $y \in T^j$, and y projects on $z \in T^k$, then x projects on z

$$\forall T^i, T^j, T^k, x, y, z((T^k \subset T^j \subset T^i \wedge x \in T^i \wedge y \in T^j \wedge z \in T^k \wedge \updownarrow(x, y) \wedge \updownarrow(y, z)) \rightarrow \updownarrow(x, z))$$

Notice that we cannot substitute $\prec$ for $\subset$ in the above formula. Consider a temporal universe consisting of `months`, `weeks`, and `days`. The week from December 29, 2003, to January 4, 2004, belongs to the decomposition of December 2003 (as well as of January 2004) and the 3rd of January 2003 belongs to the decomposition of such a week, but not to that of December 2003.

downward/upward transitivity - case 1 if $T^j \subset T^k \subset T^i$, $x \in T^i$ projects on $y \in T^j$, and y projects on $z \in T^k$, then x projects on z

$$\forall T^i, T^j, T^k, x, y, z((T^j \subset T^k \subset T^i \wedge x \in T^i \wedge y \in T^j \wedge z \in T^k \wedge \updownarrow(x, y) \wedge \updownarrow(y, z)) \rightarrow \updownarrow(x, z))$$

As in the case of downward transitivity, we cannot substitute $\prec$ for $\subset$ in the above formula. Consider a temporal universe consisting of `years`, `months`, and `weeks`. The week from December 29, 2003, to January 4, 2004, belongs both to the decomposition of the year 2003 (as well as of the year 2004) and to the decomposition of the month of January 2004, but such a month does not belong to the decomposition of the year 2003.

order preservation the linear order of layers is preserved by the projection relation. For every pair T^i, T^j, the projection intervals are ordered, but they can possibly meet (weak order preservation)

$$\forall T^i, T^j, x, y, x', y'((x \in T^i \wedge y \in T^i \wedge x' \in T^j \wedge y' \in T^j \wedge \\ \updownarrow(x, x') \wedge \updownarrow(y, y') \wedge x \ll y) \rightarrow (x' \ll y' \vee x' = y'))$$

where $x \ll y$ iff for some $i \in M$ and $\alpha > 0$, $\mathrm{DIS}_i(x, \alpha, y)$. Weak order preservation encompasses both the case of two months that share a week and the case of two months that belong to the same year.

From refinement (cases 1 and 2), symmetry and weak order preservation, it follows that, for any pair of layers T^i, T^j, with $T^j \prec T^i$, any point of T^j projects on either one or two points of T^i (*abstraction*). Moreover, from refinement (case 2), symmetry, and weak order preservation, it follows that it is never the case that, given any pair of layers T^i, T^j, with $T^j \prec T^i$, two consecutive points of T^j are both projected on the same two points of T^i.

If $T^j \subset T^i$, the projection intervals of the elements of T^i over T^j are ordered and disjoint, that is, we must substitute $x' \ll y'$ for $x' \ll y' \vee x' = y'$ (*strong order preservation*).

convexity for any ordered pair of layers T^i, T^j (either $T^i \prec T^j$ or $T^j \prec T^i$), the projection relation associates any point of T^i with an interval of contiguous points of T^j

$$\forall T^i, T^j, x, y, w, z((x \in T^i \wedge y \in T^j \wedge z \in T^j \wedge w \in T^j \wedge \\ y \ll w \wedge w \ll z \wedge \updownarrow(x, y) \wedge \updownarrow(x, z)) \rightarrow \updownarrow(x, w))$$

In some situations, the layers of the temporal universe can be assumed to (pairwise) satisfy the property of homogeneity.

homogeneity for every pair of (discrete) layers ordered by granularity, the projection relation associates the same number of points of the finer layer with every point of the coarser one

$$\forall T^i, T^j, x, y, x', x'' \exists y', y''((T^j \prec T^i \wedge x \in T^i \wedge y \in T^i \wedge x' \in T^j \wedge x'' \in T^j \wedge \\ x' \neq x'' \wedge \updownarrow(x, x') \wedge \updownarrow(x, x'')) \rightarrow (y' \in T^j \wedge y'' \in T^j \wedge y' \neq y'' \wedge \updownarrow(y, y') \wedge \updownarrow(y, y'')))$$

and

$$\forall T^i, T^j, x, y, y' \exists x'((T^j \prec T^i \wedge x \in T^i \wedge y \in T^i \wedge \\ y' \in T^j \wedge \updownarrow(y, y')) \rightarrow (x' \in T^j \wedge \updownarrow(x, x')))$$

Other interesting properties of the projection relation can be derived from the above ones, including *total covering*, *contiguity*, *seriality* (any point x can be projected on any layer T^i), *upward transitivity* (if $T^k \subset T^j \subset T^i$, $x \in T^k$ projects on $y \in T^j$, and y projects on $z \in T^i$, then x projects on z), and *downward/upward transitivity - case 2* (if $T^j \subset T^i \subset T^k$, $x \in T^i$ projects on $y \in T^j$, and y projects on $z \in T^k$, then x projects on z).

To turn a two-sorted frame $\mathbf{F}$ into a *two-sorted model* $\mathbf{M}$, we first add the interpretations for context and algebraic terms, and the valuation for atomic temporal formulas. The interpretation for context terms is given by a function $h : C \cup Y \rightarrow \mathcal{T}$; that for algebraic terms is given by a function $g : A \cup X \to D$, which is automatically extended to all terms from $T(A \cup X)$. The valuation V for propositional variables is defined as in *MTL*. An atomic formula of the form $\alpha = \beta$ (resp. $\alpha < \beta$) is *true* in a model $\mathbf{M} = (\mathbf{F}; V, g, h)$ whenever $g(\alpha) = g(\beta)$ (resp. $g(\alpha) < g(\beta)$). Analogously, $c \prec c'$ (resp. $c \subset c'$) is *true* in $\mathbf{M}$ whenever $h(c) \prec h(c')$ (resp. $h(c) \subset h(c')$). Next, the *truth* of the temporal formulas $\Delta_\alpha \phi$, $\Delta^c \phi$, and $\Diamond \phi$ is defined by the following clauses:

$$\begin{array}{rcl}
\mathbf{M}, i \Vdash \Delta_\alpha \phi & \text{iff} & \text{there exists } j \text{ such that } \mathrm{DIS}(i, g(\alpha), j) \text{ and } \mathbf{M}, j \Vdash \phi; \\
\mathbf{M}, i \Vdash \Delta^c \phi & \text{iff} & \mathrm{CONT}(i, h(c)) \text{ and } \mathbf{M}, i \Vdash \phi; \\
\mathbf{M}, i \Vdash \Diamond \phi & \text{iff} & \text{there exists } j \text{ such that } \updownarrow (i, j) \text{ and } \mathbf{M}, j \Vdash \phi.
\end{array}$$

The semantic clauses for the dual operators ∇_α, ∇^c, and $\Diamond$, as well as for the derived operator Δ^c_α, can be easily derived from the above ones. Note that $\Delta^c \phi$ (resp. $\nabla^c \phi$) conventionally evaluates to false (resp. true) outside the context c. Finally, to evaluate the quantified formula $\forall x\, \phi$, with $x \in X$ (resp. $\forall y\, \phi$, with $y \in Y$), at a point i, we write $g =_x g'$ (resp. $h =_y h'$) to state that the assignments g and g' (resp. h and h') agree on all variables except maybe x (resp. y). We have that $(\mathbf{F}; V, g, h), i \Vdash \forall x\, \phi$ iff $(\mathbf{F}; V, g', h), i \Vdash \phi$, for all assignments g' such that $g =_x g'$. Analogously for $\forall y\, \phi$.

The notions of satisfiability, validity, and logical consequence given for *MTL* can be easily generalized to *MLTL*. Furthermore, the layered structure of *MLTL*-frames makes it possible to define the notions of *local* satisfiability, validity, and logical consequence by restricting the general notions of satisfiability, validity, and logical consequence to a specific layer.

The following examples show how *MLTL* allows one to specify temporal conditions involving different time granularities (the application of *MLTL* to the specification of complex real-time systems is discussed in [Montanari, 1996]). In the simplest case (case (i)), *MLTL* specifications are obtained by contextualizing formulas and composing them by means of logical connectives. The projection operator is needed when displacements over different layers have to be composed (case (ii)). Finally, contextual and projection operators can be paired to specify nested quantifications (cases (iii)-(vi)).

Example 3.4.3. *Consider the temporal conditions expressed by the following sentences:*

(i) men work every month and eat every day;

(ii) in 20 seconds 5 minutes will have passed from the occurrence of the fault;

(iii) some days the plant works every hour;

(iv) some days the plant remains inactive for several hours;

(v) every day the plant is in production for some hours;

(vi) the plant is monitored by the remote system every minute of every hour.

They can be expressed in MLTL *by means of the following formulas:*

(i) $\forall x_{man}(\forall \alpha \nabla^{month}_{\alpha} \mathtt{work}(x_{man}) \wedge \forall \beta \nabla^{day}_{\beta} \mathtt{eat}(x_{man}))$;

(ii) $\Delta^{second}_{20} \Diamond \Delta^{minute}_{-5} \mathtt{fault}$;

(iii) $\exists\alpha\Delta_{\alpha}^{day}\Box\nabla^{hour}\texttt{work(plant)}$;

(iv) $\exists\alpha\Delta_{\alpha}^{day}\Diamond\Delta^{hour}\texttt{inactive(plant)}$;

(v) $\forall\alpha\nabla_{\alpha}^{day}\Diamond\Delta^{hour}\texttt{in\_production(plant)}$;

(vi) $\forall\alpha\nabla_{\alpha}^{hour}\Box\nabla^{minute}\texttt{monitor(remote-system, plant)}$.

As a matter of fact, it is possible to give a stronger interpretation of condition (ii), which is expressed by the formula:

(ii') $\Delta_{20}^{second}\Diamond\Delta_{-5}^{minute}\texttt{fault} \wedge \forall\alpha(0 \leq \alpha < 20 \rightarrow \neg\Delta_{\alpha}^{second}\Diamond\Delta_{-5}^{minute}\texttt{fault})$.

The problem of finding an axiomatization of validity in *MLTL* is addressed in [Ciapessoni *et al.*, 1993; Montanari, 1996]. The idea is to pair axioms and rules of *(Q-)MTL*, which are used to express the properties of the displacement operator with respect to every context, with additional axiom schemata and rules governing the behavior of the contextual and projection operators as well as the relations between these operators and the displacement one. First, the axiomatic system for *MLTL* must constrain $\prec$ to be a total order and $\subset$ to be a partial order that refines $\prec$, that is, for every pair of contexts c, c' we have that if $c \subset c'$, then $c \prec c'$, but not necessarily vice versa. Moreover, it must express the basic logical properties of the contextual and projection operators:

(AxNC)	$\nabla^c(\phi \rightarrow \psi) \rightarrow (\nabla^c\phi \rightarrow \nabla^c\psi)$	(normality of ∇^c);
(AxNP)	$\Box(\phi \rightarrow \psi) \rightarrow (\Box\phi \rightarrow \Box\psi)$	(normality of $\Box$);
(AxNEC)	$\Delta^c\phi \rightarrow \phi$	("necessity" for Δ^c);
(AxIC)	$\nabla^c\nabla^c\phi \equiv \nabla^c\phi$	(idempotency of ∇^c);
(AxCCD)	$\nabla^c\nabla_\alpha\phi \equiv \nabla_\alpha\nabla^c\phi$	(commutativity of ∇^c and ∇_α),

together with the rules:

(C-NEC)	$\vdash \phi \longrightarrow \vdash \nabla^c\phi$	(necessitation rule for ∇^c);
(P-NEC)	$\vdash \phi \longrightarrow \vdash \Box\phi$	(necessitation rule for $\Box$).

Notice that the projection operators $\Diamond$ and $\Box$ behave as the usual modal operators of possibility and necessity, while the contextual operators Δ^c and ∇^c are less standard (a number of theorems that account for the behavior of the contextual operators are given in [Montanari, 1996]). The set of axioms must also include the Barcan formula for the contextual and projection operators:

(AxBFC)	$\forall x\nabla^c\phi \rightarrow \nabla^c\forall x\phi$, with $x \neq c$	(Barcan formula for ∇^c);
(AxBFP)	$\forall x\Box\phi \rightarrow \Box\forall x\phi$	(Barcan formula for $\Box$),

as well as the counterparts of axioms (AxAD1)-(AxAD4) for the contextual operator. Similar axioms must be used to constrain the relationships between context terms, ordered by $\prec$ or $\subset$, and the displacement and contextual operators. Finally, we add a number of axioms that express the properties of the temporal structure, that is, the structural properties of the contextualization and projection relations. As an example, the axiom $\forall c_1, c_2, c_3((c_3 \subset c_2 \subset c_1 \wedge \nabla^{c_1}\Box\nabla^{c_3}\phi) \rightarrow \nabla^{c_1}\Box\nabla^{c_2}\Box\nabla^{c_3}\phi)$ can be added to constrain the projection relation to be downward transitive. Different classes of structures (e.g., homogeneous and non-homogeneous) can be captured by different sets of axioms. A sound axiomatic system for *MLTL* is reported in [Montanari *et al.*, 1992]. No completeness proof is given. In principle, one can try to directly prove it by building a canonical model for *MLTL*. However, even though there seem to be no specific technical problems to solve, the process of canonical model construction is undoubtedly very demanding in view of the size and complexity of the *MLTL* axiom system. As a matter of fact, one can follow an alternative approach, based on the technique proposed by Finger and Gabbay in [Finger and Gabbay, 1996], which views temporal logics for time granularity as combinations of simpler temporal logics, and specifies what constraints such combinations must satisfy to guarantee the transference of logical properties (including completeness results) from the component logics to the combined ones. In Section 3.4.3 we shall present temporal logics for time granularity which are obtained as suitable combinations of existing linear and branching temporal logics.

We conclude the section with a discussion of two classical problems about granularity conversions. The first problem has already been pointed out at the beginning of the section: given the truth value of a formula with respect to a certain layer, can we constrain (and how) its truth value with respect to the other layers? In [Montanari and Policriti, 1996], Montanari and Policriti give an example of a proposition which is true at every point of a given layer, and false with respect to every point of another one. It follows that, in general, we can record the links explicitly provided by the user, but we cannot impose any other constraint about the truth value of a formula with respect to a layer different from the layer it is associated with. Accordingly, *MLTL* makes it possible to write formulas involving granularity changes, but the proposed axiomatic systems do not impose any general constraint on the relations among the truth values of a formula with respect to different layers. Nevertheless, from a practical point of view, it makes sense to look for general rules expressing *typical* relations among truth values. In [Ciapessoni *et al.*, 1993], Ciapessoni et al. introduce two consistency rules that respectively allow one to project simple *MLTL* formulas, that is, *MLTL* formulas devoid of any occurrence of the displacement, contextual, and projection operators, from coarser to finer layers (downward temporal projection) and from finer to coarser ones (upward temporal projection). For any given pair of layers T^i, T^j, with $T^j \prec T^i$, any point $x \in T^i$, and any simple formula ϕ, *downward temporal projection* states that if ϕ holds at x, then there exists at least one $y \in T^j$ such that $\updownarrow (x, y)$ and ϕ holds at y, while *upward temporal projection* states that if ϕ holds at every $y \in T^j$ such that $\updownarrow (x, y)$, then ϕ holds at x. Formally, downward temporal projection is defined by the formula $\forall c_1, c_2(c_2 \subset c_1 \rightarrow \nabla^{c_1}(\phi \rightarrow \Diamond\Delta^{c_2}\phi))$, while upward temporal projection is defined by the formula $\forall c_1, c_2(c_2 \subset c_1 \rightarrow \nabla^{c_1}(\Box\nabla^{c_2}\phi \rightarrow \phi))$. It is not difficult to show that the two formulas are *inter-deducible* [Montanari, 1996]. (Downward) temporal projection captures the *weakest semantics* that can be attached to a statement with respect to a layer finer than the original one, provided that the statement is not wholistic. In most cases, however, such semantics is too weak, and additional user qualifications are needed. Various domain-specific categorizations of statements have been proposed in the literature [Roman, 1990; Shoham, 1988], which allow one to classify statements according to their behavior under temporal projection, e.g., events, properties, facts, and processes. In [Montanari, 1994], Montanari proposes some specializations of the *MLTL* projection operator $\Diamond$ that allow one to define different types of temporal projection, distinguishing among statements that hold at one and only one point of the decomposition interval (*punctual*), statements that hold at every point of such an interval (*continuous and pervasive*), statements that hold over a scattered sequence of sub-intervals of the decomposition interval (*bounded sequence*), and so on.

The second problem is the synchronization problem. We introduced this problem in Section 3.2, where we showed that the interpretations of the statements "tomorrow I will eat" and "dinner will be ready in one hour" with respect to a layer finer than the layer they explicitly refer to differ a lot. It is not difficult to show that even the same statement may admit different interpretations with respect to different finer layers (a detailed example can be found in [Montanari, 1996]). In general, the synchronization problem arises when logical formulas which state that a given fact holds at a point y of a layer T^i at distance α from the current point x need to be interpreted with respect to a finer layer T^j. There exist at least two possible interpretations for the original formula with respect to T^j (for the sake of simplicity, we restrict our attention to facts encoded by simple *MLTL* formulas, with a punctual interpretation under temporal projection, and we assume the temporal universe to be homogeneous). The first interpretation maps x (resp. y) into an arbitrary point x' (resp. y') of its decomposition interval, thus allowing the distance α' between x' and y' to vary. If x precedes y, we get the minimum (resp. maximum) value for α' when x' is the last (resp. first) element of the decomposition interval for x and y' is the first (resp. last) element of the decomposition interval for y. The second interpretation forces the mapping for y to conform to the mapping for x. As an example, if x is mapped into the first element of its decomposition interval, then y is mapped into the first element of its decomposition interval as well. As a consequence, there exists only one possible value for the distance α'. The first interpretation can be easily expressed in *MLTL* (it is the interpretation underlying the semantics of the projection operator). In order to enable *MLTL* to support the second interpretation, two extensions are needed: (i) we must replace the notion of current point by the notion of *vector* of current points (one for each layer); (ii) we must define a new projection operator that maps the current point of T^i into the current point of T^j, for every pair of layers T^i, T^j. Such extensions are accomplished in [Montanari, 1994]. In particular, it is possible to show that the new projection operator is second-order definable in terms of the original one, and that both projection operators are (second-order) definable in terms of a third simpler projection operator that maps every point into the first elements of its decomposition (and abstraction) intervals.

3.4.2 Monadic theories of time granularity

We move now from the temporal logic setting to the classical one, focusing our attention on monadic theories of time granularity. First, we introduce the relational structures for time granularity; then we present the theories of such structures and we analyze their decision problem. At the end, we briefly study the definability and decidability of meaningful binary predicates for time granularity with respect to such theories and some fragments of them.

Relational structures for time granularity

We begin with some preliminary definitions about finite and infinite sequences and trees (we assume the reader to be familiar with the notation and the basic notions of the theory of formal languages). Let A be a finite set of symbols and A^* be its Kleene closure. The length of a string $x \in A^*$, denoted by $|x|$, is defined in the usual way: $|\epsilon|$=0, $|xa| = |x| + 1$. For any pair $x, y \in A^*$, we say that x is a *prefix* of y, denoted by $x <_{pre} y$, if $xw = y$ for some $w \in A^+ (= A^* \setminus \{\epsilon\})$. The *prefix* relation $<_{pre}$ is a partial ordering over A^*. If A is totally ordered, a total ordering over A^* can be obtained from the one over A as follows. Let $<$ be

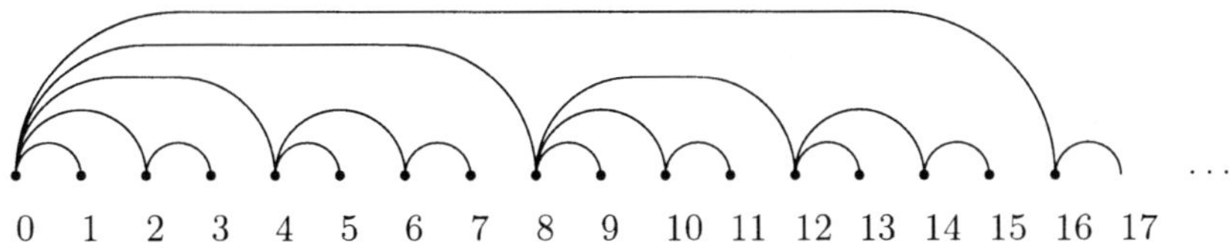

Figure 3.1: The structure of the relation $\mathtt{flip}_2$.

the total ordering over A. For every $x, y \in A^*$, we say that x lexicographically precedes y with respect to $<$, denoted $x <_{lex} y$, if either $x <_{pre} y$ or there exist $z \in A^*$ and $a, b \in A$ such that $za \leq_{pre} x$, $zb \leq_{pre} y$, and $a < b$. The *lexicographical* relation $<_{lex}$ is a total ordering over A^*.

A *finite sequence* is a relational structure $s = \langle I, < \rangle$, where I is an initial segment of the natural numbers $\mathbb{N}$ and $<$ is the usual ordering over $\mathbb{N}$. Given a *finite* set of monadic predicate symbols $\mathcal{P}$, a $\mathcal{P}$-labeled finite sequence is a relational structure $s_{\mathcal{P}} = \langle s, (\overline{P})_{P \in \mathcal{P}} \rangle$, where $s = \langle I, < \rangle$ and, for every $P \in \mathcal{P}$, $\overline{P} \subseteq I$ is the set of elements labeled with P (note that $\overline{P} \cap \overline{Q}$, with $P, Q \in \mathcal{P}$, can obviously be nonempty). An *infinite sequence* (ω-sequence for short) is a relational structure $s = \langle \mathbb{N}, < \rangle$ and a $\mathcal{P}$-labeled ω-sequence $s_{\mathcal{P}}$ is an ω-sequence s expanded with the sets $\overline{P}$, for $P \in \mathcal{P}$. For the sake of simplicity, hereafter we shall use the symbol P to denote both a monadic predicate and its interpretation; accordingly, we shall rewrite $s_{\mathcal{P}}$ as $\langle s, (P)_{P \in \mathcal{P}} \rangle$. In the following, we shall take into consideration three binary relations over $\mathbb{N}$, namely, $\mathtt{flip}_k$, $\mathtt{adj}$, and $2\times$. Let $k \geq 2$. The binary relation $\mathtt{flip}_k$ is defined as follows. Given $x, y \in \mathbb{N}$, $\mathtt{flip}_k(x, y)$, also denoted $\mathtt{flip}_k(x) = y$, if $y = x - z$, where z is the least power of k with non-null coefficient in the k-ary representation of x. Formally, $\mathtt{flip}_k(x) = y$ if $x = a_n \cdot k^n + a_{n-1} \cdot k^{n-1} + \ldots + a_m \cdot k^m$, $0 \leq a_i \leq k - 1$, $a_m \neq 0$, and $y = a_n \cdot k^n + a_{n-1} \cdot k^{n-1} + \ldots + (a_m - 1) \cdot k^m$. For instance, $\mathtt{flip}_2(18, 16)$, since $18 = 1 \cdot 2^4 + 1 \cdot 2^1$, $m = 1$, and $16 = 1 \cdot 2^4 + 0 \cdot 2^1$, while $\mathtt{flip}_2(16, 0)$, since $16 = 1 \cdot 2^4$, $m = 4$, and $0 = 0 \cdot 2^4$. Note that there exists no y such that $\mathtt{flip}_2(0, y)$. The structure of $\mathtt{flip}_2$ is depicted in Figure 3.1. The relation $\mathtt{adj}$ is defined as follows: $\mathtt{adj}(x, y)$, also denoted $\mathtt{adj}(x) = y$, if $x = 2^{k_n} + 2^{k_{n-1}} + \ldots + 2^{k_0}$, with $k_n > k_{n-1} > \ldots > k_0 > 0$, and $y = x + 2^{k_0} + 2^{k_0 - 1}$. For instance, $\mathtt{adj}(12, 18)$, since $12 = 2^3 + 2^2$, $k_0 = 2$, and $18 = 12 + 2^2 + 2^1$, while there exists no y such that $\mathtt{adj}(13, y)$, since $13 = 2^3 + 2^2 + 2^0$ and $k_0 = 0$. Finally, for any pair $x, y \in \mathbb{N}$, it holds that $2 \times (x, y)$ if $y = 2x$.

Finite and infinite (k-ary) trees are defined as follows. Let $k \geq 2$ and T_k be the set $\{0, \ldots k - 1\}^*$. A set $D \subseteq T_k$ is a (k-ary) *tree domain* if:

1. D is *prefix closed*, that is, for every $x, y \in T_k$, if $x \in D$ and $y <_{pre} x$, then $y \in D$;
2. for every $x \in T_k$, either $xi \in D$ for every $0 \leq i \leq k - 1$ or $xi \notin D$ for every $0 \leq i \leq k - 1$.

Note that, according to the definition, the whole T_k is a tree domain. A *finite tree* is a relational structure $\kappa = \langle D, (\downarrow_i)_{i=0}^{k-1}, <_{pre} \rangle$, where D is a finite tree domain, for every $0 \leq i \leq k-1$, $\downarrow_i$ is the i-th *successor relation* over D such that $\downarrow_i (x, y)$, also denoted $\downarrow_i (x) = y$, if $y = xi$, and $<_{pre}$ is the prefix ordering over D defined as above. The elements of D are

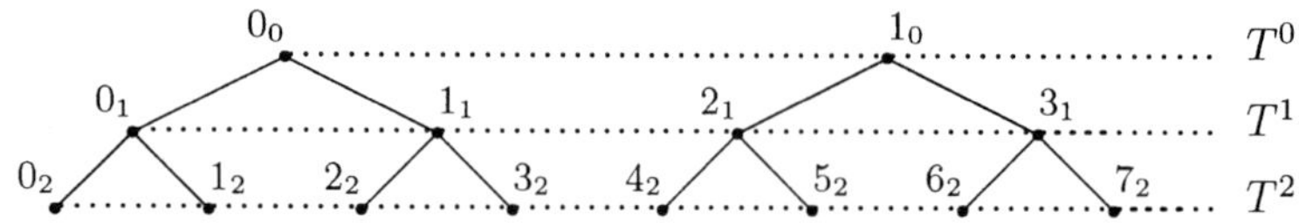

Figure 3.2: The 2-refinable 3-layered structure.

called *nodes*. If $\downarrow_i (x) = y$, then y is said the i-th *son* of x. The lexicographical ordering $<_{lex}$ over D is defined with respect to the natural ordering $<$ over $\{0, \ldots k-1\}$ such that $0 < 1 < \ldots < k-1$. A *path* P in κ is a subset of D whose nodes can be written as a sequence $x_0, x_1, \ldots$ such that, for every $i > 0$, there exists $0 \leq j \leq k-1$ with $x_i = \downarrow_j (x_{i-1})$. We shall denote by $P(i)$ the i-th element x_i of the path P. A *full path* is a maximal path with respect to set inclusion. A *chain* is any subset of a path. The *root* of κ is the node ϵ. A *leaf* of κ is an element $x \in D$ devoid of sons. A node which is not a leaf is called an *internal node*. The *depth* of a node $x \in D$ is the length of the (unique) path from the root ϵ to x. The *height* of κ is the maximum of the depths of the nodes in D. κ is *complete* if every leaf has the same depth. A $\mathcal{P}$-labeled finite tree is a relational structure $\kappa = \langle D, (\downarrow_i)_{i=0}^{k-1}, <_{pre}, (P)_{P\in\mathcal{P}}\rangle$, where the tuple $(D, (\downarrow_i)_{i=0}^{k-1}, <_{pre})$ is a finite tree and, for every $P \in \mathcal{P}$, $P \subseteq D$ is the set of nodes labeled with P. As for infinite trees, we are interested in *complete* infinite trees over the tree domain T_k. The complete *infinite tree* over T_k is the tuple $\kappa = \langle T_k, (\downarrow_i)_{i=0}^{k-1}, <_{pre}\rangle$. Paths, full paths, and chains are defined as for finite trees. A $\mathcal{P}$-labeled infinite tree is an expansion of the complete infinite tree over T_k with monadic predicates P, for $P \in \mathcal{P}$.

Relational structures for time granularity consists of a (possibly infinite) number of distinct layers/domains (we shall use the two terms interchangeably). We focus our attention on n-layered structures, which include a fixed finite number n of layers, and ω-layered structures, which feature an infinite number of layers.

Let $n \geq 1$ and $k \geq 2$. For every $0 \leq i < n$, let $T^i = \{j_i \mid j \geq 0\}$. The *$n$-layered temporal universe* is the set $\mathcal{U}_n = \bigcup_{0 \leq i < n} T^i$. The ($k$-refinable) *$n$-layered structure* ($n$-LS for short) is the relational structure $\langle \mathcal{U}_n, (\downarrow_j)_{j=0}^{k-1}, < \rangle$. Such a structure can be viewed as an infinite sequence of complete (k-ary) trees of height $n-1$, each one rooted at a point of the coarsest layer T^0 (see Figure 3.2). The sets T^i, with $0 \leq i < n$, are the layers of the trees. For every $0 \leq j \leq k-1$, $\downarrow_j$ is the j-th *successor relation* over $\mathcal{U}_n$ such that $\downarrow_j (x, y)$ (also denoted $\downarrow_j (x) = y$) if y is the j-th son of x. Hereafter, to adhere to the common terminology in the field, we shall substitute the term projection for the term successor. Note that for all x belonging to the finest layer T^{n-1} there exist no $0 \leq j \leq k-1$ and $y \in \mathcal{U}_n$ such that $\downarrow_j (x) = y$. Finally, $<$ is a total ordering over $\mathcal{U}_n$ given by the *pre-order* (root-left-right in the binary trees) visit of the nodes (for elements belonging to the same tree) and by the total linear ordering of trees (for elements belonging to different trees). Formally, for any pair $a_b, c_d \in \mathcal{U}_n$, we have that $\downarrow_j (a_b) = c_d$ if $b < n-1$, $d = b+1$, and $c = a \cdot k + j$. The total ordering $<$ is defined as follows:

1. if $x = a_0$, $y = b_0$, and $a < b$ over $\mathbb{N}$, then $x < y$;

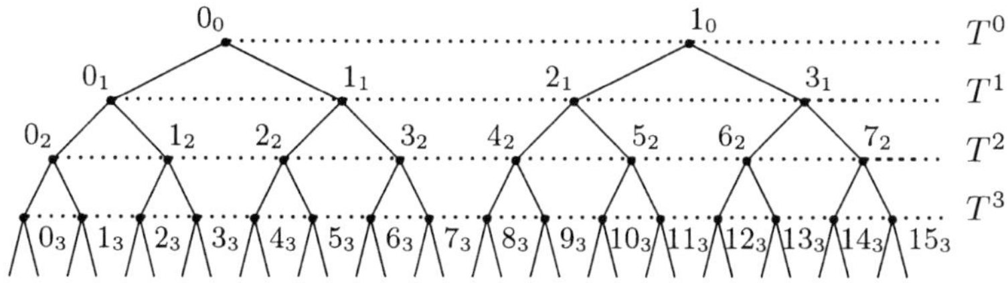

Figure 3.3: The 2-refinable downward unbounded layered structure.

2. for all $x \in \mathcal{U}_n \setminus T^{n-1}$, $x <\downarrow_0 (x)$, and $\downarrow_j (x) <\downarrow_{j+1} (x)$, for all $0 \le j < k-1$;
3. if $x \in \mathcal{U}_n \setminus T^{n-1}$, $x < y$, and not $\texttt{ancestor}(x, y)$, then $\downarrow_{k-1} (x) < y$;
4. if $x < z$ and $z < y$, then $x < y$,

where $\texttt{ancestor}(x, y)$ if there exists $0 \le j \le k-1$ such that $\downarrow_j (x) = y$ or there exist $0 \le j \le k-1$ and z such that $\downarrow_j (z) = y$ and $\texttt{ancestor}(x, z)$. A *path* over the n-LS is a subset of the domain whose elements can be written as a sequence $x_0, x_1, \ldots x_m$, with $m \le n-1$, in such a way that, for every $i = 1, \ldots m$, there exists $0 \le j < k$ for which $x_i =\downarrow_j (x_{i-1})$. A *full path* is a maximal path with respect to set inclusion. A *chain* is any subset of a path. A $\mathcal{P}$-labeled n-LS is a relational structure $\langle \mathcal{U}_n, (\downarrow_i)_{i=0}^{k-1}, <, (P)_{P \in \mathcal{P}} \rangle$, where the tuple $(\mathcal{U}_n, (\downarrow_i)_{i=0}^{k-1}, <)$ is the n-LS and, for every $P \in \mathcal{P}$, $P \subseteq \mathcal{U}_n$ is the set of points labeled with P.

As for ω-layered structures, we focus our attention on the (k-refinable) downward unbounded layered structure (DULS for short), which consists of a coarsest domain together with an infinite number of finer and finer domains, and the (k-refinable) upward unbounded layered structure (UULS for short), which consists of a finest temporal domain together with an infinite number of coarser and coarser domains. Let $\mathcal{U} = \bigcup_{i \ge 0} T^i$ be the *ω-layered temporal universe*. The DULS is a relational structure $\langle \mathcal{U}, (\downarrow_i)_{i=0}^{k-1}, < \rangle$. It can be viewed as an infinite sequence of complete (k-ary) infinite trees, each one rooted at a point of the coarsest domain T^0 (see Figure 3.3). The sets T^i, with $i \ge 0$, are the layers of the trees. The definitions of the projection relations $\downarrow_j$, with $0 \le j \le k-1$, and the total ordering $<$ over $\mathcal{U}$ are close to those for the n-LS. Formally, for any pair $a_b, c_d \in \mathcal{U}$, we have that $\downarrow_j (a_b) = c_d$ if and only if $d = b+1$ and $c = a \cdot k + j$, while the total ordering $<$ is defined as follows:

1. if $x = a_0$, $y = b_0$, and $a < b$ over $\mathbb{N}$, then $x < y$;
2. for all $x \in \mathcal{U}$, $x <\downarrow_0 (x)$, and $\downarrow_j (x) <\downarrow_{j+1} (x)$, for all $0 \le j < k-1$;
3. if $x < y$ and not $\texttt{ancestor}(x, y)$, then $\downarrow_{k-1} (x) < y$;
4. if $x < z$ and $z < y$, then $x < y$.

A *path* over the DULS is a subset of the domain whose elements can be written as an infinite sequence $x_0, x_1, \ldots$ such that, for every $i \ge 1$, there exists $0 \le j < k$ for which $x_i =\downarrow_j (x_{i-1})$. A *full path* is a maximal (infinite) path with respect to set inclusion. A *chain* is

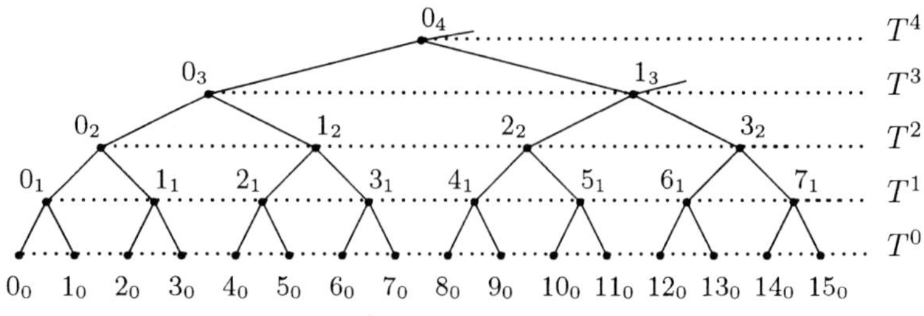

Figure 3.4: The 2-refinable upward unbounded layered structure.

any subset of a path. A $\mathcal{P}$-labeled DULS is a relational structure $\langle \mathcal{U}, (\downarrow_i)_{i=0}^{k-1}, <, (P)_{P\in\mathcal{P}}\rangle$, where the tuple $(\mathcal{U}, (\downarrow_i)_{i=0}^{k-1}, <)$ is the DULS and, for every $P \in \mathcal{P}$, $P \subseteq \mathcal{U}$ is the set of points labeled with P.

The UULS is a relational structure $\langle \mathcal{U}, (\downarrow_i)_{i=0}^{k-1}, <\rangle$. It can be viewed as a complete (k-ary) infinite tree generated from the leaves (Figure 3.4). The sets T^i, with $i \geq 0$, are the layers of the tree. For every $0 \leq j \leq k-1$, $\downarrow_j$ is the j-th *projection relation* over $\mathcal{U}$ such that $\downarrow_j (x, y)$ (also denoted by $\downarrow_j (x) = y$) if y is the j-th son of x. The total ordering $<$ over $\mathcal{U}$ is induced by the *in-order* (left-root-right in the binary tree) visit of the treelike structure. Formally, for every $a_b, c_d \in \mathcal{U}$, $\downarrow_j (a_b) = c_d$ if $b > 0$, $d = b - 1$, and $c = a \cdot k + j$. The total ordering $<$ is defined as follows:

1. for all $x \in \mathcal{U} \setminus T^0$, $\downarrow_0 (x) < x$, $x <\downarrow_1 (x)$, and $\downarrow_j (x) <\downarrow_{j+1} (x)$, for every $0 < j < k-1$;
2. if $x < y$ and not $\texttt{ancestor}(x, y)$, then $\downarrow_{k-1} (x) < y$;
3. if $x < y$ and not $\texttt{ancestor}(y, x)$, then $x <\downarrow_0 (y)$;
4. if $x < z$ and $z < y$, then $x < y$.

A *path* over the UULS is a subset of the domain whose elements can be written as an infinite sequence $x_0, x_1, \ldots$ such that, for every $i \geq 1$, there exists $0 \leq j < k$ such that $x_{i-1} =\downarrow_j (x_i)$. A *full path* is a maximal (infinite) path with respect to set inclusion. A *chain* is any subset of a path. It is worth noting that every pair of paths over the UULS may differ on a finite prefix only. A $\mathcal{P}$-labeled UULS is obtained by expanding the UULS with a set $P \subseteq \mathcal{U}$, for any $P \in \mathcal{P}$.

Theories of time granularity

We are now ready to introduce the theories of time granularity. They are systems of monadic second-order (MSO for short) logic that allow quantification over arbitrary sets of elements. We shall study the properties of the full systems as well as of some meaningful fragments of them. We shall show that some granularity theories can be reduced to well-know classical MSO theories, such as the MSO theory of one successor and the MSO theory of two successors, while other granularity theories are proper extensions of them.

Definition 3.4.1. *(The language of monadic second-order logic)*

Let $\tau = c_1, \ldots, c_r, u_1, \ldots, u_s, b_1, \ldots, b_t$ *be a finite alphabet of symbols, where* $c_1, \ldots, c_r$ *(resp.* $u_1, \ldots, u_s$, $b_1, \ldots, b_t$*) are constant symbols (resp. unary relational symbols, binary relational symbols), and let* $\mathcal{P}$ *be a finite set of uninterpreted unary relational symbols. The second-order language with equality* $\text{MSO}[\tau \cup \mathcal{P}]$ *is built up as follows:*

1. atomic formulas *are of the forms* $x = y$, $x = c_i$, *with* $1 \leq i \leq r$, $u_i(x)$, *with* $1 \leq i \leq s$, $b_i(x, y)$, *with* $1 \leq i \leq t$, $x \in X$, $x \in P$, *where* x, y *are individual variables,* X *is a set variable, and* $P \in \mathcal{P}$*;*

2. formulas *are built up from atomic formulas by means of the Boolean connectives* $\neg$ *and* $\wedge$*, and the quantifier* $\exists$ *ranging over both individual and set variables.*

In the following, we shall write $\text{MSO}_{\mathcal{P}}[\tau]$ for $\text{MSO}[\tau \cup \mathcal{P}]$; in particular, we shall write $\text{MSO}[\tau]$ when $\mathcal{P}$ is meant to be the empty set. The first-order fragment of $\text{MSO}_{\mathcal{P}}[\tau]$ will be denoted by $\text{FO}_{\mathcal{P}}[\tau]$, while its path (resp. chain) fragment, which is obtained by interpreting second-order variables over paths (resp. chains), will be denoted by $\text{MPL}_{\mathcal{P}}[\tau]$ (resp. $\text{MCL}_{\mathcal{P}}[\tau]$). We focus our attention on the following theories:

1. $\text{MSO}_{\mathcal{P}}[<]$ and its first-order fragment interpreted over finite and ω-sequences;

2. $\text{MSO}_{\mathcal{P}}[<, \texttt{flip}_k]$ (as well as its first-order fragment), $\text{MSO}_{\mathcal{P}}[<, \texttt{adj}]$, and $\text{MSO}_{\mathcal{P}}[<, 2\times]$ interpreted over ω-sequences;

3. $\text{MSO}_{\mathcal{P}}[<_{pre}, (\downarrow_i)_{i=0}^{k-1}]$ and its first-order, path, and chain fragments interpreted over finite and infinite trees;

4. $\text{MSO}_{\mathcal{P}}[<, (\downarrow_i)_{i=0}^{k-1}]$ and its first-order, path, and chain fragments interpreted over the n-LS, the DULS, and the UULS.

We preliminarily introduce some notations and basic properties that will help us in comparing the expressive power and logical properties of the various theories. Most definitions and results are given for full MSO theories with uninterpreted unary relational symbols, but they immediately transfer to their fragments, possibly devoid of uninterpreted unary relational symbols.

Let $\mathcal{M}(\varphi)$ be the set of models of the formula φ. We say that $\text{MSO}_{\mathcal{P}}[\tau_1]$ can be *embedded* into $\text{MSO}_{\mathcal{P}}[\tau_2]$, denoted $\text{MSO}_{\mathcal{P}}[\tau_1] \rightarrow \text{MSO}_{\mathcal{P}}[\tau_2]$, if there is an *effective* translation tr of $\text{MSO}_{\mathcal{P}}[\tau_1]$-formulas into $\text{MSO}_{\mathcal{P}}[\tau_2]$-formulas such that, for every formula $\varphi \in \text{MSO}_{\mathcal{P}}[\tau_1]$, $\mathcal{M}(\varphi) = \mathcal{M}(tr(\varphi))$. For instance, it is easy to prove that $\text{FO}_{\mathcal{P}}[<_{pre}, (\downarrow_i)_{i=0}^{k-1}] \rightarrow \text{MPL}_{\mathcal{P}}[<_{pre}, (\downarrow_i)_{i=0}^{k-1}] \rightarrow \text{MCL}_{\mathcal{P}}[<_{pre}, (\downarrow_i)_{i=0}^{k-1}] \rightarrow \text{MSO}_{\mathcal{P}}[<_{pre}, (\downarrow_i)_{i=0}^{k-1}]$ (the same holds for their counterparts devoid of $\mathcal{P}$), where all theories are interpreted over trees. The condition 'X is a path' can indeed be written in the monadic chain logic, and the condition 'X is a chain' can be expressed in the MSO logic. It is also easy to show that the monadic path logic over paths is as expressive as the monadic path logic over full paths. Moreover, we say that $\text{MSO}_{\mathcal{P}}[\tau_1]$ is *as expressive as* $\text{MSO}_{\mathcal{P}}[\tau_2]$, written $\text{MSO}_{\mathcal{P}}[\tau_1] \rightleftarrows \text{MSO}_{\mathcal{P}}[\tau_2]$, if both $\text{MSO}_{\mathcal{P}}[\tau_1] \rightarrow \text{MSO}_{\mathcal{P}}[\tau_2]$ and $\text{MSO}_{\mathcal{P}}[\tau_2] \rightarrow \text{MSO}_{\mathcal{P}}[\tau_1]$. It is immediate to see that if $\text{MSO}_{\mathcal{P}}[\tau_1] \rightarrow \text{MSO}_{\mathcal{P}}[\tau_2]$ and $\text{MSO}_{\mathcal{P}}[\tau_2]$ is decidable (resp. $\text{MSO}_{\mathcal{P}}[\tau_1]$ is undecidable), then $\text{MSO}_{\mathcal{P}}[\tau_1]$ is decidable (resp. $\text{MSO}_{\mathcal{P}}[\tau_2]$ is undecidable) as well.

Besides decidability issues, we are interested in definability ones. Let β be a relational symbol. We say that β is *definable* in $\text{MSO}_{\mathcal{P}}[\tau]$ if $\text{MSO}_{\mathcal{P}}[\tau \cup \{\beta\}] \rightarrow \text{MSO}_{\mathcal{P}}[\tau]$. If the addition of β to a decidable theory $\mathrm{MSO}_{\mathcal{P}}[\tau]$ makes the resulting theory $\mathrm{MSO}_{\mathcal{P}}[\tau \cup \{\beta\}]$ undecidable, we can conclude that β is not definable in $\mathrm{MSO}_{\mathcal{P}}[\tau]$. The opposite does not hold in general: the predicate β may not be definable in $\mathrm{MSO}_{\mathcal{P}}[\tau]$, but the extension of $\mathrm{MSO}_{\mathcal{P}}[\tau]$ with β may preserve decidability. In such a case, we obviously cannot reduce the decidability of $\mathrm{MSO}_{\mathcal{P}}[\tau \cup \{\beta\}]$ to that of $\mathrm{MSO}_{\mathcal{P}}[\tau]$.

The decidability of $\mathrm{MSO}_{\mathcal{P}}[<]$ over finite sequences has been proved in [Büchi, 1960; Elgot, 1961], while its decidability over ω-sequences has been shown in [Büchi, 1962] ($\mathrm{MSO}_{\mathcal{P}}[<]$ over ω-sequences is the well-known MSO theory of one successor $S1S$).

Theorem 3.4.2. *(Decidability of* $\mathrm{MSO}_{\mathcal{P}}[<]$ *over sequences)*
$\mathrm{MSO}_{\mathcal{P}}[<]$ *over finite (resp. infinite) sequences is non-elementarily decidable.*

The theory $\mathrm{MSO}_{\mathcal{P}}[<, \mathtt{flip}_k]$ ($S1S^k$ for short), interpreted over ω-sequences, has been studied by Monti and Peron in [Monti and Peron, 2000]. Such a theory properly extends $S1S$. Moreover, the unary predicate $\mathtt{pow}_k$ such that $\mathtt{pow}_k(x)$ if x is a power of k can be easily expressed as $\mathtt{flip}_k(x) = 0$. Hence, $S1S^k$ is at least as expressive as the well-known (decidable) extension of $\mathrm{MSO}_{\mathcal{P}}[<]$ with the predicate $\mathtt{pow}_k$ [Elgot and Rabin, 1966]. The decidability of $S1S^k$ has been proved by showing that it is the logical counterpart of the class of ω-sequences languages (ω-languages for short) recognized by systolic (k-ary) tree automata. The class of the languages of finite sequences recognized by systolic tree automata was originally investigated by Culik II et al. in [Culik II *et al.*, 1984]. In [Monti and Peron, 2000], Monti and Peron extend the notion of systolic tree automaton to deal with ω-languages. They prove that the class of systolic tree ω-languages is a proper extension of the class of regular ω-languages (that is, ω-languages recognized by Büchi automata), that maintains the closure properties of regular ω-languages as well as the decidability of the emptiness problem. The correspondence between systolic tree ω-languages and $S1S^k$ is established by means of a generalization of Büchi's Theorem.

Theorem 3.4.3. *(Decidability of* $\mathrm{MSO}_{\mathcal{P}}[<, \mathtt{flip}_k]$ *over* ω*-sequences)*
$\mathrm{MSO}_{\mathcal{P}}[<, \mathtt{flip}_k]$ *over* ω*-sequences is non-elementarily decidable.*

The theories $\mathrm{MSO}_{\mathcal{P}}[<, \mathtt{adj}]$ and $\mathrm{MSO}_{\mathcal{P}}[<, 2\times]$, interpreted over ω-sequences, have been investigated in [Monti and Peron, 2001]. $\mathrm{MSO}_{\mathcal{P}}[<, \mathtt{adj}]$ is a proper extension $\mathrm{MSO}_{\mathcal{P}}[<, \mathtt{flip}_2]$. Unfortunately, unlike $\mathrm{MSO}_{\mathcal{P}}[<, \mathtt{flip}_2]$, it is undecidable.

Theorem 3.4.4. *(Undecidability of* $\mathrm{MSO}_{\mathcal{P}}[<, \mathtt{adj}]$ *over* ω*-sequences)*
$\mathrm{MSO}_{\mathcal{P}}[<, \mathtt{adj}]$ *over infinite sequences is undecidable.*

Since $\mathrm{MSO}_{\mathcal{P}}[<, 2\times]$ is at least as expressive as $\mathrm{MSO}_{\mathcal{P}}[<, \mathtt{adj}]$, its decision problem is undecidable as well.

Theorem 3.4.5. *(Undecidability of* $\mathrm{MSO}_{\mathcal{P}}[<, 2\times]$ *over* ω*-sequences)*
$\mathrm{MSO}_{\mathcal{P}}[<, 2\times]$ *over* ω*-sequences is undecidable.*

The theories $\mathrm{MSO}_{\mathcal{P}}[<_{pre}, (\downarrow_i)_{i=0}^{k-1}]$, interpreted over infinite (k-ary) trees, are the well-known MSO theories of k successors (SkS for short). The decidability of SkS over finite trees has been shown in [Doner, 1970; Thatcher and Wright, 1968]. The decidability of the MSO theory of the infinite binary tree $S2S$ has been proved in [Rabin, 1969]. Such a result can be easily generalized to the MSO theory of the infinite k-ary tree SkS, for any $k > 2$ (and even to $S\omega S$ over countably branching trees) [Thomas, 1990].

Theorem 3.4.6. *(Decidability of* $\mathrm{MSO}_{\mathcal{P}}[<_{pre}, (\downarrow_i)_{i=0}^{k-1}]$ *over trees)*
$\mathrm{MSO}_{\mathcal{P}}[<, (\downarrow_i)_{i=0}^{k-1}]$ *over finite (resp. infinite) trees is non-elementarily decidable.*

The decidability of $\mathrm{MSO}_{\mathcal{P}}[<, (\downarrow_i)_{i=0}^{k-1}]$ over the n-LS has been proved in [Montanari and Policriti, 1996] by reducing it to $S1S$. Such a reduction is accomplished in two steps. First, the n-layered structure is flattened by embedding all its layers into the finest one; then, metric temporal information is encoded by means of a finite set of unary relations. This second step is closely related to the technique exploited in [Alur and Henzinger, 1993] to prove the decidability of a family of real-time logics*. It relies on the *finite-state character* of the involved metric temporal information, which can be expressed as follows: every temporal property that partition an infinite set of states/time points into a finite set of classes can be finitely *modeled* and hence it is decidable.

Theorem 3.4.7. *(Decidability of* $\mathrm{MSO}_{\mathcal{P}}[<, (\downarrow_i)_{i=0}^{k-1}]$ *over the* n-LS)
$\mathrm{MSO}_{\mathcal{P}}[<, (\downarrow_i)_{i=0}^{k-1}]$ *over the n-LS is non-elementarily decidable.*

The decidability of $\mathrm{MSO}_{\mathcal{P}}[<, (\downarrow_i)_{i=0}^{k-1}]$ over both the DULS and the UULS has been shown in [Montanari *et al.*, 1999]. The decidability of the theory of the DULS has been proved by embedding it into SkS. The infinite sequence of infinite trees of the k-refinable DULS can indeed be appended to the rightmost full path of the infinite k-ary tree. The encoding of the 2-refinable DULS into the infinite binary tree is shown in Figure 3.5. Suitable definable predicates are then used to distinguish between the nodes of the infinite tree that correspond to elements of the original DULS, and the other nodes. As an example, in the case depicted in Figure 3.5 we must differentiate the auxiliary nodes belonging to the rightmost full path of the tree from the other ones. Finally, for $0 \leq j \leq k-1$, the j-th projection relation $\downarrow_j$ can be interpreted as the j-th successor relation and the total order $<$ can be naturally mapped into the lexicographical ordering $<_{lex}$ (it is not difficult to show that $<_{lex}$ can be defined in SkS).

Theorem 3.4.8. *(Decidability of* $\mathrm{MSO}_{\mathcal{P}}[<, (\downarrow_i)_{i=0}^{k-1}]$ *over the* DULS)
$\mathrm{MSO}_{\mathcal{P}}[<, (\downarrow_i)_{i=0}^{k-1}]$ *over the DULS is non-elementarily decidable.*

The decidability of the theory of the UULS has been proved by reducing it to $S1S^k$. For the sake of simplicity, we describe the basic steps of this reduction in the case of the 2-refinable UULS (the technique can be generalized to deal with any $k > 2$). An embedding of $MSO[<, \downarrow_0, \downarrow_1]$ into $S1S^2$ can be obtained as follows. First, we replace the 2-refinable ULLS by the so-called *concrete* 2-refinable ULLS, which is defined as follows:

- for all $i \geq 0$, the i-th layer T^i is the set $\{2^i + n2^{i+1} : n \geq 0\} \subseteq \mathbb{N}$;

*The relationships between the theories of n- and ω-layered structures and real-time logics have been explored in detail by Montanari et al. in [Montanari *et al.*, 2000]. Logic and computer science communities have traditionally followed a different approach to the problem of representing and reasoning about time and states. Research in logic resulted in a family of (metric) tense logics that take *time* as a primitive notion and define (*timed*) *states* as sets of atomic propositions which are true at given time points, while research in computer science concentrated on the so–called (real-time) temporal logics of programs that take *state* as a primitive notion, and define *time* as an attribute of states. Montanari et al. show that the theories of time granularity provide a unifying framework within which the two approaches can be reconciled. States and time-points can indeed be uniformly referred to as elements of the (decidable) theories of the DULS and the UULS. In particular, they show that the theory of timed state sequences, underlying real-time logics, can be naturally recovered as an abstraction of such theories.

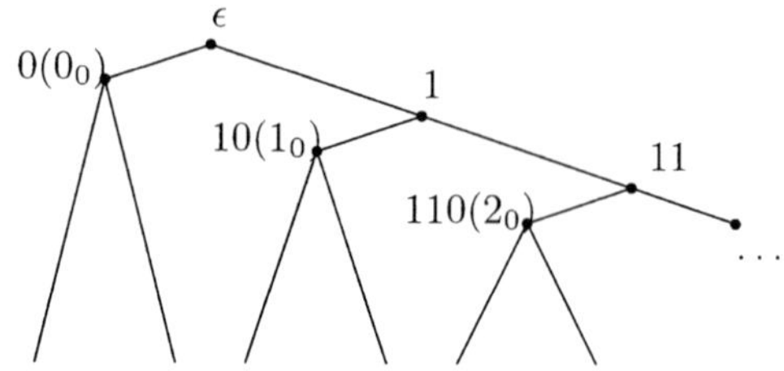

Figure 3.5: The encoding of the 2-refinable DULS into $\{0,1\}^*$.

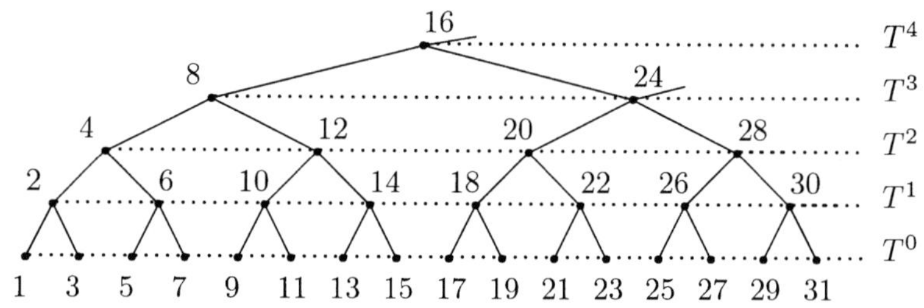

Figure 3.6: The concrete 2-refinable UULS.

- for every element $x = 2^i + n2^{i+1}$ belonging to T^i, with $i \geq 1$, $\downarrow_0(x) = 2^i + n2^{i+1} - 2^{i-1} = 2^{i-1} + 2n2^i$ and $\downarrow_1(x) = 2^i + n2^{i+1} + 2^{i-1} = 2^{i-1} + (2n+1)2^i$;
- $<$ is the usual ordering over $\mathbb{N}$.

A fragment of this concrete structure is depicted in Figure 3.6. Notice that all odd numbers are associated with layer T^0, while even numbers are distributed over the remaining layers. Notice also that the labeling of the concrete structure does not include the number 0*. It is easy to show that the two structures are isomorphic by exploiting the obvious mapping that associates each element of the 2-refinable UULS with the corresponding element of the concrete structure, preserving projection and ordering relations. Hence, the two structures satisfy the same $MSO[<, \downarrow_0, \downarrow_1]$-formulas. Next, we can easily encode the concrete 2-refinable UULS into $\mathbb{N}$. Both relations $\downarrow_0$ and $\downarrow_1$ can indeed be defined in terms of $\texttt{flip}_2$ as follows. For any given even number x,

$$\begin{array}{lll} \downarrow_0(x) = y & \text{iff} & y < x \wedge \texttt{flip}_2(y) = \texttt{flip}_2(x) \wedge \\ & & \neg\exists z(y < z \wedge z < x \wedge \texttt{flip}_2(z) = \texttt{flip}_2(x)); \\ \downarrow_1(x) = y & \text{iff} & \texttt{flip}_2(y) = x \wedge \neg\exists z(y < z \wedge \texttt{flip}_2(z) = x). \end{array}$$

By exploiting such a correspondence, it is possible to define a translation τ of $MSO[<, \downarrow_0, \downarrow_1]$ formulas (resp. sentences) into $S1S^2$ formulas (resp. sentences) such that, for any formula

*In [Montanari *et al.*, 2002a], Montanari et al. show that it is convenient to consider 0 as the label of the first node of an imaginary additional finest layer, whose remaining nodes are not labeled. In such a way the node with label 0 turns out to be the left son of the node with label 1.

(resp. sentence) $\phi \in MSO[<, \downarrow_0, \downarrow_1]$, ϕ is satisfiable by (resp. true in) the UULS if and only if $\tau(\phi) \in S1S^2$ is satisfiable by (resp. true in) $\langle \mathbb{N}, <, \mathtt{flip}_2 \rangle$.

Theorem 3.4.9. *(Decidability of* $\mathrm{MSO}_{\mathcal{P}}[<, (\downarrow_i)_{i=0}^{k-1}]$ *over the* UULS*)*
$\mathrm{MSO}_{\mathcal{P}}[<, (\downarrow_i)_{i=0}^{k-1}]$ *over the UULS is non-elementarily decidable.*

In [Montanari and Puppis, 2004b], Montanari and Puppis deal with the decision problem for the MSO logic interpreted over an ω-layered temporal structure devoid of both a finest layer and a coarsest one (we call such a structure totally unbounded, TULS for short). The temporal universe of the TULS is the set $\mathcal{U}_n = \bigcup_{i \in \mathbb{Z}} T^i$, where $\mathbb{Z}$ is the set of integers; the layer T^0 is a distinguished intermediate layer of such a structure. It is not difficult to show that $\mathrm{MSO}_{\mathcal{P}}[<, (\downarrow_i)_{i=0}^{k-1}]$ over both the DULS and the UULS can be embedded into $\mathrm{MSO}_{\mathcal{P}}[<, (\downarrow_i)_{i=0}^{k-1}, L_0]$ over the TULS (L_0 is a unary relational symbol used to identify the elements of T^0). The solution to the decision problem for $\mathrm{MSO}_{\mathcal{P}}[<, (\downarrow_i)_{i=0}^{k-1}, L_0]$ proposed by Montanari and Puppis extends Carton and Thomas' solution to the decision problem for the MSO theories of residually ultimately periodic words [Carton and Thomas, 2002]. First, they provide a tree-like characterization of the TULS and, taking advantage of it, they define a non-trivial encoding of the TULS into a vertex-colored tree that allows them to reduce the decision problem for the TULS to the problem of determining, for any given Rabin tree automaton, whether it accepts such a vertex-colored tree. Then, they reduce this latter problem to the decidable case of regular trees by exploiting a suitable notion of tree equivalence [Montanari and Puppis, 2004a].

Theorem 3.4.10. *(Decidability of* $\mathrm{MSO}_{\mathcal{P}}[<, (\downarrow_i)_{i=0}^{k-1}, L_0]$ *over the* TULS*)*
$\mathrm{MSO}_{\mathcal{P}}[<, (\downarrow_i)_{i=0}^{k-1}, L_0]$ *over the TULS is non-elementarily decidable.*

Notice that, taking advantage of the above-mentioned embedding, such a result provides, as a by-product, an alternative (uniform) decidability proof for the theories of the DULS and the UULS.

The definability and decidability of a set of binary predicates in monadic languages interpreted over the n-LS, the DULS, and the UULS have been systematically explored in [Franceschet *et al.*, 2003]. The set of considered predicates includes the equi-level (resp. equi-column) predicate constraining two time points to belong to the same layer (resp. column) and the horizontal (resp. vertical) successor predicate relating a time point to its successor within a given layer (resp. column), which allow one to express meaningful properties of time granularity [Montanari, 1996]. The authors investigate definability and decidability issues for such predicates with respect to $\mathrm{MSO}[<, (\downarrow_i)_{i=0}^{k-1}]$ and its first-order, chain, and path fragments $\mathrm{FO}[<, (\downarrow_i)_{i=0}^{k-1}]$, $\mathrm{MPL}[<, (\downarrow_i)_{i=0}^{k-1}]$, and $\mathrm{MCL}[\tau]$ of $\mathrm{MSO}[<, (\downarrow_i)_{i=0}^{k-1}]$ (as well as their $\mathcal{P}$-variants $\mathrm{FO}_{\mathcal{P}}[<, (\downarrow_i)_{i=0}^{k-1}]$, $\mathrm{MPL}_{\mathcal{P}}[<, (\downarrow_i)_{i=0}^{k-1}]$, and $\mathrm{MCL}_{\mathcal{P}}[<, (\downarrow_i)_{i=0}^{k-1}]$). Figure 3.7 summarizes the relationships between the expressive powers of such formal systems (an arrow from $\mathcal{T}$ to $\mathcal{T}'$ stands for $\mathcal{T} \to \mathcal{T}'$). From Theorems 3.4.7, 3.4.8, 3.4.9, and 3.4.10, it immediately follows that all the formalisms in Figure 3.7, when interpreted over the n-LS, the DULS, the UULS, and the TULS are decidable.

The outcomes of the analysis of the equi-level, equi-column, horizontal successor, and vertical successor predicates can be summarized as follows. First, the authors show that all these predicates are not definable in the MSO language over the DULS and the UULS, and that their addition immediately leads the MSO theories of such structures to undecidability.

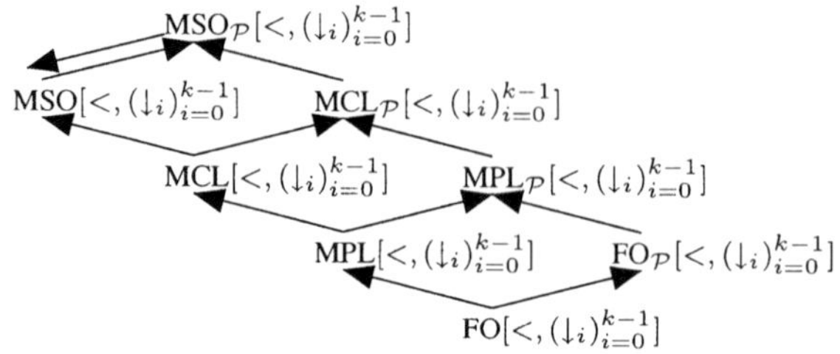

Figure 3.7: A hierarchy of monadic formalisms over layered structures.

As for the n-LS, the status of the horizontal (equi-level and horizontal successor) and vertical (equi-column and vertical successor) predicates turns out to be quite different: while horizontal predicates are easily definable, vertical ones are undefinable and their addition yields undecidability. Then, the authors study the effects of adding the above predicates to suitable *fragments* of the MSO language, such as its first-order, path, and chain fragments, possibly admitting uninterpreted unary relational symbols. They systematically explore all the possibilities, and give a number of positive and negative results. From a technical point of view, (un)definability and (un)decidability results are obtained by reduction from/to a wide spectrum of undecidable/decidable problems. Even though the complete picture is still missing (some decidability problems are open), the achieved results suffice to formulate some general statements. First, all predicates can be added to monadic first-order, path, and chain fragments, devoid of uninterpreted unary relational symbols, over the n-LS and the UULS preserving decidability. In the case of the DULS, they prove the same result for the equi-level and horizontal successor predicates, while they do not establish whether the same holds for the equi-column and vertical successor predicates. Moreover, they prove that the addition of the equi-column or vertical successor predicates to monadic first-order fragments over the ω-layered structures, with uninterpreted unary relational symbols, makes the resulting theories undecidable. The effect of such additions to the n-layered structure is not known. As for the equi-level predicate, they only prove that adding it to the monadic path fragment over the DULS, with uninterpreted unary relational symbols, leads to undecidability. Finally, as far as the MSO language over the UULS is concerned, they establish an interesting connection between its extension with the equi-level (resp. equi-column) predicate and systolic ω-languages over Y-trees (resp. trellis) [Gruska, 1990].

3.4.3 Temporalized logics and automata for time granularity

In the previous section, we have shown that monadic theories of time granularity are quite expressive, but they have not much computational appeal because their decision problem is *non-elementary*. This roughly means that it is possible to algorithmically check the truth of sentences, but the complexity of the algorithm grows very rapidly and it cannot be bounded. Moreover, the corresponding automata (Büchi sequence automata for the theory of the n-LS, Rabin tree automata for the theory of the DULS, and systolic tree automata for the theory of the UULS) do not directly work over layered structures, but rather over collapsed structures into which layered structures can be encoded. Hence, they are not natural and intuitive tools to specify and check properties of time granularity. In this section, we outline a different approach that connects monadic theories of time granularity back

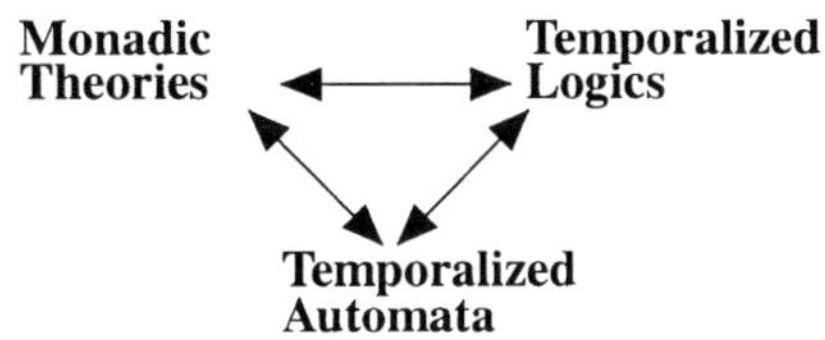

Figure 3.8: From monadic theories to temporalized logics via temporalized automata.

to temporal logic [Franceschet and Montanari, 2001a; Franceschet and Montanari, 2001b; Franceschet and Montanari, 2004]. Taking inspiration of methods for logic combinations (a short description of these methods can be found in [Franceschet *et al.*, 2004]), Franceschet and Montanari reinterpret layered structures as *combined structures*. This allows them to define suitable combined temporal logics and combined automata over layered structures, respectively called temporalized logics and temporalized automata, and to study their expressive power and computational properties by taking advantage of the transfer theorems for combined logics and combined automata. The outcome is rewarding: the resulting combined temporal logics and automata directly work over layered structures; moreover, they are expressively equivalent to monadic systems, and they are elementarily decidable.

Finding the temporal logic counterpart of monadic theories is a difficult task, involving a non-elementary blow up in the length of formulas. Ehrenfeucht games have been successfully exploited to deal with such a correspondence problem for first-order theories [Immerman and Kozen, 1989] and well-behaved fragments of second-order monadic ones, e.g., the path fragment of the monadic second-order theory of infinite binary trees [Hafer and Thomas, 1987]. As for the theories of time granularity, in [Franceschet and Montanari, 2003] Franceschet and Montanari show that an expressively complete and elementarily decidable combined temporal logic counterpart of the path fragment of the MSO theory of the DULS can be obtained by means of suitable applications of Ehrenfeucht games. Ehrenfeucht games have also been used by Montanari et al. to extend Kamp's theorem to deal with the first-order fragment of the MSO theory of the UULS [Montanari *et al.*, 2002a]. Unfortunately, these techniques produce rather involved proofs and they do not naturally lift to the full second-order case. A little detour is needed to deal with such a case. Instead of trying to establish a direct correspondence between MSO theories of time granularity and temporal logics, Franceschet and Montanari connect them via automata [Franceschet and Montanari, 2004] (cf. Figure 3.8). Firstly, they define the class of temporalized automata, which can be proved to be the automata-theoretic counterpart of temporalized logics, and they show that relevant properties, such as closure under Boolean operations, decidability, and expressive equivalence with respect to temporal logics, transfer from component automata to temporalized ones. Then, on the basis of the established correspondence between temporalized logics and automata, they reduce the task of finding a temporal logic counterpart of the MSO theories of the DULS and the UULS to the easier one of finding temporalized automata counterparts of them. The mapping of MSO formulas into automata (the difficult direction) can indeed greatly benefit from automata closure properties.

As a by-product, the alternative characterization of temporalized logics for time granularity as temporalized automata allows one to reduce logical problems to automata ones. As it is well-known in the area of automated system specification and verification, such a reduction presents several advantages, including the possibility of using automata for both system modeling and specification, and the possibility of checking the system on-the-fly (a detailed account of these advantages can be found in [Franceschet and Montanari, 2001b]).

3.4.4 Coda: time granularity and interval temporal logics

As pointed out in [Montanari, 1996], there exists a natural link between structures and theories of time granularity and those developed for representing and reasoning about time intervals. Differently-grained temporal domains can indeed be interpreted as different ways of partitioning a given discrete/dense time axis into consecutive disjoint intervals. According to this interpretation, every time point can be viewed as a suitable interval over the time axis and projection implements an intervals-subintervals mapping. More precisely, let us define *direct constituents* of a time point x, belonging to a given domain, the time points of the immediately finer domain into which x can be refined, if any, and *indirect constituents* the time points into which the direct constituents of x can be directly or indirectly refined, if any. The mapping of a given time point into its direct or indirect constituents can be viewed as a mapping of a given time interval into (a specific subset of) its subintervals.

The existence of such a natural correspondence between interval and granularity structures hints at the possibility of defining a similar connection at the level of the corresponding theories. For instance, according to such a connection, temporal logics over DULSs allow one to constrain a given property to hold true densely over a given time interval, where P densely holds over a time interval w if P holds over w and there exists a direct constituent of w over which P densely holds. In particular, establishing a connection between structures and logics for time granularity and those for time intervals would allow one to transfer decidability results from the granularity setting to the interval one. As a matter of fact, most interval temporal logics, including Moszkowski's Interval Temporal Logic (ITL) [Moszkowski, 1983], Halpern and Shoham's Modal Logic of Time Intervals (HS) [Halpern and Shoham, 1991], Venema's CDT Logic [Venema, 1991a], and Chaochen and Hansen's Neighborhood Logic (NL) [Chaochen and Hansen, 1998], are highly undecidable. Decidable fragments of these logics have been obtained by imposing severe restrictions on their expressive power, e.g., the *locality* constraint in [Moszkowski, 1983].

Preliminary results can be found in [Montanari *et al.*, 2002b], where the authors propose a new interval temporal logic, called Split Logic (SL for short), which is equipped with operators borrowed from HS and CDT, but is interpreted over specific interval structures, called *split-frames*. The distinctive feature of a split-frame is that there is at most one way to chop an interval into two adjacent subintervals, and consequently it does not possess *all* the intervals. They prove the decidability of SL with respect to particular classes of split-frames which can be put in correspondence with the first-order fragments of the monadic theories of time granularity. In particular, *discrete* split-frames with maximal intervals correspond to the n-layered structure, discrete split-frames (with unbounded intervals) can be mapped into the upward unbounded layered structure, and *dense* split-frames with maximal intervals can be encoded into the downward unbounded layered structure.

3.5 Qualitative time granularity

Granularity operators for qualitative time representation have been first provided in [Euzenat, 1993; Euzenat, 1995a]. These operators are defined in the context of relational algebras and they apply to both point and interval algebras. They have the advantage of being applicable to fully qualitative and widespread relational representations. They account for granularity phenomena occurring in actual applications using only qualitative descriptions.

After a short recall of relation algebras (Section 3.5.1), a set of six constraints applying to the granularity operators is defined (Section 3.5.2). These constraints are applied to the well-known temporal representation of point and interval algebras (Section 3.5.3). Some general results of existence and relation of these operators with composition are also given (Section 3.5.4).

3.5.1 Qualitative time representation and granularity

The qualitative time representation considered here is a well-known one:

1. it is based on an algebra of binary relations $\langle 2^{\Gamma}, \cup, \circ, ^{-1} \rangle$ (see Chapter 1); we focus our attention on the point and interval algebras [Vilain and Kautz, 1986; Allen, 1983]);
2. this algebra is augmented with a neighborhood structure (in which $N(r, r')$ means that the relationships r and r' are neighbors) [Freksa, 1992];
3. last, the construction of an interval algebra [Hirsh, 1996] is considered (the conversion of a quadruple of base relationships R into an interval relation is given by $\Rightarrow R$ and the converse operation by $\Leftarrow r$ when it is defined).

In such an algebra of relations, the situations are described by a set of possible relationships holding between entities (here points or intervals).

As an example, imagine several witnesses of an air flight incident with the witness from the ground (g) saying that "the engine stopped working (W) and the plane went [immediately] down", the pilot (p) saying that "the plane worked correctly (W) until there has been a misfiring period (M) and, after that, the plane lost altitude", and the (unfortunately out of reach) "blackbox" flight data recorder (b) revealing that the plane had a short misfiring period (M) and a short laps of correct behavior before the plane lost altitude (D).
If these descriptions are rephrased in the interval algebra (see Figure 3.9), this would correspond to three different descriptions: $g = \{WmD\}$, $p = \{WmM, MmD\}$ and $b = \{WmM, MbD\}$. Obviously, if any two of these descriptions are merged, the result is an inconsistent description. However, such inconsistencies arise because the various sources of information do not share the same precision and not because of intrisically contradictory descriptions. It is thus useful to find in which way the situations described by g and p can be coarse views of that expressed by b.

The qualitative granularity is defined through a couple of operators for converting the representation of a situation into a finer or coarser representation of the same situation. These operators apply to the relationships holding between the entities and transform these relationship into other plausible relationships at a coarser (with upward conversion denoted by $\uparrow$) or finer (with downward conversion denoted by $\downarrow$) granularity. When the conversion is not oriented, i.e., when we talk about a granularity change between two layers, but it is not necessary to know which one is the coarser, a neutral operator is used (denoted by $\rightarrow$).

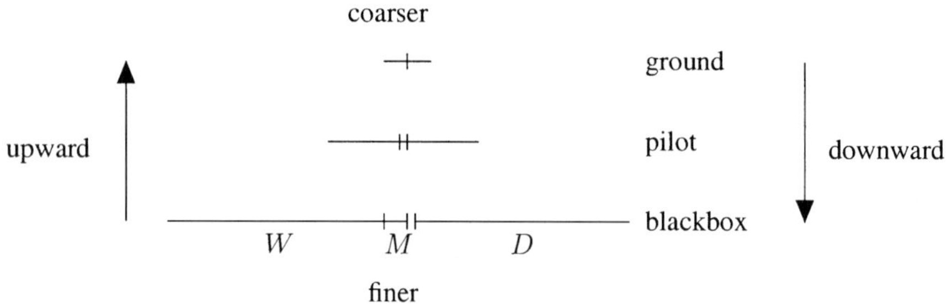

Figure 3.9: The air flight incident example.

Before turning to precisely define the granularity conversion, the assumptions underlying them must be clear. First of all, the considered language is qualitative and relational. Each layer represents a situation in the unaltered language of the relational algebra. This has the advantage of considering any description of a situation as being done under a particular granularity. Thus the layers are external to the language. The descriptions considered here are homogeneous (i.e., the language is the same for all the layers). The temporal structure is given by the algebra itself. The layers are organised as a partial order $\langle \mathcal{T}, \prec \rangle$ (sometimes it is known that a layer is coarser than another). In the example of Figure 3.9, it seems clear that $b \prec p \prec g$. It is not assumed that they are aligned or decomposed into homogeneous units, but the constraints below can enforce contiguity. The only operators considered here are the projection operators. The contextualisation operator is not explicit since (by opposition to logical systems) it cannot be composed with other operators. However, sometimes the notation ${}_{g} \rightarrow_{g'}$ is used, providing a kind of contextualisation (by specifying the concerned granularities). The displacement operator is useless since the relational language is not situated (or absolute, i.e., it does not evaluate the truth of a formula at a particular moment, but rather evaluates the truth of a temporal relationship between two entities).

3.5.2 Generic constraints on granularity change

Anyone can think about a particular set of projection operators by imagining the effects of coarseness. But here we provide a set of properties which should be satisfied by any system of granularity conversion operators. In fact, the set of properties is very small. Next section shows that they are sufficient for restricting the number of operators to only one (plus the expected operators corresponding to identity and conversion to everything).

Constraints below are given for unit relations (singletons of the set of relations). The operators on general relations are defined by:

$$\rightarrow R = \cup_{r \in R} \rightarrow r \tag{3.2}$$

Self-conservation

Self-conservation states that whatever be the conversion, a relationship must belong to its own conversion (this corresponds to the property named reflexivity when the conversion is a relation).

$$r \in \rightarrow r \qquad \text{(self-conservation)} \tag{3.3}$$

It is quite a sensible and minimal property: the knowledge about the relationship can be less precise, but it must have a chance to be correct. Moreover, in a qualitative system, it is possible that nothing changes through granularity if the (quantitative) granularity step is small enough. Not requiring this property would disable the possibility that the same situation looks the same under different granularity. Self-conservation accounts for this.

Neighborhood compatibility

A property considered earlier is the *order preservation* property — stated in [Hobbs, 1985] as an equivalence: $\forall x, y, x < y \equiv (\rightarrow x) < (\rightarrow y)$. This property takes for granted the availability of an order relation ($<$) structuring the set of relationships. It states that

$$\text{if } x > y \text{ then } \neg(\rightarrow x <\rightarrow y) \qquad \text{(order preservation)}$$

However, order preservation has the shortcoming of requiring the order relation. Its algebraic generalization could be reciprocal avoidance:

$$\text{if } xry \text{ then } \neg(\rightarrow xr^{-1} \rightarrow y) \qquad \text{(reciprocal avoidance)}$$

Reciprocal avoidance is over-generalized and conflicts with self-conservation in case of auto-reciprocal relationships (i.e. such that $r = r^{-1}$). The neighborhood compatibility, while not expressed in [Euzenat, 1993], has been taken into account informally: it constrains the conversion of a relation to form a conceptual neighborhood (and hence the conversion of a conceptual neighborhood to form a conceptual neighborhood).

$$\begin{aligned} &\forall r, \forall r', r'' \in \rightarrow r, \exists r_1, \ldots r_n \in \rightarrow r : \\ &\qquad r_1 = r', r_n = r'' \text{ and } \forall i \in [1, n-1] N(r_i, r_{i+1}) \end{aligned} \qquad \text{(neighborhood compatibility)} \tag{3.4}$$

This property has already been reported by Freksa [Freksa, 1992] who considers that a set of relationships must be a conceptual neighborhood in order to be seen as a coarse representation of the actual relationship. It is weaker than the two former proposals because it does not prevent the opposite to be part of the conversion. But in such a case, it constrains a path between the relation and its converse to be in the conversion too. Neighborhood compatibility seems to be the right property, partly because, instead of the former ones, it does not forbid a very coarse granularity under which any relationship is converted in the whole set of relations. It also seems natural because granularity can hardly be imagined as discontinuous (at least in continuous spaces).

Conversion-reciprocity distributivity

An obvious property for conversion is symmetry. It states that the conversion of the relation between a first object and a second one must be the reciprocal of the conversion of the relation between the second one and the first one. It is clear that the relationships between two temporal occurrences are symmetric and thus granularity conversion must respect this.

$$\rightarrow r^{-1} = (\rightarrow r)^{-1} \qquad \text{(distributivity of} \rightarrow \text{on} {}^{-1}) \qquad (3.5)$$

Inverse compatibility

Inverse compatibility states that the conversion operators are consistent with each other, i.e., that if the relationship between two occurrences can be seen as another relationship under some granularity, then the inverse operation from the latter to the former can be achieved through the inverse operator. Stated otherwise, this property corresponds to symmetry when the operator is described as a relation.

$$r \in \bigcap_{r' \in \uparrow r} \downarrow r' \text{ and } r \in \bigcap_{r' \in \downarrow r} \uparrow r' \qquad \text{(inverse compatibility)} \qquad (3.6)$$

For instance, if someone in situation (p) of Figure 3.9 is able to imagine that, under a finer granularity (say situation b), there is some time between the misfiring period and the loss of altitude, then (s)he must be ready to accept that if (s)he were in situation (b), (s)he could imagine that there is no time between them under a coarser granularity (as in situation p).

Idempotency

A property which is usually considered first (especially in quantitative systems) is the full transitivity:

$$_g\!\rightarrow_{g'}\ _{g'}\!\rightarrow_{g''} r = _g\!\rightarrow_{g''} r \qquad \text{(transitivity)}$$

This property is too strong; it would for instance imply that:

$$_g\!\uparrow^{g'}\ {}^{g'}\!\downarrow_g r = r$$

Of course, it cannot be achieved because this would mean that there is no loss of information through granularity conversion: this is obviously false. If it were true anyway, there would be no need for granularity operators: everything would be the same under any layer. On the other hand, other transitivity such as the oriented transitivity (previously known as cumulated transitivity) can be expected:

$$_g\!\uparrow^{g'}_{g'}\!\uparrow^{g''} r = _g\!\uparrow^{g''} r \text{ and } {}^g\!\downarrow^{g'}_{g'}\!\downarrow_{g''} r = {}^g\!\downarrow_{g''} r \qquad \text{(oriented transitivity)}$$

However, in a purely qualitative calculus, the precise granularity (g) is not relevant and this property becomes a property of idempotency of operators:

$$\uparrow\uparrow r = \uparrow r \text{ and } \downarrow\downarrow r = \downarrow r \qquad \text{(idempotency)} \qquad (3.7)$$

At first sight, it could be clever to have non idempotent operators which are less and less precise with granularity conversion. However, if this applies very well to quantitative data, it does not apply for qualitative: the qualitative conversion applies equally for a large granularity conversion and for a small one which is ten times less. If, for instance, in a particular situation, a relationship between two entities is r, in a coarser representation it is r' and in an even coarser representation it is r'', then r'' must be a member of the upward conversion of r.

This is because r'' is indeed the result of a qualitative conversion from the first representation to the third. Thus, qualitatively, $\uparrow\uparrow=\uparrow$.

If there were no idempotency, converting a relationship directly would give a different result than when doing it through ten successive conversions.

Representation independence

Since the operation allowing one to go from a relational space to an interval relational space has been provided (by $\Leftarrow$ and $\Rightarrow$), the property constraining the conversion operators can also be given at that stage: representation independence states that the conversion must not be dependent upon the representation of the temporal entity (as an interval or as a set of bounding points). Again, this property must be required:

$$\rightarrow r = \Leftarrow\rightarrow\Rightarrow r \text{ and } \rightarrow r = \Rightarrow\rightarrow\Leftarrow r \qquad \text{(representation independence)} \tag{3.8}$$

It can be though of as a distributivity:

$$\Rightarrow\rightarrow r = \rightarrow\Rightarrow r \text{ and } \Leftarrow\rightarrow r = \rightarrow\Leftarrow r$$

Note that, since $\Leftarrow$ requires that the relationship between bounding points allows the result to be an interval, there could be some restrictions on the results (however, these restrictions correspond exactly to the vanishing of an interval which is out of scope here).

The constraints (3.3, self-conservation) and (3.7, idempotence), together with the definition of the operators for full relations (3.2), characterise granularity operators as closure operators.

Nothing ensures that these constraints lead to a unique couple of operators for a given relational system.

Definition 3.5.1. *Given a relational system, a couple of operators up-down satisfying 3.3-3.7 is a coherent granularity conversion operator for that system.*

For any relation algebra there are two operators which always satisfy these requirements: the identity function (Id) which maps any relation into itself (or a singleton containing itself) and the non-informative function (Ni) which maps any relation into the base set of the algebra. It is noteworthy that these functions must then be their own inverse (i.e., they are candidates for both $\uparrow$ and $\downarrow$ at once). These solutions are not considered anymore below.

The framework provided so far concerns two operators related by the constraints, but there is no specificity of the upward or downward operator (this is why constraints are symmetric). By convention, if the system contains an equivalence relation (defined as e such that $e = e \circ e = e^{-1}$ [Hirsh, 1996]), the operators which maps this element to a strictly broader set is denoted as the downward operator. This meets the intuition because the coarser the view the more indistinguishable the entities (and they are then subject to the equivalence relation).

3.5.3 Results on point and interval algebras

From these constraints, it is possible to generate the possible operators for a particular relation algebra. This is first performed for the point algebra and the interval algebra in which it turns out that only one couple of non-trivial operators exists. Moreover, these operators satisfy the relationship between base and interval algebra.

Granularity for the point algebra

Proposition 3.5.1. *Table 3.1 defines the only possible non auto-inverse upward/downward operators for the point algebra.*

relation: r	$\uparrow r$	$\downarrow r$
$<$	$<=$	$<$
$=$	$=$	$<=>$
$>$	$>=$	$>$

Table 3.1: Upward and downward granularity conversions for the point algebra.

These operators fit intuition very well. For instance, if the example of Figure 3.9 is modeled through bounding points (x^- for the left endpoint and x^+ for the right endpoint) of intervals W^+, M^-, M^+ and D^-, it is represented in (b) by $W^+ = M^-$ (the engine stops working when it starts misfiring), $M^- < M^+$ (the beginning of the misfire is before its end), $M^+ < D^-$ (the end of the misfiring period is before the beginning of the loss of altitude) in (p) by $M^+ = D^-$ (the misfiring period ends when the loss of altitude begins) and in (g) by $M^- = M^+$ (the misfiring period does not exist anymore). This is possible by converting $M^+ < D^-$ into $M^+ = D^-$ ($= \in \uparrow <$) and $M^- = M^+$ into $M^- < M^+$ ($< \in \downarrow =$).

Granularity for the interval algebra

Since the temporal interval algebra is a plain interval algebra, the constraint 3.8 can be applied for deducing its granularity operators. This provides the only possible operators for the interval algebra. Table 3.2 shows the automatic translation from points to intervals:

r	$\uparrow r$				$\uparrow r$	$\downarrow r$				$\downarrow r$
b	$<=$	$<=$	$<=$	$<=$	bm	$<$	$<$	$<$	$<$	b
d	$>=$	$<=$	$>=$	$<=$	$dsfe$	$>$	$<$	$>$	$<$	d
o	$<=$	$<=$	$>=$	$<=$	$osmef^{-1}$	$<$	$<$	$>$	$<$	o
s	$=$	$<=$	$>=$	$=$	se	$<=>$	$<$	$>$	$<$	osd
f	$>=$	$<=$	$>=$	$=$	fe	$>$	$<$	$>$	$<=>$	$o^{-1}fd$
m	$<=$	$<=$	$=$	$<=$	m	$<$	$<$	$<=>$	$<$	bmo
e	$=$	$<=$	$>=$	$=$	e	$<=>$	$<$	$>$	$<=>$	$of^{-1}d^{-1}s$ $es^{-1}dfo^{-1}$

Table 3.2: Transformation of upward and downward operators between points into interval relation quadruples.

The conversion table for the interval algebra is given below. The corresponding operators enjoy the same properties as the operators for the point algebra.

Proposition 3.5.2. *The upward/downward operators for the interval algebra of Table 3.3 satisfy the properties 3.3 through 3.7.*

r	$\uparrow r$	$\downarrow r$	r^{-1}	$\uparrow r^{-1}$	$\downarrow r^{-1}$
b	bm	b	b^{-1}	$b^{-1}m^{-1}$	b^{-1}
d	$dfse$	d	d^{-1}	$d^{-1}s^{-1}f^{-1}e$	d^{-1}
o	$of^{-1}sme$	o	o^{-1}	$o^{-1}s^{-1}fem^{-1}$	o^{-1}
s	se	osd	s^{-1}	$s^{-1}e$	$d^{-1}s^{-1}o^{-1}$
f	fe	dfo^{-1}	f^{-1}	$f^{-1}e$	$d^{-1}f^{-1}o$
m	m	bmo	m^{-1}	m^{-1}	$o^{-1}m^{-1}b^{-1}$
e	e	$of^{-1}d^{-1}ses^{-1}dfo^{-1}$			

Table 3.3: Upward and downward granularity conversion for the interval algebra.

Proposition 3.5.3. *The upward/downward operators for the interval algebra of Table 3.3 are the only ones that satisfy the property 3.8 with regard to the operators for the point algebra of Table 3.1.*

If one wants to generate possible operators for the interval algebra, many of them can be found. But the constraint that this algebra must be the interval algebra (in the sense of [Hirsh, 1996]) of the point algebra restricts drastically the number of solutions.

The reader is invited to check on the example of Figure 3.9, that what has been said about point operators is still valid: the situation (b) is described by $W\{m\}M$ (the working period meets the misfiring one), $M\{b\}D$ (the misfiring period is anterior to the loss of altitude), in (p) by $M\{m\}D$ (the misfiring period meets the loss of altitude) and in (g) where the misfiring period does not appear anymore by $W\{m\}D$ (the working period meets the loss of altitude). This is compatible with the idea that, under a coarser granularity, b can become m ($m \in\uparrow b$) and that under a finer granularity m can become b ($b \in\downarrow m$).

The upward operator does not satisfy the condition 3.4 for B-neighborhood (in which objects are translated continuously [Freksa, 1992]) as it is violated by d, s, and f and C-neighborhood (in which the objects are continuously expanded or contracted by preserving their center of gravity [Freksa, 1992]) as it is violated by o, s, and f. This is because the corresponding neighborhoods are not based upon independent limit translations while this independence has been used for translating the results from the point algebra to the interval algebra.

It is noteworthy that the downward operator corresponds exactly to the closure of relationships that Ligozat [Ligozat, 1990] introduced in his own formalism. This seems natural since this closure, just like the conversion operators, provides all the adjacents relationships of a higher dimension.

3.5.4 General results of existence and composition

We provide here general results about the existence of granularity operators in algebra of binary relations. Then, the relationships between granularity conversion and composition, i.e., the impact of granularity changes on inference results, are considered.

Existence results for algebras of binary relations

The question of the general existence of granularity conversion operators corresponding to the above constraints can be raised. Concerning granularity conversion operators different from Id and Ni, two partial results have been established [Euzenat, 2001]. The first one shows that there are small algebras with no non-trivial operators:

Proposition 3.5.4. *The algebra based on two elements a and a^{-1} such that $N(a, a^{-1})$ has no granularity conversion operators other than identity and non-informative map.*

A more interesting result is that of the existence of operators for a large class of algebras. In the case of two auto-inverse operators (e.g., $=$ and $\neq$), there must exist conversion operators as shown by proposition 3.5.5. Proposition 3.5.5 exhibits a systematic way of generating operators from minimal requirements (but does not provide a way to generate all the operators). It only provides a sufficient, but not necessary, condition for having operators.

Proposition 3.5.5. *Given a relation algebra containing two relationships a and b such that $N(a, b)$ (it is assumed that neighborhood is converse independent, i.e., $N(a^{-1}, b^{-1})$), there exists a couple of upward/downward granularity operators defined by :*

if a and b are auto-inverse $\downarrow a = \{a, b\}$, $\uparrow b = \{a, b\}$, *the remainder being identity;*

if a only is auto-inverse $\downarrow a = \{a, b, b^{-1}\}$, $\uparrow b = \{a, b\}$, $\uparrow b^{-1} = \{a, b^{-1}\}$, *the remainder being identity;*

if a and b are not auto-inverse $\downarrow a = \{a, b\}$, $\uparrow b = \{a, b\}$, $\downarrow a^{-1} = \{a^{-1}, b^{-1}\}$, $\uparrow b^{-1} = \{a^{-1}, b^{-1}\}$, *the remainder being identity.*

There can be, in general, many possible operators for a given algebra. Proposition 3.5.5 shows that the five core properties of Section 3.5.2 are consistent. Another general question about them concerns their independence. It can be answered affirmatively:

Proposition 3.5.6. *The core properties of granularity operators are independent.*

This is proven by providing five systems satisfying all properties but one [Euzenat, 2001].

Granularity and composition

The composition of symbolic relationships is a favored inference means for symbolic representation systems. One of the properties which would be interesting to obtain is the independence of the results of the inferences from the granularity level (equation 3.9). The distributivity of $\rightarrow$ on $\circ$ denotes the independence of the inferences from the granularity under which they are performed.

$$\rightarrow (r \circ r') = (\rightarrow r) \circ (\rightarrow r') \qquad \text{(distributivity of} \rightarrow \text{over} \circ) \qquad (3.9)$$

This property is only satisfied for upward conversion in the point algebra.

Proposition 3.5.7. *The upward operator for the point algebra satisfies property 3.9.*

It does not hold true for the interval algebra. Let three intervals x, y and z be such that xby and ydz. The application of composition of relations gives $x\{b\ o\ m\ d\ s\}z$ which, once upwardly converted, gives $x\{b\ m\ e\ d\ f\ s\ o\ f^{-1}\}z$. By opposition, if the conversion is first applied, it returns $x\{b\ m\}y$ and $y\{d\ f\ s\ e\}z$ which, once composed, yields $x\{b\ o\ m\ d\ s\}z$. The interpretation of this result is the following: by first converting, the information that there exists an interval y forbidding x to finish z is lost; however, if the relationships linking y to x and z are preserved, then the propagation will take them into account and recover the lost precision: $\{b\ m\ e\ d\ f\ s\ o^{-1}\} \circ \{b\ o\ m\ d\ s\} = \{b\ o\ m\ d\ s\}$. In any case, this cannot be enforced since, if the length of y is so small that the conversion makes it vanish, the correct information at that granularity is the one provided by applying first the composition: x can meet the end of z under such a granularity. However, if equation 3.9 cannot be achieved for upward conversion in the interval algebra, upward conversion is super-distributive over composition.

Proposition 3.5.8. *The upward operator for the interval algebra satisfies the following property:*

$$(\uparrow r) \circ (\uparrow r') \subseteq \uparrow (r \circ r') \qquad \text{(super-distributivity of } \uparrow \text{ over } \circ)$$

A similar phenomenon appears with the downward conversion operators (it appears both for points and intervals). Let x, y and z be three points such that $x > y$ and $y = z$. On the one hand, the composition of relations gives $x > z$, which is converted to $x > z$ under the finer granularity. On the other hand, the conversion gives $x > y$ and $y{<}{=}{>}z$ because, under a more precise granularity, y could be close but not really equal to z. The composition then provides no more information about the relationship between x and z ($x{<}{=}{>}z$). This is the reverse situation as before: it takes into account the fact that the non-distinguishability of two points cannot be ensured under a finer grain. Of course, if everything is converted first, then the result is as precise as possible: downward conversion is sub-distributive over composition.

Proposition 3.5.9. *The downward operators for the interval and point algebras satisfy the following property:*

$$\downarrow (r \circ r') \subseteq (\downarrow r) \circ (\downarrow r') \qquad \text{(sub-distributivity of } \downarrow \text{ over } \circ)$$

These two latter properties can be useful for propagating constraints in order to get out of them the maximum of information quickly. For instance, in the case of upward conversion, if no interval vanishes, every relationship must be first converted and then composed.

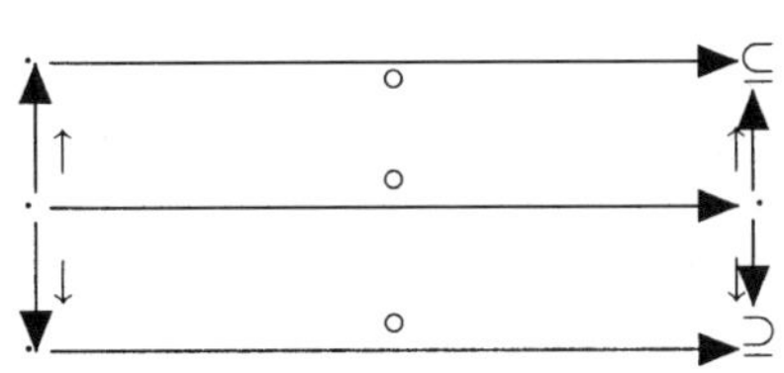

Figure 3.10: A diagrammatic summary of Propositions 3.5.9 and 3.5.8.

These properties have been discovered independently in the qualitative case [Euzenat, 1993] and in the set-theoretic granularity area through an approximation algorithm for quantitative constraints [Bettini *et al.*, 1996].

3.5.5 Granularity through discrete approximation

The algebra of relations can be directly given or derived as an interval algebra. It can also be provided by axiomatizing properties of objects or generated from properties of artefacts. Bittner [Bittner, 2002] has taken such an approach for generating sets of relations depending on the join of related objects. He has adapted a framework for qualitatively approximating spatial position to temporal representation. This framework can be used in turn for finding approximate relations between temporal entities which can be seen as relations under a coarser granularity.

Qualitative temporal relations

This work is based on a new analysis of the generation of relations between two spatial areas. These relations are characterized through the "intersection" (or meet) between the two regions. More precisely, the relation is characterized by the triple:

$$\langle x \wedge y \not\approx \bot, x \wedge y \approx x, x \wedge y \approx y \rangle$$

The items in these triples characterize the non emptiness of $x \wedge y$ (1st item) and its relation to x and y (2nd and 3rd items). So the values of this triple are relations (this approach is inspired from [Egenhofer and Franzosa, 1991]). These values are taken out of a set of possible relations Ω. This generates several different sets of relations depending on the kind of relations used:

- boundary insensitive relations (RCC5);
- one-dimensional boundary insensitive relations between intervals (RCC_1^9);
- one-dimensional boundary insensitive relations between non convex regions (RCC_1^9);
- boundary sensitive relations (RCC8);
- one-dimensional boundary sensitive relations (RCC_1^{15}).

Some of these representations are obviously refinement of others. In that sense, we obtain a granular representation of a temporal situation by using more or less precise qualitative relationships. This can also be obtained by using other kinds of temporal representations (RCC8 is less precise than Allen's algebra of relations).

As an example, RCC_1^9 considers regions x and y corresponding to intervals on the real line. The set Ω is made of FLO, FLI, T, FRI, FRO. FLO indicates that no argument is included in the other (O) and there is some part of the first argument left (L) of the second one, FLI indicates that the second argument is included in the first one and there is some part of the first argument left (L) of the second one, T corresponds to the equality of the intersection with the interval, and FRI and FRO are the same for the right hand bound. This provides the relations of Table 3.4.

$x \wedge y \not\sim \perp$	$x \wedge y \sim x$	$x \wedge y \sim y$	Allen
FLO	FLO	FLO	b m
FRO	FRO	FRO	b^{-1} m^{-1}
T	FLO	FLO	o
T	FRO	FRO	o^{-1}
T	T	FLI	d s
T	T	FRI	d f
T	FLI	T	d^{-1} f^{-1}
T	FRI	T	d^{-1} s^{-1}
T	T	T	e

Table 3.4: The relations of RCC_1^9.

The relations in these sets are not always jointly exhaustive and pairwise disjoint. For instance, RCC_1^9 is exhaustive but not pairwise disjoint, simply because d and d^{-1} appear in two lines of the table.

Qualitative temporal locations

The framework as it is developed in [Bittner and Steel, 1998] considers a space, here a temporal domain, as a set of places T_0. Any spatial or temporal occurrence will be a subset of T_0. So, with regard to what has been considered in Section 3.3, the underlying space is aligned and structured.

An approximation is based on the partition of T_0 into a set of cells K (i.e., $\forall k, k' \in K, k \subseteq T_0, k \cap k' = \emptyset$ and $\cup_{k \in K} k = T_0$). The localization of any temporal occurrence is then approximated by providing its relation to each cell. The location of $x \subseteq T_0$ is a function $\rho_x : K \longrightarrow \Omega'$ from the set of cells to a set of relations Ω' (which may but have not to correspond to Ω or a RCC_q^p defined above). The resulting approximation is thus dependent on the partition K and the set of relations Ω'.

From this, we can state that two occurrences x and y are indistinguishable under granularity $\langle K, \Omega' \rangle$ if and only if $\rho_x = \rho_y$. This formulation is typical from the set-theoretic approach to temporal granularity used in a strictly qualitative domain.

We can also define the interpretation of an area of the set of cells ($X : K \longrightarrow \Omega$) as the set of places it approximates:

$$[X] = \{x \subseteq T_0 | \rho_x = X\}$$

Relations between approximations and granularity

It is clear that the approximation of a region x can be considered as its representation $\uparrow x$ under the granularity $\langle K, \Omega' \rangle$ (i.e., ρ_x). In the same vein, the interpretation of approximation $[X]$ corresponds to the conversion of this region to the finer granularity $\downarrow X$. In that respect we are faced with two discrete and aligned granularities.

The following question can be raised: given a relation $r \in RCC_q^p$ between x and y, the approximations $\uparrow x$ and $\uparrow y$, and $\uparrow r$ holding between $\uparrow x$ and $\uparrow y$, what can be said of the relationship between r and $\uparrow r$? The approximate relation $\uparrow r$ holding between X and Y is characterized as $SEM(X,Y)$ and defined as:

$$SEM(X,Y) = \{r \in RCC_q^p | x \in [X], y \in [Y], xRy, \text{ and } r \in R\}$$

The author goes on to define a syntactic operator ($SYN(X,Y)$) for determining the relationships between approximate regions. This operator must be as close as possible to $SEM(X,Y)$. It is defined by replacing in the equations defining the relations of the considered set, the region variables (x and y) by approximation variables (X and Y) and the meet operation by upper or lower bounds for the meet operation. This provides a pair of values for the relations between X and Y depending on whether they have been computed with the upper and lower meet.

It is now possible to obtain the relations between granular representations of the entities by considering that $x \uparrow r\ y$ can be obtained in the usual way (but for obtaining $\uparrow r$ we need to consider all the possible granularities, i.e., all the possible K and all the possible Ω'). $X \downarrow r\ Y$ is what should be obtained by $SEM(X,Y)$ and approximated by $SYN(X,Y)$.

Hence, a full parallel can be made between the above-described work on qualitative granularity and this work on discrete approximation in general. Unfortunately, the systems developed in [Bittner, 2002] do not include Allen's algebra. The satisfaction of the axioms by this scheme has not been formally established. However, one can say that self-conservation and idempotence are satisfied. Neighborhood compatibility depends on a neighborhood structure, but $SYN(X,Y)$ is very often an interval in the graph of relations (which is not very far from a neighborhood structure). It could also be interesting to show that when RCC_1^{15} relations correspond to Allen's ones, the granularity operators correspond.

In summary, this approximation framework has the merit of providing an approximated representation of temporal places interpreted on the real line. The approximation operation itself relies on aligned granularities. This approach is entirely qualitative in its definition but can account for orientation and boundaries.

3.6 Applications of time granularity

Time granularity come into play in many classes of applications with different constraints. Thus, the contributions presented below not only offer an application perspective, but generally provide their own granular formalism. The fact that there are no applications to multi-agent communication means that the agents currently developed communicate with agents of the same kind. With the development of communicating programs, it will become necessary to consider the compatibility of two differently grained descriptions of what they perceive.

3.6.1 Natural language processing, planning, and reasoning

The very idea of granularity in artificial intelligence comes from the field of natural language understanding [Hobbs, 1985]. In [Gayral, 1992] Gayral and Grandemange take into account the same temporal unit under a durative or instantaneous aspect. Their work is motivated by problems in text understanding. A mechanism of upward/downward conversion is introduced and modeled in a logical framework. It only manages symbolic constraints and it converts the entities instead of their relationships. The representation they propose is based on a notion of composition and it allows the recursive decomposition of beginning and ending bounds of intervals into new intervals. The level of granularity is determined during text understanding by the election of a distinguished individual (which could be compared with a focus of attention) among the set of entities and the aspect (durative vs. instantaneous) of that individual. Unlike most of the previously-described approaches, where granularity is considered orthogonal to a knowledge base, in Gayral and Grandemange's work the current granularity is given relatively to the aspect of a particular event. A link between the two notions can be established by means of the decomposition relation between entities (or history [Euzenat, 1993]). Time granularity in natural language processing and its relation with the durative/instantaneous aspects have been also studied by other authors. As an example, Becher et al. model granularity by means of time units and two basic relations over them: precedence and containment (alike the set-theoretic approach, Section 3.3) [Becher *et al.*, 1998]. From a model of time units consisting of a finite sequence of rational numbers, the authors build an algebra of relations between these units, obtaining an algebraic account of granularity.

In [Badaloni and Berati, 1994], Badaloni and Berati use different time scales in an attempt to reduce the complexity of planning problems. The system is purely quantitative and it relies on the work presented in Section 3.3. The NatureTime [Mota *et al.*, 1997] system is used for integrating several ecological models in which the objects are modeled under different time scales. The model is quantitative and it explicitly defines (in Prolog) the conversions from a layer to another. This is basically used during unification when the system unifies the temporal extensions of the atoms. Combi et al. [Combi *et al.*, 1995] applied their multi-granular temporal database to clinical medicine. The system is used for the follow-up of therapies in which data originate from various physicians and the patient itself. It allows one to answer (with possibility of undefined answers) to various questions about the history of the patient. In this system (like in many other) granularity usually means "converting units with alignment problems".

3.6.2 Program specification and verification

In [Ciapessoni *et al.*, 1993], Ciapessoni et al. apply the logics of time granularity to the specification and verification of real-time systems. The addition of time granularity makes it possible to associate coarse granularities with high-level modules and fine granularities with the lower level modules that compose them. In [Fiadeiro and Maibaum, 1994], Fiadeiro and Maibaum achieve the same practical goal by considering a system in which granularity is defined a posteriori (it corresponds to the granularity of actions performed by modules, while in the work by Ciapessoni et al. the granularity framework is based on a metric time) and the refinement (granularity change) takes place between classical logic theories instead of inside a specialized logical framework (as in Section 3.4.1). It is worth pointing out that both contributions deal with refinement, in a quite different way, but they do not take into account upward granularity change. Finally, in [Broy, 1997], Broy introduces the notion of temporal refinement into the description of software components in such a way that the behavior of these components is temporally described under a hierarchy of temporal models.

3.6.3 Temporal Databases

Time granularity is a long-standing issue in the area of temporal databases (see Chapter 14). As an evidence of the relevance of the notion of time granularity, the database community has released a "glossary of time granularity concepts" [Bettini *et al.*, 1998a]. As we already pointed out, the set-theoretic formalization of granularity (see Section 3.3) has been settled in the database context. Moreover, besides theoretical advances, the database community contributed some meaningful applications of time granularity. As an example, in [Bettini *et al.*, 1998b] Bettini et al. design an architecture for dealing with granularity in federated databases involving various granularities. This work takes advantage of extra information about the database design assumptions in order to characterize the required transformations. The resulting framework is certainly less general than the set-theoretic formalization of time granularity reported in Section 3.3, but it brings granularity to concrete databases applications. Time granularity has also been applied to data mining procedures, namely, to procedures that look for repeating collection of events in federated databases [Bettini *et al.*, 1998d] by solving simple temporal reasoning problems involving time granularities (see Section 3.3). An up-to-date account of the system is given in [Bettini *et al.*, 2003].

3.6.4 Granularity in space

(Spatial) granularity plays a major role in geographic information systems. In particular, the granularity for the Region Connection Calculus [Randell *et al.*, 1992; Egenhofer and Franzosa, 1991] has been presented in that context [Euzenat, 1995b]. Moreover, the problem of generalization is heavily related to granularity [Muller *et al.*, 1995]. Generalization consists in converting a terrain representation into a coarser map. This is the work of cartographers, but due to the development of computer representation of the geographic information, the problem is now tackled in a more formal, and automated, way.

In [Topaloglou, 1996], Topaloglou et al. have designed a spatial data model based on points and rectangles. It supports aligned granularities and it is based on numeric constraints. The treatment of granularity consists in tolerant predicates for comparing objects of different granularities which allow two objects to be considered as equals if they only deviate from the granularity ratio.

In [Puppo and Dettori, 1995; Dettori and Puppo, 1996], Puppo and Dettori outline a general approach to the problem of spatial granularity. They represent space as a cell complex (a set of elements with a relation of containment and the notion of dimension as a map to integers) and generalization as a surjective mapping from one complex cell into another. One can consider the elements as simplexes (points of dimension 1, segments of dimension 2 bounded by two points, and triangles of dimension 3 bounded by three segments). This notion of generalization takes into account the possible actions on an object: preservation, if it persists with the same dimension under the coarser granularity, reduction, if it persists at a lower dimension, and immersion, if it disappears (it is then considered as immersed in another object). The impact of these actions on the connected objects is also taken into account through a set of constraints, exactly like it has been done in Section 3.5.2. This should be totally compatible with the two presentations of granularity given here. Other transformations, such as exaggeration (when a road appears larger than it is under the map scale) and displacement, have been taken into account in combination with generalization, but they do not fit well in the granularity framework given in Section 3.2. Last, it must be noted that these definitions are only algebraic and that no analytical definitions of the transformations have been given.

Other authors have investigated multi-scale spatial databases, where a simplified version of the alignment problem occurs [Rigaux and Scholl, 1995]. It basically consists in the requirement that each partition of the space is a sub-partition of those it is compared with (a sort of spatial alignment).

Finally, some implementations of multi-resolution spatial databases have been developed with encouraging results [Devogele *et al.*, 1996]. As a matter of fact, the addressed problem is simpler than that of generalization, since it consists in matching the elements of two representations of the same space under different resolutions. While generalization requires the application of a (very complex) granularity change operator, this problem only requires to look for compatibility of representations. Tools from databases and generalization can be used here.

3.7 Related work

We would like to briefly summarize the links to time granularity coming from a variety of research fields and to provide some additional pointers to less-directly related contributions which have not been fully considered here due to the lack of space. Relationships with research in databases have been discussed in Sections 3.3 and 3.6.3. Granularity as a phenomenon that affects space has been considered in Section 3.6.4. The integration of a notion of granularity into logic programming is dealt with in [Mota *et al.*, 1997; Liu and Orgun, 1997] (see Section 3.6.1 and see also Chapter 13). Work in qualitative reasoning can also be considered as relevant to granularity [Kuipers, 1994] (see Chapter 20).

The relationships between (time) granularity and formal tools for abstraction have been explored in various papers. As an example, Giunchiglia et al. propose a framework for abstraction which applies to a structure $\langle L, A, R \rangle$, where L is a language, A is a set of axioms, and R is a set of inference rules [Giunchiglia *et al.*, 1997]. They restrict abstraction to A, because the granularity transformations are constrained to remain within the same language and the same rules apply to any abstraction. One distinctive feature of this work is that it is oriented towards an active abstraction (change of granularity) in order to increase the performance of a system. As a matter of fact, using a coarse representation reduces the problem size by getting rid of details. The approaches to time granularity we presented in this chapter are more oriented towards accounting for the observed effects of granularity changes instead of creating granularity change operators which preserve certain properties.

Concluding remarks

We would like to conclude this chapter by underlining the relevance and complexity of the notion of time granularity. On the one hand, when some situations can be seen from different viewpoints (of designers, observers, or agents), it is natural to express them under different granularities. On the other hand, problems immediately arise from using multiple granularity, because it is difficult to assign a proper (or, at least, a consistent) meaning to these granular representations.

As it can be seen from above, a lot of work has already been devoted to granularity. This research work has been developed in various domains (e.g., artificial intelligence, databases, and formal specification) with various tools (e.g., temporal logic, set theory, and algebra of relations). It must be clear that the different approaches share many concepts and results, but they have usually considered different restrictions. The formal models have provided constraints on the interpretations of the temporal statements under a particular granularity, but they did not provide an univocal way to interpret them in a specific application context.

On the theoretical side, further work is required to formally compare and/or integrate the various proposals. On the application side, if the need for granularity handling is acknowledged, it is not very developed in the solutions. There are reasons to think that this will change in the near future, drained by applications such as federated databases and agent systems, providing new problems to theoretical research.

Handbook of Temporal Reasoning in Artificial Intelligence
Edited by M. Fisher, D. Gabbay and L. Vila

Chapter 4

Modal Varieties of Temporal Logic

Howard Barringer & Dov Gabbay

This chapter provides a rudimentary introduction to a number of different systems of temporal logic that have been developed from a modal logic basis. We assume that the reader has some familiarity with propositional and first order logic but assume no background in modal logic, although some reference to modal logic does occasionally occur. Our purpose is to take a tour through a few key "modal" forms of temporal logic, from linear to branching and from points to intervals, present their salient properties and features, for example, syntactic and semantic expressiveness, inference systems, satisfiability and decidability results, and provide sufficient insight into these families of logics to support the interested reader in undertaking further study or to use such logics in practice. The field is vast and there are many other important systems of temporal logic we could have developed; space is limited however and we have therefore focussed primarily on the development on the modal forms of linear time temporal logics.

4.1 Introduction

Most interesting systems, be they computational, physical, biological, mental, social, and so on, are dynamic and evolve with time. In order to help understand such evolving systems, specialised languages and logics have been developed over the centuries to reason about and model their dynamic, or temporal, behaviour. Although Aristotle and many later philosophers made major contributions to the debate on the relation between time, truth and possibility, it should be emphasised that much of the formal development of temporal logic has occurred within the last half century, following Prior's seminal work on tense logics. Furthermore, it is the application of temporal logics for reasoning about computational systems that has been the major stimulus for the explosion of research in temporal logics and reasoning over the past three decades. The field is vast and an introductory chapter such as this can only dance lightly across some aspects of the area. Hence here we have chosen to focus on a particular kind of temporal logic, one in which time is effectively abstracted away and special logical operators are used to shift one's attention from one moment to another; we refer to these as modal varieties of temporal logic.

So let us begin our brief tour by asking rhetorically "What is required in order to reason about a system that evolves over time?" Put quite simply, one needs

1. a logic $\mathcal{L}_S$ to reason about the state of the system at some moment in time, and

2. a logic $\mathcal{L}_T$ to reason about how the states of the system at different moments in time are related.

The combination of these two logics, say $\mathcal{L}_T(\mathcal{L}_S)$, which we denote this way since $\mathcal{L}_T$ will be built based upon $\mathcal{L}_S$, we might then think of as a temporal logic. Our interest in this chapter is, however, focussed on the temporal aspects of the logic $\mathcal{L}_T(\mathcal{L}_S)$ and for the sake of simplicity we will in general be treating the logic $\mathcal{L}_S$ as a propositional one.

To address the question of what the logic $\mathcal{L}_T$ might be, we need to model the notion of a system whose states are time-dependent and, in the process of doing so, show how the different temporal states are connected. For a fairly general situation a set of system states together with some connection matrix would suffice. As a simple introductory example, let us construct a temporal logic $\mathcal{L}_T(\mathcal{L}_S)$ that can describe some properties of, and hence be used to reason about certain aspects of, a system S that evolves in discrete times steps, $t_0, t_1, t_2, \ldots, t_n, \ldots$. We will draw the time points, t_n, from the set of natural numbers and the connection matrix will comply with the usual arithmetic ordering on the numbers. We will take the state logic $\mathcal{L}_S$ to be a propositional logic based on a stock of propositions, PROP, that are used to characterise the state of the system. The logic $\mathcal{L}_T$ however, is a one-sorted first-order logic, where quantification is restricted to individuals ranging over the sort of natural numbers; $\mathcal{L}_T$ will also possess necessary arithmetic functions and relations, e.g. $+$, $-$, $<$, etc. Importantly, however, we equip $\mathcal{L}_T$ with a two-place predicate $holds$ that determines whether a formula of $\mathcal{L}_S$ (describing the makeup of the state) holds at a particular time point t. Effectively, the embedding of $\mathcal{L}_S$ in $\mathcal{L}_T$ makes formulae of $\mathcal{L}_S$ terms of $\mathcal{L}_T$. Assuming p and q are propositions from PROP, the following formulae of $\mathcal{L}_T$ are examples of the use of the $holds$ predicate:

$holds(p, t)$	is true if and only if the proposition p is true at t
$holds(p \wedge q, t)$	is true if and only if the formula $p \wedge q$ is true at t
$holds(\neg p \wedge q, t+1)$	is true if and only if $\neg p \wedge q$ is true at $t+1$, i.e. p is false and q is true at the $t+1$

We can then construct formulae such as

(i) $\forall t \cdot holds(p, t) \Rightarrow holds(\neg p \wedge q, t+1)$

(ii) $\forall r \cdot holds(p, r) \Rightarrow \exists s \cdot (r < s \wedge holds(\neg p, s) \wedge \forall t \cdot s < t \Rightarrow holds(\neg p, t))$

The two diagrams below represent an example state evolution that satisfies, respectively, each of the properties above. In the pictorial representation of the state space the absence of p (resp. q) from the "state" is used to indicate that p (resp. q) is false in that state, whereas, of course, presence of p (resp. q) indicates that the proposition holds true. The formula in (i) captures the property that whenever proposition p is true, p will be false in the next moment of time and q will be true. Hence we see in the first evolution that since p is given true at t_1, it is false at t_2 but q must be true at t_2.

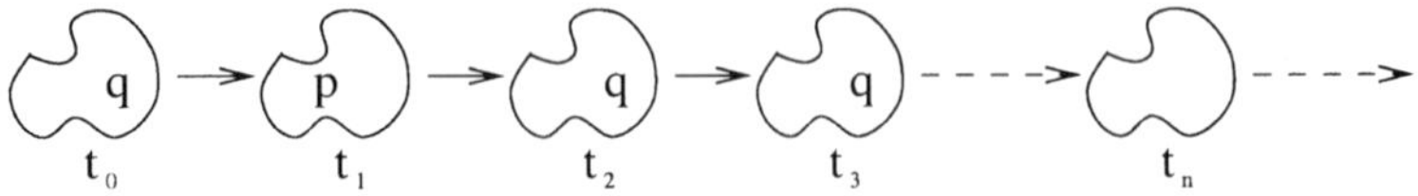

The formula in (ii) characterises a system evolution such that if ever the proposition p becomes true, say at time r, then there will be a time beyond r from which the proposition p will always be false.

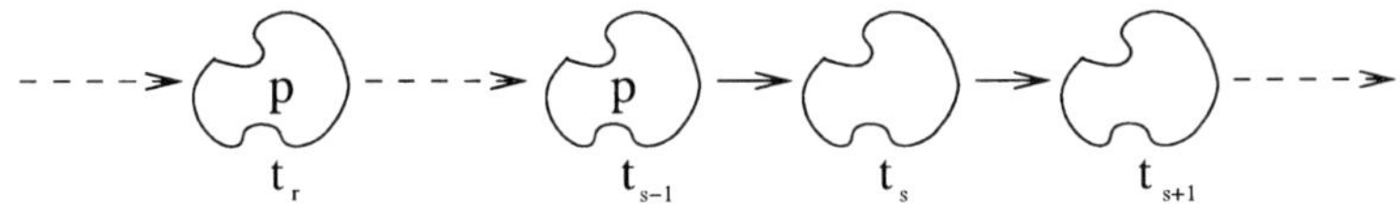

The definition of the *holds* predicate must ensure that the following equivalences hold.

$$\begin{array}{lcl} holds(p \wedge q, t) & \Leftrightarrow & holds(p,t) \wedge holds(q,t) \\ holds(p \vee q, t) & \Leftrightarrow & holds(p,t) \vee holds(q,t) \\ holds(\neg p, t) & \Leftrightarrow & \neg holds(p,t) \\ \vdots & \Leftrightarrow & \end{array}$$

Rather than continue with the use of a meta predicate "holds", we can let the temporal logic $\mathcal{L}_T$ be based on unary predicates $p()$ for each proposition p of $\mathcal{L}_S$ with the proviso that for every time point t

$$p(t) \text{ iff } holds(p,t)$$

must hold for all t. The example formulae from above become:

$$\begin{array}{l} \forall t \cdot p(t) \Rightarrow \neg p(t+1) \wedge q(t+1) \\ \forall r \cdot p(r) \Rightarrow \exists s \cdot (r < s \wedge \neg p(s) \wedge \forall t \cdot s < t \Rightarrow \neg p(t)) \end{array}$$

This approach is easily extended to, say, predicate logic for $\mathcal{L}_S$ which results in $\mathcal{L}_T$ being a two-sorted logic - one sort for the time points, and the other capturing the sort of $\mathcal{L}_S$.

One awkwardness with the above form of temporal logic is that it can often be rather difficult to "see the wood for the trees", i.e. to recognise the temporal relations, or connections, being characterised by a given formula. It is not that *natural* a representation. Indeed, although the logic is certainly well able to model a rich expressive set of temporal phenomena, *model* is the key word and the resulting logical expressions do not clearly resemble the concise linguistic temporal patterns we can speak and write. Consider the following statement:

> The dollar has been falling and will continue to fall whilst there is uncertainty in the state of the government.

Let the unary predicate p denote that the dollar is falling and let q denote certainty in the state of the government. A first-order modelling of the above statement will go something like the following, where the individual n represents the current time point (i.e. now):

$$\begin{array}{l} \exists t \cdot t < n \wedge \forall s \cdot t < s < n \Rightarrow p(s) \\ \quad \wedge \\ p(n) \\ \quad \wedge \\ (\forall t \cdot n < t \Rightarrow p(t) \\ \quad \vee \\ \exists t \cdot n < t \wedge q(t) \wedge \forall s \cdot n < s < t \Rightarrow p(s)) \end{array}$$

The first conjunct captures the fact that the dollar has been falling, the second conjunct that the dollar is still falling, and the third conjunct captures that the dollar will continue to fall whilst there is uncertainty in the state of the government. This latter expression captures the fact that either the dollar continues to fall in perpetuity or there is a future in which there is certainty in the government (q) but up to then the dollar had been falling.

As is clear, the formula is cluttered with quantifications and constraints on the time point variables*. The modal varieties of temporal logic, especially tense logic†, overcome these problems through the use of modalities (temporal/tense modal operators). The since-until tense logic (of Kamp), for example, could be used to capture the falling dollar statement as below

$$p \textbf{ since true } \wedge p \wedge p \textbf{ unless } q$$

which is abundantly clearer than the first order logic representation‡. The formula p **unless** q captures the property that either p will hold into the future until q holds or if q never holds at some future point then p will hold forever into the future.

In the following pages of this chapter, we will develop basic systems of the modal varieties of temporal logic. At the start of this subsection we observed that a set of states together with a connection matrix (i.e. a binary relation on states) would suffice to model the notion of time dependent states, where the connection matrix defines the temporal flows. Such a structure is rather similar to a modal frame and in Section 4.2 we introduce the notion of temporal frames and different characterisations of temporal flows.

In order to abstract away from the detail of the temporal model, modal temporal operators (or better, temporal modalities) are defined that can be used to express properties over the network of time-dependent states. Initially we introduce just four primitive temporal modalities:

$\boxplus$	in every future moment	$\boxminus$	in every past moment
$\diamondplus$	in some future moment	$\diamondminus$	in some past moment

For the natural number model of time we were using above, we will define that the formula $\boxplus p$ holds at time point s if and only if for every t, $s < t$ implies that p holds at time t, i.e. p holds in all future moments of s. Whereas, the formula $\diamondplus p$ holds at time point s if and only if there is some time t such that $s < t$ and p holds at t, i.e. p holds in some future moment of s. Similarly for the past time operators $\boxminus$ and $\diamondminus$. So instead of defining $\mathcal{L}_T$ as a sorted predicate logic, $\mathcal{L}_T$ is, effectively, defined as a multi-modal language - the syntactic and semantic details of these operators are defined in Section 4.2.2. From this basis, Section 4.3 introduces a minimal temporal logic and considers correspondence properties in Section 4.3.1, e.g. if the formula $\diamondplus \diamondplus \varphi \Rightarrow \diamondplus \varphi$ is valid for a temporal frame, then the forwards accessibility relation is transitive, etc..

Although we show in Section 4.3.1 that the temporal operators $\boxplus$, $\diamondplus$, and past time mirrors, are sufficient to characterise a large number of different frame properties§, we show in Section 4.4 that this set is not expressive enough and a range of richer temporal logics is then presented. Section 4.4 restricts attention to linear temporal logics, so in Section 4.5 we explore briefly some aspects of branching time logics. The presentation on modal temporal systems up to that stage primarily focuses on point-based temporal structures and so in Section 4.6 we explore some elements of interval temporal logics using, however, point-based models. We conclude with some pointers to further reading.

*And it gets worse when one adds in the necessary formulae that characterise the temporal sort

†Developed for the study of tense in natural language

‡One should note that some advantages will occur through the use of a well-understood first order logic

§some second-order properties as well

4.2 Temporal Structures

We begin by introducing the general notion of a *temporal frame*, $\mathcal{F}$, a structure comprising a set of time points, T, and two binary relations, R_f and R_b, on T, i.e. $\subseteq T \times T$.

$$\mathcal{F} = (T, R_f, R_b)$$

R_f relates time points that are connected in a forwards direction of time, i.e. given time points t_1 and t_2 ($\in T$) if $t_1 R_f t_2$ then t_1 is an earlier time than t_2. Similarly, R_b relates time points that are connected in a backwards direction of time, i.e. given time points t_1 and t_2 ($\in T$) if $t_1 R_b t_2$ then t_1 is a later time than t_2. These binary relations thus determine the temporal flow, that is, the progression of time from one moment to another. The temporal frame, on the other hand, represents a specific model of time and is characterised by the properties of its set of time points T and its binary (flow) relations. For example, for a model of discrete time, where time is clocked forward in explicit jumps, one could simply choose the set T to be a discrete set (of appropriate size).

In many models, or views, of time (or temporal flow) there is no need to have both relations, R_f and R_b, distinguished as it is usual that one is the inverse of the other and hence one *earlier than* relation will suffice*. Where this is the case, without loss of generality, we will denote temporal frames as just pairs $\mathcal{F} = (T, R_f)$.

For the temporal flows of time that we will mainly consider in this chapter, i.e. just linear and branching acyclic flows, we add the further constraint that the binary relations should be asymmetric and transitive. The reason for requiring $R_f(R_b)$ to be transitive should be clear given that we intend to model abstractions of real time, i.e. as 1/1/00 is earlier than 2/1/00† which is earlier than 3/1/00, 1/1/00 is also earlier than 3/1/00. Then transitivity combined with asymmetry precludes any cycles in the temporal flow.

The following four examples illustrate a few simple cases of temporal frames.

Example 4.2.1 (Natural Number Time). *The temporal frame*

$$\mathcal{F}_{\mathbb{N}} = (\mathbb{N}, <)$$

where $<$ is the usual less than ordering on numbers represents a model of natural number time, i.e. time that has a beginning, is discrete, linear and future serial (without future end). This model is often used as a temporal abstraction of computation, where each "time point" corresponds to some discrete computation state.

Example 4.2.2 (Real Time). *For those not in favour of the Big Bang theory, the temporal frame*

$$\mathcal{F}_{\mathbf{R}} = (\mathbf{R}, <)$$

can represent a continuous linear flow of time, without beginning or end; again $<$ is the usual less than ordering on real numbers.

Example 4.2.3 (Days of the Week). *The following frame could be used for a crude model of the days of the week.*

$$\mathcal{F}_{\text{Days}} = (\text{Days}, <_{\text{Days}})$$

---

*That is, if in our general abstractions of time, $\forall t_1, t_2 \in T \cdot t_1 R_f t_2 \equiv t_2 R_b t_1$ we only need one relation.

†Assuming the English date format dd/mm/yy.

where

$$\begin{array}{lcl} \text{Days} & = & \{\textbf{Sun}, \textbf{Mon}, \textbf{Tue}, \textbf{Wed}, \textbf{Thu}, \textbf{Fri}, \textbf{Sat}\} \\ <_{\text{Days}} & = & \{ \quad (\textbf{Sun}, \textbf{Mon}), (\textbf{Sun}, \textbf{Tue}), (\textbf{Sun}, \textbf{Wed}), \ldots, (\textbf{Sun}, \textbf{Sat}) \\ & & \quad\quad (\textbf{Mon}, \textbf{Tue}), (\textbf{Mon}, \textbf{Wed}), (\textbf{Mon}, \textbf{Thu}), \ldots, (\textbf{Mon}, \textbf{Sat}) \\ & & \quad\quad (\textbf{Tue}, \textbf{Wed}), (\textbf{Tue}, \textbf{Thu}), (\textbf{Tue}, \textbf{Fri}), \ldots, (\textbf{Tue}, \textbf{Sat}) \\ & & \quad\quad \vdots \\ & & \quad\quad (\textbf{Fri}, \textbf{Sat}) \\ & & \} \end{array}$$

So with our week beginning on Sunday and ending on Saturday, we have the usual, or expected, orderings that Monday comes before Tuesday, Tuesday before Thursday, etc., but note that Saturday no longer comes before Sunday!

Example 4.2.4 (Database Updates). *As a rather different example*where one might wish not to maintain R_f and R_b as inverses, consider a typical situation in database updating. First assume a discrete set of database states and then take the forwards temporal flow as database updates. As there may well be certain updates that can't be undone (i.e. rolled back), one might choose to model this as discontinuities in the backwards temporal flow.*

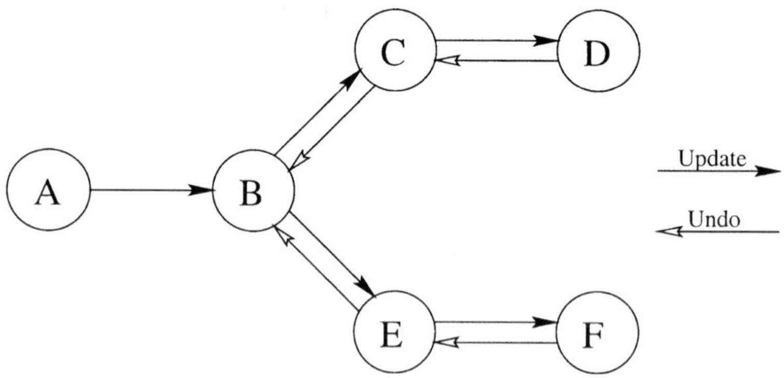

To keep the above picture uncluttered the full transitive relations for Update and Undo have not been shown, only their principal elements. More formally, it represents the temporal frame

$$\mathcal{F}_{DB} = (States, Update, Undo)$$

where

$$\begin{array}{lcl} States & = & \{A, B, C, D, E\} \\ Update & = & \{ \quad (A, B), (A, C), (A, D), (A, E), (A, F) \\ & & \quad\quad (B, C), (B, D), (C, D), \\ & & \quad\quad (B, E), (B, F), (E, F) \\ & & \} \\ Undo & = & \{ \quad (D, C), (D, B), (C, B) \\ & & \quad\quad (F, E), (F, B), (E, B) \\ & & \} \end{array}$$

*And perhaps a little contrived from a purely temporal standpoint

As can be clearly seen, the update from state A to B represents a commit which can not be undone.

So far temporal frames appear very similar to (multi-)modal frames; in that context the set of possible worlds is the set of time points, and the accessibility relation is the earlier/later than relation. The principal difference is that we have restricted the accessibility relation to be transitive. In light of this it is not unreasonable to ask whether the frame of Example 4.2.4 is really a temporal frame, rather than a multi-modal frame? Not wishing to embark upon such philosophical discussion here, in what follows we will assume not. Indeed, we will adopt the following minimal requirements for temporal frames.

Invertibility: now is in the past of every future moment and now is in the future of every past moment;

Antisymmetry: a future moment of some moment in time can not also be a past moment of that moment, and vice-versa;

Transitivity: a future moment of a future moment of now is also a future moment of now, and similarly for the past.

Figure 4.1: Minimal Constraints for Temporal Frames

The above constraints characterise what we generally take for granted when we reason about time, at least the temporal flow in which we live. Obviously, one might dream up models of circular time, where one's past can be reached by going into the future (indeed it might even be possible one day by backward time travel, though if it were we might have had some sign about it already!). We will stick with the intuitive, natural, minimal constraints and henceforth we shall use "$<$" to denote the "earlier than/later than" temporal binary relation on time points.

4.2.1 Temporal Frame Properties

In the above section we presented a few specific illustrations of different temporal frames by choosing particular sets of time points and temporal relations. The set of time points in each had well known properties, e.g. the discreteness of the natural numbers and integers, the continuity of the reals. It is more useful, however, to give formal, logical, characterisations of the frame properties and then characterise *classes* of temporal frames according to their properties. For example, we may be interested in the class of all asymmetric, transitive, weakly dense temporal frames (which includes the frames $(\mathbb{Q}, <)$, $(\mathbf{R}, <)$, etc.). Table 4.1 presents a number of interesting frame properties together with a formal characterisation in predicate logic (first order for all but the wellfoundedness property).
The first three properties, namely **irreflexivity**, **asymmetry** and **transitivity**, are clear. For the others, however, a brief explanation is in order. **Future (past) seriality** characterises the property that time has no ending (beginning). **Maximal (minimal) points** characterises that time does have some ends (beginnings). Beware that maximal (minimal) points do not characterise future (past) finiteness of time. The time may be branching and the property requires

*This and the mirror property are often referred to as right (resp. left) linearity

Property	Formal Characterisation
irreflexivity	$\forall t \in T \cdot \neg(t < t)$
asymmetry	$\forall s, t \in T \cdot \neg(s < t \wedge t < s)$
transitivity	$\forall s, t, u \in T \cdot s < t \wedge t < u \Rightarrow s < u$
future serial	$\forall s \in T \cdot \exists t \in T \cdot s < t$
past serial	$\forall s \in T \cdot \exists t \in T \cdot t < s$
maximal points	$\exists s \in T \cdot \neg \exists t \in T \cdot s < t$
minimal points	$\exists s \in T \cdot \neg \exists t \in T \cdot t < s$
connectedness	$\forall s, t \in T \cdot s < t \vee s = t \vee t < s$
weak future connectedness*	$\forall s, t, u \in T \cdot (s < t \wedge s < u) \Rightarrow (t < u \vee t = u \vee u < t)$
weak past connectedness	$\forall s, t, u \in T \cdot (t < s \wedge u < s) \Rightarrow (t < u \vee t = u \vee u < t)$
successors	$\forall s \in T \cdot \exists t \in T \cdot s < t \wedge \neg \exists u \in T \cdot s < u \wedge u < t$
predecessors	$\forall s \in T \cdot \exists t \in T \cdot t < s \wedge \neg \exists u \in T \cdot t < u \wedge u < s$
weakly dense	$\forall s, u \in T \cdot s < u \Rightarrow \exists t \in T \cdot s < t \wedge t < u$
weakly dense with breaks	$\forall s, t, u \in T \cdot s < t < u \Rightarrow \exists v \in T \cdot s < v < t \vee t < v < u$
wellfoundedness	$\forall P \cdot \exists t \in T \cdot P(t) \Rightarrow$ $\exists t \in T \cdot (P(t) \wedge \forall s \in T \cdot (s < t \Rightarrow \neg P(s)))$

Table 4.1: Temporal Frame Properties

only that some point is a dead end (beginning) and thus some paths through the structure may be serial. **Connectedness** characterises that every pair of different time points are ordered by the temporal relation. Finiteness of time, on the other hand, has to be characterised by a second order property (**wellfoundedness** in the table).

The temporal frame of Example 4.2.1 (Natural Number Time) satisfies the properties irreflexivity, asymmetry, transitivity, future seriality, minimal points, connectedness, weak future connectedness, weak past connectedness, successors, predecessors and wellfoundedness.

The temporal frame of Example 4.2.2 (Real Time) satisfies irreflexivity, asymmetry, transitivity, future seriality, past seriality, connectedness, weak future connectedness, weak past connectedness and weak density.

Note that the temporal frame $(\mathbb{Q}, <)$ that is based on the rationals also satisfies the list given just above for the real time frame. However, it should be remembered that the temporal frame $(\mathbf{R}, <)$ also satisfies a completeness property[†], which is not the case for the rationals.

4.2.2 Temporal Language, Models and Interpretations

Let us now introduce our base temporal logic language. As indicated in the previous section, we wish to use temporal modalities $\boxplus$, $\boxminus$, $\oplus$ and $\ominus$. More formally, let the temporal language $\mathcal{L}_{(\boxplus, \boxminus)}$ be the set of formulas defined inductively by the following formation rules:

[†]i.e. $\forall P \cdot \exists s \in T \cdot P(s) \wedge \exists s \in T \cdot \neg P(s) \wedge (\forall s \in T \cdot \forall t \in T \cdot (P(s) \wedge \neg P(t) \Rightarrow s < t)) \Rightarrow \exists s \in T \cdot (P(s) \wedge \forall t \in T \cdot (s < t \Rightarrow \neg P(t))) \vee \exists s \in T \cdot (P(s) \wedge \forall t \in T \cdot (t < s \Rightarrow \neg P(t)))$

(i) p is in $\mathcal{L}_{(\boxplus,\boxminus)}$ for any atomic proposition p drawn from the stock, PROP;

(ii) If φ and ψ are formulae in $\mathcal{L}_{(\boxplus,\boxminus)}$, then so are the Boolean combinations $\neg\varphi$, $\varphi \wedge \psi$, $\varphi \vee \psi$, $\varphi \Rightarrow \psi$ and $\varphi \Leftrightarrow \psi$ in $\mathcal{L}_{(\boxplus,\boxminus)}$;

(iii) If φ is a formula of $\mathcal{L}_{(\boxplus,\boxminus)}$, then $\boxplus\varphi$, $\boxminus\varphi$, $\diamondplus\,\varphi$ and $\diamondminus\,\varphi$ are also formulae in $\mathcal{L}_{(\boxplus,\boxminus)}$.

Thus, assuming that Lhb, Lhs, Lgdg are atomic propositions and hence drawn from the stock PROP, the following are examples of formulae in $\mathcal{L}_{(\boxplus,\boxminus)}$

Lhb	$\diamondplus$ Lhb	Lhb $\wedge\ \neg$Lhs
$\diamondplus$ (Lhb $\wedge$ $\diamondplus$ Lgdg)	$\diamondminus$ Lhs	$\diamondplus$ (Lgdg $\wedge$ $\diamondminus$ (Lhb $\wedge$ $\diamondminus$ Lhs))
$\diamondminus$ (Lhs $\wedge\ \neg$Lhb)	$\diamondplus$ ($\neg$Lgdg $\wedge\ \neg$Lhb $\wedge\ \neg$Lhs)	$\neg\boxminus$Lhs
$\neg\boxplus$ $\diamondplus$ Lhb	$\diamondminus$ $\boxminus\neg$Lhs	$\boxplus$(Lgdg $\Rightarrow$ $\diamondminus$ Lhs)

Semantics A model for a logical formula must provide the information necessary to interpret fully that formula. We have seen how temporal frames, and properties placed upon them, can provide an underlying temporal structure, or network of time points, over which the temporal connectives of the language will be interpreted. In addition to the temporal frame, a valuation function is required for the propositions of the language. In the case of propositional logic, where formulae are effectively interpreted in a single world, the valuation function is just a truth valuation function. For the temporal logic case, propositions may have different interpretations at different points in time - i.e. they are not statically interpreted. Thus the valuation function must provide the set of time points at which any given proposition holds true. A model for temporal logic formulae is therefore taken as a structure combining a temporal frame with a valuation function.

$$M = (\underbrace{T, <}_{\text{temporal frame}},\ \underbrace{V}_{\substack{\text{valuation function}\\ \text{PROP} \to 2^T}})$$

We can now define the interpretation of formulae of the temporal language $\mathcal{L}_{(\boxplus,\boxminus)}$ in the above model structure. Let $\models$ be a satisfaction relation between a model time-point pair (M, s) and a temporal formula φ, i.e. $M, s \models \varphi$ means that φ is true in model M at time point s. As is to be expected the interpretation is defined inductively over the structure of the temporal formulae.

- For φ being an atomic proposition p drawn from PROP, we have

  $$M, s \models p \ \textbf{iff}\ \ s \in V(M)(p)$$

  We use the notation $V(M)$ to denote the valuation function of the model M. $V(M)(p)$ thus yields the set of time points at which the proposition p holds true. Thus the model M satisfies p at time point s if and only if s is a time point at which the proposition holds true according to the valuation.

  As it is only the interpretation of proposition symbols which requires access to the valuation, for notational convenience, the reference to the model M is dropped from the interpretations for propositional and temporal connectives making it clear, especially in the case of temporal connectives, that their interpretation is dependent upon the particular time point in the model M.

- Assuming that ψ and ϕ are formulae of $\mathcal{L}_{(\boxdot,\boxminus)}$, for the propositional connectives the inductive cases are standard as below.

$$\begin{array}{lll} s \models \phi \wedge \psi & \textbf{iff} & s \models \phi \text{ and } s \models \psi \\ s \models \phi \vee \psi & \textbf{iff} & s \models \phi \text{ or } s \models \psi \\ s \models \neg\phi & \textbf{iff} & \text{it is not the case that } s \models \phi \\ \vdots & \vdots & \vdots \end{array}$$

- The interesting cases are for the temporal connectives, $\boxplus$, $\boxminus$, $\diamondplus$ and $\diamondminus$.

$$\begin{array}{lll} s \models \boxplus\varphi & \textbf{iff} & \text{for every } t, s < t \text{ implies } t \models \varphi \\ s \models \boxminus\varphi & \textbf{iff} & \text{for every } t, t < s \text{ implies } t \models \varphi \\ s \models \diamondplus\varphi & \textbf{iff} & \text{there exists some } t, s < t \text{ and } t \models \varphi \\ s \models \diamondminus\varphi & \textbf{iff} & \text{there exists some } t, t < s \text{ and } t \models \varphi \end{array}$$

Note that:

$\boxplus$, always in the future, has the usual modal interpretation. Namely, for $\boxplus\phi$ to be true at point $s \in T$ in a model $(T, <, V)$, then ϕ must be true at all points $t \in T$ reachable by $<$ from s.

$\diamondplus$, sometime in the future, also has the normal modal interpretation. So, $\diamondplus\phi$ is true at $s \in T$ in model $(T, <, V)$ if and only if there is a point $t \in T$ reachable from s by $<$ (i.e. later than s) at which ϕ is true.

The past time connectives $\boxminus$ and $\diamondminus$ have mirror definitions.

Example 4.2.5 (Interpretation exercises). *Assume a model M with time points $\{A, B, C, D\}$ and the relation $<$ given as below*

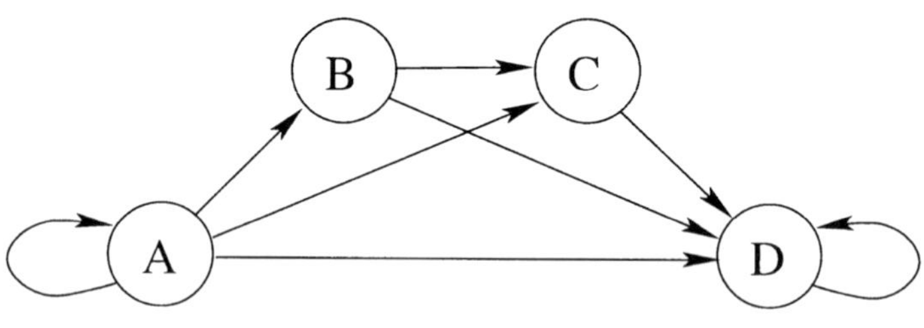

and the valuation V is

$$p \mapsto \{A, C, D\}, q \mapsto \{A, B\}, r \mapsto \{B, C, D\}$$

1. *Consider the interpretation of the formula $\diamondplus\boxplus r$ at node (time point) A. For it to be true at A in the given model, we must be able to move to a node (time point) in the network, say n at which $\boxplus r$ is true. For the latter formula to be true, all (future) reachable nodes must have r true. Choose the node n to be node B. This clearly satisfies the constraints.*

   Notice that the formula $\boxplus r$ is not true at A. A is reachable from itself, and as r is not true at A, it will contradict the requirement that r is true at all (future) reachable nodes.

2. *Now consider the interpretation of $\boxminus(p \wedge q)$ at node A. Here we require that the formula $p \wedge q$ be true in all nodes which precede, i.e. can reach node A. There is only one node preceding node A and that is just node A. Since both p and q are true in A, so is $\boxminus(p \wedge q)$.*
3. *For $\diamondminus\, r$ to be true at A, there needs to be a node that can reach A at which r evaluates true. The only node which can reach A is A itself. r is not true at A and therefore neither is $\diamondminus\, r$.*
4. *Consider $\boxplus r$ at D. This requires that r be true in reachable nodes from D. Similar to the above, the only reachable node from D is D itself. However in this case r evaluates true at D, therefore $\boxplus r$ is true at D.*
5. *For $\diamondminus\, \boxplus r$ to be true at D we must be able to find a node in D's past at which $\boxplus r$ is true. One could choose node B or C. Note that node A will* not *do as r is not necessarily true in the future, A is in the future of itself.*
6. *Finally consider $\boxminus(p \vee q)$ at node D. Since all nodes in the model satisfy $p \vee q$, all nodes that can reach D must also satisfy $p \vee q$. Therefore $\boxminus(p \vee q)$ is true at node D.*

Now that we have defined the interpretation of temporal formulae against our model structures we are in a position to define other (standard) notions, e.g. validity. Like other modal logics we define three notions of validity:

Definition 4.2.1 (Model Validity). *A formula φ is said to be model valid if it holds true at every time point of the model M. Formally,*

$$M \models \varphi \text{ iff for every } t \in T(M),\ M, t \models \varphi$$

We'll refer to formulae being M-valid.

Definition 4.2.2 (Frame Validity). *A formula φ is said to be frame valid if it is model valid for every model of the frame, i.e. it holds true for possible valuation and at every possible time point of the temporal frame.*

$$F \models \varphi \text{ iff for every } M = (F, V),\ M \models \varphi$$

As above, we refer to a formula being F-valid. Clearly frame validity implies model validity, but not vice-versa.

And finally it is useful to define validity for a class of frames (satisfying some property, e.g. discrete frames). Obviously a formula is valid (in the unrestricted sense) if it is valid for all possible frames.

Definition 4.2.3 (Class Validity). *A formula φ is said to be valid wrt a class C of frames F if it is frame valid for each F in C, i.e.*

$$C \models \varphi \text{ iff for every frame } F \in C,\ F \models \varphi$$

Example 4.2.6 (Exercise in validity). *Consider the model $M = (\mathbb{N}, <, V)$ where $V(p) = \mathbb{N}$, i.e. atomic propositions are true everywhere, the following five formulae are all M-valid*

$$p \quad \boxplus p \quad \diamondplus\, p \, \boxminus p \quad \boxplus\, \diamondplus\, p \quad \boxplus\, \boxminus p$$

One might be led to the false conclusion that since every proposition is true everywhere in this particular model, every temporal formula will also be true. This isn't the case because our model has an asymmetry between the future and the past whereas in our language $\mathcal{L}_{(\boxplus, \boxminus)}$ the past time connectives are proper mirrors of their future counterparts. Indeed the *formula* $\diamondminus\, p$ *is not valid on* M. *Why not? Because at time point 0,* $\diamondminus\, p$ *is false (and for all other points it is true).*

Consider a dense temporal frame F, *such as* $(\mathbf{R}, <)$, *i.e. for any two points* u, v, *there is always a point* w *such that* $u < w$ *and* $w < v$ *(*w *lies strictly between* u *and* v*). The temporal formula* $\diamondplus\, \phi \Rightarrow \diamondplus\, \diamondplus\, \phi$ *is frame valid for* F.

Indeed for the class of weakly dense frames, i.e. for any two points u, v, *there is always a point* w *such that* $u < w$ *and* $w < v$, *the above formula* $\diamondplus\, \phi \Rightarrow \diamondplus\, \diamondplus\, \phi$ *is class valid.*

The usual notion of validity, namely a formula ϕ *is valid iff it is true in all models, still applies. Indeed, the formula would be valid for all possible frames, etc. Tautologies, e.g.* $\varphi \Rightarrow \varphi$ *are clearly examples of valid temporal formulae. A more interesting temporal example is the formula* $\diamondplus\, \diamondplus\, \phi \Rightarrow \diamondplus\, \phi$. *It is temporally valid since we have defined temporal frames to be those that satisfy a minimal number of constraints (Figure 4.1), in particular, temporal frames are transitive; the given formula is valid on every transitive frame (see later Section 4.3.1 on temporal correspondences). However, we generally apply validity in a restricted context, namely relative to a particular frame, or class of frames.*

4.3 A Minimal Temporal Logic

In the above section we introduced minimal constraints that should hold on a frame for the frame to be referred to as temporal, namely invertibility, antisymmetry and transitivity of the ordering relation. In this section we reflect these constraints in our temporal language $\mathcal{L}_{(\boxplus, \boxminus)}$ and define as a result the minimal temporal logic*, K_T. Similar to the minimal constraints on temporal frames, we require:-

A now is in the past of every future moment and now is in the future of every past moment.

B a future moment of a future moment of now is also a future moment of now. Similarly for past.

K If, in all future moments $\phi \Rightarrow \psi$ is true and in all future moments ϕ holds true
Then, in all future moments ψ will hold true. Similarly for the past.

The conditions **A** and **B** are indeed met by our given notion of temporal frame $(T, <)$. In particular, requirement **A** (invertibility) is clearly satisfied by virtue of just using the relation $<$ as the accessibility (or earlier/later than) relation. Of course if two relations had been given (as in some presentations of temporal logic), say $\xrightarrow{+}$ and $\xleftarrow{-}$ then we would require the model constraint,

$$\forall t_1, t_2 \in T \cdot t_1 \xrightarrow{+} t_2 \Leftrightarrow t_1 \xleftarrow{-} t_2$$

Requirement **B** is simply a transitivity condition. Again, $<$ is given as a transitive relation and also usually taken as irreflexive. The requirement **K** is a normality condition, again similar to that usually required of modal logics.

We'll present temporal logics via axioms and inference rules†. In fact, all the temporal systems we'll consider will be classical and hence include all "propositional" tautologies.

*This is similar in spirit to the way that a minimal modal logic, system K, is developed.

†In actual fact we use finite sets of axiom and inference rule schemata, and an axiomatisation is obtained by taking all substitution instances over the appropriate alphabets.

The requirements **A** and **B** correspond to the formulae Cf, Cp and 4f, 4p, respectively, treated as axioms. The normality constraint **K** is captured by the axioms Kf, Kp. Thus the axiom schemata (where ϕ, ψ, φ, etc., are meta-variables) together with "necessitation" inference rules for $\boxplus$ and $\boxminus$, and Modus Ponens gives what is referred to as the **Minimal Temporal Logic—K_T**.

Axioms:

Tautologies	
Cf	$\varphi \Rightarrow \boxplus \diamondminus \varphi$
Cp	$\varphi \Rightarrow \boxminus \diamondplus \varphi$
$4f$	$\diamondplus \diamondplus \varphi \Rightarrow \diamondplus \varphi$
$4p$	$\diamondminus \diamondminus \varphi \Rightarrow \diamondminus \varphi$
Kf	$\boxplus(\varphi \Rightarrow \psi) \Rightarrow (\boxplus\varphi \Rightarrow \boxplus\psi)$
Kp	$\boxminus(\varphi \Rightarrow \psi) \Rightarrow (\boxminus\varphi \Rightarrow \boxminus\psi)$

Inference Rules:

MP $$\frac{\vdash \varphi \qquad \vdash \varphi \Rightarrow \psi}{\vdash \psi}$$

$\boxplus - Gen$ $$\frac{\vdash \varphi}{\vdash \boxplus\varphi}$$

$\boxminus - Gen$ $$\frac{\vdash \varphi}{\vdash \boxminus\varphi}$$

Example 4.3.1 (Transitivity). *Above we stated that the axiom $4f$ characterises transitive frames - let us formally establish that property. Firstly we consider the easier case, namely given an arbitrary transitive frame we prove that the formula $4f$ is indeed valid for that frame. Then we'll prove that if $4f$ is frame valid, then the frame's accessibility relation is transitive.*

only if case: *Let $F = (T, <)$ be an arbitrary transitive frame. We show that $4f$ is frame valid. Let V be an arbitrary valuation and s, t and u arbitrary members of T such that $s < t$ and $t < u$. Assume that $((T, <), V), u \models \varphi$. Therefore by the interpretation definition for $\diamondplus$, we have $((T, <), V), t \models \diamondplus \varphi$. By similar reasoning, we have $((T, <), V), s \models \diamondplus \diamondplus \varphi$. By the definition of $\Rightarrow$, for the formula $4f$ to be true at s, we must show that $((T, <), V), s \models \diamondplus \varphi$. By the transitivity of the frame F, as $s < t$ and $t < u$, we have that $s < u$. Since we were given that φ held at time point u, we thus have $\diamondplus \varphi$ holding at s. Hence $4f$ holds at time point s. Since both V and s were arbitrary, $4f$ is frame valid. Hence the desired result.*

if case: *Now we are given that for some frame $F = (T, <)$, the formula $4f$ is F-valid. Thus for arbitrary valuation function V and arbitrary time point s, we have $((T, <), V), s \models \diamondplus \diamondplus \varphi \Rightarrow \diamondplus \varphi$. We need only consider the case when the antecedent of $4f$ is true. Without loss of generality, assume a valuation V such that φ is only true at time point u. Since $\diamondplus \diamondplus \varphi$ holds at s, there must also be a time point t, such that $s < t$ and $t < u$ such that $\diamondplus \varphi$ holds at t. By the frame validity of $4f$, it must also be the case that $\diamondplus \varphi$ holds at time point s. Therefore by the interpretation definition for $\diamondplus$, it must be the case that $s < u$. Therefore we have established that the accessibility relation $<$ is transitive. Hence the result.*

A similar proof can be produced for $4p$. We leave that as an exercise for the reader and also the proof to establish that the axioms $Cf(Cp)$ correspond to the invertibility properties.

More modalities

For notational convenience, in Table 4.2 we define the following additional temporal modalities in terms of the existing modalities and connectives. Of course this expansion in the number of temporal modalities does not increase the semantic expressiveness of the temporal logic, but it does improve the syntactic compactness and structural expressiveness of the language. Later in section 4.4 we consider extending the semantic expressiveness of the language.

$$
\begin{array}{lcl}
\boxed{\pm}\varphi & \stackrel{def}{=} & \boxed{-}\varphi \wedge \varphi \wedge \boxed{+}\varphi \\
\langle\pm\rangle\varphi & \stackrel{def}{=} & \langle-\rangle\varphi \vee \varphi \vee \langle+\rangle\varphi \\
\Box\varphi & \stackrel{def}{=} & \varphi \wedge \boxed{+}\varphi \\
\Diamond\varphi & \stackrel{def}{=} & \varphi \vee \langle+\rangle\varphi \\
\blacksquare\varphi & \stackrel{def}{=} & \varphi \wedge \boxed{-}\varphi \\
\blacklozenge\varphi & \stackrel{def}{=} & \varphi \vee \langle-\rangle\varphi
\end{array}
$$

Table 4.2: More temporal modalities

So now we've introduced five variations of the "box" modality and five variations of "diamond" modality. It is useful to remember the variations as follows:

$\boxed{+}$ takes one everywhere reachable in the *strict* future (not including the present)

$\boxed{-}$ takes one everywhere reachable in the *strict* past (not including the present)

$\Box$ takes one everywhere reachable in the present and future

$\blacksquare$ takes one everywhere reachable in the present and past

$\boxed{\pm}$ takes one everywhere that is reachable, be it in the past, present or future.

Similarly for the diamond modality taking one somewhere ....

Duals and Mirrors

The observant reader will have noted that our temporal logic is propositionally classical - look back at the interpretation definition for the boolean connectives again if you're not convinced (page 128). This therefore leads to notions of temporal duality that are similar to those for classical propositional and predicate calculus, i.e. where $\wedge$ and $\vee$ are duals, and $\forall$ and $\exists$ are duals. Indeed we refer to $\langle+\rangle$ as the dual temporal modality of $\boxed{+}$ and vice-versa. This is because the temporal formula $\boxed{+}\varphi \equiv \neg\langle+\rangle\neg\varphi$ is valid (i.e. true for all models). We'll establish one direction of the equivalence here and leave the other as an easy exercise. For convenience we omit the detailed reference to the model structure. Picking an arbitrary time point s, if $\boxed{+}\varphi$ is true at s, then by definition φ is true at all t, s.t. $s < t$. Therefore there is no w, $s < w$ s.t. $\neg\varphi$ is true, in other words, by the interpretation definition of $\Diamond^{+}$, $\neg \Diamond^{+} \neg\varphi$ holds at time s. Hence the result. The other direction is just as straightforward.

Clearly we have the following pairs of temporal modalities as duals of each other: $\boxminus$ and $\Diamond^{-}$; $\blacksquare$ and $\blacklozenge$; $\Box$ and $\Diamond$; $\boxed{\pm}$ and $\Diamond^{\pm}$.

Note that the complement of a temporal formula consisting of a prefix of temporal modalities, say T_i, applied to formula ϕ, can always be written as the string of the duals of the prefix T_i applied to $\neg\phi$. So for example, the complement of $\Diamond^{-} \Diamond^{-} \boxplus \Diamond^{-} \boxplus \boxminus \phi$ would be $\boxminus \boxminus \Diamond^{+} \boxminus \Diamond^{-} \Diamond^{-} \neg\phi$.

We also introduce the notion of a *Mirror* image of a temporal formula. It is obtained by interchanging the past connectives with their future counterparts, and vice-versa. For example assuming that φ is some boolean combination of atomic propositions,

$$\Diamond^{+} \Box\varphi \Rightarrow \Diamond^{+} \varphi$$

has mirror image

$$\Diamond^{-} \blacksquare\varphi \Rightarrow \Diamond^{-} \varphi$$

The mirror image of a formula can be thought of as just the formula's reflection about now. The inductive definition of mirror is left as an exercise.

4.3.1 Temporal Correspondences

In Section 4.2.1 we showed how classes of temporal frames can be specified by first-order properties over the frame, and in Example 4.3.1 we established that the axiom $4f$ of the minimal temporal logic K_T does indeed determine transitive frames. In this section we refer back to more of the frame properties listed in Table 4.1 and show how, for many, each can be characterised by a temporal formula. The existence of such characteristic formulae leads to one way to develop different forms of temporal logic. The minimal temporal logic K_T placed minimal constraints on the frames. By adding further axioms, each corresponding to specific properties such as seriality, or weak density, etc., we can obtain richer forms of temporal logic. Does this always work? That is to say, as axioms are added to the system, is the resulting logic complete with respect to the union of the properties represented by the axioms? In the final subsection we provide an example where this is not the case.

transitivity The formula $\Diamond^{+} \Diamond^{+} \varphi \Rightarrow \Diamond^{+} \varphi$ (or its mirror) has already been considered. A different formulation is $\Diamond^{+} \varphi \Rightarrow \boxminus \Diamond^{+} \varphi$ (or its mirror). We'll establish one direction of the proof, namely showing the formula is valid on transitive frames, leaving the other direction as an exercise. So consider an arbitrary transitive frame $F = (T, <)$, with valuation V and some time point t. If $\Diamond^{+} \varphi$ is false at t, then the original formula is true. More interestingly, if $\Diamond^{+} \varphi$ is true at t, then there is some point u beyond t such that φ holds true at u. For $\boxminus \Diamond^{+} \varphi$ to hold true at t, we require, by the interpretation definition of $\boxminus$ that for every time point s strictly before t we have $\Diamond^{+} \varphi$ holding true. This is almost trivially the case since by the transitivity of the accessibility relation, $<$, from $s < t$ and $t < u$ we have that $s < u$ - and hence the desired result.

weak future connectedness We characterised this frame property as

$$\forall s, t, u \in T \cdot (s < t \wedge s < u) \Rightarrow (t < u \vee t = u \vee u < t)$$

Three possible temporal logic formulas determining such frames are as follows.

$$\diamondplus \varphi \wedge \diamondplus \psi \Rightarrow \diamondplus (\diamondplus \varphi \wedge \psi) \vee \diamondplus (\varphi \wedge \psi) \vee \diamondplus (\varphi \wedge \diamondplus \psi)$$

$$\text{or} \quad \boxplus(\Box\varphi \Rightarrow \psi) \vee \boxplus(\Box\psi \Rightarrow \varphi)$$

$$\text{or} \quad \boxed{\pm}\varphi \Rightarrow \boxminus\boxplus\varphi \text{ together with Cp and Cf}$$

The correspondence with the first given formula should be clear. Take a future connected frame. If φ and ψ are both true in the future, say at points v and w, respectively, then if $w < v$ we must have by definition of $\diamondplus$ that $(\diamondplus \varphi \wedge \psi)$ holds at w and hence $\diamondplus (\diamondplus \varphi \wedge \psi)$ holds at u. The other two cases are similar. They are the only possibilities. The argument for the other direction is as straightforward but omitted for sake of space! Proofs of the other two formulae are also left as exercises.

We refer to temporal formulae corresponding to weak future (resp. past) connectedness, as WFC (and WPC). When both of these formulae are added as axioms to K_T, the resulting temporal logic is complete with respect to total orders.

connectedness This is a stronger property than WFC, or WPC, and captures that for every pair of time points, either one comes before the other, or vice-versa, or they are both the same point, i.e. $\forall t, u \in T \cdot (t < u \vee t = u \vee u < t)$*. Interestingly, there is no temporal formula that characterises the class of connected frames. The proof of this is by contradiction. Suppose φ is such a characteristic formula, then by definition it is valid on the connected frames $F_1 = (T_1, <_1)$ and $F_2 = (T_2, <_2)$ whose sets of time points T_1 and T_2 are disjoint. By definition of frame validity, φ is valid on the frame $F_3 = (T_1 \cup T_2, <_1 \cup <_2)$. Unfortunately, F_3 is not connected since T_1 and T_2 are disjoint sets. Thus φ can not be a characteristic formula and there is no such characterisation.

future seriality This means that time is endless in the future direction, i.e. $\forall s \in T \cdot \exists t \in T \cdot s < t$. The temporal formulae

$$\boxplus\varphi \Rightarrow \diamondplus \varphi$$

or even

$$\diamondplus \, \mathbf{true}$$

characterise this frame property. Considering the first formula. Suppose there was an end to time, i.e. there is a point in time from which there are no other reachable points. Since the given formula is valid, it must be true at that end-point. Furthermore, at

*Some authors refer to this property as "comparability" since every pair of elements are comparable. We prefer the term "connectedness" because it fits better with the notion of fully connected networks of time points.

that end-point it must be the case that $\boxplus\varphi$ is also true (vacuously), since there are no other points. That therefore means that $\Diamond_{+}\varphi$ must be true at the end-point. But this is contradictory, since there are no points which can be reached from the end-point. Hence the original assumption that the frame was bounded in the future is therefore false.

The alternative formulation, $\Diamond_{+}$ **true**, is perhaps more straightforward.

past seriality Similar to above, the mirror image of a formula characterising future seriality will determine past serial frames, i.e. those with no beginning. Thus, $\boxminus\varphi \Rightarrow \Diamond_{-}\varphi$.

maximal and minimal points The addition of an axiom for future (past) seriality clearly forces the frames for which the temporal logic is valid to be endless in the future (past). The absence of such axioms, however, does not imply boundedness. The constraint for maximal (minimal) points will help, namely:

$$\exists s \in T \cdot \neg\exists t \in T \cdot s < t$$

The temporal formula

$$\boxplus\mathbf{false} \vee \Diamond_{+}\boxplus\mathbf{false}$$

captures this constraint. Informally, either there is no future (first disjunct) or we can move to a future point that is the end (second disjunct). The mirror captures minimal points.

weakly dense (not to be confused with *weekly dense*!) This property is such that if two points s and u are related, i.e. $s < u$, then one can always find a time point in between. The frame property is:

$$\forall s, u \in T \cdot s < u \Rightarrow \exists t \in T \cdot s < t \wedge t < u$$

In our temporal logic this is neatly characterised by:

$$\Diamond_{+}\varphi \Rightarrow \Diamond_{+}\Diamond_{+}\varphi$$

To see this fact, consider a frame that has some discreteness embedded within it. In particular there will be two points e and b such that $e < b$ and for which there are no points m in between e and b. For the formula $\Diamond_{+}\varphi \Rightarrow \Diamond_{+}\Diamond_{+}\varphi$ to be valid on this frame, the formula must be true for all models based upon that frame. Choose a valuation such that φ evaluates to true only at point b and hence the evaluation of $\Diamond_{+}\varphi$ at point e must be true. Thus $\Diamond_{+}\Diamond_{+}\varphi$ must be true also at e, and therefore there is a point beyond e such that $\Diamond_{+}\varphi$ is true. Take that point to be the nearest future time point to e, i.e. time point b. But $\Diamond_{+}\varphi$ is false at b since b is the only point that makes φ true. And hence the formula $\Diamond_{+}\varphi \Rightarrow \Diamond_{+}\Diamond_{+}\varphi$ is not valid on this frame. Clearly the formula is valid on weakly dense frames.

weakly dense with breaks The frame used as a counterexample immediately above was indeed a weakly dense frame with one break. These frames are characterised by the following property.

$$\forall s, t, u \in T \cdot s < t < u \Rightarrow \exists v \in T \cdot s < v < t \vee t < v < u$$

Informally, pick any three ordered time points, there may be a discreteness on only one side of the middle point for clearly if there were no points in between either s and t, or t and u, the property would be false. Here is a temporal formula corresponding to this property.

$$\diamondplus\,(\varphi \wedge \diamondplus\,\psi) \Rightarrow \diamondplus\,(\diamondplus\,\varphi \vee \diamondplus\,\diamondplus\,\psi)$$

We leave the proof of correspondence to the reader. Clearly this formula holds on a frame with single gaps between dense regions, so consider the validity on a frame with two consecutive gaps between otherwise dense regions.

immediate successors The constraint

$$\forall s \in T \cdot \exists u \in T \cdot s < u \wedge \neg \exists t \in T \cdot s < t \wedge t < u$$

defines frames whose points have immediate successors, i.e. a necessary condition (but not sufficient) for obtaining discrete frames. The temporal formula

$$\varphi \wedge \boxminus\varphi \Rightarrow \diamondplus\,\boxminus\varphi$$

corresponds to this property. Suppose a frame F at point s does not have an immediate successor, i.e. $\forall u \in T \cdot s < u \Rightarrow \exists t \in T \cdot s < t < u$, the given formula is not valid on that frame. Consider a valuation that makes φ true for time point s and all its preceding points, and false elsewhere. Since the right neighbourhood of s is dense, $\diamondplus\,\boxminus\varphi$ will be false. Hence the formula can not be valid on such a frame. Clearly the formula is valid on frames with immediate successors.

The mirror image of this formula characterises immediate predecessors.

irreflexivity This was the first frame property presented in table 4.1 of the previous section. Unfortunately there is no axiom that corresponds to this particular property, however, when other constraints are placed, one can result in frames that are irreflexive, amongst other properties. For example, add Löb's axiom to transitive, weakly future connected frames. If it were the case that for some point $s \in T$, $s < s$, there would be a potentially infinite chain of stability - but this is contradicted by Löb's well-foundedness property implying that there is always some first point at which a property becomes true. Hence there can not be any such cycles in the relation, thus the frames must also now be irreflexive.

As one further example of correspondence, if we add to our minimal temporal logic K_T, axioms for weak future (past) connectedness, WFC (WPC), and a weakened version of immediate successors (to cater for possible boundedness), the resulting temporal logic is complete with respect to discrete total orders (see Figure 4.2).

Cf	φ	$\Rightarrow$	$\boxplus \Diamond^{-} \varphi$
Cp	φ	$\Rightarrow$	$\boxminus \Diamond^{+} \varphi$
$4f$	$\Diamond^{+} \Diamond^{+} \varphi$	$\Rightarrow$	$\Diamond^{+} \varphi$
$4p$	$\Diamond^{-} \Diamond^{-} \varphi$	$\Rightarrow$	$\Diamond^{-} \varphi$
Kf	$\boxplus(\varphi \Rightarrow \psi)$	$\Rightarrow$	$(\boxplus\varphi \Rightarrow \boxplus\psi)$
Kp	$\boxminus(\varphi \Rightarrow \psi)$	$\Rightarrow$	$(\boxminus\varphi \Rightarrow \boxminus\psi)$
WFC	$\Diamond^{+} \varphi \wedge \Diamond^{+} \psi$	$\Rightarrow$	$\Diamond^{+} (\Diamond^{+} \varphi \wedge \psi) \vee \Diamond^{+} (\varphi \wedge \psi) \vee \Diamond^{+} (\varphi \wedge \Diamond^{+} \psi)$
WPC	$\Diamond^{-} \varphi \wedge \Diamond^{-} \psi$	$\Rightarrow$	$\Diamond^{-} (\Diamond^{-} \varphi \wedge \psi) \vee \Diamond^{-} (\varphi \wedge \psi) \vee \Diamond^{-} (\varphi \wedge \Diamond^{-} \psi)$
IS	$(\varphi \wedge \boxminus\varphi)$	$\Rightarrow$	$(\boxplus\mathbf{false} \vee \Diamond^{+} \boxminus\varphi)$
IP	$(\varphi \wedge \boxplus\varphi)$	$\Rightarrow$	$(\boxminus\mathbf{false} \vee \Diamond^{-} \boxplus\varphi)$

Figure 4.2: Axioms for discrete temporal logic over total orders

4.3.2 A consistent but incomplete logic

We have been busy demonstrating correspondences between frame properties and temporal axioms. We now present an example (due to Thomason 1972) of a temporal logic which is consistent, i.e. it has models, but which is not determined by any class of frames. Consider the smallest temporal logic containing:

Löb	$\Diamond^{-} \varphi$	$\Rightarrow$	$\Diamond^{-} (\varphi \wedge \neg \Diamond^{-} \varphi)$
WFC	$\Diamond^{+} \varphi \wedge \Diamond^{+} \psi$	$\Rightarrow$	$\Diamond^{+} (\Diamond^{+} \varphi \wedge \psi) \vee \Diamond^{+} (\varphi \wedge \psi) \vee \Diamond^{+} (\varphi \wedge \Diamond^{+} \psi)$
FS	$\Diamond^{+} \mathbf{true}$		
STAB	$\boxplus \Diamond^{+} \varphi$	$\Rightarrow$	$\Diamond^{+} \boxplus\varphi$

This is a consistent logic, but there are no frames for which it is valid.

To show that the above logic has a model, i.e. is consistent, consider $M = (\mathbb{N}, <, V)$ where $V(p) = \{\}$ for all p in PROP. The frame $(\mathbb{N}, <)$ validates all axioms apart from STAB*. However, it can be shown, for any φ, that the set of points at which φ is true in M is either finite, or cofinite. Therefore, φ either eventually stabilises as false (the finite case) or eventually stabilises as true. This corresponds to either $\boxplus \Diamond^{+} \varphi$ being false everywhere or $\Diamond^{+} \boxplus\varphi$ being true everywhere. Thus STAB is M-valid. We now establish that there is no frame which validates the above logic. Note first that Löb (i.e. Löb's axiom) determines transitive, wellfounded frames; WFC ensures that the frame is weakly future connected; and FS guarantees there are no future end-points. Suppose a frame validates the logic. The set of reachable points (i.e. via $<$), P_s, from s is connected and forms a strict total ordering which by the future seriality, FS, has no final element. Take a subset Q of P_s such that neither Q nor $P_s - Q$ has an end point. Make the valuation of φ be that subset Q. Thus $\boxplus \Diamond^{+} \varphi$ is true at s in M, but $\Diamond^{+} \boxplus\varphi$ is clearly false at s. But this contradicts the assumption that the frame validates the logic.

*In modal logic, this axiom is often referred to as McKinsey's axiom; see [Goldblatt, 1991] where the axiom is shown to be the smallest formula (not equivalent to one) that is not canonical - the McKinsey axiom is not valid in the canonical frame for the smallest normal modal logic containing it.

4.4 A Range of Linear Temporal Logics

The penultimate example of the previous section presented a temporal logic for discrete total orders, i.e. frames that are antisymmetric, transitive, (weakly) future and past connected, together with immediate successors and predecessors. If we remove the requirement for discreteness the resulting system is the smallest temporal logic closest to what we can call a linear temporal logic (often referred to as tense logic). Strictly speaking, it is the smallest temporal logic for total orders but it does not determine a linear order. A frame validating the axioms of this particular logic for total orders may be the union of a set of disjoint frames, each being a total order. The problem is essentially that which was raised when attempting to characterise connectedness. Indeed our logics can not distinguish the individual total orders in the set. Since we can't tell the difference between such parallel flows and a single linearly-ordered set of time points, we will treat the logic over such frames as a linear temporal logic.

In this section we will first define a few examples of linear temporal logics using the $\mathcal{L}_{(\boxplus, \boxminus)}$ language, then begin to explore the expressiveness of the temporal modalities. We will conclude the section with the introduction of a temporal logic based on fixed point operators - the temporal μ-calculus.

In the presentations of temporal logics that follow, we will focus attention on the temporal axioms additional to the minimal temporal logic. But recall that an axiomatisation of the logic is built from a base of propositional tautologies together with inference rules for Modus Ponens and temporal necessitation (backwards and forwards), as in Figure 4.3.

Axioms:

$Taut$	φ	Propositional tautologies
Cf	$\varphi \Rightarrow \boxplus \ominus \varphi$	
Cp	$\varphi \Rightarrow \boxminus \oplus \varphi$	
$4f$	$\oplus \oplus \varphi \Rightarrow \oplus \varphi$	
$4p$	$\ominus \ominus \varphi \Rightarrow \ominus \varphi$	
Kf	$\boxplus(\varphi \Rightarrow \psi) \Rightarrow (\boxplus\varphi \Rightarrow \boxplus\psi)$	
Kp	$\boxminus(\varphi \Rightarrow \psi) \Rightarrow (\boxminus\varphi \Rightarrow \boxminus\psi)$	
WFC	$\oplus \varphi \wedge \oplus \psi \Rightarrow$ $\oplus(\oplus \varphi \wedge \psi) \vee \oplus(\varphi \wedge \psi) \vee \oplus(\varphi \wedge \oplus \psi)$	
WPC	$\ominus \varphi \wedge \ominus \psi \Rightarrow$ $\ominus(\ominus \varphi \wedge \psi) \vee \ominus(\varphi \wedge \psi) \vee \ominus(\varphi \wedge \ominus \psi)$	

Inference Rules:

MP $$\frac{\vdash \varphi \qquad \vdash \varphi \Rightarrow \psi}{\vdash \psi}$$

$\boxplus - Gen$ $$\frac{\vdash \varphi}{\vdash \boxplus\varphi}$$

$\boxminus - Gen$ $$\frac{\vdash \varphi}{\vdash \boxminus\varphi}$$

Figure 4.3: The Smallest Linear Temporal Logic

4.4.1 Linear temporal logics

We take as the starting point for linear systems the minimal system K_T with just weak connectedness (future and past). This logic is the smallest *linear* temporal logic.

Now by adding further axioms, each being a temporal formula corresponding to particular constraints on temporal frames, one can define linear temporal logics over discrete structures, dense structures, finite but unbounded structures, infinite structures, etc. For example, by adding to the above logic formulae corresponding to past and future seriality as axioms, namely

PS $\diamondminus\,\mathbf{true}$ FS $\diamondplus\,\mathbf{true}$

we obtain a linear temporal logic that is infinite in the past and infinite in the future. But note this is only in the sense that one can make infinitely many moves via the temporal relation into the past, respectively future, from any given point in time. Within the class of frames determined by this logic is the frame that has the set of points in the real open interval $(0, 1)$ together with the usual $<$ ordering on points as well as the frame that has the natural numbers with the usual ordering. To constrain the logic to, say, weakly dense models, the following formulae should be added as axioms.

WDF $\diamondplus\varphi \Rightarrow \diamondplus\diamondplus\varphi$ WDP $\diamondminus\varphi \Rightarrow \diamondminus\diamondminus\varphi$

On the other hand, to move towards natural number time, we need to add constraints for discreteness, i.e. immediate predecessors and successors.

IP $(\varphi \wedge \diamondminus\varphi) \Rightarrow \diamondplus\boxminus\varphi$ IS $(\varphi \wedge \diamondplus\varphi) \Rightarrow \diamondminus\boxplus\varphi$

Note that if the temporal flow is not constrained to be serial in the past and/or future the above axioms would require weakening to allow for the beginning, respectively end, of time, i.e.

WIP $(\varphi \wedge \diamondminus\varphi \wedge \diamondplus\,\mathbf{true}) \Rightarrow \diamondplus\boxminus\varphi$
WIS $(\varphi \wedge \diamondplus\varphi \wedge \diamondminus\,\mathbf{true}) \Rightarrow \diamondminus\boxplus\varphi$

Modalities for Next and Previous

Even though the logic above determines discrete frames, this does not mean that the logic is expressive enough to be able to define a general next-time (respectively, previous-time) temporal modality, one that would move forwards (backwards) one step in time to the next (previous) moment in time. The proof that such a temporal modality is not expressible, i.e. definable, in $\mathcal{L}_{(\boxplus,\boxminus)}$, proceeds as follows. We pose two models, which clearly could be distinguished by a logic with a next time connective. By distinguished, we mean that a formula can be given which has a different truth value at related time points of the different models. We then establish that the models can not be distinguished by the logic without next, i.e. that the models are zig-zag equivalent. If that is the case, then clearly "next" can not be definable in the logic without next, otherwise the models would still be distinguishable. So consider the two models M_v and M_w

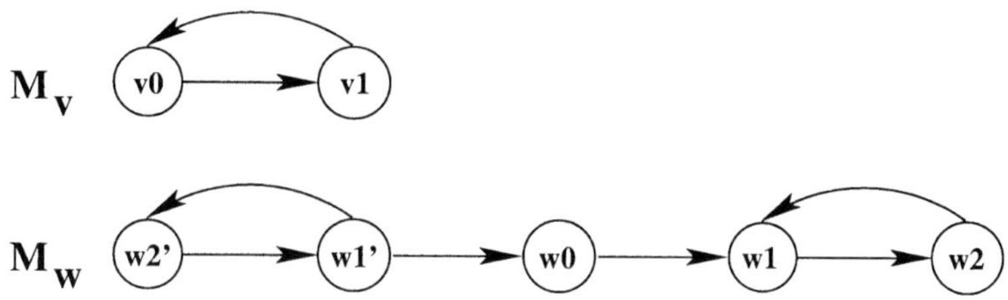

where $V(p) = \{$v1 $\}$, $W(p) = \{$w2' , w2 $\}$ and $V(x) = W(x) = \{\}$ for all $x \neq p$. We claim that for any formula φ, M_V, v0 $\models \varphi$ iff M_W, w0 $\models \varphi$. To prove this, however, we need to establish a stronger result, namely

i.	v1 $\models \varphi$ **iff** w2' $\models \varphi$	iii.	v0 $\models \varphi$ **iff** w1' $\models \varphi$
ii.	v1 $\models \varphi$ **iff** w2 $\models \varphi$	iv.	v0 $\models \varphi$ **iff** w0 $\models \varphi$
		v.	v0 $\models \varphi$ **iff** w1 $\models \varphi$

which effectively shows that the point v0 is equivalent to w1' , w0 and to w1 , and that point v1 is equivalent to w2' and to w2 .

Without loss of generality, assume the temporal language has only one atom, namely p. We will establish the results by inducting over the depth of temporal connectives. (Note, of course, that the depth of $\boxplus\varphi$ is one plus the depth of φ and the depth of a purely propositional formula is zero.)

Basis: The valuation of any purely propositional formula φ at some point t is only dependent on the valuations of propositions at t. Thus:

i.	v1 $\models \varphi$ **iff** w2' $\models \varphi$	iii.	v0 $\models \varphi$ **iff** w1' $\models \varphi$
ii.	v1 $\models \varphi$ **iff** w2 $\models \varphi$	iv.	v0 $\models \varphi$ **iff** w0 $\models \varphi$
		v.	v0 $\models \varphi$ **iff** w1 $\models \varphi$

since v0 has the same valuation for p as w1' , w0 and w1 , and v1 has the same valuation for p as w2' and w2 .

Inductive step: Assume the result holds for all formulae φ with temporal connective depth less than or equal to k. We now show that the result holds for all formulae with depth $k+1$.

Wlog, consider formulae only of shape $\boxplus\varphi$ where φ has maximum depth k. The argument for other temporal connectives will be similar. Then the other cases to be considered can be handled using those forms.

By definition v0 $\models \boxplus\varphi$ implies both v0 $\models \varphi$ and v1 $\models \varphi$. Therefore by the inductive assumption, it implies w2' $\models \varphi$, w1' $\models \varphi$, w0 $\models \varphi$, w1 $\models \varphi$ and w2 $\models \varphi$. But from these we can obtain, w1' $\models \boxplus\varphi$, w0 $\models \boxplus\varphi$ and w1 $\models \boxplus\varphi$, which is as required.

Similarly v1 $\models \boxplus\varphi$ implies both w2' $\models \boxplus\varphi$ and w2 $\models \boxplus\varphi$.

The argument for the converses proceeds along similar lines.

Now we need to introduce next-time and previous-time modalities into our logic and show that the models M_V and M_W can be distinguished. For convenience, let us first introduce a relation $\mathcal{N}$ from $<$ of the temporal frame.

$$m\mathcal{N}n \textbf{ iff } m < n \wedge \neg\exists t \cdot m < t < n$$

Thus, for discrete frames $\mathcal{N}$ relates adjacent time points, but for dense frames (with no gaps) this relation is empty. It is, in effect, a one-step relation*. A temporal modality for next-time, $\bigcirc$, is thus defined as:

$$F, s \models \bigcirc\varphi \textbf{ iff } \text{for all } t \cdot s\mathcal{N}t \text{ implies } F, t \models \varphi$$

We read this temporal modality as "in the next moment", or "tomorrow", etc. Similarly, we define a temporal modality for taking a step backwards in time, $\bullet$, which we read as "in the previous moment", or "yesterday", and so forth.

$$F, s \models \bullet\varphi \textbf{ iff } \text{for all } t \cdot t\mathcal{N}s \text{ implies } F, t \models \varphi$$

Let the language $\mathcal{L}_{(\bigcirc, \bullet)}$ be $\mathcal{L}_{(\boxplus, \boxminus)}$ extended in the obvious way with the next and previous time modalities. Are the two models posed above distinguishable with this logic? For $\mathcal{L}_{(\boxplus, \boxminus)}$ we had shown that the point v0 was indistinguishable from the points w1' , w0 and w1 . But for the formula $\bigcirc p \wedge \bullet p$, for example, clearly distinguishes them. It is true at point v0 , but is clearly false in w1' , w0 and w1 . We have thus established that $\mathcal{L}_{(\bigcirc, \bullet)}$ is more expressive than $\mathcal{L}_{(\boxplus, \boxminus)}$.

Example 4.4.1 (Next time relationships). *Consider a temporal frame $F = (\mathbf{Z}, <)$. The following formulae (and the corresponding mirror formulae)*†

$$\begin{array}{llcl}
i. & \neg\bigcirc\varphi & \Leftrightarrow & \bigcirc\neg\varphi \\
ii. & \bigcirc(\varphi \Rightarrow \psi) & \Rightarrow & (\bigcirc\varphi \Rightarrow \bigcirc\psi) \\
iii. & \Box\varphi & \Leftrightarrow & \varphi \wedge \bigcirc\Box\varphi \\
iv. & \Diamond\varphi & \Leftrightarrow & \varphi \vee \bigcirc\Diamond\varphi \\
v. & \bigcirc\bullet\varphi & \Leftrightarrow & \bullet\bigcirc\varphi
\end{array}$$

are all valid *on F. We sketch the proof of (i) and (iii), respectively, and leave the others as an exercise. Considering the $\Rightarrow$ direction of (i), for any point s, $s \models \neg\bigcirc\varphi$ implies that it is not the case that $s \models \bigcirc\varphi$. By definition of $\bigcirc$, this implies that it is also not the case that $s + 1 \models \varphi$. In other words, it is the case that $s + 1 \models \neg\varphi$. Therefore, by definition of $\bigcirc$, $s \models \bigcirc\neg\varphi$. The $\Leftarrow$ direction of (i) is as straightforward. For the $\Rightarrow$ direction of (iii), $s \models \Box\varphi$ means that $t \models \varphi$, for every t such that $s \leq t$. Thus $s \models \varphi$ and for every t such that $s + 1 \leq t$ $t \models \varphi$. Hence $s \models \bigcirc\Box\varphi$. Similarly, for the $\Leftarrow$ direction of (iii). If $s \models \varphi$ and $s + 1 \models \Box\varphi$ then clearly for every t such that $s \leq t$, $t \models \varphi$. Hence the result.*

The above equivalences are of particular interest for they indicate that one might be able to define natural number based temporal logic in terms of $\bigcirc$, $\Box$, instead of using $\boxplus$. Indeed, the formula $\neg\bigcirc\varphi \Rightarrow \bigcirc\neg\varphi$ characterises, in a certain sense, linearity‡. The other direction characterises seriality and discreteness.

*Some presentations of linear discrete temporal logics actually start with such a next time relation as the frame relation, then define the usual frame relation (used in $\boxplus$ definitions, etc) as the transitive closure of the step relation.

†Recall that $\Box\varphi \stackrel{def}{=} \varphi \wedge \boxplus$ and that $\Diamond\varphi \stackrel{def}{=} \varphi \vee \Diamond\!\!\!\!+\, \varphi$, i.e. they are the reflexive versions.

‡Actually, branching models would be acceptable, however, the logic would not be able to distinguish the different paths.

For a while

We will now introduce another temporal modality that is easily definable over our model structures; the future (past) version captures the property that a formula holds true within the future (past) vicinity of the current point. Such a modality would be useful in natural language representation, for example, for expressing temporal adverbials such as "for a while". Formally, we define

$$M, s \models \widetilde{\boxplus}\varphi \ \textbf{iff} \ \exists t \cdot s < t \wedge \forall u \cdot s < u \wedge u < t \Rightarrow M, u \models \varphi$$

and then read $\widetilde{\boxplus}\varphi$ as "φ holds uninterruptably for a while immediately in the future". The past time mirror of this connective has obvious definition. An interesting question is whether this temporal modality can be defined in either $\mathcal{L}_{(\boxplus, \boxminus)}$ or $\mathcal{L}_{(\bigcirc, \bullet)}$? If it can't we have shown yet another weakness in the expressibility of this particular temporal modal logic. The answer, not unsurprisingly, is that such modalities are not definable in $\mathcal{L}_{(\boxplus, \boxminus)}$. We will proceed here to sketch the proof for the first question, is $\widetilde{\boxplus}$ expressible in $\mathcal{L}_{(\boxplus, \boxminus)}$, leaving the second as an exercise for the interested reader.

We follow a similar approach to that above in showing that $\bigcirc$ was not expressible in $\mathcal{L}_{(\boxplus, \boxminus)}$. So we need to find a pair of models that can not be distinguished by any formula in $\mathcal{L}_{(\boxplus, \boxminus)}$, then show that a formula of $\mathcal{L}_{(\boxplus, \boxminus, \widetilde{\boxplus}, \widetilde{\boxminus})}$ is able to distinguish them. We pose two models M_V and M_W based on the temporal frame $F = (\mathbf{R}^+, <)$ with the valuations V and W, respectively, for proposition letter p (again, without loss of generality, assume only one proposition letter).

$$V(p) = \{0, 1, 2, \ldots\} \qquad W(p) = \{\tfrac{1}{2}, \tfrac{1}{4}, \tfrac{1}{8}, \ldots\} \cup V(p)$$

An inductive proof over the structure of formulae of $\mathcal{L}_{(\boxplus, \boxminus)}$ will easily establish that for any $\mathcal{L}_{(\boxplus, \boxminus)}$ formula φ

$$M_V, 0 \models \varphi \ \textbf{iff} \ M_W, 0 \models \varphi$$

However, it is fairly easy to see that the formula $\widetilde{\boxplus}\neg p$ does indeed distinguish these two models at time point 0, i.e.

$$\text{i.} \quad M_V, 0 \models \widetilde{\boxplus}\neg p \qquad \text{ii.} \quad M_W, 0 \not\models \widetilde{\boxplus}\neg p$$

The formula $\widetilde{\boxplus}\neg p$ holds at 0 in M_V since p is false in the open interval $(0, 1)$. However, in M_W the same is not the case. For any point t within the open interval $(0, 1)$, we have infinitely many points s, $0 < s < t$, such that $M_W, s \models p$, i.e. there is no point s, $0 < s < 1$ such that p is stable over $(0, s]$.

The tense modalities: Until and Since

As one further extension, we define the until and since temporal connectives. These are generally referred to as tense logic modalities because their introduction came principally from a logical formalisation of tense in natural language.

$$
\begin{array}{lll}
M, s \models \varphi\, \mathcal{U}^+ \psi & \text{iff} & \text{there is } u \cdot s < u \text{ and } M, u \models \psi \text{ and} \\
 & & \quad \text{for all } t \cdot s < t < u \text{ implies } M, t \models \varphi \\
M, s \models \varphi \ \textbf{since}^- \ \psi & \text{iff} & \text{there is } u \cdot u < s \text{ and } M, u \models \psi \text{ and} \\
 & & \quad \text{for all } t \cdot u < t < s \text{ implies } M, t \models \varphi
\end{array}
$$

The formula $\varphi\mathcal{U}^+\psi$ is read as φ will hold until ψ holds (similarly for since). As we will indicate, they have formally been shown to be very expressive. Indeed first of all notice that a language based on until and since, i.e. $\mathcal{L}_{(\mathcal{U}^+,\ \mathcal{S}^-)}$ contains both $\mathcal{L}_{(\boxplus,\ \boxminus)}$ and $\mathcal{L}_{(\boxplus,\ \boxminus,\ \tilde{\boxplus},\ \tilde{\boxminus})}$. The following equivalences are straightforward to establish:

$$
\begin{array}{lllllll}
\diamondplus\,\varphi & \Leftrightarrow & \mathbf{true}\ \mathcal{U}^+\ \varphi & \qquad & \diamondminus\,\varphi & \Leftrightarrow & \mathbf{true\ since}^-\ \varphi \\
\tilde{\boxplus}\varphi & \Leftrightarrow & \varphi\mathcal{U}^+\ \mathbf{true} & & \tilde{\boxminus}\varphi & \Leftrightarrow & \varphi\ \mathbf{since}^-\ \mathbf{true}
\end{array}
$$

However, we really need to establish that $\mathcal{L}_{(\mathcal{U}^+,\ \mathcal{S}^-)}$ is strictly more expressive than the previous language $\mathcal{L}_{(\boxplus,\ \boxminus,\ \tilde{\boxplus},\ \tilde{\boxminus})}$. The approach is as before. We must provide two models that can be distinguished by formulas of $\mathcal{L}_{(\mathcal{U}^+,\ \mathcal{S}^-)}$ but not by formulas of $\mathcal{L}_{(\boxplus,\ \boxminus,\ \tilde{\boxplus},\ \tilde{\boxminus})}$. Consider models M_V and M_W formed from the frame (**R**, $<$) with valuations V and W for two propositions, p and q, as:

$$
\begin{array}{lll}
V(p) & = & \{\pm1, \pm2, \pm3, \ldots\} \\
W(p) & = & \{\pm2, \pm3, \ldots\} \\
V(q) & = & W(q) = \{\ldots(-5,-4), (-3,-2), (-1,+1), (+2,+3), (+4,+5)\ldots\} \\
 & & \text{i.e. the union of open intervals}
\end{array}
$$

We can show, via an inductive argument over the structure of formulae, that for any φ constructed from just $\boxplus$, $\boxminus$, $\tilde{\boxplus}$, $\tilde{\boxminus}$ temporal connectives,

$$M_V, 0 \models \varphi \text{ iff } M_W, 0 \models \varphi$$

But it should be clear that

$$M_V, 0 \models q\mathcal{U}^+\ p \text{ and } M_W, 0 \not\models q\mathcal{U}^+\ p$$

because in model M_V p is true at time point 1 and q holds over the interval $(0, 1)$. However, in model M_W the first point in the future of 0 at which p holds is time point 2 and q does not hold over the open interval $(0, 2)$ for it is false over the closed interval $[1, 2]$.

Since and Until in Linear Discrete Frames

If we restrict attention to linear discrete frames, a collection of connectives, which have been shown most useful for describing properties of computational systems, can be defined as below.

$$
\begin{array}{rcl@{\qquad}rcl}
\odot\varphi & \stackrel{def}{=} & \mathbf{false}\ \mathcal{U}^+\ \varphi & \bullet\!\!\!\circ\,\varphi & \stackrel{def}{=} & \mathbf{false\ since}^-\ \varphi \\
\bigcirc\varphi & \stackrel{def}{=} & \neg\odot\neg\varphi & \bullet\varphi & \stackrel{def}{=} & \neg\bullet\!\!\!\circ\neg\varphi \\
\Diamond\varphi & \stackrel{def}{=} & \varphi \vee \mathbf{true}\ \mathcal{U}^+\ \varphi & \blacklozenge\,\varphi & \stackrel{def}{=} & \varphi \vee \mathbf{true\ since}^-\ \varphi \\
\Box\varphi & \stackrel{def}{=} & \neg\Diamond\neg\varphi & \blacksquare\varphi & \stackrel{def}{=} & \neg\blacklozenge\neg\varphi \\
\varphi\ \mathbf{until}\ \psi & \stackrel{def}{=} & \psi \vee \varphi \wedge (\bigcirc\psi \vee \varphi\mathcal{U}^+\ \psi) & \varphi\ \mathbf{since}\ \psi & \stackrel{def}{=} & \psi \vee \varphi \wedge (\bullet\psi \vee \varphi\ \mathbf{since}^-\ \psi) \\
\varphi\mathcal{W}\psi & \stackrel{def}{=} & \varphi\ \mathbf{until}\ \psi \vee \Box\varphi & \varphi\mathcal{Z}\psi & \stackrel{def}{=} & \varphi\ \mathbf{since}\ \psi \vee \blacksquare\varphi
\end{array}
$$

The above definitions are fairly self-explanatory, but let us dwell on a few of them. First of all we have defined a "strong" version of the next-time modality, $\odot$. We refer to this as a strong version of next because $\odot\varphi$ is existential in nature, i.e. if it holds, then there is a next moment of time and φ holds there. It is defined in terms of $\mathcal{U}^+$ by noting that φ holds eventually in the strict future, i.e. beyond now, but that **false** holds strictly between now and when φ holds. Because **false** never holds, there can't be any points in between now and when φ holds, so it must be a next moment in time. The universal version, or weak version, of next, e.g. as in $\bigcirc\varphi$, may be vacuously true - in the situation that there is no next moment - or true if φ holds in all next moments (the model may be branching in the general case). The universal version of next is obtained from the existential one in the obvious way. Thus when interpreted in linear discrete frames, the formula $\odot\mathbf{true}$ characterises that there is a next moment, whereas $\bigcirc\mathbf{false}$ can only be true at the end of time. The past mirrors of strong and weak next, i.e. strong and weak previous, temporal modalities are defined in a similar manner.

A non-strict modality for eventually in the future, i.e. allowing $\Diamond\varphi$ to be satisfied by φ holding now, is defined by noting that either φ holds now or, via the strict until, φ holds in the future (with **true** holding in between). The non-strict always in the future is simply the dual of the non-strict eventually in the future.

A non-strict version of until, φ **until** ψ, can be satisfied by ψ holding now or φ holding now together with either ψ holding at the next moment or φ will hold strictly until ψ. We can note that from this definition the following equivalence holds

$$\varphi\ \mathbf{until}\ \psi \Leftrightarrow \psi \vee \varphi \wedge \bigcirc(\varphi\ \mathbf{until}\ \psi)$$

In computational and specification contexts it has also been found useful to define a weak version of the until connective, $\mathcal{W}$ - read as unless, which is universal in nature and doesn't force ψ to be true, but in the situation that ψ is never true, φ must be true for ever.

Future-time Linear Discrete Temporal Logic

Restricting attention to a future fragment of the since-until temporal language over linear discrete frames, e.g. $(\mathbb{N}, <)$, we obtain the logic that was used in the early work of Manna and Pnueli for the global description of program properties, see for example [Pnueli, 1977; Manna and Pnueli, 1992; Manna and Pnueli, 1995]. The following is an axiomatisation for the logic.

The given axiomatisation follows, effectively, the approach that we've taken before - namely start with a minimal system and add constraints to restrict to the frame(s) of interest. Thus we take all tautologies as axioms. The first axiom about next is essentially the K axiom of modal logic. The second axiom about next provides commutativity of next and negation; it also determines future seriality and discreteness (in one direction) and future linearity (for the other), as explained below. The essence of the final axiom for unless is that it determines the formula $\varphi\mathcal{W}\psi$ as a solution to the implication $\xi \Rightarrow \psi \vee \varphi \wedge \bigcirc\xi$. Correspondingly, the inference rule of interest is $\mathcal{W}$-introduction. This captures the fact that $\varphi\mathcal{W}\psi$ is a maximal solution to the above-mentioned implication*. We will give discussion on that matter in Section 4.4.5 where we consider the more general fixed point temporal logic. The other future-time modalities that we introduced earlier can be defined as below.

$$\begin{array}{llll}
\Box\varphi & \stackrel{def}{=} \varphi\mathcal{W}\,\mathbf{false} & \boxplus\varphi & \stackrel{def}{=} \bigcirc\Box\varphi \\
\Diamond\varphi & \stackrel{def}{=} \neg\Box\neg\varphi & \diamond\!\!\!+\,\varphi & \stackrel{def}{=} \bigcirc\Diamond\varphi \\
\varphi\ \mathbf{until}\ \psi & \stackrel{def}{=} \neg(\neg\psi\,\mathcal{W}(\neg\psi \wedge \wedge\varphi)) & \varphi\,\mathcal{U}^{+}\psi & \stackrel{def}{=} \bigcirc(\varphi\ \mathbf{until}\ \psi)
\end{array}$$

*Solutions are ordered by implication; thus **false** is the minimum element of the ordering and the maximum element is **true**.

Axioms

$\vdash w$ tautology

$\vdash \bigcirc(\varphi \Rightarrow \psi) \Rightarrow (\bigcirc\varphi \Rightarrow \bigcirc\psi)$

$\vdash \bigcirc\neg\varphi \Leftrightarrow \neg\bigcirc\varphi$

$\vdash \varphi \mathcal{W} \psi \Rightarrow \psi \vee \varphi \wedge \bigcirc(\varphi \mathcal{W} \psi)$

Inference Rules

Modus Ponens $\dfrac{\vdash \varphi \qquad \vdash \varphi \Rightarrow \psi}{\vdash \psi}$

$\bigcirc$ – Gen $\dfrac{\vdash \varphi}{\vdash \bigcirc\varphi}$

$\mathcal{W}$ – Intro $\dfrac{\vdash \xi \Rightarrow \psi \vee \varphi \wedge \bigcirc\xi}{\vdash \xi \Rightarrow \varphi \mathcal{W} \psi}$

Note:

$i \models \varphi \mathcal{W} \psi$ iff there is $k \cdot i \leq k$ and $k \models \psi$ and
for all $j \cdot i \leq j < k$ implies $j \models \varphi$
or for all $k \cdot i \leq k$ implies $k \models \varphi$

Figure 4.4: Axiomatisation for Future-time Linear Discrete Temporal Logic

The definition of **until** may look slightly odd at first, however, it has in fact been defined as the dual of $\mathcal{W}$, just as $\Diamond$ is defined as the dual of $\Box$. Some further equivalences and explanation are given below in the paragraph "Until-Unless duality".

Theorem 4.4.1. *The logic $\mathcal{L}_{(\mathcal{W},\bigcirc)}$ is sound with respect to temporal frames* $(\mathbb{N}, <)$, *i.e.*

if $F \vdash \varphi$ then $F \models \varphi$

We will not work through the soundness proof leaving that as an exercise. However, let us just note the interesting properties of the axiom $\neg\bigcirc\varphi \Leftrightarrow \bigcirc\neg\varphi$.

Consider $\neg\bigcirc\varphi \Rightarrow \bigcirc\neg\varphi$ as an axiom on the class of discrete frames. We show that the frames must be future linear. First remember that $\bigcirc$ has a universal interpretation, namely: $s \models \bigcirc\varphi$ if and only if for all t, $s\mathcal{N}t$ implies $t \models \varphi$. Thus, by definition, $s \models \neg\bigcirc\varphi$ implies that it is not the case that φ holds for all successors of s, i.e. there is at least one successor t where φ is false. But $s \models \bigcirc\neg\varphi$ implies, by definition, that φ is false in all successors of s. Therefore, as the given implication is axiomatic, our language can not distinguish between the successors: the branching model is thus zig-zag equivalent to a linear model. Hence the axiom determines, in essence, future linearity.

Consider next $\bigcirc\neg\varphi \Rightarrow \neg\bigcirc\varphi$ as an axiom on the class of discrete frames. We show that the frames validating the formula must be future serial. Suppose s is an endpoint. For any valuation of φ, $s \models \bigcirc\neg\varphi$ is true: there is no successor to the point s and thus $\bigcirc\varphi$ is vacuously true. But by the axiom, $\neg\bigcirc\varphi$, must also hold at s. But this formula is false at s as $\bigcirc\varphi$ must be true at an endpoint, which therefore contradicts the assumption that s is an endpoint. The class of frames is thus future serial.

Propositional logic has the following deduction theorem

$$\frac{\varphi_1, \ldots, \varphi_n \vdash \psi}{\varphi_1, \ldots, \varphi_{n-1} \vdash \varphi_n \Rightarrow \psi}$$

where $\varphi_1, \ldots, \varphi_n \vdash \psi$ means that ψ is a theorem under the assumptions that $\varphi_1, \ldots, \varphi_n$ are also theorems. Suppose this were to hold in modal systems.

Assume $\vdash \varphi$. By the necessitation rule, $\vdash \Box\varphi$ is also a theorem, thus $\varphi \vdash \Box\varphi$. Therefore by the (proposed) deduction theorem, $\vdash \varphi \Rightarrow \Box\varphi$. But this is not valid — consider the model $M = (\mathbb{N}, <, V)$ such that $V(p) = \{0\}$. Clearly this invalidates $p \Rightarrow \Box p$.

The problem is that theoremhood in modal systems corresponds to truth in all worlds of all models of a class of frames. The movement of a premise assumption across the turnstile effectively weakens the assumption to it being true at a world, rather than at all worlds of a model. Thus modal deduction must ensure that the box is introduced. Hence

$$\frac{\varphi_1, \ldots, \varphi_n \vdash \psi}{\varphi_1, \ldots, \varphi_{n-1} \vdash \Box\varphi_n \Rightarrow \psi}$$

The given counterexample then deduces that $\vdash \Box p \Rightarrow \Box p$

Theorem 4.4.2. *The logic $\mathcal{L}_{(\mathcal{W},\bigcirc)}$ is complete with respect to temporal frames* $(\mathbb{N}, <)$, *i.e.*

if $F \models \varphi$ then $F \vdash \varphi$

Completeness proofs are generally notoriously much harder to establish than their soundness counterparts. In modal logic there are several standard techniques for establishing completeness. We don't have the space to investigate such methods. However, one approach that has been used for this particular temporal logic over the natural numbers builds on the fact that the logic is decidable. By that we mean an algorithm can be given which will give a yes/no answer to the problem "Is φ (in $\mathcal{L}_{(\mathcal{W},\bigcirc)}$) valid for the frame $(\mathbb{N}, <)$?" Again, we don't have space to give detailed proof of the decision procedure, however, we will outline the mechanism later. Completeness can be shown by establishing that the steps taken by the semantic procedure can be encoded as a proof using the given axiomatisation.

Until-Unless duality The definition of until as the dual of the unless gives the following immediate equivalences.

$$\begin{array}{lcl} \neg(\varphi \ \textbf{until}\ \psi) & \Leftrightarrow & (\neg\psi)\,\mathcal{W}\,(\neg\psi \wedge \neg\varphi) \\ \neg(\varphi\,\mathcal{W}\,\psi) & \Leftrightarrow & (\neg\psi)\ \textbf{until}\ (\neg\psi \wedge \neg\varphi) \end{array}$$

The first equivalence above is by definition; the second one is derived from the first via renaming of propositions. An inference rule for the introduction of **until** can be obtained from the $\mathcal{W}$-intro inference rule and defines φ **until** ψ as the minimal solution to the implication $\psi \vee (\varphi \wedge \bigcirc X) \Rightarrow X$.

$\psi \vee (\varphi \wedge \bigcirc X) \Rightarrow X$	Assumption
$\neg X \Rightarrow \neg(\psi \vee (\varphi \wedge \bigcirc X))$	PR
$\neg X \Rightarrow (\neg\psi \wedge \neg\varphi) \vee (\neg\psi \wedge \bigcirc\neg X)$	PR
$\neg X \Rightarrow (\neg\psi)\,\mathcal{W}\,(\neg\psi \wedge \varphi)$	$\mathcal{W}$-Intro
$\neg((\neg\psi)\,\mathcal{W}\,(\neg\psi \wedge \varphi)) \Rightarrow X$	PR
$\varphi\ \textbf{until}\ \psi \Rightarrow X$	by **until** definition to yield conclusion

thus establishing the rule

$$\textbf{until}\ \text{-Intro}\quad \frac{\vdash \psi \vee \varphi \wedge \bigcirc \xi \Rightarrow \xi}{\vdash \varphi\ \textbf{until}\ \psi \Rightarrow \xi}$$

Furthermore, it is relatively straightforward to establish that φ **until** $\psi \Leftrightarrow \varphi \mathcal{W} \psi \wedge \Diamond\psi$, which could have been taken as an alternative definition. The $\Rightarrow$ direction of the equivalence is trivially proved by showing that $\varphi \mathcal{W} \psi \wedge \Diamond\psi$ is a solution to the implication $\psi \vee (\varphi \wedge \bigcirc X) \Rightarrow X$. In a similar way, the $\Leftarrow$ direction can be proved by showing that $\neg(\varphi$ **until** $\psi) \wedge \varphi \mathcal{W} \psi$ is a solution to the implication $X \Rightarrow \neg\psi \wedge \bigcirc X$, thus proving that $\neg(\varphi$ **until** $\psi) \wedge \varphi \mathcal{W} \psi \Rightarrow \square\neg\psi$ and hence that $\varphi \mathcal{W} \psi \wedge \Diamond\psi \Rightarrow \varphi$ **until** ψ.

Incorporating the Past It is relatively straightforward to adapt the axiomatisation of $\mathcal{L}_{(\mathcal{W},\bigcirc)}$ to an axiomatisation for $\mathcal{L}_{(\mathcal{W},\ \mathcal{Z},\bigcirc,\bullet)}$ which is sound and complete with respect to the frame $(\mathbf{Z},<)$. The temporal modality $\mathcal{Z}$ is the past time mirror of the unless modality $\mathcal{W}$ and is pronounced "zince" (the existential, or strong, version being the since modality **since**). First of all include the past time mirrors of the $\mathcal{L}_{(\mathcal{W},\bigcirc)}$ axioms and rules, then introduce the "cancellation" axioms for next and last. Note that the cancellation axioms simply capture the fact that now is in the past, in fact yesterday, of tomorrow, and vice-versa. The result is listed in Figure 4.5.

And now what must be done in order to obtain an axiomatisation of the logic $\mathcal{L}_{(\mathcal{W},\ \mathcal{Z},\bigcirc,\bullet)}$ that is complete with respect to the frame $(\mathbb{N},<)$, i.e. where the past is always bounded (non serial past). Clearly, the requirement that $\bullet\neg\varphi \Rightarrow \neg\bullet\varphi$ can not hold. However, the commutativity in this direction must hold at all points other than the beginning point. The beginning point can be characterised by remembering that it is the only point at which "yesterday false" can be true. Similarly, beware the axiom $\bullet\bigcirc\varphi \Rightarrow \bigcirc\bullet\varphi$: at the beginning point, $\bullet\bigcirc\mathbf{false}$ is true and $\bigcirc\bullet\mathbf{false}$ is clearly false; however, at all other points the implication holds. Finally, one must remember to ensure that the frame is bounded in the past, i.e. add that as an axiom. Such past linear-time temporal logics were introduced for specification purposes, see for example [Barringer and Kuiper, 1984], [Lichtenstein *et al.*, 1985], [Koymans and Roever, 1985].

Decidability of $\mathcal{L}_{(\mathcal{W},\bigcirc)}$

Importantly for automation purposes, the propositional temporal logics we introduce in this chapter are all decidable, albeit of varying space and time complexity. The temporal logic $\mathcal{L}_{(\mathcal{W},\bigcirc)}$ over the natural numbers in PSPACE-complete. Given a formula φ of $\mathcal{L}_{(\mathcal{W},\bigcirc)}$ the decision procedure works by attempting to construct a model for $\neg\varphi$. If the process is unsuccessful, i.e. no models can be constructed, then clearly the original formula φ is valid. If on the other hand a model, or set of models, can be constructed, then clearly φ is invalid. The correctness of the decision result relies upon the small model property, or finite model property, of $\mathcal{L}_{(\mathcal{W},\bigcirc)}$. This property establishes that if a formula φ has a model, then it has model that can be represented finitely. For example, although the formula $\square\Diamond p$ has a model in natural number time where the proposition p has as valuation the set of points $\{i|i \text{ is prime}\}$, its models can in fact be represented by a two state structure in which one of the states has p true and must be visited infinitely often on infinite paths through the structure, with either of the states may be a starting state.

Axioms:

$\vdash w$	tautologies
$\vdash \bigcirc(\varphi \Rightarrow \psi) \Rightarrow (\bigcirc\varphi \Rightarrow \bigcirc\psi)$	K for next
$\vdash \bullet(\varphi \Rightarrow \psi) \Rightarrow (\bullet\varphi \Rightarrow \bullet\psi)$	K for last
$\vdash \bigcirc\neg\varphi \Leftrightarrow \neg\bigcirc\varphi$	commutativity of not & next
$\vdash \bullet\neg\varphi \Leftrightarrow \neg\bullet\varphi$	commutativity of not & last
$\vdash \varphi \mathcal{W} \psi \Rightarrow \psi \vee \varphi \wedge \bigcirc(\varphi \mathcal{W} \psi)$	unless "definition" as fixpoint
$\vdash \varphi \mathcal{Z} \psi \Rightarrow \psi \vee \varphi \wedge \bullet(\varphi \mathcal{Z} \psi)$	zince "definition" as fixpoint
$\vdash \bigcirc\bullet\varphi \Leftrightarrow \varphi$	next-last cancellation
$\vdash \bullet\bigcirc\varphi \Leftrightarrow \varphi$	last-next cancellation

Inference Rules:

MP $$\frac{\vdash \varphi \qquad \vdash \varphi \Rightarrow \psi}{\vdash \psi}$$

$\bigcirc$ – Gen $$\frac{\vdash \varphi}{\vdash \bigcirc\varphi}$$

$\bullet$ – Gen $$\frac{\vdash \varphi}{\vdash \bullet\varphi}$$

$\mathcal{W}$ – Intro $$\frac{\vdash \xi \Rightarrow \psi \vee \varphi \wedge \bigcirc\xi}{\vdash \xi \Rightarrow \varphi \mathcal{W} \psi}$$

$\mathcal{Z}$ – Intro $$\frac{\vdash \xi \Rightarrow \psi \vee \varphi \wedge \bullet\xi}{\vdash \xi \Rightarrow \varphi \mathcal{Z} \psi}$$

Figure 4.5: Axiomatisation for Future and Past

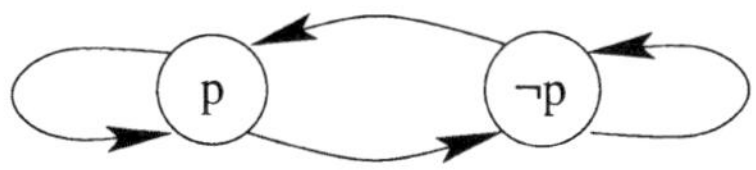

Note that such an abstraction of satisfying models, if used as a recogniser, would indeed recognise the model where p is made true only on prime indices.

There are numerous descriptions of the basic decision/satisfiability procedure for linear temporal logic in the literature and we refer the reader to any of these for detailed proofs and constructions (for example, [Gough, 1984; Lichtenstein and Pnueli, 1985; Vardi and Wolper, 1986]). In essence, the model construction proceeds by building states, each labelled by sub-formulas of the formula under test that hold there, and the next-time relation between states. The determination of the next-time relation comes from the the fact that any formula of $\mathcal{L}_{(\mathcal{W},\bigcirc)}$ can be separated into a disjunction of conjunction of states formulas and next-time formulas (see also the Section 4.4.2).

4.4.2 More on Expressiveness

We have seen, for certain temporal frames, $\mathcal{L}_{(\boxplus,\boxminus)} < \mathcal{L}_{(\boxplus,\boxminus,\widetilde{\boxplus},\widetilde{\boxminus})} < \mathcal{L}_{(\mathcal{U}^+,\mathcal{S}^-)}$, i.e. starting from a minimal logic based on $\boxplus$ and $\boxminus$, we've been able to add new temporal modalities, not expressible in the previous ones, that have gained expressiveness within particular classes of frames. We've presented this in a fairly natural and intuitive way, however, there was little logical strategy. So questions of expressive completeness, or even connective completeness, should be considered. In boolean logic, we know there are only 16 different binary connectives (there are only 16 combinations 2×2 tables of boolean values). It is easy to show that each of these 16 binary connectives can be expressed in terms of, say, just negation and conjunction, or negation and disjunction, or implication and falsity, etc. We have a notion of functional completeness. Turning to our temporal connectives, we introduced $\widetilde{\boxplus}$ and $\widetilde{\boxminus}$ as new temporal connectives and then showed that they could not be expressed in terms of $\boxplus$ and $\boxminus$. Similarly for the $\mathcal{U}^+$ and $\mathcal{S}^-$ connectives. So it is natural to ask whether there is some similar notion to functional completeness for our temporal logics. First we must note that functional completeness is the wrong notion — it clearly is inapplicable. However, what we're trying to get at is a formal notion of expressiveness. For that some well understood base is required. We fix on a first order language which can be interpreted over essentially the same models as our temporal languages, and then formally compare expressiveness with respect to the known base.

Let $\mathcal{L}_1$ be such a first order language with $=, <$ and unary predicates $q_i, i \in \mathbb{N}$. We interpret $\mathcal{L}_1$ in models similar to those for $\mathcal{L}_{(\mathcal{U}^+,\mathcal{S}^-)}$, i.e. structures $(T, <, Q_i)$ where $Q_i \subseteq T$ for $i \in \mathbb{N}$.

There is a natural transformation of $\mathcal{L}_{(\mathcal{U}^+,\mathcal{S}^-)}$ formulae φ into $\mathcal{L}_1$ formulae, $\varphi^*(t)$ s.t. φ is true at t iff $\varphi^*(t)$ is true. The transformation follows the semantic descriptions given earlier. Thus T_f^t is defined as:

$$
\begin{array}{lll}
T_f^t(p) & \stackrel{def}{=} & p(t) \\
T_f^t(\varphi \wedge \psi) & \stackrel{def}{=} & T_f^t(\varphi) \wedge T_f^t(\psi) \\
\vdots & & \\
T_f^t(\varphi \mathcal{U}^+ \psi) & \stackrel{def}{=} & \exists s \cdot t < s \wedge T_f^t(\psi) \wedge (\forall u \cdot t < u \wedge u < s \Rightarrow T_f^t(\varphi)) \\
etc & &
\end{array}
$$

Variable s, above, must be chosen so not to capture others.

Definition 4.4.1. *The logic $\mathcal{L}_{(\mathcal{U}^+, \mathcal{S}^-)}$ is said to be expressively complete wrt $\mathcal{L}_1$ if there exists a transformation from $\mathcal{L}_1$ to $\mathcal{L}_{(\mathcal{U}^+, \mathcal{S}^-)}$.*

Remember that the transformation must preserve truth, i.e. letting $\varphi_1(t)$ be a formula of $\mathcal{L}_1$ and φ be the temporal logic formula resulting from the transformation, then $\varphi_1(t)$ is true iff φ is true at t.

Theorem 4.4.3. *(due to Kamp/Gabbay/G.P.S.S.) The logic $\mathcal{L}_{(\mathcal{U}^+, \mathcal{S}^-)}$ is expressively complete wrt a 1st order language over complete linear orders.*

The expressive completeness of the since until language was first due to Kamp and was presented in his PhD thesis of 1968 [Kamp, 1968]. The particular work is not the easiest of reads, which therefore made the details of the result rather inaccessible. However, it is a very important and surprising result. What is so special about $\mathcal{U}^+$ and its mirror is that this restricted form of quantification can capture the arbitrary, unrestricted, form of quantification allowed by the 1st order language.

Others have since produced more understandable proofs, but ones which are still not that easy. Indeed Gabbay, in [Gabbay, 1981], produced a more interesting result which was based on a syntactic separation property of temporal languages (discussed in the next section).

Gabbay, Pnueli, Shelah and Stavi ([Gabbay *et al.*, 1980]) produced yet another proof of expressive completeness, more readable than Kamp's original.

Define a first order formula $\varphi(t)$ as a *future formula* if all quantification is restricted to the future of t, i.e. $\exists y \cdot t < y$

Theorem 4.4.4. *(due to Gabbay, Pnueli, Shelah and Stavi) The logic $\mathcal{L}_{(\mathcal{U}^+)}$ is expressively complete wrt the future formulae of $\mathcal{L}_1$.*

Gabbay's Separation Result

Consider $\mathcal{L}_{(\mathcal{U}^+, \mathcal{S}^-)}$ over frames $(\mathbb{N}, <)$. Define the subsets of $\mathcal{L}$, wff^0 – pure present formulae, wff^0 – pure past formulae, and wff^+ – pure future formulae. The separation result was produced simply as a means to establishing a more approachable proof of expressive completeness of temporal languages. Indeed Gabbay succeeded in providing a more general route than Kamp, as well as being more accessible.

Theorem 4.4.5. Separation Theorem *(due to Gabbay). Any formula φ of $\mathcal{L}_{(\mathcal{U}^+, \mathcal{S}^-)}$ can be written as a boolean combination of formulae from $wff^- \cup wff^0 \cup wff^+$.*

Theorem 4.4.6. *(due to Gabbay). Given $\mathcal{L}$ as a temporal language with $\oplus$, $\ominus$ and the separation property, $\mathcal{L}$ is expressively complete (over complete linear orders).*

However, the separation result is of more interest than just as a tool for improving difficult, or even unreachable, proofs; it is a result of importance in its own right. For example, it is a basis for creating models which satisfy temporal formulae, and consequentially a basis for temporal logic programming. Because of this, we look at the proof of separation in a little more depth.

The key idea behind the proof of the separation theorem is the use of a systematic procedure that extracts nested occurrences of $\mathcal{U}^+$, resp. $\mathcal{S}^-$, from within a $\mathcal{S}^-$, resp. $\mathcal{U}^+$, formula until there are no nestings of $\mathcal{U}^+$ within $\mathcal{S}^-$ and vice versa. For $\mathcal{U}^+$ within $\mathcal{S}^-$, there are eight basic cases to handle. Let φ and ψ stand for arbitrary formulae and letters a and b, etc., denote propositional atoms. The eight cases are:-

1.	$\varphi\,\mathcal{S}^-\,(\psi \wedge a\mathcal{U}^+\,b)$	2.	$\varphi\,\mathcal{S}^-\,(\psi \wedge \neg(a\mathcal{U}^+\,b))$
3.	$(\varphi \vee a\mathcal{U}^+\,b)\,\mathcal{S}^-\,\psi$	4.	$(\varphi \vee \neg(a\mathcal{U}^+\,b))\,\mathcal{S}^-\,\psi$
5.	$(\varphi \vee a\mathcal{U}^+\,b)\,\mathcal{S}^-\,(\psi \wedge a\mathcal{U}^+\,b)$	6.	$(\varphi \vee \neg(a\mathcal{U}^+\,b))\,\mathcal{S}^-\,(\psi \wedge a\mathcal{U}^+\,b)$
7.	$(\varphi \vee a\mathcal{U}^+\,b)\,\mathcal{S}^-\,(\psi \wedge \neg(a\mathcal{U}^+\,b))$	8.	$(\varphi \vee \neg(a\mathcal{U}^+\,b))\,\mathcal{S}^-\,(\psi \wedge \neg(a\mathcal{U}^+\,b))$

Other nested $\mathcal{U}^+$ forms reduce to one of the 8 schema for atomic $\mathcal{U}^+$ formula. For example, consider $\varphi\,\mathcal{S}^-\,(a\mathcal{U}^+\,(p\mathcal{U}^+\,q))$, however, this can be viewed as a formula of shape 1 above. Replace the sub-formula $p\mathcal{U}^+\,q$ by pq say, and note that the formula ψ in 1 is **true**.

For each of the above shapes, one can provide an equivalent formula of form $E_1 \vee E_2 \vee E_3$ where each E_i is a boolean combination of pure past, present and pure future formulae. An inductive proof can then establish that separation can occur for all formulae.

In the following we establish the first of the above eliminations. Let $E \stackrel{def}{=} \varphi\,\mathcal{S}^-\,(\psi \wedge a\mathcal{U}^+\,b)$. We can write E as the disjunction of $E_1E_2E_3$ such that the E_i contain no nested $\mathcal{U}^+$, in fact in a separated form,

$$\models E \Leftrightarrow E_1 \vee E_2 \vee E_3$$

In order to construct the formulae E_i, consider a model for $\varphi\,\mathcal{S}^-\,(\psi \wedge a\mathcal{U}^+\,b)$.

E_1	:	$y < n$	:	$\varphi\,\mathcal{S}^-\,(b \wedge \varphi \wedge (\varphi \wedge a)\,\mathcal{S}^-\,\psi)$
E_2	:	$y = n$	:	$b \wedge (\varphi \wedge a)\,\mathcal{S}^-\,\psi$
E_3	:	$y > n$	:	$a\mathcal{U}^+\,b \wedge a \wedge (\varphi \wedge a)\,\mathcal{S}^-\,\psi$

Let n be the point in the model at which we are evaluating the formula (which we will assume to be true). By definition of the $\mathcal{S}^-$ connective, there is a point before n, say p, at which $\psi \wedge a\mathcal{U}^+\,b$ holds. Consider then the formula $a\mathcal{U}^+\,b$ at point p. Clearly there is a point beyond p at which b holds, name that point y. y must either be earlier than, equal to, or later than the point n. We thus have three cases, the first of which is illustrated below.

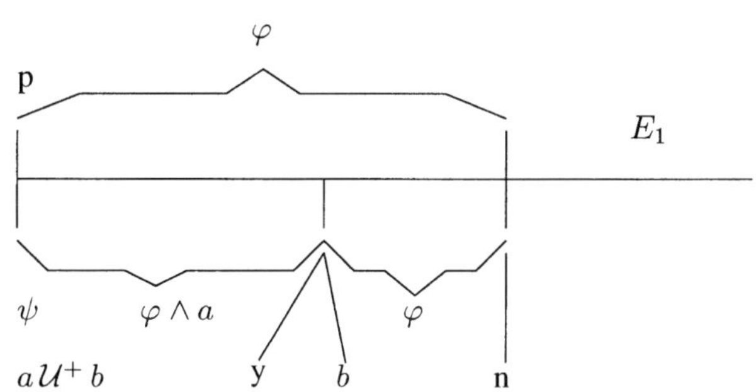

So consider the first case, i.e. y<n. We can describe the situation, from n, as φ holding back to y, at which $b \wedge \varphi$ hold and from there $\varphi \wedge a$ hold back to p at which ψ holds. This is a pure past formula. The situation when y=n can be given as a boolean combination of pure past and present time formulas. The case for y>n as a boolean combination of pure past, present, and pure future formulas. We are thus done, since the original formula is equivalent to one of these three, i.e. the disjunction of the three cases, which is a boolean combination of pure past, present and pure future formulas.

4.4.3 Is $\mathcal{L}_{(\mathcal{U}^+,\ \mathcal{S}^-)}$ expressive enough?

In the previous section we've identified the expressiveness of the $\mathcal{L}_{(\mathcal{U}^+,\ \mathcal{S}^-)}$ logic as begin equivalent to the first order language of linear order: we've precisely answered the question of how expressive the language is. However, when considering applications of temporal logic, questions relating to whether this logic is expressive enough are still likely to arise. Of course, we can continue increasing expressiveness until we can distinguish every feature of some proposed model - we very much doubt, however, whether such a logic would be useful! Indeed there is always some trade-off. For us, one important trade-off is between expressiveness and complexity of the decision process (or, worse still, how undecidable a logic may be). So one natural question arises: how much richer, or more expressive, can we make our temporal language whilst maintaining decidability? Further interesting extensions can be made, and there is a need for such. Wolper was one of the first to propose a decidable extension of the until temporal language that fulfilled a need in program specification. We proceed by highlighting his example, then introduce two alternative extensions to the until language of more or less equivalent expressiveness.

Regular properties

Consider the statement "the clock ticked on every even moment of time": can such a statement be expressed in some way in the until/since version of linear discrete temporal logic? To make a little more precise whilst capturing the essence of the example let us rephrase the problem as:- construct a temporal formula of the logic $\mathcal{L}_{(\mathcal{W},\mathcal{O})}$ that characterises that atom p holds in every even moment of the frame $(\mathbb{N}, <)$. As a first attempt, consider the formula $\Box(p \Rightarrow \bigcirc\bigcirc p) \wedge p$. If this formula is true at the first moment in time, i.e. time point 0 in the frame, it will clearly give that the atomic proposition p will be true there and at every even moment thereafter, as in the diagram below.

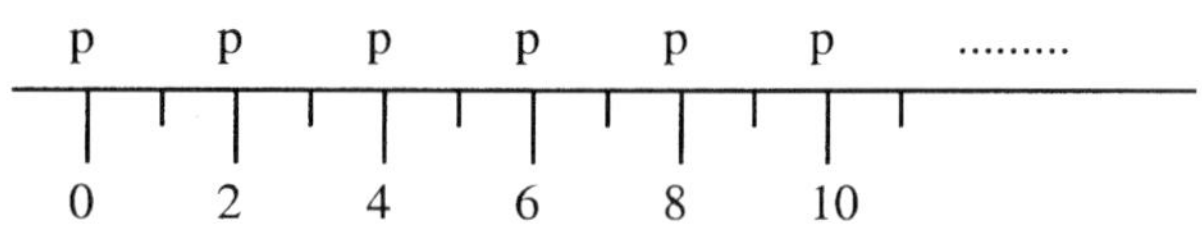

However, this formula asserts that the subformula $p \Rightarrow \bigcirc\bigcirc p$ holds at every moment in time. Therefore if p happens to be true at some odd moment in time, it will be true on every odd moment thereafter as well, as depicted in the next diagram.

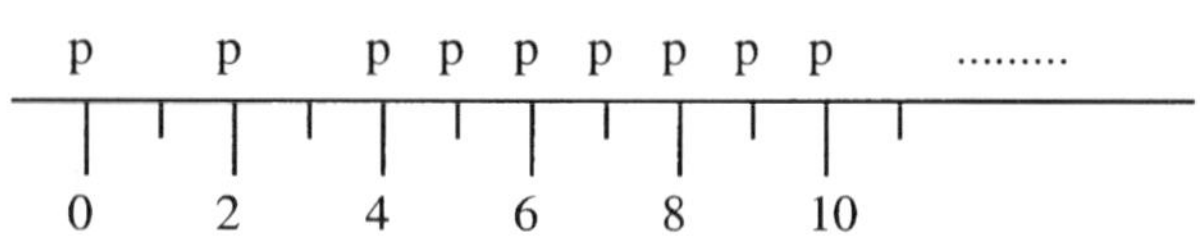

Such a situation is rather undesirable because no constraints should be placed on p on odd moments of time, for example, the situation in the next diagram should be perfectly acceptable.

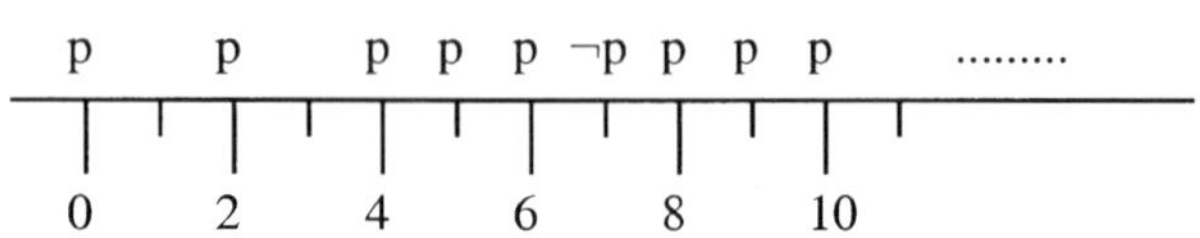

Well, no matter how hard one tries to characterise of this particular evenness property, failure is guaranteed. Not unsurprisingly, there are related properties which are expressible. For example, consider the stronger constraint that the atomic proposition p is to be true on just the even moments of time (and hence nowhere else). The following formula of $\mathcal{L}_{(\mathcal{W},\mathcal{Z},\bigcirc,\bullet)}$ will characterise the constraint*.

$$\square((p \Rightarrow \bigcirc\neg p) \wedge (\neg p \Rightarrow \bigcirc p) \wedge (\bullet\mathbf{false} \Rightarrow p))$$

Wolper [Wolper, 1983] introduced an extension of linear discrete temporal logic, aptly named Extended Temporal Logic, or ETL, in which one could define new temporal connectives based on regular grammars. Wolper further established that the logic was complete (although see [Banieqbal and Barringer, 1986]) with respect to ω-regular languages, precisely those accepted by finite state Buchi-automata. Importantly, ETL was thus a decidable extension. The essence of ETL is to define n-ary grammar operators, with production rules of the form $V_i = u_j V_k$ where V_i, V_k, etc., are non-terminal symbols and letters u_j denote terminal symbols. With respect to linear discrete models, a grammar operator, say $g_i(p_1, \ldots, p_n)$ holds at a point t in the model if and only if there is an expansion $u_{i0}u_{i1}\ldots$ of the non-terminal V_i such that each parameter, p_{im}, obtained by substitution of p_j for $u_j, j = 1, \ldots, n$, holds at $t + m$.

Motivational examples Consider the production rule $V_1 = u_1 V_1$ and the evaluation of the grammar operator $g_1(p)$ at s. It defines that the proposition p must hold on every moment t, $t \geq s$, in other words $g_1(p)$ is equivalent to $\square p$. On the other hand, consider the evaluation of $\neg g_1(\neg p)$ at s, which can only be satisfied on a model that does not have p false in every moment t, $t \geq s$ - in other words it corresponds to $\diamond p$.

Given the production rules, $V_1 = u_1 V_1$, $V_1 = u_2 V_2$ and $V_2 = u_3 V_2$, the formula $g_1(p, q, \mathbf{true})$ will correspond to $p \,\mathcal{W}\, q$: there is an unwinding of V_1 that has just u_1 for ever, and there are unwindings that have finite iteration of u_1 fby u_2 fby infinite iteration of u_3. On the other hand $\neg g_1(\neg q, \neg(p \vee q), \mathbf{true})$ corresponds to $\neg(\neg q \,\mathcal{W}\, \neg(p \vee q))$, i.e. p **until** q.

Finally consider the production rules, $V_1 = u_1 V_2$ and $V_2 = u_2 V_1$, then the evenness property, i.e. p should be true in every even moment from now, can be characterised by the formula $g(p, \mathbf{true})$.

Rather than examine ETL in detail, in the next sections we prefer to introduce Quantified Propositional Temporal Logic and the Fixed Point Temporal Logic, both syntactically more convenient extensions of linear temporal logic.

4.4.4 Quantified Propositional Temporal Logic

Consider the temporal logic $\mathcal{L}_{(\square,\blacksquare,\bigcirc,\bullet)}$, i.e. the propositional temporal logic built using just the temporal modalities, $\square$, $\bigcirc$ and their past time counterparts. This is not the most expressive temporal logic we have seen so far, however, this is rich enough for our purposes.† The extension we now make is to introduce quantification over atomic propositions, which then yields quantified propositional temporal logic, QPTL. The following are examples of QPTL formulae:

p	$\bigcirc(p \Rightarrow q)$	$\bigcirc\square(p \Rightarrow \bigcirc q)$
$\exists x \cdot (p \Rightarrow x)$	$\exists x \cdot \square(p \equiv \bigcirc x)$	$\exists x \cdot \square(x \Rightarrow p \wedge \bigcirc\bigcirc x) \wedge x$

*The past is required in order to characterise the first point in time.

†In fact, our extension will subsume the other logics we have seen so far.

The interpretation of QPTL formulae is pretty routine. The first three examples, which have no quantification, are interpreted as before. Thus p is true in a model $M = (T, <, V)$ at time point t if t is a member of $V(p)$, etc. On the other hand, the formula $\exists x \cdot (p \Rightarrow x)$ is true at time point t if one can make an assignment to the proposition x that will make the formula $p \Rightarrow x$ true at time point t, i.e. make x true at t. The formula $\exists x \cdot \Box(p \Leftrightarrow \bigcirc x)$ will be true at t if an assignment can be made to proposition x that will make $\Box(p \equiv \bigcirc x)$ true at t, which requires that the valuation of x at every point $s > t$ is the same as the valuation of proposition p at each points $s - 1$. More formally, we have the following semantic definition for existential quantification.

$$M \models_t \exists x \cdot \varphi(x) \quad \text{iff} \quad \text{there exists } M' = (T(M), <, V') \text{ s.t.} \\ V' \text{ differs from } V(M) \text{ just on } x \text{ and } M' \models_t \varphi(x)$$

Universal quantification is then defined in the usual way in terms of existential quantification, namely:

$$\forall x \cdot \varphi(x) \stackrel{def}{=} \neg \exists x \cdot \neg \varphi(x)$$

Consider now the evaluation of the formula $\exists x \cdot \Box(x \Rightarrow p \wedge \bigcirc\bigcirc x) \wedge x$ in model $M = (\mathbb{N}, <, V)$ where $V(p) = \{0, 2, 4, 6, \ldots\} \cup \{3, 7\}$. Let the given formula be denoted by $\exists x \cdot \varphi(x)$. For $M \models_0 \exists x \cdot \varphi(x)$ to hold we must find an assignment for x, V_x, such that for M updated by V_x, i.e. M', we have $M' \models_0 \varphi(x)$. From the definition of formula $\varphi(x)$, since x must be true at time point 0 and the fact that whenever x is true, say at t, it must also be true at $t + 2$, an assignment for x must have $V(x) = \{0, 2, 4, 6, \ldots\}$. For the formula $\varphi(x)$ to be true, we must also have p true whenever x is true, i.e. $V(x) \subseteq V(p)$, which is the case. Therefore $M \models_0 \exists x \cdot \Box(x \Rightarrow p \wedge \bigcirc\bigcirc x) \wedge x$. Of course, the formula we've just evaluated characterises the evenness property of the above section.

Theorem 4.4.7. *The temporal logic $\mathcal{L}_{(\mathcal{W},\bigcirc)}$ is contained in QPTL.*

In order to establish this result we need to show how any $\mathcal{L}_{(\mathcal{W},\bigcirc)}$ formula, say φ can be represented by a formula in QPTL, say ψ, such that $M \models_t \varphi$ if and only if $M \models_t \psi$ for all t in $M(T)$. The proof follows by induction over the structure of formulae. We need to consider only the $\mathcal{W}$ case, since other formula have direct correspondents. Assume that $tr(A)$, $tr(B)$ are QPTL formulae equivalent to $\mathcal{L}_{(\mathcal{W},\bigcirc)}$ formulae A and B. We assert that the QPTL formula

$$\exists x \cdot \Box(x \Leftrightarrow (tr(B) \vee tr(A) \wedge \bigcirc x)) \wedge x \wedge maximal(x) \\ \text{where } maximal(x) \stackrel{def}{=} \forall y \cdot \Box(y \Leftrightarrow (tr(B) \vee tr(A) \wedge \bigcirc y)) \Rightarrow \Box(y \Rightarrow x)$$

is true on just the models that $A \mathcal{W} B$ is true, and vice-versa. The first clause of the translation corresponds, in a sense, to the axiom that defines $A \mathcal{W} B$ is a solution to the equation $x = B \vee A \wedge \bigcirc x$, and the formula $maximal(x)$ corresponds to the unless introduction inference rule characterising that the formula $A \mathcal{W} B$ is a maximal solution to the equation.

Theorem 4.4.8. *QPTL is decidable, with non-elementary complexity.*

An axiomatisation for QPTL is given in [Kesten and Pnueli, 1995] and shown to be complete with respect to left bounded linear discrete models; the logic is equipped with both past and future temporal modalities.

4.4.5 A Fixed Point Temporal Logic

Another approach to extending the expressiveness of, say, future time temporal logic has been to start with a language with just one temporal modality (next) and then allow recursively defined formulas. Such languages have been found most natural for describing computations (particularly in a compositional fashion). We will exemplify this approach here in the context of linear discrete temporal logic. Our presentation follows that of [Banieqbal and Barringer, 1987], but see [Vardi, 1988; Kaivola, 1995] for alternative presentations. We construct a temporal language νTL (over $(\mathbb{N}, <)$) from a propositional logic, e.g.

p	atomic propositions	x	proposition (recursion) variables
$\neg$	negation	$\bigcirc$	next time temporal modality
$\wedge$	and	ν	fixed point constructor
$\vdots$	$\vdots$		

Open well formed formulae, owff, are defined inductively by

$p \in$ owff, $x \in$ owff
if $\varphi, \psi \in$ owff, then so are $\neg\varphi, \varphi \wedge \psi, \ldots, \bigcirc\varphi$
if $\chi(x) \in$ owff, with proposition variable x free, then $\nu x.\chi(x) \in$ owff

Closed well formed formulae, wff, are then open well formed formulas that have no free proposition variables. We take the language νTL to be the set of closed well formed formulae.

In order to define the semantics of νTL formulas we adopt a slightly different viewpoint. In essence, we are just changing our view so that we think of the sets of models that satisfy a temporal formula. This enables us to apply standard techniques to construct solutions to recursive definitions. For ease of presentation we will restrict our logic to a linear discrete temporal frame structure $(\mathbb{N}, <)$, thus a model $M = (\mathbb{N}, <, V)$ over which we have the successor function $(+1)$. Let U_M denote the set of all such possible models and let $\mathcal{M}^i_f$ be the set of models which satisfy the νTL formula f at time i. Then, by induction over the structure of formulae we have the following definition.

$$\begin{array}{lcllcl} \mathcal{M}^i_p & = & \{M | M, i \models p\} & \mathcal{M}^i_{\bigcirc\varphi} & = & \mathit{Shift}(\mathcal{M}^i_\varphi) \\ \mathcal{M}^i_{\varphi\wedge\psi} & = & \mathcal{M}^i_\varphi \cap \mathcal{M}^i_\psi & \mathcal{M}^i_{\neg\varphi} & = & \overline{\mathcal{M}^i_\varphi} \text{ i.e. } U_M - \mathcal{M}^i_\varphi \end{array}$$

where we define the set theoretic function *Shift* as

$$\begin{array}{lcl} \mathit{Shift}(\mathcal{M}) & = & \{(\mathbb{N}, <, V') | (\mathbb{N}, <, V) \in \mathcal{M} \text{ and } V' = shift(V)\} \\ \mathit{shift}(V)(p) & = & \{i+1 | i \in V(p)\} \text{ for any proposition } p \end{array}$$

Thus $\mathcal{M}^i_p$ is just the set of models which have proposition p true at time point i. Note that no constraint is placed on the valuation of any other proposition, or on the valuation of p at any point other than i. Slightly more interestingly, $M^i_{\bigcirc\varphi}$ is defined as the set of models that satisfy φ at $i+1$, although this is achieved through the auxiliary function *Shift* that literally shifts the evaluation of every proposition forwards by one moment. Thus the set of models $\mathcal{M}^i_{\bigcirc p}$ will be the $Shift$ of the set of models each having p true at i, resulting in the set of models that have p true at $i+1$. The definitions of the boolean connectives follows their set theoretic counterparts, from which it follows, of course, that $\mathcal{M}^i_{\neg\varphi} = \{M | M, i \not\models \varphi\}$.

Let us now consider the fixed point form $\nu x.f(x)$. First note that if g is a νTL formula then so is $f(g) = f[g/x]$, the result of substituting g for the free occurrences of x in $f(x)$. From the definition above, $\mathcal{M}^i_{f(g)}$ depends solely on $\mathcal{M}^i_g$, hence one can construct a function F on sets of models, corresponding to f, such that, for any given formula g we have,

$$\mathcal{M}^i_{f(g)} = F(\mathcal{M}^i_g)$$

Consider the sets $\mathcal{M}^i$ such that $\mathcal{M}^i = F(\mathcal{M}^i)$. If there is a maximum set among them, i.e. one which contains all the others, then we say that $\nu x.f(x)$ exists and that $\mathcal{M}^i_{\nu x.f(x)}$ is that set. It follows that since we then have

$$\mathcal{M}^i_{\nu x.f(x)} = F(\mathcal{M}^i_{\nu x.f(x)}) = \mathcal{M}^i_{f(\nu x.f(x))}$$

we have that

$$\nu x.f(x) = f(\nu x.f(x))$$

Thus $\nu x.f(x)$ is a solution to $x = f(x)$ and every other solution y satisfies $y \Rightarrow \nu x.f(x)$. We consider the necessary conditions for its existence a little below.

Examples Consider the following examples of fixed point formulae.

1. $\nu x.p \wedge \bigcirc x$.

   If the above is true at i in some model M, then M has p true at i and all points beyond in the future. Let $f(x) = p \wedge \bigcirc x$ and thus $F(\mathcal{M}^i) = \{M | i \in V(M)(p), M \in Shift(\mathcal{M}^i)\}$. Since we identify $\mathcal{M}^i$ with $F(\mathcal{M}^i)$, the maximal set $\mathcal{M}^i$ that is a solution must have a valuation for p that is the set of all $j \geq i$, i.e. p is true at i and all points beyond. This is the same as the previous semantics of $\Box p$. Thus we can indeed define $\Box\varphi \stackrel{def}{=} \nu x.\varphi \wedge \bigcirc x$.

2. $\nu x.p \wedge \bigcirc\bigcirc x$.

   If this is true at i then p has to be true at all points $i + 2 * j$ for $j \geq 0$, i.e. p has to be true at all even moments beyond i.

3. $\neg\nu x.\neg p \wedge \bigcirc x$.

   If this is true at i, then there is a $j \geq i \in V(p)$, otherwise p would be false everywhere beyond (and including) i, i.e. p is true sometime in the future.

4. $\nu x.q \vee p \wedge \bigcirc x$.

   If this formula is true at i, it characterises models that have p holding forwards from i until at least q (which may never occur, in which case p holds for ever from i).

A small extension The first of the above examples showed that the formula $\nu x.p \wedge \bigcirc x$ corresponds to the $\mathcal{L}_{(\mathrm{W},\bigcirc)}$ formula $\Box p$. In a similar way that we defined $\Diamond\varphi$ as $\neg\Box\neg\varphi$, so we can define a minimal fixed point formula. Indeed, let

$$\mu x.f(x) \stackrel{def}{=} \neg\nu x.\neg f(\neg x)$$

when the right-hand side formula exists. Thus we have

$$\neg f(\mu x.f(x)) \Leftrightarrow \neg f(\neg \nu x.\neg f(\neg x)) \Leftrightarrow \nu x.\neg f(\neg x)$$

And therefore $\mu x.f(x)$ is a fixed point of f, i.e. $f(\mu x.f(x)) = \mu x.f(x)$. Indeed, it can be shown that $\mu x.f(x)$ is a minimal solution. If $f(g) = g$ then $\neg f(\neg(\neg g)) = \neg g$, hence $\neg g \Rightarrow \nu x.\neg f(\neg x)$, i.e. $\neg \nu x.\neg f(\neg x) \Rightarrow g$ and thus $\mu x.f(x) \Rightarrow g$. Therefore $\mu x.f(x)$ is minimal.

Note we can define:

$$\begin{array}{llllll} \Box\varphi & \stackrel{def}{=} & \nu x.\varphi \wedge \bigcirc x & \Diamond\varphi & \stackrel{def}{=} & \mu x.\varphi \vee \bigcirc\varphi \\ \varphi \mathcal{W} \psi & \stackrel{def}{=} & \nu x.\psi \vee \varphi \wedge \bigcirc x & \varphi \ \mathbf{until}\ \psi & \stackrel{def}{=} & \mu x.\psi \vee \varphi \wedge \bigcirc x \end{array}$$

Existence of fixed points Consider the following νTL formula, $\nu x.p \wedge \bigcirc\neg x$. Let M be a model satisfying p and $Shift(M) = M$. We must have that M satisfies x if and only if M satisfies $\neg x$. But this is a contradiction. Therefore the given formula denotes no set of models, i.e. there is no solution to the equation $y = p \wedge \bigcirc\neg y$. On the other hand, the equation $y = p \wedge x \wedge \bigcirc\neg y$ has solutions but no unique maximal solution - **false** is a solution. So, the issue to be explored is under what conditions do maximal and minimal fixed point formula exist?

We call f monotone if whenever $x \Rightarrow y$ we have that $f(x) \Rightarrow f(y)$. For such functions, the fixed points always exist and can be constructed by approximation. Given a formula x, we define, for ordinal α and β, $f^\alpha_\wedge$ and $f^\alpha_\vee$ inductively as follows.

$$f^\alpha_\wedge(x) = \begin{cases} f(f^{\alpha-1}_\wedge(x)) & \text{if } \alpha \text{ is not limiting} \\ \bigwedge_{\beta<\alpha} f^\beta_\wedge(x) & \text{if } \alpha \text{ is limiting} \end{cases}$$

$$f^\alpha_\vee(x) = \begin{cases} f(f^{\alpha-1}_\vee(x)) & \text{if } \alpha \text{ is not limiting} \\ \bigvee_{\beta<\alpha} f^\beta_\vee(x) & \text{if } \alpha \text{ is limiting} \end{cases}$$

And then $\nu x.f(x) = f^\alpha_\wedge(\mathbf{true})$ for some ordinal α, and $\mu x.f(x) = f^\alpha_\vee(\mathbf{false})$ for some ordinal β.* Let us exemplify the construction. Consider the evaluation of formula $\nu x.p \wedge \bigcirc x$ in model M at time point i. There is some ordinal α such that $M, i \models f^\alpha_\wedge(\mathbf{true})$ where $f(x) = p \wedge \bigcirc x$: clearly $f(x)$ in x. Let $\mathcal{M}^0$ be the set of models M^0 that satisfy $f^0(\mathbf{true})$ at time point i, i.e. the formula $\mathbf{true}$. And then $\mathcal{M}^1$ be the set of models M^1 that satisfy $f^1(\mathbf{true})$, namely $p \wedge \bigcirc\mathbf{true}$, at time point i. Consider the first limiting ordinal ω: the set of models satisfying $f^\omega(\mathbf{true})$ will be intersection of the sets $\mathcal{M}^n$ for all $n \in \mathbb{N}$. Each model in this set will have p true at every time point $j \geq i$. Further iteration over this set of models does not cause change in the set. Therefore we have indeed found the set of models satisfying the maximal fixed point of f. These are, of course, precisely those models satisfying $\Box p$ at i.

As one further example, consider the maximal and the minimal solutions to the equation $f(x) = q \vee p \wedge \bigcirc x$. First note that $f(x)$ is monotone in x. The construction of the maximal solution of f requires iteration again to the first limiting ordinal ω. The set of models includes those that either have q true at some point $k \in \mathbb{N}$ and then p at all points $j \geq i$ and $j < k$, or have p true at all points $j \geq i$. The latter set of models is present in the original set ($\mathbf{true}$)

*This actually presents an alternative way to define the semantics of the fixed point formulae in the case that the function f is monotone.

and never gets removed by the iteration. On the other hand, the construction of the minimal solution to f starts from the empty set and adds all models satisfying the property that q is true at some future point and p is true up to that point. The model with p true everywhere (from i) and q never true (from i onwards) is never added. The minimal fixed point formula thus corresponds to p **until** q and the maximal fixed point formula is the weak version, namely $p\,\mathcal{W}\,q$.

The examples we've shown so far have no nesting of fixed points. However, our language allows such formulae. Suppose therefore that $f(x,y)$ is monotone in both variables x and y; it can be shown that

$$\text{if } x \Rightarrow x' \text{ then } \nu y.f(x,y) \Rightarrow \nu y.f(x',y)$$

It follows that a general condition for monotonicity of $f(x)$ is that x must occur under an even number of negations. If this is the case for all bound variables of a fixed point formula, then the fixed point does exist. For example, $\nu x.(a \wedge \bigcirc \neg \nu y.(\neg x \wedge \bigcirc y))$ is defined, x appears under two negations, the innermost being applied direct to x, then another encompassing negation applied to the immediately surrounding ν formula. The use of negation applied to bound variables, in such cases, can be avoided by the use of minimal fixed point formulae. The example just given can be rewritten as $\nu x.(a \wedge \bigcirc \mu y.(x \vee \bigcirc y))$. Indeed, if a formula f has no negation symbols applied to bound variables, then the formula $\neg f$ can also be written without negation applied to bound variables.

Decidability The propositional temporal fixed point logic, νTL, over linear discrete frames $(\mathbb{N},<)$, is decidable. A decision procedure for the logic was given in [Banieqbal and Barringer, 1987] and relied on the property that if a formula is satisfiable then it is satisfiable on an eventually periodic model, which only requires iteration (of recursion formulas) up to the first limiting ordinal ω to show satisfaction. An alternative approach to the problem was adopted in [Vardi, 1988]. See also the decidability results on the propositional μ-calculus [Streett and Emerson, 1984].

Axioms:

$\vdash w$ tautology

$\vdash \bigcirc(\varphi \Rightarrow \psi) \Rightarrow (\bigcirc\varphi \Rightarrow \bigcirc\psi)$

$\vdash \bigcirc\neg\varphi \Leftrightarrow \neg\bigcirc\varphi$

$\vdash \nu x.\chi(x) \Leftrightarrow \chi(\nu x.\chi(x))$

Inference Rules:

Modus Ponens

$\bigcirc$ – Gen $\dfrac{\vdash \varphi}{\vdash \bigcirc\varphi}$

ν – Intro $\dfrac{\vdash \xi \Rightarrow \chi(\xi)}{\vdash \xi \Rightarrow \nu x.\chi(x)}$

Figure 4.6: Axiomatisation for νTL.

Proof System for νTL Consider a fixed point temporal logic over linear discrete frames $(\mathbb{N}, <)$. The proof system given in Figure 4.6 follows the approach for the $\mathcal{L}_{(\mathcal{W},\mathcal{O})}$ system. Soundness is straightforward; on the other hand, completeness remained an open problem for several years, although a solution has been given in [Kaivola, 1995].

4.5 Branching Time Temporal Logic

We have just examined a range of temporal logics that all possess, one way or another, a constraint for linearity - each model will be structurally indistinguishable (in a zig-zag sense) from some linearly ordered structure. Let us restrict attention to a future-time linear discrete temporal logic, i.e. one that can only reason forwards into the future, so there are no past time temporal operators. Clearly the removal of the linearity constraint for such a logic will yield a temporal logic whose models may have a branching structure, i.e. each time point may have more than one immediate successor. Such a logic will also admit models where different branches rejoin at some future time, see Figure 4.7 for example. This may

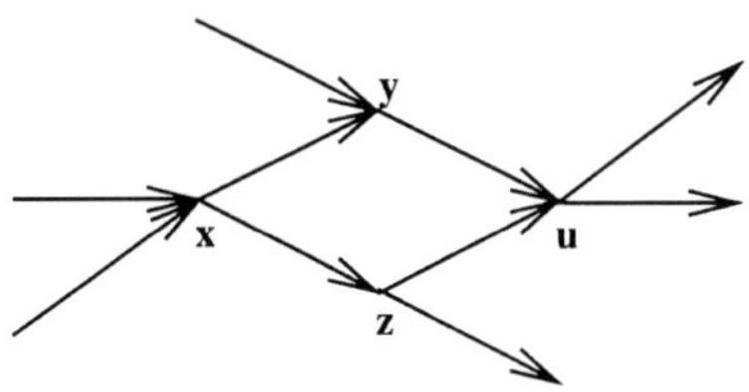

Figure 4.7: A Non Linear Structure

be quite acceptable for the desired use of the logic, however, there are obviously situations where it would not be so. Can we constrain the logic such that the determined models are pure tree structures, i.e. with only a linear past? This is a straightforward exercise using past time modalities for we simply keep a formula such as WPC present as an axiom, but how can it be expressed without the past? The first order formula

$$\forall y, z. \neg(y < z \vee z < y \vee y = z) \Rightarrow \neg\exists u. y < u \wedge z < u$$

certainly rules out backward branching, but this is not expressible with only future time modalities. Weakening the above formula by moving the two unrelated points into the future of a reference point, i.e. now, just as was done with weak future (past) connectedness, will in part solve the problem. For example, in Figure 4.7 the point u is preceded by two distinct unrelated points, y and z, i.e. there is no way to move from y to z or vice-versa; y and z can both be reached, however, from x. Indeed, the formulation will be quite adequate for all those situations where there is an initial point to the temporal flow. Thus we have

$$\forall x, y, z. x < y \wedge x < z \wedge \neg(y < z) \wedge \neg(z < y) \wedge \neg(y = z) \Rightarrow \neg\exists u. y < u \wedge z < u$$

which has corresponding temporal formula

$$\begin{array}{l} \diamondplus Y \wedge \diamondplus Z \wedge \neg \diamondplus (Y \wedge \diamondplus Z) \wedge \neg \diamondplus (Z \wedge \diamondplus Y) \wedge \neg \diamondplus (Y \wedge Z) \Rightarrow \\ \quad \neg(\diamondplus U \wedge \diamondplus (Y \wedge \diamondplus U) \wedge \diamondplus (Z \wedge \diamondplus U)) \end{array}$$

and hence the structure of Figure 4.7 would not be admissible. It should be emphasised that our concern over ruling out all branching past temporal flows without resort to past time modalities is, perhaps, somewhat academic since those backward branching models not ruled out will not be distinguishable from backward linear models using a future only language. Thus we have a future-time temporal logic determining forward branching tree structures.

Now let us consider the effect of the temporal modalities introduced in the previous section when interpreted over future branching discrete tree structures*. Assume a frame structure $(T, <)$ where T denotes a set of discrete nodes and $<$ is an asymmetric, transitive relation from which a successor relation $\mathcal{N}$ is defined. Additionally, assume that the frame satisfies the first of the above constraints.

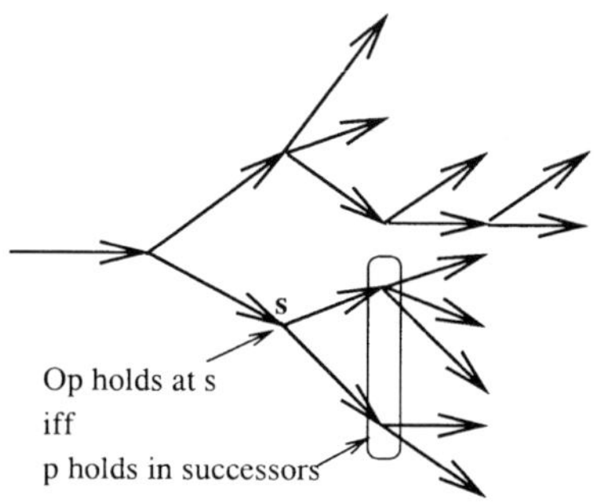

Figure 4.8: Branching tree

Recall that the next time modality $\bigcirc$ was defined as a universal, or weak, next, namely:

$$M, s \models \bigcirc\varphi \quad \textbf{iff} \quad \forall t.s\mathcal{N}t \Rightarrow M, t \models \varphi$$

and thus, on a branching model, φ has to be true in all the successors of s for $\bigcirc\varphi$ to hold at s. So in Figure 4.8, φ must be true in both the successors of point s in order for $\bigcirc\varphi$ to hold at s. Given the universal interpretation to $\bigcirc$ it follows that the $\boxplus$ modality then reaches all possible future states from the given valuation state, whereas its dual modality, $\diamondplus$, will find some future state, as illustrated in figure 4.9 below. Suppose, however, one wished to express a property about every state on some path through a computation tree, or that some property at some future state of every possible computation path, as in Figure 4.10. Is the language of $\mathcal{L}(\mathcal{W}, \bigcirc)$ expressive enough to do so? Well, the answer is no. Within the language we do have the dual of the $\bigcirc$ modality, i.e. $\odot$ an existential, or strong, next defined by $\neg\bigcirc\neg$: $\odot\varphi$ is true at node s if and only there is at least one successor t where φ holds. In order to obtain a modality to capture that a particular property holds at each moment along some path, we would clearly need to use the strong version of next. The languages of QPTL, the fixed point temporal logic, and ETL are all, indeed, rich enough to do so, when interpreted over branching structures. Because we have already shown how to translate from one to the other† we'll just demonstrate expression of these different modalities with νTL.

* Such a structure is often used as a basis for a model of the possible computation states of a program

† Of course, our presentation only considered these languages over linear structures, however, interpretation over non linear structures is a straightforward exercise

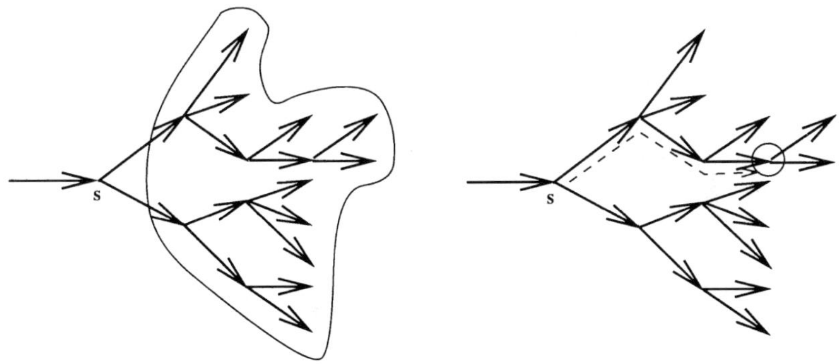

Figure 4.9: $\boxplus$ and $\diamondplus$ on trees

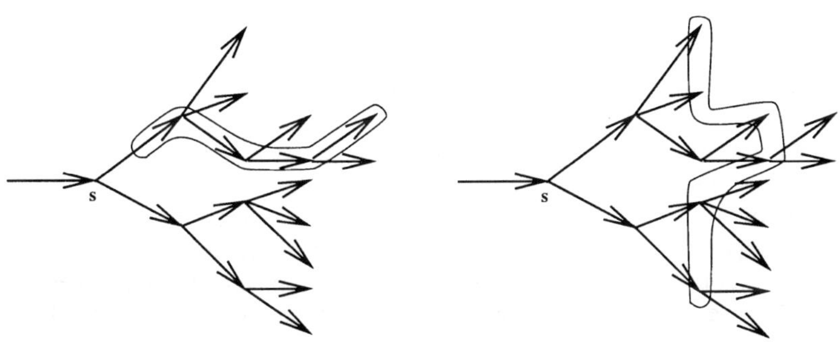

Figure 4.10: Paths and cuts on trees

The fixed point formula

$$\nu x.\varphi \wedge \odot x$$

could be used to express the suggested property. $M, s \models \nu x.\varphi \wedge \odot x$ if and only if there is some infinite path σ starting from s (i.e. $\sigma_0 = s$) such that $M, \sigma_i \models \varphi$ for every $i > 0$. The weaker formula, on the other hand,

$$\nu x.[\varphi \wedge (\odot \mathbf{true} \Rightarrow \odot x)]$$

would be satisfied on a future finite path, provided φ holds at each moment along it of course. The "cut", or wave front, property can be expressed by using the dual of $\nu x.\varphi \wedge \odot x$, namely by the formula

$$\mu x.[\varphi \vee (\odot \mathbf{true} \wedge \bigcirc x)]$$

which requires the minimal fixed point to hold in every successor of some point s if it doesn't get satisfied at s itself, and hence eventually (because it's minimal) along every path from s.The recognition of the usefulness of a language with such modalities led researchers to develop the branching time temporal logic CTL [Clarke and Emerson, 1981b], i.e. Computation Tree Logic, and an important number of extensions. It was a key development which spearheaded the now widely accepted use of model-checking as an automated verification technique, [Clarke *et al.*, 1983; Clarke *et al.*, 1986; Clarke *et al.*, 1999; Clarke and Schlingloff, 2001].

4.6 Interval-based Temporal Logic

So far, the temporal logics that we've introduced have been point-based, be they over discrete or dense structures, linear or branching temporal flows, etc.; propositions are given truth values at each individual time-point in the model. Although for the majority of applications of temporal logics in computational contexts point-based logics are quite appropriate, there are applications, particularly those dealing with representation of natural phenomena and their interactions over time, where an interval-based valuation of propositions can be more natural and intuitive. For example, "the door is closing" is a proposition that if true will always be true over some interval of time. Of course, because intervals can be, and very often are, modelled by sets of points, there is an argument that takes the line that point-based models are quite sufficient. We don't wish to explore or contribute to that particular debate*, but will take as a starting point to interval logics an extension to the point-based linear discrete temporal logic $\mathcal{L}_{(W,O)}$ that enables, model theoretically (and formulaically), the sequential composition of models (and hence the composition of temporal formulas viewed as denoting intervals). This approach will lead naturally to a brief introduction to Moszkowski's work on ITL [Moszkowski, 1986]. It would have then been appropriate to review the modal system of Halpern and Shoham, [Halpern and Shoham, 1991], where intervals are adopted as the primitive underlying temporal object (from which points can be derived), then finally make comparison with Allen's interval temporal logic [Allen, 1983; Allen, 1984; Allen and Hayes, 1989; Allen, 1991b; Allen and Ferguson, 1994]; however, space does not permit further exposition here and we merely strongly recommend this area to the interested readers.

*Interested readers may follow this up through, for example, Galton's chapter in [Galton, 1987]

4.6.1 Introducing the chop

For simplicity of exposition, consider $\mathcal{L}_{(\mathcal{W},\mathcal{O})}$ over possibly bounded natural number time, i.e. temporal frames $F = (N, <)$ for $N = \mathbb{N}$ or $\{0..i | i \in \mathbb{N}\}$ together with the successor relation $\mathcal{N}$. Furthermore, it will be easier to consider such natural number time models M represented by sequences σ of states (providing valuations to atomic propositions). We thus use the notation $\sigma, i \models \varphi$ to denote that the formula φ is satisfied in the sequence (model) σ at index (time point) i. We will add to the language of $\mathcal{L}_{(\mathcal{W},\mathcal{O})}$ a modality that will correspond to the fusion of two sequences. Consider two sequences σ_1 and σ_2 the first of which is finite and the second may be infinite such that the end state of the first sequence σ_1 is the beginning state of the second sequence σ_2; we then define the fusion of σ_1 with σ_2 as

$$\sigma_1 \circ \sigma_2 \stackrel{def}{=} \iota\sigma \text{ s.t. } \sigma_1 < \sigma \text{ and } \sigma_2 = \sigma^{(|\sigma_1|-1)}$$

If one views a sequence as a point-based representation of an interval then the fusion of two sequences corresponds to their join where the last and first elements are fused together, i.e. they are the same. In a computational context this corresponds to the sequential composition of two particular computations. We now introduce a temporal modality, $\mathcal{C}$ that will achieve the effect of fusion. Informally, the formula $\phi\,\mathcal{C}\,\psi$ will be true for some sequence model at i if and only if the sequence can be cut, or chopped, at $j > i$ such that ϕ holds on the prefix sequence up to and including j and ψ holds on the suffix sequence from j onwards. More formally

$$\begin{array}{lll} \sigma, i \models \phi\,\mathcal{C}\,\psi & \textbf{iff} & \text{either there exists } \sigma_1, \sigma_2 \text{ s.t.} \\ & & \qquad \sigma = \sigma_1 \circ \sigma_2 \text{ and } \sigma_1, i \models \phi \text{ and } \sigma_2, 0 \models \psi \\ & & \text{or } |\sigma| = \omega \text{ and } \sigma, i \models \phi \end{array}$$

This particular chop temporal modality was first introduced in order to ease the presentation of compositional temporal specifications, see [Barringer *et al.*, 1984], and was motivated by the fusion operator used in PDL [Harel *et al.*, 1980; Harel *et al.*, 1982] (see also [Chandra *et al.*, 1981a]) and by its use in Moszkowski's ITL [Moszkowski, 1986]. Its use arose in the following way. Suppose the formula ϕ characterises the (temporal) behaviour of some program P, and ψ characterises program Q, then the formula $\phi\,\mathcal{C}\,\psi$ will characterise the temporal behaviour of the sequential composition of P and Q, i.e. $P; Q$, the program that first executes P and then, when complete, executes Q. An iterated version of chop, $\mathcal{C}^*$, was also introduced in [Barringer *et al.*, 1984]; informally $\phi\,\mathcal{C}^*\psi$ denoted the maximal solution to the implication $x = \psi \vee \phi\,\mathcal{C}\,x$ and was used to obtain a compositional temporal semantics for loops. A sound and complete axiomatisation of the logic $\mathcal{L}_{(\mathcal{W},\mathcal{C},\mathcal{O})}$ was presented in [Rosner and Pnueli, 1986].

Examples To give a flavour of the linear temporal logic with chop we examine a few formulae and models in which they're satisfied. To provide a little more intuitiveness with the temporal formula, we define the following special proposition **fin**, which is true only at the end of an interval*.

$$\textbf{fin} \stackrel{def}{=} \bigcirc\textbf{false}$$

*As we are working with a future only logic we are unable to write down a formula that uniquely determines the beginning point. This is not a major problem, for we can either extend the logic with such a proposition **beg** or allow past time modalities. We will not bother to do so in this brief exposition.

Recall that the modality $\bigcirc$ has universal interpretation, hence it is vacuously true at an "end of time", but since **false** is true nowhere, **fin** is uniquely true at an end point*.

(i) $(p \,\mathcal{C}\, q) \Rightarrow p \wedge q$
(ii) $(p \wedge \mathbf{fin}\, \mathcal{C}\, q) \Rightarrow p \wedge q$
(iii) $(\Box p)\, \mathcal{C}\, (p\ \mathbf{until}\ q) \Rightarrow p\ \mathbf{until}\ q$
(iv) $(p\ \mathbf{until}\ q) \Rightarrow [((\Box p)\, \mathcal{C}\, q) \vee ((\Box p)\, \mathcal{C} \bigcirc q) \vee q]$

Which of the above formulae are valid for the linear discrete frames? The first is obviously invalid: consider a frame with just two points and construct a model with p is true only at the first point and q true in the second - $p \,\mathcal{C}\, q$ is clearly true at the first point in the model, but p and q aren't both true at that point. The second formula, however, is valid over linear discrete frames. Any model σ which satisfies the formula $p \wedge \mathbf{fin}\, \mathcal{C}\, q$ at, say, index i will have p true at i. It must also have q true at i because σ can be decomposed as two sequences, σ_1 and σ_2 such that the length of σ_1 is $i + 1$ (**fin** is true at i), thus the ith state of σ_1 is also its last state and hence the first state of σ_2; therefore q, which is true on σ_2, will also be true on σ_1 at i and hence σ at i.

The third and fourth formulas above are also valid and we leave as a simple exercise for the reader.

ITL

Moszkowski's Interval Temporal Logic (ITL), as in [Moszkowski, 1986], is essentially a point-based discrete linear-time temporal logic defined over finite sequences. In other words, the basis is the above choppy logic defined to be restricted to finite sequences. The finiteness of the intervals enabled Moszkowski, however, to develop ITL more easily as a low-level programming language - Tempura. Temporal modalities (constructs) are defined to mimic imperative programming features, such as assignment, conditional, loops, etc., and model (interval) construction became the interpretation mechanism. For example, an assignment modality can be defined in the following way.

$$\begin{array}{lcl}
\mathbf{empty} & \stackrel{def}{=} & \neg \odot \mathbf{true} \\
e_1\, \mathbf{gets}\, e_2 & \stackrel{def}{=} & \Box(\neg \mathbf{empty} \Rightarrow ((\odot e_1) = e_2) \\
\mathbf{stable}\, e & \stackrel{def}{=} & e\, \mathbf{gets}\, e \\
\mathbf{fin}\phi & \stackrel{def}{=} & \Box(\mathbf{empty} \Rightarrow \phi) \\
e_1 \rightarrow e_2 & \stackrel{def}{=} & \exists V.((\mathbf{stable}\, V) \wedge (V = e_1) \wedge \mathbf{fin}(e_2 = V))
\end{array}$$

empty is true on empty intervals, i.e. at all points in a model where there are no future states (it corresponds to our earlier use of the **fin**). $e_1\, \mathbf{gets}\, e_2$ is true at some state in an interval when the value of expression e_1 is the value the expression e_2 in the following state of the interval (thus $x\, \mathbf{gets}\, x - 2$ is true at state s is the value of x has decreased by 2 in the next state). $\mathbf{stable}\, e$ is true whenever the value of the expression e is stable over the interval, i.e. e's value remains the same. $\mathbf{fin}\, \phi$ is true anywhere within an interval if the formula ϕ is true at the end state of the interval. Finally, the temporal assignment, $e_1 \rightarrow e_2$ holds for an interval of states if the value of e_2 at the end of the interval is the value of e_1 at the start

*Similarly, if the temporal logic were equipped with the $\bullet$ modality, also with universal interpretation, we could define the proposition **beg**.

- the stability requirement on the value V is necessary as quantification in ITL is defined for non-rigid variables. In similar ways, other imperative style programming constructs can be defined as temporal formulas, with the result that, syntactically, a Tempura formula can appear just like an imperative program.

This ITL/Tempura approach therefore provided a uniform approach to the specification and implementation of programs. Within the formal methods community of computer science there are many critics of this standpoint, however, putting aside some of these more philosophical considerations, Moszkowski's ITL marked the start of an important avenue of temporal logic applications, namely, executable temporal logic. The collection [Barringer *et al.*, 1996] and the volume introduced by [Fisher and Owens, 1995a] describe alternative approaches to executable temporal logics.

4.7 Conclusion and Further Reading

The range of modal varieties of temporal logic is now vast and, as will become abundantly clear to the interested reader as she delves further into the field, this chapter has barely entered the field. Its focus has primarily been limited to the development of discrete linear-time temporal logics from a modal logic basis, although it introduced the idea of branching and interval structures; of course, these latter areas warrant whole chapters, or even books, to themselves. And then there is the issue of temporal logics over dense structures, such as used in [Barringer *et al.*, 1986; Gabbay and Hodkinson, 1990] and the whole rich field of real-time, or metric, temporal logics, for example see [Alur and Henzinger, 1991; Bellini *et al.*, 2000] for two brief surveys. There are, today, a number of excellent expositions on temporal logic, from historical accounts such as [Ohrstrom and Hasle, 1995], early seminal monographs such as [Prior, 1967; Rescher and Urquhart, 1971], various treatise and handbooks such as [van Benthem, 1983; Benthem, 1984; Benthem, 1988b; Benthem, 1988a; van Benthem, 1991; Blackburn *et al.*, 2001; Gabbay *et al.*, 1994a; Gabbay *et al.*, 1994b; Goldblatt, 1987], shorter survey or handbook chapters such as [Burgess, 1984; Stirling, 1992; Benthem, 1995; Emerson, 1990], expositions on the related dynamic and process logics such as [Harel, 1979; Harel, 1984; Harel *et al.*, 1980; Harel *et al.*, 1982] to application-oriented expositions such as [Gabbay *et al.*, 2000] and then [Kroger, 1987; Manna and Pnueli, 1992; Manna and Pnueli, 1995] for specific coverage of linear-time temporal logic in program specification and verification, and [Clarke *et al.*, 1999] on model checking, [Moszkowski, 1986; Fisher and Owens, 1995b; Barringer *et al.*, 1996] on executable temporal logic.

We trust the reader will enjoy delving more deeply into these logics and their applications through the remaining chapters of this volume and the abundant associated, technical, literature in the field.

Handbook of Temporal Reasoning in Artificial Intelligence
Edited by M. Fisher, D. Gabbay and L. Vila

Chapter 5

Temporal Qualification in Artificial Intelligence

Han Reichgelt & Lluis Vila

We use the term *temporal qualification* to refer to the way a logic is used to express that temporal propositions are true or false at different times. Various methods of temporal qualification have been proposed in the AI community. Beginning with the simplest approach of adding time as an extra argument to all temporal predicates, these methods move to different levels of representational sophistication. In this chapter we describe and analyze a number of approaches by looking at the syntactical, semantical and ontological decisions they make. From the ontological point of view, there are two issues: (i) whether time receives full ontological status or not and (ii) what the temporally qualified expressions represent: *temporal types* or *temporal tokens*. Syntactically, time can be explicit or implicit in the language. Semantically a line is drawn between methods whose semantics is based on standard first-order logic and those that move beyond the semantics of standard first-order logic to either higher-order semantics, possible-world semantics or an *ad hoc* temporal semantics.

5.1 Introduction

Temporal reasoning in artificial intelligence deals with *relationships* that hold at some times and do not hold at other times (called *fluents*), *events* that occur at certain times, *actions* undertaken by an actor at the right time to achieve a goal and *states* of the world that are true or hold for a while and then *change* into a new state that is true at the following time. Consider the following illustrative example that will be used throughout the chapter:

> "On 1/4/04, SmallCo sent an offer for selling goods g to BigCo for price p with a 2 weeks expiration interval. BigCo received the offer three days later* and it has been effective since then. A properly formalized offer becomes effective as of it is received by the offered and continues to be so until it is accepted by the offered or it expires (as indicated by its expiration interval). Anybody who makes an offer is committed to the offer as long as the offer is effective. Anybody who receives an offer is obliged to send a confirmation to the offerer within two days."

*A more realistic and up-to-date examples might be an e-trading scenario where the messages are received 2 or 3 seconds after being sent. However, the essential representation issues and results would not be affected.

This narrative contains instances of the temporal phenomena mentioned above:

- *fluents* such as "x being effective from time t to time t'". In this case, the beginning and the end and the duration are not fully determined but the beginning is. This fluent may also hold on a set of non-overlapping intervals of time.
- *Actions* such as "an agent x sending an object or message y to agent z at time t". This also may happen more than once for the same x, y and z, with t being the only distinctive feature.
- *Events* such as "x receiving y on time t". Both executed actions and events potentially are causes of some change in the domain. In this case, the event causes the offer to be effective as of the reception time.
- *States* such as the state before "1/Apr/04" and the state right after receiving the offer where the offer is effective and various obligations hold.

Additionally, we observe other kinds of temporal phenomena such as:

- Temporal features of an object or the object itself. For instance "the manager of SmallCo" can be a different person at different times or even "SmallCo" could denote different companies at different times depending on our timeframe.
- Temporal relations between events and fluents such as "The offer is effective as of it is received by the offered and will be so until it is accepted by the offered or it expires" or "sending an object causes the receiving party to receive it between 1 and 4 days later."
- Temporal relations between fluents such as "the offerer is committed to the offer as long as the offer is effective" or "an offer cannot be effective and expired at the same time".

Notice that references to time objects may appear in a variety of styles: absolute ("1/Apr/04"), relative ("two days later"), instantaneous (`now`), durative ("the month of march"), precise ("exactly 2 days"), vague ("around 2 days"), etc.

This example illustrates the issues that must be addressed in designing a formal language for temporal reasoning*, namely the *model of time* i.e. the set or sets of time objects (points, intervals, etc.) that time is made of with their structure, the *temporal ontology* i.e. the classification of different temporal phenomena (fluents, events, actions, etc.), the *temporal constraints language*, i.e. the language for expressing constraints between time objects, the *temporal qualification* method and the *reasoning system*. Research done on models of time, temporal ontologies, and temporal constraints is reviewed in the various chapters of this volume. In this chapter we will focus on **Temporal Qualification**:

> By a temporal qualification method we mean the way a logic (which we shall call the *underlying logic* of our temporal framework) is used to express the above temporal phenomena that happen at specific times.

---

*The presentation is biased towards the standard definition of first-order logic (FOL), although nothing prevents the situation of the elements described here in the context of a different logic, including non-standard semantics for FOL, modal logics and higher-order logics.

One may either adopt a well-known logic equipped with a well-defined model and proof theory as the underlying logic or define a language with a non-standard model theory and develop a proof theory for it.

The temporal qualification method is a central issue in defining a temporal reasoning framework and it is closely related to the other issues mentioned above. As said, most of these issues are discussed in detail in other chapters of this volume. We discuss them here up to level needed to make our presentation self-contained and to be able to discuss the advantages and shortcomings of each temporal qualification approach.

5.1.1 Temporal Reasoning Issues

The Model of Time

Modeling time as a mathematical structure requires deciding (i) the class or classes of the basic objects that time is composed of, such as instants, intervals, etc. (i.e. the *time ontology*) and (ii) the properties of these time sets, such as dense vs. discrete, bounded vs. unbounded, partial vs total order, etc. (i.e. the *time topology*).

This issue is discussed in chapter *Theories of Time and Temporal Incidence* in this handbook and we shall remain silent on what the best model of time is. When introducing a temporal qualification method we shall merely assume we are given a *time structure*

$$\langle \mathcal{T}_1, \ldots, \mathcal{T}_{n_t}, \mathcal{F}_{time}, \mathcal{R}_{time} \rangle$$

where each $\mathcal{T}_i$ is a non-empty set of time objects, $\mathcal{F}_{time}$ is a set of functions defined over them, and $\mathcal{R}_{time}$ is a set of relations over them. For instance, when formalizing our example we shall take a time structure with three sets: a set of *time points* that is isomorphic to the natural numbers (where the grain size is one day), the *set of ordered pairs* of natural numbers and a set of *temporal spans* or durantions that is isomorphic to the integers. $\mathcal{F}_{time}$ contains functions on these sets $\mathcal{R}_{time}$ contains relations among them

The decision about the model of time to adopt is independent of the temporal qualification method although it has an impact on the formulas one can write and the formulas one can prove. The temporal qualification method one selects will determine how the model of time adopted will be embedded in the temporal reasoning system. The completeness of a proof theory depends on the availability of a theory that captures the properties of the model of time and allows the proof system to infer all statements valid in the time structure. Such a theory, the *theory of time*, may have the form of a set of axioms written in the temporal language that will include symbols denoting functions in $\mathcal{F}_{time}$ and relations in $\mathcal{R}_{time}$. For example, the transitivity of ordering relationship (denoted by $<_1$) over $\mathcal{T}_1$ can be captured by the axiom

$$\forall\, t_1, t_2, t_3\, [t_1 \leq_1 t_2 \wedge t_2 \leq_1 t_3 \rightarrow t_1 \leq_1 t_3]$$

However, depending on the time structure and the expressive power of underlying logic it may be impossible to write a complete set of axioms in our language.

An alternative way to capture the theory of time is through an appropriate set of inference rules, typically at least one for each temporal function and relation, which indicate how these expressions can be used in generating proofs. Of course, this choice requires much more effort than the previous one.

Temporal Constraints Language

A second issue that needs to be addressed in designing a temporal reasoning system is the temporal constraints language, the language used to denote constraints between temporal objects. Temporal constraints are logical combinations of atoms built from *time constants* (possibly of different nature, such as "1/Apr/04" or "2 days") denoting time objects in $\mathcal{T}_1, \ldots, \mathcal{T}_{n_t}$, *time functions* that denote functions in $\mathcal{F}_{time}$ and *time predicates* symbols denoting relations in $\mathcal{R}_{time}$.

Temporal Ontology and the Theory of Temporal Incidence

As discussed in two previous chapters in this book ("Eventualities" by A. Galton and partly "Theories of Time and Temporal Incidence" by Ll. Vila) temporal statements can be classified in various classes (as illustrated by the different temporal phenomena in our example), each associated with a pattern of temporal incidence. Different temporal ontologies have been proposed in different contexts, such as natural language understanding and commonsense reasoning. In most cases, the result of such ontological studies is a classification of temporal relations into a number of classes $\mathcal{E}_1, \ldots, \mathcal{E}_{e_n}$ (e.g. fluents, events, etc.) that we call *temporal entities*. Each class is usually accompanied by a temporal incidence pattern that is characterized by one or more axioms written in our logical language through some sort of *temporal incidence meta-predicates*. We call the set of these axioms the *theory of temporal incidence*.

For instance, to formalize our example we decide to have a temporal ontology with the following temporal entities: $\mathcal{E}_{events}$ is the class of *events* or *accomplishments* such as "sending a legal object on time t" that occur either at a time point, i.e. one day or during a time span (several days) and $\mathcal{E}_{fluents}$ is the class of temporal relationships such as "the offer being effective as of t" that hold homogeneously throughout a number of days. Whereas the occurrence of an event over an interval is *solid*, i.e. if it occurs on a interval it does not hold on any interval that overlaps with it, the holding of a fluent over an interval is *homogeneous*, i.e. if it holds during an interval it also holds over any subinterval. For example, if we had the meta-predicate HOLDS^3, then for each fluent $R^k \in \mathcal{E}_{fluents}$

$$\begin{array}{l}\forall\, t_1, t_2, x_1, \ldots, x_k\; [\, \text{HOLDS}(t1, t2, R^k(x_1, \ldots, x_k)) \rightarrow \\ \quad \forall\, t_3, t_4\; [\, (t_3, t_4) \subseteq (t_1, t_2) \rightarrow \text{HOLDS}(t3, t4, R^k(x_1, \ldots, x_k))]\,]\end{array}$$

Although these issues are out of the scope of this chapter, we must bear in mind that the temporal qualification method determines how the temporal incidence axioms are written and formulas derived from them.

5.1.2 Temporal Qualification Issues

We are now in a position to focus on the issues that are determined by a temporal qualification method. In fact, it can be argued that any method of temporal qualification method can be regarded as the set of decisions made with respect to these issues:

- *The distinction between temporal and atemporal individuals.* As illustrated by the example, a distinction ought to be made between atemporal individuals (i.e. individuals that are independent of time such as the color green, the number 3, ...) and individuals whose existence depends on time such as "contract c1-280-440" or "the SmallCo company".

- *The distinction between temporal and atemporal functions.* The introduction of time also leads to the need to make a semantic distinction between temporal functions and classical functions, possibly co-existing in the same logic. We define a *temporal function* as a function whose value can be different at different times, for example "the manager of". We shall call $\mathcal{F}_t$ the set of temporal function symbols and $\mathcal{F}_\infty$ the set of atemporal function symbols.

- *The distinction between temporal and atemporal relations.* Similarly, a temporal logic ought to make a semantic distinction between relations whose truth-value can be different at different times, such as "agent a_1 sends an offer to a_2 to sell g" and those whose truth-value is independent of time such as "a contract is a legal document" and "an offer is properly formalized". Notice that the *time relations* mentioned above are in fact atemporal relations. We shall call $\mathcal{R}_t$ the set of temporal function symbols and $\mathcal{R}_\infty$ the set of atemporal predicate symbols.

- *The distinction between temporal occurrences and temporal types of occurrences.* By a temporal occurrence (namely **temporal token**) we mean a particular temporal relation that is true at a specific time (e.g. "at time t agent a_1 sends an offer to a_2 to sell g") as opposed to a **temporal type** that denotes the set of all the occurrences of a temporal relation (e.g. the set of all specific sending events of type "agent a_1 sends an offer to a_2 to sell g").

- *The specification of time and temporal incidence theories.* As we explained above, the time and temporal incidence theories are fairly independent of the temporal qualification method but our temporal qualification method ought to provide the flexibility and expressiveness needed to specify the axioms in one's time and temporal incidence theories.

- *The specification of nested temporal relations.* A "nested" temporal relation relates objects or other relations that in turn are temporal. For example, "an agent is committed for a period to send a confirmation of a certain offer". The committment, the send action and the offer are all temporal relations.

- *The specification of relations between temporal relations or their occurrences.* The paradigmatic example of this is the causal relation between two temporal relations where the first causes the latter to hold. Other examples are incompatibility between temporal relations and correlations between temporal relations.

Although in this chapter we focus on temporal qualification in AI, temporal qualification is an issue in any formal temporal representation. In this section we give a brief overview of temporal qualification in different areas, ending with temporal qualification in AI where we introduce the approaches that will be discussed in detail in the following sections.

5.1.3 Temporal Qualification in Logic

Classical Logics. Classical logics have proven useful for reasoning about domains that are atemporal (such as mathematics) or in domains where time is not a relevant feature and can be abstracted away (e.g. a diagnostic system in a domain where the times of the relevant symptoms do not affect the result of the diagnosis). However, in many domains time cannot be disregarded if we want our logical system to be correct and complete. Logicians have studied different theories to model time and designed various temporal logics. In such logics, statements are no longer timelessly true or false but are true or false at a certain time. Temporality may be inherent in any component of the formula: functions, predicates or logical connectives. Moreover, as soon as we have a time domain, it is natural to *quantify* over time individuals.

A simple approach to formulating a temporal logic is as a particular first-order logic (FOL) with a time theory. Temporal functions and predicates are supplemented with an additional argument representing the time at which they are evaluated and time is characterized by a set of first-order axioms. Standard FOL syntax and semantics are preserved and, therefore, standard FOL proof theory is also valid. However, time axioms complicate matters. On the one hand, as discussed above, the completeness of the theorem prover depends on the existence of a complete first-order axiomatization for the intended time structures. On the other hand, the time axioms may easily lead to an explosion of the search space to be explored by the theorem prover.

It is convenient to move to a **many-sorted logic** [Cohn, 1987; Walther, 1987; Manzano, 1993; Cimatti *et al.*, 1998a] since it naturally allows one to distinguish between time and non-time individuals. Many-sorted logics do not extend FOL's expressive power (it is well-known that a many-sorted first-order logic can be translated to standard FOL) but it provides several advantages. The notation is more efficient as formulas are more readable, more "elegant" and some $\rightarrow$ can be dropped yielding more compact formulas. Semantics also can be regarded as a simple extension of FOL. Many-sorted logic therefore preserves the most interesting logical properties of FOL while it provides some potential for making reasoning more efficient. A formula parser can perform "sort checking" and some of the reasoning involving the sortal axioms can be moved into the unification algorithm. Although this leads to a more expensive unification step, this is typically more than off-set by the reduction in the search space that can be achieved through the elimination of the sortal axioms from the theory.

Modal Logics. An alternative way to incorporate time is by complicating the model theory, along the lines of modal logic. Using the common Kripke-style possible world semantics for modal logics, each *possible world* represents a different time while the *accessibility relationship* becomes a temporal ordering relationship between possible worlds. Different modal temporal logics are obtained by (i) imposing different properties on the accessibility relationship, and (ii) choosing different domain languages (e.g. propositional, first-order, ...). In order to provide an efficient notation, modal varieties of temporal logic use a number of temporal modal operators, operators that are applied to propositions in the domain logic and change the time with respect to which the proposition is to be interpreted. Traditionally, four primitive *modal temporal operators* are defined: F (at some future time), P (at some past time), G (at any future time) and H (at any past time). Hence $F\varphi$ denote that the formula φ is true at some future time. Other common temporal modalities are p UNTIL q (p is true until q is true), p SINCE q (p has been true since q has been true) or AT(t) p (p is true at time t).

5.1.4 Temporal Qualification in Databases

From a purely logical point of view, classical database applications [Ahn, 1986; Tansel *et al.*, 1993; Chomicki, 1994] have followed the first approach outlined in the previous section. In addition to the original relations and a data domain for the values of the attributes, the temporal database includes a temporal domain. Typically, temporal databases use an instant-based approach to time. Some kind of mathematical structure is imposed on instants: usually one that is isomorphic to the natural numbers. A temporal database can be abstractly defined in a number of different ways [Chomicki, 1994].

The Model-theoretic View. A database is abstractly viewed as a two-sorted first-order language. Each relation P of arity n gives rise to a predicate R with arity $n+1$, where the additional argument is a time argument. Its intended meaning is as follows:

$$(a_1, \ldots, a_n, t) \in R \text{ if and only if } P(a_1, \ldots, a_n) \text{ holds at time } t$$

All a_i are constant symbols denoting elements in a data domain. The set of constant symbols is possibly extended with some symbols denoting elements in the temporal domain. The theory may also add some time function and relation symbols, such as a function symbol $t{+}1$ to denote the time immediately following t or the relation $<$ to denote temporal ordering.

Some databases require multiple temporal dimensions. The usual case is that a single temporal domain is assumed. The relational predicates are then given two temporal arguments to indicate that the relation holds between two points in time (interval timestamps), or a number of time arguments used to model multiple kinds of time. For example, in the so-called *bi-temporal databases*, one set of temporal arguments refers to the *valid time* (the time when the relation is true in the real world) and another to the *transaction time* (the time when the relation was recorded in the database) [Snodgrass and Ahn, 1986]. The different interpretations of multiple temporal attributes databases are captured by *integrity constraints*. For example, a constraint may state that the beginning of an interval always precedes its end or that transaction time is not before valid time.

The Timestamp View. Moving to concrete databases (database that are to be implemented and therefore must allow for a finite representation), the most useful view is the timestamp view. In this view, each tuple is supplemented with a timestamp formula possibly representing an infinite set of times. A timestamp formula is a first-order formula with one free variable in the language of the temporal domain, e.g. $0 < t < 3 \vee 10 < t$. Different temporal databases result from different decisions about what subsets can be defined by timestamp formulas. An interesting temporal domain is the Presburger arithmetic as it allows one to describe periodic sets and therefore has obvious application in calendars and repeating events.

It is not clear whether timestamps could be defined in a language richer than the first-order theory of the time domain [Chomicki, 1994]. However, there are some approaches that extend the timestamp view by associating timestamps not to tuples but to attribute values [Tansel, 1993]. Such approaches increase data expressiveness and temporal flexibility but pay for this through increased query complexity, and hence decreased efficiency.

Temporal Query Languages. While the temporal arguments approach has been predominant in temporal databases a wide variety of languages have been explored for querying them. These range from logic programs with a single instantaneous temporal argument to temporal logics with modal operators such as SINCE, UNTIL, etc. Readers interested in temporal query languages are referred to the relevant chapter on this subject in this volume.

Temporal Qualification in Computer Systems

Computer systems can be regarded as a sequence of states. Each state is characterized by a set of propositions stating what is true at that time. Interesting reasoning tasks such as system specification, verification and synthesis can be stated in terms of logical properties that must hold at some times/states in the future when the system starts at a certain initial state.

In this context, it is appropriate to model time as an ordered, discrete sequence of time points and the dominant temporal qualification approach is modal logics. The reasons are that temporal modal operators allow one to easily express relative temporal references (e.g.,"the value of variable a is x until this assignment statement is executed"). Modal operators also provide a very efficient notation for various levels of nested temporal references (e.g. "p will have been true until then"). Also, the semantics fits the discrete time model very well. Since modal temporal logic is discussed at length in other chapters in this volume, we will not expand on this discussion here and merely refer the reader to these other chapters.

5.1.5 Temporal Qualification in AI

It has been recognized that AI problems such as natural language understanding, commonsense reasoning, planning, autonomous agents, etc. make greater demands on the expressive power of temporal logics than many other areas in computer science. For example, the temporal reasoning that autonomous agents have to undertake typically requires both relative and absolute temporal references. Autonomous agents also often require reasoning about different possible futures and, if they are to engage in abductive reasoning, they may have to consider different possible pasts in order to determine which past is the best explanation for the current state of affairs.

All techniques that have been employed in temporal databases and/or computer science have also been applied in AI:

- The method of *temporal arguments* has been an appealing method to many AI researchers because of its simplicity, the ability to use standard FOL theorem proving techniques, and the fact that its expressiveness is not as limited as has commonly been claimed [Bacchus *et al.*, 1991] if we allow temporal arguments in functions as well as in predicates.

- *Temporal Modal logics* have been appealing to those interested in formalizing natural language (the so-called *tense logics*) and formal knowledge representation.

However, it is a third family of techniques that attracted much of the attention from AI researchers, specially during the 80s and 90s, namely the *reified approach*. In the reified approach, one "reifies" temporal propositions and introduces names for them. One then uses temporal incidence predicates to express that the named proposition is true at a certain time, or over a certain interval. Classical examples of this approach are the *situation calculus* [McCarthy and Hayes, 1969; Reiter, 2001; Shanahan, 1987], McDermott's logic for plans [McDermott, 1982], Allen's interval logic [Allen, 1984], *event calculus* [Kowalski and Sergot, 1986; Shanahan, 1987], the *time map manager* [Dean and McDermott, 1987], Shoham's logic for time and change [Shoham, 1987] Reichgelt's temporal reified logic [Reichgelt, 1989] and token reified logics [Vila and Reichgelt, 1996].

The attraction of the reified approach is to a large extent due to the fact that the inclusion of names for such entities as actions, events, properties and states in the formalism allows one to predicate and quantify over such entities, something that is not allowed in either the method of temporal arguments or in temporal modal logic. This expressive power is important in many AI applications. Even our seemingly simple example includes examples of propositions that require quantification. The proposition "An offer remains valid until it either expires or is withdraw" is most naturally regarded as involving a quantification over expiration and withdrawal events. Other examples of propositions that are best regarded as involving quantification over events and/or states include propositions such as "whenever company X is in need of cleaning services, it issues a tender document", or "State-funded agencies can only issue contracts after an open and transparent tendering process".

Although reified logics have proven very popular, they have come under attack from different angles. First, temporal reified systems have often been presented without a *precise formal semantics*. While temporal reified logics in general remain first-order, the introduction of names for events and states, and some meta-predicates to assert their temporal occurrence, means that one cannot simplistically rely on the standard semantics for first-order logic to provide a rich enough semantics for a temporal reified logic. In some cases, like Shoham's reified logic, the apparent increased expressive power is not superior to that of the standard, easy-to-define method of temporal arguments [Bacchus *et al.*, 1991]. Second, in the cases in which the expressiveness advantage is clear, the price to pay is a logic that may end being far too complex. Third, reified temporal logics also received criticisms from the ontological point view, Galton [Galton, 1991], for example, considers them *"philosophically suspect and technically unnecessary"*, as they seem to advocate the introduction of *temporal types* in the ontology. One way to escape from this criticism is to move to an ontology of temporal propositions based on *temporal tokens*. A temporal token is not to be interpreted as a type of temporal propositions but as a particular temporal instance of a temporal proposition. Such ontology has been used as the basis for some alternative temporal qualification methods such as *temporal token arguments* or *temporal token reification*.

5.1.6 Outline

In the following sections we describe in detail the most relevant methods of temporal qualification in AI that we briefly introduced in the previous subsection. We look at the syntactical, semantical and ontological decisions they make. As we have seen, syntactically we distinguish between those that represent times as additional arguments and those that introduce specific temporal operators. Semantically, the main distinction is between those methods that stay within standard first-order logics and those that move to some sort of non-standard semantics, either defined from scratch or by adapting some known non-classical semantics such as modal logics. Finally, from the ontological point of view, we distinguish between the methods that only give full ontological status to time from the ones that, in addition, include in the ontology denotations for temporal propositions, either as *temporal types* or as *temporal tokens*.

Each method is illustrated by formalizing our trading example. The reader should recall that we assume we are given the following:

- **A model of time.** The *time structure* composed of the three time subdomains and a number of functions and relations (see Section 5.1.1)
- **Temporal Entities and Temporal Incidence Theory.** We have two temporal entities $\mathcal{E}_{events}$ and $\mathcal{E}_{fluents}$ (see Section 5.1.1).

We analyze the advantages and shortcomings of each method according to a set of representational, computational and engineering criteria. Among the representation criteria, we shall first look at the **expressiveness** of the language. In particular, it is important for our temporal qualification method to be able to represent the various types of propositions and axioms indicated in previous sections. The comparison will be informal and illustrated by our example. Second, we shall look at the **notational efficiency**. For a host of reasons, it is important that one is able to formalize knowledge into formulas that are compact, readable and elegant. Third, it is desirable to have an **ontology** that is clean and not unnecessarily complex. One wants to make sure that one avoids undesirable entities in one's ontology. For example, an ontology that requires one to postulate the existence of both types and tokens is suspect. On the other hand, one also wants to make sure that the entities that one postulates in one's ontology are rich enough to enable one to express whatever temporal knowledge one wants to express. A second type of criteria are **theorem proving** criteria such as soundness and completeness of the proof theory, efficiency of any theorem provers, as well as the possibility of using implementation technique to improve the efficiency of the theorem prover. Finally, we also bear in mind what one might call "engineering criteria", such as **modularity** of the method. Often temporal reasoning is but one aspect of the reasoning that the system is expected to undertake. For example, an autonomous agent needs to be able to reason not only about time but also about the intentions of other agents that it is likely to have to deal with. It would therefore be advantageous if the method of temporal qualification allows one to extend the reasoning system to include reasoning about other modalities as well.

5.2 Temporal Modal Logic

One possible approach to temporal qualification in AI is the adoption of modal temporal logic (*MTL*). We already briefly discussed modal temporal logic in Section 5.1.3. Moreover, the chapter in this handbook by Barringer and Gabbay is devoted to modal varieties of temporal logic, and our discussion of this approach is therefore extremely condensed.

5.2.1 Definition

Temporal modal logics are a special case of modal logic. Starting with a normal first order logic, one adds a number of modal operators, sentential operators which, in the case of temporal modal logic, change the time at which the proposition in its scope is claimed to be true. In other words, the problem of temporal qualification is dealt with by putting a modal operator in front of a non-modal proposition. For example, one may introduce a modal operator P ("was true in the Past"). When applied to a formula ϕ, the modal operator would change the claim that ϕ is true at this moment in time to one which states that ϕ was true some time in the past. Thus, the statement "SmallCo sent offer o1 to BigCo some time in the past" would be represented as $P\ send(sco, o1, bco)$.

Modal temporal logic, as traditionally defined by philosophical logicians, is not particularly expressive. In its simplest form, modal temporal logic only allows existential and universal quantification over the past and the future. In other words, in its simplest form, modal temporal logic contains only four modal operators, namely P ("was true in the past"), H ("has always been true"), F ("will be true sometimes in the future") and G ("is always going to be true"). Clearly, this is insufficient for Artificial Intelligence, or indeed Computer Science. For example, none of the propositions in our example could be expressed in such an expressive poor formalism. It is for this reason that a number of authors (e.g., Fischer, 1991; Reichgelt, 1989) have introduced a number of additional modal operators, such as UNTIL , SINCE and a model operator scheme AT, which takes a name for a temporal unit as argument and returns a modal operator. Alternatively, one can, as Barringer and Gabbay do in an earlier chapter in this handbook, introduce a unary predicate $p()$ for each proposition p in the original -propositional- language and stipulate that $p(t)$ holds if p is true at time point t. Thus, $p(t)$ is essentially a different notation for AT$(t)p$. One advantage of the AT operator is that it is easier to see how it can be used in a full first-order logic.

Modal temporal logic inherits its model theory from generic modal logic. The standard model theory for such logics relies on the notion of a possible world, as introduced in this context by Kripke (1963). In Kripke semantics, primitive expressions, such as constants and predicates, are evaluated with respect to a possible world. Non-modal propositions can then be assigned truth values with respect to possible worlds using the standard way of doing this in first-order logic (e.g., $p \vee q$ is true in a possible world w if either p is true in w or q is true in w or both are). The semantics for modal propositions is defined with the help of an accessibility relation between possible worlds. In modal temporal logic, an intuitive way of defining possible worlds is as points in time, and the accessibility relation between possible worlds as an ordering relation between possible worlds. We then say that for example the proposition Pp is true in a possible world w if there is a possible world w', which is temporally before w and in which p is true. With this in mind, the definition of the semantics for other modal operators is relatively natural.

The only complication to this picture is caused by an introduction of a possible AT operator scheme. Since this operator requires a name for a temporal unit as an argument, the language has to be complicated to include names for such temporal units, and the semantics has to be modified to ensure that such temporal units receive their proper denotation. Obviously, the most appropriate way to deal with this complication is to assign possible worlds as the designation of names for temporal units, and to include an additional clause in the semantics that states that the proposition AT$(t)p$ is true if p is true in the possible world denoted by t.

5.2.2 Analysis

We defined a number of representational desiderata on any temporal logic. One of the criteria is the **notational efficiency** (conciseness, naturalness, readability, elegance, ...). Compared to other temporal formalisms discussed in this chapter, modal temporal logic scores well on this criterion since the temporal operators produce concise and natural temporal expressions. Another issue is the **modularity** with respect to other knowledge modalities such as knowledge and belief operators. It is straightforward to combine the syntax and semantics of a modal temporal logic with a modal logic to represent, say, knowledge. Syntactically, such a change merely involves adding a knowledge modal operator; semantically, it involves adding an accessibility relation for this new modality. The model theory now contains two accessibility operators, one used for temporal modalities, the other for epistemic modalities.

As far as cleanness of the **ontology** is concerned, the main concern is the notion of a possible world. There is a significant amount of philosophical literature on whether possible worlds are ontologically acceptable or suspect. Without wanting to delve into this literature, it seems to us that a possible world can simply be regarded as a model for a non-modal first order language, and that this makes the notion ontologically unproblematic. There are of course additional arguments about the identity of individuals across possible worlds, but it again seems to us that this problem can be solved relatively easily by insisting that the same set of individuals be used for each possible world.

Where modal temporal logic is less successful is in its ability to represent the various sentences and axioms in our example. To formalize the statement "An offer becomes effective when is received by the offered and continues to be so until it is accepted by the offered or the offer expires" we introduce several predicates. Let $E(x)$ denote "the offer x is effective", $R(x)$ denote "the offer x is received" $A(x)$ denote "the offer x is accepted" and $X(x)$ denote "the offer x expires". The classic since-until tense logic can be used to express the example as

$$\begin{array}{l} \forall\, x_a, y_a, x_o \\ \quad [\, E(o(x_a, y_a, x_o))\ \textrm{SINCE}\ R(y_a, o(x_a, y_a, x_o)) \wedge \\ \quad E(o(x_a, y_a, x_o))\ \textrm{UNTIL}\ (A(y_a, x_o(x_a, y_a, x_o)) \vee E(x_o(x_a, y_a, x_o)))] \end{array}$$

The problem is that modal temporal logic does not allow one to quantify over occurrences of a particular event. Thus, a proposition like "every time a company makes an offer, it is committed to that offer until it either expires or has been accepted" would be impossible to express.

Although the semantics for modal temporal logics is well understood, it has to be admitted that the implementation of **automated theorem provers** for modal temporal logic is not straightforward. One could of course try to adopt a theorem prover developed for general modal logic. However, such theorem provers in general do not allow for particularly complex accessibility relationships between possible worlds. Most merely allow accessibility relations to be serial, transitive, reflexive or some combination of these. However, such properties are clearly not enough if one were to introduce intervals as one's temporal units. In other words, using a general theorem prover as a reasoning mechanism for modal temporal logic is only likely to be successful if one uses points as one's temporal units. A more promising approach would be to develop theorem provers specifically for temporal modal logic, ,a topic of ongoing research and discussed in other chapters in this volume.

5.3 Temporal Arguments

The oldest and probably most widely used approach to temporal qualification is the method of temporal arguments (*TA*) as introduced in Section 5.1.3. The idea of the temporal arguments approach is to start with a traditional logical theory but to add additional arguments to predicates and function symbols to deal with time. In order to reflect the fact that the domain now contains both "normal individuals" and times, the theory is often formulated as an instance of a many-sorted first-order logic with equality.

5.3.1 Definition

For a given time structure $\langle \mathcal{T}_1, \ldots, \mathcal{T}_{n_t}, \mathcal{F}_{time}, \mathcal{R}_{time} \rangle$ with its FOL axiomatization and a classification of temporal entities $\{\mathcal{E}_1, \ldots, \mathcal{E}_{e_n}\}$, with each class accompanied by a temporal incidence axiomatization. We define the temporal arguments method as a many-sorted logic with the time sorts $T_1, \ldots, T_{n_t}$, one for each time set, and a number of non-time sorts $U_1, \ldots, U_n$.

Syntax. The vocabulary is composed of the following symbols:

- a set of function symbols $\mathbf{F} = \{f^{\langle D_1, \ldots, D_n \mapsto R \rangle}\}$. If $n = 0$, f denotes a single individual from sort R, otherwise f denotes a function $D_1 \times \ldots \times D_n \mapsto R$ and depending of the nature of the D_i, we distinguish between:
  - *Time functions* $\mathbf{F}_{time}$ whose domain and range are time sorts.
  - *Temporal functions* $\mathbf{F}_t$ whose range is a non-time sort and whose domain includes both time and non-time sorts.
  - *Atemporal functions* $\mathbf{F}_\infty$ whose domain and range are domain sorts.

  Time, temporal and atemporal terms are defined in the usual way.
- a set of predicates $\mathbf{P} = \{P^{\langle D_1, \ldots, D_n \rangle}\}$. If $n = 0$, P denotes a propositional atom, otherwise P denotes a relation defined over $D_1, \ldots, D_n$ and depending on whether D_i are time or a non-time sorts we distinguish between:
  - *Time predicates* $\mathbf{P}_{time}$ whose arguments are all time sorts.
  - *Temporal predicates* $\mathbf{P}_t$ whose arguments include both time and domain sorts.
  - *Atemporal predicates* $\mathbf{P}_\infty$ whose arguments do not include any time sort.
- a set of variable symbols for each sort.

We have three classes of basic formula: atomic temporal formulas, atomic atemporal formulas and temporal constraints.

We also have the standard connectives and quantifiers.

Semantics. The semantics is the standard semantics of many-sorted logics. Notice that time gets full ontological status as we have one or more time sorts, but that temporal entities and temporal formulas receive no special treatment.

5.3.2 Formalizing the Example

Having assumed the models of time and temporal incidence indicated in 5.1, we define the following **sorts**: T_{point} for time points, T_{int} for time intervals, and T_{span} for time spans or durations, A for agents, O for legal objects, G for trading goods, S for legal status and $\$$ for money. Our **vocabulary** includes the following symbols:

- a set of constants for each sort: day constants = $\{1/8/04, \mathsf{now}, \ldots\}$, time interval constants = $\{3/04, 2004, \ldots\}$, time span constants = $\{3d, 2w, 1y, \ldots\}$, the constant now, agent constants = $\{John, jane, bco, sco, \ldots\}$, legal object constants = $\{o_1, o_2, \ldots\}$, etc.

- the following sets of function symbols:
  - $\mathbf{F}_{time} = \{\mathtt{Next}^{\langle T_{\text{point}} \mapsto T_{\text{point}} \rangle}, +_T^{\langle T_{\text{point}}, T_{\text{span}} \mapsto T_{\text{point}} \rangle}, -_T^{\langle T_{\text{point}}, T_{\text{point}} \mapsto T_{\text{span}} \rangle},$
    $\mathtt{begin}^{\langle T_{\text{int}} \mapsto T_{\text{point}} \rangle}, \mathtt{end}^{\langle T_{\text{int}} \mapsto T_{\text{point}} \rangle},$
    $\mathtt{duration}^{\langle T_{\text{int}} \mapsto T_{\text{span}} \rangle}, \mathtt{interval}^{\langle T_{\text{point}}, T_{\text{point}} \mapsto T_{\text{int}} \rangle}, \ldots\}$
  - $\mathbf{F}_t = \{\mathit{manager}^{\langle T_{\text{int}}, A \mapsto A \rangle}\}$
  - $\mathbf{F}_\infty = \{\mathit{sale}^{\langle G, P \mapsto O \rangle}, \mathit{offer}^{\langle A, A, O, T_{\text{span}} \mapsto O \rangle}\}$
- the following sets of predicates:
  - $\mathbf{P}_{time} = \{\leq^{\langle T_{\text{point}}, T_{\text{point}} \rangle}, =^{\langle T_{\text{point}}, T_{\text{point}} \rangle}, \mathtt{Meets}, overlaps, \ldots^{T_{\text{int}} \times T_{\text{int}}}, \ldots\}$
  - $\mathbf{P}_t = \mathbf{P}_{event} \cup \mathbf{P}_{fluent}$
    * $\mathbf{P}_{event} = \{\mathit{send}^{\langle T_{\text{point}}, A, A, O \rangle}, \mathit{Receive}^{\langle T_{\text{point}}, A, O \rangle}, \mathit{Accept}^{\langle T_{\text{point}}, A, O \rangle}, \mathit{Expire}^{\langle T_{\text{point}}, O \rangle}\}$
    * $\mathbf{P}_{fluent} = \{\mathit{effective}^{\langle T_{\text{point}}, T_{\text{point}}, O \rangle}, \mathit{accepted}^{\langle T_{\text{point}}, T_{\text{point}}, O \rangle}, \mathit{Expired}^{\langle T_{\text{point}}, T_{\text{point}}, O \rangle}\}$
  - $\mathbf{P}_\infty = \{\mathit{Correct\_form}^{\langle O \rangle}, \leq_\$^{\langle P, P \rangle}$ (that denotes the $\leq$ relation between prices)$\}$
- and a set of variable symbols for each sort.

The statements in the example can be formalized as follows:

1. "On 1/4/04 SmallCo sent an offer to BigCo for selling goods g for price p with a 2 weeks expiration interval."
   $\mathit{send}(1/4/04, \mathit{sco}, \mathit{bco}, \mathit{offer}(\mathit{sco}, \mathit{bco}, \mathit{sale}(g, p), 2w))$

2. "BigCo received the offer three days later and it has been effective since then."
   $\mathit{Receive}(1/4/04 + 3d, \mathit{bco}, \mathit{offer}(\mathit{sco}, \mathit{bco}, \mathit{sale}(g, p), 2w)) \wedge$
   $\mathit{effective}(1/4/04 + 3d, \mathtt{now}, \mathit{offer}(\mathit{sco}, \mathit{bco}, \mathit{sale}(g, p), 2w))$

3. "A properly formalized offer becomes effective when it is received by the offered ..."
   $\forall\, t_1 : T_{\text{point}}, x_a, y_a : A, x_o : O, ts : T_{\text{span}},$
   $[\, \mathit{Correct\_form}(\mathit{offer}(x_a, y_a, x_o, ts)) \wedge \mathit{Receive}(t_1, y_a, \mathit{offer}(x_a, y_a, x_o, ts) \rightarrow$
   $\exists t_2 : T_{\text{point}} \,[\, \mathit{effective}(t_1, t_2, \mathit{offer}(x_a, y_a, x_o, ts) \wedge t_1 \leq t_2 \,]$
   $]$

4. "...(an effective offer) continues to be so until it is accepted by the offered or the offer expires (as indicated by its expiration interval)."
   $\forall\, t_1, t_2 : T_{\text{point}}, x_a, y_a : A, x_o : O, ts : T_{\text{span}}$
   $[\, \mathit{effective}(t_1, t_2, \mathit{offer}(x_a, y_a, x_o, ts)) \wedge t_1 \leq t_2 \rightarrow$
   $\exists t_3 : T_{\text{point}} \,[\mathit{Accept}(t_3, y_a, \mathit{offer}(x_a, y_a, x_o, ts)) \wedge t_1 < t_3 \leq t_1 + ts] \vee$
   $(t_2 = t_1 + ts \wedge \mathit{Expire}(t2, \mathit{offer}(x_a, y_a, x_o, ts)))$
   $]$

5. "Anybody who makes an offer is committed to the offer as long as the offer is effective."
   $\forall\, t_1, t_2 : T_{\text{point}}, x_a : A$
   $[\, \mathit{effective}(t_1, t_2, \mathit{offer}(x_a, \_, \_, \_)) \rightarrow \mathit{Committed}(t_1, t_2, x_a, \mathit{offer}(x_a, \_, \_, \_)) \,]$

6. "Anybody who receives an offer is obliged to send a confirmation to the offerer within two days."
$\forall\, t : T_{\text{point}}, x_a, y_a : A, x_o : O$
$[\, \textit{Receive}(t, y_a, x_a, x_o) \rightarrow \textit{Obliged}(t, t + 2d, y_a, ???) \,]$

The "???" in the last formula indicates that it is not clear how to express that y_a is obliged to "send a confirmation of x_o to x_a" since in standard FOL we cannot predicate or quantify over propositions*. In addition to this example, there are few further general statements whose formalization is interesting to consider:

1. Time axioms: "The ordering between instants is transitive":
$\forall\, t_1, t_2, t_3 : T_{\text{point}}\, [\, t_1 \leq t_2 \wedge t_2 \leq t_3 \rightarrow t_1 \leq t_3 \,]$

2. Temporal Incidence axioms such as "Fluents hold homogeneously":
$\forall\, t_1, t_2, t_3, t_4 : T_{\text{point}}, x_1 : S_1, \ldots, x_n : S_n,$
$[\, P(t_1, t_2, x_1, \ldots, x_n) \wedge t_1 \leq t_3 \leq t_4 \leq t_2 \wedge t_1 \neq t_4 \rightarrow P(t_3, t_4, x_1, \ldots, x_n) \,]$
This an "axiom schema" that is a shorthand for a potentially large set of axioms, one for each fluent predicate P in the language.

The previous examples are instances of relations holding between temporal entities, which can be important in some applications. In common-sense reasoning and planning, for instance, it is important to specify the CAUSE relationship:

> "Whenever an offer is effective it *causes* the agent who made the offer to be committed to it as long as the offer is effective."

Again, it is not clear how to express this piece of knowledge in the method of temporal arguments since it requires the predicate **causes** to take as argument the proposition $\textit{effective}(t_1, t_2, \textit{offer}(x_a, y_a, x_o, ts))$ which is beyond standard many-sorted FOL. A similar problem arises when we attempt to formalize like the following properties:

- "Whenever a cause occurs its effects hold."
- "Causes precede their effects."

5.3.3 Theorem Proving

Defining a temporal logic as a standard many-sorted logic has the advantage that we can use the various reasoning systems available for many-sorted logics [Cohn, 1987; Walther, 1987; Manzano, 1993; Cimatti *et al.*, 1998b]. For a desired time model, it may be impossible to define a set of axioms that completely captures that model. For instance, we have taken the "set of integers" as our duration subdomain. But it is well-known that there is no complete axiomatization of the integers in first-order logic if the language includes addition. Therefore, it is important to choose a temporal structure that can be characterized fully in first-order logic, such as *"unbounded linear orders"*, *"totally ordered fields"* or some of the theories discussed in chapter "Theories of Time and Temporal Incidence".

Having a complete axiomatics and therefore a complete proof theory, though, is merely the beginning of the story. We must bear in mind that, while many-sorted logics often allow

*The reader might come up with the idea of turning temporal predicates into terms in order to be able to take them as proper predicate arguments. This is the idea of temporal reified logics that we discuss below.

one to delete sortal axioms, such as "All offers are legal documents", the inclusion of a number of time sorts and predicate symbols with a specific meaning (as determined by the properties of the model of time adopted) requires one to add a potentially large number of axioms that capture the nature of the temporal incidence theory. These axioms can be a heavy load for our theorem prover as they often lead to a significant increase in the size of the search space. This problem may lead to the unavoidable effort in developing a specialized temporal theorem prover.

5.3.4 Analysis

The method of temporal arguments has a number of advantages over other approaches to temporal qualification. First, the **ontology** that one is committed to is relatively straightforward. In addition to "normal" objects, one merely has to add time objects to one's ontology. Compared to the ontologies that underlie the other approaches to temporal quantification, the ontology is both parsimonious and clean. Moreover, again in contrast with some of the approaches discussed in this chapter, the system does not make any ontological commitments itself, and one is therefore completely free to make the ontology as parsimonious as the application allows.

Second, despite it seeming simplicity, the **expressive power** of languages embodying the temporal arguments approach exceeds that of many other approaches to temporal quantification. The inclusion of additional temporal arguments in predicate and function symbols allows one both to express information about individuals and their properties at specific times and to quantify over times. Moreover, it is straightforward to include purely temporal axioms explicitly in one's theories. However, this is not to say that the method of temporal arguments gives one all the desired expressive power. For example, as we indicated in the previous section, since it stays within the expressive limitations of first-order logic, it is not possible to express temporal incidence properties for all temporal entities in class (fluents, events and so on) or any other property or relation about temporal entities such as "event e at time t causes fluent f to be true at time t'".

Third, the **notation** is perhaps not as efficient as some of the alternatives, specifically modal logic. Many of the modal temporal operators are a notational shortcut for existential or universal quantification. For example, the modal operator F provides an existential quantification over future times. Since no such notational shortcuts exist in systems based on the method of temporal arguments, the expression of sentences becomes more tedious in such systems. This is true in particular of sentences that require embedded temporal quantification, such as "The contract will have been signed by then".

Fourth, as we already indicated in the previous section, the fact that the method of temporal arguments is based on a standard first-order logic means that one can use the tried and tested **theorem proving** methods for such systems, which is not the case of methods based on a temporal logic with a non-standard temporal semantics. Moreover, setting up the system as an instance of a multi-sorted logic allows one to take advantage of the more efficient theorem provers developed for such logic. However, it is important to mention that the fact that one is forced to include explicit axioms describing temporal structures in one's theories has detrimental effects on the performance of the actual theorem provers. Many of the additional axioms lead to an combinatorial explosion of the search space and therefore significantly increase the time required to find a proof. For example, some axioms, such as for every point in time, there is a later point in time, are recursive and, unless carefully controlled, lead to an infinite search space.

Finally, since the arguments that are added to the predicate and function symbols denote time, the method of temporal arguments does not easily lend itself to the **modular** inclusion of other modalities, such as epistemic or deontic modalities.

The methods that we discuss below have been developed to overcome some of the shortcomings associated with the method of temporal arguments. One way of increasing the expressive power of the formalism without moving to a higher-order logic is through the addition of some vocabulary and a complication in the ontology. The *temporal token arguments* is one such approach.

5.4 Temporal Token Arguments

The temporal token argument method (*TTA*) was introduced in early AI temporal databases such as the *Event Calculus* [Kowalski and Sergot, 1986] and Dean's *Time Map Manager* [Dean and McDermott, 1987] and later presented in [Galton, 1991] in deeper detail. It is based on the simple idea, common in the database community, of introducing a key to identify every tuple in a relation. Here, a tuple of a temporal relation represents an instance of that relation holding at a particular time or time span. Therefore, we introduce a key that identifies a temporal instance of the relation, namely a *temporal token*, which shall receive full ontological status.

5.4.1 Definition

Given a time structure $\langle \mathcal{T}_1, \ldots, \mathcal{T}_{n_t}, \mathcal{F}_T, \mathcal{R}_T \rangle$ and a set of *temporal entities* $\{\mathcal{E}_1, \ldots, \mathcal{E}_{n_e}\}$, we define a standard many-sorted first order language with the following *sorts*: one time sort $T_1, \ldots, T_{n_t}$ for each set of time objects, a number of non-time sorts $U_1, \ldots, U_n$ and one token sort $E_1, \ldots, E_{n_e}$ whose union is called $tokens$ for each temporal entity.

Syntax. The syntax is very similar to the temporal arguments method but instead of having extra time arguments in our temporal predicates, the extra argument is a single *temporal token* term. Token terms also appear as arguments to (i) time functions, and (ii) the temporal incidence predicates introduced below. The vocabulary is extended accordingly:

- *Function symbols*: In addition to the function symbol sets introduced in our discussion of the method of temporal arguments, we have a set of **time-token** functions that map tokens to their relevant times.
- *Predicate symbols*: *Temporal predicates* no longer have any time argument, but instead have a single token argument from the sort of the temporal entity denoted by the temporal predicate. Thus, $\textit{effective}(t_1, t_2, \textit{offer}(\_))$ becomes $\textit{effective}(tt_1, \textit{offer}(\_))$ where tt_1 is a constant symbol of the new E_{fluent} sort.

  Time predicates and *Atemporal predicates* remain the same. However, we incorporate one new **Temporal Incidence Predicate (TIP)** for each temporal entity $\mathcal{E}_i$. TIPs take as sole their argument a term of the temporal sort E_i. Given our temporal ontology we have 2 TIPs: $\textsc{Holds}(tt_1)$ expresses that the fluent token tt_1 holds throughout the time interval denoted by the term $\texttt{interval}(tt_1)$ and $\textsc{Occurs}(\textit{event token})$ for event occurrences.

Semantics. The standard many-sorted first-order semantics is preserved with both time domains, non-time domains and temporal token domains with the usual interpretation of function and predicate symbols. Time and temporal incidence theories are incorporated as a set of first order axioms.

Token Incidence Theory. The specific semantics of temporal tokens may yield some additional temporal incidence axioms. An example is the so-called "maximality of fluent tokens". For efficiency reasons, one is interested in adopting the following convention:

> "A fluent token denotes a *maximal* piece of time where that fluent is true."

A consequence of this is the following property "Any two intervals associated with the same fluent are either identical or disjoint." Thus, in practice in can be interesting to define some additional incidence predicates such as $\textsc{Holds}_{at}{}^2$ and $\textsc{Holds}_{on}{}^2$ which are shorthands for

$$\textsc{Holds}_{at}(\mathit{fluent}, t) \equiv \exists f : E_{\text{fluent}}\ (fluent(f) \wedge \textsc{Holds}(f) \wedge i \in \texttt{interval}(f))$$
$$\textsc{Holds}_{on}(\mathit{fluent}, I) \equiv \exists f : E_{\text{fluent}}\ (fluent(f) \wedge \textsc{Holds}(f) \wedge I \subseteq \texttt{interval}(f))$$

respectively, where f is a variable of the *fluent token* sort E_{fluent} and $fluent(f)$ denotes the atomic proposition fluent with the extra temporal token argument f.

5.4.2 Formalizing the Example

We illustrate the approach by formalizing the example. We make the same assumptions as before and we will frequently refer to the formalization of this example in *TA* method.

In addition to the **sorts** defined in the *TA* example, we introduce sorts for tokens of each temporal entity: E_{event} for event tokens and E_{fluent} for fluent tokens. In turn, our vocabulary will include event token constants and fluent token constants. Besides the usual functions, we have the following **time-token functions**: $t_{:}E_{\text{token}} \mapsto T_{\text{point}}$, $\texttt{begin} : E_{\text{token}} \mapsto T_{\text{point}}$, $\texttt{end} : E_{\text{token}} \mapsto T_{\text{point}}$ and $\texttt{interval} : E_{\text{token}} \mapsto T_{\text{int}}$.

In addition to the time and atemporal predicates from the previous formalization, the *temporal predicates* now are as follows:

- *Events*: $\mathit{send}^{\langle E_{\text{event}}, A, A, O\rangle}$ (where the last argument denotes the event token of this particular send event), $\mathit{Receive}^{\langle E_{\text{event}}, A, A, O\rangle}$, and $\mathit{Accept}^{\langle E_{\text{event}}, A, O\rangle}$.

- *Fluents*: $\mathit{effective}^{\langle E_{\text{fluent}}, O\rangle}$ (where the first argument denotes the fluent token of a particular period where the legal object O is effective), $\mathit{accepted}^{\langle E_{\text{fluent}}, O\rangle}$ and $\mathit{Expired}^{\langle E_{\text{fluent}}, O\rangle}$.

As in the *TA* method, we have four classes of basic formula: atomic atemporal formula, atomic temporal formula, temporal constraints and temporal incidence formula.

The statements in the example can be formalized as follows:

1. "On 1/4/04, SmallCo sent an offer to BigCo for selling goods g for price p with a 2 weeks expiration interval."
   $\mathit{send}(s_1, \mathit{sco}, \mathit{bco}, \mathit{offer}(\mathit{sco}, \mathit{bco}, \mathit{sale}(g, p), 2w)) \wedge \textsc{Occurs}(s_1) \wedge t_{(}s_1, 1/4/04)$

2. "BigCo received the offer three days later and it has been effective since then."
$$\begin{aligned}&Receive(r_1, bco, offer(sco, bco, sale(g,p), 2w)) \wedge \textsc{Occurs}(r_1) \wedge \\ &t_(r_1) = 1/4/04 + 3d \wedge \\ &effective(e_1, offer(sco, bco, sale(g,p), 2w)) \wedge \textsc{Holds}(e_1) \wedge \\ &t_(r_1) = \texttt{begin}(e_1) \wedge \texttt{end}(e_1) = now\end{aligned}$$

3. "A properly formalized offer becomes effective when is received by the offered ..."
$$\begin{aligned}&\forall\, tt_1 : E_{\text{event}}, ts : T_{\text{span}}, x_a, y_a : A,\ x_o : O \\ &\quad [\ Correct\_form(offer(x_a, y_a, x_o, ts)) \wedge \\ &\quad Receive(tt_1, y_a, x_a, offer(x_a, y_a, x_o, ts)) \wedge \textsc{Occurs}(tt_1) \rightarrow \\ &\quad \exists\, tt_2 : E_{\text{fluent}} \\ &\qquad [\ effective(tt_2, offer(x_a, y_a, x_o, ts)) \wedge \textsc{Holds}(tt_2) \wedge tt_1 \texttt{ Meets } tt_2\ ] \\ &\quad]\end{aligned}$$

4. "...(an effective offer) continues to be so until it is accepted by the offered or the offer expires (as indicated by its expiration interval)."
$$\begin{aligned}&\forall\, tt_1 : E_{\text{fluent}}, x_a, y_a : A,\ x_o : O,\ ts : T_{\text{span}} \\ &\quad [\ effective(tt_1, offer(x_a, y_a, x_o, ts)) \wedge \textsc{Holds}(tt_1) \rightarrow \\ &\quad \exists tt_2 : E_{\text{event}} \\ &\qquad [Accept(tt_2, y_a, offer(x_a, y_a, x_o, ts)) \wedge \textsc{Occurs}(tt_2) \wedge \\ &\qquad \texttt{begin}(tt_1) < t_(tt_2) \leq \texttt{begin}(tt_1) + ts] \\ &\quad \vee \\ &\quad (\texttt{end}(tt_1) = \texttt{begin}(tt_1) + ts \wedge \\ &\quad \exists tt_2 : E_{\text{event}} \\ &\qquad [Expire(tt_2, offer(x_a, y_a, x_o, ts)) \wedge \textsc{Occurs}(tt_2) \wedge \\ &\qquad \texttt{end}(tt_1) = t_(tt_2)]) \\ &\quad]\end{aligned}$$

5. "Anybody who makes an offer is committed to the offer as long as the offer is effective."
$$\begin{aligned}&\forall\, tt_1 : E_{\text{fluent}}, x_a, y_a : A, x_o : O, ts : T_{\text{span}} \\ &\quad [\ effective(tt_1, offer(x_a, y_a, x_o, ts)) \wedge \textsc{Holds}(tt_1) \rightarrow \\ &\quad \exists\, tt_2 : E_{\text{fluent}} \\ &\qquad [\ Committed(tt_2, x_a, offer(x_a, y_a, x_o, ts)) \wedge \textsc{Holds}(tt_2) \wedge \\ &\qquad \texttt{interval}(tt_1) = \texttt{interval}(tt_2)\ ]\ ]\end{aligned}$$

6. "Anybody who receives an offer is obliged to send a confirmation to the offerer within two days."
$$\begin{aligned}&\forall\, tt_1 : E_{\text{event}}, x_a, y_a : A, x_o : O, ts : T_{\text{span}} \\ &\quad [\ Receive(tt_1, y_a, offer(x_a, y_a, x_o, ts)) \wedge \textsc{Occurs}(tt_1) \rightarrow \\ &\quad \exists tt_2 : E_{\text{event}} \\ &\qquad [Obliged(x_a, tt_2) \wedge send(tt_2, y_a, x_a, conf(x_o)) \wedge \\ &\qquad t_(tt_1) \leq t_(tt_2) \leq t_(tt_1) + 2d\ ]\ ]\end{aligned}$$

Observe that we express that x_a is obliged to a temporal proposition by using a temporal token of that proposition. In general, the additional flexibility of temporal tokens allows us (i) to talk about temporal occurrences that may or may not happen, and (ii) to express that an agent is obliged to that event. This is not possible in the *TA* method.

The more general statements are formalized as follows:

- Time axioms are expressed as usual:
  $\forall\, t_1, t_2, t_3 : T_{\text{point}}[\, t_1 \leq t_2 \wedge t_2 \leq t_3 \rightarrow t_1 \leq t_3 \,]$

- Temporal Incidence axioms become more compact since we can quantify over all the instances of a given entity (e.g. all fluents) independently of their particular meaning. It is no longer necessary to have an "axiom schema". For instance the "homogeneity of fluent holding" is stated by:
  $\forall\, tt : E_{\text{fluent}}, I : T_{\text{int}}\ [\, holds(tt) \wedge I \subseteq \texttt{interval}(tt) \rightarrow \text{HOLDS}_{on}(tt, I)\,]$

- "It is necessary for an offer to be properly written to be effective".
  $\forall\, tt : E_{\text{fluent}}, x_o : O\ [\mathit{effective}(tt, x_o) \wedge \text{HOLDS}(tt) \rightarrow \mathit{Correct\_form}(x_o)]$

- "Whenever an offer is effective it *causes* the agent who made the offer to be committed to it for as long as the offer is effective."
  $\forall\, tt_1 : E_{\text{fluent}}, x_a, y_a : A, x_o : O, ts : T_{\text{span}}$
  $[\, \mathit{effective}(tt_1, \mathit{offer}(x_a, y_a, x_o, ts)) \wedge \text{HOLDS}(tt_1) \rightarrow$
  $\exists tt_2 : E_{\text{fluent}}$
  $[\, \text{CAUSE}(tt_1, tt_2) \wedge \mathit{Committed}(tt_2, \mathit{offer}(x_a, y_a, x_o, ts)) \wedge \texttt{interval}(tt_1, tt_2)\,]\,]$

- "Whenever a cause occurs its effects hold."
  $\forall\, tt_1 : E_{\text{event}}, tt_2 : E_{\text{fluent}}$
  $[\text{OCCURS}(tt_1) \wedge \text{CAUSE}(tt_1, tt_2) \rightarrow \text{HOLDS}(tt_2)]$

- "Causes precede their effects."
  $\forall\, tt_1 : E_{\text{event}}, tt_2 : E_{\text{fluent}}$
  $[\, \text{CAUSE}(tt_1, tt_2) \rightarrow (\text{OCCURS}(tt_1) \rightarrow \text{HOLDS}(tt_2) \wedge t_(tt_1) \leq \texttt{begin}(tt_2)\,]$

5.4.3 Analysis

TTA has several advantages. The extra objects, i.e. the temporal tokens, introduced in the language gives the **notation** increased flexibility and helps overcome some of the expressiveness problems that we identified in the *TA* method. First, as the example shows, as temporal tokens are used as argument of other predicates they are useful to express nested temporal references. Second, different levels of time are supported by diversifying the time-token functions. For instance, we may have $\texttt{begin}_{\text{v}}(tt_1)$ to refer to *valid time* and $\texttt{begin}_{\text{t}}(tt_1)$ to refer to *transaction time*. Third, at the implementation level, a different temporal constraint network instance is maintained for each time level. Every temporal term will be mapped to a node in its corresponding constraint network.

However, the increased notation flexibility causes the notation to be more baroque and sometimes awkward (compare the formalization of our example here with the formalizations obtained by other methods). To improve notational *conciseness* we can define some syntactic sugar that allows the omission of token symbols whenever they are not strictly necessary.

Another advantage of this approach is its **modularity**. A clear separation is made between the temporal and other information as a atomic temporal formulas are linked to time through time-token functions like begin and end. However, token symbols can also be used as the link to other modalities as the deontic modalities of commitment and obligation illustrated by the example.

5.5 Temporal Reification

Temporal reification (*TR*) was motivated by the desire to extend the expressive power of the temporal arguments approach while remaining within the limits of first order logic. It is achieved by: (i) complicating the underlying ontology and (ii) representing temporal propositions as terms in order to be able to predicate and quantify over them.

In essence, in reified temporal logic, both time objects and temporal entities receive full ontological status and one introduces in the language terms referring to them. The *Temporal Incidence Predicates* are used to associate a temporal entity with its time of occurrence and allow a direct and natural axiomatization of the given temporal incidence properties, as illustrated in the example below.

Syntax. Reified temporal logics are in fact relatively straightforward to construct from a standard first order language. First, it is useful to move to a sorted logic in which we make a distinction between temporal entities, normal individuals and temporal units. Second, for each n-place function symbol in the first order language, one introduces a corresponding n-place function symbol in the reified language. Its sortal signature is that it maps n normal individuals into a normal individual. For each n-place predicate in the original language, one also introduces a n-place function symbol in the language. However, its sortal signature is different. It takes as input n normal individuals and maps them into a temporal entity.

Semantics. Interestingly, not many authors worried about providing a clear model-theoretic semantics for their formalism, either because they were not interested in doing so, or because they believed that reified temporal logic would simply inherit its semantics from first order predicate calculus. It was not until [Shoham, 1987] that the semantics of reified temporal logics became an issue. Shoham observed that reified temporal logic are very similar to formalizations of the model theory for modal temporal logic in a first order logic and proposed to formulate the semantics for reified temporal logic in these terms. It is not clear that the actual framework proposed by Shoham actually achieved this. For example, [Vila and Reichgelt, 1996] argue that Shoham's formalism is more appropriately regarded as being a hybrid between a modal temporal logic and a system in the tradition of the temporal arguments method. As a matter of fact, Shoham's is subsumed by the *TA* method [Bacchus *et al.*, 1991]. Nevertheless, Shoham's insight was the inspiration for Reichgelt [Reichgelt, 1989] who indeed formulated a reified temporal logic.

5.5.1 Formalizing the Example

We make the same assumptions and we shall be continuously referring to the formalization of this example made with the temporal arguments method in our attempt to formalize the example in reified temporal logic.

Besides the **sorts** T_{point} for time instants, T_{int} for time intervals, T_{span} for durations, A for agents, etc. we now have additional sorts, one for each temporal entity: E_{event} for events and E_{fluent} for fluents. Notice that, although we use the same names that *TTA* , there are ontological differences since here they denote temporal types whereas in *TTA* they denote temporal tokens.

Our **vocabulary** is composed of:

- For each sort, a set of constant symbols, including event constants and fluent constants.
- We have time, temporal and atemporal function symbols as in the temporal arguments approach except that the set of temporal functions (where we have functions like $\mathit{offer}^{\langle A,A,O,T \mapsto O \rangle}$) is extended with new temporal functions produced by temporal reification, one for each temporal relation (which in the temporal arguments is represented by a temporal predicate):
  - $E_{\text{event}} = \{\mathit{send}^{\langle A,A,O \mapsto E_{\text{event}} \rangle}, \mathit{Receive}^{\langle A,O \mapsto E_{\text{event}} \rangle}, \mathit{Accept}^{\langle A,O \mapsto E_{\text{event}} \rangle}, \mathit{Expire}^{\langle O \mapsto E_{\text{event}} \rangle}\}$
  - $E_{\text{fluent}} = \{\mathit{effective}^{\langle O \mapsto E_{\text{fluent}} \rangle}, \ldots\}$
- the following sets of predicates:
  - $\mathbf{P}_{time} = \leq^{\langle T,T \rangle}, =^{\langle T,T \rangle}, \ldots$
  - $\mathbf{P}_{\infty} = \leq_{\$}^{\langle P,P \rangle}$ (that denotes the $\leq$ relation between prices).
- and a set of variable symbols for each sort.

The statements in the example may be formalized as follows:

1. "On 1/4/04, SmallCo sent an offer to BigCo for selling goods g for price p with a 2 weeks expiration interval."
   $\text{OCCURS}(1/4/04, \mathit{send}(\mathit{sco}, \mathit{bco}, \mathit{offer}(\mathit{sco}, \mathit{bco}, \mathit{sale}(g,p), 2w)))$
2. "BigCo received the offer three days later and it has been effective since then."
   $\text{OCCURS}(1/4/04 + 3d, \mathit{Receive}(\mathit{bco}, \mathit{offer}(\mathit{sco}, \mathit{bco}, \mathit{sale}(g,p), 2w))) \wedge$
   $\text{HOLDS}(1/4/04 + 3d, now, \mathit{effective}(\mathit{offer}(\mathit{sco}, \mathit{bco}, \mathit{sale}(g,p), 2w)))$
3. "A properly formalized offer becomes effective when is received by the offered ..."
   $\forall t_1 : T_{\text{point}}, x_a, y_a : A,$
   $[\,\mathit{Correct\_form}(\mathit{offer}(x_a, y_a, \_, \_)) \wedge \text{OCCURS}(t_1, \mathit{Receive}(y_a, \mathit{offer}(x_a, y_a, \_, \_))) \rightarrow$
   $\exists t_2 : T_{\text{point}}\,[\,\text{HOLDS}(t_1, t_2, \mathit{effective}(\mathit{offer}(x_a, y_a, \_, \_)))]$
   $]$
4. "...(an effective offer) continues to be so until it is accepted by the offered or the offer expires (as indicated by its expiration interval)."
   $\forall t_1, t_2 : T_{\text{point}}, x_a, y_a : A, x_o : O, ts : T_{\text{span}}$
   $[\,\text{HOLDS}(t_1, t_2, \mathit{effective}(\mathit{offer}(x_a, y_a, x_o, ts))) \rightarrow$
   $\exists t_3 : T_{\text{point}}\,[t_1 < t_3 \leq t_1 + ts \wedge \text{OCCURS}(t_3, \mathit{Accept}(y_a, x_o))] \vee$
   $(t_2 = t_1 + ts \wedge \text{OCCURS}(t_2, \mathit{Expire}(offer(x_a, y_a, x_o, ts))))$
   $]$
5. "Anybody who makes an offer is committed to the offer as long as the offer is effective."
   $\forall t_1, t_2 : T_{\text{point}}, x_a : A, x_o : O$
   $[\,\text{HOLDS}(t_1, t_2, \mathit{effective}(\mathit{offer}(x_a, \_, \_, \_))) \rightarrow$
   $\text{HOLDS}(t_1, t_2, \mathit{Committed}(x_a, \mathit{offer}(x_a, \_, \_, \_)))\,]$

6. "Anybody who receives an offer is obliged to send a confirmation to the offerer within two days."
$\forall\, t : T_{\text{point}}, x_a, y_a : A, x_o : O,$
$[\textsc{Occurs}(t, \mathit{Receive}(y_a, \mathit{offer}(x_a, y_a, x_o, \_))) \rightarrow$
$\textsc{Holds}(t, t + 2d, \mathit{Obliged}(y_a, \mathit{send}(y_a, x_a, \mathit{conf}(\mathit{offer}(x_a, y_a, x_o, \_)))))]$

The last formula is legal but the resulting formalization is somewhat obscure. It expresses that the obligation holds between t and $t+2d$. However, it fails to express that the obligation is to send the confirmation between t and $t+2d$. The more general statements are formalized as follows:

- Time axioms are expressed as usual:
$\forall\, t_1, t_2, t_3 : T_{\text{point}}\; [\, t_1 \leq t_2 \wedge t_2 \leq t_3 \rightarrow t_1 \leq t_3\,]$

- Temporal incidence axioms become more compact since we can quantify over all the instances of a given entity (e.g. all fluents) independently of their particular meaning (and it is no longer necessary to have an "axiom schema"). For instance the "homogeneity of fluent holding" is stated as:
$\forall\, t_1, t_2, t_3, t_4 : T_{\text{point}}, f : E_{\text{fluent}}$
$[\, \textsc{Holds}(t_1, t_2, f) \wedge t_1 \leq t_3 \leq t_4 \leq t_2 \wedge t_1 \neq t_4 \rightarrow \textsc{Holds}(t_3, t_4, f)\,]$

- "It is necessary for an offer to be properly written to be effective".
$\forall\, t, t' : T_{\text{point}}, x_o : O\;\; [\textsc{Holds}(\mathit{effective}(t, t', x_o)) \rightarrow \mathit{Correct\_form}(x_o)]$

- "Whenever an offer is effective it *causes* the agent who made the offer to be committed to it for as long as the offer is effective."
$\forall\, t_1, t_2 : T_{\text{point}}, x_a, y_a : A, x_o : O, ts : T_{\text{span}}$
$[\, \textsc{Cause}(\mathit{effective}(t_1, t_2, \mathit{offer}(x_a, y_a, x_o, ts)),$
$\mathit{Committed}(t_1, t_2, x_a, \mathit{offer}(x_a, y_a, x_o, ts)))\,]$

- "Whenever a cause occurs its effects hold."
$\forall\, e : E_{\text{event}}, f : E_{\text{fluent}}\; [\, \textsc{Occurs}(e) \wedge \textsc{Cause}(e, f) \rightarrow \textsc{Holds}(f)\,]$

- "Causes precede their effects."
$\forall\, e : E_{\text{event}}, f : E_{\text{fluent}}$
$[\, \textsc{Cause}(e, f) \rightarrow (\textsc{Occurs}(e) \rightarrow \textsc{Holds}(f) \wedge t_(e) < \texttt{begin}(f))\,]$

5.5.2 Full Temporal Reified Logic

In the previous section we have restricted ourselves to reification of atomic propositions. However, as the following examples illustrate, it may be necessary to reify also non-atomic propositions (as first discussed in [McDermott, 1982; Allen, 1984]):

1. "The offer was sent between t_1 and t_2 but is not effective from t_1 to t_2".
$\textsc{Holds}(t_1, t_2, \mathit{sent}(o_1) \wedge \neg \mathit{effective}(o_1))$

2. "From t_1 to t_2 all offers offered by agent a_1 have been frozen."
$\textsc{Holds}(t_1, t_2, \forall x_a : A, x_o : O, ts : T_{\text{span}}\; [\mathit{frozen}(\mathit{offer}(a_1, y_a, x_o, ts))]$

3. "As of 1/may/04, when an offer is sent, the offerer will have to pay a tax within the next 3 days."
   $\text{HOLDS}(1/may/04, +\infty,$
   $\quad \forall x_a, y_a : A, x_o : O, ts : T_{\text{span}}$
   $\quad [send(x_a, y_a, offer(x_a, y_a, x_o, ts)) \rightarrow Obligation(pay(x_a, tax), t?, t?)]$

In order to deal with such examples, we need to expand our language and include a function symbol for each logical connective or quantifier. Thus, as example 1 above shows, the language has to contain a function symbol $\wedge$ which takes as input two fluents and returns another fluent. *Reichgelt's reified temporal logic* illustrates this approach. It provides a full formalization of Shoham's insight that reified temporal logic can be regarded as a formalization of modal temporal logic. Reichgelt's reified temporal logic therefore takes as its starting point modal temporal logic, and formaluates the semantics for such logics in a first-order language. The resulting system, however, becomes rather baroque as it needs to include terms to refer both to the semantic entities that are introduced in modal temporal logic, and terms to refer to the expressions in the modal temporal logic. Thus, a full reified logic would need to codify such statements as "Fp(a) is true at time t if and only if there is a time t' later than t at which the individual denoted by a is an element of the set denoted by P" and this requires the full reified logic to have expressions to refer to times ("t, t' "), expressions to refer to individuals ("the individual denoted by a") and denotations of predicates ("the set denoted by P"), as well as expressions to refer to expressions in the modal temporal logic that is used as its starting point ("the expression a"). The semantics for a full reified logic becomes correspondingly complex, as it needs to include normal individuals and points in time, as well as entities corresponding to the linguistic entities that make up the underlying modal temporal logic. Reichgelt's logic is therefore more of academic interest, rather than of any practical use. However, the system shows that one can indeed use Shoham's proposal to regard reified temporal logics as a formalization of the semantics of modal temporal logic in a complicated, sorted but classical first-order logic.

5.5.3 Advantages and Shortcomings of Temporal Reified method

As illustrated by the example, the temporal reification method provides a fairly natural and efficient notation and an expressive power clearly superior to the methods of temporal arguments as it allows one quantify over temporal relations satisfactorily.

However temporal reified approaches have been criticized on two different direction. On the one hand, because the **ontologies** they commit one to. In the example $\text{OCCURS}(1/4/04+3d, \mathit{Receive}(bco, \mathit{offer}(sco, bco, \mathit{sale}(g,p), 2w))) \wedge$ $\text{HOLDS}(1/4/04+3d, now, \mathit{effective}(\mathit{offer}(sco, bco, \mathit{sale}(g,p), 2w)))$ we observe that, in both cases, the non-time arguments to the temporal incidence predicate stand for a type of event or fluent, respectively. There are two objections against the introduction of event and state types. The first is ontological. Thus, taking his lead from [Davidson, 1967], and following a long tradition in ontology, A. Galton [Galton, 1991] argues that a logic which forces one to reify event *tokens* instead of event *types*, would be preferable on ontological grounds. Using Occam's razor, Galton argues that one should not multiply the entities in one's ontology without need, and that, unless one is a die-hard Platonist, one would prefer an ontology based on particulars rather than universals. A second argument against the introduction of types is that the resulting logic may have expressiveness shortcomings. Haugh [Haugh, 1987] talks about the "individuation and counting of the events of a particular type". One cannot, for instance, refer to the set of multiple effects originated by a single event causing them. Also, one cannot quantify over causes and the related set of the effects each produces in order to assert general constraints between them.

On the other hand, temporal reification has been criticized as an unnecessary technical complication, specially in the case that it is not defined as a standard many-sorted logic and we have to develop a new model theory and a complete proof theory. Some researchers look at the *temporal token arguments* method a the ideal alternative since it avoid both criticisms and seem to retain the expressiveness adavantages, in particular in quatifying over predicates as shown in the *TTA* section.

5.6 Temporal Token Reification

The temporal token reification approach is motivated by the attempt of achieving the expressiveness advantages of temporal reification and the ontological and technical advantages of temporal tokens shown by the temporal token arguments approach which avoids having to reify temporal types.

The primary intuition behind *Temporal Token Reification* (*TTR*) is that one reifies temporal tokens rather than temporal types. However, rather than making names for event tokens an additional argument to a predicate (like in the temporal token arguments approach), it proposes to introduce "meaningful" names for temporal tokens. This allows one to talk and quantify about "parts of a token" as well as over all tokens and thus express express general temporal properties.

5.6.1 Definition

The logical language of *TTR* is a many-sorted FOL with the same sorts as *TTA* : $T_1, \ldots, T_{n_t}$, one for each time set, a number of non-time sorts $U_1, \ldots, U_n$ and one token sort $E_1, \ldots, E_{n_e}$ for each temporal entity.

Syntax The vocabulary is defined accordingly:

- *Function symbols:* In addition to the time and atemporal function symbols of *TTA* , we have a set of additional a $m + n$-place function symbol for each n-place temporal relation, where the first m arguments are of a time sort and the last n arguments of some non-time or token sort. The output is an entity of some type E_i.

  We also have the usual *time-token function* symbols, whose input argument is of sort E_i and whose output argument is of sort T_j. For instance, `begin` denotes the starting point of a temporal token and their definition is straightforward. Thus

  $$\texttt{begin}(f(\ldots, t, t')) = t$$

  where $f(\ldots, t, t')$ is a term referring to a temporal token.

Finally, the language contains the 1-place function symbol TYPE. It takes as argument the name of a temporal token and returns a function from pairs of points in time into the set of event or state tokens respectively. Hence,

$$\textsc{Type}(f(\ldots, t, t'))$$

is basically syntactic sugar for

$$\lambda x \lambda y f(\ldots, x, y)$$

- *Predicate symbols:* As *TTA* , *TTR* makes *TIPs* 1-place. It contains one TIP each E_i with its only argument being the name for an temporal entity. For instance, the predicates HOLDS or OCCURS simply state that a fluent token indeed holds, or that an event token indeed occurs.

Semantics The semantics of the *TTR* is relatively straightforward as well and *TTR* function and predicate symbols are mapped onto the appropriate functions and relations respecting the signature of the symbol.

5.6.2 Formalizing the Example

To formalize the example, we use the same sorts and the vocabulary as in the temporal reification example with the following additions:

- $\mathbf{F}_{time} = \{\mathtt{end}^{\langle E_{\text{fluent}}, T_{\text{point}}, T_{\text{point}} \mapsto T_{\text{point}} \rangle}, \mathtt{begin}^{\langle E_{\text{fluent}}, T_{\text{point}}, T_{\text{point}} \mapsto T_{\text{point}} \rangle}\}$ where $f(\ldots, t, t')$ is a term referring to a fluent-token.
- $\mathbf{F}_t = \mathbf{F}_{event} \cup \mathbf{F}_{fluent}$
  - $\mathbf{F}_{event} = \{send^{\langle T_{\text{point}}, A, A, O \mapsto E_{\text{event}} \rangle}, Receive^{\langle T_{\text{point}}, A, O \mapsto E_{\text{event}} \rangle}, Accept^{\langle T_{\text{point}}, A, O \mapsto E_{\text{event}} \rangle}, Expire^{\langle T_{\text{point}}, O \mapsto E_{\text{event}} \rangle}\}$
  - $\mathbf{F}_{fluent} = \{effective^{\langle O, T_{\text{point}}, T_{\text{point}} \mapsto E_{\text{fluent}} \rangle}\}$
- $\mathbf{P}_t = \emptyset$
- $\mathbf{P}_\infty = \{\leq_\$^{\langle P,P \rangle}\}$ (that denotes the $\leq$ relation between prices).
- and a set of variable symbols for each sort.

The statements in the example can be formalized as follows:

1. "On 1/4/04, SmallCo sent an offer for selling goods g to BigCo for price p with a 2 weeks expiration interval."
   $\textsc{Occurs}(send(1/4/04, sco, bco, offer(sco, bco, sale(g, p), 2w)))$
2. "BigCo received the offer three days later and it has been effective since then."
   $\textsc{Occurs}(Receive(1/4/04 + 3d, bco, offer(sco, bco, sale(g, p), 2w))) \wedge$
   $\textsc{Holds}(effective(1/4/04 + 3d, \text{now}, offer(sco, bco, sale(g, p), 2w)))$

3. "A properly formalized offer becomes effective when is received by the offered..."
   $\forall\, t_1 : T_{\text{point}}, x_a, y_a : A, x_o : O, ts : T_{\text{span}}$
   $[\ \textit{Correct\_form}(\textit{offer}(x_a, y_a, x_o, ts)) \wedge$
   $\text{OCCURS}(\textit{Receive}(t_1, y_a, \textit{offer}(x_a, y_a, x_o, ts))) \rightarrow$
   $\exists t_2\ [\text{HOLDS}(\textit{effective}(t_1, t_2, \textit{offer}(x_a, y_a, x_o, ts))) \wedge t_1 \leq t_2]\ ]$

4. "...(an effective offer) continues to be so until it is accepted by the offered or the offer expires (as indicated by its expiration interval)."
   $\forall\, t_1, t_2 : T_{\text{point}}, x_a, y_a : A, x_o : O, ts : T_{\text{span}}$
   $[\ \text{HOLDS}(\textit{effective}(t_1, t_2, \textit{offer}(x_a, y_a, x_o, ts))) \wedge t_1 \leq t_2 \rightarrow$
   $\exists t_3 : T_{\text{point}}[\textit{Accept}(t_3, y_a, \textit{offer}(x_a, y_a, x_o, ts)) \wedge t_1 < t_3 \leq t_1 + ts]\ \vee$
   $(t_2 = t_1 + ts \wedge \text{OCCURS}(\textit{Expire}(t2, \textit{offer}(x_a, y_a, x_o, ts))))\ ]$

5. "Anybody who makes an offer is committed to the offer as long as the offer is effective."
   $\forall\, t_1, t_2 : T_{\text{point}}, x_a : A$
   $[\text{HOLDS}(\textit{effective}(t_1, t_2, \textit{offer}(x_a, \_, \_, \_))) \rightarrow$
   $\text{OCCURS}(\textit{Committed}(t_1, t_2, x_a, \textit{offer}(x_a, \_, \_, \_)))]$

6. "Anybody who receives an offer is obliged to send a confirmation to the offerer within two days."
   $\forall\, t_1 : T_{\text{point}}, x_a : A, x_o : O,$
   $[\text{OCCURS}(\textit{Receive}(t_1, y_a, \textit{offer}(x_a, y_a, x_o, \_))) \rightarrow$
   $\text{HOLDS}(\textit{Obliged}(t, t + 2d, y_a, \textit{send}(y_a, \textit{conf}(\textit{offer}(x_a, y_a, x_o, \_)))))$
   $]$

The additional statements are formalized as follows:

- Time axioms: "The ordering between instants is transitive":
  $\forall\, t_1, t_2, t_3 : T_{\text{point}}\ [\ t_1 \leq t_2 \wedge t_2 \leq t_3 \rightarrow t_1 \leq t_3\ ]$

- Temporal Incidence axioms such as "Fluents hold homogeneously":
  $\forall f : E_{\text{fluent}}, t_1, t_2, t_3, t_4 : T_{\text{point}}$
  $[\ \text{HOLDS}(\text{TYPE}(f)(< t_1, t_2 >)) \wedge t_1 \leq t_3 \leq t_4 \leq t_2 \wedge t_1 \neq t_4 \rightarrow$
  $\text{HOLDS}(\text{TYPE}(f)(< t_3, t_4 >))\ ]$

- "It is necessary for an offer to be properly written to be effective".
  $\forall\, t_1, t_2 : T_{\text{point}}, x_o : O$
  $[\text{HOLDS}(\textit{effective}(t_1, t_2, x_o)) \rightarrow \textit{Correct\_form}(x_o)]$

- "Whenever an offer is effective it *causes* the agent who made the offer to be committed to it for as long as the offer is effective."
  $\forall\, t_1, t_2 : T_{\text{point}}, x_a, y_a : A, x_o : O, ts : T_{\text{span}}$
  $[\text{CAUSE}(\textit{effective}(t_1, t_2, \textit{offer}(x_a, y_a, x_o, ts)),$
  $\textit{Committed}(t_1, t_2, x_a, \textit{offer}(x_a, y_a, x_o, ts)))]$

- "Whenever a cause occurs its effects hold."
  $\forall\, e : E_{\text{event}}, f : E_{\text{fluent}}$
  $[\ \text{OCCURS}(e) \wedge \text{CAUSE}(e, f) \rightarrow \text{HOLDS}(f)\ ]$

- "Causes precede their effects."
  $\forall\, e : E_{\text{event}}, f : E_{\text{fluent}}$
  $[\ \textsc{Cause}(e, f) \rightarrow (\textsc{Occurs}(e) \rightarrow \textsc{Holds}(f) \wedge t_(e) \leq \texttt{begin}(f))\ ]$

5.7 Concluding Remarks

In this chapter we have identified the relevant issues around the temporal qualification method which is central in the definition of a temporal reasoning system in AI. We have described the most relevant temporal qualification methods, illustrated them with a rich example and analysed advantages and shortcomings with respect to a number of representational and reasoning efficiency criteria. The various methods are schematically presented in Figure 5.1.

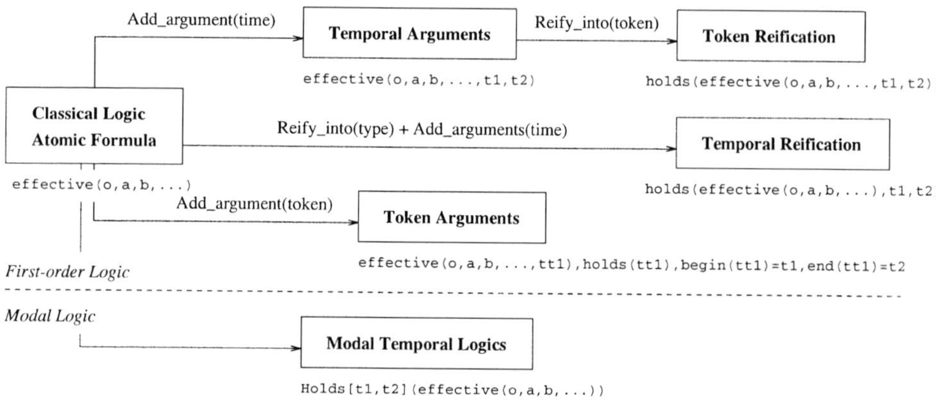

Figure 5.1: Temporal qualification methods in AI.

Temporal arguments is the classical and most straightforward method that turns out to be more expressive than has traditionally been recognized. It is enough for many applications except for those where one needs to represent nested temporal references or one needs to quantify over temporal propositions. In fact, the subsequent methods are a response to this limitation in a more or less sophisticated manner. *Temporal Token Arguments*, while using a language very similar to that of the method of temporal arguments, moves to a token-based ontology and introduces names for temporal token in the language. This provides a good deal of represenation flexibility. The other two approaches are based on reification. Reification allows one to quantify over temporal entities, resulting in significantly increased expressiveness. The increased expressiveness allows one to express statements like "receiving an offer causes to be obliged to send a confirmation" or " causes never preced their effects" which is not possible in the temporal argumentn method.

Technically, the temporal reification methods are not necessarily complex. However, the system becomes highly complex if one insists on reification of non-atomic formulas, as shown in [Reichgelt, 1987; Reichgelt, 1989]. However, in many cases, this is not necessary: some temporal reified logics can be defined as a many-sorted logic with the appropriate time and temporal incidence axiomatizations. However, it is important to be aware that these axioms can be a source of high inefficiency for the theorem prover.

Constraint Manipulation

Handbook of Temporal Reasoning in Artificial Intelligence
Edited by M. Fisher, D. Gabbay and L. Vila

Chapter 6

Computational Complexity of Temporal Constraint Problems

Thomas Drakengren & Peter Jonsson

This chapter surveys results on the computational complexity of temporal constraint reasoning. The focus is on the satisfiability problem, but also the problem of entailed relations is treated. More precisely, results for formalisms based upon relating time points and/or intervals with qualitative and/or metric constraints are reviewed. The main purpose of the chapter is to distinguish between tractable and NP-complete cases.

6.1 Introduction

The purpose of this chapter is to survey results on the computational complexity of temporal constraint reasoning. To keep the presentation reasonably short, we make a few assumptions:

1. We assume that time is linear, dense and unbounded. This implies that, for instance, we do not consider branching, discrete or finite time structures.

2. We focus on the satisfiability problem, that is, the problem of deciding whether a set of temporal formulae has a model or not. However, we also treat the problem of entailed relations, in the context of Allen's algebra.

3. Initially, we follow standard mathematical praxis and allow temporal variables to be unrelated, *i.e.*, we allow problems where variables may not be explicitly tied by any constraint. In the final section, we study some cases where this assumption is dropped.

Our main purpose is to distinguish between problems that are solvable in polynomial time and problems that are not*. As a consequence, we will not necessarily present the most efficient algorithms for the problems under consideration. We will instead emphasize simplicity and generality, which means that we will use standard mathematical tools whenever possible.

This chapter begins, in Section 6.2, with an in-depth treatment of *disjunctive linear relations* (DLR), here serving two purposes:

*Assuming $P \neq NP$, of course.

1. DLRs will be used as a unifying formalism for temporal constraint reasoning, since it subsumes most approaches that have been proposed in the literature.

2. DLRs will be used extensively for dealing with metric time.

We continue in Section 6.3 by introducing Allen's interval algebra, and presenting all tractable subclasses of that algebra. We also provide some results on the complexity of computing entailed relations.

Section 6.4 is concerned with *point-interval* relations, in which time points are related to intervals. A complete enumeration of all maximal tractable subclasses is given, together with algorithms for solving the corresponding problems.

In Section 6.5, the problem of handling metric time is studied. Extensions to Horn DLRs are considered, as well as methods based on arc and path consistency.

Finally, Section 6.6 contains some "non-standard" techniques in temporal constraint reasoning. We consider, for instance, temporal reasoning involving durations, and the implications of not allowing unrelated variables.

6.2 Disjunctive Linear Relations

6.2.1 Definitions

Definition 6.2.1. Let $X = \{x_1, \ldots, x_n\}$ be a set of real-valued variables, and α, β linear polynomials (polynomials of degree one) over X, with rational coefficients. A *linear relation* over X is a mathematical expression of the form $\alpha R \beta$, where $R \in \{<, \leq, =, \neq, \geq, >\}$.

A *disjunctive linear relation* (DLR) over X is a disjunction of a nonempty finite set of linear relations. A DLR is said to be *Horn* if at most one of its disjuncts is not of the form $\alpha \neq \beta$.

The *satisfiability* problem for a finite set D of DLRs, denoted DLRSAT(D), is the problem of checking whether there exists an assignment M of variables in X to real numbers, such that all DLRs in D are satisfied in M. Such an M is said to be a *model* of D. The satisfiability problem for finite sets H of Horn DLRs is denoted HORNDLRSAT(H). □

Example 6.2.1.

$$x + 2y \leq 3z + 42.3$$

is a linear relation,

$$(x + 2y \leq 3z + 42.3) \vee (x > \frac{3}{12})$$

is a disjunctive linear relation, and

$$(x + 2y \leq 3z + 42.3) \vee (x \neq \frac{3}{12})$$

is a Horn disjunctive linear relation.

In principle, the framework of DLRs makes it unnecessary to distinguish between qualitative and metric information. Nevertheless, when it comes to identifying tractable subclasses, the distinction is still convenient.

6.2.2 Algorithms and Complexity

In this section, we present the two main results for computing with DLRs. We also provide a polynomial-time algorithm for checking the satisfiability of Horn DLRs.

Proposition 6.2.2. The problem DLRSAT is NP-complete.

Proof. The satisfiability problem for propositional logic, which is known to be NP-complete, can easily be coded as DLRs. For the details, see [Jonsson and Bäckström, 1998].

Proposition 6.2.3. HORNDLRSAT is solvable in polynomial time.

Proof. See [Jonsson and Bäckström, 1998] or [Koubarakis, 1996].

We will present a polynomial-time algorithm for HORNDLRSAT in Algorithm 6.2.9. In order to understand it, some auxiliary concepts are needed.

Definition 6.2.4. A linear relation $\alpha R \beta$ is said to be *convex* if R is not the relation $\neq$.

Let γ be a DLR. We let $\mathcal{C}(\gamma)$ denote the DLR where all nonconvex relations in γ have been removed, and $\mathcal{NC}(\gamma)$ the DLR where all convex relations in γ have been removed.

We say that γ is *convex* if $\mathcal{NC}(\gamma) = \emptyset$, and that γ is *disequational* if $\mathcal{C}(\gamma) = \emptyset$. If γ is convex or disequational we say that γ is *homogeneous*, and otherwise it is said to be *heterogeneous*. We extend these definitions to sets of relations in the obvious way; for example, if Γ is a set of DLRs and all $\gamma \in \Gamma$ are Horn, then Γ is Horn. □

The algorithm for deciding satisfiability of Horn DLRs is based on linear programming techniques, so we begin by providing the basic facts for that. The linear programming problem is defined as follows.

Definition 6.2.5. Let A be an arbitrary $m \times n$ matrix of rational numbers and let $x = (x_1, \ldots, x_n)$ be an n-vector of variables over the real numbers. Then an instance of the *linear programming* (LP) problem is defined by $\{\min\ c^{\mathrm{T}}x$ subject to $Ax \leq b\}$, where b is an m-vector of rational numbers, and c an n-vector of rational numbers. The computational problem is as follows:

1. Find an assignment to the variables $x_1, \ldots, x_n$ such that the condition $Ax \leq b$ holds, and $c^{\mathrm{T}}x$ is minimal subject to these conditions, or
2. Report that there is no such assignment, or
3. Report that there is no lower bound for $c^{\mathrm{T}}x$ under the conditions.

□

Analogously, we can define an LP problem where the objective is to maximize $c^{\mathrm{T}}x$ under the condition $Ax \leq b$. We have the following theorem.

Theorem 6.2.6. The linear programming problem is solvable in polynomial time.

Proof. Several polynomial-time algorithms have been developed for solving LP. Well-known examples are the algorithms by [Khachiyan, 1979] and [Karmarkar, 1984].

Definition 6.2.7. Let A be a satisfiable set of DLRs and let γ be a DLR. We say that γ *blocks* A if $A \cup \{d\}$ is unsatisfiable for any $d \in \mathcal{NC}(\gamma)$. □

Lemma 6.2.8. Let A be an arbitrary $m \times n$ matrix of rational numbers, b an m-vector of rational numbers and $x = (x_1, \ldots, x_n)$ an n-vector of variables over the real numbers. Let α be a linear polynomial over $x_1, \ldots, x_n$ and c a rational number. Deciding whether the system $S = \{Ax \leq b, \alpha \neq c\}$ is satisfiable or not is a polynomial-time problem.

Proof. Consider the following instances of LP:

$$\text{LP1} = \{\min \alpha \text{ subject to } Ax \leq b\}$$

$$\text{LP2} = \{\max \alpha \text{ subject to } Ax \leq b\}$$

If either LP1 or LP2 has no solutions, then S is not satisfiable. If both LP1 and LP2 yield the same optimal value c, then S is not satisfiable, since every solution y to LP1 and LP2 satisfies $\alpha(y) = c$. Otherwise S is obviously satisfiable. Since we can solve the LP problem in polynomial time by Theorem 6.2.6, the result follows.

Algorithm 6.2.9. (Alg-HORNDLRSAT(Γ))

input Set Γ of DLRs

1 $A \leftarrow \{\gamma \mid \gamma \in \Gamma \text{ is convex}\}$
2 **if** A is not satisfiable **then**
3   **reject**
4 **if** $\exists \beta \in \Gamma$ that blocks A **then**
5   **if** β is disequational **then**
6   **reject**
7   **else**
8   Alg-HORNDLRSAT($(\Gamma - \{\beta\}) \cup \mathcal{C}(\beta)$)
9 **accept**

□

Theorem 6.2.10. Algorithm 6.2.9 correctly solves HORNDLRSAT in polynomial time.

Proof. The test in line 2 can be performed in polynomial time using linear programming, and the test in line 4 can be performed in polynomial time by Lemma 6.2.8. Thus, the algorithm runs in polynomial time. The correctness proof can be found in [Jonsson and Bäckström, 1998].

6.2.3 Subsumed Formalisms

Several formalisms can easily be expressed as DLRs, but more importantly, most proposed tractable temporal formalisms are subsumed by the Horn DLR formalism.

For the following definitions, let x, y be real-valued variables, c, d rational numbers, and $\mathcal{A}$ Allen's algebra [Allen, 1983] (see Section 6.3 for its definition). It is trivial to see that the

DLR language subsumes Allen's algebra. Furthermore, it subsumes the universal temporal language by Kautz and Ladkin, defined as follows.

Definition 6.2.11. (Universal temporal language) The *universal temporal language* [Kautz and Ladkin, 1991] consists of $\mathcal{A}$, augmented with formulae of the form $-cr_1(x - y)r_2d$, where $r_1, r_2 \in \{<, \leq\}$, and x, y are endpoints of intervals. □

DLRs also subsume the *qualitative algebra* (QA) by [Meiri, 1996]. In QA, a qualitative constraint between two objects O_i and O_j (each may be a point or an interval), is a disjunction of the form

$$(O_i r_1 O_j) \vee \ldots \vee (O_i r_k O_j)$$

where each one of the $r_i's$ is a *basic relation* that may exist between two objects. There are three types of basic relations.

1. *Interval-interval* relations that can hold between a pair of intervals. These relations correspond to Allen's algebra.
2. *Point-point* relations that can hold between a pair of points. These relations correspond to the point algebra [Vilain, 1982].
3. *Point-interval* and *interval-point* relations that can hold between a point and an interval and vice-versa. These relations were introduced by [Vilain, 1982].

Obviously, DLRs subsume QA. Meiri also considers QA extended with metric constraints of the following two forms, $x_1, \ldots, x_n$ being time points or endpoints of intervals.

1. $(c_1 \leq x_1 \leq d_1) \vee \ldots \vee (c_1 \leq x_n \leq d_1)$;
2. $(c_1 \leq x_n - x_1 \leq d_1) \vee \ldots \vee (c_1 \leq x_n - x_{n-1} \leq d_1)$.

Also this extension to QA can easily be expressed as DLRs. It has been shown that the satisfiability problems for all of these formalisms are NP-complete [Vilain *et al.*, 1990; Kautz and Ladkin, 1991; Meiri, 1996]. In retrospect, the different restrictions imposed on these formalisms seem quite artificial when compared to DLRs, especially since they do not reduce the computational complexity of the problem.

Next, we review some of the formalisms that are subsumed by Horn DLRs.

Definition 6.2.12. (Point algebra formulae, pointisable algebra) A *point algebra formula* [Vilain, 1982] is an expression xRy, where x and y are variables, and R is one of the relations $<, \leq, =, \neq, \geq$ and $>$.

The *pointisable algebra* [van Beek and Cohen, 1990] is the set of relations in $\mathcal{A}$ which can be expressed as point algebra formulae. □

We denote satisfiability problem for point algebra formulae by $\text{PASAT}(H)$, for a set H of point algebra formulae.

Definition 6.2.13. (Continuous endpoint formula, continuous endpoint algebra) A *continuous endpoint formula* [Vilain *et al.*, 1990] is a point algebra formula xRy where R is not the relation $\neq$.

The *continuous endpoint algebra* [Vilain *et al.*, 1990] is the set of relations in $\mathcal{A}$ which can be expressed as continuous endpoint formulae. □

The following formalism subsumes those of the previous two definitions.

Definition 6.2.14. (ORD-Horn algebra) An *ORD clause* is a disjunction of relations of the form xRy, where $R \in \{\leq, =, \neq\}$. The *ORD-Horn* subclass $\mathcal{H}$ [Nebel and Bürckert, 1995] is the set of relations in $\mathcal{A}$ that can be written as ORD clauses containing only disjunctions, with at most one relation of the form $x = y$ or $x \leq y$, and an arbitrary number of relations of the form $x \neq y$. □

Definition 6.2.15. (Koubarakis formula) A *Koubarakis formula* [1992] is a formula of one of the following forms:

1. $(x - y)Rc$
2. xRc
3. A disjunction of formulae of the form $(x - y) \neq c$ or $x \neq c$,

where $R \in \{\leq, \geq, \neq\}$. □

Definition 6.2.16. (Simple temporal constraint) A *simple temporal constraint* [Dechter *et al.*, 1991] is a formula on the form $c \leq (x - y) \leq d$. □

Definition 6.2.17. (Simple metric constraint) A *simple metric constraint* [Kautz and Ladkin, 1991] is a formula on the form $-cR_1(x - y)R_2d$ where $R_1, R_2 \in \{<, \leq\}$. □

Definition 6.2.18. (PA/single-interval formula) A *PA/single-interval* formula [Meiri, 1996] is a formula on one of the following forms:

1. $cR_1(x - y)R_2\, d$, where $R_1, R_2 \in \{<, \leq\}$
2. xRy where $R \in \{<, \leq, =, \neq, \geq, >\}$

□

Definition 6.2.19. (TG-II formula) A *TG-II* formula [Gerevini *et al.*, 1993] is a formula on one of the following forms:

1. $c \leq x \leq d$,
2. $c \leq x - y \leq d$
3. xRy where $R \in \{<, \leq, =, \neq, \geq, >\}$

□

Besides these classes, other temporal classes that can be expressed as Horn DLRs have been identified by different authors. Examples include the approach by [Barber, 1993], the subclass $\mathcal{V}^{23}$ for relating points and intervals [Jonsson *et al.*, 1999] (see Section 6.4), and the temporal part of TMM by [Dean and Boddy, 1988].

Not all known tractable classes can be modeled as Horn DLRs (in any obvious way*), however. Examples of this are [Golumbic and Shamir, 1993] and Drakengren and Jonsson [1997a; 1997b].

*Linear programming is a P-complete problem, so in principle, all polynomial-time computable problems can be transformed into Horn DLRs.

Basic relation		Example	Endpoints
x before y	$\prec$	xxx	$x^+ < y^-$
y after x	$\succ$	yyy	
x meets y	m	xxxx	$x^+ = y^-$
y met-by x	m^{-1}	yyyy	
x overlaps y	o	xxxx	$x^- < y^- < x^+$,
y overl.-by x	o^{-1}	yyyy	$x^+ < y^+$
x during y	d	xxx	$x^- > y^-$,
y includes x	d^{-1}	yyyyyyy	$x^+ < y^+$
x starts y	s	xxx	$x^- = y^-$,
y started by x	s^{-1}	yyyyyyy	$x^+ < y^+$
x finishes y	f	xxx	$x^+ = y^+$,
y finished by x	f^{-1}	yyyyyyy	$x^- > y^-$
x equals y	$\equiv$	xxxx	$x^- = y^-$,
		yyyy	$x^+ = y^+$

Table 6.1: The thirteen basic relations. The endpoint relations $x^- < x^+$ and $y^- < y^+$ that are valid for all relations have been omitted.

6.3 Interval-Interval Relations: Allen's Algebra

6.3.1 Definitions

Allen's interval algebra [Allen, 1983] is based on the notion of *relations between pairs of intervals*. An interval x is represented as a tuple $\langle x^-, x^+\rangle$ of real numbers with $x^- < x^+$, denoting the left and right endpoints of the interval, respectively, and relations between intervals are composed as disjunctions of *basic interval relations*, which are those in Table 6.1. Denote the set of basic interval relations **B**. Such disjunctions are represented as *sets* of basic relations, but using a notation such that, for example, the disjunction of the basic intervals $\prec$, m and f^{-1} is written $(\prec\ \mathsf{m}\ \mathsf{f}^{-1})$. Thus, we have that $(\prec\ \mathsf{f}^{-1}) \subseteq (\prec\ \mathsf{m}\ \mathsf{f}^{-1})$. The disjunction of all basic relations is written $\top$, and the empty relation is written $\perp$ (this is also used for relations between interval endpoints, denoting "always satisfiable" and "unsatisfiable", respectively). The algebra is provided with the operations of *converse, intersection and composition* on intervals, but we shall need only the converse operation explicitly. The converse operation* takes an interval relation i to its converse i^{-1}, obtained by inverting each basic relation in i, *i.e.*, exchanging x and y in the endpoint relations shown in Table 6.1.

By the fact that there are thirteen basic relations, we get $2^{13} = 8192$ possible relations between intervals in the full algebra. We denote the set of all interval relations by $\mathcal{A}$. Subclasses of the full algebra are obtained by considering subsets of $\mathcal{A}$. There are $2^{8192} \approx 10^{2466}$ such subclasses. Classes that are closed under the operations of intersection, converse and composition are said to be *algebras*.

The problem of *satisfiability* (ISAT) of a set of interval variables with relations between them is that of deciding whether there exists an assignment of intervals on the real line for

*The notation varies for this operation. However, we believe that the standard notation for inverse relations is the best and simplest choice.

the interval variables, such that all of the relations between the intervals are satisfied. This is defined as follows.

Definition 6.3.1. (ISAT($\mathcal{I}$)) Let $\mathcal{I} \subseteq \mathcal{A}$ be a set of interval relations. An instance of ISAT($\mathcal{I}$) is a labelled directed graph $G = \langle V, E \rangle$, where the nodes in V are interval variables and E is a subset of $V \times \mathcal{I} \times V$. A labelled edge $\langle u, r, v \rangle \in E$ means that u and v are related by r.

A function M taking an interval variable v to its interval representation $M(v) = \langle x^-, x^+ \rangle$ with $x^-, x^+ \in \mathbb{R}$ and $x^- < x^+$, is said to be an *interpretation* of G.

An instance $G = \langle V, E \rangle$ is said to be *satisfiable* if there exists an interpretation M such that for each $\langle u, r, v \rangle \in E$, $M(u) r M(v)$ holds, *i.e.*, the endpoint relations required by r (see Table 6.1) are satisfied by the assignments of u and v. Then M is said to be a *model* of G.

We refer to the *size* of an instance G as $|V| + |E|$. □

6.3.2 Complexity Results

A complete classification of the computational complexity of ISAT(X) has been presented by Krokhin *et al.* [2003]. The classification provides no new tractable subclasses; interestingly, it turns out that all existing tractable subclasses of Allen's algebra had been published in earlier papers [Nebel and Bürckert, 1995; Drakengren and Jonsson, 1997b; Drakengren and Jonsson, 1997a]. For the complete classification, the lengthy proof uses results from a number of earlier publications, *cf.* [Krokhin *et al.*, 2001; Drakengren and Jonsson, 1998; Nebel and Bürckert, 1995].

Next, we present the main result and the tractable subclasses; after that we present the polynomial-time algorithms for the tractable subclasses.

Theorem 6.3.2. Let X be a subset of $\mathcal{A}$. Then ISAT(X) is tractable iff X is a subset of the ORD-Horn algebra (Definition 6.2.14), or of one of the 17 subalgebras defined below. Otherwise, ISAT(X) is NP-complete.

Proof. See [Krokhin *et al.*, 2003].

Definition 6.3.3. (Subclasses $A(r, b)$ [Drakengren and Jonsson, 1997b])
Let $b \in \{\mathsf{s}, \mathsf{s}^{-1}, \mathsf{f}, \mathsf{f}^{-1}\}$, and r one of the relations

$(\prec\ \mathsf{d}^{-1}\ \mathsf{o}\ \mathsf{m}\ \mathsf{s}\ \mathsf{f}^{-1})$
$(\prec\ \mathsf{d}^{-1}\ \mathsf{o}\ \mathsf{m}\ \mathsf{s}^{-1}\ \mathsf{f}^{-1})$
$(\prec\ \mathsf{d}\ \mathsf{o}\ \mathsf{m}\ \mathsf{s}\ \mathsf{f})$
$(\prec\ \mathsf{d}\ \mathsf{o}\ \mathsf{m}\ \mathsf{s}\ \mathsf{f}^{-1})$

containing b. First define the subclasses $A_1(b)$, $A_2(r, b)$ and $A_3(r, b)$ by

$$A_1(b) = \{r' \cup (b\, b^{-1}) | r' \in \mathcal{A}\},$$

$$A_2(r, b) = \{r' \cup (b) | r' \subseteq r\}$$

and

$$A_3(r, b) = \{r' \cup (\equiv) | r' \in A_2(r, b)\} \cup \{(\equiv)\}.$$

Then set

$$B = A_1(b) \cup A_2(r, b) \cup A_3(r, b)$$

and finally define the subclass $A(r, b)$ by

$$A(r, b) = B \cup \{x^{-1} | x \in B\} \cup \{(\,)\}.$$

□

For an explicit enumeration of the sets $A(r, b)$, see [Drakengren and Jonsson, 1997b].

Definition 6.3.4. (Subclass $A_\equiv$ [Drakengren and Jonsson, 1997b]) Define the subclass $A_\equiv$ to contain every relation that contains $\equiv$, and the empty relation ( ). □

Definition 6.3.5. (Subclasses $S(b)$, $E(b)$ [Drakengren and Jonsson, 1997a]) Set $r_s = (\succ \; \mathsf{d} \; \mathsf{o}^{-1} \; \mathsf{m}^{-1} \; \mathsf{f})$, and $r_e = (\prec \; \mathsf{d} \; \mathsf{o} \; \mathsf{m} \; \mathsf{s})$. Note that r_s contains all basic relations b such that whenever IbJ for interval variables I, J, $I^- > J^-$ has to hold in any model, and symmetrically, r_e is equivalent to $I^+ < J^+$ holding in any model.

First, for $b \in \{\succ, \mathsf{d}, \mathsf{o}^{-1}\}$, define $S(b)$ to be the set of relations r, such that either of the following holds:

$$\begin{array}{rcccl} (b\,b^{-1}) & \subseteq & r & & \\ (b) & \subseteq & r & \subseteq & r_s \cup (\equiv \; \mathsf{s}\,\mathsf{s}^{-1}) \\ (b^{-1}) & \subseteq & r & \subseteq & {r_s}^{-1} \cup (\equiv \; \mathsf{s}\,\mathsf{s}^{-1}) \\ & & r & \subseteq & (\equiv \; \mathsf{s}\,\mathsf{s}^{-1}). \end{array}$$

Then, by switching the starting and ending points of intervals, $E(b)$ is defined, for $b \in \{\prec, \mathsf{d}, \mathsf{o}\}$, to be the set of relations r, such that either of the following holds:

$$\begin{array}{rcccl} (b\,b^{-1}) & \subseteq & r & & \\ (b) & \subseteq & r & \subseteq & r_e \cup (\equiv \; \mathsf{f}\,\mathsf{f}^{-1}) \\ (b^{-1}) & \subseteq & r & \subseteq & {r_e}^{-1} \cup (\equiv \; \mathsf{f}\,\mathsf{f}^{-1}) \\ & & r & \subseteq & (\equiv \; \mathsf{f}\,\mathsf{f}^{-1}). \end{array}$$

□

Definition 6.3.6. (Subclasses S^*, E^* [Drakengren and Jonsson, 1997a]) Let r_s and r_e be as in Definition 6.3.5, and define S^* to be the set of relations r, such that either of the following holds:

$$\begin{array}{rcccl} (\equiv \; \mathsf{f}\,\mathsf{f}^{-1}) & \subseteq & r & & \\ (\mathsf{f}\,\mathsf{f}^{-1}) & \subseteq & r & \subseteq & r_s \cup {r_s}^{-1} \\ (\equiv \; \mathsf{f}) & \subseteq & r & \subseteq & r_s \cup (\equiv \; \mathsf{s}\,\mathsf{s}^{-1}) \\ (\equiv \; \mathsf{f}^{-1}) & \subseteq & r & \subseteq & {r_s}^{-1} \cup (\equiv \; \mathsf{s}\,\mathsf{s}^{-1}) \\ (\mathsf{f}) & \subseteq & r & \subseteq & r_s \\ (\mathsf{f}^{-1}) & \subseteq & r & \subseteq & {r_s}^{-1} \\ (\equiv) & \subseteq & r & \subseteq & (\equiv \; \mathsf{s}\,\mathsf{s}^{-1}) \\ & & r & = & \bot \end{array}$$

Symmetrically, replacing f by s (and their inverses), $(\equiv \; \mathsf{s}\,\mathsf{s}^{-1})$ by $(\equiv \; \mathsf{f}\,\mathsf{f}^{-1})$, and r_s by r_e, we get the subclass E^*. □

6.3.3 Algorithms

We will now present the tractable algorithms for the subclasses of Allen's algebra presented in the previous section. The proofs of the following claims can be found in [Drakengren and Jonsson, 1997a; Drakengren and Jonsson, 1997b].

- Algorithm 6.3.8 correctly solves $\textsc{ISat}(\mathcal{A}(r,b))$ in polynomial time.
- Algorithm 6.3.9 correctly solves $\textsc{ISat}(\mathcal{A}_{\equiv})$ in polynomial time.
- Algorithm 6.3.12 correctly solves $\textsc{ISat}(\mathcal{S}(b))$ and $\textsc{ISat}(\mathcal{S}^*)$ in polynomial time, and exchanging starting and ending points in the algorithm, also $\textsc{ISat}(\mathcal{E}(b))$ and $\textsc{ISat}(\mathcal{E}^*)$ can be solved in polynomial time.

A definition is needed to understand Algorithm 6.3.8.

Definition 6.3.7. (Strong component) A subgraph C of a graph G is said to be a *strong component* of G if it is maximal such that for any nodes a, b in C, there is always a path in G from a to b. □

Algorithm 6.3.8. (Alg-$\textsc{ISat}(\mathcal{A}(r,b))$)

input Instance $G = \langle V, E \rangle$ of $\textsc{ISat}(\mathcal{A})$

Redirect the arcs of G so that all relations are in $A_1(b) \cup A_2(r,b) \cup A_3(r,b)$
Let G' be the graph obtained from G by removing arcs which are not labelled by some relation in $A_2(r,b) \cup A_3(r,b)$
Find all strong components C in G'
for every arc e in G whose relation does not contain $\equiv$
    if e connects two nodes in some C **then**
        reject
accept

□

Algorithm 6.3.9. (Alg-$\textsc{ISat}(\mathcal{A}_{\equiv})$)

input Instance $G = \langle V, E \rangle$ of $\textsc{ISat}(\mathcal{A})$

if some arc in G is labelled by ( ) **then**
    reject
else
    accept

□

A few definitions are needed for Algorithm 6.3.12. The observant reader might notice that some of the definitions differ slightly from the original ones [Drakengren and Jonsson, 1997a]. However, the changes were only done in order to improve the presentation; it is easy to see that they are equivalent (and cleaner).

Definition 6.3.10. **(*sprel*(r), *eprel*(r), *sprel*$^+(r)$, *eprel*$^-(r)$)** Take the relation $r \in \mathcal{A}$, let u and v be interval variables, and consider the instance S of $\textsc{Isat}(\{r\})$ which relates u and v with the relation r only. Define the relation *sprel*(r) on real numbers to be the implied relation between the starting points of u and v. That is, for basic relations, we define (the quotation marks are only to avoid notational confusion; the actual relations are intended)

$$\begin{array}{rcl} sprel(\equiv) & = & \text{“}=\text{”} \\ sprel(\prec) & = & \text{“}<\text{”} \\ sprel(\mathsf{d}) & = & \text{“}>\text{”} \\ sprel(\mathsf{o}) & = & \text{“}<\text{”} \\ sprel(\mathsf{m}) & = & \text{“}<\text{”} \\ sprel(\mathsf{s}) & = & \text{“}=\text{”} \\ sprel(\mathsf{f}) & = & \text{“}>\text{”} \\ sprel(r^{-1}) & = & (sprel(r))^{-1}, \end{array}$$

and for disjunctions, *sprel*(r) is the relation corresponding to $\bigvee_{b \in r} sprel(b)$. For example, *sprel*$((\prec \succ))$ = “$\neq$”. Symmetrically, we define *eprel*(r) to be the implied relation between ending points given r. Note that *sprel*(r) and *eprel*(r) have to be either of $<$, $\leq$, $=$, $\geq$, $>$, $\neq$, $\top$ or $\bot$. Further, we define specialisations of these, by

$$sprel^+(r) = sprel(r \cap (\equiv \ \mathsf{f}\,\mathsf{f}^{-1}))$$

and

$$eprel^-(r) = eprel(r \cap (\equiv \ \mathsf{s}\,\mathsf{s}^{-1})),$$

i.e., the implied relations on starting (ending) points by r, given that the ending (starting) points are known to be equal. □

Definition 6.3.11. **(Explicit starting (ending) point relations)** Let $\mathcal{I} \subseteq \mathcal{A}$, and define the function *expl*$^-$ on instances $G = \langle V, E \rangle$ of $\textsc{Isat}(\mathcal{I})$ by setting

$$expl^-(G) = \{u^- sprel(r) v^- \mid \langle u, r, v \rangle \in E\}.$$

expl$^-(G)$ is said to be obtained from G by *making starting point relations explicit*.

Symmetrically, using *eprel* and ending points instead of *sprel* and starting points, *expl*$^+(G)$ is said to be obtained from G by *making ending points explicit*. □

6.3.4 Computing Entailed Relations

Given an instance Θ of $\textsc{Isat}(\mathcal{I})$ and two distinguished nodes X and Y, we define an instance of the *entailed relation problem* ($\textsc{Ient}$) to be the triple $\langle \Theta, X, Y \rangle$, and the computational task as follows: find the smallest set R of basic relations such that $\Theta \cup X(\mathbf{B} - R)Y$ is not satisfiable*. $\textsc{Ient}$ is polynomially equivalent to a number of other computational problems

*An equivalent definition of the computational task is the following: find the largest set R of basic relations such that XRY holds in all models of Θ. This is the standard notion of entailment.

Algorithm 6.3.12. (Alg-ISAT($S(b)$), Alg-ISAT(S^*))

input Instance $G = \langle V, E\rangle$ of ISAT($\mathcal{A}$)

```
H ← expl⁻(G)
if not PASAT(H) then
    reject
K ← ∅
for each ⟨u, r, v⟩ ∈ E
    if not PASAT(H ∪ {u⁻ ≠ v⁻}) then
        K ← K ∪ {u⁻ = v⁻}
    else
        K ← K ∪ {u⁻ ≠ v⁻}
P ← {u⁺eprel⁻(r)v⁺ | ⟨u, r, v⟩ ∈ E ∧ u⁻ = v⁻ ∈ H ∪ K}
if not PASAT(P) then
    reject
accept
```

□

such as the *minimum labelling problem** (MLP) where one computes the entailed relation between *all* pairs of variables.

For the ORD-Horn algebra, it turns out that computing entailed relations is a polynomial-time problem, as proved by [Nebel and Bürckert, 1995]. We state the simple proof here.

Theorem 6.3.13. IENT($\mathcal{H}$) is solvable in polynomial time.

Proof. Let $\langle \Theta, X, Y\rangle$ be an instance of IENT($\mathcal{H}$). Using a polynomial-time algorithm for ISAT($\mathcal{H}$), one can check whether $\Theta \cup (X(B_i)Y)$ is satisfiable for each $B_i \in \mathbf{B}$. The set of basic relations for which the test succeeds is the relation between X and Y which is entailed by Θ.

It is easy to see that if IENT($\mathcal{I}$) can be solved in polynomial time, then ISAT($\mathcal{I}$) is a polynomial-time problem.

Next, we show that the converse does not hold in general. Let $r_1 = (\mathsf{m}\,\mathsf{m}^{-1}\,\mathsf{s}\,\mathsf{s}^{-1}\,\mathsf{f}\,\mathsf{f}^{-1})$ and $r_2 = \mathcal{B} - \{\equiv\}$.

Lemma 6.3.14. Let A, B, X be intervals such that

1. $A(\prec)B$;
2. Xr_1A; and
3. Xr_2B.

Then, in any model I,

$$[I(X^-), I(X^+)] \in \{\ [I(A^-), I(B^-)], [I(A^-), I(B^+)],$$
$$[I(A^+), I(B^-)], [I(A^+), I(B^+)]\ \}.$$

*This problem is denoted ISI in [Nebel and Bürckert, 1995].

Proof. Easy exercise.

Theorem 6.3.15. If S is a subclass containing r_1 and r_2, then $\text{IENT}(\mathcal{S})$ is NP-complete.

Proof. We establish this by a polynomial-time reduction from the NP-complete problem of 4-COLOURABILITY. Let $G = \langle V, E \rangle$ be an arbitrary graph, and construct a set of interval formulae as follows:

1. Introduce two auxiliary interval variables A and B;
2. For each $w \in V$, introduce an interval variable W and the relations Wr_1A, Wr_2B;
3. For each $(w_1, w_2) \in E$, add the relation $W_1r_2W_2$.

Let r be the entailed relation between A and B in Θ. We claim that $\prec \in r$ iff G is 4-colourable.

if: Let $f : V \to \{1, 2, 3, 4\}$ be a legal colouring of the vertices in G. We incrementally construct a model I of Θ such that $A(\prec)B$. First, arbitrarily choose I such that $I(A)(\prec)I(B)$. For each $w \in V$, let

1. $I(W) = [I(A^-), I(B^-)]$ iff $f(w) = 1$;
2. $I(W) = [I(A^-), I(B^+)]$ iff $f(w) = 2$;
3. $I(W) = [I(A^+), I(B^-)]$ iff $f(w) = 3$;
4. $I(W) = [I(A^+), I(B^+)]$ iff $f(w) = 4$.

It is easy to see that I is a model of Θ.

only-if: Let I be a model of Θ such that $I(A)(\prec)I(B)$. By Lemma 6.3.14 and the construction of Θ, we know that for each $w \in V$,

$$I(W) \in \{[I(A^-), I(B^-), [I(A^-), I(B^+)], [I(A^+), I(B^-)], [I(A^+), I(B^+)]\}.$$

Furthermore, if $(w_1, w_2) \in E$, then $I(W_1) \neq I(W_2)$, and thus G is 4-colourable.

Corollary 6.3.16. Define $A(r, b)$ as in Definition 6.3.3. Then $\text{IENT}(A(r, b))$ is NP-complete.

Proof. $r_1, r_2 \in A(r, b)$ for all possible choices of r and b.

6.4 Point-Interval Relations: Vilain's Point-Interval Algebra

The point-interval algebra [Vilain, 1982] is based on the notions of *points*, *intervals* and *binary relations* on these. Where Allen's algebra is used for expressing relations between intervals, and the point algebra is used for expressing relations between points, the point-interval algebra allows points to be related to intervals. Thus, the relations in this algebra relate objects of different types, making it useful for combining the world of points with the world of intervals. That is exactly how it is used in Meiri's [1996] qualitative algebra.

Basic relation		Example	Endpoints
p before I	b	p III	$p < I^-$
p starts I	s	p III	$p = I^-$
p during I	d	p III	$I^- < p < I^+$
p finishes I	f	p III	$p = I^+$
p after I	a	p III	$p > I^+$

Table 6.2: The five basic relations of the $\mathcal{V}$-algebra. The endpoint relation $I^- < I^+$ that is required for all relations has been omitted.

6.4.1 Definitions

A point p is a variable interpreted over the set of real numbers $\mathbb{R}$. An interval I is represented by a pair $\langle I^-, I^+\rangle$ satisfying $I^- < I^+$, where I^- and I^+ are interpreted over $\mathbb{R}$. We assume that we have a fixed universe of variable names for points and intervals. Then, a $\mathcal{V}$-*interpretation* is a function M that maps point variables to $\mathbb{R}$ and interval variables to $\mathbb{R} \times \mathbb{R}$, and which satisfies the previously stated restrictions. We extend the notation by denoting the first component of $M(I)$ by $M(I^-)$ and the second by $M(I^+)$.

Given an interpreted point and an interpreted interval, their relative positions can be described by exactly one of five *basic point-interval relations*, where each basic relation can be defined in terms of its endpoint relations (see Table 6.2). A formula of the form pBI, where p is a point, I an interval and B is a basic point-interval relation, is said to be satisfied by a $\mathcal{V}$-interpretation if the interpretation of the points and intervals satisfies the endpoint relations specified in Table 6.2.

To express indefinite information, unions of the basic relations are used, yielding 2^5 distinct binary *point-interval* relations. Naturally, a set of basic relations is to be interpreted as a disjunction of its member relations. A point-interval relation is written as a list of its members, *e.g.*, (b d a). The set of all point-interval relations is denoted by $\mathcal{V}$. We denote the empty relation $\perp$ and the universal relation $\top$.

A formula of the form $p(B_1, \ldots, B_n)I$ is said to be a *point-interval* formula. Such a formula is said to be satisfied by a $\mathcal{V}$-interpretation M if pB_iI is satisfied by M for some i, $1 \le i \le n$. A set Θ of point-interval formulae is said to be $\mathcal{V}$-*satisfiable* if there exists an $\mathcal{V}$-interpretation M that satisfies every formula of Θ. Such a satisfying $\mathcal{V}$-interpretation is called a $\mathcal{V}$-*model* of Θ. The reasoning problem we will study is the following:

INSTANCE: A finite set Θ of point-interval formulae.
QUESTION: Does there exist a $\mathcal{V}$-model of Θ?

We denote this problem $\mathcal{V}$-SAT. In the following, we often consider restricted versions of $\mathcal{V}$-SAT, where relations used in the formulae in Θ are taken only from a subset $\mathcal{S}$ of $\mathcal{V}$. In this case we say that Θ is a set of formulae over $\mathcal{S}$, and use a parameter in the problem description to denote the subclass under consideration, *e.g.* $\mathcal{V}$-SAT($\mathcal{S}$).

6.4.2 Complexity Results

The restriction of expressiveness only to allow relations between points and intervals does not reduce computational complexity when compared to Allen's algebra.

Theorem 6.4.1. Deciding satisfiability in the point-interval algebra is NP-complete.

Proof. See [Meiri, 1996].

However, the reduction of expressiveness makes it easier to completely classify which subclasses are tractable and which are not: a complete classification of tractability in the point-interval algebra was done by [Jonsson *et al.*, 1999]. It turns out that there are only five maximal tractable subclasses, named $\mathcal{V}^{23}$, $\mathcal{V}^{20}_{\mathtt{s}}$, $\mathcal{V}^{20}_{\mathtt{f}}$, $\mathcal{V}^{17}_{\mathtt{s}}$ and $\mathcal{V}^{17}_{\mathtt{f}}$. See Table 6.3 for a presentation of these subclasses.

6.4.3 Algorithms

We will now present the tractable algorithms for the subclasses presented in the previous section; the correctness proofs and complexity analyses can be found in [Jonsson *et al.*, 1999].

- Algorithm 6.4.2 correctly solves satisfiability for $\mathcal{V}^{23}$ in polynomial time*.
- Algorithm 6.4.3 correctly solves satisfiability for $\mathcal{V}^{20}_{\mathtt{s}}$ in polynomial time.
- Algorithm 6.4.3, exchanging starting and ending points of intervals, correctly solves satisfiability for $\mathcal{V}^{20}_{\mathtt{f}}$ in polynomial time.
- Algorithm 6.4.4 correctly solves satisfiability for $\mathcal{V}^{17}_{\mathtt{s}}$ in polynomial time.
- Algorithm 6.4.4 correctly solves satisfiability for $\mathcal{V}^{17}_{\mathtt{f}}$ in polynomial time.

Algorithm 6.4.2. (Alg-$\mathcal{V}$-$SAT(\mathcal{V}^{23})$)

input Instance $G = \langle V, E\rangle$ of $\mathcal{V}$-$SAT(\mathcal{V}^{23})$

```
1  Transform G into an equivalent set P of point-algebra formulae
2  if PASAT(P) then
3      accept
4  else
5      reject
```

□

*The set $\mathcal{V}^{23}$ is exactly the set of relations which can be expressed in the point-algebra, so line 1 can be performed in linear time.

	$\mathcal{V}^{23}$	$\mathcal{V}_{\mathrm{s}}^{20}$	$\mathcal{V}_{\mathrm{f}}^{20}$	$\mathcal{V}_{\mathrm{s}}^{17}$	$\mathcal{V}_{\mathrm{f}}^{17}$
$\perp$	•	•	•	•	•
(b)	•	•	•		
(s)	•	•		•	
(b s)	•	•	•	•	
(d)	•				
(b d)	•		•		
(s d)	•			•	
(b s d)	•		•	•	
(f)	•		•		•
(b f)			•		•
(s f)				•	•
(b s f)			•	•	•
(d f)	•				•
(b d f)	•		•		•
(s d f)	•			•	•
(b s d f)	•		•	•	•
(a)	•	•	•		
(b a)		•	•		
(s a)		•		•	
(b s a)		•	•	•	
(d a)	•	•			
(b d a)	•	•	•		
(s d a)	•	•		•	
(b s d a)	•	•	•	•	
(f a)	•	•	•		•
(b f a)		•	•		•
(s f a)		•		•	•
(b s f a)		•	•	•	•
(d f a)	•	•			•
(b d f a)	•	•	•		•
(s d f a)	•	•		•	•
$\top$	•	•	•	•	•

Table 6.3: The maximal subclasses of $\mathcal{V}$ which have a polynomial-time satisfiability problem.

Algorithm 6.4.3. (Alg-$\mathcal{V}$-$SAT(\mathcal{V}_{\text{s}}^{20})$)

input Instance $G = \langle V, E \rangle$ of $\mathcal{V}$-$SAT(\mathcal{V}_{\text{s}}^{20})$

Define $f : \{\mathtt{b}, \mathtt{s}, \mathtt{d}, \mathtt{f}, \mathtt{a}\} \rightarrow \{<, =, >\}$ such that $f(\mathtt{b}) =$ " $<$",
$f(\mathtt{s}) =$ " $=$" and $f(\mathtt{d}) = f(\mathtt{f}) = f(\mathtt{a}) =$ " $>$".
Let $P = \{v(\bigcup_{r \in R} f(r))w \mid (v, R, w) \in E\}$.
if PASAT(P) **then**
    accept
else
    reject

□

Algorithm 6.4.4. (Alg-$\mathcal{V}$-$SAT(\mathcal{V}_{\text{s}}^{17})$)

input Instance $G = \langle V, E \rangle$ of $\mathcal{V}$-$SAT(\mathcal{V}_{\text{s}}^{17})$

if G contains $\perp$ **then**
    reject
else
    accept

□

6.5 Formalisms with Metric Time

We will now examine known tractable formalisms allowing for metric time, and which are not subsumed by the Horn-DLR framework. By formalisms allowing metric time, we mean formalisms with the ability to express statements such as "X happened at time point 100" or "X happened at least 50 time units before Y". Note that Allen's algebra cannot express this, while the Horn DLRs can.

The first example is an extension to the continuous endpoint formulae, and the second is a method for expressing metric time in the sub-algebras $S(\cdot)$, $E(\cdot)$, S^* and E^*.

6.5.1 Definitions

Definition 6.5.1. (Augmented (continuous) endpoint formula) An *augmented (continuous) endpoint formula* [Meiri, 1996] is

1. a (continuous) point algebra formula; or
2. a formula of the type $x \in \{[d_1^-, d_1^+], \ldots, [d_n^-, d_n^+]\}$,
   where $d_1^-, \ldots, d_n^-, d_1^+, d_n^- \in \mathbb{Q}$ and $d_i^- \leq d_i^+, 1 \leq i \leq n$.

□

If there is a need for unbounded intervals, $\mathbb{Q}$ can be replaced by $\mathbb{Q} \cup \{-\infty, +\infty\}$ in the previous definition. Note that the definition allows for discrete domains by setting the left and right endpoint of the intervals equal. A set Γ of augmented endpoint formulae is satisfiable if there exists an assignment I to the variables that

1. satisfies (in the ordinary sense) the point algebra formulae; and
2. if $x \in \{[d_1^-, d_1^+], \ldots, [d_n^-, d_n^+]\} \in \Gamma$, then $I(x) \in \bigcup\{[d_1^-, d_1^+], \ldots, [d_n^-, d_n^+]\}$.

We will now return to the interval satisfiability problem (Definition 6.3.1), and extend it to allow for metric information on starting points of intervals.

Definition 6.5.2. (M-ISAT($\mathcal{I}$)) Let $\langle V, E\rangle$ be an instance of ISAT($\mathcal{I}$) and H a finite set of DLRs over the set $\{v^+, v^- \mid v \in V\}$ of variables, v^- representing starting points and v^+ ending points of intervals v.

An instance of the problem of *interval satisfiability with metric information* for a set $\mathcal{I}$ of interval relations, denoted M-ISAT($\mathcal{I}$), is a tuple $Q = \langle V, E, H\rangle$.

An *interpretation* M for Q is an interpretation for $\langle V, E\rangle$. Since we now need to refer to starting and ending points of intervals, we extend the notation such that $M(v^-)$ obtains the starting point of the interval $M(v)$, and similarly for $M(v^+)$.

An instance Q is said to be *satisfiable* if there exists a model M of $\langle V, E\rangle$ such that the DLRs in H are satisfied, with values for all v^- and v^+ by $M(v^-)$ and $M(v^+)$, respectively. □

In order to obtain tractability, the following restrictions are imposed (the definitions differ slightly from the original ones).

Definition 6.5.3. (M_s-ISAT($\mathcal{I}$), M_e-ISAT($\mathcal{I}$)) Let $\langle V, E, H\rangle$ be an instance of M-ISAT($\mathcal{I}$) where the DLRs of H are restricted in two ways: first, H may only contain Horn DLRs and second, H may not contain any variables v^+, where $v \in V$, *i.e.*, it may only relate starting points of intervals. The set of such instances is denoted M_s-ISAT($\mathcal{I}$), and is said to be the problem of *interval satisfiability with metric information on starting points*.

Symmetrically, by exchanging starting and ending points, we get the problem of *interval satisfiability with metric information on ending points*, denoted M_e-ISAT($\mathcal{I}$). □

6.5.2 Complexity Results

Theorem 6.5.4. Deciding the satisfiability of augmented endpoint formulae is NP-complete, while deciding satisfiability of augmented continuous endpoint formulae is a polynomial-time task.

Proof. See [Meiri, 1996]. A set of augmented continuous endpoint formulae is satisfiable iff it is arc and path consistent; explicit algorithms can be found in Meiri's paper.

Theorem 6.5.5. M_s-ISAT($S(b)$), M_e-ISAT($E(b)$), M_s-ISAT(S^*) and M_e-ISAT(E^*) are polynomial-time problems, for $b \in \{\succ, \mathsf{d}, \mathsf{o}^{-1}\}$.

Proof. See [Drakengren and Jonsson, 1997a]. A polynomial-time algorithm is presented in Algorithm 6.5.7 for the case of M_s-ISAT; an algorithm for the case of M_e-ISAT is easily obtained by exchanging starting and ending points of intervals.

The restriction that we cannot express starting and ending point information at the same time is essential for obtaining tractability, once we want to go outside the ORD-Horn algebra.

Proposition 6.5.6. Let $S \subseteq \mathcal{A}$ such that S is not a subset of the ORD-Horn algebra, and let *SE* be the set of instances $Q = \langle V, E, H\rangle$ of M-ISAT(S), where H may contain only DLRs $u^+ = v^-$ for some $u, v \in V$. Then the satisfiability problem for *SE* is NP-complete.

Proof. See [Drakengren and Jonsson, 1997a].

Algorithm 6.5.7. (Alg-M_s-ISAT$(\mathcal{I})$)

```
input Instance Q = ⟨V, E, H⟩ of M_s-ISAT(A)

H' ← H ∪ expl⁻(⟨V, E⟩)
if not HORNDLRSAT(H') then
    reject
K ← ∅
for each ⟨u, r, v⟩ ∈ E
    if not HORNDLRSAT(H' ∪ {u⁻ ≠ v⁻}) then
        K ← K ∪ {u⁻ = v⁻}
    else
        K ← K ∪ {u⁻ ≠ v⁻}
P ← {u⁺ eprel⁻(r) v⁺ | ⟨u, r, v⟩ ∈ E ∧ u⁻ = v⁻ ∈ H' ∪ K}
if not PASAT(P) then
    reject
accept
```

□

6.6 Other Approaches to Temporal Constraint Reasoning

6.6.1 Unit Intervals and Omitting $\top$

Most results on Allen's algebra that we have presented so far rely on two underlying assumptions:

1. The top relation is always included in any sub-algebra*; and
2. Any interval model is regarded as a valid model of a set of Allen relations.

These assumptions are not always appropriate. For instance, there are examples of graph-theoretic applications where there is no need to use the top relations, *e.g.*, interval graph recognition [Golumbic and Shamir, 1993]. Similarly, there are scheduling and physical mapping applications where it is required that the intervals must be of length 1 [Pe'er and Shamir, 1997].

The implications of such "non-standard" assumptions have not been studied in any greater detail in the literature. However, for a subclass known as $\mathcal{A}_3$ (defined by [Golumbic and Shamir, 1993]), the picture is very clear, as we will see.

*In other words, we allow variables that are not explicitly constrained by any relation.

	Δ_1	Δ_2	Δ_3
$\perp$	•	•	•
$(\prec)$	•	•	•
$(\succ)$	•	•	•
$(\prec\succ)$		•	•
$(\cap)$	•	•	
$(\prec\cap)$	•		
$(\succ\cap)$	•		
$\top$	•		•

Table 6.4: Maximal tractable subclasses of $\mathcal{A}_3$.

Let $\cap$ denote the Allen relation ($\equiv$ d d^{-1} o o^{-1} m m^{-1} s s^{-1} f f^{-1}), that is, the relation stating that two intervals have at least one point in common (they have a nonempty intersection). Let $\mathcal{A}_3$ denote the following set of Allen relations*:

$$\{\perp, (\prec), (\succ), (\prec\succ), (\cap), (\prec\cap), (\succ\cap), \top\}.$$

The maximal tractable subclasses of $\mathcal{A}_3$ have been identified by [Golumbic and Shamir, 1993] and [Webber, 1995], and they are presented in Table 6.4. Note that $\top$ is not a member of Δ_2. The maximal tractable subclasses of $\mathcal{A}_3$ under the additional assumption that all intervals are of unit length have been identified by [Pe'er and Shamir, 1997]. These subclasses can be found in Table 6.5†.

Some of the maximal tractable subclasses of $\mathcal{A}_3$ are related to the tractable subclasses presented in Sections 6.2 and 6.3. For instance, $\Delta'_1 \subset \Delta_1 \subset \mathcal{H}$ and $\Delta_3 \subset S(\succ)$. It should be noted that satisfiability in the ORD-Horn-algebra can be decided in polynomial time even under the unit interval assumption. Given a set of ORD-Horn relations, convert them to Horn DLRs and add constraints of the type $x^+ - x^- = 1$ for each interval $I = [x^-, x^+]$. The resulting set of formulae is also a set of Horn DLRs, and thus the satisfiability can be decided in polynomial time.

6.6.2 Point-Duration Relations

Reasoning about durations has recently obtained a certain amount of interest, *cf.* [Condotta, 2000; Pujari and Sattar, 1999; Wetprasit and Sattar, 1998; Navarrete and Marin, 1997b].

We will present the framework by [Navarrete and Marin, 1997b] due to its appealing simplicity, and since many of the other methods build on it. Navarrete and Marin have proposed a formalism for reasoning about durations in the point algebra, and they have provided certain tractability results. Below, we present their approach and slightly generalize their tractability result.

Definition 6.6.1. A *point-duration network* (PDN) is a tuple $\Sigma = \langle N_P, N_D\rangle$ where

*Here, the relations are to be viewed as "macro relations", so that $(\prec\ \cap)$ denotes the Allen relation ($\prec\ \equiv$ d d^{-1} o o^{-1} m m^{-1} s s^{-1} f f^{-1}).

†[Golumbic and Shamir, 1993] and [Pe'er and Shamir, 1997] agree on the definition of Δ_2 and Δ_3 but they define Δ_1 differently. By Δ_1, we mean Δ_1 in the sense of [Golumbic and Shamir, 1993] and by Δ'_1, we mean Δ_1 in the sense of [Pe'er and Shamir, 1997].

	Δ_1'	Δ_2	Δ_3
$\perp$	•	•	•
$(\prec)$		•	•
$(\succ)$		•	•
$(\prec\succ)$		•	•
$(\cap)$	•	•	
$(\prec\cap)$	•		
$(\succ\cap)$	•		
$\top$	•		•

Table 6.5: Maximal tractable subclasses of $\mathcal{A}_3$ under the unit interval assumption.

1. N_P is a set of PA formulae over a set $P = \{x_1, \ldots, x_n\}$ of *point variables*;
2. N_D is a set of PA formulae over a set $D = \{d_{ij} \mid 1 \leq i < j \leq n\}$ of *duration variables*;

□

A PDN $\Sigma = \langle N_P, N_D \rangle$ is satisfiable if there exists an assignment I to the variables in N_P such that

1. $I(x_i) r I(x_j)$ whenever $x_i r x_j \in N_P$; and
2. $|I(x_i) - I(x_j)| r |I(x_k) - I(x_m)|$ whenever $d_{ij} r d_{km} \in N_D$.

Theorem 6.6.2. Deciding whether a PDN is satisfiable or not is NP-complete.

Proof. See [Navarrete and Marin, 1997b].

In order to obtain tractability, [Navarrete and Marin, 1997b] define a restriction of a PDN.

Definition 6.6.3. (Simple PDN [Navarrete and Marin, 1997b]**)** A PDN is said to be *simple* if the following holds:

- Only the relations $<, >$ or $=$ are allowed in N_P and N_D;
- For each $x_i, x_j \in P$, $x_i r x_j \in N_P$ for some r; and
- For each $d_i, d_j \in D$, $d_i r d_j \in N_D$ for some r.

□

It is important to note that this definition does not allow two variables to be unrelated. Furthermore, they show that deciding the satisfiability of simple PDNs is a polynomial-time problem. We now intend to weaken their restriction in two steps, still obtaining tractability. The tool for this will be the Horn DLRs.

Definition 6.6.4. (Point-simple PDN) A PDN is said to be *point-simple* if the following holds:

- Only the relations $<, >$ or $=$ are allowed in N_P; and
- For each $x_i, x_j \in P$, $x_i r x_j \in N_P$ for some r.

□

Note that there are no requirements on the formulae in N_D; thus durations may be related with arbitrary PA relations, including the $\top$ relation.

We now show how the satisfiability problem for point-simple PDNs can be solved in polynomial time, by a straightforward reduction to Horn DLRs.

Let $\Sigma = \langle N_P, N_D \rangle$ be a point-simple PDN. Construct a set Θ of Horn DLR formulae incrementally as follows: Check whether N_P is satisfiable or not. If it is not satisfiable, report that Σ is not satisfiable. Otherwise, let Θ initially equal N_P.

For each formula $d_{ij} r d_{km} \in N_D$, check whether $x_i < x_j$, $x_i > x_j$ or $x_i = x_j$ is in N_P. Since Σ is point-simple, at least one of these relations is in N_P. By observing that N_P is satisfiable, exactly one of the relations is in N_P. Note the following:

1. if $x_i < x_j \in N_P$, then $d_{ij} = |x_i - x_j| = x_j - x_i$;
2. if $x_i > x_j \in N_P$, then $d_{ij} = |x_i - x_j| = x_i - x_j$;
3. if $x_i = x_j \in N_P$, then $d_{ij} = |x_i - x_j| = 0$;

Continue by checking whether $x_k < x_m$, $x_k > x_m$ or $x_k = x_m$, and decide the value of d_{km} as above. Now, it is easy to convert the relation $d_{ij} r d_{km}$ to a Horn DLR.

As an example, assume that $d_{ij} < d_{km}$, $x_i > x_j$ and $x_k < x_m$. The corresponding Horn DLR then will be $x_i - x_j < x_m - x_k$. Add the Horn DLR to Θ and note that Σ is satisfiable iff Θ is satisfiable. The transformation from point-simple PDNs to Horn DLRs can easily be performed in polynomial time, and thus we have shown that deciding satisfiability of point-simple PDNs is a polynomial-time solvable problem.

We are in the position to make one more generalization, still retaining tractability.

Definition 6.6.5. (Horn-simple PDN) We say that $\Sigma = \langle N_P, N_D \rangle$ *Horn-simple* if Σ satisfies all the requirements for being point-simple, except that N_D is allowed to contain arbitrary Horn DLRs over D, instead of requiring PA formulae. □

Theorem 6.6.6. Deciding whether a Horn-simple PDN is satisfiable or not is a polynomial-time problem.

Proof. The above transformation from N_D relations to Horn DLR point relations simply replaces duration variables d_{ij} by either $x_i - x_j$, $x_j - x_i$ or 0. If a Horn DLR ϕ is in N_D, then the transformed formula will obviously be a Horn DLR too, but now over the point variables.

Handbook of Temporal Reasoning in Artificial Intelligence
Edited by M. Fisher, D. Gabbay and L. Vila

Chapter 7

Indefinite Constraint Databases with Temporal Information: Representational Power and Computational Complexity

Manolis Koubarakis

We develop the scheme of indefinite constraint databases using first-order logic as our representation language. When this scheme is instantiated with temporal constraints, the resulting formalism is more expressive than standard temporal constraint networks. The extra representational power allows us to express temporal knowledge and queries that have been impossible to express before. To make our claim more persuasive, we survey previous works on querying temporal constraint networks and show that they can be viewed as an instance of the scheme of indefinite constraint databases. Then we study the computational complexity of the proposed scheme when constraints are temporal, and carefully outline the boundary between tractable and intractable query answering problems.

7.1 Introduction

The last fifteen years have been very productive for research in temporal reasoning. Researchers have defined various formalisms, most notably *temporal constraint networks* [Allen, 1983], and studied algorithms for consistency checking, finding a solution and computing the minimal network [Vilain and Kautz, 1986; Vilain *et al.*, 1990; van Beek and Cohen, 1990; Dechter *et al.*, 1991; Meiri, 1991; van Beek, 1992; Ladkin and Maddux, 1994; Nebel and Bürckert, 1995; Brusoni *et al.*, 1995a; Gerevini and Schubert, 1995a; Koubarakis, 1995; Koubarakis, 1997a; Koubarakis, 1996; Jonsson and Bäckström, 1996; Jonsson and Bäckström, 1998; Delgrande *et al.*, 1999; Staab, 1998; Koubarakis, 2001]. There have also been various implementations of temporal reasoning systems based on the theoretical models [Gerevini and Schubert, 1995a; Gerevini *et al.*, 1993; Yampratoom and Allen, 1993; Stillman *et al.*, 1993; Brusoni *et al.*, 1997]. All these implementations use a temporal constraint network as the underlying formalism for representing temporal information.

When temporal constraint networks are used to represent temporal information their nodes represent the times when certain facts are true, or when certain events take place, or when events start or end. By labeling nodes with appropriate natural language expressions (e.g., $breakfast$ or $walk$) and arcs by temporal relations, temporal constraint networks can be queried in useful ways. For example the query "Is it possible (or certain) that event $walk$ happened after event $breakfast$?" or "What are the known events that come after event $breakfast$?" can be asked [Brusoni *et al.*, 1994; Brusoni *et al.*, 1997; van Beek, 1991]. However, other kinds of queries cannot be asked even though the knowledge required to answer them might be available. These kinds of queries usually involve non-temporal as well as temporal information e.g., "Who is certainly having breakfast before taking a walk?". This problem arises because temporal constraint networks do not have the required expressive power for representing all kinds of knowledge needed in a real application.

This situation has been understood by temporal reasoning researchers, and application-oriented systems where temporal reasoners were combined with more general knowledge representation systems have been implemented. These systems include EPILOG*, Shocker†, Telos [Mylopoulos *et al.*, 1990] and TMM [Dean and McDermott, 1987; Dean, 1989; Schrag *et al.*, 1992; Boddy, 1993]. EPILOG uses the temporal reasoner Timegraph [Gerevini and Schubert, 1995a], Shocker uses TIMELOGIC, Telos uses a subclass of Allen's interval algebra [Allen, 1983] while TMM uses networks of difference constraints [Dechter *et al.*, 1991].

In parallel with these developments the state of the art in algorithms for temporal constraint networks has improved dramatically and our understanding of the theoretical and practical issues involved has matured. As a result, some researchers [van Beek, 1991; Koubarakis, 1993; Koubarakis, 1994b; Brusoni *et al.*, 1994; Brusoni *et al.*, 1997; Brusoni *et al.*, 1995b; Brusoni *et al.*, 1995a; Brusoni *et al.*, 1999] have actively pursued the combination of these two strands of research to develop representational frameworks and systems that offer sophisticated query languages for temporal constraint networks. These efforts can be understood to proceed on the footsteps of TMM [Dean and McDermott, 1987; Dean, 1989] the first temporal reasoning system to augment a temporal constraint network with a Prolog-like language for representing other kinds of useful non-temporal knowledge.

This chapter proposes the *scheme of indefinite constraint databases* as the formalism that can unify the proposals of [van Beek, 1991; Koubarakis, 1993; Koubarakis, 1994b; Brusoni *et al.*, 1994; Brusoni *et al.*, 1995b; Brusoni *et al.*, 1997; Brusoni *et al.*, 1995a; Brusoni *et al.*, 1999]. The proposed formalism is a *scheme* because it can be instantiated with various kinds of constraints defined by a first-order language. When the constraints chosen are temporal, the resulting formalism is more expressive than the corresponding temporal constraint networks. To make our claim more persuasive, we show how previous research on querying temporal constraint networks [van Beek, 1991; Brusoni *et al.*, 1994; Brusoni *et al.*, 1995b; Brusoni *et al.*, 1997] can be viewed as an instance of the scheme of indefinite constraint databases. The same is true for previous research on querying temporal databases with relative and indefinite information [Koubarakis, 1993; Koubarakis, 1994b; Brusoni *et al.*, 1995a; Brusoni *et al.*, 1999].

This chapter shows that in order to achieve the required expressive power and functionality, we must be prepared to go from temporal constraint networks (or conjunctions of temporal constraints) to *first order theories of temporal constraints* as studied in [Ladkin, 1988; Koubarakis, 1994a]. We identify *variable elimination* (and its logical analogue *quantifier elimination*) as the main technical tool needed by the proposed framework (theses concepts have been mostly ignored by temporal constraint network research). We show that query evaluation in the proposed formalism can be viewed as quantifier elimination in a first order

*See `www.cs.rochester.edu/research/epilog/`.

†See `www.cs.rochester.edu/research/kr-tools.html`.

language of temporal constraints.

Recently we have made the same arguments in the field of constraint-based extensions of relational databases [Koubarakis, 1997b]. In this chapter we develop similar machinery in a first-order logic setting. In addition we show explicitly how the proposed scheme subsumes earlier proposals.

After exploring the representational power of the proposed framework, we turn to the study of its computational properties. Using the data complexity measure [Vardi, 1982], we study the complexity of query answering in the proposed scheme when constraints range over well-known temporal constraint classes. Our analysis carefully outlines the boundary between tractable and hard computational problems.

The chapter is organized as follows. Section 7.2 introduces the temporal constraint languages that we will study. Section 7.3 introduces the problems of deciding the satisfiability of a set of constraints, and performing variable or quantifier elimination. Section 7.4 introduces the proposed formalism: the scheme of indefinite constraint databases. Sections 7.5, 7.6 and 7.7 show that the formalisms of [van Beek, 1991; Koubarakis, 1993; Koubarakis, 1994b; Brusoni *et al.*, 1994; Brusoni *et al.*, 1997; Brusoni *et al.*, 1995b; Brusoni *et al.*, 1995a; Brusoni *et al.*, 1999] are subsumed by the scheme of indefinite constraint databases. Section 7.8 studies the complexity of query answering in the proposed scheme. Finally, Section 7.9 presents our conclusions and discusses future work.

7.2 Constraint Languages

We start by introducing some concepts useful for the developments in forthcoming sections. We will deal with many-sorted first order languages [Enderton, 1972]. For each first-order language $\mathcal{L}$ we will define a structure $\mathcal{M}_{\mathcal{L}}$ that will give the *intended interpretation* of formulas of $\mathcal{L}$ (this is called the *intended structure* for $\mathcal{L}$). The theory $Th(\mathcal{M}_{\mathcal{L}})$ (i.e., the set of sentences of $\mathcal{L}$ that are true in $\mathcal{M}_{\mathcal{L}}$) will also be considered. Finally, for each language $\mathcal{L}$ a special class of formulas called $\mathcal{L}$ *constraints* will be defined.

The rest of this section defines several progressively more complex first order temporal constraint languages.

7.2.1 The language PA

The language PA is a very simple language that we can use for talking about temporal phenomena. The logical symbols of PA include: parentheses, a countably infinite set of variables, the equality symbol $=$ and the standard sentential connectives. There is only one non-logical symbol: the predicate symbol $<$. The intended structure $\mathcal{M}_{PA}$ has the set of rational numbers $\mathcal{Q}$ as its domain, and interprets predicate symbol $<$ as the relationship "less than" over the rational numbers. We will freely use other defined predicates like $\leq$ and $\neq$.

PA *constraints* are exactly the constraints of the well-known *Point Algebra* **PA** defined in [Vilain and Kautz, 1986; van Beek and Cohen, 1990; van Beek, 1992; Ladkin and Maddux, 1994].

Example 7.2.1. *The following is a set of PA constraints:*

$$e_1 < e_2,\ e_2 \leq e_3,\ e_3 = e_4,\ e_4 \neq e_5$$

Researchers have also considered the sub-algebra of **PA** which does not include the relation $\neq$. This algebra is called the *Convex Point Algebra* (**CPA**) [Vilain *et al.*, 1990].

7.2.2 The language IA

The language IA is a first order language that allows us to make similar distinctions to the ones allowed by PA. The difference is that IA is a language for *intervals*. The logical symbols of IA include: parentheses, a countably infinite set of variables and the standard sentential connectives. IA has 13 predicate symbols inspired from [Allen, 1983]:

$$before,\ after,\ meets,\ met\text{-}by,\ during,\ over,\ overlaps,$$

$$overlapped\text{-}by,\ starts,\ started\text{-}by,\ finishes,\ finished\text{-}by,\ equal$$

The intended structure $\mathcal{M}_{IA}$ has the set of intervals over $\mathcal{Q}$ as its domain [Ladkin, 1988]. Predicates are interpreted as binary relations over intervals in the obvious way [Ladkin, 1988].

IA *constraints* are exactly the constraints of the *Interval Algebra* **IA** defined in [Allen, 1983] and subsequently studied by [van Beek and Cohen, 1990; Ladkin and Maddux, 1994; Ladkin, 1988; Nebel and Bürckert, 1995] and others.

Example 7.2.2. *Let us consider the following example from [van Beek, 1991]:*

> *"Fred was reading the paper while eating his breakfast. He put the paper down and drank the last of his coffee. After breakfast he went for a walk."*

The above paragraph asserts the following IA constraints among events breakfast, paper, coffee *and* walk*:*

$$breakfast\ before\ walk,$$

$$coffee\ during\ breakfast,$$

$$paper\ overlaps\ breakfast \lor paper\ overlapped\text{-}by breakfast \lor$$

$$paper\ starts\ breakfast \lor paper\ started\text{-}by\ breakfast \lor$$

$$paper\ during\ breakfast \lor paper\ over\ breakfast \lor paper\ finishes\ breakfast \lor$$

$$paper\ finished\text{-}by\ breakfast \lor paper\ equals\ breakfast,$$

$$paper\ overlaps\ cofee \lor paper\ starts\ coffee \lor paper\ during\ coffee$$

Interval algebra researchers have also considered a sub-algebra of **IA** called **SIA**. **SIA** includes only relations which translate into conjunctions of endpoint relations in **PA** [van Beek and Cohen, 1990].

7.2.3 The language LIN

The language LIN is also a first order language (LIN comes from *lin*ear). The logical symbols of LIN include: parentheses, a countably infinite set of variables, the equality symbol $=$ and the standard sentential connectives. The non-logical symbols of LIN include: a countably infinite set of constants (one for each rational numeral), the binary function symbols $+$ and $*$ (the symbol $*$ can only be applied to a variable and a constant) and the binary predicate symbol $<$.

The intended structure $\mathcal{M}_{LIN}$ has the set of rational numbers $\mathcal{Q}$ as its domain. $\mathcal{M}_{LIN}$ assigns to each constant symbol an element of $\mathcal{Q}$, to function symbol $+$, the addition operation for rational numbers, to function symbol $*$ the multiplication operation for rational numbers, and to predicate symbol $<$, the relation "less than" over $\mathcal{Q}$.

LIN constraints are the well-known class of linear constraints known from linear programming [Schrijver, 1986]. LIN constraints are useful for temporal reasoning because they allow the representation of *quantitative* temporal information (e.g., the duration of interval I is less than 5 minutes, event A lasts at least 5 hours more than event B etc.).

We will pay particular attention to a special subclass of LIN constraints called HDL constraints. *HDL constraints* or *Horn disjunctive linear constraints* have been defined originally in [Koubarakis, 1996; Jonsson and Bäckström, 1996]. Later their properties have also been studied in detail in [Cohen *et al.*, 1997; Jonsson and Bäckström, 1998; Cohen *et al.*, 2000; Koubarakis, 2001].

Definition 7.2.1 ([Koubarakis, 1996; Jonsson and Bäckström, 1996]). *A* Horn-disjunctive linear constraint *or an HDL* constraint *is a formula of LIN of the form $d_1 \vee ... \vee d_n$ where each d_i, $i = 1, ..., n$ is a weak linear inequality or a linear in-equation and the number of inequalities among d_1, ..., d_n does not exceed one.*

Example 7.2.3. *The following is a set of HDL constraints:*

$$x_1 - x_2 \leq 5,\ 3x_1 + x_2 \leq 3,$$

$$x_4 + 4x_5 \neq 6,\ x_1 - x_5 \neq 2 \vee x_6 \neq 7,$$

$$4x_1 + 3x_2 - 5x_5 \leq 5 \vee x_1 - x_2 \neq 4 \vee x_3 + 3x_4 \neq 5$$

Interval algebra researchers have also considered a sub-algebra of **IA** called **ORD-Horn**. **ORD-Horn** includes only relations which translate into conjunctions of endpoint relations that are HDL constraints [Nebel and Bürckert, 1995].

7.2.4 The language $LATER$

The language $LATER$ is a first-order language inspired by the temporal reasoning system LATER [Brusoni *et al.*, 1994; Brusoni *et al.*, 1997; Console and Terenziani, 1999]. It has three sorts: $\mathcal{P}$ for time points, $\mathcal{I}$ for time intervals and $\mathcal{DUR}$ for durations. The constant symbols of $LATER$ include *dates* and *times* of the form

$$month/day/year\ hour : minute$$

and *durations* of the form

$$days : hours : minutes$$

(followed by the word $days, hours$ or $minutes$). Times with the smallest duration are of sort $\mathcal{P}$ while everything else is of sort $\mathcal{I}$. Durations are of sort $\mathcal{DUR}$. $LATER$ has two function symbols $start$ and end with sort $\mathcal{I} \rightarrow \mathcal{P}$.

The predicate symbols of $LATER$ have been defined in detail in [Brusoni *et al.*, 1994; Brusoni *et al.*, 1997]. They include the *convex* predicates of **PA** ($<$, $\leq$, $>$, $\geq$, $=$) [Vilain and Kautz, 1986], the 13 basic predicates of **IA** [Allen, 1983] and the 10 basic point-to-interval predicates of [Meiri, 1991]. There are also functions (e.g., $start$, end) and predicates (e.g., $lasting$, $lasting\ at\ least$, $since$, $until$, at) that can be used to assert durations of intervals and locations of points on the time line.

The intended structure $\mathcal{M}_{LATER}$ interprets dates as integer elements of $\mathcal{Q}$ and durations as positive integers. The interpretation of function and predicate symbols is the obvious one.

$LATER$ *constraints* have been defined in detail in [Brusoni *et al.*, 1994; Brusoni *et al.*, 1997]. They offer a nice temporal reasoning framework since they include many useful classes of qualitative and metric temporal constraints. However, because disjunctive relations are *carefully controlled*, the expressive power of $LATER$ constraints is not greater than the expressive power of *difference constraints* as studied in [Dechter *et al.*, 1989; Brusoni *et al.*, 1995b]. The complete set of functions and predicates can be found in [Brusoni *et al.*, 1997; Brusoni *et al.*, 1994].

Example 7.2.4. *The following set of* $LATER$ *constraints provides information about the working hours of Tom, Mary and Ann:*

$$TomWork\ since\ 1/1/1995\ 14:15,\quad TomWork\ until\ 1/1/1995\ 18:30$$

$$TomWork\ before\ MaryWork,\quad MaryWork\ lasting\ at\ least\ 4:40\ hours$$

$$start(AnnWork)\ at\ 1/1/1995,\quad AnnWork\ lasting\ 3:00\ hours,$$

$$end(AnnWork)\ before\ 1/1/1995\ 18:00$$

7.2.5 Other Languages

Temporal reasoning researchers have studied other languages of temporal constraints. The following languages deserve being mentioned here even though they are not defined in detail; the careful reader will probably have no difficulty in doing so after consulting the relevant publications.

Dechter, Meiri and Pearl [Dechter *et al.*, 1989] have studied the language $DIFF$ of *difference constraints*. $DIFF$ deals only with points, and allows us to express constraints on the location of points on the rational line (e.g., $x < 2$) or on the distance of one point from another (e.g., $5 \leq x - y \leq 8$). [Koubarakis, 1995; Gerevini and Cristani, 1995; Koubarakis, 1997a] have extended the work of Dechter, Meiri and Pearl to consider in-equations of the form $x - y \neq r$ (r is a rational constant) as basic constraints. Our definition of $DIFF$ *constraints* will not include such in-equations.

Meiri, Kautz and Ladkin [Meiri, 1991; Kautz and Ladkin, 1991] have previously studied the language $QMPIA$ (Meiri's term) that deals with points and intervals and mixes qualitative and metric constraints between points and intervals. More precisely, $QMPIA$ allows IA constraints between intervals, PA constraints between points and $DIFF$ constraints between points or interval endpoints. Our class of $QMPIA$ *constraints* includes all the *qualitative/metric point-to-point/interval-to-interval/point-to-interval* constraints considered in

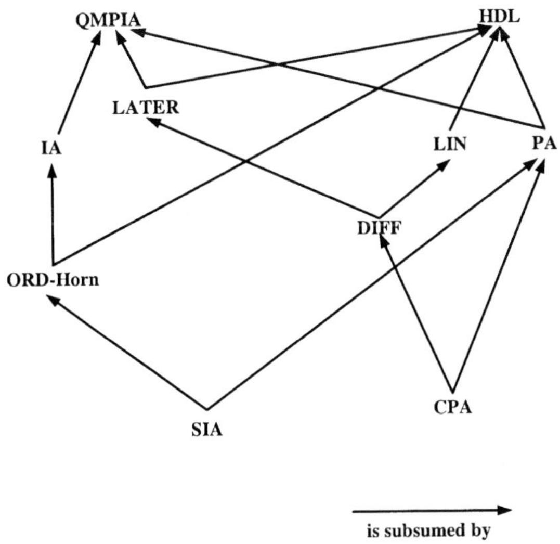

Figure 7.1: Subsumption relations between temporal constraint classes

[Meiri, 1991]. [Meiri, 1991] studies $QMPIA$ constraints using *general temporal constraint networks.*

7.2.6 Relationships Between Classes of Temporal Constraints

Several relationships hold between the classes of temporal constraints defined in the above sections. They are captured in Figure 7.1 as stated in the following theorem.

Theorem 7.2.1. *The subsumption relations of Figure 7.1 hold. Subsumption relations between a class of interval constraints (e.g.,* **SIA***) and a class of point constraints (e.g., PA) mean that each constraint in the first class can be expressed by a conjunction of constraints in the second class. Classes not connected by an arrow are incomparable.*

This section has defined several temporal constraint languages and constraint classes. We now turn to some interesting related problems in constraint-based reasoning.

7.3 Satisfiability, Variable Elimination & Quantifier Elimination

In the framework presented in this chapter, two problems are important: deciding the satisfiability of a set of constraints, and performing variable or quantifier elimination. Satisfiability of temporal constraints has been studied by the research community continuously since [Allen, 1983]. Unfortunately, variable and quantifier elimination have not been paid the attention they deserve except in the work of the present author [Koubarakis, 1994a; Koubarakis, 1995; Koubarakis, 1996; Koubarakis, 1997b; Koubarakis, 1997a]. This section is an introduction to these important problems.

Definition 7.3.1. *Let C be a set of $\mathcal{L}$ constraints in variables $x_1, \ldots, x_n$. The* solution set *of C, denoted by $Sol(C)$, is the following relation:*

$$\{(x_1^0, \ldots, x_n^0) : (x_1^0, \ldots, x_n^0) \in domain(\mathcal{M}_\mathcal{L})^n \text{ and}$$

$$\text{for every } c \in C, \ (x_1^0, \ldots, x_n^0) \text{ satisfies } c\}.$$

Each member of $Sol(C)$ is called a solution *of C.*

Definition 7.3.2. *A set of constraints (in some language $\mathcal{L}$) is called* satisfiable *or* consistent *if and only if its solution set is nonempty.*

Example 7.3.1. *The set of constraints of Example 7.2.1 is satisfiable. Tuple $(1, 2, 3, 3, 5)$ is one of its solutions.*

A lot of previous research has concentrated on the complexity of checking the satisfiability of a set of temporal constraints, and has identified tractable and possibly intractable constraint classes (e.g., see [Vilain *et al.*, 1990; van Beek, 1992; Dechter *et al.*, 1991; Gerevini and Schubert, 1994b; Nebel and Bürckert, 1995; Koubarakis, 1996; Jonsson and Bäckström, 1996; Jonsson and Bäckström, 1998]). The following theorem summarises two core results.

Theorem 7.3.1.

1. *Deciding the satisfiability of a set of HDL constraints can be done in PTIME [Koubarakis, 1996; Jonsson and Bäckström, 1996]. As a result, the same is true for all temporal constraint classes of Figure 7.1 that are subsumed by HDL constraints.*
2. *Deciding the consistency of a set of IA constraints is NP-hard (so the same is true for $QMPIA$ constraints) [Vilain* et al.*, 1990].*

Let us now define the operations of quantifier and variable elimination. Quantifier elimination is an operation from mathematical logic [Enderton, 1972]. Variable elimination is an algebraic operation [Schrijver, 1986]. As we will see below, quantifier elimination algorithms utilize variable elimination algorithms as subroutines. In the scheme of indefinite constraint databases introduced in Section 7.4, the operation of quantifier elimination is very useful because it can be used for query evaluation.

Definition 7.3.3. *Let Th be a theory in some first order language $\mathcal{L}$. Th* admits elimination of quantifiers *iff for every formula ϕ there is a disjunction ϕ' of conjunctions of $\mathcal{L}$ constraints such that $Th \models \phi \equiv \phi'$.*

This definition is stronger than the traditional one where ϕ' is simply required to be quantifier-free [Enderton, 1972]. We require ϕ' to be in the above form because we do not want to deal with negations of $\mathcal{L}$ constraints.

Let Th be a theory in some first order language $\mathcal{L}$, and let ϕ be a formula. If Th admits elimination of quantifiers, then a quantifier-free formula ϕ' equivalent to ϕ can be computed in the following standard way [Enderton, 1972]:

1. Compute the prenex normal form $(Q_1 x_1) \cdots (Q_m x_m) \psi(x_1, \ldots, x_m)$ of ϕ.

2. If Q_m is $\exists$ then let $\theta_1 \vee \cdots \vee \theta_k$ be a disjunction equivalent to $\psi(x_1, \ldots, x_m)$ where the θ_i's are conjunctions of $\mathcal{L}$ constraints. Then *eliminate variable* x_m from each θ_i to compute θ'_i using a *variable elimination* algorithm for $\mathcal{L}$ constraints. The resulting expression is $\theta'_1 \vee \cdots \vee \theta'_k$.

   If Q_m is $\forall$ then let $\theta_1 \vee \cdots \vee \theta_k$ be a disjunction equivalent to $\neg\psi(x_1, \ldots, x_m)$ where the θ_i's are conjunctions of $\mathcal{L}$ constraints. Then *eliminate variable* x_m from each θ_i to compute θ'_i as above. The resulting expression is $\neg(\theta'_i \vee \cdots \vee \theta'_k)$.

3. Repeat step 2 to eliminate all remaining quantifiers and obtain the required quantifier-free formula.

Step 2 of the above algorithm assumes the existence of a variable elimination algorithm for conjunctions (or, equivalently, *sets*) of $\mathcal{L}$ constraints. The operation of variable elimination can be defined as follows.

Definition 7.3.4. *The operation of* variable elimination *takes as input a set C of $\mathcal{L}$ constraints with set of variables X and a subset Y of X, and returns a new set of constraints C' such that $Sol(C') = \Pi_{X \setminus Y}(Sol(C))$ where Π_Z is the standard operation of projection of a relation on a subset Z of its set of columns.*

For the class of linear constraints defined above variable elimination can be performed using Fourier's algorithm. Fourier's algorithm can be summarized as follows [Schrijver, 1986]. Any weak linear inequality involving a variable x can be written in the form $x \leq r_u$ or $x \geq r_l$ i.e., it gives an upper or a lower bound on x. Thus if we are given two linear inequalities, one of the form $x \leq r_u$ and the other of the form $x \geq r_l$, we can eliminate x and obtain the inequality $r_l \leq r_u$. Obviously, $r_l \leq r_u$ is a logical consequence of the given inequalities. In addition, any solution of $r_l \leq r_u$ can be extended to a solution of the given inequalities (simply by choosing for x any value between the values of r_l and r_u). Following this observation, Fourier's elimination algorithm forms all pairs $x \leq r_u$ and $x \geq r_l$, eliminates x and returns the resulting constraints. The generalization of this algorithm to strict linear inequalities is obvious.

Example 7.3.2. *Let C be the following set of linear constraints:*

$$x_3 \leq x_1,\ x_5 < x_1,\ x_1 - x_2 \leq 2,\ x_4 \leq x_5$$

The elimination of variable x_1 from C using Fourier's algorithm results in the following set:

$$x_3 - x_2 \leq 2,\ x_5 - x_2 < 2,\ x_4 \leq x_5.$$

The following theorem is easy.

Theorem 7.3.2. *Let $\mathcal{L}$ be any of the languages defined in Section 7.2. The theory $Th(\mathcal{M}_{\mathcal{L}})$ admits quantifier elimination.*

Proof. Algorithms can be developed that eliminate variables from sets of PA, IA, HDL, $LATER$ and $QMPIA$ constraints. For PA and HDL the algorithms are provided in [Koubarakis, 1995; Koubarakis, 1997a] and [Koubarakis, 1996]. For the rest of the classes variable elimination algorithms can be readily developed using similar techniques. The existence of quantifier elimination algorithms follows easily (see also [Koubarakis, 1994a]). □

It is not difficult to see that the above quantifier elimination algorithm has exponential complexity even for theories with polynomial time variable elimination algorithms. Luckily more sophisticated quantifier elimination algorithms exist and have been studied by computational complexity theorists in the 70s and 80s [Fischer and Rabin, 1974; Ferrante and Rackoff, 1975; Ferrante and Geiser, 1977; Stockmeyer, 1977; Reddy and Loveland, 1978; Ferrante and Rackoff, 1979; Berman, 1980; Bruss and Meyer, 1980; Furer, 1982; Sontag, 1985] and more recently by constraint database researchers [Kanellakis *et al.*, 1990; Koubarakis, 1997b].

The presentation of preliminary concepts is now complete. We can therefore proceed to define the scheme of indefinite constraint databases.

7.4 The Scheme of Indefinite Constraint Databases

In this section we present the scheme of indefinite constraint databases originally proposed in [Koubarakis, 1997b]. We follow the spirit of the original proposal but use first order logic instead of relational database theory.

We assume the existence of a many-sorted first-order language $\mathcal{L}$ with a fixed intended structure $\mathcal{M}_{\mathcal{L}}$. Let us also assume that $Th(\mathcal{M}_{\mathcal{L}})$ *admits quantifier elimination* (Section 7.3 has defined this concept precisely). For the purposes of this chapter $\mathcal{L}$ can be any of the languages of Section 7.2 e.g., the language LIN.

Let us now consider, as an example, the information contained in the following two sentences:

> Mary took a walk in the park. After walking around for a while, she met Fred and started talking to him.

The information in the above sentences is about activities (e.g., walking, talking), constraints on the times of their occurrence (e.g., after) and, finally, other information about real-world entities (e.g., names of persons). Temporal constraint networks [Allen, 1983; van Beek, 1992; Dechter *et al.*, 1991] can be used to represent such information by capturing temporal constraints in their edges and storing all other information as node labels.

In the scheme of indefinite constraint databases information like the above is represented by utilising a first-order temporal language like LIN and extending it to represent non-temporal information. Let us now show how to do this formally in an abstract setting by considering an arbitrary many-sorted first order language $\mathcal{L}$ with the properties discussed above.

7.4.1 From $\mathcal{L}$ to $\mathcal{L} \cup \mathcal{EQ}$ and $(\mathcal{L} \cup \mathcal{EQ})^*$

Let $\mathcal{EQ}$ be a fixed first order language with only equality (=) and a countably infinite set of constant symbols. The intended structure $\mathcal{M}_{\mathcal{EQ}}$ for $\mathcal{EQ}$ interprets $=$ as equality and constants as "themselves". $\mathcal{EQ}$ is a very simple language which can only be used to represent knowledge about things that are or are not equal. $\mathcal{EQ}$ *constraints* or *equality constraints* are formulas of the form $x = v$ or $x \neq v$ where x is a variable, and v is a variable or a constant.

We now consider the language $\mathcal{L} \cup \mathcal{EQ}$. The set of sorts for $\mathcal{L} \cup \mathcal{EQ}$ will contain the special sort $\mathcal{D}$ (for terms of $\mathcal{EQ}$) and all the sorts of $\mathcal{L}$. The intended structure for $\mathcal{L} \cup \mathcal{EQ}$ is $\mathcal{M}_{\mathcal{L} \cup \mathcal{EQ}} = \mathcal{M}_{\mathcal{L}} \cup \mathcal{M}_{\mathcal{EQ}}$.

Finally, we define a new first order language $(\mathcal{L} \cup \mathcal{EQ})^*$ by augmenting $\mathcal{L} \cup \mathcal{EQ}$ with a countably infinite set of *database predicate symbols* $p_1, p_2, \ldots$ of various arities. These predicate symbols can be used to express thematic information i.e., information with no special temporal or spatial semantics (e.g., the name of the person who went for a walk is Mary). The indefinite constraint databases and queries defined below are formulas of $(\mathcal{L} \cup \mathcal{EQ})^*$.

Example 7.4.1. *Let $\mathcal{L}$ be the language LIN defined in Section 7.2. Let $walk$ be a ternary database predicate symbol with arguments of sort $\mathcal{D}$, $\mathcal{Q}$ and $\mathcal{Q}$ respectively. The following is a formula of the language $(LIN \cup \mathcal{EQ})^*$ capturing the fact that somebody took a walk during some unknown interval of time:*

$$(\exists x/\mathcal{D})(\exists t_1/\mathcal{Q})(\exists t_2/\mathcal{Q})(t_1 < t_2 \wedge walk(x, t_1, t_2))$$

7.4.2 Databases And Queries

In this section the symbols $\overline{\mathcal{T}}$ and $\overline{\mathcal{T}}_i$ will denote vectors of sorts of $\mathcal{L}$. Similarly, the symbol $\overline{\mathcal{D}}$ will denote a vector with all its components being the sort $\mathcal{D}$.

Indefinite constraint databases and queries are special formulas of $(\mathcal{L} \cup \mathcal{EQ})^*$ and are defined as follows.

Definition 7.4.1. *An* indefinite constraint database *is a formula $DB(\overline{\omega})$ of $(\mathcal{L} \cup \mathcal{EQ})^*$ of the following form:*

$$\bigwedge_{i=1}^{m} (\forall \overline{x_i}/\overline{\mathcal{D}})(\forall \overline{t_i}/\overline{\mathcal{T}}_i)(\bigvee_{j=1}^{l_i} Local_j(\overline{x_i}, \overline{t_i}, \overline{\omega}) \equiv p_i(\overline{x_i}, \overline{t_i})) \ \wedge$$

$$ConstraintStore(\overline{\omega})$$

where

- *$Local_j(\overline{x_i}, \overline{t_i}, \overline{\omega})$ is a conjunction of $\mathcal{L}$ constraints in variables $\overline{t_i}$ and Skolem constants $\overline{\omega}$, and $\mathcal{EQ}$ constraints in variables $\overline{x_i}$.*

- *$ConstraintStore(\overline{\omega})$ is a conjunction of $\mathcal{L}$ constraints in Skolem constants $\overline{\omega}$.*

The second component of the above formula defining a database is a *constraint store*. This store is a conjunction of $\mathcal{L}$ constraints and corresponds to a constraint network. $\overline{\omega}$ is a vector of *Skolem constants* denoting entities (e.g., points and intervals in time or points and regions in a multi-dimensional space) about which *only partial knowledge* is available. This partial knowledge has been coded in the constraint store using the language $\mathcal{L}$.

The first component of the database formula is a set of equivalences *completely defining* the database predicates p_i (this is an instance of the well-known technique of predicate completion in first order databases [Reiter, 1984]).

These equivalences may refer to the Skolem constants of the constraint store. In temporal reasoning applications, the constraint store will contain the temporal constraints usually captured by a constraint network, while the predicates p_i will encode, in a flexible way, the events or facts usually associated with the nodes of this constraint network.

For a given database DB the first conjunct of the database formula will be denoted by

$$EventsAndFacts(DB)$$

and the second one by

$$ConstraintStore(DB)\,.$$

For clarity we will sometimes write sets of conjuncts instead of conjunctions. In other words a database DB can be seen as the following pair of sets of formulas:

$$(EventsAndFacts(DB),\; ConstraintStore(DB)).$$

We will feel free to use whichever definition of database fits our needs in the rest of this chapter.

The new machinery in the indefinite constraint database scheme (in comparison with relational or Prolog databases) is the Skolem constants in

$$EventsAndFacts(DB)$$

and the constraint store which is used to represent "all we know" about these Skolem constants. Essentially this proposal is a combination of constraint databases (without indefinite information) as defined in [Kanellakis *et al.*, 1990], and the marked null values proposal of [Imielinski and Lipski, 1984; Grahne, 1991]. Similar ideas can also be found in the first order databases of [Reiter, 1984].

Let us now give some examples of indefinite constraint databases. The constraint language used is LIN.

Example 7.4.2. *The following is an indefinite constraint database which formalises the information in the paragraph considered at the beginning of this section.*

$$\begin{gathered}
(\ \{\ (\forall x/\mathcal{D})(\forall t_1,t_2/\mathcal{Q})((x = Mary \wedge t_1 = \omega_1 \wedge t_2 = \omega_2) \equiv walk(x,t_1,t_2)),\\
(\forall x/\mathcal{D})(\forall y/\mathcal{D})(\forall t_3,t_4/\mathcal{Q})\\
((x = Mary \wedge y = Fred \wedge t_3 = \omega_3 \wedge t_4 = \omega_4) \equiv talk(x,y,t_3,t_4))\ \},\\
\{\ \omega_1 < \omega_2,\ \omega_1 < \omega_3,\ \omega_3 < \omega_2,\ \omega_3 < \omega_4\ \}\ )
\end{gathered}$$

This database contains information about the events $walk$ and $talk$ in which Mary and Fred participate. The temporal information expressed by order constraints is indefinite since we do not know the exact constraint between Skolem constants ω_2 and ω_4.

Example 7.4.3. *Let us consider the following planning database used by a medical laboratory for keeping track of patient appointments for the year 1996.*

$$\begin{gathered}
(\ \{\ (\forall x,y/\mathcal{D})(\forall t_1,t_2/\mathcal{Q})\\
(((x = Smith \wedge y = Chem1 \wedge t_1 = \omega_1 \wedge t_2 = \omega_2)\vee\\
(x = Smith \wedge y = Chem2 \wedge t_1 = \omega_3 \wedge t_2 = \omega_4)\vee\\
(x = Smith \wedge y = Radiation \wedge t_1 = \omega_5 \wedge t_2 = \omega_6)) \equiv treatment(x,y,t_1,t_2))\ \},\\
\{\ \omega_1 \geq 0,\ \omega_2 \geq 0,\ \omega_3 \geq 0,\ \omega_4 \geq 0,\ \omega_5 \geq 0,\ \omega_6 \geq 0,\\
\omega_2 = \omega_1 + 1,\ \omega_4 = \omega_3 + 1,\ \omega_6 = \omega_5 + 2,\ \omega_2 \leq 91,\ \omega_3 \geq 91,\ \omega_4 \leq 182,\\
\omega_3 - \omega_2 \geq 60,\ \omega_5 - \omega_4 \geq 20,\ \omega_6 \leq 213\ \}\ )
\end{gathered}$$

In this example the set of rationals $\mathcal{Q}$ is our time line. The year 1996 is assumed to start at time 0 *and every interval* $[i, i+1)$ *represents a day (for* $i \in \mathcal{Z}$ *and* $i \geq 0$*). Time intervals will be represented by their endpoints. They will always be assumed to be of the form* $[B, E)$ *where* B *and* E *are the endpoints.*

The above database represents the following information:

1. *There are three scheduled appointments for treatment of patient Smith. This is represented by three conjuncts within the disjunction defining the extension of the predicate* $treatment$.

2. *Chemotherapy appointments must be scheduled for a single day. Radiation appointments must be scheduled for two consecutive days. This information is represented by constraints* $\omega_2 = \omega_1 + 1$, $\omega_4 = \omega_3 + 1$, *and* $\omega_6 = \omega_5 + 2$.

3. *The first chemotherapy appointment for Smith should take place in the first three months of 1996 (i.e., days 0-91). This information is represented by the constraints* $\omega_1 \geq 0$ *and* $\omega_2 \leq 91$.

4. *The second chemotherapy appointment for Smith should take place in the second three months of 1996 (i.e., days 92-182). This information is represented by constraints* $\omega_3 \geq 91$ *and* $\omega_4 \leq 182$.

5. *The first chemotherapy appointment for Smith must precede the second by at least two months (60 days). This information is represented by constraint* $\omega_3 - \omega_2 \geq 60$.

6. *The radiation appointment for Smith should follow the second chemotherapy appointment by at least 20 days. Also, it should take place before the end of July (i.e., day 213). This information is represented by constraints* $\omega_5 - \omega_4 \geq 20$ *and* $\omega_6 \leq 213$.

Let us now define queries. The concept of query defined here is more expressive than the query languages for temporal constraint networks proposed in [Brusoni *et al.*, 1994; Brusoni *et al.*, 1997; van Beek, 1991], and it is similar to the concept of query in TMM [Schrag *et al.*, 1992].

Definition 7.4.2. A first order modal query *over an indefinite constraint database is an expression of the form* $\overline{x}/\overline{\mathcal{D}}, \overline{t}/\overline{\mathcal{T}} : \; OP\ \phi(\overline{x}, \overline{t})$ *where* OP *is the modal operator* $\Diamond$ *or* $\Box$, *and* ϕ *is a formula of* $(\mathcal{L} \cup \mathcal{EQ})^*$. *The constraints in formula* ϕ *are only* $\mathcal{L}$ *constraints and* $\mathcal{EQ}$ *constraints.*

Modal queries will be distinguished in *certainty* or *necessity* queries ($\Box$) and *possibility* queries ($\Diamond$).

Example 7.4.4. *The following query refers to the database of Example 7.4.2 and asks "Who was the person who possibly had a conversation with Fred during this person's walk in the park?":*

$$x/\mathcal{D} : \; \Diamond(\exists t_1, t_2, t_3, t_4/\mathcal{Q})$$
$$(walk(x, t_1, t_2) \wedge talk(x, Fred, t_3, t_4) \wedge t_1 < t_3 \wedge t_4 < t_2)$$

Let us observe that each query can only have *one* modal operator which should be placed in front of a formula of $(\mathcal{L} \cup \mathcal{EQ})^*$. Thus we do not have a full-fledged modal query language like the ones in [Levesque, 1984; Lipski, 1979; Reiter, 1988]. Such a query language can be beneficial in any application involving indefinite information but we will not consider this issue in this chapter.

We now define the concept of an answer to a query.

Definition 7.4.3. *Let q be the query $\overline{x}/\overline{\mathcal{D}}, \overline{t}/\overline{\mathcal{T}} : \Diamond\phi(\overline{x}, \overline{t})$ over an indefinite constraint database DB. The answer to q is a pair $(answer(\overline{x}, \overline{t}),\ \emptyset)$ such that*

1. *$answer(\overline{x}, \overline{t})$ is a formula of the form*

$$\bigvee_{j=1}^{k} Local_j(\overline{x}, \overline{t})$$

   where $Local_j(\overline{x}, \overline{t})$ is a conjunction of $\mathcal{L}$ constraints in variables $\overline{t}$ and $\mathcal{EQ}$ constraints in variables $\overline{x}$.

2. *Let V be a variable assignment for variables $\overline{x}$ and $\overline{t}$. If there exists a model M of DB which agrees with $\mathcal{M}_{\mathcal{L}\cup\mathcal{EQ}}$ on the interpretation of the symbols of $\mathcal{L} \cup \mathcal{EQ}$, and M satisfies $\phi(\overline{x}, \overline{t})$ under V then V satisfies $answer(\overline{x}, \overline{t})$ and vice versa.*

We have chosen the notation $(answer(\overline{x}, \overline{t}),\ \emptyset)$ to signify that *an answer is also a database* which consists of a single predicate defined by the formula $answer(\overline{x}, \overline{t})$ and the empty constraint store. In other words, no Skolem constant (i.e., no uncertainty) is present in the answer to a modal query. Although our databases may contain uncertainty, we know for sure what is possible and what is certain.

Example 7.4.5. *The answer to the query of Example 7.4.4 is $(x = Mary,\ \emptyset)$.*

The definition of answer in the case of certainty queries is the same as Definition 7.4.3 with the second condition changed to:

2. *Let M be any model of DB which agrees with $\mathcal{M}_{\mathcal{L}\cup\mathcal{EQ}}$ on the interpretation of the symbols of $\mathcal{L} \cup \mathcal{EQ}$. Let V be a variable assignment for variables $\overline{x}$ and $\overline{t}$. If M satisfies $\phi(\overline{x}, \overline{t})$ under V then V satisfies $answer(\overline{x}, \overline{t})$ and vice versa.*

Definition 7.4.4. *A query is called* closed *or* yes/no *if it does not have any free variables. Queries with free variables are called* open.

Example 7.4.6. *The query of Example 7.4.4 is open. The following is its corresponding closed query:*

$$: \Diamond(\exists x/\mathcal{D})(\exists t_1, t_2, t_3, t_4/\mathcal{Q})$$
$$(walk(x, t_1, t_2) \wedge talk(x, Fred, t_3, t_4) \wedge t_1 < t_3 \wedge t_4 < t_2)$$

By convention, when a query is closed, its answer can be either $(true, \emptyset)$ (which means yes) or $(false, \emptyset)$ (which means no).

Example 7.4.7. *The answer to the query of Example 7.4.6 is $(true, \emptyset)$ i.e., yes.*

Let us now give some more examples of queries.

Example 7.4.8. *Let us consider the database of Example 7.4.3 and the query "Find all appointments for patients that can possibly start at the 92th day of 1996". This query can be expressed as follows:*

$$\{\, x, y/\mathcal{D} : \ \diamond(\exists t_1, t_2/\mathcal{Q})(treatment(x, y, t_1, t_2) \wedge t_1 = 92) \,\}$$

The answer to this query is the following:

$$(\,(x = Smith \wedge y = Chem2) \vee (x = Smith \wedge y = Radiation),\ true\,)$$

Example 7.4.9. *The following query refers to the database of Example 7.4.3 and asks "Is it certain that the first Chemotherapy appointment for Smith is scheduled to take place in the first month of 1996?":*

$$:\ \square(\exists t_1, t_2/\mathcal{Q})(treatment(Smith, Chem1, t_1, t_2) \wedge 0 \leq t_1 < t_2 \leq 31)$$

The answer to this query is no.

7.4.3 Query Evaluation is Quantifier Elimination

Query evaluation over indefinite constraint databases can be viewed as quantifier elimination in the theory $Th(\mathcal{M}_{\mathcal{L}\cup\mathcal{EQ}})$. $Th(\mathcal{M}_{\mathcal{L}\cup\mathcal{EQ}})$ admits quantifier elimination. This is a consequence of the assumption that $Th(\mathcal{M}_{\mathcal{L}})$ admits quantifier elimination (see beginning of this section) and the fact that $Th(\mathcal{M}_{\mathcal{EQ}})$ admits quantifier elimination (proved in [Kanellakis *et al.*, 1995]). The following theorem is essentially from [Koubarakis, 1997b].

Theorem 7.4.1. *Let DB be the indefinite constraint database*

$$\bigwedge_{i=1}^{m} (\forall \overline{x_i}/\overline{\mathcal{D}})(\forall \overline{t_i}/\overline{\mathcal{T}}_i)(\bigvee_{j=1}^{l_i} Local_j(\overline{x_i}, \overline{t_i}, \overline{\omega}) \equiv p_i(\overline{x_i}, \overline{t_i})) \ \wedge$$

$$ConstraintStore(\overline{\omega})$$

and q be the query $\overline{y}/\overline{\mathcal{D}}, \overline{z}/\overline{\mathcal{T}} \ : \ \diamond\phi(\overline{y}, \overline{z})$. The answer to q is $(answer(\overline{y}, \overline{z}),\ \emptyset)$ where $answer(\overline{y}, \overline{z})$ is a disjunction of conjunctions of $\mathcal{EQ}$ constraints in variables $\overline{y}$ and $\mathcal{L}$ constraints in variables $\overline{z}$ obtained by eliminating quantifiers from the following formula of $\mathcal{L}_{=}$:

$$(\exists \overline{\omega}/\overline{\mathcal{T}}')(ConstraintStore(\overline{\omega}) \wedge \psi(\overline{y}, \overline{z}, \overline{\omega}))$$

In this formula the vector of Skolem constants $\overline{\omega}$ has been substituted by a vector of appropriately quantified variables with the same name ($\overline{\mathcal{T}}'$ is a vector of sorts of $\mathcal{L}$). $\psi(\overline{y}, \overline{z}, \overline{\omega})$ is obtained from $\phi(\overline{y}, \overline{z})$ by substituting every atomic formula with database predicate p_i by an equivalent disjunction of conjunctions of $\mathcal{L}$ constraints. This equivalent disjunction is obtained by consulting the definition

$$\bigvee_{j=1}^{l_i} Local_j(\overline{x_i}, \overline{t_i}, \overline{\omega}) \equiv p_i(\overline{x_i}, \overline{t_i})$$

of predicate p_i in the database DB.

If q is a certainty query then $answer(\overline{y}, \overline{z})$ is obtained by eliminating quantifiers from the formula

$$(\forall \overline{\omega}/\overline{T}')(ConstraintStore(\overline{\omega}) \supset \psi(\overline{y}, \overline{z}, \overline{\omega}))$$

where $ConstraintStore(\overline{\omega})$ and $\psi(\overline{y}, \overline{z}, \overline{\omega})$ are defined as above.

Example 7.4.10. *Using the above theorem, the query of Example 7.4.4 can be answered by eliminating quantifiers from the formula:*

$$\begin{array}{c}(\exists \omega_1, \omega_2, \omega_3, \omega_4/\mathcal{Q}) \\ (\omega_1 < \omega_2 \wedge \omega_1 < \omega_3 \wedge \omega_3 < \omega_2 \wedge \omega_3 < \omega_4 \wedge \\ (\exists t_1, t_2, t_3, t_4/\mathcal{Q})((x = Mary \wedge t_1 = \omega_1 \wedge t_2 = \omega_2) \wedge \\ (x = Mary \wedge t_3 = \omega_3 \wedge t_4 = \omega_4) \wedge t_1 < t_3 \wedge t_4 < t_2)\end{array}$$

The result of this elimination is the formula $x = Mary$.

Answering queries by the above method is mostly of theoretical interest. For implementations of this scheme more efficient alternatives have to be considered.

Let us close this section by pointing out that what we have defined is a *database scheme*. Given various choices for $\mathcal{L}$ (e.g., $\mathcal{L} = LIN$), one gets a *model* of indefinite constraint databases (e.g., the model of indefinite LIN constraint databases). Examples of such instantiations will be seen repeatedly in the forthcoming Sections 7.5, 7.6 and 7.7 where we demonstrate that the proposals of [van Beek, 1991; Brusoni *et al.*, 1994; Brusoni *et al.*, 1995b; Brusoni *et al.*, 1997; Brusoni *et al.*, 1995a; Brusoni *et al.*, 1999; Koubarakis, 1993; Koubarakis, 1994b] are subsumed by the scheme of indefinite constraint databases.

7.5 The LATER System

In [Brusoni *et al.*, 1994; Brusoni *et al.*, 1997; Brusoni *et al.*, 1995b] sets of $LATER$ constraints are considered as knowledge bases with indefinite temporal knowledge, and are queried in sophisticated ways using a first-order modal query language. This section will show that query answering in the LATER system is really an instance of the scheme of indefinite constraint databases.

We will first specify a method for translating a LATER knowledge base KB (i.e., a set of $LATER$ constraints) to an *indefinite $LATER$ constraint database DB*. The translation is done in two steps. First, for each symbolic point or interval I in KB, we introduce a fact $happens_I(\omega_I)$ in $EventsAndFacts(DB)$ where $happens_I$ is a new database predicate and ω_I is a new Skolem constant of appropriate sort. Then, for each constraint c between symbolic intervals I and J in KB, we introduce the same constraint between Skolem constants ω_I and ω_J in $ConstraintStore(DB)$.

Example 7.5.1. *The following is the indefinite $LATER$ constraint database which corresponds to the* LATER *knowledge base of Example 7.2.4.**

$$(\ \{\ happens_{TomWork}(\omega_{TomWork}),\ happens_{MaryWork}(\omega_{MaryWork}),$$

*In this and the next section we do not follow Definition 7.4.1 precisely for reasons of clarity and prefer to write sets of conjuncts instead of conjunctions. Also, when it comes to $EventsAndFacts(DB)$, we write positive atomic formulas of first order logic and mean the *completions* of these formulas [Reiter, 1984].

$happens_{AnnWork}(\omega_{AnnWork})\ \}$,

$\{\ \omega_{TomWork}\ Since\ 1/1/1995\ 14:15,\ \ \omega_{TomWork}\ Until\ 1/1/1995\ 18:30,$

$\omega_{TomWork}\ Before\ \omega_{MaryWork},\ \ \omega_{MaryWork}\ Lasting\ At\ Least\ 4:40\ hours,$

$start(\omega_{AnnWork})\ At\ 1/1/1995,\ \ \omega_{AnnWork}\ Lasting\ 3:00\ hours,$

$end(\omega_{AnnWork})\ Before\ 1/1/1995\ 18:00\ \}\ )$

Now it is easy to translate queries over a LATER knowledge base to first order modal queries over an indefinite $LATER$ constraint database. We will consider all types of queries presented in [Brusoni *et al.*, 1994; Brusoni *et al.*, 1995b; Brusoni *et al.*, 1997].

1. *WHEN queries.* A WHEN query is of the form

   $$WHEN\ T\,?$$

   where T is a symbolic point or interval in the queried LATER knowledge base. For the case of intervals, the corresponding query in our framework is

   $$x/\mathcal{I}:\ happens_T(x)$$

   and similarly for points.

   Example 7.5.2. *The query*

   $$WHEN\ TomWork\,?$$

   is translated into

   $$x/\mathcal{I}:\ happens_{TomWork}(x)$$

   and has the following answer over the database of Example 7.2.4:

   $$(\ \{x=\omega_{TomWork}\},$$

   $$\{\ \omega_{TomWork}\ Since\ 1/1/1995\ 14:15,\ \ \omega_{TomWork}\ Until\ 1/1/1995\ 18:30\ \}\ )$$

2. *MUST queries.* A MUST query in its simplest form is

   $$must\ c(I,J)\,?$$

   where I, J are symbolic time intervals and c is a temporal constraint in LATER (similarly for points). The corresponding query in our framework is

   $$:\ \Box(\exists x,y/\mathcal{I})(happens_I(x)\wedge happens_J(y)\wedge c(x,y))$$

   The extension to arbitrary MUST queries is straightforward.

Example 7.5.3. *The query*

$$MUST\ overlaps(AnnWork, MaryWork)\ ?$$

can be translated into

$$:\ \Box(\exists x, y/\mathcal{I})(happens_{AnnWork}(x) \wedge happens_{MaryWork}(y) \wedge Overlaps(x, y))$$

The answer to this query over the LATER *KB of Example 7.2.4 is*

$$(false,\ \emptyset)$$

which means NO.

3. *MAY queries.* The translation is similar to MUST queries but now the modal operator $\Diamond$ is used.

4. *Hypothetical queries.* The query language of our framework does not support hypothetical queries. They can be simulated by updating the database with an appropriate set of constraints and then asking a query.

7.6 Van Beek's Proposal for Querying IA Networks

In [van Beek, 1991] van Beek went beyond the typical reasoning problems studied for **IA** networks and considered them as knowledge bases about events that can be queried in more sophisticated ways. This section will show that van Beek's efforts can also be subsumed by our framework.

In [van Beek, 1991] an **IA** knowledge base is a set of Interval Algebra constraints among appropriately named event constants (see Example 7.2.2). We will first specify a method for translating an **IA** knowledge base KB to an indefinite IA constraint database DB. The translation is done in two steps. First, for each event e in KB, we introduce the facts

$$event(e),\ \ happens(e, \omega_e)$$

in $EventsAndFacts(DB)$ where $event$ and $happens$ are database predicates and ω_e is a new Skolem constant of sort $\mathcal{I}$.* Then, for each constraint c between events e_1 and e_2 in KB, we introduce the same constraint between events ω_{e_1} and ω_{e_2} in $ConstraintStore(DB)$.

Example 7.6.1. *The following is the indefinite IA constraint database corresponding to the IA constraints of Example 7.2.2:*

$$(\ \{\ event(breakfast),\ event(paper),\ event(coffee),\ event(walk),$$

$$happens(breakfast, \omega_{breakfast}),\ happens(paper, \omega_{paper}),$$

$$happens(coffee, \omega_{coffee}),\ happens(walk, \omega_{walk})\ \},$$

$$\{\ \omega_{breakfast}\ before\ \omega_{walk},$$

*Let $\mathcal{I}$ be the only sort of language IA.

ω_{coffee} *during* $\omega_{breakfast}$,

ω_{paper} *overlaps* $\omega_{breakfast} \vee \cdots \vee \omega_{paper}$ *equals* $\omega_{breakfast}$,

ω_{paper} *overlaps* $\omega_{coffee} \vee \omega_{paper}$ *starts* $\omega_{coffee} \vee \omega_{paper}$ *during* ω_{coffee} })

The first component of the above pair asserts the existence of four events and their times. The second component asserts "all we know" about these times in the form of IA constraints.

It is easy to translate queries over an **IA** KB to first order modal queries over an indefinite IA constraint database. We will consider all types of queries presented in [van Beek, 1991].

1. *Possibility* and *certainty* queries. These are very similar to MAY and MUST queries in LATER. The translation to our framework is also very similar. A certainty (resp. possibility) query is a formula of the form

   $$OP\ \phi(e_1, \ldots, e_n)?$$

   where OP is $\Box$ (resp. $\Diamond$), and ϕ is a quantifier free formula of IA with free variables $e_1, \ldots, e_n$. In our framework the corresponding query is

   $$: OP\ (\exists x_1, \ldots, x_N/\mathcal{D})(\exists t_1, \ldots, t_n/\mathcal{I})$$

   $$(event(x_1) \wedge \cdots \wedge event(x_n) \wedge happens(x_1, t_1) \wedge \cdots \wedge happens(x_2, t_2) \wedge$$

   $$\phi(t_1, \ldots, t_n))$$

2. *Aggregation questions*. An aggregation question is of the form

   $$x_1, \ldots, x_n :\ x_1 \in E \wedge \cdots \wedge x_n \in E \wedge OP\ \phi(x_1, \ldots, x_n)$$

   where E is the set of all events in the KB, OP is the modal operator $\Diamond$ or $\Box$ and ϕ is a quantifier free first order formula of IA.

   The corresponding query in our framework is

   $$x_1, \ldots, x_n/\mathcal{D} :\ OP\ (\exists t_1, \ldots, t_n/\mathcal{I})$$

   $$(event(x_1) \wedge \cdots \wedge event(x_n) \wedge happens(x_1, t_1) \wedge \cdots \wedge happens(x_2, t_2) \wedge$$

   $$\phi(t_1, \ldots, t_n))$$

   Example 7.6.2. *The following* **IA** *KB provides information about a patient's visits to the hospital during the period 1990-1991:*

   1990 *meets* 1991,

   visit4 during 1990, *visit5 during* 1990,

$$visit6\ during\ 1991, \quad visit7\ during\ 1991,$$

$$visit4\ before\ visit5, \quad visit5\ before\ visit6, \quad visit6\ before\ visit7$$

The aggregation query

$$x : \ x \in Visits \wedge \Box(x\ during\ 1991)$$

where $Visits$ is the set of all events can be translated into the following query in our framework:

$$x/\mathcal{D} : \ (\exists t/\mathcal{I})(event(x) \wedge happens(x,t) \wedge \Box(x\ during\ 1991))$$

Note that calendars are not part of IA. To deal with them we follow our approach for $LATER$: calendar primitives (e.g., years) can be introduced as terms of the language and interpreted accordingly.

If the above query is executed over the indefinite IA constraint database which corresponds to KB (it is easy to construct this database as it was done in Example 7.6.1) then it has the following answer:

$$(\{x = visit1, \ x = visit7\}, \ \emptyset)$$

7.7 Other Proposals

In [Brusoni *et al.*, 1995a; Brusoni *et al.*, 1999] the LATER team extended the relational model of data with the temporal reasoning facilities of LATER. In their proposal, a relational database stores non-temporal information about events and facts which times are constrained by a set of $LATER$ constraints.

Earlier (and independently) similar work had been done by Koubarakis in [Koubarakis, 1993; Koubarakis, 1994b] where the model of indefinite temporal constraint databases was first defined as an extension of the relational data model.

The above data models and query languages are instantiations of the scheme of indefinite constraint databases presented in this chapter. The model of [Brusoni *et al.*, 1995a; Brusoni *et al.*, 1999] is essentially the model of *indefinite $LATER$ constraint databases*. Similarly the model of [Koubarakis, 1993; Koubarakis, 1994b] is the model of *indefinite $DIFF$ constraint databases.* The only notable difference is that in this chapter we have developed our framework using first-order logic while Koubarakis, Brusoni, Console, Pernici and Terenziani use the relational data model.

Another related effort is of course TMM [Dean and McDermott, 1987; Schrag *et al.*, 1992] that can be seen to be an *ancestor* of all of the above systems. TMM has a very expressive representation language so it cannot be presented under the umbrella of the proposed scheme. However, if we omit *persistence assumptions, projection rules* and *dependencies* from the TMM formalism then the resulting subset is subsumed by indefinite $DIFF$ constraint databases.

Now that we have investigated the representational power of the indefinite constraint database scheme in detail, we turn to its computational properties and ask the following question: What is the computational complexity of the proposed scheme when constraints encode temporal information? In particular, do we stay within PTIME when the classes of constraints utilised for representing temporal information have satisfiability and variable elimination problems that can be solved in PTIME? These questions are answered in the following section.

7.8 Query Answering in Indefinite Constraint Databases

In this section, we study the computational complexity of evaluating possibility and certainty queries over indefinite constraint databases when constraints belong to the temporal languages studied in Section 7.2. The complexity of query evaluation will be measured using the notion of *data complexity* originally introduced by database theoreticians [Vardi, 1982]. When we use data complexity, we measure the complexity of query evaluation as a function of the database size only; the size of the query is considered *fixed*. This assumption is reasonable and it has also been made in previous work on querying temporal constraint networks [van Beek, 1991]. For the purposes of this chapter the *size* of the database under the data complexity measure can be defined as the number of symbols of a binary alphabet that are used for its encoding.

We already know that evaluating possibility queries over indefinite constraint databases can be NP-hard even when we only have equality and inequality constraints between atomic values [Abiteboul *et al.*, 1991]; similarly evaluating certainty queries is co-NP-hard. It is therefore important to seek *tractable* instances of query evaluation.;

The rest of this chapter does not consider equality constraints (from language $\mathcal{EQ}$) as they have been used in the definition of databases (Definition 7.4.1) and queries (Definition 7.4.2). This can be done without loss of generality because they do not change our results in any way. We reach tractable cases of query evaluation by restricting the classes of $\mathcal{L}$ constraints, databases and queries we allow. The concepts of query type and database type introduced below allow us to make these distinctions.

7.8.1 Query Types

A *query type* is a tuple of the following form:

$$Q(OpenOrClosed, Modality, FO\text{-}Formula\text{-}Type, Constraints)$$

The first argument of a query type can take the values $Open$ or $Closed$ and distinguishes between open and closed queries. The argument *Modality* can be $\Diamond$ or $\Box$ representing possibility or necessity queries respectively.

The third argument $FO\text{-}Formula\text{-}Type$ can take the values

$$FirstOrder,\ PositiveExistential \text{ or } SinglePredicate.$$

The value $FirstOrder$ denotes that the first-order expression part of the query can be an *arbitrary* first-order formula. Similarly, $PositiveExistential$ denotes that the first order part of the query is a *positive existential* formula i.e., it is of the form $(\exists \overline{x}/\overline{s})\phi(\overline{x})$ where ϕ involves only the logical symbols $\wedge$ and $\vee$. Finally, $SinglePredicate$ denotes that the query is of the form $\overline{u}/\overline{s}_1 : \ OP\ (\exists \overline{t}/\overline{s}_2)p(\overline{u}, \overline{t})$ where $\overline{u}$ and $\overline{t}$ are vectors of variables, $\overline{s}_1,\ \overline{s}_2$ are vectors of sorts, p is a database predicate symbol and OP is a modal operator.

The fourth argument $Constraints$ denotes the class of constraints that are used in the query. Definition 7.4.2 allows queries to contain any constraint from the class of $\mathcal{L}$ constraints. This section will also consider restricting query constraints to members of any constraint class $\mathcal{C}$ such that $\mathcal{C}$ is a subclass of the class of $\mathcal{L}$ constraints.

7.8.2 Database Types

A *database type* is a tuple of the following form:

$$DB(Arity, LocalCondition, ConstraintStore)$$

Argument $Arity$ denotes the maximum arity of the database predicates. It can take values

$$Monadic,\ Binary,\ Ternary, \ldots, N\text{-}ary \text{ (i.e., arbitrary)}.$$

Argument $LocalCondition$ denotes the constraint class used in the definition of the database predicates. Finally, argument $ConstraintStore$ denotes the class of constraints in the constraint store. Definition 7.4.1 allows the local conditions and the constraint store to contain any constraint from the class of $\mathcal{L}$ constraints. This section will also consider restrictions to members of any constraint class $\mathcal{C}$ such that $\mathcal{C}$ is a subclass of the class of $\mathcal{L}$ constraints.

7.8.3 Constraint Classes

In the rest of this section we will refer to certain constraint classes which we summarize below for ease of reference. Some of these classes have already been introduced in Section 7.2. Others are defined for the first time.

- $HDL, LIN, IA, SIA, ORD\text{-}Horn, PA$ and CPA defined earlier.
- $UTVPI$ and $UTVPI^{\neq}$.

  A $UTVPI$ *constraint* is a LIN constraint of the form $\pm x_1 \sim c$ or $\pm x_1 \pm x_2 \sim c$ where x_1, x_2 are variables ranging over the rational numbers, c is a rational constant and $\sim$ is $\leq$. The class of UTVPI$^{\neq}$ is obtained when $\sim$ is also allowed to be $\neq$.

  The following are some examples of $UTVPI^{\neq}$ constraints:

  $$-x_1 \leq 12,\ x_1 + x_2 \leq 2,\ x_3 - x_2 \leq 0.5,\ x_3 + x_2 \neq 6$$

  $UTVPI$ constraints are a natural extension of $DIFF$ constraints studied in [Dechter *et al.*, 1989]. They are also a subclass of $TVPI$ *constraints* [Shostak, 1981; Jaffar *et al.*, 1994]. $TVPI$ is an acronym for linear inequalities with at most *T*wo *V*ariables *P*er *I*nequality. In a similar spirit, $UTVPI$ is an acronym for $TVPI$ constraints with *U*nit coefficients.

  The class of $UTVPI^{\neq}$ constraints was first studied in [Koubarakis and Skiadopoulos, 1999; Koubarakis and Skiadopoulos, 2000].

- $2d\text{-}IA$ and $2d\text{-}ORD\text{-}Horn$.

  The class $2d\text{-}IA$ is a generalization of IA in two dimensions and it is based on the concept of *rectangle* in $\mathcal{Q}^2$ [Guesgen, 1989; Papadias *et al.*, 1995; Balbiani *et al.*,

1998]. Every rectangle r can be defined by a 4-tuple $(L_x^r, L_y^r, U_x^r, U_y^r)$ that gives the coordinates of the lower left and upper right corner of r. There are 13^2 basic relations in $2d\text{-}IA$ describing all possible configurations of 2 rectangles in $\mathcal{Q}^2$.

$2d\text{-}ORD\text{-}Horn$ is the subclass of $2d\text{-}IA$ which includes only these relations R with the property

$$r_1 \; R \; r_2 \equiv \phi(r_1, r_2) \wedge \psi(r_1, r_2)$$

where

- ϕ is a conjunction of $ORD\text{-}Horn$ constraints on variables L_x^r and U_x^r.
- ψ is a conjunction of $ORD\text{-}Horn$ constraints on variables L_y^r and U_y^r.

The above classes of constraints refer to *spatial* objects. It is interesting to consider them in this section because some interesting results for these can easily be obtained by the corresponding results for the temporal classes.

- $LINEQ$. This is the subclass of LIN which contains only linear equalities.
- $SORD$. This is the sub-algebra of PA which contains only the relations $\{<, >\}$. In other words, $SORD$ is the class of *strict order* constraints.
- $WORD$. This is the sub-algebra of PA which contains only the relations $\{\leq, \geq\}$. In other words, $WORD$ is the class of *weak order* constraints.
- $ORD\text{-}CON$. This is the subclass of LIN which contains only constraints of the form $x \sim r$ where x is a variable, r is a *rational constant* and $\sim$ is $<$, $>$, $\leq$, or $\geq$.
- $UTVPI\text{-}EQ$. This is the subclass of $UTVPI$ which contains only equality constraints.
- $RAT\text{-}EQUAL$. This is the subclass of $LINEQ$ which contains only equality constraints of the form $x = v$ where x is a variable and v is a *variable or a rational constant* (ordinary or Skolem).
- $RAT\text{-}EQUAL\text{-}CON$. This is the subclass of $RAT\text{-}EQUAL$ which contains only equality constraints of the form $x = a$ where x is a variable and a is a *rational constant* (ordinary or Skolem).

  Among other things, this class is useful for specifying databases of type

  $$DB(A, RAT\text{-}EQUAL\text{-}CON, \mathcal{C})$$

  where A is an arity and $\mathcal{C}$ is a constraint class. In databases of this type, predicates are defined by completions (in the sense of [Reiter, 1984]) of formulas of the form $p(\overline{a}, \overline{\omega})$ where $\overline{a}$ is a vector of rational constants and $\overline{\omega}$ is a vector of Skolem constants. For example, the database

  $$(\; \{\; (\forall t_1, t_2, t_3/\mathcal{Q})((t_1 = \omega_1 \wedge t_2 = \omega_2 \wedge t_3 = 1) \equiv p(t_1, t_2, t_3)) \;\}, \\ \{\; \omega_1 < \omega_2 \;\} \;)$$

is of type

$$DB(3\text{-}ary, RAT\text{-}EQUAL\text{-}CON, SORD).$$

These databases are typical of the kind of databases encountered in temporal and spatial problems involving indefinite information (where information about non-temporal entities like *Mary* and *Fred* of Example 7.4.2 has been abstracted away).

- $NONE$. This is the class which contains only the trivial constraints $true$ and $false$. This class is useful for specifying queries with database predicates but no constraints. Also, it is useful for specifying databases of the form

$$(EventsAndFacts(DB),\ ConstraintStore(DB))$$

where $ConstraintStore(DB) = \emptyset$ (i.e., there might be Skolem constants but we know nothing about them).

Now that we have introduced the constraints classes that we will consider, we are ready to present our results. Proofs are omitted and can be found in [Koubarakis and Skiadopoulos, 2000].

7.8.4 PTIME Problems

The following theorem gives our main PTIME upper bound.

Theorem 7.8.1. *The evaluation of*

(a) $Q(Closed, \Diamond, PositiveExistential, HDL)$ *queries over* $DB(N\text{-}ary, HDL, HDL)$ *databases,*

(b) $Q(Closed, \Box, PositiveExistential, LINEQ)$ *queries over* $DB(N\text{-}ary, LINEQ, HDL)$ *databases,*

(c) $Q(Open, \Diamond, PositiveExistential, UTVPI^{\neq})$ *queries over* $DB(N\text{-}ary, UTVPI^{\neq}, UTVPI^{\neq})$ *databases and*

(d) $Q(Open, \Box, SinglePredicate, NONE)$ *queries over* $DB(N\text{-}ary, UTVPI\text{-}EQ \cup UTVPI^{\neq}_{\leq 1}, UTVPI^{\neq})$ *databases*

can be performed in PTIME.

The above theorem is very interesting. It shows how classes with tractable satisfiability and/or variable elimination problems can be combined with a logical database framework to obtain a much more expressive representational framework where query answering still remains tractable. The reader should notice the restrictions on the queries and databases that enable tractability.

Let us now consider databases and queries involving higher-order objects i.e., intervals and rectangles and derive a similar result.

Theorem 7.8.2. *The evaluation of*

(a) $Q(Closed, \diamond, PositiveExistential, ORD\text{-}Horn)$ *queries over* $DB(N\text{-}ary, ORD\text{-}Horn, ORD\text{-}Horn)$ *databases,*

(b) $Q(Closed, \diamond, PositiveExistential, 2d\text{-}ORD\text{-}Horn)$ *queries over* $DB(N\text{-}ary, 2d\text{-}ORD\text{-}Horn, 2d\text{-}ORD\text{-}Horn)$ *databases,*

(c) $Q(Open, \diamond, PositiveExistential, SIA)$ *queries over* $DB(N\text{-}ary, SIA, SIA)$ *databases*

can be performed in PTIME.

Theorem 7.8.2(b) is an interesting result for rectangle databases with indefinite information over $\mathcal{Q}^2$. This result can be generalized to $\mathcal{Q}^n$ if one defines an appropriate algebra $nd\text{-}ORD\text{-}Horn$.

7.8.5 Lower Bounds

The theorems of the previous section gave us restrictions on queries, databases and constraint classes that enable us to have tractable query answering problems. We now consider identifying the precise boundary between tractable and intractable query answering problems for indefinite constraint databases with linear constraints. We start our inquiry by considering whether the results of Theorem 7.8.1 can be extended to more expressive classes of queries.* For example, can we allow negation in the queries (equivalently, can we allow arbitrary first order formulas) and still get results like Theorem 7.8.1(a) or 7.8.1(b)? The following theorem shows that the answer to this question is negative.†

Theorem 7.8.3 ([Abiteboul *et al.*, 1991]). *Let* DBC *be the set of databases of type*

$$DB(4\text{-}ary, RAT\text{-}EQUAL\text{-}CON, NONE)$$

with the additional restriction that every Skolem constant occurs at most once in any member of DBC*. Then:*

1. *There exists a query* $q \in Q(Closed, \diamond, FirstOrder, RAT\text{-}EQUAL)$ *such that deciding whether* $q(db) = yes$ *is NP-complete even when db ranges over databases in the set* DBC*.*

2. *There exists a query* $q \in Q(Closed, \Box, FirstOrder, RAT\text{-}EQUAL)$ *such that deciding whether* $q(db) = yes$ *is co-NP-complete even when db ranges over databases in the set* DBC*.*

Theorem 7.8.1(a) and (b) together with the above theorem establish a clear separation between tractable and possibly intractable query answering problems. The presence of negation in the query language can easily lead us to computationally hard query evaluation problems (NP-complete or co-NP-complete) even with very simple input databases.

Another issue that we would like to consider is whether one can improve Theorem 7.8.1(b) with a class which is more expressive than $LINEQ$ (for example LIN). The following result shows that this is not possible; even the presence of strict order constraints in the query is enough to lead us away from PTIME.

*Similar issues arise for Theorem 7.8.2. The results of this section can easily be generalised to this case.

†The theorem has been proved in [Abiteboul *et al.*, 1991] for equality constraints over any countably infinite domain thus it holds for the domain of rational numbers too.

Theorem 7.8.4 ([van der Meyden, 1992]). *There exists a query in*

$$Q(Closed, \Box, Conjunctive, SORD)$$

with co-NP-hard data complexity over

$$DB(Binary, RAT\text{-}EQUAL\text{-}CON, SORD)$$

databases.

Note that for the above theorem to be true, $SORD$ constraints must be present *both in the database and in the query.* Otherwise, as Theorems 7.8.5 and 7.8.6 imply, conjunctive query evaluation can be done in PTIME.

Theorem 7.8.5. *Evaluating* $Q(Closed, \Box, PositiveExistential, NONE)$ *queries over*

$$DB(N\text{-}ary, RAT\text{-}EQUAL\text{-}CON, HDL)$$

databases can be done in PTIME.

Theorem 7.8.6. *Evaluating* $Q(Closed, \Box, Conjunctive, LIN)$ *queries over*

$$DB(N\text{-}ary, RAT\text{-}EQUAL\text{-}CON, NONE)$$

databases can be done in PTIME.

A final issue that the careful reader might be wondering about is whether Parts (c) and (d) of Theorem 7.8.1 can be extended. Let us consider Part (c) first. Theorem 7.8.3 shows that we should not expect to stay within PTIME if we move away from positive existential queries. So the only way that this result could be improved is by discovering a class $\mathcal{C}$ such that $UTVPI^{\neq} \subset \mathcal{C} \subset HDL$ and $VAR\text{-}ELIM(\mathcal{C})$ is in PTIME. This is therefore an interesting open problem; its solution will also be very interesting to linear programming researchers [Hochbaum and Naor, 1994; Goldin, 1997].

Let us now consider whether we can improve Theorem 7.8.1(d). The following result shows that this is *not* possible by extending the class of constraints allowed in the definitions of the database predicates so that *more than one* non $UTVPI\text{-}EQ$ constraints are allowed in each conjunction.*

Theorem 7.8.7. *There exists a query in* $Q(Closed, \Box, SinglePredicate, NONE)$ *with co-NP-hard data complexity over*

$$DB(Monadic, RAT\text{-}EQUAL\text{-}CON \cup WORD_{\leq 2}, SORD)$$

databases.

The following theorem complements the previous one by showing that the query answering problem considered in Theorem 7.8.1 (d) becomes co-NP-hard if we slightly extend the class of queries considered (more precisely, if we consider conjunctive queries with *two* conjuncts that are database predicates and no constraints).

---

*Since our result is negative, it is enough to consider closed queries.

Theorem 7.8.8. *There exists a query q in* $Q(Closed, \Box, Conjunctive, NONE)$ *with co-NP-hard data complexity over databases in the class*

$$DB(Monadic, RAT\text{-}EQUAL\text{-}CON \cup WORD_{\leq 1}, SORD).$$

The query q has exactly two conjuncts that are database predicates.

We can now conclude that it is unlikely that Theorem 7.8.1(d) can be improved except with the discovery of a class of constraints $\mathcal{C}$ such that $UTVPI^{\neq} \subset \mathcal{C} \subset HDL$ and $VAR\text{-}ELIM(\mathcal{C})$ is in PTIME (this is similar to what we concluded for Theorem 7.8.1(c)).

Let us close this section by summarising what we have achieved. The main tractability result of this section is Theorem 7.8.1. The rest of this section has focused on establishing that this theorem outlines very precisely the frontier between tractable and intractable query processing problems in indefinite constraint databases with Horn disjunctive linear constraints. The two cases left open by our results can only be resolved after answering an important open question in the area of linear programming (i.e., whether there exists a class of constraints $\mathcal{C}$ such that $UTVPI^{\neq} \subset \mathcal{C} \subset HDL$ and $VAR\text{-}ELIM(\mathcal{C})$ is in PTIME [Hochbaum and Naor, 1994; Goldin, 1997]).

7.9 Concluding remarks

We presented the scheme of indefinite constraint databases using first-order logic as our representation language. We demonstrated that when this scheme is instantiated with temporal constraints, the resulting formalism is more expressive than the standard machinery of temporal constraint networks. Previous proposals by [van Beek, 1991] and [Brusoni *et al.*, 1997] served to validate our claims.

We have also studied the problem of query evaluation for indefinite constraint databases when constraints encode temporal information. As it might be expected the problem of evaluating first-order possibility or certainty queries over indefinite temporal constraint databases turns out to be hard (NP-hard for possibility queries and co-NP-hard for certainty queries if we use the data complexity measure). Fortunately, there are many useful cases when query evaluation is tractable.

The reader of this chapter is invited to consider the application of similar ideas to spatial constraint databases and their use in querying geographical, image and multimedia databases (e.g., "Give me all the images where there is an olive tree *to the left* of a house"). The main technical challenge here is to develop variable and quantifier elimination algorithms for interesting classes of spatial constraints. Some recent interesting work in this area appears in [Skiadopoulos, 2002].

Finally, implementation techniques for models based on our proposal are urgently needed. Not much has been done in this area with the exception of work by the LATER and TMM groups [Brusoni *et al.*, 1999; Dean, 1989].

Handbook of Temporal Reasoning in Artificial Intelligence
Edited by M. Fisher, D. Gabbay and L. Vila

Chapter 8

Processing Qualitative Temporal Constraints

Alfonso Gerevini

In this chapter we provide an overview of the main techniques for processing qualitative temporal constraints. We survey a collection of algorithms for solving fundamental reasoning problems in the context of Allen's Interval Algebra, Vilain and Kautz's Point Algebra, and of other tractable and intractable classes of temporal relations. These problems include determining the satisfiability of a given set S of constraints; finding a consistent instantiation of the variables in S; deducing new (implicit) constraints from S, and computing the minimal network representation of S.

8.1 Introduction

Reasoning about qualitative temporal information has been an important research field in artificial intelligence (AI) for two decades, and it has been applied in the context of various AI areas. Such areas include knowledge representation (e.g., [Schmiedel, 1990; Miller, 1990; Schubert and Hwang, 1989; van Beek, 1991; Artale and Franconi, 1994]), natural language understanding (e.g., [Allen, 1984; Miller and Schubert, 1990; Song and Cohen, 1988]), commonsense reasoning (e.g., [Allen and Hayes, 1985]), diagnostic reasoning and expert systems (e.g., [Nökel, 1991; Brusoni *et al.*, 1998]), reasoning about plans (e.g., [Allen, 1991a; Tsang, 1986; Kautz, 1987; Kautz, 1991; Weida and Litman, 1992; Song and Cohen, 1996; Yang, 1997]) and scheduling (e.g., [Rit, 1986]).

Qualitative temporal information can often be represented in terms of temporal constraints among point or interval variables over a linear, continuous and unbound time domain (e.g., the rational numbers). In the following we give an example from an imaginary trains transportation domain, that will be used through the rest of the chapter to illustrate the prominent approaches to reasoning about qualitative temporal information expressible as binary temporal constraints.

Suppose that we want to represent the temporal information contained in the following simple story (see Figure 8.1):*

- *during its travel from city* `C1` *to city* `C2`*, train* `T1` *stopped first at the station* `S1` *and then at station* `S2`*;*

*This is a revised and extended version of an example that we gave in [Gerevini, 1997].

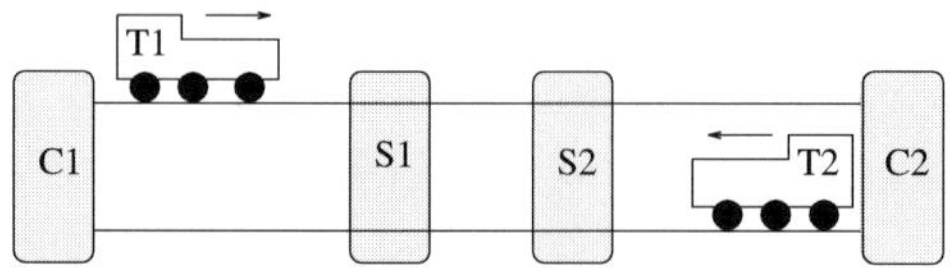

Figure 8.1: Pictorial description of the trains example

- *train* T2 *traveled in the opposite direction of* T1 *(i.e., from* C2 *to* C1*);*
- *during its trip,* T2 *stopped first at* S2 *and then at* S1*;*
- *when* T2 *arrived at* S1, T1 *was stopping there too;*
- T1 *and* T2 *left* S1 *at different times;*
- T1 *arrived at* C2 *before* T2 *arrived at* C1.

These sentences contain some explicit qualitative information about the ordering of the time intervals during which the events described occurred. In particular:

- from the first sentence we can derive that the intervals of time during which T1 stopped at S1 (at(T1,S1)) and at S2 (at(T1,S2)) are *contained* in the interval of time during which T1 traveled from C1 to C2 (travel(T1,C1,C2));
- from the second sentence we can derive that at(T1,S1) is *before* at(T1,S2);
- from the third and the fourth sentences we can derive that at(T2,S1) and at(T2,S2) are *during* travel(T2,C2,C1) and that at(T2,S2) is *before* at(T2,S1);
- from the fourth sentence we can derive that the starting time of at(T1,S1) *precedes* the starting time of at(T2,S1) and that the starting time of at(T2,S1) *precedes* the end time of at(T1,S1);
- from the fifth sentence we can derive that at(T1,S1) and at(T2,S1) cannot finish at the same time (i.e., that the end times of at(T1,S1) and at(T2,S1) are different time points); and,
- finally, from the last sentence we can derive the constraint that the end time of travel(T1,C1,C2) is *before* the end time of travel(T2,C2,C1).*

Suppose that in addition we know that no more than one train can stop at S2 at the same time (say, because it is a very small station). Then we also have that

- at(T2,S2) is *disjoint* from at(T1,S2).

*Despite when T2 arrived at S1 T1 was still there, it is possible that T2 had to stay at S1 enough time to allow T1 to arrive at C2 before the arrival of T2 at C1.

Relation	Inverse	Meaning
$I\ before\ (b)\ J$	$J\ after\ (a)\ I$	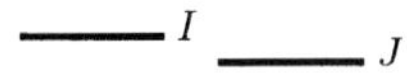
$I\ meets\ (m)\ J$	$J\ met\text{-}by\ (mi)\ I$	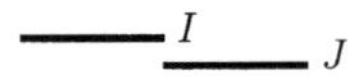
$I\ overlaps\ (o)\ J$	$J\ overlapped\text{-}by\ (oi)\ I$	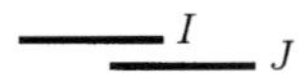
$I\ during\ (d)\ J$	$J\ contains\ (c)\ I$	
$I\ starts\ (s)\ J$	$J\ started\text{-}by\ (si)\ I$	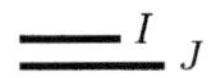
$I\ finishes\ (f)\ J$	$J\ finished\text{-}by\ (fi)\ I$	
$I\ equal\ (eq)\ J$	$J\ equal\ I$	

Figure 8.2: The thirteen basic relations of IA. IA contains 2^{13} relations, each of which is a disjunction of basic relations.

In terms of relations in Allen's Interval Algebra (IA) [Allen, 1983] (see Figure 8.1), the temporal information that we can derive from the story include the following constraints (assertions of relations) in IA, where **B** is the set of all the thirteen basic relations:*

(1) `at(T1,S1)` {during} `travel(T1,C1,C2)`
`at(T1,S2)` {during} `travel(T1,C1,C2)`

(2) `at(T2,S1)` {during} `travel(T2,C2,C1)`
`at(T2,S2)` {during} `travel(T2,C2,C1)`

(3) `at(T1,S1)` {before} `at(T1,S2)`
`at(T2,S2)` {before} `at(T2,S1)`

(4) `at(T1,S1)` {overlaps, contains, finished-by} `at(T2,S1)`

(5) `at(T1,S1)` **B** − {equal, finishes, finished-by} `at(T2,S1)`

(6) `travel(T1,C1,C2)` {before, meets, overlaps, starts, during}
`travel(S2,C2,C1)`

(7) `at(T2,S2)` {before, after} `at(T1,S2)`

A set of temporal constraints can be represented with a *constraint network* [Montanari, 1974], whose vertices represent interval (point) variables, and edges are labeled by the relations holding between these variables. Figure 8.3 gives a portion of the constraint network

*We specify such constraints using the set notation. Each set of basic relations denotes the *disjunction* of the relations in the set. E.g., I {before, after} J means $(I\ before\ j) \vee (I\ after\ j)$. Note, however, that when we consider a set of constraints (assertions of relations), such a set should be interpreted as the conjunction of the constraints forming it.

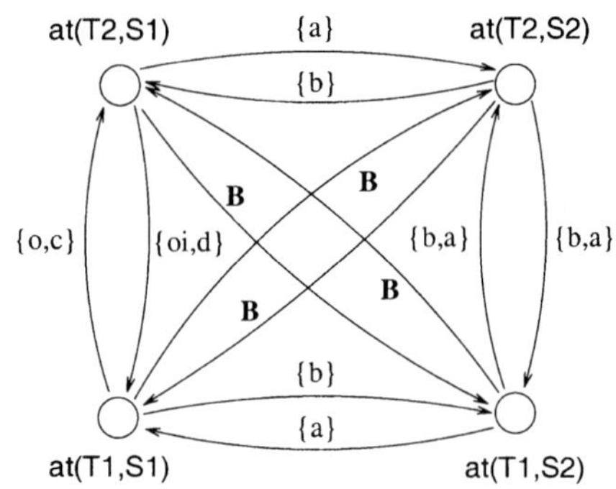

Figure 8.3: A portion of the interval constraint network for the trains example. Since the constraints between `at(T2,S1)` and `at(T1,S2)` are not explicit, they are assumed to be the universal relation **B**.

representing the temporal information of the trains example formalized using relations in IA. (The names of the relations are abbreviated using the notation introduced in Figure 8.1.)

By reasoning about the temporal constraints provided by the previous simple story, we can determine that the story is temporally consistent; we can deduce new constraints that are implicit in the story, such as that `travel(T1,C1,C2)` and `travel(T2,C2,C1)` must have more than one common time point, i.e. that

$$\texttt{travel(T1,C1,C2)}\ \mathbf{B} - \{\mathrm{b, a, m, mi}\}\ \texttt{travel(T2,C2,C1)}$$

holds; we can strengthen explicit constraints (e.g., we deduce that `at(T2,S2)` must be before `at(T1,S2)`, ruling out the possibility that `at(T2,S2)` is after `at(T1,S2)`, because `at(T2,S2)` {after} `at(T1,S2)` is *not* feasible); finally, we can determine that the ordering and interpretation of the interval endpoints in Figure 8.4 is consistent with all the (implicit and explicit) temporal constraints in the story.

Note that, if the supplementary information that `T1` stopped at `S2` *before* `T2` were provided, then the story would be temporally *in*consistent. This is because the explicit temporal constraints in the story imply that `T2` left `S2` before `T1` left `S1`, which precedes the arrival of `T1` at `S2`.

More in general, given a set of qualitative temporal constraints, fundamental reasoning tasks include:

- *Determining consistency* (satisfiability) of the set.
- *Finding a consistent scenario*, i.e., an ordering of the temporal variables involved that is consistent with the constraints provided, or *a solution*, i.e., an interpretation of all the temporal variables involved that is consistent with the constraints provided.
- *Deducing new constraints* from those that are known and, in particular, *computing the strongest relation* that is entailed by the input set of constraints between two particular

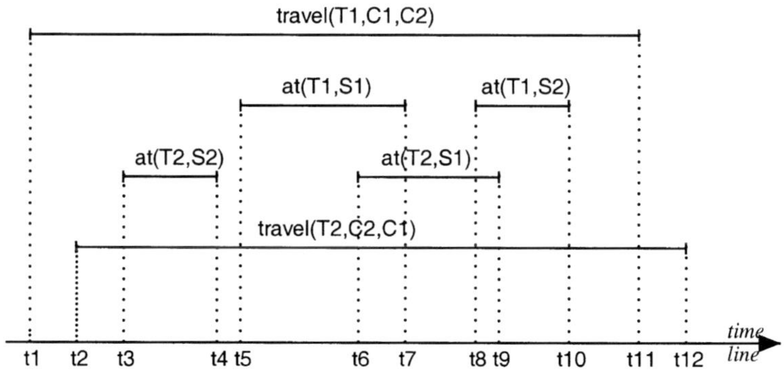

Figure 8.4: A consistent ordering (scenario) and an interpretation (solution) for the interval endpoints in the trains example.

variables, between one particular variable and all the others, or between every temporal variable and every other variable.*

Clearly, consistency checking and finding a solution (or a consistent scenario) are related problems, since finding a solution (consistent scenario) for an input set of constraints determines that the set is consistent. Finding a consistent scenario and finding a solution are strictly related as well, since from a solution for the first problem we can easily derive a solution for the second, and viceversa.

A solution for a set of constraints is also called a *consistent instantiation* of the variables involved, and an *interval realization*, if the variables are time intervals [Golumbic and Shamir, 1993].

In the context of the constraint network representation, the problem of computing the strongest entailed relations between all the pairs of variables corresponds to the problem of computing the *minimal network* representation.† Figure 8.5 gives the minimal network representation of the constraints in Figure 8.3.

The minimal network of an input set of constraints can be implemented as a matrix M, where the entry M$[i, j]$ is the strongest entailed relation between the ith-variable and the jth-variable. Therefore, once we have the minimal network representation, we can derive in constant time the strongest entailed relation between every temporal variable and every other temporal variable.

In some alternative graph-based approaches, the task of computing the strongest entailed relation between two particular variables v and w is sometimes called "querying" the relation between the two vertices of the graph representing v and w. Here we will also call this task "computing the *one-to-one* relation between v and w". Finally, we will call the problem of

*A relation R_1 is stronger than a relation R_2 if R_1 implies R_2 (e.g., "$<$" implies "$\leq$").

†Moreover, note that in the literature this problem is also called computing the "deductive closure" of the constraints [Vilain *et al.*, 1990], computing the "minimal labels" (between all pairs of intervals or points) [van Beek, 1990], the "minimal labeling problem" [Golumbic and Shamir, 1993], and computing the "feasible [basic] relations" [van Beek, 1992].

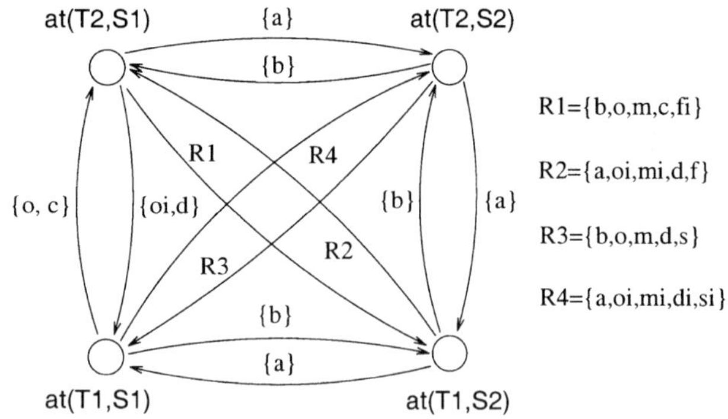

Figure 8.5: The minimal network of the constraint network in Figure 8.3

computing the strongest entailed relation between a (source) variable s and all the others "computing the *one-to-all* relations for s".

All these reasoning tasks are NP-hard if the assertions are in the Interval Algebra [Vilain *et al.*, 1990], while they can be solved in polynomial time if the assertions are in the Point Algebra (PA) ([Ladkin and Maddux, 1988; Vilain *et al.*, 1990; van Beek, 1990; van Beek, 1992; Gerevini and Schubert, 1995b]), or in some subclasses of IA, such as Nebel and Bürckert's ORD-Horn algebra [Nebel and Bürckert, 1995].

Table 8.1 summarizes the computational complexity of the best algorithms, known at the time of writing, for solving fundamental reasoning problems in the context of the following classes of qualitative temporal relations: PA, PA^c, SIA, SIA^c, ORD-Horn, IA, and $\mathcal{A}_3$. PA consists of eight relations between time points, $<, \leq, =, \geq, >, \neq, \emptyset$ (the empty relation) and ? (the universal relation); PA^c is the (convex) subalgebra of PA containing all the relations of PA except $\neq$; SIA consists of the set of relations in IA that can be translated into conjunctions of relations in PA between the endpoints of the intervals [Ladkin and Maddux, 1988; van Beek, 1990; van Beek and Cohen, 1990]; SIA^c is the (convex) subalgebra of SIA formed by the relations of IA that can be translated into conjunctions of relations in PA^c; ORD-Horn is the (unique) maximal tractable subclass of IA containing all the thirteen basic relations [Nebel and Bürckert, 1995]; finally, $\mathcal{A}_3$ [Golumbic and Shamir, 1993] is a class of relations formed by all the possible disjunctions of the following three interval relations: the basic Allen's relations *before* and *after*, and the IA relation $intersect$, which is defined as follows

$$intersect \equiv \mathbf{B} - \{\text{before, after}\}.$$

In the next sections, we will describe the main techniques for processing qualitative temporal constraints, including the algorithms concerning Table 8.1. We will consider the constraint network approach as well as some other graph-based approaches. Section 8.2 concerns the relations in the Point Algebra; Section 8.3 concerns the relations in tractable subclasses of the Interval Algebra; Section 8.4 concerns the relations of the full Interval Algebra; finally, Section 8.5 gives the conclusions, and mention some issues that at the time

Problem	PA^c/SIA^c	PA/SIA	ORD-Horn	IA	$\mathcal{A}_3$
Consistency	$O(n^2)$	$O(n^2)$	$O(n^3)$	exp	exp
Consistent scenario	$O(n^2)$	$O(n^2)$	$O(n^3)$	exp	exp
Minimal network	$O(n^3)$	$O(n^4)$	$O(n^5)$	exp	exp
One-to-one relations	$O(n^2)$	$O(n^2)$	$O(n^3)$	exp	exp
One-to-all relations	$O(n^2)$	$O(n^3)$	$O(n^4)$	exp	exp

Table 8.1: Time complexity of the known best reasoning algorithms for PA^c/SIA^c, PA/SIA, ORD-Horn, IA and $\mathcal{A}_3$, in terms of the number (n) of temporal variables involved."exp" means exponential.

of writing deserve further research.

8.2 Point Algebra Relations

The Point Algebra is a relation algebra [Tarski, 1941; Ladkin and Maddux, 1994; Hirsh, 1996] formed by three basic relations: $<, >$ and $=$. The operations unary converse (denoted by $\cdot^{\smile}$), binary intersection ($\cap$) and binary composition ($\circ$) are defined as follows:

$$\begin{array}{lrcl} \forall x, y: & xR^{\smile}y & \leftrightarrow & yRx \\ \forall x, y: & x(R \cap S)y & \leftrightarrow & xRy \ \wedge \ xSy \\ \forall x, y: & x(R \circ S)y & \leftrightarrow & \exists z : (xRz) \ \wedge \ (zSy). \end{array}$$

Table 8.2 defines the relation resulting by composing two relations in PA. Any set (conjunction) of interval constraints in SIA can be translated into a set (conjunction) of constraints in PA. For example, the interval constraints

`at(T1,S1)` {overlaps, contains, finished-by} `at(T2,S1)`
`at(T1,S1)` **B** − {equal, finishes, finished-by} `at(T2,S1)`

in the example given in the previous section can be translated into the following set of interval endpoint constraints

{ `at(T1,S1)`$^-$ < `at(T1,S1)`$^+$,
`at(T2,S1)`$^-$ < `at(T2,S1)`$^+$,
`at(T1,S1)`$^-$ < `at(T2,S1)`$^-$,
`at(T2,S1)`$^-$ < `at(T1,S1)`$^+$,
`at(T1,S1)`$^+$ ≠ `at(T2,S1)`$^+$ },

where `at(T1,S1)`$^-$ denotes the starting time of `at(T1,S1)`, and `at(T1,S1)`$^+$ denotes the end time of `at(T1,S1)` (analogously for `at(T2,S1)`).

However, note that not all the constraints of the trains example can be translated into a set of constraints in PA. In particular, in addition to the $<$-constraints ordering the endpoints of the intervals involved, constraint (7) requires either a *disjunction* of constraints involving four interval endpoints,

$\circ$	$<$	$>$	$=$	$\leq$	$\geq$	$\neq$	?
$<$	$<$	?	$<$	$<$	?	?	?
$>$	?	$>$	$>$	?	$>$	?	?
$=$	$<$	$>$	$=$	$\leq$	$\geq$	$\neq$	?
$\leq$	$<$	?	$\leq$	$\leq$	?	?	?
$\geq$	?	$>$	$\geq$	?	$\geq$	?	?
$\neq$	?	?	$\neq$	?	?	?	?
?	?	?	?	?	?	?	?

Table 8.2: Composition table for PA relations

$$[\texttt{at(T1,S2)}^+ < \texttt{at(T2,S2)}^-] \vee [\texttt{at(T2,S2)}^+ < \texttt{at(T1,S2)}^-],$$

or two disjunctions involving three interval endpoints each [Gerevini and Schubert, 1994b]:

$$[\texttt{at(T1,S2)}^- < \texttt{at(T2,S2)}^-] \vee [\texttt{at(T2,S2)}^+ < \texttt{at(T1,S2)}^-],$$
$$[\texttt{at(T2,S2)}^- < \texttt{at(T1,S2)}^-] \vee [\texttt{at(T1,S2)}^+ < \texttt{at(T2,S2)}^-].$$

Some techniques for handling such "non-pointizable" interval constraints will be considered in Section 8.5.

8.2.1 Consistency Checking and Finding a Solution

The methods for finding a solution of a tractable set of qualitative constraints are typically based on first determining the consistency of the set, and then, if the set turns out to be consistent, using a technique for deriving a consistent scenario. A solution can be derived from a consistent scenario in linear time by simply assigning to each variable a number consistent with the order of the variables in the scenario.

Van Beek proposed a method for consistency checking and finding a consistent scenario for a set of constraints in PA consisting of the following steps [van Beek, 1992]:

1. Represent the input set of constraints as a labeled directed graph, where the vertices represent point variables, and each edge is labeled by the PA-relation of the constraint between the variables represented by the vertices connected by the edge.

2. Compute the strongly connected components (SCC) of the graph as described in [Cormen *et al.*, 1990], ignoring edges labeled "$\neq$". Then, check if any of the SCCs contains a pair of vertices connected by an edge with label "$<$" or "$\neq$". The input set of constraints is consistent if and only if such a SCC does *not* exist.

3. If the set of the input constraints is consistent, then collapse each SCC into an arbitrary vertex v within that component. Such a vertex represents an equivalent class of point variables (those corresponding to the vertices in the collapsed component).

4. Apply to the directed acyclic graph (DAG) obtained in the previous step an algorithm for topologically sorting its vertices [Cormen *et al.*, 1990], and use the resulting vertex ordering as a consistent scenario for the input set of constraints.

Both steps 1–2 (consistency checking) and steps 3–4 (finding a consistent scenario) can be computed in $O(n^2)$ time and space. For more details, the interested reader may see [Tarjan, 1972; van Beek, 1990; Cormen *et al.*, 1990; Gerevini and Schubert, 1994a].

8.2.2 Path Consistency and Minimal PA-networks

Path consistency is an important property for a set of constraints on which, as we will see, some reasoning algorithms rely. Enforcing path consistency to a given set of constraints corresponds to enforcing path consistency to its constraint network representation. This task requires deriving a (possibly) new *equivalent* network in which, for every 3-vertex subnetwork formed by vertices i, j, and k, the relation R_{ik} labeling the edge from i to k is stronger than the composition of the relations R_{ij} and R_{jk} labeling the edges from i to j, and from j to k, respectively. I.e., in a path-consistent network we have that

$$\forall i, j, k \;\; R_{ik} \subseteq R_{ij} \circ R_{jk},$$

where i, j and k are different vertices (variables) of the network. Two networks are equivalent when the represented variables admit the same set of consistent interpretations (solutions) in both the representations. Also, recall that the relations of PA (and of IA) form an algebra, and hence they are closed under the operation of composition, as well as under the operations of converse and intersection. For more details on the algebraic characterization of PA and IA, the interested reader may consult [Tarski, 1941; Ladkin and Maddux, 1994; Hirsh, 1996].

Several algorithms for enforcing path consistency are described in the literature on temporal constraint satisfaction (e.g., [Allen, 1983; van Beek, 1992; Vilain *et al.*, 1990; Ladkin and Maddux, 1994; Bessière, 1996]). Typically these algorithms require $O(n^3)$ time on a serial machine, where n is the number of temporal variables, while on parallel machines the complexity of iterative local path consistency algorithms lies asymptotically between n^2 and $n^2 log\ n$ [Ladkin and Maddux, 1988; Ladkin and Maddux, 1994]. Some path consistency algorithms require $O(n^2)$ space, while others require $O(n^3)$ space.

Figure 8.2.2 gives a path consistency algorithm which is a variant of the algorithm given by van Beek and Manchak in [van Beek and Manchak, 1996], which in turn is based on Allen's original algorithm for interval algebra relations [Allen, 1983]. Note that this is a general algorithm that can be applied not only to point relations in PA, but also to the interval relations in IA, as well as to other classes of binary qualitative relations, such as the spatial relations of the Region Connection Calculus RCC-8 [Randell *et al.*, 1992; Renz and Nebel, 1997; Gerevini and Renz, 1998].

The time complexity of this path consistency algorithm applied to a PA-network is $O(n^3)$, where n is the number of the temporal variables; the space complexity is $O(n^2)$. In order to derive from the input network C an equivalent path-consistent network, the algorithm checks whether the following conditions hold (steps 9 and 17)

(a) $R_{ik} \neq R_{ik} \cap R_{ij} \circ R_{jk}$,

(b) $R_{kj} \neq R_{kj} \cap R_{ki} \circ R_{ij}$.

If (a) holds, then R_{ik} is updated (strengthened), and the pair (i, k) is added to a list L to be processed in turn, provided that (i, k) is not already on L. Similarly, if (b) holds, then R_{kj}

Algorithm: PATH-CONSISTENCY(C)
Input: a $n \times n$ matrix C representing a network of constraints over n variables.
Output: either a path-consistent network equivalent to C or *false*.

```
L ← {(i, j) | 1 ≤ i < j ≤ n}
while (L is not empty) do
   select and delete an item (i, j) from L
   for k ← 1 to n, k ≠ i and k ≠ j, do
      t ← R_ik ∩ R_ij ∘ R_jk
      if t is the empty relation then
          return false
      else
          if t ≠ R_ik then
              R_ik ← t
              R_ki ←INVERSE(t)
              L ← L ∪ {(i, k)}
          t ← R_kj ∩ R_ki ∘ R_ij
          if t is the empty relation then
              return false
          else
              if t ≠ R_kj then
                  R_kj ← t
                  R_jk ←INVERSE(t)
                  L ← L ∪ {(k, j)}
 return C
```

Figure 8.6: A path consistency algorithm. R_{ij} indicates the relation between the i-th variable and the j-th variable which is stored as the entry $C[i, j]$ of C. The function INVERSE implements the unary operation inverse.

is updated (strengthened), and the pair (k, j) is added to L to be processed in turn, provided that (k, j) is not already on L. The algorithm iterates until no more relations (labels on the network edges) can be updated, or a relation is reduced to the empty relation. In the later case the algorithm returns *false* (the network is inconsistent); in the former case, when the algorithm terminates, it returns a path-consistent network equivalent to C.

Enforcing path consistency to a set of PA-constraints is a sound and complete method for determining the consistency of the set [Ladkin and Maddux, 1988; Ladkin and Maddux, 1994]: the set is consistent if and only if a path consistency algorithm applied to the set does not revise a relation to be the empty relation.

An interesting question is whether a path-consistent network of PA-constraints is also a minimal network. The answer is positive only for constraints in PA^c (i.e., the class containing all the relations of PA except "$\neq$"), while for constraints in PA this is not the case. This is because a path-consistent network of PA constraints can contain subnetworks that are

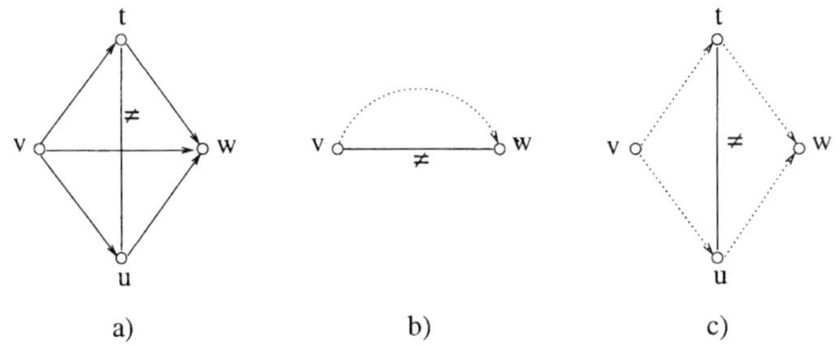

Figure 8.7: a) van Beek's forbidden graph; b) and c) the two kinds of implicit $<$ relation in a TL-graph. Edges with no labels are assumed to be labeled "$\leq$". Dotted arrows indicate paths, solid lines $\neq$-edges. In each of the graphs there is an implicit $<$ relation between v and w.

instances of a particular path-consistent PA-network that is not minimal. Such a subnetwork, called "forbidden subgraph", was identified by van Beek [van Beek, 1992] and it is depicted in Figure 8.7.a). This network is not minimal because the relation "$=$" between v and w is not feasible: there exists no solution for the set of constraints represented by the network in which the variables v and w are interpreted as the same time point.

Gerevini and Schubert proved that any path-consistent network of constraints in PA that contains no forbidden graphs is minimal [Gerevini and Schubert, 1995b].* Van Beek proposed an algorithm based on this property for computing the minimal network of a set of PA-constraints whose time complexity is $O(n^3 + m \cdot n^2)$, where m is number of input $\neq$-constraints [van Beek, 1992] (which is $O(n^2)$). This algorithm consists of two main steps:

- the first step computes a path-consistent network representing the input constraints, which can be accomplished in $O(n^3)$ time;
- the second step identifies and reduces all the forbidden graphs that are present in the path-consistent network. The time complexity of this step is $O(m \cdot n^2)$.

It is worth noting that the forbidden subgraph can be seen as a special case of the "metric forbidden graphs" identified by Gerevini and Cristani [Gerevini and Cristani, 1996] for the class of constraints STP$^{\neq}$, which subsumes PA and the class of metric constraints in Dechter, Meiri and Pearl's STP framework [Dechter *et al.*, 1991].

8.2.3 One-to-all Relations for PA

Figure 8.8 gives the algorithm proposed by van Beek and Cohen for computing one-to-all relations (OAC). The input of OAC is a matrix C representing a consistent network of constraints, and a vertex (a temporal variable) s of the network; the output is C with the constraints between s and every other variable (possibly) revised.

*This was first claimed (without a correct proof) by van Beek and Cohen in [van Beek and Cohen, 1990].

Algorithm: OAC(s, C)
Input: a source vertex s and a consistent constraints network stored in C
Output: C revised to compute one-to-all relations for s

```
L ← V − {s}   (V is the set of the vertices in the network)
while (L is not empty) do
    select and delete a vertex v from L s.t. the cost of R_sv is minimum
    for t in V do
        l ← R_st ∩ R_sv ∘ R_vt
        if l ≠ R_st then
            R_st ← l
            L ← L ∪ {t}
return C
```

Figure 8.8: Van Beek and Cohen's algorithm for computing one-to-all relations.

Algorithm: OAC-2(s, C)
Input: a source vertex s and a consistent constraint network stored in C
Output: C revised to compute one-to-all relations for s

```
for each relation R_si (1 ≤ i ≤ n, i ≠ s) do
    for each basic relation r in R_si do
        t ← R_si
        R_si ← r
        if C is not consistent then
            R_si = R_si − {r}
        else R_si = t
return C
```

Figure 8.9: A cubic time algorithm for computing one-to-all relations for a (consistent) set of constraints in PA.

OAC takes $O(n^2)$ time and is an adaptation of Dijkstra's algorithm for computing the shortest path from a single source vertex to every other vertex [Cormen *et al.*, 1990]. The algorithm maintains a list of vertices that are processed following an order determined by the "costs" of the relative relation with the source vertex. In principle, these costs can be arbitrarily defined without affecting the worst-case time complexity of the algorithm. However, in practice the order in which the vertices are selected from the list can significantly affect the number of iterations performed by the algorithm. Van Beek and Cohen proposed a weighting scheme for computing the costs of the relations which halves the number of iterations of the algorithm, compared with the number of iterations determined by a random choice of the next vertex to be processed. (For more details the interested reader may see [van Beek and Cohen, 1990].)

Unfortunately, while the previous algorithm is complete for constraints in PA^c, it is not complete for constraints in PA [van Beek and Cohen, 1990]. It appears then that the (current) best method for computing one-to-all constraints for PA is based on independently checking the feasibility of each of the basic relations between the source variable (vertex) and every other variable (vertex). This algorithm is given in Figure 8.9. It is easy to see that the algorithm is correct and complete for the full PA, and that, since it performs $O(n)$ consistency checks (each of which requires $O(n^2)$ time – see Section 8.2.1), the time complexity of the algorithm is $O(n^3)$.

8.2.4 Efficient Graph-based Approaches

The techniques based on the constraint network representation are often elegant, simple to understand and easy to implement. On the other hand, their computational costs (both in time and space) can be inadequate for applications in which efficient temporal reasoning is an important issue.

Some alternative approaches based on graph algorithms have been proposed with the aim of addressing scalability, and supporting efficient reasoning for large data sets. Such techniques are especially suitable for managing "sparse" temporal data bases, i.e., sets of PA-constraints whose size is significantly lower than $(n^2 - n)/2$, where n is the number of the temporal variables involved.

Currently, the most effective of these graph-based methods are the approaches using *ranked temporally labeled graphs* [Gerevini and Schubert, 1995a; Delgrande *et al.*, 2001], *timegraphs* [Miller and Schubert, 1990; Gerevini and Schubert, 1995a], or *series-parallel graphs* [Delgrande and Gupta, 1996; Delgrande *et al.*, 2001]. In the following we will give a general overview of each of them. Another important related method is Ghallab and Mounir Alaoui's *indexed time table* [Ghallab and Mounir Alaoui, 1989]. However, this approach is incomplete for the full Point Algebra, because it can not detect some $<$-constraints that are implied via $\neq$-constraint [Gerevini and Schubert, 1995a]. Moreover, as claimed in [Delgrande *et al.*, 2001], the general idea underlying Ghallab and Mounir Alaoui's method seems subsumed by a variant of the approach based on series-parallel graphs.

In a graph-based approach, instead of precomputing all the constraints that are implicit in the set of input constraints (i.e., computing their minimal network representation), we build a graph representation with some particular data structures that support efficient deduction of constraints at *query time*. In two of the three approaches that we consider here, temporal information is partitioned into a set of specialized graph representations (either chains or series-parallel graphs [Valdes *et al.*, 1982]), that are connected by a metagraph data structure. Queries involving variables within the same specialized representation can be answered in constant time by using special purpose algorithms, while in the general case they require a search on the metagraph.

The time chain representation is particularly suitable for story comprehension and planning applications [Miller and Schubert, 1990; Gerevini and Schubert, 1995a]; the series-parallel graph representation can be used, for instance, to model the qualitative temporal evolution of process execution [Delgrande *et al.*, 2001].

Experimental results conducted using TimeGraph-II, a temporal reasoning system based on timegraphs [Gerevini *et al.*, 1995], show that building a timegraph can be much faster than computing the minimal network representation [Gerevini and Schubert, 1995a]. Moreover, for domains that exhibit structure, in terms of time chains or series-parallel graphs, querying the strongest entailed relations is very efficient [Gerevini and Schubert, 1995a; Delgrande *et al.*, 2001].

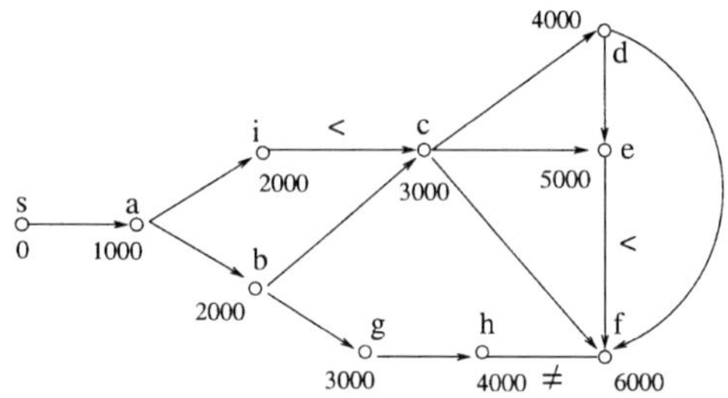

Figure 8.10: An example of TL-graph with ranks. Edges with no label are assumed to be labeled "$\leq$".

Ranked Temporally Labeled Graphs

A *temporally labeled graph* (*TL-graph*) is a graph with at least one vertex and a set of labeled edges, where each edge (v, l, w) connects a pair of distinct vertices v, w. The edges are either directed and labeled $\leq$ or $<$, or undirected and labeled $\neq$.

Every vertex of a TL-graph has at least one name attached to it, and if a vertex has more than one name, then they are alternative names for the same time point. The name sets of any two vertices are required to be disjoint. Figure 8.10 shows an example of TL-graph. A path in a TL-graph is called a $\leq$-path if each edge on the path has label $<$ or $\leq$. A $\leq$-path is called a $<$-path if at least one of the edges has label $<$.

A TL-graph $\mathcal{G}$ contains an *implicit* $<$ relation between two vertices v_1, v_2 when the strongest relation entailed by the set of constraints from which $\mathcal{G}$ has been built is $v_1 < v_2$ and there is no $<$-path from v_1 to v_2 in $\mathcal{G}$. Figures 8.7.b) and 8.7.c) show the two possible TL-graphs which give rise to an implicit $<$ relation. All TL-graphs with an implicit $<$ relation contain one of these graphs as subgraph.

An acyclic TL-graph without implicit $<$ relations is an *explicit* TL-graph. In order to make explicit a TL-graph containing implicit $<$ relations, we can add new edges with label $<$ [Gerevini and Schubert, 1995a]. For example, in Figure 8.7 we add the edge $(v, <, w)$ to the graph. An important property of an explicit TL-graph is that it entails $v \leq w$ if and only if there is a $\leq$-path from v to w; it entails $v < w$ if and only if there is a $<$-path from v to w, and it entails $v \neq w$ if and only if there is a $<$-path from v to w or from w to v, or there is an edge $(v, \neq, w)$.

Given a set S of c PA-constraints, clearly we can construct a TL-graph $\mathcal{G}$ representing S in $O(c)$ time. In order to check consistency of S and transform $\mathcal{G}$ into an equivalent acyclic TL-graph, we can use van Beek's method for PA (see Section 8.2.1). If the TL-graph is consistent, each SCC is collapsed into an arbitrary vertex v within that component. All the cross-component edges entering or leaving the component are transferred to v.* The edges within the component are eliminated and a supplementary set of alternative names for v is generated.

*When there is more than one edge from different collapsed vertices to the same vertex z that is not collapsed, the label on the edge from x to z is the intersection of the labels on these edges and the label on the current edge from x to z (if any). Similarly for multiple edges from the same vertex z to different collapsed vertices.

In order to query the strongest relation between two variables (vertices) of a TL-graph , there are two possibilities depending on whether (a) we preprocess all $\neq$-relations to make implicit $<$-relations explicit before querying, or (b) we identify implicit $<$-relations by handling $\neq$-relations at query time, using a more elaborated query algorithm [Delgrande *et al.*, 2001]. For generic TL-graphs, option (b) seems more appropriate than (a), because making implicit $<$ relations explicit can be significantly expensive (it requires $O(m \cdot n^2)$ time, where m is the number of input $\neq$-constraints and n the number of the temporal variables). However, as we will briefly discuss in the next section, for a TL-graph that is suitable for the timegraph representation, making $<$ relations explicit can be much faster.

Let $\mathcal{G}$ be a TL-graph with e edges representing a set S of c PA-constraints with no $\neq$-constraint ($e \leq m$). The strongest entailed relation R between two variables v_1 and v_2 in S can be determined in $O(e)$ time by two main steps: (1) check whether v_1 and v_2 are represented by the same vertex of $\mathcal{G}$ (in such a case R is "$=$"); if this is not the case, then (2) search for a $<$-path between the vertices representing v_1 and v_2 (or for a $\leq$-path, if there is no $<$-path). Such a search can be accomplished, for instance, by using the single-source-longest-paths algorithm given in [Cormen *et al.*, 1990].

When S contains $\neq$-constraints, and they pre-processed to make the TL-graph representing S explicit, the query algorithm is the same as above, except for the following addition: if the graph contains an $\neq$-edge between v_1 and v_2, then R is "$\neq$". Alternatively, if the TL-graph is not made explicit before querying, we can handle $\neq$-constraints as proposed in [Delgrande *et al.*, 2001]. During the search for a path from v_1 to v_2, we identify the set $V_{\leq} = \{w \mid v_1 \leq w,\ w \leq v_2\}$ by making the vertices of the graph according to whether they lie on a $\leq$-path from v_1 to v_2. (Similarly when searching for a path from v_2 to v_1.) If $x \neq y \in S$ and $x, y \in V_{\leq} \cup \{v_1, v_2\}$, then the TL-graph entails $v_1 < v_2$. The time complexity of the resulting query procedure is linear with respect to the number of the input constraints.

A *ranked* TL-graph is a simple but powerful extension of an acyclic TL-graph. In a ranked TL-graph, each vertex (time point) has a *rank* associated with it. The *rank* of a vertex v can be defined as the length of the longest $\leq$-paths to v from a source vertex s of the TL-graph representing the "universal start time", times a distance increment k [Ghallab and Mounir Alaoui, 1989; Gerevini and Schubert, 1995a]. s is a special vertex with no predecessor and whose successors are the vertices of the graph that have no other predecessor. The ranks for an acyclic TL-graph can be computed in $O(n + e)$ time using a slight adaptation of the DAG-longest-paths algorithm [Cormen *et al.*, 1990].

The use of the ranks can significantly speed up the search for a path from a vertex p to another vertex q: the search can be pruned whenever a vertex with a rank greater than or equal to the rank of q is reached. For instance, during the search of a path from a to g in the ranked TL-graph of Figure 8.10, when we reach vertex c, we can prune the search from this vertex, because the ranks if its successors are greater than the rank of g. Thus, it suffices to visit at most three nodes (i, c and b) before reaching g from a. The advantage of using ranks to prune the search at query time has been empirically demonstrated in [Delgrande *et al.*, 2001].

The experimental analysis in [Delgrande *et al.*, 2001] indicates that the use of a ranked TL-graph is the best approach when the graph is sparse and temporal information does not exhibit structure that can be "encapsulated" into specialized graph representations, like time chains or series-parallel graphs.

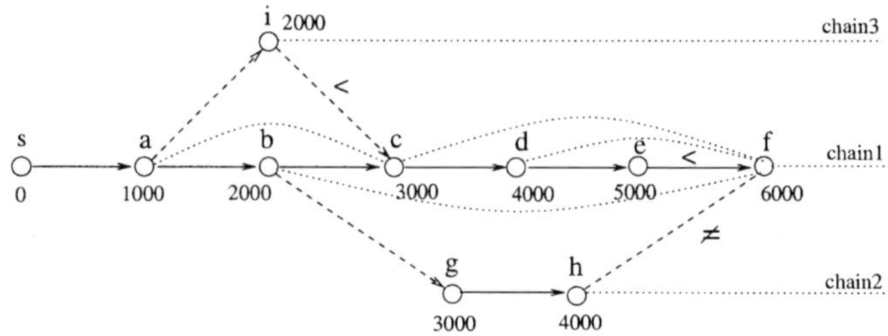

Figure 8.11: The timegraph of the TL-graph of Figure 8.10, with transitive edges and auxiliary edges omitted. Edges with no label are assumed to be labeled "$\leq$".

Timegraphs

A *timegraph* is an acyclic TL-graph partitioned into a set of *time chains*, such that each vertex is on one and only one time chain. A time chain is a $\leq$-path, plus possibly *transitive edges* connecting pairs of vertices on the $\leq$-path. Distinct chains of a timegraph can be connected by *cross-chain edges*. Vertices connected by cross-chain edges are called *metavertices*. Cross-chain edges and certain auxiliary edges connecting metavertices on the same chain are called *metaedges*. The metavertices and metaedges of a timegraph T form the *metagraph* of T.

Figure 8.11 shows the timegraph built from the TL-graph of Figure 8.10. All vertices except d and e are metavertices. The edges connecting vertices a to i, i to c, b to g, h with f, are metaedges. Dotted edges are special links called *nextgreaters* that are computed during the construction of the timegraph and that indicate for each vertex v the nearest descendant v' of v on the same chain as v such that the graph entails $v < v'$.

As in a ranked TL-graph, each vertex (time point) in a timegraph has rank associated with it. The main purpose of the ranks is to allow the computation of the strongest relation entailed by the timegraph between two vertices on the same chain in constant time. In fact, given two vertices v_1 and v_2 on the same chain such that the rank of v_2 is greater than the rank of v_1, if the rank of the nextgreater of v_1 is lower that the rank of v_2, then the timegraph entails $v_1 < v_2$, otherwise it entails $v_1 \leq v_2$. For example, the timegraph of Figure 8.11 entails $a < d$ because a and d are on the same chain, and the rank of the nextgreater of a is lower than the rank of d.

In general, the ranks in a timegraph are very useful to speed up path search both during the construction of the timegraph and at query time.

Given a set S of constraints in PA, in order to build a timegraph representation of S, we start from a TL-graph $\mathcal{G}$ representing S. The construction of the timegraph from $\mathcal{G}$ consists of four main steps: consistency checking, ranking of the graph (assigning to each vertex a rank), formation of the chains of the metagraph, and making explicit the implicit $<$ relations.

We have already described the first two steps in Section 8.2.4. The third step, the formation of the chains, consists of partitioning the TL-graph into a set of time chains ($\leq$-paths), deriving from this partition the metagraph and doing a first-pass computation of the nextgreater links. The first two subtasks take time linear in $n + e$, while the last may require an $O(\hat{e})$ metagraph search for each of the $\hat{n}$ metavertices, where $\hat{e}$ is the number of cross-chain edges in the timegraph.

The fourth step, making explicit all the implicit $<$ relations, can be the most expensive task in the construction of a timegraph. This is the same as in van Beek's approach for eliminating the forbidden graphs in a path-consistent network of PA-constraints (see Section 8.2.2). However, the data structures provided by a timegraph allow us to accomplish this task more efficiently in practice. A final operation is the revision of nextgreater links, to take account of any implicit $<$ relations made explicit by the fourth step.

Figures 8.7.b) and 8.7.c) show the two cases of implicit $<$ relations. The time complexity of the algorithm for handling the first case in the timegraph approach is $O(\hat{e}_{\neq} \cdot (\hat{e} + \hat{n}))$, where $\hat{e}_{\neq}$ is the number of cross-chain edges with label $\neq$.

In order to make implicit $<$ relations of the second kind (Figure 8.7.c) explicit, and removing redundant $\neq$-edges, a number of $\neq$ diamonds of the order of $e_{\neq} \cdot n^2$ may need to be identified in the worst case, where $e_{\neq}$ is the number of edges labeled "$\neq$" in the TL-graph. However, for timegraphs only a subset of these needs to be considered. In fact it is possible to limit the search to the *smallest* $\neq$ diamonds, i.e., the set of diamonds obtained by considering for each edge $(v, \neq, w)$ only the *nearest common descendants* of v and w ($NCD(v, w)$) and their *nearest common ancestors* ($NCA(v, w)$). This is a consequence of the fact that, once we have inserted a $<$ edge from each vertex in $NCA(v, w)$ to each vertex in $NCD(v, w)$, we will have explicit $<$-paths for all pairs of "diamond-connected" vertices. Overall, the worst-case time complexity of the fourth step is $O(\hat{e}_{\neq} \cdot (\hat{e} + \hat{n}))$.

Regarding querying the strongest entailed relations between two vertices (time points) p_1 and p_2 in a timegraph, there are four cases in which this can be accomplished in constant time. The first case is the one where p_1 and p_2 are alternative names of the same point. The second case is the one where the vertices v_1 and v_2 corresponding to p_1 and p_2 are on the same time chain. The third case is the one where v_1 and v_2 are not on the same chain and have the same rank, and there is no $\neq$ edge between them (the strongest entailed relation is ?). The fourth case is the one where p_1 and p_2 are connected by a $\neq$-edge (the strongest entailed relation is $\neq$).

In the remaining cases an explicit search of the graph needs to be performed. If there exists at least one $<$-path from v_1 to v_2, then the answer is $v_1 < v_2$. If there are only $\leq$-paths (but no $<$-paths) from v_1 to v_2, then the answer is $v_1 \leq v_2$. (Analogously for the paths from v_2 to v_1.) Such a graph search can be accomplished in $O(h + \hat{e} + \hat{n})$ time, where h is the constant corresponding to the time required by the four special cases.

Series-Parallel Graphs

In this section we describe Delgrande and Gupta's SPMG approach based on structuring temporal information into *series-parallel graphs* [Valdes *et al.*, 1982]. A series-parallel graph (SP-graph) is a DAG with one source s and one sink t, defined inductively as follows [Valdes *et al.*, 1982; Delgrande *et al.*, 2001]:

- *Base case.* A single edge (s, t) from s to t is a series-parallel graph with source s and sink t.

- *Inductive case.* Let G_1 and G_2 be series-parallel graphs with source and sink s_1, t_1 and s_2, t_2, respectively, such that the sets of vertices of G_1 and G_2 are disjoint. Then,

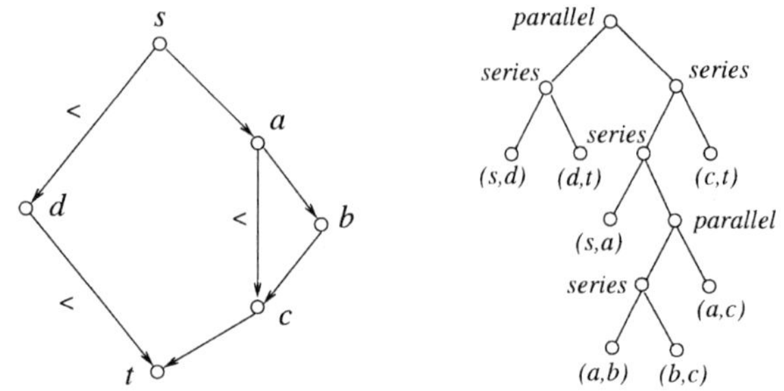

Figure 8.12: An example of an SP-graph with its decomposition tree. Edges with no label are assumed to be labeled "$\leq$".

- *Series step.* The graph constructed by taking the disjoint union of G_1 and G_2 and identifying s_2 with t_1 is a series-parallel graph with source s_1 and sink t_2 constructed using a *series step.*

- *Parallel step.* The graph constructed by taking the disjoint union of G_1 and G_2 and identifying s_1 with s_2 (call this vertex s) and t_1 with t_2 (call this vertex t) is a series-parallel graph with source s and sink t constructed using a *parallel step.*

In SPMG, each edge of a SP-graph is labeled either $<$ or $\leq$, and represents either a $<$-constraint or a $\leq$-constraints, respectively ($\neq$-constraints are not explicitly represented in the graph). Moreover, in any SP-graph G with e edges and n vertices, we have $e \leq 2n$. Figure 8.12 gives an example of a simple SP-graph, together with its *decomposition tree.* Any SP-graph G can be decomposed into the decomposition tree of G, that is implicitly given by the definition of SP-graph. Internal nodes of the tree are labeled "series" or "parallel", while leaf nodes are labeled by edges of G. The decomposition tree of a SP-graph can be computed in linear time [Valdes *et al.*, 1982].

Using the decomposition tree of a SP-graph G, SPMG efficiently "compiles" G to derive some information supporting constant time queries on G. This processing requires $O(n)$ time, and consists of two main steps: computing a *planar embedding* of G, and computing the *functions* $\mathcal{S}$ *and* $\mathcal{A}$ for the vertices of G. A planar embedding of G is an assignment to each vertex v of a co-ordinate (x_v, y_v) on the integer plan such that, for any other vertex w, there is a path from v to w if and only if $x_v < x_w$ and $y_v < y_w$. Figure 8.13 shows an example of planar embedding. In this example, since the co-ordinates of a are both lower than the corresponding co-ordinates of t, we can derive that there is a $\leq$-path from a to t.

By using the planar embedding, we can answer queries of type $\leq$ in constant time, but we cannot answer queries of type $<$, because the planar embedding does not distinguish $<$-paths and $\leq$-paths in the SP-graph. The $\mathcal{S}$ and $\mathcal{A}$ functions of G have this purpose: given two vertices x, y such that in G there is a $\leq$-path from x to y, we have that G contains a $<$-path from x to y if and only if $\mathcal{A}(x) < \mathcal{S}(w)$. For example, since in Figure 8.13 $\mathcal{A}(a) < \mathcal{S}(t)$, the SP-graph under consideration has a $<$-path from a to t, entailing $a < t$.

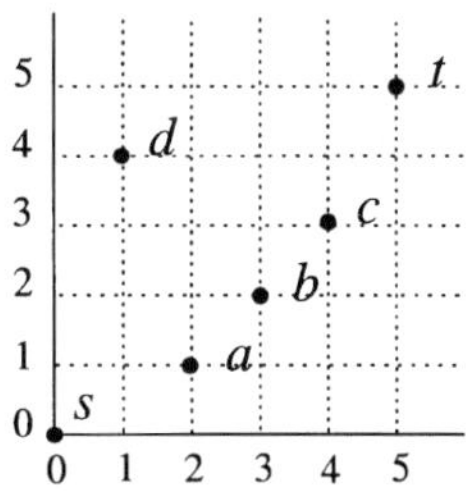

$\mathcal{S}(s) = 0$	$\mathcal{A}(s) = 0$
$\mathcal{S}(t) = 2$	$\mathcal{A}(t) = 2$
$\mathcal{S}(a) = 0$	$\mathcal{A}(a) = 0$
$\mathcal{S}(b) = 0$	$\mathcal{A}(b) = 2$
$\mathcal{S}(c) = 1$	$\mathcal{A}(c) = 2$
$\mathcal{S}(d) = 1$	$\mathcal{A}(d) = 1$

Figure 8.13: A planar embedding and the $\mathcal{S}, \mathcal{A}$ values for the SP-graph of Figure 8.12.

For every vertex v of G, $\mathcal{S}(v)$ is defined as the maximum number of $<$-edges on any path from the source vertex of G to v, while $\mathcal{A}(v)$ is defined as follows. If v is the sink of G or there exists a vertex w such that G has an $<$-edge from v to w, then $\mathcal{A}(v) = \mathcal{S}(v)$; otherwise $\mathcal{A}(v)$ is the minimum value over values in the set $\{\mathcal{A}(w) \mid G$ contains a $\leq$-edge from v to $w\}$. Figure 8.13 gives an example of $\mathcal{S}$ and $\mathcal{A}$.

Given a (consistent) acyclic TL-graph G, SPMG constructs a *series-parallel metagraph* (SP-metagraph) G' for G as follows. First G is partitioned into a set of maximal series-parallel subgraphs, and each of these SP-graphs is collapsed into a single metaedge of G'. A metaedge from u to v represents a SP-graph with source u and vertex v, and its label is the intersection of the labels of all paths from u to l in G. Any $\neq$-edge in G connecting two vertices x, y in the same SP-subgraph may be replaced with a $<$-edge (if there is a path from x to y); otherwise the edge is a $\neq$-metaedge of the metagraph.

Then, each metaedge in the metagraph thus derived, is processed to compute a planar embedding for the corresponding SP-graph and its $\mathcal{A}$ and $\mathcal{S}$ functions. This allows SPMG to answer queries involving vertices "inside" the same metaedge in constant time. In order to answer queries between vertices of the metagraph, SPMG uses a path-search algorithm that, like in TL-graphs and timegraphs, can exploit ranks for pruning the search. The time complexity of such an algorithm is linear in the number of vertices and edges forming the metagraph. $\neq$-edges are handled at query time, as described for TL-graphs. To compute the strongest entailed relation between two vertices that are internal to two different metaedges, SPMG combines path-search on the metagraph and lookup inside the two SP-graphs associated with the metaedges. For more details on constructing and querying a SP-metagraph, the interested reader may see [Delgrande *et al.*, 2001].

An experimental analysis conducted in [Delgrande *et al.*, 2001] shows that SPMG is very efficient for sparse TL-graphs that are suited for being compiled into SP-metagraph representation. Furthermore, the performance of SPMG degrades gracefully for the randomly generated (without forcing any structure) data sets considered in the experimental analysis.

8.3 Tractable Interval Algebra Relations

IA is a relation algebra [Tarski, 1941; Ladkin and Maddux, 1994; Hirsh, 1996] in which the operators converse, intersection and compositions are defined as we have described for

PA in Section 8.2. In the context of IA, the main reasoning tasks are intractable. However, several tractable subclasses of IA have been identified. Among them, the most studied in terms of algorithm design are the convex simple interval algebra (SIA^c), the simple interval algebra (SIA) and the ORD-Horn algebra. In terms of the set of relations contained in these subalgebras of IA, we have that

$$\mathrm{SIA}^c \subset \mathrm{SIA} \subset \text{ORD-Horn}.$$

ORD-Horn is a maximal tractable subclass of IA formed by the relations in IA that can be translated into conjunctions of (at most binary) disjunctions of interval endpoint constraints in $\{\leq, =, \neq\}$ (or simply in $\{\leq, \neq\}$, given that any $=$-constraint can be expressed by two $\leq$-constraints), where at most one disjunct (PA-constraint) is of type "$=$" or "$\leq$". For example, the IA-constraint

$$I \; \mathbf{B} - \{starts\} \; J$$

can be translated into the following set of constraints between of I and J:

$$\{I^- < I^+, \; J^- < J^+, \; I^- \neq J^- \vee J^+ \leq I^+\},$$

where I^- and I^+ are the starting point and the end point of I, respectively (analogously for J^- and J^+).

Other maximal tractable subclasses of IA have been identified [Drakengren and Jonsson, 1997b; Krokhin *et al.*, 2003]. However, such classes are probably less interesting than ORD-Horn, because they do not contain all the basic relations of IA, and hence they cannot express definite information about the ordering of two temporal intervals. (For more details on these classes, the interested reader may see the chapter on computational complexity of temporal constraint problems in this book).

Finally, Golumbic and Shamir studied some interesting tractable subclasses of IA, which are restrictions of the set of relations forming the intractable class $\mathcal{A}_3$ [Golumbic and Shamir, 1993]. In particular, they show that, for some of these tractable subclasses, the problem of deciding consistency is equivalent to some well-known polynomial graph-theoretic problems; while for the other tractable subclasses they present new polynomial graph-based techniques. Golumbic and Shamir illustrate also some interesting applications of temporal reasoning involving their classes of relations.

In the rest of this section we will focus on the main techniques for processing constraints in SIA^c, SIA and ORD-Horn.

8.3.1 Consistency Checking and Finding a Solution

Consistency checking (finding a consistent scenario/solution) for a set of constraints in SIA^c and SIA can be easily reduced to consistency checking (finding a consistent scenario/solution) for an equivalent set of constraints in PA^c and PA respectively. Hence, these tasks can be performed by using the method described in Section 8.2.1, which requires $O(n^2)$ time.

Concerning ORD-Horn constraints, it has been proved that path consistency guarantees consistency [Nebel and Bürckert, 1995]: given a set Ω of constraints in ORD-Horn, the path

$\circ$	b	bi	d	di	o	oi	m	mi	s	si	f	fi
b	b	**B**	b d o m s	b	b	b d o m s	b	b d o m s	b	b	b d o m s	b
bi	**B**	bi	bi d oi mi fi	bi	bi d oi mi fi	bi	bi d oi mi fi	bi	bi d oi mi fi	bi	bi	bi
d	b	bi	d	**B**	b d o m s	bi d oi mi f	b	bi	d	bi d oi mi f	d	b d o m s
di	b di o m fi	bi di oi mi si	d di s si f fi o oi eq	di	di o fi	di oi si	di o fi	di oi fi	di o fi	di	di oi si	di
o	b	bi di oi mi si	d o s	b di o m fi	b o m	eq d di o oi s si f fi	b	di oi si	o	di oi fi	d o s	b o m
oi	b di o m fi	bi	d oi f	bi di oi mi si	eq d di o oi s si f fi	bi oi mi	di o fi	bi	d oi f	bi oi mi	oi	di oi si
m	b	bi di oi mi si	d o s	b	b	d o s	b	eq f fi	m	m	d o s	b
mi	b di o m fi	bi	d oi f	bi	d oi f	bi	eq s si	bi	d oi f	bi	mi	mi
s	b	bi	d	b di o m fi	b o m	d oi f	b	mi	s	eq s si	d	b o m
si	b di o m fi	bi	d oi f	di	di o fi	oi	di oi fi	mi	eq s si	si	oi	di
f	b	bi	d	bi di oi mi si	d o s	bi oi mi	m	bi	d	bi oi mi	f	eq f fi
fi	b	bi di oi mi si	d o s	di	o	di oi s	m	di oi s	o	di	eq f fi	fi

Table 8.3: Allen's composition table for IA (the basic relation "eq" is omitted). The composition of eq and any basic relation r is r.

consistency algorithm of Figure 8.2.2 is a complete procedure for deciding the consistency of Ω in cubic time.*

Other path consistency algorithms for processing IA-constraints have been proposed in the temporal reasoning literature. For a comparison of some of the most representative see [Bessière, 1996].

In practice, the efficiency of a path consistency algorithm applied to a set of constraints in IA may significantly depend on the time spent for constraint composition. Allen [Allen, 1983] originally proposed calculating the $2^{13} \times 2^{13}$ possible compositions of IA-relations dynamically, using a table storing the 13×13 compositions of the basic relations of IA (see Table 8.3). The composition of two arbitrary relations R_1 and R_2 in IA is the union of all the compositions $r_i \circ r_j$, such that r_i and r_j are basic relations in R_1 and R_2, respectively.

Other significantly improved methods have been proposed since then by Hogge [Hogge, 1987] and by Ladkin and Reinefeld [Ladkin and Reinefeld, 1997]. Ladkin and Reinefeld showed that their method of storing all the possible compositions in a table (requiring about 64 megabytes of memory) is much faster than any alternative previously proposed.

Van Beek and Manchak [van Beek and Manchak, 1996] studied other efficiency improvements for a path consistency algorithm applied to a set of IA-constraints obtained by using some techniques that reduce the number of composition operations to be performed, or by using particular heuristics for ordering the constraints to be processed (e.g., the pairs on the list L of the algorithm in Figure 8.2.2). Finally, another useful technique for improving path consistency processing in IA-networks is presented by Bessière in [Bessière, 1996].

Concerning the problem of finding a scenario/solution for a set of ORD-Horn constraints,

* We have introduced this algorithm in the context of PA, but the same algorithm can be used also for constraints in IA. Of course, for IA-constraints the algorithm uses a different composition table and a different INVERSE function.

two different approaches have been proposed. Given a path consistent set Ω involving variables $x_1, \ldots, x_n$, Ligozat proved that we can find a solution for Ω in the following way [Ligozat, 1996]: iteratively choose instantiations of x_i, for $1 \leq i \leq n$, in such a way that for each i, the interval assigned to x_i has the maximal number of endpoints distinct from the endpoints of the intervals assigned to x_k, $k = 1, \ldots i-1$, allowed by the constraints between x_i and x_k. Operatively, from this result we can derive the following simple method for finding a scenario: iteratively refine the relation R of a constraint xRy to a basic relation among those in R, preferring relations that impose a maximal number of different endpoints for x and y; each time a relation is refined, we enforce path-consistency to the resulting set of constraints. Each refinement transforms the network to a tighter equivalent network, and the method is guaranteed to be backtrack free.* Although Ligozat in his paper does not give a complexity analysis, it can be proved that his method takes $O(n^3)$ time [Bessière, 1997; Gerevini, 2003a].

The second method was proposed by Gerevini and Cristani [Gerevini and Cristani, 1997]. Their technique is based on deriving form a path-consistent set Ω of constraints in ORD-Horn a particular set Σ of constraints over PA involving the endpoints of the interval variables in Ω. From a consistent scenario (solution) for Σ we can then easily derive a consistent scenario (solution) for Ω. The time complexity of this method is $O(n^2)$, if the input set of constraints is known to be path-consistent, while in the general case it is $O(n^3)$, because before applying the method we need to process Ω with a path consistency algorithm.

8.3.2 Minimal Network and One-to-all Relations

A path-consistent network of constraints over SIA^c is minimal [Vilain and Kautz, 1986; Vilain *et al.*, 1990]. However, path consistency is not sufficient to ensure minimality when the constraints of the set are in SIA, and thus neither when they are in ORD-Horn, which is a superclass of SIA.†

Regarding ORD-Horn, Bessière, Isli and Ligozat proved that path consistency is sufficient to compute the minimal network representation for two subclasses of ORD-Horn, one of which covers more than 60% of the relations in ORD-Horn [Bessière *et al.*, 1996]. Actually, their results in [Bessière *et al.*, 1996] are stronger than this. They show that, for these subclasses of ORD-Horn, path consistency ensures *global consistency* [Dechter, 1992]. A globally consistent set of constraints implies that its constraint network is minimal and, furthermore, that a consistent scenario/solution can be found in a backtrack free manner [Dechter, 1992].

The minimal network representation for a set S of constraints in SIA can be computed in three main steps:

1. Translate S into an equivalent set S' of interval endpoint constraints over PA;

2. Compute the minimal network representation of S' by using the method described in Section 8.2.2;

3. Translate the resulting PA-constraints back into the corresponding interval constraints over SIA.

*A constraint network $\mathcal{N}$ is tighter than another equivalent network $\mathcal{N}'$ when every constraint represented by $\mathcal{N}$ is stronger than the corresponding constraint of $\mathcal{N}'$.

†An example of path-consistent set of constraints in IA that is not minimal is given in [Allen, 1983].

The time complexity of this procedure is dominated by step 2, which takes $O(n^3 + m \cdot n^2)$ time (see Section 8.2.2).

Unfortunately, this method cannot be applied to a set Ω of constraints over ORD-Horn, because the translation of Ω can include *disjunctions* of PA-constraints. It appears that at the time of writing the following simple method, based on solving a set of consistency checking instances, is the most efficient way for computing the minimal network of Ω (in terms of worst-case time complexity).

Minimal Network Representation for ORD-Horn. For each basic relation $r \in R$ involved in each constraint xRy of Ω, we refine xRy to xry and we check the consistency of the resulting set Ω'. r belongs to the relation of the constraint between x and y in the minimal network of Ω if and only if Ω' is consistent.

Since this method performs $O(n^2)$ consistency checks, it is clear that its worst-case time complexity is $O(n^5)$. It has been conjectured that this is the best that we can do for ORD-Horn [Nebel and Bürckert, 1995] (in terms of worst-case complexity), and it appears that at the time of writing no proof exists for this claim yet.

Concerning the problem of computing one-to-all relations, the algorithm OAC that we have presented in the context of PA (see Figure 8.8) is complete for SIA^c, but it is incomplete for SIA.

When the input constraints belong to SIA, or to a larger class, the problem of computing one-to-all relations can be solved by using the algorithm OAC-2 (see Figure 8.9). It is easy to see that, since consistency checking for a set of constraints in SIA can be accomplished in $O(n^2)$ time, OAC-2 applied to a set of SIA-constraints requires $O(n^3)$ time. Similarly, OAC-2 applied to a set of ORD-Horn constraints requires $O(n^4)$ time, because consistency checking requires $O(n^3)$ time.

Finally, in Section 8.4.2 we will consider an extension of the timegraph approach called *disjunctive timegraphs*. This extension adds a great deal of expressiveness power, including the ability to represent constraints in ORD-Horn. A disjunctive timegraph representing a set of constraints in ORD-Horn can be polynomially processed for solving the problems of consistency checking, finding a scenario/solution and computing one-to-one relations.

8.4 Intractable Interval Algebra Relations

In this section we present some techniques for processing intractable classes of IA-relations, i.e., classes for which the main reasoning problems are NP-hard, and hence that cannot be solved in polynomial time (assuming P $\neq$ NP).

The ORD-Horn class, though computationally attractive, is not practically adequate for all AI applications because it does not contain disjointness relations such as *before or after*, which are important in planning and scheduling. Figure 8.14 gives a list of the disjointness relations in IA, together with their translation in terms of PA-constraints between interval endpoints.

For example, these relations can be useful to express the constraint that some planned actions cannot be scheduled concurrently, because they contend for the same resources (agents, vehicles, tools, pathways, and so on). In the context of the trains example given in Section 8.1, the constraint

$$
\begin{array}{lcl}
I\ \{\text{before,after}\}\ J & \Leftrightarrow & I^+ < J^- \vee J^+ < I^- \\
I\ \{\text{before,met-by}\}\ J & \Leftrightarrow & I^+ < J^- \vee J^+ = I^- \\
I\ \{\text{meets,after}\}\ J & \Leftrightarrow & I^+ = J^- \vee J^+ < I^- \\
I\ \{\text{meets,met-by}\}\ J & \Leftrightarrow & I^+ = J^- \vee J^+ = I^- \\
I\ \{\text{before,after,meets}\}\ J & \Leftrightarrow & I^+ \leq J^- \vee J^+ < I^- \\
I\ \{\text{before,after,met-by}\}\ J & \Leftrightarrow & I^+ < J^- \vee J^+ \leq I^- \\
I\ \{\text{before,meets,met-by}\}\ J & \Leftrightarrow & I^+ \leq J^- \vee J^+ = I^- \\
I\ \{\text{meets,after,met-by}\}\ J & \Leftrightarrow & I^+ = J^- \vee J^+ \leq I^- \\
I\ \{\text{before,after,meets,met-by}\}\ J & \Leftrightarrow & I^+ \leq J^- \vee J^+ \leq I^-
\end{array}
$$

Figure 8.14: The nine disjointness relations of IA and the corresponding translation into disjunctions of PA-constraints between interval endpoints. (The complete translation of each interval relation between I and J into a set of point relations also contains the endpoint constraints $I^- < I^+$ and $J^- < J^+$.)

$$\texttt{at(T2,S2)}\ \{\text{before, after}\}\ \texttt{at(T1,S2)},$$

which is used to express the information that two trains cannot stop at station S2 at the same time, cannot be expressed using only ORD-Horn relations. Moreover, as indicated in [Gerevini and Schubert, 1994b], reasoning about disjoint actions or events is important also in natural language understanding. Finally, Golumbic and Shamir [Golumbic and Shamir, 1993] discuss an application of reasoning about interval relations to a problem in molecular biology, where disjointness relations are used to express that some pairs of segments of DNA are disjoint [Benzen, 1959].

Unfortunately, adding any of the disjunctive relation of Figure 8.14 to ORD-Horn (as well as to SIA, SIA^c and to the simple class formed by only the thirteen relations of IA) leads to intractability.*

In general, the problem of deciding the satisfiability of a set of constraints in IA (called ISAT for IA in [Golumbic and Shamir, 1993]) is NP-complete [Vilain and Kautz, 1986; Vilain *et al.*, 1990]. The hard to solve instances of ISAT for IA appear around a *phase transition* concerning the probability of satisfiability that was identified and investigated by Ladkin and Reinefeld [Ladkin and Reinefeld, 1992] and by Nebel [Nebel, 1997].

A phase transition is characterized by some critical values of certain order parameters of the problem space [Cheeseman *et al.*, 1991]. Specifically, Ladkin and Reinefeld observed a phase transition of ISAT for IA in the range $6 \leq q \times n \leq 15$ for $q \geq 0.5$, where q is the ratio of non-universal constraints (i.e., those different from the disjunction of all the thirteen basic relations), and n is the number of the interval variables involved in the constraints.

Nebel characterized the phase transition in terms of the average degree (d) of the constraint network representing the input set of constraints. For example, when the average number of basic relations forming a constraint (i.e., its "label size") is 6.5, the phase transition shown in Figure 8.4 is centered in $d = 9.5$. (For more details, the interested reader may

*It should be noted that there exist some tractable classes containing {before, after} [Krokhin *et al.*, 2003; Golumbic and Shamir, 1993]. However, these classes do not contain all the basic relations of IA, and hence they are limited in terms of the definite temporal information that can be expressed. This may significantly affect the applicability of these classes.

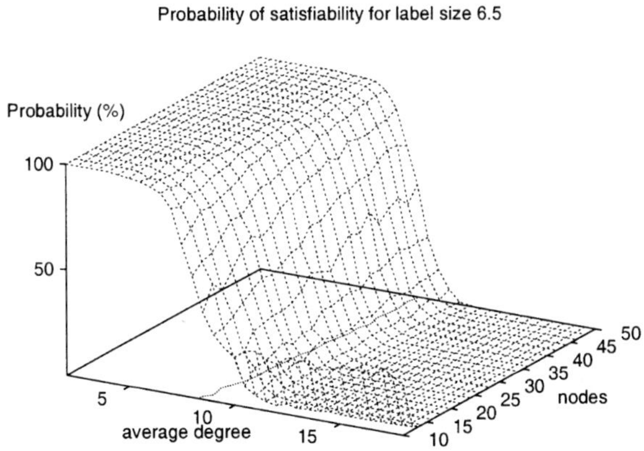

Figure 8.15: Nebel's Phase transition of ISAT for IA when the label size is 6.5.

see [Nebel, 1997; Ladkin and Reinefeld, 1992]).

8.4.1 Backtracking and Path Consistency

Typically, the algorithms for processing intractable classes of relations in IA are based on search methods that use backtracking [Bitner and Reingold, 1975; Shanahan and Southwick, 1989]. Ladkin and Reinefeld [Ladkin and Reinefeld, 1992] proposed a method for determining the consistency of a set of constraints in IA that is based on chronological backtracking, and that uses path consistency algorithms as a forward checking and pruning technique. At the time of writing their algorithm, which has also been investigated by van Beek and Manchak [van Beek and Manchak, 1996] and by Nebel [Nebel, 1997], appears to be the known fastest (complete) method for handling constraints in the full IA, using the constraint network representation.*

Figure 8.16 gives Ladkin and Reinefeld's algorithm as formulated by Nebel in [Nebel, 1997]. The input set of constraints is represented by a $n \times n$ matrix, where each entry C_{ij} contains the IA-relation between the interval variables i and j ($1 \leq i, j \leq n$). Split is a tractable subset of IA (e.g., ORD-Horn). The larger is Split, the lower is the average branching factor of the search.

Nebel proved that the algorithm is complete when Split is SIA^c, SIA, or ORD-Horn [Nebel, 1997]. He also analyzed experimentally the backtracking scheme of Figure 8.16 when Split is chosen to be one of the above tractable sets, showing that the use of ORD-Horn leads to better performance on average. However, it turned out that there are other algorithmic features that affect the performance of the backtracking algorithm more significantly than the choice of which kind of Split to use. These features regard the heuristics for ordering the constraints to be processed, and the kind of path consistency algorithm used at step 1 (this can be either based on a weighted queue scheme, such as the algorithm of

*Another recent powerful approach is the one proposed in [Thornton *et al.*, 2002; Thorthon *et al.*, 2004], that uses local search techniques for fast consistency checking. This method can outperform backtracking-based methods. However, as any local search approach, it is incomplete.

Algorithm: IA-CONSISTENCY(C)
Input: A matrix C representing a set Θ of constraints in IA
Output: *true* if Θ is satisfiable, *false* otherwise

```
C ← PATH-CONSISTENCY(C)
if C = false then
    return false
else choose an unprocessed relation C_ij and
    split C_ij into R_1, ..., R_k s.t. all R_l ∈ Split (1 ≤ l ≤ k)
    if no relation can be split then
        return true
    for l ← 1 to k do
        C_ij ← R_l
        if IA-CONSISTENCY(C) then
            return true
    return false
```

Figure 8.16: Ladkin and Reinefeld's backtracking algorithm for consistency checking of IA-constraints [Ladkin and Reinefeld, 1992; Nebel, 1997].

Figure 8.2.2, or an algorithm based on an iterative scheme which uses no queue, such as the algorithm PC-1 [Montanari, 1974; Mackworth, 1977]).[*]

As shown by Nebel, from these design choices and the kind of tractable set used as Split, we can derive different search strategies that on some problem instances have complementary performance. These strategies can be orthogonally combined to obtain a method that can solve (within a certain time limit) more instances than those solvable using the single strategies. (For more details, the interested reader may see [Nebel, 1997]).

Concerning the problems of computing the minimal network representation, one-to-all relations and one-to-one relations, at the time of writing no specialized algorithm is known. However, each of these problems can be easily reduced to a set of instances of the consistency checking problem, which can be solved by using the backtracking algorithm illustrated above. For example, in order to determine the one-to-one relation between two intervals I and J, we can check the feasibility of each basic relation r contained in the stipulated relation R between I and J in the following way: first we replace R with r, and then we run IA-CONSISTENCY to check the consistency of the modified network.

The problem of computing a consistent scenario (solution) can be reduced to the problem of consistency checking. In fact, a consistent scenario (solution) for an input set of constraints exists only if the set is consistent and, in such a case, IA-CONSISTENCY has the "side effect" of reducing it to a set of *tractable* constraints (depending on the value of Split, these constraints can be, for example, in SIA^c, SIA, or ORD-Horn). A consistent scenario (solution) for this tractable set is also a scenario (solution) for the input set of constraints, and can it be determined by using the techniques described in Section 8.3.1.

[*] PC-2 [Mackworth, 1977] is another important path-consistency algorithm that has been used in the context of temporal reasoning (e.g., [van Beek and Cohen, 1990]). A disadvantage of PC-2 is that it requires $O(n^3)$ space, while the other algorithms that we have mentioned requires $O(n^2)$ space, where n is the number of the variables in the input set of (qualitative) temporal constraints.

8.4.2 Disjunctive Timegraphs

We now consider an alternative method for representing and processing intractable relations in IA, which is based on an extension of the timegraph approach illustrated in Section 8.2.4.

A *disjunctive timegraph* ($\mathcal{D}$-timegraph) is a pair $\langle T, D\rangle$, where T is a timegraph and D a set of constraints in PA (PA-disjunctions) involving only point-variables in T (see Figure 8.17). Considering our trains example in Section 8.1, each of the temporal constraints 1–7 can be expressed using a $\mathcal{D}$-timegraph. More in general, the disjunctions of a $\mathcal{D}$-timegraph add a great deal of expressive power to a timegraph, including the ability to represent relations in ORD-Horn, disjointness of temporal intervals (see Figure 8.14). Moreover, A $\mathcal{D}$-timegraph can represent other relations not belonging to IA or PA, such as Vilain's point-interval relations [Vilain, 1982],* point-interval disjointness relations [Gerevini and Schubert, 1994b] and some 3-interval and 4-interval relations [Gerevini and Schubert, 1995a] such as

$$I\,\{\text{before}\}\,J\ \vee\ K\,\{\text{before}\}\,H.^{\dagger}$$

The current algorithms for processing the disjunctions of a $\mathcal{D}$-timegraph are specialized for binary disjunctions, and hence not every relation in IA is representable (because there are some relations that require ternary disjunctions). In principle, the techniques presented in [Gerevini and Schubert, 1995a] can be extended to deal with arbitrary disjunctions.

A $\mathcal{D}$-timegraph $\langle T, D\rangle$ is *consistent* if it is possible to select one of the disjuncts for each PA-disjunction in D in such a way that the resulting collection of selected PA-constraints can be consistently added to T. This set of selected disjuncts is called an *instantiation* of D in T, and the task of finding such a set is called *deciding* D relative to T.

Once we have an instantiation of D, we can easily solve the problem of finding a consistent scenario by adding the instantiation to T and using a topological sort algorithm [Cormen *et al.*, 1990]. In order to check whether a relation R between two time points x and y is entailed by a $\mathcal{D}$-timegraph $\langle T, D\rangle$, we can add the constraint $x\overline{R}y$ to T (where $\overline{R}$ is the negation of R), obtaining a new timegraph T', and then check if (a) T' is consistent, and (b) D can be decided relative to T' (if T' is consistent). The original $\mathcal{D}$-timegraph entails xRy just in case one of (a), (b) does *not* hold. This gives us a method for computing one-to-one relations, one-to-all relations, as well as the minimal network representation using the $\mathcal{D}$-timegraph approach.

Deciding a set of binary PA-disjunctions is an NP-complete problem [Gerevini and Schubert, 1994b]. However, in practice this task can be efficiently accomplished by using a method described in [Gerevini and Schubert, 1994a; Gerevini and Schubert, 1995a]. Given a disjunctive timegraph $\langle T, D\rangle$, the method for deciding D relative to T consists of two phases:

*Vilain's class of point-interval relations is formed by 2^5 relations obtained by considering all the possible disjunctions of five basic relations between a point and an interval.

†Point-interval disjointness can be used to state that a certain time point (perhaps an instantaneous action, or the beginning or end of an action) must not be within a certain interval (another action, or the interval between two actions). This kind of constraints is fundamental, for example, in nonlinear planning (e.g., [Chapman, 1987; Pednault, 1986b; Sacerdoti, 1975; Tate, 1977; Weld, 1994; Yang, 1997]), where an earlier action may serve to achieve the preconditions of a later one, and no further action should be inserted between them which would subvert those preconditions.

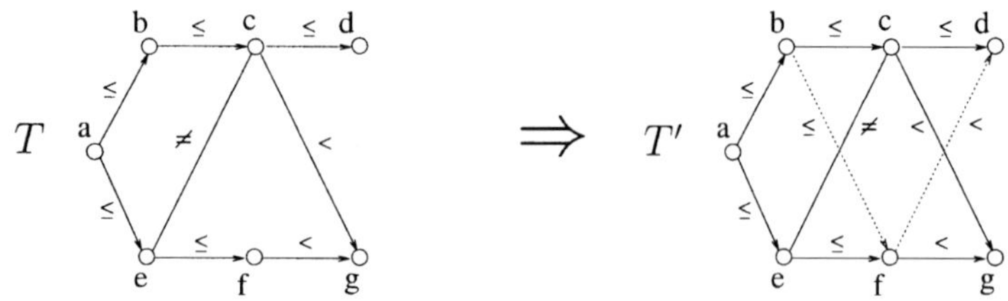

$$D : \begin{cases} D(1) : f < a \vee f < d \\ D(2) : b < f \vee a < g \\ D(3) : g \le a \vee b \le f \\ D(4) : d < g \vee b < d \\ D(5) : b \neq e \vee b < d \end{cases} \Longrightarrow \quad D' : \; D(5) : b \neq e \vee b < d$$

Figure 8.17: An example of $\mathcal{D}$-timegraph $\langle T, D \rangle$ from [Gerevini and Schubert, 1995a]. The $\mathcal{D}$-timegraph $\langle T', D' \rangle$ is equivalent to $\langle T, D \rangle$, and is obtained by applying the pruning rules to the disjunctions in D using T.

- a preprocessing phase, which prunes the search space by reducing D to a subset D' of D, producing a timegraph T' such that D has an instantiation in T if and only if D' has an instantiation in T';
- a search phase, which finds an instantiation of D' in T' (if it exists) by using backtracking.

Preprocessing uses a set of efficient *pruning rules* exploiting the information provided by the timegraph to reduce the set of the disjunctions to a logically equivalent subset. For example, the "T-derivability" rule says, informally, that if the timegraph entails one of the disjuncts of a certain disjunction, then such a disjunction can be removed without loss of information; the "T-resolution" rule says that if the timegraph entails the negation of one of the two disjuncts of a disjunction, then this disjunction can be reduced to the other disjunct (called "T-resolvent"), which can then be added to the timegraph (provided that the timegraph does not entail also the negation of the second disjunct); finally the "T-tautology" rule can be used to detect whether a disjunction can be eliminated because it is a tautology with respect to the information entailed by the timegraph. (For more details on these and other rules, the interested reader may see [Gerevini and Schubert, 1995a].)

Various strategies are possible for preprocessing the set of disjunctions using the pruning rules. The simplest strategy is the one in which the rules are applied to each disjunction once, and the set of T-resolvents generated is added to the timegraph at the end of the process. For example, the $\mathcal{D}$-timegraph $\langle T', D' \rangle$ of Figure 8.17 can be obtained from $\langle T, D \rangle$ by following this simple strategy.*

A more complete strategy, though more computationally expensive, is to add the T-resolvents to the graph as soon as they are generated, and to iterate the application of the

*D(1) and D(3) are eliminated by T-resolution, D(2) by T-derivability and D(4) by T-tautology.

rules till no further disjunction can be eliminated. This strategy is still polynomial, and it is complete for the class of PA-disjunctions translating a set of interval relations in ORD-Horn [Gerevini and Schubert, 1995a]. In general, the choice of the preprocessing strategy depends on how much effort one wants to dedicate to the preprocessing step and how much to the search step.

Once the initial set of disjunctions has been processed by applying the pruning rules, if this processing has not been sufficient to decide consistency, then the search for an instantiation of the remaining disjunctions is activated. Gerevini and Schubert proposed a search algorithm specialized for binary disjunctions of strict inequalities, which can express the practically important relation *before or after*, as well as point-interval disjointness (i.e., exclusion of a point form an interval). The algorithm is based on a "partially selective backtracking" technique, which combines chronological backtracking and a form of selective backtracking [Gerevini and Schubert, 1995a; Bruynooghe, 1981; Shanahan and Southwick, 1989].

The experimental results presented in [Gerevini and Schubert, 1995a] show that the $\mathcal{D}$-timegraph approach is very efficient especially when the timegraph is not very sparse (i.e., "enough" non-disjunctive temporal information is available), and the number of disjunctions is relatively small with respect to the number of input PA-constraints represented in the timegraph. For more difficult cases (sparse timegraphs with few PA-constraints and numerous PA-disjunctions) a "forward propagation" technique can be included into the basic search algorithm. Such a technique can dramatically reduce the number of backtracks.

8.5 Concluding Remarks

The ability to efficiently represent and process temporal information is an important issue in AI, as well as in other discipline of computer science (e.g., [Song and Cohen, 1991; Lascarides and Oberlander, 1993; Hwang and Schubert, 1994; Snodgrass, 1990; Kline, 1993; Kline, 1993; Özsoyŏglu and Snodgrass, 1995; Orgun, 1996; Golumbic and Shamir, 1993]). In this chapter we have surveyed a collection of techniques for processing qualitative temporal constraints, focusing on fundamental reasoning tasks, such as consistency checking, finding a solution (or consistent scenario), and deducing (or querying) new constraints from those that are explicitly given.

We believe that this style of temporal reasoning is relatively mature and has much to offer to the development of practical applications. However, at the time of writing there are still some important aspects that deserve further research. These include the following:

- The design and experimental evaluation of efficient methods for *incremental* qualitative temporal reasoning, both in the context of the general constraint network approach and of specialized graph-based representations like timegraphs or series-parallel graphs. In fact, in many applications we are interested in *maintaining* certain properties (e.g., consistency, the minimal network representation or the time chain partition of a TL-graph), rather then recomputing them from scratch each time a new constraint is asserted, or an existing constraint is retracted. Some studies in this direction for metric constraints are presented in [Bell and Tate, 1985; Cervoni *et al.*, 1994; Gerevini *et al.*, 1996], while other more recent studies focusing on qualitative constraints are described in [Delgrande and Gupta, 2002; Gerevini, 2003a; Gerevini, 2003b].

- The study of alternative algorithms for dealing with intractable classes of temporal constraints, such as *anytime* algorithms (e.g., [Boddy and Dean, 1994; Hansen and Zilberstein, 1996; Zilberstein, 1996]), and algorithms based on local search techniques. As we have already mentioned, an interesting example of such techniques for qualitative temporal reasoning is given in [Thorthon *et al.*, 2004].

- The study of new methods for representing and managing qualitative relations involving non-convex intervals, which, for example, can be useful in the representation of periodic events (e.g., [Leban *et al.*, 1986; Poesio and Brachman, 1991]).*

- The design of new efficient representations and algorithms for managing combined qualitative and metric temporal information. In particular, the integration of metric constraints involving deadlines, durations and absolute times into the timegraph representation is a promising research direction for addressing scalability in temporal reasoning with qualitative and metric information.†

- The study of new algorithms for handling Interval Algebra relations extended with qualitative relations about the relative duration of the involved intervals (e.g, I overlaps J and the duration of I is shorter that the duration of J). An interesting calculus for dealing with this type of temporal constraints has been proposed and studied in [Pujari *et al.*, 1999; Kumari and Pujari, 2002; Balbiani *et al.*, 2003]. Hoewever, it appears that this calculus has not yet been fully investigated from an algorithmic point of view.

- The integration of qualitative temporal reasoning and other types of constraint-based reasoning, such as qualitative spatial reasoning, into a uniform framework. For instance, the Spatio-Temporal Constraint Calculus is a recent approach for spatio-temporal reasoning integrating Allen's Interval Algebra and the Region Connection Calculus RCC-8 [Randell *et al.*, 1992; Bennett *et al.*, 2002a; Gerevini and Nebel, 2002]. The development of efficient reasoning algorithms for such a combined calculus is an important direction for future research.

*In this chapter we have not treated this type of qualitative constraints. The interested reader can see other chapters in this book.

†These metric constraints were handled in the original implementation of timegraphs [Schubert *et al.*, 1987; Miller and Schubert, 1990], but $\neq$ and PA-disjunctions were not handled, and also $<$ and $\leq$ relations entailed via metric relations were not extracted in a deductively complete way.

Reasoning Techniques

Handbook of Temporal Reasoning in Artificial Intelligence
Edited by M. Fisher, D. Gabbay and L. Vila

Chapter 9

Theorem-Proving for Discrete Temporal Logic

Mark Reynolds & Clare Dixon

This chapter considers theorem proving for discrete temporal logics. We are interested in deciding or at least enumerating the formulas of the logic which are valid, that is, are true in all circumstances. Most of the techniques for temporal theorem-proving have been extensions for methods developed for classical logics but completely novel techniques have also been developed. Initially we concentrate on discrete linear-time temporal logics, describing axiomatic, tableau, automata and resolution based approaches. The application of these approaches to other temporal logics is discussed.

9.1 Introduction

Readers of this handbook will be aware of the wide variety of useful tasks which require reasoning about time. There are many applications of temporal reasoning tasks to problems of changing knowledge, to planning, to processing natural language, to managing the interchange of information, and to developing complex systems.

There are a wide variety of temporal logics available in which such reasoning can be carried out. Depending on the task at hand, time might be thought of as linear or branching, point or interval based, discrete or dense, finite or infinite etc. Equally, the atemporal world may be able to be modelled in a simple propositional language or we may need a full first-order structure or something even more complicated. To reason about change we may need only to be able to describe the relationship between one state and the next, or we may need eventualities, or to talk about the past, or complex fixed-point languages or even alternative histories.

One of the simplest temporal logics which is still widely applicable is the propositional linear temporal logic PLTL, which uses a few simple future-time operators to describe the changes in the truth values of propositional atoms over a one step at a time, natural numbers model of time. The most important temporal operator is Kamp's "Until". We will concentrate on this language which gives a good idea of some of the important general problems and solutions in reasoning about temporal logics.

There are several distinct reasoning tasks needed for the applications of temporal logic. The most general is that of theorem-proving. Here we are interested in deciding whether a given formula in a particular temporal language is valid, or perhaps we might just want to be able to successively list all the validities of the logic. By a formula being valid, we mean a formula which is true at all times in all possible models. Knowing which formulae are valid has all sorts of uses such as being able to determine consequences, and helping determine truth in particular structures.

In surveying the methods for theorem-proving in PLTL, we identify four alternative general approaches. The fact that each approach has its devotees and its large body of research literature shows that even this specific problem is very useful but not entirely straightforward. We will mention briefly how each approach might (or might not) be able to be generalized to be used on other temporal logics.

After introducing the PLTL logic and a few related logics, we will examine theorem-proving approaches based on axiom systems, tableaux, automata and then resolution.

9.2 Syntax and Semantics

9.2.1 Linear Temporal Logics

The logic used in this chapter is Propositional Linear Temporal Logic (PLTL). PLTL is based on a natural numbers model of time, i.e. it is a countable linear sequence of discrete steps. The language, classical propositional logic augmented with future-time temporal connectives (operators) was introduced in [Gabbay *et al.*, 1980]. It is possible to add some past-time operators but, as shown in [Gabbay *et al.*, 1980], with natural numbers time, this does not add expressiveness. Future-time temporal connectives include '$\Diamond$' *sometime in the future*, '$\Box$' *always in the future*, '$\bigcirc$' *in the next moment in time*, '$\mathcal{U}$' *until*, and '$\mathcal{W}$' *unless (weak until)*. We can assume that $\bigcirc$ and $\mathcal{U}$ are the primitive connectives and the rest can be defined as abbreviations, but it is often convenient to instead assume that all of these are primitive.

PLTL formulae are constructed using the following connectives and proposition symbols.

- A set $\mathcal{P}$ of propositional symbols.
- Propositional and temporal constants **true** and **false**.
- Propositional connectives, $\neg$, $\vee$, $\wedge$, $\rightarrow$, and $\leftrightarrow$.
- Future-time temporal connectives, $\bigcirc$, $\Diamond$, $\Box$, $\mathcal{U}$, and $\mathcal{W}$.

The set of well-formed formulae of PLTL, WFF, is inductively defined as the smallest set satisfying:

- Any element of $\mathcal{P}$ is in WFF
- **true** and **false** are in WFF
- If A and B are in WFF then so are

$$\begin{array}{lllll} \neg A & A \vee B & A \wedge B & A \rightarrow B & A \leftrightarrow B \\ \Diamond A & \Box A & A \mathcal{U} B & A \mathcal{W} B & \bigcirc A \end{array}$$

A *literal* is defined as either a proposition or the negation of a proposition.

PLTL is interpreted over natural numbers time. Models of PLTL can be represented as a sequence of *states*

$$\sigma = \langle s_0, s_1, s_2, s_3, \ldots \rangle$$

where each state, s_i, is a set of propositions, representing those propositions which are satisfied in the ith moment in time. As formulae in PLTL are interpreted at a particular state in the sequence (i.e. at a particular moment in time), the notation

$$(\sigma, i) \models A$$

denotes the truth (or otherwise) of formula A in the model σ at state index $i \in \mathbb{N}$. For any formula A, model σ and state index $i \in \mathbb{N}$, either $(\sigma, i) \models A$ holds or $(\sigma, i) \models A$ does not hold, denoted by $(\sigma, i) \not\models A$. For example, a proposition symbol, 'p', is satisfied in model σ and at state index i if, and only if, p is one of the propositions in state s_i, i.e.,

$$(\sigma, i) \models p \quad \text{iff} \quad p \in s_i.$$

The semantics of the temporal connectives are defined as follows

$$\begin{array}{l}
(\sigma, i) \models \bigcirc A \text{ iff } (\sigma, i+1) \models A; \\
(\sigma, i) \models \Diamond A \text{ iff there exists a } j \geq i \text{ s.t. } (\sigma, j) \models A; \\
(\sigma, i) \models \Box A \text{ iff for all } j \geq i \text{ then } (\sigma, j) \models A; \\
(\sigma, i) \models A \mathcal{U} B \text{ iff there exists a } k \geq i \text{ s.t. } (\sigma, k) \models B \\
\qquad\qquad \text{and for all } i \leq j < k \text{ then } (\sigma, j) \models A; \\
(\sigma, i) \models A \mathcal{W} B \text{ iff } (\sigma, i) \models A \mathcal{U} B \text{ or } (\sigma, i) \models \Box A.
\end{array}$$

Equivalently, we could define PLTL in terms of the primitive operators $\bigcirc$ and $\mathcal{U}$. The other operators can be seen as abbreviations:

$$\begin{array}{l}
\textbf{true} \equiv p \vee \neg p, \text{ for some fixed atom } p \\
\textbf{false} \equiv \neg\textbf{true} \\
\Diamond A \equiv \textbf{true} \mathcal{U} A \\
\Box A \equiv \neg(\textbf{true} \mathcal{U} (\neg A)) \\
A \mathcal{W} B \equiv (A \mathcal{U} B) \vee (\Box A)
\end{array}$$

There are two slightly different pairs of notions of satisfiability and validity which are used for linear temporal logics.

The *floating* versions are as follows. We say that a formula α of PLTL is *satisfiable* iff there is some sequence σ of states and some $i < \omega$ such that $(\sigma, i) \models \alpha$. We say that α is *valid* iff for all sequences σ of states, for all $i < \omega$, $(\sigma, i) \models \alpha$. This is the notion of validity which most of the algorithms in this chapter are trying to capture.

The other notions of validity and satisfiability are the *anchored* ones seen in [Manna and Pnueli, 1992], for example. In the anchored approach we say that a formula α of PLTL is *satisfiable* iff there is some sequence σ of states such that $(\sigma, 0) \models \alpha$. We say that α is *valid* iff for all sequences σ of states, $(\sigma, 0) \models \alpha$. Note that for PLTL, without past-time temporal operators, the set of anchored and floating valid formulas coincide. In line with current usage we will use the anchored notion of validity when we look at resolution based theorem-proving techniques.

Other temporal logics arise by varying the language or the models (frames) of time or both. For example, on the natural numbers time we can, perhaps for reasons of rendering conditions in a natural way, introduce past-time operators. These might include yesterday (of which there can be two versions when time has a beginning) and *since*, the mirror image of until. See [Gabbay *et al.*, 1980], for example. It is also possible to follow, various authors such as [Wolper, 1983] and [Kozen, 1982] and allow more general connectives defined via regular expressions or fixed-point operators.

There are many applications where the natural numbers time model is too restrictive. If time has an infinite past, when perhaps we want to reason about facts in an historical database, then we might want to use an integers model of time (see, for example, [Reynolds, 1994]). If several agents or processes act in parallel or a complicated external environment is involved, then a dense model of time might be appropriate (see, for example, [Barringer *et al.*, 1986] or [Gabbay *et al.*, 1994a]).

9.2.2 Branching Temporal Logics

If we want to consider various alternative histories, or courses of action, or paths of computation then branching time logics are sensible to use. The main languages here are the purely branching Computational Tree Logic CTL and the combined branching-linear "full" Computational Tree Logic CTL*. CTL* computation tree logic, was first described in [Emerson and Sistla, 1984] and [Emerson and Halpern, 1986]. By using a slightly unusual semantics based on paths through transition structures, CTL* is able to extend, in expressiveness, both the computation tree logic, CTL, of [Clarke and Emerson, 1981a], a simple branching logic, and the standard PLTL. The formulae of CTL are also formulae of CTL* so we will return to this less expressive logic later.

The language of CTL* is used to describe several different types of structures and so there are really several different closely related logics. Standard CTL*, which we describe, is the logic of R-generable sets of paths on transition structures.

We fix a countable set $\mathcal{L}$ of atomic propositions.

Formulas are evaluated in *transition structures*. A structure is a triple $M = (S, R, g)$ where:

S	is the non-empty set of *states*
R	is a total binary relation $\subseteq S \times S$ (i.e. for every $s \in S$, there is some $t \in S$ such that $(s, t) \in R$)
g	$: S \to \wp\mathcal{L}$ is a labelling of the states with sets of atoms (i.e. $\wp\mathcal{L}$ is the powerset of $\mathcal{L}$)

A *fullpath* in M is an infinite sequence $\langle s_0, s_1, s_2, ...\rangle$ of states of M such that for each i, $(s_i, s_{i+1}) \in R$.

For the fullpath $b = \langle s_0, s_1, s_2, ...\rangle$, and any $i \geq 0$, we write b_i for the state s_i and $b_{\geq i}$ for the fullpath $\langle s_i, s_{i+1}, s_{i+2}, ...\rangle$.

The formulae of CTL* are built from **true** and the atomic propositions in $\mathcal{L}$ recursively using classical connectives $\neg$ and $\wedge$ as well as the temporal connectives $\bigcirc$, **until** and **E**: if α and β are formulae then so are $\bigcirc\alpha$, α **until** β and $\mathbf{E}\alpha$.

As well as the linear abbreviations, $\vee$, $\rightarrow$, $\leftrightarrow$ $\Diamond$ and $\Box$, we have $\mathbf{A}\alpha \equiv \neg\mathbf{E}\neg\alpha$.

Truth of formulae is evaluated at fullpaths in structures. We write $M, b \models \alpha$ iff the formula α is true of the fullpath b in the structure $M = (S, R, g)$. This is defined formally recursively by:

$M, b \models$ **true**		
$M, b \models p$	iff	$p \in g(b_0)$, any $p \in \mathcal{L}$
$M, b \models \neg\alpha$	iff	$M, b \not\models \alpha$
$M, b \models \alpha \wedge \beta$	iff	$M, b \models \alpha$ and $M, b \models \beta$
$M, b \models \bigcirc\alpha$	iff	$M, b_{\geq 1} \models \alpha$
$M, b \models \alpha$ **until** β	iff	there is some $i \geq 0$ such that $M, b_{\geq i} \models \beta$ and for each j, if $0 \leq j < i$ then $M, b_{\geq j} \models \alpha$
$M, b \models \mathbf{E}\alpha$	iff	there is some fullpath b' such that $b_0 = b'_0$ and $M, b' \models \alpha$

We say that α is valid in CTL* iff for all transition structures M, for all fullpaths b in M, we have $M, b \models \alpha$.

We say that α is satisfiable in CTL* iff for some transition structure M and for some fullpath b in M, we have $M, b \models \alpha$. Clearly α is satisfiable in a transition structure iff $\neg\alpha$ is not valid.

Some presentations of CTL* proceed by via the definition of a certain subset of the formulae which only depend, for their truth, on an evaluation point rather than fullpath. We identify such a set. We will call a formula a *state* formula if it is a boolean combination of atoms and formulae of the form $\mathbf{E}\beta$. It is easy to show that the truth of a state formula depends only on the initial state of a path and not on the rest of the path.

CTL is a sub-language of CTL* which contains only the atoms and formulae of the form $\mathbf{E}\bigcirc\alpha$, $\mathbf{A}\bigcirc\alpha$, $\mathbf{E}(\alpha$ **until** $\beta)$ and $\mathbf{A}(\alpha$ **until** $\beta)$ (for α and β from CTL) and their boolean combinations. The semantics of CTL formulae is as in CTL*. Each CTL formula is a state formula.

9.2.3 Other Temporal Logics

There are many other forms of temporal logic with practical applications. We will briefly mention first-order temporal languages in the sections below. See also [Hodkinson *et al.*, 2000] and [Gabbay *et al.*, 1994a]. We will occasionally cite references to work on combined temporal-modal languages. However, we will not consider interval based temporal reasoning here.

9.3 Axiom Systems and Finite Model Properties

Traditional techniques for theorem proving are based on axiom systems. In fact, before the advent of Kripke semantics, logics themselves were defined via axiom systems. Today, practical applications more frequently give rise to semantically defined temporal logics and so some work must be done to show their equivalence with syntactic systems. That is, we must show that the syntactic axiom system is sound and complete for the logic: the formulae which can be derived are exactly the validities of the logic.

Axiom systems can be seen as descriptions of a semi-decision procedure for enumerating validities. As such, they are not as useful as a complete decision procedure which determines whether any given formula is a validity or not. However, an axiom system can give useful insights into a logic, can provide an intuitive method for manual theorem-proving and can provide a basis for showing that other syntactic theorem-proving methods are correct.

Also, as we describe in Section 9.3.4 below, axiom systems can sometimes be combined with powerful finite model properties to demonstrate that logics are decidable and to give an initial, albeit usually inefficient, decision procedure.

Because the methods covered in this section are not usually the most efficient for automated theorem-proving we will not go into much detail here.

9.3.1 Hilbert Systems

Hilbert style axiom systems were invented for classical logic by Frege [Frege, 1972]. Early modal and temporal logics were often presented in this way (see, for example, [Prior, 1957]). After the advent of Kripke semantics, much effort was put into showing the equivalence of axiom systems and semantically defined modal and temporal logics. See, for example, [van Benthem, 1983].

Hilbert style axiom systems usually consist of a certain number of axioms, which vary considerable between logics, and a few rules of inference which are usually the same or similar for different logics. There is a procedure for deriving *theorems* which we describe below. The aim is for the theorems of the system to be exactly the validities of the logic.

The first axiomatization for PLTL was given in [Gabbay *et al.*, 1980]. We assume that $\bigcirc$ and $\mathcal{U}$ are primitive, $\Diamond$ and $\Box$ are abbreviations.

The inference rules are modus ponens and generalization:

$$\frac{A, A \rightarrow B}{B} \qquad \frac{A}{\Box A}$$

The axioms are all substitution instances of the following:

(1) all classical tautologies,
(2) $\Box(A \rightarrow B) \rightarrow (\Box A \rightarrow \Box B)$
(3) $\bigcirc \neg A \leftrightarrow \neg \bigcirc A$
(4) $\bigcirc(A \rightarrow B) \rightarrow (\bigcirc A \rightarrow \bigcirc B)$
(5) $\Box A \rightarrow A \wedge \bigcirc \Box A$
(6) $\Box(A \rightarrow \bigcirc A) \rightarrow (A \rightarrow \Box A)$
(7) $(A \mathcal{U} B) \rightarrow \Diamond B$
(8) $(A \mathcal{U} B) \leftrightarrow (B \vee (A \wedge \bigcirc(A \mathcal{U} B)))$

We assume that the reader understands the concept of a substitution instance of an axiom or a rule. A proof of A_n in this system is a finite sequence $A_1, ..., A_n$ of formulae of PLTL such that for each $i = 1, ..., n$, either A_i is a substitution instance of an axiom or there is $j, k < i$ such that

$$\frac{A_j, A_k}{A_i} \quad \text{or} \quad \frac{A_j}{A_i}$$

is a substitution instance of a rule.

If there is a proof of A then we say that A is a theorem and we write $\vdash A$. We say that A is *inconsistent* iff $\vdash A \rightarrow$ **false**. Otherwise A is consistent.

A straightforward induction on the lengths of proof gives us the following result, which is defined as the *soundness* of the axiom system:

Theorem 9.3.1. *If* $\vdash A$ *then* A *is valid in PLTL.*

The converse result is called *completeness* of the axiom system and is generally harder to show. In fact, there are also different forms of completeness and this should really be called *weak completeness*. See [Gabbay *et al.*, 1994a] for more details.

The system is complete:

Theorem 9.3.2. *If A is valid in PLTL then* $\vdash A$.

Proof. We give a sketch. The details are left to the reader: or see [Gabbay *et al.*, 1980]. Note that our axioms and even connectives are slightly different than those used in the original. It is enough to show that if A is consistent then A is satisfiable.

There is a common technique, (originally due to Henkin [Henkin, 1949] in a non-modal context), of forming a model of a consistent formula in a modal logic out of the maximal consistent sets of formulae. These are the infinite sets of formulae which are each maximal in not containing some finite subsets whose conjunction is inconsistent. In our case this model will not be a standard ω-sequence but a structure with a more general definition of truth for the temporal connectives.

Let $\mathcal{C}$ contain all the maximally consistent sets of formulae. This is a non-standard model of A with truth for the connectives defined via the following (accessibility) relations: for each $\Gamma, \Delta \in \mathcal{C}$, say $\Gamma R_+ \Delta$ iff $\{B \mid \bigcirc B \in \Gamma\} \subseteq \Delta$ and $\Gamma R_< \Delta$ iff $\{B \mid \bigcirc \Box B \in \Gamma\} \subseteq \Delta$. For example, if we call this model M then for each $\Gamma \in \mathcal{C}$, we define $M, \Gamma \models p$ iff $p \in \Gamma$ for any atom p and $M, \Gamma \models \bigcirc B$ iff there is some $\Delta \in \mathcal{C}$, such that $\Gamma R_+ \Delta$ and $M, \Delta \models B$. The truth of formulas of the form B_1 **until** B_2 is defined via paths through $\mathcal{C}$ in a straightforward way.

A technique due to Lindenbaum shows us that there is some $\Gamma_0 \in \mathcal{C}$ with $A \in \Gamma_0$. Using this and the fact that $R_<$ is the transitive closure of R_+, we can indeed show that $M, \Gamma_0 \models A$.

There is also a common technique for taking this model and factoring out by an equivalence relation to form a finite but also non-standard model. This is the method of *filtration*. See [Gabbay *et al.*, 1994a].

To do this in our logic, we first limit ourselves to a finite set of interesting formulae:

$$\mathrm{cl}(A) = \{B, \neg B, \bigcirc B, \bigcirc\neg B, \Diamond B, \Diamond\neg B \mid B \text{ is a subformula of } A\}.$$

Now we define $C = \{\Gamma \cap \mathrm{cl}(A) | \Gamma \in \mathcal{C}\}$ and we impose a relation $R_\bigcirc$ on C via $aR_\bigcirc b$ iff there exist $\Gamma, \Delta \in \mathcal{C}$ such that $a = \Gamma \cap \mathrm{cl}(A)$, $b = \Delta \cap \mathrm{cl}(A)$ and $\Gamma R_+ \Delta$.

To build an ω-model of A we next find an ω-sequence σ of sets from C starting at $\Gamma_0 \cap \mathrm{cl}(A)$ and proceeding via the $R_\bigcirc$ relation in such a way that if the set Γ appears infinitely often in the sequence then each of its $R_\bigcirc$-successors do too. We can turn σ into an ω-structure τ via $p \in \tau_i$ iff $p \in \sigma_i$ (for all atoms p). This is enough to give us a truth lemma by induction on all formulae $B \in \mathrm{cl}(A)$: namely, $B \in \sigma_i$ iff $\sigma, i \models B$. Immediately we have $\sigma, 0 \models A$ as required. □

9.3.2 Other temporal logics

Axiom systems for various logics using just Prior's '$\Diamond$' and its past-time version are summarized in [van Benthem, 1983]. Axioms for logics with until and since over various models of time, such as integers, or reals, or various classes of models of time, such as the class of all linear orders can be found in [Lichtenstein *et al.*, 1985; Venema, 1991b; Reynolds, 1994; Gabbay and Hodkinson, 1990; Burgess, 1982; Reynolds, 1992]. For fixed-point logics see [Barringer *et al.*, 1986].

It has been long known that no (recursive) axiomatization exists for first-order temporal logic over natural numbers time (see [Gabbay *et al.*, 1994a]) but see [Szalas, 1987] and [Reynolds, 1996] for related results. However, the *monodic* fragment of FOTL, has been shown to have completeness and sometimes even decidability properties [Hodkinson *et al.*, 2000]. A first-order temporal logic -formula ϕ is called *monodic* if any subformulae of the form $\mathcal{T}\psi$, where $\mathcal{T}$ is one of $\bigcirc$, $\square$, $\diamond$ (or $\psi_1\mathcal{T}\psi_2$, where $\mathcal{T}$ is one of $\mathcal{U}$, $\mathcal{W}$), contains at most one free variable. The set of valid *monodic* formulae is finitely axiomatisable. By restricting the first-order part to decidable fragments, for example the guarded fragment or the two variable fragment, we obtain decidable monodic first-order temporal logic. Other decidable, non-monodic fragments of FOTL have been identified, see for example [Pliuškevičius, 2001]. This and related papers define saturation-style calculi based on sequents.

Interval temporal logic can not be axiomatized either [Halpern and Shoham, 1986].

An axiomatization for CTL is given in [Emerson and Halpern, 1985]. In this chapter we have a slightly simpler language with $\diamond$ being an abbreviation so we can give a slightly simpler axiomatization than the original in [Emerson and Halpern, 1985]. The axioms are all substitution instances of the following:

(1) all (substitution instances of) classical tautologies,
(2) $\mathbf{E}\bigcirc(A \vee B) \leftrightarrow \mathbf{E}\bigcirc A \vee \mathbf{E}\bigcirc B$
(3) $\mathbf{A}\bigcirc A \leftrightarrow \neg\mathbf{E}\bigcirc\neg A$
(4) $\mathbf{E}(A\mathcal{U}B) \leftrightarrow B \vee (A \wedge \mathbf{E}\bigcirc\mathbf{E}(A\mathcal{U}B))$
(5) $\mathbf{A}(A\mathcal{U}B) \leftrightarrow B \vee (A \wedge \mathbf{A}\bigcirc\mathbf{A}(A\mathcal{U}B))$
(6) $\mathbf{E}\bigcirc\mathbf{true} \wedge \mathbf{A}\bigcirc\mathbf{true}$

The inference rules are:

$$\frac{A \rightarrow B}{\mathbf{E}\bigcirc A \rightarrow \mathbf{E}\bigcirc B} \qquad \frac{C \rightarrow (\neg B \wedge \mathbf{E}\bigcirc C)}{C \rightarrow \neg\mathbf{A}(A\mathcal{U}B)}$$

$$\frac{C \rightarrow (\neg B \wedge \mathbf{A}\bigcirc(C \vee \neg\mathbf{E}(A\mathcal{U}B)))}{C \rightarrow \neg\mathbf{E}(A\mathcal{U}B)} \qquad \frac{A, A \rightarrow B}{B}$$

To prove the completeness of this system as in [Emerson and Halpern, 1985] we can use the axioms to follow some reasoning about the progress of a tableau-style decision procedure also presented in that paper. It is straightforward to show that the axioms are sound. To show completeness we need to show that any consistent formula, say ϕ, has a model. The decision procedure (described briefly below) works with states which are subsets of a certain finite closure set defined from ϕ: mainly the subformulas of ϕ and their negations but also a few other formulas. Each state is supposed to represent the set of all formulas in the closure set which are true at a particular point in a potential model. The decision procedure gradually eliminates states which it establishes can not represent points in such a way. The procedure may halt finding no state containing ϕ, when ϕ is not satisfiable, or it may halt with a set of states from which a model of ϕ can be constructed. The completeness proof shows that we can find a consistent state (i.e. the axiom system can not derive falsity from the conjunction of formulas in the state) containing ϕ and that this state is never eliminated during the progress of the decision procedure. Then we have the desired result.

An axiomatization of CTL* is given in [Reynolds, 2001] with the use of a interesting but rather complex inference rule inspired by the use of automata. A simpler, more traditional axiomatization is given in [Reynolds, 2003] for CTL* with an extended language including past-time temporal operators.

9.3.3 Gentzen Systems

Gentzen systems [Gentzen, 1934] provide an alternative way of describing systematic intuitive derivations of the validities of a logic. It can be argued that Gentzen systems provide a more modular approach to derivation which is closer to natural reasoning. However, from an overall theorem-proving point of view, many of the logical and computational aspects of Gentzen systems are similar to those for Hilbert systems and so we refer readers elsewhere for the details. A good starting point might be [Paech, 1988] which contains a sound and complete Gentzen system for a logic equivalent to PLTL. Note that the system presented in [Paech, 1988], like most Gentzen systems for temporal logic, contains a species of what is known as the cut rule, and being thus not cut-free, is not in the most desirable style for theorem-proving.

9.3.4 Finite Model Properties

The main draw back of axiom systems as theorem-proving techniques is that they only form semi-decision procedures. We can certainly use a system to enumerate the theorems of the logic but they are not also nontheorem-refuting techniques. They do not give us a way of determining whether a formula is not a validity.

Fortunately, for many logics it is possible to complement an axiom system with a simple nontheorem-refuting technique based on an exhaustive search through possible models. Suppose that every satisfiable formula in the logic has a finite model (i.e. one containing a finite number of worlds). Then we say that the logic has the *finite model property*. In that case, if ϕ is not a validity of the logic then we are guaranteed to eventually find a model for $\neg\phi$ if we start an exhaustive search through all finite structures. It is possible to enumerate all the finite structures in the language of the formula that we are interested in.

Suppose we have an axiomatization for a logic with the finite model property. Now, in parallel, we run an exhaustive search through all proofs for a proof of ϕ and an exhaustive search through all finite structures for a model of $\neg\phi$. This is a decision procedure for the validity of ϕ. One of the two processes is guaranteed to terminate.

Unfortunately, many useful temporal logics do not have the finite property or, at least, seem to lack the finite model property at first sight. Models for PLTL formulae, by definition, have infinitely many states. However, we saw in the completeness proof for the Hilbert system above that there are more general semantics for the formulae of PLTL and in fact, the proof shows that any satisfiable formula does have a finite non-standard model: the model built from consistent sets of formulas, and factored out by the closure set $\mathrm{cl}(\phi)$.

It is no use just finding any non-standard model for a PLTL formula because formulae which are unsatisfiable in PLTL also have non-standard models. Extra conditions need to be applied to the interpretation of the propositions or to the accessibility relations to ensure that the satisfiability of the formula in the non-standard model implies satisfiability in some ω-structure.

In fact, with PLTL formulae we can prove a *bounded* model property: if the formula is satisfiable (in an ω-structure) then it is satisfiable in a non-standard model of size the order of an exponential in its length. See [Sistla and Clarke, 1985] for details. This immediately allows us to bypass the use of an axiom system altogether and still get a decision procedure for validity. Given ϕ, search through all appropriate non-standard models up to size $O(|\phi|)$ for a model of $\neg\phi$. There is such a model iff ϕ is not a validity of PLTL.

Finite model properties for many modal and temporal logics are given in [Popkorn, 1994]. An extended technique (using so-called *mosaics*) has recently been used to give a decision procedure for a combined temporal-modal logic in [Reynolds, 1998].

9.4 Tableau

9.4.1 Introduction

One of the most popular methods for temporal logic theorem-proving is using tableaux. These constructions have several nice properties: we can give them a rule based definition and so present them in an intuitive way showing their relation to inference systems; we can find elements of semantic structures within them and so easily find models for satisfiable formulae; and we can often put tight limits on their size and so have a good idea of the complexity of reasoning using them.

Tableaux have many connections with Gentzen proof systems [Gentzen, 1934]. It is true that tableau rules for particular logics often look very like upside down rules of proof from cut-free Gentzen sequent systems for the same logic. The connection is described in [Zeman, 1973], [Rautenberg, 1979] and [Fitting, 1983]. We have seen that Gentzen systems for Temporal Logics usually have to rely on a cut rule. However, there are important reasons to avoid cut style rules and to ensure termination of proofs in tableau systems and so most of what we cover here has little to do with Gentzen systems.

Tableaux, in the form of *semantic tableaux*, were invented, for classical propositional logic, in [Beth, 1955] and [Hintikka, 1955]. See [Smullyan, 1968] and [Hodges, 1984] for more recent descriptions of tableau approaches to classical logic.

Proposals for tableau approaches to modal logics were made in [Hughes and Cresswell, 1968]. Other early work here includes [Zeman, 1973]. Since then there has been a great amount of work in this area. See, for example, [Rautenberg, 1983] and [Fitting, 1983]. [Goré, 1997] contains a useful and detailed survey.

The first detailed descriptions of tableau methods for PLTL appeared in [Wolper, 1983]. Other early approaches include those in [Manna and Wolper, 1984], [Lichtenstein and Pnueli, 1985], and [Lichtenstein *et al.*, 1985]. An early overview appears in [Wolper, 1985], a more recent one in [Emerson, 1996].

9.4.2 Basics

We first briefly review tableaux for propositional logic. See, for example, [Hodges, 1984] for more details. These tableaux can be viewed as finite trees with nodes labelled by sets of formulae. To test a formula ϕ for satisfiability we try to construct a tableau with $\{\phi\}$ labelling the root. Movement along branches represents steps in adding consequences to the label sets. Branching itself represents choice between alternatives. There is a notion of closure of a branch indicating that the particular choices made along that branch are inconsistent. If all the branches are closed then we say that the tableau is closed and we can conclude that the original formula is unsatisfiable. If a branch can not be closed then we can use it to build a model of the formula: so it is satisfiable.

The rules for determining the labels of successor nodes involve only very simple consequences. If we suppose that the formulae of the language are built from atoms using just $\neg$

and $\wedge$, then there are just three rules:

- a node with label Σ containing $\neg\neg\alpha$ is allowed to have a unique successor labelled by $\Sigma \cup \{\alpha\}$;
- a node with label Σ containing $\alpha \wedge \beta$ is allowed to have a unique successor labelled by $\Sigma \cup \{\alpha, \beta\}$;
- a node with label Σ containing $\neg(\alpha \wedge \beta)$ is allowed to have exactly two successors, one labelled $\Sigma \cup \{\neg\alpha\}$ and one labelled $\Sigma \cup \{\neg\beta\}$.

These rules are nondeterministic, i.e. the same label may appear at different places with different successor labels. For example, a node labelled with $\{\neg\neg p, \neg(q \wedge r)\}$ can have either one or two successor nodes.

We say that a branch is closed iff there is some formula α with both α and $\neg\alpha$ appearing in the leaf node of that branch. If all the branches are closed then we say that the tableau is closed. If the original formula has a closed tableau then we can show that the formula is not satisfiable.

We can write the successor rules, and the rules for closing a branch in the following succinct form:

$$\frac{\Sigma; \alpha; \neg\alpha}{\textbf{false}} \qquad \frac{\Sigma; \neg\neg\alpha}{\Sigma; \alpha} \qquad \frac{\Sigma; \alpha \wedge \beta}{\Sigma; \alpha; \beta} \qquad \frac{\Sigma; \neg(\alpha \wedge \beta)}{\Sigma; \neg\alpha | \Sigma; \neg\beta}$$

The notation is fairly self-explanatory. Strings such as $\Sigma; \alpha \wedge \beta$ represent the set union of the set Σ and the singleton $\{\alpha \wedge \beta\}$. This means that even if a rule "uses" a formula, the formula can still appear in the successor label. For example,

$$\frac{\{\gamma, \alpha \wedge \beta\} \cup \{\alpha \wedge \beta\}}{\{\gamma, \alpha \wedge \beta, \alpha, \beta\}}$$

is an instance of the third rule.

The formulae appearing in labels will all be subformulae of ϕ, or their negations. This is called the *subformula property*. It can guarantee termination. In particular, if we terminate on repeated labels along branches (and in that case say that the branch is open) then the overall process is guaranteed to terminate. Further, suppose that we keep a record of what formulae we "use" —i.e. break up into subformulae— at each step. If we do use it then we say that a formula is marked. If we make sure we mark all possible formulae in a branch then we can also show that whether the process terminates in closure or not is independent of the choice of rules used along the way. Thus we have a sound and complete decision procedure.

Note that in many presentations of these tableaux, nodes are labelled by single formulae rather than sets of formulae. The approach turns out to be equivalent, though, as the rules for extending a tableau from a node act to use any formula which has appeared along the branch leading up to the node. We do not use this approach as it gets a little confused in modal-temporal applications.

In tableaux for modal logics there are several differences. Again we use them to test satisfiability of a formula. Again branching indicates alternatives. Again, one step along a branch corresponds to adding a simple consequence. The labels of nodes can be thought of as representing a set of formulae which we know hold simultaneously in one "possible" world. Thus we can find propositional consequences, add them to the label at the successor node, and still know that the formulae in the new label all hold in this hypothetical world.

The important difference with modal tableaux is that movement along the branch now can also represent movement along the accessibility relation to another possible world. Tableau rules which allow this are sometimes called *transition rules* as opposed to *static rules* which, like the rules for propositional logic, only add consequences about the current world. A typical transition rule allows unwrapping of a formula of the form $\Diamond\alpha$ (where $\Diamond$ is a modal diamond) in a label Σ so that α itself appears in the successor label. Of course, any formula of the form $\Box\beta \in \Sigma$ must also contribute β to the new label. It can be seen that we have to be very careful to exhaust all possible contradictions in the "old" world before throwing the formulae there away and moving on to the next world. There are many variations on these ideas for many different modal logics. See [Hughes and Cresswell, 1968] and [Goré, 1997] for details.

In tableaux for temporal logics, we have a similar situation. Again we label the nodes with sets of subformulae of the original formula ϕ. Again, branching represents choice. Again, one step along a branch represents deriving a particularly simple consequence. As in the modal case, these consequences may be local, i.e. adding a formula to what we know is true at some "current" world, or the consequence might involve moving to an accessible world.

In tableaux for temporal logic there are some extra problems. The most important is that we often have to deal with two interrelated modalities: tomorrow $\bigcirc$ and until **until**. The tableau can proceed in a one step at a time process using $\bigcirc$ in much the same way as a modal $\Diamond$. However, we must ensure that eventualities such as $\Diamond p$ do eventually get "fulfilled". We see how to do this in the next subsection.

9.4.3 A tableau system for PLTL

Let us look, in some detail, at a typical tableau system for PLTL and mention some common variations as we present it. The ideas presented here are gathered from [Wolper, 1983] and [Vardi, 1996].

We assume that the basic connectives in the language are $\neg$, $\wedge$, $\bigcirc$ and **until**. The other symbols are abbreviations. Suppose that we want to test the formula ϕ for satisfiability.

With a bit of care we can show that we need only consider the formulae which are subformulae of ϕ and their negations. Thus we require that the labels are subsets of the closure set

$$\mathbf{clos}\phi = \{\psi, \neg\psi | \psi \text{ is a subformula of } \phi\}.$$

Notice that the closure set is not closed under taking negations of formulae. In several parts of the procedure we do, however, need it to be. This turns out not to be a problem though. Suppose that $\psi \in \mathbf{clos}\phi$ but $\neg\psi$ is not in $\mathbf{clos}\phi$. It follows that ψ is of the form $\neg\chi$. It can be checked that χ, which is in $\mathbf{clos}\phi$ can be used for $\neg\psi$. By restricting attention to this closure set we have the subformula property and this helps ensure termination.

The basic rules we might want to use are the four propositional rules along with: two new static rules:

$$\frac{\Sigma; \alpha \ \mathbf{until}\ \beta}{\Sigma; \alpha | \Sigma; \beta} \text{ and } \frac{\Sigma; \neg(\alpha \ \mathbf{until}\ \beta)}{\Sigma; \neg\beta}$$

and two transition rules:

$$\frac{\Sigma; \neg\beta, \alpha \ \mathbf{until}\ \beta}{\bigcirc\Sigma; \alpha \ \mathbf{until}\ \beta}, \text{ and } \frac{\Sigma; \bigcirc\alpha}{\bigcirc\Sigma; \alpha},$$

where $\bigcirc\Sigma$ should contain all the formulae (in our closure set) which should hold at any successor state to one where Σ holds. A moments consideration suggests

$$\begin{aligned}\bigcirc\Sigma = & \quad \{\beta|\bigcirc\beta \in \Sigma\}\\ \cup & \quad \{\neg\beta|\neg\bigcirc\beta \in \Sigma\}\\ \cup & \quad \{\gamma\ \mathbf{until}\ \beta|\neg\beta, \gamma\ \mathbf{until}\ \beta \in \Sigma\}\\ \cup & \quad \{\neg(\gamma\ \mathbf{until}\ \beta)|\gamma, \neg(\gamma\ \mathbf{until}\ \beta) \in \Sigma\}\\ \cup & \quad \{\mathbf{true}|\mathbf{true} \in \Sigma\}.\end{aligned}$$

There are several serious problems with such a proposal. One, as we have mentioned, is to do with eventualities. We will come back to that later. Another problem is that we may throw away crucial information without using it. Consider the following example of one label and a valid successor label according to the second transition rule:

$$\frac{\{p \wedge \neg p, \bigcirc q\}}{\{q\}}.$$

We have to be careful about using the transition rules in a decision procedure because, as we see from the example, formulae can be lost from the label and so be unable to contribute to finding contradictions. This means that we need to be sure that there are no such contradictions before using a transition rule. Thus we need to keep track of which boolean formulae (i.e. formulae of the form $\neg\neg\alpha$, $\neg(\alpha \wedge \beta)$ or $\alpha \wedge \beta$) have been decomposed (i.e. used) by a rule higher up the branch without a subsequent use of a transition rule.

We can mark the boolean formulae which have been decomposed since the last use of a transition rule and only allow the use of a transition rule when all boolean formulae are marked. We also have to use the new static rules on formulae of the form α **until** β or $\neg(\alpha$ **until** $\beta)$ before allowing a transition.

An alternative approach to using marking, and one we will use is to do away with static rules altogether or, rather, to hide their activity. Instead we notice that actually we only want to apply transition rules to label sets which are maximally propositionally consistent in $\mathbf{clos}\phi$. We want to consider the label sets as each being the set of all formulae (from $\mathbf{clos}\phi$) true at a point in a potential model of ϕ. Our transition rules, the only rules we have now, will take us to the possible successors of such a complete label set. In any model the set of formulae true at any point will be consistent and, for each formula α, either α will be in the set or $\neg\alpha$ will be. To enforce maximal propositional consistency of the labels, we just need require that, for any label set $\Sigma \subseteq \mathbf{clos}\phi$:

- for all $\alpha \in \mathbf{clos}\phi$, $\alpha \in \Sigma$ iff $\neg\alpha \notin \Sigma$; and
- if $\alpha \wedge \beta \in \Sigma$ then $\alpha \in \Sigma$ and $\beta \in \Sigma$.

Let $PC(\phi)$ be the set of such label sets.

There are some other conditions to do with the temporal operators, which we can call *coherence* conditions, on the label sets which we can apply easily and which help us avoid consideration of impossible sets. For example, we could require that for each label set $\Sigma \subseteq \mathbf{clos}\phi$, if α **until** $\beta \in \Sigma$ then either $\alpha \in \Sigma$ or $\beta \in \Sigma$. Other possibilities include ruling out the almost immediate contradiction of $\bigcirc p$ and $\bigcirc\neg p$ being in the label and ruling out the only eventual contradiction of both α **until** β and $\neg$(**true until** β) being in it. But, as we will see, the tableau will take care of these in a more systematic way. So we do not insist on these conditions.

The relation between a node in the tableau and any successor node corresponds exactly to the relation between states and successor states. In particular, we define a relation R between labels from $PC(\phi)$ by $\Sigma_1 R \Sigma_2$ iff:

- if $\bigcirc\alpha \in \mathbf{clos}\phi$ then $\bigcirc\alpha \in \Sigma_1$ iff $\alpha \in \Sigma_2$; and
- if α **until** $\beta \in \mathbf{clos}\phi$ then α **until** $\beta \in \Sigma_1$ iff ($\beta \in \Sigma_1$ or (both $\alpha \in \Sigma_1$ and α **until** $\beta \in \Sigma_2$)).

Then, all the possible successors of a label $\Sigma_1 \in PC(\phi)$ are just the Σ_2 such that $\Sigma_1 R \Sigma_2$. This gives us a rule with a very long denominator producing a lot of branching. Remember, though, that it is effectively summing up a whole sub-tree of static rule applications.

With this approach, we have a slight problem of deciding where to start the tableau. Clearly it will do to connect some token start node to all the $\Sigma \in PC(\phi)$ such that $\phi \in \Sigma$. If there is no such label set then we can immediately say that ϕ is unsatisfiable.

With the transitivity inherent in some of the temporal connectives we have another problem with our simplistic tableau proposal, namely, non-terminating, looping branches. It is clear from examples such as $\Sigma = \{\Box\bigcirc p, \bigcirc p, p\}$ that these can be generated. It is also clear that these might reflect legitimate repetitive ω-sequence models for PLTL formulae. The simple solution here is to declare these branches open and stop extending them.

Now we almost have a tableau decision procedure. There is one more problem to overcome: this is a problem with eventualities. Instead of tackling that directly here with the current approach we will make a sensible but quite radical simplification.

It might be noticed that we will have very large trees: exponentially wide in fact. That is, if the length of ϕ is n, then nodes in the tree might have of the order of 2^n successors. To see this consider that there are of the order of n subformulae of ϕ and a set in $PC(\phi)$ will contain either the subformula or its negation. With branches being exponentially long, as well, this means a lot of repetition in the tree.

In order to avoid this it is sensible to represent the labels and their successor relation in a graph. The graph is simply $(PC(\phi), R)$: the nodes are the labels and there is a directed edge along each instance of the R relation. Branches of what was our tableau tree have now become paths in the graph, i.e. sequences (finite or countably long) $\langle \Sigma_0, \Sigma_1, ...\rangle$ with each $\Sigma_i R \Sigma_{i+1}$. A branch starting at the root now becomes such a sequence with $\phi \in \Sigma_0$.

In what follows we will call $(PC(\phi), R)$ the *initial* tableau structure because we are going to do some further work on it.

In fact, if there is a Σ_0 containing ϕ then the structure we now have looks superficially like the non-standard model which forms the basis of the axiomatic completeness proof in [Gabbay *et al.*, 1980]. In that proof we could find an ω-model of ϕ within the non-standard structure. So can we stop the procedure now and say we know that there is a model of ϕ lying in the structure somewhere?

The answer is no. The initial tableau structure we have defined generally includes so many extra labels that it will take us quite a bit of extra work to decide whether there is an ω-model hidden within it. In fact, it is just as hard to decide whether it has a non-standard model hidden within it. The extra sets are those which are propositionally consistent but not consistent with the [Gabbay *et al.*, 1980] axioms.

So we still have to decide whether there is an ω-model of ϕ within the initial tableau. To be clear about what this means let us first define the *state* corresponding to a label $\Sigma \in PC(\phi)$ to be $s = L \cap \Sigma$ where L is the set of propositional atoms appearing in ϕ. We want to try to find a ω-long path $\langle \Sigma_0, \Sigma_1, ...\rangle$ in $(PC(\phi), R)$ such that $\phi \in \Sigma_0$ and if $s_i = L \cap \Sigma_i$ then for all $i < \omega$, for all $\alpha \in \Sigma_i$, $\langle s_i, s_{i+1}, ...\rangle \models \alpha$. The latter condition can be called a truth lemma condition. We will then have $\langle s_0, s_1, ...\rangle \models \phi$. It is straight forward to show that the existence of such a model for ϕ is equivalent to the satisfiability of ϕ.

It is easiest not to look directly for such a model but to start from the initial tableau structure and proceed to repeatedly throw away nodes which can not be part of such an ω-model. Eventually we may end up throwing away so much that we know that there could not have been an ω-model within the initial tableau. Alternatively, we will end up with a new tableau from which nothing more can be discarded and we will show that then we know that there is a model within it.

First it is clear that we can throw away any node which has no successor. Note that if our closure set does not contain temporal connectives and so we have label sets such as $\{p, q\}$, then these sets do actually have successors. This discarding process should be repeated. Thus we will eventually lose any explicitly eventually contradictory labels such as $\{\bigcirc p, \bigcirc\neg p\}$.

Also, if we ever throw away all the nodes containing ϕ then we can stop and know that ϕ is unsatisfiable. Call this a halt and fail condition.

If we just applied these two procedures repeatedly until we can do so no longer but we had not halted and failed then we know that the resulting tableau contains an ω-sequence of nodes (connected by edges) and starting with a node containing ϕ. However, this may not form a model for ϕ. The reason we can not necessarily prove a truth lemma is that "eventualities may be unfulfilled". This means that there may be a label Σ_j say, in the sequence, containing α **until** β, but there may be no state Σ_i with $j \leq i$ and $\beta \in \Sigma_i$. It is easy to show that this is the only problem that such a potential model will have.

The simplest approach to ensuring that eventualities are fulfilled is to add another way of discarding labels from the graph. We discard any label whose eventualities can not be fulfilled in the current structure. We must look along all paths emanating from the chosen state to check that the eventualities of the chosen label are all fulfilled eventually along some particular path. It is not sufficient to fulfill one eventuality along one path and another on another. We need only search a finite distance down any path as there is no point continuing past repeated states. This checking procedure should be combined with the other checks so that they are all repeated until none of them can operate. Then, if the process has not halted and failed then it halts and succeeds.

It is straight forward to prove that this procedure terminates: every task is finite and we are reducing the size of the tableau each time we make a change to it. We can show that the procedure takes exponential time in the length of the formula. The reducing procedure takes polynomial time in the size of the initial tableau and that is exponential in size.

To show that the procedure is correct we need to show that it succeeds if and only if the formula ϕ is satisfiable. First consider ϕ being satisfiable: say that $\sigma \models \phi$. Let $\Sigma_i = \{\psi \in \mathbf{clos}\phi | (\sigma, i) \models \psi\}$. It is easy to show that that no label Σ_i is ever discarded in the procedure. Hence we have success.

For the converse suppose that the procedure succeeds for ϕ and that ϕ only uses atoms from the finite set L. Let $G \subseteq PC(\phi)$ be the set of nodes left in the tableau at termination. Choose any node Σ_0 from G which contains ϕ. We define sequences $0 = i_0 < i_1 < ... < \omega$ and $\langle \Sigma_0, \Sigma_1, ...\rangle$ from G recursively. Suppose that we have chosen Σ_{i_j}. If Σ_{i_j} contains a formula of the form α **until** β but also contains $\neg\beta$ then we say that it contains an unfulfilled eventuality. If it doesn't contain an unfulfilled eventuality then just put $i_{j+1} = i_j + 1$ and choose any R-successor of Σ_{i_j} in G as $\Sigma_{i_{j+1}}$. Otherwise, find a path $\Sigma_{i_j}, \Sigma_{i_j+1}, ..., \Sigma_{i_{j+1}}$

in (G, R) along which all the eventualities of Σ_{i_j} are fulfilled. This gives us i_{j+1} and $\Sigma_{i_{j+1}}$.

It is not hard to show that all eventualities in labels along the sequence $\langle \Sigma_0, \Sigma_1, ...\rangle$ do get fulfilled. This includes those that appear in some Σ_k with $i_j < k < i_{j+1}$. It is then straight forward to define $s_i = \Sigma_i \cap L$ and show that $\langle s_0, s_1, ...\rangle \models \phi$.

As described above, many of the PLTL tableau in the literature such as [Gough, 1984; Wolper, 1985] have two distinct phases:-

- the construction of the graph to satisfy propositional constraints and next-time constraints;
- a deletion procedure to check for finite paths and unfulfilled eventualities.

The deletion phase may only be carried out once the construction phase has been completed, which may be expensive.

Tableau algorithms for PLTL have been suggested that avoid these separate two phases for example [Schwendimann, 1998a]. Here, the tableau algorithm constructs cyclic tree-like structures (trees with edges allowed back to states on the same branch) rather than graphs. As well as containing finite sets of formulae, states hold information about currently satisfied eventualities, unfulfilled eventualities, and the branch history. The check for loops is carried out locally and is incorporated into the rules of the calculus. The advantage being that the whole structure does not need to be constructed before deletions can take place. For example if we want to show a formula Φ is valid, we negate and attempt to construct a tableau for $\neg\Phi$. If an open branch is detected early in the construction it saves the construction of the remaining branches and we can declare $\neg\Phi$ is satisfiable and therefore Φ is not valid. Further, only one branch needs to be kept in memory at once. This algorithm has been implemented as part of the Logics Workbench version 1.1 [Jäger *et al.*, 2002].

9.4.4 Other Temporal Logics

The above technique can be generalized for past operators over natural numbers or integers. For example a tableau for PLTL extended to allow past time operators over natural numbers is given in [Kesten *et al.*, 1997] and extended to allow past time operators over integers is given in [Gough, 1984].

Branching-Time Temporal Logics

A very similar tableau method has been shown in [Emerson and Halpern, 1985] and [Emerson and Clarke, 1982] to decide validity in the branching logic CTL. There are variants on this, an efficient version using AND and OR nodes is described in [Emerson, 1996]. We sketch an inefficient alternative approach which is simpler to present.

Suppose that we are to decide ϕ. Let $\mathbf{clos}(\phi)$ contain all the subformulas of ϕ and their negations. The idea is, as in a variant of PLTL tableaux described above, based on pruning away a graph of maximally propositionally consistent (MPC) subsets of the closure set.

Start with all MPC subsets and define the following binary relation between them. Put $\Sigma_1 R \Sigma_2$ iff:

- if $\mathbf{A}\bigcirc\alpha \in \mathbf{clos}\phi$ then $\mathbf{A}\bigcirc\alpha \in \Sigma_1$ implies $\alpha \in \Sigma_2$;
- if $\neg\mathbf{E}(\bigcirc\alpha) \in \mathbf{clos}\phi$ then $\neg\mathbf{E}(\bigcirc\alpha) \in \Sigma_1$ implies $\neg\alpha \in \Sigma_2$;

- if $\mathbf{A}(\alpha \ \mathbf{until} \ \beta) \in \mathbf{clos}\phi$ then $\mathbf{A}(\alpha \ \mathbf{until} \ \beta) \in \Sigma_1$ implies ($\beta \in \Sigma_1$ or (both $\alpha \in \Sigma_1$ and $\mathbf{A}(\alpha \ \mathbf{until} \ \beta) \in \Sigma_2$));
- if $\neg\mathbf{E}(\alpha \ \mathbf{until} \ \beta) \in \mathbf{clos}\phi$ then $\neg\mathbf{E}(\alpha \ \mathbf{until} \ \beta) \in \Sigma_1$ implies ($\neg\beta \in \Sigma_1$ and (either $\neg\alpha \in \Sigma_1$ or $\neg\mathbf{E}(\alpha \ \mathbf{until} \ \beta) \in \Sigma_2$)).

The pruning process is as follows and again, if ϕ does not appear in any labels then halt and fail. There is a local pruning process as well as pruning based on eventualities which is described below. Locally prune Σ, i.e. remove it from the graph, if there is any of the following criteria which it does not meet.

- if $\mathbf{E}\bigcirc\alpha \in \Sigma$ then there is Σ' still in the graph with $\Sigma R \Sigma'$ such that $\alpha \in \Sigma'$;
- if $\neg\mathbf{A}\bigcirc\alpha \in \Sigma$ then there is Σ' still in the graph with $\Sigma R \Sigma'$ such that $\neg\alpha \in \Sigma'$;
- if $\mathbf{E}(\alpha \mathcal{U} \beta) \in \Sigma$ then $\beta \in \Sigma$ or (both $\alpha \in \Sigma$ and there is Σ' still in the graph with $\Sigma R \Sigma'$ such that $\mathbf{E}(\alpha \mathcal{U} \beta) \in \Sigma'$); and
- if $\neg\mathbf{A}(\alpha \mathcal{U} \beta) \in \Sigma$ then $\neg\beta \in \Sigma$ and (either $\neg\alpha \in \Sigma$ or there is Σ' still in the graph with $\Sigma R \Sigma'$ such that $\neg\mathbf{A}(\alpha \mathcal{U} \beta) \in \Sigma'$).

The other pruning activity carried out is to remove any labels which contain eventualities which are not fulfillable in the current graph. An eventuality is a formula of the form $\mathbf{E}(\alpha \mathcal{U} \beta)$ or $\mathbf{A}(\alpha \mathcal{U} \beta)$. Suppose such an eventuality appears in Σ. To check fulfillability of the former eventuality we just look for a path of labels (connected via R) from Σ to Σ' containing β. To check the latter we look for a subtree (itself having every node satisfying the local pruning criteria) rooted at Σ with β in every one of the leaf labels.

When all pruning checks are made and no more nodes removed then the tableau process halts with success.

The completeness proof for this algorithm is mostly straightforward but taking care of eventualities of the second form above is interesting. Basically, copies of fulfilling subtrees need to be made and glued together to build a model of a formula from a successfully constructed tableau.

There is no known tableau method of deciding validity in CTL*.

First-Order Temporal Logics

A tableau for first order temporal logics is described in [McGuire, 1995] which uses time-reification i.e. a translation into first-order classical logic. Tableaux for decidable fragments of monodic first-order temporal logics are described in [Kontchakov *et al.*, 2003]. This paper provides a general framework for devising tableaux for these logics. The temporal and the first-order parts of the logic are separated and dealt with by using tableau algorithms for PLTL, for example [Wolper, 1985], and available (classical) first-order tableaux respectively.

9.5 Automata

Automata are finite state machines which are very promising objects to help with deciding the validity of temporal formulae. In some senses they are like formulae: they are finite objects and they distinguish some temporal structures–the ones which they accept– from other temporal structures in much the same way that formulae are true (at some point) in some structures are not in others. In other senses automata are like structures: they contain states and relate each state with some successor states. Being thus mid-way between formulae and structures allows automata to be used to answer questions–such as validity– about the relation between formulae and structures.

An automata is called *empty* iff it accepts no structures and it turns out to be relatively easy to decide whether a given automaton is empty or not. This is surprising because empty automata can look quite complicated in much the same way as unsatisfiable formulae can. This fact immediately suggests a possible decision procedure for temporal formulae. Given a formula we might be able to find an automaton which accepts exactly the structures which are models of the formula. If we now test the automaton for emptiness then we are effectively testing the formula for unsatisfiability. Validity of a formula corresponds to emptiness of an automaton equivalent to the negation of the formula.

This is the essence of the incredibly productive automata approach to theorem proving. We first look in detail at the case of PLTL on natural numbers time.

9.5.1 Automata for Infinite Linear Structures

The idea of (finite state) automata developed from pioneering attempts by Turing to formalize computation and by Kleene ([Kleene, 1956]) to model human psychology. The early work (see, for example, [Rabin and Scott, 1959]) was on finite state machines which recognized finite words. Such automata have provided a formal basis for many applications from text processing and biology to the analysis of concurrency. There has also been much mathematical development of the field. See [Perrin, 1990] for a survey.

The pioneer in the development of automata for use with infinite linear structures is Büchi in [Büchi, 1962]. He was interested in proving the decidability of a very restricted second-order arithmetic, $S1S$, which we will return to below. By the time that temporal logic was being introduced to computer scientists in [Pnueli, 1977], it was well known (see [Kamp, 1968]) that temporal logic formulae can be expressed in the appropriate second-order logic and so via $S1S$ we had the first decision procedure for PLTL.

As well as describing this round-about and inefficient procedure below we will also survey the important advances made since about 1984 when effort has been put into making much better use of automata. There are now several useful ways of using the automata stepping stone for deciding the validity of PLTL formulae.

The general idea is to translate the temporal formula into an automaton which accepts exactly the models of the formula and then to check for emptiness of the automaton. Variations arise when we consider that there are several different types of automata which we could use and that the translation from the formula can be done in a variety of ways.

Let us look at the automata first.

Büchi

For historical reasons we will switch now to a language Σ of letters rather than keep using a language of propositional atoms. The nodes of trees will be labelled by a single letter from Σ. In order to apply the results in this section we will later have to take the alphabet Σ to be 2^P where P is the set of atomic propositions.

A Σ *(linear) Büchi automaton* is a 4-tuple $A = (S, T, S_0, F)$ where

- S is a finite non-empty set called the set of *states*,
- $T \subseteq S \times \Sigma \times S$ is the *transition table*,
- $S_0 \subseteq S$ is the *initial state set* and
- $F \subseteq S$ is the *set of accepting states*.

A *run* of A on an ω-structure σ is a sequence of states $\langle s_0, s_1, s_2, ...\rangle$ from S such that $s_0 \in S_0$ and for each $i < \omega$, $(s_i, \sigma_i, s_{i+1}) \in T$. We assume that automata never grind to a halt: i.e. we assume that for all $s \in S$, for all $a \in \Sigma$, there is some $s' \in S$ such that $(s, a, s') \in T$.

We say that the automaton accepts σ iff there is a run $\langle s_0, s_1, ...\rangle$ such that $s_i \in F$ for infinitely many i.

One of the most useful results about Büchi automata, is that we can complement them. That is given a Büchi automaton A reading from the language Σ we can always find another Σ Büchi automata $\overline{A}$ which accepts exactly the ω-sequences which A rejects. This was first shown by Büchi in [Büchi, 1962] and was an important step on the way to his proof of the decidability of $S1S$–as we will see in Section 9.5.2 below. The automaton $\overline{A}$ produced by Büchi's method is double exponential in the size of A but more recent work in [Sistla *et al.*, 1987] shows that complementation of Büchi automata can always be singly exponential.

As we will see below, it is easy to complement an automaton if we can find a deterministic equivalent. This means an automaton with a unique initial state and a transition table $T \subseteq S \times \Sigma \times S$ which satisfies the property that for all $s \in S$, for all $a \in \Sigma$, there is a unique $s' \in S$ such that $(s, a, s') \in T$. A deterministic automaton will have a unique run on any given structure.

Two automata are equivalent iff they accept exactly the same structures.

The problem with Büchi automata is that it is not always possible to find a deterministic equivalent. A very short argument (see Example 4.2 in [Thomas, 1990]) shows that the non-deterministic $\{a, b\}$ automaton which recognizes exactly the set

$$L = \{\sigma | a \text{ appears only a finite number of times in } \sigma\}$$

can have no deterministic equivalent.

One of our important tasks is to decide whether a given automaton is empty i.e. accepts no ω-structures. For Büchi automata this can be done in linear time ([Emerson and Lei, 1985]) and co-NLOGSPACE ([Vardi and Wolper, 1994]). We simply need to find a finite sequence of states $\langle s_0, s_1, ..., s_n, s_{n+1}, ..., s_m\rangle$ such that $s_0 \in S_0$, for each $i \leq m$ there is some $a_i \in \Sigma$ with $(s_i, a_i, s_{i+1}) \in T$ (we put $s_{m+1} = s_n$), and some $j \geq n$ with $s_j \in F$. Such a sequence clearly determines an ultimately periodic ω-structure which is accepted by the automaton and exists iff the automaton accepts any structure. A linear time algorithm finding strongly connected components in graphs [Cormen *et al.*, 1990] can be used to check whether such a finite sequence exists. Equally, a non-deterministic algorithm need just guess each state in turn and only keep the s_n and the current s_i and s_{i+1} in memory, to show the same.

Muller or Rabin

The lack of a determinisation result for Büchi automata led to a search for a class of automata which is as expressive as the class of Büchi automata but which is closed under finding deterministic equivalents. Muller automata were introduced by Muller in [Muller, 1963] and in [Rabin, 1972] variants, now called Rabin automata, were introduced.

The difference is that the accepting condition can require that certain states do not come up infinitely often. There are several equivalent ways of formalizing this. The Rabin method is, for a Σ-automata with state set S, to use a set $\mathcal{F}$, called the set of *accepting pairs*, of pairs of sets of states from S, i.e. $\mathcal{F} \subseteq \wp(S) \times \wp(S)$.

We say that the Rabin automaton $A = (S, S_0, T, \mathcal{F})$ accepts σ iff there is some run $\langle s_0, s_1, s_2, ...\rangle$ (as defined for Büchi automata) and some pair $(U, V) \in \mathcal{F}$ such that no state in V is visited infinitely often but there is some state in U visited infinitely often.

An equivalent method, for the automata $A = (S, S_0, T, \phi)$ is to use a formula ϕ from the propositional language with atoms from S. We say that A accepts σ iff there is a run $\rho = \langle s_0, s_1, ...\rangle$ as defined before with $\rho \models \phi$. We define $\models$ inductively as usual for the propositional logic with the valuation on the atom s being $\rho \models s$ iff s appears infinitely often in ρ.

In fact, Rabin automata add no expressive power compared to Büchi automata, i.e. for every Rabin automaton there is an equivalent Büchi automaton. The translation [Choueka, 1974] is straightforward and, as it essentially just involves two copies of the Rabin automata in series with a once-only non-deterministic transition from the first to the second, it can be done in polynomial time. The converse equivalence is obvious.

Complemented pairs, or Street, automata have also been defined [Street, 1982]. These have acceptance criteria defined by a set of pairs of sets of states as for Rabin acceptance but the condition is complementary. We say that the Street automaton $A = (S, S_0, T, \mathcal{F})$ accepts σ iff there is some run $\langle s_0, s_1, s_2, ...\rangle$ such that for all pairs $(U, V) \in \mathcal{F}$ if some state in U is visited infinitely often then there is also some state in V visited infinitely often.

The most important property of the class of Rabin automata is that it is closed under determinisation. In [McNaughton, 1966], McNaughton, showed that any Büchi automaton has a deterministic Rabin equivalent. There are useful accounts of McNaughton's theorem in [Thomas, 1990] and [Hodkinson, 2000]. McNaughton's construction is doubly exponential. It follows from McNaughton's result that we can find a deterministic equivalent of any Rabin automaton: simply first find a Büchi equivalent and then use the theorem.

Safra [Safra, 1988] has more recently given a much more efficient procedure for finding a deterministic Rabin equivalent for any given Büchi automaton. If the Büchi automaton has n states then the construction gives a deterministic Rabin equivalent with $2^{O(n \log n)}$ states and $O(n)$ accepting pairs.

The determinisation result gives us an easy complementation result for Rabin automata. Given a Rabin automata we can without loss of generality assume it is deterministic. The complementary automata to the deterministic $(S, \{s_0\}, T, \phi)$ is just $(S, \{s_0\}, T, \neg\phi)$.

To decide whether Rabin automata are empty can be done with almost the same procedure we used for Büchi case. Alternatively, one can determinise the automaton A, and translate the deterministic equivalent into a deterministic Rabin automaton A' recognizing ω-sequences from the one symbol alphabet $\{a_0\}$ such that A' accepts some sequence iff A does. It is very easy to tell if A' is empty.

Alternating Automata

Alternation, as invented in the contexts of Turing Machines in [Chandra *et al.*, 1981b] and finite automata in [Brzozowski and Leiss, 1980] and [Chandra *et al.*, 1981b], provide a much more succinct way of expressing automata than even nondeterminism. The idea is to allow the requirement of several successor states (going on to produce accepting runs) after a given state as well as just the existence of one accepting continuation. Many of the useful results for alternating automata on ω-structures are presented in [Vardi, 1994].

For a set S, let $\mathcal{B}^+(S)$ be the set of positive Boolean formulae over S, that is the set of formulae built from atoms in S via $\wedge$ and $\vee$. We also allow *truth* and *false*. Given a subset $R \subseteq S$ we say that R satisfies $\phi \in \mathcal{B}^+(S)$ iff the propositional truth assignment V satisfies ϕ where V assigns true to atoms in R and false to the other atoms in S.

An *alternating* (Büchi) automaton is $A = (S, s_0, \rho, F)$ where S is the set of states, $s_0 \in S$ is the initial state, $\rho : S \times \Sigma \to \mathcal{B}^+(S)$ is the *transition function* and $F \subseteq S$ is the set of accepting states.

Runs of alternating automata on ω-structures are actually labelled trees. The trees we are interested in in the context of A are S-labelled trees which each may be thought of as some prefix-closed set of finite sequences of letters from S. For example, if aba is in the set then its parent is ab. Formally, a run of A on the ω-structure σ is a prefix-closed set T of finite S sequences such that if $\overline{s} = s_0 s_1 ... s_n \in T$ and the children of $\overline{s}$ are exactly $\{s^\frown a_1, ..., s^\frown a_j\}$ then $\{a_1, ..., a_j\}$ satisfies $\rho(s_n, \sigma_n)$.

A run is accepting iff on each infinite branch of T there is some state in F which appears infinitely often. Note that runs may have finite branches: $s = \langle s_0, s_1, ..., s_n \rangle$ may have no children if $\rho(s_n, \sigma_n) = truth$.

It is straightforward to rewrite any given Büchi automaton as an equivalent alternating automaton. It is quite a bit harder to show the converse: see [Miyano and Hayashi, 1984]. The size of the Büchi automaton B is exponential in the size of the alternating automaton A as we have to use (pairs of) sets of states from A to be states of B.

An easy check for emptiness of alternating automata is via the equivalent Büchi automaton.

9.5.2 Translating formulae into Automata

The first step in using automata to decide a temporal formula is to translate the temporal formula into an equivalent automata: i.e. one that accepts exactly the models of the formula. There are direct ways of making this translation. However, it is also worth presenting some of the methods which use a stepping stone in the translation: either a second-order logic or an alternating automata.

Direct

A direct construction of an automaton for a PLTL formula is given in [Emerson and Sistla, 1984]. The transition diagram of the automaton is essentially just the tableau graph for the formula given above. To be precise, suppose that we have PLTL formula ϕ which, without loss of generality, we want to be satisfied at the start of time. The states of the automaton are $S = PC(\phi) \cup \{s_0\}$ where the unique initial state s_0 is just some special state outside the tableau. The nondeterministic transition table is given by $(s, \sigma_i, s') \in T$ iff either both $s = s_0$ and $\phi \in s'$ or sRs' where R is the successor relation on tableau nodes.

The intuitive idea is that for any structure σ, there is a run of the automaton on σ such that the formulas of $\mathbf{clos}(\phi)$ which are true at the ith state of σ are exactly those in the ith state of the run. The acceptance criteria is used to indicate which structures are (initial) models of ϕ.

To define a nondeterministic Rabin automaton $A = (S, \{s_0\}, T, \mathcal{F})$ which accepts exactly the models σ with $\sigma, 0 \models \phi$ we need only make sure that all eventualities appearing as formulas in the states are fulfilled in the model being read. To do this we enumerate the eventualities in the closure set as $\alpha_j \mathcal{U} \beta_j$ as $j = 1, ..., m$ and we have m pairs in $\mathcal{F}$. The jth pair (U_j, V_j) corresponds to the jth eventuality using the complemented pairs acceptance condition: U_j contains the states which contain the eventuality, say $\alpha \mathcal{U} \beta$, while V_j witnesses β, i.e. contains the states which contain β.

We can easily build, from A, an equivalent nondeterministic Büchi automaton for σ. The states of this are just states of A paired with an $m + 1$-valued counter. The counter lets us witness the fulfillment of the m eventualities in sequence. See [Emerson and Sistla, 1984] for details.

The similar procedure in [Reynolds, 2000] directly gives a deterministic tableau-style automaton for the language with past-time operators.

Via $S1S$

There are slightly different ways of defining the second-order logic of one successor. We can regard it as an ordinary first-order logic interpreted in a structure which actually consists of sets of natural numbers. The signature contains the 2-ary subset relation $\subseteq$ and a 2-ary ordering relation symbol $succ$. Subset is interpreted in the natural way while $succ(A, B)$ holds for sets A and B iff $A = \{n\}$ and $B = \{n + 1\}$ for some number n. To deal with a temporal structure using atoms from L we also allow the symbols in L as constant symbols in the language: given an ω-structure σ, the interpretation of the atom p is just the set of times at which p holds.

A well-known and straightforward translation gives an $S1S$ version of any temporal formula. We can translate any temporal formula α using atoms from L into an $S1S$ formula $(*\alpha)(x)$ with a free variable x:

$$\begin{array}{rcl} *p & = & (x = p) \\ *(\neg\alpha) & = & \neg(*\alpha) \\ *(\alpha \wedge \beta) & = & *\alpha \wedge *\beta \\ *(\bigcirc\alpha) & = & \forall y((*\alpha)(y) \rightarrow \forall uv(succ(u, v) \wedge (u \subseteq x) \rightarrow (v \subseteq y)) \\ *(\alpha \mathcal{U} \beta) & = & \forall ab((*\alpha)(a) \wedge (*\beta(b)) \rightarrow \\ & & (J(a, b, x) \wedge ((\forall y(J(a, b, y) \rightarrow (x \subseteq y)))) \\ \text{where } J(a, b, z) & = & (b \subseteq z) \wedge \forall uv(succ(u, v) \wedge (v \subseteq z) \wedge (u \subseteq a) \rightarrow (u \subseteq z)) \end{array}$$

An easy induction (on the construction of α) shows that $\sigma \models (*\alpha)(S)$ iff S is the set of times at which α holds.

The translation of $S1S$ into an automaton is also easy, given McNaughton's result: it is via a simple induction. Suppose that the $S1S$ sentence uses constants from the finite set P. We proceed by induction on the construction of the sentence The automaton for $p \subseteq q$ simply keeps checking that $p \rightarrow q$ is true of the current state and falls into a fail state sink if not. The other base cases, of $p = q$ and $succ(p, q)$ are just as easy. Conjunction requires a standard construction of conjoining automata using the product of the state sets. Negation can be done using McNaughton's result to determinise the automaton for the negated subformula. It is easy to find the complement of a deterministic automaton. The case of an existential quantification, for example, $\exists y \rho(y)$, is done by simply using non-determinism to guess the truth of the quantified variable at each step.

The overall complexity is determined by the determinisation procedure and, as shown in [Safra, 1988], it is single exponential.

Via alternating automata

The easy translation from PLTL to an alternating Büchi automaton is described in [Muller *et al.*, 1988], [Vardi, 1994] and [Vardi, 1996]. Suppose that we are given a formula ϕ using only atoms from the finite set P. The alternating Büchi automaton $A = (S, s_0, \rho, F)$ recognizes ω-sequences of elements of 2^P. The set S of states of the corresponding automaton is just the set of subformulae of ϕ and their negations. The transition function ρ is defined to make $\rho(s, a)$ equal to the positive boolean combination of subformulae of ϕ which must hold in the next time instant to guarantee that the formula s holds in at the current time if the current state is given by $a \subseteq P$. For example, $\rho(p, a)$ is $\mathbf{true}$ if $p \in a$ and $\mathbf{false}$ otherwise; $\rho(\bigcirc\alpha, a) = \alpha$; and $\rho(\alpha \mathcal{U} \beta, a) = \rho(\beta, a) \vee (\rho(\alpha, a) \wedge (\alpha \mathcal{U} \beta))$.

A run T of A on an ω-sequence σ may have infinite branches eventually continually labelled by $\neg(\alpha \mathcal{U} \beta)$. As $\rho(\neg(\alpha \mathcal{U} \beta), a) = \rho(\neg\beta, a) \wedge (\rho(\neg\alpha, a) \vee (\neg(\alpha \mathcal{U} \beta)))$, this ensures that $\neg\beta$ eventually holds at each time instant in σ and so $\neg(\alpha \mathcal{U} \beta)$ does too. Thus we define F to contain exactly any states of the form $\neg(\alpha \mathcal{U} \beta)$. However, there may also be infinite branches eventually continually labelled by $\alpha \mathcal{U} \beta$. These must not be accepted as there is no guarantee that β will eventually hold in σ.

The size of the alternating automaton is clearly linear in the size of ϕ.

We have already seen that there is an exponentially complex procedure for finding an equivalent Büchi automaton for a given Alternating automaton. Thus we have, overall, an exponentially complex translation from PLTL formula into a non-deterministic Büchi automaton.

9.5.3 Deciding validity of PLTL

Putting together the results above gives us several alternative approaches to deciding validity of PLTL formulae.

For example, consider the route to a Büchi automaton, via an alternating automaton or otherwise. Given a formula ϕ, we can, in polynomial time, construct an alternating automaton accepting exactly the models of ϕ. We have seen that we can then construct an equivalent Büchi automaton A with exponentially greater size. Thus the size of the state set of A will be exponential in the size of ϕ.

We have seen that to decide whether this automaton is non-empty can be achieved in NLOGSPACE. Putting the two steps together gives us a procedure which takes exponential time in the length of the formula.

The important observation in [Vardi and Wolper, 1994] is that we can make the Büchi automata "on the fly" while testing its non-emptiness. This means that we need not store the whole description of the automaton in memory at any moment: we need only check a polynomial number of states (in the size of ϕ) and then (nondeterministically) move on to another such small group of states. This gives us a PSPACE algorithm. From the results of [Sistla and Clarke, 1985], we know this is best possible as a decision procedure.

9.5.4 Other Logics

The decision algorithm above using the translation into the language $S1S$ can be readily extended to allow for past operators or fixed point operators or both to appear in the language. This is because formulae using these operators can be expressed in $S1S$.

Several interesting changes can be made to the definition of automata to enable then to cope with sequences which are infinite in both directions. See [Nivat and Perrin, 1986] and [Perrin and Schupp, 1986]. Perhaps such extended automata can help decide validity of past and future time temporal logics with integer models of time.

Automata do not seem well suited to reasoning about dense time or general linear orders.

The same strategy as we used for PLTL also works for the decidability of branching time logics such as CTL*. The only difference is that we must use tree automata. Thus, the method proceeds by finding a tree automaton equivalent to a given branching time temporal formula and then testing the automaton for emptiness. As in the linear case, there are several ways of filling in the details.

Let us have a quick look at tree automata. For a particular $k > 0$, the k-ary infinite tree, $\mathcal{T}_k$, is just the set of all sequences from the alphabet $\Delta_k = \{\beta_0, ..., \beta_{k-1}\}$ including the empty sequence ε. We write $\sigma^\wedge\rho$ for the concatenation of sequence σ followed by sequence ρ. If Σ is a finite alphabet then a k-ary Σ-tree is a pair $(\mathcal{T}_k, \nu)$ where ν is a map from $\mathcal{T}_k$ into Σ. Call ν a Σ-labelling of $\mathcal{T}_k$.

A k-ary *Σ-tree automaton* is a 4-tuple $M = (S, T, S_0, \mathcal{F})$ where

- S is a finite non-empty set called the set of *states*,
- $T \subseteq S \times \Sigma \times \Delta_k \times S$ is the *transition table*,
- $S_0 \subseteq S$ is the *initial state set* and
- $\mathcal{F}$ is a set of subsets of S called the *acceptance condition*.

Tree automata get to work on k-ary Σ-trees. Below we use a game to define whether or not the tree automaton M accepts the tree $L = (\mathcal{T}_k, \nu)$.

The game $\Gamma(M, L)$ is played between the automaton M and a player called *Pathfinder* on the tree L. The game goes on for ω moves (starting at move 1). The ith move consists of M choosing a state q_i from S followed by Pathfinder choosing a direction $\delta_i \in \Delta_k$. M must choose q_i so that:

- $q_1 \in S_0$,
- and for each $i \geq 1$, $(q_i, \nu(\delta_1^\wedge ...^\wedge\delta_{i-1}), \delta_i, q_{i+1}) \in T$.

We can view a play of the game as being directed along the branch $\delta_1^\wedge\delta_2^\wedge...$ of $\mathcal{T}_k$. We will say that M is in state q_i at node $\delta_1^\wedge ...^\wedge\delta_{i-1}$ of this branch. Provided M can always find a state q_i, into which to move on the ith move, a play of the game gives rise to a whole sequence $q_1, q_2, q_3, ...$ of states along the branch $\delta_1^\wedge\delta_2^\wedge....$ The criterion for deciding the winner of a play is determined by this sequence as follows. We say that M has won the play $q_1\delta_1q_2\delta_2...$ if and only if the set of states which come up infinitely often in $q_1, q_2, q_3, ...$ is in $\mathcal{F}$. Otherwise Pathfinder has won. If M can not move at any stage we also deem that Pathfinder has won. We say that M *accepts* L if and only if there is a winning strategy for the player M in the game $\Gamma(M, L)$. This means there must be some function f which tells M which state to move into at each node $x \in T_k$ in such a way that playing $f(\varepsilon), f(\delta_1), f(\delta_1^\wedge \delta_2), \ldots$ wins the play for M along the branch $\delta_1^\wedge \delta_2^\wedge \ldots$

Using the techniques of [Gurevich and Shelah, 1985], one can translate a branching time temporal formula into a equi-satisfiable formula in the monadic language of two-successors, $S2S$, which is interpreted over the binary tree. We can then use Rabin's famous decidability result [Rabin, 1969] for $S2S$, using tree automata.

As in the linear case, this translation into a second-order logic turns out to be an inefficient approach. Let us briefly describe the more efficient approach in [Emerson and Jutla, 1988] which is built upon a translation from CTL* formulas to Rabin tree automata given in [Emerson and Sistla, 1984]. This latter translation gives an automaton which has number of transitions double exponential in the length of the formula but the number of accepting pairs is only exponential in the length of the formula. The automaton accepts exactly the models of the formula. The translation proceeds by first finding for a given CTL* formula ϕ an (essentially) equivalent formula (with only a linear increase in length) in which the depth of nesting of path quantifiers (**A** or **E**) is at most two: i.e. we have conjunctions and disjunctions of formulas of the forms $\mathbf{A}\psi$, $\mathbf{A}\Box\psi$, $\mathbf{E}\psi$ where ψ contains no path quantifiers. For each such subformula, an equivalent tree automata (of appropriate size) is found and then these are all combined using a cross-product construction. The case of the $\mathbf{A}\psi$ formula is the difficult one and a tableau construction for ψ is first used, then a nondeterministic (linear) Buchi automaton equivalent to ψ is found from it. Because of its particular form this is able to be determinised with only a single exponential blow-up in number of states. Finally a tree automaton for $\mathbf{A}\psi$ can be described.

In [Emerson and Jutla, 1988] a new efficient algorithm is given for testing non-emptiness of Rabin tree automata. It is shown that there is an algorithm that runs in time $O((mn)^{3n})$ which is polynomial in the size m of the transition table and exponential in the number of accepting pairs. The algorithm depends on the observation in [Emerson, 1985] that a Rabin tree automaton is non-empty iff it accepts (in a certain sense) some finite labelled graph contained within a graph of its transitions. This condition can be formulated in terms of the truth of a temporal logic formula capturing the pairs acceptance criteria. To check for such a graph within the transition graph we use the mu-calculus style fix point characterization of the temporal subformulas of this acceptance formula.

Putting together the complexity result in [Emerson and Sistla, 1984] with their own emptiness test, [Emerson and Jutla, 1988] can thus describe a decision procedure for CTL* of deterministic double exponential time complexity in the length of the formula. This agrees with the lower bound found in [Vardi and Stockmeyer, 1985].

In [Bernholtz, 1995] there is a direct translation from any CTL* formula into an equivalent alternating automaton (of a certain restricted form). This gives an alternative decision procedure for CTL*.

9.6 Resolution

9.6.1 Introduction

Resolution was proposed as a proof procedure by Robinson in 1965 [Robinson, 1965] for propositional and first-order logics. Resolution was claimed to be "machine-oriented" as it was particularly suitable for proofs to be performed by computer having only one rule of inference that may have to be applied many times. To check the validity of a logical formula Φ, it is negated and $\neg\Phi$ is translated into a normal form, $\tau(\neg\Phi)$. The resolution inference rule (see below) is applied repeatedly to the set of conjuncts of $\tau(\neg\Phi)$ and new inferences added to the set. If a contradiction (**false**) is derived then $\neg\Phi$ is unsatisfiable and the original formula Φ must therefore be valid. The process of determining the unsatisfiability of the negation of a formula is known as *refutation*. The resolution proof procedure is *refutation complete* for classical logic as, when applied to an unsatisfiable formula, the procedure is guaranteed to produce **false**.

Classical (clausal) resolution as applied to propositional logic requires formulae to be in a particular form, Conjunctive Normal Form (CNF), before resolution rules may be applied. A formula in CNF may be represented as

$$C_1 \wedge C_2 \wedge \ldots \wedge C_m$$

where each C_i, known as a *clause*, is a disjunction of literals. Pairs of clauses are resolved using the classical (propositional) resolution rule

$$\frac{\begin{array}{l} A \vee p \\ B \vee \neg p \end{array}}{A \vee B}$$

where A and B are disjunctions of literals and $A \vee B$ is known as the *resolvent*. Resolvents are added to the set of clauses, C, and the resolution rule is applied to pairs of clauses in C until an empty resolvent (denoting **false**) is derived or no further resolvents can be generated.

Non-clausal (i.e. where the translation into a normal form is not necessary) versions of resolution have also been described, see for example [Murray, 1982]. Generally the advantages of avoiding having to rewrite formulae into special normal forms are that the resulting normal forms may be longer than the original, the procedure may be costly in the terms of processing and applying such a translation may lose the underlying structure of the formula that could be useful guiding the search. The main disadvantage is that many resolution rules must be defined to cope with all combinations of operators and sometimes it is not clear which rule should be applied. When considering the application of resolution to temporal logics both clausal and non-clausal approaches have been adopted and will be discussed below.

When applying resolution to temporal logics we must make sure that the literals being resolved do actually occur at the same moment in time. In some cases a form of the classical resolution rule can be applied to temporal logic formulae directly. For example, in PLTL, pairs of complementary literals within the context of the $\Box$–operator can be resolved using the following rule.

$$\frac{\begin{array}{l} A \vee \Box p \\ B \vee \Box \neg p \end{array}}{A \vee B}$$

Generally, though, this is not the case and the problem of how to resolve two complementary literals occurring in *different* temporal contexts arises. For example we should not try to resolve a literal p true in the next moment ($\bigcirc p$) with its negation $\neg p$ in the moment following that ($\bigcirc\bigcirc\neg p$). However, in some cases formulae involving different temporal operators may still be resolved. For example, pairs of formulae including the $\Box$ and $\Diamond$–operators may be resolved using the following temporal resolution rule.

$$\frac{\begin{array}{c} A \vee \Box p \\ B \vee \Diamond \neg p \end{array}}{A \vee B}$$

On the whole, though, this is not possible. We may not be able to resolve formulae enclosed within the same temporal operator for example the formulae $A \vee \Diamond p$ and $B \vee \Diamond \neg p$, have no resolvent.

Although it would appear sensible to be able to resolve clauses which have complementary literals enclosed in the $\Box$ and $\Diamond$–operators as above, further complications occur due to induction between the $\Box$ and $\bigcirc$ formulae. For example, the formula

$$\Box(a \rightarrow \bigcirc a) \wedge a \wedge l \wedge \Box(a \rightarrow \bigcirc l)$$

implies $\Box l$ although this is not immediately obvious, and so this formula should resolve with $\Diamond \neg l$.

Such difficulties in how to apply resolution to temporal logics have led to only a few such methods being suggested. The two main ways are clausal systems, i.e. those that require translation to a normal form [Cavalli and Fariñas del Cerro, 1984; Fisher, 1991; Venkatesh, 1986] and non-clausal [Abadi, 1987]. We begin by describing the clausal approaches.

9.6.2 Clausal Resolution for PLTL

In this section we consider two main approaches that require a clausal form. A third clausal temporal resolution system is described in [Cavalli and Fariñas del Cerro, 1984]. However as it does not deal with full PLTL we leave its discussion until Section 9.6.4.

Resolution Based on SNF

This method, first described in [Fisher, 1991] and expanded in [Fisher *et al.*, 2001] is clausal and depends on the translation to a normal form that removes most of the temporal operators. Next, two types of resolution rules are applied, one essentially the classical (propositional) resolution rule known as *step resolution* and the other the resolution of an eventuality ($\Diamond p$) with sets of formulae that together imply $\Box \neg p$. Note, here the anchored version of validity is used, i.e. α is *valid* iff for all sequences σ of states, $(\sigma, 0) \models \alpha$.

The normal form, *Separated Normal Form* or SNF, reduces the number of temporal operators to a core set and requires the resultant formulae to be of a particular form. This is done by the introduction of new propositions to rename subformulae and to simulate the removed temporal operators. For example the formula $x \rightarrow \bigcirc \Box p$ is translated into SNF by the SNF formulae

$$\begin{array}{ccccccc} x & \rightarrow & \bigcirc t & \quad & t & \rightarrow & \bigcirc t \\ x & \rightarrow & \bigcirc p & \quad & t & \rightarrow & \bigcirc p \end{array}$$

where t is a new proposition symbol and there is an external $\Box$ operator surrounding the conjunction of these formulae. The normal form uses an additional operator, $\mathbf{start}$, to those given in Section 9.2. The operator $\mathbf{start}$ only holds at the beginning of time, i.e. for a model σ and state index i the semantics of $\mathbf{start}$ is

$$(\sigma, i) \models \mathbf{start} \text{ iff } i = 0;$$

and is used in the normal form to identify clauses that are true at the beginning of time. Details of the translation into the normal form are given in [Fisher, 1991; Fisher *et al.*, 2001]. The transformation into SNF preserves satisfiability and so any contradiction generated from a formula in SNF implies a contradiction in the original formula [Fisher *et al.*, 2001].

Formulae in SNF are of the general form

$$\Box \bigwedge_i A_i$$

where each A_i is known as a *clause* and must be one of the following forms where each particular k_a, k_b, l_c, l_d and l represent literals.

$$\begin{array}{rclr}
\mathbf{start} & \rightarrow & \bigvee_c l_c & \text{(an } \textit{initial } \Box\text{–clause)} \\
\bigwedge_a k_a & \rightarrow & \bigcirc \bigvee_d l_d & \text{(a } \textit{global } \Box\text{–clause)} \\
\bigwedge_b k_b & \rightarrow & \Diamond l & \text{(a } \textit{global } \Diamond\text{–clause)}
\end{array}$$

The outer '$\Box$' connective, that surrounds the conjunction of clauses is usually omitted. Similarly, for convenience, the conjunction is dropped and the set of clauses A_i is considered. Different variants of the normal form have been suggested some using a last-time formula on the left hand side of the global clauses and a disjunction of literals on the right hand side of the global $\Box$-clause, others allowing an additional clause of the form $\mathbf{start} \rightarrow \Diamond l$. These are essentially the same.

To apply the temporal resolution rule one or more of the global $\Box$ clauses may be combined, thus a variant on SNF called merged-SNF (SNF_m) [Fisher, 1991], is also defined. Given a set of clauses in SNF, the relevant set of SNF_m clauses may be generated by repeatedly applying the following rule.

$$\begin{array}{rcl}
A & \rightarrow & \bigcirc C \\
B & \rightarrow & \bigcirc D \\
\hline
(A \wedge B) & \rightarrow & \bigcirc(C \wedge D)
\end{array}$$

Thus, SNF_m represents all possible conjunctive combinations of SNF clauses.

Once a formula has been transformed into SNF, both step resolution and temporal resolution can be applied. Step resolution effectively consists of the application of the standard classical resolution rule to formulae representing constraints at a particular moment in time, together with simplification rules, subsumption rules, and rules for transferring contradictions within states to constraints on previous states. The step resolution rule is a form of classical resolution applied between $\Box$–clauses, representing constraints applying to the same moment in time. Pairs of initial $\Box$–clauses, or global $\Box$–clauses, may be resolved using the following (step resolution) rules.

$$\begin{array}{rcl}
\mathbf{start} & \rightarrow & A \vee p \\
\mathbf{start} & \rightarrow & B \vee \neg p \\
\hline
\mathbf{start} & \rightarrow & A \vee B
\end{array}
\qquad\qquad
\begin{array}{rcl}
C & \rightarrow & \bigcirc(A \vee p) \\
D & \rightarrow & \bigcirc(B \vee \neg p) \\
\hline
(C \wedge D) & \rightarrow & \bigcirc(A \vee B)
\end{array}$$

Clauses with $\bigcirc$**false** on the right hand side are removed and replaced by an additional pair of clauses as follows.

$$\{A \to \bigcirc \textbf{false}\} \quad \longrightarrow \quad \left\{ \begin{array}{rcl} \textbf{start} & \to & \neg A \\ \textbf{true} & \to & \bigcirc(\neg A) \end{array} \right\}$$

Thus, if by satisfying A in the previous moment in time a contradiction is produced, then A must never be satisfied. The new constraints therefore represent $\square\neg A$. The step resolution process terminates when either no new resolvents are generated or **false** is derived by generating one of the following unsatisfiable formulae

$$\begin{array}{rcl} \textbf{start} & \to & \textbf{false} \\ \textbf{true} & \to & \bigcirc\textbf{false}. \end{array}$$

Temporal resolution allows the resolution of a $\diamond$, for example a clause with $\diamond\neg l$ on the right hand side, with sets of merged clauses that together imply $\square l$. The rule requires that the set of merged clauses satisfy certain criterion to ensure that this is actually the case. The detection of such a set of clauses is non-trivial and algorithms to detect these sets are given in [Dixon, 1996; Dixon, 1998]. The temporal resolution rule is given by

$$\begin{array}{rcl} A_0 & \to & \bigcirc B_0 \\ \dots & \to & \dots \\ A_n & \to & \bigcirc B_n \\ C & \to & \diamond l \\ \hline C & \to & \bigwedge_{i=0}^{n} (\neg A_i)\, \mathcal{W}\, l \end{array}$$

where each $A_i \to \bigcirc B_i$ is in SNF$_m$ and with the side conditions

$$\begin{array}{l} \text{for all } i,\ 0 \le i \le n \ \text{ implies } B_i \to \neg l \\ \text{for all } i,\ 0 \le i \le n \ \text{ implies } B_i \to \bigvee_{j=0}^{n} A_j \end{array}$$

The resolvent states that once C has occurred then l must occur (i.e. the eventuality must be satisfied) before

$$\bigvee_{i=0}^{n} A_i$$

can be satisfied. The '$\mathcal{W}$' connective is used as we already have a clause guaranteeing that $\diamond l$ *will* occur. The resolvent must be translated into SNF.

Proofs that the translation into SNF preserves satisfiability are given in [Fisher *et al.*, 2001]. The completeness of this set of resolution rules is shown in [Fisher *et al.*, 2001]. The most complex part of this system is the search for the set of clauses to use in the application of the temporal resolution rule. This area is discussed in [Dixon, 1996; Dixon, 1998].

Forward Reasoning Resolution

Venkatesh [Venkatesh, 1986] describes a clausal resolution method for PLTL for future-time operators including $\mathcal{U}$. First, formulae are translated into a normal form containing a restricted nesting of temporal operators. The normal form is

$$\bigwedge_{i=1}^{n} C_i \wedge \bigwedge_{j=1}^{m} \Box C_j^{'}$$

where each C_i and $C_j^{'}$ (known as *clauses*) is a disjunction of formulae of the form

$$\bigcirc^k l,\ \bigcirc^k \Box l,\ \bigcirc^k \Diamond,\ \bigcirc^k (l' \mathcal{U}\, l)$$

(known as *principal terms*) for l and l' literals, $k \geqslant 0$ and $\bigcirc^k$ denoting a series of k $\bigcirc$–operators. To translate into the normal form temporal equivalences are used to ensure that negations are applied only to propositions, the $\bigcirc$–operator is distributed over conjunctions and disjunctions, and rules are applied to ensure a CNF-like structure. Renaming is carried out, similar to that in translation to SNF previously described, to remove the nesting of temporal operators not allowed in the normal form. For example to translate $\bigcirc(\Box F)$ into the normal form, where F is a temporal formula, we can replace it by $\bigcirc(\Box t) \wedge \Box(t \leftrightarrow F)$ where t is a new proposition symbol. The translation to the normal form is shown to preserve the satisfiability of the temporal formula.

Next *resolution*, *unwinding* and SKIP operations are defined. The resolution rule, defined on clauses, is similar to that for classical propositional logic

$$\frac{\begin{array}{c} A \vee p \\ B \vee \neg p \end{array}}{A \vee B}$$

where p is a proposition and A and B are disjunctions of principal terms. Unwinding, applied to clauses, allows the replacement of literals enclosed within the $\Box$, $\Diamond$ or $\mathcal{U}$ operators by a component applying to the current moment and a component applying to the next moment, i.e.

$$\begin{array}{rcl} A \vee \Diamond l & \rightarrow & A \vee l \vee \bigcirc \Diamond l \\ A \vee \Box l & \rightarrow & \left\{ \begin{array}{l} A \vee l \\ A \vee \bigcirc \Box l \end{array} \right\} \\ A \vee (l \mathcal{U}\, l') & \rightarrow & \left\{ \begin{array}{l} A \vee l' \vee l \\ A \vee l' \vee \bigcirc (l \mathcal{U}\, l') \end{array} \right\} \end{array}$$

Finally the operation SKIP, defined on clauses where each term in the clause is of the form $\bigcirc T$ where T is a principal term. SKIP deletes a next operator from each term, for example

$$\text{SKIP}(\bigcirc l \vee \bigcirc\bigcirc\bigcirc \Box l' \vee \bigcirc \Diamond l'') = (l \vee \bigcirc\bigcirc \Box l' \vee \Diamond l'').$$

Resolution proofs are displayed in columns separating the clauses that hold in each state. To determine unsatisfiability, the principal terms (except $\bigcirc^k l$) in each clause are *unwound* to split them into present and future parts. Next, classical style resolution is carried out between complementary literals relating to the present parts of the clauses in each column or state. Then, any clauses in a state that contain only principal terms with one or more next operators are transferred to the next state and the number of next operators attached to each term is reduced by one. This process is shown to be complete for clauses that contain no eventualities. Formulae that contain eventualities that are delayed indefinitely due to unwinding are eliminated and this process is shown to be complete.

9.6.3 Non Clausal

A non-clausal temporal resolution system for PLTL is described in [Abadi and Manna, 1985]. The system is developed first for fragments of the logic including the temporal operators $\bigcirc$, $\square$, and $\diamond$ and then extended for $\bigcirc$, $\square$, $\diamond$, $\mathcal{W}$* and $\mathcal{P}$. The binary operator $\mathcal{P}$ is known as *precedes* where $u\mathcal{P}v = \neg((\neg u)\,\mathcal{W}\,v)$. This system is further described in [Abadi, 1987; Abadi and Manna, 1990] where it extended to first order temporal logic.

The propositional system for $\bigcirc$, $\square$, and $\diamond$ has rules for simplification, distribution, cut, resolution, modality and induction. Simplification rules include rules that apply negations to formulae, rules that simplify formulae containing **false**, and the weakening rule that allows the deletion of a conjunct that is considered useless. The distribution rule allows the distribution of $\wedge$ over $\vee$. The cut rule allows the introduction of rules of the form $u \vee \neg u$ and is not necessary for the completeness of the propositional system (but is necessary for the first-order system). The resolution rule is of the form

$$A < u, \ldots, u >, B < u, \ldots, u > \longrightarrow A < \textbf{true} > \vee B < \textbf{false} >$$

where $A < u, \ldots, u >$ denotes that u occurs one or more times in A. Here occurrences of u in A and B are replaced with **true** and **false** respectively. To ensure the rule is sound each u that is replaced must be in the scope of the same number of $\bigcirc$-operators, and must not be in the scope of any other modal operator in A or B, i.e. they must apply to the same moment in time. The modality rules apply to formulae in the scope of the temporal operators. For example the $\square$-rule allows any formula $\square u$ to be rewritten as $u \wedge \bigcirc\square u$. The induction rule deals with the interaction between $\bigcirc$ and $\square$ and is of the form

$$w, \diamond u \longrightarrow \diamond(\neg u \wedge \bigcirc(u \wedge \neg w)) \text{ if } \vdash \neg(w \wedge u).$$

Informally this means that if w and u cannot both hold at the same time and if w and $\diamond u$ hold now then there must be a moment in time (now or) in the future when u does not hold and at the next moment in time u holds and w does not. A proof editor has been developed for the propositional system with the $\bigcirc$, $\square$, and $\diamond$ operators. Although not fully automatic, such a tool assists the user in the correct application of the proof rules. The resolution system is then extended to allow for the operators $\mathcal{W}$ and $\mathcal{P}$ also.

Completeness is shown relative to a tableau procedure for PLTL derived from that given in [Wolper, 1985] by proving that if a formula $\neg u$ is found unsatisfiable by the tableau decision procedure then there is a refutation for $\neg u$.

9.6.4 Extension to Other Logics

PLTL without the $\mathcal{U}$ operator

A clausal resolution method for a subset of the PLTL temporal operators described in Section 9.2, namely $\bigcirc$, $\square$ and $\diamond$ (i.e. excluding $\mathcal{U}$ and $\mathcal{W}$), is outlined in [Cavalli and Fariñas del Cerro, 1984]. Such logics have been shown to be less expressive than full PLTL [Gabbay *et al.*, 1980]. The method described rewrites formulae to a complicated normal form and then applies a series of temporal resolution rules.

A formula, F, is said to be in Conjunctive Normal Form (CNF), if it is of the form

$$F = C_1 \wedge C_2 \wedge \ldots \wedge C_n$$

*Abadi denotes $\mathcal{W}$, *unless* (or *weak until*), as $\mathcal{U}$.

where each C_j is called a *clause* and is of the following form.

$$\begin{array}{rcl} C_j & = & L_1 \vee L_2 \vee \ldots \vee L_n \vee \Box D_1 \vee \Box D_2 \vee \ldots \vee \Box D_p \\ & \vee & \Diamond A_1 \vee \Diamond A_2 \vee \ldots \vee \Diamond A_q \end{array}$$

Here each L_i is a literal preceded by a string of zero or more $\bigcirc$–operators, each D_i is a disjunction of the same general form as the clauses and each A_i is a conjunction where each conjunct possesses the same general form as the clauses. It is shown that F' the normal form of a formula F is equivalent to F. The translation does not require renaming (as the methods described in Section 9.6.2) and therefore generates no new propositions. Translation into the normal form is carried out by using classical logic equivalences and by applying some temporal logic equivalences such as the distribution of the $\bigcirc$ operator over conjunction or disjunction.

The resolution rules are split into three types

1. classical operators
2. temporal operators
3. transformation operators

denoted by Σ_1, Σ_2, and Σ_3 (or Γ) respectively. Resolution rules are of the form that $\Box x$ and $\Diamond y$ can be resolved if x and y are resolvable and the resolvent will be the resolvent of x and y with a $\Diamond$–operator in front.
Classical operations allow classical style resolution to be performed, for example

$$\Sigma_1(p, \neg p) = \emptyset \quad \text{(where } \emptyset \text{ denotes the empty set or } \textbf{false}\text{)}$$
And $(p, \neg p)$ is resolvable.

The temporal resolution rules allow resolution between formulae in the context of certain operators, for example

$$\Sigma_2(\Box E, \triangle F) = \triangle \Sigma_i(E, F) \quad \text{(provided that } \triangle \text{ is one of } \Box, \Diamond, \text{ or } \bigcirc\text{)}$$
And if (E, F) is resolvable then $(\Box E, \triangle F)$ is resolvable;

where Σ_i denotes that an operation of type i is being applied where $i = 1, 2$ or 3.
A resolution rule (Γ) is provided that operates on just a single argument to allow resolution within the context of the $\Diamond$ operator. Here $\mathcal{E}(X)$ denotes that X is a subformula of $\mathcal{E}$.

$$\Gamma(\mathcal{E}(\Diamond(D \wedge D' \wedge F))) = \mathcal{E}(\Diamond(\Sigma_i(D, D') \wedge F))$$
And if (D, D') is resolvable then $\mathcal{E}(\Diamond((D \wedge D') \wedge F))$ is resolvable;

The transformation rules allow rewriting of some formulae, to enable the continued application of the resolution rules, for example

$$\Sigma_3(\Box E, F) = \Sigma_i(\Box\Box E, F)$$
And if $(\Box\Box E, F)$ is resolvable then $(\Box E, F)$ is resolvable.

There are three rules of inference given where $R(C_1, C_2)$ (or $R(C_1)$) is a resolvent of C_1 and C_2 ((C_1)). If $C_1 \vee C$ and $C_2 \vee C'$ are clauses then the resolution inference rules are

$$\frac{C_1 \vee C \quad C_2 \vee C'}{R(C_1, C_2) \vee C \vee C'}$$

if C_1 and C_2 are resolvable and

$$\frac{C_1 \vee C}{R(C_1) \vee C}$$

if C_1 is resolvable. The following inference rule can also be applied (for $\mathcal{E}(D \vee D \vee F)$ a clause) to carry out simplification.

$$\frac{\mathcal{E}(D \vee D \vee F)}{\mathcal{E}(D \vee F)}$$

Formulae are refuted by translation to clausal form and repeated application of the inference rules. Resolution only takes place between clauses in the context of certain operators outlined in the resolution rules. It is proved that there is a refutation of a set of clauses using this method if and only if the set of clauses is unsatisfiable.

Branching-Time Temporal Logics

The method described in Section 9.6.2 has been extended to deal with the branching-time temporal logic CTL [Bolotov and Fisher, 1997]. Recall in CTL each temporal operator must be paired with a path operator (i.e. $\mathbf{A}$ or $\mathbf{E}$) so $(\mathbf{A}\,\Box p) \wedge (\mathbf{E}(p\,\mathcal{U}\,r))$ is a formula of CTL but $\mathbf{E}((\mathbf{A}\,\Box p) \wedge (\mathbf{E}(p\,\mathcal{U}\,r)))$ is not. Due to this the normal form is extended to allow path operators on the right hand side of clauses containing a temporal operator. Hence there become two global $\Box$-clauses and two global $\Diamond$-clauses one for each path operator. Similarly the external $\Box$-operator surrounding the set of clauses becomes $\mathbf{A}\,\Box$. The translation to a $\mathbf{E}$-global clause generates a label or index attached to the clause to indicate the path where this clause holds.

The set of step resolution rules are extended to allow for the path operator for example

$$\begin{array}{rcl} C & \rightarrow & \mathbf{A}\bigcirc(A \vee p) \\ D & \rightarrow & \mathbf{A}\bigcirc(B \vee \neg p) \\ \hline (C \wedge D) & \rightarrow & \mathbf{A}\bigcirc(A \vee B) \end{array} \qquad \begin{array}{rcll} C & \rightarrow & \mathbf{A}\bigcirc(A \vee p) & \\ D & \rightarrow & \mathbf{E}\bigcirc(B \vee \neg p) & \langle i \rangle \\ \hline (C \wedge D) & \rightarrow & \mathbf{E}\bigcirc(A \vee B) & \langle i \rangle \end{array}$$

where $\langle i \rangle$ is the label or index. Two $\mathbf{E}$-global clauses may be resolved if the indices match. Similarly the temporal resolution rule is extended. Correctness of the system is shown in relation to the axiom system of CTL.

First-Order Temporal Logics

This system outlined in Section 9.6.3 has been extended to first-order temporal logic in [Abadi, 1987; Abadi and Manna, 1990]. The system for $\bigcirc$, $\Box$, $\Diamond$, $\mathcal{W}$ and $\mathcal{P}$ is extended for first-order temporal logic (FOTL). Rules for skolemisation are given based on skolemisation in classical logics. Restrictions relating to the use of universal and existential operators in the scope of certain temporal operators to ensure the soundness of skolemisation rules are enforced. The resolution rule is based on that given for PLTL allowing for unification and again restrictions are imposed relating to quantification and ensuring that resolution is performed on formulae that occur in the same moment in time. Notions of completeness are discussed. It is shown that while all effective proof systems for FOTL are incomplete, a slight extension to the resolution system is as powerful as Peano arithmetic.

A clausal resolution calculus for monodic first-order temporal logic based on that described in Section 9.6.2 is described in [Degtyarev *et al.*, 2003] with associated soundness and completeness results. The calculus is not particularly practical as the resolution rules require the complex combination of clauses. A calculus which is more suitable for implementation for the expanding domain case (i.e. where the domain over which first-order terms can range can increase at each temporal step) is described in [Konev *et al.*, 2003]. Here, rather than requiring the maximal combination of clauses, smaller inference steps are carried out, similar to the step resolution inference rules for PLTL described in Section 9.6.2, but extended to the first-order setting.

9.7 Implementations

Several theorem provers have been implemented for linear time temporal logics. An early tableau-based theorem prover for PLTL, called DP, was been developed at the University of Manchester [Gough, 1984]. The tableau algorithm is of the two phase style, constructing a graph and then performing deletions upon the graph. Also implemented is DPP a tableau-based theorem prover for PLTL with infinite past. Both are implemented in Pascal.

The Logics Workbench [Heuerding *et al.*, 1995; Jäger *et al.*, 2002], a theorem-proving system for various modal logics available over the Web, has a module for dealing with PLTL. The *model* function of this module includes a C++ implementation of the one-pass tableau calculus [Schwendimann, 1998a; Schwendimann, 1998b], described previously in Section 9.4. Further, the *satisfiability* function incorporates a tableau requiring the two phase, construction of a pre-model and then deletion of unfulfilled eventualities (by analysing strongly connected components), style algorithm outlined in Section 9.4. This is described in [Janssen, 1999].

The STeP system [Bjorner *et al.*, 1995], based on ideas presented in [Manna and Pnueli, 1995], and providing both model checking and deductive methods for PLTL-like logics, has been used in order to assist the verification of concurrent and reactive systems based on temporal specifications. This contains a tableau decision procedure based on [Kesten *et al.*, 1997]. The tableau procedure described in [Kesten *et al.*, 1997] generates the two phase style of tableau with a graph construction phase followed by a phase requiring the detection of a suitable path through the graph from an initial state where all the eventualities that are encountered along the path are satisfied. The algorithm is described for a propositional linear-time logic with finite past but allowing both past and future-time operators. During the graph construction the structure is progressively refined to satisfy the next-time formulae (formulae with $\bigcirc$ as the main operator) of states and the previous-time formulae (formulae with *in the previous moment* as the main operator) of states. The satisfaction of eventualities is carried out by identifying suitable strongly connected components.

The TRP++ system [Hustadt and Konev, 2003; Konev, 2003] is a C++ implementation of the resolution method for PLTL described in Section 9.6.2. Clauses are translated into a ("near propositional") first-order representation where propositions are represented as unary predicates whose argument represents the time at which the predicate holds. That is 0 for initial clauses, the variable, x, for the left hand side of step clauses and the function successor of x, $s(x)$, for the right hand side of step clauses. Initial and step resolution inferences are carried out using ordered resolution. For loop search, a version of the BFS Algorithm [Dixon, 1998] is implemented again based on step resolution following the ideas in [Dixon, 2000].

Efficient data structures and indexing of clauses are also used.

Some implementations of PLTL decision procedures have been systematically compared in [Hustadt and Schmidt, 2002; Hustadt and Konev, 2002]. Both use two classes of formulae which are randomly generated but of particular forms, being dependent on a number of input parameters. The two classes of formulae were chosen with the expectation that the tableaux-based algorithms would outperform the resolution algorithm(s) on one set and vice versa on the other set. Both compare TRP, an earlier Prolog-based (resolution) implementation of TRP++, with the one pass tableau calculus [Schwendimann, 1998a; Schwendimann, 1998b] implemented as the *model* function of the PLTL module of the Logics Workbench, Janssen's tableau [Janssen, 1999] implemented in the *satisfiability* function of the Logics Workbench, and the tableau decision procedure based on [Kesten *et al.*, 1997] found in STeP. The C++ version of the resolution-based theorem prover, TPR++, is also compared with these provers in [Hustadt and Konev, 2002]. Results show that, as expected, the resolution based theorem provers TRP and TRP++, in general, outperform the tableau provers on one of the classes. On the other class one of the tableau provers (the Logic's Workbench *model* function) outperforms TRP and TRP++ as expected, but contrary to expectation, TRP and TRP++ perform better, in general, than the other two tableau algorithms (on this class).

9.8 Concluding Remarks

This chapter has outlined theorem proving methods based on axiomatization, tableaux, automata and resolution. Initially for each method the focus has been on PLTL with a summary of how the basic methods may be extended for other logics. Research effort has been applied into making these approaches more efficient both theoretically and practically. We have also summarised some of the implementations based on these methods.

Whilst research into axiomatizations for particular logics will continue we feel that research into each of the other three methods will also thrive. In particular in applying these methods to different logics, the development of more efficient implementations, the discovery of a range of suitable heuristics and strategies, their application to real world problems and incorporation in software tools for use in industry. Indeed, companies are already using tools such as model checkers for example to detect bugs in hardware designs. Rather than one particular method being dominant we expect interest in all methods to continue where one approach may be better in some situations and another in others. For particular tasks where efficiency is crucial we expect the emergence of highly optimised theorem provers to carry out this specific task, in the field of modal logic theorem proving see for example the FaCT system [Horrocks, 1998] a description logics classifier with a highly optimised tableaux subsumption algorithm.

Handbook of Temporal Reasoning in Artificial Intelligence
Edited by M. Fisher, D. Gabbay and L. Vila

Chapter 10

Probabilistic Temporal Reasoning

Steve Hanks & David Madigan

Research in probabilistic temporal reasoning is devoted to building models of systems that change stochastically over time. Probabilistic dynamical systems have been studied in Statistics, Operations Research, and the Decision Sciences, though usually not with the emphasis on computational inference models and structured representations that characterizes much work in AI. At the same time, a related body of work in the AI literature has developed probabilistic extensions to the deterministic temporal reasoning representations and algorithms that have been studied actively in AI from the field's inception.

This chapter develops a unifying view of probabilistic temporal reasoning as it has been studied in the optimization, statistical, and AI literatures. It discusses two main bodies of work, which differ on their fundamental views of the problem:

- as a probabilistic extension to rule-based deterministic temporal reasoning models
- as a temporal extension to atemporal probabilistic models.

The chapter covers both representational and computational aspects of both approaches.

10.1 Introduction

Most systems worth modelling have some aspects of dynamics and some aspects of uncertainty. In many AI contexts, either or both of these aspects have been abstracted away, often because it was thought that probabilistic dynamic models were either impossible to elicit and construct, prohibitively expensive to use computationally, or both. Recent techniques for building structured representations for reasoning under uncertainty have made probabilistic reasoning more tractable, thus opening the door for effective probabilistic temporal reasoning.

This chapter surveys various systems, formal and computational, that have aspects of both uncertainty and dynamics. These systems tend to differ widely in how they define and attack the problem.

In providing a unified view of probabilistic temporal reasoning systems, we will address three main questions:

- *What is the formal model?* That is, how does the system represent system state, change, time, uncertainty? What kinds of change and uncertainty can the system express in principle, and how? What inference questions does the system address?

- *What is the representation?* Formal models can be implemented in many ways, and the representation for state, change, and uncertainty will affect the efficiency of inference.

- *What is the algorithm?* The formal model defines the inference task, and the representation specifies how the information is stored. How is the representation exploited to answer temporal queries?

10.2 Deterministic Temporal Reasoning

Temporal reasoning in the AI literature addresses the problem of inferring the *state* of a system at various points in time as it changes in response to *events*. This work has typically made strong certainty or complete-information assumptions, for example that the system's initial state is known, all events are known, the effects of events are deterministic and known, and any additional information provided about the system's state is complete and accurate.

Work in probabilistic temporal reasoning tries to relax some or all of these assumptions, addressing situations where the reasoner has partial information about the state and events, and where subsequent information can be incomplete and noisy.

We will begin with a summary of the deterministic problem, based on the Yale Shooting Problem example [Hanks and McDermott, 1987]. The problem consists of the following information, tracking the state of a single individual and a single gun

- The state is described fully by the propositions
  - A (the individual is alive)
  - L (the gun is loaded)
  - M (the gun has powder marks)

- The following events can potentially occur:
  - shoot: if the gun is loaded, this event makes A false, makes L false, and makes M true
  - load: if the gun is not loaded, makes L true, otherwise has no known effects
  - unload: if the gun is loaded, makes L false, otherwise has no known effects
  - wait: this event has no known effects

The effects of events are often described using logical axioms, which might take the following form for the events listed above:

$$\forall t.\ \text{true-at}(\mathsf{L}, t) \wedge \text{occurs-at}(\mathsf{shoot}, t) \Rightarrow \neg\text{true-at}(\mathsf{A}, t+\epsilon) \wedge \neg\text{true-at}(\mathsf{L}, t+\epsilon) \wedge \text{true-at}(\mathsf{M}, t+\epsilon) \quad (10.1)$$

$$\forall t.\ \neg\text{true-at}(\mathsf{L}, t) \wedge \text{occurs-at}(\mathsf{load}, t) \Rightarrow \text{true-at}(\mathsf{L}, t+\epsilon) \quad (10.2)$$

$$\forall t.\ \text{true-at}(\mathsf{L}, t) \wedge \text{occurs-at}(\mathsf{unload}, t) \Rightarrow \neg\text{true-at}(\mathsf{L}, t+\epsilon) \quad (10.3)$$

where $t + \epsilon$ is the instant immediately following t*.

One can pose inference problems of the following form: given (1) information about the occurrence of events at various points of time, and (2) direct information about the system's state at various point of time, infer the system's state at other points in time. The *prediction* or *projection* problem is the special case where the initial state and the nature and timing of events is known, and the system's state after the last event is of interest. In the *explanation* problem, information is provided about events and about the system's final state, and questions are asked about the system's initial state or more generally about earlier states. Both of these problems are special cases of the general problem of finding truth values for *all* state variables at *all* points in time, consistent with the constraints on event behavior—equations (10.1)–(10.3) above—and (partial) information about the system's state at *any* point in time.

This version of the temporal reasoning problem implicitly makes strong assumptions about the timing and duration of events, most notably that events occur instantaneously and affect the world immediately. In making these assumptions we ignore the large body of work on reasoning about durations, delays, and event timing summarized in [Schwalb and Vila, 1998]. We adopt this version of the problem because it provides an easy bridge to the extant literature on probabilistic temporal reasoning, most of which makes these same assumptions. Some work has been done on reasoning with incomplete information about the timing and duration of events, which will be discussed below.

The original version of the Yale Shooting Problem is a projection problem:

- Initially (at t_1) A is true, and L is false. The initial state of M is not known.
- Load occurs at time t_1, shoot occurs at $t_2 > (t_1 + \epsilon)$, and wait occurs at $t_3 > (t_2 + \epsilon)$
- The system's final state is to be predicted, particularly the state of A at some point $t_4 > (t_3 + \epsilon)$

A commonly studied explanation problem is to add the information that A was observed true at t_4, and ask about the state of A or L at various intermediate time points. The technical difficulties associated with this problem are discussed in Section 10.6.1.

Graphical models Suppose it is known what events *occur* at what times. An event can occur but can *fail*, if its preconditions are not met. From this information and the event axioms (equations (10.1)–(10.3) above), we can build a *graphical model* representing the temporal scenario. The graphical model contains a node for each state variable at each relevant point in time—immediately before and immediately after the occurrence of each attempted event—along with a node representing the possibly successful occurrence of each event. Figure 10.1 shows the structure given only the information about event occurrences and the axiomatic information about their preconditions and effects.

Each node in this graph can be assigned a truth value. In the case of a proposition node, assigning a value of true simply means that the proposition was true at that time. In the case of an event node, a true value means that the event's precondition was true (the event occurred successfully).

*The semantics of these logics typically model time points either as integers or as reals. The choice is unimportant for the analysis in this chapter. In the case of integer time points, $\epsilon \equiv 1$, and in both cases the notation $[t_i, t_j]$ refers to the closed interval between t_i and $t_j \geq t_i$

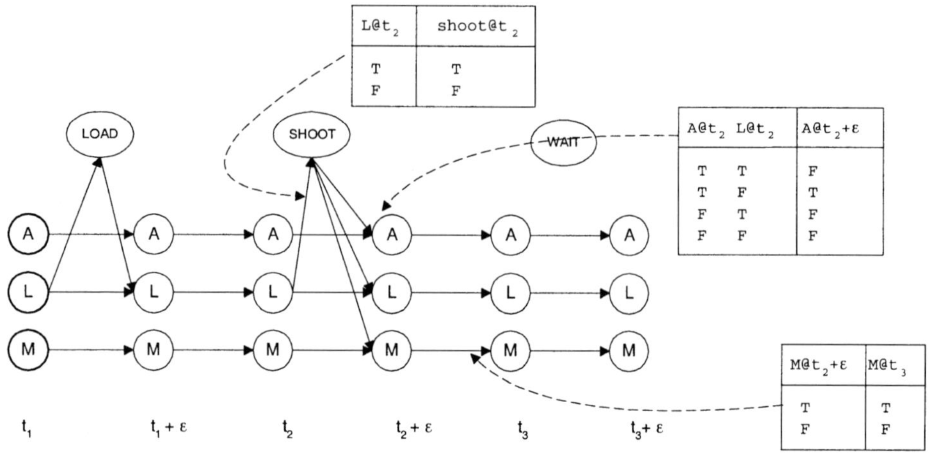

Figure 10.1: A structural graphical model for deterministic temporal reasoning

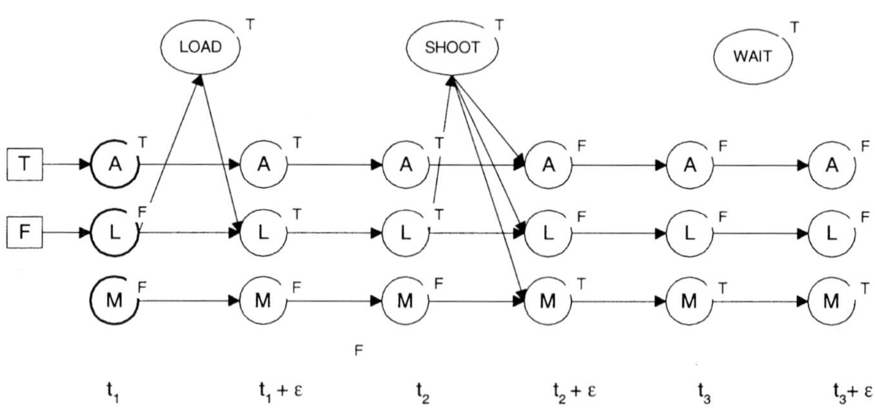

Figure 10.2: A deterministic model with evidence and inferred truth values

In a deterministic setting, information or evidence takes the form of assigning a truth value to a node in the graph as is done with A and L in the initial state in Figure 10.2. At this point the temporal reasoning problem amounts to solving a constraint-satisfaction problem: given restrictions on truth-value assignments imposed by the evidence, by the event axioms, and by persistence assumptions (discussed below), find a consistent truth assignment for every node in the graph. Figure 10.2 shows the same structural model with partial information about the initial state and a consistent assignment of truth values to the nodes. The assignment need not be unique—in the example, the initial value of M was assigned arbitrarily.

Arcs in the graph represent dependencies among node values as suggested in the truth tables in Figure 10.1. These describe the effects of events, the effects of not acting, and other dependencies among state variables. There are three types of dependencies (constraints), discussed in turn.

Causal constraints There are two sorts of causal constraints—the arrows linking events and propositions at proximate times—which describe an event's preconditions and its effects. These are equivalent to the event axioms, Equations (10.1)–(10.3). For example, the dependencies linking A and shoot enforce the constraints described in Equation (10.1) describing the event's immediate effects. The fact that there are only two arrows into the node representing $\mathsf{A}@t_2+\epsilon$ means that the variable's value can be determined (only) from the previous state of A, $\mathsf{A}@t_2$, along with information about whether shoot occurred successfully at t_2. The truth table for this variable, pictured in Figure 10.1 reflects the implicit assumption that no event other than shoot occurs between t_2 and $t_2 + \epsilon$.

Persistence constraints The arcs from a proposition at one time point to the same proposition at the next time point were not mentioned explicitly in the problem description. These are called *persistence constraints*, and are equivalent to logical *frame axioms*. Persistence constraints enforce the common-sense notion that a proposition will change state *only* if an event causes it to do so. In the deterministic framework it is difficult to reason about events that *might* have occurred but were not *known* to occur, thus the assumption is made that the known events are the *only* events that occur, and thus no state variable changes truth value over an interval $[t_i + \epsilon, t_{i+1}]$, regardless of how much time elapses. Thus the truth tables for the persistence constraints always indicate that proposition P is true at t_{i+1} if and only if it was true at $t_i + \epsilon$.

There is a second implicit assumption in the diagram, which is that at a time point t_i, where an event is known to occur, the known event is the *only* event that occurs at that instant. Thus A will be false at $t_2 + \epsilon$ if and only if shoot was successful in making it false, or if it was already false. No event other than shoot can occur at t_2 to change A's state.

There has been much research in the deterministic temporal reasoning literature on persistence constraints and the frame problem. This work, and its connection to probabilistic temporal reasoning, is discussed in Section 10.6.1.

Synchronic constraints Suppose that one observed over time that L was false whenever M was true. It might be convenient to note this observation explicitly in the graph, using an arc from M to L at every time point t. This is called a *synchronic* constraint, as it constrains the

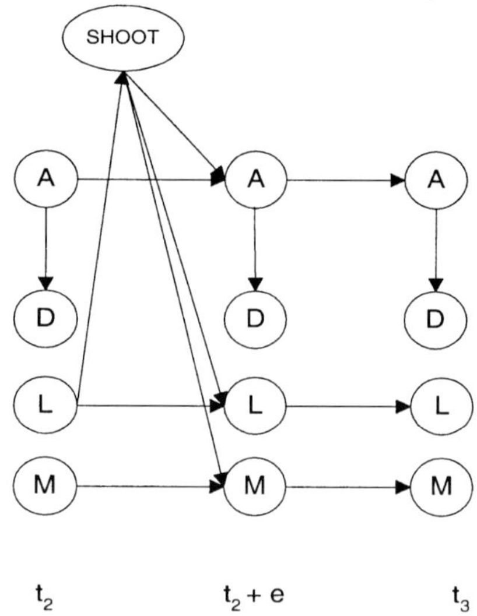

Figure 10.3: Syntactic synchronic constraints represent a definitional relationship between two propositions

values of two state variables at the same point in time. The causal and persistence constraints are *diachronic* constraints, as they relate the values of state variables at different time points.

Synchronic constraints are generally not formally necessary. For example, the relationship between M and L might be explained as follows:

1. initially M is always true
2. the only event that makes M true is shoot, which also makes L false
3. the only event that makes L true is load, but load never occurs after shoot occurs.

But all of these facts can be represented using diachronic constraints only—the synchronic constraints are redundant, though they might allow certain inferences to be made more efficiently. With redundancy also comes the possibility of contradiction: if an event were ever added that made M true without changing L, or if a load event ever occurred after a shoot, then the causal constraints would contradict the synchronic constraints.

Synchronic constraints are often used to represent simple syntactic *synonymy* or *antonymy* relationships: two propositions that *by definition* have the same or opposite states, and are included in the ontology simply for convenience. For example, we might introduce a state variable D, which is meant to be true if and only if A is false at the same time. This dependency can be enforced without explicit synchronic arcs in the graph, by ensuring that D and A are initially in opposite states, and that every action that makes A false makes D true, and vice versa. At best this method can be cumbersome, and subject to error. At worst it would be impossible to infer the relationship between A and D without the constraint, for example, if all that is known is that A is false at time t_4.

It may therefore be more convenient to represent the synchronic constraint between A and D explicitly. In Figure 10.3, D is given a special status as an antonym for A: its state is determined *only* by the state of A at the same time point. Causal and persistence axioms are allowed to refer to A directly, but not to D, thus avoiding the potential inconsistency noted above. A is called the *primitive* variable and D is called the *derived* variable [Lifschitz, 1987].

In most deterministic temporal reasoning literature, synchronic constraints representing simple syntactic relationships are treated specially in this way, and event-induced synchronic constraints are not handled at all, since they add no expressive power to the model and are a possible source of inconsistency.* Synchronic constraints are more common in the probabilistic temporal reasoning literature, and are discussed again in Section 10.4.1.

Summary When the nature and order of events is known, a temporal reasoning problem can be represented as a graph where the nodes represent temporally scoped state variables and events. The arcs represent causal relationships (diachronic or synchronic) between the variables. The graph in Figure 10.1 was constructed from a set of axioms characterizing the domain, and has the following significant features:

- Causal relationships between variables caused by known events (the causal constraints) are all mediated through the event itself, and are not reflected in synchronic relationships among the state variables.
- Each state variable "persists" independently: whether or not a variable V changes state in the interval $[t_i, t_j]$ never depends on the state of another variable W.
- Events occur independently: the occurrence or non-occurrence of an event at one time does not affect whether subsequent events occur, though it may affect whether a subsequent event *succeeds*.

We now turn to various ways in which deterministic models for temporal reasoning can be given a probabilistic semantics which allows reasoning about incomplete information, stochastic events, and noisy observation information.

10.3 Models for Probabilistic Temporal Reasoning

We will consider several models for building probabilistic versions of these dynamic scenarios. We begin with models like the one above where events or actions are represented explicitly in the graph, and where the timing of the events is known. We begin by exploring the case where there is uncertainty as to *what* event occurs at a particular time. As a special case this allows reasoning about an event that might or might not occur.

In this section we will consider a simpler version of the example: the only state variables are A and L, the possible events are load, shoot, and wait, events occur at times t_1 and t_2, and the temporal distance between t_1 and t_2 is known with certainty. Figure 10.4 shows the equivalent graphical model. It is identical in structure to the deterministic version, except

*See [Ginsberg and Smith, 1988a] for an exception: a formal system that allows synchronic and diachronic constraints to be mixed. They treat the case where blocking an air duct causes a room to become stuffy (a state variable), representing this as a synchronic constraint between blocked and stuffy.

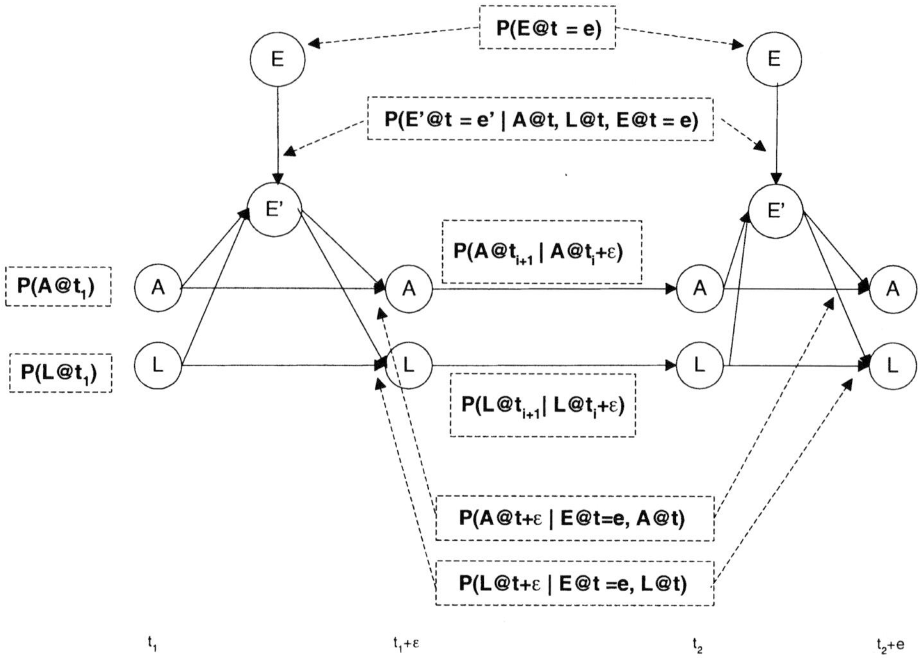

Figure 10.4: A probabilistic temporal model recording dependencies between events and states

for the additional event node E' (explained below), and the nature of the parameters noted on the figure analogous to the truth tables in Figure 10.1.
The main differences between this graph and the graph in Figure 10.1 are

- In Figure 10.4 there can be uncertainty as to *which* event occurred, so the event node is a random variable that ranges over all possible event types, whereas in Figure 10.1 the event type was fixed. In Figure 10.4 there are two nodes representing each event, a random variable representing which event occurred, and a second random variable representing that event's effects.
- Nodes in the graphs are assigned probabilities rather than truth values.
- The constraints on the arcs represent probabilistic dependencies rather than deterministic dependencies.

We will introduce the following uncertainty in the model:

- Initially (at t_1), A is true with probability 0.9 and L is true with probability 0.5
- The load event makes L true with probability 0.8. It never causes L to become false, but with probability 0.2 it changes nothing.

- If L is true when shoot occurs, then with probability 0.75 A and L both become false, and with probability 0.25 L becomes false but A remains unchanged. If L is false when shoot occurs, then with probability 1 the event changes nothing.
- L can spontaneously become false, with probability .001, when wait occurs.
- Although it is known that events occur only at times t_1 and t_2, there is uncertainty as to what event occurs at those times. At time t_1, load occurs with probability 0.8 and wait occurs with probability 0.2. At time t_2, shoot occurs with probability 0.8, load occurs with probability 0.1, and wait occurs with probability 0.1.

Let $\mathbf{P}(\mathsf{A}@t_i)$ be the probability that state variable A is true at time t_i given all available evidence and $\mathbf{P}(\mathsf{E}@t_i = e)$ be the probability that the event occurring at time t_i is the event e. The following model parameters are required:

- Probabilities describing the initial state of A and L: $\mathbf{P}(\mathsf{A}@t_1)$ and $\mathbf{P}(\mathsf{L}@t_1)$
- Probabilities describing which events occur: $\mathbf{P}(\mathsf{E}@t_i = e)$ for each i
- Probabilities describing the possible effects of an event that has occurred: $\mathbf{P}(\mathsf{E}'@t_1 = e' \mid \mathsf{E}@t_i = e)$
- Probabilities describing the immediate effects of the events on the state variables: $\mathbf{P}(\mathsf{A}@t_i + \epsilon \mid \mathsf{E}'@t_i = e', \mathsf{A}@t_i)$ and $\mathbf{P}(\mathsf{L}@t_i + \epsilon \mid \mathsf{E}'@t_i = e', \mathsf{L}@t_i)$
- Probabilities describing what happens to the state variables during the time interval $[t_1+\epsilon, t_2]$, an interval during which no event is known to occur: $\mathbf{P}(\mathsf{A}@t_{i+1} \mid \mathsf{A}@t_i+\epsilon)$ and $\mathbf{P}(\mathsf{L}@t_{i+1} \mid \mathsf{L}@t_i + \epsilon)$

10.3.1 Model structure

Each arc in the graph represents an explicit quantifiable probabilistic influence between the nodes it connects, for example that the value of $\mathsf{E}'@t$ directly affects the value of $\mathsf{L}@t + \epsilon$. The absence of arcs in the graph implies certain probabilistic *independencies*. For example, information about the state of $\mathsf{A}@t_1$ provides no additional information about the state of $\mathsf{L}@t_1$. The variables $\mathsf{A}@t_1 + \epsilon$ and $\mathsf{L}@t_1 + \epsilon$ are probabilistically dependent, since the value of E' $@t_1$ affects both, but become probabilistically independent if the value of $E@t_1$ is known*. It is again a significant feature of this model that there are no synchronic dependencies in the graph: all correlations between propositions at a single point in time, for example the relationship between $\mathsf{A}@t_1 + \epsilon$ and $\mathsf{L}@t_1 + \epsilon$, are caused by prior events.

Another significant feature of this model is that there is no way to represent dependencies over the occurrences of events, e.g. that shoot is more likely to occur at t_2 provided that load occurred at t_1† Section 10.4 will discuss the case where the distribution over event occurrences is state dependent.

*These relationships depend on there being no evidence about temporally subsequent nodes in the graph. See [Cowell *et al.*, 1999], [Pearl, 1988] or [Charniak, 1991] for information about the exact set of independencies implied by this graph structure.

†It is the case, however, that information about what event occurred at t_1 along with information about what is true at $t_2 + \epsilon$ *does* affect the posterior distribution over the event that occurred at t_2.

10.3.2 Model parameters

In the previous section, the inference problem was defined as that of finding an assignment of truth values to every node in the graph, consistent with the explicit constraints. In the probabilistic case the problem is to construct a probability distribution over all nodes in the graph—the state of A and L at t_1, $t_1+\epsilon$, t_2, and $t_2+\epsilon$, and the value of E and E' at t_1 and t_2, again consistent with the explicit probabilistic constraints and any available evidence. The question then arises: what probabilistic constraints are necessary to ensure a consistent and unique distribution exists?

Fundamental results from the general theory of probabilistic graphical models [Pearl, 1988] guarantee that the following parameters are necessary and sufficient to define a unique probability distribution over the nodes:

- Marginal (unconditional) probabilities for those nodes without parents: **P**(A@t_1) and **P**(L@t_2), and $\mathbf{P}(E@t_1 = e)$.
- A conditional probability table for each non-parent node conditioned on all possible values of its immediate parents. For example, the probability that A is true at $t_1 + \epsilon$ must be specified for all six combinations of the possible values for $E@t_1$ (load, shoot, wait) and the possible values of A@t_1 (True, False).

We discuss each class of parameters in turn.

Initial probabilities

Marginal probabilities for **P**(A@t_1) and **P**(L@t_1) are provided under the assumption that the values of these variables are probabilistically independent. Thus it is impossible to state that 85% of the time both A and L will initially be true, but 15% of the time they will both be false. This is due to our assumption that events cause all correlations. If such dependencies need to be represented, an "initial event" can be defined that induces the desired dependency.

Events and their effects

We reason about the effects of events in three stages:

- what event occurred
- what effects did the event have, given that it occurred
- what is the new state, given those effects

The first is determined by the marginal probability **P**(E@t_i = e). Note the assumption that this distribution is state independent. For the example, we have the following probabilities from the problem statement:

e	t_1	t_2
load	0.8	0.1
shoot	0.0	0.8
wait	0.2	0.1

The deterministic event representation was based on the idea of a *precondition*: if the event's precondition was true when it occurred, it was said to have *succeeded*, and it effected state changes. The effects of an event with a false precondition was not defined or the event was implicitly assumed to have no effects. In the present model, the concept of precondition and success is replaced by a more general notion of an event's effects depending on *context* (the prevailing state at the time of occurrence). There is no concept of a precondition: an event can occur under any circumstances, but its effects will depend on the context, and must be specified for all contexts.

Consider shoot for example, which was described above as having three possible outcomes depending on whether L is true. This event can be viewed as three "sub-events" shoot − 1, shoot − 2, and shoot − 3, each analogous to a deterministic event:

Event	Context	Probability	Effects
shoot − 1	L	0.75	-A, -L
shoot − 2	L	0.25	-L
shoot − 3	¬L	1.00	

where +A means that the event causes A to be true regardless of its previous state, −A means that the event causes A to be false, and the absence of A in the effects list means that the event leaves A's state unchanged.

Thus the event shoot occurs exogenously, but there can still be uncertainty as to which of shoot-1, shoot-2, and shoot-3 occurs, and that uncertainty is context dependent. These are the probabilities $\mathbf{P}(\mathsf{E}'@t_i = e^i \mid \mathsf{E}@t = e, \mathcal{S}@t)$ where $\mathcal{S}$ is some subset of the state variables.

Once the nature of the sub-event is known, the resulting state $\mathcal{S}@t+\epsilon$ is determined with certainty by the sub-event's list of effects. In other words, the quantity $\mathbf{P}(\mathcal{S}@t+\epsilon \mid E'@t = e', \mathcal{S}@t)$ is deterministic, analogous to the truth tables in Figure 10.1. Therefore the state update is performed according to the following formula:

$$\mathbf{P}(\mathcal{S}@t_i + \epsilon \mid E'@t_i = e^i, \mathcal{S}@t_i)\mathbf{P}(E'@t_i = e^i \mid \mathcal{S}@t_i, E@t_i = e)\mathbf{P}(E@t_i = e)$$

As in the deterministic case it is assumed that ϵ is short enough that no other event occurs in the interval $[t, t+\epsilon]$, though probabilistic information about simultaneous events could easily be added to the model.

Alternative event models This event model ("probabilistic STRIPS operators" or PSOs) was introduced in [Hanks, 1990], and adopted in the design of the Buridan probabilistic planner [Kushmerick *et al.*, 1995]. It is well suited to situations in which events tend to change the state of several variables simultaneously, but suffers from the complexity of specifying events and sub-events, and the fact that the event probabilities are context dependent.

An alternative model works directly with context-independent events. The event probability measures only the probability that shoot occurs rather than wait or load, and does not measure the probability that shoot-1 occurs given shoot, for example. This moves the event's context dependence into the arcs governing how state variables change as a result of the event. Figure 10.5 shows two possible models. The leftmost is the PSO model described above, the second is a model that treats events as atomic and context independent. The additional complexity in the second model arises as a result of the fact that shoot tends either to change both A and L simultaneously, or to leave both unchanged. Thus load's state at $t+\epsilon$

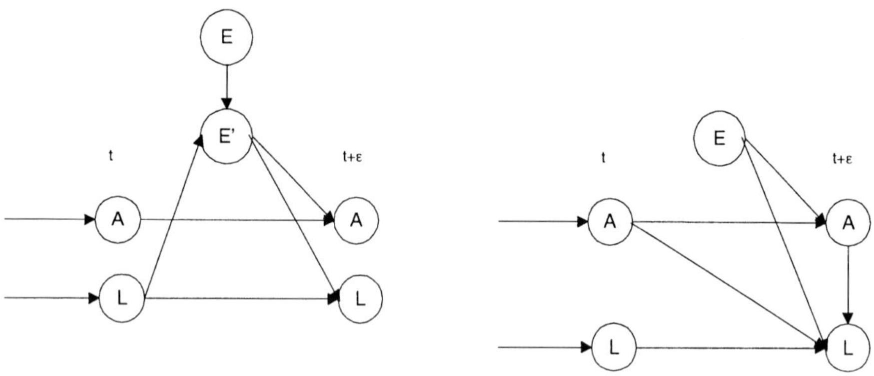

Figure 10.5: Alternative graphical models for representing the effects of events

depends on its prior state, whether or not shoot occurred, and whether A *changed state* from true to false (since if it did, load must have changed too). The synchronic arc from A to L is to allow reasoning about whether or not A changed state as a result of the event.

There are many different representations for events (see [Boutilier *et al.*, 1995b] for one alternative). Since most of them are formally equivalent [Littman, 1997], the choice of a particular model would be made for reasons of parsimony or convenience of elicitation. See [Boutilier *et al.*, 1995a] for a more extensive comparison of event models.

"Persistence" probabilities

The last set of parameters describe the likelihood of state changes between the times events are known to occur. They are $\mathbf{P}(\mathsf{P}@t_{i+1} \mid \mathsf{P}@t_i + \epsilon)$ and $\mathbf{P}(\mathsf{P}@t_{i+1} \mid \neg\mathsf{P}@t_i + \epsilon)$, for each state variable P and each event time t_i. Again note that these dependencies are isolated to single propositions: knowing the state of L at t_i or whether L changes state between t_i and t_{i+1} does not affect the likelihood that A changes state in that interval of time. If there was a source of change known to change both simultaneously, it would have to be modeled as an explicit event that might or might not occur during the interval.

In the deterministic case these constraints were handled using either a monotonic or nonmonotonic closure axiom: the axiom(s) state that the known events are the only events, thus no proposition changes state between $t_i + \epsilon$ and t_{i+1}. In the probabilistic case the model accounts for the possibility that unknown events can occur during these intervals, thus there should be *some* likelihood that P changes state during $[t_i + \epsilon, t_{i+1}]$, and furthermore that probability will typically depend at least on the interval's duration.

Persistence probabilities are typically specified using *survival functions*, which express the probability of a state-changing event occurring within an interval $[t, t + \delta]$ [Dean and Kanazawa, 1989]. These functions are often used as follows to express the persistence probabilities:

$$\begin{aligned} \mathbf{P}(\mathsf{P}@t + \delta \mid \mathsf{P}@t) &= \epsilon^{-\alpha\delta} \\ \mathbf{P}(\mathsf{P}@t + \delta \mid \neg\mathsf{P}@t) &= \epsilon^{-\beta\delta} \end{aligned}$$

where $\alpha, \beta > 0$, α measures the rate at which P will "spontaneously" become false and β

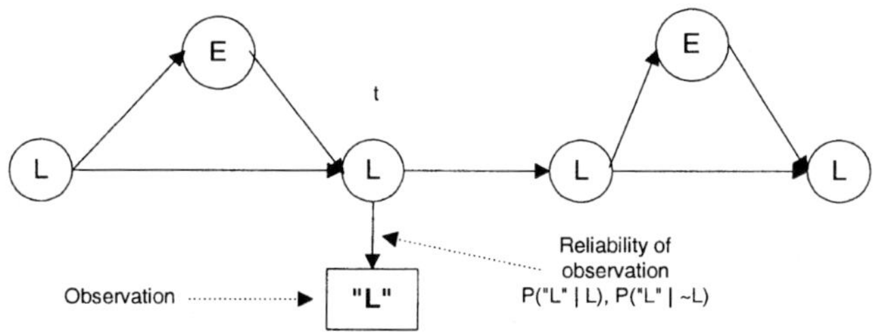

Figure 10.6: Adding evidence to the probabilistic graphical model

measures the rate at which P will "spontaneously" become true.

One problem with using this functional form is that it confuses information about a state *change* with information about the proposition's *new state*. That is, one might be certain that the proposition will change state at least once during an a long interval, but still might be unsure as to what its eventual state will be, as it might change several times.

In some cases the difference is unimportant: knowing that A changes state from true to false implies knowledge about its state at the end of the interval, since the probability of a state change back to true is 0.

In contrast, consider the problem of predicting whether or not a pet will be in a particular room. Over a long interval of time it is virtually certain that the pet will leave the room, but it might well return and leave several times over a long interval $[t, t+\delta]$, thus certainty about a state change does not amount to certainty about the new state, and the simple survivor function model will be inappropriate for reasoning about situations characterized by large values for δ.

This particular form of the survivor function is still appropriate if δ is small enough that the probability of a *second* state change in the interval is improbable. In that case, information about the state change *is* equivalent to information about the new state. In the present model, however, the δ parameter represents temporal spacing between known events, and is not under our control, thus survivor functions of the above form might not be appropriate. Section 10.3.5 discusses two potential solutions to the problem: instantiating the model at more time points so the maximum δ makes the survivor model appropriate, and adopting a variant of the survivor model that explicitly differentiates between the probability of state changes and the proposition's state conditioned on the fact that it changed one or more times.

10.3.3 Evidence

We have not yet discussed the details of how to incorporate evidence about what facts are true or what events occurred. In the deterministic model, evidence took the form of knowing the value of various propositions at various points in time: the values of various nodes could be constrained to be true or false (see Figure 10.2). Evidence can likewise be placed on nodes in the probabilistic graphical model, with the added feature that information can be uncertain: the relationship between the evidence and the node's value is probabilistic rather than being limited to a deterministic setting of the node's value.

Figure 10.6 shows a case where evidence is received about the state of L at time t. As in Figure 10.2, an additional node is used to incorporate evidence into the graph, and the link between it and L's actual state quantifies the relationship between the evidence and L's actual state. In this model, the relationship between state and observation is state independent, though this assumption could easily be relaxed.

Two parameters are required to quantify this relationship $\mathbf{P}(\text{"L"}@t \mid \mathsf{L}@t)$ and $\mathbf{P}(\text{"L"}@t \mid \neg\mathsf{L}@t)$, where "L" represents the *observation* that L was true at t, which might or might not reflect its true state at that time. These parameters reflect the probability that the evidence would have been observed assuming that L was true and false, respectively. The value of the "L" node can be set to true—the fact that the observation *was made* is definitely true—and the propagation algorithms take care of the rest.

10.3.4 Inference

We have now discussed all parameters required to complete the model, and note that standard methods for probabilistic inference in graphical models [Pearl, 1988; Dawid, 1992] can be applied, which calculates probabilities for all variables and events at all points in time (i.e. for all nodes in the graph). These algorithms are "bi-directional" in that they consider the effect of forward causation (the effect of evidence on subsequent variables, mediated by the causal rules), and backward explanation (the effect of evidence on prior variables, again mediated by the rules). Using standard algorithms can be computationally expensive, however, and Section 10.5 discusses various methods for performing the inference efficiently.

10.3.5 Constructing the model

Most schemes for probabilistic temporal reasoning provide some method for constructing an appropriate network from model fragments representing the causal influences, event probabilities, and persistence probabilities. These pieces can be network fragments [Dean and Kanazawa, 1989], symbolic rules [Hanks and McDermott, 1994], or statements in a logic program database [Ngo *et al.*, 1995].

Since the model intersperses possible event occurrences with persistence intervals, the question arises as to which time points should appear explicitly in the graph. Not placing an event node at time t amounts to assigning a probability of zero to the occurrence of an event at that time, which could result in inaccurate predictions. On the other hand, the time required for the inference task grows exponentially with the number of nodes in the worst case [Cooper, 1990] is proportional to the size of the graph, so more nodes means costlier inference. This issue is particularly important when information about the occurrence of events is vague—if at *most* time points there is *some* probability that *some* event might occur.

A second consideration in constructing the graph was noted in Section 10.3.2: if survival functions are used for the persistence probabilities, and if there is the possibility of a proposition changing state more than once, then the interval between explicit events must be chosen so the probability of a second state change in the persistence interval is sufficiently small.

The most common approach to constructing the graph, [Dean and Kanazawa, 1989] for example, is to instantiate it on a fixed time grid. A fixed time duration dt is chosen, and the model is instantiated at regular time points $t_1,\ t_1 + \mathsf{dt},\ t_1 + 2\mathsf{dt},\ \ldots$ where t_1 is the first known time point: the time at which the first known event occurs, where the initial conditions are known, or the earliest time point at which temporal information is desired.

This approach is simple, and if dt is chosen to be sufficiently small, will lead to an accurate predictive model. The problem with this approach is mainly computational: dt must be chosen to satisfy the single-state-change assumptions for the *fastest-changing* state variable, and the model must be instantiated for all state variables at all time points, not just those temporally close to the occurrence of known events. This can lead to huge graphs containing long intervals of time where most or all of the state variables are extremely unlikely to change values. A projection or explanation algorithm must nonetheless compute probabilities for all events and all state variables at all time points.

In cases where there is a good model of when events occur, one might be able to instantiate event nodes only at times where events are likely to occur. The danger is that exponential survivor functions may be inappropriate given the longer interval between event instances.

An alternative model [Hanks and McDermott, 1994] instantiates the graph only at times when events are likely to occur, say $\{t_1, t_2, \ldots, t_n\}$, which may be widely separated and irregularly spaced. Then two sets of persistence parameters are provided:

- The probability that a state variable P will undergo *at least one* state change in the interval $[t_i, t_{i+1}]$. This parameter depends only on $|t_{i+1} - t_i|$ (the time elapsed between t_i and t_{i+1}), and an exponential function is often appropriate.
- The probability that P will be true at t_{i+1} *provided* it changed state in the interval $[t_i, t_{i+1}]$.

This model has the advantage of parsimony, and also reflects a common-sense notion that many propositions have a "default" probability we can rely on when our explicit causal model breaks down. So the default probability for A is 0—if it changes state at all it will be to false, and will remain at false. On the other hand, the pet-prediction problem discussed in Section 10.3.2 is handled properly in that if the pet is assumed to move once, its position is predicted by the default probability, which is duration-independent.

Observation-based instantiation In some situations instantiation of the graph will be dictated by the environment itself. The model developed in [Nicholson and Brady, 1994] is an explicit-event model designed to monitor the location of moving objects. State variables store the objects' predicted position and heading, and the events correspond to reports from the sensors that an object has moved from one region to another. Thus the events *indicate* rather than *initiate* change, and are observed asynchronously. In the paper the assumption is made that the probability of a change in position over an interval is independent of the length of the interval, thus obviating the need for reasoning about unpredicted changes across irregularly spaced intervals. Work reported in [Goodwin *et al.*, 1994] is similar in that its events are actually observations of the state rather than change-producing occurrences. The work by Goodwin is oriented toward reasoning about how long propositions tend to persist, and does not involve a predictive model of how and when state variables might change state.

10.3.6 Summary

We have now developed a model for temporal reasoning that admits uncertainty about the initial state, about the effects of events, about the reliability of evidence, and about how the system changes due to unmodelled events that might occur over time. Inference methods are available to solve standard prediction and explanation problems.

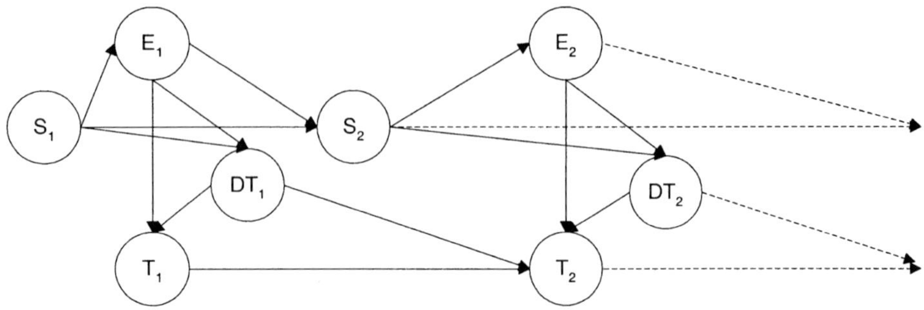

Figure 10.7: In a semi-Markov model the event times are also random variable

We now discuss two relaxations to the model: cases in which there is a probabilistic model concerning the timing of events, and cases in which the system's state can influence the nature of subsequent events.

10.4 Probabilistic Event Timings and Endogenous Change

The work presented above assumed that although the exact nature of events was uncertain, their timing was known. A common relaxation of this model is to view the system as a *semi-Markov* process, in which the times at which events occur are also modeled as random variables. The models considered above were simple Markov processes: the system's current state is sufficient to predict (probabilistically) the system's next state, but the transition *time* is deterministic and instantaneous. A semi-Markov process assumes that both the nature of and the elapsed time to transition are unknown, but can be predicted probabilistically from the current state.

Semi-Markov processes are also amenable to graphical representations, though with increased complexity (Figure 10.7). S_i is the system's state when the ith event occurs, E_i is the event that occurs, T_i is the time at which the ith event occurs, and DT_i is the elapsed time between the ith and $(i+1)^{st}$ events. In this model (similar to one proposed in [Berzuini *et al.*, 1989]), both the time at which the ith event occurred (T_i) and the transition time of the ith event (DT_i) are represented explicitly, and the current state and the nature of the next event are sufficient to predict its duration.

An alternative temporal model that was proposed in [Berzuini *et al.*, 1989] and similarly in [Kanazawa, 1991] changes the interpretation of nodes in the graph. Instead of being random variables of the form P@t ("P is true at t") with range {true, false}, the nodes are taken to be the *times* at which events occur (random variables that range over the reals), so a node might then represent "the time at which P becomes true."

Instantaneous events are represented as a single node in the graph `occur(E)`, and facts (fluents) that hold over an interval of time are represented by instants representing when they begin and cease to be true along with a "range" node representing the interval of time over which they persist. Figure 10.8 shows an example where Q is known to be true at $t = 0$, event E_1 occurs making Q false and P true, followed by E_2 which makes P false.

This representation makes it easy to determine whether a particular variable is true at a

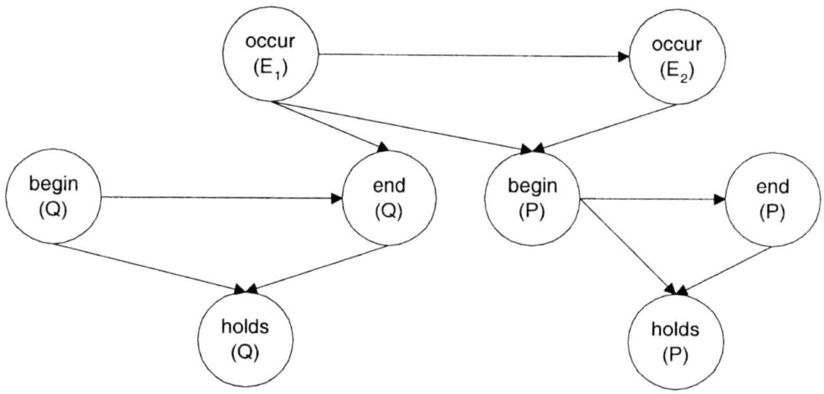

Figure 10.8: The "network of dates" model represents events and states implicitly but the time of occurrence explicitly

point in time, but it can be expensive to discover whether *combinations* of variables are true simultaneously (as must commonly be done in establishing the context needed to predict an event's effects). Also, neither Berzuini nor Kanazawa explain how the framework handles variables that change state several times over the course of a sequence of events, which is the central to the temporal reasoning problems commonly discussed in the literature.

The hidden Markov model framework has been successfully applied in contexts such as these. See, for example, [Ghahramani and Jordan, 1996] and [Smyth *et al.*, 1997]. There has also been recent work Bayesian analysis of hidden semi-Markov models [Scott, 2002].

Endogenous change

Berzuini addresses another problem, which is that the timing of one event can affect whether or not a subsequent event occurs. For example, a pump might or might not burn out (an event) depending on whether or not it first runs dry (another event), which in turn depends on whether a "refill" event occurs before the "runs dry" event. This sort of situation is not handled well by the models developed in Section 10.3, where the basic event probabilities are exogenous and state independent. Berzuini develops a theory whereby one event can *inhibit* the occurrence of a subsequent "potential" event, an event that might or might not occur. Non-occurrence is handled simply by letting its time of occurrence be infinitely large.

Event inhibition is just one aspect of a larger problem, which is that the system's state can affect the occurrence, nature, and timing of subsequent events. This problem is generally called *endogenous change*, as the system's state can endogenously cause changes whereas in the models discussed above, all change is effected by events that occur exogenously—they are specified externally and their occurrence is not affected by the system's state.

The probabilistic model developed in this work can be extended to an endogenous-change model simply by allowing event-occurrence and persistence probabilities to depend on the state as well. The main problem is how to build and instantiate models of this sort: how and when should the model be instantiated to capture changes in state caused by endogenous events?

It is common to view the system's endogenous change as being driven by a set of interacting *processes* which eventually will cause a state change [Barahona, 1994; Hanks *et al.*, 1995]. Taking an example from the latter source, consider a medical trauma case where the patient has suffered a blow to the head and to the abdominal cavity. These are both exogenous events, but they both initiate endogenous change. The former causes the brain to begin to swell, which if left unchecked will lead to dilated pupils and eventually to loss of consciousness. The latter might cause internal bleeding, which will quickly cause a drop in blood pressure, light headedness, and eventually will also cause loss of consciousness. Administering fluids will tend to slow this process.

The next endogenous event might therefore be a change in state of the pupils, or the blood pressure, followed by another endogenous change if consciousness is lost. The fact that two forces lead to loss of consciousness might or might not make it occur sooner. And interventions (exogenous events) could change the nature of the change as well.

There are two main problems associated with reasoning about endogenous change: how to build the endogenous model, and how to make predictions efficiently. [Barahona, 1994] introduces model-building techniques based on ideas from qualitative physics, and a simulation technique called *interval constraining*. In [Hanks *et al.*, 1995] a system is presented where the endogenous model is built by aggregating sub-models for the various forces acting on the system. The inference technique, based on *sequential imputation*, is discussed in Section 10.5. [Aliferis and Cooper, 1996] develop a formalism called Modifiable Temporal Belief Networks that allows expressing endogenous causal mechanisms through an extension to standard temporal Bayesian networks; they do not discuss inference algorithms.

10.4.1 Implicit event models

The models considered to this point have assumed that the source of change in the system, the modeled events, could be predicted or observed, and their effects on the system assessed accurately. This is consistent with the deterministic temporal reasoning literature, and appropriate for most planning and control applications.

In contrast, consider a case where observable exogenous interventions are rare, but one is allowed to observe all or part of the system state at various points in time. Medical scenarios are good examples, since exogenous events (interventions) are rare relative to the significant unobserved endogenous events that occur. In this case the explicit-event model may not be adequate to reason about the system, since so little information about the occurrence or effects of events is available.

An implicit-event model also depicts the system at various points in time, but there are no intervening causal events to provide the structure for predicting change. One primary difference between explicit- and implicit-event models is the role played by synchronic constraints (probabilistic dependencies among variables at a single point in time). While these dependencies are ubiquitous in real systems, it was unnecessary to represent them explicitly in the explicit-event models developed above, since it was reasonable to assume that all synchronic dependencies were caused by the modelled events. In implicit-event models, the absence of events means that observed synchronic dependencies must be noted explicitly in the model.

Figure 10.9 compares an abstract explicit-event model (a) with an implicit-event model (b). In the implicit-event case we see a sequence of static (synchronic) probabilistic models representing the system state at points of observation, connected by some number of

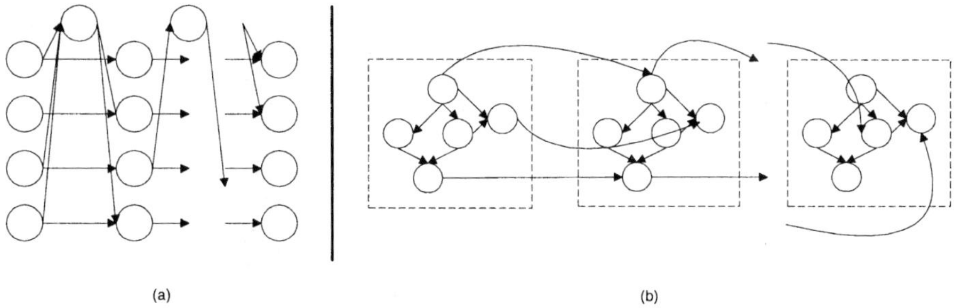

Figure 10.9: Explicit-event and implicit-event models have fundamentally different structure

diachronic constraints. Two main questions thus arise:

- What should the synchronic model look like at various points in time, and in particular should the synchronic model be the *same* at every time point?
- What diachronic constraints should be added to connect the static models, and in particular should the pattern of diachronic connections be the same at every time point?

The work presented in [Provan, 1993] is an example of how implicit-event models are built. The paper presents a dynamic model for diagnosing acute abdominal pain, which is based primarily on a static model constructed by a domain expert. The static model is duplicated at various time slices, presumably including those in which observations about the patient's state are made. There is no procedure presented for determining which diachronic arcs should be included in the model. The paper points out that models of this sort can be too big to support efficient inference, and presents several techniques for reducing the model's size. As such, it answers neither of the questions posed above.

Another example of an implicit-event model is presented in [Dagum and Galper, 1993], designed to predict sleep-apnea episodes. The input in this work is a sequence of 34,000 data points representing a patient's state measured at closely spaced regular time intervals. Each data point consists of four readings: heart rate, chest volume, blood oxygen concentration, and sleep state. The problem is to predict the onset of sleep apnea before it occurs.

This problem is an interesting contrast to the explicit-event models studied above, in that no explicit information about events is available and the state information is insufficient to build an effective process model, but large amounts of observational data are available.

In this case a k-stage temporal model—both synchronic and diachronic components—is learned from the observational data*, where k is a user-supplied parameter.

The value of state variable X_i at time t is then predicted by combining the value predicted by the diachronic model with the value predicted by the synchronic model. If $\pi(X_{it})$ is the set of all synchronic dependencies involving X_i and $\theta(X_{it})$ is the set of all diachronic dependencies involving X_i, then the value of X_{it} is computed according to the formula:

$$\mathbf{P}(X_{it} \mid \pi(X_{it}), \theta(X_{it})) = (1 - \alpha_{it})\mathbf{P}(X_{it} \mid \pi(X_{it})) + \alpha_{it}\mathbf{P}(X_{it} \mid \theta(X_{it}))$$

*The paper also alludes to "refining the model with knowledge of cardiovascular and respiratory physiology, during the process of model fitting and diagnostic checking," but does not explain this refinement process.

where α_{it} determines how strongly the new prediction depends on prior information mediated by the diachronic model as opposed to current information mediated by the synchronic model. Although α is time dependent, the paper does not mention how it might vary over time.

Summary At this point in time there is a stark contrast between temporal reasoning work based on explicit-event versus implicit-event models. The former is mainly concerned with building probabilistic models from more primitive components (rules, model fragments, logical axioms) that represent a causal or functional model of the system. The key issues here are what form the primitives take, and how they are pieced together to produce an accurate and efficient predictive model of the domain. In contrast, the implicit-event work has been oriented more toward providing special-purpose solutions to particular problems, and toward developing techniques to aid a human analyst in constructing these special-purpose models from data. There is less emphasis on causal or process models, and on automated model construction. In the current literature on implicit-event models, there is no generally satisfactory answer to the two questions posed at the beginning of this section—what should the synchronic model look like, and what diachronic constraints are appropriate—particularly regarding how the diachronic part of the model is built.

10.5 Inference Methods for Probabilistic Temporal Models

As we mentioned in Section 10.3.4, standard algorithms for probabilistic inference in graphical models apply directly to the kinds of models we have been discussing–see, for example, [Jensen, 2001], [Pearl, 1988], [Cowell *et al.*, 1999], or [Dawid, 1992]. However, as modeling progresses temporally, inference becomes increasingly intractable.

10.5.1 Adaptations to standard propagation algorithms

A number of authors have described variants on the standard algorithms that take advantage of the temporal nature of the models–key references include [Kjaerulff, 1994], [Provan, 1993], and [Dagum and Galper, 1993]. Though these references differ somewhat in their specific implementations, the essential idea is to maintain a model "window" containing a modest number of time slices. Computations in this window are carried out using standard algorithms; as time progresses, the window moves forward, relying on the Markov properties of the model–the past is conditionally independent of the future given the present–to maintain inferential veracity. This windowing idea enables standard algorithms to be applied to infinitely large models.

Here we sketch the elements of Kjaerulff's algorithm using a simple example. Figure 10.10 shows a stochastic temporal model with six time slices labeled one to six. Kjaerulff's algorithm decomposes the basic model into zero or more backward smoothing models each focusing on a single time slice, a window model containing one or more time slices, and a forecast model containing zero or more time slices. Figure 10.11 shows a decomposition for our simple example. Note that the forecast model contains not only time slices five and six, but also the vertices from time slice four required to render slices five and six conditionally independent of the remainder of the model. Similarly, the backward smoothing models contain the vertices required to render them conditionally independent of future models.

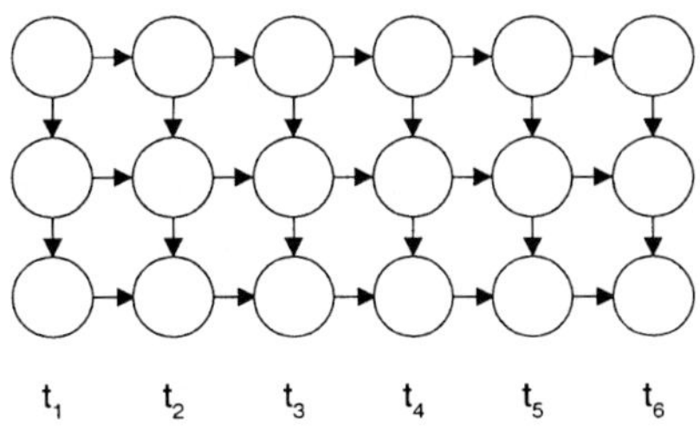

Figure 10.10: A simple dynamic belief network on a fixed time grid

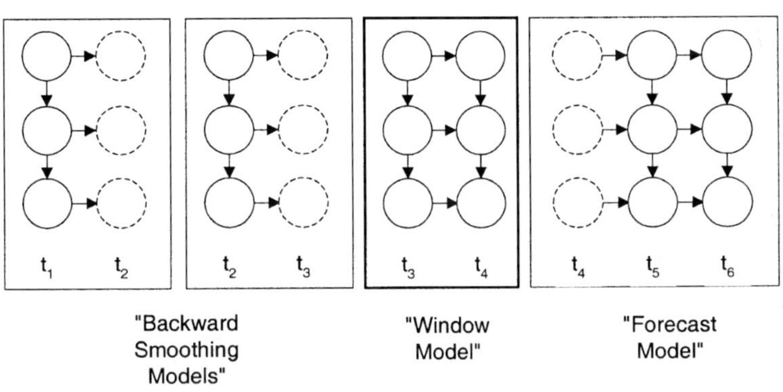

Figure 10.11: The Simple Dynamic Belief Network Decomposed

The algorithm ensures that the window model has absorbed all evidence from previous time slices; inference within the window them uses standard algorithms to further condition on evidence pertaining to the time slices within the window. "Backward smoothing" is a process whereby evidence is passed backwards from the window to the previous time slices using a message passing approach. "Forecasting" is carried out using a Monte Carlo algorithm.

Perhaps the most challenging aspect of Kjaerulff's algorithm involves moving the window. This he accomplishes by first expanding the model and the window, and then reducing the window and dispatching some time slices from the window to the backward smoothing model. Thus, window expansion by, say, k new time slices consists of (a) adding k new consecutive time slices to the forecast model, (b) moving the k oldest time slices of the forecast model to the time window, and (c) "compiling"* the newly expanded window. Window reduction involves elimination of vertices from the window and an updating of the remaining probability to reflect evidence from the eliminated variables–see [Kjaerulff, 1994] for details. We note that there are close connections between Kjaerulff's algorithm and the forwards-backwards algorithm used in Hidden Markov Modeling [Smyth *et al.*, 1997].

Unfortunately, the computations involved in window expansion and reduction, as well as the computations required within the window can quickly become intractable. Several authors have proposed approximate inference algorithms - see, for example, [Boyen and Koller, 1998] or [Ghahramani and Jordan, 1996]. Recently the stochastic simulation approach has attracted considerable attention and we discuss this next.

10.5.2 Stochastic simulation

Stochastic simulation methods† for temporal models provide considerable flexibility and apply to very general classes of dynamic models. The state-of-the-art has progressed rapidly in recent years and we refer the reader to [Doucet *et al.*, 2001] for a comprehensive treatment. In what follows, we draw heavily on [Liu and Chen, 1998]. [Kanazawa *et al.*, 1995] also provide an overview but less general in scope. We note that while our focus in this Chapter is on probabilistic inference for stochastic temporal models, the methods described here also apply to statistical learning for temporal models, as well as applications such as protein structures simulation, genetics, and combinatorial optimization. We start with a general definition:

Definition 10.5.1. *A sequence of evolving probability distributions* $\pi_t(\mathbf{x_t})$, *indexed by discrete time* $t = 0, 1, 2, \ldots$, *is called a* probabilistic dynamic system.

The state variable $\mathbf{x}_t$ can evolve in several ways but generally in what we consider $\mathbf{x}_t$ will increase in dimension over time, i.e., $\mathbf{x}_{t+1} = (\mathbf{x}_t, x_{t+1})$, where x_{t+1} can be a multidimensional component. [Liu and Chen, 1998] describe three generic tasks in systems such as these: (a) prediction: $\pi_t(x_{t+1} \mid \mathbf{x}_t)$; (b) updating: $\pi_{t+1}(\mathbf{x}_t)$ (i.e., updating previous states given new information); and (c) new estimation: $\pi_{t+1}(x_{t+1})$ (i.e., what we can say about x_{t+1} in the light of new information)?

The models described in this Chapter fit into this general framework. More specifically they are *State Space Models*. Such models comprise two parts: (1) the observation equation,

*The standard Lauritzen-Spiegelhalter algorithm involves "moralization" and triangulation of the DAG to create an undirected hypergraph in which computations take place. This process (which is NP-hard) is often called compilation.

†Also known as Monte Carlo methods.

which can be formulated as $y_t \sim f_t(\cdot \mid x_t, \phi)$; and (2) the state equation, $x_t \sim q_y(\cdot \mid x_{t-1}, \theta)$. The y_t are observations and the x_t are the observed or unobserved states. Of interest at any time t is the posterior distribution of $\mathbf{x}_t \equiv (\phi, \theta, x_1, \ldots, x_t)$. Hence the target distribution at time t is:

$$\pi_t(\mathbf{x}_t) = p(\phi, \theta, x_1, \ldots, x_t \mid \mathbf{y}_t) \propto p(\theta, \phi) \prod_{s=1}^{t} f_s(y_s \mid x_s, \phi) q_s(x_s \mid x_{s-1}, \theta).$$

These models arise in, for example, signal processing, speech recognition, multi-target tracking problems, computer vision, DNA sequence analysis, and financial stochastic volatility models.

Simple Monte Carlo methods for dynamic systems such as these require, for each time t, random samples drawn from $\pi_t(\mathbf{x}_t)$. Many applications require more general schemes such as importance sampling. Even then, most published methods assume that all of the random draws obtained at time t are discarded when the system evolves from π_t to π_{t+1}. *Sequential* Monte Carlo methods, on the other hand, "re-use" the samples obtained at time t to help construct random samples at time $t+1$, and offer considerable computational efficiencies. The basic idea dates back at least to [Hendry and Richard, 1990]. See also [Kong *et al.*, 1994] and [Berzuini *et al.*, 1997]. Here we reproduce the general formulation of [Liu and Chen, 1998]. We begin with a definition:

Definition 10.5.2. *A set of random draws and weights* $(x^{(j)}, w^{(j)}), j = 1, 2, \ldots$ *is said to be* properly weighted *with respect to* π *if:*

$$\lim_{m \to \infty} \frac{\sum_{j=1}^{m} h(x^{(j)}) w^{(j)}}{\sum_{j=1}^{m} w^{(j)}} = E_\pi(h(X))$$

for any integrable function h.

The basic idea here is that we can come up with very general schemes for sampling x_t's and associated weights, so long as the weighted average of these x's is the same as the average of x's drawn from the correct distribution (i.e., π). In particular, we do not have to draw the x_t's from π_t, but instead can draw them from a more convenient distribution, say g_t. Liu and Wong's Sequential Importance Sampling (SIS) proceeds as follows:

Let $S_t = \{\mathbf{x}_t^{(j)}, j = 1, \ldots, m\}$ denote a set of random draws that are properly weighted by the set of weights $W_t = \{\mathbf{w}_t^{(j)}, j = 1, \ldots, m\}$ with respect to π_t. Let H_{t+1} denote the sample space of X_{t+1}, and let g_{t+1} be a trial distribution. Then the SIS procedure consists of recursive applications of the following SIS steps. For $j = 1, \ldots, m$,

(A) Draw $X_{t+1} = x_{t+1}^{(j)}$ from $g_{t+1}(x_{t+1} \mid \mathbf{x}_t^{(j)})$; attach it to $\mathbf{x}_t^{(j)}$ to form $\mathbf{x}_{t+1} = (\mathbf{x}_t^{(j)}, x_{t+1}^{(j)})$.

(B) Compute

$$u_{t+1}^{(j)} = \frac{\pi_{t+1}(\mathbf{x}_{t+1}^{(j)})}{\pi_t(\mathbf{x}_t^{(j)}) g_{t+1}(x_{t+1}^{(j)} \mid \mathbf{x}_t^{(j)})}$$

and let $w_{t+1}^{(j)} = u_{t+1}^{(j)} w_t^{(j)}$.

It is easy to show that $(\mathbf{x}_{t+1}^{(j)}, w_{t+1}^{(j)})$ is a properly weighted sample of π_{t+1}.

For State Space models with known (ϕ, θ), Liu and Chen suggest the following trial distribution:

$$g_{t+1}(x_{t+1} \mid \mathbf{x}_t) \propto f_{t+1}(y_{t+1} \mid x_{t+1}, \phi) q_{t+1}(x_{t+1} \mid x_t, \theta)$$

with

$$u_{t+1} = \int f_{t+1}(y_{t+1} \mid x_{t+1}, \phi) q_{t+1}(x_{t+1} \mid x_t, \theta) dx_{t+1}.$$

Hanks et. al. [Hanks *et al.*, 1995] describe a particular implementation of this scheme, called *sequential imputation*. Other choices of g are possible - see, for example, [Berzuini *et al.*, 1997]. [Liu and Chen, 1998] describe various elaborations of the basic scheme including re-sampling steps and *Local SIS* and go on to describe a generic Monte Carlo algorithm for probabilistic dynamic system. Recent work on these so-called "particle filters" by Gilks and Berzuini [Gilks and Berzuini, 2001] is especially ingenious.

In summary, stochastic simulation methods apply to very general classes of models and extend to both learning algorithms as well as probabilistic inference. This flexibility does come at a computational cost however; while SIS is considerably more efficient than non-sequential Monte Carlo methods, the ability of the algorithm to scale to, for example, thousands of variables, remains unclear.

10.5.3 Incremental model construction

The techniques discussed above were based on the implicit assumption that a (graphical) model was constructed in full prior to solution. Furthermore, the algorithms computed a probability value for every node in the graph, thus providing information about the state of every system variable at every point in time. For many applications this information is not necessary: all that is needed is the value of a few *query variables* that are relevant to some prediction or decision-making situation. Work on incremental model construction starts with a compositional representation of the system in the form of rules, model fragments, or other knowledge base, and computes the value of a query expression trying to instantiate only those parts of the network necessary to compute the query probability accurately. In [Ngo *et al.*, 1995], the underlying system representation takes the form of sentences in a temporal probabilistic logic, and constructs a Bayesian network for a particular query. The resulting network, which should include only those parts of the network relevant to the query, can be solved by standard methods or any of the special-purpose algorithms discussed above.

In [Hanks and McDermott, 1994] the underlying system representation consists of STRIPS-like rules with a probabilistic component (Section 10.3.2). The system takes as input a query formula along with a *probability threshold*. The algorithm does not compute the exact probability of the query formula; rather it answers whether or not that probability is less than, greater than, or equal to, the threshold. The justification for this approach is that in decision-making or planning situations, the exact value of the query variables is usually unimportant—all that matters is what side of the threshold the probability lies. For example, a decision rule for planning an outing might be to schedule the trip only if the probability of rain is below 20%.

The algorithm in [Hanks and McDermott, 1994] works as follows: suppose the query formula is a single state variable P@t, and the input threshold is τ. The algorithm computes an estimate of P@t based on its current set of evidence. (Initially the evidence set is empty, and estimate is the prior for P@t). The estimate is compared to the threshold, and the algorithm computes an answer to the question "what evidence would cause the current estimate of P@t to change with respect to τ?"

Evidence and rules can be irrelevant for a number of reasons. First, they can be of the wrong sort (positive evidence about P and rules that make P true are both irrelevant if the current estimate is already greater than τ). A rule or piece of evidence can also be too tenuous to be interesting, either because it is temporally too remote from the query time point, or because its "noise" factor is too large. In either case, the evidence or rule can be ignored if its effect on the current estimate is weak enough that even if it were considered, it would not change the current estimate from greater than τ to less than τ, or vice versa.

Once the relevant evidence has been characterized, a search through the temporal database is initiated. If the search yields no evidence, and the current qualitative estimate is returned. If new evidence is found, the estimate is updated and the process is repeated.

There is an aspect of dynamic model construction in [Nicholson and Brady, 1994] as well, though this work differs from the first two in that it constructs the network in response to incoming observation data rather than in response to queries.

For work on learning dynamic probabilistic model structure from training data, see, for example, [Friedman *et al.*, 1998], and the references therein.

10.6 The Frame, Qualification, and Ramification Problems

No survey of temporal reasoning would be complete without considering the classic frame, qualification, and ramification problems. These problems, generally studied in the deterministic arena, have been central to temporal reasoning research since the problem was first discussed in the AI literature. Does a probabilistic model provide any leverage in solving these problems?

10.6.1 The frame problem

The frame problem [McCarthy and Hayes, 1969; Shanahan, 1987] refers to the need to represent the "common-sense law of inertia," that a variable does not change state unless compelled to do so, say by the occurrence of a causally relevant event. In the shooting scenario discussed in this chapter, common sense says that the L proposition should not change as a result of the wait event occurring, even though there may be no axioms explicitly stating which state variables wait does *not* change.

There is a practical and an epistemological aspect to the problem. As a practical matter, in most theories, most events leave most variables unchanged. Therefore it is unnecessarily inconvenient and expensive to have to state these facts explicitly. And even if the tedium could be engineered away, the user may lack the insight and detailed information about the domain necessary to build a deterministic model—one where every change and non-change is accounted for properly and explicitly. A complete and correct event model may be impossible.

Probabilistic theories in themselves do not constitute a solution to the practical problem of enumerating frame axioms, but neither do they stand in the way of a solution. Just as deterministic STRIPS operators embody the assumption that all variables not mentioned should remain unchanged, structured probabilistic action representations like the probabilistic STRIPS operators discussed in Section 10.3.2 can do the same. The practical side of the frame problem is addressed by choosing appropriately structured representations, irrespective of the model's underlying semantics. See [Boutilier and Goldszmidt, 1996] for an extensive analysis of the role of structured action representation in ameliorating the problem of specifying frame axioms.

The epistemological problem acknowledges the fact that information about events and their effects will typically be incomplete. As a result, inferences can be incorrect and might be contradicted by subsequent information that exposes gaps in the reasoner's knowledge. In terms of the frame problem this means that persistence inferences (e.g. that A persists across a wait event or over a period of time where no event is known to occur) should be defeasible: they might need to be retracted if contradicted by subsequent evidence (an observation that A was in fact false).

A probabilistic model confronts this problem directly. First, it provides an explicit representation for incomplete information about events and their effects, and separates what is known about the domain (information about event occurrences and their effects) from what is not known (the probabilistic components of the event description, and the probabilistic persistence assumptions). Second, it requires *quantifying* the extent to which the model is believed complete: noise terms in the event descriptions measure confidence in the ability to predict their effects, event and persistence probabilities measure confidence in the ability to predict the occurrence of events and the extent to which modeled events are sufficient to explain all changes.

It is instructive to point out why the Yale Shooting Problem does not arise in the probabilistic model. The problem originally arose in attempting to solve the frame problem using one defeasible rule: prefer scenarios that minimize the number of "unexplained" changes. The problem was that there were two scenarios minimal in that regard, one (intuitive) scenario in which load made L true, shoot made A false, and wait left A false, and another (unintuitive) scenario in which load made L true, L spontaneously became false shortly thereafter, and shoot left A true. Since both scenarios involved two state changes, the nonmonotonic logic frameworks were unable to identify the intuitive scenario as preferable to the unintuitive one.

Both scenarios are possible under the probabilistic framework, but there is an *explicit* model parameter measuring the likelihood of L spontaneously changing from true to false, which can be considered relative to the likelihood that shoot causes a state change. If this change is (relatively) unlikely, then the intuitive scenario will be assigned a higher probability. Thus the problem is solved at the expense of having to be explicit and numeric about one's beliefs.

10.6.2 The qualification problem

The qualification problem [Shoham and McDermott, 1988; Ginsberg and Smith, 1988b] involves the practical and epistemological difficulty of verifying the preconditions of events. The most common example involves a rule predicting that turning the key to the car will cause the car to start, *provided* there is fuel, spark, oxygen available, no obstruction in the tailpipe, and so on, *ad infinitum*. The practical problem is that verifying all these preconditions can be expensive; the epistemological problem is that enumerating necessary and sufficient conditions for an event's having a particular effect will generally be impossible.

The epistemological part of the qualification problem amounts to admitting that the *stated* necessary and sufficient conditions might be incomplete. Once again, this problem can be addressed deterministically by allowing the event axioms to be defeasible [Shoham, 1988]: "if all of an event's *stated* preconditions are met, then *defeasibly* conclude that the event will have its predicted effects." In other words, there is some possibility that there is some unknown precondition that will prevent the event from having its predicted effects.

The probabilistic model addresses this possibility in that it requires an explicit numeric account of the likelihood that an event will have its effects, conditioned on the fact that its context (precondition) holds in the world. That is, the event specification describes the likelihood that an effect will not be realized even though the context holds, and also the likelihood that an effect will be realized even though the context does not hold.

Although the probabilistic framework does not itself address the "practical" qualification problem (the computational difficulty of verifying the known context), it allows computational schemes that do address the problem. Suppose that the inference task specified *how certain* a decision maker must be that an event produce a particular effect. In that case, it might be possible to avoid verifying every contextual variable, because one could demonstrate that the effect was *sufficiently certain* even if a particular precondition turned out to be false. This mode of reasoning, which is enabled because the probabilistic framework allows the notion of *sufficiently certain* to be captured explicitly, is discussed in Section 10.5.3 and in more detail in [Hanks and McDermott, 1994].

10.6.3 The ramification problem

The ramification problem concerns reasoning about an event's "indirect effects." An example from [Ginsberg and Smith, 1988a] is that moving an object on top of a ventilation duct has the immediate effect of obstructing the duct, and in addition has the secondary effect of making the room stuffy. They express this relationship as a synchronic rule of the form "obstructed duct implies stuffy room" which is true at all time points. The technical question is whether formal temporal reasoning frameworks, particularly those that solve the frame and qualification problems nonmonotonically, handle the synchronic constraint properly. For example, if the inference that the vent was blocked was arrived at defeasibly, and if subsequent evidence reveals that the duct was in fact clear, will the (defeasible) inference that the room is stuffy be retracted as well?

As we have seen, probabilistic temporal reasoning systems have not addressed the interplay between synchronic and diachronic constraints in any meaningful way, and generally a probabilistic model will use one but not the other.

On the other hand, the example above could more properly be handled in a framework that treats the stuffiness as an endogenous change in the model rather than as a synchronic invariant. In that case work on endogenous change models (Section 10.4) would be relevant, though the probabilistic semantics sheds no additional light on the problem.

In summary, these classic problems have both epistemological and computational aspects. Probabilistic models address the epistemological issues directly in that they require the modeler to quantify his confidence in the model's coverage of the domain, a concept that can be difficult to capture in a satisfying manner with a nonmonotonic logics.

Probabilistic models can exacerbate the computational problems worse in that there are simply more parameters to assess. On the other hand, a numeric model admits approximation algorithms and other techniques for providing "accurate enough" answers, which could make inference easier (Section 10.5.3).

10.7 Concluding Remarks

We have presented a variety of approaches to building and computing with models of probabilistic dynamical systems. Most of this work adopts one of the following sets of assumptions:

- (Explicit-event models) A good predictive model of the domain is available and the important causal events are observable or controlled. As a result the events can be included explicitly in the model, the predictive model determines the diachronic dependencies, and synchronic dependencies are rare. The emphasis is on eliciting realistic causal models of the domain, and building the model on demand from smaller fragments.
- (Implicit-event models) Observational data about the system's state are plentiful, though one cannot count on observing or predicting the causally relevant events, and in many cases a compelling causal model will not be available. The absence of explicit events means that both synchronic and diachronic dependencies are important, and the challenge is determining the network's structure. This is typically viewed as a learning task, and success is measured by how well the model fits the available data rather than whether the model is physically plausible.

The main challenges facing the field at this point involve

- more expressive models
- automated model construction
- integrating explicit- and implicit-event models
- scaling to larger problems

First, the models studied in this chapter have been propositional. Although it is unlikely that efficient general-purpose algorithms will emerge for systems as powerful as first-order probabilistic temporal logics [Haddawy, 1994], computing with models that allow limited quantification seems possible.

Second, several automated model construction techniques were studied in the chapter, but most either assumed known exogenous events, or adopted the time-grid approach to building the model which is likely to be infeasible for large models instantiated over long periods of time. Building parsimonious models on demand, especially in situations where endogenous change is common, is a key challenge for making the technology widely useful.

Third, we noted the disparity between explicit- and implicit-event approaches. Clearly no situation will fit either approach perfectly, and a synthesis will again produce more widely applicable systems.

Finally, realistic system models may have thousands of state variables evaluated over long intervals of time. The need to make inferences from these models in reasonable time poses severe challenges for current and future probabilistic reasoning algorithms.

Handbook of Temporal Reasoning in Artificial Intelligence
Edited by M. Fisher, D. Gabbay and L. Vila

Chapter 11

Temporal Reasoning with iff-Abduction

Marc Denecker & Kristof Van Belleghem

Abduction can be defined as reasoning from observations to causes. In the context of dynamic systems and temporal domains, an important part of the background knowledge consists of causal information. The chapter shows how in the context of event calculus, different reasoning problems in a broad class of temporal reasoning domains can be mapped to abductive reasoning problems. The domains considered may contain different forms of uncertainty, such as uncertainty on the events, the initial state and on effects of nondeterministic actions. The problems considered include prediction, ambiguous prediction, postdiction, ambiguous postdiction and planning problems. We consider also applications of integrations of abduction and constraint programming for reasoning in continuous change applications and resource planning.

11.1 Introduction

Abduction has been proposed as a reasoning paradigm in AI for fault diagnosis [Charniak and McDermott, 1985], natural language understanding [Charniak and McDermott, 1985], default reasoning [Eshghi and Kowalski, 1989], [Poole, 1988]. In the context of logic programming, abductive procedures have been used for planning [Eshghi, 1988a], [Shanahan, 1989], [Missiaen, 1991a; Missiaen *et al.*, 1995], knowledge assimilation and belief revision [Kakas and Mancarella, 1990a; Kakas *et al.*, 1992], database updating [Kakas and Mancarella, 1990b]. [Denecker *et al.*, 1992] showed the role of an abductive system for forms of reasoning, different from planning, in the context of temporal domains with uncertainty.

The term abduction was introduced by the logician and philosopher C.S. Pierce (1839-1914) [Peirce, 1955] who defined it as the process of forming a hypothesis that explains given observed phenomena [Pople, 1973; Shanahan, 1989]. Often Abduction is defined as "inference to the best explanation" where *best* refers to the fact that the generated hypothesis is subjected to extra quality conditions such as (a form of) minimality or maximality criterion. There are different views on what an explanation is. One view is that a formula explains an observation iff it *logically entails* this observation. A more correct view is that an explanation gives a *cause* for the observation [Josephson and Josephson, 1994]. For example, *the street is wet* may logically entail that *it has rained* but is not a cause for it and it would be unnatural to define the first as an abductive explanation for the second. Another more illustrative example is cited from [Psillos, 1996]: the disease *paresis* is caused by a latent untreated form of syphilis, although the probability that latent untreated syphilis leads to paresis is only 25%. Note that the directionalities of logical entailment and causality here are opposite: syphilis is the cause of paresis but does not entail it, while paresis entails syphilis but does not cause it. Yet a doctor can *explain* paresis by the hypothesis of syphilis while paresis cannot account for an *explanation* for syphilis.

The term abduction has been used to cover hypothetical reasoning in a range of different settings, from human scientific discovery in philosophical treatments of human cognition to formally defined reasoning principles in formal and computational logic. In a formal logic, abduction is often defined as follows. Given a logical theory $\mathcal{T}$ representing the expert knowledge and a formula Q representing an observation on the problem domain, an abductive solution is a formula $\mathcal{E}$ such that

- $\mathcal{E}$ is satisfiable* w.r.t. $\mathcal{T}$ and
- it holds that† $\mathcal{T} \models \mathcal{E} \rightarrow Q$

In general, $\mathcal{E}$ may be subjected to further restrictions: the aforementioned minimality criteria, but more importantly criteria on the form of the explanation formula.

This formal definition implements the logical entailment view on abductive explanations. However, in many applications of abduction in AI, the theory $\mathcal{T}$ describes explicit *causality information*. This is notably the case in model-based diagnosis and in temporal reasoning, where theories describe effects of actions. By restricting the explanation formulas to the predicates describing primitive causes in the domain, an explanation formula which entails an observation gives a cause for the observation. Hence, for this class of theories, the logical entailment view implements the causality view on abductive inference.

Abduction is a form of hypothetical reasoning. Making hypotheses makes only sense when there is uncertainty, that is when $\mathcal{T}$ does not entirely fix the state of affairs of the domain of discourse. Abduction is a versatile and informative way of reasoning on *incomplete knowledge* and on uncertainty, on knowledge which does not fully describe the state of affairs in the world. In the presence of incomplete information, deduction is the reasoning paradigm to determine whether a statement is true in all possible states of affairs; abduction returns possible states of affairs in which the observation would be true or would be caused. Hence, abduction is strongly related to model generation and satisfiability checking: it is a refinement of these forms of reasoning. By definition, the existence of an abductive answer proves the satisfiability of the observation. But abduction returns more informative answers, in the sense that it describes one, or in general a class of possible states of affairs in which the observation is valid.

In the context of temporal reasoning, Eshghi [Eshghi, 1988a] was the first to use abduction. He used abduction to solve planning problems in the Event Calculus [Kowalski and Sergot, 1986]. This approach was further explored by Shanahan [Shanahan, 1989], Missiaen et al. [Missiaen *et al.*, 1992; Missiaen *et al.*, 1995], [Denecker *et al.*, 1992] and [Jung *et al.*, 1996]. Planning in the event calculus can be seen as a variant of reasoning from *observations* to causes. Here, the *observation* corresponds to the desired final state. The effect rules describing effects of actions provide the causality information. The causes are the actions to be performed to transform the given initial state into a final goal state. In Event Calculus, predicates describe the occurrences of actions and their order (event = occurrence of an action). An abductive explanation for a goal representing the final state is expressed in terms

*If $\mathcal{E}$ contains free variables, $\exists(\mathcal{E})$ should be satisfiable w.r.t. $\mathcal{T}$.

†Or, more general, if Q and $\mathcal{E}$ contain free variables: $\mathcal{T} \models \forall(\mathcal{E} \rightarrow Q)$.

of these primitive predicates and provides a *plan* (or possibly a set of plans) to reach the intended final state. In [Denecker *et al.*, 1992], this approach was further refined and extended by showing how abduction could be used also for other forms of reasoning than planning, including (ambiguous) postdiction and ambiguous prediction. This paper also clarified the role of total versus partial order, and showed how to implement a correct partial order planner by extending the abductive solver with a constraint solver CLP(LO) for the theory of total order (or linear order).

This chapter aims at presenting the above research results in a simple and unified context. One part of the section is devoted to representing different forms of uncertainty in the context of event calculus and showing how abduction can be used to solve different sorts of tasks in such representations. The tasks that will be considered are *(ambiguous) prediction, (ambiguous) postdiction* and *planning* problems.

We will consider uncertainty on the following levels:

- on the initial state,
- on the order of a known set of events,
- on the set of events,
- on the effect of (indeterminate) events

A prediction problem is one in which the state at a certain point must be determined given information on the past. A prediction problem is *ambiguous* if the final state of the system cannot be uniquely determined. An ambiguous prediction problem arises when the initial state is only partially known, or when knowledge about the sequence of actions previous to the state to be predicted is not or only partially available, or when some of these actions have a nondeterministic effect. In a postdiction problem, the problem is to infer some information about the initial state or the events using complete or partial information on the state of affairs at later stages. A postdiction problem is ambiguous if the initial state is not uniquely determined by the final state. In a planning problem, the set of events is unknown and must be derived to transform an initial state into a desired final state. In all these cases, we illustrate how abductive reasoning can help to explore the space of possible evolutions of the world. We consider also applications of integrations of abduction and constraint programming for reasoning in continuous change applications and resource planning.

The outline of the chapter is as follows. In Section 11.2 we motivate the choice for first order logic as a representation language. Section 11.3 briefly discusses how to compute abduction. Section 11.4 introduces a simple variant of event calculus, and in several subsections, different kinds of uncertainty are introduced and different applications of abduction are shown. Section 11.5 proposes a partial order planner based on an integration of abduction and a constraint solver for the theory of linear order. Section 11.6 considers applications of an integration of CLP(R) and abduction for reasoning on continuous change and resource planning. Section 11.7 briefly explores the limitations of abductive reasoning.

11.2 The logic used: FOL + Clark Completion = OLP-FOL

We will use classical first order logic (FOL) to represent temporal domains. For a long time, FOL was considered to be unsuitable for temporal reasoning. As McCarthy and Hayes pointed out in [McCarthy and Hayes, 1969], the main problem in temporal reasoning is the so-called frame problem: the problem of describing how actions affect certain properties and what properties are unaffected by the actions. At the end of the seventies, FOL was believed to be inappropriate for solving the frame problem due to its monotonicity [McCarthy and Hayes, 1969]. These problems have been the main motivation for non-monotonic reasoning [McCarthy, 1980; McDermott and Doyle, 1980; Reiter, 1980a].

However, in the beginning of the 90-ties, several authors proposed solutions for the frame problem based on Clark completion, also called explanation closure [Schubert, 1990; Reiter, 1991]. The principle is simple and well-known. Given a set of implications:

$$\forall \overline{X}_i.p(\overline{t}_i) \leftarrow \Psi_i$$

that we think of as an exhaustive enumeration of the cases in which p is true. The *completed definition* of this predicate is the formula:

$$\forall \overline{X}.p(\overline{X}) \leftrightarrow (\exists \overline{X}_1.\overline{X} = \overline{t}_1 \wedge \Psi_1) \vee .. \vee (\exists \overline{X}_n.\overline{X} = \overline{t}_n \wedge \Psi_n)$$

A variant of completion is used in Reiter's situation calculus [Reiter, 1991], currently one of the best explored temporal reasoning formalisms. Also temporal reasoning approaches in logic programming as in [Shanahan, 1989; Denecker *et al.*, 1992; Sadri and Kowalski, 1995] can be understood as classical logic approaches using completion.

Completion plays a crucial role in the theories that we will consider, both on the declarative level and the reasoning level. The logic theories considered here essentially consist of completed definitions and other first order logic axioms. Completed definitions will be written as sets of implications or rules, in uncompleted form, as in:

$$\left\{ \begin{array}{l} p(\overline{t}_1) \leftarrow \Psi_1 \\ .. \\ p(\overline{t}_n) \leftarrow \Psi_n \end{array} \right\}$$

Sometimes, when a definition consists of ground atoms, we will write also:

$$p \stackrel{\triangle}{=} \{\ p(\overline{t}_1), .., p(\overline{t}_n)\ \}$$

We call such a set of rules a *definition*. A theory consisting of (completed) definitions and FOL axioms will be denoted as in:

$$\left[\begin{array}{c} \left\{ \begin{array}{l} p(f(X)) \leftarrow \forall Z.q(X,Z) \\ .. \\ p(b)) \leftarrow \end{array} \right\} \\ \vdots \\ \forall X.p(X) \rightarrow \exists Z.q(X,Z) \end{array} \right]$$

Unless explicitly mentioned, we always include the Clark Equality Theory (CET) [Clark, 1978] or the unique names axioms [Reiter, 1980b]. Hence, we assume that two different terms represent different objects.

We assume the reader to be familiar with syntax and model semantics of classical logic. Some denotational conventions: variables start with a capital; constants and functors with a small letter; free variables in a rule or an axiom are assumed to be universally quantified. Predicates which have a completed definition, will be called *defined*, otherwise, they are called *open*. So, in a FOL theory without completed definitions, all predicates are open.

Often some further syntactical restrictions will be applied. Define a *normal clause* $p(\bar{t}) \leftarrow F$ as one in which F is a conjunction of literals, i.e. of atoms $q(\bar{s})$ or negated atoms $\neg q(\bar{s})$. As often, the conjunction symbol is denoted by the comma. A normal definition is a set of normal clauses with the same predicate in the head. A *normal axiom* is a denial of the form $\leftarrow l_1, .., l_n$ in which l_i are positive or negative literals; its logical meaning is given by the formula $\forall(\neg l_1 \vee .. \vee \neg l_n)$. A *normal theory* consists of normal definitions (one definition per defined predicate) and normal axioms. Important is that every definition and FOL axiom can be transformed in an equivalent normal one using a simple transformation, the Lloyd-Topor transformation [Lloyd and Topor, 1984].

By the denotational convention of representing a definition as a set of rules without explicit completion, normal theories syntactically and semantically correspond to Abductive Logic Programs or Open Logic Programs [Denecker, 1995]* under the 2-valued completion semantics of [Console *et al.*, 1991]. As a consequence of this, abductive procedures designed in the context of ALP can serve as special purpose abductive reasoners for FOL but tuned to definitions.

11.3 Abduction for FOL theories with definitions

The abduction that will be used here is tuned to the presence of completed definitions; we will refer to it as iff-abduction. Given a theory $\mathcal{T}$ containing definitions and FOL axioms and an observation Q, iff-abduction generates an explanation formula Ψ for Q consisting only of open predicates such that $\mathcal{T} \models \Psi \rightarrow Q$ and Ψ is consistent with $\mathcal{T}$. Essentially the computation of this Ψ can be thought of as a process of repeatedly substituting defined atoms in Q by their definition (and possibly dropping disjuncts from the definition) until an explanation formula Ψ in terms of the open predicates can be derived which entails the observation Q. In case $\mathcal{T}$ contains FOL axioms, the FOL axioms are reduced simultaneously with the query such that the resulting explanation formula also entails the FOL axioms. This form of abduction related to completed definitions was first extensively described in [Console *et al.*, 1991]. It shows strong correspondence with *goal regression* [Reiter, 1991], a reasoning technique for situation calculus based on rewriting using completed definitions.

Though iff-abduction implements the entailment view on abduction (see Section 11.1), it will generate causes for observations when the set of definitions is designed appropriately. Indeed, the design of the definitions may have subtle, extra-logical influence on the abductive reasoning. Consider the following example. We represent the fact that *streets are wet iff it rains*, and *it rains iff there are saturated clouds*. Each of these two simple equivalences can be denoted as definitions in two different directions. For example, this information can be represented as the following theories. Both consist of two definitions:

$$[\ \{\ streets\_wet \leftarrow rain\ \}\ ,\ \{\ rain \leftarrow saturated\_clouds\ \}\ ]$$

but also as:

$$[\ \{\ rain \leftarrow streets\_wet\ \}\ ,\ \{\ saturated\_clouds \leftarrow rain\ \}\ ]$$

*These two terms refer to different knowledge theoretic interpretations of syntactically the same formalism. Whereas ALP is defined as the study of abductive reasoning in logic programs, OLP-FOL is defined as a logic to express definitions and axioms, and as a sub-formalism of FOL with completed definitions. See [Denecker, 1995].

Both theories are logically equivalent; nevertheless, in both cases iff-abduction will generate different answers for the same queries. For example, the observation $streets\_wet$ will be explained by $saturated\_clouds$ in the first theory, but by itself as a primitive fact in the second theory. Satisfactory causal abductive explanations will only be generated using theories with definitions where the direction of are lined up with the causal arrow.

The above example shows that extra-logical aspects may be involved in the design of definitions. The directionality of the definitions determines the reduction and rewriting process. By designing the definitions along the arrow of causality, iff-abduction will implement the causality view on abduction, although its formal characterisation corresponds to the logical entailment view of abduction. Correct use of iff-abduction imposes a methodological requirement: that rules in the definition follow the direction of causality.

Another example shows the distinction between definition rules and logical implications. We represent that *one is walking implies that one is alive; to be born causes that one is alive.* Obviously, the first implication is not a causal rule, while the second one is. Consider the following theory:

$$\left[\left\{ \begin{array}{l} alive \leftarrow born \\ alive \leftarrow walking \end{array} \right\} \right]$$

Given this theory, two iff-abduction explanations for $alive$ are $born$ and $walking$. Only the first one is a causal explanation; the second one is not. This leads to a second methodological requirement: non-causal implications should not be added together with causal rules in one definition.

A correct representation is:

$$[\ \{\ alive \leftarrow born\ \}\ , alive \leftarrow walking\ ]$$

In this example, the solution generated by iff-abduction for $alive$ is $born$; for $walking$ it is $walking \wedge born$. These are natural and intended answers. Indeed, what the implication represents is that $alive$ is a necessary precondition for $walking$; the definition expresses that to be born is the only cause for being alive. Hence, to be born is a necessary (but not sufficient) precondition for being walking*

We discuss some restrictions of iff-abduction.

First, note that so far we assumed a set of causal rules to be exhaustive. Only if a set of rules provides an exhaustive enumeration of the causes, this set of rules can be correctly interpreted as a definition. Assume that for a certain observable p, only an incomplete set of causes represented by a set of rules $p \leftarrow \Psi_1, ..., p \leftarrow \Psi_n$ is known. Because this set is incomplete and there may be other causes for p, the completion of this set is incorrect. To abductively explain p, we want explanations using each of these rules but also others in which p is caused by some unknown cause. The latter solution will not be obtained if the set of known causes is interpreted as a definition.

*Note that in this example, there seems to be a conflict between the causality view and the logical entailment view on abduction. In the second view, the hypothesis $walking$ is a correct explanation for $alive$, while clearly it is not a cause for it. Iff-abduction is consistent with the causality view and will only generate the explanation $born$. Though iff-abduction does not generate the explanation $walking$, it is still consistent with the logical entailment view in the weaker sense that it generates a logically more general solution. Indeed, $born$ is logically more general than $walking$ because the theory entails $walking \rightarrow born$; the set of possible states of affairs in which $walking$ is true is a subset of the set of states of affairs in which $born$ is true.

There is a simple technique to extend iff-abduction in case of incomplete knowledge on causal effects. One possibility is that one introduces a new symbol, e.g. $open\_p$, adds the rule

$$p \leftarrow open\_p$$

to the rule set of p and adds the FOL axiom

$$open\_p \rightarrow \neg\Psi_1 \wedge .. \wedge \neg\Psi_n$$

to the theory. $open\_p$ can be thought of as the sub-predicate of p caused by the unknown causes of p. This sort of translation was originally mentioned in [Kakas *et al.*, 1992]. Iff-abduction will then produce answers using the known causes, but will also generate answers in terms of the unknown causes.

Second, answers generated by iff-abduction logically entail the explained observation. Recall the syphilis example of Section 11.1: causal explanations do not necessarily entail the observation. In Section 11.4.3, we will see examples with a similar flavor, involving actions with nondeterministic effects.

Also this sort of causal explanation can be easily implemented with iff-abduction. We illustrate it with the example of the introduction. Syphilis possibly causes paresis and it is the only cause. We could think of this situation as that paresis is caused by syphilis in combination with some other unnoticeable primitive cause. For this residual part of the cause, we introduce a new predicate, here simply bad_luck. With this new concept in mind, the following definition is a correct representation, obeying the methodological requirement for representing causal rules using definitions:

$$\{\ paresis \leftarrow untreated\_syphilis, bad\_luck\ \}$$

In the area of Abductive Logic Programming, algorithms have been designed which compute iff-abduction for completed definitions or for sets of rules under stronger semantics such as stable and well-founded semantics. For an overview of these abductive algorithms, we refer to [Denecker and De Schreye, 1998]. The most direct implementation of iff-abduction is the algorithm of [Console *et al.*, 1991]; it is based on rewriting a formula by substituting the righthand-side of their completed definition for defined atoms until a formula is obtained in which only open predicates occur. There are several problems which makes this algorithm unsuitable for many abductive computations. One is that it is only applicable to non-recursive (sets of) definitions; another one is that this algorithm does not provide integrated consistency checking of the generated answer formula. Improved implementations of iff-abduction are found in SLDNFA [Denecker and De Schreye, 1992; Denecker and De Schreye, 1998] and the iff-procedure [Fung and Kowalski, 1997]. Both algorithms can be seen as extensions of the SLDNF-algorithm [Lloyd, 1987] which provides the underlying procedural semantics for most current Prolog systems. Another algorithm which extends abduction with CLP is ACLP [Kakas *et al.*, 2000]. More recently, [Kakas *et al.*, 2001] proposed the Asystem, which is an integration of SLDNFA and ACLP. Here we will focus on SLDNFA; below, we describe the answers generated by SLDNFA and its correctness results. In Section 11.3.1, we give a brief overview of the algorithm.

The abductive answers that will be considered here have a particular simple form. Given is a OLP-FOL theory $\mathcal{T}$ consisting of definitions $\mathcal{D}$ and FOL axioms T, and a query Q to be explained.

Definition 11.3.1. *A ground abductive answer is a pair of a set Δ of ground atomic definitions for all open predicates, possibly containing skolem constants, and a substitution θ such that:*

- $\mathcal{D} \cup \Delta \models \forall(\theta(Q))$,
- $\mathcal{D} \cup \Delta \models T$ *and*
- $\mathcal{D} \cup \Delta$ *is consistent.*

Note that the existence of a ground abductive answer proves the consistency of $\exists(Q)$.

In many cases, the open predicates capture the essential, primitive features of the problem domain. These concepts are the features in terms of which the others can be defined. As a consequence, the set Δ, which gives an exhaustive enumeration of all primitive open predicates, can be considered as a simple description of a scenario in which the observation would be true.

Computations of SLDNFA or of the iff-procedure return possibly complex explanation formulas* in a normal form, out of which an answer in the form of a ground atomic answer can be straightforwardly extracted. The correctness theorem states a slightly weaker result than required in Definition 11.3.1: in general it cannot be proven that $\mathcal{D} \cup \Delta$ is consistent w.r.t. 2-valued semantics; however, $\mathcal{D} \cup \Delta$ is consistent w.r.t. to a 3-valued completion semantics.

Inconsistency of (sets of) definitions is due to negative cyclic dependencies. An obvious example is the definition $\left\{ \; p \leftarrow \neg p \; \right\}$. From a theoretical point of view, abductive reasoners used for reasoning in 2-valued logics should perform consistency checking of the definitions. Whereas iff-abduction through rewriting using definitions only accesses and expands definitions relevant for the explanandum, consistency checking of a theory including many definitions requires that also irrelevant definitions are processed. This can be very costly. Fortunately, this general consistency checking is unnecessary in many cases. Indeed, for a broad class of definitions, consistency is known to hold†. For example, this is the case with hierarchical and acyclic rule sets [Apt, 1990]. Also the definitions used in the temporal theories considered in the following sections, have the consistency property. The following definition formalises the consistency property.

Definition 11.3.2. *Given is a theory $\mathcal{D}$ consisting of definitions, $\mathcal{J}$ a class of interpretations of the function symbols and the open predicates. T is iff-definitional w.r.t. $\mathcal{J}$ iff for each $J \in \mathcal{J}$, there exists a unique model M of $\mathcal{D}$ that coincides with J on the function and open symbols.*

Theorem 11.3.1. *Let $\mathcal{D}$ be an acyclic set of definitions [Apt, 1990], $\mathcal{J}$ the class of Herbrand interpretations of the function symbols and the open predicates. $\mathcal{D}_{eff}$ is iff-definitional w.r.t. $\mathcal{J}$.*

This theorem is proven in [Apt, 1990]‡.

---

*These formulas Ψ satisfy the property that $\mathcal{D} \models \forall(\Psi \rightarrow Q)$ and $\mathcal{D} \models \exists(\Psi)$ w.r.t. 3-valued completion semantics.

†In certain applications of logic programming (often under stable semantics), negative cyclic dependencies are explicitly exploited to represent integrity constraints. For such applications, reasoners are needed that do perform consistency checking of the definitions.

‡[Apt, 1990] proves that the 2-valued completion of a acyclic logic program has a unique Herbrand model.

Theorem 11.3.2. *Let $\mathcal{T} = \mathcal{D} \cup T$ be a theory, $\mathcal{D}$ a set of definitions which is iff-definitional w.r.t. to a class $\mathcal{J}$ of interpretations of open and function symbols. Let (θ, Δ) be an SLDNFA-answer generated for a query Q. If there exists a model of Δ among $\mathcal{J}$ then (θ, Δ) is a correct ground abductive answer for Q w.r.t. $\mathcal{T}$.*

Proof. The correctness theorem of SLDNFA states that*:

- $\mathcal{D} \cup \Delta \models \forall(\theta(Q))$;
- $\mathcal{D} \cup \Delta \models T$.

It suffices to prove that $\mathcal{D} \cup \Delta$ is consistent. But this is trivial, since there is a model of Δ among $\mathcal{J}$ and this model can be extended to a unique model of $\mathcal{D}$, since $\mathcal{D}$ is iff-definitional w.r.t. $\mathcal{J}$. □

Whereas the role of abduction is to search for one or for a class of possible state of affairs of the problem domain which satisfy a certain property, the role of deduction is show that all possible states of affairs satisfy a given property. An important property of SLDNFA and iff-procedure is that they have the *duality property*. Given a theory $\mathcal{T}$ and a query Q to be explained, they satisfy the following property:

Definition 11.3.3. *If failure occurs in finite time then it holds that $\mathcal{T} \models \forall(\neg Q)$.*

This duality property is at the same time a completeness result for iff-abduction.

The duality property is important: it implies that these algorithms can be used not only for abduction but also for deduction tuned to iff-definitions. If the abductive reasoner fails finitely on the query $\neg Q$, then this is a proof for Q†. In the applications below, this duality property will be exploited for theorem-proving.

Note that we view these abductive procedures as special purpose reasoners to reason on FOL theories with completed definitions. So, we avoid all epistemological problems concerning the role of LP and ALP in knowledge representation, on the nature of negation as failure and more of these.

11.3.1 An algorithm for iff-abduction

The SLDNFA procedure is an abductive procedure for normal theories‡. We will call the conjunctions in $\mathcal{PG}$ a *positive goal*, a normal axiom in $\mathcal{NG}$ a *negative goal*. Both positive and negative goals may have -possibly shared- free variables. SLDNFA also maintains a store of abduced open atoms. The algorithm tries to reduce goals in $\mathcal{PG}$ to the empty goal and tries to build a finitely failed tree for the goals in $\mathcal{NG}$. Initially, $\mathcal{NG}$ contains all normal FOL axioms, and $\mathcal{PG}$ contains the initial query. At each step in the computation, one goal and a literal in it is selected and a corresponding computation step is performed. Below we sketch the steps:

*In [Denecker and De Schreye, 1998], these two results are proven for 3-valued semantics. However, because a 2-valued model of the completion is also a model in 3-valued completion, these results hold also for 2-valued completion.

†Though deduction in FOL is semi-decidable, SLDNFA and the iff-procedure are not complete for deduction.

‡Recall that these consist of normal axioms and one definition per defined predicate consisting of normal rules.

- When an open atom A is selected in a positive goal $A \wedge Q$, A is stored in the set Δ and Q is substituted for $A \wedge Q$ in $\mathcal{PG}$.

- When a defined atom A is selected in a positive query $A \wedge Q$, then one of the rules $H \leftarrow B$ defining the predicate of A is selected, the most general unifier θ of A and H is computed, and $A \wedge Q$ is replaced by $\theta(B \wedge Q)$ in $\mathcal{PG}$. Also, because θ may bind free variables, θ is applied on all formulas involved in $\mathcal{PG}, \mathcal{NG}$ and Δ.

- When a negative literal $\neg A$ is selected in a positive goal $\neg A \wedge Q$, the latter goal is replaced by Q in $\mathcal{PG}$ and $\leftarrow A$ added to $\mathcal{NG}$. Analogously, when a negative literal $\neg A$ is selected* in a negative goal $\forall \overline{X}. \leftarrow A, Q$, then the computation proceeds nondeterministically by either deleting the negative goal and adding A to $\mathcal{PG}$, or substituting $\forall \overline{X}.Q$ for the negative goal $\forall \overline{X}. \leftarrow A, Q$ in $\mathcal{NG}$.

- Assume a defined atom A is selected in a negative goal $\forall \overline{X}. \leftarrow A, Q$. In that case, all resolvents of $\forall \overline{X}. \leftarrow A, Q$ and all rules $H \leftarrow B$ of the definition of A are computed and are added to $\mathcal{NG}$. However, in these resolution steps, the free variables of the negative goal on one hand and the universal variables of the negative goal and the variables of the rules on the other hand must be treated differently. We illustrate this with a simple example. Consider the definition:

$$\{\ p(f(g(Z), V)) \leftarrow q(Z, V)\ \}$$

and the execution of the query $\neg p(f(X, a))$, where X is a free variables. Below, the selected atom at each step is underlined. Only the modified sets $\mathcal{PG}, \mathcal{NG}$ and Δ at each step are given. Initially $\mathcal{NG}$ and Δ are empty.

$$\begin{array}{ll} \mathcal{PG} = \{\underline{\neg p(f(X,a))}\}\ ,\ \mathcal{NG} = \{\}\ ,\ \Delta = \{\} & \textit{Switch to } \mathcal{NG} \\ \mathcal{PG} = \{\}\ ,\ \ \mathcal{NG} = \{\leftarrow \underline{p(f(X,a))}\} & \textit{Negative resolution} \end{array}$$

To solve the negative goal $\leftarrow p(f(X, a))$, the terms $f(X, a)$ and $f(g(Z), V)$ must be unified. Note that if we make the *default assumption* that $\forall Z. \leftarrow X = g(Z)$, then the unification fails and therefore $\neg p(f(X, a))$ succeeds. So, this assumption $\forall Z. \leftarrow X = g(Z)$ yields a solution. But in general, X may appear in other goals; to succeed these goals, it may be necessary to unify X with other terms at a later stage. Assume that due to some unification, X is assigned a term $g(t)$. In that case, we must retract the default assumption and investigate the new negative goal $\leftarrow q(t, a)$. Otherwise, if all other goals have been solved, we can conclude the SLDNFA-refutation as a whole by returning $\forall Z.X \neq g(Z)$ as a constraint on the generated solution. As we will show, adding these constraints explicitly may be avoided by substituting a new skolem constant for the variable X.

SLDNFA obtains this behavior as follows. First the unification algorithm is executed on the equality $f(X, a)) = f(g(Z), V)$, producing $\{V = a, X = g(Z)\}$. The part with universally quantified variables $\{V = a\}$ is applied as in normal resolution. The part with the free variables $\{X = g(Z)\}$ which contains the negation of the default

*$\neg A$ may be selected only when A contains no universally bound variables. Otherwise, the computation terminates in error. This error state is called *floundering negation.*

assumption, is added as a residual atom to the resolvent and the resulting resolvent $\forall Z. \leftarrow X = g(Z), q(Z, a)$ is added to $\mathcal{NG}$. The selection of the entire goal can be delayed as long as no value is assigned to X. When such an assignment occurs and for example the term $g(t)$ is assigned to X, then the goal $\leftarrow g(t) = g(Z), q(Z, a)$ reduces to the negative goal $\leftarrow q(t, a)$ which then needs further investigation. Otherwise, no further refutation is needed.

- Finally consider the case that an open atom A is selected in a negative goal $\forall \overline{X}. \leftarrow A, Q$. We must compute the failure tree obtained by resolving A with all abduced atoms in Δ. The main problem is that the final Δ may not be totally known when the goal is selected. We illustrate the problem with an example. Consider the program with open predicate r:

$$q \leftarrow r(X), \neg p(X)$$
$$p(X) \leftarrow r(b)$$

Below, an SLDNFA refutation for the query $r(a) \wedge \neg q$ is given.

$\mathcal{PG} = \{\underline{r(a)} \wedge \neg q\}$	*Abduction*
$\mathcal{PG} = \{\underline{\neg q}\}, \quad \Delta = \{r(a)\}$	*Switch to* $\mathcal{NG}$
$\mathcal{PG} = \{\}, \quad \mathcal{NG} = \{\leftarrow \underline{q}\}$	*Negative resolution*
$\mathcal{NG} = \{\leftarrow \underline{r(X)}, \neg p(X)\}$	*Selection of abducible atom*

If r was a defined predicate then at this point we should resolve the selected goal with each clause of the definition of r. Instead, we are computing a definition for r in Δ. Therefore, the atom $r(X)$ must be resolved with all facts already abduced or to be abduced about r. The problem now is that the set $\{r(a)\}$ is incomplete: indeed, it is easy to see that the resolution of the goal with $r(a)$ will ultimately lead to the abduction of $r(b)$. Hence, the failure tree cannot be computed completely at this point of the computation.

SLDNFA interleaves the computation of this failure tree with the construction of Δ. This can be implemented by storing the tuple $((\forall \overline{X}. \leftarrow A, Q)\ ,\ D)$ where D is the set of abduced atoms which have already been resolved with A. Below, the set of these tuples is denoted $\mathcal{NAG}$. We illustrate this strategy on the example. At the current point in the computation, $\mathcal{NAG}$ is empty and the only abduced fact that can be resolved with the selected goal is $r(a)$. The tuple $((\forall X. \leftarrow r(X), \neg p(X)), \{r(a)\})$ is saved in $\mathcal{NAG}$ and the resolvent $\leftarrow \neg p(a)$ is added to $\mathcal{NG}$:

$\mathcal{NG} = \{\leftarrow \underline{\neg p(a)}\}, \quad \mathcal{NAG} = \{((\forall X. \leftarrow r(X), \neg p(X)), \{r(a)\})\}$	
	Switch to $\mathcal{PG}$
$\mathcal{PG} = \{\underline{p(a)}\}, \quad \mathcal{NG} = \{\}$	*Positive resolution*
$\mathcal{PG} = \{\underline{r(b)}\}$	*Abduction*
$\mathcal{PG} = \{\}, \quad \Delta = \{r(a), \underline{r(b)}\}$	$\mathcal{NAG}$ *goal selected*

Due to the abduction of $r(b)$, another branch starting from the goal in $\mathcal{NAG}$ has to be explored:

$\mathcal{NG} = \{\leftarrow \underline{\neg p(b)}\}$, $\mathcal{NAG} = \{((\forall X. \leftarrow r(X), \neg p(X)), \{r(a), r(b)\})\}$
Switch to $\mathcal{PG}$
$\mathcal{PG} = \{\underline{p(b)}\}$, $\mathcal{NG} = \{\}$ *Positive resolution*
$\mathcal{PG} = \{\underline{r(b)}\}$ *Abduction*
$\mathcal{PG} = \{\}$

At this point, a solution is obtained: all positive goals are reduced to the empty goal, the set of negative goals is empty and with respect to Δ, a complete failure tree has been constructed for the negative goal in $\mathcal{NAG}$.

In general, the computation may end when the set $\mathcal{PG}$ is empty, each negative goal in $\mathcal{NG}$ contains an irreducible equality atom $X = t$ with X a free variable, and for each tuple $((\forall \overline{X}. \leftarrow A, Q), D)$ in $\mathcal{NAG}$, D contains all abduced atoms of Δ that unify with A. A ground abductive answer can be straightforwardly derived from such an answer, by substituting all free variables by skolem constants, and mapping Δ to a set of definitions for all open predicates.

11.4 A linear time calculus

Kowalski and Sergot proposed the original event calculus (EC) [Kowalski and Sergot, 1986] as a formalism for reasoning about events with duration, about properties initiated and terminated by these events and maximal time periods during which these properties hold*. Most subsequent developments of the EC used a simplified variant of the original EC based on time points instead of time periods. This simplified event calculus EC was applied to problems such as database updates [Kowalski, 1992], planning [Eshghi, 1988a; Missiaen *et al.*, 1995], explanation and hypothetical reasoning [Shanahan, 1989; Provetti, 1996], modeling temporal databases [Van Belleghem *et al.*, 1994], air traffic management [Sripada *et al.*, 1994], protocol specification [Denecker *et al.*, 1996].

Here, we will use the Event Calculus as defined in [Shanahan, 1987]. In this event calculus, the ontological primitive is the *time point* rather than the event. The basic predicates of the language of the calculus are listed below. The language includes sorts for time points, fluents, actions and for other domain dependent objects:

- $happens(a, t)$: an action a occurs at time t.
- $t_1 < t_2$: time point t_1 precedes time point t_2.
- $holds(p, t)$: the fluent p holds at time t.
- $clipped(e, p, t)$: the fluent p is terminated during the interval $]e, t[$.
- $clipped(p, t)$: the fluent p is terminated before t.
- $poss(a, t)$: the action preconditions of action a hold at time t.
- $initially(p)$: p is true initially.

*The original event calculus included rules $e \leftarrow F$ which derived the existence of an event e previous to some observed fact F caused by e. Such rules do not match the causality arrow. As a consequence, abductive reasoning in the form described here is quite useless because it would explain certain events in terms of facts caused by them.

- $initiates(a, p, t)$: an action a at time t is a cause for the fluent p to become true*.
- $terminates(a, p, t)$: an action a at time t is a cause for p to become false†.
- $incompatible(a_1, a_2, t)$: actions a_1, a_2 cannot occur simultaneously at time t.

Definition 11.4.1. *A state formula in time variable T is any formula Ψ in which T is the only variable of sort time and each occurrence of T in Ψ is free and occurs in an atom $holds(p, T)$ with p a fluent term.*

The EC theories considered here consist of the following parts:

$\mathcal{T}_{per}$: this is the law of inertia and consists of the following definition for the predicate $holds$‡

$$\left\{ \begin{array}{lll} holds(P,T) \leftarrow & initially(P) \wedge & \\ & \neg \exists T_1, A.\ happens(A, T_1) \wedge T_1 < T \wedge & \\ & \qquad terminates(A, P, T_1) & \\ holds(P,T) \leftarrow & happens(A, E) \wedge E < T \wedge initiates(A, P, E) \wedge & \\ & \neg \exists T_1, A_1.\ happens(A_1, T_1) \wedge E < T_1 < T \wedge & \\ & \qquad terminates(A_1, P, T_1) & \end{array} \right\}$$

$\mathcal{T}_{TO}$: a theory expressing that $<$ is a strict linear or total order on the time points. The axioms express antisymmetry, transitivity and linearity:

$$\begin{array}{l} \leftarrow T_0 < T_1, T_1 < T_0 \\ T_0 < T_2 \leftarrow T_0 < T_1 \wedge T_1 < T_2 \\ T_0 < T_1 \vee T_0 = T_1 \vee T_1 < T_0 \end{array}$$

The original EC and many proposals using variants of the EC require implicitly or explicitly that time is a partial order but the linearity requirement is absent. In Section 11.4.2, we argue that a number of anomalies reported in [Denecker *et al.*, 1992] and in [Missiaen *et al.*, 1995] in the context of planning in Event Calculus are solved by adding this theory§.

---

*Note that p may be already true at time t.

†p may be false at time t.

‡Transforming these rules to normal form using the Lloyd-Topor transformation would introduce two new predicates $clipped/2$ and $clipped/3$:

$$\left\{ \begin{array}{ll} holds(P,T) \leftarrow initially(P) \wedge \neg clipped(P,T) & \\ holds(P,T) \leftarrow \quad happens(A, E) \wedge E < T \wedge initiates(A, P, E) \wedge & \\ \qquad \neg clipped(E, P, T) & \end{array} \right\}$$

$$\{\ clipped(E, P, T) \leftarrow happens(A, T1) \wedge E < T1 < T \wedge terminates(A, P, T1)\ \}$$

$$\{\ clipped(P, T) \leftarrow happens(A, T1) \wedge T1 < T \wedge terminates(A, P, T1)\ \}$$

§Note that the axioms of $\mathcal{T}_{TO}$ are satisfied in approaches such as [Shanahan, 1987] in which time is isomorphic with the natural numbers or real numbers. As a consequence, in these approaches, the anomalies discussed in Section 11.4.2 do not appear.

$\mathcal{D}_{eff}$: this theory consists of definitions for $initiates$ and $terminates$. They consists of *effect rules* of the form:

$$initiates(a, p, T) \leftarrow \Psi$$
$$terminates(a, p, T) \leftarrow \Psi$$

where Ψ is a state formula in T, p a fluent term, a an action term. Ψ, p and a may share variables.

These rules describe initiating and terminating effects of actions. As usual in temporal reasoning, we assume that these rules exhaustively describe the effects of the actions on the fluents; under this assumption, the completion of the rule sets of the predicates $initiates$ and $terminates$ hold.

$\mathcal{T}_{pre}$: the action precondition theory consists of the action precondition axiom $\mathcal{A}_{pre}$ which expresses that $poss(A, T)$ is a necessary precondition for an action A to happen at time T:

$$happens(A, T) \rightarrow poss(A, T)$$

and a definition $\mathcal{D}_{poss}$ of the predicate $poss$ consisting of rules of the form:

$$poss(a, T) \leftarrow \Psi$$

with a an action term, Ψ a state formula in T. a and Ψ may share free variables. We assume that this set of rules exhaustively enumerates the situations in which an action may occur.

$\mathcal{T}_{state}$: the state constraint theory consists of axioms of the form:

$$\forall T. \Psi[T]$$

where $\Psi[T]$ is a state formula in T. They express that the property Ψ is satisfied at each time point.

$\mathcal{T}_{conc}$: the concurrency theory consists of the axiom $\mathcal{A}_{conc}$:

$$\leftarrow happens(A_1, T), happens(A_2, T), incompatible(A_1, A_2, T)$$

and a definition $\mathcal{D}_{incompatible}$ consisting of rules

$$incompatible(A_1, A_2, T) \leftarrow \Psi$$

where Ψ is a state formula in T. Unless stated otherwise, we exclude concurrent actions entirely for simplicity reasons by defining $incompatible$ as follows:

$$\{\ incompatible(A_1, A_2, T) \leftarrow \neg A_1 = A_2\ \}$$

$\mathcal{T}_{nar}$**:** the theory describing the narrative. This theory is a possibly incomplete description of the initial state, of a number of events (action occurrences) and their order and of a number of other user defined predicates. $\mathcal{T}_{nar}$ does not contain predicates $holds$, $clipped$, $initiates$, $terminates$, $poss$, $incompatible$. This theory may consists of definitions and of FOL axioms, depending on whether complete knowledge is available or not.

We illustrate the domain dependent axioms in the case of the Turkey Shooting problem [Hanks and McDermott, 1987]:

$$\begin{array}{l} \{\ initiates(load, loaded, E) \leftarrow \ \} \\ \left\{ \begin{array}{l} terminates(shoot, alive, E) \leftarrow holds(alive, E) \\ terminates(shoot, loaded, E) \leftarrow \end{array} \right\} \\ \left\{ \begin{array}{l} poss(load, T) \leftarrow \\ poss(wait, T) \leftarrow \\ poss(shoot, T) \leftarrow \end{array} \right\} \end{array}$$

In the case of the YTS, complete knowledge is available on initial state and events. $\mathcal{T}_{nar}$ consists of three definitions*:

$$\begin{array}{l} \{\ initially(alive) \leftarrow \ \} \\ happens \triangleq \{\ happens(load, t_0), happens(wait, t_1), happens(shoot, t_2)\ \} \\ < \triangleq \{\ t_0 < t_1 < t_2 < t_3\ \} \end{array}$$

All predicates have a definition; the resulting EC is an executable logic program (under completion semantics). The theory entails $\neg holds(alive, t_3)$; this can be verified by running Prolog on the query $\neg holds(alive, t_3)$; the query succeeds.

The following theorem is important. It allows to prove the consistency of a broad class of EC's and the consistency of abductive solutions generated by SLDNFA and iff-procedure w.r.t. 2 valued semantics.

Theorem 11.4.1. *Let $\mathcal{T}$ be any event calculus. Let $\mathcal{J}$ be the class of interpretations I that satisfy $\mathcal{T}_{TO}$ and in which $happens$ is interpreted by a finite set of atoms.*

The set of definitions $\{\mathcal{D}_{holds}, \mathcal{D}_{initiates}, \mathcal{D}_{terminates}, \mathcal{D}_{poss}, \mathcal{D}_{incompatible}\}$ in $\mathcal{T}$ is iff-definitional w.r.t. the class $\mathcal{J}$.

This theorem was proved in [Shanahan, 1987].

In the following subsections, we show how iff-abduction is a powerful instrument to explore different forms of uncertainty.

11.4.1 Uncertainty on the initial state

A well-known benchmark example with uncertainty on the initial state is the Murder Mystery [Baker, 1989]: *initially the turkey is alive; there is a shooting followed by a waiting event; then the turkey is dead.* The problem associated with the Murder Mystery scenario is the postdiction problem of inferring that initially, the gun must have been loaded. Baker used this problem to show a problem with chronological minimization.

*Here a sequence $t_1 < .. < t_n$, denotes the transitive closure $\{t_i < t_j | 1 \leq i < j \leq n\}$.

In this problem there is full knowledge on the events and their order but there is incomplete information on the initial situation. In our representation, $initially$ is the only open predicate. The domain independent information and the general domain knowledge with the $\mathcal{D}_{eff}, \mathcal{P}_{poss}, \mathcal{D}_{conc}$ are as in the YTS solution. The definitions of $happens$, and $<$, and the FOL axioms are*:

$$happens \triangleq \{ \ happens(shooting, t_1), happens(waiting, t_2) \ \}$$
$$< \triangleq \{ \ t_1 < t_2 < t_3 \ \}$$
$$initially(alive) \wedge \neg holds(alive, t_3)$$

Note that here the FOL constraint $\neg holds(alive, t_3)$ is phrased in terms of a defined predicate and indirectly constrains the state of the open predicate $initially$.

The above representation is correct and provides a correct solution to the postdiction problem. SLDNFA yields one abductive solution for the query $true$†; the generated answer is:

$$initially \triangleq \{ \ initially(alive), initially(loaded) \ \}$$

Note that this answer does not prove that the gun is initially loaded; it only asserts that it is *possible* that the gun is initially loaded. However, the stronger conclusion holds that it is necessary the gun is loaded initially. SLDNFA can prove this. The algorithm fails finitely on the query $\neg initially(loaded)$. From the duality property, it follows that this EC entails $initially(loaded)$.

11.4.2 Uncertainty on the order of events

One way in which our event calculus differs from other variants is that it contains the theory of linear/total order as fundamental axiom‡. In [Kowalski and Sergot, 1986], it is argued that one of the advantages of event calculus over situation calculus is that the time precedence of events can be a partial order representing an incompletely known order of events. However, as argued in [Denecker *et al.*, 1992], such a representation leads to incorrect results when action effects are interfering. An example illustrates the problem: *initially the light is off; at two different times* t_1, t_2, *a light switch is flipped; the order of* t_1, t_2 *is unknown*. The prediction problem to be solved is to infer that the light is off at the final state t_3. We specify the domain as follows:

$$\{ \ initiates(switch, on, T) \leftarrow \neg holds(on, T) \ \}$$
$$\{ \ terminates(switch, on, T) \leftarrow holds(on, T) \ \}$$
$$\{ \ poss(switch, T) \leftarrow \ \}$$
$$happens \triangleq \{ \ happens(t_1, switch), happens(t_2, switch) \ \}$$
$$< \triangleq \{ \ t_1 < t_3, t_2 < t_3 \ \}$$
$$initially \triangleq \{\}$$

*Transforming the FOL axiom to normal form yields:

$$\leftarrow \neg initially(alive)$$
$$\leftarrow holds(alive, t_3)$$

†Note that it would also be natural to drop $\neg holds(alive, t_3)$ from the theory and to give it as an observation to be explained as input to the abductive procedure. This makes no difference whatsoever.

‡As mentioned earlier, any approach in which time is interpreted by the natural numbers or the real numbers under standard order implicitly contains the linearity axiom.

Note that the definition of $<$ entails $\neg t_1 < t_2 \wedge \neg t_2 < t_1$; moreover by the Clark Equality Theory, $t_1 \neq t_2$. As a consequence, the linearity axiom of $\mathcal{T}_{TO}$ is violated.

The above theory augmented with the persistence theory $\mathcal{T}_{per}$ contains definitions for all predicates and corresponds to a logic program. This theory entails $holds(on, t_3)$; Prolog succeeds on the query $holds(on, t_3)$. Hence the theory fails to solve the prediction problem.

The cause for this anomaly is the fact that $<$ is a non-linear partial order, in particular that it entails $\neg t_1 < t_2 \wedge \neg t_2 < t_1 \wedge (\neg t_1 = t_2)$. Because of this fact, the intervals $]-\infty, t_1[= \{t|t < t_1\}$ and $]t_1, t_3[= \{t|t_1 < t < t_3\}$ are empty. Because on is false initially and $]-\infty, t_1[$ is empty, on is false at t_1 and hence $switch$ initiates on at t_1; because $]t_1, t_3[$ is provably empty, there is no termination of on during this interval, hence $holds(on, t_3)$ can be derived.

Representing a partially known order of events by a provably non-linear partial order is in general not a correct strategy to represent incomplete knowledge on the order of events*. A more correct representation of the narrative is obtained by dropping the definition of $<$ and including the FOL axiom $t_1 < t_3 \wedge t_2 < t_3$ and $\mathcal{T}_{TO}$. This way, the uncertainty on the order of time points is represented by the fact that the resulting theory has models in which $t_1 < t_2$ and others in which $t_2 < t_1$. However, in all models, $<$ is a total order and a linearisation of the set of *known* order atoms.

Definition 11.4.2. *A linearisation of a partial order $<$ on a domain D is any total order $<_t$ on D which includes the partial order. I.e. if $t < t'$ then $t <_t t'$.*

Abductive reasoning on the query $\neg holds(on, t_3)$ yields two solutions:

$$< \triangleq \{\ t_1 < t_2 < t_3\ \}$$

and

$$< \triangleq \{\ t_2 < t_1 < t_3\ \}$$

The existence of these solutions only proves that it is possible that the light is off at t_3. However, the theory augmented with $\mathcal{T}_{TO}$ entails that it is necessary that the light is off at t_3. SLDNFA fails finitely on the query $holds(on, t_3)$. By the duality property, it follows that this EC entails $\neg holds(on, t_3)$.

Observe here that in each linearisation of the partial order $\{t_2 < t_3, t_1 < t_3\}$, it holds that $holds(on, t_3)$ is false, while in the partial order itself, the atom $holds(on, t_3)$ is true.

11.4.3 Unknown effects and nondeterminism

Another way in which uncertainty can arise in temporal domains is by the presence of actions with nondeterministic effects: the outcome of such an action is not uniquely determined by the circumstances and the way in which it is executed.

The state of the world at all times of a domain involving nondeterministic actions is dependent on the initial state, the occurring actions and their order, and information determining for each nondeterministic action occurrence which of the possible outcomes it has.

*This problem with partial order time occurs also in the context of planning. The problem with the light switch scenario is similar to the anomalies reported in [Missiaen, 1991b; Missiaen *et al.*, 1995] on the planning approaches in [Eshghi, 1988a; Shanahan, 1989; Missiaen, 1991b]. In Section 11.4.2, we come back to this issue.

Typically the latter information is unknown, otherwise we are not talking about nondeterminism. As before, abduction can often be used to fill some gaps in the described knowledge.

First of all, we need a syntax to represent nondeterministic actions. We assume that each action has a known set of possible outcomes, one of which will be realized whenever the action occurs. This can be represented at a high level by a rule of the form:

$$A \textbf{ causes } E_1 \mid \ldots \mid E_n \textbf{ if } \Psi$$

in which the E_i are the possible outcomes of action A if it is executed when Ψ holds. The symbol | denotes a disjunction.

As an example, consider the Russian turkey shooting problem, which involves a nondeterministic action of spinning the chamber of the gun. If the gun is loaded, this action may or may not unload it:

$$spin \textbf{ causes } \neg loaded \mid true \textbf{ if } loaded$$

where $true$ denotes just the empty effect.

Note the correspondence between this problem and the *syphilis-possibly-causes-paresis* problem of Section 11.1. The technique to represent this nondeterministic causation is the one proposed in Section 11.3. A translation of nondeterministic rules of the above type to the presented calculus needs to find a way around the disjunctions, as the calculus does not allow for disjunctive rules*. Such a translation can be achieved by introducing "degree of freedom" predicates. These are open predicates of which the truth or falsehood determine the outcome of each nondeterministic action occurrence. As such, they represent exactly the information usually missing in a nondeterministic domain.

As an example, the above rule represents one nondeterministic action with two possible outcomes (among which the empty effect). Hence, there is one degree of freedom and only one predicate needs to be introduced. If this predicate is true at a certain time, the execution of the action at that time has the effect of unloading the gun. If it is false, the action has no effect and the gun remains loaded. Adopting the turkey's point of view, we call this predicate $good\_luck$. It is parameterized with a time point, to indicate that the action may have different outcomes at different times. The translation of the nondeterministic effect rule now becomes

$$terminates(spin, loaded, T) \leftarrow holds(loaded, T), good\_luck(T).$$

In the other case, i.e. when $holds(loaded, T), \neg good\_luck(T)$ is true, the action has its second possible outcome. However, this is no effect at all. For this reason there is no second rule in this case.

Degree of freedom predicates explicitly represent the missing knowledge which would determine the outcome of nondeterministic actions. As a result, abduction can be used to derive information on these predicates and hence on the way nondeterministic actions turn out. A simple example in the turkey world is the following postdiction problem: we have a sequence of actions of loading, spinning, and shooting, and we observe that after the shooting the turkey is still alive. Does this tell us anything about the outcome of spinning?

*Moreover the intended disjunction is not really standard disjunction at the level of the calculus, but a precise discussion of this issue is off-topic. Suffice it to say that the translation we provide interprets the disjunction in the right way.

Formally, we get the following definitions:

$$happens \triangleq \{\ happens(load, t_1), happens(spin, t_2), happens(shoot, t_3)\ \}$$

$$< \triangleq \{\ t_1 < t_2 < t_3 < t_4\ \}$$

and no information on the initial state. The observation $holds(alive, t_4)$ can only be explained if $holds(loaded, t_3)$ is false and $initially(alive)$ true. Since t_1 initiates $loaded$ and the action $spin$ is the only other action between t_1 and t_3, $spin$ must have terminated $loaded$ again, and so $good\_luck(t_2)$ is abduced. In addition, also $initially(alive)$ must be abduced to justify the observation $holds(alive, t_4)$.

Another benchmark example which can be interpreted as a problem involving unknown effects of actions is the stolen car example [Baker, 1989]. Someone parks his car at a rather unsafe location, leaves it there for two nights, and comes back the third day to find his car gone. In one representation, the two nights can be represented by two $wait$ actions. In this formulation of the problem, there is complete knowledge on the initial state, on the events and on their order. Normally the wait action has no effect. However, given the observation that the car is stolen in the final state and assuming that we have full knowledge of the events that occur, an intended conclusion is that one of the wait events had an (abnormal) effect of terminating $parked$.

A problem of this sort involves default reasoning. The desired non-monotonic property of the problem representation is that without the observation that $parked$ is false in the final state, it entails that $parked$ is true in this state; with the observation included in the theory, it should entail that one of the wait effects has terminated $parked$.

By FOL's monotonicity, it follows that a default of this sort cannot be represented in FOL. For example, the following EC:

$$initially \triangleq \{\}$$

$$\{\ initiates(park, parked, T) \leftarrow\ \}$$

$$terminates \triangleq \{\}$$

$$\{\ poss(wait, T) \leftarrow\ \}$$

$$happens \triangleq \{\ happens(park, t_1), happens(wait, t_2), happens(wait, t_3)\ \}$$

$$< \triangleq \{\ t_1 < t_2 < t_3 < t_4\ \}$$

entails $holds(parked, t_4)$ and hence is inconsistent with $\neg holds(parked, t_4)$. Note that this EC defines all predicates. The query $holds(parked, t_4)$ can be proven by Prolog.

One way to overcome this problem is not to take the closure of the effect rules for $initiates$ and $terminates$. The resulting theory is consistent with $holds(parked, t_4)$ but does not entail it. An abductive solution for this query is:

$$terminates \triangleq \{\}$$

$$initiates \triangleq \{ \ initiates(park, parked, t_i) \mid 1 \le i \le 4 \ \}$$

The theory is also consistent with $\neg holds(parked, t_4)$. An abductive solution for this query is:

$$\{ \ terminates(wait, park, t_2) \leftarrow \ \}$$

$$initiates \triangleq \{ \ initiates(park, parked, t_i) \mid 1 \le i \le 4 \ \}$$

An analogous solution exists with $terminates(wait, park, t_3)$.

SLDNFA fails on the query:

$$\neg holds(parked, t_4) \wedge \neg terminates(wait, parked, t_2) \wedge \\ terminates(wait, parked, t_3)$$

By the duality property, this entails that the theory entails the negation of this query, being:

$$\neg holds(parked, t_4) \rightarrow \ terminates(wait, parked, t_2) \vee \\ terminates(wait, parked, t_3)$$

An alternative solution based on nondeterministic events could be the following: we introduce two types of "waiting" actions $wait\_night$ and $wait\_day$, assuming that during any night, cars can get stolen ($parked$ is terminated). As such, $wait\_night$ is a nondeterministic action with two possible outcomes. Effect rules are now

$$\{ \ initiates(park, parked, T) \leftarrow \ \}$$

$$\{ \ terminates(wait\_night, parked, T) \leftarrow holds(parked, T), bad\_luck(T) \ \}$$

where $bad\_luck(T)$ is an open predicate.

The above scenario is now represented as

$$happens \triangleq \left\{ \begin{array}{l} happens(park, t_1), \\ happens(wait\_night, t_2), \\ happens(wait\_day, t_3), \\ happens(wait\_night, t_4) \end{array} \right\}$$

$$< \triangleq \{t_1 < t_2 < t_3 < t_4 < t_5\}$$

The observation $\neg holds(parked, t_5)$ can now be explained in only two ways: by abducing either $bad\_luck(t_2)$ or $bad\_luck(t_4)$. In other words, the car is definitely stolen, but it is not certain during which night this has happened. The theory augmented with the observation entails:

$$terminates(wait\_night, parked, t_2) \vee terminates(wait\_night, parked, t_4)$$

and also:

$$bad\_luck(t_2) \vee bad\_luck(t_4)$$

SLDNFA proves these formulas by failing on their negation.

11.4.4 Combining uncertainty on events and initial state

In [Sadri and Kowalski, 1995], the following simple example was used to demonstrate some errors with existing versions of event calculus. Consider the following scenario:: *at time* t_1 *Bob gives a book at Mary; at time* $t_2 > t_1$, *John gives the book at Tom.* The complexity of this simple scenario lies in the fact that it combines state constraints and action preconditions with uncertainty on initial state and on events. The definitions of $initiates, terminates$ and $poss$ are:

$$\{ \ initiates(give(X, O, Y), has(Y, O), T) \leftarrow \ \}$$

$$\{ \ terminates(give(X, O, Y), has(X, O), T) \leftarrow \ \}$$

$$\{ \ poss(give(X, O, Y), T) \leftarrow holds(has(X, O), T) \wedge X \neq Y \ \}$$

In this problem, there is also the state constraint that in each state an object has at most one owner:

$$\forall T.holds(has(X, O), T) \wedge holds(has(Y, O), T) \rightarrow X = Y$$

The information on the predicates $initially$, $<$, $happens$ describing the narrative, is incomplete. The EC based on the completion of the set of known $initially$ and $happens$ atoms entails the negative literals $\neg holds(has(bob, book), t_1)$ and $\neg holds(has(john, book), t_2)$, hence is inconsistent with the action preconditions of the known $give$ actions. A correct representation is given by the FOL axioms:

$$happens(give(bob, book, mary), t_1)$$

$$happens(give(john, book, tom), t_2)$$

$$t_1 < t_2 < t_3$$

An abductive solution with minimal cardinality for the query $true$ is given by:

$$happens \triangleq \left\{ \begin{array}{l} happens(give(bob, book, mary), t_1), \\ happens(give(mary, book, john), t'), \\ happens(give(john, book, tom), t_2) \end{array} \right\}$$

$$initially \triangleq \{ \ initially(has(bob, book)) \ \}$$

$$< \triangleq \{t_1 < t' < t_2 < t_3\}$$

The theory entails*:

$$holds(has(bob, book), t_1)$$

$$holds(has(mary, book), t_2)$$

$$\exists X, T.happens(give(X, book, john), T) \wedge t_1 < T < t_2$$

*The current implementation of SLDNFA cannot prove these theorems and loops, due to control problems.

$$\exists X, T.happens(give(mary, book, X), T) \wedge t_1 < T < t_2$$

An intended conclusion of this theory could be also that Tom has the book at t_3. One could argue that since no information is available that suggests or implies that Tom has given the book away after receiving it, a human expert will often infer by default that such an action has not happened. The current theory does not entail the absence of this action, and hence does not entail that Tom has the book at t_3. However, as Poole pointed out in [Poole, 1988], default reasoning of this kind can be performed by abductive reasoning. Indeed, observe that in the abductive solutions which have minimal cardinality or are minimal w.r.t. set inclusion, an action $happens(give(tom, book, x), t'')$ with $t_2 < t'' < t_3$ will be absent.

11.5 A constraint solver for $\mathcal{T}_{TO}$

In the context of temporal reasoning, abduction was introduced originally for planning in the Event Calculus [Eshghi, 1988a]. A planning problem is formulated as an EC describing effects of actions, action preconditions, the initial state and by a goal describing the desired goal state. Subject of the search is a sequence of actions that transforms the initial into the goal state. The predicates describing this sequence are $happens$ and $<$; they are subject of the planning search; a fortiori these predicates are open predicates in the EC describing the planning domain.

As reported in [Missiaen *et al.*, 1995], early abductive planning systems ([Eshghi, 1988a; Shanahan, 1989; Missiaen *et al.*, 1992]) sometimes generated erroneous partial plans, in which two interfering actions (such as flipping a switch) are assumed to be unrelated in time. While these erroneous plans logically entail the desired final state, linearisations of these plans did not in general. As a consequence, real execution of the computed plan produces an erroneous final state.

In principle, this problem is solved by including the axiom of total order in the EC. Using this technique, an abductive procedure will generate only linear plans. Unfortunately, linear planning is very inefficient. In general, in a plan many events do not interfere with each other. A linear planner is inefficient because it generates an exponential number of permutations of these *independent* events. In general, it would be desirable to get *partial plans* which satisfy the correctness criterion given in [Missiaen, 1991b]: the goal state must be provable from each linearisation of the plan. Such a partial plan leaves open the order of independent events. Compared to a partial planner, the number of plans computed by a linear planner is exponential in the number of independent pairs of events.

To solve this problem, [Denecker *et al.*, 1992] proposed an extension SLDNFA-LO with a simple constraint solver for $<$, checking the satisfiability of the abduced $<$ atoms against the theory of total order. This solver is based on a simple idea. Procedurally, it computes the transitive closure of the abduced $<$ facts. When an atom $t_1 < t_2$ is abduced, it is checked whether t_1 and t_2 are different and whether the symmetric atom $t_2 < t_1$ does not already occur in the precedence relationship. If one of these situations happens, the abduction step fails. Otherwise, the atom is abduced and the transitive closure of the extended relation is computed.

In addition to this, when SLDNFA-LO selects an atom $t_1 < t_2$ in a negative goal, it makes this atom false by abducing the symmetric atom $t_2 < t_1$. When later $t_1 < t_2$ occurs in a negative goal, the abduction of $t_1 < t_2$ fails. As a result, a derivation never depends on the absence of two symmetric precedence facts.

Example 11.5.1. *A first example illustrates how SLDNFA-LO avoids erroneous derivations as in the light switch problem of Section 11.4.2. To avoid lengthy derivations and goals, consider a simplified version:*

$$\left\{ \begin{array}{l} light\_off \leftarrow e_1 < e_2 \\ light\_off \leftarrow e_2 < e_1 \end{array} \right\}$$

Without the totality axiom, the empty answer is an abductive answer for the goal $\neg light\_off$. In this answer e_1 and e_2 are two different time points unrelated in time; in this answer, the totality axiom is violated. SLDNFA-LO correctly fails to find a solution for this goal because it realizes that if not $e_1 < e_2$, then necessarily $e_2 < e_1$ (since by CET, $e_1 \neq e_2$). The SLDNFA-LO tree is given in Figure 11.1.

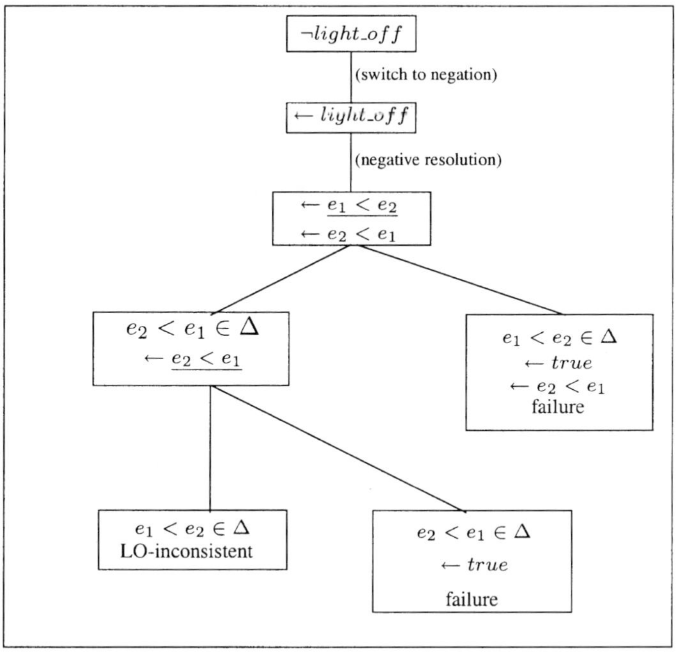

Figure 11.1: Failed SLDNFA-LO-tree for $\neg light\_off$

Example 11.5.2. *A second example illustrates how SLDNFA-LO can generate correct partial plans. Consider a simplified planning problem with four fluents p, q, r, s. An action e_0 initiates p, e_1 initiates q if s holds and e_2 initiates r and terminates s. Initially s is true, and in the goal state p, q and r are true. Clearly, any sequence of the three actions in which e_1 precedes e_2 is a solution. Without sacrificing the essence of the problem, we simplify the EC:*

$$\{\ holds(P) \leftarrow init(E, P)\ \}$$

$$\{\ clip(P, E) \leftarrow happens(C), C < E, term(C, P)\ \}$$

$$\left\{\begin{array}{l} init(e_0, p) \leftarrow \\ init(e_1, q) \leftarrow \neg clip(s, e_1) \\ init(e_2, r) \leftarrow \end{array}\right\}$$

$$\{\ term(e_2, s) \leftarrow\ \}$$

$$happens \stackrel{\triangle}{=} \{happens(e_0), happens(e_1), happens(e_2)\}$$

The derivation is presented in Figure 11.2.

$holds(p) \wedge holds(q) \wedge holds(r)$

| (positive resolution)

$init(E, p) \wedge holds(q) \wedge holds(r)$

E/e_0 | (positive resolution)

$holds(q) \wedge holds(r)$

| (positive resolution)

$holds(q) \wedge init(E', r)$

E'/e_2 | (positive resolution)

$holds(q)$

| (positive resolution)

$init(E'', q)$

E''/e_1 | (positive resolution)

$\neg clip(s, e_1)$

| (switch to negation)

$\leftarrow clip(s, e_1)$

| (negative resolution)

$\leftarrow happens(C), C < e_1, term(C, s)$

| (negative resolution)

$\leftarrow e_0 < e_1, term(e_0, s)$ $\quad \leftarrow e_1 < e_1, term(e_1, s)$ $\quad \leftarrow e_2 < e_1, term(e_2, s)$

| (negative resolution)

$\leftarrow e_1 < e_1, term(e_1, s)$ $\quad \leftarrow e_2 < e_1, term(e_2, s)$

| (negative resolution)

$\leftarrow e_2 < e_1, term(e_2, s)$

| (negative resolution)

$\leftarrow e_2 < e_1$

|

$\Delta \leftarrow e_1 < e_2$

success

Figure 11.2: SLDNFA-LO-derivation for $holds(p) \wedge holds(q) \wedge holds(r)$

Note that in the negative goals $\leftarrow e_i < e_1, term(e_i, s)$, only e_2 possibly terminates s. Depending on whether we select first the $term(e_i, s)$ atom or $e_i < e_1$, we obtain more or less instantiated plans. The derivation in Figure 11.2 selects $term(e_i, s)$ atoms first and produces a partial plan $\Delta = \{e_1 < e_2\}$.

Given a theory $\mathcal{T}$ consisting of definitions $\mathcal{D}$ and FOL axioms T and a query Q, SLDNFA-LO generates a tuple $(\Delta, S_<, \theta)$ where Δ is a set of definitions for all open predicates except

$<$, $S_<$ is a set of $<$-atoms describing a partial order and θ a substitution. In [Denecker, 1993], the following correctness theorem is proven for SLDNFA-LO.

Theorem 11.5.1. *It holds that*

- $\mathcal{D} \cup \Delta \cup S_< \cup \mathcal{T}_{TO} \models \forall(\theta(Q))$
- $\mathcal{D} \cup \Delta \cup S_< \cup \mathcal{T}_{TO} \models T$

Moreover, let $\Delta_<$ be a linearisation of $S_<$. Then it holds that:

- $\mathcal{D} \cup \Delta \cup \{\Delta_<\} \models \forall(\theta(Q))$
- $\mathcal{D} \cup \Delta \cup \{\Delta_<\} \models T$
- $\mathcal{D} \cup \Delta \cup \{\Delta_<\} \models \mathcal{T}_{TO}$

11.5.1 Partial Order Planning with Event Calculus

The following example shows an application of SLDNFA-LO for partial order planning. The EC below axiomatizes a block world problem with two robots, $karel$ and $karolien$. Both robots can perform two actions: picking up one block (from the table or from another block) and putting a clasped block on the table or on top of another block. As long as both robots operate on different blocks and locations and build different towers of blocks, their actions do not interfere. As a consequence, a partial order planner should be able to generate partial plans.

The relevant fluents in the block world domain are:

- $on(B, L)$: block B is on location L; a location is a block or the table;
- $clear(L)$: L is a clear location; i.e. something can be put on L; note that this property can be derived in terms of the on fluent: a block is clear iff nothing is on it (and the table is always clear);
- $clasped(B, R)$: robot R has clasped block B;
- $free\_robot(R)$: robot R holds nothing; note that the robot is free iff there is no block B such that $clasped(B, R)$.

One of the nice properties of the iff-formalism and of EC is that one can easily define fluents in terms of other fluents. We extend the definition $\mathcal{D}_{holds}$ with the following rules defining the fluents $clear$ in terms of on, and $free\_robot$ in terms of $clasped$:

$$\left\{\begin{array}{l} holds(clear(table), E) \leftarrow \\ holds(clear(B), E) \leftarrow block(B) \wedge \ \neg\exists B'.holds(on(B', B), E) \ \wedge \\ \qquad\qquad\qquad\qquad\qquad\qquad\qquad\quad \neg\exists R.holds(clasped(B, R), E) \\ holds(free\_robot(R), E) \leftarrow \neg\exists B.holds(clasped(B, R), E) \end{array}\right.$$

Observe that the rules defining fluents $clear$ and $free\_robot$ do not represent causal rules. Instead they represent definitions of concepts. Effects on these derived fluents are not explicitly represented; they are implicitly represented by the following rules describing the effects on the primitive fluents on and $clasped$:

$$\left\{\begin{array}{l} initiates(put(X, Y, R), on(X, Y), T) \leftarrow \\ initiates(pick(X, R), clasped(X, R), T) \leftarrow \end{array}\right\}$$

$$\left\{\begin{array}{l} terminates(pick(X,R),on(X,Y),T) \leftarrow \\ terminates(put(X,Y,R),clasped(X,R),T) \leftarrow \end{array}\right\}$$

$$\left\{\begin{array}{l} poss(put(B,L,R),E) \leftarrow \\ \quad block(B) \wedge location(L) \wedge B \neq L \wedge robot(R) \wedge \\ \quad holds(clasped(B,R),E) \wedge holds(clear(L),E) \\ poss(pick(B,R),E) \leftarrow \\ \quad block(B) \wedge robot(R) \wedge \\ \quad holds(free\_robot(R),E) \wedge holds(clear(B),E) \end{array}\right\}$$

One robot can perform only one action at the same time. The two robots can perform actions simultaneously provided that they do not operate on the same block or location. It turns out that in this domain, it is easier to define when actions can occur concurrently than to define when actions cannot occur concurrently. Therefore, we substitute the following axiom for the concurrency theory $\mathcal{T}_{conc}$:

$$happens(A_1,T), happens(A_2,T) \rightarrow A_1 = A_2, compatible(A_1,A_2,T)$$

$$\left\{\begin{array}{l} compatible(put(B_1,L_1,R_1),put(B_2,L_2,R_2),T) \leftarrow \\ \quad R_1 \neq R_2, L_1 \neq L_2 \\ compatible(pick(B_1,R_1),pick(B_2,R_2),T) \leftarrow \\ \quad R_1 \neq R_2, B_1 \neq B_2 \\ compatible(put(B_1,L_1,R_1),pick(B_2,R_2),T) \leftarrow \\ \quad R_1 \neq R_2, B_1 \neq B_2, L_1 \neq B_2 \end{array}\right\}$$

The remaining axioms define locations, blocks and the initial state. A simple planning problem in which partial order planning is possible is one in which two towers must be build.

$$\left\{\begin{array}{l} location(B) \leftarrow block(B) \\ location(table) \leftarrow \end{array}\right\}$$

$$block \triangleq \{block(a), block(b), block(c), block(d)\}$$

$$robot \triangleq \{robot(karel), robot(karolien)\}$$

$$initially \triangleq \left\{\begin{array}{l} initially(on(a,table)), initially(on(b,table)), \\ initially(on(c,table)), initially(on(d,table)) \end{array}\right\}$$

Assume that the goal state is the following one:

$$holds(on(a,b),t_f) \wedge holds(on(c,d),t_f)$$

A solution generated by SLDNFA-LO is:

$$happens \triangleq \left\{\begin{array}{l} happens(pick(a,karel),t_1), \\ happens(put(a,b,karel),t_2), \\ happens(pick(c,karolien),t_3), \\ happens(put(c,d,karolien),t_4) \end{array}\right\}$$

$$t_1 < t_2 < t_f, t_3 < t_4 < t_f$$

Each linearisation of this partial order yields a correct plan.

11.6 Reasoning on continuous change and resources

In this section, some examples show that an integration of iff-abduction with CLP(R) is able to solve more sophisticated problems in the context of reasoning on continuous change. In [Bruneel and Clarebout, 1994], an integration of SLDNFA and CLP(R) was described and an implementation of a prototype was presented. This system integrates iff-abduction and reasoning about linear equations and inequalities. A more recent system combining abduction and finite domain constraint solving CLP(FD) is the Asystem [Kakas *et al.*, 2001].

Below, two simple applications involving real number entities are given. The first example uses Shanahan's extension of EC for continuous change [Shanahan, 1990]. The example was presented in [Bruneel and Clarebout, 1994] and is a variant of one in [Shanahan, 1990]. *There is a barrel b and two water pipes p_1, p_2, two taps tap_1, tap_2 connecting respectively p_1 to b and p_2 to b. Initially b is empty and both taps are closed. The problem is to find a plan to fill b with a content of 100 liter.*

The definition of $holds$ contains one extra rule which describes a fluent P affected by an on going process $Process$. The value of P at time T is a function of the start of the $Process$ and the time T. This function is described by the predicate $trajectory(Process, T_i, T, P)$, where T_i is the initiation time of the process:

$$\left\{\begin{array}{ll} holds(P,T) \leftarrow & happens(A,T_1) \wedge T_1 < T \wedge initiates(A,P,T_1) \wedge \\ & \neg\exists T_2, A_2.\ happens(A_2,T_2) \wedge T_1 < T_2 < T \wedge \\ & \qquad terminates(A_2,P,T_2) \\ holds(P,T) \leftarrow & happens(A,T_1) \wedge T_1 < T \wedge \\ & initiates(A, Process, T_1) \wedge \\ & trajectory(Process, T_1, T, P) \wedge \\ & \neg\exists T_2, A_2.\ happens(A_2,T_2) \wedge T_1 < T_2 < T \wedge \\ & \qquad terminates(A_2, Process, T_2) \end{array}\right\}$$

The term $filling(B, Fl)$ represents the process that the barrel B is being filled at a speed of Fl liters per second. If the process starts at time T_i and the initial level of B at T_i is L_i, then at time T, the level of the barrel is $L_i + Fl * (T - T_i)$. The following definition expresses this:

$$\left\{\begin{array}{l} trajectory(filling(B, Fl), T_i, T, level(B, L)) \leftarrow \\ \quad holds(level(B, L_i), T_i) \wedge \\ \quad L = L_i + Fl * (T - T_i) \end{array}\right\}$$

The following definitions of $initiates$, $terminates$ and $poss$ assume that no simultaneous opening or closing actions occur.

$$\left\{\begin{array}{l} initiates(open\_tap(Tap), open(Tap), T) \leftarrow \\ initiates(open\_tap(Tap), filling(B, Fl), T) \leftarrow \\ \qquad flow(Tap, Fl) \wedge connects(Tap, B1, B) \wedge \\ \qquad \neg\exists Fl_1.holds(filling(B, Fl_2), T) \\ initiates(open\_tap(Tap), filling(B, Fl), T) \leftarrow \\ \qquad flow(Tap, Fl_1) \wedge connects(Tap, B1, B) \wedge \\ \qquad holds(filling(B, Fl_2), T) \wedge Fl = Fl_1 + Fl_2 \\ initiates(close\_tap(Tap), filling(B, Fl), E) \leftarrow \\ \qquad flow(Tap, Fl_1) \wedge connects(Tap, B_1, B) \wedge \\ \qquad holds(filling(B, Fl_2), E) \wedge Fl = Fl_2 - Fl_1 \end{array}\right\}$$

$$\left\{ \begin{array}{l} terminates(open\_tap(Tap), filling(B, Fl), T) \leftarrow \\ \quad holds(filling(B, Fl)), T) \wedge connects(Tap, X, B) \\ terminates(close\_tap(Tap), open(Tap), T) \leftarrow \\ terminates(close\_tap(Tap), filling(B, Fl), T) \leftarrow \\ \quad holds(filling(B, Fl)), T) \wedge connects(Tap, X, B) \\ terminates(open\_tap(Tap), level(L), T) \leftarrow holds(level(L), T) \end{array} \right\}$$

$$\left\{ \begin{array}{l} poss(open\_tap(Tap), T) \leftarrow tap(Tap) \wedge \neg holds(open(Tap), T) \\ poss(close\_tap(Tap), T) \leftarrow tap(Tap) \wedge holds(open(Tap), T) \end{array} \right\}$$

$$tap \stackrel{\triangle}{=} \{\ tap(tap_1), tap(tap_2)\ \}$$

$$flow \stackrel{\triangle}{=} \{\ flow(tap_1, 5), flow(tap_2, 3)\ \}$$

$$connects \stackrel{\triangle}{=} \{\ connects(tap_1, p_1, b), connects(tap_2, p_2, b)\ \}$$

$$initially \stackrel{\triangle}{=} \{\ initially(level(b, 0))\ \}$$

The goal state is to have the barrel filled with 100 liter (of water):

$$holds(level(b, 100), t_{end}),$$

Among the solutions generated by the system is:

$$happens \stackrel{\triangle}{=} \{\ happens(open\_tap(tap_1), t_1)\ \}$$

$$t_{end} = t_1 + 20$$

Another generated solution is

$$happens \stackrel{\triangle}{=} \{\ happens(open\_tap(tap_1), t_1), happens(open\_tap(tap_2), t_2)\ \}$$

$$t_1 < t_2 \wedge 100 = 5 * (t_2 - t_1) + 8 * (t_{end} - t_2)$$

In this solution, first tap_1 and then tap_2 is opened. The constraint on t_1, t_2 and t_{end} expresses a class of solutions.

A second example is a simple planning example in the context of a domain in which actions need certain resources. The aim of the example is to show that with iff-abduction and CLP(R), more complex planning problems can be tackled in which not only the actions are unknown and must be computed but also the initial state. A solution to such a planning problem consists of a plan of actions and a set of constraints on the unspecified initial state. The example is a variant of an example in [Bruneel and Clarebout, 1994]. The goal state is to have a bread of a given weight. The planner should compute a plan and also the needed quantities of ingredients in the initial state. The formalism used is the EC as defined in Section 11.4. The following EC assumes that no simultaneous kneading actions occur.

$$\left\{ \begin{array}{l} initiates(baking, bread(B), T) \leftarrow holds(paste(B), T) \\ initiates(kneading(ID), paste(ID), T) \leftarrow \\ initiates(kneading(ID), flour(A_f - Q_f), T) \leftarrow \\ \quad weight(ID, W) \wedge flour\_quant(W, Q_f) \wedge holds(flour(A_f), T) \\ initiates(kneading(ID), water(A_w - Q_w), T) \leftarrow \\ \quad weight(ID, W) \wedge water\_quant(W, Q_w) \wedge holds(water(A_w), T \\ initiates(kneading(ID), yeast(A_y - Q_y), T) \leftarrow \\ \quad weight(ID, W) \wedge yeast\_quant(W, Q_y) \wedge holds(yeast(A_y), T) \end{array} \right\}$$

$$\left\{\begin{array}{l} terminates(baking, paste(B), T) \leftarrow holds(paste(B), T) \\ terminates(kneading(P), flour(A_f), T) \leftarrow holds(flour(A_f), T) \\ terminates(kneading(P), water(A_w), T) \leftarrow holds(water(A_w), T) \\ terminates(kneading(P), yeast(A_y), T) \leftarrow holds(yeast(A_y), T) \end{array}\right\}$$

$$\left\{\begin{array}{l} poss(baking, T) \leftarrow \\ poss(kneading(ID), T) \leftarrow \\ \quad weight(ID, W) \wedge \\ \quad flour\_quant(W, Q_f) \wedge holds(flour(A_f), T) \wedge Q_f \leq A_f \wedge \\ \quad water\_quant(W, Q_w) \wedge holds(water(A_w), T) \wedge Q_w \leq A_w \wedge \\ \quad yeast\_quant(W, Q_y) \wedge holds(yeast(A_y), T) \wedge Q_y \leq A_y \end{array}\right\}$$

The goal is to obtain a bread of 2kg. The goal is formulated as:

$$holds(bread(b), t_{end}) \wedge weight(b, 2)$$

An answer generated by iff-abduction with CLP(R) is

$$happens \triangleq \{\ happens(kneading(b), t_1), happens(baking, t_2)\ \}$$

$$weight \triangleq \{\ weight(b, 2)\ \}$$

$$initially \triangleq \{\ initially(flour(f)), initially(water(w)), initially(yeast(y))\ \}$$

$$t_1 < t_2 < t_{end}$$

$$f \geq 1.3 \wedge w \geq 0.64 \wedge y \geq 0.6$$

The latter constraints assert that in the initial state, the amounts of flour, water and yeast must be larger than the one needed for the bread.

11.7 Limitations of iff-abduction

In the previous sections, iff-abduction was often used as a tool to prove theorems in event calculus. Sometimes natural and intended properties of a domain description cannot be proven using iff-abduction. This problem is caused by the weak axiomatization of temporal domains in First Order Event Calculus. We illustrate the problem.

Consider the following formalisation of a light switch domain. Initially the light is off. A switch action flips the status of the light from off to on and vice versa. A formalisation with fluents *on*, *off* is as follows:

$$\left\{\begin{array}{l} initiates(switch, on, T) \leftarrow holds(off, T) \\ initiates(switch, off, T) \leftarrow holds(on, T) \end{array}\right\}$$

$$\left\{\begin{array}{l} terminates(switch, on, T) \leftarrow holds(on, T) \\ terminates(switch, off, T) \leftarrow holds(off, T) \end{array}\right\}$$

$$\{\ poss(switch, T) \leftarrow\ \}$$

$$initially \triangleq \{ \ initially(off) \ \}$$

An expected property of this domain is the state constraint that either on or off holds at any time point.

One easily verifies that after any finite sequence of switch actions, either on or off holds. Hence, there exists no finite abductive solution for the query:

$$\neg holds(off, T) \wedge \neg holds(on, T)$$

Neither does there exists a finite abductive solution for the query:

$$holds(off, T) \wedge holds(on, T)$$

However, no sound iff-abductive procedure satisfying the duality property will be able to fail finitely on any of both goals. Indeed, if the procedure failed finitely on the first query, then by the duality property it would have proven that

$$\forall T.holds(off, T) \vee holds(on, T)$$

Likewise, if it failed on the second query, it would have proven that

$$\forall T.\neg holds(on, T) \vee \neg holds(off, T)$$

However, there exists models of this EC in which these state constraints are violated. Below, we construct such a model.

Consider an interpretation I in which time is interpreted by the positive real numbers. In the interval $[0, 1]$ an infinite number of $switch$ actions happen at time points $1 - \frac{1}{n}$ for each natural number $n > 0$. I interprets $happens$ as follows:

$$happens_I \triangleq \{happens(switch, 1 - \frac{1}{n}) | 0 < n \in I\!N\}$$

This interpretation of $happens$ can be extended to a model of the EC in the following way. At time 0, off holds. In the interval $]0, \frac{1}{2}]$, on holds. In the interval $]\frac{1}{2}, \frac{1}{3}]$, off holds. In the subsequent intervals, on and off alternate.

At the interval $[1, \infty[$, both on and off are false. Indeed, for any time $t \geq 1$, it holds that between each time point $1 - \frac{1}{n}$ with a $switch$ initiating on, and t, there is an intermediate time point $1 - \frac{1}{n+1} \in]1 - \frac{1}{n}, t[$ with a $switch$ terminating on. Likewise, for any time $t \geq 1$, it holds that between any time $1 - \frac{1}{n}$ initiating off and time t, a switch action happens at $1 - \frac{1}{n+1}$ which terminates off. By the definition of $holds$, both on and off must be false*.

*Formally, the interpretations of $holds$, $initiates$ and $terminates$ in this model are as follows:

$$\begin{aligned} holds_I \triangleq\ & \{holds(off, 0)\} \cup \\ & \{holds(on, t) | \exists\, 0 < n \in I\!N : 1 - \tfrac{1}{2n-1} < t \leq 1 - \tfrac{1}{2n}\} \cup \\ & \{holds(off, t) | \exists\, 0 < n \in I\!N : 1 - \tfrac{1}{2n} < t \leq 1 - \tfrac{1}{2n+1}\} \end{aligned}$$

$$\begin{aligned} initiates_I \triangleq\ & \{initiates(switch, on, 0)\} \cup \\ & \{initiates(switch, off, t) | \exists\, 0 < n \in I\!N : 1 - \tfrac{1}{2n-1} < t \leq 1 - \tfrac{1}{2n}\} \cup \\ & \{initiates(switch, on, t) | \exists\, 0 < n \in I\!N : 1 - \tfrac{1}{2n} < t \leq 1 - \tfrac{1}{2n+1}\} \end{aligned}$$

$$\begin{aligned} terminates_I \triangleq\ & \{terminates(switch, off, 0)\} \cup \\ & \{terminates(switch, on, t) | \exists\, 0 < n \in I\!N : 1 - \tfrac{1}{2n-1} < t \leq 1 - \tfrac{1}{2n}\} \cup \\ & \{terminates(switch, off, t) | \exists\, 0 < n \in I\!N : 1 - \tfrac{1}{2n} < t \leq 1 - \tfrac{1}{2n+1}\} \end{aligned}$$

The existence of such a model shows that though the state constraint is intuitively valid, it cannot be proven from the EC. The problem is caused by the fact that the axiomatization is not strong enough to eliminate models with an infinite number of actions in finite time. However, there exists a stronger axiomatization of time and actions which guarantees that in a finite interval there is only a finite number of subsequent actions. In this axiomatization, the above EC entails the above state constraint. This axiomatization is based on a second order inductive definition semantics. A further discussion of this topic is out of scope.

11.8 Concluding Remarks

This chapter studied the use of abduction for diverse forms of reasoning on temporal theories. The basis for this work is a first order logic variant of the event calculus, which uses iff-completion to solve the frame problem. We showed how different forms of incomplete temporal knowledge can be represented in it. We discussed two different views of abduction: in the logical entailment view, abduction generates hypotheses that logically entail the observations to be explained; we argued that a more correct view is the causality view, in which abduction generates potential *causes* of the observations. We discussed how by following some methodological rules regarding the representation of causal rules, abduction in the logical entailment view can be used to implement abduction in the causality view. The chapter showed the use of abduction as a very informative form of hypothetical query answering in a broad class of temporal reasoning problems. We considered also applications of integrations of abduction and constraint programming for reasoning in continuous change applications and resource planning.

Handbook of Temporal Reasoning in Artificial Intelligence
Edited by M. Fisher, D. Gabbay and L. Vila

Chapter 12

Temporal Description Logics

Alessandro Artale & Enrico Franconi

Temporal extensions of Description Logics (DL) are relevant to capture the evolving behaviour of dynamic domains, and they have been extensively considered in the literature. Several approaches for representing and reasoning with time dependent concepts have been proposed. In this chapter a summary of the temporal logic based approaches and of the concrete domain based approaches will be presented. The chapter will be organised according to the adopted ontologies of time: point-based and interval-based.

12.1 Introduction

In the Description Logic literature, several approaches for representing and reasoning with time dependent concepts have been proposed. These temporal extensions differ from each others in different ways.

- They differ on the ontology of time, whether they adopt a point-based or an interval-based notion of time. Point-based temporal description logics are usually obtained from the combination with a tense logic [Gabbay *et al.*, 1994a]. Interval-based temporal description logics are usually obtained from the combination with some restriction of the interval temporal logic $\mathcal{HS}$ [Halpern and Shoham, 1991], which is undecidable in its full power.
- They differ on the way of adding the temporal dimension, i.e., whether an explicit notion of time is adopted in which temporal operators are used to build new formulæ, or temporal information is only implicit in the language by embedding a *state-change* based language – e.g., by resorting to a STRIPS-like style of representation – to represent sequences of events; see, for example [Devanbu and Litman, 1996].
- In the case of an explicit representation of time, there is a further distinction between an *external* and an *internal* point of view; this distinction has been introduced by Finger and Gabbay [1992].
    - In the *external* method the very same individual can have different "snapshots" in different moments of time that describe the various states of the individual at these times. In this case, a temporal logic can be seen in a modular way: while an atemporal part of the language describes the "static" aspects, the temporal part relates the different snapshots describing in such a way the "dynamic" aspects.

- In the *internal* method the different states of an individual are seen as different individual components: an individual is a collection of temporal "parts" each one holding at a particular moment. An example of this is the temporal Description Logic based on concrete domains.

In this chapter a general framework will be introduced encompassing only the explicit approaches. After having introduced Description Logics and their relationship with modal logics, Section 12.4 will consider the point-based tense logical extension of Description Logics, concluding with decidability and complexity results. Section 12.5 analyses the interval-based extension, which has a worst computational behaviour. The concrete domains approach will be covered in Section 12.6, and it will be compared with the previous ones. A complete survey of the approaches not covered in this chapter can be found in [Artale and Franconi, 2001].

12.2 Description Logics

In this Section we give a brief introduction to the $\mathcal{ALCQIFO}$ description logic, which will serve as the basic representation language for the non-temporal information. With respect to the formal apparatus, we will follow the standard concept language formalism whose extensions have been summarised in [Donini *et al.*, 1996; Calvanese *et al.*, 2001]. In this perspective, Description Logics are considered as a *structured* fragment of predicate logic.

The basic types of a concept language are *concepts*, *roles*, *features*, and *individual constants*. A concept is a description gathering the common properties among a collection of individuals; from a logical point of view it is a unary predicate ranging over the domain of individuals. Inter-relationships between these individuals are represented either by means of roles (which are interpreted as binary relations over the domain of individuals) or by means of features (which are interpreted as partial functions over the domain of individuals). Individual constants denote single individuals.

According to the syntax rules of Figure 12.1, *concepts* (denoted by the letters C and D) are built out of *atomic concepts* (denoted by the letter A), *roles* (denoted by the letter R), and *features* (denoted by the letter p), and *individual constants* (denoted by the letter a). Roles are built out of *atomic roles* (denoted by the letter T) and *features*. Features are built out of *atomic features* (denoted by the letter f). $\mathcal{ALC}$ is the minimal description language including full negation and disjunction – i.e., propositional calculus – and it is a notational variant of the propositional multi-modal logic $\mathbf{K_m}$ [Schild, 1991] (see Section 12.3). In this Section, we will consider the $\mathcal{ALCQIFO}$ Description Logic, extending $\mathcal{ALC}$ with qualified cardinality restrictions ($\mathcal{Q}$), inverse roles ($\mathcal{I}$), features ($\mathcal{F}$), and individual enumerations ($\mathcal{O}$). The top part of Figure 12.1 defines the $\mathcal{ALC}$ sublanguage, while the lower parts define its extensions. Both the abstract and the concrete syntax are shown in the Figure.

Let us now consider the formal semantics of $\mathcal{ALCQIFO}$. We define the *meaning* of concepts as sets of individuals—as for unary predicates—and the meaning of roles as sets of pairs of individuals—as for binary predicates. Formally, an *interpretation* is a pair $\mathcal{I} = \langle \Delta^{\mathcal{I}}, \cdot^{\mathcal{I}} \rangle$ consisting of a set $\Delta^{\mathcal{I}}$ of individuals (the *domain* of $\mathcal{I}$) and a function $\cdot^{\mathcal{I}}$ (the *interpretation function* of $\mathcal{I}$) mapping every concept to a subset of $\Delta^{\mathcal{I}}$, every role to a subset of $\Delta^{\mathcal{I}} \times \Delta^{\mathcal{I}}$, every feature to a partial function from $\Delta^{\mathcal{I}}$ to $\Delta^{\mathcal{I}}$, and every individual constant to an element of $\Delta^{\mathcal{I}}$, such that the equations in Figure 12.2 are satisfied. The additional

C, D	$\rightarrow$	$A \mid$	A	(atomic conc.)
		$\top \mid$	`top`	(top)
		$\bot \mid$	`bottom`	(bottom)
		$\neg C \mid$	(`not` C)	(complement)
		$C \sqcap D \mid$	(`and` $C\ D\ \ldots$)	(conjunction)
		$C \sqcup D \mid$	(`or` $C\ D\ \ldots$)	(disjunction)
		$\forall R.C \mid$	(`all` $R\ C$)	(univ. quantifier)
		$\exists R.C \mid$	(`some` $R\ C$)	(exist. quantifier)
		$\geqslant nR.C \mid$	(`atleast` $n\ R\ C$)	(min cardinality)
		$\leqslant nR.C \mid$	(`atmost` $n\ R\ C$)	(max cardinality)
		$p : C \mid$	(`in` $p\ C$)	(selection)
		$\uparrow p \mid$	(`undefined` p)	(undefinedness)
		$p \downarrow q \mid$	(`same` $p\ q$)	(agreement)
		$p \uparrow q \mid$	(`not-same` $p\ q$)	(disagreement)
		$\{a_1, \ldots, a_n\}$	(`one-of` $\mathrm{a}_1 \ldots \mathrm{a}_\mathrm{n}$)	(enumeration)
R	$\rightarrow$	$T \mid$	T	(atomic role)
		$R^{-1} \mid$	(`inverse` R)	(inverse role)
		p	p	(feature)
p, q	$\rightarrow$	$f \mid$	f	(atomic feature)
		$p \circ q$	(`compose` $p\ q$)	(path)

Figure 12.1: Syntax rules for $\mathcal{ALCQIFO}$

$$
\begin{aligned}
\top^{\mathcal{I}} &= \Delta^{\mathcal{I}} \\
\bot^{\mathcal{I}} &= \emptyset \\
(\neg C)^{\mathcal{I}} &= \Delta^{\mathcal{I}} \setminus C^{\mathcal{I}} \\
(C \sqcap D)^{\mathcal{I}} &= C^{\mathcal{I}} \cap D^{\mathcal{I}} \\
(C \sqcup D)^{\mathcal{I}} &= C^{\mathcal{I}} \cup D^{\mathcal{I}} \\
(\forall R.C)^{\mathcal{I}} &= \{x \in \Delta^{\mathcal{I}} \mid \forall y. R^{\mathcal{I}}(x,y) \Rightarrow C^{\mathcal{I}}(y)\} \\
(\exists R.C)^{\mathcal{I}} &= \{x \in \Delta^{\mathcal{I}} \mid \exists y. R^{\mathcal{I}}(x,y) \wedge C^{\mathcal{I}}(y)\} \\
\\
(\geqslant n R.C)^{\mathcal{I}} &= \{x \in \Delta^{\mathcal{I}} \mid \sharp\{y \in \Delta^{\mathcal{I}} \mid R^{\mathcal{I}}(x,y) \wedge C^{\mathcal{I}}(y)\} \geq n\} \\
(\leqslant n R.C)^{\mathcal{I}} &= \{x \in \Delta^{\mathcal{I}} \mid \sharp\{y \in \Delta^{\mathcal{I}} \mid R^{\mathcal{I}}(x,y) \wedge C^{\mathcal{I}}(y)\} \leq n\} \\
\\
(p : C)^{\mathcal{I}} &= \{x \in \mathsf{dom} p^{\mathcal{I}} \mid C^{\mathcal{I}}(p^{\mathcal{I}}(x))\} \\
(\uparrow p)^{\mathcal{I}} &= \Delta^{\mathcal{I}} \setminus \mathsf{dom} p^{\mathcal{I}} \\
(p \downarrow q)^{\mathcal{I}} &= \{x \in \mathsf{dom} p^{\mathcal{I}} \cap \mathsf{dom} q^{\mathcal{I}} \mid p^{\mathcal{I}}(x) = q^{\mathcal{I}}(x)\} \\
(p \uparrow q)^{\mathcal{I}} &= \{x \in \mathsf{dom} p^{\mathcal{I}} \cap \mathsf{dom} q^{\mathcal{I}} \mid p^{\mathcal{I}}(x) \neq q^{\mathcal{I}}(x)\} \\
\\
\{a_1, \ldots, a_n\}^{\mathcal{I}} &= \{a_1^{\mathcal{I}}, \ldots, a_n^{\mathcal{I}}\} \\
\\
(R^{-1})^{\mathcal{I}} &= \{(x,y) \in \Delta^{\mathcal{I}} \times \Delta^{\mathcal{I}} \mid R^{\mathcal{I}}(y,x)\} \\
(p \circ q)^{\mathcal{I}} &= p^{\mathcal{I}} \circ q^{\mathcal{I}}
\end{aligned}
$$

Figure 12.2: Extensional semantics of $\mathcal{ALCQIFO}$

unique name assumption should be fulfilled: $a^{\mathcal{I}} \neq b^{\mathcal{I}}$ if $a \neq b$. The semantics of the language can also be given by stating equivalences among expressions of the language and open First Order Logic formulæ. An atomic concept A, an atomic role T, an atomic feature f are mapped respectively to the open formulæ $F_A(x) = A(x)$, $F_T(x) = T(x,y)$, $F_f(x) = f(x,y)$ – with f a functional relation, also written $f(x) = y$ – and x, y denoting the free variables; an individual constant a is represented by means of the corresponding constant a. Figure 12.3 gives the transformational semantics of $\mathcal{ALCQIFO}$ expressions in terms of equivalent FOL well-formed formulæ. A concept C, a role R and a path p correspond to the FOL open formulæ $F_C(x)$, $F_R(x,y)$, and $F_p(x,y)$, respectively. It is worth noting that, using the standard model-theoretic semantics, the extensional semantics of Figure 12.2 can be derived from the transformational semantics of Figure 12.3.

As an example of a concept, we can consider the concept of HAPPY FATHER, defined using the atomic concepts `Man`, `Doctor`, `Rich`, `Famous` and the roles `CHILD`, `FRIEND`. The concept HAPPY FATHER can be expressed in $\mathcal{ALCQIFO}$ as

$$\texttt{Man} \sqcap (\exists \texttt{CHILD}.\top) \sqcap \forall \texttt{CHILD}.(\texttt{Doctor} \sqcap \exists \texttt{FRIEND}.(\texttt{Rich} \sqcup \texttt{Famous})),$$

i.e., those men having some child and all of whose children are doctors having some friend who is rich or famous.

A *knowledge base*, in this context, is a finite set Σ of two types of *formulæ*: *terminological axioms* (TBox) and *assertional axioms* (ABox). For an atomic concept A, and (possibly complex) concepts C, D, terminological axioms are of the form $A \doteq C$ (concept definition), $A \sqsubseteq C$ (primitive concept definition), $C \sqsubseteq D$ (general inclusion statement). An interpretation $\mathcal{I}$ satisfies the formula $C \sqsubseteq D$ if and only if the interpretation of C is included in the

$$
\begin{array}{rl}
\top^{\mathcal{I}} \sim & \textsf{true} \\
\bot^{\mathcal{I}} \sim & \textsf{false} \\
(\neg C)^{\mathcal{I}} \sim & \neg F_C(x) \\
(C \sqcap D)^{\mathcal{I}} \sim & F_C(x) \wedge F_D(x) \\
(C \sqcup D)^{\mathcal{I}} \sim & F_C(x) \vee F_D(x) \\
(\forall R.C)^{\mathcal{I}} \sim & \forall z.F_R(x,z) \Rightarrow F_C(z) \\
(\exists R.C)^{\mathcal{I}} \sim & \exists z.F_R(x,z) \wedge F_C(z) \\
\\
(\geqslant nR.C)^{\mathcal{I}} \sim & \exists^{\geq n} z.F_R(x,z) \wedge F_C(z) \\
(\leqslant nR.C)^{\mathcal{I}} \sim & \exists^{\leq n} z.F_R(x,z) \wedge F_C(z) \\
\\
(p : C)^{\mathcal{I}} \sim & \exists z.F_p(x,z) \wedge F_C(z) \\
(\uparrow p)^{\mathcal{I}} \sim & \neg\exists z.F_p(x,z) \\
(p \downarrow q)^{\mathcal{I}} \sim & \exists z.F_p(x,z) \wedge F_q(x,z) \\
(p \uparrow q)^{\mathcal{I}} \sim & \exists z_1, z_2.F_p(x,z_1) \wedge F_q(x,z_2) \wedge z_1 \neq z_2 \\
\\
\{a_1, \ldots, a_n\}^{\mathcal{I}} \sim & x = a_1 \vee \ldots \vee x = a_n \\
\\
(R^{-1})^{\mathcal{I}} \sim & F_R(y,x) \\
(p \circ q)^{\mathcal{I}} \sim & \exists z.F_p(x,z) \wedge F_q(z,y)
\end{array}
$$

Figure 12.3: FOL semantics of $\mathcal{ALCQIFO}$

interpretation of D, i.e., $C^{\mathcal{I}} \subseteq D^{\mathcal{I}}$. It is clear that the last kind of axiom is a generalisation of the first two: concept definitions of the type $A \doteq C$ – where A is an atomic concept – can be reduced to the pair of axioms $(A \sqsubseteq C)$ and $(C \sqsubseteq A)$. For example, the abovementioned concept could be used to explicitly define the concept `HappyFather`:

$$
\begin{aligned}
\texttt{HappyFather} \doteq\ & \texttt{Man} \sqcap (\exists\texttt{CHILD}.\top) \sqcap \\
& \forall\texttt{CHILD}.(\texttt{Doctor} \sqcap \exists\texttt{FRIEND}.(\texttt{Rich} \sqcup \texttt{Famous}))
\end{aligned}
$$

Extensional knowledge is expressed by means of an ABox which is formed by a finite set of *assertional axioms*, i.e. formulæ on individual constants. An assertion is an axiom of the form $C(a)$, $R(a, b)$ or $p(a, b)$, where a and b are individual constants. A formula $C(a)$ is satisfied by an interpretation $\mathcal{I}$ iff $a^{\mathcal{I}} \in C^{\mathcal{I}}$, $P(a, b)$ is satisfied by $\mathcal{I}$ iff $(a^{\mathcal{I}}, b^{\mathcal{I}}) \in P^{\mathcal{I}}$, and $p(a, b)$ is satisfied by $\mathcal{I}$ iff $p^{\mathcal{I}}(a^{\mathcal{I}}) = b^{\mathcal{I}}$.

For example, the individual constant `john`, as defined by the following *ABox*, could be recognised as an `HappyFather`:

```
Man(john), CHILD(john,bill),
Doctor(bill), FRIEND(bill,peter), Rich(peter).
```

An interpretation $\mathcal{I}$ is a *model* of a knowledge base Σ iff every formula in Σ is satisfied by $\mathcal{I}$. If Σ has a model, then it is *satisfiable*; thus, checking for KB satisfiability is deciding whether there is at least one model for the knowledge base. Σ *logically implies* a formula ϕ (written $\Sigma \models \phi$) if ϕ is satisfied by every model of Σ. In particular, we say that a concept C is *subsumed* by a concept D in a knowledge base Σ (written $\Sigma \models C \sqsubseteq D$) if $C^{\mathcal{I}} \subseteq D^{\mathcal{I}}$ for every model $\mathcal{I}$ of Σ. We say that an individual constant a is an *instance of* a concept C in a knowledge base Σ (written $\Sigma \models C(a)$) if $a^{\mathcal{I}} \in C^{\mathcal{I}}$ for every model $\mathcal{I}$ of Σ.

For example, the concept

$\texttt{Person} \sqcap (\exists\texttt{CHILD}.\texttt{Person})$

denoting the PARENT class – i.e., the persons having at least a child which is a person – subsumes the concept HappyFather with respect to the following knowledge base Σ:

$\texttt{Doctor} \doteq \texttt{Person} \sqcap \exists\texttt{DEGREE}.\texttt{Phd},$
$\texttt{Man} \doteq \texttt{Person} \sqcap \texttt{sex} : \texttt{Male},$

i.e., every happy father is also a person having at least one child, given the background knowledge that men are male persons, and that doctors are persons.

A concept C is satisfiable, given a knowledge base Σ, if there is at least one model $\mathcal{I}$ of Σ such that $C^{\mathcal{I}} \neq \emptyset$, i.e. $\Sigma \not\models C \doteq \bot$. For example, the concept

$(\exists\texttt{CHILD}.\texttt{Man}) \sqcap (\forall\texttt{CHILD}.(\texttt{sex} : \neg\texttt{Male}))$

is unsatisfiable with respect to the above knowledge base Σ. In fact, an individual whose children are not male cannot have a child being a man.

Concept subsumption can be reduced to concept satisfiability since C is subsumed by D in Σ if and only if $(C \sqcap \neg D)$ is unsatisfiable in Σ.

The various sublanguages of $\mathcal{ALCQIFO}$ have different computational properties. Deciding any of knowledge base satisfiability, concept satisfiability, and logical implication in $\mathcal{ALCQIO}$ is NEXPTIME-complete [Tobies, 2000]. Deciding knowledge base satisfiability, concept satisfiability, and logical implication in $\mathcal{ALCQI}$, $\mathcal{ALCQO}$, $\mathcal{ALCIO}$ is EXPTIME-complete [Calvanese *et al.*, 2001]. Checking concept satisfiability, concept subsumption and instance checking with empty knowledge bases in $\mathcal{ALCF}$ is PSPACE-complete [Hollunder *et al.*, 1990]. Deciding knowledge base satisfiability, concept satisfiability, and logical implication in the full $\mathcal{ALCQIFO}$ is undecidable – it is already undecidable in $\mathcal{ALCF}$ [Lutz, 1999a].

12.3 Correspondence with Modal Logics

Schild [Schild, 1991] proved the correspondence between $\mathcal{ALC}$ and the propositional normal multi-modal logic $\mathbf{K_m}$ [Goldblatt, 1987; Halpern and Moses, 1985]. $\mathbf{K_m}$ is the simplest normal multi-modal logic interpreted over Kripke structures: there are no restrictions on the accessibility relations. Informally, an $\mathcal{ALC}$ individual corresponds to a $\mathbf{K_m}$ possible world, and an $\mathcal{ALC}$ concept corresponds to a $\mathbf{K_m}$ propositional formula, which is interpreted as the set of possible worlds over which the formula holds. The existential and universal quantifiers correspond to the possibility and necessity operators over different accessibility relations R: $\Box_R\,\psi$ is interpreted as the set of all the possible worlds such that in every R-accessible world ψ holds; $\Diamond_R\,\psi$ is interpreted as the set of all the possible worlds such that in some R-accessible world ψ holds. Thus, roles correspond to the accessibility relations between worlds. Figure 12.4 shows the correspondence between an $\mathcal{ALC}$ concept C and a $\mathbf{K_m}$ propositional formula ψ_C. It is easy to see that both the notion of model and the reasoning problems in $\mathcal{ALC}$ have obvious counterparts in $\mathbf{K_m}$.

$\mathcal{ALC}$	$\mathbf{K_m}$
C denotes a set of individuals	ψ_C denotes a set of worlds
R denotes a set of pairs of individuals	R is an accessibility relation
A	A
$C \sqcap D$	$\psi_C \wedge \psi_D$
$C \sqcup D$	$\psi_C \vee \psi_D$
$\neg C$	$\neg \psi_C$
$\forall R.C$	$\Box_R\, \psi_C$
$\exists R.C$	$\Diamond_R\, \psi_C$

Figure 12.4: Correspondence between $\mathcal{ALC}$ concepts and $\mathbf{K_m}$ formulæ.

In [Calvanese *et al.*, 2001] a very expressive Description Logic – $\mathcal{ALCQI}_{reg}$ – is defined which extends the expressivity of $\mathcal{ALCQI}$ with *regular expressions* over roles, and prove its correspondence with of *CPDL*, i.e. the propositional dynamic modal logic *PDL* with the converse operator, extended with *graded modalities*. Deciding knowledge base satisfiability, concept satisfiability, and logical implication in $\mathcal{ALCQI}_{reg}$ is EXPTIME-complete [Calvanese *et al.*, 2001]. The sublanguage $\mathcal{ALC}_{reg}$ which is in correspondence with *PDL* is often called $\mathcal{C}$, and $\mathcal{ALCQI}_{reg}$ is called $\mathcal{CIQ}$.

12.4 Point-based notion of time

This Section illustrates how to extend Description Logics with a point-based notion of time. In order to intuitively understand the meaning of the temporal operators that are being added to the Description Logic, let us consider as an example a simple definition of the temporally dependent concept Mortal:

$\texttt{Mortal} \doteq \texttt{LivingBeing} \sqcap \Diamond^+ \neg \texttt{LivingBeing}$

The concept denotes the set of pairs $\langle t, a \rangle$ where a is a kind of LivingBeing at the time t, and there exists an instant $v > t$ where a is no more a LivingBeing.

The operator *universal future*, $\Box^+$, is the dual of $\Diamond^+$. Given a time point t, the concept $\Box^+ C$ denotes the set of individuals which are of kind C at every time $v > t$. With this operator, the definition of a mortal can be refined by saying that from a certain future time, $v > t$, he/she will never be alive again:

$\texttt{Mortal} \doteq \texttt{LivingBeing} \sqcap \Diamond^+ \Box^+ \neg \texttt{LivingBeing}$

This definition is still incomplete since does not tell anything about the time between t – when the mortal is alive – and v – when a mortal dies. At each time w with $t < w < v$, a mortal can be dead or alive. For this purpose the binary operator *until*, $\mathcal{U}$, can be used. At time t, the concept $C\ \mathcal{U}\ D$ denotes all those individuals which are of kind D at some time $v > t$ and which are of kind C for all times w with $t < w < v$. Thus, a mortal can be redefined as a living being who is alive *until* he dies:

`Mortal` $\doteq$ `LivingBeing` $\sqcap$ (`LivingBeing` $\mathcal{U}$ ($\neg$`LivingBeing` $\sqcap$ $\Box^+\neg$`LivingBeing`))

More formally, complex temporal concepts can be expressed using the following syntax.

Definition 12.4.1. *The* tense-logical extension *of a concept language $\mathcal{L}$, called $\mathcal{L}_{\mathcal{US}}$, is the least set containing all concepts, roles and formulæ of $\mathcal{L}$, such that $C\ \mathcal{U}\ D, C\ \mathcal{S}\ D$ are concepts of $\mathcal{L}_{\mathcal{US}}$ if C and D are concepts of $\mathcal{L}_{\mathcal{US}}$, and such that $R_1\ \mathcal{U}\ R_2, R_1\ \mathcal{S}\ R_2$ are roles of $\mathcal{L}_{\mathcal{US}}$ if R_1 and R_2 are roles of $\mathcal{L}_{\mathcal{US}}$. If ϕ and ψ are formulæ of $\mathcal{L}_{\mathcal{US}}$ then so are $\neg\phi, \phi \wedge \psi, \phi\, \mathcal{U}\, \psi, \phi\, \mathcal{S}\, \psi$. The sublanguage of $\mathcal{L}_{\mathcal{US}}$ without temporal roles is called $\mathcal{L}^-_{\mathcal{US}}$.*

The $\mathcal{L}_{\mathcal{US}}$ semantics naturally extends with time the standard non-temporal semantics of $\mathcal{L}$ [Baader and Ohlbach, 1995; Wolter and Zakharyaschev, 1998a]. A temporal structure $\mathcal{T} = (\mathcal{P}, <)$ is assumed, where $\mathcal{P}$ is a set of (time) points and $<$ is a strict linear order on $\mathcal{P}$. A $\mathcal{L}_{\mathcal{US}}$ *temporal interpretation* over $\mathcal{T}$ is a pair $\mathcal{M} = \langle \mathcal{T}, \mathcal{I} \rangle$, where $\mathcal{I}$ is a function associating to each t in $\mathcal{T}$ a standard non-temporal $\mathcal{L}$ interpretation, $\mathcal{I}(t) \doteq \langle \Delta^{\mathcal{I}}, \cdot^{\mathcal{I}(t)} \rangle$, such that it satisfies: the standard semantic definitions of $\mathcal{L}$ for each t in $\mathcal{T}$; the rigid designator hypothesis, $a^{\mathcal{I}(w)} = a^{\mathcal{I}(v)}$ for any $w, v \in \mathcal{T}$; plus the following*

$$(C\ \mathcal{U}\ D)^{\mathcal{I}(t)} = \{x \in \Delta^{\mathcal{I}} \mid \exists v.(v > t) \wedge D^{\mathcal{I}(v)}(x) \wedge \forall w.(t < w < v) \rightarrow C^{\mathcal{I}(w)}(x)\}$$
$$(C\ \mathcal{S}\ D)^{\mathcal{I}(t)} = \{x \in \Delta^{\mathcal{I}} \mid \exists v.(v < t) \wedge D^{\mathcal{I}(v)}(x) \wedge \forall w.(v < w < t) \rightarrow C^{\mathcal{I}(w)}(x)\}$$

If the temporal structure is linear and discrete, it is possible to define the missing temporal operators: Existential Future ($\Diamond^+$), Existential Past ($\Diamond^-$), Universal Future ($\Box^+$), Universal Past ($\Box^-$), Next Instant ($\oplus$), Previous Instant ($\ominus$), as $\Diamond^+ C \doteq \top\, \mathcal{U}\, C$, $\Diamond^- C \doteq \top\, \mathcal{S}\, C$, $\oplus\, C \doteq \bot\, \mathcal{U}\, C$, $\ominus\, C \doteq \bot\, \mathcal{S}\, C$, $\Box^+ C \doteq \neg\Diamond^+\neg C$, $\Box^- C \doteq \neg\Diamond^-\neg C$.

In addition, a language could be extended with *global roles* whose interpretation does not change in time: $R^{\mathcal{I}(w)} = R^{\mathcal{I}(v)}$ for any $w, v \in \mathcal{T}$.

Definition 12.4.2. *Given a formula ϕ, an interpretation $\mathcal{M} \doteq \langle \mathcal{T}, \mathcal{I} \rangle$, and a time point $t \in \mathcal{T}$, the satisfiability relation $\mathcal{M}, t \models \phi$ is defined inductively by:*

$$
\begin{array}{lll}
\mathcal{M}, t \models C \doteq D & \textit{iff} & C^{\mathcal{I}(t)} = D^{\mathcal{I}(t)} \\
\mathcal{M}, t \models C \sqsubseteq D & \textit{iff} & C^{\mathcal{I}(t)} \subseteq D^{\mathcal{I}(t)} \\
\mathcal{M}, t \models C(a) & \textit{iff} & C^{\mathcal{I}(t)}(a^{\mathcal{I}(t)}) \\
\mathcal{M}, t \models R(a,b) & \textit{iff} & R^{\mathcal{I}(t)}(a^{\mathcal{I}(t)}, b^{\mathcal{I}(t)}) \\
\mathcal{M}, t \models \phi \wedge \psi & \textit{iff} & \mathcal{M}, t \models \phi \wedge \mathcal{M}, t \models \psi \\
\mathcal{M}, t \models \neg\phi & \textit{iff} & \mathcal{M}, t \not\models \phi \\
\mathcal{M}, t \models \phi\, \mathcal{U}\, \psi & \textit{iff} & \exists v.(v > t) \wedge \mathcal{M}, v \models \psi \wedge \forall w.(t < w < v) \rightarrow \mathcal{M}, w \models \phi \\
\mathcal{M}, t \models \phi\, \mathcal{S}\, \psi & \textit{iff} & \exists v.(v < t) \wedge \mathcal{M}, v \models \psi \wedge \forall w.(v < w < t) \rightarrow \mathcal{M}, w \models \phi
\end{array}
$$

A formula ϕ is satisfiable *if there is an interpretation $\mathcal{M}$ and a time point t such that $\mathcal{M}, t \models \phi$. A formula is* valid *if for each time point $t \in \mathcal{T}$ then $\mathcal{M}, t \models \phi$.*

We show now how all the relevant reasoning problems can be reduced to satisfiability of formulæ. A concept C is *satisfiable* if there exists $\mathcal{M}$ and t such that $\mathcal{M}, t \models \neg(C \doteq \bot)$ – indeed, this means that there exists an interpretation $\mathcal{I}$ such that $C^{\mathcal{I}(t)} \neq \emptyset$ for some t. The *local logical implication* problem from a finite set of formulæ Σ (a KB) is defined as follows: $\Sigma \models^l \phi$, if for every $\mathcal{M}$ and every time point t then if $\mathcal{M}, t \models \Sigma$ then also

*We omit the similar definitions for the temporal roles.

$\mathcal{M}, t \models \phi$, i.e. $\Sigma \models^l \phi$ if and only if the formula $((\bigwedge \Sigma) \wedge \neg\phi)$ is not satisfiable. The *global logical implication* problem is defined as follows: $\Sigma \models \phi$, if for every interpretation $\mathcal{M}$ such that $\mathcal{M}, t \models \Sigma$ for every t then also $\mathcal{M}, t \models \phi$ for every t. Global logical implication is reducible to local logical implication (and then to a satisfiability problem): $\Sigma \models \phi$ if and only if $\Sigma \cup \{\Box^+\psi \mid \psi \in \Sigma\} \cup \{\Box^-\psi \mid \psi \in \Sigma\} \models^l \phi$.
Note that – as expected – axioms in Description Logics are represented as valid formulæ in a temporal Description Logic, and the classical logical implication problem in Description Logics is reformulated in a temporal Description Logics as a global logical implication.

Theorem 12.4.1. *Finite Model Property*
If $\mathcal{L}$ includes $\mathcal{ALC}$, then $\mathcal{L}^-_{\mathcal{U}}$ does not have the finite model property [Wolter and Zakharyaschev, 1998a].

Theorem 12.4.2. *Decidability*

1. *If $\mathcal{L}$ includes $\mathcal{ALC}$, then the problem of formula satisfiability for $\mathcal{L}_{\mathcal{U}}$ and $\mathcal{L}^-_{\mathcal{U}}$ with global roles is undecidable in any unbounded linear order [Wolter and Zakharyaschev, 1999].*
2. *The problem of formula satisfiability is decidable for the following languages:*
   - *$\mathcal{CIQ}^-_{\mathcal{US}}$, $\mathcal{CIO}^-_{\mathcal{US}}$, $\mathcal{CQO}^-_{\mathcal{US}}$ and $\mathcal{DLR}^-_{\mathcal{US}}$ in $\langle\mathcal{N}, <\rangle$ and in $\langle\mathcal{Z}, <\rangle$ [Wolter and Zakharyaschev, 1998b; Artale and Franconi, 2000],*
   - *$\mathcal{CIQ}^-_{\diamond}$, $\mathcal{CIO}^-_{\diamond}$ and $\mathcal{CQO}^-_{\diamond}$ in $\langle\mathcal{Q}, <\rangle$ [Wolter and Zakharyaschev, 1998b],*
3. *Concept satisfiability in $\mathcal{ALC}^-_{\mathcal{U}}$ with global roles with empty KBs, $\emptyset \not\models C \doteq \bot$, is decidable in $\langle\mathcal{N}, <\rangle$ [Wolter, 2000].*

Theorem 12.4.3. *Complexity*

1. *Concept satisfiability in $\mathcal{ALC}^-_{\mathcal{U}}$ with empty KBs, $\emptyset \not\models C \doteq \bot$, is PSPACE-complete in $\langle\mathcal{N}, <\rangle$ [Schild, 1993].*
2. *Concept satisfiability in $\mathcal{CF}^-_{\mathcal{U}}$ with empty KBs, $\emptyset \not\models C \doteq \bot$, is EXPTIME-complete in $\langle\mathcal{N}, <\rangle$ [Schild, 1993].*
3. *Formula satisfiability in $\mathcal{ALC}^-_{\mathcal{U}}$ and $\mathcal{ALCQI}^-_{\mathcal{US}}$ is EXPSPACE-complete in $\langle\mathcal{N}, <\rangle$ [Morurovic* et al., *2000; Artale and Franconi, 2000].*

A tableau algorithm for formula satisfiability in $\mathcal{ALC}^-_{\mathcal{U}}$ with *expanding domains* has been developed in [Sturm and Wolter, 2000].

Let us consider now a fully worked out example using $\mathcal{ALCQI}^-_{\mathcal{US}}$, involving the concepts `Project`, `Employee`, `Manager`, and `Works-for`, and the roles `HAS-PRJ` and `HAS-EMP`.

- The concept `Works-for` denotes the event of an employee working for a project:

  $\texttt{Works-for} \sqsubseteq \exists\texttt{HAS-PRJ}.\texttt{Project} \sqcap \exists\texttt{HAS-EMP}.\texttt{Employee} \sqcap$
  $\qquad \leqslant 1\texttt{HAS-PRJ}.\top \sqcap \leqslant 1\texttt{HAS-EMP}.\top$

- Every project has somebody working for it:

  $\texttt{Project} \sqsubseteq \exists\texttt{HAS-PRJ}^{-1}.\texttt{Works-for}$

Relation	Abbr.	Inverse
before(i,j)	b	a
meets(i,j)	m	mi
overlaps(i,j)	o	oi
starts(i,j)	s	si
during(i,j)	d	di
finishes(i,j)	f	fi

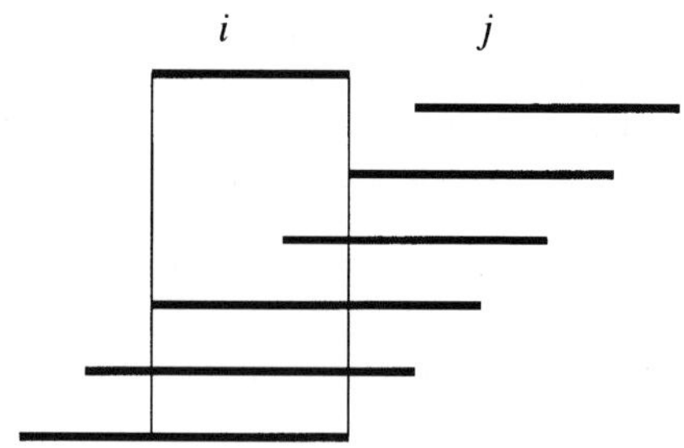

Figure 12.5: The Allen's interval relationships.

- Managers are employees:

  $\texttt{Manager} \sqsubseteq \texttt{Employee}$

- Managers are exactly those employees who do not work for a project:

  $\texttt{Manager} \doteq \forall \texttt{HAS-EMP}^{-1}.\neg \texttt{Works-for}$

- A manager becomes qualified after a period when she/he was just an employee:

  $\texttt{Manager} \sqsubseteq \texttt{Qualified}\mathcal{S}(\texttt{Employee} \sqcap \neg \texttt{Manager})$

It turns out that the following formulæ are logically implied by Σ:

- For every project, there is at least an employee who is not a manager:

  $\Sigma \models \texttt{Project} \sqsubseteq \exists(\texttt{HAS-PRJ}^{-1} \circ \texttt{HAS-EMP}).\neg \texttt{Manager}$

- A manager worked in a project before managing some (possibly different) project:

  $\Sigma \models \texttt{Manager} \sqsubseteq \Diamond^{-} \exists(\texttt{HAS-EMP}^{-1} \circ \texttt{HAS-PRJ}).\texttt{Project}$

$\mathcal{ALCQI}_{\mathcal{US}}$ has been used to encode and reason with temporal conceptual data models in databases [Artale and Franconi, 1999].

12.5 Interval-based notion of time

This section illustrates how to extend Description Logics with an interval-based notion of time. In order to intuitively understand the meaning of the temporal operators that are being added to the Description Logic, let us reconsider in this context the example of the temporally dependent concept Mortal:

$\texttt{Mortal} \doteq \texttt{LivingBeing} \sqcap \langle \text{met-by} \rangle \neg \texttt{LivingBeing}$

The definition states that a LivingBeing at the reference interval will not be alive at some other interval *met by* the reference one. In this logic, the temporal operators make use of the Allen's interval algebra [Allen, 1991a], as summarised in Figure 12.5.

Definition 12.5.1. *The* Allen's interval extension *of a concept language $\mathcal{L}$, called $\mathcal{L}_{\mathcal{A}}$, is the least set containing all concepts and roles of $\mathcal{L}$, such that $\langle\alpha\rangle C$, $[\alpha]C$ are concepts of $\mathcal{L}_{\mathcal{A}}$ if C is a concept of $\mathcal{L}_{\mathcal{A}}$, and α is one of the Allen's interval relations (Figure 12.5): before (*b*), meets (*m*), during (*d*), overlaps (*o*), starts (*s*), finishes (*f*), equal (=), after (*a*), met-by (*mi*), contains (*di*), overlapped-by (*oi*), started-by (*si*), finished-by (*fi*).*
$\mathcal{L}_{\mathcal{AF}}$ is the combination of the fragment of $\mathcal{L}_{\mathcal{A}}$ where existential temporal modalities $\langle\alpha\rangle C$ are only allowed at the top level of concepts and no universal temporal modalities $[\alpha]C$ are allowed, with global functional roles and with explicit variables in the language denoting temporal intervals à la Prior (see [Artale and Franconi, 1998] for details).

The $\mathcal{L}_{\mathcal{A}}$ semantics naturally extends with time the standard non-temporal semantics of $\mathcal{L}$. A linear and unbounded temporal structure $\mathcal{T} = (\mathcal{P}, <)$ is assumed, where $\mathcal{P}$ is a set of time points and $<$ is a strict linear order on $\mathcal{P}$. The *interval set* of a structure $\mathcal{T}$ is defined as the set $\mathcal{T}^{\star}_{<}$ of all closed proper intervals $[t_1, t_2] \doteq \{t \in \mathcal{P} \mid t_1 \leq t \leq t_2\}$ in $\mathcal{T}$. An $\mathcal{L}_{\mathcal{A}}$ *temporal interpretation* over $\mathcal{T}^{\star}_{<}$ is a pair $\mathcal{M} \doteq \langle \mathcal{T}^{\star}_{<}, \mathcal{I}\rangle$, where $\mathcal{I}$ is a function associating to each $i = [t_1, t_2] \in \mathcal{T}^{\star}_{<}$ a standard non-temporal $\mathcal{L}$ interpretation, $\mathcal{I}(i) \doteq \langle \Delta^{\mathcal{I}}, \cdot^{\mathcal{I}(i)}\rangle$, such that it satisfies the standard semantic definitions of $\mathcal{L}$ for each i in $\mathcal{T}^{\star}_{<}$, plus the following

$$\begin{aligned}
(\langle\alpha\rangle C)^{\mathcal{I}(i)} &= \{x \in \Delta^{\mathcal{I}} \mid \exists j.\, \alpha(j,i) \wedge C^{\mathcal{I}(j)}(x)\}\\
([\alpha]C)^{\mathcal{I}(i)} &= \{x \in \Delta^{\mathcal{I}} \mid \forall j.\, \alpha(j,i) \rightarrow C^{\mathcal{I}(j)}(x)\}
\end{aligned}$$

where $\alpha(i,j)$ is understood from Figure 12.5. An interpretation $\mathcal{M} \doteq \langle \mathcal{T}^{\star}_{<}, \mathcal{I}\rangle$ is a *model* for a concept C if $C^{\mathcal{I}(i)} \neq \emptyset$ for some $i \in \mathcal{T}^{\star}_{<}$. If a concept has a model then it is *satisfiable*. C is subsumed by D, i.e. $C \sqsubseteq D$, if $C^{\mathcal{I}(i)} \subseteq D^{\mathcal{I}(i)}$ for every interpretation $\mathcal{M}$ and every $i \in \mathcal{T}^{\star}_{<}$.

Theorem 12.5.1. *Decidability*

1. *If $\mathcal{L}$ includes $\mathcal{ALC}$, then the problems of concept satisfiability and concept subsumption with empty KB for $\mathcal{L}_{\mathcal{A}}$ are undecidable in any unbounded linear order [Halpern and Shoham, 1991; Bettini, 1997].*

2. *The problems of concept satisfiability and concept subsumption with empty KB are decidable for $\mathcal{ALCF}_{\mathcal{AF}}$ in an unbound, dense, linear order [Artale and Franconi, 1998].*

Theorem 12.5.2. *Complexity*

1. *Concept satisfiability and concept subsumption with empty KB for $\mathcal{F}_{\mathcal{AF}}$ and $\mathcal{FU}_{\mathcal{AF}}$* * *are NP-complete in an unbound, dense, linear order [Artale and Franconi, 1998],*

2. *Concept satisfiability with empty KB for $\mathcal{ALCF}_{\mathcal{AF}}$ is PSPACE-complete in an unbound, dense, linear order [Artale and Lutz, 1999].*

Let us consider now an example in the block domain using $\mathcal{ALCF}_{\mathcal{AF}}$. A stacking action involves two blocks (the parameters of the action), which should be both clear at the beginning; the central part of the action consists of holding one block; at the end, the blocks are one on top of the other, and the bottom one is no longer clear. The definition involves the concepts

*Where $\mathcal{F}$ is the pure positive feature Description Logic, and $\mathcal{FU}$ extends it with disjunction; see [Artale and Franconi, 1998] for details.

Stack, Clear and Hold, the feature ON, and the global functional roles *OBJECT1* and *OBJECT2*:

$$\begin{aligned}\texttt{Stack} \doteq & \langle\mathsf{overlaps}\rangle\exists \mathit{OBJECT1}.\texttt{Clear} \sqcap \\ & \langle\mathsf{finished\text{-}by}\rangle\exists \mathit{OBJECT2}.\texttt{Clear} \sqcap \\ & \langle\mathsf{finishes}\rangle\exists \mathit{OBJECT1}.(\texttt{Hold} \sqcap \neg\texttt{Clear}) \sqcap \\ & \langle\mathsf{met\text{-}by}\rangle(\mathit{OBJECT1} \circ \mathrm{ON} \downarrow \mathit{OBJECT2} \sqcap \exists \mathit{OBJECT1}.\texttt{Clear})\end{aligned}$$

The expression $\langle\mathsf{overlaps}\rangle\exists \mathit{OBJECT1}.\texttt{Clear}$ means that the first parameter of the action should be a Clear block at an interval overlapping the reference interval of the Stack action. The expression $\langle\mathsf{met\text{-}by}\rangle(\mathit{OBJECT1} \circ \mathrm{ON} \downarrow \mathit{OBJECT2} \sqcap \exists \mathit{OBJECT1}.\texttt{Clear})$ indicates that at an interval met by the reference one the object on which *OBJECT1* is placed is *OBJECT2* and *OBJECT1* is clear.

$\mathcal{ALCF}_{\mathcal{AF}}$ has been used to encode and reason with actions, events, and plans in Artificial Intelligence, in particular to solve the problem of *plan recognition* [Artale and Franconi, 1998].

12.6 Time as Concrete Domain

In the concrete domain extension of Description Logics [Baader and Hanschke, 1991], abstract individuals (i.e., elements of an abstract domain $\Delta^{\mathcal{I}}$) can now be related to values in a *concrete domain* (e.g., a temporal structure) via features. Furthermore, tuples of concrete values identified by such features can be constrained to satisfy an n-ary predicate over the concrete domain (e.g., an ordering relation).

Definition 12.6.1. *Concrete Domain A concrete domain is a pair* $\mathcal{D} = (\mathsf{dom}(\mathcal{D}), \mathsf{pred}(\mathcal{D}))$ *that consists of a set* $\mathsf{dom}(\mathcal{D})$ *(the domain), and a set of predicate symbols* $\mathsf{pred}(\mathcal{D})$*. Each predicate symbol* $P \in \mathsf{pred}(\mathcal{D})$ *is associated with an arity* n *and an* n*-ary relation* $P^{\mathcal{D}} \subseteq \mathsf{dom}(\mathcal{D})^n$*. A concrete domain* $\mathcal{D}$ *is called* admissible *iff (1)* $\mathsf{pred}(\mathcal{D})$ *is closed under negation and contains a unary predicate name* $\top_{\mathcal{D}}$ *for* $\mathsf{dom}(\mathcal{D})$*, and (2) satisfiability of finite conjunctions over* $\mathsf{pred}(\mathcal{D})$ *is decidable.*

Definition 12.6.2. *The* concrete domain extension *of a concept language* $\mathcal{L}$*, called* $\mathcal{L}_{\mathcal{D}}$*, is the least set containing all concepts, roles and formulæ of* $\mathcal{L}$*, such that* $\exists(p_1, \ldots, p_n).P$ *are concepts of* $\mathcal{L}_{\mathcal{D}}$ *if* p_i *are paths of atomic features of* $\mathcal{L}$ *and* P *is a* n*-ary predicate symbol of the concrete domain* $\mathcal{D}$*. If* $o_1 \ldots o_n$ *are names for concrete individuals of* $\mathcal{D}$ *and* P *is a* n*-ary predicate symbol of the concrete domain* $\mathcal{D}$ *then* $P(o_1, \ldots, o_n)$ *is an ABox formula of* $\mathcal{L}_{\mathcal{D}}$*. The further extension of* $\mathcal{L}_{\mathcal{D}}$ *adding complex roles, called* $\mathcal{L}_{\mathcal{RD}}$*, is the least set containing all concepts, roles and formulæ of* $\mathcal{L}_{\mathcal{D}}$*, such that* $\exists(p_1, \ldots, p_n)(q_1, \ldots, q_m).P$ *are roles of* $\mathcal{L}_{\mathcal{RD}}$ *if* p_i*,* q_j *are paths of atomic features of* $\mathcal{L}_{\mathcal{D}}$ *and* P *is a* $(n+m)$*-ary predicate symbol of the concrete domain* $\mathcal{D}$*.*

The $\mathcal{L}_{\mathcal{RD}}$ semantics naturally extends with concrete domains the standard semantics of $\mathcal{L}$ [Baader and Hanschke, 1991]. A concrete domain $\mathcal{D} = (\mathsf{dom}(\mathcal{D}), \mathsf{pred}(\mathcal{D}))$ is assumed, with $\mathsf{dom}(\mathcal{D}) \cap \Delta^{\mathcal{I}} = \emptyset$. A $\mathcal{L}_{\mathcal{RD}}$ *interpretation* extends the interpretation $\mathcal{I}$ of $\mathcal{L}$ by mapping every atomic feature f to a partial function $f^{\mathcal{I}} : \Delta^{\mathcal{I}} \rightarrow \Delta^{\mathcal{I}} \cup \mathsf{dom}(\mathcal{D})$, such that it satisfies the standard semantic definitions of $\mathcal{L}$ plus

$$\begin{aligned}(\exists(p_1,\ldots,p_n).P)^{\mathcal{I}} &= \{x \in \Delta^{\mathcal{I}} \mid \langle p_1^{\mathcal{I}}(x),\ldots,p_n^{\mathcal{I}}(x)\rangle \in P^{\mathcal{D}}\}\\ (\exists(p_1,\ldots,p_n)(q_1,\ldots,q_m).P)^{\mathcal{I}} &= \{(x,y) \in \Delta^{\mathcal{I}} \times \Delta^{\mathcal{I}} \mid \\ &\quad (p_1^{\mathcal{I}}(x),\ldots,p_n^{\mathcal{I}}(x),q_1^{\mathcal{I}}(y),\ldots,q_m^{\mathcal{I}}(y)) \in P^{\mathcal{D}}\}\end{aligned}$$

The semantics of the additional ABox statements involving concrete predicates follows the obvious intuition.

In this framework, assuming a concrete domain composed by temporal intervals and the Allen's predicates – proved admissible by [Lutz, 1999b] – the concept of Mortal can be defined as follows:

$$\begin{aligned}\texttt{Mortal} \doteq\ & \texttt{ALIVE-STATE} : \texttt{LivingBeing} \sqcap \texttt{DEAD-STATE} : (\neg\texttt{LivingBeing})\sqcap\\ & \exists(\texttt{ALIVE-STATE} \circ \texttt{HAS-TIME}, \texttt{DEAD-STATE} \circ \texttt{HAS-TIME}).\texttt{meets}\end{aligned}$$

i.e., a mortal is any individual having the property of being alive at some temporal interval that meets some other temporal interval at which the same individual has the property of being dead.

Theorem 12.6.1. *Decidability and Complexity*

- *If $\mathcal{L}$ includes $\mathcal{ALC}$, then the problem of logical implication for $\mathcal{L}_{\mathcal{D}}$ is undecidable in any unbounded, dense, linear ordered concrete domain $\mathcal{D}$ [Baader and Hanschke, 1992].*
- *If $\mathcal{L}$ includes $\mathcal{ALC}$, then the problems of concept satisfiability, concept subsumption, and instance checking with empty TBox for $\mathcal{L}_{\mathcal{RD}}$ are undecidable [Haarslev* et al.*, 1998].*
- *The problems of concept satisfiability, concept subsumption, and instance checking with empty TBox for $\mathcal{ALCF}_{\mathcal{D}}$ are PSPACE-complete in any concrete domain $\mathcal{D}$, provided that satisfiability in $\mathcal{D}$ is in PSPACE [Lutz, 1999b].*

We introduce now an example which shows that the $\mathcal{ALC}_{\mathcal{D}}$ Description Logic is more suitable to describe properties of temporal objects (e.g., intervals) rather than properties of objects varying in time (like in the Mortal example). In [Baader and Hanschke, 1991] the Allen's interval relations is internally defined using the set of real numbers $\Re$ together with the predicates $\leq, \leq, \geq, \geq, =, \neq$ as the concrete admissible domain. The Interval concept can be defined as an ordered pair of real numbers by referring to the concrete predicate $\leq$ applied to the features LEFT-HAS-TIME and RIGHT-HAS-TIME:

$$\texttt{Interval} \doteq \exists(\texttt{LEFT-HAS-TIME}, \texttt{RIGHT-HAS-TIME}).\leq$$

Allen's relations are binary relations on two intervals and are represented by the Pair concept which uses the features FIRST and SECOND:

$$\texttt{Pair} \doteq \exists\texttt{FIRST}.\texttt{Interval} \sqcap \exists\texttt{SECOND}.\texttt{Interval}$$

Now Allen's relation can be easily defined as concepts:

$$\begin{aligned}\texttt{C-Equals} &\doteq \texttt{Pair} \sqcap \exists(\texttt{FIRST} \circ \texttt{LEFT-HAS-TIME}, \texttt{SECOND} \circ \texttt{LEFT-HAS-TIME}). =\\ &\qquad\quad \sqcap \exists(\texttt{FIRST} \circ \texttt{RIGHT-HAS-TIME}, \texttt{SECOND} \circ \texttt{RIGHT-HAS-TIME}). =\\ \texttt{C-Before} &\doteq \texttt{Pair} \sqcap \exists(\texttt{FIRST} \circ \texttt{RIGHT-HAS-TIME}, \texttt{SECOND} \circ \texttt{LEFT-HAS-TIME}). \leq\\ \texttt{C-Meets} &\doteq \texttt{Pair} \sqcap \exists(\texttt{FIRST} \circ \texttt{RIGHT-HAS-TIME}, \texttt{SECOND} \circ \texttt{LEFT-HAS-TIME}). =\\ &\ldots\end{aligned}$$

As an example of $\mathcal{ALC}_{\mathcal{RD}}$, we can define the BEFORE role as being the counterpart of the concrete predicate before in the abstract domain, and use it for defining a new concept NoBefore, as the class of objects which do not have any BEFORE-related object:

$$\texttt{BEFORE} \equiv \exists(\texttt{HAS-TIME})(\texttt{HAS-TIME}).\mathsf{before}$$
$$\texttt{NoBefore} \doteq \forall\texttt{BEFORE}.\bot$$

Let us compare the above definition with a similar one in $\mathcal{ALC}_{\mathcal{A}}$

$$\texttt{NoBefore} \doteq [\mathsf{before}]\bot$$

Assuming that in both cases the temporal structure is isomorphic to the real numbers $\Re$, while the concept NoBefore in the concrete domain approach is satisfiable, denoting all the objects of the *abstract* domain having no BEFORE-related objects, the concept NoBefore in $\mathcal{ALC}_{\mathcal{A}}$ is clearly unsatisfiable. The reason is that in $\mathcal{ALC}_{\mathcal{RD}}$ we can only quantify over the abstract domain and not over the concrete one, i.e., we can only quantify over the abstract objects which may *possibly* have a specific temporal facet lifted up from the concrete domain. On the other hand, in $\mathcal{ALC}_{\mathcal{A}}$ both the abstract objects and the temporal elements are first-class citizens, resulting in a language where it is possible to quantify on both abstract objects and temporal elements.

A partial study on the relative expressive power between the languages $\mathcal{ALCF}_{\mathcal{AF}}$ and $\mathcal{ALCF}_{\mathcal{D}}$ has been conducted [Artale and Lutz, 1999]. In particular, it has been proved how the satisfiability of a $\mathcal{ALCF}_{\mathcal{AF}}$ concept can be reduced to the satisfiability of some corresponding concept in the language $\mathcal{ALCF}_{\mathcal{D}}$. The limit of this result is that the encoding preserves only satisfiability, and it does not clarify the real relationships between the two languages with respect to the problems of subsumption and logical implication.

A program* is consistent if it has an answer set not containing contradictory literals. As was shown in [Gelfond, 1994] if a program is consistent then all of its answer sets are consistent. A ground literal l is said to be *entailed* by a DLP Π, written as $\Pi \models l$, if it belongs to all of its answer sets.

In our further discussion we will need the following proposition about DLPs:

Proposition 13.2.1 ([Baral and Gelfond, 1994]). For any answer set S of a disjunctive logic program Π:

(a) For any ground instance of a rule of the type (13.2) from Π, if

$\{l_{k+1} \dots l_m\} \subseteq S$ and

$\{l_{m+1} \dots l_n\} \cap S = \emptyset$

then there exists an i, $0 \leq i \leq k$ such that $l_i \in S$.

(b) If S is a consistent answer set of Π and $l_i \in S$ for some $0 \leq i \leq k$ then there exists a ground instance of a rule from Π such that

$\{l_{k+1} \dots l_m\} \subseteq S$, and

$\{l_{m+1} \dots l_n\} \cap S = \emptyset$, and

$\{l_0 \dots l_k\} \cap S = \{l_i\}$. □

We now review the definitions of "splitting" and "signing" which we use to analyze properties of the programs obtained by translating a domain description.

Definition 13.2.3 ([Turner, 1994]). Let Π be a DLP such that no rule in it has empty heads. Let S be a set of literals in the language of Π such that no literals in $head(\Pi)$ appears complemented in $head(\Pi)$. Let $\overline{S}$ denote $Lit \setminus S$. S is said to be a *signing* for Π if each rule $r \in \Pi$ satisfies the following two conditions:

(i) $head(r) \cup pos(r) \subset S$ and $neg(r) \subset \overline{S}$, or
$head(r) \cup pos(r) \subset \overline{S}$ and $neg(r) \subset S$

(ii) If $head(r) \subset S$, then $head(r)$ is a singleton.

If a program has a signing, we say that it is signed. □

Definition 13.2.4 ([Turner, 1994]). Let Π be a program. If S is a signing for Π, then

$h_S(\Pi) = \{r \in \Pi \ : \ head(r) \subset S\}$,

$h_{\overline{S}}(\Pi) = \{r \in \Pi \ : \ head(r) \subset \overline{S}\}$. □

Proposition 13.2.2 (Based on the restricted monotonicity theorem in [Turner, 1994]). Let Π_1 and Π_2 be programs in the same language, both with signing S. If $h_{\overline{S}}(\Pi_1) \subseteq h_{\overline{S}}(\Pi_2)$ and $h_S(\Pi_2) \subseteq h_S(\Pi_1)$, then

if $\Pi_1 \models l$ and $l \in \overline{S}$ then $\Pi_2 \models l$. □

*Henceforth by "program" we mean a disjunctive logic program.

Definition 13.2.5 (Splitting set [Lifschitz and Turner, 1994]). A *splitting set* for a program Π is any set U of literals such that for every rule $r \in \Pi$, if $head(r) \cap U \neq \emptyset$ then $lit(r) \subset U$. If U is a splitting set for Π, we also say that U splits P. The set of rules $r \in \Pi$ such that $lit(r) \subset U$ is called the $bottom$ of Π relative to the splitting set U and denoted by $b_U(\Pi)$. The subprogram $\Pi \setminus b_U(\Pi)$ is called *the top of* Π relative to U. □

Definition 13.2.6 (Partial evaluation [Lifschitz and Turner, 1994]). The partial evaluation of a program Π with splitting set U w.r.t. a set of literals X is the program $e_U(\Pi, X)$ defined as follows. For each rule $r \in \Pi$ such that:

$$(pos(r) \cap U) \subset X \quad \wedge \ (neg(r) \cap U) \cap X = \emptyset$$

put in $e_U(\Pi, X)$ all the rules r' that satisfy the following property:

$$head(r') = head(r), \ pos(r') = pos(r) \setminus U, \ neg(r') = neg(r) \setminus U$$

□

Definition 13.2.7 (Solution [Lifschitz and Turner, 1994]). Let U be a splitting set for a program Π. A solution to Π w.r.t. U is a pair $\langle X, Y \rangle$ of literals such that:

- X is an answer set for $b_U(\Pi)$;
- Y is an answer set for $e_U(\Pi \setminus b_U(\Pi), X)$;
- $X \cup Y$ is consistent.

□

Lemma 13.2.1 (Splitting Lemma [Lifschitz and Turner, 1994]). Let U be a splitting set for a program Π. A set A of literals is a consistent answer set for Π if and only if $A = X \cup Y$ for some solution $\langle X, Y \rangle$ to Π w.r.t. U. □

The concept of a well-moded program due to Dembinski and Maluszynski [Dembinski and Maluszynski, 1985] has proven to be useful for establishing various properties of logic programs. We will be using it in this chapter and hence to be self-complete we will define it here. We first need the following terminology:

By a *mode* for an n-ary predicate symbol p we mean a function d_p from $\{1, \ldots, n\}$ to the set $\{+, -\}$. If $d_p(i)$ = '+' the i is called an *input* position of p and if $d_p(i)$ = '-' the i is called an *output* position of p. We write d_p in the form $p(d_p(1), \ldots, d_p(n))$. Intuitively, queries formed by predicate p will be expected to have input positions occupied by ground terms. To simplify the notation, when writing an atom as $p(u, v)$, we assume that u is the sequence of terms filling in the input positions of p and that v is the sequence of terms filling in the output positions. By $l(u, v)$ we denote expressions of the form $p(u, v)$ or *not* $p(u, v)$; $var(s)$ denotes the set of all variables occurring in s. Assignment of modes to the predicate symbols of a program Π is called *input-output specification*.

A rule $p_0(t_0, s_{m+1}) \leftarrow l_1(s_1, t_1), \ldots, l_m(s_m, t_m)$ is called *well-moded* w.r.t. its input output specification if for $i \in [1, m + 1]$, $var(s_i) \subseteq \bigcup_{j=0}^{i-1} var(t_j)$. In other words, a rule is well-moded if

i) every variable occurring in an input position of a body goal occurs either in an input position of the head or in an output position of an earlier body goal;

ii) every variable occurring in an output position of the head occurs in an input position of the head, or in an output position of a body goal.

A program is called well-moded w.r.t. its input-output specification if all its rules are.

In our analysis we will also be needing the following notion of acyclic programs [Apt, 1990].

Definition 13.2.8 ([Apt, 1990]). A general logic program Π is *acyclic* if there exists a mapping $| \ |$ from the Herbrand base of Π to the the set of natural numbers such that for every $A_0 \leftarrow A_1, \ldots, A_m, not\ A_{m+1}, \ldots, not\ A_n$ in the ground version of Π, and for every $1 \leq i \leq n$: $|A_0| > |A_i|$. □

13.2.1 Abductive logic programs

An alternative approach for reasoning with incomplete information is the formulation of abductive logic programs [Kakas and Mancarella, 1990a; Denecker and De Schreye, 1993; Baral and Gelfond, 1994], where predicates about which incompleteness is allowed is referred to as the *abducible* predicates or *open predicates*. An abductive logic program is a triple $\langle \Pi, A, O \rangle$, where A is the set of open predicates, Π is a general logic program with atoms of non-open predicates in its heads and O is a set of first order formulas. O is used to express *observations* and *constraints* in an abductive logic program. Abductive logic programs are characterized as follows:

Definition 13.2.9. Let $\langle \Pi, A, O \rangle$ be an abductive logic program. A set M of ground atoms is a *generalized stable model* of $\langle \Pi, A, O \rangle$ if there is a set of ground atoms Δ made up of predicates in A, such that M is a stable model of $\Pi \cup \Delta$ and M satisfies O.

For an atom f, we say $\langle \Pi, A, O \rangle \models_{abd} f$, if f belongs to all generalized stable models of $\langle \Pi, A, O \rangle$. For a negative literal $\neg f$, we say $\langle \Pi, A, O \rangle \models_{abd} \neg f$, if f does not belong to any of the generalized stable models of $\langle \Pi, A, O \rangle$. □

13.3 Action Languages: basic notions

Our description of dynamic domains will be based on the formalism of action languages. Such languages, first introduced in [Gelfond and Lifschitz, 1993], can be thought of as formal models of the part of the natural language that are used for describing the behavior of dynamic domains. An *action language* can be represented as the sum of two distinct parts: an "*action description language*", and an "*action query language*".

A set of propositions in an *action description language* describes the effects of actions on states. Mathematically, it defines a transition system with nodes corresponding to possible states and arcs labeled by actions from the given domain. An arc (σ_1, a, σ_2) indicates that execution of an action a in state σ_1 may result in the domain moving to the state σ_2. By a *path or history* of a transition system T we mean a sequence $\sigma_0, a_1, \sigma_1, \ldots, a_n, \sigma_n$ such that for any $1 \leq i < n$, $(\sigma_i, a_{i+1}, \sigma_{i+1})$ is an arc of T. σ_0 and σ_n are called initial and final states of the path (or history) respectively.

An *action query language* serves for expressing properties of paths in a given transition system. *The syntax* of such a language is defined by two classes of syntactic expressions: *axioms* and *queries*. *The semantics* of an action query language is defined by specifying, for every transition system T, every set Γ of axioms, and every query Q, whether Q is a consequence of Γ in T.

In the next three sections we define a simple action language $\mathcal{L}_0$ which can be viewed as the sum of an action description language $\mathcal{A}_0$ and a query description language $\mathcal{Q}_0$. We assume a fixed signature Σ_0 which consists of two disjoint and nonempty sets of symbols, a set $\mathbf{F}$ of fluents, and a set $\mathbf{A}$ of actions. Signatures of this kind will be called *action signatures*. By fluent literals we mean fluents and their negations. Negation of $f \in \mathbf{F}$ will be denoted by $\neg f$. A set S of fluent literals is called complete (w.r.t. $\mathbf{F}$) if for any $f \in \mathbf{F}$ we have $f \in S$ or $\neg f \in S$. A *state* is represented by a complete and consistent set of fluent literals of Σ_0. A fluent literal l is said to be true or said to hold in a state s, if $l \in s$. A set S of fluent literals is said to be true or said to hold in a state s, if all element of S hold in s.

13.4 Action description language $\mathcal{A}_0$

Consider a fixed action signature Σ_0. The syntax of $\mathcal{A}_0$ is characterized by the following definition.

Definition 13.4.1. In the language $\mathcal{A}_0$,

1. A fluent literal is an expression of the form f or $\neg f$ where f is a fluent name,
2. Propositions (called *causal laws*) are expressions of the form

$$impossible\_if(a, [l_1, \ldots, l_n]) \tag{13.3}$$

$$causes(a, l_0, [l_1, \ldots, l_n]) \tag{13.4}$$

   where a is an action name and l's are fluent literals. The former are called *executability conditions*, and the latter are called *dynamic causal laws*. Intuitively, the proposition (13.3) means that the action a is impossible to execute in a state s if the set of fluent literals $\{l_1, \ldots, l_n\}$ hold in s. Similarly, the proposition (13.4) means that if an action a is executed in a state s such that the set of fluent literals $\{l_1, \ldots, l_n\}$ hold in s then the fluent literal l_0 will hold in the subsequent state.

3. An *action description* is a set of causal laws. □

Given an action description $\mathcal{D}$, the semantics of $\mathcal{A}_0$ defines the transition system that is "described" by $\mathcal{D}$. More precisely

Definition 13.4.2. The transition system $T = \langle \mathcal{S}, \mathcal{R} \rangle$ *described* by $\mathcal{D}$ is defined as follows:

1. $\mathcal{S}$ is the collection of all complete and consistent sets of fluent literals of Σ_0,

2. $\mathcal{R}$ is the set of all triples (σ, a, σ'), where $\sigma, \sigma' \in \mathcal{S}$, such that $\mathcal{D}$ does not contain a proposition of the form $impossible\_if(a, [l_1, \ldots, l_n])$ with $[l_1, \ldots, l_n] \subseteq \sigma$ and

$$E(a, \sigma) \subseteq \sigma' \subseteq E(a, \sigma) \cup \sigma \tag{13.5}$$

where $E(a, \sigma)$ stands for the set of all fluent literals l_0 for which there is a dynamic causal law $causes(a, l_0, [l_1, \ldots, l_n])$ in $\mathcal{D}$ such that $[l_1, \ldots, l_n] \subseteq \sigma$.

3. For any $\sigma \in \mathcal{S}$, if there is no proposition of the form $impossible\_if(a, [l_1, \ldots, l_n])$ with $[l_1, \ldots, l_n] \subseteq \sigma$ then there exists a σ' such that $(\sigma, a, \sigma') \in \mathcal{R}$. (Note that this (σ, a, σ') must satisfy condition (2).)

We say that an action a is *prohibited* in a state σ if there is no σ' such that $(\sigma, a, \sigma') \in \mathcal{R}$. The transition system T described by $\mathcal{D}$ is called the *causal model* of $\mathcal{D}$. A domain description with no causal model is called *inconsistent*. □

Intuitively, (13.5) together with the requirement that σ' be complete and consistent says that the immediate effects of action a in state σ must be in σ', and in addition (accounting for inertia) all other fluents in σ must remain unchanged in σ'. Moreover, for $\mathcal{A}_0$, σ' satisfying (13.5), if exists, is unique. An example of a domain description that is inconsistent is $\{causes(a, f, [\ ]), causes(a, \neg f, [\ ])\}$. That is because for an arbitrary σ there does not exist a σ' such that (σ, a, σ') satisfies the condition (2). Thus condition (3) is violated.

Example 13.4.1. Let us consider a collection of vehicles which can move between different locations. The corresponding signature Σ_0 consists of two sets of object constants, $v_1, \ldots, v_n$ and $l_1, \ldots, l_m$; the set of fluents of the form $at(v, l)$ which stands for "the vehicle v is located at location l", and a set of actions $move(v, l_1, l_2)$ where l_1 and l_2 are different locations. The effects of these actions can be defined by the following set $\mathcal{D}_0$ of causal laws:

$$\mathcal{D}_0 \left\{ \begin{array}{l} causes(move(v, l_1, l_2), at(v, l_2), [\,]). \\ causes(move(v, l_1, l_2), \neg at(v, l_3), [\,]). \\ impossible\_if(move(v, l_1, l_2), [\neg at(v, l_1)]). \\ \text{where } v\text{'s are vehicles and } l_1, l_2, \text{ and } l_3 \text{ are locations and } l_3 \neq l_2. \end{array} \right.$$

To actually specify these causal laws to a computer program we will use a DLP. We assume the existence of complete lists of vehicles and locations given by collection of atoms $vehicle(v_1), \ldots$ and $location(l_1), \ldots$, and define the causal laws by rules with variables:

$$\Pi_{\mathcal{D}_0} \left\{ \begin{array}{rl} causes(move(V, L_1, L_2), at(V, L_2), [\,]) :- & vehicle(V), \\ & location(L_1), \\ & location(L_2). \\ & \\ causes(move(V, L_1, L_2), \neg at(V, L_3), [\,]) :- & vehicle(V) \\ & location(L_1), \\ & location(L_2), \\ & location(L_3), \\ & L_3 \neq L_2. \\ & \\ impossible\_if(move(V, L_1, L_2), [\neg at(V, L_1)]) :- & vehicle(V) \\ & location(L_1), \\ & location(L_2). \end{array} \right.$$

We say a causal law $c \in D_0$ iff it is entailed by the above program.

The Figure 13.1 shows the transition system T_0 described by $\mathcal{D}_0$. (For simplicity we assumed that the signature of $\mathcal{D}_0$ contains names for one vehicle and two locations.)

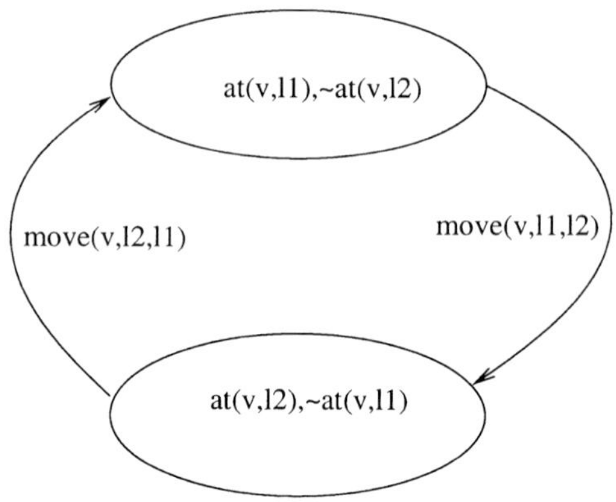

Figure 13.1: Transition system T_0

It is worth noticing that according to our description there are states in which a vehicle can occupy more than one location. Similarly, one location may contain more than one vehicle. Later we show how these possibilities – if necessary – can be eliminated. □

13.5 Query description language $\mathcal{Q}_0$

The query language $\mathcal{Q}_0$ over an action signature Σ_0 consists of two types of expressions: axioms and queries. Axioms of $\mathcal{Q}_0$ are of the form

$$initially(l) \tag{13.6}$$

where l is a fluent literal. A collection of axioms describes the set of fluents which are true in (the state corresponding to) the initial situation*. A set of axioms of $\mathcal{Q}_0$ is said to be *initial state complete* if for all fluents f either $initially(f)$ or $initially(\neg f)$ is in the set.

A query of $\mathcal{Q}_0$ is a statement of the form

$$holds\_after(l, \alpha) \tag{13.7}$$

where l is a fluent literal and α is a sequence of actions. The statement says that α is executable in the initial situation and, if it were executed, then the fluent literal l would be true afterwards. To give the semantics of $\mathcal{Q}_0$ we need the following definition.

*By situation we mean an executable sequence of actions. The initial situation corresponds to the empty sequence.

Definition 13.5.1. Let T be a transition system over action signature Σ_0. We say that

(i) a history $\sigma_0, a_1, \sigma_1, \ldots, a_n, \sigma_n$ *satisfies* an axiom $initially(l)$ if $l \in \sigma_0$,

(ii) a query $Q = holds\_after(l, [a_n, \ldots, a_1])$ is a *consequence* of a set Γ of axioms with respect to T if, for every history H of T of the form $\sigma_0, a_1, \sigma_1, \ldots, a_n, \sigma_n$ that satisfies all axioms in Γ, $l \in \sigma_n$. In this case we say Q holds in H.

Let $\mathcal{D}$ be an action description and T be the transition system defined by $\mathcal{D}$. We say that a query Q is a *consequence* of a set Γ of axioms in $\mathcal{D}$ (symbolically, $\Gamma \models_{\mathcal{D}} Q$) if Q is a consequence of Γ with respect to T. □

To illustrate the definition let us consider the following example.

Example 13.5.1. Let $\mathcal{D}_0$ be the action description from Example 13.4.1 and consider the set Γ_0 of axioms of the form

$$\Gamma_0 \begin{cases} (a)\ initially(at(v_1, l_1)), initially(at(v_2, l_2)), \ldots \\ (b)\ initially(\neg at(v_i, l_j)), \text{where } i \neq j. \end{cases}$$

Obviously, Γ_0 gives a *complete* description of the initial situation. I.e., there is only one state in T_0 which satisfies all the axioms from Γ_0. It can then be shown that

(i) $\Gamma_0 \models_{\mathcal{D}_0} holds\_after(at(v_1, l_3), [move(v_1, l_1, l_3)])$,

(ii) $\Gamma_0 \models_{\mathcal{D}_0} holds\_after(\neg at(v_1, l_i), [move(v_1, l_1, l_3)])$, for any location l_i different from l_3,

(iii) $\Gamma_0 \models_{\mathcal{D}_0} holds\_after(at(v_2, l_2), [move(v_1, l_1, l_3)])$, and

(iv) $\Gamma_0 \models_{\mathcal{D}_0} holds\_after(\neg at(v_2, l_i), [move(v_1, l_1, l_3)])$, for any location l_i different from l_2.

Similar to Example 13.4.1 the axioms of Γ_0 can be more concisely defined by replacing facts of the form (b) by the DLP below:

$$\Pi_{\Gamma_0} \begin{cases} initially(at(v_1, l_1)). \\ initially(at(v_2, l_2)). \\ \ldots \\ initially(\neg at(V, L)) \text{ :- } vehicle(V), \\ \qquad location(L), \\ \qquad not\ initially(at(V, L)). \end{cases}$$

□

In the next section we give additional DLP rules that are needed to compute $\models_{\mathcal{D}_0}$ with respect to Γ_0.

13.6 Answering queries in $\mathcal{L}(\mathcal{A}_0, \mathcal{Q}_0)$

In this section we address the question of computing the consequences of axioms of $\mathcal{Q}_0$. We limit ourselves to sets of axioms which are initial state complete. (We will lift this restriction in Section 13.9.) The consequences of an action description $\mathcal{D}$ and a set Γ of axioms will be computed by a general logic program Π_{00} together with $\mathcal{D}$ and Γ as a set of facts. Π_{00} consists of the following rules:

1. Executability of Actions:

$$\Pi^1_{00} \begin{cases} impossible([A|S]) & :- \\ & \quad impossible(S). \\ impossible([A|S]) & :- \\ & \quad impossible\_if(A, P), \\ & \quad holds\_after\_list(P, S). \\ executable(S) & :- \\ & \quad not\ impossible(S). \end{cases}$$

The atom $holds\_after\_list(p, s)$ says that the sequence s of actions is executable in the initial situation and, if it were to be executed, then all fluent literals from the list p would necessarily be true afterwards. The statement $impossible(s)$ ($executable(s)$) says that the sequence s of action can not (can) be executed in the initial situation. Intuitively, the use of negation as failure in the third rule is justified by the completeness of information about impossibility of actions and about truth and falsity of fluents. Formal justification for these and other axioms will be provided by Proposition 13.6.1 below.

2. The Effect Axioms:

$$\Pi^2_{00} \begin{cases} holds\_after(L, [\,]) & :- \\ & \quad initially(L). \\ holds\_after(L, [A|S]) & :- \\ & \quad executable([A|S]), \\ & \quad causes(A, L, C), \\ & \quad holds\_after\_list(C, S). \end{cases}$$

These axioms define the effects of actions on a state (corresponding to a situation) based on causal laws and on truth and falsity of fluents.

3. The List Axioms:

$$\Pi^3_{00} \begin{cases} holds\_after\_list([], \_). & \\ holds\_after\_list([L|Rest], S) & :- \\ & \quad holds\_after(L, S), \\ & \quad holds\_after\_list(Rest, S). \end{cases}$$

The axioms in this group define the auxiliary relation $holds\_after\_list(p, \alpha)$.

4. The Inertia Axiom:

$$\Pi^4_{00} \left\{ \begin{array}{ll} holds\_after(L, [A|S]) & :- \\ & executable([A|S]), \\ & holds\_after(L, S), \\ & not\ ab(L, A, S). \end{array} \right.$$

This is the inertia axiom mentioned in the introduction. It has a form of default which says that *normally*, things remain as they are. The atom $ab(l, a_n, [a_{n-1}, \ldots, a_1])$ says that the inertia axiom shall not be applied to establish the truth value of l after the execution of $[a_1, \ldots, a_{n-1}, a_n]$. This is a common way of representing defaults in a logic programming framework, where we represent 'normally ps are qs', but r's are an exception to this rule, by writing:

$$q(X) \leftarrow p(X), not\ ab(X)$$
$$ab(X) \leftarrow r(X)$$

5. Cancellation Axioms

$$\Pi^5_{00} \left\{ \begin{array}{ll} ab(L, A, S) & :- \\ & contrary(L, NL), \\ & causes(A, NL, C), \\ & holds\_after\_list(C, S) \end{array} \right.$$

The above axiom stops the application of the inertia axiom – that establishes the truth of a fluent literal l in situation $[a|s]$, if there are causal laws which cause l to become false in the situation $[a|s]$.

6. Auxiliary

$$\Pi^6_{00} \left\{ \begin{array}{ll} contrary(neg(F), F) & :- \\ & fluent(F). \\ contrary(F, neg(F)) & :- \\ & fluent(F). \end{array} \right.$$

The following proposition gives conditions for soundness and completeness of $\Pi_{00} \cup \mathcal{D} \cup \Gamma$ with respect to the entailment $\models_{\mathcal{D}}$ from a set of complete and consistent axioms Γ. Given a consistent (but possibly incomplete) set of axioms Γ, by $c(\Gamma)$ we denote the set $\{\Gamma'$: such that $\Gamma \subseteq \Gamma'$ and Γ' is complete $\}$. In the following proposition and through the rest of this paper, for a logic program Π, we will often denote the set $\{Q : \Pi \cup \Gamma \cup \mathcal{D} \models Q\}$ by $\Pi(\Gamma \cup \mathcal{D})$.

Proposition 13.6.1. For any consistent action description $\mathcal{D}$ and an initial state complete set of axioms Γ, $\Gamma \models_{\mathcal{D}} holds\_after(l, s)$ iff $holds\_after(l, s) \in \Pi_{00}(\mathcal{D} \cup \Gamma)$. □

sketch. The proof follows from the following two lemmas. In each of these two lemmas $\mathcal{D}$ is a consistent action description and Γ is an initial state complete set of axioms. □

Lemma 13.6.1 ([Apt, 1990]). $\Pi_{00}(\mathcal{D} \cup \Gamma)$ is acyclic. □

Proof:
The following level mapping $|\ |$ shows that the program $\Pi_{00} \cup \Gamma \cup \mathcal{D}$ satisfies the conditions for acyclicity.

Let c be the number of fluent literals in the language plus 1; p be a list of fluent literal, f be a fluent literal, and s be a sequence of actions.

For any action a, $|a| = 1$, $|[\ ]| = 1$, and for any list $[a|r]$ of actions $|[a|r]| = |r| + 1$.

Also, for any fluent literal f, $|f| = 1$, $|[\ ]| = 1$, and for any list $[f|p]$ of fluent literals $|[f|p]| = |p| + 1$.

$|holds\_after\_list(p, s)| = 6c * |s| + |p| + 4$

$|holds\_after(f, s)| = 6c * |s| + |f| + 4$

$|executable(s)| = 6c * |s| + 3$

$|impossible(s)| = 6c * |s| + 2$

$|ab(f, a, s)| = 6c * |s| + 5c + |f| + 1$

$|contrary(f, g)| = 1$, and all other atoms are mapped to 0. □

From the properties of acyclic programs [Apt, 1990] it follows that $\Pi_{00} \cup \mathcal{D} \cup \Gamma$ has a unique answer set.

Lemma 13.6.2. Let $H = \sigma_0, a_1, \sigma_1, \ldots a_n, \sigma_n$ be a history of the transition system defined by $\mathcal{D}$ that satisfy the axioms in Γ and let M be the answer set of $\Pi_{00} \cup \mathcal{D} \cup \Gamma$. Then, for all i, $0 \le i \le n$, $f \in \sigma_i$ iff $holds\_ater(f, [a_i, \ldots, a_1])$* is true in M. □

Proposition 13.6.1 reduces the question of computing the consequence relation $\models_{\mathcal{D}}$ to computing entailment with respect to the logic program $\Pi_{00} \cup \mathcal{D} \cup \Gamma$. Computation with respect to a logic program depends on the interpreter used for making inferences. Since Prolog is the most popular logic programming language to date, we now consider using the Prolog interpreter, and view the program $\Pi_{00} \cup \mathcal{D} \cup \Gamma$ as a Prolog program with variables.

Proposition 13.6.2. The program $\Pi_{00} \cup \Gamma \cup \mathcal{D}$ is computable by the Prolog interpreter. I.e., The inference due to the Prolog interpreter on $\Pi_{00} \cup \Gamma \cup \mathcal{D}$ viewed as a Prolog program is sound and complete with respect to the answer set semantics of $\Pi_{00} \cup \Gamma \cup \mathcal{D}$. □

sketch. Let us start by listing the questions which need to be addressed to prove this proposition. First it is well known that for some programs the Prolog interpreter may produce unsound results. This may happen because of *the absence of the occur-check* which, in some cases, is necessary for soundness of the SLDNF resolution, or because the *interpreter may flounder*, i.e. may select for resolution a goal of the form *not* q where q contains an uninstantiated variable. Second, the interpreter *may fail to terminate*. Even if we show that for any $X \in \Pi_{00}$ and ground query q, the interpreter which takes $\Pi_{00} \cup X$ and q as an input terminates, does not flounder, and does not require the occur-check, the soundness of our result is guaranteed only with respect to the *unsorted* grounding of Π_{00}, i.e. the grounding of Π_{00} by

*When $i = 0$, the list $[a_i, \ldots, a_1]$ denotes the empty list $[\ ]$.

terms of signature Σ_u obtained from signature Σ_0 by removing types and type information. In what follows we briefly discuss how these questions can be addressed. In particular we give hints about why (i) the program is occur-check free, (ii) it does not flounder, and (iii) it terminates. A proof based on our hints will be similar to the proofs in Section 7 of [Baral *et al.*, 1997]. □

- *Occur-check free:* To show that our program is occur-check free we use the result by Apt and Pellegrini in [Apt and Pellegrini, 1994] where they showed that if Π is well-moded [Dembinski and Maluszynski, 1985] for some input-output specification and there is no rule in Π whose head contains more than one occurrence of the same variable in its output positions then Π is occur-check free w.r.t. any ground query q. It can be shown that the following input-output specification, where '+' denotes input and '-' denotes output, indeed satisfies the above property. (For further details on this property please see [Dembinski and Maluszynski, 1985; Apt and Pellegrini, 1994; Baral *et al.*, 1997].)

  $impossible(+)$
  $executable(+)$
  $holds\_after(-,+)$
  $holds\_after\_list(-,+)$
  $ab(+,+,+)$
  $contrary(+,-)$
  $initially(-)$
  $causes(+,-,-)$
  $impossible\_if(+,-)$
  $fluent(+)$

- *Does not flounder:* To show this property we can use another theorem from [Apt and Pellegrini, 1994] which was also independently discovered by Stroetman [Stroetman, 1993]: if Π is well-moded (for some input-output specification) and all predicate symbols occurring under *not* in Π are moded completely by input then a ground query $\pi(q)$ to Π does not flounder. The only two predicate symbols occurring under *not* in $\Pi_{00} \cup \Gamma \cup \mathcal{D}$ are $impossible$ and ab, and as required by the above mentioned condition, they both are moded completely by input.

- *Terminates:* Since $\Pi_{00} \cup \mathcal{D} \cup \Gamma$ is acyclic (From Lemma 13.6.1), termination follows as a property of acyclic programs [Apt, 1990]. □

To conclude the proof it suffices to apply the main result of [McCain and Turner, 1994] which reduces entailment in typed groundings of programs to entailment in their untyped groundings. □

13.7 Query language $\mathcal{Q}_1$

In this section we expand query language $\mathcal{Q}_0$ to be able to talk about the events that have actually taken place and about hypothetical actions that may be part of a history. The letters $t_0, t_1, \ldots$ are called *actual situations* and used to denote time points in the actual evolution of the system. If such evolution is caused by consecutive actions $a_1, \ldots, a_n$ then t_0 corresponds to the initial situation and t_k where $k \leq n$ corresponds to the end of the execution of $a_1, \ldots, a_k$.

The domain's past evolution is described by a set Γ of axioms in the query language $\mathcal{Q}_1$, which are expressions of the form

$$occurs\_at(a, t_k) \tag{13.8}$$

$$holds\_at(l, t_k) \tag{13.9}$$

The axiom (13.8) says that the action a has been executed in actual situation t_k; the axiom (13.9) indicates that l is true after a sequence of k consecutive actions has been actually executed. The proposition $initially(l)$ will be often used as a shorthand for $holds\_at(l, t_0)$. The axioms of Γ can be viewed as *observations*. Besides the actual situations, we have a special situation t_c that we refer to as the *current situation*, or the *current moment of time*. If there is a situation t_k with an axiom $occurs\_at(a, t_k)$, such that for every axiom in Γ with a situation t_i in it, $i \leq k$, then t_c is the situation t_{k+1}, otherwise t_c is the situation t_{max}, where max is the maximum j, such that there is an axiom about t_j in Γ.

Queries of $\mathcal{Q}_1$ are expressions of the form (13.9)

and of the form

$$currently(l) \tag{13.10}$$

$$holds\_after(l, [a_n, \ldots, a_1], t). \tag{13.11}$$

The query (13.10) states that l holds at the current moment of time. The query (13.11) is hypothetical and is read as: "sequence $a_1, \ldots, a_n$ of actions is executable in the situation t, and if it were executed, then fluent literal l would be true afterwards. If t is an actual situation that happened in the past and the sequence $a_1, \ldots, a_n$ is different from the one that actually occurs at t then the corresponding query expresses a counterfactual. If $t = t_c$ then the query expresses a hypothesis about the system's future behavior. The following definitions refines the intuition behind the meaning of propositions of $\mathcal{Q}_1$.

Definition 13.7.1. Let T be a transition system, $H = \sigma_0, a_1, \sigma_1, \ldots, a_n, \sigma_n$ be a history of T, and Σ be a *situation map*, a mapping from situations to positive integers such that $i < j$ implies $\Sigma(t_i) < \Sigma(t_j)$, $\Sigma(t_0) = 0$ and for all t_i, $\Sigma(t_i) \leq \Sigma(t_c)$. We say that

- (H, Σ) *satisfies* an axiom $occurs\_at(a, t_k)$ if $a = a_{\Sigma(t_k)+1}$,
- (H, Σ) *satisfies* an axiom $holds\_at(l, t_k)$ if $l \in \sigma_{\Sigma(t_k)}$.

A pair (H, Σ) of history H of T and a situation map Σ is called a *model* of a set of axioms Γ if (H, Σ) satisfies all axioms from Γ and there does not exist a proper prefix H' of H such that for some situation map Σ', the pair (H', Σ') satisfies all axioms from Γ. Γ is called *consistent* if it has a model.

- a query $holds\_at(l, t_k)$ is a *consequence* of a set Γ of axioms with respect to T if, for every pair of history $\sigma_0, a_1, \sigma_1, \ldots, a_n, \sigma_n$ and situation map Σ of T that is a model of Γ, $l \in \sigma_{\Sigma(t_k)}$;
- a query $currently(l)$ is a *consequence* of a set Γ of axioms with respect to T if, for every pair of history $\sigma_0, a_1, \sigma_1, \ldots, a_n, \sigma_n$ and situation map Σ of T that is a model of Γ, $l \in \sigma_{\Sigma(t_c)}$;
- a query $holds\_after(l, [a'_m, \ldots, a'_1], t_k)$ is a *consequence* of a set Γ of axioms with respect to T if, for every pair of history $\sigma_0, a_1, \sigma_1, \ldots, a_n, \sigma_n$ and situation map Σ of T that is a model of Γ, $a'_1, \ldots, a'_m$ is executable in $\sigma_{\Sigma(t_k)}$ and for any history $\sigma_0, a_1, \sigma_1, \ldots, \sigma_{\Sigma(t_k)-1}, a_{\Sigma(t_k)}, \sigma'_0, a'_1, \sigma'_1, \ldots, a'_m, \sigma'_m$ of T such that $\sigma'_0 = \sigma_{\Sigma(t_k)}$, $l \in \sigma'_m$.

As before, $\Gamma \models_{\mathcal{D}} Q$ will mean that the query Q is the consequence of Γ in the transition system T described by the action description $\mathcal{D}$. □

It can be shown that if a history $H = \sigma_0, a_1, \sigma_1, \ldots, a_n, \sigma_n$ and situation map Σ of T is a model of Γ then $\Sigma(t_c) = n$, as otherwise the part of the history after $\sigma_{\Sigma(t_c)}$ can be eliminated from the history without affecting the truth of the axioms, thus contradicting the conditions of being a model.

Example 13.7.1. Let $\mathcal{D}_0$ be the action description from Example 13.4.1 and consider the set Γ_1 of axioms of the form

$$\Gamma_1 \left\{ \begin{array}{l} initially(at(v_1, l_1)). \\ initially(at(v_2, l_2)). \\ \ldots \\ initially(\neg at(V, L)) \ :- \\ \qquad vehicle(V), \\ \qquad location(L), \\ \qquad not\ initially(at(V, L)). \\ occurs\_at(move(v_1, l_1, l_2), t_0). \end{array} \right.$$

It can be shown that

$\Gamma_1 \models_{\mathcal{D}_0} currently(at(v_1, l_2))$

$\Gamma_1 \models_{\mathcal{D}_0} currently(\neg at(v_1, l_1))$

$\Gamma_1 \models_{\mathcal{D}_0} currently(at(v_2, l_2))$

$\Gamma_1 \models_{\mathcal{D}_0} holds\_after(at(v_1, l_1), [move(v_2, l_2, l_3)], t_0)$

$\Gamma_1 \models_{\mathcal{D}_0} holds\_after(at(v_2, l_2), [move(v_2, l_2, l_3)], t_0)$

$\Gamma_1 \models_{\mathcal{D}_0} holds\_after(at(v_2, l_2), [move(v_2, l_2, l_3)], t_1)$

The last two queries contain counterfactual and hypothetical statements respectively. Let us now consider $\Gamma_2 = \Gamma_1 \cup \{holds\_at(at(v_2, l_3), t_2)\}$. Clearly,

$\Gamma_2 \models_{\mathcal{D}_0} currently(\neg at(v_2, l_2))$

This demonstrates that the consequence relation of $\mathcal{Q}_1$ is nonmonotonic with respect to Γ. This is of course not surprising because the definition of the corresponding consequence relation incorporates the closed world assumption which roughly says that *no actions occur except those needed to explain observations of* Γ. Notice also that the only possible history which satisfies axioms from Γ_2 starts at the fully defined initial state σ_0 and consists of the two actions $move(v_1, l_1, l_2)$ and $move(v_2, l_2, l_3)$. If we were to allow queries of the form (13.8) we would be able to conclude that Γ_2 entails $occurs\_at(move(v_2, l_2, l_3))$. □

In the rest of this paper, when using $\mathcal{Q}_1$, we will make some completeness assumptions.

- (i) Γ specifies a *complete initial situation*, and
- (ii) for all models (H, Σ) of Γ, with $H = \sigma_0, a_1, \sigma_1, \ldots, a_n, \sigma_n$

  $\Sigma(t_i) = i$ and
  $occurs\_at(a_j, t_i) \in \Gamma$ iff $\Sigma(t_i) = j - 1$.

  In the above case we say that Γ specifies a *complete observation about the history* with respect to the transition system T.

Thus if a set of axioms Γ and a transition system T satisfy the above two assumptions then they have exactly one model (H, Σ), with $H = \sigma_0, a_1, \sigma_1, \ldots, a_n, \sigma_n$, where $\sigma_0 = \{l : initially(l) \in \Gamma\}$, and for $1 \leq i \leq n$, $occurs\_at(a_i, t_{i-1}) \in \Gamma$ and $\Sigma(t_i) = i$.

13.8 Answering queries in $\mathcal{L}(\mathcal{A}_0, \mathcal{Q}_1)$

As in $\mathcal{L}(\mathcal{A}_0, \mathcal{Q}_0)$ the queries in $\mathcal{L}(\mathcal{A}_0, \mathcal{Q}_1)$ will be answered by computing a program Π_{01} – similar to that of Π_{00} – together with action description $\mathcal{D}$ and axioms Γ.

The program Π_{01} will consist of the following rules:

1. Executability of Actions:

$$\Pi^1_{01} \left\{ \begin{array}{lll} impossible([A|S], T) & :- & \\ & & impossible(S, T). \\ impossible([A|S], T) & :- & \\ & & impossible\_if(A, P), \\ & & holds\_after\_list(P, S, T). \\ executable(S, T) & :- & \\ & & not\ impossible(S, T). \end{array} \right.$$

These axioms are similar to that of Π_{00}. The difference is the existence of the new parameter T which stands for an actual situation.

The statement $impossible([a_n, \ldots, a_1], t)$ says that the sequence $a_1, \ldots, a_n$ of actions cannot be executed in the actual situation t. The meaning of $possible$ and $hold\_after$ are also similar.

2. The Effect Axioms:

$$
\Pi_{01}^2 \left\{
\begin{array}{lll}
holds\_after(L, [\,], t_0) & :- & \\
 & & initially(L). \\
holds\_after(L, [A|S], T) & :- & \\
 & & executable([A|S], T), \\
 & & causes(A, L, C), \\
 & & holds\_after\_list(C, S, T). \\
 & & \\
holds\_after(L, [\,], T) & :- & \\
 & & holds\_at(L, T). \\
holds\_at(L, T_k) & :- & \\
 & & next(T_k, T_{k-1}), \\
 & & occurs\_at(A, T_{k-1}) \\
 & & holds\_after(L, [A], T_{k-1}). \\
currently(L) & :- & \\
 & & current(T), \\
 & & holds\_at(L, T). \\
current(T_k) & :- & \\
 & & next(T_k, T_{k-1}), \\
 & & occurs\_at(A, T_{k-1}), \\
 & & nothing\_happend(T_k). \\
something\_happend(T) & :- & \\
 & & occurs\_at(A, T). \\
nothing\_happend(T) & :- & \\
 & & \text{not } something\_happend(T).
\end{array}
\right.
$$

The first axiom in this group is similar to the corresponding axiom in Π_{00}. The second and the third axioms express the relationship between relations $holds\_after$ and $holds\_at$. The last four axioms define the current situation. The use of negation as failure is justified by our completeness assumption and is responsible for the non-monotonicity of our program with respect to queries of the form $currently(L)$.

3. The List Axioms: (Similar to Π_{00}^3.)

$$
\Pi_{01}^3 \left\{
\begin{array}{lll}
holds\_after\_list([], \_, T). & & \\
holds\_after\_list([L|Rest], S, T) & :- & \\
 & & holds\_after(L, S, T), \\
 & & holds\_after\_list(Rest, S, T).
\end{array}
\right.
$$

4. The Inertia Axiom: (Similar to Π_{00}^4.)

$$
\Pi_{01}^4 \left\{
\begin{array}{lll}
holds\_after(L, [A|S], T) & :- & \\
 & & executable([A|S]), \\
 & & holds\_after(L, S, T), \\
 & & \text{not } ab(L, A, S, T).
\end{array}
\right.
$$

5. Cancellation Axioms: (Similar to Π_{00}^5).)

$$\Pi_{01}^5 \begin{cases} ab(L, A, S, T) & :- \\ & contrary(L, NL), \\ & causes(A, NL, C), \\ & holds\_after\_list(C, S, T) \end{cases}$$

6. Auxiliary rules Π_{01}^6: Same as Π_{00}^6.

The following proposition gives conditions for soundness and completeness of $\Pi_{01} \cup \mathcal{D} \cup \Gamma$.

Proposition 13.8.1. For any consistent action description $\mathcal{D}$, a consistent set of axioms Γ that specifies a complete initial situation and also a complete observation of the history with respect to the transition system of $\mathcal{D}$, and a query Q of $\mathcal{Q}_1$, $\Gamma \models_{\mathcal{D}} Q$ iff $\Pi_{01} \cup \mathcal{D} \cup \Gamma \models Q$. □

The proof of the above proposition is similar to the proof in [Baral *et al.*, 1997].

As in Section 13.6 we can show that the Prolog interpreter's inferencing by viewing $\Pi_{01} \cup \mathcal{D} \cup \Gamma$ as a Prolog program is sound and complete with respect to its answer set semantics. The proof of this results is similar to the proof of Proposition 13.6.2 and the proofs in Section 7 of [Baral *et al.*, 1997]. It will require us to show the following:

- *Occur-check free:* It can be shown that the following input-output specification, where '+' denotes input and '-' denotes output, satisfies the well-moded property that guarantees that the program is occur-check free.

  $impossible(+, +)$
  $executable(+, +)$
  $holds\_after(-, +, +)$
  $holds\_after\_list(-, +, +)$
  $ab(+, +, +, +)$
  $contrary(+, -)$
  $initially(-)$
  $causes(+, -, -)$
  $impossible\_if(+, -)$
  $holds\_at(-, +)$
  $currently(-)$
  $current(-)$
  $something\_happened(+)$
  $nothing\_happened(+)$
  $next(-, -)$
  $occurs\_at(-, -)$
  $fluent(+)$

- *Does not flounder:* To show this property, as in the proof sketch of Proposition 13.6.2 we can use the theorems from [Apt and Pellegrini, 1994; Stroetman, 1993] which states: if Π is well-moded (for some input-output specification) and all predicate symbols occurring under *not* in Π are moded completely by input then a ground query

$\pi(q)$ to Π does not flounder. The only predicate symbols occurring under *not* in $\Pi_{01} \cup \mathcal{D} \cup \Gamma$ are $impossible$, ab, and $something\_happened$ and as required by the above mentioned condition, they both are moded completely by input.

- *Terminates:* To prove termination, we can use the acyclicity condition of [Apt, 1990]. We can show the acyclicity of $\Pi_{01} \cup \mathcal{D} \cup \Gamma$ by defining the following level mapping $|\ |$.

  Let c be the number of fluent literals in the language plus 1; p be a list of fluent literal, f be a fluent literal, s be a sequence of actions, t_i's be time points and t_{max} be the current time plus 1.

  For any action a, $|a| = 1$, $|[\,]| = 1$, and for any list $[a|r]$ of actions $|[a|r]| = |r| + 1$.

  For any fluent literal f, $|f| = 1$, $|[\ ]| = 1$, and for any list $[f|p]$ of fluent literals $|[f|p]| = |p| + 1$.

  For any time point t_i, $|t_i| = i + 1$.

  $|holds\_after\_list(p, s, t)| = 10c * |t| + 4c * |s| + |p| + 4$

  $|holds\_after(f, s, t)| = 10c * |t| + 4c * |s| + |f| + 4$

  $|executable(s)| = 10c * |t| + 4c * |s| + 3$

  $|impossible(s)| = 10c * |t| + 4c * |s| + 2$

  $|ab(f, a, s, t)| = 10c * |t| + 4c * (|s| + 1) + |f| + 1$

  $|holds\_at(f, t)| = 10c * |t| + |f| + 3$

  $|currently(L)| = 15ct_{max}$

  $|current(t)| = |t| + 3$

  $|nothing\_happened| = |t| + 2$

  $|something\_happened(t)| = |t| + 1$

  $|contrary(f, g)| = 1$, and all other atoms are mapped to 0.

□

13.9 Incomplete axioms

In this section we discuss how to answer a query Q when the corresponding set Γ of axioms is incomplete. For simplicity we limit our discussion to the language $\mathcal{L}(\mathcal{A}_0, \mathcal{Q}_0)$. First let us notice that the program Π_{00} from Section 13.6 can not be used for this purpose. Indeed, consider the following example:

Example 13.9.1. Let $\mathcal{D}_0$ be the action description from Example 13.4.1 and consider the set Γ_3 of axioms of the form

$$\Gamma_3 \begin{cases} initially(at(v_1, l_1)). \\ initially(\neg at(v_1, l_2)). \\ initially(at(v_2, l_2)). \\ initially(\neg at(v_2, l_1)). \end{cases}$$

Let us also assume that our domain contains exactly three vehicles, v_1, v_2 and v_3, and two locations l_1 and l_2. The axioms specify positions of v_1 and v_2 and say nothing about the position of v_3. It can be shown that $\Pi_{00} \cup \mathcal{D} \cup \Gamma_3)$ entails query

$$Q = holds\_after(at(v_3, l_1), move(v_3, l_2, l_1))$$

and hence the answer to Q is *yes*. The answer is incorrect, since Γ_3 has a model in which v_3 is initially located at position l_1. The action $move(v_3, l_2, l_1)$ is impossible in this position and hence $\Pi_{00} \cup \mathcal{D}_0 \cup \Gamma_3$ should entail neither Q nor $\neg Q$.

□

13.9.1 A sound but (possibly) incomplete formulation

There are several possible ways to modify Π_{00} to make it sound. The first modification, Π_{001}, is obtained from Π_{00} by replacing two groups of axioms as follows:

1. Executability of Actions:

$$\Pi^1_{001} \begin{cases} may\_be\_impossible([A|S]) & :- \\ & may\_be\_impossible(S). \\ may\_be\_impossible([A|S]) & :- \\ & impossible\_if(A, P), \\ & not\ fail\_after(P, S). \\ executable(S) & :- \\ & not\ may\_be\_impossible(S). \end{cases}$$

2. Cancellation Axioms

$$\Pi^5_{001} \begin{cases} ab(L, A, S) & :- \\ & contrary(L, NL), \\ & causes(A, NL, C), \\ & not\ fail\_after(C, S). \end{cases}$$

and adding the axiom

3. Falsification Axiom

$$\Pi^7_{001} \begin{cases} fail\_after(C, S) & :- \\ & member(L, C), \\ & contrary(NL, L), \\ & holds\_after(NL, S). \end{cases}$$

Thus, let Π_{001} be the set of axioms $\Pi^1_{001} \cup \Pi^2_{00} \cup \Pi^3_{00} \cup \Pi^4_{00} \cup \Pi^5_{001} \cup \Pi^6_{00} \cup \Pi^7_{001}$.

It can be checked that neither query Q from Example 13.9.1 nor its negation is entailed by $\Pi_{001} \cup \mathcal{D}_0 \cup \Gamma_3$ and hence the answer to Q is *unknown*. The correctness of this answer is not an accident as it can be shown that Π_{001} is sound with respect to the consequence relation in $\mathcal{L}(\mathcal{A}_0, \mathcal{Q}_0)$.

Proposition 13.9.1. For any consistent action description $\mathcal{D}$, consistent set of axioms Γ, and a query Q of $\mathcal{Q}_0$, if $Q \in \Pi_{001}(\mathcal{D} \cup \Gamma)$ then $\Gamma \models_{\mathcal{D}} Q$. □

sketch. From Definition 13.5.1 and Proposition 13.6.1 we have that to prove this proposition it suffices to show that if

$$Q \in \Pi_{001}(\mathcal{D} \cup \Gamma) \tag{13.12}$$

then

$$Q \in \bigcap_{\hat{\Gamma} \in c(\Gamma)} \Pi_{00}(\mathcal{D} \cup \hat{\Gamma}) \tag{13.13}$$

Using the splitting set theorem we can simplify program Π_{001} by removing all the occurrences of literals formed by predicate symbols $causes$ and $contrary$. It can be checked that the resulting program is signed and therefore, according to Proposition 13.2.2, monotonic. To conclude the proof it suffices to check that for a complete set of axioms $\hat{\Gamma}$, $\Pi_{001}(\mathcal{D} \cup \hat{\Gamma}) = \Pi_{00}(\mathcal{D} \cup \hat{\Gamma})$. □ □

The following example shows that for some action descriptions Π_{001} is incomplete.

Example 13.9.2. Let $\mathcal{D}_1$ be an action description
$causes(a, f, [p])$.
$causes(a, f, [\neg p])$.

Then $\emptyset \models_{\mathcal{D}_1} holds\_after(f, [a])$ while $holds\_after(f, [a]) \notin \Pi_{001}(\mathcal{D}_1)$ can be checked.
□

13.9.2 Soundness and completeness results for STRIPS action descriptions

Now let us consider *STRIPS action descriptions*, i.e. action descriptions consisting of causal laws of the form $causes(a, l_0, [\,])$ and $impossible\_if(a, [l_1, \ldots, l_n])$.* Notice that the action description from Example 13.9.1 belongs to this class.

Proposition 13.9.2. For any consistent STRIPS action description $\mathcal{D}$, any consistent set of axioms Γ, and a query Q of $\mathcal{Q}_0$, $Q \in \Pi_{001}(\mathcal{D} \cup \Gamma)$ iff $\Gamma \models_{\mathcal{D}} Q$. □

*This is an extension of a standard STRIPS representation language [Poole *et al.*, 1998]. Add and delete lists of this language correspond to causal laws of the type $causes(a, f, [\,])$ and $causes(a, \neg f, [\,])$ respectively. The precondition statement of STRIPS for an action a consists of a collection $p_1, \ldots, p_n$ of atomic fluents that need to be true for the action to be executable. In our action description language this corresponds to n statements of the form $impossible(\neg p_i)$ for all $1 \leq i \leq n$. Unlike the original STRIPS representation the STRIPS action descriptions allows to specify the effects of actions for incomplete descriptions of states.

sketch. It can be shown that for any Γ, $\Pi_{001}(\mathcal{D} \cup \Gamma)$ is categorical, i.e., it has a unique answer set. Let us denote this set by $A(\Gamma)$. The *if* part of the program follows immediately from Proposition 13.9.1. To prove the *only if* part we will first demonstrate that for any sequence α of actions

$$\text{if } executable(\alpha) \in \bigcap_{\hat{\Gamma} \in c(\Gamma)} A(\hat{\Gamma}) \text{ then } executable(\alpha) \in A(\Gamma) \tag{13.14}$$

We use induction on the length $|\alpha|$ of α. The base, $|\alpha| = 0$, follows immediately from the executability axioms (Π^1_{001}) of Π_{001}. Let $\alpha = [a|\beta]$,

$$executable(\alpha) \in \bigcap_{\hat{\Gamma} \in c(\Gamma)} A(\hat{\Gamma}) \tag{13.15}$$

and assume that (13.14) holds for β. Suppose now that

$$executable(\alpha) \notin A(\Gamma) \tag{13.16}$$

From (13.15) and the Executability axioms of Π_{001} we can conclude that

$$executable(\beta) \in \bigcap_{\hat{\Gamma} \in c(\Gamma)} A(\hat{\Gamma}) \tag{13.17}$$

By inductive hypotheses this implies that

$$executable(\beta) \in A(\Gamma) \tag{13.18}$$

From (13.16), (13.18), and the Executability axioms we conclude that there are fluent literals $l_1, \ldots, l_n$ such that

$$impossible\_if(a, [l_1, \ldots, l_n]) \in \mathcal{D} \tag{13.19}$$

and

$$fail\_after([l_1, \ldots, l_n], \beta) \notin A(\Gamma) \tag{13.20}$$

From (13.20) and the Falsification axiom we conclude that for any l_i $(1 \leq i \leq n)$

$$holds\_after(\overline{l_i}, \beta) \notin A(\Gamma) \tag{13.21}$$

Let

$$M = \{l_j : l_j \text{ satisfies (13.21) and } holds\_after(l_j, \beta) \notin A(\Gamma)\} \tag{13.22}$$

be the set of all fluent literals from the body of the causal law (13.19) whose truth values after the execution of β are undetermined. Since $\mathcal{D}$ is the STRIPS action description we can check (using the Effect, Inertia, and Cancellation axioms) that for any $\gamma = [a_1|\gamma_1]$ if

$$executable(\gamma) \in A(\Gamma) \text{ and } holds\_after(l, \gamma_1) \in A(\Gamma)$$

then

$$holds\_after(l, \gamma) \in A(\Gamma) \text{ or } holds\_after(\bar{l}, \gamma) \in A(\Gamma) \tag{13.23}$$

i.e., once the value of a fluent literal becomes determined it stays determined. From this observation and the construction of M we conclude that for any $l_j \in M$

$$initially(\overline{l_j}) \notin \Gamma \tag{13.24}$$

and for any action a_k from β

$$causes(a_k, l_j, [\,]) \notin \mathcal{D} \text{ and } causes(a_k, \overline{l_j}, [\,]) \notin \mathcal{D} \tag{13.25}$$

Let us now consider an extension $\hat{\Gamma}_0$ of Γ containing statements $initially(l_j)$ for any $l_j \in M$. From (13.16) we have that the body of (13.19) contains no contrary literals. This, together with (13.24) implies that $\hat{\Gamma}_0$ is consistent. From construction of $\hat{\Gamma}_0$, (13.25), and the Inertia axiom we have that

$$holds\_after(l_j, \beta) \in A(\hat{\Gamma}_0) \tag{13.26}$$

for all $l_j \in M$ and hence

$$executable(\alpha) \notin A(\hat{\Gamma}_0) \tag{13.27}$$

which contradicts our assumption (13.15). Hence

$$executable(\alpha) \in A(\Gamma) \tag{13.28}$$

To complete the proof we again use induction on α. The base case is obvious. Consider

$$holds\_after(l, [a|\beta]) \in \bigcap_{\hat{\Gamma} \in c(\Gamma)} A(\hat{\Gamma}) \tag{13.29}$$

This implies that

$$executable([a|\beta]) \in \bigcap_{\hat{\Gamma} \in c(\Gamma)} A(\hat{\Gamma}) \tag{13.30}$$

and hence, by (13.14),

$$executable(\alpha) \in A(\Gamma) \tag{13.31}$$

To show that

$$holds\_after(l, [a|\beta]) \in A(\Gamma) \tag{13.32}$$

we first consider the case when

$$causes(a, l, [\,]) \in \mathcal{D} \tag{13.33}$$

Then (13.29) follows immediately from (13.31) and the effect axioms. If (13.33) does not hold then (13.29) implies that

$$holds\_after(l, \beta) \in \bigcap_{\hat{\Gamma} \in c(\Gamma)} A(\hat{\Gamma}) \tag{13.34}$$

and hence, by the inductive hypothesis,

$$holds\_after(l, \beta) \in A(\Gamma) \tag{13.35}$$

Now (13.32) follows immediately from (13.31), (13.35), and the Inertia axioms. □ □

13.9.3 A general sound and complete formulation

The next modification of Π_{001} is obtained by adding to Π_{001} the following Initial Situation Axioms.

$$initially(l) :- not\ initially(\bar{l}) \tag{13.36}$$

for every fluent literal l. Let us denote the resulting program by Π_{002}. Intuitively, the addition of these axioms corresponds to forcing the program to consider possible values of all fluents in the initial situation and do reasoning by cases, if necessary. To better understand these rules let us go back to action description $\mathcal{D}_1$ from Example 13.9.2. It can be checked that the program $\Pi_{002}(\mathcal{D}_1)$ has two answer sets, A_1 and A_2. Suppose that A_1 does not contain $initially(p)$. Then by rule (13.36), it must contain $initially(\neg p)$. Using the second causal law from Example 13.9.2 and the effect axioms we can conclude that A_1 contains $holds\_after(f, [a])$.

Similarly we can show that A_2 contains $initially(p), holds\_after(f, [a])$, and therefore $holds\_after(f, [a]) \in \Pi_{002}(\mathcal{D}_1)$. This informal argument can easily be made precise. Moreover, the answer to a query $holds\_after(f, [a])$ can be computed by an extension of XSB, called SLG [Chen *et al.*, 1995] which allows reasoning with multiple answer sets. The following theorem shows that Π_{002} adequately represents entailment relation of $\mathcal{L}(\mathcal{A}_0, \mathcal{Q}_0)$.

Proposition 13.9.3. For any consistent action description $\mathcal{D}$ of $\mathcal{A}_0$, any consistent set of axioms Γ, and a query Q of $\mathcal{Q}_0$, $Q \in \Pi_{002}(\mathcal{D} \cup \Gamma)$ iff $\Gamma \models_{\mathcal{D}} Q$. □

Proof: Follows from using the splitting lemma (Lemma 13.2.1) and Proposition 13.6.1.

13.9.4 A sound and complete formulation using disjunction

Let us obtain Π_{003} from Π_{002} by replacing (13.36) by the following.

$$initially(f)\ \textbf{or}\ initially(neg(f)) \leftarrow \tag{13.37}$$

We can now show that the following holds.

Proposition 13.9.4. For any consistent action description $\mathcal{D}$ of $\mathcal{A}_0$, any consistent set of axioms Γ, and a query Q of $\mathcal{Q}_0$, $Q \in \Pi_{003}(\mathcal{D} \cup \Gamma)$ iff $\Gamma \models_{\mathcal{D}} Q$. □

Proof: Follows from using splitting and Proposition 13.6.1.

An alternative approach is to use the formulation of abductive logic programs [Kakas and Mancarella, 1990a; Denecker and De Schreye, 1993] for which an interpreter [Denecker and De Schreye, 1998] exists. Other alternatives were suggested in [Kartha, 1993; Dung, 1993].

13.9.5 A sound and complete formulation using abduction

$$\Pi^2_{004} \left\{ \begin{array}{lll} holds\_after(L, [\,]) & :- & \\ & & fluent(L), \\ & & initially(L). \\ holds\_after(L, [A|S]) & :- & \\ & & fluent(L), \\ & & executable([A|S]), \\ & & causes(A, L, C), \\ & & holds\_after\_list(C, S). \\ holds\_after(neg(L), S) & :- & \\ & & fluent(L), \\ & & executable(S), \\ & & not\ holds\_after(L, S), \end{array} \right.$$

$$\Pi^4_{004} \left\{ \begin{array}{lll} holds\_after(L, [A|S]) & :- & \\ & & fluent(L), \\ & & executable([A|S]), \\ & & holds\_after(L, S), \\ & & not\ ab(L, A, S). \end{array} \right.$$

$$\Pi^5_{004} \left\{ \begin{array}{lll} ab(L, A, S) & :- & \\ & & fluent(L), \\ & & contrary(L, NL), \\ & & causes(A, NL, C), \\ & & holds\_after\_list(C, S). \end{array} \right.$$

Let Π_{004} be the general logic program consisting of Π^1_{00}, Π^2_{004}, Π^3_{00}, Π^4_{004}, Π^5_{004}, and Π^6_{00}. Given a set of axioms Γ, let Γ^* denote the conjunction of atoms in the following set: $\{initially(f)$: $initially(f) \in \Gamma$ and f is a fluent $\} \cup \{\neg initially(f)$: $initially(neg(f)) \in \Gamma$ and f is a fluent $\}$. Let C be the following formula $\forall f. \neg initially(neg(f))$. Let us now consider the abductive logic program $\langle \Pi_{004} \cup \mathcal{D}, \{initially\}, \Gamma^* \wedge C \rangle$. Intuitively, the constraint $\Gamma^* \wedge C$ force $\Delta \subset atoms(initially)$ to be facts about positive fluents only, and in such a way that it is consistent with Γ.

Proposition 13.9.5. For any consistent action description $\mathcal{D}$ of $\mathcal{A}_0$, any consistent set of axioms Γ, and a query Q of $\mathcal{Q}_0$,

$\langle \Pi_{004} \cup \mathcal{D}, \{initially\}, \Gamma^* \wedge C \rangle \models_{abd} Q$ iff $\Gamma \models_{\mathcal{D}} Q$. □

sketch. The proof follows from the following three lemmas. In each of these lemmas $\mathcal{D}$ is a consistent action description and Γ is a consistent (but possibly incomplete) set of axioms. □

Lemma 13.9.1. Let $H = \sigma_0, a_1, \sigma_1, \ldots a_n, \sigma_n$ be a history of the transition system of $\mathcal{D}$ that satisfy the axioms in Γ and let M be a generalized stable model of $\langle \Pi_{004} \cup \mathcal{D}, \{initially\}, \Gamma^* \wedge C \rangle$ such that $\sigma_0 = \{f : initially(f) \in M\} \cup \{\neg f : initially(f) \notin M\}$. Let $[a_0, \ldots, a_1]$ denote the list $[\,]$. Then,
For all i, $0 \leq i \leq n$, $f \in \sigma_i$ iff $holds\_ater(f, [a_i, \ldots, a_1])$ is true in M. □

The above lemma can be proved by induction on i.

Lemma 13.9.2. For every history $H = \sigma_0, a_1, \sigma_1, \ldots a_n, \sigma_n$ of the transition system of $\mathcal{D}$ that satisfy the axioms in Γ there exists a generalized stable model M_H of $\langle \Pi_{004} \cup \mathcal{D}, \{initially\}, \Gamma^* \wedge C \rangle$ such that $\sigma_0 = \{f : initially(f) \in M_H\} \cup \{\neg f : initially(f) \notin M_H\}$. □

Lemma 13.9.3. For every generalized stable model M of $\langle \Pi_{004} \cup \mathcal{D}, \{initially\}, \Gamma^* \wedge C \rangle$ there exists a history $H_M = \sigma_0, a_1, \sigma_1, \ldots a_n, \sigma_n$ of the transition system of $\mathcal{D}$ that satisfy the axioms in Γ such that $\sigma_0 = \{f : initially(f) \in M\} \cup \{\neg f : initially(f) \notin M\}$ □

13.10 Action description language $\mathcal{A}_1$

In this section we consider an extension $\mathcal{A}_1$ of action description language $\mathcal{A}_0$ from Section 13.4. As before we consider a fixed action signature Σ_0. Propositions of $\mathcal{A}_1$ are expressions of the form

$$impossible\_if(a, [l_1, \ldots, l_n]) \tag{13.38}$$

$$causes(a, l_0, [l_1, \ldots, l_n]) \tag{13.39}$$

$$causes(l_0, [l_1, \ldots, l_n]) \tag{13.40}$$

The first two propositions are exactly those allowed in $\mathcal{A}_0$. The last proposition says that, in the action domain being described, whenever $l_1, \ldots, l_n$ are caused, l_0 is caused. Propositions of this form are called *static causal laws** To better understand the use of these laws for representing knowledge about effects of actions let us go back to Example 13.4.1. The transition diagram of the domain description $\mathcal{D}_0$ from this example contains states in which the same vehicle occupies more than one location. This possibility can be eliminated if we assume that a vehicle in our domain can not be in two locations at the same time. This information can be represented in $\mathcal{A}_1$ by static causal laws of the form

$$causes(\neg at(v, l_1), [at(v, l_2)])$$

where v is a vehicle and l_1 and l_2 are different locations. As before, this can be written as a logic programming rule

$$\begin{array}{lll} causes(\neg at(V, L_1), [at(v, L_2)]) & :- & \\ & & vehicle(V) \\ & & location(L_1) \\ & & location(L_2) \\ & & diff(L_1, L_2). \end{array}$$

Inclusion of this law makes the dynamic causal law

$$causes(move(v, l_1, l_2), \neg at(v, l_3), [\,]).$$

*The paper [Marek and Truszczyński, 1994] was perhaps the first work that inspired later logic programming and default logic based formulations of static causal laws [Baral, August 1994; Baral, 1997; Baral, 1995; McCain and Turner, 1995; McCain and Turner, 1997; Turner, 1997]. Alternative formulations of causality while reasoning about actions were suggested in [Lin, 1995; Thielscher, 1997; Lifschitz, 1997].

of $\mathcal{D}_0$ redundant and therefore it can be removed. Let us consider an action description $\mathcal{D}_2$ of $\mathcal{A}_1$ given below:

$$\mathcal{D}_2 \left\{ \begin{array}{l} causes(move(v, l_1, l_2), at(v, l_2), [\,]). \\ causes(\neg at(v, l_1), [at(v, l_2)]) \\ impossible\_if(move(v, l_1, l_2), [\neg at(v, l_1)]). \\ \text{where } v\text{'s are vehicles and } l_1, andl_2 \text{ are locations and } l_1 \neq l_2. \end{array} \right.$$

Intuitively, $\mathcal{D}_2$ describes the same transition diagram as in Figure 13.1, if we assume a single vehicle v and two locations l_1 and l_2.

We are now ready to define the semantics of $\mathcal{A}_1$ (based on the characterization in [McCain and Turner, 1995]) that uses the following terminology and notations. A set s of literals is closed under a set Z of static causal laws if s includes the head, l_0, of every static causal law (13.40) such that $\{l_1, \ldots, l_n\} \subseteq S$. The set $Cn_Z(s)$ of *consequences* of s under Z is the set of all literals that contain s and is closed under Z. Let $\mathcal{D}$ be an action description in $\mathcal{A}_1$. The transition system $T = \langle \mathcal{S}, \mathcal{R} \rangle$ *described* by $\mathcal{D}$ is defined as follows.

1. $\mathcal{S}$ is the collection of all complete and consistent sets of fluent literals of Σ_0 closed under the static laws of $\mathcal{D}$,

2. $\mathcal{R}$ is the set of all triples (σ, a, σ') such that $\mathcal{D}$ does not contain a proposition of the form $impossible\_if(a, [l_1, \ldots, l_n])$ such that $[l_1, \ldots, l_n] \subseteq \sigma$ and

$$\sigma' = Cn_Z(E(a, \sigma) \cup (\sigma \cap \sigma')) \tag{13.41}$$

   where Z is the set of all static causal laws of $\mathcal{D}$, and $E(a, \sigma)$ is the set of the heads l_0 of dynamic causal laws $causes(a, l_0, [l_1, \ldots, l_n]$ of $\mathcal{D}$ such that $\{l_1, \ldots, l_n\} \subseteq s$. The argument of $Cn(Z)$ in (13.41) is the union of the set $E(a, s)$ of the "direct effects" of a with the set $s \cap s'$ of facts that are "preserved by inertia". The application of $Cn(Z)$ adds the "indirect effects" to this union.

The following example shows that addition of static causal laws substantially increases expressive power of our language.

Example 13.10.1. Let $\mathcal{D}_3$ be an action description

$causes(a, f, [\,]).$
$causes(\neg g_1, [f, g_2]).$
$causes(\neg g_2, [f, g_1]).$

The transition system T_2 described by $\mathcal{D}_3$ is represented by Figure 13.2.

The diagram is nondeterministic and therefore cannot be described by a domain description of $\mathcal{A}_0$. □

We now give some conditions which guarantee that an action description $\mathcal{D}$ of $\mathcal{A}_1$ is deterministic, i.e., describes a deterministic transition system. Let R be a collection of static causal laws of $\mathcal{D}$. For any action a and a state σ, by $E^*(a, \sigma)$ we will denote the closure of direct effects, $E(a, \sigma)$, of executing a in σ with respect to R. We will say that $\mathcal{D}$ is *separable* if for any a and σ such that a is executable in σ, if $r \in R$ and $body(r) \cap E^*(a, \sigma) \neq \emptyset$ then $body(r) \subseteq E^*(a, \sigma)$.

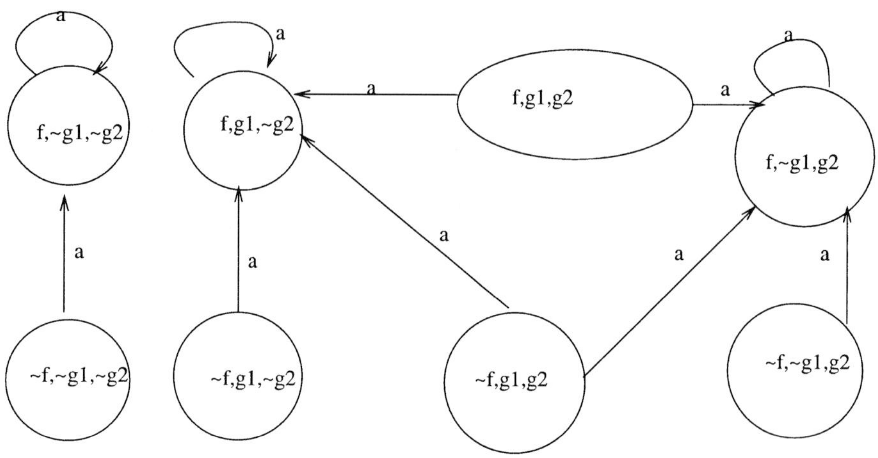

Figure 13.2: Transition Diagram

Proposition 13.10.1. Any separable action description $\mathcal{D}$ of $\mathcal{A}_1$ is deterministic. □

Proof. Let $T = \langle \mathcal{S}, \mathcal{R} \rangle$ be a transition system described by $\mathcal{D}$. We need to show that for any action a and states $\sigma, \sigma^1, \sigma^2 \in \mathcal{S}$ if

1. $(\sigma, a, \sigma^1) \in \mathcal{R}$ and $(\sigma, a, \sigma^2) \in \mathcal{R}$ then

2. $\sigma^1 = \sigma^2$.

From definition (13.41) of $\mathcal{R}$ and the assumption (1) we have

3. $\sigma^1 = Cn_Z(E(a, \sigma) \cup (\sigma \cap \sigma^1))$

which is equivalent to

4. $\sigma^1 = Cn_Z(E^*(a, \sigma) \cup (\sigma \cap \sigma^1))$.

By separability of $\mathcal{D}$ (4) is equivalent to

5. $\sigma^1 = E^*(a, \sigma) \cup Cn_Z(\sigma \cap \sigma^1)$.

Since σ and σ_1 are states they are closed under the rules of Z and hence (5) is equivalent to

6. $\sigma^1 = E^*(a, \sigma) \cup (\sigma \cap \sigma^1)$.

Similarly, we can show that

7. $\sigma^2 = E^*(a, \sigma) \cup (\sigma \cap \sigma^2)$.

To prove (2) let us assume that $l \in \sigma^1$. By (6) we have that

8. $l \in E^*(a, \sigma)$ or

9. $l \in \sigma$.

If (8) holds then from (7) we have that $l \in \sigma_2$. If (8) does not hold then we have (9). Since states are complete and consistent sets of literals this implies that $l \in \sigma^2$. This completes the proof. □

13.11 Answering queries in $\mathcal{L}(\mathcal{A}_1, \mathcal{Q}_0)$ and $\mathcal{L}(\mathcal{A}_1, \mathcal{Q}_1)$

In this section we illustrate the use of logic programming for computing consequences of domain descriptions of $\mathcal{L}(\mathcal{A}_1, \mathcal{Q}_0)$ and $\mathcal{L}(\mathcal{A}_1, \mathcal{Q}_1)$. As in Section 13.6 we assume that $\mathcal{D}$ is consistent and make some completeness assumptions about Γ. The corresponding programs Π_{10} and Π_{11} are obtained from Π_{00} and Π_{01} respectively by adding the following rules:

- Π_{10} is Π_{00} plus the following two rules.

$$\begin{aligned} holds\_after(L, S) \;:-\; & executable(S), \\ & causes(L, C), \\ & holds\_after\_list(C, S). \end{aligned}$$

$$\begin{aligned} ab(L, A, S) \;:-\; & contrary(L, NL), \\ & causes(NL, C), \\ & holds\_after\_list(C, [A|S]) \end{aligned}$$

- Π_{11} is Π_{01} plus the following two rules.

$$\begin{aligned} holds\_after(L, S, T) \;:-\; & executable(S, T), \\ & causes(L, C), \\ & holds\_after\_list(C, S, T). \end{aligned}$$

$$\begin{aligned} ab(L, A, S, T) \;:-\; & contrary(L, NL), \\ & causes(NL, C), \\ & holds\_after\_list(C, [A|S], T) \end{aligned}$$

Proposition 13.11.1. For any consistent action description $\mathcal{D}$ of $\mathcal{A}_1$, any consistent set of axioms Γ that specifies a complete initial situation, and a query Q of $\mathcal{Q}_0$, $Q \in \Pi_{10}(\mathcal{D} \cup \Gamma)$ iff $\Gamma \models_{\mathcal{D}} Q$. □

Proposition 13.11.2. For any consistent action description $\mathcal{D}$ of $\mathcal{A}_1$, a consistent set of axioms Γ that specifies a complete initial situation and also a complete observation of the history with respect to the transition system of $\mathcal{D}$, and a query Q of $\mathcal{Q}_1$, $Q \in \Pi_{11}(\mathcal{D} \cup \Gamma)$ iff $\Gamma \models_{\mathcal{D}} Q$. □

The proofs of Propositions 13.11.1 and 13.11.2 are similar to that of Propositions 13.6.1 and 13.8.1 respectively.

As before this does not work if Γ is not complete. The complete initial situation assumption can be removed by expanding Π_{11} by the rules:

$$\begin{aligned} initially(l) \ \ :- & \\ & contrary(l, \bar{l}), \\ & \textit{not } initially(\bar{l}) \end{aligned}$$

where $contrary(l, \bar{l})$ holds iff l and $\bar{l}$ are contrary fluent literals. The resulting program will be denoted by Π_{110}.

Proposition 13.11.3. For any consistent action description $\mathcal{D}$ of $\mathcal{A}_1$, a consistent set of axioms Γ that specifies a complete observation of the history with respect to the transition system of $\mathcal{D}$, and a query Q of $\mathcal{Q}_1$, $Q \in \Pi_{110}(\mathcal{D} \cup \Gamma)$ iff $\Gamma \models_{\mathcal{D}} Q$. □

Proof: Follows from using splitting and Proposition 13.11.2.

The difficulty of the computation of $\Pi_{11} \cup \mathcal{D} \cup \Gamma$ and $\Pi_{110} \cup \mathcal{D} \cup \Gamma$ is dependent on whether D describes a deterministic transition diagram. If it does then there will be a single stable model of the program and we can use the XSB interpreter. Otherwise, there may be multiple stable models of the program and we would have to use interpreters such as the Smodels and DLV systems.

13.12 Planning using model enumeration

The DLPs in the previous sections are most appropriate for *verifying* if a particular fluent literal is true after the execution of a sequence of actions. They can be used for planning by using interpreters that do answer extraction. In this section we show how the DLPs can be adapted so that planning can be done through model enumeration.

In the model enumeration approach [Subrahmanian and Zaniolo, 1995] each stable model of our program corresponds to a particular hypothetical evolution of the world. We guess a minimal plan length for a given goal and that information is part of the program. The stable models where the goal is not true at the guessed plan length are eliminated by adding appropriate constraints to the program. The stable models that are not weeded out give us plans that achieve the given goals at the guessed plan length. To make sure that each stable model of our program corresponds to a possible evolution of the world we have executability axioms, effect axioms, inertia axioms, etc., with the modification that instead of situations we use plan length or time as the basis of how the world evolves. This approach to planning has recently been called as *answer-set planning* [Lifschitz, 1999], where *answer-sets* is a more general term for stable models. Answer-set planning is a particular instance of the more general notion of *answer set programming* where queries with respect to a logic program are answered through the bottom-up approach of generating answer sets and evaluating the query with respect to them rather than through the top down approach of unification and resolution. One advantage of the answer set programming [Marek and Truszczyński, 1999; Niemelä, 1999; Eiter *et al.*, 2000b] approach is that it takes advantage of multiplicity of answer sets by treating them as a solution space, and allows us to implement the brave semantics (i.e., entailment with respect to some answer set rather than all answer sets) of logic programs.

We now give an example of how planning is done with respect to our vehicle example. In Section 13.12.1 we describe a downtown with one-way streets and do planning to go from one location to another. In Section 13.12.2 we allow observations, and do planning from the current situation.

13.12.1 Navigating a downtown with one-way streets

Consider the one-way streets in Anymetro USA given in Figure 13.3. The driver of vehicle v would like to go from the point l_3 to point l_2. Following are the domain dependent and domain independent axioms that the driver has.

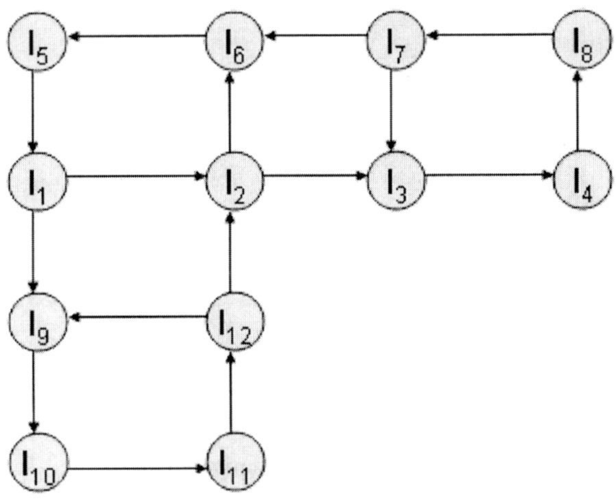

Figure 13.3: One-way streets in downtown Anymetro, USA

1. The domain dependent part

   (a) The initial street description:

   $initially(edge(l_1, l_2)).$

   $initially(edge(l_2, l_3)).$

   $initially(edge(l_3, l_4)).$

   $initially(edge(l_4, l_8)).$

   $initially(edge(l_8, l_7)).$

$initially(edge(l_7, l_6)).$

$initially(edge(l_6, l_5)).$

$initially(edge(l_5, l_1)).$

$initially(edge(l_2, l_6)).$

$initially(edge(l_7, l_3)).$

$initially(edge(l_1, l_9)).$

$initially(edge(l_9, l_{10})).$

$initially(edge(l_{10}, l_{11})).$

$initially(edge(l_{11}, l_{12})).$

$initially(edge(l_{12}, l_2)).$

$initially(edge(l_{12}, l_9)).$

(b) The initial position of the vehicle

$initially(at(v, l_3)).$

(c) The goal state

$finally(at(v, l_2)).$

(d) When actions are not executable

$impossible\_if(move(V, L1, L2), neg(at(V, L1))).$

$impossible\_if(move(V, L1, L2), neg(edge(L1, L2))).$

(e) The effect of actions

$causes(move(V, L1, L2), at(V, L2)).$

$causes(move(V, L1, L2), neg(at(V, L1))).$

2. The domain independent part

(a) Defining $goal(T)$: The goal is true in time T.

$$
\begin{aligned}
not\_goal(T) :- \quad & time(T), \\
& finally(X), \\
& not\ holds(X, T). \\
goal(T) :- \quad & time(T), \\
& not\ not\_goal(T).
\end{aligned}
$$

(b) Eliminating models which do not have a plan of the given length.

$:- \quad not\ goal(length).$

(c) Defining contrary

$$contrary(F, neg(F)).$$
$$contrary(neg(F), F).$$

(d) What holds in time point 1.

$$\begin{aligned} holds(F,1) &:- \; initially(F). \\ holds(neg(F),1) &:- \; not\ holds(F,1). \end{aligned}$$

(e) Effect axiom

$$\begin{aligned} holds(F, T+1) :- \;& T < length, \\ & executable(A,T), \\ & occurs(A,T), \\ & causes(A,F). \end{aligned}$$

(f) Inertia

$$\begin{aligned} holds(F, T+1) :- \;& contrary(F,G), \\ & T < length, \\ & holds(F,T), \\ & not\ holds(G, T+1). \end{aligned}$$

(g) We need rules that define executability in terms of the $impossible\_if$ conditions given in the domain dependent part. These rules are:

$$\begin{aligned} not\_executable(A,T) &:- \; impossible\_if(A,B), \\ &\quad\;\; holds(B,T) \\ executable(A,T) &:- \; not\ not\_executable(A,T). \end{aligned}$$

(h) What actions are possible at each time point? A simple formulation of this could be to encode that at any time point all executable actions are possible if the goal is not reached.

$$\begin{aligned} possible(A,T) :- \;& action(A), \\ & executable(A,T), \\ & not\ goal(T). \end{aligned}$$

(i) Occurrences of actions

$$\begin{aligned} occurs(A,T) &:- \; action(A), \\ &\quad\;\; possible(A,T), \\ &\quad\;\; not\ not\_occurs(A,T). \\ not\_occurs(A,T) &:- \; action(A), \\ &\quad\;\; action(AA), \\ &\quad\;\; occurs(AA,T), \\ &\quad\;\; A \neq AA. \end{aligned}$$

When the above program is given to the interpreter Smodels [Niemelä and Simons, 1997] one of the stable models that is generated has the following literals describing a plan.

$occurs(move(v, l_3, l_4), 1).$
$occurs(move(v, l_4, l_8), 2).$
$occurs(move(v, l_8, l_7), 3).$

$occurs(move(v, l_7, l_6), 4).$
$occurs(move(v, l_6, l_5), 5).$
$occurs(move(v, l_5, l_1), 6).$
$occurs(move(v, l_1, l_2), 7).$

We refer to the domain independent part of the above program as $\Pi_{00.planning}$. The following proposition states the correctness of the program $\Pi_{00.planning}$ for planning when we are given a consistent domain description and an initial state complete set of axioms.

Proposition 13.12.1. Let D be a consistent domain description in $\mathcal{A}_0$ and Γ be an initial state complete set of axioms in $\mathcal{Q}_0$. Let $length$ be a positive integer and G be a set of fluent literals that we want to be true in the goal state.

(i) If there is a sequence of actions $a_1, \ldots, a_{length}$ such that for each literal l in G, $\Gamma \models_D holds\_after(l, [a_{length}, \ldots, a_1])$, then $\Pi_{00.planning} \cup D \cup \Gamma \cup \{finally(l) : l \in G\}$ has an answer set with $\{occurs(a_1, 1), \ldots, occurs(a_{length}, length)\}$ as the set of facts about $occurs$ in it.

(ii) If $\Pi_{00.planning} \cup D \cup \Gamma \cup \{finally(l) : l \in G\}$ has an answer set with $\{occurs(a_1, 1), \ldots, occurs(a_{length}, length)\}$ as the set of facts about $occurs$ in it then for each literal l in G, $\Gamma \models_D holds\_after(l, [a_{length}, \ldots, a_1])$. □

A specific instance of the above proposition is the case where Γ consists of the rules in part 1(a) and 1(b) above and $\mathcal{D}$ consists of the rules in part 1(d) and 1(e) above.

13.12.2 Downtown navigation: planning while driving

Consider the case that an agent uses the planner in the previous section and makes a plan. It now executes part of the plan, where it moves from l_3 to l_4 and l_4 to l_8, and then hears in the radio that *an accident occurred between point* l_1*and* l_2 and that section of the street is blocked. The agent now has to make a new plan from where it is to its destination. To be able to encode observations and make plans from the current situation we need to add the following to our program in the previous section.

1. The domain dependent part

   (a) The observations

   $occurs\_at(move(v, l_3, l_4), 1).$

   $occurs\_at(move(v, l_4, l_8), 2).$

   $occurs\_at(acc(l_1, l_2), 3).$

   (b) Exogenous actions

   $causes(acc(X, Y), neg(edge(X, Y))).$

2. The domain independent part

   (a) Relating $occurs\_at$ and $occurs$

   $occurs(A, T) :- \quad occurs\_at(A, T).$

With these additions one of the plans generated by Smodels is as follows:

$occurs(move(v, l_8, l_7), 4).$
$occurs(move(v, l_7, l_6), 5).$
$occurs(move(v, l_6, l_5), 6).$
$occurs(move(v, l_5, l_1), 7).$
$occurs(move(v, l_1, l_9), 8).$
$occurs(move(v, l_9, l_{10}), 9).$
$occurs(move(v, l_{10}, l_{11}), 10).$
$occurs(move(v, l_{11}, l_{12}), 11).$
$occurs(move(v, l_{12}, l_2), 12).$

Although it does not matter in the particular example described above, we should separate the set of actions to $agent\_actions$ and $exogenous\_actions$, and in the planning module require that while planning we only use $agent\_actions$. This can be achieved by replacing the two rules about $occurs$ by the following rules.

$$\begin{array}{rl} occurs(A,T) :- & occurs\_at(A,T). \\ occurs(A,T) :- & agent\_action(A), \\ & possible(A,T), \\ & not\ not\_occurs(A,T). \\ not\_occurs(A,T) :- & not\ occurs(A,T). \\ :- & occurs(A,T), occurs(AA,T), A \neq AA. \end{array}$$

13.13 Concluding Remarks

In this chapter we presented a series of logic programming (with stable model semantics and its generalizations) based action theories with increasing expressibility, and with special emphasis on (i) using an independent automata based semantics for defining correctness, (ii) developing executable programs, and (iii) dealing with incompleteness. These aspects have been among our main interests in the last 8-9 years. Some of the other aspects of logic programming based reasoning about actions that we and other researchers worked on but which we did not discuss here are: reasoning about concurrent actions [Baral and Gelfond, 1997], reasoning with narratives [Baral *et al.*, 1997; Pinto and R.Reiter, 1993], using action theories to develop an agent architecture [Baral *et al.*, 1997], and reasoning about resources [Holldobler and Thielscher, 1993]. An important work which we would like mention here is [Lin, 1997] where Lin gives semantics of the cut operator of Prolog using an action theory.

Amongst the emerging areas, one of the most important is the area of model based planning using logic programming. Starting with the development of the S-models [Niemelä and Simons, 1997] and the work by Dimopolous et al. [Dimopoulos *et al.*, 1997], there has been a lot of recent research [McCain and Turner, 1998; Lifschitz, 1999; Erdem and Lifschitz, 1999; Baral and Gelfond, 2000] in this area. In Section 13.12 we gave a quick introduction to this.

In terms of related future and ongoing work, some of the questions that are being currently addressed and not elaborated in this chapter are: (i) using domain knowledge[Son *et al.*, 2001] and heuristics [Balduccini *et al.*, 2000; Gelfond, 2001] in model based planning using logic programming. (ii) using action theories to develop a notion of diagnosis [Baral and

Gelfond, 2000; Gelfond *et al.*, 2001], (iii) using interpreters that can accommodate disjunctive logic programs (such as the DLV interpreter [Eiter *et al.*, 2000a]) to develop planners that generate plans with sensing actions, and (iv) developing more general results about when a transition function is deterministic.

Applications

Handbook of Temporal Reasoning in Artificial Intelligence
Edited by M. Fisher, D. Gabbay and L. Vila

Chapter 14

Temporal Databases

Jan Chomicki & David Toman

Time is ubiquitous in information systems. Almost every enterprise faces the problem of its data becoming out of date. However, such data is often valuable, so it should be archived and some means of accessing it should be provided. Also, some data may be inherently historical, e.g., medical, cadastral, or judicial records. Temporal databases provide a uniform and systematic way of dealing with historical data.

This chapter develops *point-based* data models and query languages for temporal databases in the relational framework. The models provide a separation between the conceptual data (*what* is stored in the database) and the way the data is compactly represented in the temporal relations (*how* it is stored). This approach leads to a clean and elegant data model while still providing an efficient implementation path. The foundations of the approach can be traced to the *constraint database* technology [Kanellakis *et al.*, 1995]: constraint representation is used as the basis for a space-efficient representation of temporal relations.

14.1 Introduction

We first study how logics of time can be used as *query* and *integrity constraint* languages in the above setting and the differences resulting from choosing a particular logic as a query language for temporal data. Consequently, model-theoretic notions, particularly *formula satisfaction in a fixed model*, are of primary interest. This is in sharp contrast with most major application areas of temporal reasoning, where the major issues are *satisfiability* and *validity*. For this reason, the formalisms studied are usually propositional which is insufficient in the database setting. However, decidable fragments of the logics underlying temporal queries have been studied for the purposes of *schema* design and reasoning about integrity constraints.

While considerable effort has been expended on the development of temporal databases and query languages, there is still no universal consensus on how *temporal features* should be added to the standard relational model. On the surface, there appear to be many candidates for an acceptable temporal data model and query language, e.g., TQuel [Snodgrass, 1987] or TSQL2 [Snodgrass, 1995], or one of TSQL2's variants, such as ATSQL [Snodgrass *et al.*, 1995], SQL/Temporal [Snodgrass *et al.*, 1996] (the latest temporal extension of SQL3 proposed to the ISO and ANSI standardization committees). However, none of them has been adopted as the standard language of temporal databases in practice, and none has established the theoretical foundations for management of time-dependent data. This is in stark contrast with the relational model, where the relational calculus (first-order logic) has became the consensus language. In part, the reason for the limited acceptance of earlier temporal models, and their negligible contribution to the development of practical applications, is an extremely (and often unnecessarily) complex syntax *without* comprehensive theoretical foundations.

This chapter provides a formal foundation for temporal data models and query languages based on logics that have been developed over the last ten years [Chomicki, 1994; Chomicki and Toman, 1998; Toman, 1996; Toman, 1997; Toman and Niwinski, 1996; Toman, 2003c]. In our simple *point-based* approach to managing temporal data, temporal attributes naturally range over individual points in time. This approach can serve as an alternative foundation for existing temporal data models and shows that all *well-founded* queries definable in the former approaches can be equivalently and conveniently formulated using a point-based temporal query language. Moreover, the chapter introduces techniques for compact encoding of temporal data and efficient query evaluation procedures with computational properties comparable to standard relational queries.

The chapter is organized as follows: The first part focuses on temporal data models and query languages. Section 14.2 introduces the necessary notions of time ontology and time domain used in the rest of the chapter. Section 14.3 shows several ways to introduce time into the standard relational model and defines the fundamental notions of *temporal databases*. It also shows how such databases naturally arise as *histories* of ordinary relational databases. Section 14.4 discusses issues connected with database design and temporal integrity constraints. Section 14.5 introduces several *query languages* for temporal databases. Section 14.6 describes techniques needed for efficient *query evaluation* over compact representations of temporal databases. Section 14.7 discusses various temporal extensions of SQL, the standard query language of relational databases, that have been proposed over the past 25 years in the framework of abstract and concrete temporal databases and query languages. Section 14.8 outlines issues related to updating temporal databases. The second part of the chapter, Sections 14.9, 14.10, and 14.11, focus on the *limitations* of simple linearly-ordered, first-order temporal data models and queries evaluated in a single model (or, equivalently, under the closed world assumption) and on different ways of overcoming these limitations: Section 14.9 discusses more complex models of time, Section 14.10 discusses *non-first-order* extensions of temporal query languages, and Section 14.11 considers the implications connected with relaxing the closed world assumption. Section 14.12 contains brief conclusions.

14.2 Structure of Time

We first introduce a number of fundamental concepts and distinctions that are used throughout the chapter. First, there is a choice of *temporal ontology*. However, and in contrast to rather complex temporal ontologies commonly used for *reasoning* about time, we use a very simple notion of time in this chapter—a linear ordering of time instants.

Definition 14.2.1 (Temporal Domain). *A single-dimensional linearly ordered temporal domain is a structure* $\mathrm{T}_P = (T, <)$, *where* T *is a set of time instants and* $<$ *is a linear order on* T.

The subscript in T_P underlines that this is indeed a domain of time *points* and distinguishes it from the domain of *intervals*, T_I, introduced in Section 14.6.1.
In addition to linear ordering, we may consider whether time is discrete or dense and whether it is bounded or unbounded. These choices are orthogonal to the development of this chapter and the majority of the results continue to hold independent of the above choices.

While considering only linear order may seem limiting at first, we shall see that, since the temporal data models and the associated temporal query languages discussed in this chapter are considerably more powerful than those used for *reasoning* about time, we can *model* most of the additional structure often associated with a time ontology in a uniform framework of temporal databases. For example, the question of whether time is single-dimensional or multi-dimensional (i.e., whether truth of facts is associated with a single time instant or with multiple instants) will be a property of the temporal data model rather than of the time ontology. Note that multiple time dimensions can occur naturally if, for example, multiple kinds of time (e.g., transaction time vs. valid time [Snodgrass and Ahn, 1986]) are required in an application. Similarly, other extensions of the simple model time, such as temporal durations, calendars, etc., and their representation in our framework are discussed in Section 14.9.

Finally, there is a choice of *linear* vs. *nonlinear* time, i.e., whether time should be viewed as a single line or rather as a tree [Emerson, 1990; Hodkinson *et al.*, 2002], or even an acyclic graph [Wolper, 1989]. Although the branching-time view is potentially applicable to some database problems like version control or workflows, there has been very little work in this area. Therefore, in this chapter we concentrate on temporal domains that are linearly ordered sets.

14.3 Abstract Data Models and Temporal Databases

It is useful to introduce a distinction between the *abstract*, representation-independent meaning of a temporal database and its *concrete*, finite representation. This section focuses on the abstract databases while Section 14.6 will explore the concrete ones.

A standard relational database is a *first-order structure* built from a *data domain* D, usually equipped with a built-in equality (diagonal) relation. This domain is extended to a *relational database* by adding to it a finite instance $(\mathbf{r}_1, \ldots, \mathbf{r}_k)$ of a user-defined relational database schema $\rho = (r_1, \ldots, r_k)$ over D. Intuitively, a database (instance) D *believes* that a fact $r_i(a_1, \ldots, a_k)$ is *true* whenever the elements $a_1, \ldots, a_k$ are r_i-related (i.e, $a_1, \ldots, a_k \in \mathbf{r}_i^{\mathrm{D}}$) in the instance D and false otherwise. This is equivalent to the *closed world assumption* (CWA).

14.3.1 1NF Models

First we consider temporal data models that associate truth of facts with *individual time instants*. This, in database terminology, is equivalent to the *first normal form* requirement [Codd, 1971]: the requirement that relations only relate atomic values. Note that while this requirement may not be fully met by some of the temporal models below at the *syntactic level*, all the models are equivalent to (or subsumed by) such a model.

One obtains an abstract temporal database by linking a standard relational database with a temporal domain. There are several alternative ways of achieving this [Chomicki, 1994]

Booking		
Meeting	*Room*	*Time*
DB Group	DC1331	06-Jan-04.10:00
DB Group	DC1331	06-Jan-04.10:01
DB Group	DC1331	06-Jan-04.10:02
...	...	...
DB Group	DC1331	16-Jan-04.11:59
Intro to Databases	MC4042	06-Jan-04.10:00
...	...	...
Intro to Databases	MC4042	06-Jan-04.11:19
Intro to Databases	MC4042	08-Jan-04.10:00
...	...	...
Intro to Databases	MC4042	08-Jan-04.11:19

Figure 14.1: A Fragment of a Timestamp Instance of the `Booking` relation from Example 14.3.1.

that we discuss next.

The Timestamp Model

This is defined by augmenting all tuples in relations with an additional temporal attribute.

Definition 14.3.1 (Abstract Timestamp Temporal Database). *A relational symbol R_i is a* temporal extension *of the symbol r_i if it contains all attributes of r_i and a single additional attribute t of sort T_P (w.l.o.g. we assume it is the first attribute). The sort of the attributes of R_i is $\mathrm{T}_P \times \mathrm{D}^{\mathrm{arity}(r_i)}$.*

A timestamp temporal database *is a first-order structure $\mathrm{D} \cup \mathrm{T}_P \cup \{\mathbf{R}_1 \ldots, \mathbf{R}_k\}$, where $\mathbf{R}_i$ are* temporal relations— *instances of the temporal extensions R_i. In addition we require that the set $\{\mathbf{a} : (t, \mathbf{a}) \in \mathbf{R}_i\}$ be finite for every $t \in \mathrm{T}_P$ and $0 < i \leq k$.*

Note that at this point there are no cardinality restrictions imposed on the number of time instants in the instances of abstract temporal relations; we address issues connected with the actual finite representation of these relations in Section 14.6. In the rest of the chapter we use the following example to illustrate various concepts.

Example 14.3.1. *Consider a database recording room bookings for meetings in a university. A relational schema* `booking`*(Meeting, Room) links meetings to rooms. We assume that rooms are identified by their room numbers and meetings have distinct descriptions (names). Thus our temporal database, assuming the use of the timestamp model, contains a single relational schema with three attributes,*

`Booking`*(Meeting, Room, Time).*

A tuple (a, b, t) in an instance of this relation denotes the fact that a meeting a is in a room b at time t. For simplicity in this chapter we assume that time is measured in minutes. An example instance of this schema is shown in Figure 14.1. To distinguish between non-temporal *relations and (the derived) timestamp relations we capitalize the name of the later. The granularity of time in our examples is one minute (more on granularities in Section 14.9).*

It is important to understand that, e.g., the "DB group" meeting has booked room DC1331 for *every* time instant between 06-Jan-04.10:00 and 06-Jan-04.11:59. This set of tuples, depending on properties of the time domain, can be infinite (e.g., when dense time domain is considered). There are several things to note about the example: an instance of the `Booking` relation represents *complete information* about meeting schedule; in particular it contains information about meetings that have already finished (e.g., for accounting and evaluation purposes) as well as about meetings scheduled in the future (e.g., to avoid over-booking of rooms). This is necessary, for example, if we want to schedule another meeting in the future, as we need to make sure no other meeting conflicts with it. For this purpose we need to query the database for *empty rooms* at the particular future time we desire and such a query is *only possible* utilizing the closed-world assumption.

Second, we assume that distinct meetings have distinct names. Thus the same meeting (e.g., a class) can meet in several different rooms at different times. Moreover the meeting times may not be continuous (as is common, e.g., for classes). If we wish to distinguish between *instances* of a particular meeting we need to use distinguished names (or an additional attribute).

The Snapshot Model

The abstract temporal databases in this model are defined as a mapping of the temporal domain to the class of standard relational databases. This gives a Kripke structure with the temporal domain serving as the accessibility relation.

Definition 14.3.2 (Abstract Snapshot Temporal Database). *A* snapshot temporal database *over* D, T_P, *and* ρ *is a map* $DB : \mathrm{T}_P \to \mathcal{DB}(\mathrm{D}, \rho)$, *where* $\mathcal{DB}(\mathrm{D}, \rho)$ *is the class of finite relational databases over* D *and* ρ.

It is easy to see that snapshot and timestamp abstract temporal databases are merely different views of the same data and thus can represent the same class of temporal databases. Formally, a snapshot temporal database D corresponds to a timestamp temporal database D' if and only if

$$\forall x_1, \ldots, x_k . \mathbf{r}^{D(t)}(x_1, \ldots, x_k) \Leftrightarrow \mathbf{R}^{D'}(t, x_1, \ldots, x_k),$$

for all r (and R) in the schema of D (D'), where $\mathbf{r}^{D(t)}$ ($\mathbf{R}^{D'}$) are the instances of the relations r (R) in D (D'), respectively, where $k = \text{arity}\, r$. This correspondence allows us to move freely between the two models.

Example 14.3.2. *A snapshot representation of the instance in Figure 14.1 is shown in Figure 14.2.*

Note that the relationship between the timestamp and snapshot models is essentially currying and uncurrying [Barendregt, 1984] (the correspondence is exact if the relations are considered to be boolean functions from tuples to the set $\{\text{true}, \text{false}\}$).

Thus, in the rest of the chapter we use the timestamp abstract temporal databases as the common underlying temporal data model. Also, let us reiterate that the abstract data models are used solely at the *conceptual* level; relations will likely be stored in a different, more space-efficient format, e.g., one that uses time intervals (see Section 14.6).

Time	booking
06-Jan-04.10:00	{ (DB Group,DC1331), (Intro to Databases,MC4042) }
06-Jan-04.10:01	{ (DB Group,DC1331), (Intro to Databases,MC4042) }
...	
06-Jan-04.11:19	{ (DB Group,DC1331), (Intro to Databases,MC4042) }
06-Jan-04.11:20	{ (DB Group,DC1331) }
...	
06-Jan-04.11:59	{ (DB Group,DC1331) }
06-Jan-04.12:00	{ }
...	
06-Jan-04.12:00	{ }
08-Jan-04.10:00	{ (Intro to Databases,MC4042) }
...	
08-Jan-04.11:19	{ (Intro to Databases,MC4042) }

Figure 14.2: A Fragment of a Snapshot Instance of the `Booking` relation.

Relational Database Histories

Relational databases are updatable and it is natural to consider sequences of database states resulting from the updates.

Definition 14.3.3 (Finite History). *A* history *over a database schema ρ and a data domain D is a sequence $H = (D_0, \ldots, D_n)$ of database instances (called* states*) such that*

1. *all the states $D_0, \ldots, D_n$ share the same schema ρ and the same data domain* D,
2. *D_0 is the initial instance of the database,*
3. *D_i results from applying an update to D_{i-1}, $i \geq 1$,*

There is a clear correspondence between histories over D and ρ and snapshot temporal databases over D, $\mathbb{N}$ (natural numbers), and ρ (see Definitions 14.3.2 and 14.3.1). Consequently, any query language for abstract temporal databases can also be used to query database histories. However, there is a difference in the restrictions placed on updates: while there are no a priori limitations placed on snapshot temporal database updates (they can involve any snapshot), histories are *append-only* (the past cannot be modified). This property is often associated with *transaction time* databases—temporal databases in which time instants correspond to *commitment* time of transactions; the *append-only* nature of such databases corresponds to the requirement of *durable transactions*. Indeed, transaction-time temporal databases can be viewed as finite histories of standard relational databases.

14.3.2 Multiple Temporal Dimensions

So far we have considered only single-dimensional temporal databases: temporal relations were allowed only a single temporal attribute. To motivate the introduction of multiple temporal dimensions in the context of temporal databases, consider the following examples:

- *Bitemporal* databases: with each tuple in a relation two kinds of time are stored—the valid time (when a particular tuple is true) and the transaction time (when the particular tuple was inserted/deleted in the database) [Jensen *et al.*, 1993].
- *Spatial* databases: multiple dimensions over an interpreted domain can be used for representing *spatial data* where multiple dimensions serve as coordinates of points in a k-dimensional Euclidean space.

Most of the data modeling techniques require only fixed-dimensional data. However, the true need for arbitrarily large dimensionality of data models originates in the requirement of having a first-order complete query language (see Theorem 14.5.5 in Section 14.5). Thus, there are two cases to consider:

- temporal models with a fixed number of dimensions (> 1), and
- temporal models with a varying number of temporal dimensions without an upper bound.

The representation of multiple temporal dimensions in abstract temporal databases is quite straightforward: we simply index relational databases by the elements of an appropriate self-product of the temporal domain (in the case of snapshot temporal databases), or add the appropriate number of temporal attributes (in the case of timestamp temporal databases).

14.3.3 Non 1NF Temporal Models

Several temporal data models associate relationships between data values—truth of facts recorded in the database— with *sets* of time instants (rather than with a single time instant). These models are no longer in first normal form (N1NF) and are often called *temporally grouped* models [Clifford *et al.*, 1993; Clifford *et al.*, 1994].

Example 14.3.3. *The instance of the* Booking *relation from Figure 14.1 represented in the N1NF (temporally grouped) model is as follows*

Booking		
Meeting	*Room*	*Time*
DB group	*DC1331*	{*06-Jan-04.10:00, 06-Jan-04.10:01, …,06-Jan-04.11:59*}
Intro to Databases	*MC4042*	{*06-Jan-04.10:00,…,06-Jan-04.11:19, 08-Jan-04.10:00,…,08-Jan-04.11:19*}

However, the set-based attributes can be *flattened*, perhaps by introducing additional surrogate keys, to obtain a 1NF temporal database containing the same information [Clifford *et al.*, 1993; Wijsen, 1999]. Without introducing additional keys, however, this transformation can be lossy.

Example 14.3.4. *Consider a fragment of a N1NF temporal relation*

booking(*DB group, DC1331,* {*06-Jan-04.10:00,…,06-Jan-04.11:59*})
booking(*DB group, DC1331,* {*09-Jan-04.10:00,…,09-Jan-04.11:59*})

The meetings in this design are no longer identified by their names, but rather by their name and the set of all meeting times. The same information, however, can be captured by explicitly identifying meetings. Also, such an assumption prevents *us from representing a situation where a particular meeting takes place in two different rooms at two different times.*

Note that the difference between 1NF and N1NF models is intrinsic to these models and can be exhibited *without* introducing temporal aspects into the picture. Also, the differences at the level of abstract databases do not necessarily impact the way the relations are actually stored at the concrete (or physical) level; indeed both of the above examples may be simply two different views of the same physical design.

Another salient point is that a common assumption made by various temporal data models when using the N1NF representation is that facts associated with sets of time instants are also implicitly true at all time instants contained in these sets (as in the above example). This, however, may not be the case in general, as demonstrated by the following example.

Example 14.3.5. *First consider the following two tuples in an instance of a N1NF temporal database:*

`Booking`*(DB group, DC1331, [06-Jan-04.10:00, 06-Jan-04.11:59])*
`Booking`*(AI meeting, MC5114, [06-Jan-04.09:00, 06-Jan-04.10:59])*

In this case the sets (represented by intervals in this case) serve as encodings of their internal points: the database group indeed meets in the DC1331 room every time instant between 06-Jan-04.10:00 and 06-Jan-04.11:59; similarly for the AI meeting. Thus, a meaningful question is whether these two meetings conflict, i.e., whether there is a time instant related to both meetings. On the other hand, consider another fragment of a temporal database:

`Electricity`*(Jones A., 40, [15-May-03.00.00, 14-Jun-03.23:59])*
`Electricity`*(Smith J., 35, [01-May-03.00.00, 31-May-03.23:59])*

The intervals in this example do not *represent the collections of their internal points, but rather the names of the sets themselves (or points in a 2-dimensional space). Thus applying set-based operations on these sets, e.g., computing their intersection, does not have a clear meaning.*

This example also clarifies the difference between two distinct uses of intervals in temporal databases:

1. intervals as encodings of the extents of convex 1-dimensional sets, or
2. intervals as (otherwise uninterpreted) names for such sets.

These two approaches assume completely different *meaning* to be assigned to the same construct (often a pair of time instants) in different contexts. Note that in Sections 14.5 and 14.6 we use solely the first paradigm.

An interesting observation at this point is that the keys introduced in the flattening transformation essentially represent *names* of sets of time instants. This idea, however, can be formalized using a 1NF temporal model, e.g., the timestamp model: we simply add an *abstract relation* that links names of sets of time instants with their extents (essentially the *membership relation*). For example, to describe intervals, the relation would look as follows:

$$\mathsf{SETS}(n,t) := \{('[t_1,t_2]',t) : t_1 \le t \le t_2\}$$

Note that $'[t_1, t_2]'$ is now an otherwise uninterpreted element of the *data domain*. Similarly we can introduce constants (as singleton sets), calendars, etc. It has to be understood that association of other data values with names of sets does not say anything about the truth of facts with respect to the time instants belonging to these sets. Also, the extents of these sets do not have to be closed under set operations, e.g., an intersection or union of the extents of two such sets, while it always exists, may not have a *name**. Similar approach can be used to introduce names for other sets, e.g., singleton sets for constants, periodic sets for time granularities (see Section 14.9), etc.

The Parametric Model

This model [Clifford *et al.*, 1994] considers the values stored in individual fields of tuples in the database to be functions of time. It is easy to see that every instance of a relation r represented in a parametric temporal database D can be represented in the timestamp model as an instance D' as follows:

$$\mathbf{R}^{D'} = \{(t, f_1(t), \ldots, f_k(t)) : (f_1, \ldots, f_k) \in \mathbf{r}^D, t \in \mathrm{T}_P\}$$

Note that this transformation loses the *identity* of the tuples [Clifford *et al.*, 1993]. However, introducing tuple identifiers as outlined in the previous section alleviates this deficiency. Wijsen [Wijsen, 1999] also argues that this transformation indeed simplifies further technical development of integrity constraints and queries.

Moreover, if the functions used in the parametric model are *total*, then there are instances of a timestamp database containing a single unary relation, e.g., $\mathbf{R} = \{(0,a),(1,b),(1,c)\}$, that cannot be represented using the parametric model (since the number of tuples at time 0 differs from the number of tuples at time 1). Thus we need to allow partial functions and/or life-span attributes to regain the expressiveness of the simple 1NF model. We do not consider the parametric model in this chapter any further.

14.4 Temporal Database Design

The equivalence between snapshot and timestamp temporal databases (Definitions 14.3.1 and 14.3.2) makes it possible to view the design of temporal database schemas as a special case of the design of relational database schemas.

14.4.1 Temporal Functional Dependencies

Jensen et al. [Jensen *et al.*, 1996] propose a formal framework for temporal database design that encompasses and generalizes earlier approaches in this area. We provide here a purely

*This issue resurfaces when one attempts to define an interval-based temporal data model as a restriction of the N1NF model: since unions of intervals are not necessarily describable as intervals the notion of temporal elements is needed to maintain closure under boolean operations.

relational reconstruction of that framework, eliminating at the same time its inherent technical limitations. We use the timestamp model and assume first a single temporal dimension with temporal domain T_P.

The cornerstone of the approach of [Jensen *et al.*, 1996] is the notion of *temporal functional dependency* (temporal FD). A temporal FD $X \xrightarrow{T} Y$ holds in a snapshot temporal relation DB if the (classical) FD $X \rightarrow Y$ holds in every snapshot of DB. Viewing DB as a timestamp database TDB, this is equivalent to the classical FD $X\ T \rightarrow Y$ holding in TDB.

Example 14.4.1. *Assume the relation* `booking` *with attributes Meeting and Room from Example 14.3.1. The temporal FD Meeting* $\xrightarrow{T}$ *Room expresses the fact that every meeting is held in a single room at any given time. In the corresponding timestamp relation* `Booking`*, the above condition is captured by the FD Meeting Time* $\rightarrow$ *Room.*

Avoiding the introduction of a new notion of a *temporal FD* has numerous advantages. First, one can use the classical notions of FD inference (Armstrong axioms), dependency closure, keys, normal forms, and lossless decompositions *without any change*. In [Jensen *et al.*, 1996], new notions of temporal keys, temporal normal forms, etc. are derived as temporal versions of their relational analogues. Second, it is no longer necessary to restrict temporal relations to being *finite* (as in [Jensen *et al.*, 1996]) in order to test satisfaction of temporal FDs. It is enough for such relations to be *finitely representable* (in the sense of the constraint databases [Kanellakis *et al.*, 1995]). Every classical FD can be written as a first-order sentence and evaluated as a relational calculus query over any finitely representable relation. Third, one can now mix temporal and non-temporal FDs.

Example 14.4.2. *The dependency Meeting* $\rightarrow$ *Room in the timestamp relation* `Booking` *is non-temporal and expresses the property that for every specific meeting the same room is always booked.*

With multiple temporal dimensions, the advantages of the relational framework are even more pronounced. For concreteness, we assume two such dimensions: *valid time (VT)* and *transaction time (TT)*. Timestamp relations will now have zero, one (*TT* or *VT*), or two (*TT VT*) temporal attributes. Now we can have, in addition to non-temporal FDs, three kinds of temporal FDs formulated as classical FDs: transaction-time ($X\ TT \rightarrow Y$), valid-time ($X\ VT \rightarrow Y$), and bitemporal ($X\ TT\ VT \rightarrow Y$).

Example 14.4.3. *The bitemporal dependency captured by the FD*

$$Meeting\ TT\ VT \rightarrow Room$$

expresses the constraint that the record at any time of the room booked for a meeting at any time is uniquely determined. *This is a very weak constraint. If we want to say that* the room booked for a meeting at any time is uniquely determined, *we need to use the FD Meeting VT* $\rightarrow$ *Room which captures a valid-time dependency.*

Jensen et al. [Jensen *et al.*, 1996] considered the presence of two temporal dimensions but didn't analyze the consequences of this fact for FDs and other concepts of database design. There are essentially two choices. The first is to limit the attention to bitemporal dependencies. But then valid- and transaction-time FDs become inexpressible, and as a consequence one will not be able to define relational normal forms that truly capture all kinds of FD-related temporal redundancies. For example, the FD *Meeting VT* $\rightarrow$ *Room* (Example 14.4.3) identifies a potential redundancy, which should be removed during the database design process.

The second choice is to allow three kinds of temporal FDs: $X \overset{TT}{\rightarrow} Y$, $X \overset{VT}{\rightarrow} Y$, and $X \overset{TT\,VT}{\longrightarrow} Y$. But then one can no longer talk about, e.g., temporal keys, but only about valid-time, transaction-time or bitemporal keys. The framework becomes so complicated that it is unlikely to be of any use.

The relational framework does not suffer from any of those problems. The classical notion of FD is fine enough to capture all the varieties of temporal dependencies. At the same time, the framework does not require any conceptual extensions.

We should mention that temporal functional dependencies have been generalized to multiple temporal granularities [Wang *et al.*, 1997] and to the object-oriented setting [Wijsen, 1999].

14.4.2 Constraint-generating Dependencies

If we consider the first-order formulation of temporal functional dependencies in timestamp databases, we notice that the formulas obtained in this way contain *equalities* between temporal variables. It is natural to consider a generalization of such dependencies that allows not only equalities but also arbitrary *constraints* over the given temporal domain. Then we can formulate integrity constraints like "the transaction time of a given tuple should always be greater than or equal to the valid time of this tuple." Note that the constraints over the temporal domain are not used here to represent infinite sets (as in constraint databases [Kanellakis *et al.*, 1995]) but rather to obtain a more expressive language of integrity constraints.

This idea was first formulated in [Ginsburg and Hull, 1983; Ginsburg and Hull, 1986] and then formalized in [Baudinet *et al.*, 1999] using the notion of a *constraint-generating dependency* (CGD). Baudinet et al. [Baudinet *et al.*, 1999] described a general reduction of the implication problem for such dependencies to the problem of validity of universal formulas in the appropriate constraint theory. Complexity results for restricted classes of CGDs were also given. A similar idea was studied in the temporal database context in [Wijsen, 1998].

14.5 Abstract Temporal Queries

Most logic-based query languages have their semantics defined in terms of abstract temporal databases—they will be termed *abstract* as well. Other languages whose semantics is defined in terms of *concrete databases* will be appropriately called *concrete*. Here we discuss abstract databases and query languages—the concrete ones are discussed in Section 14.6.

Since databases are inherently first-order structures, in this chapter we are primarily interested in temporal extensions of *first-order* logic (relational calculus).

A natural first-order query language over such databases — the relational calculus — coincides with *first-order logic* over the vocabulary $(=, r_1, \ldots, r_k)$ of the extended structure. An answer to a query in relational calculus is the set of valuations (tuples) that make the query true in the given relational database. Domain independent relational calculus queries (those that depend only on the instance of ρ and not on the underlying domain of values D) can be equivalently expressed in *relational algebra* [Codd, 1972]. In this way the relational model provides both a natural declarative paradigm for representing and querying information stored in a relational database and the possibility of efficient implementation of queries through relational algebra.

Following are several temporal queries we may ask over our sample temporal database.

- *find all meetings that always meet in the same room.*
- *find all rooms in which the last meeting was 'DB group'.*
- *find all meetings with a scheduled break (or multi-part meetings, such as classes).*

We discuss two major approaches to introducing time into relational query languages. Both of them are developed in the context of *abstract* temporal databases and thus lead to abstract query languages. The first approach uses modal temporal connectives and implicit temporal contexts; the second adds explicit variables (attributes) and quantifiers over the temporal domain. We report on the relative expressive power of these extensions.

The two different ways of linking time with a relational database (Definitions 14.3.2 and 14.3.1) lead to two different temporal extensions of the relational calculus (first-order logic). The snapshot model gives rise to *temporal connectives*, while the timestamp model introduces explicit attributes and quantifiers for handling time. The first approach is appealing because it *encapsulates* all the interaction with the temporal domain inside the temporal connectives. In this way the manipulation of the temporal dimension is completely hidden from the user, as it is performed on implicit temporal attributes.

14.5.1 First-order Temporal Logic

Historically, many different variants of temporal logic based on different sets of connectives have been developed [Gabbay *et al.*, 1994a]. Some connectives, such as $\diamond$ (*"sometime in the future"*), $\square$ (*"always in the future"*), or **until** are well-known and have been universally accepted. But in general any appropriate first-order formula in the language of the temporal domain (or, as we will see in Section 14.10, even a second-order one) can be used to define a temporal connective.

Definition 14.5.1 (First-order Temporal Connectives). *Let*

$$O ::= t_i < t_j \mid O \wedge O \mid \neg O \mid \exists t_i.O \mid X_i$$

be the first-order language of T_P *extended with the propositional variables* X_i*. We define a* (k-ary) temporal connective *to be an* O*-formula with exactly one free variable* t_0 *and* k *free propositional variables* $X_1, \ldots, X_k$*. We assume that* t_i *is the only temporal variable free in the formula to be substituted for* X_i*.*

We define Ω *to be a finite set of definitions of temporal connectives comprising: pairs of names* $\omega(X_1, \ldots, X_k)$ *and (definitional)* O*-formulas* ω^* *for temporal connectives.*

We call the variables t_i the *temporal contexts*: t_0 defines the outer temporal context of the connective that is made available to the surrounding formula; the variables $t_1, \ldots, t_k$ define the temporal contexts for the subformulas substituted for the propositional variables $X_1, \ldots, X_k$.

The above definition allows only *first-order* temporal connectives. This is sufficient to define the common temporal connectives **since**, **until**, and their derivatives.

Example 14.5.1. *The common temporal connectives are defined as follows:*

$$X_1 \textbf{ until } X_2 \triangleq \exists t_2.t_0 < t_2 \wedge X_2 \wedge \forall t_1(t_0 < t_1 < t_2 \rightarrow X_1)$$
$$X_1 \textbf{ since } X_2 \triangleq \exists t_2.t_0 > t_2 \wedge X_2 \wedge \forall t_1(t_0 > t_1 > t_2 \rightarrow X_1)$$

Other commonly used temporal connectives, sometime in the future, $\Diamond$, always in the future, $\Box$, sometime in the past, $\blacklozenge$, *and* always in the past, $\blacksquare$, *are defined in terms of* **since** *and* **until** *as follows:*

$$\Diamond X_1 \triangleq \text{true } \textbf{until } X_1 \qquad \Box X_1 \triangleq \neg\Diamond\neg X_1$$
$$\blacklozenge X_1 \triangleq \text{true } \textbf{since } X_1 \qquad \blacksquare X_1 \triangleq \neg\Diamond\neg X_1$$

For a discrete linear order we also define the $\bigcirc$ *(next) and* $\bullet$ *(previous) operators as*

$$\bigcirc X_1 \triangleq \exists t_1.t_1 = t_0 + 1 \wedge X_1 \qquad \bullet X_1 \triangleq \exists t_1.t_1 + 1 = t_0 \wedge X_1$$

Clearly, all of the above connectives are definable in the first-order language of T_P *(the successor* $+1$ *and the equality* $=$ *on the domain* T_P *are first-order definable in the theory of discrete linear order).*

The connectives **since**, $\blacklozenge$, $\blacksquare$, *and* $\bullet$ *are called the* past temporal connectives *(as they refer to the past) and* **until**, $\Diamond$, $\Box$, *and* $\bigcirc$ *the* future temporal connectives.

We discuss the use of more expressive language in the definition of temporal connectives, e.g., monadic second-order logic over the signature of T_P, to define a richer class of temporal connectives in Section 14.10.

The modal query language—first-order temporal logic—is defined to be the original single-sorted first-order logic (relational calculus) extended with a finite set of temporal connectives.

Definition 14.5.2 (First-order Temporal Logic: syntax). *Let* Ω *be a* finite *set of (names of) temporal connectives.* First-order Temporal Logic (FOTL) L^{Ω} *over a schema* ρ *is defined as:*

$$F ::= r(x_{i_1}, \ldots, x_{i_k}) \mid x_i = x_j \mid F \wedge F \mid \neg F \mid \omega(F_1, \ldots, F_k) \mid \exists x.F$$

where $r \in \rho$ *and* $\omega \in \Omega$.

A standard linear-time temporal logic can be obtained from this definition using the temporal connectives from Example 14.5.1:

Example 14.5.2. *The standard FOTL language* $L^{\{\textbf{since},\textbf{until}\}}$ *is defined as*

$$F ::= r(x_{i_1}, \ldots, x_{i_k}) \mid x_i = x_j \mid F \wedge F \mid \neg F \mid F_1 \textbf{ since } F_2 \mid F_1 \textbf{ until } F_2 \mid \exists x.F$$

where **since** *and* **until** *are the names for the connectives defined in Example 14.5.1.*

Example 14.5.3. *We show here how various temporal connectives are used to formulate the queries over the temporal database introduced in Example 14.3.1.*

- *find all meetings that always meet in the same room.*

$$\blacklozenge\Diamond\exists y(\mathtt{booking}(x, y) \wedge \blacksquare\Box\forall z(\mathtt{booking}(x, z) \implies y = z))$$

- *find all rooms in which the last meeting was 'DB group'.*

$$(\neg\exists y.\texttt{booking}(y,x))\ \textbf{since}\ \texttt{booking}(\texttt{DB group},x)$$

Note that this query returns all time instants at which the above statement is true for room x.

- *find all meetings with a scheduled break.*

$$\blacklozenge\exists y.\texttt{booking}(x,y)\wedge\neg\exists y.\texttt{booking}(x,y)\wedge\Diamond\exists y.\texttt{booking}(x,y).$$

The standard way of giving semantics to such a language is as follows.

Definition 14.5.3 (FOTL: semantics). *Let DB be a snapshot temporal database over* D, T_P, *and* ρ, φ *a formula of* L^Ω, $t\in\mathrm{T}_P$, *and* θ *a valuation. We define a relation* $DB,\theta,t\models\varphi$ *by induction on the structure of* φ*:*

$$\begin{array}{ll}
DB,\theta,t\models r_j(x_{i_1},\ldots,x_{i_k}) & \text{if } r_j\in\rho,\ (\theta(x_{i_1}),\ldots,\theta(x_{i_k}))\in\mathbf{r}_j^{DB(t)}\\
DB,\theta,t\models x_i=x_j & \text{if } \theta(x_i)=\theta(x_j)\\
DB,\theta,t\models\varphi\wedge\psi & \text{if } DB,\theta,t\models\varphi \text{ and } DB,\theta,t\models\psi\\
DB,\theta,t\models\neg\varphi & \text{if not } DB,\theta,t\models\varphi\\
DB,\theta,t\models\exists x_i.\varphi & \text{if there is } a\in D \text{ such that } DB,\theta[x_i\mapsto a],t\models\varphi\\
DB,\theta,t\models\omega(F_1,\ldots,F_k) & \text{if } \mathrm{T}_P,[t_0\mapsto t]\models\omega^* \text{ where}\\
 & \quad\mathrm{T}_P,\delta\models X_i \text{ is interpreted as } DB,\theta,\delta(t_i)\models F_i
\end{array}$$

where $\mathbf{r}_i^{DB(t)}$ *is the interpretation of the predicate symbol* r_i *in* DB *at time* t.

We assume the rigid interpretation of constants (they do not change over time). The answer to a query φ over DB *is the set of tuples* $\varphi(DB):=\{(t,\theta_{|FV(\varphi)}):DB,\theta,t\models\varphi\}$ *where* $\theta_{|FV(\varphi)}$ *is the restriction of* θ *to the free variables of* φ.

Example 14.5.4. *The above definition can be applied to the standard language* $L^{\{\mathbf{since},\mathbf{until}\}}$ *for which it gives the usual semantics of the* **since** *and* **until** *connectives:*

$$D,\theta,t_0\models\varphi\ \textbf{until}\ \psi \text{ if } \exists t_2.t_2>t_0\wedge D,\theta,t_2\models\psi\wedge\forall t_1.t_2>t_1>t_0\rightarrow D,\theta,t_1\models\varphi.$$

There are even more restricted versions of FOTL. Gabbay, et al. [Gabbay *et al.*, 1994a] introduce first-order temporal logics where the temporal connectives are always outside of the first-order quantifiers. While such logics may provide sufficient expressive power for some applications, they are generally weaker than L^Ω (for the same set of temporal connectives Ω).

14.5.2 Two-sorted First-order Logic

The second natural extension of the relational calculus to a temporal query language is based on explicit variables and quantification over the temporal domain T_P. It is just the two-sorted version (variables are temporal or non-temporal) of first-order logic (2-FOL) over D and T_P, with the limitation that the predicates can have only one temporal argument [Bacchus *et al.*, 1991].

Definition 14.5.4 (2-FOL: syntax). *The two-sorted first-order language L^P over a database schema ρ is defined by:*

$$M ::= R(t_i, x_{i_1}, \ldots, x_{i_k}) \mid t_i < t_j \mid x_i = x_j \mid M \wedge M \mid \neg M \mid \exists x_i.M \mid \exists t_i.M$$

where R is the temporal extension of r for $r \in \rho$. We use t_i to denote temporal variables and x_i to denote data (non-temporal) variables.

Similarly to FOTL we can use 2-FOL to formulate temporal queries:

Example 14.5.5. *The query find all meetings with a scheduled break can be formulated in 2-FOL using the following formula:*

$$\exists t_1, t_2 . t_1 < t < t_2 \wedge \exists y.\texttt{Booking}(x, y, t_1) \wedge \neg\exists y.\texttt{Booking}(x, y, t) \\ \wedge \exists y.\texttt{Booking}(x, y, t_2).$$

Note that, similarly to the FOTL query in Example 14.5.3, the query returns names of meetings with a break together with the time of the break; should we require the names alone we would need to use an additional existential quantifier for t.

The semantics for this language is defined in the standard way, similarly to the semantics of relational calculus [Abiteboul *et al.*, 1995].

Definition 14.5.5 (2-FOL: semantics). *Let DB be a timestamp temporal database over* D, T_P, *and ρ, φ a formula in L^P, and θ a two-sorted valuation. We define the satisfaction relation $DB, \theta \models \varphi$ as follows:*

$$\begin{array}{ll}
DB, \theta \models R_j(t_i, x_{i_1}, \ldots, x_{i_k}) & \text{if } R_j \in \rho, (\theta(t_i), \theta(x_{i_1}), \ldots, \theta(x_{i_k})) \in \mathbf{R}_j^{DB} \\
DB, \theta \models t_i < t_j & \text{if } \theta(t_i) < \theta(t_j) \\
DB, \theta \models x_i = x_j & \text{if } \theta(x_i) = \theta(x_j) \\
DB, \theta \models \varphi \wedge \psi & \text{if } DB, \theta \models \varphi \text{ and } DB, \theta \models \psi \\
DB, \theta \models \neg\varphi & \text{if not } DB, \theta \models \varphi \\
DB, \theta \models \exists t_i.\varphi & \text{if there is } s \in \mathrm{T}_P \text{ such that } DB, \theta[t_i \mapsto s] \models \varphi \\
DB, \theta \models \exists x_i.\varphi & \text{if there is } a \in \mathrm{D} \text{ such that } DB, \theta[x_i \mapsto a] \models \varphi
\end{array}$$

where $\mathbf{R}_j^{DB}$ is the interpretation of the predicate symbol R_j in the database DB.
An L^P query is an L^P formula with exactly one free temporal variable.
An answer to an L^P query φ over DB *is the set $\varphi(DB) := \{\theta_{|FV(\varphi)} : DB, \theta \models \varphi\}$ where $\theta_{|FV(\varphi)}$ is the restriction of the valuation θ to free variables of φ.*

The restriction to a single temporal attribute in the signature of queries guarantees closure over the universe of single-dimensional temporal relations. Note that this restriction applies only to queries, not to subformulas of queries.

Expressive Power

In the remainder of this section we compare the expressive power of FOTL and 2-FOL. First we define a mapping $\mathrm{Embed} : L^{\Omega} \to L^P$ to show that the L^{Ω} formulas can be expressed in the L^P language:

Definition 14.5.6 (Translation). *Let* Embed *be a mapping of* L^{Ω} *formulas to* L^P *formulas defined as follows:*

$$\begin{array}{lcl}
\mathrm{Embed}(r_i(x_1,\ldots,x_{v_i})) & = & R_i(t_0,x_1,\ldots,x_{v_i}) \\
\mathrm{Embed}(x_i = x_j) & = & x_i = x_j \\
\mathrm{Embed}(F_1 \wedge F_2) & = & \mathrm{Embed}(F_1) \wedge \mathrm{Embed}(F_2) \\
\mathrm{Embed}(\neg F) & = & \neg\,\mathrm{Embed}(F) \\
\mathrm{Embed}(\exists x.F) & = & \exists x.\,\mathrm{Embed}(F) \\
\mathrm{Embed}(\omega(F_1,\ldots,F_k)) & = & \omega^*(\mathrm{Embed}(F_1)[t_0/t_1],\ldots,\mathrm{Embed}(F_k)[t_0/t_k])
\end{array}$$

where $\omega(X_1,\ldots,X_k)$ *is the name of* ω^* *in* Ω *and* $F[t_0/t_i]$ *is a substitution of* t_i *for* t_0 *in* F.

We know that we can freely move between snapshot and timestamp representations (see Definitions 14.3.2 and 14.3.1). Definition 14.5.6 allows us to translate queries in L^{Ω} to queries in L^P while preserving their semantics.

Theorem 14.5.1. *Let* D_1 *be a snapshot temporal database and* D_2 *an equivalent timestamp database. Then* $D_1, \theta, s \models \varphi \Leftrightarrow D_2, \theta[t_0 \mapsto s] \models \mathrm{Embed}(\varphi)$ *for all* $\varphi \in L^{\Omega}$.

Therefore Definition 14.5.6 can also be used to define the semantics of L^{Ω} queries over timestamp temporal databases. Also, it shows that L^P is at least as expressive as L^{Ω} (denoted by $L^{\Omega} \sqsubseteq L^P$). What is the relationship in the other direction? While both snapshot and timestamp temporal models are equivalent in their ability to represent temporal databases equivalently, the derived query languages differ in expressive power*. The separation results are as follows:

Theorem 14.5.2 ([Kamp, 1971]). $L^{\{\mathbf{since},\mathbf{until}\}} \sqsubset L^{\{\mathbf{since},\mathbf{until},\mathbf{now}\}} \sqsubseteq L^P$ *for dense linearly ordered time (*$\sqsubset$ *denotes the "strictly weaker than" relationship of languages).*

The proof of this fact uses structures that cannot be modeled as abstract temporal databases because they are infinite in both the data and temporal dimensions. Moreover, the proof technique does not consider arbitrary temporal connectives and discrete linear orders. The following results show that $L^{\Omega} \sqsubset L^P$ holds in general:

Theorem 14.5.3 ([Abiteboul *et al.*, 1996]). $L^{\{\mathbf{since},\mathbf{until}\}} \sqsubset L^P$ *over the class of finite timestamp temporal databases.*

Theorem 14.5.4 ([Toman and Niwinski, 1996; Bidoit *et al.*, 2004; Toman, 2003c]). $L^{\Omega} \sqsubset L^P$ *over the class of timestamp temporal databases for an arbitrary finite set of first-order temporal connectives* Ω.

In both cases L^{Ω} is shown not to be able to express the query "are there two distinct time instants at which a unary relation R contains exactly the same values?" On the other hand, this query can be easily expressed in L^P using the formula

$$\exists t_1, t_2.t_1 < t_2 \wedge \forall x.R(t_1,x) \Leftrightarrow R(t_2,x).$$

This formula can be also expressed in a temporal logic in which connectives are allowed to refer to two temporal contexts simultaneously, $L^{\Omega(2)}$ (see Section 14.5.4).

*This is a major difference from the propositional case where linear-time temporal logic has the same expressive power as the monadic first-order logic over linear orders [Kamp, 1968].

14.5.3 Temporal Relational Algebras

The separation results (Theorems 14.5.3 and 14.5.4) have several *unpleasant* consequences. In particular, a single-dimensional first-order complete temporal query language cannot be *subquery closed*. This means that in general we cannot define all queries to be combinations of simpler single-dimensional queries. This fact also prevents us from decomposing large queries into views (virtual relations defined by queries). An even more serious problem is that there is no relational algebra defined over the universe of single-dimensional temporal relations that is able to express all first-order temporal queries.

Similarly to relational algebra, a *Temporal Relational Algebra* is a (finite) set of (first-order definable) operators of the form

$$\mathrm{Op} : \mathcal{R} \times \ldots \times \mathcal{R} \longrightarrow \mathcal{R}$$

defined on the universe of single-dimensional temporal relations $\mathcal{R}$ that conform to the data model of temporal databases.

Example 14.5.6 ([Tuzhilin and Clifford, 1990]). *A temporal relational algebra (TRA) is a set of algebraic operators $\pi_V, \sigma_F, \bowtie, \cup, -, \mathcal{S}, \mathcal{U}$ over the universe of single dimensional temporal relations defined by:*

$$\begin{array}{ll}
\pi_V(R) & = \{t, \theta_{|V} : DB, \theta, t \models R\} \\
\sigma_F(R) & = \{t, \theta_{|FV(R)} : DB, \theta, t \models R \wedge F\} \\
R \bowtie S & = \{t, \theta_{|FV(R) \cup FV(S)} : DB, \theta, t \models R \wedge S\} \\
R \cup S & = \{t, \theta_{|FV(R) \cup FV(S)} : DB, \theta, t \models R \vee S\} \\
R - S & = \{t, \theta_{|FV(R) \cup FV(S)} : DB, \theta, t \models R \wedge \neg S\} \\
\mathcal{S}(R, S) & = \{t, \theta_{|FV(R) \cup FV(S)} : DB, \theta, t \models R \textbf{ since } S\} \\
\mathcal{U}(R, S) & = \{t, \theta_{|FV(R) \cup FV(S)} : DB, \theta, t \models R \textbf{ until } S\}
\end{array}$$

Additional TRA operators, $\blacklozenge$, $\lozenge$, $\blacksquare$, and $\square$ can be derived from the above operators similarly to Example 14.5.1.

The above definition allows us to translate (range restricted [Chomicki *et al.*, 2001]) formulas in $L^{\{\textbf{since},\textbf{until}\}}$ to TRA.

Example 14.5.7. *The query find all rooms in which the last meeting was 'DB group' is expressed in TRA as follows:*

$$\begin{array}{r}
\mathcal{S}(\blacklozenge(\pi_{\mathrm{Room}}(\sigma_{\mathrm{Meeting}=DB\ group}(\mathtt{Booking}))) - \pi_{\mathrm{Room}}(\mathtt{Booking})), \\
\pi_{\mathrm{Room}}(\sigma_{\mathrm{Meeting}=DB\ group}(\mathtt{Booking})))
\end{array}$$

Note that to guarantee the range-restrictions of attributes, we had to rewrite the original formula. Full account of such rewrites was developed by Chomicki et al. [Chomicki et al.*, 2001].*

However, this is also the reason why TRA with an arbitrary finite set of first-order definable operators cannot express all first-order queries (an immediate consequence of Theorems 14.5.3 and 14.5.4). This fact causes major problems when implementing query processors for temporal query languages, as the common (and efficient) implementations inherently depend on the equivalence of relational algebra and calculus to be able to execute all queries, [Abiteboul *et al.*, 1995; Ullman, 1989].

14.5.4 Multiple Temporal Dimensions

The difficulty with defining a complete temporal relational algebra closed over a single-dimensional temporal data model is probably the most compelling reason for considering temporal data models with multiple temporal dimensions. The question we need to answer here is whether a fixed number of temporal dimensions, e.g., two dimensions used in the bitemporal data model, can lead to a closed algebra. We consider this problem in the following setting: we first define multidimensional temporal query languages by essentially following the development of Section 14.5.

It is easy to see that the language L^P is inherently multi-dimensional: we simply abandon the restriction on the number of free temporal variables in queries. To define the multidimensional counterpart of L^Ω we first define the *multidimensional temporal connectives*.

Definition 14.5.7 (Multidimensional Temporal Connective). *A* k-ary m-dimensional temporal connective *is a formula in the first-order language of the temporal domain T with exactly m free variables $t_0^1, \ldots, t_0^m$ and k free predicate variables $X_1, \ldots, X_k$ (we assume that $t_i^1, \ldots, t_i^m$ are the only temporal variables free in the formula substituted for X_i).*

Similarly to Definition 14.5.1 we define Ω to be a finite set of temporal connectives definitions: pairs of names $\omega(X_1, \ldots, X_k)$ and definitions of temporal connectives ω^*.

The language $L^{\Omega(m)}$ is a first-order logic extended with a finite set $\Omega(m)$ of m-dimensional temporal connectives. The semantics of $L^{\Omega(m)}$ queries is defined using the satisfaction relation

$$DB, \theta, t_1, \ldots, t_m \models \varphi$$

similarly to Definition 14.5.3: the only difference is that now we use m evaluation points $t_1, \ldots, t_m$ instead of a single evaluation point t. This definition can be used to define most of the common multi-dimensional temporal logics, e.g., the temporal logic with the *now* operator [Kamp, 1971], the Vlach and Åqvist system [Åqvist, 1979], and most of the interval logics [Allen, 1984; van Benthem, 1983]. To compare the expressive power of temporal logics with respect to the dimension of the temporal connectives we use the following observation. The $L^{\Omega(m)}$ language can be used over an n-dimensional temporal database for $n < m$ by modifying the definition of the satisfaction relation as follows:

$$DB, \theta, s_1, \ldots, s_m \models R(t_1, \ldots, t_n, \mathbf{x}) \text{ if } (s_1, \ldots, s_n, \theta(\mathbf{x})) \in \mathbf{R}$$

Similarly we can assume that all temporal formulas from $L^{\Omega(n)}$ can be used as subformulas in $L^{\Omega(m)}$. Thus $L^{\Omega(m)} \sqsubseteq L^{\Omega(m+1)}$ over m-dimensional temporal databases. It is also easy to see that a natural extension of the Embed map to m dimensions, Embed_m, gives us $L^{\Omega(m)} \sqsubseteq L^P$. The following theorem shows that the inclusions are proper:

Theorem 14.5.5 ([Toman and Niwinski, 1996; Toman, 2003c]). $L^{\Omega(m)} \sqsubset L^{\Omega(m+k)}$ *for $m > 0$ and an arbitrary finite set of m-dimensional temporal connectives $\Omega(m)$ where k is the maximal quantifier depth of any connective in Ω.*

As a consequence $L^{\Omega(m)} \sqsubset L^P$ for all $m > 0$. Thus L^P is the only first-order complete temporal query language (among the languages discussed in this chapter). On the other hand, for any fixed query $\varphi \in L^P$ we can find an $m > 0$ such that there is an equivalent query in $L^{\Omega(m)}$. Thus, e.g., the query that was used to separate FOTL from 2-FOL in Section 14.5 can be expressed in $L^{\Omega(2)}$.

14.5.5 N1NF Data and Queries

First-order nested query languages (without second-order quantifiers or the power-set constructor) are expressively equivalent to standard first-order queries in the 1NF model [Abiteboul *et al.*, 1995]. Thus, save the possibility of avoiding additional key attributes, the *one-level* nesting in the temporal dimension does not add expressive capabilities to the more natural 1NF temporal models.

14.6 Space-efficient Encoding for Temporal Databases

In the second part we concentrate on *concrete* temporal databases: space efficient encodings of abstract temporal databases necessary from the practical point of view. First we explore in detail the most common encoding of time based on intervals and the associated concrete query languages. We introduce semantics-preserving translations of abstract temporal query languages into their concrete counterparts. We also introduce a generalization of such encodings using *constraints*. We conclude the section with a brief discussion of SQL-derived temporal query languages.

While abstract temporal databases provide a natural semantic domain for interpreting temporal queries, they are not immediately suitable for he implementation, as they are possibly infinite (e.g., when the database contains a fact holding for all time instants). Even for finite abstract temporal databases a direct representation may be extremely space inefficient: tuples are often associated with a large number of time instants (e.g., a validity interval). In addition, changes in the *granularity* of time may affect the size of the stored relations.

Our goal in this section is to develop a compact *encoding* for a subclass of abstract temporal databases that makes it possible to compactly represent such databases in finite space.

14.6.1 Interval Encoding of Temporal Databases

The most common approach to such an encoding is to use *intervals* as codes for convex 1-dimensional sets of time instants. The choice of this representation is based on the following empirical observation: Sets of time instants describing the validity of a particular fact in the real world can be often described by an interval or a finite union of intervals. We briefly discuss other encodings at the end of this section. For simplicity from now on we assume a discrete integer-like structure of time. However, dense time can also be accommodated by introducing open and half-open intervals. All the results in this section carry over to the latter setting.

Definition 14.6.1 (Interval-based Domain $\mathrm{T_I}$). *Let $\mathrm{T}_P = (T, <)$ be a discrete linearly ordered point-based temporal domain. We define the set*

$$I(T) = \{(a, b) : a \leq b, a \in T \cup \{-\infty\}, b \in T \cup \{\infty\}\}$$

where $<$ is the order over T_P extended with $\{(-\infty, a), (a, \infty), (-\infty, \infty) : a \in T\}$ (similarly for $\leq$). We denote the elements of $I(T)$ by $[a, b]$ (the usual notation for intervals). We also define four relations on the elements of $I(T)$:

$$([a,b] <_{--} [a',b']) \Leftrightarrow a < a' \quad ([a,b] <_{+-} [a',b']) \Leftrightarrow b < a'$$
$$([a,b] <_{-+} [a',b']) \Leftrightarrow a < b' \quad ([a,b] <_{++} [a',b']) \Leftrightarrow b < b'$$

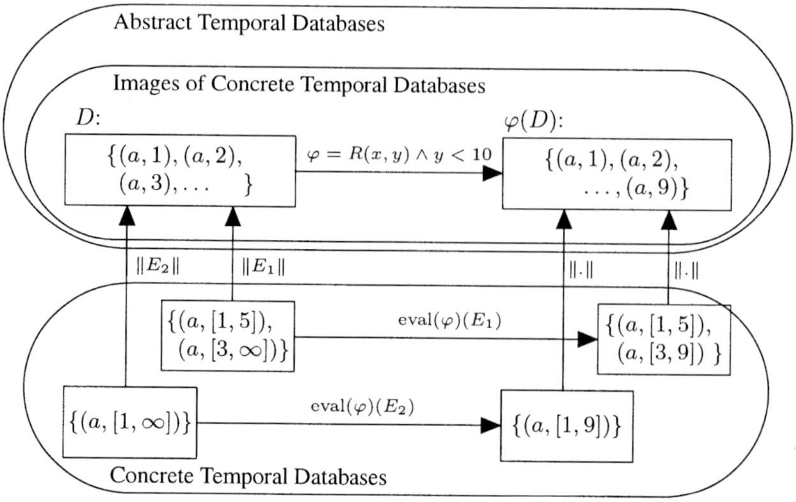

E_1 and E_2 are concrete temporal databases that represent the abstract temporal database D.

Figure 14.3: Abstract and Concrete Timestamp Temporal Databases

for $[a,b],[a',b'] \in I(T)$. *The structure* $\mathrm{T}_I = (I(T), <_{--}, <_{+-}, <_{-+}, <_{++})$ *is the* Interval-based Temporal Domain (corresponding to T_P).

A concrete (timestamp) temporal database is defined analogously to the abstract (timestamp) temporal database. The only difference is that the temporal attributes range over intervals (T_I) rather than over the individual time instants (T_P).

Definition 14.6.2 (Concrete Temporal Database). *A* concrete temporal database *is a finite first-order structure* $\mathrm{D} \cup \mathrm{T}_I \cup \{\mathbf{R}_1 \ldots, \mathbf{R}_k\}$, *where* $\mathbf{R}_i$ *are the* concrete temporal relations *which are finite instances of* R_i *over* D *and* T_I.

Clearly the values of the interval attributes can be encoded as pairs of their endpoints which are elements of $T \cup \{-\infty, \infty\}$. However, it is important to understand that both T_P and T_I model *the same* structure of time instants, a single-dimensional linearly ordered timeline. This requirement is the crucial difference between the use of intervals in temporal databases and in various interval-based logics (cf. Section 14.5.4). The meaning of concrete temporal databases is defined by a mapping to the class of abstract temporal databases.

Example 14.6.1. *A concrete representation of the instance in Figure 14.1 based on the interval encoding is shown below:*

Booking		
Meeting	*Room*	*Time*
DB group	*DC1331*	*[06-Jan-04.10:00,06-Jan-04.11:59]*
Intro to Databases	*MC4042*	*[06-Jan-04.10:00,06-Jan-04.11:19]*
Intro to Databases	*MC4042*	*[08-Jan-04.10:00,08-Jan-04.11:19]*

Definition 14.6.3 (Semantic Mapping $\|.\|$). *Let* D_1 *be an abstract temporal database and* D_2 *be a concrete temporal database over the same schema* ρ. *We say that* D_2 encodes D_1 *if*

$$\mathbf{R}_i^{D_1}(t, \mathbf{x}) \Leftrightarrow \exists I \in T_I.\mathbf{R}_i^{D_2}(I, \mathbf{x}) \wedge t \in I$$

for all r_i *in* ρ, $t \in T_P$, *and* $\mathbf{x} \in D^{\text{arity}(r_i)}$, *where* $\mathbf{R}_i^D$ *is the interpretation of the relation symbol* R_i *in the database* D. *This correspondence defines a map* $\|.\|$ *from the class of the concrete temporal databases to the class of the abstract temporal databases as an extension of the mapping of the relations in* D_2 *to the relations in* D_1.

Note that $\|.\|$ is neither injective nor onto. Therefore there is no unique *canonical* concrete temporal database that encodes a given abstract temporal database. If only a single temporal dimension is allowed, however, we can define a *canonical* form for concrete temporal relations using *coalescing*: A single-dimensional temporal relation is *coalesced* if every fact is associated only with maximal non-overlapping intervals. A concrete temporal database is *coalesced* if all the user-defined relations are coalesced. Unfortunately, such a canonical normal form does *not* generalize to higher dimensions and Theorems 14.5.3 and 14.5.4 show that we cannot restrict our attention to the single-dimensional case.

14.6.2 Concrete Temporal Query Languages

The simplest query language over concrete temporal databases is the two-sorted first-order logic where variables and quantifiers of the temporal sort range over the domain T_I rather than T_P.

Definition 14.6.4 (Interval-based Language $\mathbf{L^I}$). *Let* ρ *be a database schema and*

$$L ::= R_i(I, \mathbf{x}) \mid L \wedge L \mid \neg L \mid \exists x.L \mid \exists I.L \mid x_1 = x_2 \mid I_1^* < I_2^*$$

where R_i *is the temporal extension of* $r_i \in \rho$ *and* $I^* \in \{I^+, I^-\}$.

L^I uses $I_1^* < I_2^*$ instead of the symbols $<_{--}, <_{+-}, <_{-+}, <_{++}$ from the *actual* structure of T_I. However, it is easy to see that, e.g., $I^- < J^-$ can be expressed as $I <_{--} J$, etc., and the new notation is thus merely syntactic sugar. We could also equivalently use Allen's algebra operators [Allen, 1983]. The resulting language is equivalent to L^I.

We assume the usual Tarskian semantics for formulas in L^I. Therefore L^I is fairly easy to implement using standard relational techniques. However, it is crucial to understand that this semantics of L^I is *not* point-based—the elements of T_I correspond to points in the two-dimensional plane (cf. Section 14.5.4). Thus L^I can not be immediately used as a query language over interval-based encodings of *point-based* abstract temporal databases because, among other things, it can easily express representation-dependent queries. Consider the following example:

Example 14.6.2. *Let* D_1, D_2 *be two concrete temporal databases over the schema* $(r(x))$ *defined by* $\mathbf{R}^{D_1} = \{([0,2], a), ([1,3], a)\}$ and $\mathbf{R}^{D_2} = \{([0,3], a)\}$.
Then the formula $\exists I, J.\exists x(R(I,x) \wedge R(J,x) \wedge I \neq J)$ *is true in* D_1 *but false in* D_2.

This observation leads to the following definition:

Definition 14.6.5 ($\|.\|$-generic Queries). *Let* $\|.\|$ *be the semantics mapping and* $\varphi \in L^I$. *Then we say that* φ is $\|.\|$-generic *if* $\|D_1\| = \|D_2\|$ *implies* $\|\varphi(D_1)\| = \|\varphi(D_2)\|$ *for all concrete temporal databases* D_1, D_2.

In other words, no well-behaved query should distinguish between two equivalent, but differently represented temporal databases. Most interval-based query languages (e.g., TQuel or SQL/Temporal; cf. Section 14.7) are directly based on the language L^I (or one of its variants). This choice inherently leads to the possibility of expressing non $\|.\|$-generic queries.

Compilation of Abstract Query Languages

A desirable solution is to use one of the abstract query languages for querying the encoded temporal databases. However, the semantics of these languages is defined over the class of abstract temporal databases (and we cannot simply apply the queries to the images of the concrete temporal databases under $\|.\|$, as this would completely defy the purpose of using the concrete encodings and we would have to face the possibility of handling infinite relations). Thus we need to evaluate abstract queries directly over the concrete encodings. This goal is achieved using *compilation techniques* that transform abstract queries to formulas in L^I while *preserving meaning* under $\|.\|$:

Theorem 14.6.1 ([Toman, 1996]). *There is a (recursive) mapping $F : L^P \to L^I$ such that $\varphi(\|\mathrm{D}\|) = \|F(\varphi)(\mathrm{D})\|$ for all $\varphi \in L^P$ and all concrete temporal databases* D.

Moreover we can show that when using the interval-based encoding L^P can express all $\|.\|$-generic queries in L^I:

Theorem 14.6.2 ([Toman, 1996]). *For every $\|.\|$-generic $\varphi \in L^I$ there is $\psi \in L^P$ such that $\|\varphi(\mathrm{D})\| = \psi(\|\mathrm{D}\|)$ for all concrete temporal databases* D.

Thus, considering $\|.\|$-generic queries, there is no advantage of basing a temporal query language on L^I.

The mapping from Theorem 14.6.1 can be also used for L^Ω by composing it with the Embed map from Definition 14.5.6. However, we may ask, is there is a more direct way from L^Ω to L^I? The following theorem gives a direct mapping of L^Ω to ATSQL (which is essentially a SQL version of L^I; cf. Section 14.7):

Theorem 14.6.3 ([Böhlen *et al.*, 1996a; Chomicki *et al.*, 2001]). *There is a (recursive) mapping $G : L^\Omega \to L^I$ such that $\varphi(\|\mathrm{D}\|) = \|F(\varphi)(\mathrm{D})\|$ for all $\varphi \in L^\Omega$ and all* coalesced *concrete temporal databases* D.

This mapping is considerably simpler than the indirect way through L^P. However, we pay the price for simplicity by having to maintain coalesced temporal relations, including all intermediate results during the bottom-up evaluation of the query. Note that the use of coalescing is possible due to the inherent single-dimensionality of L^Ω.

The mappings defined in Theorems 14.6.1 and 14.6.3 bring up an interesting point: what are the images of the temporal connectives themselves? It turns out that the results of such translations can be considered to be the equivalents of the original connectives that operate on concrete temporal relations, as shown in the example below.

Example 14.6.3. *Let* **UNTIL** $= \lambda r.\lambda s.F \circ \mathrm{Embed}(r\ \mathbf{until}\ s)$ *and ϕ and ψ two queries in L^Ω. Then*

$$(\phi\ \mathbf{until}\ \psi)(\|\mathrm{D}\|) = \|(F \circ \mathrm{Embed}(\phi)\ \mathbf{UNTIL}\ F \circ \mathrm{Embed}(\psi))(\mathrm{D})\|$$

for all concrete temporal databases D.

A similar trick can be used to define the remaining temporal connectives. For coalesced databases we can use G in place of $F \circ \text{Embed}$. This definition can be used to define an algebra over concrete relations that preserves the $\|.\|$ mapping and is thus suitable for implementing L^{Ω}.

14.6.3 Concrete Multi-dimensional Temporal Databases

Similarly to the single-dimensional case, storing the abstract multi-dimensional temporal databases directly may induce enormous space requirements. Thus we need to use encodings for multiple temporal dimensions. However, the introduction of multiple dimensions brings new challenges. The choice of encoding for sets of points in the multidimensional space is often much more involved than taking products of the encoding designed for the single-dimensional case. Assume that we attempt to represent the sets of points by hyper-rectangles—the multi-dimensional counterparts of intervals. It is easy to see that we can write first-order queries that do not preserve closure over this encoding:

Example 14.6.4. *Consider the query* $\varphi(t_1, t_2) = R(t_1) \wedge R(t_2) \wedge t_1 < t_2$. *This query evaluated over the database* $R = \{([1, 10])\}$ *returns a triangle-like region where, for all the points in the region, the first coordinate is less then the second coordinate.*

There are several ways of dealing with this issue:

- We can choose a *multi-dimensional temporal logic* where all the introduced connectives preserve closure over the chosen encoding.
- We can introduce closure restriction for formulas in L^P, [Chomicki *et al.*, 1996; Toman, 1997; Chomicki *et al.*, 2003a]. Such a restriction is designed to guarantee *attribute independence* of the free variables in the query and subsequently closure over an encoding obtained by taking an appropriate number of Cartesian (self-)products of the single-dimensional encoding.
- We can use a more general encoding using constraints in some suitable constraint language [Kanellakis *et al.*, 1995; Libkin *et al.*, 2000].

Another problem with using a multi-dimensional view of time is that it is much harder to define *normal forms* for temporal relations: in the single-dimensional case the coalesced relations provide a unique normal form (for the interval based encoding). However in two or more dimensions, such a normal form does not exist anymore (even when we only use hyper-rectangles).

14.6.4 Other Encodings

While the interval-based encoding of temporal databases is the most common in the literature, it is not the only possible approach. Another way to look at this problem is as follows: consider having

- a *finite* relation (with one or more temporal attributes), and
- a view that defines another (abstract) temporal relation in terms of the given relation.

Note that the instance of the relation defined by the view is not necessarily finite. We can think of the given finite relation as the *finite encoding* of an abstract temporal relation defined in terms of the view.

Example 14.6.5 (Interval Encoding Revisited). *Consider a finite instance of a relation* $R(t_1, t_2, x)$ *where the first two attributes are temporal attributes and the last attribute is a data attribute. In addition consider the view*

$$r(t, x) := \{(t, x) : \exists t_1, t_2. R(t_1, t_2, x) \wedge t_1 \leq t \leq t_2\}$$

It is easy to see that instances of R *are essentially the concrete relations based on the interval encodings corresponding to instances the abstract relation* r*. The view provides an explicit version of the semantic mapping in Definition 14.6.3.*

This approach, however, allows us to define many different mappings between abstract temporal relations and their concrete counterparts. Bettini et al. [Bettini *et al.*, 1998e] use this approach to study *temporal semantic assumptions* in temporal databases (in the setting of temporal granularities). Examples of temporal assumptions considered are:

- values of certain attributes *persist* until the value is replaced by another value later (with respect to the flow of time),
- values of a certain attribute are computed as an average, interpolation, etc., of the closest values preceding and following w.r.t. the flow of time;
- values of a certain attribute are computed as the sum of last three values; etc.

Note that the views define *abstract relations* and thus their instances may be infinite in general, even though it is defined on top of a finite relation. Thus the queries that define these views do not have to be range-restricted.

Example 14.6.6 (Persistence). *Consider a relation* $R(t, x, y)$ *where the first attribute is a temporal attribute and the last two attributes are data attributes. Then the view*

$$\begin{aligned} r(t, x, y) := \{(t, x, y) : \exists t_1. R(t_1, x, y) \wedge t_1 \leq t \\ \wedge \forall t_2, y_2. R(t_2, x, y_2) \implies (t_2 < t_1 \vee t_2 > t)\} \end{aligned}$$

defines an abstract temporal relation in which, for a given value x*, the value for* y persists *until changed.*

The same approach can be applied to define an abstract temporal relation from a log of insertions into and deletions from a temporal relation.

The association of abstract relations with their concrete encodings based on views has been studied extensively in the data integration community under the *global-as-a-view* (GAV) paradigm [Lenzerini, 2002]. Thus, query evaluation is essentially based on view expansion followed by the approach outlined in Section 14.6.2. Note however, that to interpret the *results of queries* we need to specify or derive the temporal assumptions associated with the (finite) answer. One option here is to use the interval encoding as the default assumption.

14.7 SQL and Derived Temporal Query Languages

Up to this point we have only discussed temporal query languages based on logic. In this section we focus on the proposals for temporal extensions of more practical query languages, especially SQL [ISO, 1992]. When designing such an extension several obstacles need to be overcome:

1. The semantics of SQL and other practical languages are commonly based on a bag (duplicate) semantics rather than on a set (Tarskian) semantics. Therefore we need to design our extension to be consistent with the semantics of the language we started with. This also means that we need to deal with various non first-order features of the original language, e.g., with aggregation (the ability to count the number of tuples in a relation or to compute the sum of values in an attribute of the relation over all tuples).

2. We need to design the extension in a way that consistently supports the chosen model of time. This point is often not emphasized enough and many of the proposals drift from the intended model of time in order to accommodate extra features. However, such design decisions lead to substantial problems in the long run, especially when a precise semantics of the extension has to be spelled out (this is one of the reasons why only informal semantics exist for many of these languages).

3. To obtain a feasible solution we need to use a compact encoding of temporal databases introduced in Section 14.6. Therefore we need an *efficient* query evaluation procedure for the chosen class of *concrete databases*.

We would like to point out that vast majority of practical temporal query languages assume a *point-based model of time* (i.e., the truth of facts is associated with single time instants rather than with sets of time instants) [Chomicki, 1994]. Unfortunately (and also in most cases) the *syntax* is based on the syntax of L^I or some of its variants, e.g., languages that use Allen's interval algebra operators [Allen, 1983]. This discrepancy leads to a tension between the syntactic constructs used in the language and the intended semantics of queries. While we focus mostly on temporal extensions of SQL, our observations are general enough to apply to temporal extensions of other query languages, e.g., TQuel [Snodgrass, 1987].

Example 14.7.1. *We demonstrate the differences between the approaches using the following query:* List all meetings with a scheduled break. *This query can be easily formulated in temporal logic as follows:*

$$\blacklozenge\exists y.\texttt{booking}(x,y) \land \neg\exists y.\texttt{booking}(x,y) \land \Diamond\exists y.\texttt{booking}(x,y).$$

This query could be equivalently expressed using future (or past) temporal connectives only.

The temporal extensions of SQL can be divided into two major groups, treated below, based on the *syntactic constructs* added to support temporal queries.

14.7.1 Abstract Temporal Extensions of SQL

We first consider extensions of SQL based on abstract temporal query languages.

Extensions based on on L^P

While query languages based on L^P were often considered to be inherently inefficient, recent results (especially Theorem 14.6.1, [Toman, 1996]) allow us to define a *point-based* extension of SQL that can be efficiently evaluated over the concrete interval-based temporal databases. The proposed language, SQL/TP, is a clean temporal extension of SQL [Toman, 1997]:

- The syntax and semantics of SQL/TP are defined as a natural extension of SQL with an additional data type based on the point-based temporal domain T_P (i.e., a linearly ordered set of time instants).
- The use of Theorem 14.6.1 also avoids the problems outlined later in the chapter in Example 14.7.4: the result of the F map is an ordinary query in L^I (or SQL). Therefore it can be efficiently evaluated over the concrete temporal databases based on interval encoding of timestamps (like any other SQL query).

The SQL/TP proposal also includes a definition of meaningful duplicate semantics and aggregation operations that are compatible with standard SQL [Toman, 1997]. The query from Example 14.7.1 can be formulated in SQL/TP in the expected way:

```
select r1.Meeting
from   Booking r1, Booking r2
where  r1.Meeting = r2.Meeting
  and  r1.time < r2.time
  and  not exists ( select *
                    from   Booking r3
                    where  r3.Meeting = r1.Meeting
                      and  r1.time < r3.time
                      and  r3.time < r2.time )
```

It is easy to see that the above formulation is is very similar to the declarative formulation of the query in the language L^P or in temporal logic.

Languages based on L^Ω

Another possible temporal extension of SQL can be based on the language L^Ω for some finite set of temporal connectives Ω. The temporal connectives can be introduced in the language similarly to set operations, e.g., the `union` operation.

Example 14.7.2 (SQL/{since, until}). *The extended language is defined as follows. Every SQL query is also an SQL/*{**since**, **until**} *query. Standard SQL queries are evaluated pointwise at every time instant. In addition if* `Q1` *and* `Q2` *are two queries (fullselects) then*

```
Q1 since Q2          Q1 until Q2
```

are also SQL/{**since**, **until**} *queries. The semantics of this language is based on a natural extension of Definition 14.5.3.*

This language is a natural temporal extension of ATSQL's *sequenced semantics* [Snodgrass *et al.*, 1995]. We can use Theorem 14.6.3 to evaluate queries in this language efficiently over coalesced interval-encoded concrete temporal databases, [Böhlen *et al.*, 1996a; Chomicki *et al.*, 2001]. Note that in this case all temporal relations have only one temporal attribute and therefore we can use coalescing.

Alternatively we can compose the mappings defined in Definition 14.5.6 with Theorem 14.6.1 to obtain a query evaluation procedure for $\mathbf{L}^{\Omega}$. This time we do not have to enforce coalescing of the concrete temporal relations as Theorem 14.6.1 allows evaluation of queries over *all* concrete temporal databases based on interval encoding. Chen et al. [Chen and Zaniolo, 1999] used this approach to define a *universal* way of temporalizing other query languages, such as QBE and Datalog.

14.7.2 Concrete Temporal Extensions of SQL

Next, we consider temporal extensions of SQL based on the concrete temporal query languages.

Extensions of SQL based on L^I

This group contains the majority of the proposals, in particular SQL/Temporal to the ANSI/ISO SQL standardization group [Snodgrass *et al.*, 1996], and ATSQL [Snodgrass *et al.*, 1995], the *applied* version of TSQL2 [Snodgrass, 1993], and the recent temporal extension of Informix (TIP) [Yang *et al.*, 2000]. All these languages are directly based on L^I with Allen's algebra operators expressed in SQL syntax and using bag (duplicate) semantics.

Let us try to formulate the query from Example 14.7.1 in such a language, e.g., TSQL2 or its successor, SQL/Temporal. The solution that most people come up with is the query below (we use an intuitive and simplified syntax to make our point; for full details on syntax of SQL/Temporal see [Snodgrass *et al.*, 1995; Snodgrass *et al.*, 1996]):

Example 14.7.3. *Query from Example 14.7.1 in SQL/Temporal:*

```
select r1.Meeting
from   Booking r1, Booking r2
where  r1.Meeting = r2.Meeting
  and  r1.time before r2.time
```

Note that the `time` *attributes range over intervals and the* `before` *relationship denotes the before relationship between two intervals. For a similar example in TQuel see [Chomicki, 1994].*

Strangely enough, this query accesses the relation `Booking` only twice while the original query in Example 14.7.1 references the relation three times. This is often considered to be a "feature" of the L^I-based proposals and is attributed to the use of interval-based temporal attributes. It is also appealing due to savings in the query evaluation cost. However, closer scrutiny reveals that the above SQL/Temporal query is incorrect. Indeed, it returns all meetings that were held consecutively in three different rooms without a break. This result is consistent with the *two-dimensional* interval-based semantics of L^I. Similarly we can show many innocent-looking queries to be non-generic (in sense of Definition 14.6.5) and therefore necessarily incorrect with respect to their intended meaning. On the other hand access to interval endpoints (the *non-sequenced semantics* [Snodgrass *et al.*, 1996]) is essential to write non-trivial temporal queries in SQL/Temporal.

There are two principal approaches that try to avoid this incorrect and unexpected behavior by modifying the semantics of the above languages.

Coalescing

The first (and historically oldest) approach is based on *coalescing*: an assumption that the timestamps are represented by maximal non-overlapping intervals (see Section 14.6). This is also the assumption commonly made when queries like the one in Example 14.7.3 are formulated. The coalescing attempts to produce a *normal form* of temporal relations over which the semantics of queries could be (uniquely) defined. The formal justification of this approach lies in realizing that the intended semantics of the language is point-based and therefore we can evaluate queries over any of the $\|.\|$-equivalent temporal databases (one of which is the coalesced one). For a detailed discussion of coalescing in temporal databases see [Böhlen *et al.*, 1996b].

The most prominent representatives of this approach are TQuel [Snodgrass, 1987; Snodgrass, 1993], and TSQL2 [Snodgrass, 1995; Snodgrass *et al.*, 1994]. However:

- Coalescing does not solve the problem with the query in Example 14.7.3. The query would only work if the `Booking` relation was coalesced *after* projecting out the attribute *Room*. This is not done in the (informal) semantics of TQuel nor TSQL2. It also means that the performance gain attributed to the use of interval valued attributes does not exist as we need to re-coalesce temporal relations on the fly.
- While coalescing preserves $\|.\|$-equivalence in the set-based semantics, it is incompatible with the use of duplicate semantics as it inherently removes duplication. This is the main reason why the newer proposals, e.g., SQL/Temporal or ATSQL, do not use coalescing in order to preserve compatibility with SQL's duplicate semantics.

The most serious problem with coalescing-based approaches is exposed by Theorems 14.5.3 and 14.5.4: the theorems show that we cannot evaluate all first-order queries using only one temporal dimension. This result is fatal to the coalescing-based approaches since a canonical representation of temporal relations no longer exists and $\|.\|$-equivalent concrete relations can be distinguished using a first-order query in, for example, SQL/Temporal. We call such queries *representation dependent*. Even very simple queries, e.g., counting the number of regions along the axes, give different results depending on the particular representation.

Folding and Unfolding

The second approach is based on two additional operations: *fold* and *unfold* [Lorentzos, 1993; Lorentzos and Mitsopoulos, 1997]. These two operations allow us to convert a concrete temporal relation with interval-based timestamps to a temporal relation with point-based timestamps explicitly. An appropriate use of these two operations in in queries, e.g., defining

$$R \text{ } p\text{-}diff \text{ } S := fold(unfold(R) - unfold(S)),$$

and then using the *p-diff* operator in place of set difference, would make the above query work, as the semantics is now defined essentially on the unfolded temporal relations and therefore is equivalent to the point-based semantics of L_P. However, a direct use of these operations, which is generally allowed in such languages as *unfold* is part of the syntax, is prohibitively expensive as shown in the following example.

Example 14.7.4. *Consider a temporal relation R containing a single tuple $(a, [-2^n, 2^n])$ for some $n > 0$. Clearly, this relation can be stored in $2n + |a|$ bits. However, unfolding this relation gives us $\{(a, i) : -2^n \leq i \leq 2^n\}$. This relation needs space $2^n \cdot |a|$ which is* exponential *in the size of the original relation R.*

Such a cost would clearly disqualify approaches employing these operators as a basis for a practical temporal query language. Note also that while the unfolding can be represented by a first-order query

$$\mathit{unfold}(R) = \{(t, \mathbf{a}) : \exists I.R(I, \mathbf{a}) \wedge t \in I\},$$

there cannot be an equivalent *range-restricted* query (i.e., a query in which variables range only over values *present in the concrete database*) that defines this operator: the variable t is not *range-restricted* in the definition.

IXSQL [Lorentzos and Mitsopoulos, 1997] tries to combat the use of the *unfold* operation by defining a *normal form* of temporal relations and introducing an additional efficient *normalization operator* [Lorentzos *et al.*, 1995] into the query language. This operator essentially converts IXSQL's temporal relations to $\|.\|$-equivalent normal forms and reinforces the fact that the meaning of the temporal relations is indeed point-based while intervals serve as a representational tool. The normalization operator is similar to the one used by Toman [Toman, 1996] to prove Theorem 14.6.1 and later extended to handle duplicates and aggregation in translations of SQL/TP queries to SQL/92 [Toman, 1997].

Similarly to SQL/TP (and unlike the TSQL2 family of languages) IXSQL treats temporal values simply as an additional data type and allows varying numbers of temporal attributes to be used by a relational schema. Date, while using a syntactic variant of IXSQL [Date *et al.*, 2003], considers this approach superior based on the principle of *least departure from the relational foundations* as defined by Codd [Codd, 1972]. However, the true necessity of multiple temporal dimensions (and thus the need for an arbitrary number of temporal attributes) originates from Theorems 14.5.3, 14.5.4, and 14.5.5 and is necessary to guarantee relational completeness.

14.8 Updating Temporal Databases

In addition to storing and retrieving information, most applications of information systems also require the ability to *modify* the stored data. Temporal databases are no different. Here we again take advantage of the representation-independent nature of abstract temporal databases to define *database updates*. Indeed, from the conceptual point of view, updating an abstract temporal database is no different from updating a standard relational database. Thus the standard SQL-style statements for inserting, deleting, and modifying contents of relation instances can be used. There is, however, one small difference: in general, the instances of abstract temporal relations may be infinite and thus cannot be *populated* by inserting single tuples (this is always sufficient in the case of standard relational databases).

Example 14.8.1. *Continuing with our running example, making a new booking of a room for a meeting can be achieved as follows:*

```
INSERT into Booking (
   SELECT 'DBgroup', 'DC1331', t
   FROM   unit
   WHERE  '23-Jan-04.14.00' <= t <= '23-Jan-04.16.00' )
```

where `unit` *is an auxiliary table that contains a single tuple**. *The inner query produces a set*

$$\{(DB\ group, DC1331, t) : \textit{23-Jan-04.14.00} \le t \le \textit{23-Jan-04.16.00}\}$$

that is added to the instance of `Booking` *as representing another scheduled meeting. Deletion, e.g., creating a 20 minute break in the middle of the above meeting, is achieved analogously by the following statement:*

```
DELETE from Booking
    WHERE  Meeting = 'DBgroup'
      AND  Room = 'DC1331'
      AND  '23-Jan-04.14.50' <= t <= '23-Jan-04.15.10'
```

In this case the set

$$\{(DB\ group, DC1331, t) : \textit{23-Jan-04.14.50} \le t \le \textit{23-Jan-04.15.10}\}$$

is removed from the abstract instance of the `Booking` *relation.*

Similar examples can be shown for SQL's `UPDATE` statement.

14.8.1 Updates and Concrete Temporal Databases

In addition to being able to *express* the update requests on the abstract level, and similarly to queries, the effects of the updates must be mapped faithfully into the concrete representation. This is reasonably easy when *interval encoding* is used for concrete databases:

- to make insertions, simply add the appropriate set of concrete tuples to the concrete relation;
- deletions and updates are more complex: we first use techniques similar to those used for mapping L_P queries to the L_I language to identify and remove the affected concrete tuples. However, since a single concrete tuple may represent multiple abstract ones and the deletion may only affect a subset of those tuples, a new tuple(s) may have to be reinserted into the concrete relation to compensate for this situation.

Example 14.8.2. *The insertion in Example 14.8.1, assuming an underlying concrete representation based on interval encoding, is realized by adding a concrete tuple,*

$$(DB\ group, DC1331, [\textit{23-Jan-04.14.00}, \textit{23-Jan-04.16.00}])$$

to the instance of the concrete representation of the relation `Booking`. *While the insertion (save enforcement of integrity constraints) is relatively straightforward, a deletion (and update/modification) is slightly more complex due to the use of the concrete encoding. The deletion in Example 14.8.1 is performed in two steps:*

1. *Tuples* `Booking`$(DB\ group, DC1331, J)$*, for* $I \cap J \neq \emptyset$ *are removed,*
2. *Tuples* `Booking`$(DB\ group, DC1331, J')$ *for* $J' \in (J - I)$ *are reinserted*†,

*As SQL does not allow `SELECT` blocks without a `FROM` clause.

†Note that subtracting an interval from another interval may yield a set of intervals, as in our example.

where $I = [23\text{-}Jan\text{-}04.14.50, 23\text{-}Jan\text{-}04.15.10]$. *The two steps can be commuted to avoid the need for auxiliary relations. In our example, this leads to the deletion of the tuple*

$$(DB\ group, DC1331, [23\text{-}Jan\text{-}04.14.00, 23\text{-}Jan\text{-}04.16.00])$$

and to the insertion of the tuples

$$(DB\ group, DC1331, [23\text{-}Jan\text{-}04.14.00, 23\text{-}Jan\text{-}04.14.49])$$
$$(DB\ group, DC1331, [23\text{-}Jan\text{-}04.15.11, 23\text{-}Jan\text{-}04.16.00]).$$

Also, the situation becomes more complex if the mapping between the abstract and concrete representations is specified by a view. In this case, we are facing the view update problem and, depending on the complexity of the view definition, some of the updates may not be allowed.

14.8.2 Append-only Databases and Data Expiration

The situation in the case of append-only (or *transaction-time*) temporal databases is slightly different: here the *updates* are (at least conceptually) realized by adding a *new* state to an already existing (finite) history, yielding an *extended history* which is still finite. Such a history represents an abstract temporal database under the *persistence* assumption (cf. Section 14.6.4). However, in this scenario data accumulates over time and there is no apriori mechanism that allows us to remove/delete no longer needed parts of the history. To combat this problem various *data expiration* techniques have been developed. There are two main approaches to expiring data.

Administrative Approaches. These approaches identify data based on *policies* [Jensen, 1995; Skyt *et al.*, 2003] which can be considered view specifications over the original history: all data not in the view extent are *expired*. Query answering then reduces to answering queries (formulated over the original history) using data in these views only. This problem has been extensively studied in the information integration area and is often referred to as *answering queries over views* [Levy *et al.*, 1995] or the LAV (local as a view) approach [Lenzerini, 2002].

Query-driven Approaches. These approaches base their decisions of what data to expire on identifying parts of database histories that can be safely removed without affecting answers to a given set of queries [Chomicki, 1995; Toman, 2001; Toman, 2003a; Toman, 2003b].

Data expiration techniques can be compared by measuring the size of the residual data (the amount of data retained after the expiration operation completes on a history) in terms of the length of the original history, the size of the active data domain, the queries, etc. Chomicki [Chomicki, 1995] and Toman [Toman, 2001; Toman, 2003b] show that for the past fragment of FOTL and the 2-FOL queries, respectively, the size of the residual data can be made independent of the length of the history, while preserving answers to a fixed set of queries. On the other hand Toman [Toman, 2003b] shows that such techniques cannot exist, e.g., for the future fragment of the fixpoint TL and for various duplicate-preserving temporal query languages.

14.9 Complex Structure of Time

So far we have only considered the simplest temporal domains possible: linearly ordered sets of time instants. In this section we consider relaxing this restriction.

14.9.1 Complex Temporal Domains

Often, a temporal domain has also a distinguished element 0 (the beginning of time). The standard temporal domains are: natural numbers $\mathbb{N} = (N, 0, <)$, integers $\mathbb{Z} = (Z, 0, <)$, rationals $\mathbb{Q} = (Q, 0, <)$, and reals $\mathbb{R} = (R, 0, <)$. However, additional structure can be added to the temporal domain; among the more common extensions considered are the

- Durations and Temporal Distances, and
- Periodic Sets.

The first extension can be achieved by introducing a fragment of linear arithmetic into the signature of the temporal domain. Similarly, the later extension adds the *modulo* k predicates to the signature.

14.9.2 Impact on Integrity Constraints and Database Design

The additional structure of the temporal domain yields new classes of integrity constraints available to users. Indeed, the linear order of time has already enabled the use of *order dependencies* (see Section 14.4.2). Following that approach, the new interpreted predicates in the signature of the complex temporal domain lead to more complex constraint dependencies.

The additional structure is also essential for specifying *calendars* and *time granularities* [Bettini *et al.*, 2000], for example an *hour* can be defined as

$$hour(t, t') = t \equiv_{60} 0 \wedge t \leq t' < t + 60,$$

where $hour(t, t')$ holds whenever t is the first minute of the hour (which is used to identify hours) and t' is a time instant within the hour t. This also leads to the definition of functional dependencies that take granularity of time into account. Such dependencies constrain attribute values (Y) to depend on another values (X) *within a particular time granule*, e.g., an hour (denoted $R : X \rightarrow_{hour} Y$) and can be captured by a formula in the extended signature as follows:

$$\forall \overline{x}, \overline{y_1}, \overline{y_2}, t_1, t_2. \exists t. R(\overline{x}, \overline{y_1}, t_1) \wedge hour(t, t_1) \wedge R(\overline{x}, \overline{y_1}, t_2) \wedge hour(t, t_2) \rightarrow (\overline{y_1} = \overline{y_2})$$

Such dependencies, in turn, lead to the definition of *temporal normal forms*, e.g., TBCNF, and the development of decision procedures for logical implication [Wang *et al.*, 1997; Wijsen, 1999].

14.9.3 Impact on Query Languages

The impact of such extensions on the abstract query languages is minimal: the new predicate symbols in the signature of the temporal domain are used in exactly the same way as the linear order symbol $<$ has been used so far. This, in the case of temporal logics, leads to the ability to define additional temporal connectives. For example, in temporal domains with constants it is natural to consider bounded versions of such connectives, e.g., $\Box_{[k_1,k_2]}A$, meaning that A is true in the future between time k_1 and time k_2, [Alur and Henzinger, 1991; Koymans, 1989]. Bounded temporal connectives can be defined like the unbounded ones using first-order formulas (Definition 14.5.1). In fact, for discrete time they can even be directly simulated using the unbounded connectives together with $\bullet$ and $\circ$. However, bounded connectives are quite useful and have been applied to the specification of real-time integrity constraints [Chomicki, 1995], and real-time logic programs [Brzoska, 1993; Brzoska, 1995]. Their advantage is that they are also meaningful in a slightly different semantic model of histories, in which the value of the clock in a state does not have to coincide with the index of the state in a history.

14.9.4 Impact on Concrete Temporal Databases

In order to introduce the additional structure of the temporal domain into the *concrete* temporal query languages, we need to consider how the added predicates affect the concrete temporal databases first. A careful analysis of Definition 14.6.1 reveals that the intervals are essentially quantifier-free formulas in the language of linear order with exactly one free variable. This idea can be generalized to more general structures [Kanellakis *et al.*, 1995]: Let (T, σ) be a point-based temporal domain with the signature σ. Then we can define the set of formulas $C_\sigma = \{\phi(t) : \phi \in L_\sigma \wedge FV(\phi) = \{t\}\}$ where L_σ is the set of finite conjunctions of atomic formulas in the language of σ. This set can serve as the basis of the temporal domain for the class of concrete temporal databases, similar to intervals in Definition 14.6.1. An example of an alternative encoding is the use of *periodic constraints* [Kabanza *et al.*, 1995; Toman and Chomicki, 1998], or *linear arithmetic constraints* [Kanellakis *et al.*, 1995]. Concrete queries over such complex encodings are increasingly hard to write (cf. the problems we encountered in the case of linear order only). Thus the need for using abstract query languages in this setting is even more crucial.

14.10 Beyond First-order Logic

We survey here a number of temporal query languages whose expressive power goes beyond that of first-order logic. Most of these languages have only recently been proposed and thus their relative expressive power is not completely known and implementation techniques (in particular compilation to concrete query languages) have yet to be developed. In all likelihood such an implementation will require the development of more powerful concrete query languages, as currently available languages like TQuel or TSQL2 are not sufficiently expressive to serve as targets of the compilation.

14.10.1 Second-order Temporal Connectives

Definition 14.5.1 of temporal connectives can be extended with *monadic* second-order quantification over the temporal domain (quantification over subsets of the domain). This gives extra expressive power. For example, the modality "any time at an even distance from now" can be defined as

$$\equiv_2^0 X_1 \triangleq \exists t_1.X_1 \wedge \exists S.t_0 \in S \wedge t_1 \in S \wedge closed(S)$$
$$\wedge \forall S'.(t_0 \in S' \wedge closed(S') \Rightarrow S \subseteq S')$$

where $closed(S) \triangleq \forall t.(t \in S \Rightarrow t+2 \in S) \wedge (t+2 \in S \Rightarrow t \in S)$. If $\mathbb{N}$ is the temporal domain, the above extension is identical in expressive power to ETL, an extension of temporal logic where temporal connectives are defined using regular languages. ETL was first proposed in [Wolper, 1983], in the propositional case and generalized to the first-order case in [Abiteboul *et al.*, 1996]. The latter paper shows that the expressive power of ETL is incomparable to that of L^P. For other temporal domains, the expressive power of temporal logic with monadic second-order connectives has not yet been studied.

14.10.2 Fixpoints

A number of temporal fixpoint query languages have recently been proposed by [Abiteboul *et al.*, 1999]:

- TS-FIXPOINT: the extension of L^P with inflationary fixpoints,
- T-FIXPOINT: the extension of temporal logic with inflationary fixpoints and some additional constructs, such as moves back and forth in time, and local and non-inflationary variables (for details, see [Abiteboul *et al.*, 1999]),

Corresponding non-inflationary versions of those languages have also been proposed. It was shown in [Abiteboul *et al.*, 1999], that TS-FIXPOINT is at least as expressive as T-FIXPOINT and that the relationship in the other direction depends on unresolved questions in complexity theory. On the other hand, T-FIXPOINT is more expressive than L^P. These languages appear to be mainly of theoretical interest. Fixpoint temporal logic μTL [Vardi, 1988], has been extensively used in program verification, although only in the propositional case.

14.11 Beyond the Closed World Assumption

So far we only considered semantics for temporal queries based on the *closed world assumption* (CWA). Under this assumption, temporal databases hold complete information about truth. An alternative that is more commonly considered by AI approaches is to treat the relational structures representing temporal databases as incomplete specifications and use the *open world assumption* (OWA) to answer queries. However, even for closed formulas in any of the abstract query languages we have considered so far, query processing essentially reduces to the satisfiability problem for formulas in these languages which, in all the cases, is highly undecidable.

14.11.1 Infinite Database Histories and Potential Answers

Even restricting the scope of the OWA to *append-only* temporal databases does not alleviate the decidability problems. Consider finite histories introduced in Definition 14.3.3 to be *finite prefixes* of infinite (or complete) histories. Queries, then, are evaluated with respect to the infinite histories (using the same semantic definitions as in Section 14.5, the only difference is in allowing an infinite temporal domain for the history). However, as only a finite portion (a prefix) of the history is available at a particular (finite) point in time, we need to define answers to queries with respect to *possible completions* of the prefix to a complete history.

Definition 14.11.1. *Let H be a finite history, Q a query (in an appropriate query language), and θ a substitution. We say that*

- *θ is a potential answer for Q with respect to H if there is an infinite completion H' of H such that $H', \theta \models Q$.*
- *θ is a certain answer for Q with respect to H if for all infinite completions H' of H we have $H', \theta \models Q$.*

The notion of *potential answer* is a direct generalization of the notion of *potential constraint satisfaction* [Chomicki, 1995].

Unfortunately, the above definition leads to *undecidable satisfiability problems* even for closed formulas in the temporal query languages introduced in Section 14.5. Indeed, potential/certain satisfaction is closer to the general satisfiability/validity problems that to satisfaction in a fixed model. Therefore potential/certain satisfaction is not useful as a basis for query evaluation. The negative results are as follows:

Proposition 14.11.1 ([Gabbay *et al.*, 1994a]). *The satisfaction problem for two dimensional propositional temporal logic over the natural numbers-based time domain is not decidable.*

This proposition rules out the temporal relational calculus. For weaker query languages based on single-dimensional temporal logic, or its Past and Future fragments, the results are as follows:

Proposition 14.11.2 ([Chomicki, 1995]). *For past formulas potential constraint satisfaction is undecidable.*

Proposition 14.11.3 ([Chomicki and Niwinski, 1995]). *For future temporal logic formulas (with a single quantifier in the scope of temporal connectives), potential constraint satisfaction is undecidable.*

14.11.2 Decidable Fragments

To regain ability to effectively evaluate queries under the OWA, the only option is to restrict the query languages themselves. Decidable fragments of first-order logic (i.e., languages in which the satisfiability problem is decidable) have been extensively studied. In the temporal setting, Hodkinson et. al. [Hodkinson *et al.*, 2000] have introduced the *monodic temporal extensions* of several decidable fragments of first-order logic. The *monodicity* restriction stipulates that temporal subformulas of formulas in L^{Ω}, i.e., subformulas rooted by a temporal connective, may contain at most one free variable over the data domain (in addition to the requirement that the first-order portion of the formula belongs to an appropriate decidable fragment). Their technique has been successfully applied to a variety of logics, e.g., to the $\mathcal{ALC}$ and $\mathcal{DLR}$ description logics [Artale and Franconi, 2001], to the guarded, packed, and two variable fragments [Hodkinson, 2002]. In addition, the complexity of the decision procedures for these fragments has been studied [Hodkinson *et al.*, 2003]. Decidability and complexity of fixpoint variants of these results have been studied by Franconi and Toman [Franconi and Toman, 2003].

14.11.3 Temporal Logic Programming

Another way to escape the limitations of temporal logic is to keep its syntax but use different semantics for its Horn subset. This is analogous to the move from first-order logic to logic programming. Indeed, several proposals have been made by [Abadi and Manna, 1989; Baudinet, 1992; Baudinet, 1995; Brzoska, 1991; Brzoska, 1993; Brzoska, 1995], to extend the language of Horn clauses with temporal connectives in such a way that there is still some notion of least model and resolution-based operational semantics. Not surprisingly, those languages can usually be translated to the standard logic programming languages. For instance, the temporal connectives in Templog, [Abadi and Manna, 1989; Baudinet, 1992; Baudinet, 1995], can be simulated in Prolog using an additional predicate argument that can contain the successor function symbol [Baudinet *et al.*, 1993; Chomicki and Imieliński, 1988]. In this way, there is an exact correspondence between function-free Templog and $Datalog_{1S}$, an extension of Datalog with the successor function symbol in one predicate argument. More sophisticated temporal connectives involving numeric bounds on time, [Brzoska, 1991; Brzoska, 1993; Brzoska, 1995], can be simulated using arithmetic constraints [Jaffar and Lassez, 1987]. One can also study the extensions of the above Horn clause languages with stratified negation [Apt *et al.*, 1988]. Temporal logic programming languages are directly amenable to efficient implementation using the existing logic programming technology. Recently, $Datalog_{1S}$ with negation has been used to define the operational semantics of active database systems [Lausen *et al.*, 1998]. As far as the expressive power is concerned, it is not difficult to see that $Datalog_{1S}$ is subsumed by T-FIXPOINT and is incomparable to ETL. $Datalog_{1S}$ with stratified negation strictly subsumes ETL.

14.12 Concluding Remarks

The chapter has provided mathematical foundations of temporal data management in a uniform framework. This framework allows us to formally compare and evaluate various data models and query languages proposed for managing temporal data. We believe that further work in this area, in addition to solving the remaining open problems, should focus on bridging the gap between logic and practical database systems by developing the necessary software tools and interfaces.

14.12.1 Issues not Covered in the Chapter

The chapter, however, does not cover all issues related to management of temporal data. Below we briefly discuss the main topics not covered by the chapter.

Conceptual Modeling of Temporal Data

In Section 14.4 we discuss temporal integrity constraints and the connected issues relating to temporal normal forms. However, the chapter does not cover conceptual design for temporal databases, in particular, various *Temporal ER* models; for a survey see [Gregersen and

Jensen, 1999]. A formal treatment of these issues is presented elsewhere in this volume; see Chapter 12. Also, we do not discuss data models not derived from the relational model, such as the *object oriented* (OO) data model, and their temporal variants in this chapter.

Physical Design for Temporal Databases

Another set of issues not covered by this chapter are issues related to data structures and algorithms (query operators) supporting efficient processing of temporal queries and updates. However, we have shown that most of the approaches to querying temporal data essentially end up with first-order queries over concrete temporal databases—queries that depend heavily on the use of *ordering* of time instants. Note that, for example, the translation of temporal equijoin in an abstract query language yields an order-based join on the concrete encoding. A similar situation occurs naturally when using a variant of L^I in which the WHERE condition is explicit, e.g., in the form of an interval intersection operator, or when temporal queries are formulated directly in SQL [Snodgrass, 1999]. To facilitate these operations, special-purpose physical access methods (for a survey see [Salzberg and Tsotras, 1999]) and relational operators. For example, [Zhang *et al.*, 2002] consider join methods tailored to processing ordered data.

However, many of these techniques are often limited to single or two-dimensional temporal data model. This is not sufficient for processing of general temporal queries as a consequence of Theorems 14.5.3, 14.5.4, and 14.5.5, and more general techniques such as those proposed by Lorentzos et al. [Lorentzos *et al.*, 1995] are necessary.

Time Series and Temporal Data Mining

Considerable attention has been focused on discovering *interesting patterns* in time series—sequences of values generated over time, such as stock prices. Sequences and time series can be easily modeled as database histories. However, temporal query languages considered in this chapter are not adequate for discovering patterns, correlation, and other statistically interesting phenomena in such histories. Giannotti et al. [Giannotti *et al.*, 2003] consider *logic based* languages for specifying such queries, albeit in a non-temporal setting. A thorough discussion of issues related to temporal data mining and its applications to time series, however, is beyond the scope of this chapter. For a recent overview see [Last *et al.*, 2004].

14.12.2 Extensions, Related Topics, and Future Directions

In the remainder of this section we discuss several research directions that are closely related to temporal data management. In particular, we discuss how ideas and results developed for management of temporal data can be applied in those areas.

Spatio-Temporal Databases

A very natural extension of the research presented here is to combine time and space in *spatio-temporal* databases. It has already been mentioned here that spatial databases can be treated similarly to multidimensional temporal databases. Spatio-temporal databases also fit in this framework [Geerts *et al.*, 2001]. In principle, one could use both the snapshot and the timestamp models, as well as hybrid models (for example, snapshot databases where the snapshots are spatial timestamp databases). In a pure timestamp model (temporal and spatial timestamps), [Mokhtar *et al.*, 2002] proposed a linear-constraint-based query language for databases of moving objects and [Vazirgiannis and Wolfson, 2001] described an SQL extension with abstract data types that model the trajectories of objects moving on road networks. In an earlier seminal paper in this area [Sistla *et al.*, 1997] presented a a hybrid model query language based on a combination of temporal logic and spatial relationships.

In spatio-temporal databases, it is common to query not only the past states but also the (predicted) future states of the database. It seems fair to say that the design of spatio-temporal query languages is currently at an early stage of development, and the understanding of their formal properties has not yet reached the level of maturity of understanding of the properties of temporal query languages.

Streaming Data Management

The management of *streaming data* [Babcock *et al.*, 2002], that is, query processing over sequences of data items arriving over time (*data streams*), has been the focus of recent research. Several groups are pursuing implementation of streaming data management systems (DSMS) [The STREAM Group, 2003; Chen *et al.*, 2000; Madden *et al.*, 2002]. The issues faced in this area have much in common with those encountered in temporal databases, in particular when focusing on append-only database histories. For example, the issues related to limiting the space needed to store portions of the stream—called *synopses* in the streaming literature—which are necessary for *contiguous query* processing [Arasu *et al.*, 2002] are essentially the same as those addressed by data expiration techniques for database histories (see Section 14.8.2 or [Toman, 2003b]).

The correspondence between temporal data management and data management for streaming data allows transfer of technology and results: temporal query languages, as surveyed in this chapter, offer mature and well-understood theoretical and practical foundations for the development of query languages for data streams.

Time in Document Management and XML

In contrast to the management of temporal data based on the relational model, handling time in document management systems or in XML repositories is not concerned with representing time-related information *external to the database* but rather with the evolution of a document or of a set of documents over time [Chien *et al.*, 2001; Chien *et al.*, 2002]. Thus the approaches are closer to version control systems used, for example, for managing source code of software systems. The design of temporal extensions of XML itself and of the associated query languages is in its infancy and the understanding of the issues involved is limited.

Model Checking

Model checking techniques were developed to verify temporal properties of (executions of) finite-state concurrent systems. Similarly to temporal databases, the input to a model checker is a finite encoding of all possible executions of the system (often in a form of a finite state-transition system) and a query, usually formulated in a dialect of propositional temporal logic. The techniques for verifying whether the formula is satisfied by the system are commonly based on the correspondence between propositional temporal logics and automata theory. Clarke et al. [Clarke *et al.*, 1999] provide an in depth introduction to the field. The main difference between these two approaches is that temporal databases commonly assume a fixed structure of time while model checking approaches tend to represent time explicitly using a transition system. The full understanding of the correspondence between these two fields is, however, remains to be studied.

Handbook of Temporal Reasoning in Artificial Intelligence
Edited by M. Fisher, D. Gabbay and L. Vila

Chapter 15

Temporal Reasoning in Agent-Based Systems

Michael Fisher & Michael Wooldridge

Multi-agent systems are typically composed of multiple autonomous agents, cooperating to solve problems that are beyond the ability of any one individual agent. Agents are essentially dynamic — thus temporal aspects are at the heart of both individual agents and agent-based systems. In particular, temporal reasoning explicitly occurs in a number of areas including:

1. temporal foundations of *agent theory*;
2. temporal *specification* of agents;
3. *agent execution* using temporal techniques;
4. temporal *verification* of agents; and
5. use of temporal reasoning *within* agent computation.

The last of these utilises many techniques described elsewhere in this collection; thus we will not discuss this aspect here. Instead we will expand upon the use of temporal reasoning in the first four areas. While we cannot hope to address of *all* activity in the area, we aim to provide the reader with a sense of how (and why) temporal reasoning has been, and continues to be, important in agent-based systems. (This chapter represents a combination and extension of material from [Fisher and Wooldridge, 1997], [Wooldridge, 2000] and [Fisher, 2004].)

We begin, in Section 15.1, with some background on agents and multi-agent systems followed, in Section 15.2, by some logical preliminaries. In the subsequent four sections, we consider temporal aspects of agent theories (Section 15.3), agent specification (Section 15.4), agent execution (Section 15.5), and agent verification (Section 15.6). Finally, in Section 15.7, we present some concluding remarks.

15.1 Introduction

The technology of agent-based systems provides the software developer with a powerful abstraction tool for approaching a complex and important class of software application problems for which mainstream software engineering techniques provide few sophisticated solutions. In attempting to characterise the concept of 'agent' and 'multi-agent system', our starting point is the notion of a *reactive system*:

> *Reactive systems are systems that cannot adequately be described by the* relational *or* functional *view. The relational view regards programs as functions ... from an initial state to a terminal state. Typically, the main role of reactive systems is to maintain an interaction with their environment, and they must therefore be described (and specified) in terms of their on-going behaviour ... [E]very concurrent system ... must be studied by behavioural means. This is because each individual module in a concurrent system is a reactive subsystem, interacting with its own environment which consists of the other modules. [Pnueli, 1986]*

Within such reactive systems, we consider specific (often sophisticated) components, called *agents*. While the question "what is an agent?" has spawned considerable debate in the philosophical and agent research communities [Franklin and Graesser, 1996], we choose to follow the early definition provided by Wooldridge and Jennings [1995], namely that an agent is an autonomous component that is *pro-active* (i.e., can initiate computation on its own behalf), *reactive** (i.e., can respond, in a timely manner, to environmental stimuli), and *social* (i.e., can, and often must, communicate with other agents in order to achieve its goals).

Note that multi-agent systems are reactive, in precisely this sense:

- the applications for which an agent-based approach seems well suited, (e.g., distributed sensing [Durfee, 1988]), are typically non-terminating, and therefore cannot easily be described by the functional view;
- multi-agent systems are necessarily concurrent and, as Pnueli observes (above), each agent should therefore be considered as a reactive system.

Although the fact that multi-agent systems are reactive systems in Pnueli's sense has been recognised by agent theorists (notably Singh [1994], and Rao-Georgeff [1991]) it has, as yet, had relatively little impact on the practice of multi-agent systems. In particular, the various software tools and languages that have been proposed for multi-agent development have typically employed few features that make them especially well suited to the development of reactive systems (see [Wooldridge and Jennings, 1995] for a survey of such systems).

The use of software agents is expanding rapidly, primarily within applications related to the INTERNET. While such agents are often relatively simple, more complex, *rational*, agents have been shown to particularly useful in dealing flexibly and dynamically with complex and rapidly changing environments [Wooldridge, 2002]. Yoav Shoham, for example, envisaged systems composed of multiple interacting agents (a "societal model of computation"), where the agents were directly represented (and programmed) in terms of *mental states* such as beliefs, desires, and intentions [Shoham, 1993]. The idea is that instead of directly programming an agent in terms of low-level instructions relating to its precise course of action, we give it a *goal* (or *intention*) to achieve, and give it information about its environment in the form of *beliefs*. The agent then makes a *rational* decision about what action to perform, given its beliefs and goals/intentions: it behaves in the way any rational individual would, given these beliefs and goals. This vision of rational agents has become very popular and, increasingly, such agents are constructed using complex software architectures, and applied in areas such as real-time process control [Rao and Georgeff, 1995;

*Note the two meanings of *reactive* — from two different traditions.

Jennings and Wooldridge, 1998]. A particularly impressive example is the use of a rational agent architecture as part of the real-time fault monitoring and diagnosis carried out in the Deep Space One mission [Muscettola *et al.*, 1998].

With agents beginning to be used in such critical applications, it is clear that more precise, and logically well-founded, development techniques will be required for agent-based applications in the future. However, as Bradshaw et. al. [1999] note

> *a large and ugly chasm still separates the world of formal theory and infrastructure from the world of practical ... agent-system development.*

Hence there is a need not only for clear and appropriate formal foundations, but also for a link between such foundations and software development techniques. As we will see below, this is an area where temporal logics have made a significant impact, not only providing the foundation for theories of agency (including theories of *rational agency*), but then being used for both agent execution and agent verification.

15.2 Logical Preliminaries

In this section, we will examine the logical background for representations of activity in agents, namely *modal logics* and *temporal logic*. *Combinations* of the two will be discussed in Section 15.3.1.

15.2.1 Modal Logics

In classical logic, formulae are evaluated within a single fixed world. For example, a proposition such as "it is Monday" is either *true* or *false*. Propositions are then combined using constructs such as 'and', 'if...then', 'or', 'not', the constant symbols 'true' and 'false', and a set of symbols representing atomic propositions. In *modal* logics, however, formulae are evaluated with respect to a range of *possible* worlds.

Syntax and Semantics

As well as syntactic operations for manipulating the truth and falsehood of propositions within a world, operators for navigating between worlds are required. In standard modal logics there are two such operators:

> '$[\,]\varphi$' means that φ is true in *all* worlds accessible from the current world.
>
> '$\langle\,\rangle\varphi$' means that φ is true in *some* world accessible from the current world.

Thus, the truth of propositions is dependent upon the world in which they are evaluated. But what does 'accessibility' mean? Its meaning is dependent upon the context in which the logic is to be used. For example, all of the following interpretations for $[\,]/\langle\,\rangle$ are common.

- is necessary/is possible
- believes/doesn't believe opposite
- knows/doesn't know opposite
- always in future/sometime in future (see Section 15.2.2)

Semantics

Let us make the semantics of modal formulae more precise. Such formulae are interpreted within a model ($\mathcal{M}$) comprising

- a set of worlds, W,
- a binary relation, R, on worlds in W, and,
- a propositional interpretation π of type $\pi\colon W \times \text{PROP} \rightarrow \{T, F\}$

Thus, the key part of the semantics is

$$\begin{array}{lll} \mathcal{M}, w_1 \models p & \text{iff} & \pi(w_1, p) = T \\ \mathcal{M}, w_1 \models [\,]\varphi & \text{iff} & \text{for all } w_2\text{, if } R(w_1, w_2),\ \text{then } \mathcal{M}, w_2 \models \varphi \\ \mathcal{M}, w_1 \models \langle\,\rangle\varphi & \text{iff} & \text{there exists a } w_2\text{, such that } R(w_1, w_2) \text{ and } \mathcal{M}, w_2 \models \varphi \end{array}$$

In modal logics, the properties of the accessibility relation, R, play a crucial role. So far we have considered unrestricted relations. If we now restrict the relation, we can induce interesting (and useful) effects in the logic used. There are *many* relevant properties of R, for example

- **reflexivity**: if $w_1 \in W$ then $R(w_1, w_1)$
- **transitivity**: if $R(w_1, w_2)$ and $R(w_2, w_3)$ then $R(w_1, w_3)$

Axioms and Correspondences

The core axiom of *normal* modal logics is the 'K' axiom:

$$\text{K:}\quad \vdash [\,](\varphi \Rightarrow \psi) \Rightarrow ([\,]\varphi \Rightarrow [\,]\psi)$$

Other axioms that are commonly used in modal logics include

$$\begin{array}{ll} \text{D:} & \vdash [\,]\varphi \Rightarrow \langle\,\rangle\varphi \\ \text{T:} & \vdash [\,]\varphi \Rightarrow \varphi \\ \text{4:} & \vdash [\,]\varphi \Rightarrow [\,][\,]\varphi \\ \text{5:} & \vdash \langle\,\rangle\varphi \Rightarrow [\,]\langle\,\rangle\varphi \end{array}$$

Correspondence theory [Benthem, 1984] links particular axioms to properties of R, for example

- the 'T' axiom corresponds to the reflexivity of R,
- the '4' axiom corresponds to the transitivity of R.

The logic comprising axioms K, D, 4 and 5 (unsurprisingly called 'KD45') is commonly used where accessibility represents 'belief'.

K: $[\,](\varphi \Rightarrow \psi) \Rightarrow ([\,]\varphi \Rightarrow [\,]\psi)$
i.e., belief is closed under implication

D: $[\,]\varphi \Rightarrow \neg[\,]\neg\varphi$
i.e., belief is consistent

4: $[\,]\varphi \Rightarrow [\,][\,]\varphi$
i.e., the agent believes its beliefs (termed "positive introspection")

5: $\neg[\,]\neg\varphi \Rightarrow [\,]\neg[\,]\neg\varphi$
i.e., negative introspection

Adding the 'T' axiom to KD45 gives the logic S5, which is commonly used where the accessibility relation represents 'knowledge' [Fagin *et al.*, 1996].

T: $[\,]\varphi \Rightarrow \varphi$
i.e., what the agent knows is true

Multiple Modalities

This basic modal logic foundation can be extended to utilise multiple accessibility relations, and hence multiple modalities. The semantic structure used is now

- a set of worlds, W,
- a *set* of labelled binary relations, R_i, on worlds in W, and,
- π, again of type $\pi\colon W \times \text{PROP} \rightarrow \{T, F\}$

Thus, the syntax of modal logic can now be parameterised by the labels i, j, etc:

- '$[i]\varphi$' means that φ is true in *all* worlds that are accessible via R_i from the current world.
- '$\langle i\rangle\varphi$' means that φ is true in *some* world that is accessible via R_i from the current world.

Note that modalities such as '$[i]$' are often replaced by symbols providing more intuition about the intended interpretation of the modality. For example, if $[i]$ is a modality of the KD45 type, it is often represented by B_i, denoting belief. Similarly, if $[i]$ is a modality of the S5 type, it is often represented by K_i, denoting knowledge.

Example 1 — agent i believes that agent j believes φ: $B_i B_j \varphi$

Example 2 — agent i believes that agent j knows φ: $B_i K_j \varphi$

We will generally use the $[]/\langle\rangle$ versions, but will utilise B_i, K_j, etc, where appropriate.

Thus far, we have considered only *static* aspects of systems. Let us now see how the basic modal structures can be extended with temporal modalities, in order to capture the *dynamics* of a system.

15.2.2 Propositional Linear Temporal Logic

The propositional temporal logic we use for describing agent behaviour (called PML) is fairly standard; for a fuller account of the properties and applications of such temporal logics see, for example, other chapters in this collection or [Emerson, 1990]. PML is based on a model of time that is *linear* (i.e., each moment in time has a unique successor), *bounded in the past* (i.e., there was a moment that was the 'beginning of time'), and *infinite in the future* (i.e., there are an infinite number of moments in the future).

Syntax

The language of PML contains the following symbols:

1. a countable set, Prop, of *proposition symbols*;
2. the symbol **true**;
3. the *unary propositional connective* '$\neg$' and *binary propositional connective* '$\vee$';
4. the *unary temporal connectives* '$\bullet$' and '$\bigcirc$';
5. the *binary temporal connectives* '$\mathcal{U}$' and '$\mathcal{S}$';
6. the punctuation symbols ')' and '('.

All the remaining propositional and temporal connectives are introduced as abbreviations (see below). The set of well-formed formulae of PML is defined as follows.

Definition 15.2.1. *Well-formed formulae of* PML, WFF_p, *are defined by the following rules.*

1. *All proposition symbols, together with* **true**, *are in* WFF_p;
2. *If* ϕ *is in* WFF_p *then so are* $\neg\phi$, $\bigcirc\phi$ *and* $\bullet\phi$;
3. *If* ϕ *and* ψ *are in* WFF_p *then so are* $\phi \vee \psi$, $\phi\mathcal{U}\psi$, *and* $\phi\mathcal{S}\psi$;
4. *If* ϕ *is in* WFF_p, *then so is* (ϕ).

Semantics

The meaning of the temporal connectives is quite straightforward, with formulae being interpreted at a particular moment in time. If ϕ and ψ are well-formed formulae of PML, then $\bigcirc\phi$ is satisfied at the current moment in time if ϕ is satisfied at the next moment in time, while $\phi\mathcal{U}\psi$ is satisfied now if ψ is satisfied at some future moment, and ϕ is satisfied until then. The past-time connectives are similar: $\bullet\phi$ is satisfied at the current moment in time if either there was no previous moment in time or, if there was then ϕ was satisfied at that moment; $\phi\mathcal{S}\psi$ is satsfied at the current moment in time if ψ was satisfied at some previous moment in time, and ϕ has been satisfied at every moment since then.

More formally, we define a model, $\mathcal{M}$, for PML as a structure $\langle\sigma, \pi_p\rangle$ where

- σ is the ordered set of states $s_0, s_1, s_2, \ldots$ representing 'moments' in time, and
- $\pi_p : \mathbb{N} \times \text{Prop} \rightarrow \{T, F\}$ is a function assigning T or F to each atomic proposition at each moment in time.

$$
\begin{array}{llll}
\langle \mathcal{M}, u \rangle & \models & \mathbf{true} & \\
\langle \mathcal{M}, u \rangle & \models & p & \text{iff} \quad \pi_p(u, p) = T \\
\langle \mathcal{M}, u \rangle & \models & \neg\phi & \text{iff} \quad \langle \mathcal{M}, u \rangle \not\models \phi \\
\langle \mathcal{M}, u \rangle & \models & \phi \vee \psi & \text{iff} \quad \langle \mathcal{M}, u \rangle \models \phi \text{ or } \langle \mathcal{M}, u \rangle \models \psi \\
\langle \mathcal{M}, u \rangle & \models & \bigcirc\phi & \text{iff} \quad \langle \mathcal{M}, u+1 \rangle \models \phi \\
\langle \mathcal{M}, u \rangle & \models & \bullet\phi & \text{iff} \quad \text{if } u > 0 \text{ then } \langle \mathcal{M}, u-1 \rangle \models \phi \\
\langle \mathcal{M}, u \rangle & \models & \phi\,\mathcal{U}\,\psi & \text{iff} \quad \exists v \in \mathbb{N} \cdot (u \leq v) \text{ and } \langle \mathcal{M}, v \rangle \models \psi \\
& & & \qquad \text{and } \forall w \in \{u, \ldots, v-1\} \cdot \langle \mathcal{M}, w \rangle \models \phi \\
\langle \mathcal{M}, u \rangle & \models & \phi\,\mathcal{S}\,\psi & \text{iff} \quad \exists v \in \mathbb{N} \cdot (v < u) \text{ and } \langle \mathcal{M}, v \rangle \models \psi \\
& & & \qquad \text{and } \forall w \in \{v+1, \ldots, u-1\} \cdot \langle \mathcal{M}, w \rangle \models \phi
\end{array}
$$

Figure 15.1: Semantics of PML

As usual, we use the satisfaction relation '$\models$' to give the truth value of a formula in a model $\mathcal{M}$, at a particular moment in time u. This relation is inductively defined for well-formed formulae of PML in Fig. 15.1. Note that these rules only define the semantics of the basic propositional and temporal connectives; the remainder are introduced as abbreviations (we omit the propositional connectives, as these are standard):

$$
\begin{array}{rcl}
\mathbf{start} & \stackrel{\text{def}}{=} & \bullet\mathbf{false} \\
\Diamond\phi & \stackrel{\text{def}}{=} & \mathbf{true}\,\mathcal{U}\,\phi \\
\Box\phi & \stackrel{\text{def}}{=} & \neg\Diamond\neg\phi \\
\phi\,\mathcal{W}\,\psi & \stackrel{\text{def}}{=} & \Box\phi \vee \phi\,\mathcal{U}\,\psi \\
\blacklozenge\,\phi & \stackrel{\text{def}}{=} & \mathbf{true}\,\mathcal{S}\,\phi \\
\blacksquare\phi & \stackrel{\text{def}}{=} & \neg\blacklozenge\neg\phi \\
\phi\,\mathcal{Z}\,\psi & \stackrel{\text{def}}{=} & \blacksquare\phi \vee \phi\,\mathcal{S}\,\psi
\end{array}
$$

Note that the '**start**' operator is particularly useful in that it can only ever be satisfied at the first moment in time. We will see below that this plays an important role in the definition of our normal form for PML [Fisher, 1997a].

Example Formulae

Before proceeding, we present some simple examples of PML formulae. (Note that we use ground predicates as synonyms for propositions.) First, the following formula expresses the fact that, "while METATEM is not currently famous, it will be at some time in the future":

$$\neg \mathit{famous}(\text{METATEM}) \wedge \Diamond \mathit{famous}(\text{METATEM}).$$

The second example expresses the fact that 'sometime in the past, PROLOG was famous':

$$\blacklozenge\, \mathit{famous}(\text{PROLOG}).$$

We might want to state that "if PROLOG is famous then, at some time in the future, it will cease to be famous" (i.e., that fame is not permanent):

$$famous(\text{PROLOG}) \Rightarrow \Diamond\Box\neg famous(\text{PROLOG}).$$

The final example expresses a statement that frequently occurs in human negotiation, namely "we are not friends until you apologise":

$$(\neg friends(me, you))\,\mathcal{U}\,apologise(you).$$

An advantage of using temporal logic for specifying the behaviour of an individual agent is that it provides the core elements for representing dynamic behaviour, in particular:

- a description of behaviour at the *current* moment;
- a description of transitions that might occur between current and *next* moments;
- a description of situations that *will* occur at some (unspecified) moment in the future.

While we use arbitrary PML formulae to specify agent behaviour, it is often useful to translate such formulae into a normal form. The normal form we use is called *Separated Normal Form* (SNF) as it separates past-time from present and future-time formulae. It has been used to provide the basis for clausal proof methods [Fisher, 1991; Fisher *et al.*, 2001] and execution methods [Barringer *et al.*, 1996; Fisher and Ghidini, 1999], and can be defined as follows [Fisher, 1997a]. Formulae in SNF are

$$\Box \bigwedge_{i=1}^{n} (P_i \Rightarrow F_i)$$

where each '$P_i \Rightarrow F_i$' (called a *rule*) is constructed as follows.

$$\textbf{start} \Rightarrow \bigvee_{b=1}^{r} l_b \qquad \text{(an } \textit{initial} \text{ rule)}$$

$$\bigwedge_{a=1}^{g} k_a \Rightarrow \bigcirc\left[\bigvee_{b=1}^{r} l_b\right] \qquad \text{(a } \textit{step} \text{ rule)}$$

$$\bigwedge_{a=1}^{g} k_a \Rightarrow \Diamond l \qquad \text{(a } \textit{sometime} \text{ rule)}$$

Note, here, that each k_a, l_b, or l is a literal, and that the majority of operators from PML have been "translated away".

This normal form provides a simple and intuitive description of what is true at the beginning of execution (via *initial* rules), what must be true during any execution step (via *step* rules), and what constraints exist on future execution states (via *sometime* rules). To illustrate this, we below provide a few simple examples of properties that might be represented directly as SNF rules.

- Specifying initial conditions: $\textbf{start} \Rightarrow sad$

- Defining transitions between states: $(sad \wedge \neg rich) \Rightarrow \bigcirc sad$
- Introducing new eventualities (goals):
$$\begin{array}{rcl} (\neg resigned \wedge sad) & \Rightarrow & \Diamond famous \\ sad & \Rightarrow & \Diamond happy \end{array}$$
- Introducing permanent properties: $lottery\text{-}win \Rightarrow \bigcirc\Box rich$ which, in SNF, becomes
$$\begin{array}{rcl} lottery\text{-}win & \Rightarrow & \bigcirc rich \\ lottery\text{-}win & \Rightarrow & \bigcirc x \\ x & \Rightarrow & \bigcirc rich \\ x & \Rightarrow & \bigcirc x \end{array}$$
where x is a new proposition symbol.

15.3 Temporal Aspects of Agent Theories

Agent-based systems are a growing area in both industry and academia [Wooldridge and Jennings, 1995]. In particular, the characterisation of complex distributed components as *intelligent* or *rational* agents allows the system designer to analyse applications at a much higher level of abstraction. In order to reason about such agents, a number of theories of rational agency have been developed, such as the BDI [Rao and Georgeff, 1991] and KARO [van Linder *et al.*, 1996] frameworks. These frameworks are usually represented as combined temporal and modal logics, allowing the representation of agent's behaviour directly in terms of mental attitudes [Bratman, 1990]. In addition to their use in agent theories, where the basic representation of agency and rationality is explored, these logics form the basis for agent-based formal methods. The leading agent theories and formal methods generally share similar logical properties. In particular, the logics used have:

- an *informational* component, such as being able to represent an agent's beliefs or knowledge,
- a *dynamic* component, allowing the representation of dynamic activity, and,
- a *motivational* component, often representing the agents desires, intentions or goals.

These aspects are typically represented as follows:

Information — modal logic of belief (KD45) or knowledge (S5);

Dynamism — temporal or dynamic logic;

Motivation — modal logic of intention (KD) or desire (KD).

Thus, the predominant approaches use relevant combinations. For example: Moore [1990] combines propositional dynamic logic and a modal logic of knowledge (S5); the BDI framework [Rao and Georgeff, 1991; Rao and Georgeff, 1995] uses linear or branching temporal logic, together with modal logics of belief (KD45), desire (KD), and intention (KD); Halpern et al. [Fagin *et al.*, 1996] use linear and branching-time temporal logics combined with a multi-modal (S5) logic of knowledge; and the KARO framework [van Linder *et al.*, 1996; Meyer *et al.*, 1999] uses propositional dynamic logic, together with modal logics of belief (KD45) and wishes (KD). One of the most influential approaches to developing a theory of rational agency was that of Cohen-Levesque [Cohen and Levesque, 1990]. Their formal framework combined KD45 belief modalities and a K desire modality in a linear temporal logic framework (rather similar to PML as described above). They also incorporated a framework for representing action, by using action expressions interpreted over linear temporal histories. (Possible worlds in the Cohen-Levesque framework were in fact linear temporal histories.) This foundational framework was used to define a logic of intention (in the sense of "intending to perform some action"), and was extremely influential in the multi-agent systems community, as a formal framework within which to capture theories of agency. While it may seem peculiar to characterise software components in terms of mental notions such as belief and desire, this follows a well known approach termed the *intentional stance* [Bratman, 1990]. Attributing such mental notions to agents provides us with a convenient and familiar way of describing, explaining, and predicting the behaviour of these systems. Thus, the intentional stance simply represents an *abstraction* mechanism for representing agent behaviour.

Next we will examine the formal logical background for such representations, namely combinations of multi-modal and temporal logics.

15.3.1 Modal and Temporal Combinations

Now that we have looked at (multi-) modal and temporal logics separately, the key element in logical agent theories is the combination of these logics. For example, a multi-modal logic, on its own, can be used to describe the '*mental state*' of the agent, for example using knowledge and belief. However, we usually wish to characterise the evolution and change of this state over time – this is where temporal logic comes in. Hence, we typically use combinations of modal and temporal logics [Bennett *et al.*, 2002b].

We first consider two examples showing how such combinations can be generally useful. Note that, since we are dealing with both knowledge and belief, we revert to the B_i and K_j notation rather than the $\langle k \rangle$ and $[l]$ notation in order to make the distinction explicit.

Security in Multi-Agent Systems Temporal logics of knowledge can be used to represent the information that each distributed component is aware of, for example

$$[K_{me}K_{you}key(me) \wedge K_{me}send(me, you, msg)] \Rightarrow \Diamond K_{you}contents(msg)$$

i.e.,

> *"if I know that you know my public key, and I know that I have sent you a message, then at some moment in the future you will know the contents of that message"*

Autonomous Agent Analysis

$$\left[\begin{array}{l} K_{pilot}\exists engine.\ working(engine) \wedge \\ B_{pilot}broken(left\_engine) \end{array} \right] \Rightarrow \bigcirc shutdown(left\_engine)$$

i.e.,

> *"if the pilot knows that there is at least one engine working, and believes that the left engine is broken, then the pilot will shut down the left engine next"*

As explained above, the behaviour of an agent may be specified in terms of its beliefs, desires and intentions. Thus, we are able to use combinations of modal and temporal logics to specify a range of rational agent descriptions.

BDI Example

$$B_{me} \Diamond D_{you} attack(you, me) \;\Rightarrow\; I_{me} \bigcirc attack(me, you)$$

i.e.,

> *"if I believe that you desire to attack me, then I intend to attack you at the next moment in time"*

Alternatively, using just belief and time:

$$B_{me} \Diamond B_{you} attack(you, me) \;\Rightarrow\; B_{me} \bigcirc attack(me, you)$$

As we can see, the combination of (multi-) modal and temporal logics is very powerful. The *complexity* of such logics is determined in large part by the extent of interactions between the temporal and modal components of the logic. As a general rule, the fewer interactions, the simpler the resulting system from a technical and computational standpoint. However, once we model multi-agent scenarios, we tend to introduce many axioms incorporating interactions, for example in a temporal logic of knowledge [Fagin *et al.*, 1996]

$$\begin{array}{rl} \text{(synchrony+) perfect recall:} & K_i \bigcirc \varphi \;\Rightarrow\; \bigcirc K_i \varphi \\ \text{(synchrony+) no learning:} & \bigcirc K_i \varphi \;\Rightarrow\; K_i \bigcirc \varphi \end{array}$$

Unfortunately, many of these combinations, incorporating either temporal or dynamic logic, become too complex (highly undecidable) to use in practical situations [Halpern and Moses, 1992]. Thus, much current research activity centres around developing simpler combinations of logics that can express many of the properties that may be expressed in more complex combinations, yet are simpler to mechanise. For example, some of our work in this area has involved developing a simpler logical basis for BDI-like agents [Fisher, 1997b; Fisher and Ghidini, 2002]; see Section 15.5.4.

15.4 Temporal Agent Specification

In this section, we consider some example multi-agent systems, and present descriptions of the behaviour of agents in terms of temporal formulae. (In Section 15.6, we consider the formal verification of certain properties for these example systems.) For simplicity, we provide these specifications in the notation of Concurrent METATEM, which is basically the SNF described earlier, together with some operational information required for the execution described in Section 15.5.

15.4.1 Aside: Concurrent METATEM Notation

The basic computational components of Concurrent METATEM are autonomous entities, executing independently, and having complete control over their own internal behaviour. There are two elements to each such agent: its *interface definition* and its *internal definition*.

The definition of which messages an agent recognises, together with a definition of the messages that an agent may itself produce, is provided by the *interface definition*. The interface definition for an agent, for example 'car', may be defined in the following way

$$car(go, stop, turn)[fuel, overheat]:$$

Here, $\{go,\ stop,\ turn\}$ is the set of messages the agent recognises (the 'in' list), while the agent itself is able to produce the messages $\{fuel,\ overheat\}$, (i.e., the 'out' list). Both sets correspond to predicates that occur within the *internal definition* of the agent, which is provided as a set of SNF rules describing the behaviour of the agent. (We will consider the execution mechanism in more detail in Section 15.5.)

We now consider three example agent systems (derived from those in [Fisher and Wooldridge, 1997]) and outline their temporal specifications.

15.4.2 Specification: Resource Controller

The first example system we consider is defined in Figure 15.2, and represents a very simple 'resource controller' system. This system consists of three agents: 'rp', which is a 'resource producer' that guarantees to (eventually) give a resource to any agent that asks for it, but will only allocate one resource at a time; '$rc1$', which continually asks for a resource for itself; and '$rc2$', which asks for a resource if it sees $rc1$ asking for a resource, but has not asked for one itself in the previous cycle. (Note that we will consider the properties that we might wish to verify of this system in Section 15.6.2.)

$rp(ask1, ask2)[give1, give2]:$
1. $ask1 \Rightarrow \Diamond give1;$
2. $ask2 \Rightarrow \Diamond give2;$
3. $\mathbf{true} \Rightarrow \bigcirc(\neg give1 \lor \neg give2);$
4. $\mathbf{start} \Rightarrow \neg give1;$
5. $\mathbf{start} \Rightarrow \neg give2.$

$rc1(give1)[ask1]:$
1. $\mathbf{start} \Rightarrow ask1;$
2. $ask1 \Rightarrow \bigcirc ask1.$

$rc2(ask1, give2)[ask2]:$
1. $(ask1\ \&\ \neg ask2) \Rightarrow \bigcirc ask2.$

Figure 15.2: A Simple Resource Controller System

15.4.3 Specification: An Abstract Distributed Problem Solving System

A common form of multi-agent system is based upon the idea of cooperative distributed problem solving [Smith, 1980]. Here, we consider a simple abstract distributed problem solving system, in which a single agent, called $executive$, broadcasts a problem to a group of problem solvers. Some of these problem solvers can solve the problem completely, and some will reply with a solution. We define such a system in Figure 15.3. Here, $solvera$

$$
\begin{array}{|l|}
\hline
executive(solution1)[problem1, solved1]: \\
\quad 1. \quad \mathbf{start} \Rightarrow \Diamond problem1; \\
\quad 2. \quad solution1 \Rightarrow \bigcirc solved1. \\
\hline
\end{array}
$$

$$
\begin{array}{|l|}
\hline
solvera(problem2)[solution2]: \\
\quad 1. \quad problem2 \Rightarrow \bigcirc solution2. \\
\hline
\end{array}
$$

$$
\begin{array}{|l|}
\hline
solverb(problem1)[solution2]: \\
\quad 1. \quad problem1 \Rightarrow \Diamond solution1. \\
\hline
\end{array}
$$

$$
\begin{array}{|l|}
\hline
solverc(problem1)[solution1]: \\
\quad 1. \quad problem1 \Rightarrow \Diamond solution1. \\
\hline
\end{array}
$$

Figure 15.3: A Distributed Problem Solving System

can solve a different problem from the one $executive$ poses, while $solverb$ can solve the desired problem, but does not announce this fact (as $solution1$ is not in the 'out' list for $solverb$); $solverc$ can solve the problem posed by $executive$, and will *eventually* reply with the solution. (Again, we will verify some properties of the above system in Section 15.6.2.)

15.4.4 Specification: The Contract Net

Finally, we look at a more complex multi-agent system in more detail. This system contains a group of agents cooperating via a contract net-like protocol. Throughout, we assume familiarity with the contract net protocol [Smith, 1980] and, to simplify the description, we allow temporal rules to have constraints about the present in *both* the antecedent and consequent. We also utilise first-order notation where appropriate.

In the Contract Net protocol, a *manager* agent announces a particular task (or set of tasks) that it requires to be completed. The other agents in the system each have a specific set of capabilities and can, based upon these, bid for the contract to undertake all, or part of, a particular task. We first describe the notions of *tasks* and *capabilities* that are used throughout this specification. These will be represented by *internal predicates*, i.e., the value of these predicates are local to the particular agent in which they occur.

Internal Predicates

An individual capability is simply represented as a constant. For example, if an agent is able to move, speak and jump, the capabilities of the agent would be represented by the

Predicate	Meaning
$announce(Task)$	announces that a particular task is available for bids
$bid(Task, Bidder)$	a bid for a particular task
$award(Task, Awardee)$	awards the contract for a particular task
$completed(Task, By, Result)$	signals the completion of a particular task

Table 15.1: Message Predicates

capabilities predicate within the agent's definition:

$$capabilities(Agent, [Move, Speak, Jump])$$

A task is represented simply as the function *task* applied to certain arguments:

$$task(Name, Description, Requirements, Originator)$$

where

- *Name* is the name of the task;
- *Description* is the general description of the task (we will not provide any further details regarding this);
- *Requirements* is the list of capabilities required of an agent for it to be able to carry out the task;
- *Originator* is the agent who announced the task.

In particular, we will define the predicates *competent*, *busy*, *bidded*, and *most-preferable* as follows. (We assume that each agent awarding contracts has an internal selection procedure which is characterised by the predicate *preferable*.)

$$\begin{array}{rcl} capabilities(A, Cap) \wedge (Cap \cap Req \neq \emptyset) & \Rightarrow & competent(A, task(T, D, Req, O)) \\ (\neg completed(T, \mathsf{self}, R))\, \mathcal{S}\, award(T, \mathsf{self}) & \Rightarrow & busy(\mathsf{self}) \\ (\neg award(T, A))\, \mathcal{S}\, announce(T) \wedge bid(T, X) & \Rightarrow & bidded(T, X) \\ \neg\exists Y \cdot preferable(Y, X) \wedge bidded(T, Y) & \Leftrightarrow & most\_preferable(T, X) \end{array}$$

Note that 'self' refers to the identity of the agent in which the predicates occur.

Messages

In addition to the above internal predicates, the system utilises a set of basic message predicates, which are summarised in Table 15.1.

In general, the interface to an individual agent within this system is defined as

$$agent(announce, bid, award, completed)[announce, bid, award, completed].$$

Thus, every agent is capable of being both a manager and a contractor. If we wish to introduce agent types for manager and contractor, then we might define their interfaces as follows:

$$manager(bid, completed)[announce, award]$$

$$contractor(announce, award)[bid, completed]$$

In the remainder of this section, we outline the formulae rules that can be used to describe the behaviour of a simple agent taking part in our system (adapted from [Fisher and Wooldridge, 1997]). The behaviours of the agent will be split into categories relating to *task announcement*, *bidding*, the *award* of contracts, and the *completion* of contracts.

Task Announcement

Initially, a prospective manager agent just announces its first task, using the following rule.

$$\textbf{start} \Rightarrow announce(task(task\_name, task\_desc, task\_req, \mathsf{self})) \qquad (A1)$$

If an agent has been contracted to carry out a task, yet is unable to complete it, then it must sub-contract part of the task. The rule used in this case utilises '*split*', a predicate that splits a task appropriately, given the agent's capabilities (i.e., a task is split into two tasks, the first of which the agent is able to complete, the second of which it must attempt to subcontract).

$$\left(\begin{array}{c} award(task(N, D, Req, O), \mathsf{self}) \\ \wedge\ capabilities(\mathsf{self}, Cap) \\ \wedge\ (Req - Cap \neq \emptyset) \end{array}\right) \Rightarrow \bigcirc \left(\begin{array}{c} split(task(N, D, Req, O), T1, T2) \\ \wedge\ announce(T2) \\ \wedge\ \Diamond \exists R \cdot\ result(T1, R) \end{array}\right) \qquad (A2)$$

Bidding

The first rule in the bidding process states that an agent should only define a *possible* task as one that has been announced (and not yet awarded) and which the agent has the capabilities to undertake (at least partially).

$$((\neg award(T, A))\, \mathcal{S}\, announce(T) \wedge competent(A, T)) \quad \Leftrightarrow \quad possible(A, T) \qquad (B1)$$

Given this rule, another basic property of bidding agents is that they should not bid for tasks that are not possible.

$$\neg possible(\mathsf{self}, T) \quad \Rightarrow \quad \neg bid(T, \mathsf{self}) \qquad (B2)$$

We can then add a variety of rules depending upon the behaviour required for the agent. For example, the following rules can be used in order to ensure that each agent only bids for one task at a time.

$$possible(\mathsf{self}, T) \Rightarrow \exists Y \cdot\ bid(Y, \mathsf{self}) \qquad (B3)$$

$$(bid(X, \mathsf{self}) \wedge bid(Y, \mathsf{self})) \Rightarrow (X = Y) \qquad (B4)$$

The following rule is needed if we restrict the agent's behaviour so it cannot bid while it is actively undertaking a task.

$$busy(\mathsf{self}) \quad \Rightarrow \quad \neg bid(X, \mathsf{self}) \qquad (B5)$$

Finally, if we require that an agent is able to bid for every task, at any time, we might replace rules $(B3)$, $(B4)$, and $(B5)$ by the following rule.

$$possible(\mathsf{self}, T) \quad \Rightarrow \quad bid(T, \mathsf{self}) \qquad (B6)$$

Awarding Contracts

Given that a manager agent has announced a task then, after a certain time, it must decide which bidding agent to award the contract to. To achieve this, we may simply use the following rule.

$$(bidded(T, X) \wedge most\_preferable(T, Y)) \quad \Rightarrow \quad \bigcirc award(T, Y) \qquad (W1)$$

Thus, the choice amongst those agents that have made bids for the contract is made by consulting the manager's internal list of preferences.

Task Completion

There are two rules relating to the completion of a task, the first for tasks solely carried out within the agent, the second for tasks that were partially sub-contracted.

$$\left(\begin{array}{c} (\neg completed(T, \mathsf{self}, X))\, \mathcal{S}\, award(T, \mathsf{self}) \\ \wedge\ \bullet result(T, R) \end{array} \right) \Rightarrow completed(T, \mathsf{self}, R) \qquad (C1)$$

$$\left(\begin{array}{c} (\neg completed(T, \mathsf{self}, X))\, \mathcal{S}\, award(T, \mathsf{self}) \\ \wedge\ \blacklozenge\ split(T, T1, T2) \\ \wedge\ \blacklozenge\ result(T1, R1) \\ \wedge\ \blacklozenge\ completed(T2, By, R2) \end{array} \right) \Rightarrow completed(T, \mathsf{self}, R1 \cup R2) \qquad (C2)$$

These are a little complex and utilise the past-time temporal operators '$\bullet$' ("at the last moment in time"), '$\blacklozenge$' ("at some moment in the past") and '$\mathcal{S}$' ("since"). In the first case, once the agent has produced a result (and this task has not previously been completed), the completion of the task is announced, while in the second case completion is only announced once the agent has completed its portion of the task and the sub-contractor reports completion of the remainder. (Note that we simplify the composition of results just as their union.)

This, more complex specification indicates the type of multi-agent system that may be represented using a temporal notation. Again, we might wish to verify that certain properties hold of this specification — it is this issue that we consider in Section 15.6.2.

15.5 Executing Temporal Agent Specifications

One interesting idea that has been explored in the multi-agent systems arena is that of *directly executing* agent specifications, expressed in the kinds of languages we have discussed above. Of those languages with an explicitly temporal component, perhaps the best known is METATEM [Barringer *et al.*, 1995; Barringer *et al.*, 1996]. This provides a mechanism for directly executing the temporal logic given earlier (specifically in the form of SNF) in order to animate each agent's behaviour. In the following subsections we will provide an introduction to basic temporal execution, through METATEM and Concurrent METATEM (the multi-agent version [Fisher, 1993]), and outline how the execution of temporal formulae has been extended to the direct execution of combined modal and temporal formulae.

15.5.1 Overview of Concurrent METATEM

We have seen earlier that Concurrent METATEM has a syntax for representing agent interfaces and internal rules. We next give a brief overview of the basic approach to execution.

The Concurrent METATEM language represents the behaviour of an agent as a directly executable temporal formula. Temporal logic provides a declarative means of specifying agent behaviour, which can not only represent the dynamic aspects of an execution, but also contains a mechanism for representing and manipulating the goals of the system. The concurrent operational model of Concurrent METATEM is both general purpose and intuitively appealing, being similar to approaches used both in Distributed Operating Systems [Birman, 1991] and Distributed Artificial Intelligence [Maruichi *et al.*, 1991]. While the internal execution of each agent can be achieved in a variety of languages, these can be seen as implementations of the abstract specification of the agent provided by the temporal formula. However, since temporal logic represents a powerful, high-level notation, we choose to animate the agent, at least for prototyping purposes if not for full implementation, by directly executing the temporal formula [Fisher, 1996b]. The logic we execute is exactly that defined in Section 15.2.2.

15.5.2 Executing Agent Descriptions

Given that the internal behaviour of an agent is described by a set of rules, then we utilise the *imperative future* [Barringer *et al.*, 1996] approach in order to execute these rules. This applies rules of the above form at every moment in time, using information about the history of the agent in order to constrain its future execution. Thus, as the aim of execution is to produce a model for a formula, a *forward-chaining* process is employed. The underlying (sequential) METATEM language exactly follows this approach.

Execution of such a specification, φ, is taken to mean constructing a model, $\mathcal{M}$, for φ, i.e., constructing a model $\mathcal{M}$ such that $\mathcal{M} \models_{PML} \varphi$. In our case, the execution of an agent's specification is carried out by, at each moment in time, checking the antecedants of its rules and collecting together present and future-time constraints. A choice among these constraints is then made and execution continues to the next state. Thus, this approach utilises a form of forward chaining.

The operator used to represent basic temporal indeterminacy within the language is the *sometime* operator, '$\Diamond$'. When a formula such as $\Diamond\varphi$ is executed, the system must try to ensure that φ *eventually* becomes true. As such eventualities might not be able to be satisfied immediately, we must keep a record of the unsatisfied eventualities, attempting them again as execution proceeds [Fisher and Owens, 1992]. In METATEM, execution is allowed to backtrack if a contradiction is found. However, in Concurrent METATEM backtracking is not allowed past the output of a message to the agent's environment (see below). Thus, the agent has effectively *committed* its execution after a message is output.

Single Agent Example

As an example of a simple set of rules which might be part of an agent's description, consider the following. (Note that these rules are not meant to form a meaningful program – they are only given for illustrative purposes.)

$$
\begin{array}{l}
car(go, stop, turn)[fuel, overheat]: \\
\qquad\qquad\qquad\begin{array}{rcl}
\mathbf{start} & \Rightarrow & moving \\
go & \Rightarrow & \Diamond moving \\
(moving \wedge go) & \Rightarrow & \bigcirc(overheat \vee fuel)
\end{array}
\end{array}
$$

Looking at these program rules, we see that *moving* is false at the beginning of time and whenever *go* is true in the last moment in time (for example, if a *go* message has just been received), a commitment to eventually make *moving* true is given. Similarly, whenever both *go* and *moving* are true in the last moment in time, then either *overheat* or *fuel* will be made true. As with standard logic languages, the execution of disjunctions may involve a process of backtracking. Eventualities (such as $\Diamond moving$) can be seen as goals that the agent attempts to satisfy as soon as it can.

During execution of an individual agent, if a component predicate (i.e., a predicate in the 'out' list) is satisfied, this has the side-effect of *broadcasting* the value of that proposition to all other agents. If a particular message (in the 'in' list) is received, a corresponding *environment proposition* is made true in the agent's execution.

Although the use of only broadcast message-passing may seem restrictive, not only can standard point-to-point message-passing be simulated by adding an extra 'destination' argument to each message, but also the use of broadcast message-passing as the communication mechanism gives the language the ability to define more adaptable and flexible systems [Fisher, 1994; Borg *et al.*, 1983; Birman, 1991; Maruichi *et al.*, 1991]. The default behaviour for a message is that if it is broadcast, then it will *eventually* be received at all possible receivers. Also note that, by default, the order of messages is not preserved.

Finally, not only are agents autonomous, having control over which (and how many) messages to send and receive, but they can form *groups* within the agent space. Groups are dynamic, open and first-class, and this natural structuring mechanism and has a variety of diverse applications [Fisher and Kakoudakis, 1999; Fisher *et al.*, 2003].

15.5.3 Multi-Agent Example

In this section, we provide a simple example of a multi-agent system, represented in PML, that can be executed using Concurrent METATEM. This example considers competition between three agents (representing academics) to secure funding from a *funder* agent. In order to secure funding, the agents must send *apply* messages. These are processed by the *funder* and appropriate *grant* messages are then sent out.

$$
\begin{array}{rcl}
\multicolumn{3}{l}{\textit{funder(apply)[grant]:}} \\
\textit{apply(X)} & \Rightarrow & \Diamond \textit{grant(X)}; \\
\textit{grant(X)} \wedge \textit{grant(Y)} & \Rightarrow & X{=}Y. \\
\hline
\multicolumn{3}{l}{\textit{prof1(grant)[apply]:}} \\
\mathbf{start} & \Rightarrow & \textit{apply(prof1)}; \\
\textit{apply(prof1)} & \Rightarrow & \bigcirc \textit{apply(prof1)}. \\
\hline
\multicolumn{3}{l}{\textit{prof2(apply,grant)[apply]:}} \\
\textit{apply(prof1)} & \Rightarrow & \bigcirc \textit{apply(prof2)}. \\
\hline
\multicolumn{3}{l}{\textit{prof3(grant)[apply]:}} \\
\textit{grant(prof1)} & \Rightarrow & \bigcirc \textit{apply(prof3)}.
\end{array}
$$

Figure 15.4: Competing Academics Example

The behaviour of the agents involved is presented in Figure 15.4, and is described below. Note that we, for clarity, have used the first order (over a finite domain) version of the language.

- *prof1* wants to apply at every cycle in order to maximise the chances of achieving a grant. This is achieved because in the agent's first rule, **start** is satisfied at the beginning of time, and so an *apply* message is broadcast then, thus ensuring that *apply(prof1)* is satisfied in the next moment, thus firing rule 2, and so on.
- *prof2* needs to be spurred into applying by seeing that *prof1* has applied. Thus, the agent's one rule is triggered when an appropriate *apply* is seen.
- *prof3* only thinks about applying when it sees that *prof1* has achieved some funding. Again its single rule is activated once a *grant(prof1)* message has been received.
- Finally, the *funder* will accept *apply* messages and promises to grant to each applicant at some point in the future (first rule). However, *funder* will only *grant* to at most one applicant at a time (second rule).

Thus, such agent descriptions can be executed, as can those given in Section 15.4.

15.5.4 Extending with Belief

While we have described the execution of temporal specifications of agents, it is natural also to consider the execution of combined temporal and modal descriptions. In particular, we would like to execute agent specifications given in the above temporal logics of belief. This can be achieved, but can be quite complex, and so practical limits were put on the amount of reasoning about belief that could occur. This is not only intended to improve efficiency, but is also meant to characterise *resource-boubded agents*, and such a system, based on multi-context belief logics, was described in [Fisher and Ghidini, 1999].

This approach has, over recent years, been extended with other modalities, notably *ability*. Together with ability and belief, a simple (and weak) motivational attitude is often required. Thus, in [Fisher and Ghidini, 2002], the combination of belief and eventuality was characterised as such a motivation, and termed *confidence*. Here, $[i]\Diamond\varphi$ being true implies that agent i belives that eventually φ will become true, i.e. i is *confident* in φ. The key aspect here is that an agent may be confident in something, even if that agent does not know how to make it happen — the agent can be confident in other agents making it true. Such an attitude allows us to reason about team building activities [Fisher *et al.*, 2003] as well as individual agent behaviour.

Rather than give further details on this approach, we just note a key axiom of such a system comprising ability, belief and confidence, namely

$$[i]\Diamond\varphi \wedge A_i\varphi \Rightarrow \Diamond\varphi$$

meaning that, if an agent (i) is confident in φ occurring, and is able to achieve φ, then φ will really happen at some time in the future.

15.6 Temporal Agent Verification

Next, we consider the verification of agent specifications which, in addition to being useful for checking the properties of agents, is also required in order to support the types of proof obligations generated during agent refinement. The verification of the temporal properties of individual agents can be carried out in a number of ways and we will consider three of these, namely temporal proof, proof in a temporal logic of belief and model checking.

15.6.1 Agent Verification via Temporal Proof

Given temporal specifications of the behaviour of each agent, then we can (in some cases) put these together to provide a temporal formula characterising the whole system; this is exactly the approach used in [Fisher, 1996a]. However, once we consider asynchronously executing agents, the semantics is given as a formula in the Temporal Logic of the Reals (TLR) [Barringer *et al.*, 1986], which is a temporal logic based upon the Real, rather than Natural, numbers. The density of this Real Number model is useful in representing the asynchronous nature of each agent's execution. Fortunately, decision problems in this logic can be reduced back to a problem in our discrete, linear temporal logic [Kesten *et al.*, 1994].

Thus, in order to verify a property of our agent specification, we simply need a decision procedure for the discrete, linear, propositional temporal logic. In our case, we use clausal temporal resolution [Fisher, 1991; Fisher *et al.*, 2001]. Here, in order to prove the validity of a temporal formula, say φ, we negate the formula, giving $\neg\varphi$, translate it into a set of SNF rules, and attempt to derive a contradiction using specific resolution rules. Recall that SNF comprises three different types of rule: initial rules, step rules and sometime rules. The resolution method we have developed ensures that

1. *initial resolution* occurs between initial rules,

2. *step resolution* occurs between step rules, and,

3. *temporal resolution* occurs between one sometime rule and a *set* of step rules.

The three varieties of resolution operation that act upon SNF rules are simply

INITIAL RESOLUTION:
$$\frac{\begin{array}{rcl}\textbf{start} & \Rightarrow & A \vee l \\ \textbf{start} & \Rightarrow & B \vee \neg l\end{array}}{\begin{array}{rcl}\textbf{start} & \Rightarrow & A \vee B\end{array}}$$

STEP RESOLUTION:
$$\frac{\begin{array}{rcl}C & \Rightarrow & \bigcirc(A \vee l) \\ D & \Rightarrow & \bigcirc(B \vee \neg l)\end{array}}{\begin{array}{rcl}(C \wedge D) & \Rightarrow & \bigcirc(A \vee B)\end{array}}$$

TEMPORAL RESOLUTION:
$$\frac{\begin{array}{rcl}C & \Rightarrow & \Diamond l \\ D & \Rightarrow & \bigcirc\Box\neg l\end{array}}{\begin{array}{rcl}C & \Rightarrow & (\neg D)\,\mathcal{W}\,l\end{array}}$$

Note that the temporal resolution operation is actually applied to a set of step rules that together characterise $D \Rightarrow \bigcirc\Box\neg l$ (this formula itself is not in SNF) and that the resolvent produced from this operation must still be translated into SNF.

Rather than go through this resolution method in detail, we direct the reader to [Fisher *et al.*, 2001].

15.6.2 Agent Verification via Proof in a Temporal Logic of Belief

A different approach to characterising the information that each agent has is to represent this information in terms of the agent's *beliefs* [Wooldridge., 1992]. Thus, for example, if p is satisfied in agent ag_1's computation, then we can assert that ag_1 believes p. By extending our basic temporal logic with a multi-modal KD45 dimension representing belief, we can again represent this as $[ag_1]p$, i.e., that agent ag_1 believes p. Importantly, the truth of, for example, $[ag_1]p$ is distinct from that of $[ag_2]p$. Such a temporal logic of belief can be used to *axiomatize* certain properties of Concurrent METATEM systems.

SENDING MESSAGES: $\vdash [i]P \Rightarrow \Diamond P$
(P is one of i's component propositions)

RECEIVING MESSAGES: $\vdash P \Rightarrow \bigcirc\Diamond[i]P$
(P is one of i's environment propositions)

HISTORICAL ACCURACY: $\vdash [i]A \Rightarrow \bigcirc[i]\bullet A$

RULE AVAILABILITY: $\vdash [i]\textbf{start} \Rightarrow \Box[i]R$ (R is one of i's rules)

SYNCHRONISED START: $\vdash \textbf{start} \Rightarrow [i]\textbf{start}$

Using the axiomatization of Concurrent METATEM (partially) given above, we can attempt to prove properties of, for example, the Concurrent METATEM system presented in Section 15.5.3. Some examples of the types of properties we can prove include:

1. $prof1$ believes that it will apply infinitely often;
2. the $funder$ is fair — if $prof1$ applies infinitely often, it will be successful infinitely often;

3. $prof1$ believes that it will be successful infinitely often (from (1) and (2));
4. $prof3$ believes that it will apply at some moment in the future (from (3)).

For more detailed proofs relating to this form of system, see [Fisher and Wooldridge, 1997].

We will now consider several more examples derived from the specifications provided in Section 15.4. In the proofs that follow, we use the notation $\{S\} \vdash \phi$ to represent the statement "*system S satisfies property* ϕ". Also, since most of the proof steps involve applications of the *Modus Ponens* inference rule, we will omit reference to this rule.

Again, in these cases, the clausal resolution method can be extended to combinations of modal and temporal logics. There are a variety of resolution rules characterising the specific properties of the modal extension used [Dixon *et al.*, 1998]. In addition, in [Hustadt *et al.*, 2000], a *translation* approach is used for the modal dimensions, whereby modal formulae are translated to classical first-order logic [Ohlbach, 1993] and classical resolution is carried out.

Verification: Resource Controller

We begin by proving some properties of the simple resource controller outlined in Section 15.4.2. This multi-agent system, which we shall refer to as S1, consists of three agents: a resource producer (rp), and two resource consumers ($rc1$ and $rc2$).

The first property we prove is that the agent $rc1$, once it has commenced execution, satisfies the commitment $ask1$ on every cycle.

Lemma 15.6.1. $\{S1\} \vdash \mathbf{start} \Rightarrow \Box[rc1]ask1.$

(The proof of this lemma is given in [Fisher and Wooldridge, 1997]; we shall also omit all other proofs from this section.) Using this result, it is not difficult to establish that the message $ask1$ is then sent infinitely often.

Lemma 15.6.2. $\{S1\} \vdash \Box\Diamond ask1.$

Similarly, we can show that any agent that is *listening* for $ask1$ messages, in particular rp, will receive them infinitely often.

Lemma 15.6.3. $\{S1\} \vdash \mathbf{start} \Rightarrow \Box\Diamond[rp]ask1.$

Now, since we know that $ask1$ is one of rp's environment predicates, then we can show that once both rp and $rc1$ have started, the resource will be given to $rc1$ infinitely often.

Lemma 15.6.4. $\{S1\} \vdash \mathbf{start} \Rightarrow \Box\Diamond give1.$

Similar properties can be shown for $rc2$. Note, however, that we require knowledge about $rc1$'s behaviour in order to reason about $rc2$'s behaviour.

Lemma 15.6.5. $\{S1\} \vdash \mathbf{start} \Rightarrow \Box\Diamond[rp]ask2.$

Given this, we can derive the following result.

Lemma 15.6.6. $\{S1\} \vdash \mathbf{start} \Rightarrow \Box\Diamond give2.$

Finally, we can show the desired behaviour of the system:

Theorem 15.6.1. $\{S1\} \vdash \mathbf{start} \Rightarrow (\Box\Diamond give1 \;\;\&\;\; \Box\Diamond give2).$

$solverd(problem1, solution1.2)[solution1]$:
1. $(solution1.2 \ \& \ \blacklozenge problem1) \Rightarrow \Diamond solution1.$

$solvere(problem1)[solution1.2]$:
1. $problem1 \Rightarrow \Diamond solution1.2.$

Figure 15.5: Refined Problem Solving Agents

Verification: Abstract Distributed Problem Solving System

We now consider properties of the simple distributed problem-solving system presented in Section 15.4.3. If we call this system S2, then we can prove the following.

Lemma 15.6.7. $\{S2\} \vdash \textbf{start} \Rightarrow \Diamond solution1.$

We can then use this result to prove that the system solves the required problem:

Theorem 15.6.2. $\{S2\} \vdash \textbf{start} \Rightarrow \Diamond solved1.$

We briefly consider a refinement of the above system where $solverc$ is replaced by two agents who together can solve $problem1$, but cannot manage this individually. These agents, called $solverd$ and $solvere$ can be defined in Figure 15.5.

Thus, when $solverd$ receives the problem, it cannot do anything until it has heard from $solvere$. When $solvere$ receives the problem, it broadcasts the fact that it can solve part of the problem (i.e., it broadcasts $solution1.2$). When $solverd$ sees this, it knows it can solve the other part of the problem and broadcasts the whole solution. Thus, given these new agents we can prove the following (the system is now called S3).

Theorem 15.6.3. $\{S3\} \vdash \textbf{start} \Rightarrow \Diamond solved1.$

Verification: Contract Net

We now give an outline of how selected properties of the simple Contract Net system presented in Section 15.4.4 may be established. Throughout, we will refer to this system as S4 and we will utilise first-order notation for succinctness.

Theorem 15.6.4. *If at least one agent bids for a task, then the contract will eventually be awarded to one of the bidders.*

As this is a global property of the system, not restricted to a particular agent, then it can be represented logically as follows.

$$\{S4\} \vdash \forall T \cdot \exists A \cdot (bid(T, A) \Rightarrow \exists B \cdot \Diamond award(T, B))$$

In order to prove this statement, we start with the assumption that an agent a has a task t for which it bids:

$$[a]bid(t, a).$$

Now, from the axioms governing communication between agents, we know that, if a particular predicate is a component predicate then it will eventually be broadcast (i.e., SENDING MESSAGES axiom given earlier). This, together with the above, ensures that

$$\Diamond bid(t, a). \qquad (CN1)$$

Now, we know that, once broadcast, such a message will eventually reach all agents who wish to receive messages of this form (from RECEIVING MESSAGES axiom). Thus, we can deduce that

$$bid(t, a) \Rightarrow \Diamond[m]bid(t, a)$$

where m is the manager agent for this particular task. Similarly, we can derive

$$bid(t, a) \Rightarrow \Diamond[m]bidded(t, a).$$

By the definition of contract allocation given by axiom (W1), we know that for some bidding agent p (the 'most preferable'), then the manager will eventually award the contract to p:

$$bid(t, a) \Rightarrow \Diamond[m]award(t, p).$$

Using this, together with (CN1), above, and additional axioms concerning the system, we can derive

$$\Diamond[m]award(t, p).$$

Finally, as this information is broadcast, we can derive the global statement that, given $[a]bid(t, a)$,

$$\exists B \cdot \Diamond award(t, B)$$

thus establishing the theorem.

Theorem 15.6.5. *Agents do not bid for tasks that they cannot contribute to.*

In logical terms, this is simply

$$\{\text{S4}\} \vdash \forall T \cdot \forall A \cdot (announce(T) \;\&\; \neg competent(A, T)) \Rightarrow \neg bid(T, A)$$

If we know that, for some task t and agent a, where the task t has been announced, yet the agent a is not competent to perform the task, then we know by rule $(B1)$ that

$$[a]\neg possible(a, t).$$

Then, by rule $(B2)$, we can derive the fact that agent a will not bid for the task, i.e.,

$$[a]\neg bid(t, a).$$

Theorem 15.6.6. *Agents do not bid unless they believe there has been a task announcement.*

Again, this can be formalised as

$$\{S4\} \vdash \forall T \cdot \forall A \cdot bid(T, A) \Rightarrow \blacklozenge\, announce(T).$$

In order to prove this statement, we simply show that for there to have been a bid, a particular agent a must have considered the task, t, possible:

$$[a]possible(t, a)$$

and, for this to occur, then by $(B1)$

$$[a](\neg award(t, B))\, \mathcal{S}\, announce(t)$$

which in turn implies

$$[a]\blacklozenge\, announce(t).$$

As $announce$ is an environment predicate for agent a then it must be the case that the appropriate message was broadcast at some time in the past:

$$\blacklozenge\, announce(t).$$

Theorem 15.6.7. *Managers award the contract for a particular task to at most one agent.*

This can be simply represented by

$$award(T, A) \wedge award(T, B) \Rightarrow (A = B).$$

The proof of this follows simply from $(W1)$ which states that the 'most preferable' bidder is chosen. The definition of 'most preferable' in turn utilises the linear ordering provided by the *preferable* predicate.

Using a Temporal Logic of Knowledge An alternative, but related, approach to the representation of information within distinct agents is to use the abstraction of *knowledge*, rather than belief. Thus, by extending our temporal logic with a multi-modal S5 logic, rather than the multi-modal KD45 logic used to characterise belief, we produce a *temporal logic of knowledge* [Fagin *et al.*, 1996; Dixon *et al.*, 1998]. In [Wooldridge, 1996], such a logic is used to give a knowledge-theoretic semantics to the types of Concurrent METATEM systems we are considering here.

15.6.3 Verification by Model Checking

For systems where finite-state models (or abstractions) are available, then model-checking is often used [Holzmann, 1997]. There are many scenarios in which model-checking techniques may be appropriate [Halpern and Vardi, 1991] and, indeed, model checking techniques have been developed for carrying out agent verification. In this section, we give a brief review of some of this work.

Model checking was originally introduced as a technique for verifying that finite state systems satisfy their specifications [Clarke *et al.*, 1986]. The basic idea is that a state transition graph for a finite state system S can be interpreted as a model M_S for a temporal logic: nodes in the graph correspond to instantaneous states of the system, and arcs in the graph to the execution of individual program instructions. Checking that a system S satisfies a particular property ϕ (where ϕ is expressed as a formula of temporal logic) then amounts to checking that ϕ is valid in S, i.e., that $M_S \models \phi$, where $\models$ is the satisfaction relation of the logic used to express the requirements ϕ. The problem of checking that $M_S \models \phi$ is the *model checking* problem [Clarke *et al.*, 1999]. What makes model checking so appealing as a practical approach to automated verification is that it is ostensibly 'cheaper', computationally speaking, than the corresponding proof problem for the logic. For example, the model checking problem for the well-known branching time temporal logic CTL can be solved in time $O(|M| \cdot |\phi|)$, where $|M|$ and $|\phi|$ denote the size of the model and the size of the formula to be checked in this model respectively [Emerson, 1990; Clarke *et al.*, 1999]. A number of industrial strength verification tools have been developed within the model checking community, of which the two best known are SPIN (a model checker for a linear temporal logic which is essentially PML) [Holzmann, 1997; Holzmann, 2003], and SMV (a model checker for CTL) [Clarke *et al.*, 1999].

Within the multi-agent systems community, model checking has begun to arouse considerable interest as an approach to automated verification. As we noted above, Halpern and Vardi set out a manifesto for model checking knowledge properties of systems [Halpern and Vardi, 1991], although they did not describe any implemented system to do this. Rao and Georgeff [Rao and Georgeff, 1993] described model checking algorithms for their Belief-Desire-Intention family of logics [Rao and Georgeff, 1993]. Benerecetti and colleagues described a more general approach to model checking temporal modal specifications of systems [Benerecetti *et al.*, 1998].

Wooldridge and colleagues [Wooldridge *et al.*, 2002] implemented a simple BDI agent programming system called MABLE on top of the SPIN model checker. Using MABLE, it became possible to model check simple temporal/dynamic/BDI properties of MABLE systems. The approach was based on a translation of the agent programming language into PROMELA, the model specification language of the SPIN model checker, and used fairly simple reduction of BDI modalities to predicates over data structures in the generated PROMELA model.

In parallel work, Bordini and colleagues investigated a similar approach to model checking BDI properties of rational agent programming languages, and in particular, the AgentSpeak programming language [Bordini *et al.*, 2003c]. In this work, two approaches to the verification of rational agent programs were developed [Bordini *et al.*, 2003a; Bordini *et al.*, 2003b]. Both involved viewing rational agents as being implemented/described in AgentSpeak and both utilised *model checking* in order to carry out the verification. The first translated AgentSpeak programs into PROMELA and then applied SPIN [Holzmann, 2003] to verify this translated agent code; the second translated AgentSpeak into Java and utilised the work at NASA on model checking Java using Java Pathfinder 2 [Visser *et al.*, 2000].

15.7 Concluding Remarks

Multi-agent systems can be viewed as a novel way of thinking about distributed, concurrent systems, where control is itself distributed over the nodes in the system, and where the component nodes must therefore cooperate and dynamically coordinate their activities in order to achieve there design objectives. In some cases, the component agents will be designed by different organisations, with competing or conflicting objectives, and in such cases, the ability of agents to reach agreements comes to the fore.

Although there are obvious benefits to such a distributed control regime, there are also problems. In particular, it becomes much harder to predict and explain the behaviour of such systems. As a consequence, pragmatic techniques for the verification of such systems becomes extremely important. In this chapter, we have explored some of the issues involved in the use of temporal logic to reason about — and particularly, verify — such systems. We hope to have demonstrated that temporal logic is a natural and elegant framework within which to express the dynamics of multi-agent systems, and temporal logics combined with modal operators for representing the 'mental states' of such agents — their information and aspirations — seems to be a natural and abstract way of capturing what is known about their state.

From a logical point of view, multi-agent systems present many challenges. In particular, the need for *combinations* of temporal and modal aspects, for practical associated theorem proving and model checking tools, as well as (potentially) mechanisms for the refinement and execution of such logics, poses a number of interesting and well-motivated research problems for both the logic and agent communities.

Handbook of Temporal Reasoning in Artificial Intelligence
Edited by M. Fisher, D. Gabbay and L. Vila

Chapter 16

Time in Planning

Maria Fox & Derek Long

In this chapter we proceed to examine the role that time can play in the planning problem, how time has been introduced into planning models and algorithms and planners that have handled temporal planning problems in a variety of ways.

16.1 Introduction

The classical AI Planning problem is defined as follows: given a description of a set of possible actions, an initial state and a goal condition, find an ordered collection of actions whose execution (in the given order) will lead from the initial state to a state in which the goal condition is satisfied. It is natural to suppose that this problem is intimately bound up with temporal projection, since the actions will execute in time and the coordination of those activities is clearly the heart of the planning problem. However, for most of its history planning research has been almost exclusively concerned with the *logical*, or relative, structure of the relationship between the activities in a plan, rather than with the metric temporal structure. That is, planning has been concerned with the ordering of activities — typically into a total order — in such a way that the logical executability of the plan is guaranteed.

In contrast, research in scheduling has been far more concerned with how activities should be arranged in time, both relative to one another and also relative to absolute time lines. The concerns of planning research and those of scheduling research are different. Classically, planning is concerned with *what* activities should be performed whilst scheduling is concerned with *when* and *with what* resources identified activities should be performed. This distinction is somewhat simplified for the purposes of this discussion, but it essentially characterises the classical situation. Importantly, the situation is now changing – the integration of temporal scheduling with planning has been tackled by several researchers [Cesta and Oddi, 1995; Ghallab and Laruelle, 1994; Muscettola, 1994; Vere, 1983; Kvarnströn *et al.*, 2000; Bacchus and Ady, 2001], and is increasingly a central concern of many researchers in planning.

In this chapter we will consider temporal planning in terms of the following four issues: the choice of temporal ontology, causality, the management of concurrency and continuous change. These issues have received considerable treatment in the temporal reasoning, reasoning about action and change and planning communities. However, the ways in which they have been treated vary, with different emphases being given to different issues within

```
(:action load
 :parameters (?o - object ?t - truck ?loc - location)
 :precondition (and (at ?t ?loc) (at ?o ?loc))
 :effect (and (not (at ?o ?loc)) (in ?o ?t)))
```

Figure 16.1: Simple example of an action schema written in PDDL.

The action has three parameters, the variables denoted syntactically by the prefix '?', with types given following hyphens. The pre- and post-conditions are written using propositions, with predicates and their arguments enclosed together in brackets.

the three communities. We begin by introducing the four issues and explaining why they are important in planning. We then consider each issue in detail by describing how modern planning algorithms address the issue and resolve the problems that arise. We briefly synthesise a view of the current state of the art in temporal planning and conclude the chapter by identifying some of the open issues that remain for the management of temporal domains in planning.

16.2 Classical Planning Background

A classical planning problem is represented by providing a set of action schemas, or *operators*, that can be applied by composition to a given initial state in order to produce a desired goal condition. In a propositional planning problem a finite collection of action instances can be constructed from the schema set by instantiating the variables in the schemas in all possible ways (subject to type constraints). Classical planning makes a number of simplifying assumptions: actions have instantaneous effects and time is relative; actions always have their expected outcomes; the world state is always fully known by the planner and the number of objects in any state is finite. Under these assumptions a plan is a partially (perhaps totally) ordered collection of actions which, when applied to the initial state in any order consistent with the specified partial order, produces a state satisfying the goal condition.

Action schemas are described in terms of their logical preconditions, which must be true in the state of application of any instance, and their postconditions enabling a planner to predict the effects of applying action instances to world states. For historical reasons the formal language in which action schemas are described usually has a Lisp-based or modal logic-based syntax. The current standard language for describing sets of action schemas for use by a planner is the PDDL family of Planning Domain Description Languages, originated by Drew McDermott in 1998. Figure 16.1 shows an example of a simple object-loading action expressed in PDDL.

Definition 16.2.1. *A (Classical) State is a finite set of ground atomic propositions.*

Definition 16.2.2. *A Classical Planning Problem is a 4-tuple $\langle A, O, I, G\rangle$ where A is a set of* action schemas, *O is a finite set of domain objects, I is an initial state and G is a conjunction of ground atomic proposition. The propositions in I and G are formed from predicates applied to objects drawn from O. Action schemas are grounded by instantiating variables with objects drawn from O. Ground actions are triples $\langle Pre, Add, Del\rangle$ where each element is a set of ground atomic propositions.*

Action instances are functions from State to State, defined as follows. Given an action a and a state s:

$$if \quad Pre_a \subseteq s \quad then \quad a(S) = (s \setminus Del_a) \cup Add_a$$

In classical planning preconditions are evaluated in a state under the closed world assumption. A common form for describing postconditions relies on the well-known STRIPS assumption, that all atomic propositions in the state are completely unaffected by the application of an action unless the action postconditions explicitly indicate otherwise. The STRIPS assumption provides a simple solution to the frame problem when states are described as sets of atomic propositions. The classical planning assumption is that states can be described atomically but this is not a general view of the modelling of change. Although simplifying, this assumption is surprisingly expressive [Nebel, 2000] and continues to pose many challenges for automated plan generation.

Broadly three algorithmic approaches to classical planning can be characterised. These are: state-space search; plan-space search and plan graph search. These approaches can arise in different guises (for example there are different search strategies that can be exploited within these approaches, and the nodes in the search spaces can be structurally different depending on approaches taken to representation, abstraction and other aspects of the modelling and reasoning problems). For the purposes of this chapter we restrict our attention to some of the exemplars of these approaches which have most heavily influenced the development of the field.

One of the most influential early contributions to planning was made by the seminal work of Fikes and Nilsson [Fikes and Nilsson, 1971] on the STanford Research Institute Problem Solver (STRIPS). The STRIPS system searches in a space consisting of partially developed, totally ordered plans. Each node contains the sequence of actions forming the plan so far (the plan head), the goals remaining to be achieved and the state resulting from application of the plan head to the initial state. The search heuristically prefers nodes with fewest outstanding goals and this can be managed within a variety of best-first or A* style searches.

The STRIPS strategy is hampered by the fact that decomposing the problem, by tackling each sub-goal as it arises as if it were independent of other components of the problem, sometimes results in poor quality plans. The so-called *Sussman's anomaly* [Sussman, 1990] demonstrated that the STRIPS search space does not even contain optimal solutions to non-decomposable problems and that it therefore constitutes a fundamentally limited model of the dynamics of the problem domain. This observation led to the development of *partial order planning*, an approach which delays commitment to the ordering of activities, the choice of objects to play specific roles in the developing plan, the choice of actions to apply and so on. Search takes place in a space of partial plans, with the plan development operations corresponding to ordering choices, action selections and variable bindings. When commitments are made they are enforced by means of *causal links* [Penberthy and Weld, 1992]. By delaying commitments until they are forced it is possible to integrate non-decomposable elements of a problem in order to produce optimal solutions. Nonlin [Tate, 1977], Noah [Sacerdoti, 1975] and TWEAK [Chapman, 1987] all demonstrated the ability to solve Sussman's anomaly optimally.

Partial order planning remained a key research focus within the field for many years, but it has never been possible to demonstrate the performance advantages that it was expected would result from least-commitment search. Although, in principle, least commitment search entails less backtracking over poor choices, in practice the search space is too large to search effectively without very powerful heuristic guidance. The lack of informative heuristics means that such planners tend to be severely limited in terms of the size and complexity of the problems they could solve. This situation might change as more research focusses on identifying informative heuristics for partial order planners [Younes and Simmons, 2003; Nguyen and Kambhampati, 2001].

In 1994, Blum and Furst [Blum and Furst, 1995] produced the Graphplan system. This system had a dramatic effect on the planning community, producing vastly improved behaviour compared to the then current technology. It has subsequently been the foundation of several other planning systems and remains a powerful and influential tool in many current systems.

Graphplan constructs a data structure, called a *plan graph*, consisting of alternating layers of facts and actions. Each fact layer contains all of the facts that are reachable from the initial state in as many steps as there are action layers between the initial state and that fact layer. Each action layer contains all of the actions that are applicable at the corresponding point in the plan. A vertex within an action layer represents an action all the preconditions of which are available in the preceding fact layer. Fact vertices are linked by edges to the actions that achieve them and actions are linked by edges to the precondition facts that they require. In addition to showing which facts are, in principle, achievable and at what stage in a plan they might be made true, the graph also records an important additional detail: where pairs of facts in the same layer are mutually exclusive and where pairs of actions in the same layer are mutually exclusive each of these conditions is recorded using an edge linking the affected pairs. The plan graph is an extremely efficient representation of the reachability relation on the underlying domain description, which can be constructed in time polynomial in the domain size.

A plan is found by searching in the plan graph for a sub-graph in which the goal facts are all included in a single fact layer, pairwise non-mutex, and for each fact included in the sub-graph there is an achieving action included (unless it is in the initial layer, which represents the initial state) and for each action included all of its preconditions are included. Since most interesting problems involve higher order mutual exclusion relationships, which are not visible in the plan graph, Graphplan usually fails to find a plan in the initial plan graph. In the original Graphplan algorithm search was conducted using an iterated depth-first search interleaved with extension of the plan graph. Search was conducted backwards from the goal facts, which guarantees to find the shortest concurrent plan (if a plan exists). Graphplan can produce plans very quickly when the initial plan graph does not need to be iteratively extended very far. However, this search approach has proved expensive for some problems and other search strategies have been explored [Gerevini and Serina, 2002; Baioletti *et al.*, 2000; Kautz and Selman, 1995].

The Graphplan search process can be expensive because of the need to recompute information on each iteration and to maintain, at each graph layer, records of unachievable goal sets in order to avoid needless recomputation of failing searches. The planning field has therefore moved away from the basic Graphplan approach, but has taken advantage of several of its key contributions. First, Graphplan showed that, even for quite large problem instances, it is computationally reasonable to render the domain description in a propositional form before embarking on the planning process. Surprising though it seems this has become a standard strategy in the field. Secondly, the construction of the initial plan graph provides an efficient means of obtaining apparently promising heuristics for use in other search strategies. In particular, plan graph based heuristic computations have become important for modern planning systems based on partial order search and forward state-space search.

The UNPOP system of McDermott [McDermott, 1996] and the HSP system of Geffner and Bonet [Bonet *et al.*, 1997; Bonet and Geffner, 1997] are state-space searching planners demonstrating the power of searching forward, from the initial state to a goal state, using a search strategy guided by a *relaxed* distance estimate. To estimate the distance between a state and a goal state a very simple, yet very effective, measurement is made: the number of actions required to achieve all the outstanding goals if the destructive effects of those actions are ignored. Achieving goals using actions whose destructive effects are ignored is called *relaxed planning*. The measure of outstanding work is simply the size of a relaxed plan to achieve the goals. Unfortunately, finding an optimal relaxed plan is, perhaps surprisingly, technically as hard as finding a real plan [Bylander, 1994]. Fortunately, however, it is relatively easy to find arbitrary relaxed plans, and even to find "good" relaxed plans. The work inspired by McDermott and Geffner and Bonet uses efficient techniques to construct good relaxed plans which are treated as reasonably accurate measures of the work required to complete a plan if a given choice of action is pursued.

One of the most efficient planners based on this approach is the FF system developed by Hoffmann [Hoffmann and Nebel, 2000]. This planner uses a *relaxed* plan graph (built using actions with their destructive effects ignored) and an efficient plan graph search to find good relaxed plans. Neither the heuristic exploited by HSP nor the plan graph based heuristic of FF is admissible. HSP constructs a measure of distance which assumes independence, or decomposability, of the problem so does not take advantage of positive interactions between plan steps. FF relies on extraction of a relaxed plan from a relaxed plan graph, and there is no guarantee that the plan extracted will be the shortest one available. It seems that the heuristic used by FF might be more informative because the empirical picture suggests that FF performs slightly better, in general, than HSP [Bacchus, 2001].

There have been many planners developed on these foundations, exploiting alternative search strategies and a variety of optimisations. Although forward state-space search does not seem likely to provide a useful basis for temporal extensions, because the plans produced are sequential and temporal plans must almost certainly involve concurrency, partial order planning and Graphplan-based approaches have provided important foundations for the development of temporal planning research.

As can be seen from the strategies described above, the view of change common to classical planning is based on the simple state transition model depicted in Figure 16.2. The passage of time involved in accessing a goal state from an initial state is interpreted in terms of the length of a trace within the state transition system between the two states, subject to the fact that commutative transitions can be seen as being applicable in any order and hence, in principle at least, concurrently. Such a view takes a simplified approach to concurrency and causality. The opportunity for concurrency is seen as likely to be present whenever two actions are commutative, and causality is seen simply in terms of the directions of the state transition arrows. Modelling the way in which the world changes when an action is applied presents many complex problems, concerned with causality, temporal projection, qualification, and so on, addressed over several decades by the reasoning about action community [Shanahan, 1999; Gelfond *et al.*, 1991; Giunchiglia and Lifschitz, 1998; Lifschitz, 1997; McCain and Turner, 1997]. A duality exists between actions and states, as identified by Lansky [Lansky, 1986]. This duality allows actions (or *events*, in Lansky's terms) to be seen as state changing functions, so that the view of change is entirely state-

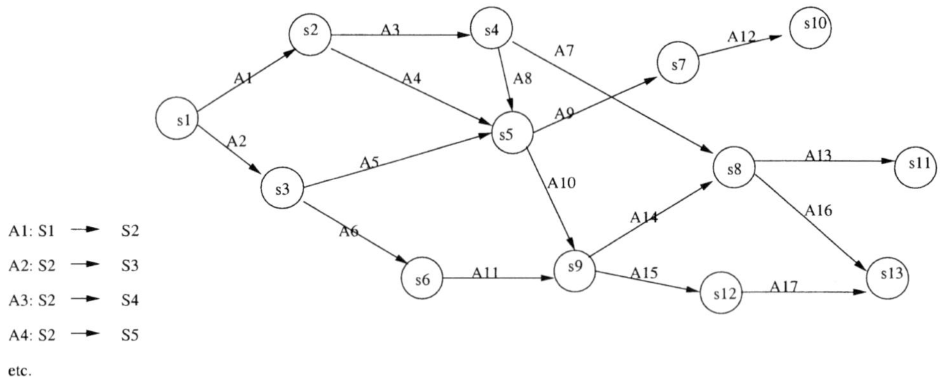

Figure 16.2: The Classical State-transition View of Planning

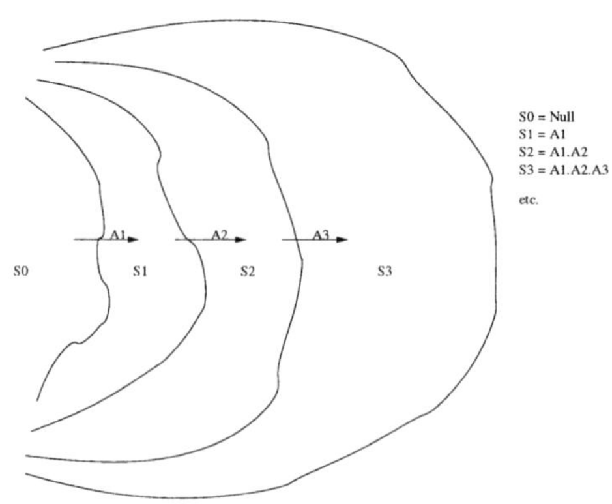

Figure 16.3: The Histories View of Change: States are explained in terms of the histories of events that produce them.

oriented and, dually, states to be seen as records of the activity that has occurred so far in the world history. Under the first interpretation, depicted in Figure 16.2, world states are seen as snapshots in time separated by action applications. Under the second, depicted in Figure 16.3, states are seen as evolving continuously, with different evolutions linked by instantaneous moments of change. An alternative view of state change during the passage of time was presented by Pednault [Pednault, 1986a]. Following McDermott [McDermott, 1982] Pednault proposed that states are *chronicles* recording all that has been true, is true and will be true in the world. Actions cause transitions between chronicles so that acting on one part of the world can cause the evolution of other parts of the world to change. This view is intuitively appealing as it accounts for the way in which the world changes of its own accord in response to, and alongside, changes made by an executive agent. The distinction between the two models is important from the point of view of understanding the semantics of action underlying modern planning approaches.

16.3 Temporal Planning

In order to discuss the way the planning field has developed towards handling domains with explicit temporal properties it is necessary to say precisely what we mean by a *temporal planning problem*. In fact there are many different ways in which explicit time might be modelled and there are different interpretations of what is meant by a temporal plan. For the purposes of this chapter we will define two temporal planning problems that have received broad treatment in the field. These problems, which are extensions of the classical planning problem defined in Definition 16.2.2, are *Temporally Extended Actions (TEA)* and *Temporally Extended Goals (TEG)*. *TEA* is the classical planning problem extended with the notion of activities taking time to have their expected effects. An additional factor is that plan quality can be measured in terms of the total time taken to achieve the specified goals, thereby encouraging concurrent activity where this can be achieved. The initial and goal state specifications remain unaffected but the construction of a plan must now take into account the additional complexity of the correct handling of concurrent action. Our definitions are intended to characterise the temporal planning problems that have received most attention in the field. They are not intended to prescribe how temporal planning should be formulated and, indeed, several of the planners discussed in this paper use alternative (although broadly equivalent) definitions. Proposals for the representation of temporal planning domains (many with accounts of reasoning with these representations) have been made by several authors, such as [Sandewall, 1994; Giunchiglia and Lifschitz, 1998; Cesta and Oddi, 1995; Vidal and Ghallab, 1996; Trinquart and Ghallab, 2001; Muscettola, 1994; Fox and Long, 2003; Bacchus and Kabanza, 1998].

Definition 16.3.1. *A Metric Temporal State is a triple $\langle t, S, v \rangle$ where t is the time at which the metric temporal state starts to hold, S is a classical state and v is a valuation assigning real values to the metric fluents of a planning problem.*

Definition 16.3.2. *A Temporally Extended Actions Problem is a 5-tuple $\langle A, O, I, G, f \rangle$ where A is a set of temporal action schemas, O is a finite set of domain objects, I is an initial Temporal Metric State and G is a propositional formula. The function f is a mapping from ground temporal actions (GTA) and Metric Temporal States (MTS) to times (to be interpreted as the* durations *of the corresponding ground temporal actions when executed from the corresponding metric temporal state). Temporal action schemas are grounded by instantiation of their variables using objects drawn from O. Thus:*

$$f : GTA \times MTS \to \mathbb{R}$$

Ground temporal actions are functions from metric temporal states (the state in which they are first applied) to an effect function. Thus, the ground temporal action, a, applied to metric temporal state m, yields the effect function:

$$a(m) = g : MTS \times [0, f(a, m)] \to MTS$$

The effect function describes the state transition induced by the temporal action at each time point during its application.

The definition given here is not explicit about the form of the effect function. This is because it is possible for an effect function to have discrete effects at some finite set of points during its period of execution and continuous effects throughout the duration of its execution.

Modern planners are able to deal with different variants of this problem and there remains considerable variation between their current approaches.

We define *TEG* to be *TEA* extended with temporally constrained goals. We do not provide a formal definition of *TEG* because the more the classical framework is extended the more variation exists between the approaches taken by different planners, and between the forms of the problem that can be successfully addressed. An informal specification of the *TEG* problem suffices for our purposes. The important extension is that goals are no longer properties of states but of trajectories, or even sets of trajectories, through metric temporal state spaces. For example, a goal specification might require a certain fact to be maintained over a specified interval or achieved by a specified deadline. The ability to express temporally extended goals brings planning closer to automated verification since safety and maintenance goals, quantified goals and other complex logical formulae can be expressed, corresponding to the representation of safety and liveness requirements in concurrent systems. Languages exist for the modelling of temporally constrained properties [Pnueli, 1977; Clarke and Emerson, 1981b; Moszkowski, 1985] and these have been extended and modified for use by planning systems [Bacchus and Kabanza, 1998; Cimatti *et al.*, 1998b; Ghallab and Laruelle, 1994]. In addition some planning systems have addressed more complex temporal planning problems (for example, temporally extended initial states allow predictable exogenous events to be expressed). However, *TEA* was the main form of temporal planning problem explored in the 3rd International Planning Competition [Long and Fox, 2003b] and considerable progress has been made towards efficient solution of the *TEA* problem. Although *TEA* is subsumed by *TEG* many researchers have considered only *TEA* so it makes sense to consider *TEA* in its own right.

Within the framework of *TEA* and *TEG* it is necessary to decide how the temporal aspects of a problem domain should be modelled. This issue returns to the question of whether the model is action-centric or object-centric, since the passage of time needs to be associated with either actions or objects states (or possibly both). In fact, this decision can be made in terms of representation of temporal domains and properties in a way separate from whether the planner performs state transitions, or constructs histories, in the development of a plan. For example, TLplan [Bacchus and Kabanza, 2000] constructs plans using a state-transition approach but it uses a modal interval based language to describe the necessary and desirable properties of the trajectories that the planner constructs [Bacchus and Kabanza, 1998].

The distinction between the state-transition view of change and the histories view nevertheless emerges in different planning systems. HSTS [Muscettola, 1994] and ASPEN [Rabideau *et al.*, 1999] organise activities along *timelines*, one timeline for each active object in the developing plan. Timelines account for the states of individual objects over the lifetime of the plan by maintaining non-intersecting intervals associated with particular states of the objects. To have a complete account of the trajectory of a specific object the union of the intervals must cover the entire timeline. This approach exemplifies the histories view of change, since timelines describe how the states of objects evolve over time and they do not emphasise the role of *action* in the development of a plan. Indeed, the distinction between action and state is seen to be irrelevant to the timeline based approach [Muscettola, 1994; Ghallab, 1996].

Maintaining timelines correctly necessitates the specification of all of the interval constraints necessary to ensure correct axiomatisation of the behaviours of the objects. For example, for a particular vehicle to be moving over a specific interval of time it is necessary to specify that that same vehicle is stationary at the time points defining the limits of the

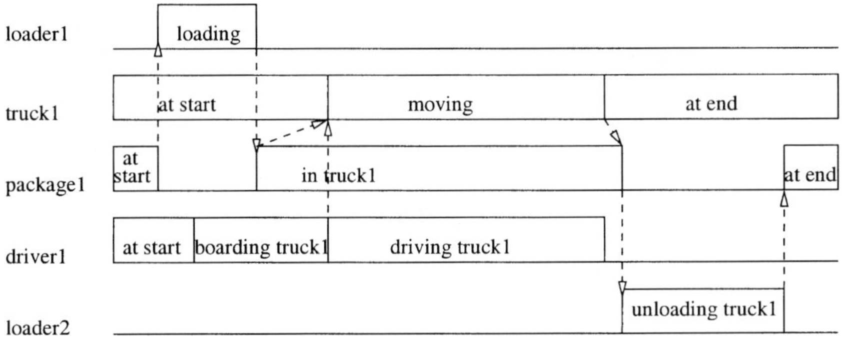

Figure 16.4: An example of a partially developed timeline-based plan.

The figure shows timelines for five domain objects, with some intervals showing the activity of the corresponding object at certain times within the respective timeline. The dotted arrows indicate temporal constraints between intervals on different timelines.

period in which it is moving. In HSTS this is achieved by defining interval relationships in the style of Allen's interval algebra [Allen, 1984] in which a moving interval is *met by* and *meets* two stationary intervals. Defining a temporal planning domain involves defining all of the necessary interval relationships that axiomatise the domain behaviour. In DDL, the language of HSTS, these are called *compatibilities*. Figure 16.4 gives a simple example of the representation of a partial timeline-based plan.

Using the timelines approach it is straightforward to constrain state changes to occur at specific times on a timeline, and then rely on constraint propagation to determine whether the timeline remains consistent as other activities are scheduled on it. This makes it possible to handle some *TEG* problems without the introduction of further reasoning mechanisms.

An alternative approach is to structure the developing plan around the notion of a partially ordered task network [Sacerdoti, 1975; Tate, 1977] and to use temporal constraint reasoning techniques to ensure temporal validity of the network at each stage of its development. This approach, which includes the causal-link based approaches of IxTeT [Ghallab and Laruelle, 1994], Deviser [Vere, 1983] and VHPOP [Younes and Simmons, 2003], takes a state transition view in which the planner builds up a partially ordered collection of states through which the active objects will pass. These states are compound representations of domain configurations and are produced by action applications to prior states. Various forms of action representation have been used in temporal planners of this nature. For example, IxTeT uses a reified logic description of the conditions that must prevail at the start or end of an action, over its entire period of execution or, in principle, over sub-intervals. The period of execution is defined as part of the action description. In this language it is possible to express that events will occur at specific points during the execution of such actions. A temporal network is needed to ensure the temporal validity of a partial plan constructed from these action descriptions. IxTeT and Deviser are capable of handling subsets of *TEG*, whilst VHPOP is a *TEA* planner.

Other approaches, whilst not based on task networks or partial ordering, share the state-transition view of change. For example, TLplan [Bacchus and Kabanza, 2000], TALplanner [Kvarnströn *et al.*, 2000], all Graphplan-based planners [Smith and Weld, 1999; Garrido *et al.*, 2002; Long and Fox, 2003a] and forward search planners [Haslum and Geffner, 2001; Do and Kambhampati, 2001] are based fundamentally on this view. This approach relies on interpreting the domain description in an action-centred way but the decision concerning whether time passes during action application or within states can still be made independently. For example, McDermott [McDermott, 2003] attaches the passage of time to states, during which processes modifying metric quantities can be active, and makes action applications instantaneous. His language reflects this choice by specifying actions as if they were instantaneous in the STRIPS sense. Time is attached to states during planning as the temporal requirements of active processes become established. Alternatively it is possible to attach temporal durations to actions in the syntax of the language but to interpret such actions as encapsulating periods of time within states, as in LPGP [Long and Fox, 2003a], which uses the durative action syntax of PDDL2.1. Indeed, the idea of a *durative action* has become almost standard for the representation of temporal domains for the research-based core of the planning community. We now describe several approaches that have been taken to the modelling of durative action and then we focus on temporal planning using this form of modelling for the remainder of the chapter.

16.3.1 Modelling Durative Actions

The first form of durative actions used in planning extended the classical action representation simply by the addition of a numeric duration. This form, shown in Figure 16.5 part (a), was first introduced by Smith and Weld [Smith and Weld, 1999] and used in the TGP planner. It was then widely used by the part of the classical planning community concerned with extensions to temporal planning [Haslum and Geffner, 2001; Garrido *et al.*, 2002]. This extension affects the semantics of action in certain ways. Preconditions must be maintained invariant over the duration of an action, since no syntactic distinction is made between those conditions needed only to initiate the action and those that must remain true over the entire period of its execution. Effects are asserted at the end of the period of execution and undefined during the action interval. This is a highly simplified form of durative action supporting only a restricted amount of concurrency. In effect, actions can overlap only if they do not interact in any way.

The form depicted in Figure 16.5 part (b) comprises an official extension to the PDDL domain description language used by the planning community since the release of the language [McDermott, 2000] in 1998. This form, described in detail in Fox and Long [Fox and Long, 2003], was used in the 3rd International Planning Competition which was primarily concerned with the ability of modern planning technology to reason with temporal domain descriptions. This form still constitutes a simplified model of time — it was necessary to avoid being over-ambitious given the state of the art in planning prior to the competition — and there remain many interesting extensions to investigate.

In this form a basic distinction is made between preconditions and invariant conditions, thereby supporting the possibility for greater exploitation of concurrency. In addition, a distinction was made between the effects that become true as soon as an action is initiated (for example, the level of water in a tank becomes non-zero as soon as a water source into it is turned on) and those that become true at the end of the durative interval. Finally, the conditions necessary for successful termination of the action are distinguished from preconditions and invariant conditions. An example of such a termination condition is that an executive

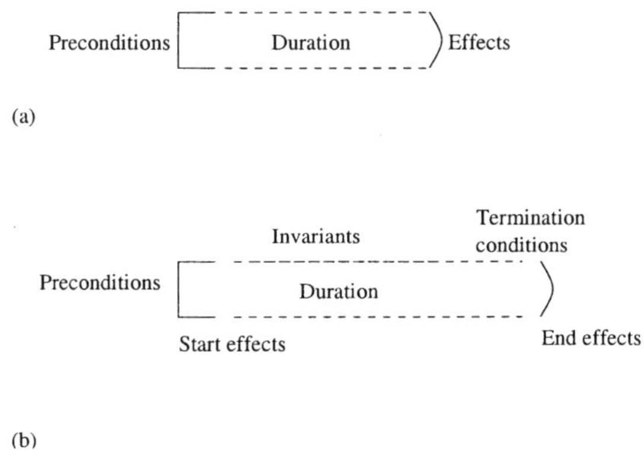

Figure 16.5: Two Durative Action Representations.
The form in part (a) is the durative action construct of TGP. The action is a black box with the preconditions and effects inaccessible during the iterval of its execution.
The form in part (b) was defined for, and used, in the 3rd International Planning Competition. The action is not black-boxed: access is available to both conditions and effects throughout the duration.

must be present to turn off the water source when the tank contains sufficient water. The executive does not need to be present throughout the filling action however, thereby allowing concurrent activity to occur.

Clearly this form of durative action could be extended to allow effects to be asserted at other points during the interval of an action. For example, perhaps the effect of the water in the tank reaching a certain temperature occurs two minutes into the filling period. The languages of IxTeT and SAPA enable the representation of intermediate effects but the formal semantics and computational properties of such representations have not been made clear. PDDL2.1 does not support the explicit modelling of such effects, instead taking the view that judicious modelling can avoid the need to make reference to many time points within an action interval, and thereby simplifying both semantics and the practical issues of reasoning. The advantages and limitations of the competition form of durative action are described in [Fox and Long, 2003].

The durative action forms shown in Figure 16.5 emphasise the representation of discretised change. It is in fact possible to use form (b) in the figure to model continuous change, by allowing the representation of time-dependent functions of those values in a way similar to that proposed by Pednault [Pednault, 1986a]. Figure 16.7 depicts how continuous change can be modelled using durative actions with these features. In fact, extensions to support time dependent functions of continuous values were provided amongst the PDDL extensions made for use in the competition, but the competition problems did not exploit them. Nevertheless, they are discussed in detail in [Fox and Long, 2003]. Such actions wrap up the effects of continuous change into temporal packages that abstract much of what is really happening in order to simplify both representation and reasoning. A better approach might be to explicitly separate the points of initiation and termination of processes, modelling the behaviour of the processes independently and distinguishing between the different ways in which active processes can terminate (by the deliberate action of the planner, for example,

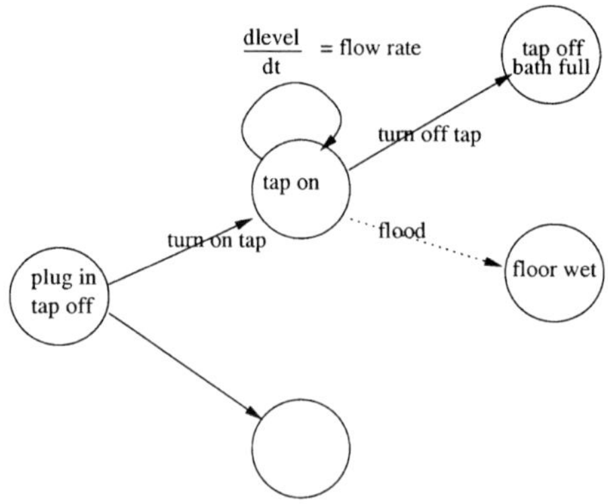

Figure 16.6: The Hybrid View of Change.

Dotted lines are events executed by the world, solid lines are actions under the control of the planner. Cycles on states are processes causing numeric change. These are labelled with the derivative describing how the numeric value (in this case, level of water in the bath) changes. The figure shows that a filling process can be terminated either by an action to turn off the tap or by the event of the bath flooding.

or by the intended or unintended intervention of the world). Fox and Long introduced an extended form of PDDL, called PDDL+, supporting the representation of actions, processes and events [Fox and Long, 2002a; Fox and Long, 2002b], and the language used by McDermott's OPTOP planner [McDermott, 2003] was strongly influenced by its features. The semantics of PDDL+, which is given by means of a mapping to hybrid automata theory [Henzinger, 1996], demonstrates that PDDL+ has the power to support the modelling of complex mixed discrete-continuous situations. Figure 16.6 shows how the integration of actions, processes and events can achieve the classical notion of state transition. Similar modelling power can be obtained in other ways, for example, using the event calculus [Kowalski and Sergot, 1986], but these are less well-integrated with the classical planning heritage.

An alternative approach to the modelling of durative action is to consider the execution of actions to be instantaneous, but to associate actions with effects that are delayed in time and to hide the underlying processes that achieves those effects. TLplan adopts this approach [Bacchus and Ady, 2001]. The notion of a delayed effect might appear as a temporal equivalent to "effect at a distance", with a similarly uneasy relationship to commonly accepted physical laws. However, it is possible to see the delayed effect as the observed consequence of a process triggered by the action, with the process itself having no discernible effect at the level of abstraction of the model prior to the delayed effect. Provided that the delayed effect can be seen as an inevitable consequence of the process triggered by the initial action, this view is both consistent and intuitively reasonable. This observation emphasises the fact that planning domain models are intended to allow planners to reason about the effects of the actions they select between in the construction of a plan, which is not necessarily the same as providing a model of the physical world within which the actions will be executed. A model can be abstracted in many ways that simplify the reasoning that the planner must perform to construct a plan and the abstraction of details of a process that cannot be

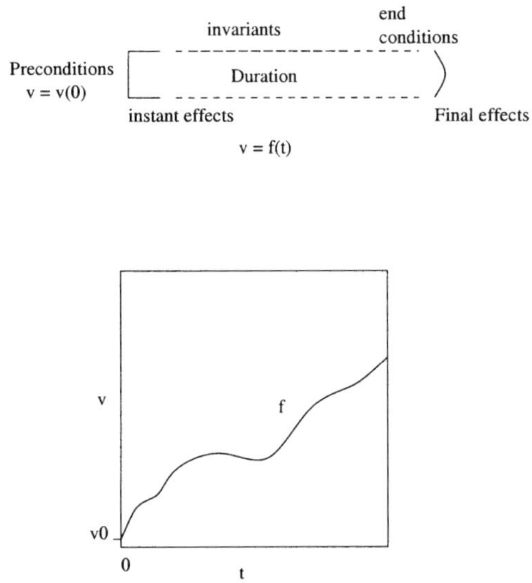

Figure 16.7: Representing time-dependent change in a durative action framework.

The value v is a continuously changing numeric quantity, with a value v(0) at the point of initiation of the durative action. The value of v is changed according to the function f and its value at any time t during the execution of the action is given by f(t).

affected by the planner during its execution is only one such possibility.

Although more sophisticated languages exist for planning, as can be observed by consideration of the languages of OPTOP, IxTeT and TLplan and of PDDL+, few planners yet exist that are capable of planning with them. The current state of the art is considered in Section 16.9. Following the 3rd International Planning Competition considerable progress has been made with the solution of the *TEA* problem, using the language depicted in Figure 16.5 part (b), and many challenges remain to be addressed by the community.

16.4 Planning and Temporal Reasoning

Four issues within the temporal reasoning community have been of particular significance in the development of temporal planning. These are: the selection of a temporal ontology; causality; the problems of modelling and reasoning about concurrency and the management of continuous change. Because of the importance of these issues in the effective exploitation of temporal planning domain models this chapter will focus on the ways in which they have been addressed in modern temporal planning approaches. We begin by giving a brief introduction to the aspects of these issues that are central to planning, then we consider in more detail how they arise, and are resolved, in algorithms designed to solve the *TEA* and *TEG* planning problems.

16.4.1 Temporal Ontology

Temporal reasoning systems all share the need to capture a model of the progression of time. The ontological primitives from which the representations of time are built vary between systems. A fundamental ontological decision concerns whether time should be modelled as interval-based or point-based. Time is most conveniently thought of as passing in intervals, while change, particularly logical change, appears to be located at points. Both interval-based [Allen, 1984] and point-based [McCarthy and Hayes, 1969] approaches to the modelling of change have been adopted in different planning systems and there are also systems that combine both interval and point-based ontologies in different components of the reasoning mechanisms [Ghallab and Laruelle, 1994; Muscettola, 1994]. A related question is whether time itself is considered to be continuous or discrete. Planning is directly concerned with change brought about by actions, so it is naturally concerned with the way in which the actions fit into the ontological structure of time. One of the questions that is directly affected by the ontological choice is how change is captured at an instant of activity: this question has been referred to as the *divided instant problem* [van Benthem, 1983].

In considering the ontological commitments made within certain planning architectures we also consider how temporal extent is managed. In a state-based model it is common to consider that states are instants of time and that time passes between the states, meaning that actions have temporal extent. Conversely, it is possible to consider the state-transitions as instantaneous and states to have temporal extent. We examine how these alternative views are manifest in particular planning systems and also how they affect the consequent reasoning with time and change.

16.4.2 Causality

Causality is a central issue in temporal reasoning. Causality is the relationship that holds between events or actions and the changes that necessarily follow them. It is a temporal relationship, since cause precedes effect. It is also a relationship that depends on levels of abstraction in models that capture it, since causes can be expressed at many different levels of granularity. Causal relations can attempt to model physical relationships derived from Newtonian physical models, or they can be abstracted to capture far less direct causal links, replacing chains of physical links with single relationships. For example, in typical models of the so-called Yale Shooting Problem [Hanks and McDermott, 1986] there is a physical causal relationship stating that pulling the trigger of a gun will cause it to fire (if the gun is loaded and functioning correctly). Causal relationships of this kind allow indirect causal relations to be inferred, such as that pulling the trigger of a gun causes the death of the person at whom the gun is aimed. Modelling and inferring these causal relationships is highly complex because of factors such as ramification and uniqueness of causal explanations.

In temporal reasoning it is often a primary objective to identify causes for observed events in order to generate explanations for observed situations. In planning, matters are typically simplified by making the assumption that the only causes of change are the actions that are selected for execution by the planner. Furthermore, the task of a planner is to construct a plan that achieves the goals, exploiting the causal relationships between action execution and change, rather than to construct explanations (although there are some parallels between these activities). The restricted objectives of temporal reasoning in a planning context simplify many of the issues surrounding causality. Nevertheless, causal behaviour underlies planning domain models and decisions about causal relationships can, therefore, affect the structure of planning problems and, as a consequence, planning algorithms. In Section 16.6 we discuss the specific ways in which causality has been addressed in planning research.

16.4.3 Concurrency

Planning is concerned with the organisation of activity: temporal planning is further concerned with how the activity is organised in time. For the temporal planning problem to be interestingly different from the classical planning problem of identifying a totally ordered sequence of actions to achieve a goal, it is necessary that there be opportunity for a planner to exploit the passage of time efficiently. This requires that there be a basis for concurrency. Concurrency complicates models of action and change because they require a representation of the possible interactions, both positive and negative, between concurrent actions. Planners are forced to reason about how actions might affect potentially parallel activities in order to construct sound plans. Planning activities that must be performed within a deadline can only be performed successfully if there is an adequate model of concurrency allowing activities to be executed in parallel.

An issue that arises in the context of concurrency is the question of synchronisation and what assumptions are made in different planning systems about how actions or states can be organised to overlap and to synchronise with one another. An example of a problem that is linked to this question is Gelfond's soup bowl problem [Gelfond *et al.*, 1991] in which, to successfully raise a bowl of soup without spilling the contents, both sides must be lifted together. To model this problem as intended it must be possible to capture the interaction between the two actions of lifting (one on each side of the bowl) and the synchronisation of those actions.

Different planning systems have approached the problem of concurrency in different ways and we will discuss how the various approaches represent compromises between tractable reasoning about planning problems and restrictions on the modelling and problem representations that the planners can use.

16.4.4 Continuous change

Temporal reasoning is tied to reasoning about change. Change can be instantaneous but it can also be more closely associated with the flow of time. In particular, when processes are executing over time, the changes that are wrought by the processes will also evolve over time. This includes processes that are caused by physical effects such as the action of forces and conservation of momentum. In traditional physical models it is usual to treat changes such as these using parameters whose values are described by continuous functions of time. In temporal logical models continuous change can be abstracted into discrete changes associated with specific points of time, or with intervals during which a changing value is undefined. Several temporal reasoning frameworks began with consideration of discrete change and, later, were extended to handle continuous change. For example, in [Shanahan, 1990] Shanahan extends the event calculus of Kowalski and Sergot [Kowalski and Sergot, 1986] to enable the modelling of continuous change.

Continuous change becomes an issue when the way that actions can affect states can be numeric as well as logical. If all change is logical the flow of time can be discretised around action effects. In this way a situation involving continuous change can be modelled as a discretised sequence of effects. For example: the situation in which a ball is dropped from the roof of a tower, and can be seen from each of the floors in the building as it passes their windows, can be modelled discretely in terms of the dropping of the ball and the fact of the visibility of the ball at each of the windows at successive points in time.

In languages in which numeric change can be modelled the situation is complicated by the need to correctly model the way that numeric quantities change over time. When multiple concurrent actions can affect the same numeric quantities this can lead to arbitrarily complex models of time. There has been a recent growth of interest in planning with continuous change although these issues have been considered in the reasoning about action community for some time.

16.5 Temporal Ontology

The representation of time has been associated with an important dichotomy between ontological foundations in intervals [Allen, 1984] or in points [McCarthy and Hayes, 1969]. This dichotomy affects planning as much as other uses of time. The state-transition semantics that is commonly used in planning lends itself to the use of a point-based ontology. However, the exploitation of concurrent activity, the management of extended activities or processes, of windows of opportunity and of periods of constrained activity all fit more readily with an interval-based ontology. As we have discussed, both ontological bases have been explored in planning while the question of whether states are points between which actions occur over time or whether actions are instantaneous transitions between states that have duration has not been given an unequivocal answer in the planning community. It is possible to be agnostic about whether states or actions have duration because classical planning assumes that the only source of change in the world is the execution of actions selected by the planner and that all change initiated by an action is completed prior to the initiation of a new action. This combination of assumptions means that the passage of time is not important in classical planning, but only the ordering of events within it.

16.5.1 Changing Fluents and the Divided Instant Problem

Although classical planning is not particularly concerned with whether states or actions have duration, there is one detail of the interface between states and actions that has to be resolved in giving a semantics to the execution of plans. The detail arises from the fact that the preconditions of an action must be tested in a state that *strictly precedes* the state in which the effects become apparent, since the effects can be, indeed usually are, inconsistent with the preconditions. If actions are considered instantaneous then there is a question over the precise truth status of propositions affected by an action at the point of action execution. The issue is not particularly problematic when plans are seen as totally ordered sequences of actions, since the precise status of propositions at the point of application of actions is not required for reasoning about what actions may follow one another — it only affects the possibility of concurrent action. Matters are not resolved by adopting the alternative view that actions have duration with states being instantaneous, since the truth values of propositions affected by the actions are then undefined during the interval of their execution. The divided instant problem [van Benthem, 1983] is the problem of determining what happens

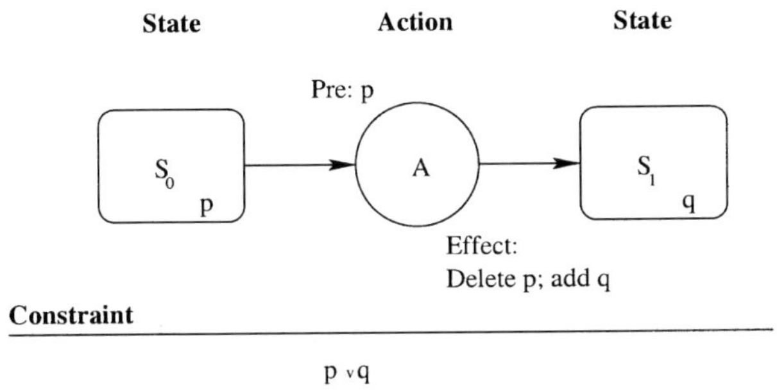

Figure 16.8: The question of truth during action execution.

at the instant of application of an action in a model in which actions are instantaneous. We generalise the problem in the following discussion to the question of what happens when an action is executed, whether the change it provokes is instantaneous or associated with a duration. It should be noted that an action with duration can still have instantaneous effects on the state at distinct points during its execution (typically the start and end points). We are concerned in the following with the way that change itself is brought about, rather than the possible linking of coordinated changes into a single action structure. Essentially, the question is what happens to a fluent (atomic) propositional variable as it changes? There are four possibilities:

1. A propositional variable always has a defined truth value. It is common to achieve this on a real time line by simply ensuring that adjacent intervals over which a proposition takes different truth values always meet with one interval being open and one being closed. Whether intervals are always half-open on the left or on the right is simply a matter of convention. It is natural, in this view, to consider state with duration and actions as instantaneous, so that change occurs at the instants on the closed boundary of the intervals.

2. A propositional variable does not have an associated truth value while undergoing change. This resolution makes no assumptions about whether change has associated duration or whether states have duration.

3. A propositional variable always has a specific truth value during change (either true or false). This approach has the virtue of simplicity, but does not have a particularly strong claim to intuitive appeal.

4. A propositional variable is considered to be both true and false during change. Although this approach offers support for concurrent activity, by allowing any constraint on the truth value of a proposition to be satisfied, it allows inconsistent constraints to be satisfied and can therefore be rejected as a plausible option.

In practice, one of the first two solutions is always adopted.

To better understand the impact of this question on planning, consider the following problem, illustrated in Figure 16.8. An action, A, is applied in a state, S_0, in which proposition p holds. It has the effect of making p false and q true, which is apparent in the following state, S_1. Suppose that a constraint is to be maintained that $p \vee q$ be true across a period

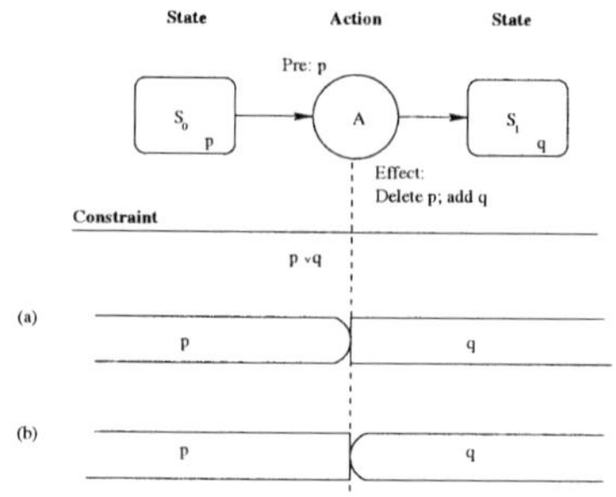

Figure 16.9: A resolution to the question of truth during action execution.

p and q true in disjoint abutting intervals, meeting at the point of application of A. In case (a) the interval is half open on the right, while in (b) it is half open on the left.

containing the application of A. The question is whether the condition is met. Notice that there is no commitment to whether states or actions have duration in this problem. Consider the impact of the four possible choices offered above:

1. In this case, at each instant in time the proposition $p \vee q$ is true, since the truth value is defined for each of p and q at each time point. The situation will be one or other of those shown in Figure 16.9. This is the approach adopted in LPGP [Long and Fox, 2003a] and Sapa [Do and Kambhampati, 2001], for example. The semantics of the PDDL language are also based on this approach, using intervals that are half open on the right [Fox and Long, 2003].

2. Using this approach, the status of p and q is unknown at the time when A is applied. Therefore, the constraint must be considered broken and the action cannot be part of a valid plan that has to maintain the constraint over the interval in which the action is being considered. This approach is used in TGP [Smith and Weld, 1999] and TP4 [Haslum and Geffner, 2001], for example.

3. With this possibility both p and q will have the same truth value when A is applied. Since this value can be selected arbitrarily (in defining the semantics of change), $p \vee q$ might be either true or false. However, if p is the proposition *doorOpen* and q is *doorClosed*, for example, then it is also reasonable to add a constraint $\neg p \vee \neg q$. In this case, one or other of the constraints will certainly be false across the interval including execution of A. This example shows that this solution can still lead to intuitively plausible concurrent effects being prevented despite propositional variables being defined throughout the plan.

16.5.2 Relative time

In classical planning models, time is treated as relative. That is, the only temporal structuring in a plan, and in reasoning about a plan, is in the ordering between actions. This is most clearly emphasised by the issues that dominated planning research in the late 1980s and early 1990s, when classical planning was mainly characterised by the exploration of partial plan spaces, in planners such as TWEAK [Chapman, 1987], UCPOP [Penberthy and Weld, 1992] and SNLP [McAllester and Rosenblitt, 1991]. Partial plans include a collection of actions representing the activity thus far determined to be part of a possible plan and a set of temporal constraints on those actions. The temporal constraints used in a partial plan are all of the form $A < B$ where A and B are time points corresponding to the application of actions. The efficient management of ordering constraints in a partial order planner depends on being able to add new constraints, to query the collection of constraints in order to determine whether a given pair of actions is already ordered (possibly by an ordering implied by the transitivity of the explicit constraints) and to remove constraints during backtracking. There is a significant challenge in implementing an efficient constraint handler that allows all of these tasks to be managed at low cost. Gerevini and Schubert produced TimeGraph in two successive versions [Gerevini *et al.*, 1995; Gerevini and Schubert, 1995a], capable of handling both ordering constraints and also separation constraints of the form $A \neq B$. Fox and Long produced Tempman [Fox and Long, 1996] which manages only ordering constraints. Each of these systems makes compromises between the relative costs of constraint addition, constraint retraction and constraint querying that make performance dependent on the context of use. Importantly, in both of these systems, and in other temporal constraint managers implemented for partial order planners, the constraints are all relative, rather than absolute: the duration between time points is not considered important. In a partial planner, a finished plan can contain a partial order on the set of actions it contains. The interpretation of the partial order can be seen as supporting possible concurrency between the actions that are required to fall between two points in a plan, but are not themselves ordered. In fact, more strictly it means that the actions in the collection can be executed in any order and lead to a state that will allow both completion of the plan and successful achievement of the goals. This need not mean that the unordered actions can be expected to lead to the same state regardless of the order of their execution and, if they do not, it is even less reasonable to suppose that they can be executed concurrently. Even if the actions commute, it is not clear that it is reasonable to suppose they can be executed concurrently, particularly because there is no indication (in classical planning problems) of whether the actions have duration and, if so, whether they are all of equal duration.

Classical linear planners [Fikes and Nilsson, 1971; Russell and Norvig, 1995] rely on the simple fact that a total ordering on the points at which actions are applied can be trivially embedded into a time line. Again, the duration between actions is not considered.

The construction of a plan involves building a collection of activities whose organisation satisfies certain constraints. These constraints include temporal constraints that govern the necessary separation or ordering of certain elements of the collection. These constraints can be expressed using either interval or point-based models. However, some constraints that can be represented as binary constraints on intervals cannot be expressed as binary constraints on points. For example, the constraint that two intervals, A and B, must not overlap is represented as a disjunction of the form:

$$A_{end} < B_{start} \vee B_{end} < A_{start}$$

which cannot be captured using a conjunction of binary constraints on the four time points representing the end-points of the two intervals.

16.5.3 Metric time

The role of time in planning becomes far more significant once metric time is introduced. With metric time it is possible to associate specific durations with actions, to set deadlines or windows of opportunity. The problems associated with relative time have still to be resolved in a metric time framework, but new problems are introduced. In particular, durations become explicit, so it is necessary to decide what the durations attach to: actions or states. Further, explicit temporal extents make it more important to confront the issue of concurrency in order to best exploit the measured temporal resources available to a planner.

In contrast to the simple ordering constraints required for relative time, metric time requires more powerful constraint management. Most metric time constraint handlers are built around the foundations laid by Dechter, Meiri and Pearl [Dechter *et al.*, 1991]. For example, IxTeT uses extensions of temporal constraint networks [Ghallab and Laruelle, 1994]. One of the earliest planners to consider the use of metric time was Deviser [Vere, 1983], which was developed from NONLIN [Tate, 1977]. In Deviser, metric constraints on the times at which actions could be applied and deadlines for the achievements of goals were both expressible and the planner could construct plans respecting metric temporal constraints on the interactions between actions. Cesta and Oddi [Cesta and Oddi, 1996] have explored various developments of temporal constraint network algorithms to achieve efficient implementation for planning and Galipienso and Sanchis [Galipienso and Sanchis, 2002] and and Tsamardinos and Pollack [Tsamardinos and Pollack, 2003] consider extensions to manage disjunctive temporal constraints efficiently, which is a particularly valuable expressive element for plan construction as was observed above, since constraints preventing overlap of intervals translate into disjunctive constraints on time points. HSTS [Muscettola, 1994] also relies on a temporal constraint manager.

The classic algorithms for handling simple temporal networks (STPs) [Dechter *et al.*, 1991] make use of the possibility to view temporal constraints as graphs. The edges of the graph represent ordering constraints and the edges can be weighted to reflect duration bounds. In this representation, negatively weighted cycles imply inconsistency in the constraints. Variants of Bellman-Ford algorithms can be used to efficiently propagate information through a graph as constraints are added, checking for negative cycles and allowing efficient determination of implied constraints.

In systems that use continuous real-valued time it is possible to make use of linear constraint solvers to handle temporal constraints. In particular, constraints dictated by the relative placement of actions with durations on a timeline can be approached in this way [Long and Fox, 2003a]. An alternative timeline that is often used is a discretised line based on integers. The advantage of this approach is that it is possible to advance time to a *next* value after considering activity at any given time point. The *next* modality can be interpreted in a continuous time framework by taking it to mean the state following the next logical change, regardless of the time at which this occurs [Bacchus and Kabanza, 1998]. In planning problems in which no events can occur other than the actions dictated by the planner and no continuous change is modelled, plans are finite structures and therefore change can occur at only a finite number of time points during its execution. This makes it possible to embed the execution of the plan into the integer-valued discrete time line without any loss of expressiveness.

16.6 Causality

Giunchiglia and Lifschitz [Giunchiglia and Lifschitz, 1998] describe two types of causal law: static and dynamic. Static laws are of the form:

$$caused \quad F \quad if \quad G$$

and dynamic laws are of the form:

$$caused \quad F \quad if \quad G \quad after \quad H$$

In both cases, F and G are *fluents* (propositions the truth values of which can change), and H can be an action identifier. Of these laws the second is fundamental to planning whilst the first is much less commonly exploited. Static causality describes the ramifications of change and can be modelled by the addition to planning problem descriptions of axioms describing the indirect effects of actions. Axioms of this kind are not heavily used because reasoning about action interactions is complicated by the presence of indirect effects.

A critical issue for planning is the tractability of domain models. A continuing challenge for the field is to find ways of expressing complex relationships without sacrificing the prospect of finding plans in practice. In classical planning all effects of actions are explicitly identified with the actions that produce them, often resulting in tractable models. The overriding concern with the tractability of the reasoning problem has necessitated a trade-off of philosophical expressiveness for practical efficiency. Although static causality has tended not to be explored in depth, dynamic causality, in which a fact is caused *after* some action has taken place, is fundamental because it describes the effects of applying actions to world states.

The notion of fluents having *default values* has not been considered in detail in planning, although it is an important factor in providing causal explanations for observed situations. For example, Giunchiglia and Lifschitz's spring-loaded door cannot be captured in a classical planning formulation. When a door is spring loaded it becomes closed without the planning agent carrying out any action to achieve that effect. Indeed, opening the door causes it to be closed after a certain amount of time has elapsed. The underlying causal model cannot be expressed in classical planning terms but can be expressed once time is introduced and actions can be executed concurrently. For example, the action of going through a door, from room A to room B, can have the precondition that the door be closed, and that the agent is in room A, and the immediate effect that it is open and that the agent is in room B. After a specified amount of time has elapsed the action has the effect that the door is once again closed. This example helps to emphasise the importance of the link between causality and time.

Planners all exploit the implicit causal relationship between the execution of actions and the realisation of their effects. In fact, the causal link between actions and their effects is typically a great simplification and, although planners can reason with planning domain models as though the actions are the causes of the changes that they describe, domain models are often not intended to be causal models. The constraints of the representational framework available for construction of planning domain models can make it very difficult to identify the causal structure underlying a planning domain. For example, consider the simple Briefcase Problem [Pednault, 1989], in which a briefcase is currently at the office, together with some other items such as a book. The actions available to the planner are to load items into and unload them from the briefcase and to carry the briefcase between locations. One way to

```
(:action load
 :parameters (?o - object ?b - briefcase ?loc - location)
 :precondition (and (at ?o ?loc) (at ?b ?loc))
 :effect (and (not (at ?o ?loc)) (in ?o ?b)))

(:action carry
 :parameters (?b - briefcase ?from ?to - location)
 :precondition (at ?b ?from)
 :effect (and (not (at ?b ?from)) (at ?b ?to)))

(:action unload
 :parameters (?o - object ?b - briefcase ?loc - location)
 :precondition (and (at ?b ?loc) (in ?o ?b))
 :effect (and (not (in ?o ?b)) (at ?o ?loc)))
```

Figure 16.10: An encoding of Pednault's briefcase problem using purely STRIPS actions.

represent this problem without using quantified effects is shown in Figure 16.10. As can be seen, this model suggests that if a plan is constructed to move a book from the office to home by loading the book into the briefcase, carrying the briefcase home and then unloading the book, it will appear to be the action of unloading that causes the book to be at home. It would be reasonable to argue that it is actually the act of carrying home the briefcase, containing the book, that causes the book to be at home. A model using quantified effects (Figure 16.11) can make this causal relationship more explicit, but a planner can adequately reason with the first model, generating a sensible plan to get the book home, despite the fact that the model is not a causal model. More generally, in planning domain descriptions actions are used to maintain a consistent model of the state of the world and achieving this can involve effects that are concerned more with managing the machinery of the model within the constraints of the domain modelling framework than they are with reflecting causal features of the domain that is being modelled. Gazen and Knoblock [Gazen and Knoblock, 1997] have shown that various features of richer expressive models (that can allow apparently more accurate causal models) can be compiled into simpler STRIPS models by utilising encoding techniques. Such techniques create models in which the causal structure is very much diluted.

As we have shown, planning domain descriptions are constructed in order for planners to reason about the construction of plans, rather than to reason about explicit causal relationships. The distinction between a causal model and a planning domain model arises in other ways. For example, in planners that make use of advice supplied alongside the domain model, such as TLPlan [Bacchus and Kabanza, 2000], SHOP [Nau *et al.*, 1999], SIPE2 [Wilkins, 1988] and O-Plan [Drabble and Tate, 1994], the advice typically constrains a planner to choose particular actions to achieve certain goals because these are considered, by the human advisor, to be the better choices. Clearly such advice is not causal and restricts a planner in order to prevent use of actions that might cause a particular effect but would not be sensible choices in the construction of a plan. It is possible to separate advice from the action model of a planning domain, but most systems that use advice do not attempt to clearly distinguish a causal model from the advice that is encoded.

As discussed above, in research into reasoning about action and change it has been common to distinguish dynamic and static causal rules. Planning systems have generally not been built to respect this distinction, but some systems, such as UCPOP [Penberthy and Weld, 1992], make use of domain axioms that are distinct from actions. The role of domain axioms

```
(:action load
 :parameters (?o - object ?b - briefcase ?loc - location)
 :precondition (and (at ?o ?loc)
                    (at ?b ?loc)
                    (not (in ?o ?b)))
 :effect (in ?o ?b))

(:action carry
 :parameters (?b - briefcase ?from ?to - location)
 :precondition (at ?b ?from)
 :effect (and (not (at ?b ?from)) (at ?b ?to)
              (forall (?o - object)
                  (when (in ?o ?b)
                      (and (not (at ?o ?from))
                           (at ?o ?to))))))

(:action unload
 :parameters (?o - object ?b - briefcase)
 :precondition (in ?o ?b)
 :effect (not (in ?o ?b)))
```

Figure 16.11: An encoding of Pednault's briefcase problem using actions with negative preconditions and quantified, conditional effects.

is usually to allow fluent propositions that are indirectly affected by different actions to be correctly managed without complicated conditional effects. Examples of situations in which axioms might be used are in modelling the flow of electricity around a circuit [Thiébaux *et al.*, 1996] or of fluid around a network of pipes [Aylett *et al.*, 1998]. In circuits the act of closing a switch might cause flow around parts of the circuit. However, to determine which parts of a circuit are affected requires knowledge of which switches are currently open or closed and how the circuit is connected. To correctly update the model to reflect which parts of the circuit are made live by closing a switch can be achieved with conditional effects, but only by making the conditional effects tie very closely to the specific circuit for which the action is to be used. Using domain axioms, the liveness condition can be modelled as an implied effect of the status of a collection of switches. In this way, the action of opening or closing a switch can describe just the direct effect on the switch itself, while its causal effects on the liveness of the circuit can be captured through the use of the domain axioms that will support inference of the circuit status from the fluent propositions recording the states of the switches. The use of domain axioms can be compiled into action encodings, as shown by Gazen and Knoblock [Gazen and Knoblock, 1997] and Garagnani [Garagnani, 2000], but models using axioms reflect more of the causal structure of the domain. This picture is complicated by concurrency, as we discuss in Section 16.7.4.

16.6.1 Exogenous events

Many planning systems assume that the only changes that can occur in the world are caused by the actions selected by the planner. In real problem domains this assumption is too simple. In practice, events occur in the world outside the direct control of the planner. There are at least two ways in which this can happen: events can occur regardless of the activities planned by and subsequently executed on behalf of a planner, such as sunrise and sunset, and events can be indirectly influenced by the actions of a planner, such as a ball hitting the ground after its planned release. Events that lie outside the control of the planner can include predictable events and also unpredictable events, perhaps representing the effects of actions made by other agents. Exogenous events are relevant to the question of causality because they break the usual assumption in planning that all causal structure is, at least implicitly, determined by the relationship between the planners selection of actions and the effects of those actions: events are produced by causal relationships that are either outside the control of the planner or are directed through chains of causation that lead from actions to the ultimate triggering of events.

Planning with unpredictable events is difficult, because the nature of planning is to attempt to predict the evolution of the world and to control it, while unpredictable events undermine the ability to control. There are various strategies available for managing this problem. One option is to build *conformant plans*. These are plans that will execute regardless of what events the world generates, within certain limits. Conformant planning has been explored, for example, using a model-checking approach to planning in the CMBP system, by Cimatti and Roveri [Cimatti and Roveri, 1999; Cimatti and Roveri, 2000] and in a planning-as-satisfiability system, C-Plan, by Castellini, Giunchiglia and Tacchella [Castellini *et al.*, 2001]. An alternative strategy is to construct *contingent plans* that attempt to exploit probabilistic predictions of the evolution of the world and to construct plans with contingent branches that can be used to handle different outcomes in the world. A Graphplan-based approach to contingent planning has been explored in the SGP system by Weld, Anderson and Smith [Weld *et al.*, 1998], while Drabble, in the Excalibur system [Drabble, 1993], and Blythe, in the Weaver system [Blythe, 1995], have also considered the treatment of unpredictable exogenous events using probabilistic models.

Where events are predictable planning is able to proceed in a more traditional manner, predicting the evolution of the world as it unfolds according to the actions of the planner. The fact that some actions can lead to further events, as for example in Thielscher's circuit problem [Thielscher, 1997], can be represented using only actions at the cost of a distortion in the model of the causal structure of the domain. Events can be seen as similar to actions, except that they happen without the planner making a choice to add them to the plan. This can be represented by adding the actions to a partial plan structure before the planning begins or else by forcing the planner to select actions through the introduction of artificial preconditions into other activities, preventing the planner from making any progress at all without initiating the event-simulating actions. This approach subverts the causal structure, as with other encoding techniques discussed above, but allows a planner to handle exogenous events with relatively little modification.

16.6.2 Causality and Non-determinism

There has been a considerable body of work exploring non-deterministic effects in planning [Cimatti and Roveri, 1999; Cimatti and Roveri, 2000; Bertoli *et al.*, 2001; Blythe, 1999; Bonet and Geffner, 2000; Majercik and Littman, 1999; Boutilier *et al.*, 1999; Onder and Pollack, 1999; Rintannen, 1999; Bresina *et al.*, 2002]. An example of an action with non-deterministic effects is tossing a coin, where the outcome is known to lie in the finite set $\{heads, tails\}$, but could be either value. The structure of plans for domains with actions such as these, and even the nature of planning itself, is not universally agreed upon. It is clear that a model using non-deterministic behaviour is often the consequence of an unwillingness or inability to supply causal explanations or causal models of the underlying behaviour. For example, one might, in principle, be able to describe the behaviour of a spinning coin in terms of the physical forces, distribution of mass and so on that govern its trajectory, but the precise details of too many of the elements that affect the tossing of a coin are simply unavailable to allow precise modelling supporting prediction of the outcome.

A different form of non-determinism, particularly relevant in temporal planning, is non-deterministic duration: actions might have durations that are modelled by probability distributions. HSTS and IXTET [Vidal and Ghallab, 1996] model the durations of intervals with end points themselves represented as intervals of uncertainty. The interpretation of uncertainty over interval end points can be as flexibility for the executive to exploit during plan execution, or else as uncertainty that the planner must allow for in building robust plans. In the former case, the intention would be to capture the fact that an executive can occasionally execute an action in less time by speeding up, or in more time by slowing down. For example, the action of driving to work might normally take fifteen minutes, but it could be stretched to twenty or twenty-five minutes by driving at a leisurely pace, or decreased to twelve or even ten minutes by driving as fast as possible. In the case where variability represents uncertainty that the planner must allow for in a plan, the action duration varies out of the control of the executive. For example, when driving to work through heavy traffic the duration of the drive action is dependent on the traffic load. There is clearly scope to represent both kinds of uncertainty in domain models, but this remains an open area of research.

16.7 Concurrency

Concurrency becomes an important issue for planning when actions are associated with duration or when goals are temporally constrained. Sometimes the ability to perform actions in parallel determines solvability of a problem, sometimes only the quality of the solution found is affected. However, the semantics of concurrent activity are more complex than when actions are linearly ordered.

16.7.1 Concurrency and Mutual Exclusion

One of the first issues that must be resolved in handling concurrent activity is to determine when concurrent activities are possible and which activities interfere or interact with one another. Interference means that the activities cannot be executed concurrently, while interaction can lead to effects that are not implied by any of the individual actions alone.

Using the simplified durative action model depicted in Figure 16.5 part (a) a strong mutual exclusion definition is needed to ensure plan validity. In TGP [Smith and Weld, 1999] actions cannot be allowed to overlap in a plan if there is any conflict between their preconditions, postconditions, or between their pre- and postconditions. For example, if an action, A, deletes the effect of another action, B, A cannot overlap with B even if its end point is later (or earlier) than the end point of B. The reason is that B is seen as a durative interval over which some process producing the effect is active, and A is seen as a durative interval over which another process, that undermines that same effect, is active. Plans in which mutually exclusive processes like this overlap are deemed invalid. Sapa [Do and Kambhampati, 2001] is also based on the view that there are processes hidden in the durative intervals of actions that are responsible for producing effects at the end points. The resulting mutual exclusion

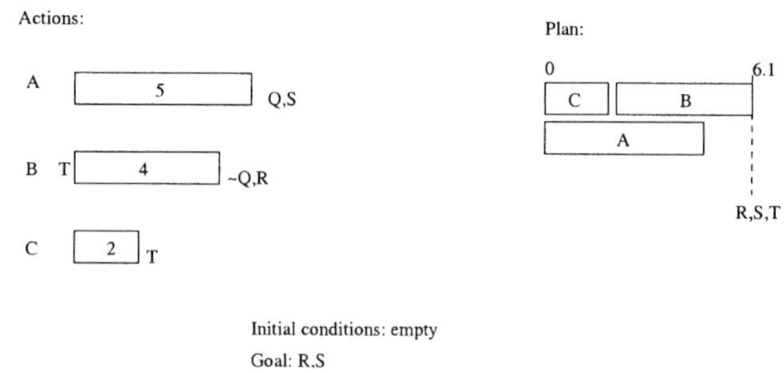

Figure 16.12: A, B and C are durative actions with durations 5, 4 and 2 respectively.

A plan is required to achieve the goals R and S from an empty initial state. Since C and A have empty preconditions they can be immediately applied concurrently. B can be applied as soon as its precondition, T, is available, resulting in a plan that achieves the goal condition after 6.1 units of time. This plan uses a separation of one tenth of a unit of time between actions B and C to avoid interactions between their end points. The need for such a separation is discussed further in Section 16.7.2. TGP would not consider this plan to be valid because of the (assumed) conflicting underlying processes producing R and S.

definition is conservative, in that some intuitively valid forms of concurrency are prohibited. Figure 16.12 depicts an example of a situation in which a plan is deemed invalid according to the mutual exclusion definition of TGP, even though in fact it appears to be a valid concurrent plan. Using the extended durative action model of Figure 16.5 part (b) it is possible to exploit more concurrency by distinguishing between those conditions and effects that are in the process of being maintained or produced throughout the interval of the action, and those that are instantaneous or temporary. Taking the example in Figure 16.12 it can be observed that, if Q is an initial effect of B instead of a final effect, and is not maintained as an invariant condition throughout the durative interval, there is no conflict between the hidden processes of A and B and the plan in Figure 16.12 can be considered valid. Thus, distinguishing between the different roles that conditions and effects can play in the definition of an action can support the exploitation of greater concurrency than is possible if these different roles are confounded by too simple a representation.

A semantics that allows actions to be applied concurrently by considering actions to initiate instantaneous change, but associating invariant conditions with the intervals over which actions execute, offers scope for far more concurrency, as this example illustrates. Nevertheless, there remains a question about precisely what activity can be concurrent at the instant of change. That is, which actions can actually be applied simultaneously, and how this is interpreted.

The question of which instantaneous actions can be executed simultaneously was also considered by Blum and Furst [Blum and Furst, 1995] in the development of Graphplan. This is because Graphplan allows actions to appear active in the same layer of the plan graph in a valid plan, implying that these actions can be executed simultaneously. In Graphplan, actions can be active in the same layer of the plan graph if they do not interfere — that is, if the delete effects of one action do not intersect with either the preconditions or positive postconditions of the other. This definition of mutual exclusivity of actions is actually important as much for the construction of plans in Graphplan as it is for the definition of concurrency, and it appears to be more of a matter of *post hoc* rationalisation than one of principle that non-mutex actions are argued to be executable in parallel. However, the idea behind the definition of mutex actions and its relationship to concurrency is important and bears striking similarity to the mechanism by which shared-memory accesses are managed in operating systems, through the use of *read* and *write* locks. If one considers actions analogous to separate processes in a multi-processing operating system and fluents as variables in shared-memory, then an action precondition demands *read-access* to all of the fluents it refers to, while action postconditions demand *write-access* to all of the fluents they refer to. Then, as in shared-memory systems, a fluent can support multiple simultaneous read-accesses, but a write-access prevents any other process from accessing the fluent. An action can, of course, refer to the same fluent in both its pre- and postconditions, just as a single process can read and then write to shared-memory, because its own memory accesses are sequenced. In the context of simultaneous action execution in planning, this interpretation is slightly more conservative than the Graphplan definition of mutual exclusion, since it implies that an action that refers to a fluent in a postcondition will require a *write-lock* for the fluent even if it does not actually change it. Similarly, two actions that are both attempting to modify a fluent in the same way are mutually exclusive under the shared-memory semantics, but not under the Graphplan definition. The shared-memory semantics has the advantage of accounting for mutual exclusion in a much wider set of cases than the Graphplan definition and a long heritage of use in concurrent programming. PDDL2.1 [Fox and Long, 2003] adopts the shared-memory semantics under the name of the *No Moving Targets* rule.

16.7.2 Synchronisation and Simultaneity

It should be noted that, in the plan depicted in Figure 16.12, the actions C and B do not exactly abut but are separated by a small interval of time. The reason for this is that C achieves a precondition for B, which makes the two activities mutually exclusive under the shared-memory semantics, requiring their separation. Another interpretation of the need for separation in this case is that there is a causal relationship between the end point of C and the start point of B. These two end points cannot, therefore, occur precisely simultaneously because causal relationships imply temporal ordering. Furthermore, precise synchronicity is impossible to achieve in reality, and the validity of a plan should not appear to rely on it being achievable, or on it being possible to ensure that the order in which the two end points actually occur will preserve the necessary causal relationship.

In fact this is controversial since the planning community has classically ignored the synchronicity issue and allowed achievement and consumption of conditions to occur at the same time in the plan. For example, TGP [Smith and Weld, 1999] allows the plan in which a vehicle moves from X to Y and then from Y to Z to start the second move action at the precise instant at which the first move action terminates. The question of how such a plan might be executed is often answered [Smith and Weld, 1999; Bacchus and Ady, 2001; McDermott, 2003] by saying that in fact the actions associated with the same point in time can be sequenced if causally necessary at the point of execution. That is, multiple actions can be executed simultaneously and yet in sequence. This device ensures that no attempt is made to move from Y to Z before Y has actually been reached. Although in this simplistic example the solution appears to work, because there is no possibility of leaving Y before it

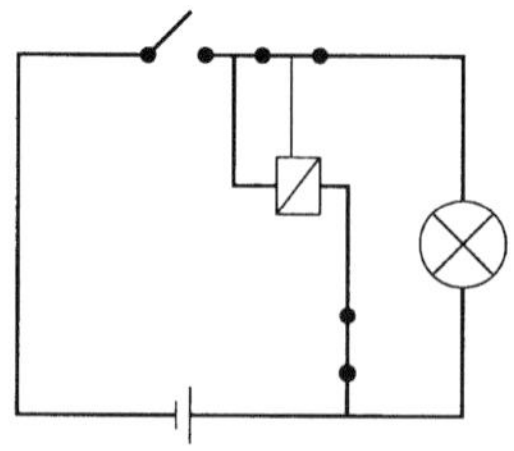

Figure 16.13: Thielscher's circuit: at different levels of abstraction the example demonstrates the problems of synchronization, concurrency, continuous change and causality.

has been reached, more complex situations can arise in which the executive might proceed with an attempt to execute a step in a plan an instant before the point at which a condition vital for the success of the action has been achieved. Indeed, if the action to leave Y is time-stamped in the plan, rather than given relative to the action moving from X to Y, then a literal interpretation of the plan by an executive could still lead to an attempt to execute the second move before the first is completed.

Relying on execution-time ordering makes it impossible to confirm the validity of a plan prior to its execution, since there is no guarantee that all causally necessary sequencing will be achievable at execution time if it was ignored at plan construction time. To enable tractable automatic validation of plans it is necessary to resolve this question in a pragmatic way. One such way is to require plans to separate coinciding end points by a non-zero amount of time as in the example in Figure 16.12. As mentioned, the community has not agreed that this is the most appropriate solution to the problem and it is, at the time of writing, a question under some discussion.

In modelling physical situations in which concurrency and synchronisation are important it is sometimes possible to abstract the level of the model so that these issues can effectively be ignored. This depends on whether the true physical behaviour of the system must be modelled for reasoning purposes, or whether it is sufficient to restrict the model to having only a high level view of the problem. An example of a problem where granularity is important is Thielscher's circuit problem [Thielscher, 1997], illustrated in Figure 16.13. Modelled coarsely this example supports a simple level of causal reasoning: closing switch 1 both creates and breaks a circuit, effectively simultaneously. The presence of the relay means that it cannot be inferred that the lamp is alight after switch 1 has been closed.

Modelling this situation coarsely is problematic because activities which are actually sequenced (the relay does not become active until switch 1 is closed) have to be treated as though they are simultaneous. The fact that the closure of switch 1 causes the relay to close, thereby breaking the circuit so that the lamp does not light, cannot be modelled without viewing events at an extremely fine level of granularity. Two events cannot be both simultaneous and causally related, therefore at an abstract level the real underlying causal structure of the system is lost. The two activities are treated as though they are in fact concurrent and in this way concurrency provides a way of abstracting from the details of the precise timing of events.

At a lower level of granularity more complex interactions occur, the modelling of which involves precise timing, synchronicity and continuous change. Closing switch 1, when switch 3 is closed, causes the relay to activate, opening switch 2. The consequence is that, despite the initial creation of a circuit for the lamp by the closure of switch 1, the lamp does not light because the circuit is broken by the opening of switch 2. The precise timing of these events is, in reality, dependent on the time it takes for the magnetic flux in the relay switch to achieve sufficient force to drag switch 2 open, the potential of the cell (and its ability to support arcing across switch 2 as it opens) and the time it takes to heat the filament of the lamp to incandescence. In practice, it is unlikely that the lamp will achieve any appearance of lighting before the circuit is broken and, for most reasoning purposes, an appropriate level of abstraction might be to ignore all of these low level physical processes and concentrate on the coarse level at which the lamp appears simply to fail to light up.

This example leads to a difficulty in the argument that causal relations cannot be modelled using simultaneous actions, since it seems that it is necessary to model the effects of closing switch 1 on the lamp and on the relay either using simultaneous events or by providing a model at a very fine granularity that accounts for cumbersome levels of detail in the underlying physical system. There are various resolutions of this problem. Firstly, only the action of closing switch 1 is initiated by the executive under the direction of the planner — the subsequent effects are actually events. Therefore, the argument that no executive could actually measure time precisely enough to synchronise simultaneous actions is not challenged: the world can react as precisely as required. The causality argument is more difficult to address — in fact, there is a causal relationship between the closure of switch 1 and the opening of the relay and this does take a non-zero amount of time to trigger. If we choose to abstract the model to a level of granularity at which the non-zero time is treated as actually zero, by putting the event of the relay opening at the same time as the switch closing, then we are simplifying the causal model. To do this can lead to temporal paradoxes: if we nest together a very large number of relays then a model in which the reaction of a relay to the flow of current is instantaneous will suggest that all the relays open simultaneously, yet the number of relays can be made large enough that the cumulative time lag can become large enough to impact on interactions with the circuit.

Despite this potential for paradox, it is often the case that we want to construct abstracted models without having to explicitly model all of the details of underlying physical processes. To work with the shared-memory semantics of mutual exclusion it is then necessary to combine the effects of the entire sequence of action and events into one atomic unit. This can be achieved by using a conditional effect, so that the action of closing switch 1 has an effect of opening switch 2, provided switch 3 is closed, and of lighting the lamp if switch 3 is open. This is not really problematic, since the abstraction is obviously intended to avoid the planner attempting to interact with the circuit at a finer grained level of activity than this model would allow. The alternative, which offers the advantage of separating the events and actions into a decomposed model, is to adopt the sequenced simultaneous activities proposed by McDermott [McDermott, 2000] and by Bacchus [Bacchus and Ady, 2001]. An adaptation of their approach could allow *events* to be sequenced, but not actions, respecting the argument that an executive cannot synchronise actions to be both simultaneous and sequenced.

It is interesting to compare the issues discussed in this section with research into timed hybrid automata [Henzinger, 1996]. Timed hybrid automata have been proposed as models of mixed discrete-continuous real-time systems, used in model-based verification systems such as HYTECH [Henzinger *et al.*, 1995]. These systems also model logical change as instantaneous and attach duration to states. The passage of time allows continuous effects to change the values of metric fluents, while the system remains in the same logical state of the underlying finite automaton. In these systems, it is possible for a cascade of transitions to occur without any time passing, since state transitions are instantaneous. Since transitions can be forced by conditions governing occupation of states, these models can also represent events triggered by actions, all occurring simultaneously and yet in sequence. The question of the robustness of trajectories in time hybrid automata, given the inherent limitations of executives in accurately measuring time, has also been observed by Henzinger and his colleagues [Gupta *et al.*, 1997], leading to the definition of *robust trajectories*. A robust trajectory is an accepting trajectory for which there is a finite non-zero interval of possible oscillations in the assignments of times to the transitions in the trajectory such that all the trajectories so defined are also accepting trajectories. This idea has practical difficulties associated with tractable verification, but is a semantically attractive treatment of the problem of inaccurate measurement of time.

16.7.3 Planning with Concurrent Actions

Various strategies have been explored for planning with concurrency. Graphplan has proved to be a convenient framework for exploiting concurrency. TGP [Smith and Weld, 1999] uses an extension of Graphplan, in which the plan graph is generalised to allow propositions and actions to be introduced at the earliest times at which they could be activated. Mutex relations are generalise to capture a the more complex exclusions over intervals that can arise between actions, between propositions and, because of the introduction of temporal duration, between actions and propositions. As has already been discussed, the conservative model of interaction used in TGP reduces its scope for exploiting concurrency.

LPG [Gerevini and Serina, 2002] uses local search to replace the original Graphplan search. In its temporal extension, LPG handles concurrency by retaining the Graphplan model, so that all actions are activated in successive layers. When the actions are durative, LPG propagates the durations through the graph in order to determine the earliest point at which facts can be achieved. Plans are constructed using the standard plan graph structure but then times are allocated to actions to respect the ordering constraints imposed by the layers of the graph, mutual exclusion relations and the earliest achievement times of propositions and actions. This approach gives remarkably efficient makespans, with good use of concurrency, at least in current benchmark problems. The definition of mutual exclusion is extended, in LPG, so that, in certain cases, actions that interfere only at their end points can be carefully overlapped allowing concurrency to be exploited in the plan structure that would be prevented if the conservative TGP model were used.

A different interpretation of the plan graph structure, from that used in either TGP or LPG, is exploited in the LPGP [Long and Fox, 2003a] planning system. In LPGP action layers are considered to represent simultaneous and instantaneous transitions. Duration is attached to the intervening fact layers, corresponding to periods of persistent state. Linear constraints are used to ensure that the fact layers that separate the instantaneous transitions representing the end points of a durative action (which will be activated in separate action layers) have the necessary duration. This approach leads to a very natural embedding of the plan graph structure into a real time-line with concurrency being represented by the parallel active actions in layers of the graph.

Alternative approaches, not based on a Graphplan foundation, exist to the management of concurrency. The timelines approach of HSTS [Muscettola, 1994] provides a natural way of handling concurrent activity. Because each object is assigned its own timeline, on which the state of that object is uniquely recorded, concurrency arises as a consequence of the parallel timelines for the different objects. The *compatibilities* that are used to describe the constraints on the relationships between intervals (called *tokens*) for each object can constrain the relationship between the tokens for one object and concurrent tokens for other objects, in order to ensure that interaction between objects is properly represented. As a consequence, concurrent activity is not only naturally represented, but is inherent within the representation of the primitive level of activity.

In temporal partial order planning, IxTeT [Vidal and Ghallab, 1996] and VHPOP [Younes and Simmons, 2003] use temporal constraint networks to allow concurrent activity, imposing constraints on the end points of actions. The solutions of STPs [Dechter *et al.*, 1991] describing the relative and absolute positions of end points of the actions leads to the emergence of concurrency where actions overlap.

Although a forward search planning strategy constructs inherently sequential plans it is possible to achieve a concurrent plan by means of post-processing of the sequential plan structure. MIPS [Edelkamp and Helmert, 2000], a forward search planner exploiting a relaxed distance heuristic, uses this approach. To exploit concurrency, plans are post-processed to lift a partial order from the totally ordered plan structure, and then a scheduling algorithm based on critical path analysis is used to embed the partial order in the real time line, exploiting concurrency. The problem of lifting a partial order from a total order in order to allow rescheduling of actions has been considered in the context of other total order planners, such as Prodigy [Veloso *et al.*, 1995]. The problem of finding an optimal partial order is combinatorially hard [Veloso *et al.*, 1990], but heuristically straightforward, using a simple greedy algorithm to identify candidate causal relationships between actions in the totally ordered plan and the preconditions required by later actions.

Concurrency can also be exploited within a hierarchical decomposition approach to planning. SHOP [Nau *et al.*, 1999] is a hierarchical task network (HTN) planner, in which the domain representation is carefully crafted to support the modelling of actions as decomposable structures, where the most abstract components represent pre-compiled plans for the achievement of the goals they support. Time could be introduced in different ways in this framework, but a recent approach [Nau *et al.*, 2003] is to attach durations to actions as *costs* and to attempt to minimise cost of plans. This approach is complicated by the fact that concurrent actions do not combine costs additively so, in this version of SHOP, a special technique is employed to count costs using a maximum value across parallel actions. This approach is interesting, although possibly somewhat limited, because concurrency and, indeed, time itself, is not represented explicitly. Instead, the costs are abstract values that are attached to the actions and interpreted as durations indirectly.

Sapa [Do and Kambhampati, 2001] and TLplan [Bacchus and Kabanza, 2000] both exploit the notion of delayed effect, with timed effects occurring as time advances according to the pending event queue. Concurrent activity in both of these systems is handled by embedding all activity, including pending events, into an absolute timeline at the outset. This simplifies the problems of reasoning about concurrency and supports the solution of many temporal planning problems. However, embedding is not a very general approach and has limited utility for the solution of complex problems in which it is not possible to predict in advance exactly where on the timeline events will occur.

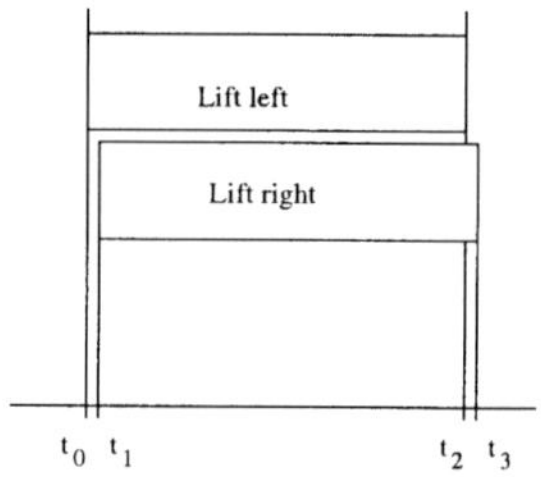

t_0 Lift left starts – left side up

t_1 Lift right starts – right side up

t_2 Lift left ends – left and right both up, so no spill

t_3 Lift right ends – left and right both up, so no spill

```
(:durative–action lift–left
 :parameters ()
 :duration (= ?duration lifting–time)
 :condition (at start (left–down))
 :effect (and (at start (not (left–down)))
              (at start (left–up))
              (at end (when (and (left–up) (right–down) (not (spilt)))
                                 (spilt))))

(:durative–action lift–right
 :parameters ()
 :duration (= ?duration lifting–time)
 :condition (at start (right–down))
 :effect (and (at start (not (right–down)))
              (at start (right–up))
              (at end (when (and (right–up) (left–down) (not (spilt)))
                                 (spilt))))
```

Figure 16.14: Modelling Gelfond's soup bowl problem using durative actions.

16.7.4 Interacting Concurrent Effects

In Gelfond's soup bowl problem [Gelfond *et al.*, 1991], concurrent actions can interact to generate effects that are not the effects of any of the actions individually. Both sides of a soup bowl must be lifted concurrently to raise the bowl without spilling the soup). In planning systems such interactions have not been explored very widely: the treatment of interference (negative interaction) between concurrent actions remains a lively area of debate and is simpler to manage than the exploitation of positive interactions. A simple treatment is to actions with conditional effects [Pednault, 1989], but care must be taken over how this approach interacts with decisions about the interference between concurrent actions. For example, an action to lift a side of a soup bowl might be modelled using the conditional effect stating that the contents of the bowl will be spilled unless the other side is also lifted. The shared-memory semantics would prevent two lifting actions from being applied simultaneously since both actions need read and write access to the states of both sides of the bowl. Using a semantics based on sequential activation of actions does not resolve this problem, since the first action applied would cause the soup to spill, even though the second action is intended to be applied simultaneously.

There are are at least two possible resolutions to the modelling problem. One approach is to remove the interactions from the operators so that each lifting action refers only to the state of the side that it affects. To ensure correctness of the domain description it is then necessary to supply a domain axiom to specify that the soup spills if only one side of the bowl is lifted. A plan to lift the bowl without spilling the soup would need to exploit the two lifting actions concurrently. This example demonstrates that the ability to express domain axioms (or causal rules) in a language that supports concurrency can result in greater expressive power than when axioms are added to languages which restrict its exploitation (by means of a strong mutual exclusion relation, for example). A second approach is to abstract the two lifting actions into one which avoids the issue but results in a less flexible model and requires the domain designer to anticipate the ways in which lifting might combine with other actions. When durative actions are used the problem can be resolved without domain axioms while maintaining the shared-memory semantics for simultaneous actions. This is achieved by making the lifting action, for a single side of the bowl, have an initial effect that

that side of the bowl is lifted and then a final conditional effect that the soup spills if only one side is lifted at the end of the durative interval. This duration is selected to coincide with the time it takes for the bowl to tip to the critical point. Figure 16.14 illustrates this solution. Note that the two lift actions cannot be synchronised exactly with one another because the shared-memory semantics rules that the end points of the two actions interfere. It is interesting to observe that this solution depends on the physically accurate temporal separation of the initiation of the lifting and the ultimate spilling of the soup.

16.8 Continuous Change

Modelling the passage of time makes it possible to consider a more complex relationship between change and time than has been traditional in planning: change that occurs continuously over a period of time. In many planning domains, continuous change can be abstracted into discrete changes at specific time points. In fact, if only propositional models are constructed then continuous change must always be abstracted in this way. Once domains encodings can exploit real-valued metric quantities then it is possible to describe continuous change using functions parameterised by time. We will refer to a continuous change directed by the passage of time as a *process*. The idea of planning with processes has been explored in several planning systems.

Some important questions arise in handling continuous change in temporal planning domains. First among these is whether it is really necessary to model it, or whether abstractions into discrete change are, in fact, adequate. Secondly, we consider the question of how continuous change is modelled and, thirdly, how it is incorporated into the planning process. Finally, there is a question over the treatment of more complex continuous change, including interacting processes.

16.8.1 The Need for Explicit Models of Continuous Change

If interaction between actions and processes is modulated to occur at specific points then it is possible to abstract process effects into sequences of discrete actions or events. For example, the problem of the falling ball passing in front of a sequence of windows of a high building during its fall can be modelled in this way, with a chain of events corresponding to the ball passing in front of each window in turn. If actions can be freely inserted into time to interact with processes at any point then this model is inadequate. An example of a situation in which this matters is the problem of the rechargeable planetary rover, drawn from [Fox and Long, 2002b]. In this problem a rover must draw on its finite, but rechargeable, power supply to move to a site of an experiment. Recharging is conducted once the rover is exposed to the sun (using solar arrays). The rover begins with insufficient power to reach the site and carry out the sampling experiment on the rock it finds there, so must recharge as part of the plan. However, matters are complicated by the fact that the experiment must be completed before the rock is too hot — it heats under the influence of the sun, following sunrise. Depending on the precise values of the parameters in this problem — the charge consumed by moving and by sampling the rock, the recharge rate, the charge capacity of the rover and the time available before the rock overheats — a planner might be able to sequence movement, recharging and sampling. If the deadline or power capacity is too constrained to allow this the planner must recharge concurrently with moving or sampling, or both. The difficulty that this introduces is

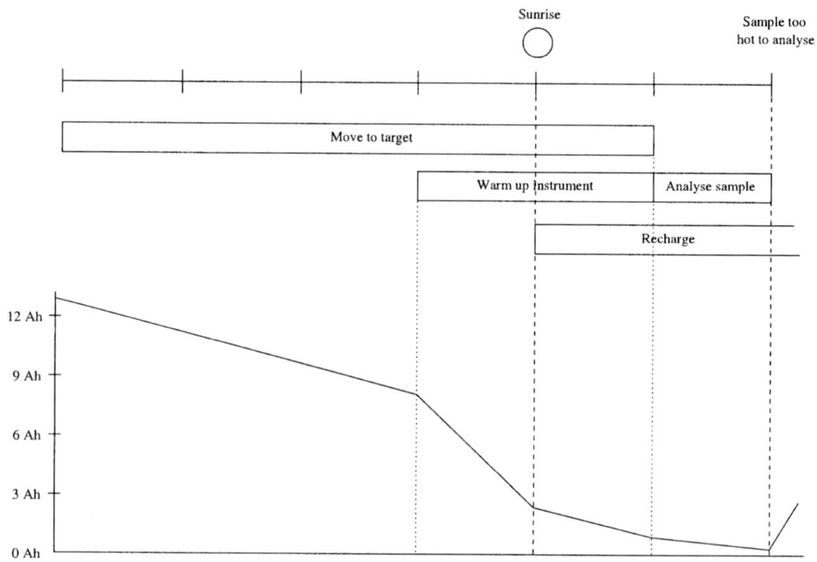

Figure 16.15: A plan with energy management by a planetary rover.

that the construction of a correct plan can require access to the current charge level at points during the movement action or sampling action, both of which are responsible for decreasing the charge continuously, in order to ensure that the invariant condition of recharging, that the charge never exceeds the capacity, is met throughout the plan and that the invariant condition of movement and sampling themselves, that the charge never reaches zero, is met throughout their execution. Figure 16.15 illustrates the concurrent activities of the rover that could allow it to achieve the goal in one version of the problem, together with the energy profile of the rover over the duration of the plan. Shanahan's water tanks [Shanahan, 1990] have similar upper and lower bound conditions that must be respected by concurrent increasing and decreasing continuous processes.

A model that gives no access to the continuously changing parameters while they are being affected by an active process prevents concurrent activity that affects the same value. In particular, the rover problem cannot be solved if the deadline and charge capacity are too constrained to allow sequential movement, recharge and sampling.

16.8.2 Modelling Continuous Change

Various researchers have considered the problem of modelling continuous change. Pednault [Pednault, 1986a] proposes explicit description of the functions that govern the continuous change of metric parameters, attached to actions that effect instantaneous change to initiate the processes. However, his approach is not easy to use in describing interacting continuous processes. For example, if water is filling a tank at a constant rate and then an additional water source is added to increase the rate of filling then the action initiating the second process must combine the effects of the two water sources. This means that the second action cannot be described simply in terms of its direct effect on the world — to increase the rate of flow into the tank — but with reference to the effects of other actions that have already affected the rate of change of the parameter. Shanahan [Shanahan, 1990] also uses this approach, with the consequence that processes are modelled as stopping and then restarting with new trajectories as each interacting action is applied.

In Zeno [Penberthy and Weld, 1994], actions have effects that are described in terms of derivatives. This approach makes it easier to describe interacting processes, but complicates the management of processes by making it necessary to solve differential equations. The complication has not deterred other authors from taking this approach: McDermott takes this approach in his process planner [McDermott, 2003].

In PDDL2.1 [Fox and Long, 2003] processes are encapsulated as continuous effects associated with durative actions (although an extended representation in which processes are explicitly modelled separately from the actions that initiate them is proposed in PDDL+ [Fox and Long, 2002a]). An example of a problem using continuous effects can be seen in Figure 16.16. The special symbol #t is used to represent the continuously changing time parameter within the context of each separate action, measuring time from the initiation of the respective durative actions. This formalism allows processes to interact in complex ways, beginning with actions that initiate continuous acceleration of processes by causing continuous change to affect the parameter representing the rate of change in another active process. Sapa [Do and Kambhampati, 2001] makes use of the PDDL2.1 formalism to describe continuous processes.

16.8.3 Planning with Continuous Processes

Planning with continuous processes is still at an early stage. Zeno [Penberthy and Weld, 1994; Penberthy, 1993] is a partial order planner that handles processes by building constraint sets from the expressions that describe the trajectories of the continuous change. The logical structure of the plan drives the plan construction process, with choices being made for development of the partial plan and then the metric constraints that these imply being propagated into the metric constraint set, Once constraints become linear, a linear constraint solver is used to confirm solvability. This interleaving of logical and metric constraint handling is a common approach in treating problems that require mixed discrete and continuous constraint sets. Its chief drawback is that metric constraints are hard to manage in general and this can mean that significant effort is devoted to the development of partial plans in which the metric constraints are actually not solvable, but for which the metric constraint solvers are not sophisticated enough to determine that this is the case.

Sapa [Do and Kambhampati, 2001] uses a forward heuristic search and can manage continuous change in a limited sense. It can evaluate the projection of certain kinds of continuous change at choice points in the development of a plan, allowing some interaction between preconditions of actions and the continuous change described by other actions. However, the progression of time in Sapa is limited to the end points of actions, so Sapa cannot currently support the extension of plans by the introduction of actions at arbitrary times when continuously changing parameters would support their preconditions. A more sophisticated use of forward heuristic search with processes is in McDermott's recent extension of OPTOP [McDermott, 2003]. This planner uses projections of processes to determine when conditions will allow introduction of potentially beneficial actions into a plan. It is currently restricted to managing linear change. The problem of carrying out forward heuristic search in the context of processes is that the finite range of possible actions that can be used to leave a state

Durative actions

```
(:durative-action generate
 :parameters (?g)
 :duration (= ?duration  100)
 :condition (over all (> (fuel-level ?g) 0))
 :effect (and (decrease (fuel-level ?g)
                        (* #t 1))
              (at end (generator-ran))))

(:durative-action refuel
 :parameters (?g ?b)
 :duration (= ?duration (/ (fuel-level ?b)
                           (refuel-rate ?g)))
 :condition (and (at start
                      (not (refueling ?g)))
             (over all (<= (fuel-level ?g)
                           (capacity ?g))))
 :effect (and (at start (refueling ?g))
          (decrease (fuel-level ?b)
                    (* #t (refuel-rate ?g)))
          (increase (fuel-level ?g)
                    (* #t (refuel-rate ?g)))
          (at end (not (refueling ?g)))))
```

Problem

```
(:objects generator barrel1 barrel2)
(:init (= (fuel-level generator) 61)
       (= (refuel-rate generator) 2)
       (= (capacity generator) 61)
       (= (fuel-level barrel1) 20)
       (= (fuel-level barrel2) 20))
(:goal (generator-ran))
```

Possible plan

```
1: (generate generator) [100]
50: (refuel generator barrel1) [10]
70: (refuel generator barrel2) [10]
```

Figure 16.16: Encoding in PDDL2.1 of a problem involving a generator with a constrained fuel supply using durative actions and a possible plan for the problem.

in propositional planning problems extends to an infinite range when one of the choices is to simply wait for some period while processes evolve. Sapa manages this problem by restricting the choice to those time points corresponding to the end points of durative actions that are already being executed, but OPTOP does not restrict the duration of processes by encapsulating them within durative actions, so cannot exploit this possibility. Instead, potentially useful actions are identified under the assumption that processes can evolve to support their preconditions and then projection is used to confirm whether and for how long processes must evolve in order to meet the necessary conditions.

16.8.4 Interacting with Continuous Processes

The introduction of continuous processes into the planning problem represents a considerable complication, even over a model that includes temporal features and supports concurrency. It is an area of active research and the community has not yet agreed on matters of representation, let alone semantics. A practical role for the development of semantics is its embodiment in a system for plan verification. Tools for automatic plan verification are intimately tied to the languages for planning domain modelling, and therefore their availability tends to be linked to how widespread is the adoption of a particular problem formalism. The development of plan verification tools for PDDL2.1 is reasonably advanced, offering validation of temporal plans including those using continuous effects [Howey and Long, 2002]. The problems that must be resolved in verifying plans with continuous change are, to some extent, a reflection of the problems that must be resolved in constructing those plans. The key problems that must be confronted include managing the interactions between multiple concurrent continuous effects and between continuous effects and invariants over intervals.

Continuous processes can interact in complex ways, because it is possible for one continuous change to modify a fluent that governs the rate of change of another process. For example, a process can accelerate the change induced by a second process. Handling these interactions leads to the need to solve systems of simultaneous differential equations describing the processes. Managing invariants over intervals that include continuous effects is complicated because checking metric invariants, such as whether a metric fluent lies within certain bounds throughout an interval, reduces to the problem of finding zeros of functions describing change within the intervals of invariants. Both of these problems imply, in general, the use of numerical methods and approximation in implementation, which re-emphasise the practical difficulties in synchronisation, precise measurement of time and robustness of plans to temporal uncertainty.

With systems such as HYTECH [Henzinger *et al.*, 1995] and Uppaal [Yi *et al.*, 1997], the model-checking community has explored the use of automatic verification techniques in real-time mixed discrete-continuous systems. Simplifying assumptions are typically made to make the systems tractable, such as the restriction of rates of change to integer constants. The question of robustness to imprecision in the measurement of time has also been considered in this context [Gupta *et al.*, 1997].

(a) (b)

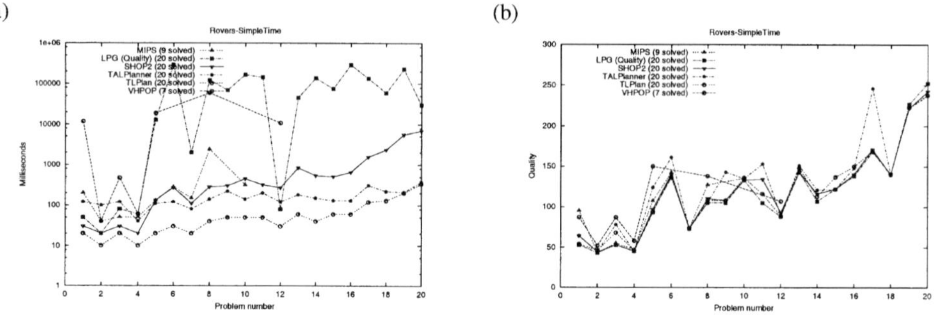

Figure 16.17: Results for problems in a SimpleTime domain, showing (a) speed and (b) quality.

16.9 An Overview of the State of the Art in Temporal Planning

In this section we present a summary of the performances, with respect to three different kinds of temporal problems, of the planners participating in the 3rd International Planning Competition. This presentation gives some insights into the state of the art in temporal planning at the time of writing. It should be taken as suggestive, rather than conclusive, because it does not take into account the capabilities of planners that did not participate in the competition.

In the 3rd International Competition, which took place in 2002, a collection of problems called *Simple Time*, were posed and were successfully handled by most of the participating planners. These problems correspond to the *TEA* subset in which there are no metric fluents and the duration of each temporal action is independent of the state in which it is applied. A further subset, called *Time*, dropped this restriction and required the durations of actions to be computed from other state information. The most complex class of problems, called *Complex*, dropped both restrictions, requiring the management of computed durations and metric fluents. None of the competition problems involved continuous change — all change was modelled in terms of step functions occurring at the start or end-points of actions.

Figure 16.17 part (a) shows how the participating planning systems performed in terms of speed on a collection of *Simple Time* problems. Part (b) shows their relative performance in terms of quality measured using a given objective function. The objective is always to minimize the function, so low quality values are good. Figure 16.18 parts (a) and (b) present speed and quality respectively, for problems in the *Time* collection. Finally, Figure 16.19 demonstrates the behaviour of the planners on *Complex* problems. The performances depicted in these figures are discussed in detail in [Long and Fox, 2003b], for any readers interested in gaining a deeper understanding of the nature of the domains and problems used.

It can be seen from all of the figures presented here that three planners consistently emerge as the best performers, in terms of both time and quality. These planners differ from the other competitors in making use of additional domain knowledge not presented as part of the official domain descriptions provided for the competitors. They constitute the so-

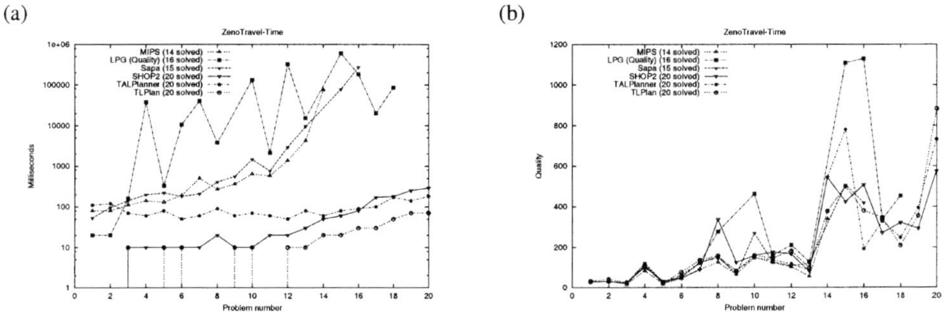

Figure 16.18: Results for problems in a Time domain, showing (a) speed and (b) quality.

called *hand-coded* planners, and are distinguished in [Long and Fox, 2003b] from the *fully automated* competitors. For the purposes of this discussion they are presented alongside the fully automated planners. We are not concerned here with *how* planners are able to address the problems posed, but only with what kinds of problems can be tackled by current planning technology.

It can be observed that the problems in *Time* and *Complex* pose significant challenges, in particular to the fully automated planners. The planning community is currently engaged in understanding and overcoming these challenges.

16.10 Concluding Remarks

Research in the planning community, in particular in the management of metric time and resources, has tended to be driven by the pragmatic requirement to produce plans at a given level of abstraction for a given family of domains. The issues we have examined in this chapter are all central to our understanding of the interactions between actions, planning and execution and the physical processes planners seek to control, yet many of them have been ignored by planning research. Until very recently the modelling languages used within planning have not had the expressive power to enable the representation of temporal relations, continuous change, concurrency or causality. Modern languages still do not directly address the challenges of accurate causal modelling. On the other hand, sophisticated plan generation algorithms exist that are capable of generating complex plans within rather impoverished models of change.

In recent years the planning community has tended to be driven by the desire to build systems that solve problems (even problems that do not bear much relation to the real world) rather than by the desire to formulate a deep understanding of what actions and plans mean or to be able to reason with models that correctly represent reality. Comprehending the philosophical implications of action and change has been seen as the domain of the knowledge representation community rather than as squarely in the domain of planning. The sequence of International Planning Competitions has encouraged this development because it places an emphasis on the efficiency of planners rather than on the philosophical validity of domain models.

(a) (b)

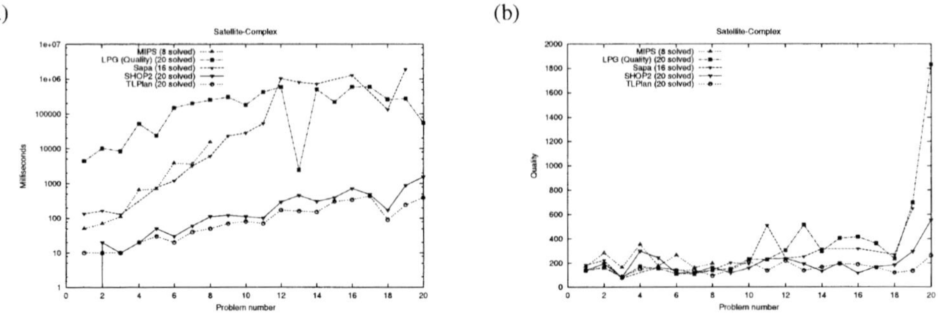

Figure 16.19: Results for problems in a Complex domain, showing (a) speed and (b) quality.

Despite this, the competition series has played a very important role in pushing forward the development of planning systems and building the basis for the scientific development of the field. The issues emphasised at each competition, and the nature of the participating planners, indicate the changing priorities of the research field and give insights into the state of the art of implemented planning systems.

The setup and results of the competition are discussed in depth in [Long and Fox, 2003b; Fox and Long, 2003]. It can be seen that the handling of simple metric constraints is now well advanced and sophisticated techniques can be used to construct plans that satisfy these constraints. These advances are aided by the development of algorithms for solving specific constraint satisfaction problems such as simple temporal networks. As far as can be observed from the competition data the management of complex metric constraints is less well advanced in the planning community and, according to this admittedly restricted view of the state of the art, the problems associated with continuous change, exogenous events and many of the more sophisticated elements of *TEG* have not yet been comprehensively tackled by the research community.

As we have emphasised throughout this chapter, the planning community has always followed a broad agenda containing several different, though closely related, directions of research. In particular there are many alternative definitions of the temporal planning problem, of what constitutes a valid temporal plan, of how the consequences of action should be modelled and inferred and of the distinction between state and action. Despite this variability the community is focussing on broadly similar temporal planning concerns: exploiting concurrency, managing continuous change and anticipating and responding to exogenous events. Whilst this work has tended to be driven by pragmatic concerns — the desire to build practical planning systems capable of producing adequate plans efficiently — there is an increasingly pressing overlap between the concerns of planning research and the wider concerns of the temporal reasoning and reasoning about action and change communities. The planning community is working to converge on an agreement about the modelling of the issues that arise in temporal and metric planning and PDDL2.1 represents a first stage of convergence. If the community can agree on a shared language, which can be used as a basis for developing extended expressive power, the pragmatic concerns of the planning community can continue to be ever more closely reconciled with the knowledge representation issues discussed in this paper.

Handbook of Temporal Reasoning in Artificial Intelligence
Edited by M. Fisher, D. Gabbay and L. Vila

Chapter 17

Time in Automated Legal Reasoning

Lluis Vila & Hajime Yoshino

Despite the ubiquity of time and temporal references in legal texts, their formalization has often been either disregarded or addressed in an *ad hoc* manner. In this chapter we address this issue from the standpoint of the research done on temporal representation and reasoning in AI. We identify the temporal requirements of legal domains and propose a temporal representation framework for legal reasoning which is independent of (i) the underlying representation language and (ii) the specific legal reasoning application. The approach is currently being used in a rule-based language for an application in commercial law*.

17.1 Introduction

Automated legal reasoning systems require a proper formalization of time and temporal information [Sergot, 1995; McCarty, 1995]. Quoting L. Thorne McCarty [McCarty, 1995]:

> "...time and action are both ubiquitous in legal domains. ..."

Notions related to time are found in major legal areas such as labor law (e.g. the time conditions to compute benefit periods), commercial law (e.g. the time of the information used to establish the validity of agreements or to calculate damages† [Blumsohn, 1991]), criminal law (e.g. the temporal information known about the various elements involved in the analysis of a criminal case) and patent law (e.g. the time constraints formulated in regulations for applying for patents). Moreover, many procedural codes associated with these statutes usually require the management of timetables based on some temporal representation.

We elaborate on two representative examples. The first example is taken from the *United Nations Convention for International Sale of Goods* (CISG)[Yoshino, 1994b].

Example 17.1.1. (CISG) Article 15: *An offer becomes effective when it reaches the offeree. An offer, even if it is irrevocable, may be withdrawn if the withdrawal reaches the offeree before or at the same time as the offer.*

*This chapter is an updated version of the paper "Time in Automated Legal Reasoning" by L. Vila and H. Yoshino, previously published in the journal *Law, Computers and Artificial Intelligence / Information and Communications Technology Law. Special Issue on Time and Evidence*, 7(3) 1998.

†This can either be before the tort, at the tort time, before the trial, until the damages have been paid or even after that.

This article contains various temporal aspects that are common in legal texts. We find denotations for events that *happen at a certain time* (e.g. "reach"), objects that have a certain *lifetime* (e.g. "offer", "withdrawal"), properties that *change over time* (e.g. "an offer is effective") and *temporal relations* (e.g. "before or at the same time").

We borrow our second example from [Poulin *et al.*, 1992].

Example 17.1.2. *The next two articles belong to the* Canadian Unemployment Insurance Law*:*
Section 9(1) *[...] A benefit period begins on the Sunday of the week in which (a) the interruption of earnings occurs, or (b) the initial claim for benefit is made, whichever the later.*
Section 7(1) *[...] the qualifying period of an insured person is the shorter of (a) the period of fifty-two weeks that immediately precedes the commencement of a benefit period under subsection 9(1), and*
(b) the period that begins on the commencement date of an immediately preceding benefit period and ends with the end of the week preceding the commencement of a benefit period under subsection 9(1).

In addition to denotations of temporal events (e.g. "interruption of earnings", "claim for benefits"), we find references to temporal units such as "qualification period" and "benefit period", and temporal relations such as "begins", "ends", "period of fifty-two weeks", "the period that precedes", "the period that immediately precedes" and a rich variety of temporal operators such as "the shorter of ...", "the Sunday of the week...", "the later of ...".

The present work belongs to the tradition of formalizing law using logic. Despite the prominent presence of temporal references in legal texts, temporal representation and reasoning is an issue that legal reasoning projects have often either disregarded or addressed in an *ad hoc* manner. This is a surprising situation given the prolific research activity in temporal reasoning in AI during the past 20 years (as shown by this volume). This may be due to the fact that, quoting Marek Sergot [Sergot, 1995], "it looks like a *huge* topic". Another reason could be the utilization of techniques traditionally disconnected from legal reasoning such as constraint satisfaction.

Our goal here is to provide a representation framework well-suited to formalizing the temporal aspects of law in its different areas. We build upon results from the research area of *temporal reasoning in AI*.

We proceed by first identifying the requirements of the legal reasoning domain (Section 17.2). Then we review related work done in computational legal reasoning (Section 17.2.4). After that we present a systematic discussion of temporal reasoning issue and analyze how it can be best addressed according to requirements identified in Section 17.3. This leads to a general framework called LTR. We show the adequacy of our proposal by revisiting the examples above.

The contribution of this chapter is twofold: (i) as a reference for analyzing the temporal representation in existing legal reasoning systems, and (ii) as the foundation in building the "temporal component" of a legal reasoning application. Temporal representation and reasoning is a very broad area and covering everything would be too ambitious for a single chapter, even if its focus is on a particular application area.

The following issues are beyond the scope of this chapter: (i) periodic occurrences, (ii) handling time associated with legal provisions, and (iii) non-monotonic temporal reasoning.

Terminology. Before going ahead we define a few terms common in the temporal reasoning literature used throughout this chapter. By *temporal expression* we mean an expression whose denotation is naturally associated with a specific time. In the above examples, "offer is effective" and "interruption of earnings" are temporal expressions. We shall distinguish between *fluents* when they are expressions that describe the state of affairs in a given domain ("offer is effective"), and *events* when they represent occurrences that may change that state ("interruption of earnings")*. A *temporal proposition* is a logical proposition representing a temporal expression and the *temporal qualification method* is the set of syntactical, semantical and ontological decisions made to to abscribe time to temporal propositions. It usually involves a number of meta-predicates such as *Holds* and *Occurs* that are called *temporal incidence predicates* (TIPs). Figure 17.1 presents a scheme of the various temporal qualification methods proposed in the literature. By *temporal relation* we mean a relation whose

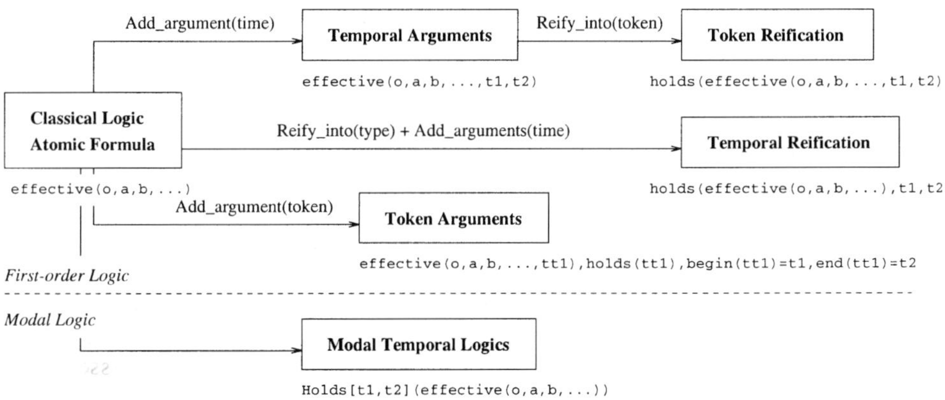

Figure 17.1: Temporal qualification methods in AI.

arguments are all temporal, and by *temporal function* a function whose range is temporal†. By *time ontology* the classes and structure of the objects (whether they are points or intervals) that time is made of. *Time theory* refers to the properties of this structure whereas *temporal incidence theory* are the properties holding between the various temporal occurrences of a given temporal expression. The reader is referred to previous chapters in this volume for detailed description of these concepts (specially in the foundations part).

17.2 Requirements

In this section we identify the requirements of a temporal representation language for formalizing law. The analysis is done at the two main general levels: *notational efficiency*, which comprises issues such as expressiveness, modularity, readability, conciseness, flexibility, ... and *computational efficiency*. Finally, we explain the issues that have not been considered in this work.

*"Offer" can be modeled as an event, if we refer to the offer object, or as a fluent if we refer to the "existence of the offer".

†As opposed to a function whose interpretation is time-dependent.

17.2.1 Notational Efficiency Requirements

Nested Temporal References. A *nested temporal reference* is a temporal expression that includes a reference to another temporal expression. Nested temporal references abound in legal texts. Let us consider a piece from Example 17.1.1:

> "An **offer**, even if it is **irrevocable**, may be **withdrawn** if the **withdrawal reaches** the **offeree** before or at the same time as the **offer**."

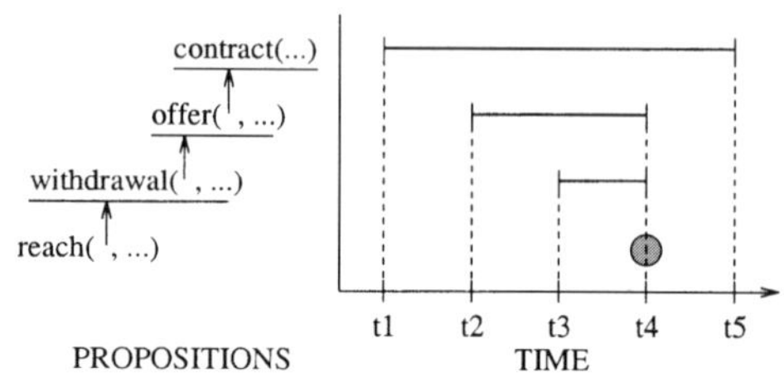

Figure 17.2: *Nested temporal reference* example.

The "reach" event makes reference to a "withdrawal" of an "offer" of a "contract", all these being temporal objects with their own associated times of occurrence (see Figure 17.2). In addition, some implicit constraints may hold among these various times. For example, the "reach" event cannot happen outside the lifetime interval of the offer.

Temporal Operators. Legal texts with temporal references often involve a (sometimes large) number of temporal operators. Example 17.1.2, for instance, involves a function that returns "the shorter of" two periods or a functions that returns the "the latest of" two dates.

Precise and Indefinite Temporal Relations. In addition to exact times and dates (e.g. 3:15pm, October 2nd 1996), many different classes of "less precise" temporal relations appear in legal texts. The following are some examples: "... before or at the same time as ...", "... during ...", "... contains or overlaps ...", "... immediately precedes ...", "... in a few days ...", "... between 2 or 3 days ...", "... either 2 or 3 days if ... or between 1 and 2 weeks if ...". These relations are called *indefinite* since they represent a set (interpreted as a disjunction) of possible times. When the set is not convex we talk about *non-convex* or *disjunctive* relations. Indefinite relations are often present in the description of legal cases (e.g. "...a few days later the message was dispatched", "the transaction took a couple of weeks", "between 9:00 and 10:00 the suspect was seen at ...").

Several Temporal Levels. Some legal applications require distinguishing between different levels of temporal information [Sergot, 1995]. A common distinction (often made in database systems [Tansel *et al.*, 1993]) is *real time* (in databases called *valid time*) vs. *belief time* (i.e. *transaction time*).

Modularity. Since legal domains usually involve knowledge related to various notions such as evidence, belief, intention, obligation, permission and uncertainty, modularity is a central issue. A desirable feature for a temporal representation is that it allows for an orthogonal combination with other knowledge modalities.

17.2.2 Computational Efficiency Requirements

The ability to efficiently encode and process temporal relations may have a high impact on the performance of the overall procedure from both points of view: space and time.

The *size* of the temporal representation is polynomial in the number of temporal propositions and the number of possible temporal relations which, in turn, depends on the model of time adopted (bounded, dense/discrete, etc.).

The *time* performance of answering temporal queries can be strongly influenced by the class of temporal relations supported. The checking consistency of a set of temporal constraints can at best be linear in the number of relations, but if the indefiniteness of temporal relations is *non-convex* it is unlikely that the problem is tractable [Vilain *et al.*, 1990; Dechter *et al.*, 1991]. In most legal scenarios the ratio *number of temporal relations vs. number of temporal propositions* is relatively low and the amount of non-convex indefiniteness is small. However, some cases are found in specific domains (such as in some criminal cases) or some tasks (e.g. *legal planning*) where multiple temporal possibilities need to be taken into consideration.

In both, easy and hard cases, the capability of efficiently answering queries about temporal relations is an important issue. In the easy case because the number of temporal propositions involved in legal scenarios may be large. In the hard case because the potential dramatic performance degradation due to the combinatorial nature of non-convex relations.

17.2.3 Issues not Addressed

Periodic Occurrences. Although not very common, some legal norms and cases require the expression of periodic events such as "pay X once every month" or "get a supply twice a week from 1/1/95 to 1/1/96". This is an issue of current research [Morris *et al.*, 1997; Wetprasit *et al.*, 1996] that we shall not address here.

The Time of Law. Law changes over time. New norms are introduced and some existing ones are derogated over time. A proper account of these changes is obviously important to correctly interpret the law [Bulygin, 1982; Chemilieu-Gendrau, 1987]. This is a fairly open issue in automated legal reasoning which could be handled by means of a temporal representation that associates time with objects more complex than atomic propositions such as rules or contexts. Our investigation here is restricted to time associated to atomic propositions.

Non-monotonic Temporal Reasoning. Rescinding agreements, withdrawing decisions, handling retro-active provisions*, ... all require non-monotonic reasoning capabilities. It can be considered a "temporal" issue since non-monotonic assumptions and inference rules can be formulated using the underlying temporal language. Moreover, there is a non-monotonic reasoning that is specificly temporal: the one that concerns assumptions about temporal relations. For instance, we may want to assume that a fluent holds over time as long as it is consistent with the rest of the information. This matter is beyond the scope of this chapter.

*Retro-active effects are also related to the issue of law change.

17.2.4 Related Work

In legal reasoning systems, time is usually represented like any other attribute. Some systems are provided with an *ad hoc* temporal representation which may range from a few built-in functions to a whole temporal subsystem.

Gardner [Gardner, 1987], for instance, proposes a system for analysis of contract formation which includes a temporal component. The ontology is composed of time points and time intervals. A distinction is made between events and states (i.e. fluents). Time is treated as another argument. All the arguments are expressed through a proposition identifier, time among them, therefore the temporal qualification method here is a sort of token arguments method. Some relevant features, however, are less developed due to the bias towards the specific application: the time unit is fixed to days, only a few point-to-point relations are considered (some temporal relations such as "follows" or "immediately" are mentioned but not supported), and issues such as temporal constraints and temporal incidence are not considered at all.

KRIP-2 [Nitta *et al.*, 1988] is a system for legal management and reasoning in patent law whose language supports temporal representation. The ontology is also based on instants and periods, and includes both convex metric and qualitative interval temporal constraints. Events are qualified with time by using the form

event(Id, class, conditions, time)

Although *Id* looks like a token symbol, it is not used for temporal qualification since *time* is also an argument.

These temporal representation approaches turn out to be adequate for the purposes of the system they are defined in. However, as a general approach to temporal representation in law they lack of some of the following: (i) an explicit identification of requirements from legal domains, (ii) a consideration of the results in temporal reasoning in AI, and (iii) a rational decision on each of the issues involved in a temporal representation framework. In previous sections we have already gone over (i) and (ii). In the next section we go over (iii) but, before that, we analyze two pieces of work that do take care of these three issues.

The first is the *event calculus* (EC) [Kowalski and Sergot, 1986], a temporal database management framework specified in PROLOG. Although not specifically intended for legal reasoning, EC has been used in several legal formalizations [Sergot, 1988; Bench-Capon *et al.*, 1988]. According to the above features, EC is described as follows:

Event Calculus	
Time Ontology	Units: Instant, period Relations: $\{<, =, >\}$
Time Theory	Not defined
Temporal Constraints	Not defined
Temporal Qualification	For fluents: *Temporal reification* For events: *Token arguments*
Temporal Incidence Theory	TIPs: `{holds, holds_at}` Axioms: holds homogeneity
Underlying language	PROLOG

The second is presented in the context of the *Chomexpert* system [Mackaay *et al.*, 1990; Poulin *et al.*, 1992], an application on the *Canadian Unemployment Insurance Law*. The features of the temporal representation language, called EXPERT/T, are summarized as follows:

EXPERT/T	
Time Ontology	Units: Instant, Period Relations: Qualitative point, qualitative interval, Qualitative point-interval, absolute dates
Time Theory	Not defined
Temporal Constraints	Point and Interval Algebras Unary metric (absolute dates)
Temporal Qualification	*Temporal reification*
Temporal Incidence Theory	TIPs: {`holds_on`, `occurs_at`} Axioms: Not defined
Underlying language	PROLOG

Although both works start from an analysis of temporal representation requirements, none of them identifies *nested temporal references*, *multiple time levels* and *modularity* as relevant issues to address. This is the reason why some of the decisions made on the temporal features are not the most well-suited for formalizing legal texts. Both proposals (in EC only for fluents) use temporal reification as the temporal qualification method. In the next section we give a number of reasons to prefer the token arguments approach. Both use PROLOG as underlying language. A shortcoming of languages purely based on logic (logic programming among them) is their inefficiency in handling constraints. Proof-driven inference procedures turn out to perform poorly in constraint processing. The integration of a constraint specialist seems the natural way to overcome this problem. EC does not provide any "machinery" for processing temporal constraints. Although the period primitive is part of the time ontology, period relations and interval algebra constraints (*a la* Allen) are not supported. EXPERT/T processes qualitative constraints using Allen's path-consistency propagation algorithm [Poulin *et al.*, 1992], but no type of metric constraints is supported.

Our approach here is based on integrating temporal constraints and the appropriate temporal qualification method into a logic-based language.

17.3 Legal Temporal Representation

In this section we analyze each temporal reasoning issue bearing in mind the requirements identified in Section 17.2.

17.3.1 Time Ontology: Instants, Periods and Durations as Dates

Time Units. Most temporal expressions in legal domains are associated with a period of time (e.g. "an offer being effective" in Example 17.1.1, or the "qualifying" and "benefit" periods in Example 17.1.2). Moreover, these expressions are often related by period relations such as "a period of validity of an offer happens during its period of existence" or "the qualifying period immediately precedes the benefit period". Hence, it is natural to include the period as a time primitive. Do we also need instants? A brief analysis of legal texts yields several cases where the notion of instant appears:

1. The endpoints of the periods above are naturally associated with instants such as the moment where "the offer becomes effective" or the time as of which "the contract is no longer valid".

2. Some *events* such as "the offer reaches the offeree" are viewed as instantaneous. These are called *instantaneous events.*

3. Norms often involve conditions about the state of a certain fluent at a certain instant. For example, "If ... and the offer is not withdrawn at the moment when it reaches the offeree and ... then ...". Notice that, even if the "reach" event is modeled as durable, the condition may still refer to the instant at the end of that period.

4. Whenever metric temporal relations are involved, they are often stated as constraints between instants, (e.g. "a document sent by mail reaches its destination between 3 and 5 days later").

Besides instants and periods, since legal domains involve numeric relations the *duration* unit is also needed.

In practice, time in legal domains is expressed in *clock/calendar units.* Accordingly we define our instant, period and duration constants in terms of *dates*, where a *date* is defined as an indexed sequence of values for clock/calendar units:

date ::= [*second*''][*minute*'][*hour*h][*day*d][*week*w][*month*m][*year*y]

For example, `00''15'21h2d10m96y`, `00''15'21h`, `21h2d10m96y`, `10w96y`, `96y` are well-formed dates. Some convenient shorthands are clock times (e.g. `00:15:21`) and calendar dates (e.g. `2/10/96`). Dates are used as both instant and duration constants. Period constants are defined as ordered pairs of dates. We use the conventional notation ()/[] to specify open/closed intervals. In addition, a set of indexed symbolic constants (`i1,i2, ...p1,p2, ...`) is included for each unit to express times not associated to any specific temporal proposition.

Granularity. The adequate time granularity may vary from one legal context to another, yet the basic structure of time and the properties of temporal constraints do not change. We address this issue by allowing the user to select the appropriate granularity. Date constants will be interpreted as either an instant or a period according to what is specified by the directive `Granularity()` which takes a clock/calendar unit as its only argument. The issues of combining various granularities or dynamically changing from one granularity to another are not addressed.

Primitive Time Units. Our proposal is based on the following primitive temporal relations: the 3 qualitative point relations $\prec$, $=$ and $\succ$, the 5 qualitative point-interval relations `Before`, `Begin`, $\in$, `End`, **after** , the 13 qualitative interval relations,

A `Before` B	B `After` A
A `Meets` B	B `Met_by` A
A `Overlaps` B	B `Overlapped_by` A
A `Starts` B	B `Started_by` A
A `During` B	B `Contains` A
A `Finishes` B	B `Finished_by` A
A `Equal` B	B `Equal` A

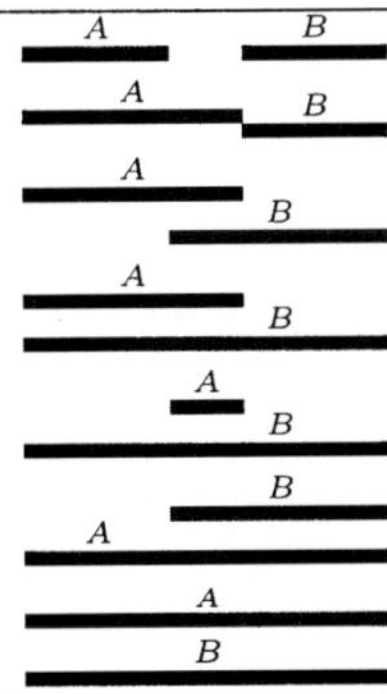

and the duration relations $=$ and $\in$ used to express unary constraints only*, for example

`duration(tt1)=52w,begin(tt2)-end(tt1)` $\in$ `[3w,4w]`

Binary duration constraints are an issue of current research [Navarrete and Marin, 1997a].

Primitive Functions. We define a set of logical functions between temporal units. Some of them are just the functional version of a temporal relation above:

`Begin, End`:	*period*	$\mapsto$ *instant*
`[],(),[),(]`:	*instant* $\times$ *instant*	$\mapsto$ *period*
`Duration`:	*period*	$\mapsto$ *duration*

Besides, a set of *interpreted*† temporal functions is required in practice. These functions are not involved in the term unification process but they are computed at inference time. This set includes functions such as the following:

- *Date arithmetics*, e.g. $+$: *date* $\times$ *date* $\mapsto$ *date*
- *Date predicates*, e.g. `is_holiday` : *date* $\mapsto$ {*t/f*}
- *Date operations*, e.g. `next_holiday` : *date* $\mapsto$ *day*
- *Date transformations*, e.g. `week_of` : *date* $\mapsto$ *week*
- *Date set operations*, e.g. `nth, latest, shorter_of` : *date-set* $\mapsto$ *date*

A list of them is given in [Vila and Yoshino, 1996].

Time Theory. Provided with the set of dates as our underlying model of time, the only structural property of time that demands a specific discussion here is the dense/discrete one. Dense models are required in domains where *continuous change* needs to be modeled such as *qualitative physics*. This is not the case of legal domains where the relevant changes are (viewed as) discrete (e.g. "signing a contract", "receiving an offer", "interruption of earnings", ...) and the dates set has a basic, indivisible granularity. Therefore we adopt a *discrete* model of time which has two consequences. At the ontological level, we add

* Although the relations are binary, only one of the arguments will be a duration variable.

† Interpreted functions are also referred as *built-in* functions or *operators*.

two instant relations that are exclusive of discrete models: `Previous`, `Next`: *instant* $\times$ *instant*[*]. At the axiomatics level, we take a discrete time theory. It is based on $\mathcal{IP}$ [Vila, 1994], a simple instant-period theory that accepts both discrete and dense models, plus a few *discreteness* axioms.

The "Immediate" Relation. Immediate is a difficult temporal term to characterize because its meaning may vary from one context to another. It may mean "in a few seconds" or "in a few hours". Even in a fixed context, it may not have a precise interpretation. Our proposal is based on regarding immediate as a qualitative relation somewhere between `Previous(Next)` and $\prec(\succ)$. This loose connection is formally specified by the following axioms over instants:

$$
\begin{array}{ll}
\mathbf{Im_1} & i \ \texttt{Immediate}\ \mathbf{after}\ i' \Rightarrow i' \prec i \\
\mathbf{Im_2} & i \ \texttt{ImmediateBefore}\ i' \Rightarrow i \prec i' \\
\mathbf{Im_3} & i \ \texttt{Previous}\ i' \Rightarrow i \ \texttt{ImmediateBefore}\ i' \\
\mathbf{Im_4} & i \ \texttt{Next}\ i' \Rightarrow i \ \texttt{Immediate}\ \mathbf{after}\ i'
\end{array}
$$

When `Immediate` is adjoined to period relations, it is interpreted as one of the following two:

1. The period relation `Meets(Met_by)`.
2. The first (last) of the *set* of periods that follow (precede) the current period.

The appropriate choice will depend on the context. It is left to the responsibility of the language user. We formalize some instances of immediate relations in the examples below.

17.3.2 Temporal Constraints

Given the indefiniteness of temporal relations in some legal domains[†] and the fact that existing temporal constraint algorithms scale down well in general, our framework includes almost all kinds temporal constraints:

- Qualitative constraints between instants
  (e.g. `begin(tt1)` $\preceq$ `begin(tt2)`)
- Metric constraints over instants
  (e.g. `begin(tt2)-begin(tt1)` $\in$ {`[2d,3d] [1w,2w]`})
- Qualitative constraints between periods
  (e.g. `period(tt3) Contains Overlaps period(tt2)`)
- Qualitative constraints between an instant and a period
  (e.g. `instant(tt2)` $\in$ `1/Oct/95`)

---

[*] These relations will also be used in their functional form as time operators (e.g. `begin(tt1)=Next(end(tt2))`).

[†] Although in most legal applications only some specific classes of temporal constraints are involved, different applications require different types of constraints. Moreover, a few domains (such as labor law) where the temporal issue is paramount and data may be imprecise, involve all kinds of temporal constraints.

- Unary metric constraints over durations

  (e.g. `duration(P1)=52w`)

Besides representing indefinite temporal relations, temporal constraints can be used to maintain a partial representation over time. Consider, for instance, a fluent `f` that is holding now. Unless we have specific information, it may cease holding any time as of the current time. It can be expressed by a constraint similar to `end(f)`$\in$ `[now,+`∞`]`.

Temporal constraints are either unary or binary and in both cases the syntax has the form

time-term temporal-relation time-term

where the types of the time terms agree with the signature of the temporal relation. In unary constraints, one of the time terms is always ground. The formal syntax of the constraints is given in [Vila and Yoshino, 1996].

Temporal constraints are processed by representing them in a constraint network and applying the available efficient techniques for processing different classes of constraints: qualitative point [Ghallab and Mounir Alaoui, 1989; van Beek, 1992; Gerevini and Schubert, 1995a; Delgrande and Gupta, 1996], qualitative interval [van Beek, 1992] and metric point [Dechter *et al.*, 1991; Schwalb and Dechter, 1997]. Also some progress has been achieved in combining metric-point and interval algebra constraints [Meiri, 1991; Kautz and Ladkin, 1991]. This currently is an area of active research and forthcoming results can be straitforwardly integrated within our framework.

17.3.3 Temporal Qualification: Token Arguments

Since *nested temporal references* are pervasive in legal domains, temporal qualification methods based on tokens are more adequate. Among the two token-based methods proposed in the literature, *token arguments* is better suited to our needs here as we shall see in a moment. In *token arguments*, something like an offer of the contract `c` from `a` to `b` is formalized as `offer(c,a,b,...,tt1)` where `tt1` is a constant symbol of the new *token* sort*. We call these atomic formula *token atoms*. To improve *readability* we emphasize the role of the token argument with some syntactic sugar: instead of `offer(c,a,b,...,tt1)` (where `tt1` is a token term) we shall write

```
tt1 : offer(c,a,b,...)
```

A set of functions, called *token temporal* functions†, that map tokens to their relevant times is defined. For example, `begin(tt1)` denotes the initial instant of the token denoted by `tt1` and `period(tt1)` its period. TIPs are used to express that the temporal proposition is true at its associated time(s) as discussed below in Section 17.3.4.

The token arguments method has several advantages:

1. Token symbols can be directly used as an argument of other predicates. In the above example, `tt1` can be used in `dispatch(tt1,a,b,...)` to express that the offer `tt1` is dispatched from `a` to `b`.

*The idea behind token arguments is similar to the *Compound Predicate Formula* approach [Yoshino, 1994a] when applied to temporal pieces of information.

†To be distiguished from the temporal functions in Section 17.3.1 with similar names but different signature.

2. Different levels of time are supported by diversifying the token temporal functions. For instance, we may have `begin_v(tt1)` to refer to *valid time* and `begin_t(tt1)` to refer to *transaction time*. At the implementation level, a different temporal constraint network instance is maintained for each time level.

3. Token symbols can be used as the link to other knowledge modalities. For instance, in a multiple agents domain, the degree of belief of a proposition `p(...)` by an agent `a` can be represented by `belief(a,tt1)` where `tt1` is a token from `tt1:p(...)`. *Deontic modalities* can be represented by predicates (such as `O` for obligation and `P` for permission) that take a token as an argument. Furthermore, we can distinguish between the time where the deontic relation holds and the time of the object in the relation. For example, consider that a legal person `a` is obligated to offer a contract `c` to `b`. We represent the offer by `tt1:offer(c,a,b,...)`, its relevant instants by `begin(tt1)` and `end(tt1)`, the obligation by `tt2:O(a,tt1)` and the beginning and end instants of the obligation by `begin(tt2)` and `end(tt2)`.

To increase notation *conciseness* we define syntactic sugar that allows omitting token symbols whenever they are not strictly necessary (i.e. whenever there are no references to them). There are two cases. In the first case two or more token atoms are collapsed into one. For instance, the facts

```
tt1:  offer(c,a,b,...)
tt2:  withdrawal(tt1)
tt3:  reach(tt2,b)
```

in a rule that does not contain other references to `tt2`, can be rewritten as

```
tt1:  offer(c,a,b,...)
tt3:  reach(withdrawal(tt1),b)
```

The second case is related with temporal incidence expressions and is explained in the next subsection.

17.3.4 Temporal Incidence

In the temporal token arguments method, TIPs take a token as their sole argument. We introduce the TIP `Holds` to express holding of fluents (e.g. `Holds(tt1)`) and `Occurs` to express occurrence of events. We call these atomic formulas *incidence atoms*.

Holds Incidence. There is a common agreement in the literature about the *homogeneity* of holding of fluents [McDermott, 1982; Allen, 1984; Shoham, 1987]. Although we agree with that, that is not the meaning that we want for our `Holds` predicate. Instead we take a quite different approach: the convention that we call *token holds maximality*:

> A fluent token denotes a maximal piece of time where that fluent is true.

A consequence of this convention is the following *Event Calculus* axiom:

> "Any two periods associated with the same fluent are either identical or disjoint."

In practice, one is interested in knowing whether the current token database entails that a certain fluent is true at a certain time. To this purpose we define the following two additional TIPs:

Holds_on (*fluent*, *period*)
Holds_at (*fluent*, *instant*)

Notice that these are neither syntactic sugar of the above nor temporal reification TIPs, but they are new TIPs with the following existential quantification meaning. Given a fluent f, a period p and an instant i:

$$\begin{aligned}\texttt{Holds\_on}(f, p) &\equiv \exists TT\ (TT{:}f \wedge \texttt{Holds}(TT) \wedge \\ &\qquad p\ \texttt{During Starts Finishes Equal period}(TT)) \\ \texttt{Holds\_at}(f, i) &\equiv \exists TT\ (TT{:}f \wedge \texttt{Holds}(TT) \wedge i \in \texttt{period}(TT))\end{aligned}$$

where TT is a variable of the *fluent token* sort.

Occurs Incidence. There is no common agreement on the characterization of the occurrence of events [Allen, 1984; Shoham, 1987; Galton, 1991]. As a matter of fact, no evidence on the need for any specific theory of events is found in practice. Occurs is used to express the actual occurrence of an event or an action and, thus, to allow describing events whose occurrence is unknown (e.g. to express the possibility or the obligation for that event to occur).

Some syntactic sugar for incidence expressions is defined to omit token symbols. The expression

```
TT:become-effective(...)
Occurs(TT)
instant(TT)=I
```

will be written as

```
Occurs(become-effective(...),I)
```

The formal syntax for incidence atoms is given in [Vila and Yoshino, 1996].

17.3.5 Underlying Language

Our proposal is independent of the underlying language, as long as it is a many-sorted language. The sorts set must include our three temporal sorts, (namely instants, periods and durations), and the two tokens sorts (namely fluent and event tokens).

In this section we address a few additional relevant features:

Negation. Negation of token and incidence atoms will be handled by the standard mechanism of the underlying language. Negation of temporal constraints is less problematic since temporal constraints exhibit the following nice property:

Proposition 17.3.1. *In a constraint language that does not restrict non-convex constraints, any negated constraint can be expressed as an equivalent non-negated constraint form.*

For example $\neg(t \leq t') \equiv t > t'$, or $\neg(t - t' \in \{[3,5]\}) \equiv t - t' \in \{[-\infty, 3), (5, +\infty]\}$. Hence negated constraints will be asserted and queried by regular constraint propagation and entailment.

Token Sets. Some applications require dealing with sets of temporal elements*. For instance, let us consider the following piece of text from Example 17.1.2:

> ...(b) the period that begins on the commencement date of an immediately preceding **benefit period** and ends with the end of the week preceding the commencement of a benefit period under subsection 9(1).

Since for a given person there might be several *benefit periods*, a possible interpretation for "immediately preceding benefit period ..." is, as noted in Section 17.3.1, "the last of all benefit periods before ...". Thus, we need to refer to the set of all those "benefit period" tokens that are `Before` ... Coping with the notion of set requires higher order expressiveness. Some research has been done on extending first order languages in this direction [Maier, 1986; Kuper, 1987; Abiteboul and Grumbach, 1988; Chen and Warren, 1989; Kifer and Lausen, 1989; Chimenti, 1990]. We restrict the development here to the context of a token-based approach where the set notion is used to specify sets of temporal tokens that satisfy a certain condition. The syntax we propose is as follows†:

`token_set` ([*temporal atom*]$^+$)

where *temporal atom* can be either a token atom, an incidence atom or a temporal constraint. The token set operator binds the token variables appearing in the token atoms (e.g. the variable `TT3` in `TT3: benefit-period(TT1)`) to all those tokens of that relation that satisfy all the conditions inside the form. For instance, the example above is formalized as

```
token_set( TT3:  benefit-period(TT1)
           period(TT3) Before Meets period(TT2) )
```

We define a number of practical operators on sets of tokens. For instance, `latest` denotes the last token of that set according to the temporal ordering. These operators can be applied on token set variables (e.g. `latest(TT3)`). Some of these operators admit an alternative first order formulation by splitting the conditions into different rules and using negation, however this approach is clearly impractical‡.

*This issue is not included in the requirements list (Section 17.2) because the notion of set is not strictly a temporal representation feature, but the notion of set of temporal elements is relevant here as we discuss in this section.

†We are not particularly happy with this syntax since it does not follow a pure declarative style, but it turns out to be adequate in practice.

‡As an exercise, you may try to use this approach to specify the operator `4th` which selects the 4th token that satisfies certain conditions.

Token Attributes. The token arguments method allows to detach time from its temporal proposition. The same can be done for the remaining attributes of the proposition to enhance language flexibility. For example, we can refer to the offerer of

```
tt1:  offer(c,a,b,...)
```

by `offerer(tt1)`. Now attribute names are represented explicitly. It requires (i) *declaring* the attributes for each predicate,

```
Attribute(what,offer)
Attribute(offerer,offer)
Attribute(offeree,offer)
...
```

for which we shall use the shorthand

```
Attributes(offer,{what,offerer,offeree,...})
```

and (ii) referring to the attributes of a particular token. Our `tt1:  offer(c,a,b,...)` can be regarded as a shorthand* for

```
what(tt1)=c
offerer(tt1)=a
offeree(tt1)=b
...
```

Summary. The set of choices that defines our proposal is summarized in the following table:

LTR		
Time Ontology	Units:	Instants, periods, durations with clock/calendar forms as constants.
	Relations:	{$\prec$, `begin`, `end`, `Next`, `Previous`, `ImmediateBefore`, `Immediate` **after** }
Time Theory	$\mathcal{IP}$ axioms + discreteness axioms + $\mathbf{Im}_{1\div4}$ axioms	
Temporal Constraints	Combined (metric) Point – Interval Constraints	
Temporal Qualification	*Token arguments*	
Temporal Incidence Theory	TIPs:	{`holds`,`occurs`,`holds_at`,`holds_on`}
	Axioms:	`holds` maximality and `holds_on` homogeneity

17.4 Examples

In this section we illustrate the application of our approach as we revisit the two examples introduced in Section 17.1. We take a rule-based language as underlying language without

*The translation will take the order of the attributes from an explicit declaration supported by the underlaying language.

making any assumption about the inference regime. A set of facts in both the body and the head of a rule is interpreted as a conjunction. The marks [[...]] indicate pieces of text that have not been formalized because either their meaning is not clear, their main emphasis is not temporal or they are merely redundant. The mark `% Implicit` indicates pieces of formal knowledge that are not directly derived from the legal text. Ontological elements resulting from a conceptualization process are emphasized in **bold**. Temporal relations are underlined.

17.4.1 Formalizing the CISG Example

The CISG is intended to provide a normative frame for international commerce. Part II of the law is devoted to the formation of contracts. For instance, it is used to determine when a contract is concluded. Queries like this can be answered in the LTR formalization we present next.

The predicate attributes used in the example are:

```
Attributes(contract,{offerer,offeree,class,type,qp-provision})
Attributes(offer,{what,offerer,offeree,is-irrevocable,
                  offer-begin,offer-end})
Attributes(acceptance,{what})

Attributes(effective,{what})
Attributes(concluded,{what})
Attributes(withdrawn,{what})
Attributes(accepted,{what})

Attributes(become-effective,{what})
Attributes(become-concluded,{what})

Attributes(reach,{what,who})
Attributes(dispatch,{what,who,to-whom,type,stamped-date})
```

A granularity of days might seem adequate for this example, however some occurrences of the "immediate" relation require moving to a finer granularity:

```
Granularity(second)
```

A law article is formalized as (a number of) rules that express the relations between occurrence of events under certain conditions and their effects in terms of the holding of derived fluents. For instance, in Example 17.1.1, "**Article 15(1)** An **offer** becomes **effective** when it **reaches** the **offeree**." is formalized as

```
If      TT1:   offer(C,OR,OE,...)
        TT2:   reach(TT1,OE)
        Occurs(TT2)
        ¬Holds_at(withdrawn(TT1),instant(TT2))     % Implicit
then    Occurs(become-effective(TT1),instant(TT2))
```

```
If      TT2:   become-effective(TT1) % Implicit
        Occurs(TT2)
then    Holds(effective(TT1),(instant(TT2),_))
```

Next we include a few additional interesting articles also from CISG part II.

Article 18(2) An **acceptance** of an **offer** becomes **effective** <u>at the moment</u> the **indication of assent reaches** the **offerer**. An **acceptance** is **not effective** if the **indication of assent** does not **reach** the **offerer** <u>within the time</u> he has fixed [[or, if no time is fixed, within a reasonable time, due account being taken of the circumstances of the transaction, including the rapidity of the means of communication employed by the offerer.]]

```
If      TT1:   offer(_,OR,_,_,OBegin,OEnd)
        TT2:   acceptance(TT1)
        TT3:   reach(TT2,OR)
        Occurs(TT3)
        instant(TT3) ∈ [OBegin,OEnd]
        Holds_at(accepted(TT1),instant(TT3))      % Implicit
then    Occurs(become-effective(TT1),instant(TT3))
```

Implicit from Article 18(2) When an acceptance of an offer of a contract becomes effective the contract becomes concluded.

```
If      TT2:   become-effective(acceptance(offer(TT1,...)))
        Occurs(TT2)
then    Occurs(become-concluded(TT1), instant(TT2))
```

```
If      TT2:   become-concluded(TT1) % Implicit
        Occurs(TT2)
then    Holds(concluded(TT1),(instant(TT2),_))
```

Article 18(2) (cont) An **oral offer** must be* **accepted** <u>immediately</u> [[unless the circumstances indicate otherwise.]]

*Notice that "must be" here does not denote obligation but a temporal constraint.

```
If      TT1:  offer(...)
        TT2:  dispatch(TT1,_,_,oral,_,_)
        Occurs(TT2)
then    offer-begin(TT1)← instant(TT2)
        offer-end(TT1)← Immediate after (instant(TT2))
```

Article 20(2) Official **holidays** or non-business days occurring during the **period for acceptance** are included in calculating the **period**. However, if a notice of **acceptance** cannot be **delivered** at the address of the **offerer** on the last day of the period because that day falls on an official holiday or a non-business day at the place of business of the **offerer**, the **period** is extended until the first business day which follows.

```
If      TT2:  offer(...)
        Is_holiday(offer-end(TT2))
then    offer-end(TT2)← next_holiday(offer-end(TT2))
```

Temporal database projection* would be sufficient to answer the intended queries. The bottom-up inference procedure would make an intensive use of the specialized modules for (i) constraint processing and (ii) token management. The result will be a temporal map composed of instants and periods for the instances of events and fluents, together with the temporal constraints holding among them. For example, given the input formalized by the following facts

```
tt1:  contract(a,b,sale,machine,_)
tt2:  offer(tt1,a,b,_,[-∞,+∞],[-∞,+∞]),
       instant(tt2)∈1/Oct/95
tt3:  dispatch(tt2)
tt4:  reach(tt2,b), instant(tt4)∈8/Oct/95
tt5:  withdrawal(tt2)
tt6:  dispatch(tt5,a), instant(tt6)∈7/Oct/95
tt7:  reach(tt5,b), instant(tt7)∈11/Oct/95
tt8:  acceptance(tt2)
tt9:  dispatch(tt8,b), instant(tt8)∈10/Oct/95
tt10:  reach(tt8,a), instant(tt10)∈12/Oct/95
```

the time map shown by Figure 17.3 would be generated. The query "Is the contract concluded" will be affirmatively answered by `YES, as of October 12 '95`. The sequence of rules involved in deriving token `tt1.2: concluded(tt2)` can be easily recorded and returned as justification.

*As in the *TMM* system [Dean and McDermott, 1987; Schrag and Boddy, 1991] for example.

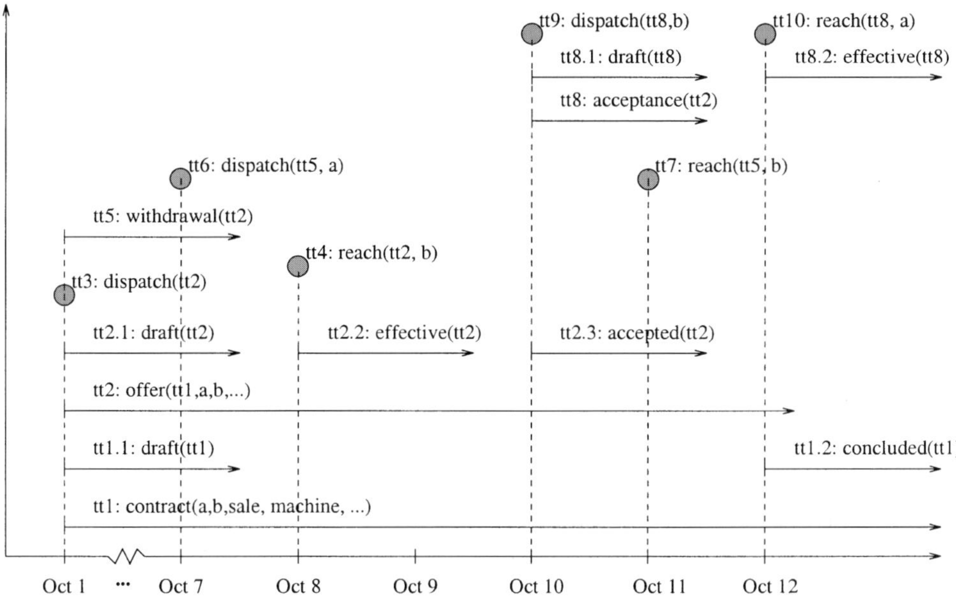

Figure 17.3: CISG example.

17.4.2 Formalizing the Canadian Unemployment Insurance Law Example

A key section of the *Canadian Unemployment Insurance Law* [Poulin *et al.*, 1992] is intended to determine whether a person is eligible for benefits or not. It involves determining a *qualifying period* (the period during which the person has been employed) and a *benefit period* (the period during which the person should receive benefits).

The following predicate attributes need to be declared:

```
Attributes(insured-person,{...})
Attributes(benefit-period,{whom})
Attributes(qualifying-period,{whom})

Attributes(interruption-of-earnings,{what})
Attributes(initial-claim,{what})
```

For a proper formalization of the temporal aspects of this act, a granularity of days is fine enough.

```
Granularity(day)
```

Next we show the sections that address the assesment of the benefit and qualifying periods and their formalization in **LTR**:

Section 7(1) [...] the **qualifying period** of an **insured person** is the shorter of: (a) the period of fifty-two weeks that immediately precedes the commencement of a **benefit period** under subsection 9(1), and
(b) the period that begins on the commencement date of an immediately preceding **benefit period** and ends with the end of the week preceding the commencement of a **benefit period** under subsection 9(1).

```
If      TT1:  insured-person()
        TT2:  benefit-period(TT1)
        duration(P1)=52w
        P1 Meets period(TT1)
        token_set( TT3:  benefit-period(TT1)
                   period(TT3) Before Meets period(TT2) )
        begin(P2)=begin(latest(TT3))
        end(P2)←end_of_week(week_before(week_of(begin(TT2))))
then    TT5:  qualifying-period(TT1)
        period(TT5)←shorter_of({P1,P2})
```

Section 9(1) [...] A **benefit period** begins on the Sunday of the week in which
(a) the **interruption of earnings** occurs, or
(b) the **initial claim** for benefit is made,
whichever the later.

```
If      TT1:  insured-person()
        TT2:  interruption-of-earnings(TT1)
        Occurs(TT2)
        TT3:  initial-claim(TT1)
        Occurs(TT3)
then    TT4:  benefit-period(TT1)
        begin(TT4)←sunday_of(week_of(latest_of(instant(TT2),
                                  instant(TT3))))
```

17.5 Concluding Remarks

We explored the representation of time and temporal information in legal domains in the tradition of using logic to formalize law. We propose **LTR**, a temporal representation framework described by the following choices on the temporal reasoning features:

LTR		
Time Ontology	Units:	Instants, periods, durations with clock/calendar forms as constants.
	Relations:	{$\prec$, `begin`, `end`, `Next`, `Previous`, `ImmediateBefore`, `Immediate` **after** }
Time Theory	$\mathcal{IP}$ axioms + discreteness axioms + $\mathbf{Im}_{1\div4}$ axioms	
Temporal Constraints	Combined (metric) Point – Interval Constraints	
Temporal Qualification	*Token arguments*	
Temporal Incidence Theory	TIPs:	{`Holds`,`Occurs`,`Holds_at`,`Holds_on`}
	Axioms:	`Holds` and `holds_on` homogeneity

Our approach is independent of the underlying representation language and the specific legal reasoning application. We discussed its adequacy wrt. the requirements identified in legal domains. **LTR** is currently being used within a rule-based language in the formalization of the *Convention for International Sale of Goods*.

In this work we did not address the issues of (i) representing periodic occurrences, (ii) temporal non-monotonic reasoning, and (iii) handling time of legal statutes. For instance, tasks that involve meta-reasoning about the validity of statutes and laws over time are out the scope of our approach. This is matter of our current research.

Handbook of Temporal Reasoning in Artificial Intelligence
Edited by M. Fisher, D. Gabbay and L. Vila

Chapter 18

Temporal Reasoning in Natural Language

Alice ter Meulen

Logicians have sometimes found inspiration for new research in the ordinary languages that we use to communicate on a daily basis and acquire naturally in childhood. The logical issues in the foundations of mathematics primarily motivated the development of mathematical logic with its emphasis on notions of proof, validity, axiomatization, (un)decidability, (in)consistency and (in)completeness. The logical analysis of selected expressions of natural languages has motivated the development of philosophical logic with its emphasis on semantic notions of presupposition, entailment, modality, conditionals and intensionality. The connections between these research programs in mathematical and philosophical logic and natural language syntax and semantics as branches of theoretical linguistics have gained in importance, since the advent of Montague Grammar and its current spin-offs in the dynamic semantics of natural language*. This chapter reviews a particularly interesting and lively area of interaction - the semantics of temporal reference and quantification and its logical properties. This topic is paradigmatic of the fruitful interaction between logic and linguistic research to develop empirically adequate models of reasoning with partial information, sharing or exchanging information, dynamic interpretation in context, belief revision, multi-agent systems and other aspects of information sharing.

Competent speakers of a natural language share an essential cognitive capacity to describe change in their world as consisting of certain events that took place and states that were the case. Based on what we explicitly assert as having happened, we automatically draw all kinds of inferences about what must have happened when. Some of these inferences arise because we attribute causal structure to the events described. Other inferences may be triggered by word meaning, world knowledge or personal prejudice, presumptions or private information. If logical modelling of such human linguistic competence is intended to contribute to our understanding of the human cognitive endowment, it must address the general question how the given information is used in such reasoning about temporal relations in natural language. Human reasoning in natural language, itself considered as a temporally extended cognitive process, exploits the order in which information is presented, which may affect the conclusions drawn from it at any time. Besides the temporal information embodied in the order of presentation, the syntactic properties of a clause and its constituents often indicate how its content may be preserved or affected by subsequent updates of the

*See [Partee, 1997] for a good overview of the development of Montague grammar.

information. Generic information in ordinary English, for instance expressed with present tense clause in *Lions have manes*, persists through virtually any update. The restrictor of the generic operator immunizes it against revision, relegating apparent counterexamples to exceptions to the generic relation between the two properties of being a lion and having manes [Carlson and Pelletier, 1995].

In contrast to generic statements, information expressed in a progressive clause as *John was reading the paper* may require adjustment as soon as the context changes, especially if information about John added later attributes to him incompatible properties, like closing his eyes or skiing down a slope. The content of this progressive clause may of course be preserved by converting it to a perfect progressive clause as *John had been reading the paper*, which remains true no matter how the context is updated. Since temporal reference (and aspect) is indexical in nature, different verbal inflection forms may be required to grasp the same content at different points in time. In developing a genuinely dynamic logic of temporal reasoning, such adjustments in verbal tense form need to be taken as reflecting systematic representational properties of natural language that we exploit in reasoning and reporting our conclusions. Competent users of ordinary English know when to adjust indexically presented information to the current context and information state. This process of adjustment is what makes human reasoning *situated*: to report content it must be adjusted to the context that was created by the interpretation and the time at which the conclusion was drawn.

In order to develop some basic intuitions regarding temporal expressions and their logical properties, this chapter first reviews various syntactic categories in English containing expressions whose content is used in temporal reasoning. These linguistic data and observations constitute the empirical domain for the subsequent logical analysis and formalization. In the second section the composition of aspectual classes is presented, which determines to a large extent how updates affect the temporal parameters of a context, constraining in turn the belief revision affected by such updates. The third section analyzes some inferential patterns using aspectual verbs and adverbs, presenting their logical behavior in a dynamic semantics. The fourth section contains a brief introduction to Dynamic Aspect Trees (DAT), data structures for temporal information, and section five compares the dynamic inferences in DAT to Discourse Representation Theory, a closely related dynamic theory of semantic representation. The final sixth section provides a summary of the chapter and discusses some open problems that may be of interest to logicians and computer scientists working on knowledge representation, belief revision, multi-agent systems and natural language semantics.

18.1 The Syntactic Categories of Temporal Expressions

In this section expressions of various syntactic categories of English are reviewed in order to analyze their temporal meaning. No comprehensive linguistic description is here attempted. The attention is focused primarily on adverbs, verbs and the tense inflection, as well as the aspectual properties of clauses, considered to determine to an important extent how temporal parameters in a context may require resetting, when information is added in an update.

English has lexicalized aspectual verbs which describe the internal temporal structure of events: their onset, e.g. *start*, *begin*, *commence*, *initiate*, *resume*, their middle e.g. *continue* and *keep*, and their ending *end*, *finish*, *terminate*, *halt*, *cease*, *complete*. The way we use such aspectual verbs in inferences and temporal reasoning exhibits their logical meaning, and determines their interaction with various forms of negation and their relations to the aspectual classes controlling the flow of information. When an event starts, obviously no stage of it has yet occurred, although other events of the same type, i.e. with the same participants doing the same thing, may have occurred earlier. But when an event continues, resumes, stops, ends or finishes, part of it has already occurred, for at least it must have started. Such an assumption of what must already be included in the context is a *presupposition*, a constraint on what the context must contain for the interpretation process to proceed. Clearly, when we interpret a clause as *Jane continued to read this book*, we do not just assume that one or another arbitrary initial stage of Jane's reading of some book has occurred. The starting stage that is presupposed must be the onset of this particular reading that she continued to do. She may well have been reading this book before and even have finished reading it. But all such stages are temporal constituents of other earlier events of her reading this book, temporally preceding the one being described as continuing. The presupposition is hence not merely existential in nature, but essentially anaphoric, i.e. bound, and contextual in character. Such anaphoric temporal presuppositions play an important role in how we use information in reasoning efficiently about temporal relations between described events.

A well-known characteristic of presuppositions is that both positive clauses and their negative counterparts entail the same presupposed information. It is illustrated in (1), where a-d, uttered with no special intonation or contrastive stress, all presuppose the same perfect tense clause in e.

(1): a. Jane stopped reading this book

b. Jane did not stop reading this book

c. Jane continued reading this book

d. Jane did not continue to read this book

e. Jane must have started to read this book

The simple past of the aspectual verbs in (1 a-d) presuppose perfect clauses containing the information about the onset of the event in (1 e). Updating a context with presupposed or entailed information does not affect the current temporal reference, determining which event is described by new information. The aspectual verbs that describe the onset of an event are regarded as having existential force in the dynamic interpretation, introducing a new first stage of the described event in the context. They describe the transition from 0 (off) to 1 (on), terminating its off-state, and starting an on-state of the given event-type.

Just as the universal quantifier in predicate logic is definable as the external negation of the existential quantifier with an internal negation, *continue/keep V-ing* is equivalent to *not start not V-ing*, preserving throughout the presupposition *have started V-ing*. So *keep* and *continue* have quantificational force, preserving the given on- or off-state of the event-type, whichever it happens to be. Pursuing this heuristic analogy with predicate logic, we see that the internally negated existential aspectual verb *start not V-ing* is lexicalized in English by those describing the suspension, ending or completion of the event, i.e. *finish, terminate, complete, halt, stop, end, cease.*

One striking difference in how we use *continue* and *keep* is in their presuppositions. *Keep V-ing* requires that the action is actually going on. For instance, you cannot keep reading, unless you are reading at this very moment. But if you continue to read this book after a break, you resume reading and then presumably keep reading it. So *continue to V* does not require that one is actually *V-ing,* as it allows the event to be resumed first, if it was interrupted. This is evident also in (2), when a story is reported in several installments.

(2): This story is to be continued/*to be kept (on)

The aspectual verb *keep* requires continuation of ongoing action, i.e. you can only keep doing something, when you are already doing it, and something can only be kept going, when it is already going on. When you continue to do something, but you happened to have stopped it now, the action must be resumed. If there is no interruption and the event is actually going on, the same information is given in using *continue* or *keep*. Using *continue* induces hence a more liberal constraint on the internal structure of the event, allowing as it were the interrupted bits and pieces of it to be collected into one single event. Within such a discontinuous, gappy or scattered event there still is one unique start and one unique finish or end, but possibly many stops, interruptions and corresponding resumptions.

Finally we should consider the semantic properties of the verbs that describe the ending of events. Events like driving home may be finished, whereas events like driving around can only be ended as in (3), unless temporal boundaries are somehow determined independently in the context.

(3): Jane finished *driving around/ driving home.

Finishing implies ending, but not vice versa, as is obvious in (4).

(4): a. They ended the meeting agreeing to finish another time.
b. *They finished the meeting agreeing to end another time.

Another semantic difference between *end* and *finish* that plays a role in inferences is the constraint on individual denoting internal arguments with *end*, e.g. (5).

(5): a. She finished the call/the apple
b. She ended the call/*the apple

Though a singular event can only be finished or ended once, it can be stopped or halted many times over and resumed later. All verbs of ending require that what is going on is not continued any longer after the described action, i.e. the action is turned off. But they differ in their ability to individuate an event, only *finish* and *stop* induce the transition between the event itself and the perfect state of its having occurred. The verb *end* merely indicates that there was no resumption after the event was last stopped, which is negative and hence stative information.

Adverbs often contain explicit temporal information, describing temporal order or inclusion relations between events with *before*, *while* or *after*, or more complex temporal relations as in *since*, *until*, *when(ever)*, or *never*. Furthermore, adverbs may measure duration in either durative adverbials as *for a while* and *weeks on end*, or containing adverbs as *in a while* and *in two weeks*. The interpretation of such temporal adverbs is quite straightforward, given a mapping from event structures to the associated interval structure on which temporal relations of precedence and overlap may be defined.

Adverbs are called aspectual, when they refer to or quantify over the internal structure of an event*. The aspectual verbs describing event internal transitions play an important role in the meaning of aspectual adverbs. They may refer to the onset of an event, as in (6a-b) and (7a-b), describing John's current action as related to its starting point, or to its end, as in (6c-d) and (7 c-d), describing John's current action as related to its termination.

*See [ter Meulen and Smessaert, 2004] for a dynamic semantics of aspectual adverbs.

(6): a. John was not yet reading.

b. John was already reading.

c. John was still reading.

d. John was not reading anymore.

Aspectual adverbs when marked in English with specific stress and high pitch prosody, here indicated with capital letters, induce additional semantic complexity, contributing information about expected alternatives in various temporal parameters, as in (7).

(7): a. John was STILL not reading.

b. John was alREADY reading.

c. John was STILL reading.

d. John was no LONGER reading.

In using such intensional aspectual adverbs the position of the current temporal reference point in the course of events is contrasted to later or earlier alternatives. With *alREADY* in (7b) and *no LONGER* in (7d) the actual course of events is evaluated by the speaker as faster than expected. With *STILL not* in (7a) and *STILL* in (7c), in contrast, the actual course of events is perceived as slower than expected. This tension between actual value and expected value is absent in the four extensional aspectual adverbs *not yet* in (6a), the unstressed use of *already* and *still* in (6b, c) and with *not... anymore* in (6d).

Besides verbs and adverbs, of course the lexical descriptive verbs or predicates also contain temporal information in their morphological inflections. The verb is either marked for the simple past tense with *-ed*, or it is marked for present tense, where future auxiliary verbs are here considered to be modal in their semantics. The perfect morphological inflection using the auxiliary *have* does not itself indicate any temporal reference, for it occurs in both past and present tense, but it carries aspectual information, describing the state that is caused by the termination of an event. E.g. *John had eaten a sandwich* is interpreted as describing the enduring state he is in since he finished eating that sandwich. The progressive morphology using the auxiliary verb *be* and the gerundive form of the verb *V-ing*, indicates that the starting point of the event is past, and the event is continuing, possibly ending in the future. E.g. *John was eating a sandwich* is interpreted as describing the state he was in after having started to eat the sandwich.

These linguistic observations regarding the syntactic categories of English which contain temporal information is primarily intended to set the stage for logical analysis. The next section will address how temporal reference is composed within a clause, consisting of the meaning of the verbal predicate and its arguments, and the way it affects temporal reference in context.

18.2 The Composition of Aspectual Classes

Ordinarily the linear order human communicators must express information in does not necessarily reflect the temporal order in which the described changes actually occurred. Well-crafted stories do not give such a play-by-play account of what happened. Quite freely jumping back and forth in time, as it were, information is encoded about what happened in an informative, coherent and useful description, relying on our cognitive abilities to reason about their temporal relations. In certain contexts the order we give to our utterances does reflect the temporal relations between the events described. But in other contexts the order of description is quite independent of the temporal order of what is described. How then does a recipient of such information reconstruct, at least up to a certain extent, what happened when? How is information about the temporal relations extracted from what we say, when it is not explicitly asserted by temporal adverbs?

Obviously the choice of verbal tense and aspect also matters a great deal in descriptions of what happened. But tenses only partly indicate in which order the events described took place. Sometimes a sequence of pure simple past tenses without any temporal adverbs mirrors the temporal order in which the events happened, as in (8).

(8): A car hit the fence. The driver was killed. The police arrived.

We immediately infer from (8) that the car hit the fence *before* the driver was killed and the police arrived *after* the car had hit the fence. Anyone who understands (8) does not need to give it much thought to realize that these adverbs describe explicitly the correct temporal relations. We often draw conclusions using overt temporal adverbials, even when the premises did not contain any.

In other contexts, however, a sequence of three simple past tense sentences does not directly reflect the temporal order, as in (9).

(9): Jane was so happy. She sang, danced and clapped her hands.

For (9) a natural interpretation, though by no means the only possible one, is to understand it as indicating that it was all happening simultaneously. Hence Jane clapped her hands, being happy, while also dancing and singing. If competent users of a language have no trouble deciding which temporal relations hold given certain descriptive information, then cognitive processes must underlie this fundamental capacity which caused the differences in the interpretation of (8) and (9). Such processes should be characterized semantically, if it is to model our temporal reasoning in natural language. It should explain how conclusions about the temporal relations between parts of a described episode are derived from the information given about it.

From these first observations we may conclude that tenses put only weak constraints on how the described events are related in time. The simple past tense itself merely requires that what is described happened before the information about it was given. Aspect contributes crucial information about the temporal architecture of the descriptive information. The observed difference in (8) and (9) is caused by a fundamental difference in aspectual class of the descriptive content of the clauses, which determines to an important extent how information we get later is related to the events we already have information about. The sentences in (8) each refer to an event no part of which is an event of the same type, but in (9) the states described obviously temporally contain sub-states of the exact same type, described by the same clauses. The first kind of event description is often called telic, from the Greek *telos*, goal. The second is called atelic, including both states and events. This difference between telic and atelic clauses determines in part how temporal reference is established in context, for shifting it requires a telic clause, if no explicit temporal adverb is used. An atelic clause leaves its context open to updates referring to other events temporally contained within the event it refers to, as in (9). In contrast, a telic clause closes the context for updates with other events temporally contained within it, unless presuppositions require temporal subordination. Instead of the traditional linguistic terminology of telic and atelic events, this chapter uses the more semantic distinction between open events for atelic ones, and closed events for telic ones, reflecting their effect on updates of their context. Open events will be represented by open nodes, or 'holes', in the Dynamic Aspect Trees system presented below, and closed events by closed nodes, or 'plugs', which visualizes their effect on updates.

Often the interpreter of a text has a certain freedom of choice to understand a next sentence as describing an event following the event described by the previous clause. The meaning of the verb or its arguments may partially constrain his choice, and knowledge of the world may always contribute additional constraints.

(10): Jane felt ill. She sat down, attempted to decipher the message and looked at her watch. She sighed. It was not even noon yet.

From (10) we infer for instance quickly that Jane already felt ill *before* noon and looked at her watch *after* sitting down and *while* feeling ill. But it is less clear whether her attempt to decipher the message temporally included her looking at her watch or that attempt ended before she looked at her watch. In the first case we would infer that she looked at her watch *while* she was still attempting to decipher the message. In the second case, she looked at her watch and sighed, no longer attempting to decipher the message. Both interpretations leave it entirely open whether she ever succeeded in deciphering the message, though both are perfectly determinate in inferring that it all happened before noon and while she was feeling ill. Such interpretive choices are pervasive in natural language texts as well as in other media for efficient communication. It is not considered the task of semantic theory to prescribe which interpretive choices should be made in such cases, nor which choice is the best, the 'most natural' or even the preferred one in a given case. Semantic theory should characterize in what contexts such interpretive options arise and what the semantic consequences are of taking any of the open options. Cognitive psychology may determine how people actually make such choices, what preferences they may have for resolving such ambiguities or what cognitive constraints may affect their choice. The DAT account of temporal reference and reasoning regards interpretation hence as an indeterministic process, and characterizes the semantically determinate consequences of interpretive options in its conditional constraints on content. Although other domains of knowledge or information may be adduced to constrain the open options further, such more general accounts of reasoning or belief revision are beyond the intended scope of this chapter. Any theory of temporal reasoning in natural language must contain a core of logical inferences based on tense and aspectual information, which may well be context-dependent and situated.

In an interpretation we must at some point decide on such options. If we choose to interpret a next tensed clause as describing a next event, we commit ourselves to certain consequences. For example, if we interpret (10) to mean that her looking at her watch made her stop deciphering the message, we must interpret the next sentence *She sighed* as describing an event occurring after she stopped. If we impute such a causal correlation to her looking at her watch and stopping to decipher the message, her sighing cannot possibly be a temporal part of her attempt to decipher the message. But if that sentence had been in a perfect tense instead, i.e. *She had sighed*, we would have been free to infer that her sighing occurred during her attempt to decipher the message, even if we adhered to the causal correlation. If, instead, we interpret her looking at her watch as occurring while she was deciphering the message, her sighing could also be simultaneous with it.

Making such interpretive decisions depends on the aspectual class we assign to the clause. The classification of inflected clauses into aspectual classes contributes essential information about the temporal relations between the events and states described. This determines the temporal architecture of the representation of the descriptive information about what happened. Other factors may induce additional interpretive constraints, including causal correlations, prior context, background assumptions, prejudices, presuppositions and the thematic roles of verbal arguments. The aspectual classes and aspectual properties assigned during the interpretation determine how the events in the described episode are temporally related. Aspect controls the dynamics of the flow of information about described episode encoded in a text.

Natural languages contain diverse linguistic means to encode the description of change as either open or closed events, or as states, where no change is considered to occur. In English the clauses in (11) are simple examples of sentences that are ordinarily, disregarding special contexts, interpreted as referring to open events or 'holes'.

(11): a. Water spread over the floor

b. I bought clothes

c. Mary walked along the river

d. John damaged his car

Events described as holes typically end rather than finish, since the descriptive information about them does not indicate what would constitute their completion. Such events last for some time and endure throughout the periods described by durative adverbial modification (e. g. *for an hour*, *three hours long*). In English, indefinite mass nouns as *water* (11a) or the bare plural *clothes* (11b) as arguments of the verb virtually enforce the interpretation of the clause as an open event in any context, since they typically allow the description of the entire event to be equally applicable to any of its temporal parts. E.g. if (11 a) describes a past event of water spreading over the floor that ended before this information was given, there must be a smaller event temporally contained within it that is also a past event of water spreading over that floor. Prepositional clauses as *along the river* in (11c) that do not describe a definite measure or container, but rather a path or a continuous change of location, may be used in descriptions of events as holes. Certain lexical verbs such as *damage* in (11d) or *patrol*, also allow the part-whole inference characteristic of open events. If a given clause is interpreted as describing a hole, its starting-point must precede the event described by any subsequent simple past clause, though states, described with perfect tenses, may temporally overlap with it. However, causal connections or other knowledge of the world may interfere with and overrule these general semantic principles determining temporal dependencies.

Plugs, represented by closed nodes, put a fairly weak constraint on the flow of information. A clause interpreted as a plug gives information about the smallest event of that type representing its descriptive content. In (12) some simple examples are given of English sentences that are typically interpreted as filters, momentarily disregarding the influence of context and background.

(12): a. The book fell on the floor

b. I bought a book

c. I drank a glass of water

d. Mary walked to the river

e. John destroyed his car

Filters are descriptions of the kind of events that may finish or get finished, and do not merely cease or end. They describe events with singular count or amount term arguments, modified by goal-describing PPs, e.g. (12a, d), or container-adverbials, as with *in an hour*, or *within a day*. Such modification does not require that the event lasted throughout the hour or the day, but expresses only that the event took place inside the specified period. Of course, in requiring that e.g. (12b) describes a smallest event of the buying of a book, it is fixed which book is being bought. I could well have bought some other books along with it. I could even have bought one of those other books within the time it took for me to buy the first one. But I could not have bought that first book within the time that I bought it, for I would then have bought the same book twice. If this sounds trivially true, one should, with Heraclitus, ponder why it is that you do not simultaneously drink water twice, even though within the time it took for you to drink some specific quantity of water, you also must drink other, smaller quantity of water. Similarly, why is it that one destroys a car only once, but can damage it often, repetitively or gradually? Holes do not give us such smallest events of the given type, only plugs do.

Aspect is concerned with the way we represent change in the world as structured. We use aspectual information to organize the descriptive information about the world, so aspectual properties are not determined by what is the case in the world. Events are in the world, but nothing about their physical structure makes them a plug or hole. We create holes and plugs to classify the reference of our descriptions, to communicate efficiently about them and to make our descriptive information hook up properly into the changing world. A plug is a semantic ticket to disregard change internal to the described event, to treat it as atomic and close off its internal structure for further description. Of course, later we may always reconsider it, return to it, and unplug it to unveil more of its internal structure.

18.3 Inferences with Aspectual Verbs and Adverbs

The familiar square of opposition of quantifiers is given in Figure 18.1. where the four corners are related by internal and external negation and two quantifiers are each others duals, related by composition of internal and external negation.

The arrows indicate monotonicity in respectively the interpretation of the noun in the noun-phrase and the interpretation of the verb-phrase, which are the left and right argument of the determiner regarded as a relation D between sets A and B. Internal negation reverses the direction of monotonicity in the right argument, external negation reverses it in both arguments. The concepts and tests are illustrated in (13).

(13): a. existential - *a, some* - left and right increasing.
a beautiful woman sings $\Rightarrow$ a woman sings.
a woman sings an aria $\Rightarrow$ a woman sings.

b. universal - *every, all* - left decreasing, right increasing.
every woman sings $\Rightarrow$ every beautiful woman sings.
every woman sings an aria $\not\Rightarrow$ every woman sings.

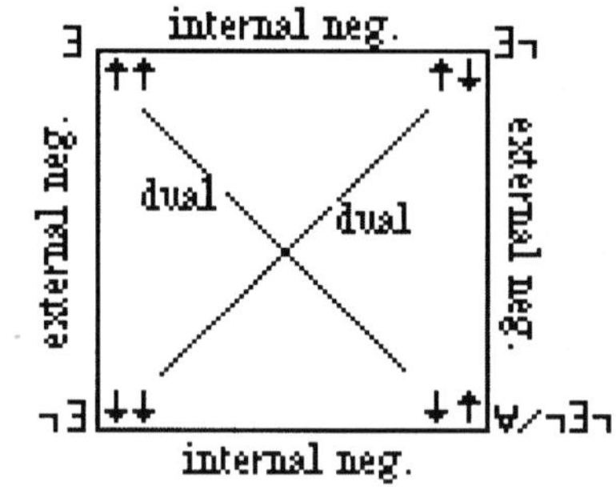

Figure 18.1: Square of logical quantifiers

c. internally negated existential - left increasing, right decreasing.
a beautiful woman is not singing ⇒ a woman is not singing.
a woman is not singing ⇒ a woman is not singing an aria.

d. externally negated existential - *no* - left and right decreasing.
no woman is singing ⇒ no beautiful woman is singing.
no woman is singing ⇒ no woman is singing an aria.

Applying this basic square to the event-external aspectual verbs, we get Figure 18.2. The aspectual verbs *start* and *finish* are existential (dynamic) in nature, and *continue*, together with the non-lexicalized position externally negating start, are universal (static).

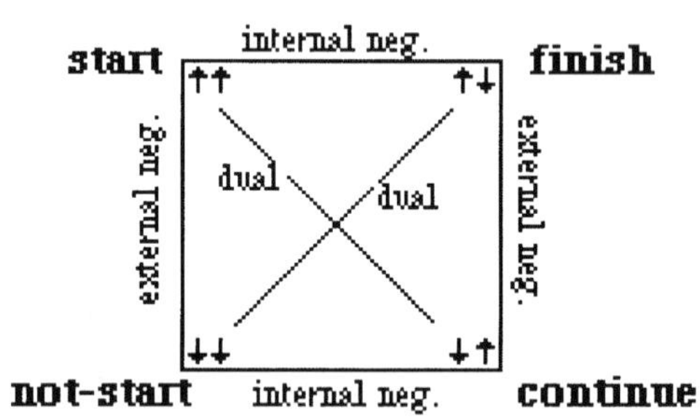

Figure 18.2: Square of event-external aspectual verbs

If we analyze these verbs semantically as relations between a contextually determined reference time *t*, and an event-type *e* and a polarity 0 (off) or 1(on), the logical equivalences in (14) follow from Figure 18.2. E.g. (14a) states that starting at t a positive phase of an event e is logically equivalent to finishing at t a negative phase of e. These equivalences may be considered meaning-postulates clarifying the interaction between the aspectual verbs and polarity reversals.

(14): a. For all t, e, [*start* (t, e, +) ⇔ *finish* (t, e, -)]

b. For all t, e, [*not start* (t, e, -) $\Leftrightarrow$ *continue* (t, e, +)]

c. For all t, e, [*continue* (t, e, +) $\Leftrightarrow$ *not finish* (t, e, +)]

d. For all t, e, [*start* (t, e, -) $\Leftrightarrow$ *not notstart* (t, e, -)]

If we consider aspectual verbs to be interpreted by relations between sets of instants, reducing an event e for simplicity to the interval I during which it takes place, the extensional set-theoretic concepts of generalized quantifier theory, originally developed for determiners as illustrated in (13), becomes available for application to the temporal domain*. First, the Conservativity of determiners D relating sets A and B, respectively the interpretation of the noun in the subject and the verb phrase, DAB = D A (A | B) (also called the 'live-on property') is reformulated as requiring consideration of intervals I which temporally intersect with the singleton set $\{t\}$, containing the contextually determined reference-time *t*, as in (15).

(15): CONS: $V(\{t\}, I) = V(\{t\}, (\{t\} \cap I))$

Although Variety, excluding the universal and the empty relation, and Extension, i.e. insensitivity to domain-extension may be adopted without modification, Quantity, requiring permutation-invariance, must be dropped as the order in the interval domain matters crucially in this analysis of aspectual verbs.

The reference-times in the left argument constitute a set partially ordered by the temporal precedence relation $\leq$, and the intervals which constitute the right argument are partially ordered by a temporal inclusion relation restricted to realizations of the same event-type, i.e. having the same relation, arguments and polarity. If at *t* an event *e* starts interval *I*, and *I* is included in *I'* (realizing the same event), then *I'* starts at *t*: *start* is right increasing. Furthermore, if at *t* an event *e* starts interval *I*, there can't be any earlier *t'* preceding *t*, whose singleton set intersects with *I*. Other reference times intersecting *I* must all be later than *t*, if *t* is to constitute the starting point of *e*: *start* is also left increasing. Similarly, if you assume that an event *e* taking place during an interval *I* has been completed or is over at *t*, and take a later time *t'*, then I must be over at *t'* too: *finish* is left-increasing. And with the same assumption taking a smaller interval I' contained in I, that I' must be over at *t* too: *finish* is right-decreasing. And again, for *continue*, if the event *e* is continuing during *I* at the reference time *t*, it must have been continuing at some earlier reference time *t'* preceding *t*, and a larger interval I' is continuing at t, i.e. you're 'amidst' of the event, as summarized in (16).

(16): a. *start* - left and right increasing
start ($\{t\}$, I) , t $\leq$ t' $\Rightarrow$ *start* ($\{t'\}$, I)
start ($\{t\}$, I) , I is included in I' $\Rightarrow$ *start* ($\{t\}$, I')

b. *finish* - left increasing, right decreasing
finish ($\{t\}$, I) , t $\leq$ t' $\Rightarrow$ *finish* ($\{t'\}$, I)
finish ($\{t\}$, I) , I' is included in I $\Rightarrow$ *finish* ($\{t\}$, I')

*See [Keenan and Westerstahl, 1997] and references cited there for the main results of generalized quantifier theory of natural language determiners. See [ter Meulen, 1990] for a first application of GQ theory to aspectual verbs,

c. *continue* - left decreasing, right increasing
continue ({t}, I) , t' ≤ t ⇒ *continue* ({t'}, I)
continue ({t}, I) , I is included in I' ⇒ *continue* ({t}, I')

The right-decreasing character of *stop* and *finish* is further attested in their triggering negative polarity *any*, as in (17).

(17): a. John stopped/ceased making any sense.

b. John finished any book he started.

Let's look at the event-internal aspectual verbs in a diagram, Figure 18.3. Note that all four positions are lexically realized, if *end* is taken in the static sense of *not resuming* . Of course, *resume* means *begin again*, and *begin* could be in the same position, if we drop the presupposition of the ongoing negative stage of the same event-type.

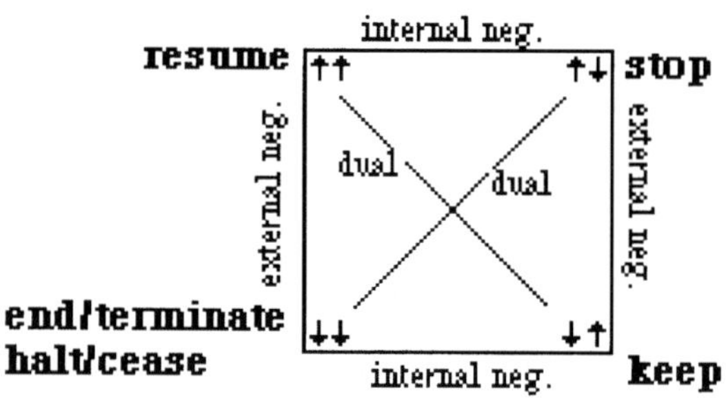

Figure 18.3: Square of event-internal aspectual verbs

The same tests are applied to this square for equivalences and entailments in (18) and (19).

(18): a. For all t, e, [*resume* (t, e, -) ⇔ *stop* (t, e, +)]

b. For all t, e, [*not resume* (t, e, -) ⇔ *keep* (t, e, +)]

c. For all t, e, [*keep* (t, e, +) ⇔ *not stop* (t, e, +)]

d. For all t, e, [*resume* (t, e, -) ⇔ *not end* (t, e, -)]

(19): a. *resume* - left and right increasing
resume ({t}, I) , t ≤ t' ⇒ *resume* ({t'}, I)
resume ({t}, I) , I is included in I' ⇒ *resume* ({t}, I')

b. *stop* - left increasing, right decreasing
stop ({t}, I) , t ≤ t' ⇒ *stop* ({t'}, I)
stop ({t}, I) , I' is included in I ⇒ *stop* ({t}, I')

c. *keep* - left decreasing, right increasing
keep ({t}, I) , t' ≤ t ⇒ *keep* ({t'}, I)
keep ({t}, I) , I is included in I' ⇒ *keep* ({t}, I')

d. *end/terminate/halt* - left decreasing, right decreasing
$end\ (\{t\}, I)\ , t' \leq t \Rightarrow end\ (\{t'\}, I)$
$end\ (\{t\}, I)$, I' is included in I $\Rightarrow end\ (\{t\}, I')$

It may need explaining why *end* in (19d) is left decreasing. Since the temporal order on the reference times is not a strict one, the given reference time will always be available to be identified with t', satisfying the constraint on its left downward monotonicity. This captures the static 'hole' nature of ending at t and remaining there, whereas finishing is a plug shifting dynamically to a later reference time at which the event which has been finished is no longer taking place.

The two squares, one for the event-external aspectual verbs in Figure 18.2, one for the event-internal ones in Figure 18.3. can be related by polarity transitions. We have already seen that *stop* is the internal negation of *start*, just as *finish*, but *stop* presupposes that the event was started and a positive stage is going on. *Finish* only presupposes that the same event-type has been realized before. You can finish something even though you have interrupted it for a while, but you cannot stop doing something unless you are right there doing it. So *finish* admits gapping over time, *stop* does not. If *stop* is the internal negation of *start* with the additional presupposition that the event is going on, we can relate the two squares in a three-dimensional cube by flipping the event-internal diagram along its vertical axis, as in Figure 18.4.

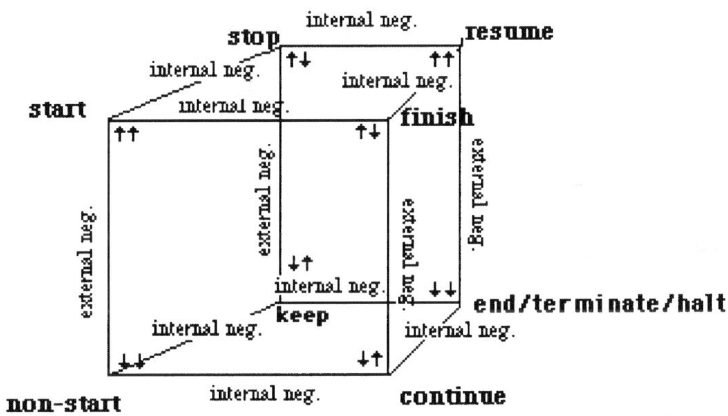

Figure 18.4: Three-dimensional square of aspectual quantifiers

It is now easy to check that the other internal negations also work as polarity reversal.

(20): a. For all t, e, [*stop* (t, e, +) $\Leftrightarrow$ *start* (t, e, -)]
b. For all t, e, [*resume* (t, e, +) $\Leftrightarrow$ *finish* (t, e, -)]
c. For all t, e, [*not resume* (t, e, +) $\Leftrightarrow$ *continue* (t, e, -)]
d. For all t, e, [*keep* (t, e, +) $\Leftrightarrow$ *not start* (t, e, -)]

Furthermore a diagonal across the top from *start* to *resume* or *begin again* is equivalent to going from *start* to *stop* to *resume*. If it did not go through *stop*, it would simply be *start* entailing *begin*. Similarly *continue* entails *keep*. The entailments across the diagonal over the top and bottom are from the front event-external to the back event-internal verbs.

It follows immediately that resuming a positive event presupposes you have started it and stopped it first. Similarly, finishing an event presupposes having started it and perhaps stopped and resumed it first. Or you end an event, by first starting it, then non-starting the negative event-type, which is equivalent to keeping the positive event going on, and then you end it. Any non-cyclic transition through the aspectual cube represents a transition, if you enter in *start* and switch polarity of the event-type when passing an internal negation and exit in *finish* (for telic events or plugs) or *end* (for atelic events or holes).

The semantic automata designed by Johan van Benthem for determiners (see van Benthem 1986) as generalized quantifiers can be applied to the aspectual verbs. It shows how the internal-external duality of the Figure 18.4 can be represented by corresponding finite state automata. The main result here is that the presuppositions of the event-internal aspectual verbs are compositionally obtained from the aspectual cube and the simple machines for the event-external verbs, accounting neatly for the projections of presuppositions.

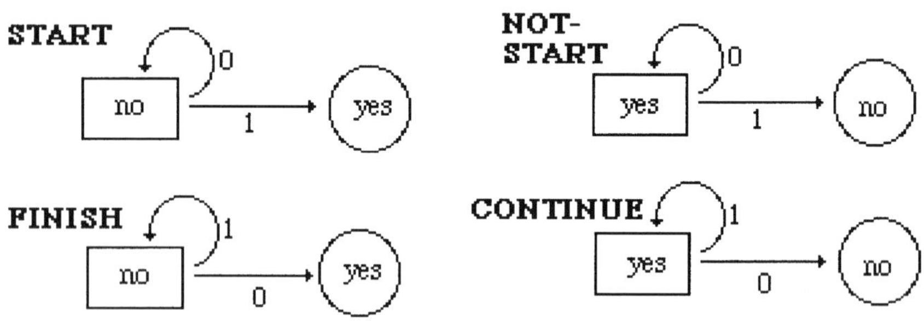

Figure 18.5: Automata for event-external aspectual verbs

In Figure 18.5 the starting-state for all machines is the square on the left, and the halting state the circle on the right. 'Yes' indicates the accepting state and 'no' the rejecting state. For the START-automaton you scan realizations of the event-type with negative polarity, rejecting until you find the first realization of the event-type with a positive polarity, then you go into the accepting halting state. It is easy to see that if we scan individuals rather than polarities of event-types, the same machine would work, for an existential quantifier is verified with at least one positive instance of the predicate you are testing for. The other automata for event-external aspectual verbs are easy to construct once you know that internal negation switches the 0 and 1 on the arrows, and external negation switches accepting and rejecting state. So the automaton for *finish* starts with checking for realizations of the event-type with positive polarity, and keeps rejecting until you get a realization of the event-type with a negative polarity, which means the event has come to an end. The presupposition of *finish*, i.e. that the same event-type has been realized with positive polarity in the representation, is indirectly captured by the fact that it rejects as long as the event-type polarity remains positive. The semantic characteristic of *finish* (and internally negated existentials) is that as long as there are positive instances, if any, the verb or quantifier is rejected, but as soon as there is a negative instance, the verb (or quantifier) is accepted. Note that the automaton for *continue* does require at least one positive realization of the event, since it does not accept or reject until you've passed the 1-loop once, assuming that acceptance requires passing at least one loop. In that precise sense *continue* has a stronger presupposition than *finish*.

To create an automaton for an event-internal aspectual verb you construct the automata for each node you pass from *start* until you reach the intended corner in the back of the aspectual cube. The automata for each verb passed is composed into a sequence of simple automata. For example, the automaton for *stop* is composed with the *start*-machine and the autmata for *finish* as in Figure 18.6 (*finish* and *stop* have the same monotonicity properties, Figure 18.4).

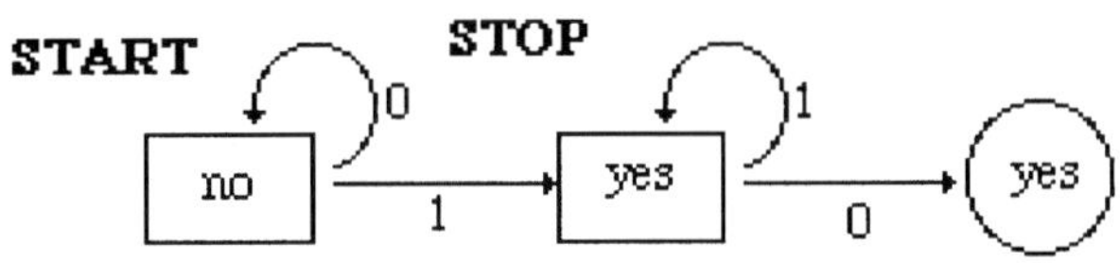

Figure 18.6: Automaton for event-internal *stop*

The computational content of aspectual verbs has been modelled in these simple automata, together with their composition based on the transitions in the cube of aspectual verbs given in Figure 18.4.

This account of aspectual verbs is incorporated in the semantics of aspectual adverbs to account for the validity of reasoning patterns involving aspectual adverbs in contexts where the temporal reference point may change. Consider the inference in (21), where the premises (21a, b) are presented in the order indicated, and (21c) is a valid conclusion (indicated by $\models$) , but (21d) is invalid (indicated by $\not\models$).

(21): a. John is STILL not asleep.

b. John fell asleep.

c. John is finally asleep.

d. $\not\models$ John is alREADY asleep.

The dynamic information in (21b) referring to John's falling asleep as a plug changes the information state created by (21a): some of it is updated, whereas other information is not affected. The valid conclusion in (21c) preserves the speaker subjective information of (21a) (*John fell asleep later than the speaker had preferred*), whereas in (21d) it is not preserved (*John fell asleep earlier than the speaker had preferred*). Established preferences, judgments of speed of change and other epistemic or evaluative attitudes are generally not affected when new factual information becomes available. The aspectual verbs have an important role to play in the dynamic semantics of aspectual adverbs, their prosodic meaning (i.e. the content which is added to the truth-conditional meaning when the prosody is marked with high pitch), and validity of dynamic inferences with such adverbs*.

*The interested reader is referred to [ter Meulen and Smessaert, 2004] for a detailed semantics of aspectual adverbs and their role in dynamic reasoning. In [ter Meulen, 2003], Ter Meulen presents a concise overview of the semantics of English aspectual adverbs.

18.4 Dynamic Semantics of Temporal Reference

To analyze how information is preserved while reasoning in time about time, the system of Dynamic Aspect Trees (DAT) was designed for ordinary English [ter Meulen, 1995; ter Meulen, 2000]. With Discourse Representation Theory (DRT) [Kamp and Reyle, 1993], and most current semantic theories of tense and aspect, it shares the assumption that tense is a double indexical, which refers to a time dependent not only upon the time the information is received, but also on the information processed earlier. Aspectual information drives the construction of the representation; in DRT the structured discourse representations, and in the DAT system the tree structure. Tree-structures of the DATs direct the reasoning during updates, incorporating causal information to constrain the temporal relations. Stative information may spread in the DAT to other nodes, locally constrained to an important extent by the DAT structure. In DRT this form of reasoning is relegated to a default logic, based on normal possible worlds, which properly belongs to a pragmatic module of the theory. DAT structure may be revised, if certain conditions obtain, to resolve a local contradiction or accommodate otherwise incompatible information. In DRT no such revision of the constructed representations is envisaged, nor may contradictions be resolved. This may be the most important difference between DRT and DAT, though the two dynamic systems otherwise share many fundamental assumptions*.

Like DRT, Dynamic Aspect Trees constitute a logical system of temporal reasoning in which dynamic information, describing change, is distinguished from stative information, describing states where no change occurs. The first affects the architecture of the tree representation by adding new nodes, carrying truth conditional descriptive content in their labels. Stative information merely adds labels to existing nodes, never affecting the structure of the DAT, but such labels may spread to other nodes, if certain structural tree conditions obtain.

In order to consider DATs as structured objects in their own right, we first specify the syntactic conditions on their wellformedness. DATs are not expressions of any logical language that encode the traditional 'logical form' of the linguistic input into a symbolic language designed to represent its meaning. Of course, it remains always possible to translate a DAT to a relational formula of some higher order logic, if this were desirable for extraneous reasons. In my opinion there are definite advantages to the visual transparency and ease of use inherent to the graphic tree representation of DATs, and the heuristic value of visual display should become apparent in the next section.

Types that label the nodes of a DAT are formed by the following rules, recursively specifying the class *TYPE*, in (22).

*The appendix in [ter Meulen, 1995] reviews the most important linguistic differences between DRT and DATs, showing that atelic event descriptions, or activities, should be distinguished from the state descriptions, though both preserve the current context.

(22): **Definition 18.4.1 (TYPE).** *a. T is a basic type in TYPE iff. T is a sequence consisting of an n-ary relation **R**, n objects* $a_1 \ldots a_n$*, and a positive or negative polarity + or -.*

b. T is a parametric or parametrized type in TYPE iff. T is a basic type in which a relation or an object is replaced by a relation parameter R or an object parameter a_i*. respectively.*

c. if T is in TYPE and x is an object parameter then x_T *is a restricted object parameter. If T contains* x_T*, T is a* restricted parametrized type *in TYPE.*

d. if x is a parameter and T is in TYPE , then $[x|T]$ *is a* role. *If T is a restricted parametrized type, all parameters in the restriction must occur in the role-type to the left of* |.[†a]

e. if T and T' are in TYPE, so is the conjoined type $\ll$ *T&T'* $\gg$ *and conditional type* $\ll T \Rightarrow T' \gg$.

f. Nothing else is in TYPE unless it is obtained by the clauses in (i) - (v).

There is a primitive notion of *compatibility* of types. Any two types are compatible iff. there is a situation that supports both within the same temporal context, called a *chronoscope*. A chronoscope is a connected path in the DAT leading from a single terminal node to its root, including the parent of every node in the chronoscope. A chronoscope is *current*, if it contains the unique current node. The current chronoscope is unique, only if the current node is terminal, which need not always be the case during DAT construction. Chronoscopes are intended to model cones of locally consistent information about an episode, satisfiable simultaneously by a set of events. Obviously, any type is compatible with itself, and incompatible with its negative counterpart containing a negative polarity or any of its entailments. Knowledge of the world and causal information in natural language supplies a host of basic (in)compatibility relations between types, encoded as conditional correlations between features in the lexicon. Two sets of types are compatible iff. their union is compatible; and a single type *T* is compatible with a set *S* of types just in case $S \cup \{T\}$ is compatible.

The DATs are simple, acyclic, directed graphs in which the top-down order reflects the temporal inclusion relation between events, and the left to right order is intended to represent the temporal precedence relation between events. Two kinds of nodes are used in DAT construction: holes and plugs. Holes are open nodes, indicating that new information may be represented as as a temporally included sub-event by a dependent node. Plugs are closed nodes, indicating that no further dependent nodes may be added[‡]. Information added to a DAT whose current node is a plug must be understood as describing later events, hence represented by right sister nodes of the given current node. The source node represents the event of receiving information, i.e. the current time. Present tense information, including the generic statements alluded to above, must label the source node or one of its ancestors, whereas past tense information will always be located to the left of the source node. Since

[†] In this paper we have not yet made any use of roles in DAT-representations. They are listed here for sake of completeness of the *TYPE* specification. The additional condition on forming roles from restricted parametric types is called the Absorption law in Gawron and Peters (1990), supported by empirical linguistic arguments based on VP anaphora.

[‡] Later this clause needs to be refined to allow for presupposition accommodation to open up a plug and add new dependent nodes. This is a restructuring operation in DATs.

future tense is treated as a static modality, ranging over later updates, no nodes in DATs are later than, i.e. to the right of the source time.

(23): **Definition 18.4.2 (DAT).** *A DAT consists of:*

(i) a finite set of nodes, N = $\{n, n', \ldots, n_m\}$

(ii) a function Δ_N *from N to N*, where N* is the set of non-repeating finite sequences of N, assigning to each node n a sequence of nodes, its children or immediate dependents* $\Delta_N(n)$.

(iii) a function Π_N *from N to N, assigning an arrow pointing to a node n from its immediately dominating node, its parent* $\Pi_N(n)$.

(iv) a subset H_N *of N, the Holes; N-*H_N *is the set* P_N *of plugs.*

(v) a function α_N *from N to the power set of TYPE, assigning to each node a set of types.*

(vi) a distinguished node c_N *in, the current node, and another distinguished node* s_N *in*P_N*, the source node.*

such that

1. $\forall n, n'$ *in N, n is in* $\Delta_N(n')$ *iff.* $\Pi_N(n) = n'$.
2. *One and only one node, the root, is its own ancestor (n is an ancestor of n' iff.* $\exists n_1, \ldots, n_m$ $(m \geq 2)$ *such that* $n_i = \Pi_N(n_i + 1), n = n_1$ *and* $n' = n_m$.
3. *The source node is the right most terminal node.*
4. *The set of all types labelling the ancestors of a node n (i.e.* $\{\cup \alpha_N(n') | n'$ *is an ancestor of n*$\}$*) is compatible with those types labelling n itself.*

The semantics of DATs is specified by embedding the trees into event structures, as given below in (25) and (26).

Information accumulation is simulated by updating a DAT. It is defined as an ordering on DATs in (24), where c is the current node from which the updating procedure is started.

(24): *Updating DATs*:

DAT D_1 is updated to DAT D_2 iff:

$$D_1 \leq D_2 = D_1 \cup \{c_{D2}\}$$

and either:

1. (Hole rule) c_{D_1} is in H_{D_1} and each of Δ_{D_2}, Π_{D_2}, H_{D_2} and α_{D_2} extends the corresponding function of D_1 with the sole exception that $\Delta_{D_2}(c_{D_1}) =< c_{D_2} >$, or
2. (Plug rule) cD_1 is in P_{D_1} and each of Δ_{D_2}, Π_{D_2}, H_{D_2} and α_{D_2} extends the corresponding function of D_1 with the sole exception that $\Delta_{D_2}(\Pi_{D_1}(c_{D_1}))$ is obtained by appending c_{D_2} to the end of $\Delta_{D_1}(\Pi_{D_1}(c_{D_1}))$, or

3. (Filter rule) $\alpha_{D_2}(c_{D_2})$ is incompatible with the types assigned to the ancestors of c_{D_1}; and $\exists D'_1 < D_2$ with the same nodes as D_1 and the same functions Δ, Π and α but with $c_{D'_1}$ as ancestor of c_{D_1} and $c_{D'_1}$ is not in $H_{D'_1}$
4. (Sticker rule) c_{D_1} is in N_{D_1} and each of Δ_{D_2}, Π_{D_2}, N_{D_2} is identical to its corresponding function of D_1, but α_{D_2} extends the corresponding function of D_1 and $c_{D_1} = c_{D_2}$, if c_{D_1} is in P_{D_1}, and otherwise α_{D_2} is extended into α_{D_3} after application of the hole or filter rule.

Define $\ll$ to be the transitive closure of $<$, i.e. $D \ll D'$ iff. there are $D_1, \ldots, D_n$ such that $D_i < D_{i+1}$, $D = D_1$ and $D' = D_n$. Let 0 be the DAT with a single node o, $\Delta_0(o) =< o >$, $\Pi_0(o) = o$, $H_0(o) = o$, $c_0(o) = o$, $\alpha_0(o) = \emptyset$. The class of *well formed* DATs consists of only those DATs D such that $0 \ll D$.

DATs are intended to be interpreted in event-structures, consisting of events with their natural temporal inclusion and precedence ordering and constrained by some special temporal conditions. We first define the notion of an event-frame.

(25): **Definition 18.4.3 (Event-frame).** *An event-frame consists of a set of events E ordered by temporal inclusion* $\rightarrow$ *(*$x \rightarrow y$ *means y is a temporal part of x)and temporal precedence* $<$ *(*$x < y$ *means x occurs before y), together with an assignment to each T in TYPE, of a set of events [[T]] , the extension of T, such that the temporal inclusion is a partial order, temporal precedence is a strict partial order and their interaction is constrained by* [a]*:*

- *monotonicity: if* $y \rightarrow x$ *and* $y < z$ *then* $x < z$.
- *convexity: if* $x < y < z$ *and* $u \rightarrow x$ *and* $u \rightarrow z$ *then* $u \rightarrow y$.

DATs are interpreted in such event-frames by embeddings, mapping nodes to events preserving the temporal relations and satisfying certain additional conditions.

(26): **Definition 18.4.4 (Embedding).** *A function f mapping a DAT into an event-frame is an embedding iff:*

1. *for every arrow* $\Pi_N(n) \rightarrow n$, $f(\Pi_N(n)) \rightarrow f(n)$
2. *if n commands n', then* $f(n) < f(n')$¶.
3. $f(n) \models T$ *where T is the type labelling n.*

The event-frames into which DATs are embedded are called *event-structures*, which are said to *support* the DATs embedded into them. They are suitable models for temporal reasoning only if they in addition satisfy a number of constraints governing the spread of stickers in the DAT, as discussed below. In reasoning with a DAT we rely on a fundamental property of the situations that support them, called *persistence*. If an event-structure supports a DAT D1, for instance, and D2 grows out of D1 by application of the construction rules, and another

§See [van Benthem, 1983] for arguments why convexity and monotonicity are the minimal principles governing the event based temporal logic. Overlap is definable (x overlaps with y iff. there is a z that is part of both). Cf [Benthem, 1995] for a good survey of possible linguistic applications of temporal logics.

¶The notion command is an adaptation of the core configurational notion of precede and command in generative syntax. It is defined here as follows: a node n commands all right sister nodes, descending from of its parent, and their dependent nodes.

event-structure supports D2, then it must also support D1. We will return to a discussion of reasoning in DATs, after presenting a simple illustration of the application of this system to an English text.

Any natural language text provides three kinds of information: *descriptive, aspectual* and *perspectival* content. The descriptive content determines the truth-conditional meaning. It classifies an event as being of a certain type or as supporting that type. It is represented in DATs by labels on nodes, encoding a relation, an appropriate number of arguments and a positive or negative polarity as a sequence, as defined above. The aspectual content of a clause tells us how its descriptive content is to be integrated within the given DAT. This aspectual information is encoded in the open or closed nodes or the stickers, representing states. Open nodes, or holes, represent descriptions of an atelic event which may apply homogeneously to any part of it. Closed nodes, or plugs, represent descriptions of a telic event which cannot be applied to any temporal part of it. Stickers are used to represent stative information, appended to nodes without introducing new ones. The perspectival content of a clause determines which node in the DAT is considered the point-of-view of the interpretation, i.e. the location of the reasoning agent drawing inferences from the represented information. It determines, for instance, the direct reference of indexicals and demonstratives, but it also affects the form with which available information is reported. The spatio-temporal location of the act of receiving the information is also included in the perspectival content, in DATs represented as the source-node, the unique right-most terminal node.

Only a single example of the representation of a text in a DAT is analyzed here, due to page limitations. Labels are simplified to aid legibility by leaving out the polarity, if positive, and using quasi English instead of the full ordered type, as defined above. The interested reader is referred to further examples in [ter Meulen, 1995] and further references. The text in (27) represented as DAT below is discussed in more detail in [ter Meulen, 2000].

(27): After dinner (plug), Jane worked on her homework (hole). She was sitting on the sofa (PROG sticker). The cat slept on her lap (hole). Suddenly the doorbell rang (plug). She got up to open the door (plug). It was John (sticker). He wanted her to come with him (sticker). He did not realize she was doing her homework (negative polarity sticker). She started to explain that he better leave (plug). First she said her homework was not done yet (plug).

DAT construction starts out with a source node, representing the event of issuing information orally or otherwise, and its parent, the root. Since the text is entirely past tense, all of its nodes are introduced to the left of the source node, i.e. describing an earlier episode. The adverbial phrase *after dinner* introduces the first, closed node, representing the completed event of having dinner*. The main clause *Jane worked on her homework* is hole, represented by an open node. The second sentence is a past progressive, represented as sticker, which, according to the sticker rule, must await the introduction of the next node to which it is to be appended. The subsequent sentence *the cat slept on her lap* introduces a hole, as it is also an atelic hole, to which the progressive sticker can now be appended. The following sentence introduces a plug representing the telic event of the ringing of the doorbell. It terminates this chronoscope and hence forces the temporal reference of information to be added to this DAT to later events. When information is entered that Jane got up to open the door, this update cannot introduce any dependent nodes as its current node is a plug. Its parent contains the

*Strictly speaking the construction rules for adverbial phrases have not yet been specified. For simplicity, I treat this adverbial phrase as if it were the indicative sentence with past tense Jane had dinner.

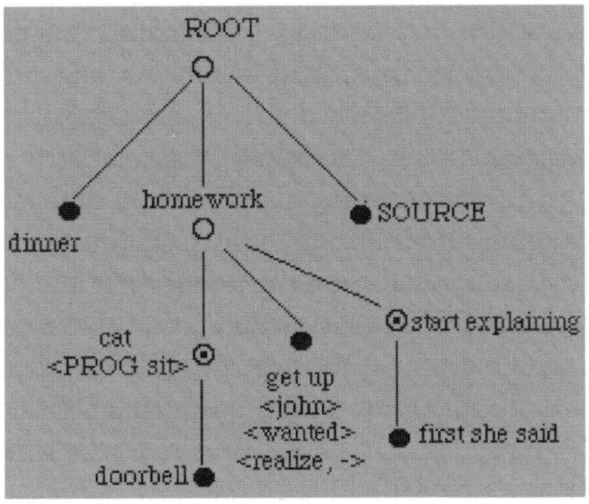

Figure 18.7: DAT for (27)

information that Jane was sitting on the sofa, which is incompatible at the level of lexical features with her getting up. Now the construction procedure backtracks to the lowest node in the chronoscope labeled with the incompatible type ≪Prog sit...≫, converts it to a plug and continues with the plug rule. It creates a new right sister node to this node, which gets labeled with the information that Jane got up.

In this DAT the entailment that the cat is no longer sleeping on Jane's lap, once she got up, is accounted for. Left sister nodes of any node n are understood to be completed before the start of n. The DAT so created supports the inference that Jane was no longer sitting on the sofa when she got up, but that she was still doing her homework. Some reasoners may be less tolerant of 'gappy events', disallowing intermissions and resumptions of events. They would probably reject the inference that Jane was doing her homework when she was getting up to open the door, and accordingly create it as a sister node to the higher homework node instead. Such divergence in possible interpretations is a positive feature of DAT construction, allowing reasoners to differ in the situated inferences they draw from one and the same text. Semantic representation should not legislate just what is or is not compatible, as such judgments may also vary among the users of natural language and may indeed depend in all kinds of ways upon the context in which the inferences are made.

Since the next three clauses introduce only stickers, they all get stacked and appended to this plug. Ordinarily stickers do not spread to right sisters of the node they are initially appended to, nor to higher parent nodes. Stative information may only be imported to other nodes according to the portability conditions of stickers discussed below. Only perfect stickers, created by perfect tense clauses, may spread towards the right onto newly introduced nodes, since this is the only kind of information that persists as such and is carried forward indefinitely into the future. Perfect stickers may also be introduced at right sisters of nodes which carry any other label.

The information that Jane started to explain that he better leave is represented by a new plug, as 'start' is a telic verb, represented as a right sister to the getting up plug. Parallel to the filler rule, which converts holes to plugs of local inconsistencies obtain, there is also a way to convert plugs to holes, if presuppositions must be accommodated. This rule has not been included in the set of DAT construction rules in (24), as it would require an excursion into the effects of presupposition accommodation, leading much beyond the scope of the present chapter. Yet it may here be illustrated briefly, as its operation is perspicuous and interesting. The final sentence of the text contains the temporal ordinal adverb, *first*. It presupposes that what she is saying is a temporal part of her explanation to John that he better leave. Of course, this presupposition itself is only reached as a conclusion after a substantial amount of reasoning about the relations between saying and explaining, taking into account that we tacitly assume that John must still be at the door and she is addressing him etc. Since the current node in the DAT at that point of the interpretation is a plug, no dependent nodes may be added. Instead, to accommodate the presupposition that what she says is part of her explanation, this plug is first converted to a hole, relabeling it with $\ll$ *explain, jane, john,* ϕ , +$\gg$ to represent the atelic event of her explaining. This conversion is supported by a natural constraint requiring the start of any event to be part of the event itself, whether it be atelic/hole or telic/plug. Aspectual verbs and ordinal adverbs typically trigger such constraints. Now the DAT may be updated by a plug representing her saying that her homework was not done yet, dependent on her explaining to John that he better leave. The exact relation between the content of what she says, i.e. that her homework is not done yet, and the fact that this plug is dependent on the hole, representing her doing her homework, is not further analyzed here. Obviously it supports the interpretation allowing gaps to occur, for her getting up to answer the doorbell and talking to John is temporally include in the event of her doing her homework. This concludes the construction of the DAT for the simple text in (27), which obviously cannot be a very natural end of the whole story. The DAT structure resulting from the interpretation of the text is now used in drawing further conclusions from it. This is discussed in more detail in the next section.

18.5 Situated Inference and Dynamic Temporal Reasoning

Constructing DATs models the processing of a natural language text, allowing for revision of the construction, if local inconsistency or presupposition accommodation requires it. Since the support relation between event-structures and DATs is persistent, the information represented at an earlier stage of construction of a DAT should always be retrievable, although the nodes may not remain directly accessible from any later node. The way the represented information may be reported in natural language conclusions depends on the DAT and its current node, as well as the relation between it and the node labelled with the descriptive information used in the conclusion. Generally, once a premise is used in growing a node, it does not automatically constitute a situated entailment at any later node. The information received is interpreted as an instruction to construct a DAT, but an inference from a DAT reports what results after executing the instruction. A given DAT may incorporate new information not only by growing new nodes, but also by plugging up holes or opening plugs. The interpretation process defines a non-monotonic update relation between DATs, because a DAT need not be preserved as a substructure of the DAT it grows into. Tracing back into the history of the construction, one should always be able to retrieve any earlier stage of the interpretation.

Reasoning with DATs is situated, as the current node must support the sticker which represents the conclusion. Conclusions are always stative and hence get represented as stickers, for they draw upon the DAT but cannot affect it in any way other than adding a sticker to the node which is current when the inference is made. Since different DATs may be constructed for the same sequence of premises, based on variation in judgments of the compatibility of predicates, different conclusions may be drawn from the same story. Stickers, representing stative conclusions, may be imported to a node according to the Sticker Portability rules in (28), informally stated.

If a state holds, it must hold during any temporal part of it. This is reminiscent of the homogeneity condition or downwards monotonicity of interval semantics*. So the first portability condition of stickers (28.1) allows for any sticker to be copied onto dependent nodes. We already discussed the rightward portability of stickers representing perfect tense descriptions of states, resulting from an event that caused them (28.2). If an event is described with a progressive clause, we infer that its starting point must be past, and its end must be later, but we cannot always locate these nodes as such in the DAT. So the corresponding inference rule must require that it is possible to update the given DAT with a corresponding start node to its left. This rule does not actually introduce such a node, unless there is no DAT structure to the left at all yet. For this purpose, the directed modalities are used in (28.3), quantifying over possible updates. Left directed modalities quantify either existentially (weak) or universally (strong) over updates of the DAT to the left, i.e. past, of the current node; right directed modalities idem over DAT structure to its right, i.e. future. From a perfect tense description we infer that the event, that caused this state, must be over now. Hence it must be located somewhere to its left (28.4). Similarly, a node representing an event should allow for the introduction of the corresponding perfect sticker, describing its resulting state, on any node to its right (28.5). Finally, since dependence between nodes models spatio-temporal inclusion, a node n which is dependent upon another node n' may carry a progressive sticker corresponding to the label at n' (28.6). Although the portability constraints in (28) by no means exhaust all the valid inferences on DATs, at least they capture a few core intuitions of how the DAT structure may guide our reasoning in time about time.

(28): *Portability constraints for stickers*

1. Any sticker may be copied to any dependent node.
2. A PERF sticker may be copied onto any right sister node.
3. A PROG sticker imports a left-directed weak modal START and a right-directed weak modality for END of that label at that node.
4. A PERF sticker imports a left-directed weak modal with that label at that node.
5. Any label may be copied onto a right sister as PERF sticker of that label.
6. A label may be imported as PROG sticker of that label on any dependent node.

Although stickers are static and hence do not affect a DAT structurally, they are not in the sense of traditional propositional logic genuine propositions. The main difference is that ordinary propositions are void of aspectual and perspectival content. They simply are functions from worlds to truth-values, and obey the usual laws of first-order propositional logic. In DATs even stative information in premises is used as an instruction to update the DAT with a sticker, which may spread to other nodes. Stickers are supported in event structures, and they do not refer to events, but rather describe states. If propositions denote truth-values, events must then be reduced to sets of moments within the interval during which that event

*Cf. [Dowty, 1979] for linguistic applications of interval semantics.

takes place. In DAT semantics events are primitive, and moments may be defined as maximally pairwise overlapping sets of events. Stickers obviously do a lot more work in this dynamic semantics than simple propositions were ever meant to do in plain vanilla propositional logic. A text consisting only of stative information with no incompatibilities in the descriptive content would not create much of a DAT, since all stickers would label the root node.

In assessing the advantages of situated reasoning over traditional notions of logical consequence, it may be useful to compare the DAT reasoning to the DRT definition in [Kamp and Reyle, 1996, p. 305].

(29): **Definition 18.5.1 (DRT Definition of logical consequence).** *A DRS K' is a logical consequence of DRS K iff any verifying embedding of the conditions in K can be extended to a verifying embedding of the conditions in K'.*
Definition. Let K, K' be pure (...) DRSs. Thus K' is a logical consequence of K $(K \models K')$ *iff the following condition holds:*
Suppose M is a model and f is a function from $U_k \cup Fr(K) \cup Fr(K')$ *into* U_M*, such that* $M \models_f K$*. Then there is a function* $g \supseteq_{UK}, f$ *such that* $M \models_g K'$*.*

A DRS is pure if and only if all reference markers used in the conditions are also declared at that level or at a super-ordinate one. The DRT analysis of tense and aspect makes essential use of reference markers for reference times, which also occur in K', the conclusion DRS. In this sense the conclusions may be related to the current reference time, although they need not be in this sense temporally situated.

The definition of situated inference makes use of the DAT structure and its unique current node, at which the sticker corresponding to the conclusion must be supported. The premises are first used to construct the DAT, and they describe the episode which constitutes the image of any embedding function of this DAT into the event structures. Given its current node, the conclusion sticker must be portable to that current node using any of the eight rules in (28). This means that on the semantic side the image of the current node, *f(c)*, under any embedding supports that sticker, if indeed the argument is a valid one, cf. (30).

(30): *DAT situated inference* [ter Meulen, 1995]
Given a DAT D for the premises $T_1 \ldots T_n$, with *c* as current node, then T is a situated inference from the premises, written $T_1, \ldots, T_n \vdash T$, when *c* supports T for any verifying embedding of that DAT into a possible event-structure E.

Definition 18.5.2 (Situated entailment). *Let D be a DAT for the premises* $T_1, \ldots, T_n$ *and let c be its current node, then* $T_1, \ldots, T_n \vdash T$ *iff. for all event-structures E and all embeddings f of D into E, if* $T_1, \ldots, T_n$ *describes f(D), then f (c) is of type T.*

DAT logic predicts the following situated entailments, which would not be logical entailments in DRT. In SDRT they could be characterized as possible default inferences, which requires the not unproblematic specification of 'normal courses of events' [Lascarides and Asher, 1993]. From (31) in DAT logic (32a) and (32b) are situated entailments, but they are not logical consequences from the DRS for (31), given in (33).

(31): Jane patrolled the neighborhood (hole). She noticed a car parked in an alley (plug). She gave it a ticket (plug).

The situated inference from (31) to (32a) requires more details of adverbial restriction than we have accounted for so far. But it is clear that in any case the *when*-clause in (32a) must refer to the right terminal node, which is also the current node. The progressive main clause in the conclusion (32a) is represented as a sticker, which can be imported on the current node by rule (28.6) from its parent node.

(32a): Jane was patrolling the neighborhood, when she ticketed the car.

The rule (28.3) supports the situated inference (32b) from (31).

(32b): Jane may end patrolling the neighborhood, after she has ticketed the car in the alley.

The right directed modal, obviously corresponding to an epistemic modal *may*, is imported onto the current node, using the progressive sticker introduced in (32a).

In (33) a somewhat simplified DRS is presented for the discourse in (31). The reference markers for the temporal reference points are t and t', which represent the temporal progression in a precedence ordering. Atelic event descriptions are treated in DRT as states, represented by a reference marker s which always includes the reference time, whereas telic event descriptions are represented by event reference markers e and e', which always are included in the reference time, set to be t and t' respectively.

(33): *DRS for (31)*

x y s t z e t' w e' r0
x = jane patrol (s, x, y) neighborhood (y) s includes t t = r0 t precedes *now* notice (e, x, z) car. . . (z) t includes e t precedes t' t' = r0 t' precedes *now* give (e, x, z, w) z = y ticket (w) t' includes e'

No temporal relation obtains in the DRS (33) between the patrolling state s and the ticketing event e, although their respective reference times are ordered as they should be and they both precede the speech time *now*. To develop an account of the inference in (32a) DRT would need to appeal to extra-logical properties, which are not structurally represented. In DATs such properties are as it were 'hard wired' into the structural properties of the trees, which may be repaired or revised, if information requiring such is received.

Some logical properties of situated entailment in DAT could usefully be considered structural rules in DAT logic. A complete set of structural rules has not yet been determined, together with a proof of the completeness and soundness of situated inference. These structural rules may be viewed as approximating the remnant of propositional logic in DAT logic, as it specifies how stickers may be manipulated. Alternatively, these structural rules may be viewed as text-manipulation constraints, governing how a text may be altered while preserving its situated inferences.

Only stickers of the same kind may be reversed in order if they are adjacent (PERM). One may add only a compatible sticker between two sentences or at their end (MON). If B is a situated inference from a perfect sticker A, then B is also a situated inference from a perfect sticker Z which has A as a situated inference (CUT). The last property may prove to be useful in characterizing adequacy of automated text summarization techniques.

PERM $\dfrac{X, A, B, Y \vdash C}{X, B, A, Y \vdash C}$ only when A, B are stickers of the same kind

MON $\dfrac{X, Y \vdash A}{X, B, Y \vdash A}$ $\dfrac{X, Y \vdash A}{X, Y, B \vdash A}$ only when B is a sticker

CUT $\dfrac{X, A, Y \vdash B \quad Z \vdash A}{X, Z, Y \vdash B}$ only when Z and A are PERF stickers

These three meta-logical properties show how DAT logic may be applied in natural language processing systems, which could be useful and an empirically significant gain over the more classical temporal logics with full evaluation procedures, which built in no such temporal reasoning structure relying on textual cohesion. The requisite proofs of the interaction between DAT construction and embedding functions into event-structures, constrained by the sticker portability conditions, still need to be provided*.

18.6 Concluding Remarks

This chapter has reviewed some logical properties of temporal reasoning in ordinary English, based on the content of adverbs, auxiliary and lexical verbs, on aspectual class and some general insights into the effects the order of presentation of the premises may have on the conclusions we draw. Obviously, there are still other syntactic categories in English which may contain expressions that carry temporal information, such as the adjectives *earlier*, *later*, and *subsequent*, or the nouns *day*, *month*, *second*, *hour* etc. A comprehensive and fully integrated account of temporal reasoning has not yet been provided for any natural language. It would be interesting to compare different languages to see how much variation exists in the way temporal dynamics is expressed and utilized in temporal reasoning, based on what must ultimately be an universal underlying logical system. The logical issues in such linguistic research are rich and clearly worth exploring for logicians.

*See also [ter Meulen, 2003] for further exposition of the DAT system and its logic.

The DAT system described in the chapter constitutes a simple and straightforward relational dynamic logic, which could be implemented in computational environments to enhance their user interface. It could be especially worthwhile to employ such implementations in temporal data bases, with question-answer dialogue interface. In the current state of the art systems, to my knowledge, no temporal questions regarding precedence and inclusion of described events can be answered, unless each clause is explicitly marked with a time and date. The fact that such explicit dating is clearly not needed in natural language information exchanges again shows how efficient and economical our reasoning in our own language is, advantages that should be simulated rather than avoided in computational systems with human user interfaces.

Handbook of Temporal Reasoning in Artificial Intelligence
Edited by M. Fisher, D. Gabbay and L. Vila

Chapter 19

Temporal Reasoning in Medicine

Elpida Keravnou & Yuval Shahar

This chapter aims to give a comprehensive and critical review of current approaches to temporal reasoning in medical applications, and to suggest future research directions. The chapter begins by presenting the relevant time representation and temporal reasoning requirements. Temporal-data abstraction constitutes a central requirement that presently receives much and justifiable attention. The role of this process is especially crucial in the context of time-oriented clinical monitoring and databases. General AI theories of time do not fully address the identified requirements for medical reasoning and key aspects of mismatch with three well-known general theories of time are pointed out.

Temporal data abstraction is then further elaborated. An exposition on the different types of temporal data abstraction is followed by a discussion on various approaches to temporal data abstraction, relating that important task to the tasks of knowledge discovery, summarization of on-line medical records, time-oriented monitoring, exploration of time-oriented clinical data, clinical-guideline-based care, and assessment of the quality of medical care.

The modeling of time in medical diagnosis and guideline-based therapy is presented next. A central relation in medical diagnosis is the causal relation, while the predominant reasoning paradigm is that of abductive reasoning. The discussion regarding time-oriented medical diagnosis focuses on the temporal semantics of causality and the integration of temporal and abductive reasoning. The discussion on time-oriented guideline-based therapy focuses on the temporal semantics of clinical guidelines and protocols and the kind of automated support required for guideline-based care. As will be seen, both the diagnostic and therapeutic tasks require a *mediator* to time-oriented clinical data that can respond to temporal queries regarding both raw data and derived concepts.

Electronic patient records and databases of such records are obligatory components of any modern hospital information system; clinicians can do without automated decision support for diagnosis and therapy, but they cannot do without a database of patient records. Time is an intrinsic characteristic of patient data, in particular, chronic patients data; thus, research in time-oriented medical databases is an important component of the overall research in temporal reasoning in medicine. The discussion on the summarization approaches of on-line medical records, presented under temporal data abstraction, gives insights into specific temporal models for the particular clinical databases. In addition, more general considerations about temporal medical databases are presented. In particular the relevant research issues under investigation are listed.

Finally, two general time ontologies, proposed by the authors, which cover most of the tasks discussed, are overviewed in more detail. These are Shahar's ontology for knowledge-based temporal-data abstraction, and Keravnou's time-object ontology for medical tasks. The chapter concludes by summarizing what has been done and suggesting issues that need further exploration.

19.1 Introduction

Medical tasks, such as diagnosis and therapy, are by nature complex and not easily amenable to formal approaches. The philosophical question "Is medicine science or art?" is frequently posed to show that expert clinicians often reach correct decisions on the basis of intuition and hindsight rather than scientific facts [Van Bemmel, 1996]. Medical knowledge is inherently uncertain and incomplete. Likewise patient data are often ridden with uncertainty and imprecision, showing serious gaps. In addition, they are often too voluminous and at a level of detail that would prevent direct reasoning by a human mind. Effective computer-based support to the performance of medical tasks poses many challenges. Thus, it is not surprising that AI researchers were intrigued with the automation of medical problem solving from the early days of AI. The technology of expert systems is largely founded on attempts to automate medical expert diagnostic reasoning. A well-known example is the Stanford Heuristic Programming Project, which resulted, among other outcomes, in the MYCIN family of rule-based medical and other expert systems [Buchanan and Shortliffe, 1984].

Physicians and other care providers are required to perform various tasks that require extensive reasoning about time-oriented patient data, such as diagnose the cause of a problem, predict its development, prescribe treatment, monitor the progress of a patient and overall manage a patient. Similarly, they often need to retrospectively analyze large amounts of time-oriented clinical data for quality assessment or research purposes. A care provider's decision should be as informed as possible. In the present age of information explosion, which everyone experiences with the advent of information communication technologies in general, and the Web in particular, the only viable means for handling large amounts of information are computer-based. The work of all care providers can benefit substantially from computer-based support. In the early days, the biggest challenge was the modeling of knowledge for the purpose of supporting tasks such as diagnosis, therapy, and monitoring. To a certain extent, this is still a challenge. But the information explosion has brought a drastic change in focus from knowledge-intensive to data-intensive applications [Horn, 2001] and from systems that *advise* to systems that *inform* [Rector, 2001]. The major challenge is no longer the deployment of knowledge for diagnostic or other purposes but the intelligent exploitation of data. The exploitation of medical data, whether they refer to clinical or demographic data, is extremely valuable and multifaceted. For starters, such an analysis can yield significant new knowledge, e.g. guidelines and protocols for the treatment of acute and chronic disorders, by summarizing all available evidence in the particular field, an approach currently referred to as *evidence-based medicine*; it also can provide accurate predictors for critical risk groups based on "low-cost" information, etc. Secondly, it aims to provide means for the intelligent comprehension of individual patients' data, whether such data are riddled with gaps, or are voluminous and heterogeneous in nature. Such data comprehension closes the gap (or conceptual distance) between the raw patient data and the medical knowledge to be applied for reaching the appropriate decisions for the patient in question.

In spite of the shift in focus from knowledge-intensive to data-intensive approaches, the ultimate objective is still the same, namely to aid care providers reach the best possible decisions for any patient, to help them see through the consequences of their decisions/actions and if necessary to take rectifying actions as timely as possibly.

The change in focus has given a new dimension of significance to clinical databases and in particular to the intelligent management and comprehension of the data represented within them. Several researchers had recognized such issues as important from the early days, but widespread recognition of the necessity to exploit medical data is a relatively recent development. Methods for abstraction, query and display of time-oriented data, lie at the heart of this research. Such methods are of relevance to all of the medical tasks mentioned above. That is why these three tasks (in particular, temporal abstraction) feature very prominently in this chapter. The various medical tasks are also discussed to a greater or lesser extent. Time considerations arise in all cases. Only in very simple applications, it would be justifiable to abstract time away. For example, in diagnostic tasks, abstracting time away would mean that dynamic situations are converted to static (snap-shot) situations, where neither the evolution of disorders, nor patient states can be modeled.

The rest of this introductory section addresses, in general, time representation and temporal reasoning requirements for medical domains, elaborating further in the case of time-oriented medical databases. The general requirements are compared against the provisions of three well-known general theories of time. Through this comparison we do not intend in any way to demean the significant contributions of these theories, which have paved the way for the development of the temporal field in AI, but rather to pinpoint the specific temporal needs of medical applications. For example, temporal-data abstraction is a key process for medical problems. None of the general theories examined, at least in its basic form, gives the necessary provisions for adequately supporting such a process.

The rest of the chapter is organized as follows. Sections 19.2 and 19.3 are concerned with temporal-data abstraction. More specifically, Section 19.2 categorizes data abstractions, and Section 19.3 presents a number of specific approaches to temporal-data abstraction. Some of these approaches have been used in the context of knowledge discovery and others for summarization of on-line medical records. Sections 19.4–19.6 discuss time representation and temporal reasoning in the context of the medical tasks of monitoring, clinical diagnosis and guideline-based therapy, respectively. In these sections the particular issues are largely presented through representative approaches proposed in the literature. The aim here is neither to give an exhaustive presentation of all relevant approaches, nor to present the temporal aspects of the selected approaches in fine technical detail. Rather, the aim is to show what the issues are and how they have been addressed in particular cases. These cases were selected so as to include both earlier as well as more recent approaches. Section 19.7 discusses temporal medical databases. Section 19.8 overviews Shahar's general ontology for temporal data abstraction and Keravnou's general ontology for medical tasks. The chapter concludes in Section 19.9, which also provides a brief summary and discussion of what has been done in temporal reasoning in medicine and what remains to be done.

19.1.1 Time Representation Requirements

Time representation requirements for medical applications are many and varied because time manifests in different ways in expressions of medical knowledge and patient information. There are two issues here: how to model time per se, and how to model time-varying situations or occurrences. Real time is infinite and dense. Modeling time as a dense or discrete number line, a model often adopted in temporal databases and other applications, may not provide the appropriate abstraction for medical applications. A richer model providing a multidimensional structure to time, through a number of interrelated, conceptual, temporal contexts, and multiple granularities, is often required. A dynamic situation (either abstract or actual) is defined through a collection of occurrences and their explicit or implicit dependencies or interactions. An occurrence describes a happening in some temporal context, where the word happening is used in a broad sense. Many representation issues apply to occurrences, such as the following:

- Absolute versus relative timelines: The existence of some occurrence can be expressed in absolute terms, relative to some fixed time point, by specifying its initiation and termination (e.g., using calendar-based time). Similarly, it can be expressed relative to the existence of other occurrences (e.g., birth, start of chemotherapy).

- Absolute and relative vagueness, duration, and incompleteness: An occurrence is associated with absolute vagueness if its initiation and/or termination cannot be precisely specified in a given temporal context; precision is relative to the particular temporal context. Absolute vagueness may be expressed in terms of quantitative constraints on the initiation, termination, or extent of the occurrence, e.g. the earliest possible and latest possible time for its initiation or termination, or the minimum and maximum for its duration. An occurrence is associated with relative vagueness if its temporal relation with other occurrences is not precisely known but can only be expressed as a disjunction of primitive relations (e.g., the vomiting occurred before or during the diarrhea period). Incompleteness in the specification of occurrences is thus a common phenomenon.

- Point and interval occurrences: An occurrence may be considered a point occurrence in some temporal context if its duration is less than the time unit, if any, associated with the particular temporal context. A point occurrence may be treated as an instantaneous and hence as a non-decomposable occurrence in the given temporal context. Thus an occurrence may be considered an interval occurrence in some temporal context if its duration is at least equal to the time unit associated with the particular temporal context. Interval occurrences can be further divided into convex and non-convex occurrences. The former indicates that the unfolding of the occurrence during the interval of its existence is characterized with some form of activity throughout that interval. The latter indicates that there could be periods of inactivity during the interval defining the lifetime of the occurrence.

- Compound occurrences: Two or more repeated instantiations of some type of occurrence, usually (but not necessarily!) in a regular fashion, may need to be collectively represented as a periodic occurrence. An abstract periodic occurrence consists of the occurrence type and the 'algorithm' governing the repetition. A specific periodic occurrence is the collation of the relevant, individual, occurrences. A temporal trend, or simply trend, is an important kind of interval occurrence. A *trend* describes a change, the direction of change, and the rate of change that takes place in the given interval of time. An example of a trend describing both direction and rate could be "blood pressure, increasing quickly." A trend is usually derived from a collection of occurrences at a lower level. A temporal pattern, or simply a pattern, is a compound occurrence, consisting of a number of simpler occurrences (and their relations). There are different kinds of patterns. A sequence of meeting trends is a commonly used kind of pattern. A periodic occurrence is another example of pattern. A set of relative occurrences, or a set of causally related occurrences, could form patterns. A compound occurrence can in fact be expressed at multiple levels of abstraction. Abstraction and refinement are therefore important structural relations between occurrences. Through refinement an occurrence can be decomposed into component occurrences and through abstraction component occurrences can be contained into a compound occurrence.

- Causality and other temporal constraints: Causality is a central relation between occurrences. Changes are explained through causal relations. Time is intrinsically related to causality. The temporal principle underlying causality is that an effect cannot precede its cause. Causally unrelated occurrences can also be temporally constrained, as already mentioned. For example, a periodic occurrence could be governed by the constraint that the distance between successive occurrences should be 4 hours.

19.1.2 Temporal Reasoning Requirements

Important (generic) functionalities for a medical temporal reasoner include the following:

- Mapping the existence of occurrences across temporal contexts, if multiple temporal contexts are supported and more than one such context is meaningful to some occurrence.

- Determining bounds for absolute existences. The initiation and termination points of absolute existences are usually expressed in (qualitative) terms which need to be translated into upper and lower bounds for the actual points within the relevant temporal context.

- Consistency detection and clipping of uncertainty. If the inferences drawn from a collection of occurrences are to be valid the occurrences must be mutually consistent. Inconsistency arises when there are overlapping occurrences that assert mutually exclusive propositions. The inconsistency can be resolved if the boundaries of the implicated occurrences can be moved so that the overlapping is eliminated. In fact the identification of such clashes usually results in narrowing the bounds for the initiation/termination of the relevant occurrences. More generally, inconsistency arises when the (disjunctive) temporal constraints relating a given set of occurrences cannot be mutually satisfied. A conflict is detected when all the possible temporal relationships between a pair of temporal entities are refuted. Temporal constraint propagation, minimization of disjunctive constraints (i.e. reducing the uncertainty), detection and resolution of conflicts are necessary functionalities, as in many other non-medical applications.

- Deriving new occurrences from other occurrences. There are different types of derivation. A predominant type is *temporal data abstraction*, which is described separately in Section 19.2. Other types include decomposition derivations (the potential components of compound occurrences are inferred), causal derivations (potential antecedent occurrences, consequent occurrences, or causal links between occurrences are derived), etc.

- Deriving temporal relations between occurrences. Often the temporal relations that hold between occurrences are significant for the given problem solving. Thus if the temporal relation between a pair of occurrences is not explicitly given, it would need to be inferred.

- Deriving the truth status of queried occurrences. This functionality brings together many of the other functionalities. A (hypothesized) occurrence, of any degree of complexity, e.g. periodic, trend, compound, etc, is queried against a set of occurrences (and temporal contexts) that are assumed to be true. The queried occurrence is derived as true (it can be logically deduced from the assumed occurrences), false (it is counter-indicated by the assumed occurrences), or unknown (possibly true or possibly false).

- Deriving the state of the world at a particular time. The previous functionality starts with a specific set of assumed occurrences and a specific queried occurrence. It is considered a necessary functionality because often problem solvers seek to establish specific information. Alternatively though, in an investigative/explorative mode, the problem solver may need to be informed about what is considered to be true at some specific time. The query may be expressed relative to another specific point in time which defaults to now, e.g. at time point t, what was/is/will be believed to be true during some specified period p? This functionality may be used to compose the set of assumed occurrences for queries of the previous type.

19.1.3 Further Requirements for Time-Oriented Medical Databases

In addition to reasoning about time-oriented medical data, it is also necessary to manage these data. As shown in Section 19.7, this involves explicit representation of several aspects of the data, such as the time in which the data were acquired (i.e., when the measurements were *valid*) and the time at which the data were recorded in the database (the *transaction time*). Databases in medical information systems need to be able to answer such queries for clinical, research, and legal purposes. An example is, "When Dr. Jones prescribed penicillin on January 14 1997, did she know at that time that the patient had an allergic reaction to penicillin that happened on January 5 1997?". The answer to that question depends on *when* the information that was valid during January 5 1997 (its *valid time*) was actually recorded (i.e., its *transaction time*) in the patient's medical record.

Furthermore, as was previously mentioned, there are often inherent uncertainties in time-oriented clinical data; the patient might report a headache that occurred "3 or 4 days ago", lasting "5 to 7 hours". It is important to be able to represent these uncertainties explicitly.

Finally, supporting multiple clinical applications (e.g., diagnosis, application of guideline-based care, quality assessment, research, administration) requires the ability to answer time-oriented queries about the patient's medical record at various levels of abstraction, even though the patient's database might include only raw data. Thus, a *temporal mediation service*, or a *temporal mediator*, as advocated by several researchers [Nguyen *et al.*, 1999; O'Connor *et al.*, 2002; Boaz and Shahar, 2003] is needed. A temporal mediator combines the functionality of *temporal reasoning* (in particular, temporal abstraction) with the capability for *temporal maintenance* (in particular, storage, query, update, and retrieval of time-oriented data). The mediator should perform its function in a manner transparent to user applications.

19.1.4 The Insufficiency of three Well-Known General Theories of Time for Medical Tasks

Three well-known general theories of time, that are justifiably credited for the sparking of widespread interest in time representation and temporal reasoning in the AI community are Allen's interval-based temporal logic [Allen, 1984], Kowalski and Sergot's event calculus [Kowalski and Sergot, 1986] and Dean and McDermott's time map manager [Dean and McDermott, 1987]. None of these general theories of time was developed with the purpose of supporting knowledge-based problem solving, let alone medical problem solving. Hence it comes as no surprise that in their basic form, none of these adequately supports the identified requirements for medical temporal reasoning discussed above (Table 19.1). The approaches do provide a useful model of time and temporal predicates, but, in the context of medical tasks, insufficient support to the semantics of the entities represented by these predicates. As a matter of fact, various extensions of Allen's logic and the event calculus have been applied to medical problems with lesser or greater success; some of these approaches are mentioned in the sequel. Such attempts resulted in revealing the rather limited expressivity of these theories with respect to medical problems. Their widespread adoption is in fact attributed to their relative simplicity. However, their lack of structuredness both with respect to a model of time as well as a model of occurrences, but more importantly their very limited support for the critical process of temporal data abstraction, renders their applicability in the context of medical problems at large, non viable. Below we quote some of the criticisms of the event calculus that was expressed by Chittaro and Dojat [Chittaro and Dojat, 1997] in their attempt to apply this general theory of time to patient monitoring. In the event calculus a change in a property is the effect of an event. In real-life a symptom may be self-limiting where no event is required to terminate its existence. The designers went around this problem by introducing so-called 'ghost' events. Another limitation encountered was that only instantaneous causality could be expressed. So delayed effects or effects of a limited persistence could not be expressed. The limited support for temporal data abstraction, the lack of multiple granularities as well as the lack of any vagueness in the expression of event occurrences, are also pointed out as issues of concern regarding the expressivity of the event calculus with respect to the realities of medical problems.

To illustrate further the points of criticism raised, we try to represent some medical knowledge in terms of these general theories. The medical knowledge in question describes (in a simplified form) the skeletal dysplasia disorder SEDC (skeletal dysplasia is a generalized abnormality of the skeleton). This knowledge is given below:

> "SEDC *presents from birth* and can be lethal. It *persists throughout the lifetime* of the patient. People suffering from SEDC exhibit the following: short stature, due to short limbs, *from birth*; mild platyspondyly *from birth*; absence of the ossification of knee epiphyses *at birth*; bilateral severe coax-vara *from birth, worsening with age*; scoliosis, *worsening with age*; wide triradiate cartilage *up to about the age of 11 years*; pear-shaped vertebral-bodies *under the age of 15 years*; variable-size vertebral-bodies *up to the age of 1 year*; and *retarded ossification* of the cervical spine, epiphyses, and pubic bones."

	Allen's Time-Interval Algebra	Kowalski & Sergot's Even Calculus	Dean & McDermott's Time-Token Manager
multiple conceptual temporal contexts	N	N	N
multiple granularities	N	N	N
absolute time	N	S	S
relative time	S	N	P
absolute vagueness	N	N	S
relative vagueness	S	N	N
duration	N	S	S
point existences	N	S	S
interval existences	S	S	S
periodic occurrences	N	N	N
temporal trends	N	N	N
temporal patterns	P	N	P
structural relations (temporal composition)	N	N	N
temporal causality	P	P	P

Key: N does Not support; P supports Partly; S Supports.

Table 19.1: Evaluation of General Theories of Time Against Medical Temporal Requirements.

The text given in italic font refers to time, directly or indirectly.

The temporal primitive of Allen's interval-based logic is the time interval and eight basic relations (plus the inverses for seven of these) are defined between time intervals. The other primitives of the logic are properties (static entities), processes and events (dynamic entities), which are respectively associated with predicates holds, occurring and occur:

$$holds(p, T) \Leftrightarrow (\forall t \; in(t, T) \Rightarrow holds(p, t))$$

$$occurring(p, t) \Rightarrow \exists t' \; in(t', t) \wedge occuring(p, t')$$

$$occur(e, t) \wedge in(t', t) \Rightarrow \neg occur(e, t')$$

The logic covers two forms of causality, event and agentive causality. Allen's logic is a relative theory of time, where time is structured as a dense time line. In order to represent the SEDC knowledge in terms of Allen's logic we need to decide which of the entities correspond to events, which to properties, and which to processes. The relevant generic events are easily identifiable. These are: $birth(P)$, $age1yr(P)$, $age11yrs(P)$, $age15yrs(P)$ and $death(P)$ which mark the birth, the becoming of 1 year of age, etc of some patient P. Deciding whether to model SEDC and its manifestations as properties or processes is not immediately apparent. In the following representation the distinction into processes and properties is decided on a rather ad hoc basis:

$$
\begin{aligned}
& occurring(SEDC(P), I) \Rightarrow \\
& \qquad occur(birth(P), B) \wedge occur(age1yr(P), O) \wedge occur(age11yrs(P), E) \\
& \wedge \quad occur(age15yrs(P), F) \wedge occur(death(P), D) \wedge started\_by(I, B) \\
& \wedge \quad finished\_by(I, D) \wedge holds(stature(P, short), I) \\
& \wedge \quad holds(ossification(P, knee\_epiphyses, absent), B) \\
& \wedge \quad occurring(scoliosis(P, worsening), I) \wedge holds(triradiate\_cartilage(P, wide), W) \\
& \wedge \quad started\_by(W, B) \wedge finished\_by(W, E) \wedge started\_by(F', B) \\
& \wedge \quad occurring(coxa\_vara(P, bilateral\_severe, worsening), I) \\
& \wedge \quad holds(vertebral\_bodies(P, pear\_shaped), F') \\
& \wedge \quad holds(vertebral\_bodies(P, variable\_size), V) \wedge started\_by(V, B) \\
& \wedge \quad finished\_by(V, O) \wedge before(F', F) \\
& \wedge \quad occurring(ossification(P, cervical\_spine, poor), I) \\
& \wedge \quad occurring(ossification(P, epiphyses, retarded), I) \\
& \wedge \quad occurring(ossification(P, pubic\_bones, retarded), I).
\end{aligned}
$$

In this formalization, a relative representation has been forced on absolute occurrences. The specified events are not consequences of the occurrence of SEDC; their role is to demarcate the relevant intervals. For this (disorder) representation to be viable, the implication should either be temporally screened against the particular patient in order to remove future or non-applicable consequences, or simply such happenings should be assumed to be true by default. A particular limitation of any relative theory of time is inability to adequately model the derivation of temporal trends, or the derivation of delays or prematurity with respect to the unfolding of some process, since the notion of temporal distance which is inherently relevant to both types of derivation is foreign to such theories of time. A statement about a trend, delay, prematurity, etc is a kind of summary statement for a collection of happenings over a period of time. Another limitation of relative theories of time is inability to model absolute vagueness. In the above representation the widening of the triradiate cartilage is expected to hold exactly up to the occurrence of the event "becoming 11 years of age" and also it is not possible to delineate a margin for the termination of the property "pear-shaped vertebral bodies"; instead its termination is expressed in a relative way by saying that this happens before the event "becoming 15 years of age" happens, which does not capture the intuitive meaning of the given manifestation.

The temporal primitive of Kowalski and Sergot's event calculus is the event. Events are instantaneous happenings which initiate and terminate periods over which properties hold. A property does not hold at the time of the event that initiates it, but does hold at the time of the event that terminates it. Default persistence of properties is modeled through negation-as-failure. Causality is not directly modeled, although a rather restricted notion of causality is implied, e.g. an event happening at time t causes the initiation of some property at time (t+1) and/or causes the termination of some (other) property at time t. The calculus can be applied both under a dense or a discrete model of time. The event calculus representation of the SEDC knowledge consists of a number of clauses like the following:

$$holds\text{–}at(ossification(P, knee\text{–}epiphyses), T)$$
$$\Leftarrow act(E, birth(P)) \wedge happens(E) \wedge time(E, T) \wedge holds\text{–}at(SEDC(P), T).$$
$$initiates(E, stature(P, short))$$
$$\Leftarrow act(E, birth(P)) \wedge happens(E) \wedge time(E, T) \wedge holds\text{–}at(SEDC(P), T).$$
$$terminates(E, stature(P, short))$$
$$\Leftarrow act(E, death(P)) \wedge happens(E) \wedge time(E, T) \wedge holds\text{–}at(SEDC(P), T).$$
$$initiates(E, coxa\text{-}vara(P, bilateral\text{–}severe, worsening))$$
$$\Leftarrow act(E, birth(P) \wedge happens(E) \wedge time(E, T) \wedge holds\text{–}at(SEDC(P), T).$$
$$terminates(E, vertebral\text{–}bodies(P, pear\text{–}shaped))$$
$$\Leftarrow act(E, age15yrs(P) \wedge happens(E) \wedge time(E, T) \wedge holds\text{–}at(SEDC(P), T).$$

Many of the criticisms discussed above with respect to Allen's logic apply to the event calculus as well. Properties in event calculus are analogous to Allen's properties. They are essentially 'static' entities. Evolving situations such as temporal trends, or retardation in the execution of some process, or more generally continuous change, cannot be adequately modeled within pure event calculus. For example, the above clause concerning coxa-vara talks about some worsening being initiated, and also, based on the various axioms of the event calculus, it can be inferred that the worsening holds at every instant of time. What is initiated is "bilateral severe coxa-vara" while the worsening of this condition is a kind of meta-level inference on the continuous progression of this condition. Furthermore, absolute vagueness is not addressed, and as with Allen's logic, the SEDC knowledge is not represented as an integral entity but as a sparse collection of 'independent' happenings.

The temporal primitive of Dean and McDermott's time map manager is the point (instant). The other temporal entity is the time-token that is defined to be an interval together with a (fact or event) type. A time-token is a static entity. It cannot be structurally analyzed and it cannot be involved in causal interactions. A collection of time-tokens forms a time map. This is a graph in which nodes denote instants of time associated with the beginning and ending of events and arcs describe relations between pairs of instants. This ontology can be applied both under a dense or a discrete model of time. Below we represent part of the SEDC knowledge as a time map. The granularity used is years and the reference point (denoted as `*ref*`) is birth. The first argument of the time-token predicate is the (fact or event) type and the second is the interval. Predicate `elt` expresses margins (bounds) for the beginnings and endings of intervals, with respect to `*ref*`.

```
((time-token (SEDC present) I))

((time-token  (coxa-vara bilateral-severe) C) )

((time-token (coxa-vara worsening) C'))

((time-token (ossification epiphyses retarded) E))

((time-token (triradiate-cartilage wide) W))

((time-token (vertebral-bodies pear-shaped) V))
```

```
. . . . . . . . .

((elt (distance (begin C) *ref*) 0 0))

((elt (distance (end C) *ref*) *pos-inf* *pos-inf*))

((elt (distance (begin C') *ref*) ? ?))

((elt (distance (end C') *ref*) ? ?))

((elt (distance (begin W) *ref*) 0 0))

((elt (distance (end W) *ref*) 10 11))

((elt (distance (begin V) *ref*) 0 0))

((elt (distance (end V) *ref*) ? 14))

((elt (distance (begin E) *ref*) ? ?))

((elt (distance (end E) *ref*) ? ?))

(
. . . . . . . . .
```

Again the SEDC process per se and its manifestations are represented as independent occurrences. The expression of absolute temporal vagueness is supported (see instances of predicate elt above), but no mechanism for translating qualitative expressions of vagueness into the relevant bounds based on temporal semantics of properties is provided. In the above representation "up to about the age of 11 years" is translated, in an ad hoc way, to the margin (10 11) while for "under the age of 15 years" it is not easy to see what the earliest termination ought to be. The points raised above regarding the representation of trends, process retardations, etc., apply here as well. Again this is because the types associated with the tokens capture either instantaneous events, or static, downward hereditary, properties.

Thus, the important reasoning process of temporal data abstraction is not supported by any of the three general theories of time considered.

19.2 Temporal-Data Abstraction

Medical knowledge-based systems involve the application of medical knowledge to patient specific data with the goal of reaching diagnoses or prognoses, deciding the best therapy regime for the patient, or monitoring the effectiveness of some ongoing therapy and if necessary applying rectification actions. Medical knowledge, like any kind of knowledge, is expressed in as general a form as possible, say in terms of associations or rules, causal models of pathophysiological states, behavior (evolution) models of disease processes, patient management protocols and guidelines, etc. Data on a specific patient, on the other hand, comprise numeric measurements of various parameters (such as blood pressure, body temperature, etc.) at different points in time. The record of a patient gives the history of the patient (past operations and other treatments), results of laboratory and physical examinations as well as the patient's own symptomatic recollections.

To perform any kind of medical problem solving, patient data have to be 'matched' against medical knowledge. For example, a forward-driven rule is activated if its antecedent can be unified against patient information; similarly, a patient management protocol is activated if its underlying preconditions can be unified against patient information, etc. The difficulty encountered here is that often the abstraction gap between the highly specific, raw patient data, and the highly abstract medical knowledge does not permit any direct unification between data and knowledge. The process of data abstraction aims to close this gap; in other words, it aims to bring the raw patient data to the level of medical knowledge in order to permit the derivation of diagnostic, prognostic or therapeutic conclusions. Hence data abstraction can be seen as an auxiliary process that aids the problem solving process per se. However it is a critical auxiliary process since the success of some medical knowledge-based system can depend on it; data abstraction involves low level processing, but this processing could be of a more 'intelligent' and computationally demanding nature, than that of the higher level reasoning process.

The significance of a data abstraction process in the context of a knowledge-based system was first perceived by Clancey in his seminal proposal on heuristic classification [Clancey, 1985]. In Clancey's work, *data abstraction* is used as the stepping stone towards the activation of nodes on a solution hierarchy. Such nodes, especially at the high levels of the hierarchy, are associated with triggers, where a trigger is a conjunction of observable items of information. In heuristic classification, data abstraction is applied in an event-driven fashion with the aim of mapping raw case data to the level of abstraction used in the expression of triggers, in order to enable the activation of triggers (i.e. their unification against data).

Obviously, a knowledge-based system that does not possess any data abstraction capabilities would require its user to express the case data at the level of abstraction corresponding to its knowledge. Such a system puts the onus on the user to perform the data abstraction process. This approach has limitations. Firstly the user, often a non-specialist himself, is burdened with the task of not only observing, measuring, and reporting data, but also of interpreting such data for the special needs of the particular problem solving. Secondly, manual abstraction is prone to errors and inconsistencies even for domains where it can be considered 'doable'. There are, however, many domains where the sheer amount of raw data renders such a thing practically impossible. In short, the usefulness of a medical knowledge-based system that does not possess data abstraction capabilities is substantially reduced.

For instance, in clinical domains, a final diagnosis is not always the main goal. What is often needed is a coherent intermediate-level interpretation of the relationships between data and events, and among data, especially when the overall context (e.g., a major diagnosis) is known. The goal is then to abstract the clinical data, which often is acquired or recorded as time-stamped measurements, into higher-level concepts, which often hold over time periods. These concepts should be useful for one or more tasks (e.g., planning of therapy or summarization of a patient's record). Thus, the goal is often to create, from time-stamped input data, interval-based temporal abstractions, such as "bone-marrow toxicity grade 2 or more for 3 weeks in the context of administration of a prednisone/azathioprine protocol for treating patients who have chronic graft-versus-host disease, and complication of bone-marrow transplantation" and more complex patterns, involving several intervals (Figure 19.1).

19.2.1 Types of Data Abstraction

The purpose of data abstraction, in the context of medical problem solving, is therefore the intelligent interpretation of the raw data on some patient, so that the derived abstract data are at the level of abstraction corresponding to the given body of knowledge. Abstract data are useful since they can be unified against knowledge.

There are different types of data abstraction. Some are rather simple and others quite complicated. The types discussed below are more for illustration; they are not meant to provide an exhaustive classification. This is due to the rather open-ended nature of data abstraction and the multitude of ways basic types can be combined to yield complex types. The common feature of all these types, even the very simple ones, is that their derivation is knowledge-driven; hence data abstraction is itself a knowledge-based process. The use of knowledge in the derivation of abstractions is the feature that distinguishes data abstraction from statistical data analysis, e.g. the derivation of trends through time-series analysis. Data abstraction is knowledge-based and heuristic while statistical analysis is 'syntactic' and algorithmic.

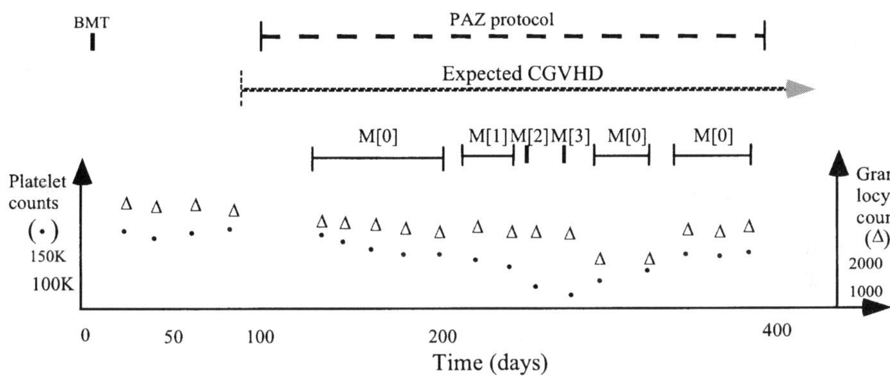

Figure 19.1: Temporal abstraction of platelet and granulocyte values during administration of a prednisone/azathioprine (PAZ) clinical protocol for treating patients who have chronic graft-versus-host disease (CGVHD).

> The time line starts with a bone-marrow–transplantation (BMT) external event. The platelet- and granulocyte-count parameters and the PAZ and BMT external events (interventions) are typical inputs. The abstraction and context intervals are typically part of the output.

•= platelet counts;	M[n] = myelotoxicity (bone-marrow–toxicity) grade n;
dashed line with bars = event;	full line with bars = closed abstraction interval;
Δ = granulocyte counts;	striped arrow = open context interval;

Before listing the types of data abstraction it is necessary to say a few words about the nature of raw patient data. Their highly specific form has already been stressed. In addition they can be noisy and inconsistent. For some domains, e.g. intensive care monitoring, the data are voluminous, while for other domains they are grossly incomplete, e.g. for medical domains dealing with skeletal abnormalities. Different medical parameters can have very different sampling frequencies and hence different time units (granularities) arise. Thus for some parameter there could be too much and very specific data, while for another parameter only very few and far between recordings. In either case, data abstraction tries to ferret out the useful (abstract) information, safeguarding against the possibility of noise; in the first case it tries to eliminate the detail while in the second case to fill the gaps, two orthogonal aims. Since noise is an unavoidable phenomenon a viable data abstraction process should perform some kind of data validation and verification which also makes use of knowledge [Horn *et al.*, 1997].

Simple types of data abstraction are atemporal and often involve a single datum, which is mapped to a more abstract concept. The knowledge underlying such abstractions often comprises concept taxonomies or concept associations. Examples of simple data abstractions are:

- Qualitative abstraction, where a numeric expression is mapped to a qualitative expression, e.g. "a temperature of 41 degrees C" is abstracted to "high fever". Such abstractions are based on simple associational knowledge such as <"a temperature of at least 40 degrees C", "high fever">.

- Generalization abstraction, where an instance is mapped to (one of) its class(es), e.g. "halothane is administered" is abstracted to "drug is administered"; the concept "halothane" is an instance of the concept class "drug". Such abstractions are based on (strict or tangled) concept taxonomies.

- Definitional abstraction, where a datum from one conceptual category is mapped to a datum in another conceptual category that happens to be its definitional counterpart in the other context. The movement here is not hierarchical within the same concept taxonomy, as it is for generalization abstractions, but it is lateral across two different concept taxonomies. The resulting concept must be more abstract than the originating concept in some sense, e.g. it refers to something more easily observable. An example of definitional abstraction is the mapping of "generalized platyspondyly" to "short trunk". "Generalized platyspondyly" is a radiological concept, the observation of which requires the taking of a radiograph of the spine; platyspondyly means flattening of vertebrae and generalized platyspondyly means the flattening of all vertebrae. "Short trunk" is a clinical concept, the observation of which does not require any special procedure. The knowledge driving such abstractions consists of simple associations between concepts across different categories.

In all the above types of data abstraction time is implicit. The abstractions refer to the same times, explicitly or implicitly, associated with the raw data. Thus in an atemporal situation, where everything is assumed to refer to 'now', we have the general implication $holds(P, D) \rightarrow holds(P, abs(D))$, where predicate holds denotes that datum D holds for patient P now and function abs embodies any of the above types of simple abstraction. Predicate holds can be extended to have a third argument giving an explicit time, thus having

$holds(P, D, T_1) \rightarrow holds(P, abs(D), T_2)$. (In the case of a basic abstraction, such as a definitional one, $T_1 = T_2$; in the case of general temporal patterns, or inducement of a context [e.g., following a drug administration] $T_1 \neq T_2$ is common). When time becomes an explicit and inherent dimension of patient data, and medical knowledge, it plays a central role in data abstraction, hence the name *temporal data abstraction*.

The dimension of time adds a new aspect of complexity to the derivation of (temporal) abstractions. In the simple types of (atemporal) data abstraction discussed above, often it is just a single datum which is mapped to a more abstract datum, although several data (with implicitly the same temporal dimension) might be mapped to one abstract concept. In temporal abstractions, however, it is a cluster of (time-stamped) data that is mapped to an abstract temporal datum. Atemporal data abstraction is "concept abstraction", going from a specific concept to a more abstract concept. Temporal data abstraction is both "concept abstraction" and "temporal abstraction". The latter encompasses different notions, such as going from discrete time-points (used in the expression of raw patient data) to continuous (convex) time-intervals or (non-convex) collections of time-intervals (used in the expression of medical knowledge), or moving from a fine time granularity to a grosser time granularity, etc. Temporal data abstraction can therefore be decomposed into concept abstraction, i.e., atemporal data abstraction, followed by temporal abstraction. The reverse sequence is not valid since the (concrete) concepts involved have to be mapped to more abstract concepts, to facilitate temporal abstractions.

Temporal data abstraction entails temporal reasoning, both of a commonsense nature (e.g. intuitive handling of multiple time granularities and temporal relations such as before, overlaps, disjoint, etc.), as well as of a specialist nature dealing with persistence semantics of concepts, etc. Examples of important types of temporal abstraction are (here a datum is assumed to be an association between a property and a temporal aspect, which often is a time-point at a given time-unit; a simple property is a tuple comprising a subject (parameter or concept) and a list of attribute value pairs):

- *Merge abstraction*, where a collection of data, all having the concatenable [Shoham, 1987] property and whose temporal aspects collectively form a (possibly overlapping) chain are abstracted to a single datum with the given property, whose temporal aspect is the maximal time-interval spanning the original data. For example three consecutive, daily, recordings of fever, can be mapped to the temporal abstraction that the patient had fever for a three-day interval. Merge abstraction is also known as *state abstraction*, since its aim is to derive maximal intervals over which there is no change in the state of some parameter.

- *Persistence abstraction*, where again the aim is to derive maximal intervals spanning the extent of some property; here, though, there could be just one datum on that property, and hence the difficulty is in filling the gaps by 'seeing' both backwards and forwards in time from the specific, discrete, recording of the given property. For example if it is known that the patient had headache in the morning, can it be assumed that he also had headache in the afternoon and/or the evening before? Also if the patient is reported to have gone blind in one eye in December 1997 can it be assumed that this situation persists now? In some temporal reasoning approaches the persistence rule is that some property is assumed to persist indefinitely until some event (e.g. a therapy) is known to have taken place and this terminates the persistence of the property. This rule is obviously unrealistic for patient data, since often symptoms have a finite existence and go away even without the administration of any therapy. Thus, persistence derivation with respect to patient data can be a complicated process, drawing from the persistence semantics of properties. These categorize properties into finitely or infinitely persisting, where finitely persisting properties are further categorized into recurring and non-recurring. In addition, ranges for the duration of finitely persisting properties may be specified, in the absence of any external factors such as treatments, etc. Thus blindness could be classified as an infinitely persistent property, chickenpox as a finitely persisting but not a recurring property, and flu as a finitely persisting, recurring, property. Persistence derivation is often context-sensitive, where contexts can also be dynamically derived (abstracted) from the raw data [Shahar, 1997]. Within different contexts, clinical propositions can have different persistence semantics. As already said, persistence can be either forward in time, to the future, or backwards in time, to the past. Thus, a certain value of hemoglobin measured at a certain time point might indicate that with high probability the value was true at least within the previous day and within the next 2 days [Shahar, 1997]. For example if it is known that the patient with the headache took aspirin at noon, it can be inferred that the persistence of headache lasted most probably (that is, above a certain probability threshold) up to about 1pm, and that with high-enough probability there was no headache up to 3pm. This is based on the derivation of the time interval spanning the persistence of the effectiveness of the event of aspirin administration; e.g., relevant knowledge may dictate that this starts about 1 hour after the occurrence of the event and lasts for about 2 hours. Such time intervals defining the persistence of the effectiveness of treatments are referred to as context intervals. Qualitative abstraction (see above) can also be context-sensitive.

- *Trend abstraction*, where the aim is to derive the significant changes and the rates of change in the progression of some parameter. Trend abstraction entails merge and persistence abstraction in order to derive the extents where there is no change in the value of the given parameter. However the difficulty is in subsequently joining everything together (which may well involve filling gaps), deciding the points of significant change and the directions of change. Again this type of abstraction is driven by knowledge. Most of the current work in temporal data abstraction concerns trend abstraction, where often the medical domain under examination involves especially difficult data such as very noisy and largely incomplete data [Larizza *et al.*, 1997].

- *Periodic abstraction*, where repetitive occurrences, with some regularity in the pattern of repetition, are derived, e.g., headache every morning, for a week, with increasing severity. Such repetitive, cyclic occurrences are not uncommon in medical domains. A periodic abstraction is expressed in terms of a repetition element (e.g., headache), a repetition pattern (e.g., every morning for a week) and a progression pattern (e.g., increasing severity) [Keravnou, 1997]. It can also be viewed as a set of time and value local constraints on the repeating element (a single time interval), and a set of global constraints on each pair of elements or even on the whole element set [Chakravarty and Shahar, 2000; Chakravarty and Shahar, 2001]. The repetition element can be of any order of complexity (e.g. it could itself be a periodic abstraction, or a trend abstraction, etc.), giving rise to very complex periodic abstractions. The period spanning the extent of a periodic occurrence is non-convex by default; i.e., it is the collection of time intervals spanning the extents of the distinct instantiations of the repetition element, and the collection can include gaps. Periodic abstraction uses the other types of data abstraction and it is also knowledge driven. Relevant knowledge can include acceptable regularity patterns, means for justifying local irregularities, etc. The knowledge-intensive, heuristic, derivation of periodic abstractions is currently largely unexplored although its significance in medical problem solving is widely acknowledged.

Table 19.2 summarizes the discussed types of data abstraction. As already mentioned these types can be combined in a multitude of ways yielding complex abstractions. As already explained, data abstraction is deployed in some problem solving system and hence the derivation of abstractions is largely done in a directed fashion. This means that the given system, in exploring its hypothesis space, predicts various abstractions which the data abstraction process is required to corroborate against the raw patient data; in this respect the data abstraction process is goal-driven. However, for the creation of the initial hypothesis space the data abstraction process needs to operate in a non-directed or event-driven fashion (as already discussed with respect to Clancey's seminal proposal [Clancey, 1985]). In the case of a monitoring system, data abstraction, which is the heart of the system, in fact operates in a largely event-driven fashion. This is because the aim is to comprehensively interpret all the data covered by the moving time window underlying the operation of the monitoring system, i.e. to derive all abstractions, of any degree of complexity, and on the basis of such abstractions the system decides whether the patient situation is static, or it is improving or worsening.

Atemporal Types
• *Qualitative Abstraction*: Converting numeric expressions to qualitative expressions. • *Generalization Abstraction*: Mapping instances into classes. • *Definitional Abstraction*: Mapping across different conceptual categories.
Temporal Types
• *Merge (or State) Abstraction*: Deriving maximal intervals for some concatenable property from a group of time-stamped data for that property. • *Persistence Abstraction*: Applying (default) persistence rules to project maximal intervals for some property, both backwards and forwards in time and possibly on the basis of a single datum. • *Trend Abstraction*: Deriving significant changes and rates of change in the progression of some parameter. • *Periodic Abstraction*: Deriving repetitive occurrences, with some regularity in the pattern of repetition.

Table 19.2: Example Data Abstraction Types

Non-directed data abstraction repeatedly applies the methods for deriving the different types of data abstraction, until no more derivations are possible. Data abstraction, operating under such a mode, can be used in a stand alone fashion, i.e., in direct interaction with the user rather than with a higher level reasoning engine; in such a case the derived abstractions should be presented to the user in a visual form. Visualization is also of relevance when a data abstraction process is not used in a stand alone fashion; since the overall reasoning of the system depends critically on the derived abstractions a good way of justifying this reasoning is the presentation of the relevant abstractions in a visual form.

In summary, the ability to automatically create interval-based abstractions of time-stamped clinical data has multiple implications:

1. Data summaries of time-oriented electronic data, such as patient medical records, have an immediate value to a human user, such as to a care provider scanning a long patient record for meaningful trends [Downes *et al.*, 1986].

2. Temporal abstractions support *recommendations* by intelligent decision-support systems, such as diagnostic and therapeutic systems [Keravnou and Washbrook, 1990].

3. Abstractions support *monitoring* of plans (e.g., therapy plans) during execution of these plans (e.g., application of clinical guidelines [Musen *et al.*, 1996]).

4. Meaningful time-oriented contexts enable generation of *context-specific abstractions*, maintenance of *several interpretations* of the same data within different contexts, and certain hindsight and foresight inferences [Shahar, 1997].

5. Temporal abstractions are helpful for *explanation* of recommended actions by an intelligent system.

6. Temporal abstractions are a useful representation for the intentions of designers of clinical guidelines, and enable real time and retrospective critiquing and quality assessment of the application of these guidelines by care providers [Shahar *et al.*, 1998].

7. Domain-specific, meaningful, interval-based characterizations of time-oriented medical data are a prerequisite for effective *visualization* and dynamic exploration of these data by care providers and researchers [Shahar and Cheng, 1999; Shahar and Cheng, 2000; Shahar *et al.*, 2003a]. Visualization and exploration of information in general, and of large amounts of time-oriented medical data in particular, is essential for effective decision making. Examples include deciding whether a patient had several episodes of bone marrow toxicity of a certain severity and duration, caused by therapy with a particular drug; or deciding if a certain therapeutic action has been effective. Different types of care providers require access to different types of time-oriented data, which might be distributed over multiple databases.

Finally, there are several points to note with respect to the *desired* computational behavior of a method that creates meaningful abstractions from time-stamped data in medical domains:

1. The method should be able to accept as input both *numeric* and *qualitative* data. Some of these data might be at *different levels of abstraction* (i.e., we might be given either raw data or higher-level concepts as primary input, perhaps abstracted by the care provider from the same or additional data). The data might also involve different forms of temporal representation (e.g., time *points* or time *intervals*).

2. The output abstractions should also be available for query purposes *at all levels of abstraction*, and should be created as time *points* or as time *intervals*, as necessary, aggregating relevant conclusions together as much as possible (e.g., "extremely high

blood pressures for the past 8 months in the context of treatment of hypertension"). The outputs generated by the method should be controlled, sensitive to the goals of the abstraction process for the task at hand (e.g., only particular types of output might be required). The output abstractions should also be sensitive to the context in which they were created.

3. Input data should be used and incorporated in the interpretation even if they arrive *out of temporal order* (e.g., a laboratory result from last Tuesday arrives today). Thus, the past can change our view of the present. This phenomenon has been called a *view update* [Shahar and Musen, 1996]. Furthermore, new data should enable us to reflect on the past; thus, the present (or future) can change our interpretation of the past, a property referred to as *hindsight* [Russ, 1989].

4. Several possible interpretations of the data might be reasonable, each depending on additional factors that are perhaps unknown at the time (such as whether the patient has AIDS); interpretation should be specific to the context in which it is applied. All reasonable interpretations of the same data relevant to the task at hand should be available automatically or upon query.

5. The method should leave room for some *uncertainty* in the input and the expected data *values*, and some uncertainty in the *time* of the input or the expected temporal pattern.

6. The method should be generalizable to other clinical domains and tasks. The domain-specific assumptions underlying it should be explicit and as declarative as possible (as opposed to procedural code), so as to enable *reuse* of the method without rebuilding the system, *acquisition* of the necessary knowledge for applying it to other domains, *maintenance* of that knowledge, and *sharing* that knowledge with other applications in the same domain.

19.3 Approaches to Temporal Data Abstraction

This section discusses a number of specific approaches to temporal data abstraction. As already mentioned temporal data abstraction is primarily used for converting the raw data on some patient to more useful information. However, it can also be used for discovering new knowledge. The latter role of temporal data abstraction is briefly addressed in this section that also overviews one of the first programs developed for this purpose, Rx. This program aimed to discover possible causal relationships by examining a time-oriented clinical database. The principal role of temporal data abstraction, summarization of patient records, is addressed more extensively, through two pioneering systems, IDEFIX and TOPAZ. Further approaches of this type, used specifically in the context of patient monitoring, are addressed in Section 19.4.

19.3.1 Data Abstraction for Knowledge Discovery

Data abstraction and more specifically temporal data abstraction can be utilized for the discovery of medical knowledge. Data is patient specific, while knowledge is patient independent, it consists of generalizations that apply across patients. Machine learning for medical domains aims to discover medical knowledge by inducing generalizations from the records of representative samples of patients. Trying to induce such generalizations directly from the raw patient data, which are recorded at the level of "the systolic blood pressure reading was 9 at 10 am on March 26th 1998", is infeasible, since at this level finding the same datum in more than one patient's record is highly unlikely. True generalizations can be more effectively discovered by comparing the patient profiles at a high level of abstraction, in terms of derived data abstractions such as periodic occurrences, trends and other temporal patterns. Different raw data can yield the same abstractions, even if they differ substantially in volume. The number of derived abstractions is relatively constant across patients with the same medical situation, and of course this number is considerably smaller than the number of raw data. Temporal data abstractions reveal the essence of the profile of a patient, hide superfluous detail, and last but not least eliminate noisy information. Furthermore, the temporal scope of abstractions such as trends and periodic occurrences are far more meaningful and prone to adequate comparison than the time-points corresponding to raw data. In addition, temporal abstractions incorporate domain-specific knowledge (e.g. meaningful ranges) that might not be learnable from the raw data itself. If the same complex abstraction, such as a nested periodic occurrence, is associated with a significant number of patients from a representative sample, it makes a strong candidate for knowledge-hood.

Current machine learning approaches do not attempt to first abstract, on an individual basis, the example cases that constitute their training sets, and then to apply whatever learning technique they employ for the induction of further generalizations. Strictly speaking every machine learning algorithm performs a kind of abstraction over the entire collection of cases; however it does not perform any abstraction on the individual cases. Cases tend to be atemporal, or at best they model time (implicitly) as just another attribute. Data abstractions on the selected cases are often manually performed by the domain experts as a preprocessing step. Such manual processing is prone to non uniformity and inconsistency, while the automatic extraction of abstractions is uniform and objective.

One of the goals behind the staging of a series of international workshops called IDAMAP (Intelligent Data Analysis in Medicine and Pharmacology) is to bring together the machine learning and temporal data abstraction communities interested in medical problems [Lavrač *et al.*, 1997].

19.3.2 Discovery in Time-Oriented Clinical Databases: Blum's Rx Project

Rx [Blum, 1982] was a program that examined a time-oriented clinical database, and produced a set of possible causal relationships among various clinical parameters. Rx used a *discovery module* for automated discovery of statistical correlations in clinical databases. Then, a *study module* used a medical knowledge base to rule out spurious correlations by creating and testing a statistical model of a hypothesis. Data for Rx were provided from the American Rheumatism Association Medical Information System (ARAMIS), a chronic-disease time-oriented database that accumulates time-stamped data about thousands of patients who have rheumatic diseases and who are usually followed for many years. The ARAMIS database evolved from the mainframe-based Time Oriented Database (TOD) [Fries, 1972]. Both databases incorporate a simple three-dimensional structure that records, in an entry indexed by the patient, the patient's visit, the clinical parameter, and the value of that parameter, if entered on that visit. The TOD was thus a *historical* database [Snodgrass and Ahn, 1986] (see Section 19.7).

The representation of data in the Rx program included *point events*, such as a laboratory test, and *interval events*, which required an extension to TOD to support diseases, the duration of which was typically more than one visit. The medical knowledge base was organized into two hierarchies: *states* (e.g., disease categories, symptoms, and findings) and *actions* (drugs).

The Rx program determined whether interval-based complex states, such as diseases, existed by using a hierarchical *derivation tree*: Event A can be defined in terms of events B_1 and B_2, which in turn can be derived from events C_{11}, C_{12}, C_{13} and C_{21}, C_{22}, and so on. When necessary, to assess the value of A, Rx traversed the derivation tree and collected values for all A's descendants [Blum, 1982].

Due to the requirements of the Rx modules — in particular, those of the study module— Rx sometimes had to assess the value of a clinical parameter when it was not actually measured — a so-called *latent* variable. One way to estimate latent variables was by using *proxy variables* that are known to be highly correlated with the required parameter. An example is estimating what was termed in the Rx project the *intensity* of a disease during a visit when only some of the disease's clinical manifestations had been measured.

The main method used to access data at time points when a value for them did not necessarily exist used *time-dependent database access functions*. One such function was *delayed-action(variable, day, onset-delay, interpolation-days)*, which returned the assumed value of *variable* at *onset-delay* days before *day*, but not if the last visit preceded *day* by more than *interpolation-days* days. Thus, the dose of prednisone therapy, 1 week before a certain visit, was concluded on the basis of the dose known at the previous visit, if that previous visit was not too far in the past. A similar *delayed-effect* function for states used interpolation if the gap between visits was not excessive. The *delayed-interval* function, whose variable was an interval event, checked that no residual effects of the interval event remained within a given carryover time interval. Other time-dependent database-access functions included functions such as *previous-value(variable, day)*, which returned the last value before *day*; *during(variable, day)*, which returned a value of *variable* if *day* fell within an episode of *variable*; and *rapidly_tapered(variable, slope)*, which returned the interval events in which the point event *variable* was decreasing at a rate greater than *slope*. All these functions and their intelligent use were assumed to be supplied by the user. Thus, Rx could have a modicum of control over *value uncertainty* and *persistence uncertainty*.

In addition, to create interval events, Rx used a parameter-specific *intra-episode gap* to determine whether visits could be joined, and an *inter-episode definition* using the medical knowledge base to define clinical circumstances under which two separate intervals of the parameter could *not* be merged. The intra-episode gap was not dependent on clinical contexts or on other parameters.

19.3.3 Summarization of On-line Medical Records

De Zegher-Geets' IDEFIX Program for Medical-Record Summarization

De Zegher Geets' IDEFIX program [de Zegher-Geets *et al.*, 1988], had goals similar to an earlier program developed by Downes [Downes *et al.*, 1986]—namely, to create an intelligent summary of the patient's current status, using an electronic medical record. IDEFIX used the ARAMIS project's database (in particular, for patients who had systemic lupus erythematosus (SLE)). This program updated the disease likelihood by using essentially a

Bayesian odds-update function. IDEFIX used probabilities that were taken from a probabilistic interpretation of the INTERNIST-1 [Miller *et al.*, 1982] knowledge base, based on Heckerman's work [Heckerman and Miller, 1986]. However, IDEFIX dealt with some of the limitations of Downs' program, such as the assumption of infinite persistence of the same abnormal attributes, and the merging of static, general, and dynamic, patient-specific, medical knowledge. IDEFIX also presented an approach for solving a problem closely related to the persistence problem—namely, that older data should be used, but should not have the same weight for concluding higher-level concepts as do new data. IDEFIX used weighted severity functions, which computed the severity of the manifestations (given clinical cut-off ranges) and then the severity of the state or disease by a linear-combination weighting scheme. (Temporal evidence, however, had no influence on the total severity of the abnormal state). Use of clinical, rather than purely statistical, severity measures improved the performance of the system—the derived conclusions were closer to those of human expert care providers looking at the same data.

The IDEFIX medical knowledge ontology included abnormal primary attributes (APAs), such as the presence of protein in the urine; abnormal states, such as nephrotic syndrome; and diseases, such as SLE-related nephritis. APAs were derived directly from ARAMIS attribute values. IDEFIX inferred abnormal states from APAs; these states were essentially an intermediate-level diagnosis. From abnormal states and APAs, IDEFIX derived and weighted evidence to deduce the likelihood and severity of diseases, which were higher-level abnormal states with a common etiology. IDEFIX used two strategies. First, it used a goal-directed strategy, in which the program sought to explain the given APAs and states and their severity using the list of known complications of the current disease (e.g., SLE). Then, it used a data-driven strategy, in which the system tried to explain the remaining, unexplained APAs using a cover-and-differentiate approach based on odds-likelihood ratios.

De Zegher-Geets added a novel improvement to Downs' program by using time-oriented probabilistic functions (TOPFs). A TOPF was a function that returned the conditional probability of a disease D given a manifestation M, $P(D/M)$, as a function of a time interval, if such a time interval was found. The time interval could be the time since M was last known to be true, or the time since M started to be true, or any other expression returning a time interval. Figure 19.2 shows a TOPF for the conditional probability that a patient with SLE has a renal complication (lupus nephritis) as time passes from the last known episode of lupus nephritis. A temporal predicate that used the same syntax as did Downs' temporal predicates, but which could represent higher-level concepts, was used to express the temporal interval for which IDEFIX looked. For instance, previous.adjacent.episode (lupus.nephritis) looked for the time since the last episode of lupus nephritis. Thus, *as time progressed, the strength of the (probabilistic) connection between the disease and the manifestation could be changed in a predefined way*. For instance, as SLE progressed in time, the probability of a complication such as lupus nephritis increased as a logarithmic function (Figure 19.2). TOPFs were one of four functions: linear increasing, exponential decreasing, exponential increasing and logarithmic. Thus, only the type and coefficients of the function had to be given, simplifying the knowledge representation.

Note that TOPFs were used to compute only *positive* evidence; *negative* evidence likelihood ratios were constant, which might be unrealistic in many domains. The derivation of diseases was theoretically based on derived states, but in practice depended on APAs and states. In addition, TOPFs did not depend on the *context* in which they were used (e.g., the patient is also receiving a certain therapy) or on the *value* of the manifestation (e.g., the severity of the last lupus-nephritis episode). TOPFs were not dependent on the *length* of time for which the manifestation was true (i.e., for how long a manifestation, such as the presence of lupus nephritis, existed).

TOPFs included an implicit strong assumption of *conditional independence* among related diseases and findings (some of which was alleviated by grouping together of related findings as disjunctions). Knowledge about APAs included an *expected time of validity* attribute, but it was also, like TOPFs, independent of the clinical context.

The *goal* of the IDEFIX reasoning module was to explain, for a particular patient visit, the various manifestations for that visit, taking as certain all previous data. There was no explicit intention of creating *interval-based abstractions*, such as "a 6-month episode of lupus nephritis" for the purposes of enabling queries by a care provider or by another program; such conclusions were apparently left to the care provider who, using the graphic display module, looked at all the visits*. Therefore, such intervals were not used explicitly by the reasoning module.

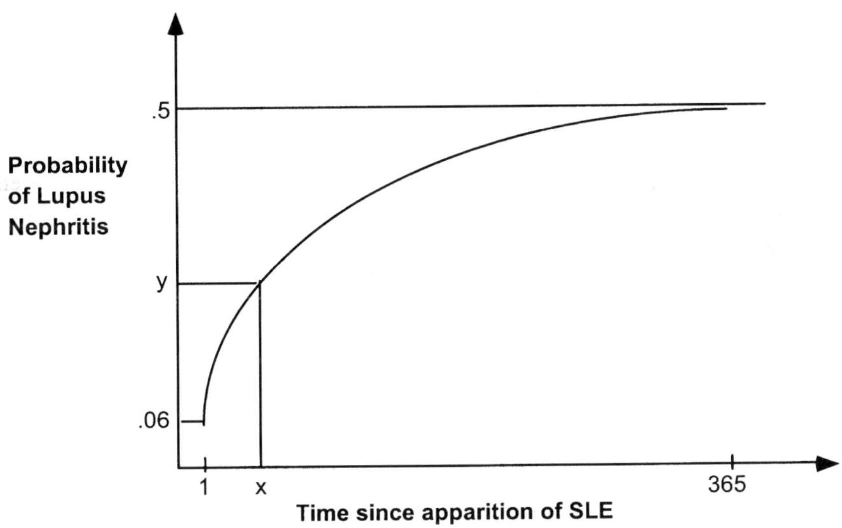

Figure 19.2: A time-oriented probabilistic function (TOPF) associated with the predicate "previous episode of lupus nephritis."

*In fact, the graphic module originally assumed infinite persistence of states, and concatenated automatically adjacent state or disease intervals, regardless of the expected duration of each state; it was modified by the introduction of an expected-length attribute that was used only for display purposes.

Kahn's TOPAZ System: An Integrated Interpretation Model

Kahn has suggested using more than one temporal model to exploit the full power of different formalisms of representing medical knowledge. Kahn [Kahn, 1991a] has implemented a temporal-data summarization program, TOPAZ, based on three temporal models:

- A numeric model represented quantitatively the underlying processes, such as bone-marrow responses to certain drugs, and their expected influence on the patient's granulocyte counts. The numeric model was based on differential equations expressing relations among hidden patient-specific parameters assumed by the model, and measured findings. When the system processed the initial data, the model represented a *prototypical-patient model* and contained general, population-based parameters. That model was specialized for a particular patient — thus turning it into an *atemporal patient-specific model* — by addition of details such as the patient's weight. Finally, the parameters in the atemporal patient-specific model were adjusted to fit actual patient-specific data that accumulate over time (such as response to previous therapy), turning the model into a *patient-specific temporal model* [Kahn, 1988].

- A symbolic interval-based model aggregated intervals that were clinically interesting in the sense that they violated expectations. The model encoded abstractions as a hierarchy of symbolic intervals. The symbolic model created these intervals by comparing population-based model predictions to patient-specific predictions (to detect surprising observations), by comparing population-based model parameters to patient-specific parameter estimates (for explanation purposes), or by comparing actual patient observations to the expected patient-specific predictions (for purposes of critiquing the numeric model). The abstraction step was implemented by context-specific rules.

- A symbolic state-based model generated text paragraphs that used the domain's language, from the interval-based abstractions, using a representation based on augmented transition networks (ATNs). The ATNs encoded the possible summary statements as a network of potential interesting states. The state model transformed interval-based abstractions into text paragraphs.

In addition, Kahn [Kahn, 1991b] designed a temporal-maintenance system, TNET, to maintain relationships among intervals in related contexts and an associated temporal query language, TQuery [Kahn, 1991c]. TNET and TQuery were used in the context of the ONCOCIN project [Tu *et al.*, 1989] to assist care providers who were treating cancer patients enrolled in experimental clinical protocols. The TNET system was extended to the ETNET system , which was used in the TOPAZ system. ETNET [Kahn, 1991b] extended the temporal-representation capabilities of TNET while simplifying the latter's structure. In addition, ETNET had the ability to associate interpretation methods with ETNET intervals; such intervals represented contexts of interest, such as a period of lower-than-expected granulocyte counts. ETNET was not only a *temporal-reasoning* system, but also a flexible *temporal-maintenance* system. Kahn noted, however, that ETNET could not replace a database-management system, and suggested implementing it on top of one.

TOPAZ used different formalisms to represent different aspects of the complex interpretation task. TOPAZ represents a landmark attempt to create a hybrid interpretation system for time-oriented data, comprising three different, integrated, temporal models.

The numeric model used for the representation of the prototypical (population-based) patient model, for the generation of the atemporal patient-specific model, and for the fitting of the calculated parameters with the observed time-stamped observations (thus adjusting the model to a temporal patient-specific model), was a complex one. It was also highly dependent on the domain and on the task at hand. In particular, the developer created a complex model just for predicting *one* parameter (granulocytes) by modeling *one* anatomical site (the bone marrow) for patients who had *one* disease (Hodgkin's lymphoma) and who were receiving treatment by *one* particular form of chemotherapy (MOPP, a clinical protocol that administers nitrogen mustard, vincristine, procarbazine, and prednisone). Even given these considerable restrictions, the model encoded multiple simplifications. For instance, all the drugs were combined into a pseudodrug to represent more simply a combined myelosupressive (bone-marrow–toxicity) effect. The model represents the decay of the drug's *effect*, rather than the decay of the actual drug *metabolites*. This modeling simplification was introduced because the two main drugs specifically toxic to the bone-marrow target organ had similar myelosuppressive (toxic to the bone marrow) effects. As Kahn notes, this assumption might not be appropriate even for other MOPP toxicity types for the same patients and the same protocols; it certainly might not hold for other cancer-therapy protocols, or in other protocol-therapy domains. In fact, it is not clear how the model can be adjusted to fit even the rather related domain of treatment of chronic Graft-Versus-Host Disease (GVHD) patients. Chronic GVHD patients suffer from similar—but not quite the same—effects due to myelosuppressive drug therapy, as well as from multiple-organ (e.g., skin and liver) involvement due to the chronic GVHD disease itself; such effects might complicate the interpretation of other drug toxicities.

In addition, many clinical domains seem to defy complete numeric modeling, e.g. the domain of monitoring children's growth. Similarly, in many other clinical domains, the parameter associations are well known, but the underlying physiology and pathology are little or incompletely understood, and cannot be modeled with any reasonable accuracy. Quantitative modeling is especially problematic in data-poor domains, where measurements are taken once a week or once a month.

TOPAZ used the patient-specific predictions, not the actual observed data, for comparisons to the expected population data. The reason for this choice was that data produced for patient-specific predictions (assuming a correct, complete, patient-specific model) should be *smoother* than actual data and should contain fewer spurious values. However, using predictions rather than observed data might make it more difficult to detect changes in patient parameters. Furthermore, the calculated, patient-specific expected values do not appear in the generated summary and therefore would not be saved in the patient's medical record. It is therefore difficult to produce an explanation to a care provider who might want a justification for the system's conclusions, at least without a highly sophisticated text-generating module.

The ETNET system was highly expressive and flexible. It depended, however, on a model of unambiguous time-stamped observations. This assumption was also made in Russ' TCS system (see Section 19.4.2) and in Shahar's RÉSUMÉ system (at least as far as the input, is concerned). In addition, TOPAZ did not handle well vertical (value) or horizontal (temporal) uncertainty, and, as Kahn remarks, it is in general difficult to apply statistical techniques to data-poor domains.

19.4 Time-Oriented Monitoring

Most clinical monitoring tasks require measurement and capture over time of numerous patient data, often on electronic media. Care providers who have to make diagnostic or therapeutic decisions based on these data may be overwhelmed by the number of data if the care providers' ability to *reason* with the data does not scale up to the data-storage capabilities. Thus, support of automated monitoring is a major task involving reasoning about time in medical applications.

Most stored clinical data include a time stamp in which the particular datum was valid; an emerging pattern over a stretch of time has much more significance than an isolated finding or even a set of findings. Experienced care providers are able to combine several significant contemporaneous findings, to abstract such findings into clinically meaningful higher-level concepts in a context-sensitive manner, and to detect significant trends in both low-level data and abstract concepts.

Thus, it is desirable to provide short, informative, context-sensitive summaries of time-oriented clinical data stored on electronic media, and to be able to answer queries about abstract concepts that summarize the data. Providing these abilities benefits both a human care provider and an automated decision-support tool that recommends therapeutic and diagnostic measures based on the patient's clinical history up to the present. Such concise, meaningful summaries, apart from their immediate value to a care provider, support an automated system's further recommendations for diagnostic or therapeutic interventions, provide a justification for the system's or for the human user's actions, and monitor not just patient data, but also therapy plans suggested by the care provider or by the decision-support system. A meaningful summary cannot use only *time points*, such as dates when data were collected; it must be able to characterize significant features over *periods* of time, such as "5 months of decreasing liver enzyme levels in the context of recovering from hepatitis."

Many of the temporal-abstraction methodologies mentioned above are intended, in part, to support the automated monitoring task. One of the problems encountered in monitoring is that of time-oriented validation of clinical data. Several methodologies have been proposed or used, including intricate schemes for detecting inconsistencies that can only be revealed over time [Horn *et al.*, 1997].

19.4.1 Fagan's VM Program: A State-Transition Temporal-Interpretation Model

Fagan's VM system was one of the first knowledge-based systems that included an explicit representation for time. It was designed to assist care providers managing patients on ventilators in intensive-care units [Fagan *et al.*, 1984]. VM was designed as a rule-based system inspired by MYCIN, but it was different in several respects: VM could reason explicitly about time units, accept time-stamped measurements of patient parameters, and calculate time-dependent concepts such as rates of change. In addition, VM relied on a state-transition model of different intensive-care therapeutic situations, or contexts (in the VM case, different ventilation modes). In each context, different expectation rules would apply to determine what, for instance, is an acceptable mean arterial pressure in a particular context. Except for such state-specific rules, the rest of the rules could ignore the context in which they were applied, since the context-specific classification rules created a context-free, "common denominator", symbolic-value environment. Thus, similar values of the same parameter that appeared in meeting intervals (e.g., ideal mean arterial pressure) could be joined and aggregated into longer intervals, even though the meaning of the value could be different, depending on the context in which the symbolic value was determined. The fact that the system changed state was inferred by special rules, since VM was not connected directly to the ventilator output.

Another point to note is that the VM program used a classification of expiration dates of parameters, signifying for how long VM could assume the correctness of the parameter's value if that value was not sampled again. The expiration date value was used to fill a good-for slot in the parameter's description. Constants (e.g., gender) are good (valid) forever, until replaced. Continuous parameters (e.g., heart rate) are good when given at their regular, expected sampling frequency unless input data are missing or have unlikely values. Volunteered parameters (e.g., temperature) are given at irregular intervals and are good for a parameter- and context-specific amount of time. Deduced parameters (e.g., hyperventilation) are calculated from other parameters, and their reliability depends on the reliability of these parameters.

VM did not use the MYCIN certainty factors, although they were built into the rules. The reason was that most of the uncertainty was modeled within the domain-specific rules. Data were not believed after a long time had passed since they were last measured; aberrant values were excluded automatically; and wide (e.g., ACCEPTABLE) ranges were used for conclusions, thus already accounting for a large measurement variability. Fagan notes that the lack of uncertainty in the rules might occur because, in clinical contexts, care providers do not make inferences unless the latter are strongly supported, or because the intensive-care domain tends to have measurements that have a high correlation with patient states.

VM could not accept data arriving out of order, such as blood-gas results that arrive after the current context has changed, and thus could not revise past conclusions. In that sense, VM could not create a valid *historical* database (see Section 19.8), although it did store the last hour of parameter measurements and all former conclusions; in that respect, VM maintained a *rollback* database of measurements and conclusions.

19.4.2 Temporal Bookkeeping: Russ' Temporal Control Structure

Russ designed a system called the temporal control structure (TCS), which supports reasoning in time-oriented domains, by allowing the domain-specific inference procedures to ignore temporal issues, such as the particular time stamps attached to values of measured variables [Russ, 1989; Russ, 1995].

The main emphasis in the TCS methodology is creating what Russ terms as a state abstraction: an abstraction of continuous processes into steady-state time intervals, when all the database variables relevant for the knowledge-based system's reasoning modules are known to be fixed at some particular value. The state-abstraction intervals are similar to VM's states, which were used as triggers for VM's context-based rules. TCS is introduced as a control-system buffer between the database and the rule environment. The actual reasoning processes (e.g., domain-specific rules) are activated by TCS over all the intervals representing such steady states, and thus can reason even though the rules do not represent time explicitly. That ignorance of time by the rules is allowed because, by definition, after the various intervals representing different propositions have been broken down by the control system into steady-state, homogeneous subintervals, there can be no change in any of the parameters relevant to the rule inside these subintervals, and time is no longer a factor.

The TCS system allows user-defined code modules that reason over the homogeneous intervals, as well as user-defined data variables that hold the data in the database. Modules define inputs and outputs for their code; Russ also allows for a memory variable that can transfer data from one module to a succeeding or a preceding interval module (otherwise, there can be no reasoning about change). Information variables from future processes are termed oracles; variables from the past are termed history.

The TCS system creates a process for each time interval in which a module is executed; the process has access only to those input data that occur within that time interval. The TCS system can chain processes using the memory variables. All process computations are considered by the TCS system as black boxes; the TCS system is responsible for applying these computations to the appropriate variables at the appropriate time intervals, and for updating these computations, should the value of any input variable change. Figure 19.3 shows a chain of processes in the TCS system.

The underlying temporal primitive in the TCS architecture is a time *point* denoting an exact date. Propositions are represented by point variables or by interval variables. Intervals are created by an abstraction process that employs user-defined procedural Lisp code inside the TCS modules to create steady-state periods, such as a period of stable blood pressure. The abstraction process and the subsequent updates are data driven. Variables can take only a single value, which can be a complex structure; the only restriction on the value is the need to provide an equality predicate.

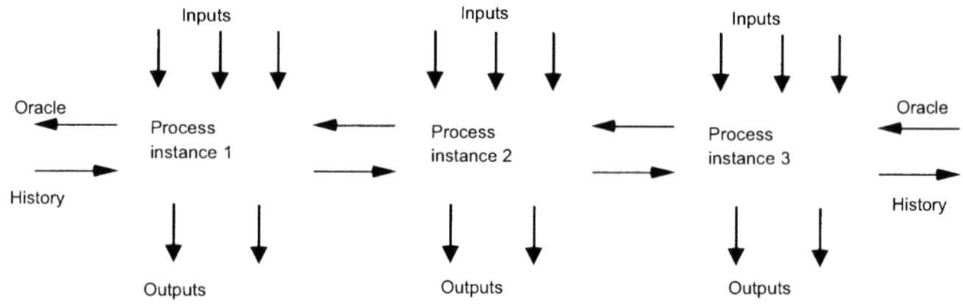

Figure 19.3: A chain of processes in the TCS system.

Each process has in it user-defined code, a set of predefined inputs and outputs, and memory variables connecting it to future processes (oracle variables) and to past processes (history variables).

A particularly interesting feature of TCS is the truth-maintenance capability of the system—that is, the abilities to maintain dependencies among data and conclusions in every steady-state interval, and to propagate the effects of a change in past or present values of parameters to all concerned reasoning modules. Thus, the TCS system creates a *historical database* that can be updated at arbitrary time points, in which all the time-stamped conclusions are valid. Another interesting property of Russ's system is the ability to reason by hindsight—that is, to reassess past conclusions based on new, present data [Russ, 1989]. This process is performed essentially by information flowing through the memory variables backward in time.

19.4.3 Haimowitz and Kohane's TrenDx System

A more recent system, demonstrating initial encouraging results, is Haimowitz and Kohane's TrenDx temporal pattern-matching system [Haimowitz and Kohane, 1996]. TrenDx focuses on using efficient general methods for representing and detecting predefined temporal patterns in raw time-stamped data.

Trend templates (TTs) describe typical clinical temporal patterns, such as normal growth development, or specific types of patterns known to be associated with functional states or disease states, by representing these patterns as *horizontal* (temporal) and *vertical* (measurement) constraints. The TrenDx system has been developed mainly within the domain of pediatric growth monitoring, although examples from other domains have been presented to demonstrate its more general potential.

For example, the growth TT declares several predefined events, such as PUBERTY ONSET; these events are constrained to occur within a predefined temporal range, e.g., puberty onset must occur within 10 to 15 years after birth. Within that temporal range, height should vary only by $\pm\delta$.

TrenDx has the rather unique ability to match *partial* patterns by maintaining an agenda of candidate patterns that *possibly* match an evolving pattern. Thus, even if TrenDx gets only one point as input, it might (at least in theory) still be able to return a few possible patterns as output. As more data points are known, the list of potential matching patterns and their particular instantiation in the data is modified. This continuous pattern-matching process might be considered a goal-directed approach to pattern matching.

A TT indeed provides a powerful mechanism for expressing the dynamics of some process, in terms of the different phases comprising it, the uncertainty governing the transitions from one phase to the next, the significant events marking these transitions and various constraints on parameter-values associated with the different phases. However, the abstraction levels are not explicit, and there is no decoupling between an intermediate level of data interpretation (derivation of abstractions) and a higher level of decision making. Data interpretation involves the selection of the TT instantiation that matches best the raw temporal data (this procedure solves the problems of noise detection and positioning of transitions). The selected TT instantiation is the final solution; thus temporal data abstraction and diagnostic-monitoring reasoning per se are tangled up into a single process. This makes the overall reasoning more efficient, but it limits the re-usability of the approach.

19.4.4 Larizza et al.'s Temporal-Abstraction Module in the M-HTP System

M-HTP [Larizza *et al.*, 1992] is a system for monitoring heart-transplant patients that has a module for abstracting time-stamped clinical data. The system generates abstractions such as Hb-decreasing, and maintains a temporal network (TN) of temporal intervals, using a design inspired by Kahn's TNET temporal-maintenance system (see above). Like TNET, M-HTP uses an object-oriented visit taxonomy and indexes parameters by visits. M-HTP also has an object-oriented knowledge base that defines a taxonomy of significant-episodes—clinically interesting concepts such as diarrhea or WBC_DECREASE. Parameter instances can have properties, such as MINIMUM. The M-HTP output includes intervals from the patient TN that can be represented and examined graphically, such as "CMV_viremia_increase" during particular dates.

The temporal model of the M-HTP system includes both time points and intervals. The M-HTP system uses a temporal query language to define the antecedent part of its rules, such as "an episode of decrease in platelet count that *overlaps* an episode of decrease of WBC count *at least for* 3 days *during* the past week implies suspicion of CMV infection".

19.4.5 Miksch et al.'s VIE-VENT System

Miksch et al. [Miksch *et al.*, 1996] have developed VIE-VENT, a system for data validation and therapy planning for artificially ventilated newborn infants. The overall aim is the context-based validation and interpretation of temporal data, where data can be of different types (continuously assessed quantitative data, discontinuously assessed quantitative data, and qualitative data). The interpretation contexts are not dynamically derived, but they are defined through schemata with thresholds that can be dynamically tailored to the patient under examination. The context schemata correspond to potential treatment regimes; which context is actually active depends on the current regime of the patient. If the interpretation of data points to an alarming situation, the higher level reasoning task of therapy assessment and (re)planning is invoked which may result in changing the patient's regime thus switching to a new context. Context switching should be done in a smooth way and again relevant thresholds are dynamically adapted to take care of this. The data abstraction process per se is fairly decoupled from the therapy planning process. Hence this approach differs from Haimowitz and Kohane's approach where the selection and instantiation of an interpretation context (trend template) represents the overall reasoning task. In VIE-VENT the data abstraction process does not need to select the interpretation context, as this is given to it by the therapy planning process.

The types of knowledge required are classification knowledge and temporal dynamic knowledge (e.g., default persistences, expected qualitative trend descriptions, etc.). Everything is expressed declaratively in terms of schemata that can be dynamically adjusted depending on the state of the patient. First quantitative point-based data are translated into qualitative values, depending on the operative context. Smoothing of data oscillating near thresholds then takes place. Interval data are then transformed to qualitative descriptions resulting in a verbal categorization of the change of a parameter over time, using schemata for trend-curve fitting. The system deals with four types of trends: very short-term, short-term, medium-term and long-term.

Overall this approach is aimed at a specific type of medical applications, and so, unlike Shahar's KBTA method, the aim is not to formulate in generic terms a reusable kernel for temporal data abstraction.

19.5 Time in Clinical Diagnosis

Although there is a large body of work in medical diagnostic systems the explicit incorporation of the temporal dimension has only recently received substantial attention. This is so for diagnostic systems in general and not just for medical diagnostic systems. In fact, the majority of approaches in temporal diagnosis involve medical domains. It is interesting to note that in most of these cases the diagnostic systems originally developed were atemporal; the temporal versions were subsequently built in an attempt to achieve significant performance enhancements.

In medical diagnosis the predominant paradigm is that of abductive reasoning since the primary entity to be modeled is a disorder process. Often normal and abnormal (disorder) processes are modeled alike. This uniformity of representation is a strength as in most realistic domains, knowledge on normality is a necessary component of diagnostic knowledge. Furthermore the predominant relationship underlying such models is that of causality. Quite naturally, the emphasis is therefore on how to integrate temporal and abductive reasoning, i.e. how to integrate time in the formation and evaluation of diagnostic hypotheses, and how to incorporate time in causality. In addition, in a temporal diagnostic system, patient data consist of temporal findings and the process of temporal data abstraction is directly relevant, as illustrated in the preceding sections.

19.5.1 The Heart Disease Program

In the Heart Disease Program (HDP) [Long, 1996], the diagnostic knowledge is represented as a Bayesian probabilistic network where the arcs represent causal relations. The issue of multiple temporal granularities is very relevant to the domain of HDP since some processes take place over minutes while others take place over months or years. A strictly probabilistic approach that was used in the early version of the system had the limitation of generating hypotheses that were impossible given the temporal relations involved. As a result temporal constraints on the causal relations were explicitly represented and the patient data became time-stamped entities. A difficulty of the particular medical domain is that the available observations are limited.

In this system the causal relation has rich temporal semantics. *Onset* is the range of time that can be assumed for the effect when it is observed while *delay* is the range of time the cause must be true before the effect can start (this includes the onset time). *Persist* is the range of time that the effect will remain if the cause ceases to be true and *max-exist* is the maximum time the cause will remain, even though the effect continues. Furthermore a causal relation is classified as *self-limiting* if the abnormality ceases by max-exist without any rectification action while a state is classified as *intermittent* if it is absent over subintervals of the interval in which it is true. Finally it is required that an effect is observable after the cause is observable and overlaps the cause. Onset, delay, max-exist, etc. are represented as time intervals where the begin and end of an interval can be expressed as the range of possible time points, with respect to the relevant granularities. The multiplicity of granularities is not handled in a systematic way.

The causal relation enables the representation of different patterns of causality such as *immediate* (the effect happens immediately), *progressive* (the effect, once it takes place, continues and often worsens), *accumulative* (when a cause is required to exist over a period of time), *corrective* (when a state causes another state to return to normality; here the causes are often therapies but they can also be pathophysiologic states such as dehydration "correcting" high blood volume). The Bayesian network used does not allow for cyclic phenomena. This is not a limitation for the particular medical domain as cyclic phenomena do not happen. Cyclic (periodic) phenomena in the patient data are treated as atomic findings in the same way as all other findings. Temporal data abstraction is not supported in HDP.

During a consultation with HDP, nodes in the Bayesian network are instantiated. This essentially means defining their observable extents in terms of time intervals (earliest and latest begin and end) where a time is expressed relative to the current point in time. The specified temporal constraints enable the derivation of such temporal extents both for a cause given its effect and vice versa. Since diagnostic reasoning is abductive reasoning the most common reasoning step is to infer a cause from an effect.

The incorporation of time enhanced the performance of HDP not only because the evaluation of hypotheses was more accurate but also because this resulted in constraining the generation of hypotheses.

19.5.2 Temporal Parsimonious Covering Theory

The parsimonious covering theory (PCT) of Peng and Reggia [Peng and Reggia, 1990] is a well known general theory of abductive diagnosis. The basic version of the theory models diagnostic knowledge in terms of a set of causes (disorders), D, a set of manifestations (M) and a causal relation, $C \subset D \times M$, relating each cause to its effects. An efficient algorithm, BIPARTITE, is defined, which incrementally constructs, in generator-set format, all the explanations of a set of occurring manifestations, $M^+ \subset M$, for some case (patient). An explanation is a subset of D which covers completely the set of occurring manifestations M^+ (i.e., every element of M^+ is an effect of at least one element of the explanation) and satisfies a specified parsimony criterion. There are three parsimony criteria which in ascending order of strictness are relevancy (every disorder in the explanation is a cause of at least one element of M^+), irredundancy (no subset of the explanation is also a cover of M^+) and minimality (the explanation has the minimum cardinality among all the covers of M^+). The preferred parsimony criterion is that of irredundancy and this is the one embedded in the BIPARTITE algorithm.

Wainer and de Melo Rezende [Wainer and de Melo Rezende, 1997] have proposed a temporal extension to the basic version of PCT, referred to as t-PCT, which they have applied to the domain of food-borne diseases. Their argument is that irredundancy as parsimony criterion is too weak to significantly reduce the number of alternative explanations.

In t-PCT each disorder is modeled, separately, as a *temporal graph*. This is a directed, acyclic, transitive, not necessarily connected, graph the nodes of which represent manifestations and the directed arcs represent temporal precedence (a directed arc from manifestation m_i to manifestation m_j means that the begin of m_i must precede the begin of m_j). A temporal graph is not necessarily a causal graph since the precedence relation does not necessarily imply causality. If there is quantitative information about the duration of a manifestation, it is associated with the corresponding node; similarly if there is quantitative information about the elapsed time between the start of two manifestations, it is associated with the corresponding arc. Durations and delays are expressed as pairs of numbers denoting minimum and maximum values. This representation allows for temporal incompleteness as not every delay or duration needs to be specified. Moreover, the precedence relation does not need to be completely specified.

A similar representation to the disorder model is used for patient information. The patient information consists of a set of actual manifestations. Again where the duration of a manifestation is known, a range for this is specified. In addition a range for the beginning of a manifestation, if known, is specified relative to some arbitrary origin. Thus it can be said, for example, that manifestation m_1 started between 2 and 3 weeks ago and it lasted for 1-2 days, and that manifestation m_2 is present but there is no information on when it started. In this example the arbitrary origin is taken to be the present point in time. Different granularities are implicated both in the representation of the diagnostic knowledge and the patient information but, like the HDP system, the multiplicity of granularities is handled in an ad hoc fashion, and not in a systematic, semantically-based, fashion.

The temporal primitive in t-PCT is the time point. An interval, $I = [I^-, I^+]$, is defined to be a non-empty, convex, set of time points; I^- gives its minimum duration and I^+ its maximum duration. When I^- equals I^+ there is no uncertainty regarding the particular temporal measure, i.e., the duration of some manifestation is known exactly, or the distance between two times (e.g. 'now' and the beginning of some manifestation) is known exactly. If $I^- > I^+$, an inconsistency is signaled since this says that the minimum of the given temporal measure exceeds its maximum.

Two binary, arithmetic, operations are defined on intervals, *intersection* and *sum*. Intersection gives the common subrange, and hence the two intervals must denote the same temporal measure, while sum propagates delays (between the begins of manifestations) along a chain of manifestations, or positions a manifestation on the time line (the sum of the delay of its begin, from some origin, and its duration). The result of an intersection operation can be an inconsistent interval (the two ranges are disjoint) but not so for sum. These operations are applied for deciding whether the model of some disorder (temporal graph) is temporally inconsistent with the patient information. Temporal inconsistency arises if (a) the actual begin of a manifestation is disjoint from the expected begin of that manifestation under the given disorder, or (b) the actual duration of a manifestation is different from its duration expected under the given disorder.

An explanation that contains a disorder that is temporally inconsistent with the patient information is removed. More specifically a set E of disorders is a temporally consistent explanation of M^+, if E covers M^+ (each element of M^+ appears in the temporal graph of at least one element of E), E satisfies a parsimony criterion (preferably irredundancy) and every disorder in E is not temporally inconsistent with the patient information. Algorithm BIPARTITE has been extended to t-BIPARTITE implementing the notion of temporal inconsistency. It is important to note that temporal inconsistency is not implemented as a filter but it is used to direct the formation of explanations.

The principal objective of t-PCT is to use time for constraining the generation of explanations beyond what is possible from the irredundancy parsimony criterion. Temporal incompleteness and uncertainty is supported but other essential representation requirements such as compound occurrences, systematic handling of multiple granularities, and temporal data abstraction are not addressed. Furthermore, the authors note that the impossibility of defining cycles is a major restriction on the expressive power of their formalism since it is not possible to represent recurring events.

More recently, t-PCT has been extended to fuzzy t-PCT [Wainer and Sandri, 1999]. Here the nodes of a disorder temporal graph are instantaneous events denoting begins and ends of manifestations and its arcs do not necessarily capture precedence. An arc is labeled with a fuzzy temporal interval giving a typical range for the particular temporal distance as well as other possible values.

19.5.3 Abstract Temporal Diagnosis

Gamper and Nejdl [Gamper and Nejdl, 1997] have developed a logic-based framework for abstract temporal diagnosis (ATD) which they have applied to the domain of hepatitis B with promising results. This framework, in contrast with the previous approaches discussed, emphasizes the need to automatically derive abstract observations over time intervals from (direct) observations at time points. This is an important aspect of the framework despite the fact that the actual temporal data abstraction mechanism used is very simplistic; the importance is in signifying the essence of temporal data abstraction in diagnostic contexts, in addition to its predominant application context, patient monitoring.

ATD is based on Allen's [Allen, 1984] time-interval based logic. More specifically the temporal primitive used is the convex time-interval. A linear and dense time structure, called *time line*, is assumed which is unbound in both directions, past and future. The time line is represented by real numbers. So intervals have explicit Begins and Ends, [B, E]. The overall time of relevance to some diagnostic problem is denoted by i_{max}, which includes all other time intervals. Time invariant properties hold throughout i_{max}. Temporal propositions are represented by introducing time as an additional argument to the relevant predicates, e.g., fever(high,i), meaning that fever is high during interval i.

The designers of ATD observe that a process-oriented ontology is more suitable for representing dynamic systems than a component-based ontology. In ATD diagnostic knowledge is represented as a set of process descriptions, one of which corresponds to normal behavior while the others represent different abnormal behaviors. The temporal evolution of a (normal or abnormal) process is expressed through a chaining sequence of states, described in terms of process state assumptions, s(p,i); this says that process p assumes state s throughout interval i. Interval i is constrained through temporal relations with other intervals such as i {starts, during, finishes, equal} [1,10] which says that i either starts, is during, finishes or is equal to the absolute interval [1,10], i.e., i is constrained to be within that period.

A process is non observable. There are, however, observable parameters (manifestations). Manifestation propositions (or simply manifestations) are expressed as m(v,i) which says that manifestation m assumes value v throughout interval i. A manifestation can assume different values over different time intervals but only one value at a time. Such mutual exclusivity constraints for manifestations as well as process states are expressed, again in first order logic, as a kind of background knowledge.

The state description model (SDM) of a process p is a logical formula $\alpha \wedge \tau_\alpha \rightarrow \beta \wedge \tau_\beta$ where α and β are conjunctions of temporal propositions (process state assumptions and/or manifestations) while τ_α and τ_β are conjunctions of temporal relations between the implicated time intervals. These temporal constraints denote the temporal behavior of the given process. The SDM formula says that if process p assumes the states as specified in α such that the temporal relations in τ_α are satisfied, the manifestations in β and the temporal relations in τ_β are predicted. So the entailment in the formula captures causality (the process states in α are possible causes for the manifestations in β) and hence it can be said that an SDM integrates the causal and temporal knowledge for the given process.

The temporal constraints included in τ_α and τ_β form a binary constraint network, where nodes are time intervals and arcs are labeled with (disjunctions) of temporal relations. Inverse relations or self-referencing are not permitted. As the temporal relations are mutually exclusive, under a consistent scenario, every arc should be labeled with a single relation. Well known, efficient constraint satisfaction algorithms, can be used for deriving feasible scenarios.

Raw patient data consist of a set of direct observations, where an observation is a measurement (v) of an observable parameter (m) at a particular time point t (with respect to the real time line). This is expressed as $m(v,i) \wedge i$ {equals} $[t,t]$. A temporal data abstraction mechanism is applied to the direct, point-based, observations in order to derive more useful abstract, interval-based, observations. As already indicated the abstraction mechanism of ATD is very simplistic; namely all parameters are considered concatenable and thus all "meeting" intervals denoting the same parameter and value are joined in order to obtain maximal validity periods for the given parameter-value. No other form of temporal abstraction is performed. Thus the distinction between concrete and abstract observations is that the former refer to time points while the latter to intervals. If at every measurement, a parameter changes value, no abstraction is possible but in reality this should not be so since once a change takes place it persists over a period of time. The sampling frequency of a parameter (temporal granularity) should be chosen so as not to miss any significant changes. Often however it is not possible to have 'complete' information on a parameter even with respect to the given sampling rate and hence one of the difficult aspects of temporal data abstraction is how to fill such gaps. An abstract observation is expressed as $m(v,i) \wedge \tau$ where τ gives the temporal constraints between the extent of interval i and the real time line and/or other abstract observations. The temporal constraints in the abstract patient information are also represented as a binary constraint network.

Since ATD is a logic-based, abductive, framework, for the derivation of explanations it is necessary to define the set of abducibles, those literals that are acceptable as explanations. These are the literals which occur only in the antecedents of SDMs, e.g. the process state assumptions. An explanation of the patient information is a conjunction of abducibles which together with the diagnostic knowledge (SMDs and background theory) entail the abstract observations denoting abnormality (derived from the patient information) and is consistent with all abstract observations. This is a typical logic-based definition of diagnosis. However it should be said that the criterion of complete coverage of abnormality observations which appears in this framework as well as in t-PCT and the following approach is a very strict one for realistic medical diagnostic problems.

19.5.4 Console and Torasso's Temporal Abductive Diagnostic Architecture

Console and Torasso [Console and Torasso, 1991b] propose a logic-based, temporal abductive, architecture for medical diagnosis. This architecture is an extension of the causal component of CHECK, an atemporal diagnostic system that was applied to the domains of cirrhosis and leprosis.

In this proposal diagnostic knowledge is represented as a single, acyclic, causal network where the arcs are associated with temporal information denoting a range (minimum and maximum) for the delay between the start of the cause and the start of the effect. These delays can be expressed with respect to various granularities and in fact some delay may involve mixed granularities such as a minimum of 1 hour and a maximum of 1 day. As in the previous approaches discussed, the multiplicity of temporal granularities is only mentioned in passing.

The temporal primitive of the proposal is the *time point*. A *time interval* is a convex set of time points. In order to allow uncertainty with respect to temporal existencies, *variable intervals* are used which are expressed as 4-tuples of time points where the first pair of time points gives the range for the begin and the second pair the range for the end of the interval. A variable interval encompasses a set of precise intervals. This is a fairly standard representation for absolute temporal uncertainty.

The nodes in the causal network define findings (manifestations), pathophysiologic states (initial and intermediary), and contextual information (c-nodes). Manifestations and contextual information are directly obtainable (observable entities) while pathophysiologic states (p-states) are non observable, possibly with the exception of some initial states, and therefore need to be inferred. Some of the p-states define diagnoses. All types of nodes are associated with a set of single-valued attributes and the value set of each attribute is expressed in linguistic terms. Instantiating such a node means assigning values to its attributes and determining its temporal extent as a (variable) time interval.

A causal arc in the network relates an antecedent to a consequent where a consequent is either a p-state or a manifestation. In the simplest form, an antecedent is a single p-state, but it can also be a conjunction of p-states and c-nodes involving at least one p-state (although the authors note that the majority of causal relations encountered in the medical domains investigated were of the simple form). Where complex causal antecedents are involved the delay information can be interpreted either in a weak way as the delay between the first point in time where all the elements in the antecedent hold and the start of the consequent, or in a strong way as the separate pairwise delays between the start of each conjunct of the antecedent and the consequent. The weak interpretation is more intuitive, but is computationally intractable, while the strong interpretation is restrictive (incomplete relative to the weak interpretation) but computationally tractable. This is because as already said, the principal step in medical diagnostic reasoning, in an abductive sense, is to infer causes from effects. Under the strong interpretation the temporal extent for each conjunct node in the antecedent can be deterministically computed (albeit as variable intervals) from the temporal extent of the consequent node and the delay information. Actually the delay information is used to compute the bounds for the start of an antecedent node from the (bounds) of the start of a consequent node (this also ensures that an effect cannot precede its cause). Bounds for the end of an antecedent node are obtained on the basis of two general temporal constraints, namely that a cause cannot 'outlive' its effect and that there cannot be a gap between the two. Under the weak interpretation the only thing that can be deterministically obtained is the temporal extent of a so called virtual state that defines the co-existence of the various nodes involved.

A causal arc can be associated with an arbitrary logical expression the validity of which in a given diagnostic situation is a necessary condition for assuming the presence of the causal arc. The authors do not explain whether such a condition can include further temporal constraints and the impression given is that such conditions express atemporal contextual factors for the materialization of the causality relation.

As mentioned above the nodes in the causal network are characterized by a set of attributes. A causal arc in fact encompasses a set of associations relating combinations of node-attribute-value triplets (for nodes from the antecedent) to combinations of attribute-value pairs for the consequent. If none of these associations is satisfied, the causal arc is again revoked. Although not explicitly discussed, it appears that the delay information of the causal arc applies to all potential combinations of attribute-values specified. Finally there can be multiple causal arcs (either with simple or complex antecedents) sharing the same consequent.

The representation of the causal relation in this proposal is rich, but from the atemporal rather than the temporal sense. In fact the authors themselves admit that the expressive power allotted to the causal relation, through complex antecedents would be uncalled for in most medical domains. Furthermore, such complex causality reverts to a collection of simple causal relations, just sharing the same consequent (and underlined by the same condition, if any) if computational reasons enforce the strong interpretation of the delay information. From the temporal perspective, this representation is not rich; the temporal semantics of a causal arc are both simple (just delay information) and restrictive (a cause cannot outlive an effect). Many causality patterns in medicine, e.g. those identified by Long in HDP cannot be expressed in this formalism from the temporal perspective.

A difference between this approach and the previous three approaches discussed is that in this architecture no general duration information for the nodes in the causal network is given. The authors emphasize that in medicine the available temporal knowledge tends to be just delay information, while temporal extents can only be dynamically inferred and constitute factual information for the particular diagnostic cases. Actual temporal extents of unobservable states may indeed need to be inferred but general knowledge about the persistences of such states can be of great assistance in such reasoning. Such general temporal knowledge *can* be available in medical domains as the HDP, t-PCT and the next approach's domains illustrate.

The authors view temporal reasoning in medical diagnosis as a temporal constraint satisfaction problem. The patient information consists of a collection of manifestation instances (findings), and their (possibly variable) temporal extents. The objective is to determine the path in the network whose delays are temporally consistent with the extents of the findings and that accounts for the findings, by propagating backwards the temporal extents of the findings. So they advocate the integration of an abductive engine with a temporal constraint satisfaction engine. As with the previous approaches the latter engine is not used as a filter but participates actively in the formation of diagnostic explanations. However unlike the previous approaches the authors consider the deployment of the temporal engine as a filter, as a cleaner solution which they would have employed had it not been the case that the abductive engine was throwing away viable explanations due to its ignorance of the temporal evolution of a pathophysiologic situation; furthermore they see the use of the temporal engine in a tightly integral fashion with the abductive engine as increasing the overall complexity. It should be said, however, that the view of abduction employed in this proposal is again the strict, logic-based, view, where all abnormality observations need to be covered and consistency with all observations is required; this view is certainly challenged by many real-life medical domains. The authors of HDP, t-PCT and ATD see the tight integration of temporal reasoning with their respective diagnostic engines as a strength of their approaches because it makes the formation of diagnostic explanations more efficient by preventing the proliferation of temporally inconsistent possibilities.

In the authors' own admission, the representation of patient information is rather restrictive; more specifically an observable parameter can attain an abnormality value during a single interval only and throughout the rest of the period of relevance to the diagnostic activity this parameter is assumed to be normal. This is very restrictive because it prevents the expression of repetitive happenings; of course periodicity is also absent at the level of diagnostic knowledge since the causal network is acyclic and each disorder is not modeled separately through its own causal model thus permitting multiple instantiations giving distinct occurrences of the same disorder. The authors indicate that in order to allow recurring happenings they would need to use nonconvex time intervals. This of course would mean a drastic reconstruction of their proposal. Apart from nonconvexity, compound occurrences and temporal data abstraction (e.g. temporal trends) would need to be supported.

More recently, members of this team have proposed a unifying framework for temporal model-based diagnosis [Brusoni *et al.*, 1998]. This work represents a significant extension to Console and Torasso's spectrum of logical definitions of model-based diagnosis [Console and Torasso, 1991a]. In temporal model-based diagnosis, the authors distinguish between *time-varying context* (observing the behavior of a system at different times), *temporal behavior* (the consequences of the fact that a system is in a specific (normal or faulty) mode manifest themselves after some time and for some time), and *time-varying behavior* (permitted transitions between faults; if this knowledge is missing any transition is permissible by default). They also distinguish between temporal entailment and temporal consistency. They conclude by giving a categorization for diagnosis, ranging from snapshot diagnosis (atemporal diagnosis performed at a point in time) to temporal diagnosis (considers temporal behavior over a specified time window, but not time-varying behavior) and general temporal diagnosis (considers both time-varying and temporal behavior, again over a specified time window). In temporal diagnosis, the assumption that a fault persists during the considered time window is made. This assumption is waved under general temporal diagnosis.

19.5.5 Temporal Abductive Diagnostic Framework Based on Time-Objects

In the approaches discussed above the emphasis is on incorporating temporal constraints on causal relations (HDP and Console and Torasso's approach), where diagnostic knowledge is modeled in terms of a single causal network, or on incorporating temporal constraints on the temporal extents of occurrences (t-PCT and ATD), where each process is modeled separately through its own temporal graph or state description model. Temporal uncertainty and incompleteness is recognized as a necessary representation aspect, which is expressed either in an absolute way (ranges for delays, durations, or temporal extents), or a relative way (disjunction of temporal relations between two intervals).

In all these approaches the occurrences are treated as indivisible entities. Moreover, such occurrences are not treated as dynamic entities, embodying time as an integral aspect, and interacting with each other; time is loosely associated with them by pairing an atemporal entity with some time interval, e.g., by including the interval as yet another argument of the relevant predicates. Recurring phenomena and periodicity in general, as well as temporal trends are not addressed, since these require compound occurrences. Temporal data abstraction is addressed in only one of the four proposals (ATD) but again what is actually provided is not a fully fledged temporal data abstraction engine. Another issue, which is only mentioned in passing, is that of multiple temporal granularities.

As already mentioned compound occurrences, temporal data abstraction and multiple granularities are identified requirements for temporal reasoning in medicine. The time-object ontology (see Section 19.8.2) aims to address these as well as the other identified requirements for temporal reasoning in medicine. The central primitives of this ontology are the time-axis enabling a multidimensional and multigranular model of time [Keravnou, 1999], and the time-object, a dynamic entity embodying time as an integral aspect, and bringing together temporal, structural and causal knowledge. A concrete, i.e. instantiated, time-object can be seen as an *agent* that is either extinguished, if its existence refers to the past, or it is alive and active, if its existence is still ongoing, or it is asleep and waiting, if its existence refers to the future. It is dynamic and exhibits a certain behavior in terms of the changes that it can bring about either to itself or to other time-objects. A change is constructive if it brings about the creation of another time-object or it is destructive if it brings about the destruction of some time-object, possibly its own self. So a time-object interacts with other time-objects in a positive (constructive) or negative (destructive) manner. Such interactions are modeled through causality. Furthermore, part of the behavior of a time-object may deal with its defense mechanisms against other time-objects with negative intentions towards it. Disorder processes, therapeutic actions and patient histories can be modeled in terms of time-objects [Keravnou, 1996a]. For example, a disorder process can be modeled as a compound time-object, the components of which are the disorder's manifestations. The behavior of a disorder time-object is to materialize its manifestations in accordance with temporal and other constraints and to 'defend' itself against therapeutic action time-objects. A therapeutic action time-object behaves with negative intentions towards disorder time-objects and their component manifestation time-objects.

In this section we overview a time-object based framework for temporal abductive diagnosis [Keravnou and Washbrook, 2001]. This represents ongoing work, the early roots of which are found in the temporal reasoning framework of the Skeletal Dysplasias Diagnostician (SDD) system [Keravnou and Washbrook, 1990].

First, disorders and their manifestations are classified as follows from the temporal perspective: (a) infinitely persistent, either with a fixed or a variable initiation margin (e.g. SEDC); (b) finitely persistent, but not recurring, again either with a fixed or a variable initiation margin (e.g. chicken pox) ; and (c) finitely persistent which can recur (here the initiation margin is variable), e.g. flu. The temporal extent of a finite persistence is either indefinite or bounded (through minimum and maximum durations).

A disorder process is modeled as an (acyclic) causal structure comprising a number of causal paths, emanating from the node denoting the disorder and terminating at nodes denoting (usually observable) manifestations. Intermediate nodes on such paths denote internal (usually unobservable) causal states; these are also temporally classified as explained above. Such a causal structure is naturally expressed as a collection of abstract time-objects; each node corresponds to a time-object and each arc to the relevant instance of relation causes. A time-object on this causal structure can be a compound object (e.g., a periodic object, or a trend object, etc.), components of which can also be compound, etc. Thus although on the outset the causal structure is acyclic, cyclic phenomena, both with respect to internal states and external manifestations, can be modeled through compound, periodic time-objects.

The overall causal network representing the diagnostic knowledge is therefore partitioned into distinct causal models for the various disorders. The partitioning is necessary in order to allow multiple, dynamic, instantiations of the same disorder, thus capturing recurring conditions. There is only one model per disorder; however the same disorder can appear as an ordinary causal state node in another disorder's model.

The relevant history of a patient consists of those assertions whose valid time is covered by the concrete time-axis corresponding to the time window of the diagnostic activity. Each selected temporal assertion corresponds to a (concrete) time-object. The number of time-objects comprising a patient history is kept to the minimum possible, by performing appropriate merges as well as other forms of temporal data abstraction on the raw time-objects. Furthermore, potential causality dependencies between these time-objects are investigated through the application of axiom A20 (see Section 19.8.2) and where a causality-link is established to hold it is appropriately instantiated. Some of the time-objects comprising the patient history are contextual and do not need any explanation; these usually assert past disorders or past or ongoing therapeutic actions.

Predicate functions *accounts-for* and *in-conflict-with*, each of which accepts two time-objects as arguments, form the basis for the definition of evaluation criteria for potential diagnostic explanations or hypothetical worlds. A hypothetical world is a collection of temporal instantiations of disorder models. Different notions of plausible and best explanation can be composed from such criteria [Keravnou and Washbrook, 2001].

A call to accounts-for or in-conflict-with is evaluated with respect to some consistent collection of time-objects and their interrelationships, the evaluation domain, e.g. the patient history, or a hypothetical world. By default this is taken to be the domain of the first argument. A time-object accounts for another time-object either directly or indirectly through one (if any) of its component time-objects, or one (if any) of its established causal consequent time-objects. For a direct accounting, the property of the first time-object implies (i.e. subsumes) the property of the second time-object, and the existence of the first time-object covers completely the existence of the second time-object. Predicate function in-conflict-with is similarly defined. For a direct conflict, the properties of the two time-objects are mutually exclusive, and their existences are not disjoint. Using the agent paradigm for a time-object, an accounting corresponds to a constructive interaction (either directly or indirectly) between the two time-objects, while a conflict corresponds to a destructive interaction. A hypothetical world to be plausible should exhibit constructive interactions with respect to the patient history and any destructive interactions between the two should not be significant.

In conclusion it can be said that medical temporal diagnosis is presently attracting much and justifiable attention. Interesting results have already materialized but further work is needed in order to address fully the temporal needs of realistic medical diagnostic problems.

19.6 Time-Oriented Guideline-Based Therapy

Since the early days of medical informatics (when that term, in fact, did not exist as such), there has been a continuing interest by information scientists in automating medical diagnosis; some of the relevant details had been explained in this chapter . However, clinicians do not always equally share that enthusiasm, feeling that *management* of patients, rather then simply *classifying* their initial problem, is the real issue. That feeling has indeed been supported by formal and informal surveys regarding the information needs of physicians.

Over the past two decades, it has become increasingly clear that supporting clinical *therapy* and continuous *management*, and in particular, enhancing the *quality* of that therapy by multiple runtime *quality-assurance* and retrospective *quality-assessment* methods, is the major new frontier. The encounter of the overwhelming majority of patients with their clinicians is not the first one. Thus, often the issue at stake is not to classify the patient as a diabetes type II patient, but rather to make the difficult decision, based on past clinical course and present clinical data, how to manage that patient. Most of the health-care costs are now spent on management of patients who suffer from chronic conditions such as cardiovascular diseases, diabetes, pulmonary diseases, and chronic infectious diseases (e.g., AIDS).

Temporal reasoning is especially important when managing patients over time. Increasingly, the most common format for doing that is to follow established clinical guidelines or protocols that specify how to best treat certain types of patients. The use of such methodologies has been shown to have significant positive effects on the behavior of care providers [Grimshaw and Russel, 1993].

19.6.1 Clinical Guidelines and Protocols

Clinical guidelines (or *Care Plans*) are a powerful method for standardization and uniform improvement of the quality of medical care. Clinical guidelines are a set of schematic plans, at varying levels of abstraction and detail, for management over extended periods of patients who have a particular clinical condition (e.g., insulin-dependent diabetes). *Clinical protocols* are typically highly detailed guidelines, often used in areas such as oncology and experimental clinical trials. *Reminders* and *alerts* can be viewed as "mini guidelines", useful mostly for representing a single rule that needs to be applied whenever the patient's record is accessed, as opposed to representation of a long-term plan [Peleg *et al.*, 2001]. Their effectiveness (as part of an automated system) in outpatient care has been demonstrated repeatedly, and more recently (especially for promoting preventive care, such as pneumococcal vaccination), also in hospital environments [Dexter *et al.*, 2001]. It is now universally agreed that conforming to state-of-the-art guidelines is the best way to improve the quality of medical care, a fact that had been rigorously demonstrated [Grimshaw and Russel, 1993], while reducing the escalating costs of medical care. Clinical guidelines are most useful at the point of care (typically, when the care provider has access to the patient's record), such as at the time of order entry by the care provider.

The application of clinical guidelines by care providers typically involves collecting and interpreting considerable amounts of data over time, applying standard therapeutic or diagnostic plans in an episodic fashion, and revising those plans when necessary. Clinical guidelines can be viewed as reusable *skeletal plans* that, when applied to a particular patient, need to be refined by a care provider over significant time periods, while often leaving considerable room for flexibility in the achievement of particular goals. Another possible view, however, is that clinical guidelines are a set of *constraints* regarding the *process* of applying the guideline (i.e., care-provider actions) and its desired *outcomes* (i.e., patient states), that is, process (care-provider *action*) and outcome (patient *state*) *intentions* [Shahar *et al.*, 1998]. These constraints are mostly *temporal*, or at least have a significant temporal dimension, since most clinical guidelines concern the care of chronic patients, or at least specify a care plan to be applied over a significant period.

Most clinical guidelines are text-based and inaccessible to the physicians who most need them. Even when guidelines exist in electronic format, and even when that format is accessible online, physicians rarely have the time and means to decide which of the multiple guidelines best pertains to their patient, and, if so, exactly what does applying that guideline to the particular patient entail. Furthermore, recent health-care organizational and professional developments often reduce guideline accessibility, by creating a significant information overload on health care professionals. These professionals need to process more data than ever, in continuously shortening periods of time. Similar considerations apply to the task of assessing the quality of clinical-guideline application.

To support the needs of health-care providers as well as administrators, and ensure continuous quality of care, more sophisticated information processing tools are needed. Due to limitations of state-of-the-art technologies, analyzing unstructured text-based guidelines is not feasible. Thus, there is an urgent need to facilitate guideline dissemination and application using machine-readable representations and automated computational methods.

Several of the major tasks involved in guideline-based care, which would benefit from automated support, include specification (authoring) and maintenance of clinical guidelines, retrieval of guidelines appropriate to each patient, runtime application of guidelines, and retrospective assessment of the quality of the application of the guidelines.

It is important to emphasize that supporting guideline-based care does not in any way imply substitution of the attending physician by a program; rather, it implies creation of a *dialog* between a care provider and an automated support system, each of which has its relative strengths. For example, physicians have better access to certain types of patient-specific clinical information (such as their odor, skin appearance, and mental state) and to general medical and commonsense knowledge. Automated systems have better and more accurate access to guideline specifications and detect more easily pre-specified complex temporal patterns in the patient's data. Thus, the key word in supporting guideline-based care is *synergy*.

19.6.2 Automated Support to Guideline-Based care

Several approaches to the support of guideline-based care permit hypertext browsing of guidelines via the World Wide Web [Barnes and Barnett, 1995] but do not directly use the patient's electronic medical record. Several simplified approaches to the task of supporting guideline-based care that *do* use the patient's data encode guidelines as elementary state-transition tables or as situation-action rules dependent on the electronic medical record, as was attempted using the Arden syntax [Sherman *et al.*, 1995]. An established (ASTM) medical-knowledge representation standard, the Arden Syntax [Hripcsak *et al.*, 1994], represents medical knowledge as independent units called Medical Logical Modules (MLMs), and separates the general medical logic (encoded in the Arden syntax) from the institution-specific component (encoded in the query language and terms of the local database).

However, rule-based approaches typically do not include an intuitive representation of the guideline's clinical logic, have no semantics for the different types of clinical knowledge represented, lack the ability to easily represent and reuse guidelines and guideline components as well as higher, meta-level problem-solving knowledge, cannot represent intended ambiguity (e.g., when there are several options and several pro and con considerations, but no single action is, or should be, clearly prescribed) [Peleg *et al.*, 2001], and do not support application of guidelines over extended periods of time, [Peleg *et al.*, 2001] as is necessary to support the care of chronic patients. On the other hand, as Peleg et al. also point out, such approaches do have the advantage of simplicity when only a single alert or reminder is called for, and the heavier machinery of higher-level languages is uncalled for and might even be disruptive. Thus, they might be viewed as complementary to complex guideline representations.

During the past 20 years, there have been several efforts to support complex guideline-based care over time in automated fashion. Examples of architectures and representation languages include ONCOCIN [Tu *et al.*, 1989], T-HELPER [Musen *et al.*, 1992], DILEMMA [Herbert *et al.*, 1995], EON [Musen *et al.*, 1996], Asgaard [Shahar *et al.*, 1998], PRO*forma* [Fox *et al.*, 1998], the guideline interchange format (GLIF) [Ohno-Machado *et al.*, 1998; Peleg *et al.*, 2001], the European PRESTIGE project [Gordon and Veloso, 1996], and the British Prodigy project [Johnson *et al.*, 2000].

Most of the approaches can be described as being *prescriptive* in nature, specifying *what* actions need to be performed and *how*. However, several systems, notably Miller's VT-Attending system [Miller, 1986], have used a *critiquing* approach, in which the physician suggests a specific therapy plan and gets feedback from the program. The Asgaard project [Shahar *et al.*, 1998] uses the *Asbru* language, which supports both an expressive, time-oriented, prescriptive specification of recommended interventions, and a set of meta-level annotations, such as process and outcome intentions of the guidelines, which support also a critiquing approach for retrospective quality assessment. Access to the original process and outcome intentions of the guideline designers supports forming an automated critique of *where*, *when*, and by *how much* the care provider seems to be deviating from the suggested process of applying the guideline, and in *what way* and *to what extent* the care provider's outcome intentions might still be similar to those of the author's (e.g., she might be using a different process to achieve the same outcome intention). Thus, effective quality assessment includes searching for a reasonable *explanation* that tries to understand the care provider's rational by comparing it to the *design rational* of the guideline's author. (It is perhaps a specific instance of a rather general observation, that critiquing an agent's actions must always include at least an attempt to understand that agent's reasons for such actions).

Other recent approaches to support guideline use at the point of care enable a Web-based connection from an electronic patient record to an HTML-based set of rules, such as is done in the ActiveGuidelines model [Tang and Young, 2000], which is embedded in a commercial electronic medical record system. However, such approaches have no standardized, sharable, machine-readable representation of guidelines that can support multiple tasks such as automated application and quality assurance, and are not intended for representation of complex care plans over time. A recent framework, GEM, enables structuring of a text document containing a clinical guideline as an *extensible markup language* (*XML*) document, using a well-defined XML schema [Shiffman *et al.*, 2000]. However, GEM is an application running on a stand-alone computer, and the framework does not support any computational tools that can interpret the resulting semi-structured text, since it does not include a formal language that provides a clear computational model. Thus, it seems that the future lies with architectures that support the full life cycle, from guideline specification by experts, through a computable representation, to a locally customized guideline; GLIF3 is one of the architectures supporting such a life cycle [Peleg *et al.*, 2001].

Furthermore, specialized architectures have been designed to support incremental markup (semi-structuring) of free-text guidelines by an expert physician, followed by full structuring of the resulting guideline into a formal, machine-comprehensible representation. The different phases exploit the domain expert's understanding of the guideline semantics and the knowledge engineer's understanding of the target guideline specification language syntax and semantics. Thus, the resultant *hybrid* guideline library includes guidelines in different formats, depending on where they are in the specification life cycle; furthermore, each guideline might be represented in a *hybrid* format that includes free text, structured text, and machine-comprehensible code. Such an architecture has been implemented successfully by the Digital Electronic GuidelinE Library (DEGEL) project [Shahar *et al.*, 2003b; Shahar *et al.*, 2003c].

In summary, there is a clear need for effective guideline-support tools at the point of care and at the point of critiquing, which will relieve the current information overload on both care providers and administrators. To be effective, these tools need to be grounded in the patient's record, must use standard medical vocabularies, should have clear semantics, must facilitate knowledge maintenance and sharing, and need to be sufficiently expressive to explicitly capture the design rational (process and outcome intentions) of the guideline's author, while leaving flexibility at application time to the attending physician and their local favorite methods.

19.7 Temporal-Data Maintenance: Time-Oriented Medical Databases

In addition to *reasoning* about time-oriented medical data, it is also necessary to consider the *management* of these data: insertion, deletion, and query–a task often referred to as *temporal-data maintenance*.

Initially, systems that were designed to manage temporal clinical data were based on the flat relational model. These systems were based on time stamping the database tuples: the date of the visit was added to the specific attribute values. Later work, such as the *Time Oriented Database* (*TOD*) project at Stanford during the 1970s by Wiederhold and colleagues, has proposed the use of a specific temporal-query language for clinical data that are structured by a temporally indexed model. The indices of the 3-dimensional structure, which came to be called the *cubic model,* included the *patient*, the *visit*, and the *clinical parameter* measured; the indexed entry was the *value* of the clinical parameter for that patient during that particular visit. Even though such languages were patient oriented and were not based on a generic data model, they were preliminary proposals for an extension of query languages so as to enable the system to retrieve complex temporal properties of stored data. Most query languages and data models used for clinical data management were application-dependent; thus, developers had to provide ad-hoc facilities for querying and manipulating specific temporal aspects of data.

Recent work on temporal clinical databases presents a more general approach and highlights the true requirements for storage and maintenance of time-oriented medical data. An issue that was explored in depth in the general temporal-database area is the one concerning what *kinds* of temporal dimensions need to be supported by the temporal database. Three different temporal dimensions have been distinguished [Snodgrass and Ahn, 1986]: (1) the *transaction time*, that is, the time at which data are stored in the database (e.g., the time in which the assertion "white blood-cell (WBC) count is 7600" was entered into the patient's medical record); (2) the *valid time*, that is, the time at which the data are true for the modeled real world entity (e.g., the time in which the WBC-count was, in fact, 7600), and (3) the *user-defined time*, whose meaning is related to the application and thus is defined by the user (e.g., the time in which the WBC count was determined in the laboratory). Using this temporal-dimension taxonomy, four kinds of databases can be defined: (a) *snapshot databases*, based on flat, timeless data models; (b) *rollback databases*, which represent explicitly only the transaction time (e.g., a series of updates to the patient's *current* address stamped by the time in which the modification was recorded), (c) *historical databases*, which represent explicitly only the valid time (thus, they represent the best current knowledge about the WBC value on 1/12/97, and allow future updates referring to data on 1/12/97, but keep no record of the updates themselves), and (d) what is now called *bitemporal databases*, which represent explicitly both transaction time and valid time and thus are both historical and rollback. Thus, in a bitemporal database it can be represented explicitly that, on January 17, 1997 (transaction time), the physician entered in the patient's record the fact that on January 12, 1997 (valid time) the patient had an allergic reaction to a sulpha-type drug. Figure 19.4 plots the transaction time and the valid time of a particular fact as two temporal axes. The *transaction* time (and associated interval) recorded in the database can be viewed as the period during which a *belief* was held about the value of the *valid* time, in which the fact *actually* held in reality.

Typically, only the *valid time*, at which the clinical data or conclusions were true, has been considered in clinical systems. However, storing also the *transaction time*, at which the data were inserted into the patient's record, has multiple benefits, such as being able to restore the state of the database that was true (i.e.: what was known) when the physician or a decision-support system decided on a particular therapeutic action, an ability that has significance both for explanation and legal purposes. Another temporal dimension of information considered recently is the *decision-time* [Gal *et al.*, 1994]: the decision time of a therapy, for example, could be different from both the valid time during which the therapy is administered and from the transaction time, at which the data related to the therapy are inserted into the database.

Bitemporal databases are thus the only representation mode that fulfills the necessary functional and legal requirements for time-oriented medical databases, although historical and rollback databases are currently most common. There are multiple advantages for the use of bitemporal databases in medical information systems, including the ability to answer both research and legal questions (e.g., "When another physician prescribed a sulpha-type medication on January 14 1997, did she know at that time that the patient had an allergic reaction to a sulpha drug on a previous date?")

19.7.1 Maintenance of both clinical raw data and their abstractions

Several recent systems allow not only the modeling of complex clinical concepts at the database level, but also the maintenance of certain inference operations at that level. For example, *active databases* [Widom and Ceri, 1996] can also store and query derived data; these data are obtained by the execution of rules that are triggered by external events, such as the insertion of patient related data [Caironi *et al.*, 1997].

Furthermore, integrity constraints based on temporal reasoning [Horn *et al.*, 1997] can often be evaluated at the database level, for example to *validate* clinical data during their acquisition. This validation, however, requires domain-specific knowledge (e.g., height is a monotonically increasing function, and should never decrease, at least for children; weight cannot increase by more then a certain number of pounds a day). As we shall see, ultimately, maintenance of both raw data and abstractions requires an integration of the temporal reasoning and temporal maintenance tasks.

19.7.2 Merging temporal reasoning and temporal maintenance: Temporal mediators

When building a time-oriented decision-support application, one needs to consider the mode of integration between the application, the data-abstraction process (essentially, a temporal-reasoning task), and the temporal-maintenance aspect of the system. Both the temporal-reasoning and the temporal-abstraction processes are needed to support clinical tasks such as diagnosis, monitoring, and therapy.

Data abstraction (see Section 19.2) is a critical auxiliary process. It is usually deployed in the context of a higher-level problem solving system, it is knowledge-based, and it operates in a goal- or event-driven fashion, or both. The knowledge used by the data abstraction

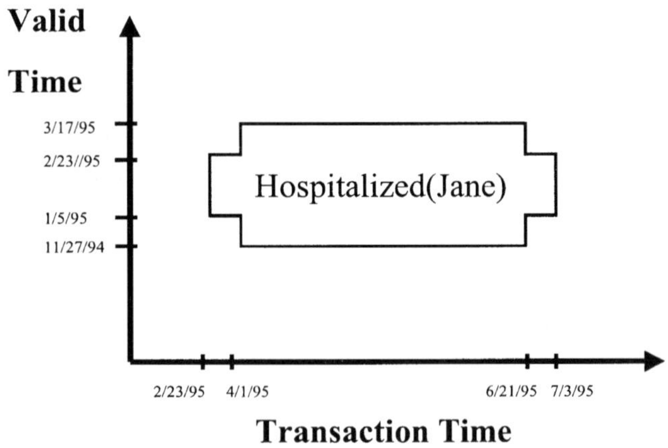

Figure 19.4: Transaction time versus valid time in a bitemporal database.

According to the database transactions, Jane was considered, between Feb. 23, 1995, to April 1, 1995 (transaction time), to have been hospitalized from Jan 5, 1995, till Feb. 23, 1995 (valid time). The (valid) period of her hospitalization was then revised, according to her claim, to have been Nov. 27, 1994, ti!l March 17, 1995. This was considered as the valid period until, on June 21, 1995, new documents were found. The hospitalization period was then recorded again as the shorter period, and stayed this way until the day this database was looked at, on July 2, 1995.

process comprises both specialist knowledge and so called 'world' knowledge, i.e. common-sense knowledge which is assumed domain and even task independent. The knowledge is organized on the basis of some *ontology* that defines the classes of concepts and the types of relations among them (see Section 19.8).

In this section we briefly discuss the mode of integration between a problem solving system and a data abstraction process. This mode can be described as *loosely coupled* or *tightly coupled* and denotes the level of generality, and thus degree of reusability, of the data abstraction process. A *loosely-coupled* process implies that the data abstraction process is domain independent (e.g. it can be integrated with any diagnostic system irrespective of its medical domain), task independent (e.g. it can be integrated with different reasoning tasks, such as diagnosis, monitoring, prognosis, etc., within the same medical domain), or both (e.g. it can be integrated with different reasoning tasks applied to different domains). A *tightly coupled* process, on the other hand, implies that the data-abstraction process is an embedded component of the problem solving system; thus, its usability outside that system is limited.

In general, one can conceive of three basic modes of integration among the temporal-data abstraction process, the temporal-data management process, a medical decision-support application (e.g., diagnosis, therapy), and a time-oriented database (Figure 19.5):

- Incorporating the abstraction process within the database: the drawbacks include relying on the database management system's language, typically simpler than a programming langauge, and forming a tight coupling to the particular syntax and semantics of the database used;

- Adding a data-management capability to the application system, assuming an inherent data-abstraction capability: the drawbacks include the problem of duplicating quite a few of the functions already inherent to a database management system, the lack of ability to take advantage of the sophisticated data-management and query-optimization techniques implemented within the database, and tight coupling to the particular application, without the ability to reuse the abstraction mechanisms elsewhere; and

- Out-sourcing both the temporal-data management and the temporal-data abstraction capabilities, by encapsulating them within an intermediate *mediator* that is independent of either.

The concept of a mediator has been proposed in the early 1990s [Wiederhold, 1992]. It is called a *mediator* because it serves as an intermediate layer of processing between client applications and databases. As a result, the mediator is tied to neither a particular application, domain, or task, nor to a particular database [Wiederhold and Genesereth, 1997]. By combining the functions of temporal reasoning and temporal maintenance within one architecture, which we refer to as a *temporal mediator* (or, more precisely, a *temporal-abstraction mediator*, since it should include also the data-abstraction capability), a transparent interface can be created to the patient's time-oriented database. An example of such an architecture was the Tzolkin temporal-mediation module [Nguyen *et al.*, 1999], which supported the EON guideline-based–therapy system [Musen *et al.*, 1996]. The Tzolkin module combined the RÉSUMÉ temporal-abstraction system [Shahar and Musen, 1996], the Chronus temporal-maintenance system [Das and Musen, 1994], and a controller into a

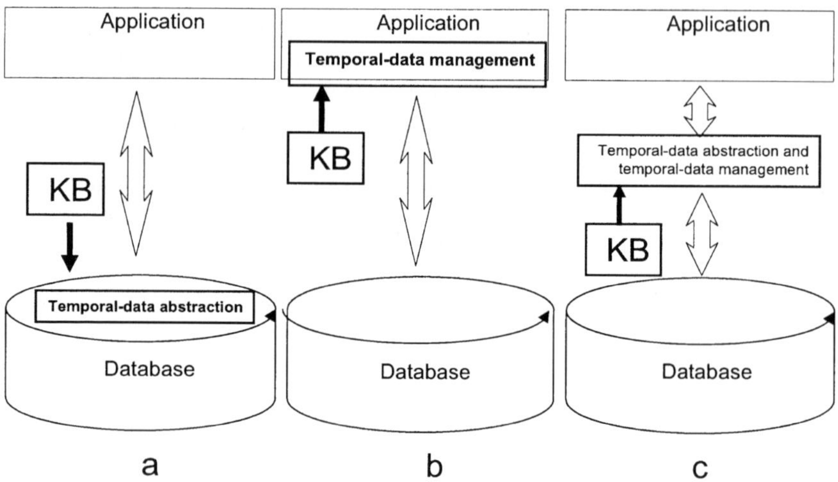

Figure 19.5: Three modes of integrating the temporal-data abstraction and temporal-data management processes with a medical decision-support application (e.g., diagnosis, therapy) and a time-oriented database.

(a) Incorporating the abstraction process within the database;

(b) adding a data-management capability to the application system, assuming an inherent data-abstraction capability;

(c) encapsulating the temporal-data management and the temporal-data abstraction capabilities within an intermediate *mediator* that is independent of either.

unified temporal-mediation server. The Tzolkin server answered complex temporal queries, regarding either raw clinical data or their abstractions, submitted by care providers or clinical decision-support applications, hiding the internal division of computational tasks from the user (or from the clinical decision-support application). When users asked complex temporal queries including abstract terms that do not exist in the database, the Tzolkin controller loaded the necessary raw data from the database, used RÉSUMÉ to abstract the data, saved the results in a temporary database, and used Chronus to access the results and answer the original temporal query. Modern architectures, such as the Chronus-2 temporal mediator [O'Connor *et al.*, 2002], which uses a highly expressive temporal-query language, and the IDAN temporal-abstraction architecture [Boaz and Shahar, 2003] have extended the temporal-mediation idea. For example, the IDAN architecture is more uniform, because a subset of the temporal- and value-constraints language used in its internal temporal-abstraction computational component, the ALMA system, is used in the query interface of the temporal-abstraction mediator's controller (the process that parses the original query and decides, with the help of the ALMA system, what data and knowledge should be used). Thus, ALMA, which is a more abstract implementation of the RÉSUMÉ system, can also process the query's temporal constraints. Unifying both tasks avoids re-implementation of the constraint-satisfaction process and the use of a temporary storage space. IDAN is also fully distributed and access multiple clinical databases, medical knowledge bases, and, in theory, multiple computational temporal-abstraction modules. An IDAN session starts by defining a particular data, knowledge, and processing configuration and then referring raw-data or abstract-concept queries to the controller [Boaz and Shahar, 2003].

Thus, the ideal situation is to have a data abstraction process that is both domain- and task- independent, and implemented within a temporal-abstraction mediator. Whether this is fully achievable remains to be seen, although some significant steps have been taken in this direction (as illustrated by the application of Shahar's KBTA method to several different medical domains and tasks, and even to several nonmedical domains and tasks (see Section 19.8.1)).

The looseness or otherwise of coupling between a data abstraction process and a problem solving system can be decided on the basis of the following questions:

Is the ontology underlying the specific knowledge domain independent? If so, then removing that knowledge and incorporating a knowledge-acquisition component that functions to fill the given knowledge base with the relevant knowledge from another domain will result in a traditional skeletal system for data abstraction, applicable to different domains for the same task.

Is the overall ontology task independent? If so, we can obtain a skeletal system for data abstraction, applicable to different tasks within the same domain.

Is the specific knowledge task independent? If so, the data abstraction process is already applicable to different tasks within the same domain.

Do generated abstractions constitute the system's main and final output? If so, the data abstraction process is strongly coupled to the problem solving system. In the spirit of the new generation of knowledge-engineering methodologies, the objective should be to form a *library* of generic data abstraction methods, with different underlying ontologies and computational mechanisms, e.g., [Shahar, 1997; Russ, 1995].

19.7.3 Visual interactive exploration of the output of a temporal-abstraction or a temporal-maintenance process

Physicians and other care providers are not database experts and should not be expected to be familiar with the internal workings of either a temporal-reasoning or a temporal-maintenance system or even with the interface to a temporal-abstraction mediator. Thus, one challenge is to provide them with easy to use, perhaps even graphic, temporal-query interfaces that enable them to take advantage of the sophisticated architectures that are being built on top of the clinical, time-oriented electronic patient records [Combi *et al.*, 1994]. Furthermore, many queries might be unnecessary if useful visualization interfaces exist. The semantics of these interfaces (e.g., deciding automatically which abstraction level of the same set of parameters to show and at what temporal granularity) might draw upon the domain-specific knowledge base. An early example was a framework for visualization of time-oriented clinical data [Cousins and Kahn, 1991], which defined a small but powerful set of domain-independent graphic operators with well defined semantics, and a domain-specific representation of reasonable temporal-granularities for a presentation of various entities in the specific clinical domain.

More sophisticated interfaces might be built by taking advantage, for instance, of formally-represented knowledge about time-oriented properties of clinical data in specific clinical areas, to build powerful graphical interfaces for visualization and exploration of multiple levels of abstractions of time-oriented clinical data. Indeed, this approach has been taken by the developers of the Knowledge-based Navigation of Abstractions for Visualization and Explanation (KNAVE) architecture [Shahar and Cheng, 1999; Shahar and Cheng, 2000], later extended into the KNAVE-II framework [Shahar *et al.*, 2003a]. The KNAVE-II visualization and exploration operators support subtasks such as *browsing* both raw data and abstract concepts; *exploration* of semantically related concepts, such as entities from which the browsed concept is abstracted or that can be derived from it; several methods of *zooming* into the data at various levels of temporal and semantic granularity; use of both calendar-based timelines as well as *clinically-significant timelines* (e.g., time since transplantation); *explanation* of derived concepts in terms of both the data they are dependent on and the specific medical knowledge used to derive them; and *dynamic sensitivity analysis* of the effects of data and knowledge modification on derived concepts.

19.8 General Ontologies for Temporal Reasoning in Medicine

As we emphasized in Section 19.2, abstraction of time-oriented medical data is a crucial temporal-reasoning task that is an implicit or explicit aspect of most diagnostic, therapeutic, quality-assessment or research-oriented applications. It also bridges the gap noted in Section 19.1.4, regarding the mismatch between general theories of temporal reasoning and the needs of medical tasks. Thus, we conclude this chapter with a detailed presentation of two temporal-data abstraction ontologies that address the issue of providing a comprehensive conceptual model for that process: Shahar's *knowledge-based temporal-abstraction* method and ontology, whose main motivation was clinical-data summarization and query for therapy and research; and Keravnou's *time-object* ontology, whose main motivation was the diagnostic task and the formal reasoning embedded in it.

19.8.1 Shahar's Knowledge-Based Temporal-Abstraction Ontology

Shahar defined a knowledge-based framework, including a formal temporal ontology [Shahar, 1997] and a set of computational mechanisms using that ontology [Shahar and Musen, 1996; Shahar, 1998; Shahar, 1999; Chakravarty and Shahar, 2000; Chakravarty and Shahar, 2001] specific to the task of creating abstract, interval-based concepts from time-stamped clinical data: the *knowledge-based temporal-abstraction* (KBTA) *method*. The KBTA method decomposes the temporal-abstraction task into five subtasks; a formal mechanism was proposed for solving each subtask (Figure 19.6). The KBTA framework emphasizes the explicit representation of the knowledge required for abstraction of time-oriented clinical data, and facilitates its acquisition, maintenance, reuse, and sharing. The KBTA method has been implemented by the RÉSUMÉ system and evaluated in several clinical domains, such as guideline-based care of oncology and AIDS patients, monitoring of children's growth, and management of patients who have insulin-dependent diabetes [Shahar and Musen, 1996].

The knowledge-based temporal-abstraction ontology

The KBTA theory defines the following set of entities:

1. The basic time primitives are *time stamps* $T \in T_i$. Time stamps are structures (e.g., dates) that can be mapped, by a time-standardization function $f_S(T_i)$, into an integer amount of any element of a set of predefined *temporal granularity units* $G_i \in \Gamma$ (e.g., DAY). A *zero-point* time stamp (the start of the positive time line) must exist. Time stamps are therefore either positive or negative shifts from the zero point measured in the G_i units. (Intuitively, the 0 point might be grounded in each domain to different absolute, "real-world," time points: the patient's age, the start of the therapy, the first day of the twentieth century.) The domain must have a time unit G_0 of the lowest granularity (e.g., second); there must exist a mapping from any integer amount of granularity units G_i into an integer amount of G_0. (The time unit G_0 can be a task-specific choice.) A finite negative or positive integer amount of G_i units is a *time measure*.

   The special symbols $+\infty$ and $-\infty$ are both time stamps and time measures, denoting the furthest future and the most remote past, respectively. Any two time stamps must belong to either a precedence relation or an equivalence relation defined on the set of pairs of time stamps. The precedence relation corresponds to a temporal order; the equivalence relation denotes temporal equivalence for the domain. The $-\infty$ time stamp precedes any other time stamp; the $+\infty$ time stamp follows (is preceded by) all other time stamps. Subtraction of any time stamp from another must be defined and should return a time measure. Addition or subtraction of a time measure to or from a time stamp must return a time stamp.

2. A *time interval* I is an ordered pair of time stamps representing the interval's end points: [*I*.start, *I*.end]. *Time points* Ti are therefore represented as zero-length intervals where *I*.start = *I*.end. Propositions can be interpreted only over time intervals.

   As will be clear from the rest of the definitions of the TA ontology, the set of points included in a time interval depends on the proposition interpreted over that interval.

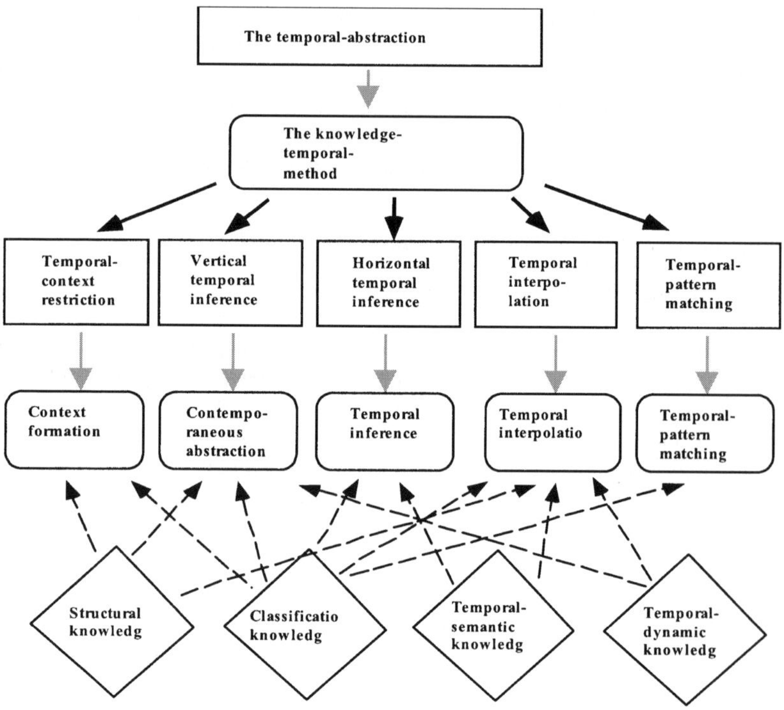

Figure 19.6: The knowledge-based temporal-abstraction (KBTA) method.

The TA *task* is decomposed by the KBTA *method* into five *subtasks*. Each subtask can be performed by one of five TA *mechanisms*. The TA mechanisms depend on four domain- and task-specific *knowledge types*. Rectangle = task; oval = method or mechanism; diamond = knowledge type; striped arrow = decomposed-into relation; full arrow = performed-by relation; dashed arrow = used-by relation.

A time interval can be closed on both sides (in the case of state-type and pattern-type parameter propositions and interpretation contexts), open on both sides (in the case of gradient- and rate-type abstractions), or closed on the left and open on the right (in the case of event propositions).

3. *interpretation context* $\Xi \in \Xi$ is a proposition. Intuitively, it represents a state of affairs that, when interpreted (logically) over a time interval, can change the interpretation (abstraction) of one or more parameters within the scope of that time interval. Thus, "the drug insulin has an effect on blood glucose during this interval" changes the interpretation of the state of the blood-glucose level, by suggesting a different definition of the value low. is-a and subcontext relations are defined over the set of interpretation contexts.*Basic* interpretation contexts are atomic propositions. An interpretation context in conjunction with one of its subcontexts can create a *composite interpretation context.* Composite interpretation contexts are interpretation contexts. Formally, the structure $<\Xi_i,\Xi_j>$ is an interpretation context, if the ordered pair (Ξ_j, Ξ_i) belongs to the sub-context relation (i.e., Ξ_j is a sub-context of Ξ_i). In general, if the structure $<\Xi_1,\Xi_2,\ldots,\Xi_i>$ is a (composite) interpretation context, and the ordered pair (Ξ_j,Ξ_i) belongs to the sub-context relation, then the structure $<\Xi_1,\Xi_2,\ldots,\Xi_i,\Xi_j>$ is a (composite) interpretation context. Intuitively, composite interpretation contexts allow us to define increasingly specific contexts (e.g., a specific drug regimen that is a part of a more general clinical protocol), or combinations of different contexts, for interpretation of various parameters. Composite interpretation contexts represent a combination of *contemporaneous* interpretation contexts whose *conjunction* denotes a new context that has significance for the interpretation of one or more parameters. Finally, *generalized* and *non-convex interpretation contexts* are special types of contexts that enable, when present, the joining of propositions formed within different context intervals. The first allows the generalization of propositions of similar type that hold in different but temporally adjacent contexts into a proposition that holds in a more general context. The second allows the aggregation of propositions of similar types that hold in similar but temporally disjoint contexts into a proposition that holds over a (temporally) non-convex interval within a corresponding non-convex context interval (e.g., blood-glucose abstractions before breakfast over several consecutive days).

4. A *context interval* is a structure $<\Xi, I>$, consisting of an interpretation context Ξ and a temporal interval *I*. Intuitively, a context interval represents an interpretation context interpreted over a time interval; the interpretation of one or more parameters is different within the temporal scope of that interval. Thus, the effects of chemotherapy form an interpretation context that can hold over several weeks, within which the values of hematological parameters might be abstracted differently.

5. An *event proposition* $e \in E$ (or an *event*, for short, when no ambiguity exists) represents the occurrence of an external volitional action or process, such as the administration of a drug (as opposed to a measurable datum, such as temperature). Events have a series a_i of *event attributes* (e.g dose) and a corresponding series N_i of *attribute values*. (Typically, events are controlled by a human or an automated agent, and thus neither are they measured data, nor can they be abstracted from the other input data.)

   An is-a hierarchy (in the usual sense) of *event schemata* (or event types) exists. Event schemata have a list of attributes a_i, where each attribute has a domain of possible values V_i, but do not necessarily contain any corresponding attribute values. Thus, an *event proposition* is an event schema in which each attribute a_i is mapped to some value $N_i \in V_i$. A PART-OF relation is defined over the set of event schemata. If the pair of event schemata (*ei*, *ej*) belongs to the part-of relation, then event schema *ei* can be a *sub-event* of an event schema *ej* (e.g., a Clinical-protocol event can have several parts, all of them Medication events).

6. An *event interval* is a structure $<e, I>$, consisting of an event proposition *e* and a time interval *I*. The time interval *I* represents the duration of the event.

7. A *parameter schema* (or a *parameter*, for short) $\pi \in \Pi$ is, intuitively, a measurable aspect or a describable state of the world, such as a patient's temperature. Parameter schemata have various *properties*, such as a domain V_π of possible symbolic or numeric values, measurement units, and a measurement scale (which can be one of nominal, ordinal, interval, or ratio, corresponding to the standard distinction in statistics among types of measurement*). Not all properties need have values in a parameter schema. An is-a hierarchy (in the usual sense) of parameter schemata exists. The combination $<\pi, \Xi>$ of a parameter π and an interpretation context Ξ is an *extended parameter schema* (or an *extended parameter*, for short). Extended parameters are parameters (e.g., blood glucose in the context of insulin action, or platelet count in the context of chemotherapy effects). Note that an extended parameter can have properties, such as possible domains of value, that are different from that of the original (non-extended) parameter (e.g., in a specific context, a parameter might have a more refined set of possible values). Extended parameters also have a special property, a $N \in V_\pi$. Values often are known only at runtime.

   Intuitively, parameters denote either input (usually raw) data, or any level of abstraction of the raw data (up to a whole pattern). For instance, the Hemoglobin level is a parameter, the White-blood–cell count is a parameter, the Temperature level is a parameter, and so is the Bone-marrow–toxicity level (which is abstracted from Hemoglobin and other parameters).

   The combination of a parameter, a parameter value, and an interpretation context—that is, the tuple $<\pi$, N, $\Xi>$ (i.e., an extended parameter and a value)—is called a *parameter proposition* (e.g., "the state of Hemoglobin has the value low in the context of therapy by AZT"). A mapping exists from all parameter propositions and the properties of their corresponding parameter (or extended parameter) schema into specific property values.

   Much of the knowledge about abstraction of higher-level concepts over time depends on knowledge of specific parameter-proposition properties, such as persistence over time of a certain parameter with a certain value within a particular context. Different TA mechanisms typically require knowledge about different parameter properties of the same parameter propositions.

*Nominal-scale parameters have values that can be listed, but that cannot be ordered (e.g., color). Ordinal-scale parameters have values that can be ordered, but the intervals among these values are not meaningful by themselves and are not necessarily equal (e.g., military ranks). Interval-scale parameters have scale with meaningful, comparable intervals, although a ratio comparison is not necessarily meaningful (e.g., temperature measured on a Celsius scale). Ratio-scale parameters have, in addition to all these properties, a fixed zero point (e.g., height); thus, a ratio comparison, such as "twice as tall," is meaningful regardless of the height measurement unit.

Primitive parameters are parameters that play the role of raw data in the particular domain in which the TA task is being solved. They cannot be inferred by the TA process from any other parameters (e.g., laboratory measurements). They can appear only in the input of the TA task.

Abstract parameters are parameters that play the role of intermediate concepts at various levels of abstraction; these parameters can be part of the output of the TA task, having been *abstracted* from other parameters and events, or they may be given as part of the input (e.g., the value of the state of Hemoglobin is moderate_anemia). There is an abstracted-into relationship between one or more parameters and an abstract parameter. Each pair of parameters that belongs to an abstracted-into relation represents only one abstraction step; that is, the abstracted-into relation is not transitive. It is also irreflexive and antisymmetric.

Constant parameters are parameters that are considered atemporal in the context of the particular interpretation task that is being performed, so their values are not expected to be time-dependent (e.g., the patient's gender, the patient's address, the patient's father's height). There are few, if any, truly constant parameters. (Indeed, using explicit semantic properties, constants can be represented as fluents with a particular set of temporal-semantic inferential properties, such as infinite persistence into the past and future, thus removing, in effect, the traditional distinction between temporal and atemporal variables.) It is often useful to distinguish between (1) *case-specific constants*, which are specific to the particular case being interpreted and which appear in the runtime input (e.g., the patient's date of birth), and (2) *case-independent constants*, which are inherent to the overall task, and which are typically prespecified or appear in the domain ontology (e.g., the local population's distribution of heights).

8. *Abstraction functions* $\theta \in \Theta$ are unary or multiple-argument functions from one or more parameters to an abstract parameter. The "output" abstract parameters can have one of several *abstraction types* (which are equivalent to the abstraction function used). We distinguish among at least three basic abstraction types: *state*, *gradient*, and *rate*. (Other abstraction functions and therefore types, such as *acceleration* and *frequency*, can be added). These abstraction types correspond, respectively, to a classification (or computational transformation) of the parameter's value, the sign of the derivative of the parameter's value, and the magnitude of the derivative of the parameter's value during the interval (e.g., low, decreasing, and fast abstractions for the Platelet-count parameter). The state abstraction is always possible, even with qualitative parameters having only a nominal scale (e.g., different values of the Skin-color parameter can be mapped into the state-abstraction value red); the gradient and rate abstractions are meaningful for only those parameters that have at least an ordinal scale (e.g., degrees of physical fitness) or an interval scale (e.g., Temperature), respectively.

   The θ abstraction of a parameter schema π is a new parameter schema $\theta(\pi)$—a parameter different from any of the arguments of the θ function (e.g., *state(Hemoglobin)*, which we will write as *Hemoglobin_state*). This new parameter has its own domain of values and other properties (e.g., scale), typically different from those of the parameters from which it was abstracted. It can also be abstracted further (e.g., *gradient(state(Hemoglobin))*).

   A special type of abstraction function (and a respective proposition type) is *pattern*: A function that creates a temporal pattern from temporal intervals, over which hold parameters, events, contexts, or other patterns (e.g., a quiescent-onset pattern of chronic graft-versus-host disease). Patterns were previously defined as a special abstract-parameter type [Shahar, 1997] but have since been recognized as an independent proposition type. Patterns have interval-based components. Local constraints on these components (e.g. duration) and global constraints among components (e.g. qualitative temporal relations) define the pattern. Patterns can be *linear* or *periodic*.

Statistics such as *minimum*, *maximum*, and *average value* are not abstraction types in this ontology. Rather, these statistics are *functions* on parameter *values* that return simply a *value* of a parameter, possibly during a time interval, often from the domain of the original parameter (e.g., the minimum Hemoglobin value within a time interval *I* can be 8.9 gr./100cc, a value from the domain of Hemoglobin values), rather than a parameter *schema*, which can have a new domain of values (e.g., the Hemoglobin_state can have the value increasing).

9. *parameter interval* is a tuple $<\pi, \nu, \Xi, I>$, where $<\pi, \nu, \Xi>$ is a parameter proposition and *I* is a time interval. If *I* is in fact a time point (i.e., *I*.start = *I*.end), then the tuple can be referred to as a *parameter point*. Intuitively, a parameter interval denotes the value ν of parameter π in the context Ξ during time interval *I*. The value of parameter π at the beginning of interval *I* is denoted as *I*.start.π, and the value of parameter π at the end of interval *I* as *I*.end.π. *Pattern intervals* are defined in a similar fashion.

10. An *abstraction* is a parameter or pattern interval $<\pi, N, \Xi, I>$, where π is an abstract parameter or pattern. If *I* is in fact a time point (i.e., *I* .start = *I*.end), the abstraction can also be referred to as an *abstraction point*; otherwise, we can refer to it as an *abstraction interval*.

11. An *abstraction goal* $\psi \in \Psi$ is a proposition that denotes a particular goal or intention that is relevant to the TA task during some interval (e.g., diagnosis).

12. An *abstraction-goal interval* is a structure $<\psi, I>$, where ψ is an abstraction goal and *I* is a time interval. Intuitively, an abstraction-goal interval represents the fact that an *intention* holds or that a TA *goal* (e.g., the goal of monitoring AIDS patients) should be achieved during the time interval over which it is interpreted. An abstraction-goal interval is used for creating correct interpretation contexts for the interpretation of data.

13. *Induction of context intervals*: Intuitively, context intervals are inferred dynamically (at runtime) by certain event, parameter, or abstraction-goal propositions being true over specific time intervals. The contexts interpreted over these intervals are said to be *induced* by these propositions (e.g., by the event "administration of 4 units of regular insulin"). Certain predefined temporal constraints must hold between the inferred context interval and the time interval over which the inducing proposition is interpreted. For instance, the effect of insulin with respect to changing the interpretation of blood-glucose values might start at least 30 minutes after the start of the insulin administration and might end up to 8 hours after the end of that administration. Two or more context-forming propositions induce a *composite interpretation context*, when the temporal spans of their corresponding induced context intervals intersect, if the

interpretation contexts that hold during these intervals belong to the sub-context relation. *Figure 19.7* shows inducement of context intervals within, after, and even before an inducing event.

Formally, a *dynamic induction relation of a context interval* (*DIRC*) is a relation on propositions and time measures, in which each member is a structure of the form $< \Xi, \varphi, ss, se, es, ee >$ (see explanation below). The symbol Ξ is the interpretation context that is induced. The symbol φ P is the *inducing proposition*: an event, an abstraction-goal, or a parameter proposition. (An event schema is also allowed, as shorthand for the statement that the relation holds for any event proposition representing an assignment of values to the event schema's arguments.) Each of the other four symbols denotes a time measure or the wildcard symbol '*'. A proposition φ that is an inducing proposition in at least one DIRC is a *context-forming proposition*.

The knowledge represented by DIRCs can be used to infer new context intervals at runtime. Intuitively, the inducing proposition is assumed, at runtime, to be interpreted over some time interval *I* with known end points. The four time measures denote, respectively, the temporal distance *ss* between the *start* point of *I* and the *start* point of the induced context interval, the distance *se* between the *start* point of *I* and the *end* point of the induced context interval, the distance *es* between the *end* of *I* and the *start* point of the context interval, and the distance *ee* between the *end* point of *I* and the *end* point of the induced context interval (see Figure 19.7). Note that, typically, only two values are necessary to define the scope of the inferred context interval (more values might create an inconsistency), so that the rest can be undefined (i.e., they can be wildcards, which match any time measure), and that sometimes only one of the values is a finite time measure (e.g., the *ee* distance might be $+\infty$). Note also that the resultant context intervals do not have to span the same temporal scope over which the inducing proposition is interpreted. There are multiple advantages to the DIRC representation, which separates propositions from the contexts that they induce [Shahar, 1997].

Exactly which basic propositions and relations exist in the ontology of the KBTA theory and problem-solving method can now be clarified. They are abstraction goals, event propositions, parameter propositions, interpretation contexts, and DIRCs.

The set of all the relevant event schemata and propositions in the domain, their attributes, and their sub-events forms the domain's *event ontology*. The set of all the potentially relevant contexts and sub-contexts of the domain, whatever their inducing proposition, defines a *context ontology* for the domain. The set of all the relevant parameters and parameter propositions in the domain and their properties forms the domain's *parameter ontology*. The set of all patterns and their properties form the domain's *pattern ontology*. These four ontologies, together with the set of abstraction-goal propositions and the set of all DIRCs, define the domain's *TA ontology*.

To complete the definition of the TA task, the existence of a set of *temporal queries* is assumed, expressed in a predefined *TA query language* that includes constraints on parameter values and on relations among start-point and end-point values among various time intervals and context intervals. That is, a temporal query is a set of constraints over the components of a set of parameter, pattern, event and context intervals, using the domains and TA ontology. Intuitively, the TA language is used (1) to define the relationship between a pattern-type abstraction and its defining component intervals, and (2) to ask arbitrary queries about the result of the TA inference process.

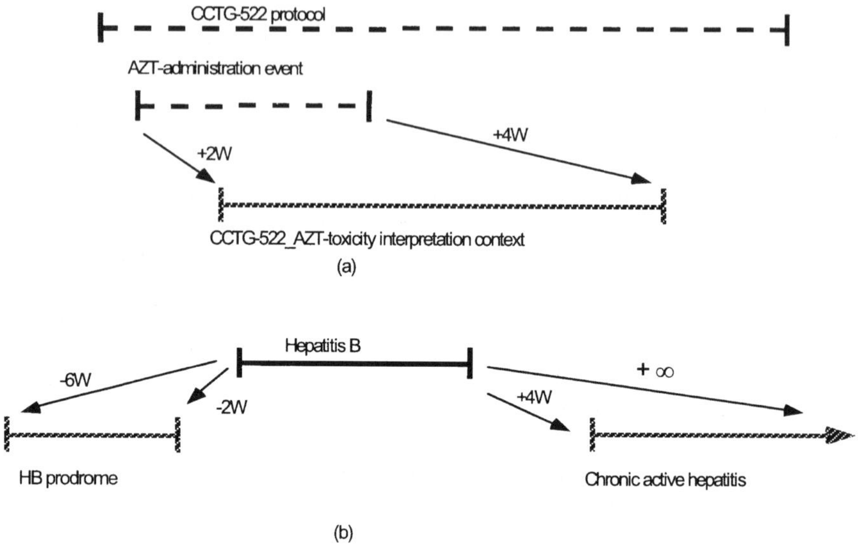

Figure 19.7: Dynamic induction relations of context intervals (DIRCs).

(a) An overlapping direct and prospective AZT-toxicity interpretation context induced by the existence of an AZT-administration event in the context of the CCTG-522 AIDS-treatment experimental protocol. The interpretation context starts 2 weeks after the start of the inducing event, and ends 4 weeks after the end of the inducing event.

(b) *Prospective* (chronic active hepatitis complication) and *retrospective* (hepatitis B prodrome) interpretation contexts, induced by the external assertion or internal conclusion of a hepatitis B abstraction interval, a context-forming abstraction.

Dashed line with bars = event interval; striped line with bars = closed context interval; striped arrow with bars = open context interval; full line with bars = closed abstraction interval.

The *TA task* solved by the KBTA method is defined as follows: Given at least one abstraction-goal interval $< \psi, I >$, a set of event intervals $< e_j, I_j >$, and a set of parameter intervals $< \pi k, \nu k, \Xi k, Ik >$ (Ξ_k) might be the empty interpretation context in the case of primitive parameters), and the domain's temporal-abstraction ontology, produce an *interpretation*—that is, a set of context intervals $< \Xi n, In >$ and a set of (new) abstractions $< \pi_m, \nu_m{}', \Xi_m, I_m >$—such that the interpretation can answer any temporal query about all the abstractions derivable from the transitive closure of the input data and the domain knowledge.

In all of the domains in which the RÉSUMÉ system has been tested, the feasibility of knowledge acquisition, representation, and maintenance was evaluated, and the methodology was applied to various clinical test cases. Both the general temporal-abstraction computational knowledge and the domain-specific temporal-abstraction knowledge were found to be reusable. The RÉSUMÉ system and its various versions had been used to support guideline-based application [Musen *et al.*, 1996] and guideline-based quality assessment of medical care [Shahar *et al.*, 1998], as well as for visualization and exploration of time-oriented patient data and their abstractions [Shahar and Cheng, 1999; Shahar and Cheng, 2000; Shahar *et al.*, 2003a]. The KBTA ontology and the have even been used to successfully model the task of critiquing traffic controller's actions [Shahar and Molina, 1998], a spatio-temporal abstraction task, further demonstrating the generality (with respect to both domain and application) of the KBTA ontology, and the domain-independence of the computational mechanisms implemented within the RÉSUMÉ system.

The Temporal-Abstraction Knowledge-Acquisition Tool

A graphical tool was constructed for automated acquisition of temporal-abstraction knowledge from medical-domain experts [Shahar *et al.*, 1999], using the *Protg* framework. The *Protg* project [Tu *et al.*, 1995] aims to develop a library of highly-reusable, domain-independent, problem-solving method. One advantage of the Protg approach is the production, given the relevant problem-solving-method and domain ontologies, of automated knowledge-acquisition tools, tailored for the selected problem-solving method and domain.

Evaluation of the temporal-abstraction knowledge-acquisition tool regarding its usability, involving experts in domains such as oncology and endocrinology, has been quite encouraging [Shahar *et al.*, 1999]. The experiments proved the feasibility of semi-automated maintenance of temporal-abstraction knowledge by expert care providers.

19.8.2 Keravnou's Time-Object Ontology for Medical Tasks

This subsection presents a time ontology that aims to comprehensively address the many and varied temporal requirements for medical, knowledge-based, problem solving, discussed in Section 19.1. The principal primitives of the proposed ontology are the time-axis and the time-object. The notion of a time-axis supports a rich, multi-dimensional, model of time, where multiple granularities are represented, while the notion of a time-object supports a natural integration of temporal and atemporal aspects of different types of occurrences.

The design goals of Keravnou's proposed time ontology are (a) to provide an adequate level of *abstraction* for medical knowledge engineering purposes; (b) to be adequately *expressive* (c) to 'force' *time* to be treated *as an integral aspect* of the particular problem solving; and (d) overall to result in a uniform and natural amalgamation of temporal knowledge with other essential types of knowledge such as structural and causal knowledge.

Ontological Primitives

The principal primitives of the ontology are the *time-axis* and the *time-object* that respectively model time per se and occurrences. The ontological classes are:

- *Tunits*, the set of *time-units* (granularities).
- *Axes*, the set of discrete *time-axes*.
- *Times(α), the sequence of literal time-values on time-axis α.*
- *Tobjects, the set of time-objects.*
- *Tobjects(α), the subset of Tobjects that have a valid existence on time-axis α.*
- *Pobjects(α), the subset of Tobjects(α) that have a point existence on time-axis α.*
- *Iobjects(α), the subset of Tobjects(α) that have an interval existence on time-axis α.*
- *Props, the set of properties.*
- *Props(μ)* ($\subseteq$Props), *the set of properties of relevance to time-unit μ.*

Time-Units and Time-Axes

Class Tunits defines the possible time-units (granularities) in descending order of grain. Let Tunits = $\{\mu_1, \mu_2, \ldots, \mu_n\}$; $\forall i < j(\mu_i \prec \mu_j)$, where the relation "$x \prec y$" stands for "x is finer in grain than y". Furthermore, μ_i is an integral multiple of μ. For example Tunits = $\{$days, weeks, years$\}$. Relation *scale (μ,μ',s)* gives the scale relation between granularities μ and μ':

Axiom A1: (scale(μ_i, μ_j, s) $\wedge$ s> 1) ($\mu_i \prec \mu_j$)

Axiom A2: (scale(μ_i, μ_j, s) $\wedge$ scale(μ_j, μ_k, s') $\Rightarrow$ scale($\mu_i, \mu_k, s \times s'$)
A time-axis, α, is expressed discretely at a specific granularity, μ (relation *gran(α,μ)* expresses this association), in terms of a chronological sequence of time-values, *Times(α)* = $\{t_1, t_2, \ldots, t_i, \ldots, t_n\}$, given with respect to the *origin* of the time-axis. Times(α) is either a finite or an infinite sequence of time-values. The origin of an *abstract* (i.e. generic) time-axis denotes a generic time-point; a *concrete* time-axis is an instantiation of an abstract time-axis where the origin gets bound to a real time-point. Example time-axes are gestation and infancy with respective granularities gestation-week and month. The basic relation between time-axes is *t-link (α,t,α',t')* that links a time-value on one time-axis with a time-value on another time-axis:

Axiom A3: t-link $(\alpha_i, t_i, \alpha_j, t_j)\Rightarrow$ $(t_i \in$ Times$(\alpha_i) \wedge t_j \in$ Times(α_j)

Axiom A4: (t-link $(\alpha, t_i, \alpha', t_i')$ $\wedge$ t-link $(\alpha, t_j, \alpha', t_j')$ $\wedge$ $(t_i \le t_j) \Rightarrow (t_i' \le t_j')$.
This axiom specifies that t-links between the same pair of time-axes cannot cross each other.

Axiom A5: t-link $(\alpha_i, t_i, \alpha_j, t_j) \wedge$ t-link $(\alpha_j, t_j, \alpha_k, t_k) \Rightarrow$ t-link $(\alpha_i, t_i, \alpha_k, t_k)$
Other relations can be expressed through t-link, such as:

Axiom A6: immediately-before$(\alpha_i, \alpha_j) \Rightarrow$ t-link $(\alpha_i, \mathit{upper\text{-}time}(\alpha_i), \alpha_j, \mathit{lower\text{-}time}(\alpha_j))$.
Functions lower-time, upper-time: Axes $\rightarrow$ Times, return the first and last element of Times (α) for their argument time-axis, α.

Axiom A7: includes$(\alpha_i, \alpha_j) \Leftrightarrow \exists t, t'$ Times(α_i) $\{$t-link $(\alpha_i, t, \alpha_j, \mathit{lower\text{-}time}(\alpha_j)) \wedge$ t-link $(\alpha_i, t', \alpha_j, \mathit{upper\text{-}time}(\alpha_j))$ $\}$

Axiom A4 ensures that $t \leq t'$. If $t = t'$, α_j corresponds to a single point on time-axis α_i. A *spanning-axis* spans a chaining sequence of other time-axes. Its sequence of time-values is the concatenation of the time-values for its component axes and hence it can have a hybrid granularity. Figure 19.8 illustrates a system of spanning and atomic axes modeling developmental periods. Spanning-axes belong to ontological class *Saxes* ($\subset$Axes). Relation *spans* defines a spanning-axis, sα:

Axiom A8: *spans*(sα,$\{\alpha_1, ..., \alpha_n\}$)$\Rightarrow$ *s*$\alpha \in$ **Saxes** $\wedge \forall \alpha_i$; (i = 1,..,n) $\alpha_i \in$ (Axes $\setminus$ $\{$s$\alpha\}$) $\wedge$ $\forall\alpha_i,\alpha_{i+1}$; i = 1,. . . ,n-1 (immediately-before (α_i,α_{i+1}))

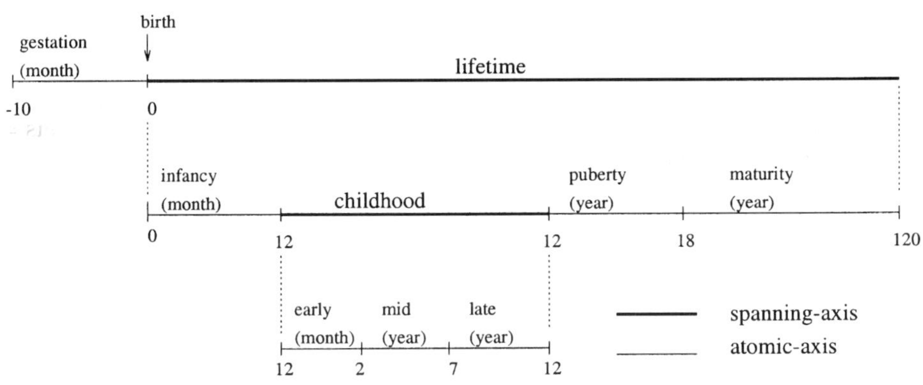

Figure 19.8: A network of abstract time-axes. Atomic-axes are denoted by thin lines and spanning-axes by thick lines.

19.8.3 Time-Objects

A time-object, τ, is a dynamic entity for which time constitutes an integral aspect. It is viewed as a tight coupling between a *property* and an *existence*, where its existence can be expressed with respect to different time-axes. Its existence with respect to the most appropriate time-axis for it, is called the time-object's *main existence*. The two central access functions for time-object entities are:

π: Tobjects $\rightarrow$ Props
ε: Tobjects Axes $\rightarrow$ Eexps

Access function π gives the property, ρ Props, of a time-object, while access function ε gives its absolute existence (lifetime) with respect to a particular time-axis. Eexps is the class of absolute existence expressions (see below). Function $\varepsilon_{\mathcal{T}}$ denotes the partial parameterization of function ε with respect to time-object τ, i.e. the first argument of the general function is fixed to the particular time-object. This notation is used below for functions and relations. A time-object has a *valid* existence on some time-axis iff the granularity of the time-axis is meaningful to the property of the time-object (see below) and the span of time modeled by the time-axis covers (possibly partially) the lifetime of the time-object. If time-object τ does not have a valid existence in the context of time-axis α, $\varepsilon_{\mathcal{T}}(\alpha)$ = (the time-object is undefined with respect to the particular temporal context). If time-object, τ, has a valid existence on some time-axis, α, its *absolute existence* on α, $\varepsilon_{\mathcal{T}}(\alpha)$, is given as:

$\varepsilon_{\mathcal{T}}(\alpha) = < t_{\rm s}, t_{\rm f}, \varsigma >$ where $t_{\rm s}, t_{\rm f} \in Times(\alpha)$;
$t_{\rm s} \leq t_{\rm f}$; and $\varsigma \in \{closed, open, open\text{-}from\text{-}left, open\text{-}from\text{-}right, moving\}$

Time-values t_s and t_f respectively give the (earliest) *start* and (latest) *finish* of the time-object on α. The third element, ς, gives the *status* of τ on α. If the status is *closed* the existence of τ with respect to α, and hence its duration, is fixed. Otherwise the status denotes openness (i.e. vagueness) on the one or both ends of the existence. In the case of openness at the start, function le-fr$_\tau(\alpha)$ gives the latest possible start. Similarly in the case of openness at the finish, function ri-fr$_\tau(\alpha)$ gives the earliest possible finish. Hence a time-object can exist as a *point-object* on some time-axis ($\tau \in$ Pobjects(α) iff $t_s = t_f$) but as an *interval-object* on another time-axis ($\tau \in$ Iobjects(α) iff $t_s < t_f$). In the former case the extent of the time-object is less than the time-unit of the particular time-axis. If a time-object has a point existence under some context, it is treated as a non decomposable entity under that context. Status *moving* is reserved for the special time-object *now* which has a point existence on any relevant concrete time-axis and functions to partition (concrete) time-objects into past, future, or ongoing.

Axiom A9: ε (*now*,α) $\neq \perp \Rightarrow$ $\{$*now* $\in$ Pobjects(α) $\wedge$ $\exists\, t \in$ Times(α) (ε(*now*, α) = $< t, t,$ *moving* $>$)$\}$
Three important types of relations are defined for time-objects, temporal, structural, and causal, relations. In this ontology Allen's set of temporal relations [Allen, 1984] has been adapted and extended to fit the discrete, multidimensional, and multi-granular, model of time. More specifically temporal relations are 3-place relations where the first argument is a time-axis, and instances of these relations may be derived from absolute existence expressions; furthermore new relations based on temporal distance are added and useful disjunctions are directly defined. For illustration the basic relation *overlaps-onto* and the useful compound relations *starts-before* and *disjoint* are defined, where $\varepsilon(\tau_i, \alpha) = < t_{si}, t_{fi}, \varsigma_i >$ and $\varepsilon(\tau_j, \alpha)$ $= < t_{sj}, t_{fj}, \varsigma_j >$:

Axiom A10: *overlaps-onto*$_\alpha(\tau_i, \tau_j) \Leftrightarrow t_{sj} > t_{si} \wedge t_{fj} > t_{fi} \wedge t_{fi} > t_{sj}$

Axiom A11: *starts-before*$_\alpha(\tau_i, \tau_j) \Leftrightarrow$ (*before*$_\alpha(\tau_i, \tau_j) \vee$ *overlaps-onto*$_\alpha(\tau_i, \tau_j) \vee$ *chains-to*$_\alpha(\tau_i, \tau_j) \vee$ *finished-by*$_\alpha(\tau_i, \tau_j) \vee$ *covers*$_\alpha(\tau_i, \tau_j)$) (i.e. iff $t_{si} < t_{sj}$)

Axiom A12: $\mathit{disjoint}_\alpha(\tau_i, \tau_j) \Leftrightarrow (\tau_i >_\alpha \tau_j \vee \tau_j >_\alpha \tau_i)$ (i.e. iff $t_{si} > t_{fj} \vee t_{sj} > t_{fi}$)
The temporal relation between a pair of time-objects can be different on different time-axes. For example two time-objects may overlap on some time-axis but may be considered concurrent on another, coarser granularity, time-axis.The time-object primitive must provide the right level of abstraction for modeling compound dynamic processes such as disease processes and therapy plans. Structural relations enabling the decomposition and composition of time-objects are therefore considered a necessary part of the time-object ontology; through such relations *structural clusters* of time-objects can be formed and hence some situation (e.g. a disorder process) can be expressed at multiple levels of abstraction. The structural relations between time-objects are *isa-component-of*, and its inverse *contains*, and *variant-component*, and its inverse *variant-contains*. The latter two express conditional containment:

Axiom A13: *contains* $(\tau_i, \tau_j) \Leftarrow$ *variant-contains* $(\tau_i, \tau_j, cs) \wedge$ *conds-hold(cs)*
A variant component can only be assumed in some situation (e.g. some patient), if the specified conditions are satisfied. Under any context where a component time-object has a valid existence, the relevant compound time-object does too, and overall a time-object exists within the one that contains it:

Axiom A14: (*isa-component-of* $(\tau_i, \tau_j) \wedge \varepsilon(\tau_i, \alpha) \neq \perp) \Rightarrow \varepsilon(\tau_j, \alpha) \neq \perp$

Axiom A15: (*isa-component-of* $(\tau_i, \tau_j) \wedge \varepsilon(\tau_j, \alpha) = \perp) \Rightarrow \varepsilon(\tau_i, \alpha) = \perp$

Axiom A16: (*isa-component-of* $(\tau_i, \tau_j) \wedge \varepsilon(\tau_i, \alpha) \neq \perp) \Rightarrow \tau_i \subseteq_\alpha \tau_j$
Temporal relation $\tau_i \subseteq_\alpha \tau_j$ means that the existence of τ_i (on α) is completely covered by the existence of τ_j. Trends and periodic occurrences are modeled as compound time-objects. The derivation of periodic occurrences is discussed in Keravnou [Keravnou, 1997]. Finally, causality. This is a very important relation, which can be naturally modeled with respect to time-objects. Time-objects are dynamic entities that can yield changes, i.e. cause the creation or termination of other time-objects. By allowing the antecedents and consequents of causal relations to be compound time-objects, complex causality can be expressed. Relation *causes* between a pair of (abstract) time-objects τ_i and τ_j specifies various constraints (temporal and other) that need to be satisfied in order for a *causality-link* to be established to hold between a pair of concrete instances of τ_i and τ_j:

Axiom A17: *causality-link* $(\tau_i, \tau_j, cf) \Leftarrow$ *causes* $(\tau_i, \tau_j, cs, cf) \wedge$ *conds-hold(cs)* $\wedge \neg$ *starts-before* (τ_j, τ_i). Argument cf denotes a certainty factor. The uncertainty is due to knowledge incompleteness.

Properties

Properties (ontology class Props), that constitute the other half of time-objects, are atomic or compound (negations, disjunctions, or conjunctions), passive or active, and some are time-invariant. Examples of properties are "sex male", "sore throat", "severe coughing", "administration of drug x", "removal of tonsils", etc. Properties have explicit temporal attributes. A property is associated with relevant granularities, e.g. "headache present" is associated with hours and days, but not months or years. This way the time-axes meaningful to a property can be defined. A property, ρ, either has an infinite persistence, *infper* (ρ), or a finite persistence, *finper* (ρ) In the latter case the following are additionally specified: whether the property can *recur*; maximum and minimum durations (*max-dur*, *min-dur*) under any of the relevant granularities, where the default is any duration; and a default margin for the initiation of any instantiation of the property, under a relevant temporal context (*earliest-init*, *latest-init*), which if not specified is assumed to be the entire extent of the particular time-axis. For example "SEDC present" is an infinitely persistent property whose earliest-init is birth. On the other hand "flu present" is a finitely persistent, recurring property, and "chicken-pox present" is a finitely persistent, but normally not a recurring property. In addition, the proposed ontology adopts the semantic attributes of properties specified by Shoham [Shoham, 1987], e.g. downward hereditary, upward hereditary, solid, gestalt, etc. For illustration the following axioms are given:

Axiom A18: $(\mathit{finper}(\pi_\tau) \wedge \varepsilon_\tau(\alpha) = < t_s, t_f, \varsigma >) \Rightarrow t_f \leq \mathit{upper\text{-}time}\,(\alpha)$

Axiom A19: $\mathit{infper}(\pi_\tau) \Rightarrow \neg\, (\exists \tau'$ Tobjects such that $\tau' \neq \tau \wedge \pi(\tau') = \pi_\tau)$

Causality, with explicit temporal constraints, is specified at the level of properties as well. Relation *cause-spec* is a 6-place relation where the first two arguments are properties, the third is a granularity, the fourth and fifth are sets of relative (TRel) and absolute (Css) temporal constraints respectively, and the last argument is a certainty factor. This relation also enables the derivation of *causality-links* between pairs of (concrete) time-objects:

Axiom A20: $\mathit{causality\text{-}link}\,(\tau_i, \tau_j, cf) \Leftarrow \mathit{cause\text{-}spec}\,(\rho_i, \rho_j, \mu, TRel, Css, cf) \wedge \pi(\tau_i) = \rho_i \wedge \pi(\tau_j) = \rho_j \wedge$
$\mathit{r\text{-}satisfied}\,(\tau_i, \tau_j, \mu, TRel) \wedge \mathit{a\text{-}satisfied}\,(\tau_i, \tau_j, \mu, Css) \wedge \neg \mathit{starts\text{-}before}\,(\tau_j, \tau_i)$. Other property relations include exclusion, necessitation, etc, for example:

Axiom A21: $\mathit{excludes}\,(\pi(\tau_i), \pi(\tau_j)) \Rightarrow \mathit{disjoint}_\alpha(\tau_i, \tau_j)$

Axioms are classified into *deductive rules* (e.g. axiom A1) and *integrity constraints* (e.g. axiom A3). The ontological primitives and their associated axioms are discussed in detail in Keravnou [Keravnou, 1996a], which also gives a detailed comparison between this ontology and the three general theories of time mentioned in Section 19.1.4. In Keravnou [Keravnou, 1996b], it is shown that medical concepts can be naturally modeled in terms of time-objects.

Implementation of the Time-Object Ontology

An object-based implementation, in Common Lisp, of the ontology has been performed. The implementation comprises three levels, a meta-level (Figure 19.9), an abstract-level and a concrete level. The top level meta-objects are the class of relation objects and the class of non-relation objects. The various axioms, classified into deductive rules and integrity constraints, are distributed among the (meta) relation objects that constitute their invocation contexts. For the declarative expression of axioms, as well as attribute constraints and various methods, an *assertion language* has been developed. This combines object-based, functional and logical features. In this language a deductive rule is formatted as

$$L \leftarrow A_1 \wedge A_2 \wedge .... \wedge A_n$$

where L is a literal and A_i; $i = 1,..,n$, is either a literal, or some attribute, repeat, or arbitrary predicate expression. Deductive rules are applied in a backward reasoning fashion for deriving literals. An integrity constraint is formatted as

$$H_1 \wedge H_2 \wedge \ldots \wedge H_n \rightarrow C_1 \wedge C_2 \wedge \ldots \wedge C_m$$

where H_i is a literal while H_i; $i = 2,..,n$ and C_j; $j = 1,..,m$ are either literals, attributes, or some repeat or arbitrary predicate expressions. Integrity constraints are applied in a forward reasoning fashion in order to detect integrity conflicts. The current status of the implementation of the ontology is discussed in Keravnou [Keravnou, 1999].

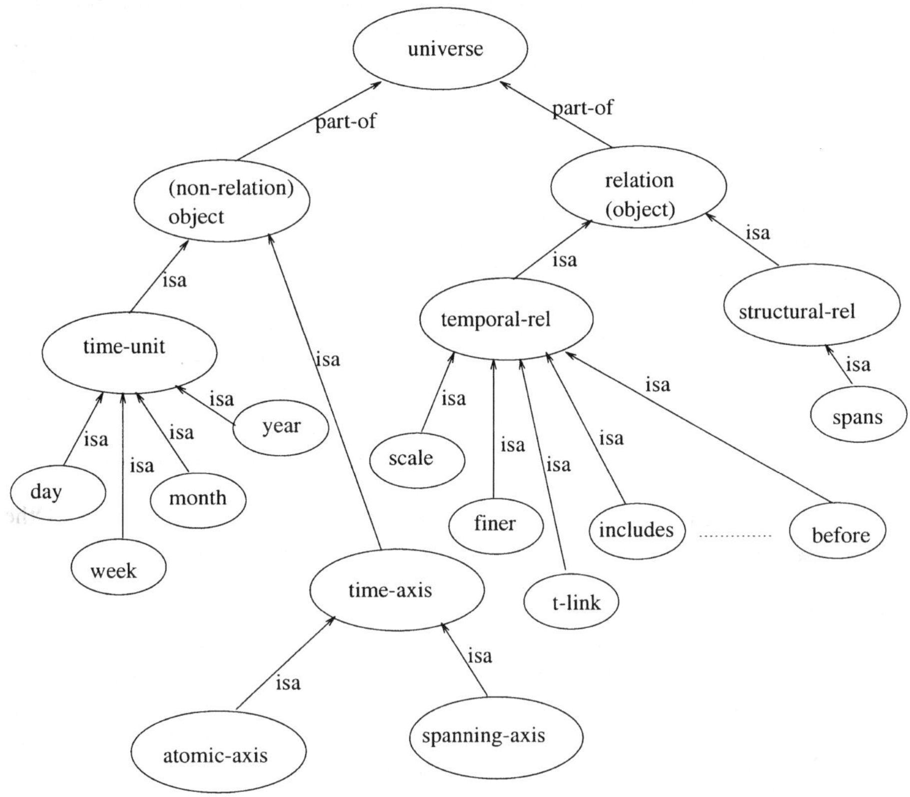

Figure 19.9: The objects comprising the meta-level of the time-object ontology . Arcs depict a type relation (IS-A,A-KIND-OF).

The time-object ontology is developed in the context of a broader effort concerning the development of a generic and reusable temporal kernel for medical knowledge-based systems. The ontology forms the ontological layer of the kernel. Higher layers provide necessary, generic, temporal reasoning functionalities dealing with mapping existences of time-objects across time-axes, detecting conflicts as well as various derivation functionalities, where temporal data abstraction derivations take central stage, culminating at functionalities for ensuring overall consistency and providing relevant query facilities for the user [Keravnou,

1996b]. When the kernel is embedded in some medical knowledge-based system additional functional layers, specific to the task at hand, would need to be incorporated. For example additional layers of relevance to a diagnostic system would be hypothesis formation and hypothesis evaluation layers, representing the abductive engine of the system.

19.9 Concluding Remarks

Time is intrinsically relevant to medical knowledge and patient data. Temporal requirements for medical reasoning are many and varied. General theories of time do not appear to be adequately expressive for the needs of real-life medical problems; in particular they do not address the crucial process of temporal data abstraction.

This chapter attempted to give as a comprehensive as possible, given the necessary space constraints, picture of past and current research in temporal reasoning in medicine, emphasizing the need to develop reusable ontologies and methods. Given that the relevant technology has sufficiently matured over the past decade or so and the general requirements for time representation and temporal reasoning in medical applications are now reasonably well understood, effort can indeed be channeled in developing reusable tools. One dimension that has been explored little so far is the emerging globality and heterogeneity of medical data which calls for the development of tools that can handle such distributed complexity as well. Care provides have made it clear that what they need are tools to provide them with the right information, in the right form and at the right time. This is why the intelligent storage, analysis, interpretation, and presentation (in visual form) of (distributed, heterogeneous) data as a means of closing the gap between data gathering and data comprehension is becoming a must. Although there is still much to be done in this respect the existing temporal data abstraction technology provides a good starting point to build from.

Early temporal reasoning proposals, although by all accounts quite successful, they were highly application specific; their re-usability was thus quite low. New proposals aim to address at least a class of medical applications, by not embedding in their workings actual specific domain knowledge but instead by operating in terms of conceptual knowledge ontologies. Hence new approaches are more generic and reusable; however, they are knowledge-driven, and hence their deployment in a new application context depends on the availability of the required knowledge. Thus once again we are faced with the traditional bottleneck of knowledge-based approaches, the acquisition of the knowledge per se. A synergy with the new generation of techniques for the discovery of the necessary knowledge is therefore called for. Such a synergy can in fact be of mutual benefit; machine learning can provide the means for discovering the knowledge for driving some temporal abstraction method, but, in addition, temporal data abstraction can provide a more objective means for pre-processing medical records for a machine-learning engine. Such potential integrations between the temporal-reasoning and knowledge discovery technologies in medicine are almost completely unexplored at present, but they may indeed provide fertile ground for research.

Temporal data abstraction was singled out in our conclusions because of its direct relevance to all medical tasks (diagnosis, monitoring, therapy management, guideline-based care, clinical research, etc). Any advances in temporal data abstraction will be of benefit to the higher reasoning performed by such tasks; this provided that data abstraction is modeled as a loosely coupled (sub) process. One solution that has been outlined here is the temporal-abstraction mediator. However, even granted a temporal-abstraction mediation service, further work is required to support the temporal reasoning inherent in the core medical tasks themselves.

Handbook of Temporal Reasoning in Artificial Intelligence
Edited by M. Fisher, D. Gabbay and L. Vila

Chapter 20

Time in Qualitative Simulation

Dan Clancy & Benjamin Kuipers

Qualitative models are abstractions of ordinary differential equation models. Their value comes from the ability to represent natural states of incomplete knowledge, and to draw useful inferences from those states of knowledge. QSIM is a representation for qualitative differential equation (QDE) models and an algorithm for qualitative simulation, producing a transition graph of qualitative states rooted in a given initial qualitative state [Kuipers, 1994]. QSIM provides the guarantee that the predicted transition graph of qualitative states describes all possible real solutions to all possible ordinary differential equation (ODE) models and initial states described by the given QDE and initial qualitative state [Kuipers, 1986]. Furthermore, as the imprecision of the state of knowledge decreases to zero, the resulting model and its predictions converge to an ordinary differential equation and its real-valued solution [Berleant and Kuipers, 1997].

Qualitative models are therefore useful whenever an agent, human or robotic, needs to reason about continuous change in spite of incomplete knowledge. Knowledge is often incomplete, of course, but especially so in common-sense reasoning about the everyday continuous world, diagnosis of broken systems, design of new systems, and scientific discovery about unknown systems.

The treatment of time in qualitative simulation attempts to bridges the gap between continuous and discrete symbolic models of time, making it possible to apply a variety of other discrete symbolic calculi for temporal inference to problems that arise in the continuous domain.

20.1 Time in Basic Qualitative Simulation

Qualitative simulation manipulates symbolic descriptions of variables, which represent time-varying quantities. The domain of each variable is described qualitatively in terms of a finite, totally order set of *landmark values* representing important (but perhaps numerically unknown) values on the extended real number line, $\Re^* = [-\infty, +\infty]$. It is convenient to assume that the domain is a closed set, so that every value can be described either as equal to a landmark value, or in an open interval bounded by two adjacent landmark values.

In order for qualitative reasoning to be possible, we must restrict variables to correspond to functions of time whose behavior is *reasonable*.

Definition 20.1.1. *Where* $[a, b] \subseteq \Re^*$, *the function* $f : [a, b] \rightarrow \Re^*$ *is a* reasonable function *over* $[a, b]$ *if*

1. *f is continuous on $[a, b]$,*
2. *f is continuously differentiable on (a, b),*
3. *f has only finitely many critical points in any bounded interval,*
4. *The one-sided limits $\lim_{t \to a^+} f'(t)$ and $\lim_{t \to b^-} f'(t)$ exist in $\Re^*$. Define $f'(a)$ and $f'(b)$ to be equal to these limits.*

The conditions on reasonable functions are designed to ensure that continuous change is described qualitatively as transitions from one qualitative value to an adjacent one, and to ensure that qualitative changes cannot take place infinitely often.

The time domain is represented by a finite sequence of landmark values, $t_0, t_1, \ldots t_n$, where it is possible that $t_n = \infty$. The possible values of time in a qualitative simulation are therefore drawn from an alternating sequence of time-points and open time-intervals:

$$t_0, (t_0, t_1), t_1, (t_1, t_2), \ldots (t_{n-1}, t_n), t_n.$$

The values of each variable in a QDE model are described in terms of the landmark values and open intervals in its domain, and in terms of the direction of change. The qualitative time-points are defined to be the points in time when there is some change in the qualitative value of one or more variables in the QDE. By definition, then, the qualitative values of all variables remain constant over each time interval (t_i, t_{i+1}). Therefore, the *qualitative states* of the QDE correspond to the time-points and time-intervals in its behavior.*

The QSIM algorithm for qualitative simulation starts from an initial qualitative state (at t_0), and predicts all possible sequences of qualitative states starting at that state, and consistent with both continuity and with the constraints in the QDE model. Unlike numerical simulation, where each state has only a single successor, under the qualitative description a state may have several different consistent successors. The result is thus a branching-time model of a disjunctive set of possible futures, where each future is described by a sequence of alternating time-points and time-intervals starting from t_0. For convenience in representing certain infinite paths, repeated qualitative states can be identified, and the branching-time tree is represented as a transition graph (Figure 20.1).

QSIM works by generating all possible successor values for each variable in each qualitative state, forming all possible combinations to define the set of successors, then filtering out all inconsistent qualitative states. Thus, each successor-generation step involves solving a new constraint satisfaction problem. Since all possible successors are generated, and only provably inconsistent ones are filtered out, we get the guarantee that all consistent solutions are predicted. (The converse is not true: it is not possible to guarantee that every inconsistent successor is detected.)

There are several consistency tests that are applied to completed states and behaviors. One of these tests is based on the properties of reasonable functions at finite and infinite values of variables, including time. The following rules allow us to examine the derivative of a variable v, and sometimes infer a temporal attribute: $t = \infty$ or $t < \infty$.

$$v(t) < \infty \text{ and } v'(t) \neq 0 \quad \rightarrow \quad t < \infty$$
$$v(t) = \infty \text{ and } v'(t) < \infty \quad \rightarrow \quad t = \infty$$

*Some approaches to qualitative reasoning include the non-standard concept of "mythical time", referring to a progression of steps in the deduction of a complete qualitative description of a single successor qualitative state. The perfect example is the cartoon character who runs past the edge of a cliff, stops horizontal motion in mid-air, realizes he is unsupported, and finally begins to fall, sometimes in several stages. QSIM does not model this process.

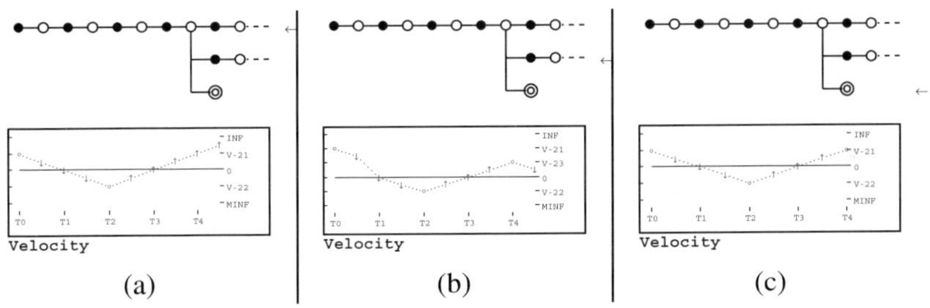

Figure 20.1: Three qualitative behaviors

The three qualitative behaviors describe one cycle of an oscillator, branching according to whether the oscillation is (a) increasing, (b) decreasing, or (c) cyclic. The tree of qualitative states grows from left to right, with each behavior alternating time-point and time-interval states. The first two behaviors are incomplete, while the third is terminated by recognizing a cycle (all variables equal to the same landmark values). The qualitative graph of $Velocity(t)$ is shown for each behavior. Meaningful qualitative values are landmark values or intervals between them, with landmark values of time on the horizontal axis and landmarks of $Velocity$ on the vertical axis. The symbol plotted ($\uparrow$, $\downarrow$, $\ominus$) represents the direction of change. Dots connecting symbols have no significance. Note that, in behavior (b), the qualitative value of $Velocity$ over the time-interval (t_0, t_1) is $\langle(0, V_{21}), dec\rangle$. The landmark V_{23} within that interval is created later, at t_4. This does not create a problem.

Once a temporal attribute has been deduced for a time-point, the qualitative value and direction of change of every variable v in the state must satisfy the following constraints.

$$t = \infty \quad \rightarrow \quad [v(t) < \infty \rightarrow v'(t) = 0]$$
$$t < \infty \quad \rightarrow \quad [v(t) = \infty \rightarrow v'(t) = \infty]$$

If a state violates any of these constraints, it is inconsistent, and removed from the predicted behavior tree.

20.1.1 Semi-Quantitative Simulation

In addition to the purely qualitative models described so far, it is possible to augment the qualitative model description with incomplete quantitative information [Kuipers, 1994, Chapter 9]. This information is typically in the form of a real bounded interval describing the real values that can possibly correspond to a particular landmark value (or certain other point-like terms), and of real-valued envelope functions bounding the possible graphs of unspecified monotonic functions. Once a qualitative behavior has been predicted, intervals and envelopes can be propagated through constraints implied by the behavior description via the laws of interval arithmetic, combining by interval intersection.

For example, we could have the qualitative relation $t_1 < t_2$, along with semi-quantitative information

$$t_1, t_2 \in [1, 10], \qquad d(t_1, t_2) = t_2 - t_1 \in [2, 3].$$

Propagation via interval arithmetic gives

$$t_1 \in [1, 8], \qquad t_2 \in [3, 10], \qquad d(t_1, t_2) \in [2, 3].$$

With each intersection, the interval bounds and envelopes never increase and may decrease, improving the precision of the resulting behavior description. If any intersection is empty, the associated term can have no consistent value, so the entire behavior is refuted, and therefore pruned out of the behavior graph. If an entire graph is refuted, the QDE model itself is inconsistent. Figure 20.2 shows two QSIM behaviors of a simple model, one consistent and one inconsistent, using semi-quantitative simulation.

This refutation-based approach to integrating quantitative observations with symbolic predictions is useful in a number of settings, including monitoring and diagnosis of continuous systems [Dvorak and Kuipers, 1989; Kay *et al.*, 2000; Rinner and Kuipers, 1999].

20.2 Time Across Region Transitions

The description of qualitative simulation so far has assumed that the QDE model remains constant throughout the history of the system, and that all changes are continuous. However, we frequently want to reason qualitatively about systems that have multiple models with different operating regions, or that include discontinuous changes.

In QSIM, a QDE may specify boundaries at which the trajectory of the system leaves the current operating region [Kuipers, 1994, Chapter 8]. Such a boundary can either terminate the simulation, or can provide a function that takes the current qualitative state (a time-point state) and returns a new time-point state representing the initial state for simulation within the QDE model for the new operating region.

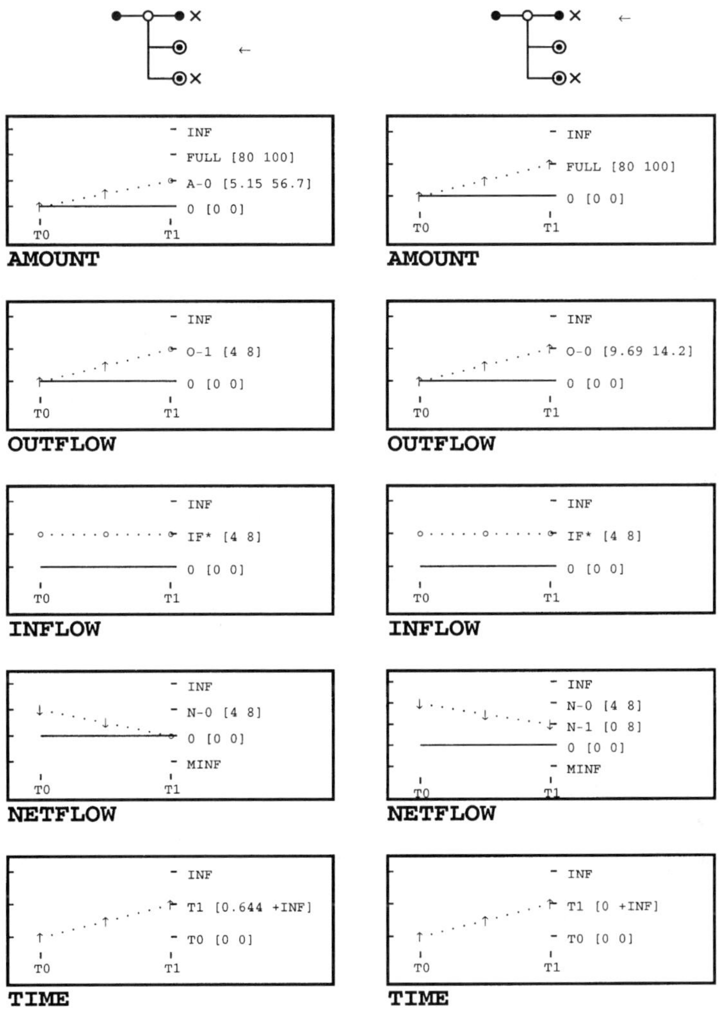

(a) Equilibrium (consistent) (b) Overflow (refuted)

Figure 20.2: Semi-quantitative simulation of a water-tank model

There are three consistent qualitative behaviors of the water-tank model: equilibrium, overflow, and equilibrium-at-full. Then we assert semi-quantitative information: $FULL \in [80, 100]$, $IF^* \in [4, 8]$, $t_0 \in [0, 0]$, and numerical upper and lower envelope functions around the unknown monotonic function $outflow = M_0^+(amount)$. The equilibrium behavior (a) is consistent, and infers weak bounds on t_1. In the overflow behavior (b), the constraint $netflow(t_1) = inflow(t_1) - outflow(t_1)$ implies the equation $if^* = n_1 + o_0$, which implies a contradiction: $[4, 8] = [0, 8] + [9.69, 14.2]$. The equilibrium-at-full behavior is refuted similarly. The refutations prune three possible behaviors down to a unique semi-quantitative prediction.

Thus, unlike the normal alternation of time-point and time-interval states, a region transition can link one time-point state to an immediate successor time-point state. If the transition takes place at time-point t_2, for example, the successor state t_2' is a distinct time-point state with the same temporal coordinates. There are two different principled interpretations for region transitions.*

Sudden Change; Negligible Time-Interval. There are few, if any, genuinely discontinuous changes in the physical world. An apparent discontinuity is typically a very fast continuous process whose detailed behavior is unimportant to the model builder. Therefore, it is represented as a discontinuous transition from an initial to a final state, and the open interval between the two is treated as having length zero [Nishida and Doshita, 1987; Iwasaki *et al.*, 1995].

For example, suppose we model a ball flying through the air and bouncing on a hard surface without loss of energy (Figure 20.3(a)). The ball is launched upward at time t_0, reaches its peak at t_1, strikes the surface at t_2, is reflected upward at t_2', reaches the next peak at t_3, strikes the surface again at t_4, and so on.

$$t_0, (t_0, t_1), t_1, (t_1, t_2), t_2 \rightarrow t_2', (t_2', t_3), t_3, (t_3, t_4), t_4 \rightarrow t_4', (t_4', t_5), \ldots$$

By the notation $t_2 \rightarrow t_2'$, we indicate that a fast process is taking place, but we are treating the extent of the interval (t_2, t_2') as negligible, and giving t_2 and t_2' the same temporal coordinates, to the resolution of the model. This is a simple form of *time-scale abstraction*.

Same Time-Point; Different Descriptions. A region transition can also represent a change in the level of description of the model, describing the very same instant in time with respect to a different set of variables and constraints.

For example, we can describe the same bouncing ball, but at the instant t_2 when the ball touches the surface moving downward, the model switches to a "compressing spring" model starting at t_2'. The ball will compress to its limit at t_3, expand again until the ball is just touching the surface moving upward at t_4, when it switches at t_4' to the "flight" model, and so on (Figure 20.3(b)).

$$t_0, (t_0, t_1), t_1, (t_1, t_2), t_2 \equiv t_2', (t_2', t_3), t_3, (t_3, t_4), t_4 \equiv t_4', (t_4', t_5), \ldots$$

The notation $t_2 \equiv t_2'$ indicates that the two qualitative states describe the same instant in time with respect to different QDE models, which may embody different modeling assumptions. For example, the "compressing spring" model may ignore the force of gravity as being negligible compared with the spring force of bounce, while gravity is the only significant force during the "flight" model.

20.3 Time-Scale Abstraction

We have seen how a discontinuous transition can be used to model a continuous behavior taking place at a much faster time-scale. More generally, if a complex system can be decomposed into mechanisms that operate at widely separated time-scales, then a particular mechanism can view a faster one as being instantaneous, and a slower one as being constant.

*Although we provide distinct notations for the two interpretations in this paper, the QSIM QDE syntax does not currently provide a way to express that distinction, so the difference remains in the mind of the model-builder.

(a) Bouncing ball viewed as reflection.

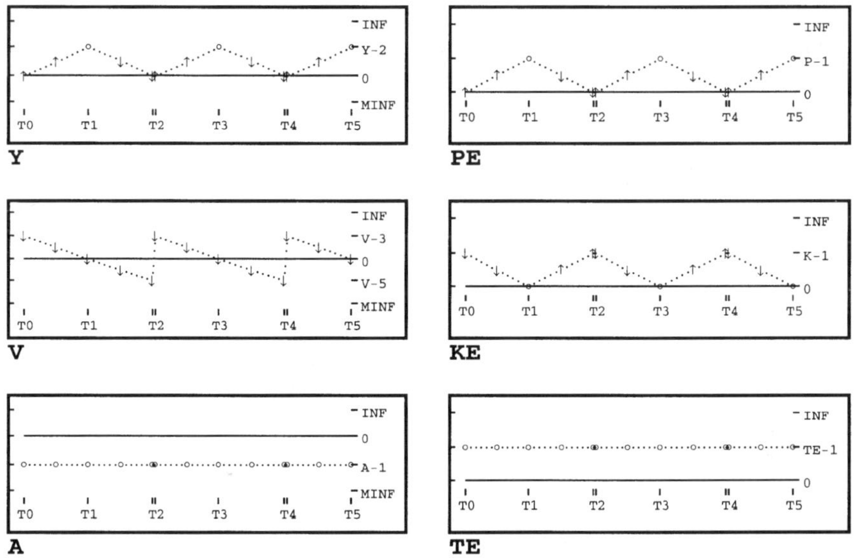

(b) Bouncing ball viewed as spring.

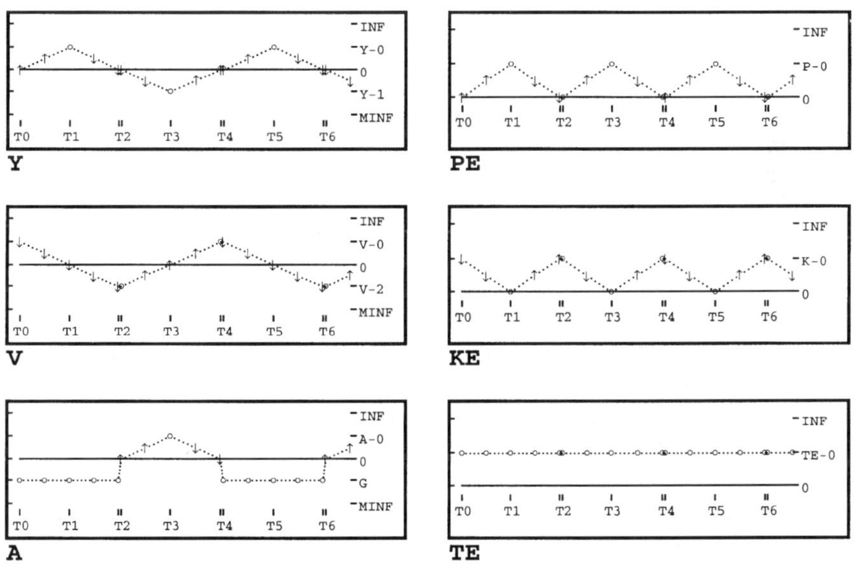

Figure 20.3: Two treatments of time across region transitions.

Region transitions can be treated either (a) as very fast processes with negligible temporal extent, or (b) as re-descriptions of the same instant in time within a new model.

How do we represent the effect of an instantaneous mechanism? Many models include functional constraints $y = f(x)$ in which a change to x is instantaneously reflected in a corresponding change to y. * Such a constraint frequently represents the equilibrium states of a faster process whose dynamic behavior is not important to the current model. For example, consider the constraint:

$$speed\_of\_car = f(position\_of\_accelerator\_pedal).$$

Such a functional constraint $y = f(x)$ is considered a *quasi-equilibrium model* of the relation between x and y. Both x and y can change, but the model assumes that the dynamic relationship between them is always in equilibrium, so the transient behavior between an initial change to x and the subsequent change to y can be abstracted away.

It is worth noting in passing that a functional constraint $y = f(x)$ can acquire a *causal order* $\Delta x \Rightarrow \Delta y$ if it is a quasi-equilibrium abstraction of a dynamic model in which x is an independent variable and y is a dependent variable. This abstraction relationship can justify an asymmetric causal order even though there is an apparent symmetry at the slower time-scale between $y = f(x)$ and its inverse $x = g(y)$.

QSIM allows the human model-builder to decompose a complex model into simpler models operating at widely different time-scales. Figure 20.4 illustrates the simulation of a complex model consisting of equilibrium mechanisms operating at three different time-scales. These issues and examples are discussed in more detail in [Kuipers, 1994, Chapters 7 and 12].

From the perspective of our previous discussion of the interpretation of region transitions, the vertical arrows in Figure 20.4 represent re-descriptions $t_i \equiv t_j$ of the same instant in time with respect to different models at different time-scales. Of course, what constitutes an "instant" is dramatically different at different time-scales (by definition). While QSIM provides means for the human model-builder to express models at different time-scales, it does not provide a formal definition of what time-scales are.

20.4 Using QSIM to Prove Theorems in Temporal Logic

As we have seen, QSIM takes a QDE and initial qualitative state, and produces a transition graph of qualitative states guaranteed to describe the real solutions to every ODE model and initial state described by the QDE and initial qualitative state. Intuitively, if every predicted behavior has some desirable property, for example stable convergence to a setpoint for a controller, then we should be able to conclude that every dynamical system described by the QDE will also have this property.

Happily, it is possible to formalize and extend this intuition. The branching-time temporal logic CTL* [Emerson, 1990] provides an appropriate language for expressing queries and conclusions about the QSIM behavior tree. We can appeal to QSIM-specific propositions for testing for particular qualitative values or properties such as quiescence, stability, cycles, or transitions. CTL* includes the usual logical connectives, temporal relations for use within a single linear-time behavior, and modal quantifiers over sets of behaviors at a branch.

---

*An important strength of qualitative modeling, not otherwise discussed in this context, is the ability to describe a function f as monotonically increasing, without knowing its exact functional form.

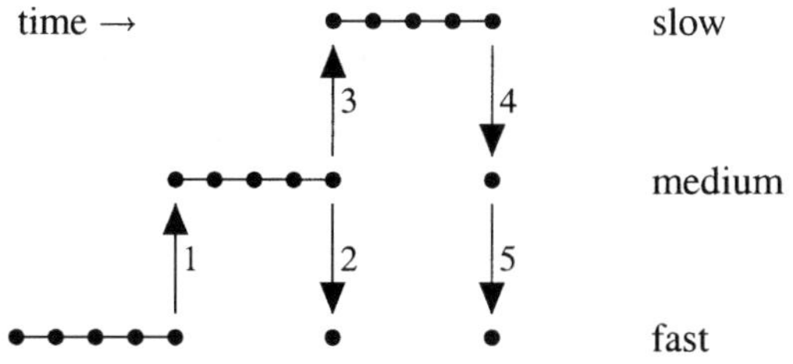

Figure 20.4: Qualitative simulation at multiple time-scales.

Each bead represents a qualitative state, so simulation produces a string of beads, and propagation of an equilibrium state produces a single bead. Changes in focus of attention take place in the sequence shown. (1) The equilibrium state of the fastest mechanism provides values for initializing a simulation of the next slower mechanism. (2) The final state of the second simulation is first used to propagate a new equilibrium state for the fastest mechanism. (3) Then values from both faster mechanisms are available to initialize the slowest mechanism. Values from the final state of the slowest mechanism are propagated to equilibrium states of (4) the intermediate and (5) the fastest mechanisms.

modal	temporal	logical	QSIM
necessarily	*until*	*and*	*qval*
possibly	*next*	*or*	*status*
	eventually	*implies*	
	always	*not*	

In order to answer queries and prove statements in CTL*, we interpret the transition graph produced by QSIM as a structure that can serve as a logical model for the CTL* statement. Combining the guarantees associated with QSIM with those associated with the model-checker, we can conclude that successfully checking any *universal* statement in CTL* against a complete qualitative state graph from QSIM proves the corresponding theorem about every ODE system described by the QDE [Shults and Kuipers, 1997]. This has been used to prove the properties of complex heterogeneous control systems [Kuipers and Åström, 1994].

It is quite possible for QSIM simulation of a large QDE model to produce a qualitative state graph that is too large for human inspection to draw useful conclusions. With this result, it is possible to use temporal logic as a query language to explore the properties of the QDE and its behaviors.

Furthermore, it is also possible to use related methods based on model-checking to exploit temporal logic statements as *inputs* to the simulation process, focusing attention on those branches of the qualitative state graph that satisfy the given temporal logic statements [Brajnik and Clancy, 1998]. This is useful to allow the model-builder to incorporate knowledge into the model that is not expressible in the QSIM language for describing QDEs, for example to specify the behavior of exogenous variables. More pragmatically, it is also useful to allow the model user to focus attention on a small portion of the qualitative state graph satisfying certain properties, rather than considering all possible behaviors.

20.5 Concluding Remarks

Qualitative simulation exploits a very rich description of time. The basic representation for time is the abstraction of the real-valued timeline to an alternating sequence of time-points and time-intervals, where the final time-point may explicitly represent $t = \infty$.

The representation for time becomes richer when we take into account the way complex models may be decomposed into a collection of simpler models, perhaps at significantly different time-scales. Sound reasoning with temporal descriptions in this context must take into account aspects of the granularity with which different models describe the world.

Since qualitative simulation is based on a rigorous abstraction of the theory of ordinary differential equations, its theory of time has a solid foundation. It can therefore be combined with the theory of temporal logic and model-checking to produce powerful tools for reasoning about the behavior of complex dynamical systems, even in the face of incomplete qualitative knowledge.

Bibliography

[Åqvist, 1979] L. Åqvist. A Conjectured Axiomatization of Two-Dimensional Reichenbachian Tense Logic. *J. Philosophical Logic*, 8:1–45, 1979.

[Abadi and Manna, 1985] M. Abadi and Z. Manna. Nonclausal Temporal Deduction. *Lecture Notes in Computer Science*, 193:1–15, 1985.

[Abadi and Manna, 1989] M. Abadi and Z. Manna. Temporal Logic Programming. *Journal of Symbolic Computation*, 8(3), 1989.

[Abadi and Manna, 1990] M. Abadi and Z. Manna. Nonclausal Deduction in First-Order Temporal Logic. *Journal of the ACM*, 37(2):279–317, 1990.

[Abadi, 1987] M. Abadi. *Temporal-Logic Theorem Proving*. PhD thesis, Department of Computing, Stanford University, 1987. STAN-CS-87-1151.

[Abiteboul and Grumbach, 1988] S. Abiteboul and S. Grumbach. A Logic-Based Language for Complex Objects. In *Proceedings of the International Conference on Extending Database Technology (EDBT)*, 1988.

[Abiteboul *et al.*, 1991] S. Abiteboul, P. Kanellakis, and G. Grahne. On the Representation and Querying of Sets of Possible Worlds. *Theoretical Computer Science*, 78(1):159–187, 1991.

[Abiteboul *et al.*, 1995] S. Abiteboul, R. Hull, and V. Vianu. *Foundations of Databases*. Addison-Wesley, 1995.

[Abiteboul *et al.*, 1996] S. Abiteboul, L. Herr, and J. Van den Bussche. Temporal Versus First-Order Logic to Query Temporal Databases. In *Proceedings of the ACM Symposium on Principles of Database Systems (PODS)*, pages 49–57, 1996.

[Abiteboul *et al.*, 1999] S. Abiteboul, L. Herr, and J. Van den Bussche. Temporal Connectives Versus Explicit Timestamps to Query Temporal Databases. *Journal of Computer and System Sciences*, 58(1):54–68, 1999.

[Ahn, 1986] I. Ahn. Towards an Implementation of Database Management Systems with Temporal Support. In *Proceedings of the 2nd International Conference on Data Engineering*, pages 374–381, 1986.

[Alferes and Pereira, 1996] J. Alferes and L. Pereira. *Reasoning With Logic Programming*. Springer Verlag, 1996.

[Aliferis and Cooper, 1996] C. Aliferis and G. Cooper. A Structurally and Temporally Extended Bayesian Belief Network Model: Definitions, Properties, and Modeling Techniques. In *Proceedings of International Conference on Uncertainty in AI (UAI)*, pages 28–38, 1996.

[Allen and Ferguson, 1994] J.F. Allen and G. Ferguson. Actions and events in interval temporal logic. *Journal of Logic and Computation*, 4(5):531–579, October 1994.

[Allen and Hayes, 1985] J. Allen and P. Hayes. A Common-Sense Theory of Time. In *Proceedings of the Nineth International Joint Conference on Artificial Intelligence (IJCAI-85)*, pages 528–531, Los Angeles CA, USA, 1985. Morgan Kaufmann.

[Allen and Hayes, 1989] J. Allen and P. Hayes. Moments and Points in an Interval-Based Temporal Logic. *Computational Intelligence*, 5(4):225–238, November 1989.

[Allen, 1983] J. F. Allen. Maintaining Knowledge About Temporal Intervals. *Communications of the ACM*, 26(11):832–843, November 1983.

[Allen, 1984] James Allen. Towards a General Theory of Action and Time. *Artificial Intelligence*, 23:123–154, 1984.

[Allen, 1991a] James F. Allen. Temporal reasoning and planning. In J. F. Allen, H. Kautz, R. N. Pelavin, and J. Tenenberg, editors, *Reasoning about Plans*, chapter 1, pages 1–67. Morgan Kaufmann, 1991.

[Allen, 1991b] J.F. Allen. Time and Time Again: The Many Ways to Represent Time. *International Journal of Intelligent Systems*, 6(4):341–356, July 1991.

[Alur and Henzinger, 1991] R. Alur and T.A. Henzinger. Logics and Models of Real-Time: A Survey. In *Real Time: Theory in Practice*, volume 600 of *Lecture Notes in Computer Science*, pages 74–106. Springer-Verlag, 1991.

[Alur and Henzinger, 1993] R. Alur and T. Henzinger. Real-Time Logics: Complexity and Expressiveness. *Information and Computation*, 104:35–77, 1993.

[Alur *et al.*, 1993] R. Alur, C. Courcoubetis, T. Henzinger, and P. Ho. Hybrid Automata: an Algorithmic Approach to the Specification and Analysis of Hybrid Systems. In *Proceedings of International Workshop on Theory of Hybrid Systems*, pages 209–229, 1993.

[Apt and Pellegrini, 1994] K. Apt and A. Pellegrini. On the Occur-Check Free Logic Programs. *ACM Transactions on Programming Languages and Systems*, 16(3):687–726, 1994.

[Apt *et al.*, 1988] K.R. Apt, H.A. Blair, and A. Walker. Towards a Theory of Declarative Knowledge. In J. Minker, editor, *Foundations of Deductive Databases and Logic Programming*, pages 89–148. Morgan Kaufmann, 1988.

[Apt, 1990] K.R. Apt. Logic Programming. In Jan van Leeuwen, editor, *Handbook of Theoretical Computer Science*, volume B, chapter 10, pages 493–574. Elsevier/MIT Press, 1990.

[Arasu *et al.*, 2002] A. Arasu, B. Babcock, S. Babu, J. McAlister, and J. Widom. Characterizing Memory Requirements for Queries over Continuous Data Streams. In *Proceedings of the ACM Symposium on Principles of Database Systems (PODS)*, pages 221–232, 2002.

[Artale and Franconi, 1994] A. Artale and E. Franconi. A Computational Account for a Description Logic of Time and Action. In *Principles of Knowledge Representation and Reasoning: Proceedings of the Fourth International Conference (KR'94)*, pages 3–14, San Francisco, CA, 1994. Morgan Kaufmann.

[Artale and Franconi, 1998] A. Artale and E. Franconi. A Temporal Description Logic for Reasoning about Actions and Plans. *Journal of Artificial Intelligence Research*, 9:463–506, 1998.

[Artale and Franconi, 1999] A. Artale and E. Franconi. Temporal Entity-Relationship Modeling with Description Logics. In *Proceedings of the International Conference on Conceptual Modeling (ER'99)*. Springer-Verlag, November 1999.

[Artale and Franconi, 2000] A. Artale and E. Franconi. Temporal Description Logics for Conceptual Modelling, July 2000. Technical report, Department of Computer Science, University of Manchester, UK.

[Artale and Franconi, 2001] A. Artale and E. Franconi. A Survey of Temporal Extensions of Description Logics. *Annals of Mathematics and Artificial Intelligence*, 30(1-4), 2001.

[Artale and Lutz, 1999] A. Artale and C. Lutz. A Correspondence between Temporal Description Logics. In *Proceedings of the 1999 Description Logic Workshop (DL'99)*, pages 145–149, 1999.

[Aylett *et al.*, 1998] R. Aylett, J. Soutter, G. Petley, and P. Chung. AI planning in a chemical plant domain. In *Proceedings of European Conference on Artificial Intelligence (ECAI)*, pages 622–626, 1998.

[Baader and Hanschke, 1991] F. Baader and P. Hanschke. A Scheme for Integrating Concrete Domains into Concept Languages. In *Proceedigns of Twelfth international Conference on Artificial Intelligence (IJCAI)*, pages 446–451, Sidney, Australia, 1991.

[Baader and Hanschke, 1992] F. Baader and P. Hanschke. Extensions of Concept Languages for a Mechanical Engineering Application. In *Proceedings of the 16th German AI-Conference (GWAI-92)*, volume 671 of *Lecture Notes in Computer Science*, pages 132–143. Springer-Verlag, 1992.

[Baader and Ohlbach, 1995] F. Baader and H-J. Ohlbach. A Multi-Dimensional Terminological Knowledge Representation Language. *Journal of Applied Non-Classical Logics*, 5:153–19, 1995.

[Babcock *et al.*, 2002] B. Babcock, S. Babu, M. Datar, R. Motwani, and J. Widom. Models and Issues in Data Stream Systems. In *Proceedings of the ACM Symposium on Principles of Database Systems (PODS)*, pages 1–16, 2002.

[Bacchus and Ady, 2001] F. Bacchus and M. Ady. Planning with Resources and Concurrency: A Forward Chaining Approach. In *Proceedings of the International Joint Conference on Artificial Intelligence (IJCAI)*, pages 417–424, 2001.

[Bacchus and Kabanza, 1996] F. Bacchus and F. Kabanza. Planning for Temporally Extended Goals. In *Proceedings of AAAI'96*, pages 1215–1222. AAAI press, 1996.

[Bacchus and Kabanza, 1998] F. Bacchus and F. Kabanza. Planning for Temporally Extended Goals. *Annals of Mathematics and Artificial Intelligence*, 22:5–27, 1998.

[Bacchus and Kabanza, 2000] F. Bacchus and F. Kabanza. Using Temporal Logic to Express Search Control Knowledge for Planning. *Artificial Intelligence*, 116(1-2):123–191, 2000.

[Bacchus *et al.*, 1991] F. Bacchus, J. Tenenberg, and J. Koomen. A Non-Reified Temporal Logic. *Artificial Intelligence*, 52(1):87–108, 1991.

[Bacchus, 2001] F. Bacchus. The AIPS'00 Planning Competition. *AI Magazine*, 22(3):47–56, 2001.

[Bach, 1986] E. Bach. The Algebra of Events. *Linguistics and Philosophy*, 9:5–16, 1986.

[Badaloni and Berati, 1994] S. Badaloni and M. Berati. Dealing with Time Granularity in a Temporal Planning System. *Lecture Notes in Computer Science*, 827:101–116, 1994.

[Baioletti *et al.*, 2000] M. Baioletti, S. Marcugini, and A. Milani. DPPlan: An Algorithm for Fast Solutions Extraction from a Planning Graph. In *Proceedings of AIPS*, pages 13–21, 2000.

[Baker, 1989] A.B. Baker. A simple solution to the Yale Shooting Problem. In R.J. Brachman, H.J. Levesque, and R. Reiter, editors, *Proceedings of the First International Conference on Principles of Knowledge Representation and Reasoning (KR-89)*, pages 11–20. Morgan Kaufmann, 1989.

[Balbiani *et al.*, 1998] P. Balbiani, J.-F. Condotta, and L.F. del Cerro. Bidimensional Temporal Relations. In *Proceedings of International Conference on Knowledge Representation and Reasoning (KR)*, June 1998.

[Balbiani *et al.*, 2003] P. Balbiani, J.F. Condotta, and G. Ligozat. On the Consistency Problem for the indu Calculus. In *Proceedings of the 10th International Symposium on Temporal Representation and Reasoning and Fourth International Conference on Temporal Logic (TIME-ICTL'03)*. IEEE Computer Society, 2003.

[Balduccini *et al.*, 2000] M. Balduccini, M. Gelfond, and M. Nogueira. A-Prolog as a Tool for Declarative Programming. In *Proceedings of the 12th International Conference on Software Engineering and Knowledge Engineering (SEKE)*, 2000.

[Banieqbal and Barringer, 1986] B. Banieqbal and H. Barringer. A Study of an Extended Temporal Logic and a Temporal Fixed Point Calculus. Technical Report UMCS-86-10-2, University of Manchester, Manchester, October 1986.

[Banieqbal and Barringer, 1987] B. Banieqbal and H. Barringer. Temporal logic with fixed points. In *Temporal Logic in Specification*, page 62. LNCS 398 Springer-Verlag, April 1987.

[Barahona, 1994] P. Barahona. A Causal and Temporal Reasoning Model and its use in Drug Therapy Applications. *Artificial Intelligence in Medicine*, 6:1–27, 1994.

[Baral and Gelfond, 1994] C. Baral and M. Gelfond. Logic programming and knowledge representation. *Journal of Logic Programming*, 19,20:73–148, 1994.

[Baral and Gelfond, 1997] C. Baral and M. Gelfond. Reasoning about Effects of Concurrent Actions. *Journal of Logic Programming*, 31(1-3):85–117, May 1997.

[Baral and Gelfond, 2000] C. Baral and M. Gelfond. Reasoning Agents in Dynamic Domains. In J. Minker, editor, *Logic Based Artificial Intelligence*. Kluwer, 2000.

[Baral *et al.*, 1997] C. Baral, M. Gelfond, and A. Provetti. Representing Actions: Laws, Observations and Hypothesis. *Journal of Logic Programming*, 31(1-3):201–243, May 1997.

[Baral, 1995] C. Baral. Reasoning about Actions : Non-deterministic effects, Constraints and Qualification. In *Proceedings of International Joint Conference on Artificial Intelligenc (IJCAI)*, pages 2017–2023, 1995.

[Baral, 1997] C. Baral. Embedding Revision Programs in Logic Programming Situation Calculus. *Journal of Logic Programming*, 30(1):83–97, Jan 1997.

[Baral, August 1994] C. Baral. Rule Based Updates on Simple Knowledge Bases. In *Proceedings of AAAI'94*, pages 136–141, August 1994.

[Barber, 1993] F. A. Barber. A Metric Time-Point and Duration-Based Temporal Model. *SIGART Bulletin*, 4(3):30–49, 1993.

[Barendregt, 1984] H. P. Barendregt. *The Lambda Calculus: Its Syntax and Semantics*, volume 103 of *Studies in Logic and the Foundations of Mathematics*. North-Holland, 1984.

[Barnes and Barnett, 1995] M. Barnes and G. Barnett. An Architecture for a Distributed Guideline Server. In R. M. Gardner, editor, *Proceedings of the Annual Symposium on Computer Applications in Medical Care (SCAMC)*, pages 233–237, New Orleans, USA, 1995. Hanley & Belfus.

[Barringer and Kuiper, 1984] H. Barringer and R. Kuiper. Hierarchical Development of Concurrent Systems in a Temporal Logic Framework. In S.D. Brookes, A.W. Roscoe, and G. Winskel, editors, *Proceedings of the NSF/SERC Seminar on Concurrency*, volume 197 of *Lecture Notes in Computer Science*, pages 35–61. Springer-Verlag, Heidleberg, 1984.

[Barringer *et al.*, 1984] H. Barringer, R. Kuiper, and A. Pnueli. Now You May Compose Temporal Logic Specifications. In *Proceedings of the 16th Symposium on Theory of Computing (STOC)*, pages 51–63. ACM, April 1984.

[Barringer *et al.*, 1986] H. Barringer, R. Kuiper, and A. Pnueli. A really abstract concurrent model and its temporal logic. In *Proceedings of the Thirteenth ACM Symposium on the Principles of Programming Languages*, pages 173–183, St. Petersberg Beach, Florida, January 1986. ACM Press.

[Barringer *et al.*, 1995] H. Barringer, M. Fisher, D. Gabbay, G. Gough, and R. Owens. METATEM: An Introduction. *Formal Aspects of Computing*, 7(5):533–549, 1995.

[Barringer *et al.*, 1996] H. Barringer, M. Fisher, D. Gabbay, R. Owens, and M. Reynolds, editors. *The Imperative Future: Principles of Executable Temporal Logics*. Research Studies Press, Chichester, United Kingdom, 1996.

[Baudinet *et al.*, 1993] M. Baudinet, J. Chomicki, and P. Wolper. Temporal Deductive Databases. In Tansel et al. [1993], pages 294–320.

[Baudinet *et al.*, 1999] M. Baudinet, J. Chomicki, and P. Wolper. Constraint-Generating Dependencies. *Journal of Computer and System Sciences*, 59(1):94–115, 1999.

[Baudinet, 1992] M. Baudinet. A Simple Proof of the Completeness of Temporal Logic Programming. In L. Fariñas del Cerro and M. Penttonen, editors, *Intensional Logics for Programming*. Oxford University Press, 1992.

[Baudinet, 1995] M. Baudinet. On the Expressiveness of Temporal Logic Programming. *Information and Computation*, 117(2):157–180, 1995.

[Becher *et al.*, 1998] G. Becher, F. Clérin-Debart, and P. Enjalbert. A Model for Time Granularity in Natural Language. In *Proceedings of International Workshop on Temporal Representation and Reasoning (TIME)*, Los Alamitos (CA US), 1998. IEEE computer society press.

[Bell and Tate, 1985] C.E. Bell and T. Tate. Use and Justification of Algorithms for Managing Temporal Knowledge in o-plan. Technical Report 531, AIAI, Edinburgh, U.K., 1985.

[Bellini *et al.*, 2000] P. Bellini, R. Mattolini, and P. Nesi. Temporal Logics for Real-Time System Specification. *ACM Computing Surveys*, 32(1):12–42, March 2000.

[Bench-Capon *et al.*, 1988] T. Bench-Capon, G. Robinson, T. Routen, and M. Sergot. Logic Programming for Large Scale Applications in Law: A Formalization of Supplementary Benefit Legislation. In Hayes, Michie, and Richards, editors, *Machine Intelligence*, pages 209–260. Oxford Univ. Press, 1988.

[Benerecetti *et al.*, 1998] M. Benerecetti, F. Giunchiglia, and L. Serafini. Model Checking Multiagent Systems. *Journal of Logic and Computation*, 8(3):401–423, 1998.

[Bennett *et al.*, 2002a] B. Bennett, A. Cohn, F. Wolter, and M. Zakharyaschev. Multi-dimensional modal logic as a framework for spatio-temporal reasoning. *Applied Intelligence*, 2002.

[Bennett *et al.*, 2002b] B. Bennett, C. Dixon, M. Fisher, E. Franconi, I. Horrocks, and M. de Rijke. Combinations of Modal Logics. *AI Review*, 17(1):1–20, 2002.

[Bennett, 1988] J. Bennett. *Events and Their Names*. Clarendon Press, Oxford, 1988.

[Benthem, 1984] J.F.A.K. van Benthem. Correspondence Theory. In D. Gabbay and F. Guenthner, editors, *Handbook of Philosophical Logic - volume II*. Reidel, Dordrecht, 1984.

[Benthem, 1988a] J.F.A.K. van Benthem. *A Manual of Intensional Logic - Second Edition, Revised and Expanded*, volume 1 of *CSLI Lecture Notes*. Center for the Study of Language and Information, Stanford University, California, 1988.

[Benthem, 1988b] J.F.A.K. van Benthem. Time, Logic and Computation. In J. W. de Bakker, W.-P. de Roever, and G. Rozenberg, editors, *Linear Time, Branching Time and Partial Order in Logics and Models for Concurrency - LNCS Vol. XXX*, pages 1–49. Springer-Verlag, Heidelberg, June 1988.

[Benthem, 1995] J.F.A.K. van Benthem. Temporal logic. In D. M. Gabbay, C. J. Hogger, and J. A. Robinson, editors, *Handbook of Logic in Artificial Intelligence and Logic Programming, Volume 4: Epistemic and Temporal Reasoning*, pages 241–350. Clarendon Press, Oxford, 1995.

[Benzen, 1959] S. Benzen. On the Topology of the Genetic Fine Structure. *Proceedings of the National Academy of Science*, 45(10):1607–1620, 1959.

[Berleant and Kuipers, 1997] D. Berleant and B. Kuipers. Qualitative and Quantitative Simulation: Bridging the Gap. *Artificial Intelligence*, 95(2):215–255, 1997.

[Berman, 1980] L. Berman. The Complexity of Logical Theories. *Theoretical Computer Science*, 11:71–78, 1980.

[Bernholtz, 1995] O. Bernholtz. *Model Checking for Branching Time Temporal Logics*. PhD thesis, The Technion, Israel, 1995.

[Bertoli *et al.*, 2001] P. Bertoli, A. Cimatti, M. Roveri, and P. Traverso. Planning in Non-Deterministic Domains under Partial Observability via Symbolic Model-Checking. In *Proceedings of International Joint Conference on Artificial Intelligence (IJCAI)*, 2001.

[Berzuini *et al.*, 1989] C. Berzuini, R. Bellazzi, and S. Quaglini. Temporal Reasoning with Probabilities. In *Proceedingsof International Conference on Uncertainty in Artificial Intelligence (UAI)*, 1989.

[Berzuini *et al.*, 1997] C. Berzuini, N.G. Best, W.R. Gilks, and C. Larizza. Dynamic Conditional Independence Models and Markov Chain Monte Carlo Methods. *Journal of the American Statistical Association*, 92:1403–1412, 1997.

[Bessière *et al.*, 1996] C. Bessière, A. Isli, and G. Ligozat. Global Consistency in Interval Algebra Networks: Tractable Subclasses. In *Proceedings of the Fifteenth European Conference on Artificial Intelligence (ECAI)*, 1996.

[Bessière, 1996] C. Bessière. A Simple Way to Improve Path-Consistency in Interval Algebra Networks. In *Proceedings of the Thirteenth National Conference of the American Association for Artificial Intelligence (AAAI)*, pages 375–380, Portland, OR, 1996.

[Bessière, 1997] C. Bessière. Personal communication, August 1997.

[Beth, 1955] E. Beth. Semantic Entailment and Formal Derivability. *Mededelingen der Koninklijke Nederlandse Akad. van Wetensch*, 18, 1955.

[Bettini *et al.*, 1996] C. Bettini, X. S. Wang, and S. Jajodia. Testing Complex Temporal Relationships Involving Multiple Granularities and its Application to Data Mining. In *Proceedings of International Conference on Principles of Database Systems (PODS)*, pages 68–78, 1996.

[Bettini *et al.*, 1998a] C. Bettini, C. Dyreson, W. Evans, R. Snodgrass, and X. S. Wang. A Glossary of Time Granularity Concepts. In O. Etzion, S. Jajodia, and S. M. Sripada, editors, *Temporal Databases: Research and Practice*, volume 1399 of *Lecture Notes in Computer Science*, pages 406–413. Springer-Verlag, 1998.

[Bettini *et al.*, 1998b] C. Bettini, X. S. Wang, and S. Jajodia. An Architecture for Supporting Interoperability among Temporal Databases. In O. Etzion, S. Jajodia, and S. M. Sripada, editors, *Temporal Databases: Research and Practice*, volume 1399 of *Lecture Notes in Computer Science*, pages 26–55. Springer-Verlag, 1998.

[Bettini *et al.*, 1998c] C. Bettini, X. S. Wang, and S. Jajodia. A General Framework for Time Granularity and its Application to Temporal Reasoning. *Annals of Mathematics and Artificial Intelligence*, 1(22):29–58, 1998.

[Bettini *et al.*, 1998d] C. Bettini, X. S. Wang, S. Jajodia, and J-L. Lin. Discovering Frequent Event Patterns with Multiple Granularities in Time Sequences. *IEEE Transactions on Knowledge and Data Engineering*, 2(10):222–237, 1998.

[Bettini *et al.*, 1998e] C. Bettini, X.S. Wang, E. Bertino, and S. Jajodia. Semantic Assumptions and Query Evaluation in Temporal Databases. *IEEE Transactions on Knowledge and Data Engineering*, 10(2):277–296, 1998.

[Bettini *et al.*, 2000] C. Bettini, S. Jajodia, and X. S. Wang. *Time Granularities in Databases, Data Mining, and Temporal Reasoning*. Springer, Berlin, Germany, 2000.

[Bettini *et al.*, 2003] C. Bettini, S. Mascetti, and V. Pupillo. GSTP: A Temporal Reasoning System Supporting Multi-Granularity Temporal Constraints. In *Proceedings of the International Joint Conference on Artificial Intelligence (IJCAI); Intelligent Systems Demonstrations*, pages 1633–1634. Morgan Kaufmann, 2003.

[Bettini, 1997] C. Bettini. Time Dependent Concepts: Representation and Reasoning Using Temporal Description Logics. *Data and Knowledge Engineering*, 22(1):1–38, 1997.

[Bidoit *et al.*, 2004] N. Bidoit, S. de Amo, and L. Segoufin. Order Independent Temporal Properties. *Journal of Logic and Computation*, 2004.

[Birman, 1991] K. P. Birman. The Process Group Approach to Reliable Distributed Computing. Techanical Report TR91-1216, Department of Computer Science, Cornell University, July 1991.

[Bitner and Reingold, 1975] J.R. Bitner and E.M. Reingold. Backtrack Programming Techniques. *Journal of the ACM*, 18:651–655, 1975.

[Bittner and Steel, 1998] T. Bittner and J. Steel. A Boundary Sensitive Approach to Qualitative Location. *Annals of Mathematics and Artificial Intelligence*, 24(1-2):93–114, 1998.

[Bittner, 2002] T. Bittner. Approximate Qualitative Temporal Reasoning. *Annals of Mathematics and Artificial Intelligence*, 36(1-2):39–80, 2002.

[Bjorner *et al.*, 1995] N. Bjorner, A. Browne, E. Chang, M. Colón, A. Kapur, Z. Manna, H. B. Sipma, and T. E. Uribe. *STeP: The Stanford Temporal Prover Educational Release Version 1.0 User's Manual.* Computer Science Department, Stanford University, California 94305, November 1995.

[Blackburn *et al.*, 2001] P. Blackburn, M. de Rijke, and Yde Venema. *Modal Logic*, volume 53 of *Cambridge Tracts in Theoretical Computer Science.* Cambridge University Press, Cambridge, England, 2001.

[Blum and Furst, 1995] A. Blum and M. Furst. Fast Planning through Plan-graph Analysis. In *Proceedings of the International Joint Conference on Artificial Intelligence (IJCAI)*, 1995.

[Blum, 1982] R.L. Blum. Discovery and Representation of Causal Relationships from a Large Time-Oriented Clinical Database: The RX Project. In D.A. Lindberg and P.L. Reichartz, editors, *Lecture Notes in Medical Informatics*, volume 19. Springer-Verlag, New York, 1982.

[Blumsohn, 1991] G. Blumsohn. *Three Essays on Law and Information in the Law of Damages.* Dissertation Information Service. UMI, 1991.

[Blythe, 1995] J. Blythe. AI Planning in Dynamic, Uncertain Domains. In *Proceedings of AAAI Spring Symposium on Extending Theories of Action*, 1995.

[Blythe, 1999] J. Blythe. An Overview of Planning Under Uncertainty. *Lecture Notes in Computer Science*, 1600:85–110, 1999.

[Boaz and Shahar, 2003] D. Boaz and Y. Shahar. Idan: A Distributed Temporal-Abstraction Mediator for Medical Databases. In *Proceedings of the Ninth Conference on Artificial Intelligence in Medicine — Europe (AIME)*, Protaras, Cyprus, 2003.

[Boddy and Dean, 1994] M. Boddy and T. Dean. Deliberation Scheduling for Problem Solving in Time-Constrained Enviroments. *Artificial Intelligence*, 67(2):245–285, 1994.

[Boddy, 1993] Mark Boddy. Temporal Reasoning for Planning and Scheduling. *SIGART Bulletin*, 4(3):17–20, 1993.

[Böhlen *et al.*, 1996a] M. Böhlen, J. Chomicki, R.T. Snodgrass, and D. Toman. Querying TSQL2 Databases with Temporal Logic. In *International Conference on Extending Database Technology (EDBT)*, Avignon, France, 1996. Springer Verlag, LNCS 1057.

[Böhlen *et al.*, 1996b] M. Böhlen, R.T. Snodgrass, and M.D. Soo. Coalescing in Temporal Databases. In *International Conference on Very Large Data Bases (VLDB)*, pages 180–191, 1996.

[Bolotov and Fisher, 1997] A. Bolotov and M. Fisher. A Resolution Method for CTL Branching-Time Temporal Logic. In *Proceedings of the Fourth International Workshop on Temporal Representation and Reasoning (TIME)*, Daytona Beach, Florida, May 1997. IEEE Computer Society Press.

[Bonet and Geffner, 1997] B. Bonet and H. Geffner. Planning as Heuristic Search: New Results. In *Proceedings of the Fourth European Conference on Planning (ECP)*. Springer-Verlag, 1997.

[Bonet and Geffner, 2000] B. Bonet and H. Geffner. Planning with Incomplete Information as Heuristic Search in Belief Space. In *Proceedings of the Fifth International Conference on AI Planning and Scheduling (AIPS)*, 2000.

[Bonet *et al.*, 1997] B. Bonet, G. Loerincs, and H. Geffner. A Robust and Fast Action Selection Mechanism for Planning. In *Proceedings of the Fourteenth National Conference on AI (AAAI)*, pages 714–719. AAAI/MIT Press, 1997.

[Bordini *et al.*, 2003a] R. Bordini, M. Fisher, C. Pardavila, and M. Wooldridge. Model Checking AgentSpeak. In *Proceedings of the Second International Joint Conference on Autonomous Agents and Multi-Agent Systems (AAMAS), Melbourne, Australia, 14–18 July*, 2003.

[Bordini *et al.*, 2003b] R. Bordini, M. Fisher, W. Visser, and M. Wooldridge. Verifiable Multi-Agent Programs. In *Proceedings of the First International Workshop on Programming Multiagent Systems: languages, frameworks, techniques and tools (PROMAS), Melbourne, Australia*, 2003.

[Bordini *et al.*, 2003c] R. Bordini, W. Visser, M. Fisher, C. Pardavila, and M. Wooldridge. Model Checking Multi-Agent Programs with CASP. In *Proceedings of the Fifteenth Conference on Computer-Aided Verification (CAV), Boulder, USA, 8–12 July*, 2003.

[Borg *et al.*, 1983] A. Borg, J. Baumbach, and S. Glazer. A Message System Supporting Fault Tolerance. In *Proceedings of the Ninth ACM Symposium on Operating System Principles*, pages 90–99, New Hampshire, October 1983. ACM. (In ACM Operating Systems Review, vol. 17, no. 5).

[Boutilier and Goldszmidt, 1996] C. Boutilier and M. Goldszmidt. The Frame Problem and Bayesian Network Action Representations. In *Proceedings of the Eleventh Biennial Canadian Conference on Artificial Intelligence*, May 1996.

[Boutilier *et al.*, 1995a] C. Boutilier, T. Dean, and S. Hanks. Planning Under Uncertainty: Structural Assumptions and Computational Leverage. In *Proceedings of the Second European Planning Workshop*, 1995.

[Boutilier *et al.*, 1995b] C. Boutilier, R. Dearden, and M. Goldszmidt. Exploiting Structure in Policy Construction. In *Proceedings of the International Joint Conference on Artificial Intelligence (IJCAI)*, 1995.

[Boutilier *et al.*, 1999] C. Boutilier, T. Dean, and S. Hanks. Decision Theoretic Planning: Structural Assumptions and Computational Leverage. *Journal of AI Research*, 11:1–94, 1999.

[Boyen and Koller, 1998] X. Boyen and D. Koller. Approximate Learning of Dynamic Models. In *Proceedings of NIPS*, pages 396–402, 1998.

[Bradshaw *et al.*, 1999] J. Bradshaw, M. Greaves, H. Holmback, T. Karygiannis, B. Silverman, N. Suri, and A. Wong. Agents for the Masses? *IEEE Intelligent Systems*, 14(2), 1999.

[Brajnik and Clancy, 1998] G. Brajnik and D. J. Clancy. Focusing Qualitative Simulation Using Temporal Logic: Theoretical Foundations. *Annals of Mathematics and Artificial Intelligence*, 22(1-2):59–86, 1998.

[Brass *et al.*, 1998] S. Brass, J. Dix, I. Niemelä, and T. Przymusinski. A Comparison of the Static and the Disjunctive Well-Founded Semantics and its Implementation. In *Proceedings of International Conference on Knowledge Representation and Reasoning (KR)*, pages 74–85, 1998.

[Bratman, 1990] M. E. Bratman. What is intention? In P. R. Cohen, J. L. Morgan, and M. E. Pollack, editors, *Intentions in Communication*, pages 15–32. MIT Press, 1990.

[Bresina *et al.*, 2002] J. Bresina, R. Dearden, N. Meuleau, D. Smith, and R. Washington. Planning under Continuous Time and Resource Uncertainty: A Challenge for AI. In *Proceedings of AIPS Workshop on Temporal Planning*, 2002.

[Bresolin *et al.*, 2004] D. Bresolin, A. Montanari, and G. Puppis. Time Granularities and Ultimately Periodic Automata. In *Ninth European Conference on Logics in Artificial Intelligence (JELIA)*, volume 3229 of *Lecture Notes in Artificial Intelligence*, pages 513–525. Springer-Verlag, 2004.

[Broy, 1997] M. Broy. Refinement of Time. *Lecture Notes in Computer Science*, 1231:44–63, 1997.

[Bruce, 1972] B. Bruce. A Model for Temporal References and its application in a Question Answering Program. *Artificial Intelligence*, 4:1–25, 1972.

[Bruneel and Clarebout, 1994] G. Bruneel and P. Clarebout. Een implementatie van SLD-NFA+CLP(R) en zijn toepassing voor het redeneren over continue verandering. Masterthesis, supervisors: M. Denecker and D. De Schreye, Dept. of Computing, K.U.Leuven, in Dutch, 1994.

[Brusoni *et al.*, 1994] V. Brusoni, L. Console, B. Pernici, and P. Terenziani. LaTeR: A General Purpose Manager of Temporal Information. In *Proceedings of the Eighth International Symposium on Methodologies for Intelligent Systems (ISMIS)*, volume 869 of *Lecture Notes in Computer Science*. Springer-Verlag, 1994.

[Brusoni *et al.*, 1995a] V. Brusoni, L. Console, B. Pernici, and P. Terenziani. Extending Temporal Relational Databases to Deal with Imprecise and Qualitative Temporal Information. In J. Clifford and A. Tuzhilin, editors, *Recent Advances in Temporal Databases (Proceedings of the International Workshop on Temporal Databases, Zürich, Switzerland, September 1995)*, Workshops in Computing. Springer, 1995.

[Brusoni *et al.*, 1995b] V. Brusoni, L. Console, and P. Terenziani. On the Computational Complexity of Querying Bounds on Differences Constraints. *Artificial Intelligence*, 74(2):367–379, 1995.

[Brusoni *et al.*, 1997] V. Brusoni, L. Console, B. Pernici, and P. Terenziani. LaTeR: An Efficient, General Purpose Manager of Temporal Information. *IEEE Expert*, 12(4):56–64, August 1997.

[Brusoni *et al.*, 1998] V. Brusoni, L. Console, P. Terenziani, and D. Theseider Dupré. A spectrum of definitions for temporal model-based diagnosis. *Artificial Intelligence*, 102(1):39–80, 1998.

[Brusoni *et al.*, 1999] V. Brusoni, L. Console, P. Terenziani, and B. Pernici. Qualitative and Quantitative Temporal Constraints and Relational Databases: Theory, Architecture, and Applications. *IEEE Transactions on Knowledge and Data Engineering*, 1(6):948–968, 1999.

[Bruss and Meyer, 1980] A.R. Bruss and A.R. Meyer. On Time-Space Classes and their Relation to the Theory of Real Addition. *Theoretical Computer Science*, 11:59–69, 1980.

[Bruynooghe, 1981] M. Bruynooghe. Solving Combinatorial Search Problems by Intelligent Backtracking. *Information Processing Letters*, 12(1), 1981.

[Brzoska, 1991] Ch. Brzoska. Temporal Logic Programming and its Relation to Constraint Logic Programming. In *Proceedings of International Logic Programming Symposium (ILPS)*, 1991.

[Brzoska, 1993] Ch. Brzoska. Temporal Logic Programming with Bounded Universal Goals. In *Proceedings of the Tenth International Conference on Logic Programming (ICLP)*, pages 239–256, 1993.

[Brzoska, 1995] Ch. Brzoska. Temporal Logic Programming in Dense Time. In *Proceedings of International Logic Programming Symposium (ILPS)*, 1995.

[Brzozowski and Leiss, 1980] J. Brzozowski and E. Leiss. Finite Automata, and Sequential Networks. *Theoretical Computer Science*, 10, 1980.

[Buchanan and Shortliffe, 1984] B.G. Buchanan and E.H. Shortliffe, editors. *Rule Based Expert Systems: The MYCIN Experiments of the Stanford Heuristic Programming Project*. Addison-Wesley, Reading, USA, 1984.

[Büchi, 1960] J. R. Büchi. Weak Second-Order Arithmetic and Finite Automata. *Z. Math. Logik Grundlag. Math.*, 6:66–92, 1960.

[Büchi, 1962] J.R. Büchi. On a Decision Method in Restricted Second Order Arithmetic. In *Logic, Methodology, and Philosophy of Science: Proceedings of 1960 International Congress*, pages 1–11. Stanford University Press, 1962.

[Bulygin, 1982] E. Bulygin. Time and Validity. In A. Martino, editor, *Deontic Logic, Computational Liguistics and Information Systems*, chapter Vol. II, pages 65–81. North-Holland, 1982.

[Burgess, 1982] J. P. Burgess. Axioms for Tense Logic I: 'Since' and 'Until'. *Notre Dame J. Formal Logic*, 23(2):367–374, 1982.

[Burgess, 1984] J.P. Burgess. Basic Tense Logic. In D. Gabbay and F. Guenthner, editors, *Handbook of Philosophical Logic, volume II*, pages 89–133. D. Reidel Publishing Company, 1984.

[Bylander, 1994] T. Bylander. The Computational Complexity of Propositional STRIPS Planning. *Artificial Intelligence*, 69(1-2), 1994.

[Caironi *et al.*, 1997] P. Caironi, L. Portoni, C. Combi, F. Pinciroli, and S Ceri. HyperCare: A Prototype of an Active Database for Compliance with Essential Hypertension Therapy Guidelines. In *Proceedings of the AMIA Annual Fall Symposium (formerly the Symposium on Computer Applications in Medical Care)*, pages 288–292, Philadelphia, USA, 1997. Hanley & Belfus.

[Calvanese *et al.*, 2001] D. Calvanese, G. De Giacomo, M. Lenzerini, and D. Nardi. Reasoning in Expressive Description Logics. In *Handbook of Automated Reasoning*, pages 1581–1634. Elsevier, 2001.

[Carlson and Pelletier, 1995] G. Carlson and J. Pelletier, editors. *The Generic Book*. University of Chicago Press, Chicago, 1995.

[Carton and Thomas, 2002] O. Carton and W. Thomas. The Monadic Theory of Morphic Infinite Words and Generalizations. *Information and Computation*, 176:51–65, 2002.

[Casati and Varzi, 1996] R. Casati and A. Varzi, editors. *Events*, volume 15 of *The International Research Library of Philosophy*. Dartmouth Publishing, Aldershot, 1996.

[Castellini *et al.*, 2001] C. Castellini, E. Giunchiglia, and A. Tacchella. C-Plan: a Conformant Planner based on Satisfiability. In *Proceedings of International Joint Conference on Artificial Intelligence*, 2001.

[Cavalli and Fariñas del Cerro, 1984] A. Cavalli and L. Fariñas del Cerro. A Decision Method for Linear Temporal Logic. In R. E. Shostak, editor, *Proceedings of the Seventh International Conference on Automated Deduction (CADE)*, volume 170 of *Lecture Notes in Computer Science*, pages 113–127. Springer-Verlag, 1984.

[Cervoni *et al.*, 1994] R. Cervoni, A. Cesta, and A. Oddi. Managing Dynamic Temporal Constraint Networks. In *Proceedings of the Second International Conference on Artificial Intelligence Planning Systems (AIPS)*, pages 196–201, Chicago, USA, 1994. AAAI press.

[Cesta and Oddi, 1995] A. Cesta and A. Oddi. A Formal Domain Description Language for a Temporal Planner. In *Topics in AI: Proceedings of the Fourth Congress of the Italian Association for AI (AI*AI)*, pages 255–260, 1995.

[Cesta and Oddi, 1996] A. Cesta and A. Oddi. Gaining Efficiency and Flexibility in the Simple Temporal Problem. In L. Chittaro, S.D. Goodwin, H.J. Hamilton, and A. Montanari, editors, *Proceedings of the Third International Workshop on Temporal Representation and Reasoning (TIME)*, 1996.

[Chakravarty and Shahar, 2000] S. Chakravarty and Y. Shahar. A Constraint-Based Specification of Periodic Patterns in Time-Oriented Data. *Annals of Mathematics and Artificial Intelligence*, 30:1–4, 2000.

[Chakravarty and Shahar, 2001] S. Chakravarty and Y. Shahar. Specification and Detection of Periodicity in Clinical Data. *Methods of Information in Medicine*, 40(5):410–420, 2001. (Reprinted in: Haux, R., and Kulikowski, C. (eds), *Yearbook of Medical Informatics 2003*, Stuttgart: F.K. Schattauer and The International Medical Informatics Association, pp.296-306).

[Chandra *et al.*, 1981a] A. Chandra, J.Y. Halpern, A. Meyer, and R. Parikh. Equations between Regular Terms and an Application to Process Logic. In *Proceedings of the Thirteenth Annual ACM Symposium on Theory of Computation (STOC)*, pages 384–390, Milwaukee, USA, 1981.

[Chandra *et al.*, 1981b] A. Chandra, D. Kozen, and L. Stockmeyer. Alternation. *Journal of the ACM*, 28:114–133, 1981.

[Chaochen and Hansen, 1998] Z. Chaochen and M. Hansen. An Adequate First Order Interval Logic. In W.P. de Roever, H. Langmaak, and A. Pnueli, editors, *Compositionality: the Significant Difference*, volume 1536 of *LNCS*, pages 584–608. Springer, 1998.

[Chapman, 1987] D. Chapman. Planning for Conjunctive Goals. *Artificial Intelligence*, 32(3):333–377, 1987.

[Charniak and McDermott, 1985] E. Charniak and D. McDermott. *Introduction to Artifical Intelligence*. Addison-Wesley, 1985.

[Charniak, 1991] E. Charniak. Bayesian Networks without Tears. *AI Magazine*, 12(4):50–63, December 1991.

[Cheeseman *et al.*, 1991] P. Cheeseman, B. Kanefsky, and W.M. Taylor. Where the *really* hard problems are. In *Proceedings of the Twelfth International Joint Conference on Artificial Intelligence (IJCAI)*, pages 331–337. Morgan Kaufmann, 1991.

[Chemilieu-Gendrau, 1987] M. Chemilieu-Gendrau. *Le Role du Temps dans la Formation du Droit International.* Droit International. Editions Pedone, 1987.

[Chen and Warren, 1989] W. Chen and D. Warren. C-logic of Complex Objects. In *Proceedings of the Eighth ACM-SIGACT-SIGMOD-SIGART Symposium on Principles of Database Systems (PODS)*, 1989.

[Chen and Zaniolo, 1999] C. X. Chen and C. Zaniolo. Universal Temporal Extensions for Database Languages. In *Proceedings of IEEE International Conference on Data Engineering*, pages 428–437, 1999.

[Chen *et al.*, 1995] W. Chen, T. Swift, and D. Warren. Efficient Top-Down Computation of Queries under the Well-Founded Semantics. *Journal of Logic Programming*, 24(3):161–201, 1995.

[Chen *et al.*, 2000] J. Chen, D. J. DeWitt, F. Tian, and Y. Wang. NiagaraCQ: A Scalable Continuous Query System for Internet Databases. In *Proceedings of the ACM SIGMOD International Conference on Management of Data*, pages 379–390, 2000.

[Chien *et al.*, 2001] S-Y. Chien, V. J. Tsotras, and C. Zaniolo. Version Management of XML Documents. *SIGMOD Record*, 30(3):46–53, 2001.

[Chien *et al.*, 2002] S-Y. Chien, V. J. Tsotras, and C. Zaniolo. Efficient Schemes for Managing Multiversion XML Documents. *The VLDB Journal*, 11(4):332–353, 2002.

[Chimenti, 1990] D. Chimenti. The IDL System Prototype. *IEEE Transactions on Knowledge and Data Engineering*, 2(1):78–90, 1990.

[Chittaro and Dojat, 1997] L. Chittaro and M. Dojat. Using a General Theory of Time and Change in Patient Monitoring: Experiment and Evaluation. *Computers in Biology and Medicine*, 27(5):435–452, 1997.

[Chomicki and Imieliński, 1988] J. Chomicki and T. Imieliński. Temporal Deductive Databases and Infinite Objects. In *Proceedings of the ACM Symposium on Principles of Database Systems (PODS)*, pages 61–73, Austin, USA, March 1988.

[Chomicki and Niwinski, 1995] J. Chomicki and D. Niwinski. On the Feasibility of Checking Temporal Integrity Constraints. *Journal of Computer and System Sciences*, 51(3):523–535, December 1995.

[Chomicki and Toman, 1998] J. Chomicki and D. Toman. Temporal Logic in Information Systems. In J. Chomicki and G. Saake, editors, *Logics for Databases and Information Systems*, pages 31–70. Kluwer, 1998.

[Chomicki *et al.*, 1996] J. Chomicki, D. Goldin, and G. Kuper. Variable Independence and Aggregation Closure. In *Proceedings of the ACM Symposium on Principles of Database Systems (PODS)*, pages 40–48, Montréal, Canada, June 1996.

[Chomicki *et al.*, 2001] J. Chomicki, D. Toman, and M. H. Böhlen. Querying ATSQL Databases with Temporal Logic. *ACM Transactions on Database Systems*, 26(2):145–178, 2001.

[Chomicki *et al.*, 2003a] J. Chomicki, D. Goldin, G. Kuper, and D. Toman. Variable Independence in Constraint Databases. *IEEE Transactions on Knowledge and Data Engineering*, 15(6):1422–1436, 2003.

[Chomicki *et al.*, 2003b] J. Chomicki, G. Saake, and R. van der Meyden, editors. *Logics for Emerging Applications of Databases*. Springer, 2003.

[Chomicki, 1994] J. Chomicki. Temporal Query Languages: A Survey. In Gabbay, D. and Ohlbach, H., editor, *First International Conference on Temporal Logic (TIME)*, volume 827 of *Lecture Notes in Artificial Intelligence*. Springer Verlag, 1994.

[Chomicki, 1995] J. Chomicki. Efficient Checking of Temporal Integrity Constraints Using Bounded History Encoding. *ACM Transactions on Database Systems*, 20(2):149–186, June 1995.

[Choueka, 1974] Y. Choueka. Theories of Automata on ω-Tapes: A Simplified Approach. *Journal of Computer and System Sciences*, 8:117–141, 1974.

[Ciapessoni *et al.*, 1993] E. Ciapessoni, E. Corsetti, A. Montanari, and P. San Pietro. Embedding Time Granularity in a Logical Specification Language for Synchronous Real-Time Systems. *Science of Computer Programming*, 20(1):141–171, 1993.

[Cimatti and Roveri, 1999] A. Cimatti and M. Roveri. Conformant Planning via Model Checking. In *Proceedings of European Conference on Planning (ECP)*, pages 21–34, 1999.

[Cimatti and Roveri, 2000] A. Cimatti and M. Roveri. Conformant Planning via Symbolic Model Checking. *Journal of AI Research*, 13:305–338, 2000.

[Cimatti *et al.*, 1998a] A. Cimatti, F. Giunchiglia, and R. W. Weyhrauch. A Many-Sorted Natural Deduction. *Computational Intelligence*, 14:134–149, 1998.

[Cimatti *et al.*, 1998b] A. Cimatti, M. Roveri, and P. Traverso. Automatic OBDD-Based Generation of Universal Plans in Non-Deterministic Domains. In *Proceedings of AAAI*, pages 875–881, 1998.

[Citrigno *et al.*, 1997] S. Citrigno, T. Eiter, W. Faber, G. Gottlob, C. Koch, N. Leone, C. Mateis, G. Pfeifer, and F. Scarcello. The DLV System: Model Generator and Application Front Ends. In *Proceedings of the Twelfth Workshop on Logic Programming*, pages 128–137, 1997.

[Clancey, 1985] W.J. Clancey. Heuristic Classification. *Artificial Intelligence*, 27(3):289–350, 1985.

[Clark, 1978] Keith L. Clark. Negation as Failure. In H. Gallaire and J. Minker, editors, *Logic and Databases*, pages 293–322. Plenum Press, 1978.

[Clarke and Emerson, 1981a] E. Clarke and E. Emerson. Synthesis of Synchronization Skeletons for Branching Time Temporal Logic. In *Proceedings of IBM Workshop on Logic of Programs*, pages 52–71, Yorktown Heights, USA, 1981. Springer, Berlin.

[Clarke and Emerson, 1981b] E.M. Clarke and E.A. Emerson. Design and Synthesis of Synchronization Skeletons using Branching Time Temporal Logic. In D. Kozen, editor, *Workshop on Logics of Programs*, volume 131 of *Lecture Notes in Computer Science*, pages 52–71. Springer-Verlag, 1981.

[Clarke and Schlingloff, 2001] E.M. Clarke and B.-H. Schlingloff. Model Checking. In A. Robinson and A. Voronkov, editors, *Handbook of Automated Reasoning*, pages 1635–1790. North-Holland, 2001.

[Clarke *et al.*, 1983] E.M. Clarke, E.A. Emerson, and A.P. Sistla. Automatic Verification of Finite State Concurrent Systems Using Temporal Logic Specifications: A Practical Approach. In *Proceedings of International Symposium on Principles of Programming Languages (POPL)*, pages 117–126. ACM Press, 1983.

[Clarke *et al.*, 1986] E.M. Clarke, E.A. Emerson, and A.P. Sistla. Automatic Verification of Finite State Concurrent Systems Using Temporal Logic Specifications. *ACM Transactions on Programming Languages and Systems*, 8(2):244–263, 1986.

[Clarke *et al.*, 1999] E. M. Clarke, O. Grumberg, and D. A. Peled. *Model Checking*. MIT Press, 1999.

[Clifford and Rao, 1988] J. Clifford and A. Rao. A Simple General Structure for Temporal Domains. In *Temporal Aspects of Information Systems*, pages 17–28. Elsevier, Amsterdam (NL), 1988.

[Clifford *et al.*, 1993] J. Clifford, A. Croker, and A. Tuzhilin. On the Completeness of Query Languages for Grouped and Ungrouped Historical Data Models. In Tansel, A. et. al., editor, *Temporal Databases: Theory, Design and Implementation*, chapter 20, pages 496–533. Benjamin/Cummings Pub. Co., 1993.

[Clifford *et al.*, 1994] J. Clifford, A. Croker, and A. Tuzhilin. On Completeness of Historical Relational Query Languages. *ACM Transactions on Database Systems*, 19(1):64–116, March 1994.

[Codd, 1971] E. F. Codd. Normalized Data Structure: A Brief Tutorial. In E. F. Codd and A. L. Dean, editors, *Proceedings of ACM-SIGFIDET Workshop on Data Description, Access and Control*, pages 1–17, San Diego, USA, 1971. ACM.

[Codd, 1972] E. F. Codd. Relational Completeness of Data Base Sub-Languages. In R. Rustin, editor, *Data Base Systems*, pages 33–64. Prentice-Hall, 1972.

[Cohen and Levesque, 1990] P. R. Cohen and H. J. Levesque. Intention is Choice with Commitment. *Artificial Intelligence*, 42:213–261, 1990.

[Cohen *et al.*, 1997] D. Cohen, P. Jeavons, and M. Koubarakis. Tractable disjunctive constraints. In *Proceedings of Constraint Programming (CP)*, volume 1330 of *Lecture Notes in Computer Science*, pages 478–490, Linz, Austria, 1997.

[Cohen *et al.*, 2000] D. Cohen, P. Jeavons, P. Jonsson, and M. Koubarakis. Building Tractable Disjunctive Constraints. *Journal of the ACM*, 47(5):826–853, 2000.

[Cohn, 1987] A.G. Cohn. A More Expressive Formulation of Many Sorted Logics. *Journal of Automated Reasoning*, 3(2):113–200, 1987.

[Combi *et al.*, 1994] C. Combi, F. Pinciroli, G. Musazzi, and C. Ponti. Managing and Displaying Different Time Granularities of Clinical Information. In J.G. Ozbolt, editor, *Proceedings of Eighteenth Annual Symposium on Computer Applications in Medical Care (SCAMC)*, pages 954–958, Philadelphia, USA, 1994. Hanley & Belfus.

[Combi *et al.*, 1995] C. Combi, F. Pinciroli, M. Cavallaro, and G. Cucchi. Querying Temporal Clinical Databases with Different Time Granularities: the GCH-OSQL Language. In *Proceedings of the Annual Symposium on Computer Applications in Medical Care (SCAMC)*, pages 326–330, New-Orleans, USA, 1995.

[Combi *et al.*, 2004] C. Combi, M. Franceschet, and A. Peron. Representing and Reasoning about Temporal Granularities. *Journal of Logic and Computation*, 14(1):51–77, 2004.

[Comrie, 1976] B. Comrie. *Aspect: an Introduction to the Study of Verbal Aspect and Related Problems*. Cambridge University Press, Cambridge, 1976.

[Condotta, 2000] J-F. Condotta. The Augmented Interval and Rectangle Networks. In A. G. Cohn, F. Giunchiglia, and B. Selman, editors, *Proceedings of the Seventh International Conference on Principles of Knowledge Representation and Reasoning (KR)*, pages 571–579, Breckenridge, CO, USA, April 2000. Morgan Kaufmann.

[Console and Terenziani, 1999] L. Console and P. Terenziani. Efficient Processing of Queries and Assertions about Qualitative and Quantitative Temporal Constraints. *Computational Intelligence*, 15(4):442–465, 1999.

[Console and Torasso, 1991a] L. Console and P. Torasso. A Spectrum of Logical Definitions of Model-Based Diagnosis. *Computational Intelligence*, 7:133–141, 1991.

[Console and Torasso, 1991b] L. Console and P. Torasso. On the Co–operation Between Abductive and Temporal Reasoning in Medical Diagnosis. *Artificial Intelligence in Medicine*, 3:291–311, 1991.

[Console *et al.*, 1991] L. Console, D. Theseider Dupre, and P. Torasso. On the Relationship Between Abduction and Deduction. *Journal of Logic and Computation*, 1(5):661–690, 1991.

[Cooper, 1990] G. Cooper. The Computational Complexity of Probabilistic Inference using Bayesian Belief Networks. *Artificial Intelligence*, 42, 1990.

[Cormen *et al.*, 1990] T.H. Cormen, C.E. Leiserson, and R.L. Rivest. *Introduction to Algorithms*. MIT Press, 1990.

[Corsetti *et al.*, 1991a] E. Corsetti, E. Crivelli, D. Mandrioli, A. Montanari, A. Morzenti, P. San Pietro, and E. Ratto. Dealing with Different Time Scales in Formal Specifications. In *International Workshop on Software Specification and Design*, pages 92–101, 1991.

[Corsetti *et al.*, 1991b] E. Corsetti, A. Montanari, and E. Ratto. Dealing with Different Time Granularities in Formal Specifications of Real-Time Systems. *Journal of Real-Time Systems*, 3(2):191–215, 1991.

[Cousins and Kahn, 1991] S.B. Cousins and M.G. Kahn. The Visual Display of Temporal Information. *Artificial Intelligence in Medicine*, 3(6):341–357, 1991.

[Cowell *et al.*, 1999] R.C. Cowell, A.P. Dawid, S.L. Lauritzen, and D.J. Spiegelhalter. *Probabilistic Networks and Expert Systems*. Springer-Verlag, NewYork, 1999.

[Culik II *et al.*, 1984] K. Culik II, A. Salomaa, and D. Wood. Systolic Tree Acceptors. *R.A.I.R.O Informatique Théorique*, 18:53–69, 1984.

[Dagum and Galper, 1993] P. Dagum and A. Galper. Forecasting Sleep Apnea with Dynamic Network Models. In *Proceedings of Conference on Uncertainty in Artificial Intelligence (UAI)*, pages 64–71, 1993.

[Dal Lago and Montanari, 2001] U. Dal Lago and A. Montanari. Calendars, Time Granularities, and Automata. In *Proceedings of the International Symposium on Spatial and Temporal Databases*, volume 2121 of *Lectures Notes on Computer Science*, pages 279–298, Los Angeles, USA, 2001.

[Dal Lago *et al.*, 2003a] U. Dal Lago, A. Montanari, and G. Puppis. Time Granularities, Calendar Algebra, and Automata. Technical Report 4, Dipartimento di Matematica e Informatica, Università di Udine, Italy, February 2003.

[Dal Lago *et al.*, 2003b] U. Dal Lago, A. Montanari, and G. Puppis. Towards Compact and Tractable Automaton-based Representations of Time Granularity. In *Proceedings of the Eighth Italian Conference on Theoretical Computer Science (ICTCS)*, volume 2841 of *LNCS*, pages 72–85. Springer, October 2003.

[Das and Musen, 1994] A.K. Das and M.A. Musen. A Temporal Query System for Protocol–Directed Decision Support. *Methods of Information in Medicine*, 33:358–370, 1994.

[Date *et al.*, 2003] C. J. Date, H. Darwen, and N. A. Lorentzos. *Temporal Data and the Relational Model*. Morgan Kaufman, 2003.

[Davidson, 1967] D. Davidson. The Logical Form of Action Sentences. In N. Rescher, editor, *The Logic of Decision and Action*. University of Pittsburgh Press, 1967.

[Davidson, 1969] D. Davidson. The Individuation of Events. In N. Rescher, editor, *Essays in Honor of Carl G. Hempel*. D. Reidel, Dordrecht, 1969. (Reprinted in D. Davidson, *Essays on Actions and Events*, Oxford, Clarendon Press, 1980, pages 163-180).

[Davis, 1992] E. Davis. Infinite Loops in Finite Time: Some Observations. In *Proceedings of the Third International Conference on Principles of Knowledge Representation and Reasoning (KR)*, pages 47–58. Morgan-Kaufmann, 1992.

[Dawid, 1992] A. P. Dawid. Applications of a General Propagation Algorithm for Probabilistic Expert Systems. *Statistics and Computing*, 2:25–36, 1992.

[de Zegher-Geets *et al.*, 1988] I.M. de Zegher-Geets, A.G. Freeman, M.G. Walker, R.L. Blum, and G. Wiederhold. Summarization and Display of On-Line Medical Records. *M.D. Computing*, 5:38–46, 1988.

[Dean and Boddy, 1988] T. Dean and M. Boddy. Reasoning About Partially Ordered Events. *Artificial Intelligence*, 36:375–399, 1988.

[Dean and Kanazawa, 1989] T. Dean and K. Kanazawa. A Model for Reasoning about Persistence and Causation. *Computational Intelligence*, 5:142–150, 1989.

[Dean and McDermott, 1987] T. Dean and D.V. McDermott. Temporal Data Base Management. *Artificial Intelligence*, 32:1–55, 1987.

[Dean, 1989] T. Dean. Using Temporal Hierarchies to Efficiently Maintain Large Temporal Databases. *Journal of ACM*, 36(4):687–718, 1989.

[Dechter *et al.*, 1989] R. Dechter, I. Meiri, and J. Pearl. Temporal Constraint Networks. In R. Brachman, H. Levesque, and R. Reiter, editors, *Proceedings of First International Conference on Principles of Knowledge Representation and Reasoning (KR)*, pages 83–93, Toronto, Canada, 1989.

[Dechter *et al.*, 1991] R. Dechter, I. Meiri, and J. Pearl. Temporal Constraint Networks. *Artificial Intelligence*, 49(1-3):61–95, 1991. Special Volume on Knowledge Representation.

[Dechter, 1992] R. Dechter. From Local to Global Consistency. *Artificial Intelligence*, 55:87–107, 1992.

[Degtyarev *et al.*, 2003] A. Degtyarev, M. Fisher, and B. Konev. Monodic Temporal Resolution. In *Proceedings of Conference on Automated Deduction (CADE)*, Lecture Notes in Computer Science. Springer, July 2003.

[Delgrande and Gupta, 1996] J.P. Delgrande and A. Gupta. A Representation for Efficient Temporal Reasoning. In *Proceedings of the Thirteenth National Conference of the American Association for Artificial Intelligence (AAAI)*, pages 381–388, Portland, OR, 1996.

[Delgrande and Gupta, 2002] J.P. Delgrande and A. Gupta. Updating $<=,<$-Chains. *Information Processing Letters*, 83(5):261–268, 2002.

[Delgrande *et al.*, 1999] J.P. Delgrande, A. Gupta, and T. Van Allen. Point Based Approaches to Qualitative Temporal Reasoning. In *Proceedings of AAAI Conference*, pages 739–744, 1999.

[Delgrande *et al.*, 2001] J. Delgrande, A. Gupta, and T. Van Allen. A Comparison of Point-based Approaches to Qualitative Temporal Reasoning. *Artificial Intelligence*, 131:135–170, 2001.

[Dembinski and Maluszynski, 1985] P. Dembinski and J. Maluszynski. AND-Parallelism with Intelligent Backtracking for Annotated Logic Programs. In V. Saraswat and K. Ueda, editors, *Proceedings of the International Symposium on Logic Programming (ILPS)*, pages 25–38, 1985.

[Demri, 2004] S. Demri. LTL over Integer Periodicity Constraints (Extended Abstract). In *Proceedings of the Seventh International Conference on Foundations of Software Science and Computation Structures (FOSSACS)*, volume 2987 of *Lecture Notes in Computer Science*, pages 121–135, Heidelberg, Germany, 2004. Springer-Verlag.

[Denecker and De Schreye, 1992] M. Denecker and D. De Schreye. SLDNFA: an Abductive Procedure for Normal Abductive Programs. In K.R. Apt, editor, *Proceedings of the International Joint Conference and Symposium on Logic Programming*, pages 686–700. MIT Press, 1992.

[Denecker and De Schreye, 1993] M. Denecker and D. De Schreye. Representing incomplete Knowledge in Abductive Logic Programming. In *Proceedings of International Logic Programming Symposium (ILPS)*, pages 147–164, Vancouver, Canada, 1993.

[Denecker and De Schreye, 1998] M. Denecker and D. De Schreye. SLDNFA: an Abductive Procedure for Abductive Logic Programs. *Journal of Logic Programming*, 34(2):111–167, 1998.

[Denecker *et al.*, 1992] M. Denecker, L. Missiaen, and M. Bruynooghe. Temporal reasoning with Abductive Event Calculus. In *Proceedings of the European Conference on Artificial Intelligence (ECAI)*. John Wiley and sons, 1992.

[Denecker *et al.*, 1996] M. Denecker, K. Van Belleghem, G. Duchatelet, F. Piessens, and D. De Schreye. A Realistic Experiment in Knowledge Representation Using Open Event Calculus: Protocol Specification. In M. Maher, editor, *Proceedings of the International Joint Conference and Symposium on Logic Programming*, pages 170–184. MIT Press, 1996.

[Denecker, 1993] M. Denecker. *Knowledge Representation and Reasoning in Incomplete Logic Programming*. PhD thesis, Department of Computer Science, K.U.Leuven, 1993.

[Denecker, 1995] M. Denecker. A Terminological Interpretation of (Abductive) Logic Programming. In V.W. Marek, A. Nerode, and M. Truszczynski, editors, *International Conference on Logic Programming and Nonmonotonic Reasoning (LPNMR)*, volume 928 of *Lecture Notes in Artificial Intelligence*, pages 15–29. Springer, 1995.

[Dettori and Puppo, 1996] G. Dettori and E. Puppo. How Generalization Interacts with the Topological and Metric Structure of Maps. In *Proceedings of International Symposium on Spatial Data Handling*, pages 27–38, 1996.

[Devanbu and Litman, 1996] P. T. Devanbu and D. J. Litman. Taxonomic Plan Reasoning. *Artificial Intelligence*, 84:1–35, 1996.

[Devogele *et al.*, 1996] T. Devogele, J. Trevisan, and L. Raynal. Building a Multi-Scale Database with Scale-Transition Relationship. In *Proceedings of International Symposium on Spatial Data Handling*, 1996.

[Dexter *et al.*, 2001] P.R. Dexter, S. Perkins, M.J. Overhage, K. Maharry, R.B. Kohler, and C.J. McDonald. A Computerized Reminder System to Increase the use of Preventive Care for Hospitalized Patients. *New England Journal of Medicine*, 345(13):965–970, 2001.

[Dimopoulos *et al.*, 1997] Y. Dimopoulos, B. Nebel, and J. Koehler. Encoding Planning Problems in Non-Monotonic Logic Programs. In *Proceedings of European Conference on Planning (ECP)*, pages 169–181, 1997.

[Dix, 1991] J. Dix. Classifying Semantics of Logic Programs. In *Proceedings of International Workshop in Logic Programming and Nonmonotonic Reasoning (LPNMR)*, pages 166–180, Washington D.C., USA, 1991.

[Dixon *et al.*, 1998] C. Dixon, M. Fisher, and M. Wooldridge. Resolution for Temporal Logics of Knowledge. *Journal of Logic and Computation*, 8(3):345–372, 1998.

[Dixon, 1996] C. Dixon. Search Strategies for Resolution in Temporal Logics. In M. A. McRobbie and J. K. Slaney, editors, *Proceedings of the Thirteenth International Conference on Automated Deduction (CADE)*, volume 1104 of *Lecture Notes in Artificial Intelligence*, pages 672–687, New Brunswick, USA, July/August 1996. Springer-Verlag.

[Dixon, 1998] C. Dixon. Temporal Resolution using a Breadth-First Search Algorithm. *Annals of Mathematics and Artificial Intelligence*, 22:87–115, 1998.

[Dixon, 2000] C. Dixon. Using Otter for Temporal Resolution. In *Advances in Temporal Logic*, volume 16 of *Applied Logic Series*, pages 149–166. Kluwer, 2000. (Proceedings the Second International Conference on Temporal Logic (ICTL).).

[Do and Kambhampati, 2001] M. Binh Do and S. Kambhampati. Sapa: a Domain-Independent Heuristic Metric Temporal Planner. In *Proceedings of European Conference on Planning (ECP)*, 2001.

[Doner, 1970] J. Doner. Tree Acceptors and Some of their Applications. *Journal of Computer and System Sciences*, 4:406–451, 1970.

[Donini *et al.*, 1996] F. M. Donini, M. Lenzerini, D. Nardi, and A. Schaerf. Reasoning in Description Logics. In G. Brewka, editor, *Principles of Knowledge Representation*, pages 191–236. CSLI Publications, Stanford, California, 1996.

[Doucet *et al.*, 2001] A. Doucet, N. DeFreitas, and N. Gordon. *Sequential Monte Carlo Methods in Practice*. Springer-Verlag, NewYork, 2001.

[Downes *et al.*, 1986] S.M. Downes, M.G. Walker, and R.L. Blum. Automated Summarization of On-line Medical Records. In R. Salamon, B. Blum, and M. Jorgensen, editors, *Proceedings of the Fifth Conference on Medical Informatics (MEDINFO)*, pages 800–804, Amsterdam, NL, 1986. North-Holland.

[Dowty, 1979] D. Dowty. *Word Meaning and Montague Grammar*. Kluwer Academic Publishers, Dordrecht, 1979.

[Drabble and Tate, 1994] B. Drabble and A. Tate. The Use of Optimistic and Pessimistic Resource Profiles to Inform Search in an Activity Based Planner. In *Proceedings of the Second Conference on AI Planning Systems (AIPS)*. AAAI Press, 1994.

[Drabble, 1993] B. Drabble. EXCALIBUR: A Program for Planning and Reasoning with Processes. *Artificial Intelligence*, 62(1):1–40, 1993.

[Drakengren and Jonsson, 1997a] T. Drakengren and P. Jonsson. Eight maximal tractable subclasses of Allen's algebra with metric time. *Journal of Artificial Intelligence Research*, 7:25–45, 1997.

[Drakengren and Jonsson, 1997b] T. Drakengren and P. Jonsson. Twenty-One Large Tractable Subclasses of Allen's Algebra. *Artificial Intelligence*, 93(1–2):297–319, 1997.

[Drakengren and Jonsson, 1998] T. Drakengren and P. Jonsson. A Complete Classification of Allen's Algebra Relative to Subsets Of Basic Relations. *Artificial Intelligence*, 106(2):205–219, 1998.

[Dung, 1993] P. Dung. Representing Actions in Logic Programming and its Application in Database Updates. In D. S. Warren, editor, *Proceedings of International Conference on Logic Programming (ICLP)*, pages 222–238, 1993.

[Durfee, 1988] E. H. Durfee. *Coordination of Distributed Problem Solvers*. Kluwer, 1988.

[Dvorak and Kuipers, 1989] D. Dvorak and B. Kuipers. Model-Based Monitoring of Dynamic Systems. In *Proceedings of the Eleventh International Joint Conference on Artificial Intelligence (IJCAI)*, pages 1238–1243, San Mateo, CA, 1989. Morgan Kaufmann.

[Dyreson and Snodgrass, 1994] C. Dyreson and R. Snodgrass. Temporal Granularity and Indeterminacy: Two Sides of the Same Coin. Technical Report 6, University of Arizona, Tucson, USA, 1994.

[Edelkamp and Helmert, 2000] S. Edelkamp and M. Helmert. On the Implementation of MIPS. In *Proceedings of Workshop on Decision-Theoretic Planning, Artificial Intelligence Planning and Scheduling (AIPS)*, pages 18–25. AAAI-Press, 2000.

[Egenhofer and Franzosa, 1991] M. Egenhofer and R. Franzosa. Point Set Topological Spatial Relations. *International Journal of Geographical Information Systems*, 5(2):161–174, 1991.

[Eiter *et al.*, 2000a] T. Eiter, W. Faber, G. Gottlob, C. Koch, C. Mateis, N. Leone, G. Pfeifer, and F. Scarcello. The DLV System. In J. Minker, editor, *Pre-prints of Workshop on Logic-Based AI*, 2000.

[Eiter *et al.*, 2000b] T. Eiter, W. Faber, N. Leone, and G. Pfeifer. Declarative problem solving in DLV. In J. Minker, editor, *Logic Based Artificial Intelligence*, pages 79–103. Kluwer Academic Publishers, 2000.

[Elgot and Rabin, 1966] C. Elgot and M. Rabin. Decidability and Undecidability of Second (First) Order Theory of Generalized Successor. *Journal of Symbolic Logic*, 31:169–181, 1966.

[Elgot, 1961] C. Elgot. Decision Problems for Finite Automata Design and Related Arithmetics. *Trans. Amer. Math. Soc.*, 98:21–52, 1961.

[Emerson and Clarke, 1982] E. Emerson and E. C. Clarke. Using Branching Time Temporal Logic to Synthesise Synchronisation Skeletons. *Science of Computer Programming*, 2, 1982.

[Emerson and Halpern, 1985] E. Emerson and J. Halpern. Decision Procedures and Expressiveness in the Temporal Logic of Branching Time. *Journal of Computer and System Sciences*, 30(1):1–24, 1985.

[Emerson and Halpern, 1986] E. Emerson and J. Halpern. 'Sometimes' and 'Not Never' Revisited: on Branching versus Linear Time. *Journal of the ACM*, 33, 1986.

[Emerson and Jutla, 1988] E. Emerson and C. Jutla. Complexity of Tree Automata and Modal Logics of Programs. In *Proceedings of the Twenty Ninth IEEE Conference on Foundations of Computer Science (FOCS)*. IEEE, 1988.

[Emerson and Lei, 1985] E. Emerson and C. Lei. Modalities for Model Checking: Branching Time Strikes Back. In *Proceedings of the Twelfth Symposium on Principles of Programming Languages (POPL)*, pages 84–96, 1985.

[Emerson and Sistla, 1984] E. Emerson and A. Sistla. Deciding Full Branching Time Logic. *Information and Control*, 61(3):175 – 201, 1984.

[Emerson, 1985] E. Emerson. Automata, Tableaux and Temporal Logics. In *Proceedings of the Workshop on Logics of Programs*, Brooklyn, USA, 1985.

[Emerson, 1990] E.A. Emerson. Temporal and modal logic. In J. van Leeuwen, editor, *Handbook of Theoretical Computer Science: Formal Models and Semantics*, chapter 16, pages 995–1072. Elsevier Science Publishers, 1990.

[Emerson, 1996] E. Emerson. Automated Temporal Reasoning for Reactive Systems. In F. Moller and G. Birtwistle, editors, *Logics for Concurrency*, pages 41–101. Springer Verlag, 1996.

[Enderton, 1972] H. B. Enderton. *A Mathematical Introduction To Logic*. Academic Press, 1972.

[Endriss, 2003] U. Endriss. *Modal Logics of Ordered Trees*. PhD thesis, Department of Computer Science, King's College London, 2003.

[Erdem and Lifschitz, 1999] E. Erdem and V. Lifschitz. Transformations of Logic Programs Related to Causality and Planning. In *Proceedings of Logic Programming and Non-Monotonic Reasoning (LPNMR)*, pages 107–116, 1999.

[Eshghi and Kowalski, 1989] K. Eshghi and R.A. Kowalski. Abduction Compared with Negation as Failure. In *Proceedings of the International Conference on Logic Programming (ICLP)*. MIT-Press, 1989.

[Eshghi, 1988a] K. Eshghi. Abductive Planning with Event Calculus. In R.A. Kowalski and K.A. Bowen, editors, *Proceedings of the Fifth International Conference and Symposium on Logic Programming*, pages 562–579, Cambridge, MA, 1988. MIT Press.

[Eshghi, 1988b] K. Eshghi. Abductive Planning with Event Calculus. In *Proceedings of International Conference on Logic Programming (ICLP)*, 1988.

[Euzenat, 1993] J. Euzenat. Représentation Granulaire du Temps. *Revue d'Intelligence Artificielle*, 7(3):329–361, 1993.

[Euzenat, 1995a] J. Euzenat. A Categorical Approach to Time Representation: First Study on Qualitative Aspects. In *Proceedings of the IJCAI Workshop on Spatial and Temporal Reasoning*, pages 145–152, 1995.

[Euzenat, 1995b] J. Euzenat. An Algebraic Approach to Granularity in Qualitative Space and Time Representation. In *Proceedings of International Joint Conference on Artificial Intelligence (IJCAI)*, pages 894–900, 1995.

[Euzenat, 2001] J. Euzenat. Granularity in Relational Formalisms with Application to Time and Space Representation. *Computational Intelligence*, 17(4):703–737, 2001.

[Evans, 1989] C. Evans. Negation-as-Failure as an Approach to the Hanks and McDermott Problem. In *Proceedings of the Second International Symposium on Artificial Intelligence*, 1989.

[Fagan *et al.*, 1984] M. Fagan, J. C. Kunz, E. A. Feigenbaum, and J. J. Osborn. Extensions to the Rule-Based Formalism for a Monitoring Task. In Buchanan and Shortliffe [1984], pages 397–423.

[Fagin *et al.*, 1996] R. Fagin, J. Halpern, Y. Moses, and M. Vardi. *Reasoning About Knowledge*. MIT Press, 1996.

[Ferrante and Geiser, 1977] J. Ferrante and J.R. Geiser. An Efficient Decision Procedure for the Theory of Rational Order. *Theoretical Computer Science*, 4(2):227–233, 1977.

[Ferrante and Rackoff, 1975] J. Ferrante and C. Rackoff. A Decision Procedure for the First Order Theory of Real Addition with Order. *SIAM Journal on Computing*, 4(1):69–76, 1975.

[Ferrante and Rackoff, 1979] J. Ferrante and C. Rackoff. *The Computational Complexity of Logical Theories*. Lecture Notes in Mathematics. Springer Verlag, 1979.

[Fiadeiro and Maibaum, 1994] J. L. Fiadeiro and T. Maibaum. Sometimes "tomorrow" is "sometime": Action Refinement in a Temporal Logic of Objects. *Lecture Notes in Computer Science*, 827:48–66, 1994.

[Fikes and Nilsson, 1971] R.E. Fikes and N.J. Nilsson. STRIPS: A New Approach to the Application of Theorem-Proving to Problem-Solving. *Artificial Intelligence*, 2(3):189–208, 1971.

[Finger and Gabbay, 1992] M. Finger and D.M. Gabbay. Adding a Temporal Dimension to a Logic System. *Journal of Logic, Language, and Information*, 1(3):203–233, 1992.

[Finger and Gabbay, 1996] M. Finger and D. Gabbay. Combining Temporal Logic Systems. *Notre Dame Journal of Formal Logic*, 37:204–232, 1996.

[Fischer and Rabin, 1974] M.J. Fischer and M.O. Rabin. Super-exponential Complexity of Presburger Arithmetic. In *Proceedings of the AMS Symposium on Complexity of Real Computational Processes*, volume III, 1974.

[Fisher and Ghidini, 1999] M. Fisher and C. Ghidini. Programming Resource-Bounded Deliberative Agents. In *Proceedings of International Joint Conference on Artificial Intelligence (IJCAI)*. Morgan Kaufmann, 1999.

[Fisher and Ghidini, 2002] M. Fisher and C. Ghidini. The ABC of Rational Agent Programming. In *Proceedings of the First International Conference on Autonomous Agents and Multi-Agent Systems (AAMAS)*, pages 849–856. ACM Press, July 2002.

[Fisher and Kakoudakis, 1999] M. Fisher and T. Kakoudakis. Flexible Agent Grouping in Executable Temporal Logic. In *Proceedings of Twelfth International Symposium on Languages for Intensional Programming (ISLIP)*. World Scientific Press, 1999.

[Fisher and Owens, 1992] M. Fisher and R. Owens. From the Past to the Future: Executing Temporal Logic Programs. In *Proceedings of Logic Programming and Automated Reasoning (LPAR)*, volume 624 of *Lecture Notes in Computer Science*, St. Petersberg, Russia, July 1992. Springer-Verlag.

[Fisher and Owens, 1995a] M. Fisher and R. Owens. An Introduction to Executable Modal and Temporal Logics. In *Executable Modal and Temporal Logics*, volume 897 of *Lecture Notes in Artificial Intelligence*, pages 1–20, Heidelberg, Germany, 1995. Springer-Verlag.

[Fisher and Owens, 1995b] M. Fisher and R. Owens, editors. *Executable Modal and Temporal Logics*, volume 897 of *Lecture Notes in Artificial Intelligence*. Springer-Verlag, February 1995.

[Fisher and Wooldridge, 1997] M. Fisher and M. Wooldridge. On the Formal Specification and Verification of Multi-Agent Systems. *International Journal of Cooperative Information Systems*, 6(1):37–65, January 1997.

[Fisher *et al.*, 2001] M. Fisher, C. Dixon, and M. Peim. Clausal Temporal Resolution. *ACM Transactions on Computational Logic*, 2(1):12–56, January 2001.

[Fisher *et al.*, 2003] M. Fisher, C. Ghidini, and B. Hirsch. Organising logic-based agents. In M. Hinchey, J. Rash, W. Truszkowski, C. Rouff, and D. Gordon-Spears, editors, *Proceedings of Second International Workshop on Formal Approaches to Agent-Based Systems (FAABS)*, volume 2699 of *Lecture Notes in Computer Science*, pages 15–27, Greenbelt, USA, October 2003. Springer.

[Fisher, 1991] M. Fisher. A Resolution Method for Temporal Logic. In *Proceedings of the Twelfth International Joint Conference on Artificial Intelligence (IJCAI)*, Sydney, Australia, 1991. Morgan Kaufman.

[Fisher, 1993] M. Fisher. Concurrent METATEM — A Language for Modeling Reactive Systems. In *Parallel Architectures and Languages, Europe (PARLE)*, volume 694 of *Lecture Notes in Computer Science*, Munich, Germany, June 1993. Springer-Verlag.

[Fisher, 1994] M. Fisher. A Survey of Concurrent METATEM — The Language and its Applications. In *First International Conference on Temporal Logic (ICTL)*, volume 827 of *Lecture Notes in Computer Science*, Bonn, Germany, July 1994. Springer-Verlag.

[Fisher, 1996a] M. Fisher. A Temporal Semantics for Concurrent METATEM. *Journal of Symbolic Computation*, 22(5/6), November/December 1996.

[Fisher, 1996b] M. Fisher. An Introduction to Executable Temporal Logics. *Knowledge Engineering Review*, 11(1):43–56, March 1996.

[Fisher, 1997a] M. Fisher. A Normal Form for Temporal Logic and its Application in Theorem-Proving and Execution. *Journal of Logic and Computation*, 7(4), July 1997.

[Fisher, 1997b] M. Fisher. Implementing BDI-like Systems by Direct Execution. In *Proceedings of International Joint Conference on Artificial Intelligence (IJCAI)*. Morgan-Kaufmann, 1997.

[Fisher, 2004] M. Fisher. Temporal Development Methods for Agent-Based Systems. To appear in *Journal of Autonomous Agents and Multi-Agent Systems*, 2004.

[Fitting, 1983] M. Fitting. *Proof Methods for Modal and Intuitionistic Logics*. Reidel, 1983.

[Forbus, 1989] K. Forbus. Introducing Actions into Qualitative Simulation. In *Proceedings of International Joint Conference on Artificial Intelligence (IJCAI)*, pages 1273–1278. Morgan Kaufmann, 1989.

[Fox and Long, 1996] M. Fox and D. Long. An Efficient Algorithm for Managing Partial Orders in Planning. *ACM SIGART Bulletin*, 7(4):3–12, 1996.

[Fox and Long, 2002a] M. Fox and D. Long. PDDL+ : Planning with Time and Metric Resources. Technical Report Department of Computer Science, Durham University, UK, 2002.

[Fox and Long, 2002b] M. Fox and D. Long. PDDL+: Modelling Continuous Time-dependent Effects. In *Proceedings of the Third International NASA Workshop on Planning and Scheduling for Space*, 2002.

[Fox and Long, 2003] M. Fox and D. Long. PDDL2.1: An extension to PDDL for expressing temporal planning domain s. *Journal of AI Research*, 20, 2003.

[Fox *et al.*, 1998] J. Fox, N. Johns, and A. Rahmanzadeh. Disseminating medical knowledge: the pro*forma* approach. *Artificial Intelligence in Medicine*, 14:157–181, 1998.

[Franceschet and Montanari, 2001a] M. Franceschet and A. Montanari. A Combined Approach to Temporal Logics for Time Granularity. In *Proceedings of the Second International Workshop on Methods for Modalities (M4M)*, 2001.

[Franceschet and Montanari, 2001b] M. Franceschet and A. Montanari. Towards an Automata-Theoretic Counterpart of Combined Temporal Logics. In *Proceedings of the Second International Workshop on Verification and Computational Logic*, pages 55–74, 2001.

[Franceschet and Montanari, 2003] M. Franceschet and A. Montanari. Branching Within Time: An Expressively Complete and Elementarily Decidable Temporal Logic for Time Granularity. *Research on Language and Computation*, 1(3-4):229–263, 2003.

[Franceschet and Montanari, 2004] M. Franceschet and A. Montanari. Temporalized Logics and Automata for Time Granularity. *Theory and Practice of Logic Programming*, 4(5-6):621–658, 2004.

[Franceschet *et al.*, 2003] M. Franceschet, A. Montanari, A. Peron, and G. Sciavicco. Definability and Decidability of Binary Predicates for Time Granularity. In *Proceedings of the Tenth International Symposium on Temporal Representation and Reasoning and of the Fourth International Conference on Temporal Logic (TIME-ICTL)*, pages 192–202. IEEE Computer Society Press, 2003.

[Franceschet *et al.*, 2004] M. Franceschet, A. Montanari, and M. de Rijke. Model Checking for Combined Logics with an Application to Mobile Systems. *Automated Software Engineering*, 11(3):287–319, 2004.

[Franceschet, 2002] M. Franceschet. *Dividing and Conquering the Layered Land.* PhD thesis, Department of Mathematics and Computer Science, University of Udine, Udine, Italy, 2002.

[Franconi and Toman, 2003] E. Franconi and D. Toman. Fixpoint Extensions of Temporal Description Logics. In *Proceedings of Workshop on Description Logics (DL)*, volume 81 of *CEUR-WS*, pages 160–167, 2003.

[Franklin and Graesser, 1996] S. Franklin and A. Graesser. Is it an Agent, or just a Program?: A Taxonomy for Autonomous Agents . In J. P. Müller, M. J. Wooldridge, and N. R. Jennings, editors, *Intelligent Agents III — Proceedings of the Third International Workshop on Agent Theories, Architectures, and Languages (ATAL)*, Lecture Notes in Artificial Intelligence. Springer-Verlag, Heidelberg, 1996.

[Frege, 1972] G. Frege. *Conceptual Notation (Begriffschrift), and Related Articles.* Oxford : Clarendon Press, 1972. (English translation, edited by T. Bynum.).

[Freksa, 1992] Christian Freksa. Temporal reasoning based on semi-intervals. *Artificial intelligence*, 54(1):199–227, 1992.

[Friedman *et al.*, 1998] N. Friedman, K. Murphy, and S. Russell. Learning the Structure of Dynamic Probabilistic Networks. In *Proceedings of International Conference on Uncertainty in AI (UAI)*, pages 139–147, 1998.

[Fries, 1972] J.F. Fries. Time oriented patient records and a computer databank. *Journal of the American Medical Association*, 222:1536–1543, 1972.

[Früehwirth, 1996] T. Früehwirth. Temporal Annotated Constraint Logic Programming. *Journal of Symbolic Computation*, 22(5/6), 1996.

[Fung and Kowalski, 1997] T.H. Fung and R. Kowalski. The IFF Proof Procedure for Abductive Logic Programming. *Journal of Logic Programming*, 33(2):151–165, 1997.

[Furer, 1982] M. Furer. The Complexity of Presburger Arithmetic with Bounded Quantifier Alternation Depth. *Theoretical Computer Science*, 18:105–111, 1982.

[Fusaoka, 1996] A. Fusaoka. Situation Calculus on a Dense Flow of Time. In *Proceedings of AAAI Conference*, pages 633–638. AAAI press, 1996.

[Gabbay and Hodkinson, 1990] D. M. Gabbay and I. M. Hodkinson. An Axiomatisation of the Temporal Logic with Until and Since over the Real Numbers. *Journal of Logic and Computation*, 1(2):229 – 260, 1990.

[Gabbay *et al.*, 1980] D. Gabbay, A. Pnueli, S. Shelah, and J. Stavi. The Temporal Analysis of Fairness. In *Proceedings of the Seventh ACM Symposium on the Principles of Programming Languages (POPL)*, pages 163–173, Las Vegas, Nevada, January 1980.

[Gabbay *et al.*, 1994a] D. Gabbay, I. Hodkinson, and M. Reynolds. *Temporal Logic: Mathematical Foundations and Computational Aspects, Volume 1*. Oxford University Press, 1994.

[Gabbay *et al.*, 1994b] D.M. Gabbay, C. Hogger, J. Robinson, and D. Nute. *Handbook of Logic in AI and Logic Programming - Volume 4: Epistemic and Temporal Reasoning*. Clarendon Press, Oxford, 1994.

[Gabbay *et al.*, 2000] D.M. Gabbay, M.A. Reynolds, and M. Finger. *Temporal Logic: Mathematical Foundations and Computational Aspects - Volume 2*, volume 40 of *Oxford Logic Guides*. Oxford University Press, 2000.

[Gabbay, 1981] D.M. Gabbay. The Separation Theorem for Temporal Logic. Technical Report DFG Project RO/245/12, University of Stuttgart, 1981.

[Gal *et al.*, 1994] A. Gal, O. Etzioni, and A. Segev. Representation of Highly-Complex Knowledge in a Database. *Journal of Intelligent Information Systems*, 3(2):185–203, 1994.

[Galipienso and Sanchis, 2002] M.I.A. Galipienso and F.B. Sanchis. Representation and Reasoning with Disjunction Temporal Constraints. In *Proceedings of Ninth International Symposium on Temporal Representation and Reasoning (TIME)*, 2002.

[Galton, 1984] A. P. Galton. *The Logic of Aspect: an Axiomatic Approach*. Clarendon Press, Oxford, 1984.

[Galton, 1987] A. Galton, editor. *Temporal Logics and Their Applications*. Academic Press, 1987.

[Galton, 1990] Antony Galton. A Critical Examination of Allen's Theory of Action and Time. *Artificial Intelligence*, 42:159–188, 1990.

[Galton, 1991] A. P. Galton. Reified Temporal Theories and How To Unreify Them. In *Proceedings of International Joint Conference on Artificial Intelligence (IJCAI)*, pages 1177–1182. Morgan Kaufmann, 1991.

[Galton, 1996a] A. P. Galton. A Note on a Lemma of Ladkin. *Journal of Logic and Computation*, 6(1):1–4, 1996.

[Galton, 1996b] A. P. Galton. An Investigation of 'Non-Intermingling' Principles in Temporal Logic. *Journal of Logic and Computation*, 6, 2:271–294, 1996.

[Gamper and Nejdl, 1997] J. Gamper and W. Nejdl. Abstract Temporal Diagnosis in Medical Domains. *Artificial Intelligence in Medicine*, 10:209–234, 1997.

[Garagnani, 2000] M. Garagnani. A Correct Algorithm for Efficient Planning with Preprocessed Domain Axioms. In M. Bramer, A. Preece, and F. Coenen, editors, *Research and Development in Intelligent Systems XVII (Proceedings of ES'2000)*. Springer-Verlag, 2000.

[Gardner, 1987] A. Gardner. *An Artificial Intelligence Approach to Legal Reasoning*. MIT Press, 1987.

[Garrido *et al.*, 2002] A. Garrido, M. Fox, and D. Long. Temporal Planning with PDDL2.1. In *Proceedings of the European Conference on Artificial Intelligence (ECAI)*, 2002.

[Gayral, 1992] F. Gayral. *Sémantique du Langage Naturel et Profondeur Variable: Une Première Approche*. PhD thesis, Université de Paris-Nord, Villetaneuse (FR), 1992.

[Gazen and Knoblock, 1997] B. Gazen and C. Knoblock. Combining the Expressivity of UCPOP with the Efficiency of Graphplan. In *Proceedings of European Conference on Planning (ECP)*, pages 221–233, 1997.

[Geerts *et al.*, 2001] F. Geerts, S. Haesevoets, and B. Kuijpers. A Theory of Spatio-Temporal Database Queries. In *Proceedings of the International Workshop on Database Programming Languages*, pages 198–212, 2001.

[Gelfond and Lifschitz, 1988] M. Gelfond and V. Lifschitz. The stable model semantics for logic programming. In R. Kowalski and K. Bowen, editors, *Logic Programming: Proc. of the Fifth Int'l Conf. and Symp.*, pages 1070–1080. MIT Press, 1988.

[Gelfond and Lifschitz, 1990] M. Gelfond and V. Lifschitz. Logic Programs with Classical Negation. In D. Warren and P. Szeredi, editors, *Proceedings of the Seventh International Conference on Logic Programming (ICLP)*, pages 579–597, 1990.

[Gelfond and Lifschitz, 1991] M. Gelfond and V. Lifschitz. Classical Negation in Logic Programs and Disjunctive Databases. *New Generation Computing*, 9:365–387, 1991.

[Gelfond and Lifschitz, 1993] M. Gelfond and V. Lifschitz. Representing Actions and Change by Logic Programs. *Journal of Logic Programming*, 17(2,3,4):301–323, 1993.

[Gelfond *et al.*, 1991] M. Gelfond, V. Lifschitz, and A. Rabinov. What are the Limitations of the Situation Calculus? In R. Boyer, editor, *Essays in honor of Woody Bledsoe*, pages 167–179. Kluwer Academic, 1991.

[Gelfond *et al.*, 2001] M. Gelfond, M. Balduccini, and J. Galloway. Diagnosing Physical Systems in A-Prolog. In T. Eiter, W. Faber, and M. Truszczyński, editors, *Proceedings of the Sixth International Conference on Logic Programming and Nonmonotonic Reasoning (LPNMR)*, pages 213–226, 2001.

[Gelfond, 1994] M. Gelfond. Logic Programming and Reasoning with Incomplete Information. *Annals of Mathematics and Artificial Intelligence*, 12:19–116, 1994.

[Gelfond, 2001] M. Gelfond. Representing knowledge in A-Prolog. In *Computational Logic: from Logic Programming to the Future, Collection of Papers in Honour of B. Kowalski*. Elsevier, 2001.

[Gentzen, 1934] G. Gentzen. Untersuchungen über das logische schliessen. *Math. Zeitschrift*, 39:176–210, 405–431, 1934.

[Gerevini and Cristani, 1995] A. Gerevini and M. Cristani. Reasoning with Inequations in Temporal Constraint Networks. Technical report, IRST - Instituto per la Ricerca Scientifica e Tecnologica, Povo TN, Italy, 1995. (A shorter version appears in the Proceedings of the Workshop on Spatial and Temporal Reasoning, IJCAI-95).

[Gerevini and Cristani, 1996] A. Gerevini and M. Cristani. On Temporal Constraint Networks with Inequations. Technical Report RT 199611-3, Dipartimento di Elettronica per l'Automazione, Università di Brescia, Italy, 1996.

[Gerevini and Cristani, 1997] A. Gerevini and M. Cristani. On Finding Solutions in Temporal Constraint Networks. In *Proceedings of the Fifteenth International Joint Conference on Artificial Intelligence (IJCAI)*, pages 1460–1465, Nagoya, Japan, 1997. Morgan Kaufmann.

[Gerevini and Nebel, 2002] A. Gerevini and B. Nebel. Qualitative Spatio-Temporal Reasoning with RCC-8 and Allen's Interval Calculus: Computational Complexity. In *Proceedings of the Seventh European Conference on Artificial Intelligence (ECAI)*, pages 312–316. IOS Press, 2002.

[Gerevini and Renz, 1998] A. Gerevini and J. Renz. Combining Topological and Qualitative Size Constraints for Spatial Reasoning. In *Proceedings of the Fourth International Conference on Principles and Practice of Constraint Programming (CP)*. Splinger Verlag, 1998.

[Gerevini and Schubert, 1994a] A. Gerevini and L. Schubert. An Efficient Method for Managing Disjunctions in Qualitative Temporal Reasoning. In *Proceedings of the Fourth International Conference on Principles of Knowledge Representation and Reasoning (KR)*, pages 215–225, San Francisco, CA, 1994. Morgan Kaufmann.

[Gerevini and Schubert, 1994b] A. Gerevini and L. Schubert. On Point-Based Temporal Disjointness. *Artificial Intelligence*, 70:347–361, 1994.

[Gerevini and Schubert, 1995a] A. Gerevini and L. Schubert. Efficient Algorithms for Qualitative Reasoning about Time. *Artificial Intelligence*, 74(2):207–248, 1995.

[Gerevini and Schubert, 1995b] A. Gerevini and L. Schubert. On Computing the Minimal Labels in Time Point Algebra Networks. *Computational Intelligence*, 11(3):443–448, 1995.

[Gerevini and Serina, 2002] A. Gerevini and I. Serina. LPG: A Planner Based on Local Search for Planning Graphs. In *Proceedings of the Sixth International Conference on AI Planning Systems (AIPS)*. AAAI Press, 2002.

[Gerevini *et al.*, 1993] A. Gerevini, L. Schubert, and S. Schaeffer. Temporal Reasoning in Timegraph I-II. *SIGART Bulletin*, 4(3):21–25, 1993.

[Gerevini *et al.*, 1995] A. Gerevini, L. Schubert, and S. Schaeffer. The Temporal Reasoning Tools TimeGraph-I-II. *International Journal of Artificial Intelligence Tools*, 4(1–2):281–299, 1995. (A shorter version appeared in *Proceedings of the Sixth IEEE Int. Conf. on Tools with Artificial Intelligence*, p. 513–520, IEEE Computer Society Press, 1994; and in *SIGART Bulletin*, ACM Press, 4(3):21-25, July 1993.).

[Gerevini *et al.*, 1996] A. Gerevini, A. Perini, and F. Ricci. Incremental Algorithms for Managing Temporal Constraints. In *Proceedings of the Eighth IEEE International Conference on Tools with Artificial Intelligence (ICTAI)*, Toulouse, France, 1996. IEEE Computer Society Press.

[Gerevini, 1997] A. Gerevini. Reasoning About Time and Actions in Artificial Intelligence: Major Issues. In O. Stock, editor, *Spatial and Temporal Reasoning*, pages 43–70. Kluwer Academic Publishers, 1997.

[Gerevini, 2003a] A. Gerevini. Incremental Tractable Reasoning about Qualitative Temporal Constraints. In *Proceedings of the Eighteenth International Joint Conference on Artificial Intelligence (IJCAI)*, pages 1283–1288. Morgan Kaufmann, 2003.

[Gerevini, 2003b] A. Gerevini. Incremental Tractable Reasoning about Qualitative Temporal Information. Technical Report 2003-12-32, Dipartimento di Elettronica per l'Automazione, Università di Brescia, Italy, 2003.

[Ghahramani and Jordan, 1996] Z. Ghahramani and M.I. Jordan. Factorial hidden Markov models. In *Proceedings of NIPS*, pages 396–402, 1996.

[Ghallab and Laruelle, 1994] M. Ghallab and H. Laruelle. Representation and Control in IxTeT, a Temporal Planner. In *Proceedings of the International Conference on Artificial Intelligence Planning and Scheduling (AIPS)*, 1994.

[Ghallab and Mounir Alaoui, 1989] M. Ghallab and A. Mounir Alaoui. Managing Efficiently Temporal Relations Through Indexed Spanning Trees. In *Proceedings of the Eleventh International Joint Conference on Artificial Intelligence (IJCAI-89)*, pages 1297–1303, San Mateo, CA, 1989. Morgan Kaufmann.

[Ghallab, 1996] M. Ghallab. On Chronicles: Representation, On-line Recognition and Learning. In *Proceedings of Interntation Conference on Knowledge Representation and Reasoning (KR)*, pages 597–606, 1996.

[Giannotti *et al.*, 2003] F. Giannotti, G. Manco, and J. Wijsen. Logical Languages for Data Mining. In Chomicki et al. [2003b], chapter 9, pages 325–361.

[Gilks and Berzuini, 2001] W.R. Gilks and C. Berzuini. Following a Moving Target — Monte Carlo Inference for Dynamic Bayesian Systems. *Journal of the Royal Statistical Society (Series B)*, 63(1):127–146, 2001.

[Ginsberg and Smith, 1988a] M. Ginsberg and D. Smith. Reasoning about Action I: A Possible Worlds Approach. *Artificial Intelligence*, 35(2):165–196, June 1988.

[Ginsberg and Smith, 1988b] M. Ginsberg and D. Smith. Reasoning about Action II: The Qualification Problem. *Artificial Intelligence*, 35(3):311–342, July 1988.

[Ginsburg and Hull, 1983] S. Ginsburg and R. Hull. Order Dependency in the Relational Model. *Theoretical Computer Science*, 26:149–195, 1983.

[Ginsburg and Hull, 1986] S. Ginsburg and R. Hull. Sort Sets in the Relational Model. *Journal of the ACM*, 33(3):465–488, 1986.

[Giunchiglia and Lifschitz, 1998] E. Giunchiglia and V. Lifschitz. An Action Language Based on Causal Explanation: Preliminary Report. In *Proceeings of the AAAI Conference*, pages 623–630, 1998.

[Giunchiglia *et al.*, 1997] F. Giunchiglia, A. Villafiorita, and T. Walsh. Theories of Abstraction. *AI Communications*, 10(2):167–176, 1997.

[Goldblatt, 1987] R. Goldblatt. *Logics of Time and Computation*, volume 7 of *CSLI Lecture Notes*. Center for the Study of Language and Information, Stanford University, California, 1987.

[Goldblatt, 1991] R. Goldblatt. The McKinsey Axiom is not Canonical. *The Journal of Symbolic Logic*, 56(2):554–562, 1991.

[Goldin, 1997] D.Q. Goldin. *Constraint Query Algebras*. PhD thesis, Dept. of Computer Science, Brown University, USA, 1997.

[Golumbic and Shamir, 1993] Martin Charles Golumbic and Ron Shamir. Complexity and algorithms for reasoning about time: A graph-theoretic approach. *Journal of the ACM*, 40(5):1108–1133, 1993.

[Goodwin *et al.*, 1994] S.D. Goodwin, E. Neufeld, and A. Trudel. Probabilistic Temporal Representation and Reasoning. *International Journal of Expert Systems*, 7(3):261–289, 1994.

[Gordon and Veloso, 1996] C. Gordon and M. Veloso. The PRESTIGE Project: Implementing Guidelines in Healthcare. In *Medical Informatics Europe*, pages 887–891. IOS Press, 1996.

[Goré, 1997] R. Goré. Tableau Methods for Modal and Temporal Logics. Technical Report TR-ARP-15-95 (revised 1997), Automated Reasoning Project, Australian National University, Canberra, Australia, 1997.

[Gough, 1984] G. D. Gough. Decision Procedures for Temporal Logic. Master's thesis, Department of Computer Science, University of Manchester, October 1984. (Also University of Manchester, Department of Computer Science, Technical Report UMCS-89-10-1.).

[Grahne, 1991] G. Grahne. *The Problem of Incomplete Information in Relational Databases*, volume 554 of *Lecture Notes in Computer Science*. Springer Verlag, 1991.

[Gregersen and Jensen, 1999] H. Gregersen and C. S. Jensen. Temporal Entity-Relationship Models - A Survey. *Knowledge and Data Engineering*, 11(3):464–497, 1999.

[Grimshaw and Russel, 1993] J.M. Grimshaw and I.T. Russel. Effects of Clinical Guidelines on Medical Practice: A Systematic Review of Rigorous Evaluation. *Lancet*, pages 1317–1322, 1993.

[Gruska, 1990] J. Gruska. Synthesis, Structure and Power of Systolic Computations. *Theoretical Computer Science*, 71(1):47–77, 1990.

[Guesgen, 1989] H.-W. Guesgen. Spatial Reasoning Based on Allen's Temporal Logic. Technical Report TR-89-094, ICSI, 1989.

[Gupta *et al.*, 1997] V. Gupta, T.A. Henziner, and R. Jagadeesan. Robust timed automata. In *Hybrid and Real-time Systems (HART)*, volume 1201 of *Lecture Notes in Computer Science*, pages 331–345. Springer-Verlag, 1997.

[Gurevich and Shelah, 1985] Y. Gurevich and S. Shelah. The Decision Problem for Branching Time Logic. *J. of Symbolic Logic*, 50:668–681, 1985.

[Haarslev *et al.*, 1998] V. Haarslev, C. Lutz, and R. Möller. Foundation of Spatiotemporal Reasoning with Description Logics. In A. Cohn, L. Schubert, and S. C. Shapiro, editors, *Proceedings of the Sixth International Conference on Principles of Knowledge Representation and Reasoning (KR)*, pages 112–123, Trento, Italy, June 1998. Morgan Kaufmann.

[Haddawy, 1994] P. Haddawy. *Representing Plans under Uncertainty: A Logic of Time, Chance, and Action.* Number 770 in Lecture Notes in Artificial Intelligence. Springer-Verlag, 1994.

[Hafer and Thomas, 1987] T. Hafer and W. Thomas. Computation tree logic CTL* and path quantifiers in the monadic theory of the binary tree. In *Proceedings of the International Colloquium on Automata, Languages and Programming (ICALP)*, volume 267 of *Lecture Notes in Computer Science*, pages 269–279, Karlsruhe, Germany, 1987. Springer.

[Haimowitz and Kohane, 1996] I.J. Haimowitz and I.S. Kohane. Managing Temporal Worlds for Medical Trend Diagnosis. *Artificial Intelligence in Medicine*, 8(3):299–321, 1996.

[Halpern and Moses, 1985] J. Y. Halpern and Y. Moses. A Guide to the Modal Logics of Knowledge and Belief. In *Proceedings of the Ninth International Joint Conference on Artificial Intelligence (IJCAI)*, pages 480–490, 1985.

[Halpern and Moses, 1992] J. Y. Halpern and Y. Moses. A Guide to Completeness and Complexity for Modal Logics of Knowledge and Belief. *Artificial Intelligence*, 54:319–379, 1992.

[Halpern and Shoham, 1986] J. Halpern and Y. Shoham. A Propositional Modal Logic of Time Intervals. In *Proceedings of International Symposium on Logic in Computer Science (LICS)*. IEEE Press, 1986.

[Halpern and Shoham, 1991] J. Y. Halpern and Y. Shoham. A Propositional Modal Logic of Time Intervals. *Journal of the ACM*, 38(4):935–962, 1991.

[Halpern and Vardi, 1991] J. Y. Halpern and M. Y. Vardi. Model Checking vs. Theorem Proving: A Manifesto. In V. Lifschitz, editor, *AI and Mathematical Theory of Computation — Papers in Honor of John McCarthy*. Academic Press, 1991.

[Hamblin, 1971] C. L. Hamblin. Instants and Intervals. *Studium Generale*, 24:127–34, 1971.

[Hamblin, 1972] C. L. Hamblin. Instants and Intervals. In J. T. Fraser, F. C. Haber, and G. H. Müller, editors, *The Study of Time*, pages 324–328. Springer-Verlag, New York, 1972.

[Hanks and McDermott, 1986] S. Hanks and D. McDermott. Default Reasoning, Nonmonotonic Logic and the Frame Problem. In *Proceedings of the American Association for AI Conference (AAAI)*, pages 328–333, 1986.

[Hanks and McDermott, 1987] S. Hanks and D. McDermott. Nonmonotonic Logic and Temporal Projection. *Artificial Intelligence*, 33(3):379–412, 1987.

[Hanks and McDermott, 1994] S. Hanks and D. McDermott. Modeling a Dynamic and Uncertain World I: Symbolic and Probabilistic Reasoning about Change. *Artificial Intelligence*, 65(2), 1994.

[Hanks *et al.*, 1995] S. Hanks, D. Madigan, and J. Gavrin. Probabilistic Temporal Reasoning with Endogenous Change. In *Proceedings of International Conference on Uncertainty in Artificial Intelligence (UAI)*, 1995.

[Hanks, 1990] S. Hanks. Projecting Plans for Uncertain Worlds. Technical Report 756, Department of Computer Science, Yale University, USA, January 1990. Ph.D. thesis.

[Hansen and Zilberstein, 1996] E.A. Hansen and S. Zilberstein. Monitoring the Progress of Anytime Problem-Solving. In *Proceedings of the Thirteenth National Conference of the American Association for Artificial Intelligence (AAAI)*, pages 1229–1234. AAAI Press/The MIT Press, 1996.

[Harel *et al.*, 1980] D. Harel, D. Kozen, and R. Parikh. Process Logic: Expressiveness, Decidability, Completeness. In *Proceedings of IEEE Symposium on Foundations of Computer Science (FOCS)*, pages 129–142, 1980.

[Harel *et al.*, 1982] D. Harel, D. Kozen, and R. Parikh. Process Logic: Expressiveness, Decidability, Completeness. *Journal of Computing System Sciences*, 25:144–170, 1982.

[Harel, 1979] D. Harel. *First-Order Dynamic Logic*, volume 68. Springer-Verlag Inc., New York, USA, 1979.

[Harel, 1984] D. Harel. Dynamic Logic. In D. Gabbay and F. Guenthner, editors, *Handbook of Philosophical Logic*, volume II: Extensions of Classical Logic, pages 497–604. D. Reidel Publishing Co., Dordrecht, 1984.

[Haslum and Geffner, 2001] P. Haslum and H. Geffner. Heuristic Planning with Time and Resources. In *Proceedings of the European Conference on Planning (ECP)*, Toledo, Spain, 2001.

[Haugh, 1987] B. A. Haugh. Non-Standard Semantics for The Method of Temporal Arguments. In *Proceedings of the Tenth International Joint Conference on Artificial Intelligence (IJCAI-87)*, pages 449–454. Morgan Kaufmann, 1987.

[Heckerman and Miller, 1986] D.E. Heckerman and R.A. Miller. Towards a Better Understanding of the INTERNIST-1 Knowledge Base. In R. Salamon, B. Blum, and M. Jorgensen, editors, *Proceedings of the Fifth Conference on Medical Informatics (MEDINFO)*, pages 27–31, New York, 1986. North-Holland.

[Hendry and Richard, 1990] D.F. Hendry and J.F. Richard. Likelihood Evaluation for Dynamic Latent Variables Models. In H.M. Amann, D.A. Belsley, and L.F. Pau, editors, *Computational Economics and Econometrics*, chapter 1. Kluwer, Dordrecht, 1990.

[Henkin, 1949] L. Henkin. The Completeness of the First-Order Functional Calculus. *J. of Symbolic Logic*, 14:159–166, 1949.

[Henzinger *et al.*, 1994] T. Henzinger, Z. Manna, and A. Pnueli. Temporal Proof Methodologies for Timed Transition Systems. *Information and Computation*, 112:273–337, 1994.

[Henzinger *et al.*, 1995] T.A. Henzinger, P-H. Ho, and H Wong-Toi. A user guide to HYTECH. In E. Brinksma, W.R. Cleaveland, K.G. Larsen, T. Margaria, and B. Steffen, editors, *Proceedings of Conference on Tools and Algorithms for the Construction and Analysis of Systems: (TACAS)*, volume 1019 of *Lecture Notes in Computer Science*, pages 41–71, 1995.

[Henzinger, 1996] T.A. Henzinger. The Theory of Hybrid Automata. In *Proceedings of the 11th Annual Symposium on Logic in Computer Science (LICS)*, pages 278–292. IEEE Computer Society Press, 1996.

[Herbert *et al.*, 1995] S.I. Herbert, C.J. Gordon, A. Jackson–Smale, and J.L. Renaud Salis. Protocols for Clinical Care. *Computer Methods and Programs in Biomedicine*, 48:21–26, 1995.

[Heuerding *et al.*, 1995] A. Heuerding, G. Jaeger, S. Schwendimann, and M. Seyfried. Propositional Logics on the Computer. In P. Baumgartner, R. Hähnle, and J. Posegga, editors, *Proceedings of Tableaux Workshop*, volume 918 of *Lecture Notes in Computer Science*, pages 310–323. Springer-Verlag, 1995.

[Hintikka, 1955] J. Hintikka. Form and Content in Quantification Theory. *Acta Philosophica Fennica*, 8:7–55, 1955.

[Hirsh, 1996] R. Hirsh. Relation Algebras of Intervals. *Artificial Intelligence*, 83(2):267–295, 1996.

[Hobbs, 1985] J. Hobbs. Granularity. In *Proceedings of International Joint Conference on Artificial Intelligence (IJCAI)*, pages 432–435, 1985.

[Hochbaum and Naor, 1994] D.S. Hochbaum and J. Naor. Simple and Fast Algorithms for Linear and Integer Programs with Two Variables per Inequality. *SIAM Journal on Computing*, 23(6):1179–1192, 1994.

[Hodges, 1984] W. Hodges. Elementary Predicate Logic. In D. Gabbay and F. Guenthner, editors, *Handbook of Philosophical Logic*. D. Reidel, Dordrecht, 1984.

[Hodkinson *et al.*, 2000] I. Hodkinson, F. Wolter, and M. Zakharyashev. Decidable Fragments of First-Order Temporal Logics. *Annals of Pure and Applied Logic*, 106:85–134, 2000.

[Hodkinson *et al.*, 2002] I. Hodkinson, F. Wolter, and M. Zakharyaschev. Decidable and Undecidable Fragments of First-Order Branching Temporal Logics. In *IEEE Symposium on Logic in Computer Science*, pages 393–402, 2002.

[Hodkinson *et al.*, 2003] I. Hodkinson, R. Kontchakov, A. Kurucz, F. Wolter, and M. Zakharyaschev. On the Computational Complexity of Decidable Fragments of First-order Linear Temporal Logics. In *Proceedings of the Joint Tenth International Symposium on Temporal Representation and Reasoning and Fourth International Conference on Temporal Logic (TIME-ICTL)*, 2003.

[Hodkinson, 2000] I. Hodkinson. Temporal Logic and Automata (Chapter 2). In *Temporal Logic: Mathematical Foundations and Computational Aspects, Vol. 2*. Oxford University Press, 2000.

[Hodkinson, 2002] I. M. Hodkinson. Monodic Packed Fragment with Equality is Decidable. *Studia Logica*, 72(2):185–197, 2002.

[Hoffmann and Nebel, 2000] J. Hoffmann and B. Nebel. The FF Planning System: Fast Plan Generation Through Heuristic Search. *Journal of AI Research*, 14:253–302, 2000.

[Hogge, 1987] J.C. Hogge. TPLAN: A Temporal Interval-based Planner with Novel Extensions. Technical Report UIUCDCS-R-87, University of Illinois, USA, 1987.

[Holldobler and Thielscher, 1993] S Holldobler and M Thielscher. Actions and Specificity. In D. Miller, editor, *Proceedings of the International Conference on Logic Programming (ICLP)*, pages 164–180, 1993.

[Hollunder *et al.*, 1990] B. Hollunder, W. Nutt, and M. Schmidt-Schaus. Subsumption Algorithms for Concept Description Languages. In *Proceedings of European Conference on Artificial Intelligence (ECAI)*, pages 348–353, 1990.

[Holzmann, 1997] G.J. Holzmann. The Model Checker Spin. *IEEE Transactions on Software Engineering*, 23(5):279–295, May 1997.

[Holzmann, 2003] G. J. Holzmann. *The Spin Model Checker: Primer and Reference Manual.* Addison-Wesley, November 2003.

[Horn *et al.*, 1997] W. Horn, S. Miksch, G. Egghart, C. Popow, and F. Paky. Effective Data Validation of High–Frequency Data: Time–Point–, Time–Interval–, and Trend–Based Methods. *Computers in Biology and Medicine*, 27(5):389–409, 1997.

[Horn, 2001] W. Horn. AI in Medicine on its way from Knowledge-Intensive to Data-Intensive Systems. *Artificial Intelligence in Medicine*, 23:3–12, 2001.

[Horrocks, 1998] I. Horrocks. The FaCT System. In *Proceedings of International Conference on Automated Reasoning with Analytic Tableaux and Related Methods (Tableaux'98)*, volume 1397 of *Lecture Notes in Computer Science*, pages 307–312. Springer-Verlag, May 1998.

[Howey and Long, 2002] R. Howey and D. Long. Validating Plans with Continuous Effects. Technical report, Department of Computer Science, University of Durham, UK, 2002.

[Hripcsak *et al.*, 1994] G. Hripcsak, P. Ludemann, T.A. Pryor, O.B. Wigertz, and P.D. Clayton. Rationale for the Arden Syntax. *Computers and Biomedical Research*, 27:291–324, 1994.

[Hrycej, 1993] T. Hrycej. A Temporal Extension of Prolog. *Journal of Logic Programming*, 15:113–145, 1993.

[Hughes and Cresswell, 1968] G. Hughes and M. Cresswell. *An Introduction to Modal Logic*. Methuen, London, 1968.

[Hustadt and Konev, 2002] U. Hustadt and B. Konev. TRP++: A Temporal Resolution Prover. In *Proceedings of 3rd International Workshop on the Implementation of Logics*, Tbilisi, Georgia, October 2002.

[Hustadt and Konev, 2003] U. Hustadt and B. Konev. TRP 2.0: A Temporal Resolution Prover. In *Proceedings of 19th International Conference on Automated Deduction (CADE)*, LNCS. Springer, July/August 2003.

[Hustadt and Schmidt, 2002] U. Hustadt and R. A. Schmidt. Scientific Benchmarking with Temporal Logic Decision Procedures. In D. Fensel, F. Giunchiglia, D. McGuinness, and M.-A. Williams, editors, *Proceedings of the Eighth International Conference on Principles of Knowledge Representation and Reasoning (KR)*, pages 533–544. Morgan Kaufmann, 2002.

[Hustadt *et al.*, 2000] U. Hustadt, C. Dixon, R. A. Schmidt, and M. Fisher. Normal Forms and Proofs in Combined Modal and Temporal Logics. In *Proceedings of the Third International Workshop on Frontiers of Combining Systems (FroCoS)*, volume 1794 of *Lecture Notes in Artificial Intelligence*. Springer-Verlag, March 2000.

[Hwang and Schubert, 1994] C.L. Hwang and L.K. Schubert. Interpreting Tense, Aspect, and Time Adverbials: A Compositional, Unified Approach. In D.M. Gabbay and H.J. Ohlbach, editors, *Proceedings of the First International Conference on Temporal Logic (ICTL)*, volume 827 of *Lecture Notes in Computer Science*, pages 237–264, Berlin, 1994. Springer-Verlag.

[Imielinski and Lipski, 1984] T. Imielinski and W. Lipski. Incomplete Information in Relational Databases. *Journal of ACM*, 31(4):761–791, 1984.

[Immerman and Kozen, 1989] N. Immerman and D. Kozen. Definability with Bounded Number of Bound Variables. *Information and Computation*, 83(2):121–139, 1989.

[ISO, 1992] ISO. Database Language SQL. ISO/IEC 9075:1992, International Organization for Standardization, 1992.

[Iwasaki and Low, 1992] Y. Iwasaki and C.M. Low. Device Modelling Environment: An Integrated Model-formulation and simulation environment for Continuous and Discrete Phenomena. In *Proceedings of the Conference on Intelligent Systems Engineering*, 1992.

[Iwasaki *et al.*, 1995] Y. Iwasaki, A. Farquhar, V. Saraswat, D. Bobrow, and V. Gupta. Modelling Time in Hybrid Systems: How Fast Is 'Instantaneous'? In *Proceedings of the Fourteenth International Joint Conference on Artificial Intelligence (IJCAI)*, pages 1773–1781. Morgan Kaufmann, 1995.

[Jackendoff, 1976] R. Jackendoff. Toward an Explanatory Semantic Representation. *Linguistic Inquiry*, 7(1):89–150, 1976.

[Jaffar and Lassez, 1987] J. Jaffar and J-L. Lassez. Constraint Logic Programming. In *Proceeidngs of ACM Symposium on Principles of Programming Languages (POPL)*, 1987.

[Jaffar and Maher, 1994] J. Jaffar and M.J. Maher. Constraint Logic Programming: A Survey. *Journal of Logic Programming*, 19(20):503–581, 1994.

[Jaffar *et al.*, 1994] J. Jaffar, M. J. Maher, P. Stuckey, and R. Yap. Beyond Finite Domains. In A. Borning, editor, *Proceedings of PPCP Conference*, volume 874 of *Lecture Notes in Computer Science*, pages 86–94. Springer Verlag, 1994.

[Jäger *et al.*, 2002] G. Jäger, P. Balsiger, A. Heuerding, S. Schwendimann, M. Bianchi, K. Guggisberg, G. Janssen, W. Heinle, F. Achermann, A. D. Boroumand, P. Brambilla, I. Bucher, and H. Zimmermann. LWB–The Logics Workbench 1.1. `http://www.lwb.unibe.ch/`, 2002. University of Berne, Switzerland.

[Janssen, 1999] G.L.J.M. Janssen. *Logics for Digital Circuit Verification: Theory, Algorithms, and Applications*. PhD thesis, Eindhoven University of Technology, Eindhoven, The Netherlands, 1999.

[Jennings and Wooldridge, 1998] N. R. Jennings and M. Wooldridge. Applications of Agent Technology. In *Agent Technology: Foundations, Applications, and Markets*. Springer-Verlag, Heidelberg, 1998.

[Jensen *et al.*, 1993] C.S. Jensen, M.D. Soo, and R.T. Snodgrass. Unification of Temporal Data Models. In *Proceedings of IEEE International Conference on Data Engineering*, 1993.

[Jensen *et al.*, 1994] C. Jensen, J. Clifford, S. Elmasri, R. Gadia, P. Hayes, S. Jajodia, C. Dyreson, F. Grandi, W. Kaefer, N. Kline, N. Lorentzos, Y. Mitsopoulos, A. Montanari, D. Nonen, E. Peressi, B. Pernici, J. Roddick, N. Sarda, M. Scalas, A. Segev, Richard Snodgrass, Mike Soo, A. Tansel, P. Tiberio, and W. Gio. A Consensus Glossary of Temporal Database Concepts. *SIGMOD record*, 23:52–64, 1994.

[Jensen *et al.*, 1996] C.S. Jensen, R.T. Snodgrass, and M.D. Soo. Extending Existing Dependency Theory to Temporal Databases. *IEEE Transactions on Knowledge and Data Engineering*, 8(4), 1996.

[Jensen, 1995] C. S. Jensen. Vacuuming. In R. T. Snodgrass, editor, *The TSQL2 Temporal Query Language*, pages 447–460. Kluwer Academic Publishers, 1995.

[Jensen, 2001] F.V. Jensen. *Bayesian Networks and Decision Graphs*. Springer-Verlag, New York, 2001.

[Johnson *et al.*, 2000] P. Johnson, S. Tu, N. Booth, B. Sugden, and I. Purves. Using Scenarios in Chronic Disease Management Guidelines for Primary Care. In M.J. Overhage, editor, *Proceedings of the AMIA Annual Symposium*. Hanley & Belfus, 2000.

[Jonsson and Bäckström, 1996] P. Jonsson and C. Bäckström. A Linear Programming Approach to Temporal Reasoning. In *Proceedings of the AAAI Conference*, pages 1235–1240. AAAI Press/MIT Press, 1996.

[Jonsson and Bäckström, 1998] Peter Jonsson and Christer Bäckström. A unifying approach to temporal constraint reasoning. *Artificial Intelligence*, 102(1):143–155, 1998.

[Jonsson *et al.*, 1999] Peter Jonsson, Thomas Drakengren, and Christer Bäckström. Computational complexity of relating time points with intervals. *Artificial Intelligence*, 109(1–2):273–295, 1999.

[Josephson and Josephson, 1994] J.R. Josephson and S.G. Josephson, editors. *Abductive Inference: Computation, Philosophy, Technology*. New York: Cambridge University Press, 1994.

[Jung *et al.*, 1996] C.G. Jung, K. Fischer, and A. Burt. Multi-Agent Planning Using an Abductive Event Calculus. Technical Report DFKI Report RR-96-04, DFKI, Germany, 1996.

[Kabanza *et al.*, 1995] F. Kabanza, J-M. Stevenne, and P. Wolper. Handling Infinite Temporal Data. *Journal of Computer and System Sciences*, 51(1):3–17, 1995.

[Kahn and Gorry, 1977] K. Kahn and G.A. Gorry. Mechanizing Temporal Knowledge. *Artificial Intelligence*, 9:87–108, 1977.

[Kahn, 1988] M.G. Kahn. *Model-Based Interpretation of Time-Ordered Medical Data*. PhD thesis, Section on Medical Information Sciences, University of California, San Francisco, USA, 1988.

[Kahn, 1991a] M.G. Kahn. Combining Physiologic Models and Symbolic Methods to Interpret Time-Varying Patient Data. *Methods of Information in Medicine*, 30:167–178, 1991.

[Kahn, 1991b] M.G. Kahn. Extensions to the Time-Oriented Database Model to Support Temporal Reasoning in Medical Expert Systems. *Methods of Information in Medicine*, 30:4–14, 1991.

[Kahn, 1991c] M.G. Kahn. TQuery: A Context-Sensitive Temporal Query Language. *Computers and Biomedical Research*, 24:401–419, 1991.

[Kaivola, 1995] R. Kaivola. Axiomatising Linear Time mu-Calculus. In *Proceedings of the Sixth International Conference on Concurrency theory (CONCUR)*, volume 962 of *LNCS*, pages 423–437. Springer-Verlag, 1995.

[Kakas and Mancarella, 1990a] A. Kakas and P. Mancarella. Generalized Stable Models: A Semantics for Abduction. In *Proceedings of European Conference on Artificial Intelligence (ECAI)*, pages 385–391, 1990.

[Kakas and Mancarella, 1990b] A.C. Kakas and P. Mancarella. Database Updates Through Abduction. In *Proceedings of the Sixteenth International Conference on Very Large Databases (VLDB)*, pages 650–661. Morgan Kaufmann, 1990.

[Kakas and Miller, 1997] A. Kakas and R. Miller. A Simple Declarative Language for Describing Narratives with Actions. *Journal of Logic Programming*, 31(1-3):157–200, April-June 1997.

[Kakas *et al.*, 1992] A. C. Kakas, R.A. Kowalski, and F. Toni. Abductive Logic Programming. *Journal of Logic and Computation*, 2(6):719–770, 1992.

[Kakas *et al.*, 2000] A.C. Kakas, A. Michael, and C. Mourlas. ACLP: Abductive Constraint Logic Programming. *Journal of Logic Programming*, 44(1-3):129–177, 2000.

[Kakas *et al.*, 2001] A. Kakas, B. Van Nuffelen, and M. Denecker. A-system : Problem Solving Through Abduction. In B. Nebel, editor, *Proceedings of Seventeenth International Joint Conference on Artificial Intelligence (IJCAI)*, volume 1, pages 591–596. Morgan Kaufmann Publishers, Inc., 2001.

[Kamp and Reyle, 1993] H. Kamp and U. Reyle. *From Discourse to Logic*. Kluwer Academic Publishers, Dordrecht, 1993.

[Kamp and Reyle, 1996] H. Kamp and U. Reyle. A Calculus for First-Order Discourse Representation Structures. *Journal of Logic, Language and Information*, 5:297–348, 1996.

[Kamp, 1968] H. Kamp. *Tense Logic and the Theory of Linear Order*. PhD Dissertation, UCLA, Los Angeles, USA, 1968.

[Kamp, 1971] H. Kamp. Formal Properties of 'now'. *Theoria*, 37:227–273, 1971.

[Kamp, 1979] H. Kamp. Events, Instants and Temporal Reference. In R. Bäuerle, U. Egli, and A. von Stechow, editors, *Semantics from Different Points of View*, pages 376–417. Springer-Verlag, 1979.

[Kanazawa *et al.*, 1995] K. Kanazawa, D. Koller, and S. Russell. Stochastic Simulation Algorithms for Dynamic Probabilistic Networks. In *Proceedings of International Conference on Uncertainty in AI (UAI)*, 1995.

[Kanazawa, 1991] K. Kanazawa. A Logic and Time Nets for Probabilistic Inference. In *Proceedings of the Ninth National Conference on Artificial Intelligence (AAAI)*, pages 360–365. MIT Press, 12–19 July 1991.

[Kanellakis *et al.*, 1990] P.C. Kanellakis, G.M. Kuper, and P.Z. Revesz. Constraint Query Languages. In *Proceedings of the Ninth ACM SIGACT-SIGMOD-SIGART Symposium on Principles of Database Systems (PODS)*, pages 299–313, 1990.

[Kanellakis *et al.*, 1995] P.C. Kanellakis, G.M. Kuper, and P.Z. Revesz. Constraint Query Languages. *Journal of Computer and System Sciences*, 51(1):26–52, August 1995.

[Karmarkar, 1984] N. Karmarkar. A New Polynomial Time Algorithm for Linear Programming. *Combinatorica*, 4:373–395, 1984.

[Kartha, 1993] G. Kartha. Soundness and Completeness Theorems for Three Formalizations of Action. In *Proceedings if International joint Conference on Artificial Intelligence (IJCAI)*, pages 724–729, 1993.

[Kautz and Ladkin, 1991] H. Kautz and P. Ladkin. Integrating Metric and Temporal Qualitative Temporal Reasoning. In *Proceedings of the Ninth (US) National Conference on Artificial Intelligence (AAAI)*, pages 241–246, Anaheim, USA, July 1991. American Association for Artificial Intelligence, AAAI Press/MIT Press.

[Kautz and Selman, 1995] H. Kautz and B. Selman. Unifying SAT-based and Graph-based Planning. In *Proceedings of the Fourteenth International Joint Conference on Artificial Intelligence (IJCAI)*, pages 318–325. Morgan Kaufmann, 1995.

[Kautz, 1987] H.A. Kautz. *A Formal Theory of Plan Recognition*. PhD thesis, Department of Computer Science, University of Rochester, Rochester, USA, May 1987. Available as Technical Report 215.

[Kautz, 1991] H.A. Kautz. A Formal Theory of Plan Recognition and its Implementation. In *Reasoning about Plans*, pages 69–126. Morgan Kaufmann, San Mateo, CA, 1991.

[Kay *et al.*, 2000] H. Kay, B. Rinner, and B. J. Kuipers. Semi-quantitative System Identification. *Artificial Intelligence*, 119:103–140, 2000.

[Keenan and Westerstahl, 1997] E. Keenan and D. Westerstahl. Generalized Quantifiers in Linguistics and Logic. In J. van Benthem and A. ter Meulen, editors, *Handbook of Logic and Language*, pages 837–893. MIT/Elsevier, 1997.

[Kenny, 1963] A. Kenny. *Action, Emotion, and Will*. Routledge and Kegan Paul, London, 1963.

[Keravnou and Washbrook, 1990] E.T. Keravnou and J. Washbrook. A Temporal Reasoning Framework used in the Diagnosis of Skeletal Dysplasias. *Artificial Intelligence in Medicine*, 2:239–265, 1990.

[Keravnou and Washbrook, 2001] E.T. Keravnou and J. Washbrook. Abductive Diagnosis using Time-Objects: Criteria for the Evaluation of Solutions. *Computational Intelligence*, 17:87–131, 2001.

[Keravnou, 1996a] E.T. Keravnou. An Ontology of Time Using Time-Axes and Time-Objects as Primitives. Technical Report TR-96-9, Department of Computer Science, University of Cyprus, Cyprus, 1996.

[Keravnou, 1996b] E.T. Keravnou. Temporal Diagnostic Reasoning based on Time-Objects. *Artificial Intelligence in Medicine*, 8:235–265, 1996.

[Keravnou, 1997] E.T. Keravnou. Temporal Abstraction of Medical Data: Deriving Periodicity. In N. Lavrač, E.T. Keravnou, and B. Zupan, editors, *Intelligent Data Analysis in Medicine and Pharmacology*, pages 61–79. Kluwer Academic Publishers, 1997.

[Keravnou, 1999] E.T. Keravnou. A Multidimensional and Multigranular Model of Time for Medical Knowledge–Based Systems. *Journal of Intelligent Information Systems*, 13:79–120, 1999.

[Kesten and Pnueli, 1995] Y. Kesten and A. Pnueli. A Complete Proof System for QPTL. In *Logics of Programs*, pages 2–12. IEEE, 1995.

[Kesten *et al.*, 1994] Y. Kesten, Z. Manna, and A. Pnueli. Temporal Verification of Simulation and Refinement. *Lecture Notes in Computer Science*, 803, 1994.

[Kesten *et al.*, 1997] Y. Kesten, Z. Manna, H. McGuire, and A. Pnueli. A Decision Algorithm for Full Propositional Temporal Logic. In *Proceedings of Conference on Computer Aided Verification (CAV)*, volume 697 of *Lecture Notes in Computer Science*, pages 97–109. Springer, 1997.

[Khachiyan, 1979] L. G. Khachiyan. A Polynomial Algorithm in Linear Programming. *Soviet Mathematics Doklady*, 20:191–194, 1979.

[Kifer and Lausen, 1989] M. Kifer and G. Lausen. F-logic: A Higher-order Language for Reasoning about Objects. In *Proceedings of Eighth ACM-SIGACT-SIGMOD-SIGART Symposium of Principles of Database Systems (PODS)*, 1989.

[Kjaerulff, 1994] U. Kjaerulff. A Computational Scheme for Reasoning in Dynamic Probabilistic Networks. In *Proceedings of International Conference on Uncertainty in AI (UAI)*, pages 121–129, 1994.

[Kleene, 1956] S. Kleene. Representation of Events in Nerve Nets and Finite Automata. In C. Shannon and J. McCarthy, editors, *Automata Studies*, pages 3–41. Princeton Univ. Press, 1956.

[Kline, 1993] N. Kline. An Update of the Temporal Database Bibliography. *SIGMOD RECORD*, 22(4):66–80, 1993.

[Konev *et al.*, 2003] B. Konev, A. Degtyarev, C. Dixon, M. Fisher, and U. Hustadt. Towards the Implementation of First-Order Temporal Resolution: the Expanding Domain Case. In *Proceedings of the Joint Tenth International Symposium on Temporal Representation and Reasoning and Fourth International Conference on Temporal Logic (TIME-ICTL)*. IEEE Press, 2003.

[Konev, 2003] B. Konev. TRP++: Temporal Resolution Prover, 2003. Department of Computer Science, University of Liverpool, UK. `http://www.csc.liv.ac.uk/~konev/trp++`.

[Kong *et al.*, 1994] A. Kong, J. Liu, and W.H. Wong. Sequential Imputations and Bayesian Missing Data Problems. *Journal of the American Statistical Association*, 89:278–298, 1994.

[Kontchakov *et al.*, 2003] R. Kontchakov, C. Lutz, F. Wolter, and M. Zakharyaschev. Temporalizing Tableaux. *Studia Logica*, 2003.

[Koubarakis and Skiadopoulos, 1999] M. Koubarakis and S. Skiadopoulos. Querying Temporal Constraint Networks in PTIME. In *Proceedings of AAAI Conference*, pages 745–750, 1999.

[Koubarakis and Skiadopoulos, 2000] M. Koubarakis and S. Skiadopoulos. Querying Temporal and Spatial Constraint Networks in PTIME. *Artificial Intelligence*, 123(1-2):223–263, 2000.

[Koubarakis, 1992] M. Koubarakis. Dense Time and Temporal Constraints with $\neq$. In Swartout and Nebel [1992], pages 24–35.

[Koubarakis, 1993] M. Koubarakis. Representation and Querying in Temporal Databases: the Power of Temporal Constraints. In *Proceedings of the Ninth International Conference on Data Engineering*, pages 327–334, April 1993.

[Koubarakis, 1994a] M. Koubarakis. Complexity Results for First-Order Theories of Temporal Constraints. In *Proceedings of the Fourth International Conference on Principles of Knowledge Representation and Reasoning (KR)*, pages 379–390. Morgan Kaufmann, San Francisco, CA, May 1994.

[Koubarakis, 1994b] M. Koubarakis. Database Models for Infinite and Indefinite Temporal Information. *Information Systems*, 19(2):141–173, March 1994.

[Koubarakis, 1995] M. Koubarakis. From Local to Global Consistency in Temporal Constraint Networks. In *Proceedings of the First International Conference on Principles and Practice of Constraint Programming (CP)*, volume 976 of *Lecture Notes in Computer Science*, pages 53–69, Cassis, France, September 1995.

[Koubarakis, 1996] M. Koubarakis. Tractable Disjunctions of Linear Constraints. In *Proceedings of the Second International Conference on Principles and Practice of Constraint Programming (CP)*, pages 297–307, Cambridge, MA, USA, August 1996.

[Koubarakis, 1997a] M. Koubarakis. From Local to Global Consistency in Temporal Constraint Networks. *Theoretical Computer Science*, 173:89–112, February 1997.

[Koubarakis, 1997b] M. Koubarakis. The Complexity of Query Evaluation in Indefinite Temporal Constraint Databases. *Theoretical Computer Science*, 171:25–60, January 1997.

[Koubarakis, 2001] M. Koubarakis. Tractable Disjunctions of Linear Constraints: Basic Results and Applications to Temporal Reasoning. *Theoretical Computer Science*, 266:311–339, September 2001.

[Kowalski and Sadri, 1997] R. Kowalski and F. Sadri. Reconciling the Event Calculus with the Situation Calculus. *Journal of Logic Programming*, 31(1-3):39–58, 1997.

[Kowalski and Sergot, 1986] R.A Kowalski and M.J. Sergot. A Logic-based Calculus of Events. *New Generation Computing*, 1(4):67–95, 1986.

[Kowalski, 1992] R.A. Kowalski. Database Updates in the Event Calculus. *Journal of Logic Programming*, 1992.

[Koymans and Roever, 1985] R. Koymans and W.-P. de Roever. Examples of a Real-Time Temporal Logic Specification. In B.T. Denvir, W.T. Harwood, M.I. Jackson, and M.J. Wray, editors, *Analysis of Concurrent Systems*, volume 207 of *Lecture Notes in Computer Science*, pages 231–251. Springer-Verlag, Berlin-Heidelberg-New York, 1985.

[Koymans, 1989] R. Koymans. *Specifying Message Passing and Time-Critical Systems with Temporal Logic*. PhD thesis, Technische Universiteit Eindhoven, Netherlands, 1989.

[Kozen, 1982] D. Kozen. Results on the Propositional μ-calculus. In *Proceeings of ICALP*, number 140 in Lecture Notes in Computer Science, pages 340–359, 1982.

[Kroger, 1987] F. Kroger. *Temporal Logic of Programs*. Springer Verlag, 1987.

[Krokhin *et al.*, 2001] A. Krokhin, P. Jeavons, and P. Jonsson. A Complete Classification of Tractability in Allen's Algebra in the Presence of a Non-Trivial Basic Relation. In B. Nebel, editor, *Proceedings of the Seventeenth International Joint Conference on Artificial Intelligence (IJCAI)*, pages 83–88, Seattle, Washington, USA, August 2001. Morgan Kaufmann.

[Krokhin *et al.*, 2003] A. Krokhin, P. Jeavons, and P. Jonsson. The Tractable Subalgebras of Allen's Interval Algebra. *Journal of the ACM*, 50(5):591–640, 2003.

[Kuipers and Åström, 1994] B. J. Kuipers and K. Åström. The Composition and Validation of Heterogeneous Control Laws. *Automatica*, 30(2):233–249, 1994.

[Kuipers, 1986] B. Kuipers. Qualitative Simulation. *Artificial Intelligence*, 26:289–338, 1986.

[Kuipers, 1988] B. Kuipers. Qualitative Simulation using Time-Scaled Abstraction. *Artificial Intelligence in Engineering*, 3(4):185–191, 1988.

[Kuipers, 1994] B. J. Kuipers. *Qualitative Reasoning: Modeling and Simulation with Incomplete Knowledge*. MIT Press, Cambridge, MA, 1994.

[Kumari and Pujari, 2002] G.V. Kumari and K. Pujari. Enforcing the Local Consistency in INDU. In *Proceedings of the International Conference on Knowledge Based Computed Systems*, 2002.

[Kuper, 1987] G. Kuper. Logic Programming with Sets. In *Proceedings of the Sixth ACM-SIGACT-SIGMOD-SIGART Symposium of Principles of Database Systems (PODS)*, 1987.

[Kushmerick *et al.*, 1995] N. Kushmerick, S. Hanks, and D. Weld. An Algorithm for Probabilistic Planning. *Artificial Intelligence*, 76:239–286, 1995.

[Kvarnströn *et al.*, 2000] J. Kvarnströn, P. Doherty, and P. Hasslum. Extending TALplanner with Concurrency and Resources. In *Proceedings of the Europena Conference on Artificila Intelligence (ECAI)*, Berlin, Germany, August 2000.

[Ladkin and Maddux, 1988] P.B. Ladkin and R. Maddux. On Binary Constraint Networks. Technical Report KES.U.88.8, Kestrel Institute, Palo Alto, USA, 1988.

[Ladkin and Maddux, 1994] P.B. Ladkin and R. Maddux. On Binary Constraint Problems. *Journal of the ACM*, 41(3):435–469, 1994.

[Ladkin and Reinefeld, 1992] P.B. Ladkin and A. Reinefeld. Effective Solution of Qualitative Interval Constraint Problems. *Artificial Intelligence*, 57(1):105–124, 1992.

[Ladkin and Reinefeld, 1997] P.B. Ladkin and A. Reinefeld. Fast Algebraic Methods for Interval Constraint Problems. *Annals of Mathematics and Artificial Intelligence*, 19:383–411, 1997.

[Ladkin, 1987] P. Ladkin. The Completeness of a Natural System for Reasoning with Time Intervals. In *Proceedings of the International Joint Conference on Artificial Intelligence (IJCAI)*, pages 462–467, 1987.

[Ladkin, 1988] P. Ladkin. Satisfying First-Order Constraints About Time Intervals. In *Proceedings of AAAI Conference*, pages 512–517, 1988.

[Lansky, 1986] A.L. Lansky. A Representation of Parallel Activity Based on Events, Structure and Causality. In M.P. Georgeff and A.L. Lansky, editors, *Proceedings of the Timberline Oregon Workshop on Reasoning about Actions and Plans*, 1986.

[Larizza *et al.*, 1992] C. Larizza, A. Moglia, and M. Stefanelli. M-HTP: A System for Monitoring Heart-Transplant Patients. *Artificial Intelligence in Medicine*, 4(2):111–126, 1992.

[Larizza *et al.*, 1997] C. Larizza, R. Bellazzi, and A. Riva. Temporal Abstractions for Diabetic Patients Management. In *Proceedings of AIME Conference*, volume 1211 of *Lecture Notes in Artificial Intelligence*, pages 319–330. Springer, 1997.

[Lascarides and Asher, 1993] A. Lascarides and N. Asher. Temporal Interpretation, Discourse Relations and Commonsense Entailment. *Linguistics and Philosophy*, 16:437–594, 1993.

[Lascarides and Oberlander, 1993] A. Lascarides and J. Oberlander. Temporal Connectives in a Discourse Context. In *Proceedings the Sixth Conference of the European Chapter of the ACL (EACL)*, pages 260–268, 1993.

[Last *et al.*, 2004] M. Last, A. Kandel, and H. Bunke, editors. *Data Mining in Time Series Databases*, volume 57 of *Machine Perception and Artificial Intelligence*. World Scientific, 2004.

[Lausen *et al.*, 1998] G. Lausen, B. Ludäscher, and W. May. On Logical Foundations of Active Databases. In J. Chomicki and G. Saake, editors, *Logics for Databases and Information Systems*, pages 389–422. Kluwer, 1998.

[Lavrač *et al.*, 1997] N. Lavrač, E.T. Keravnou, and B. Zupan, editors. *Intelligent Data Analysis in Medicine and Pharmacology*. Kluwer Academic Publishers, 1997.

[Leban *et al.*, 1986] B. Leban, D. Mcdonald, and D. Foster. A Representation for Collections of Temporal Intervals. In *Proceedings of the Fifth National Conference of the American Association for Artificial Intelligence (AAAI)*, pages 367–371, 1986.

[Lenzerini, 2002] M. Lenzerini. Data Integration: a Theoretical Perspective. In *Proceedings of the ACM Symposium on Principles of Database Systems (PODS)*, pages 233–246, 2002.

[Levesque, 1984] H.J. Levesque. Foundations of a Functional Approach to Knowledge Representation. *Artificial Intelligence*, 23:155–212, 1984.

[Levy *et al.*, 1995] A. Y. Levy, A. O. Mendelzon, Y. Sagiv, and D. Srivastava. Answering Queries Using Views. In *Proceedings of the ACM Symposium on Principles of Database Systems (PODS)*, pages 95–104, 1995.

[Libkin *et al.*, 2000] L. Libkin, G. Kuper, and J. Paredaens, editors. *Constraint Databases*. Springer, 2000.

[Lichtenstein and Pnueli, 1985] O. Lichtenstein and A. Pnueli. Checking that Finite State Concurrent Programs Satisfy their Linear Specification. In *Proceedings of the Twelfth ACM Symposium on the Principles of Programming Languages (POPL)*, pages 97–107, New Orleans, USA, January 1985.

[Lichtenstein *et al.*, 1985] O. Lichtenstein, A. Pnueli, and L. Zuck. The Glory of the Past. In *Logics of Programs*, volume 193 of *Lecture Notes in Computer Science*, pages 196–218. Springer-Verlag, Heidelberg, 1985.

[Lifschitz and Turner, 1994] V. Lifschitz and H. Turner. Splitting a Logic Program. In P. Van Hentenryck, editor, *Proceedings of the Eleventh International Conference on Logic Programming (ICLP)*, pages 23–38, 1994.

[Lifschitz, 1987] V. Lifschitz. Formal Theories of Action. In *Proceedings of the Workshop on the Frame Problem*, pages 35–37, 1987.

[Lifschitz, 1997] V. Lifschitz. On the Logic of Causal Explanation. *Artificial Intelligence*, 96:451–465, 1997.

[Lifschitz, 1999] V. Lifschitz. Answer Set Planning. In *Proceedings of International Conference on Logic Programming (ICLP)*, pages 23–37, 1999.

[Ligozat, 1990] G. Ligozat. Weak Representations of Interval Algebras. In *Proceedings of AAAI Conference*, pages 715–720, 1990.

[Ligozat, 1996] G. Ligozat. A New Proof of Tractability for ORD-Horn Relations. In *Proceedings of the Thirteenth National Conference of the American Association for Artificial Intelligence (AAAI)*, pages 715–720. AAAI Press/The MIT Press, 1996.

[Lin, 1991] Y. Lin. Two Theories of Time. *Journal of Applied Non-Classical Logics*, 1(1):37–63, 1991.

[Lin, 1995] F. Lin. Embracing Causality in Specifying the Indirect Effects of Actions. In *Proceedings of the Internationl Joint Conference on Artificial Intelligence (IJCAI)*, pages 1985–1993, 1995.

[Lin, 1997] F. Lin. Application of the Situation Calculus to Formalizing Control and Strategic Information: the Prolog Cut Operator. In *Proceedings of the Internationl Joint Conference on Artificial Intelligence (IJCAI)*, pages 1412–1418, 1997.

[Lipski, 1979] W. Lipski. On Semantic Issues Connected with Incomplete Information Databases. *ACM Transcactions on Database Systems*, 4(3):262–296, September 1979.

[Littman, 1997] M. L. Littman. Probabilistic proposition planning: Representations and complexity. In *Proceedings of AAAI Conference*, 1997.

[Liu and Chen, 1998] J. Liu and R. Chen. Sequential Monte Carlo Methods for Dynamic Systems. *Journal of the American Statistical Association*, 93, 1998.

[Liu and Orgun, 1997] C. Liu and M. Orgun. Dealing with Multiple Granularity of Time in Temporal Logic Programming. *Journal of Symbolic Computation*, 22(5):699–720, 1997.

[Lloyd and Topor, 1984] J.W. Lloyd and R.W. Topor. Making Prolog More Expressive. *Journal of Logic Programming*, 1(3):225–240, 1984.

[Lloyd, 1987] J.W. Lloyd. *Foundations of Logic Programming*. Symbolic Computation Series. Springer-Verlag, 2 edition, 1987.

[Lobo *et al.*, 1992] J. Lobo, J. Minker, and A. Rajasekar. *Foundations of Disjunctive Logic Programming*. The MIT Press, 1992.

[Long and Fox, 2003a] D. Long and M. Fox. Exploiting a Graphplan Framework in Temporal Planning. In *Proceedings of International Conference on Automated Planning and Scheduling (ICAPS)*, 2003.

[Long and Fox, 2003b] D. Long and M. Fox. The 3rd International Planning Competition: Results and Analysis. *Journal of AI Research*, 20, 2003.

[Long, 1996] W.J. Long. Temporal Reasoning for Diagnosis in a Causal Probabilistic Knowledge Base. *Artificial Intelligence in Medicine*, 8:193–215, 1996.

[Lorentzos and Mitsopoulos, 1997] N. A. Lorentzos and Y. G. Mitsopoulos. SQL Extension for Interval Data. *IEEE Transactions on Knowledge and Data Engineering*, 9(3):480–499, 1997.

[Lorentzos *et al.*, 1995] N. A. Lorentzos, A. Poulovassilis, and C. Small. Manipulation Operations for an Interval-extended Relational Model. *Data and Knowledge Engineering*, 17(1):1–29, 1995.

[Lorentzos, 1993] N. A. Lorentzos. The Interval-extended Relational Model and Its Application to Valid-time Databases. In Tansel et al. [1993], pages 67–91.

[Lutz, 1999a] C. Lutz. Complexity of Terminological Reasoning Revisited. In *Proceedings of the Sixth International Conference on Logic for Programming and Automated Reasoning (LPAR)*, pages 181–200. Springer-Verlag, 6 – 10, 1999.

[Lutz, 1999b] C. Lutz. Reasoning with Concrete Domains. In T. Dean, editor, *Proceedings of the Sixteenth International Joint Conference on Artificial Intelligence (IJCAI)*, pages 90–95, Stockholm, Sweden, 31 – 6, 1999. Morgan-Kaufmann Publishers.

[Mackaay *et al.*, 1990] E. Mackaay, D. Poulin, J. Fremont, P. Bratley, and C. Deniger. The Logic of Time in Law and Legal Expert Systems. *Ratio Juris*, 3(2):254–271, 1990.

[Mackworth, 1977] A.K. Mackworth. Consistency in Networks of Relations. *Artificial Intelligence*, 8(1):99–118, 1977.

[Madden *et al.*, 2002] S. Madden, M. A. Shah, J. M. Hellerstein, and V. Raman. Continuously Adaptive Continuous Queries over Streams. In *Proceedings of the ACM SIGMOD International Conference on Management of Data*, pages 49–60, 2002.

[Maier, 1986] D. Maier. A Logic for Objects. In *Proceedings of the Workshop on Foundations of Deductive Database and Logic Programming*, 1986.

[Majercik and Littman, 1999] S. Majercik and M. Littman. Contingent Planning under Uncertainty via Stochastic Satisfiability. In *Proceedings of Sixteenth National Conference on AI*, 1999.

[Manna and Pnueli, 1992] Z. Manna and A. Pnueli. *The Temporal Logic of Reactive and Concurrent Systems*. Springer-Verlag, Berlin, Heidelberg, New York, 1992.

[Manna and Pnueli, 1995] Z. Manna and A. Pnueli. *Temporal Verification of Reactive Systems: Safety*. Springer-Verlag, New York, 1995.

[Manna and Wolper, 1984] Z. Manna and P. Wolper. Synthesis of Communicating Processes from Temporal Logic Specifications. *ACM Transactions on Programming Languages and Systems*, 6(1):68–93, January 1984.

[Manzano, 1993] M. Manzano. *Many-Sorted Logic and its Applications in Computer Science*, chapter 1 (Introduction to Many-sorted logic; pp. 1-86). John Wiley&Sons. Chichester. (UK), tucker & meinke edition, 1993.

[Marek and Truszczyński, 1994] W. Marek and M. Truszczyński. Revision Programming, Database Updates and Integrity Constraints. In *Proceedings of Fifth International Conference in Database Theory (ICDT)*, Prague, Czechoslovakia, 1994.

[Marek and Truszczyński, 1999] W. Marek and M Truszczyński. Stable Models and an Alternative Logic Programming Paradigm. In Apt, K. and Marek, W. and Truszczyński, M. and Warren, D., editor, *The Logic Programming Paradigm: a 25-Year perspective*, pages 375–398. Springer, 1999.

[Maruichi *et al.*, 1991] T. Maruichi, M. Ichikawa, and M. Tokoro. Modelling Autonomous Agents and their Groups. In Y. Demazeau and J. P. Müller, editors, *Decentralized AI 2 – Proceedings of the* 2nd *European Workshop on Modelling Autonomous Agents and Multi-Agent Worlds (MAAMAW)*. Elsevier/North Holland, 1991.

[McAllester and Rosenblitt, 1991] D. McAllester and D. Rosenblitt. Systematic Nonlinear Planning. In *Proceedings of the Ninth National Conference on Artificial Intelligence (AAAI)*, volume 2, pages 634–639, Anaheim, California, USA, 1991. AAAI Press/MIT Press.

[McCain and Turner, 1994] N. McCain and H. Turner. Language Independence and Language Tolerance in Logic Programs. In *Proceedings of the Eleventh International Conference on Logic Programming (ICLP)*, pages 38–57, 1994.

[McCain and Turner, 1995] N. McCain and H. Turner. A causal theory of ramifications and qualifications. In *Proc. of IJCAI 95*, pages 1978–1984, 1995.

[McCain and Turner, 1997] N. McCain and H. Turner. Causal Theories of Action and Change. In H. Shrobe and T. Senator, editors, *Proceedings of the Thirteenth National Conference on Artificial Intelligence and the Eighth Innovative Applications of Artificial Intelligence Conference (AAAI)*, pages 460–465, Menlo Park, California, 1997. AAAI Press.

[McCain and Turner, 1998] N. McCain and H. Turner. Satisfiability Planning with Causal Theories. In *Proceedings of International Conference on Principles of Knowledge Representation and Reasoning (KR)*, pages 212–223, 1998.

[McCarthy and Hayes, 1969] J. McCarthy and P. J. Hayes. Some Philosophical Problems from the Standpoint of Artificial Intelligence. In B. Melzer and D. Michie, editors, *Machine Intelligence 4*. Edinburgh University Press, 1969.

[McCarthy, 1959] J. McCarthy. Programs with Common Sense. In *Proceedings of the Teddington Conference on the Mechanization of Thought Processes*, pages 75–91, London, 1959. Her Majesty's Stationery Office.

[McCarthy, 1963] J. McCarthy. Situations, Actions and Causal Laws. Technical Report Memo 2, Stanford Artificial Intelligence Project, 1963.

[McCarthy, 1980] J. McCarthy. Circumscription – A Form of Non-Monotonic Reasoning. *Artificial Intelligence*, 13:27–39, 1980.

[McCarty, 1995] L. Thorne McCarty. Some requirements on an action language for legal discourse (position paper). In *Spring Symposium Series'95: Extending Theories of Action*, pages 136–138. AAAI, 1995.

[McDermott and Doyle, 1980] D. McDermott and J. Doyle. Non-Monotonic Logic I. *Artificial Intelligence*, 13:41–72, 1980.

[McDermott, 1982] D. McDermott. A Temporal Logic for Reasoning about Processes and Plans. *Cognitive Science*, 6:101–155, 1982.

[McDermott, 1996] D. McDermott. A Heuristic Estimator for Means Ends Analysis in Planning. In B. Drabble, editor, *Proceedings of the Third International Conference on Artificial Intelligence Planning Systems (AIPS)*, pages 142–149. AAAI Press, 1996.

[McDermott, 2000] D. McDermott. The 1998 AI Planning Systems Competition. *AI Magazine*, 21(2), 2000.

[McDermott, 2003] D. McDermott. Reasoning about Autonomous Processes in an Estimated-Regression Planner. In *Proceedings of the International Conference on Automated Planning and Scheduling (ICAPS)*, 2003.

[McGuire, 1995] H. W. McGuire. *Two Methods for Checking Formulas of Temporal Logic*. PhD thesis, Department of Computer Science, Stanford University, USA, June 1995. Stanford Computer Science Technical Reports CS-TR-95-1551.

[McNaughton, 1966] R. McNaughton. Testing and Generating Infinite Sequences by Finite Automata. *Information and Control*, 9:521–530, 1966.

[Meiri, 1991] I. Meiri. Combining Qualitative and Quantitative Constraints in Temporal Reasoning. In *Proceedings of AAAI Conference*, pages 260–267, 1991.

[Meiri, 1996] I. Meiri. Combining Qualitative and Quantitative Constraints in Temporal Reasoning. *Artificial Intelligence*, 87(1–2):343–385, 1996.

[Meyer *et al.*, 1999] J.-J. Ch. Meyer, W. van der Hoek, and B. van Linder. A Logical Approach to the Dynamics of Commitments. *Artificial Intelligence*, 113:1–40, 1999.

[Miksch *et al.*, 1996] S. Miksch, W. Horn, C. Popow, and F. Paky. Utilizing Temporal Data Abstraction for Data Validation and Therapy Planning for Artificially Ventilated Newborn Infants. *Artificial Intelligence in Medicine*, 8(6):543–576, 1996.

[Miller and Schubert, 1990] S. A. Miller and L.K. Schubert. Time Revisited. *Computational Intelligence*, 6:108–118, 1990.

[Miller and Shanahan, 1994] R. Miller and M. Shanahan. Narratives in the Situational Calculus. *Journal of Logic and Computation*, 4(5):513–530, 1994.

[Miller *et al.*, 1982] R.A. Miller, H.E. Pople, and J.D. Myers. INTERNIST-I, An Experimental Computer-Based Diagnostic Consultant for General Internal Medicine. *New England Journal of Medicine*, 307:468–476, 1982.

[Miller, 1986] P. L. Miller. *Expert Critiquing Systems: Practice-Based Medical Consultation by Computer*. Springer-Verlag, New York, NY, 1986.

[Miller, 1990] B. Miller. The Rhetorical Knowledge Representation System Reference Manual. Technical Report 326, Department of Computer Science, University of Rochester, Rochester, New York, USA, 1990.

[Missiaen *et al.*, 1992] L. R. Missiaen, M. Bruynooghe, and M. Denecker. Abductive Planning with Event Calculus. Internal report, Department of Computer Science, K.U.Leuven, 1992.

[Missiaen *et al.*, 1995] L. R. Missiaen, M. Denecker, and M. Bruynooghe. CHICA, An Abductive Planning System Based on Event Calculus. *Journal of Logic and Computation*, 5(5):579–602, September 1995.

[Missiaen, 1991a] L. R. Missiaen. Localized Abductive Planning for Robot Assembly. In *Proceedings of the IEEE Conference on Robotics and Automation*, pages 605–610. IEEE Robotics and Automation Society, 1991.

[Missiaen, 1991b] L. R. Missiaen. *Localized Abductive Planning with the Event Calculus*. PhD thesis, Department of Computer Science, K.U.Leuven, 1991.

[Miyano and Hayashi, 1984] S. Miyano and T. Hayashi. Alternating Finite Automata on ω-words. *Theoretical Computer Science*, 32:321–330, 1984.

[Mokhtar *et al.*, 2002] H. Mokhtar, J. Su, and O. Ibarra. On Moving Objects Queries. In *Proceedings of the ACM Symposium on Principles of Database Systems (PODS)*, pages 188–198, 2002.

[Montanari and de Rijke, 1997] A. Montanari and M. de Rijke. Two-Sorted Metric Temporal Logic. *Theoretical Computer Science*, 183:187–214, 1997.

[Montanari and Policriti, 1996] A. Montanari and A. Policriti. Decidability Results for Metric and Layered Temporal Logics. *Notre-Dame Journal of Formal Logic*, 37:260–282, 1996.

[Montanari and Puppis, 2004a] A. Montanari and G. Puppis. Decidability of MSO theories of tree structures. In *Proceedings of the Twenty-Fourth Conference on Foundations of Software Technology and Theoretical Computer Science (FSTTCS)*, Lecture Notes in Computer Science. Springer-Verlag, 2004.

[Montanari and Puppis, 2004b] A. Montanari and G. Puppis. Decidability of the Theory of the Totally Unbounded ω-Layered Structure. In *Proceedings of the Eleventh International Symposium on Temporal Representation and Reasoning (TIME)*, pages 156–160. IEEE Computer Society Press, 2004.

[Montanari *et al.*, 1992] A. Montanari, E. Ciapessoni, E. Corsetti, and P. San Pietro. Dealing with Time Granularity in Logical Specifications of Real-Time Systems: The Synchronous Case. Technical Report 7, Dipartimento di Matematica ed Informatica, Universitá di Udine, Udine (IT), May 1992.

[Montanari *et al.*, 1999] A. Montanari, A. Peron, and A. Policriti. Theories of Omega-Layered Metric Temporal Structures: Expressiveness and Decidability. *Logic Journal of the IGPL*, 7(1):79–102, 1999.

[Montanari *et al.*, 2000] A. Montanari, A. Peron, and A. Policriti. The Taming (Timing) of the States. *Logic Journal of the IGPL*, 8(5):681–699, 2000.

[Montanari *et al.*, 2002a] A. Montanari, A. Peron, and A. Policriti. Extending Kamp's Theorem to Model Time Granularity. *Journal of Logic and Computation*, 12(4):641–678, 2002.

[Montanari *et al.*, 2002b] A. Montanari, G. Sciavicco, and N. Vitacolonna. Decidability of Interval Temporal Logics over Split-Frames via Granularity. In *Proceedings of the European Conference on Logic in Artificial Intelligence (JELIA)*, number 2424 in Lecture Notes in Artificial Intelligence, pages 259–270. Springer, 2002.

[Montanari, 1974] U. Montanari. Networks of Constraints: Fundamental Properties and Applications to Picture Processing. *Information Science*, 7(3):95–132, 1974.

[Montanari, 1994] A. Montanari. A Layered and Metric Temporal Logic for Time Granularity, Synchrony and Asynchrony. Technical Report MPI-I-94-230, Max-Plank-Institut fuer Informatik, July 1994.

[Montanari, 1996] A. Montanari. *Metric and Layered Temporal Logic for Time Granularity*. PhD thesis, University of Amsterdam, Amsterdam, Netherlands, september 1996. ILLC Dissertation Series 1996-02.

[Monti and Peron, 2000] A. Monti and A. Peron. Systolic Tree ω-Languages: The Operational and the Logical View. *Theoretical Computer Science*, 23:1–17, 2000.

[Monti and Peron, 2001] A. Monti and A. Peron. Logical Definability of Y-Tree and Trellis Systolic ω-Languages. *Acta Cybernetica*, 15:75–100, 2001.

[Moore, 1990] R. C. Moore. A Formal Theory of Knowledge and Action. In J. F. Allen, J. Hendler, and A. Tate, editors, *Readings in Planning*, pages 480–519. Morgan Kaufmann, 1990.

[Morris *et al.*, 1997] R. Morris, W. Shoaf, and L. Khatib. Domain Independent Temporal Reasoning with Recurring Events. *Computational Intelligence*, 12(3):450–477, 1997.

[Morurovic *et al.*, 2000] M. Morurovic, F. Wolter, and M. Zakharyaschev. Modalized Description Logic — How Much? Technical report, Computer Science Department, University of Leipzig, Germany, 2000.

[Moszkowski, 1983] B. Moszkowski. *Reasoning about Digital Circuits*. PhD thesis, Department of Computer Science, Stanford University, Technical Report STAN-CS-83-970, Stanford, CA, USA, 1983.

[Moszkowski, 1985] B. Moszkowski. A Temporal Logic for Multilevel Reasoning about Hardware. *IEEE Computer*, 18(2), 1985.

[Moszkowski, 1986] B. Moszkowski. *Executing Temporal Logic Programs*. Cambridge University Press, Cambridge, 1986.

[Mota *et al.*, 1997] E. Mota, D. Robertson, and A. Smaill. NatureTime: Temporal Granularity in Simulation of Ecosystems. *Journal of Symbolic Computation*, 22(5):665–698, 1997.

[Mourelatos, 1978] A. P. D. Mourelatos. Events, Processes and States. *Linguistics and Philosophy*, 2:415–434, 1978.

[Muller *et al.*, 1988] D. Muller, A. Saoudi, and P. Schupp. Weak Alternating Automata give a Simple Explanation of why most Temporal and Dynamic Logics are Decidable in Exponential Time. In *Proceedings of Third IEEE Symposium on Logic in Computer Science (LICS)*, pages 422–427. IEEE, 1988.

[Muller *et al.*, 1995] J.-C. Muller, J.-P. Lagrange, R. Weibel, and F. Salgé. Generalization: State of the Art and Issues. In J.-C. Muller, J.-P. Lagrange, and R. Weibel, editors, *GIS and Generalization*, pages 3–17. Taylor and Francis, London (GB), 1995.

[Muller, 1963] D. Muller. Infinite Sequences and Finite Machines. In *Proceedings of the Fourth Annual IEEE Symposium on Switching Circuit Theory and Logical Design*, pages 3–16, 1963.

[Murray, 1982] N. V. Murray. Completely Non-Clausal Theorem Proving. *Artificial Intelligence*, 18:67–85, 1982.

[Muscettola *et al.*, 1998] N. Muscettola, P. Nayak, B. Pell, and B. Williams. Remote Agent: To Boldly Go Where No AI System Has Gone Before. *Artificial Intelligence*, 103(1-2):5–48, 1998.

[Muscettola, 1994] N. Muscettola. HSTS: Integrating Planning and Scheduling. In M. Zweben and M.S. Fox, editors, *Intelligent Scheduling*, pages 169–212. Morgan Kaufmann, San Mateo, CA, 1994.

[Musen *et al.*, 1992] M.A. Musen, C.W. Carlson, L.M. Fagan, S.C. Deresinski, and E. H. Shortliffe. T–HELPER: Automated Support for Community–Based Clinical Research. In M.E. Frisse, editor, *Proceedings of the Sixteenth Annual Symposium on Computer Applications in Medical Care (SCAMC)*, pages 719–723. McGraw Hill, 1992.

[Musen *et al.*, 1996] M.A. Musen, S.W. Tu, A.K. Das, and Y. Shahar. EON: A Component-Based Approach to Automation of Protocol-Directed Therapy. *Journal of the American Medical Informatics Association*, 3(6):367–388, 1996.

[Mylopoulos *et al.*, 1990] J. Mylopoulos, A. Borgida, M. Jarke, and M. Koubarakis. Telos: A Language for Representing Knowledge About Information Systems. *ACM Transactions on Information Systems*, 8(4):325–362, October 1990.

[Nau *et al.*, 1999] D. Nau, Y. Cao, A. Lotem, and H. Muñoz-Avila. SHOP: Simple Hierarchical Ordered Planner. In *Proceedings of the International Joint Conference on Artificial Intelligence (IJCAI)*, 1999.

[Nau *et al.*, 2003] D. Nau, T.C. Au, O. Ilghami, U. Kuter, J.W. Murdoch, D. Woo, and F. Yaman. SHOP2: an HTN Planning Environment. *Journal of AI Research*, 2003.

[Navarrete and Marin, 1997a] I. Navarrete and R. Marin. Qualitative Temporal Reasoning with Points and Durations. In *Proceedings of International Joint Conference on Artificial Intelligence (IJCAI)*, pages 1454–1459. Morgan Kaufmann, 1997.

[Navarrete and Marin, 1997b] Isabel Navarrete and Roque Marin. Qualitative temporal reasoning with points and durations. In Martha E. Pollack, editor, *Proceedings of the Fifteenth International Joint Conference on Artificial Intelligence (IJCAI)*, Nagoya, Japan, August 1997. Morgan Kaufmann.

[Nebel and Bürckert, 1995] B. Nebel and H-J. Bürckert. Reasoning about Temporal Relations: A Maximal Tractable Subclass of Allen's Interval Algebra. *Journal of the ACM*, 42(1):43–66, 1995.

[Nebel, 1997] B. Nebel. Solving Hard Qualitative Temporal Reasoning Problems: Evaluating the Efficiency of Using the ORD-Horn Class. *CONSTRAINTS*, 1(3):175–190, 1997.

[Nebel, 2000] B. Nebel. On the Compilability and Expressive Power of Propositional Planning Formalisms. *Journal of Artificial Intelligence Research*, 12:271–315, 2000.

[Newton-Smith, 1980] W.H. Newton-Smith. *The Structure of Time*. Routledge & Heagan Paul, 1980.

[Newton, 1936] I. Newton. *Mathematical Principles of Natural Philosophy*. F. Cajori Ed., 1936.

[Ngo *et al.*, 1995] L. Ngo, P. Haddawy, and J. Helwig. A Theoretical Framework for Context-Sensitive Temporal Probability Model Construction with Application to Plan Projection. In *Proceedings on International Conference on Uncertainty in AI (UAI)*, 1995.

[Nguyen and Kambhampati, 2001] X. Nguyen and S. Kambhampati. Reviving Partial Order Planning. In *Proceedings of the International Joint Conference on Artificial Intelligence (IJCAI)*, pages 459–466, 2001.

[Nguyen *et al.*, 1999] J. Nguyen, Y. Shahar, S.W. Tu, A.K. Das, and M.A. Musen. Integration of Temporal Reasoning and Temporal-Data Maintenance into a Reusable Database Mediator to Answer Abstract, Time-Oriented Queries: The Tzolkin System. *Journal of Intelligent Information Systems*, 13(1/2):121–145, 1999.

[Nicholson and Brady, 1994] A.E. Nicholson and J.M. Brady. Dynamic Belief Networks for Discrete Monitoring. *IEEE Transactions on Systems, Man and Cybernetics*, 24(11):1593–610, November 1994.

[Niemelä and Simons, 1997] I. Niemelä and P. Simons. Smodels – An Implementation of the Stable Model and Well-Founded Semantics for Normal Logic Programs. In J. Dix, U. Furbach, and A. Nerode, editors, *Proceedings of the Fourth International Conference on Logic Programming and Non-Monotonic Reasoning (LPNMR)*, pages 420–429. Springer, 1997.

[Niemelä, 1999] I. Niemelä. Logic Programs with Stable Model Semantics as a Constraint Programming Paradigm. *Annals of Mathematics and Artificial Intelligence*, 25(3-4):241–271, 1999.

[Niézette and Stevenne, 1992] M. Niézette and J.-M. Stevenne. An Efficient Symbolic Representation of Periodic Time. In *Proceedings of the International Conference on Information and Knowledge Management (CIKM)*, pages 161–168, Baltimore, USA, 1992. ACM Press.

[Nishida and Doshita, 1987] T. Nishida and S. Doshita. Reasoning about Discontinuous Change. In *Proceedings of the Sixth (US) National Conference on Artificial Intelligence (AAAI)*, pages 643–648. AAAI press, 1987.

[Nitta *et al.*, 1988] K. Nitta, J. Nagao, and M. Tetsuya. A Knowledge Representation and Inference System for Procedural Law. *New Generation Computing*, 5:319–359, 1988.

[Nivat and Perrin, 1986] M. Nivat and D. Perrin. Ensembles Reconnaissables de mot Biinfinis. *Canadian Journal of Mathematics*, 38:513–537, 1986.

[Nökel, 1991] K. Nökel. *Temporally Distributed Symptoms in Technical Diagnosis*, volume 517. Springer-Verlag, Berlin, Heidelberg, New York, 1991.

[O'Connor *et al.*, 2002] M. J. O'Connor, S. W. Tu, and M. A. Musen. The Chronus II Temporal Database Mediator. In *Proceedings of the American Medical Informatics Association (AMIA) Annual Fall Symposium*, San Antonio, USA, 2002.

[Ohlbach, 1993] H-J. Ohlbach. Translation Methods for Non-Classical Logics – An Overview. *Journal of the IGPL*, 1(1):69–90, 1993.

[Ohno-Machado *et al.*, 1998] L. Ohno-Machado, J. Gennari, S. Murphy, and et al. The Guideline Interchange Format: A Model for Representing Guidelines. *Journal of the American Medical Informatics Association*, 5:357–72, 1998.

[Ohrstrom and Hasle, 1995] P. Ohrstrom and Per F. V. Hasle. *Temporal Logic: From Ancient Ideas to Artificial Intelligence*, volume 57 of *Studies in Linguistics and Philosophy*. Kluwer Academic Publishers, Dordrecht, The Netherlands, 1995.

[Onder and Pollack, 1999] N. Onder and M. Pollack. Conditional Probabilistic Planning: A Unifying Algorithm and Effective Search Control Mechanisms. In *Proceedings of Sixtenth (US) National Conference on Artificial Intelligence (AAAI)*, 1999.

[Orgun, 1996] M.A. Orgun. On Temporal Deductive Databases. *Computational Intelligence*, 12(2):235–259, 1996.

[Özsoyŏglu and Snodgrass, 1995] R. Özsoyŏglu and T. Snodgrass. Temporal and Real-Time Databases: A Survey. *IEEE Transactions of Knowledge and Data Engineering*, 7:513–532, 1995.

[Paech, 1988] B. Paech. Gentzen-Systems for Propositional Temporal Logics. In E. Börger, H. Kleine Büning, and M. Richter, editors, *Proceedings of Conference on Computer Science Logic (CSL)*, volume 385 of *Lecture Notes in Computer Science*, pages 240–253, 1988.

[Papadias *et al.*, 1995] D. Papadias, Y. Theodoridis, T. Sellis, and M. Egenhofer. Topological Relations in the World of Minimum Bounding Rectangles: A Study with R-trees. In *Proceedings of the ACM SIGMOD International Conference on Management of Data*, pages 92–103, 1995.

[Partee, 1997] B. Partee. Montague Grammar. In J. van Benthem and A. ter Meulen, editors, *Handbook of Logic and Language*, pages 5–91. MIT/Elsevier, 1997.

[Pearce and Wagner, 1989] D. Pearce and G. Wagner. Reasoning with Negative Information 1 – Strong Negation in Logic Programming. Technical report, Gruppe fur Logic, Wissentheorie and Information, Freie Universitat Berlin, Berlin, Germany, 1989.

[Pearl, 1988] J. Pearl. *Probablistic Reasoning in Intelligent Systems*. Morgan Kaufmann, San Mateo, CA, 1988.

[Pednault, 1986a] E. P. D. Pednault. Formulating Multiagent, Dynamic-World Problems in the Classical Planning Framework. In M.P. Georgeff and A.L. Lansky, editors, *Proceedings of the Timberline Oregon Workshop on Reasoning about Actions and Plans*, 1986.

[Pednault, 1986b] E. P. D. Pednault. Towards a Mathematical Theory of Plan Syntesis. Technical Report Ph.D. Thesis, Department of Electrical Engineering, Stanford University, Palo Alto, USA, 1986.

[Pednault, 1989] E. P. D. Pednault. ADL: Exploring the Middle Ground between STRIPS and the Situation Calculus. In *Proceedings of International Conference on Principles of Knowledge Representation and Reasoning (KR)*, pages 324–332, 1989.

[Pe'er and Shamir, 1997] I. Pe'er and R. Shamir. Satisfiability Problems on Intervals and Unit Intervals. *Theoretical Computer Science*, 175:349–372, 1997.

[Peirce, 1955] C. S. Peirce. *Philosophical Writings of Peirce*. Dover Publications, New York, 1955.

[Peleg *et al.*, 2001] M. Peleg, A. Boxwala, E. Bernstam, S.W. Tu, R.A. Greenes, and E.H. Shortliffe. Sharable Representation of Clinical Guidelines in GLIF: Relationship to the Arden Syntax. *Journal of Biomedical Informatics*, 34:170–181, 2001.

[Penberthy and Weld, 1992] J. Penberthy and D.S. Weld. UCPOP: a Sound, Complete, Partial-Order Planner for ADL. In *Proceedings of International Conference on Principles of Knowledge Representation and Reasoning (KR)*, pages 103–114, Los Altos, CA, 1992. Kaufmann.

[Penberthy and Weld, 1994] J. Penberthy and D. Weld. Temporal Planning with Continuous Change. In *Proceedings of Twelfth (US) National Conference on Artificial Intelligence (AAAI)*. AAAI/MIT Press, 1994.

[Penberthy, 1993] J. Penberthy. Planning with Continuous Change. Technical Report 93-12-01, Department of Computer Science & Engineering, University of Washington, USA, 1993.

[Peng and Reggia, 1990] Y. Peng and J.A. Reggia. *Abductive Inference Models for Diagnostic Problem Solving*. Springer–Verlag, 1990.

[Pereira *et al.*, 1990] L. Pereira, L. Caires, and J. Alferes. Classical negation in logic programs. In *7 Simposio Brasiliero de Inteligencia Artificial*, 1990.

[Perrin and Schupp, 1986] D. Perrin and P. E. Schupp. Automata on the Integers, Recurrence Distinguishability, and the Equivalence and Decidability of Monadic Theories. In *Proceedings of International Symposium on Logic in Computer Science (LICS)*, pages 301–304, Cambridge, USA, 16–18 June 1986. IEEE Computer Society.

[Perrin, 1990] D. Perrin. Finite Automata. In J. van Leeuwen, editor, *Handbook of Theoretical Computer Science*, volume B. Elsevier, Amsterdam, 1990.

[Pinto and R.Reiter, 1993] J. Pinto and R.Reiter. Temporal Reasoning in Logic Programming: A Case for the Situation Calculus. In *Proceedings of the International Conference on Logic Programming (ICLP)*, pages 203–221, 1993.

[Pinto, 1994] J. Pinto. *Temporal Reasoning in the Situation Calculus.* PhD thesis, University of Toronto, Toronto, Ontario, Canada, February 1994.

[Pliuškevičius, 2001] R. Pliuškevičius. Deduction-Based Decision Procedure for a Clausal Miniscoped Fragment of FTL. In *Proceedings of the First International Joint Conference on Automated Reasoning (IJCAR)*, volume 2083 of *Lecture Notes in Artificial Intelligence*, pages 107–120. Springer, 2001.

[Pnueli, 1977] A. Pnueli. The Temporal Logic of Programs. In *Proceedings of the Eighteenth IEEE Symposium on the Foundations of Computer Science (FOCS)*, pages 46–57, Providence, USA, 31–2 1977. IEEE Computer Society Press.

[Pnueli, 1986] A. Pnueli. Specification and Development of Reactive Systems. In *Proceeings of Information Processing Conference*. Elsevier, 1986.

[Poesio and Brachman, 1991] M. Poesio and R.J. Brachman. Metric Constraints for Maintaining Appointments: Dates and Repeated Activities. In *Proceedings of the Nineth National Conference of the American Association for Artificial Intelligence*, pages 253–259. The MIT press, 1991.

[Poole *et al.*, 1998] D. Poole, A. Mackworth, and R. Goebel. *Computational Intelligence*. Oxford University Press, 1998.

[Poole, 1988] D. Poole. A Logical Framework for Default Reasoning. *Artifical Intelligence*, 36:27–47, 1988.

[Popkorn, 1994] S. Popkorn. *First Steps in Modal Logic*. Cambridge, 1994.

[Pople, 1973] H. Pople. On the Mechanization of Abductive Logic. In *Proceedings of the Third International Joint Conference on Artificial Intelligence (IJCAI)*, pages 147–152, 1973.

[Poulin *et al.*, 1992] D. Poulin, E. Mackaay, P. Bratley, and J. Fremont. Time Server — A Legal Time Specialist. In A. Martino, editor, *Expert Systems in Law*, pages 295–312, 1992.

[Prior, 1957] A. Prior. *Time and Modality*. Oxford University Press, 1957.

[Prior, 1967] A. Prior. *Past, Present and Future*. Oxford (Clarendon Press), 1967.

[Provan, 1993] G. Provan. Tradeoffs in Constructing and Evaluating Temporal Influence Diagrams. In *Proceedings of International Conference on Uncertainty in Artificial Intelligence (UAI)*, pages 40–47, 1993.

[Provetti, 1996] A. Provetti. Hypothetical Reasoning: From Situation Calculus to Event Calculus. *Computational Intelligence*, 12(3), 1996.

[Przymusinski, 1990] T. Przymusinski. Extended Stable Semantics for Normal and Disjunctive Programs. In D. Warren and P. Szeredi, editors, *Proceedings of the Seventh International Conference on Logic Programming (ICLP)*, pages 459–477, 1990.

[Psillos, 1996] S. Psillos. Ampliative Reasoning: Induction or Abduction. In *ECAI-96 workshop on Abductive and Inductive Reasoning*, 1996.

[Pujari and Sattar, 1999] K. Pujari and A. Sattar. A New Framework for Reasoning about Points, Intervals and Durations. In Thomas Dean, editor, *Proceedings of the Sixteenth International Joint Conference on Artificial Intelligence (IJCAI)*, pages 1259–1267, Stockholm, Sweden, July 1999. Morgan Kaufmann.

[Pujari *et al.*, 1999] K. Pujari, G.V. Kumari, and A. Sattar. INDU: An Interval and Duration Network. In *Proceedings of Australian Joint Conference on Artificial Intelligence*, pages 291–303, 1999.

[Puppo and Dettori, 1995] E. Puppo and G. Dettori. Towards a Formal Model for Multi-Resolution Spatial Maps. *Lecture Notes in Computer Science*, 951:152–169, 1995.

[Rabideau *et al.*, 1999] G. Rabideau, R. Knight, S. Chien, A. Fukunaga, and A. Govindjee. Iterative Repair Planning for Spacecraft Operations in the ASPEN System. In *Proceedings of the International Symposium on Artificial Intelligence Robotics and Automation in Space (ISAIRAS)*, 1999.

[Rabin and Scott, 1959] M. Rabin and D. Scott. Finite Automata and their Decision Problem. *IBM Journal of Research*, 3:115–124, 1959.

[Rabin, 1969] M. Rabin. Decidability of Second-Order Theories and Automata on Infinite Trees. *Transactions of the American Mathematical Society*, 141:1–35, 1969.

[Rabin, 1972] M. Rabin. *Automata on Infinite Objects and Church's Problem*. American Mathematical Society, 1972.

[Randell *et al.*, 1992] D. Randell, Z. Cui, and A. Cohn. A Spatial Logic based on Regions and Connection. In *Proceedings of the Third International Conference on Principles of Knowledge Representation and Reasoning (KR)*, pages 165–176, 1992.

[Rao and Georgeff, 1991] A. S. Rao and M. P. Georgeff. Modeling Agents within a BDI-Architecture. In R. Fikes and E. Sandewall, editors, *Proceedings of the International Conference on Principles of Knowledge Representation and Reasoning (KR)*, Cambridge, Massachusetts, April 1991. Morgan Kaufmann.

[Rao and Georgeff, 1993] A. S. Rao and M. P. Georgeff. A Model-Theoretic Approach to the Verification of Situated Reasoning Systems. In *Proceedings of the Thirteenth International Joint Conference on Artificial Intelligence (IJCAI-93)*, pages 318–324, Chambéry, France, 1993.

[Rao and Georgeff, 1995] A. S. Rao and M. Georgeff. BDI Agents: from Theory to Practice. In *Proceedings of the First International Conference on Multi-Agent Systems (ICMAS)*, pages 312–319, San Francisco, USA, June 1995.

[Rautenberg, 1979] W. Rautenberg. *Klassische und Nichtklassische Aussagenlogik*. Vieweg, 1979.

[Rautenberg, 1983] W. Rautenberg. Modal Tableau Calculi and Interpolation. *Journal of Philosophical Logic*, 12:403–423, 1983.

[Rector, 2001] A. Rector. AIM: A Personal View of Where I Have Been and Where We Might Be Going. *Artificial Intelligence in Medicine*, 23:111–127, 2001.

[Reddy and Loveland, 1978] C. R. Reddy and D. W. Loveland. Presburger Arithmetic with Bounded Quantifier Alternation. In *Proceedings of the ACM Symposium on the Theory of Computing (STOC)*, pages 320–325, 1978.

[Reichgelt, 1987] H. Reichgelt. Semantics for Reified Temporal Logics. In J. Hallam and C. Mellish, editors, *Advances in Artificial Intelligence*, pages 49–61. John Wiley and Sons, 1987.

[Reichgelt, 1989] H. Reichgelt. A Comparison of First Order and Modal Logics of Time. In P. Jackson, H. Reichgelt, and F. van Harmelen, editors, *Logic-Based Knowledge Representation*, pages 143–176. MIT Press, 1989.

[Reiter, 1978] R. Reiter. On Closed World Data Bases. In H. Gallaire and J. Minker, editors, *Logic and Data Bases*, pages 119–140. Plenum Press, New York, 1978.

[Reiter, 1980a] R. Reiter. A Logic for Default Reasoning. *Artificial Intelligence*, 13:81–132, 1980.

[Reiter, 1980b] R. Reiter. Equality and Domain Closure in First-Order Databases. *Journal of the ACM*, 27:235–249, 1980.

[Reiter, 1984] R. Reiter. Towards a Logical Reconstruction of Relational Database Theory. In M. Brodie, J. Mylopoulos, and J. Schmidt, editors, *On Conceptual Modelling: Perspectives from Artificial Intelligence, Databases and Programming Languages*, pages 191–233. Springer Verlag, 1984.

[Reiter, 1988] R. Reiter. On Integrity Constraints. In *Proceedings of the Second Conference on Theoretical Aspects of Reasoning About Knowledge (TARK)*, pages 97–111, Asilomar, USA, 1988.

[Reiter, 1991] R. Reiter. The Frame Problem in the Situation Calculus: A simple Solution (Sometimes) and a Completeness Result for Goal Regression. In V. Lifschitz, editor, *Artificial Intelligence and Mathematical Theory of Computation: Papers in Honour of John McCarthy*, pages 359–380. Academic Press, 1991.

[Reiter, 2001] R. Reiter. *Knowledge in Action*. MIT press, 2001.

[Renz and Nebel, 1997] J. Renz and B. Nebel. On the Complexity of Qualitative Spatial Reasoning: A Maximal Tractable Fragment of the Region Connection Calculus. In *Proceedings of the Fifteenth International Joint Conference on Artificial Intelligence (IJCAI)*, pages 522–527. Morgan Kaufmann, 1997.

[Rescher and Garson, 1968] N. Rescher and J. Garson. Topological Logic. *Journal of Symbolic Logic*, 33:537–548, 1968.

[Rescher and Urquhart, 1971] N. Rescher and A. Urquhart. *Temporal Logic*. Library of Exact Philosophy. Springer Verlag, 1971.

[Reynolds, 1992] M. Reynolds. An Axiomatization for Until and Since over the Reals without the IRR rule. *Studia Logica*, 51:165–193, May 1992.

[Reynolds, 1994] M. Reynolds. Axiomatizing U and S over Integer Time. In D. Gabbay and H.-J. Ohlbach, editors, *Proceedings of the First International Conference on Temporal Logic (ICTL)*, volume 827 of *Lecture Notes in Artificial Intelligence*, pages 117–132, Bonn, Germany, July 1994. Springer-Verlag.

[Reynolds, 1996] M. Reynolds. Axiomatising First-Order Temporal Logic: Until and Since over Linear Time. *Studia Logica*, 57:279–302, 1996.

[Reynolds, 1998] M. Reynolds. A Decidable Logic of Parallelism. *Notre Dame Journal of Formal Logic*, 1998.

[Reynolds, 2000] M. Reynolds. More Past Glories. In *Proceedings of Fifteenth Annual IEEE Symposium on Logic in Computer Science (LICS)*, pages 229–240. IEEE, June 2000.

[Reynolds, 2001] M. Reynolds. An Axiomatization of Full Computation Tree Logic. *Journal of Symbolic Logic*, 66(3):1011–1057, 2001.

[Reynolds, 2003] M. Reynolds. An Axiomatization of PCTL*. *Information and Computation*, 2003.

[Rigaux and Scholl, 1995] P. Rigaux and M. Scholl. Multi-Scale Partitions: Application to Spatial and Statistical Databases. In *Proceedings of the Fourth International Symposium on Spatial Databases (SSD)*, volume 951 of *Lecture Notes in Computer Science*, pages 170–183. Springer-Verlag, 1995.

[Rinner and Kuipers, 1999] B. Rinner and B. Kuipers. Monitoring Piecewise Continuous Behaviors by Refining Semi-Quantative Trackers. In *Proceedings of the Sixteenth International Joint Conference on Artificial Intelligence (IJCAI)*, pages 1080–1086, 1999.

[Rintannen, 1999] J. Rintannen. Constructing Conditional Plans by a Theorem Prover. *Journal of AI Research*, 10:323–352, 1999.

[Rit, 1986] J. F. Rit. Propagating Temporal Constraints for Scheduling. In *Proceedings of the Fifth National Conference of the American Association for Artificial Intelligence (AAAI)*, pages 383–388. Morgan Kaufmann, 1986.

[Robinson, 1965] J. A. Robinson. A Machine–Oriented Logic Based on the Resolution Principle. *Journal of the ACM*, 12(1):23–41, January 1965.

[Roman, 1990] G. Roman. Formal Specification of Geographic Data Processing Requirements. *IEEE Transaction on Knowledge and Data Engineering*, 2(4):177–192, 1990.

[Rosner and Pnueli, 1986] R. Rosner and A. Pnueli. A Choppy Logic. In *Proceedings of the Symposium on Logic in Computer Science (LICS)*, pages 306–313. IEEE Computer Society, June 1986.

[Russ, 1989] T. A. Russ. Using Hindsight in Medical Decision Making. In *Proceedings of the Symposium on Computer Applications in Medical Care (SMAMC)*, pages 38–44, New York, USA, 1989. IEEE Computer Society Press.

[Russ, 1995] T. A. Russ. Use of Data Abstraction Methods to Simplify Monitoring. *Artificial Intelligence in Medicine*, 7:497–514, 1995.

[Russell and Norvig, 1995] S. Russell and P. Norvig. *Artificial Intelligence: a Modern Approach*. Prentice Hall, 1995.

[Russell, 1956] B. Russell. On Order in Time. In R.C. Marsh, editor, *Bertrand Russell: Logic and Knowledge (essays 1901–1950)*. Routledge, 1956.

[Sacerdoti, 1975] E. D. Sacerdoti. The Nonlinear Nature of Plans. In *Proceedings of the Fourth International Joint Conference on Artificial Intelligence (IJCA)*, pages 206–214, Tbilisi, Georgia, USSR, September 1975.

[Sadri and Kowalski, 1995] F. Sadri and R. Kowalski. Variants of the Event Calculus. In L. Sterling, editor, *Proceedings of the International Conference on Logic Programming (ICLP)*, 1995.

[Safra, 1988] S. Safra. On the Complexity of ω-Automata. In *Proceedings of Twenty-Ninth IEEE Symposium on the Foundations of Computer Science (FOCS)*, 1988.

[Salzberg and Tsotras, 1999] B. Salzberg and V. J. Tsotras. Comparison of Access Methods for Time-Evolving Data. *ACM Computing Surveys*, 31(2):158–221, 1999.

[Sandewall, 1994] E. Sandewall. *Features and Fluents: The Representation of Knowledge about Dynamical Systems*, volume I. Oxford University Press, 1994.

[Schild, 1991] K. Schild. A Correspondence Theory for Terminological Logics: Preliminary Report. In *Proceedings of the Twelfth International Joint Conference on Artificial Intelligence (IJCAI)*, pages 466–471, Sidney, Australia, 1991.

[Schild, 1993] K. Schild. Combining Terminological Logics with Tense Logic. In M. Filgueiras and L. Damas, editors, *Progress in Artificial Intelligence – Proceedings of the Sixth Portuguese Conference on Artificial Intelligence (EPIA)*, volume 727 of *Lecture Notes in Computer Science*, Porto, Portugal, October 1993. Springer.

[Schmiedel, 1990] A. Schmiedel. A Temporal Terminological Logic. In *Proceedings of the Eighth National Conference of the American Association for Artificial Intelligence (AAAI)*, pages 640–645. AAAI Press/The MIT Press, 1990.

[Schrag and Boddy, 1991] B. Schrag and M. Boddy. β-TMM Functional Description. Technical report, Honeywell SRC, USA, 1991.

[Schrag *et al.*, 1992] R. Schrag, M. Boddy, and J. Carciofini. Managing Disjunction for Practical Temporal Reasoning. In Swartout and Nebel [1992], pages 36–46.

[Schrijver, 1986] A. Schrijver, editor. *Theory of Integer and Linear Programming*. Wiley, 1986.

[Schubert and Hwang, 1989] L.K. Schubert and C. H. Hwang. An Episodic Knowledge Representation for Narrative Texts. In *Proceedings of the First International Conference on Principles of Knowledge Representation and Reasoning (KR)*, pages 444–458, Toronto, Canada, 1989. Morgan Kaufmann.

[Schubert *et al.*, 1987] L. K. Schubert, M. A. Papalaskaris, and J. Taugher. Accelerating Deductive Inference: Special Methods for Taxonomies, Colours, and Times. In N. Cercone and G. McCalla, editors, *The Knowledge Frontier: Essays in the Representation of Knowledge*, pages 187–220. Springer-Verlag, Berlin, Heidelberg, New York, 1987.

[Schubert, 1990] L. Schubert. Monotonic Solution of the Frame Problem in the Situation Calculus: An Efficient Method for Worlds with Fully Specified Actions. In *Knowledge Representation and Defeasible Reasoning*, pages 23–67. Kluwer Academic Press, 1990.

[Schwalb and Dechter, 1997] E. Schwalb and R. Dechter. Processing Disjunctions in Temporal Constraint Networks. *Artificial Intelligence*, 93:29–61, 1997.

[Schwalb and Vila, 1998] E. Schwalb and L. Vila. Processing Metric Temporal Constraints, 1998.

[Schwalb *et al.*, 1994] E. Schwalb, K. Kask, and R. Dechter. Temporal Reasoning with Constraints on Fluents and Events. In *Proceedings of (US) National Conference on Artificial Intelligence (AAAI)*. AAAI press, 1994.

[Schwalb *et al.*, 1996] E. Schwalb, L. Vila, and R. Dechter. Temporal Constraint Logic Programming. Technical report, UC Irvine, California, USA, 1996.

[Schwalb, 1996] E. Schwalb. Personal Communication, 1996.

[Schwendimann, 1998a] S. Schwendimann. A New One-Pass Tableau Calculus for PLTL. In H. de Swart, editor, *Proceedings of Tableaux Workshop*, volume 1397 of *Lecture Notes in Artificial Intelligence*, pages 277–291. Springer-Verlag, 1998.

[Schwendimann, 1998b] S. Schwendimann. *Aspects of Computational Logic*. PhD thesis, University of Bern, Switzerland, 1998.

[Scott, 2002] S. L. Scott. Bayesian Methods for Hidden Markov Models. Recursive Computing in the 21st Century. *Journal of the American Statistical Assoication*, 97:337–351, 2002.

[Sergot, 1988] M. Sergot. Representing Legislation as Logic Programs. In Hayes, Michie, and Richards, editors, *Machine Intelligence*, pages 209–260. Oxford University Press, 1988.

[Sergot, 1995] M. Sergot. Using Logic for Knowledge Representation in Legal Knowledge Based System. Tutorial Notes from the Fifth International Conference on Artificial Intelligence in Law, May 1995.

[Shahar and Cheng, 1999] Y. Shahar and C. Cheng. Intelligent Visualization and Exploration of Time-Oriented Clinical Data. *Topics in Health Information Systems*, 20(2):15–31, 1999.

[Shahar and Cheng, 2000] Y. Shahar and C. Cheng. Model-Based Visualization of Temporal Abstractions. *Computational Intelligence*, 16(2):279–306, 2000.

[Shahar and Molina, 1998] Y. Shahar and M. Molina. Knowledge-Based Spatiotemporal Linear Abstraction. *Pattern Analysis and Applications*, 1(2):91–104, 1998.

[Shahar and Musen, 1996] Y. Shahar and M.A. Musen. Knowledge-Based Temporal Abstraction in Clinical Domains. *Artificial Intelligence in Medicine*, 8(3):267–298, 1996.

[Shahar *et al.*, 1998] Y. Shahar, S. Miksch, and P.D. Johnson. The Asgaard Project: A Task-Specific Framework for the Application and Critiquing of Time-Oriented Clinical Guidelines. *Artificial Intelligence in Medicine*, 14:29–51, 1998.

[Shahar *et al.*, 1999] Y. Shahar, H. Chen, D. Stites, L. Basso, H. Kaizer, D. Wilson, and M.A. Musen. Semiautomated Acquisition of Clinical Temporal-Abstraction Knowledge. *Journal of the American Medical Informatics Association*, 6(6):494–511, 1999.

[Shahar *et al.*, 2003a] Y. Shahar, D. Boaz, G. Tahan, M. Galperin, D. Goren-Bar, H. Kaizer, L.V. Basso, S.B. Martins, and M.K. Goldstein. Interactive Visualization and Exploration of Time-Oriented Clinical Data using a Distributed Temporal-Abstraction Architecture. In *Proceedings of the AMIA Annual Fall Symposium*, Washington (DC), USA., 2003.

[Shahar *et al.*, 2003b] Y. Shahar, E. Shalom, A. Mayaffit, O. Young, M. Galperin, S.B. Martins, and M.K. Goldstein. A Distributed, Collaborative, Structuring Model for a Clinical-Guideline Digital-Library. In *Proceedings of the AMIA Annual Fall Symposium*, Washington (DC), USA., 2003.

[Shahar *et al.*, 2003c] Y. Shahar, O. Young, E. Shalom, A. Mayaffit, R. Moskovitch, A. Hessing, and M. Galperin. DEGEL: A Hybrid, Multiple-Ontology Framework for Specification and Retrieval of Clinical Guidelines. In *Proceedings of the Ninth Conference on Artificial Intelligence in Medicine — Europe (AIME)*, Protaras, Cyprus, 2003.

[Shahar, 1997] Y. Shahar. A Framework for Knowledge-Based Temporal Abstraction. *Artificial Intelligence*, 90(1):79–133, 1997.

[Shahar, 1998] Y. Shahar. Dynamic Temporal Interpretation Contexts for Temporal Abstraction. *Annals of Mathematics and Artificial Intelligence*, 22(1–2):159–192, 1998.

[Shahar, 1999] Y. Shahar. Knowledge-Based Temporal Interpolation. *Journal of Experimental and Theoretical Artificial Intelligence*, 11:123–144, 1999.

[Shanahan and Southwick, 1989] M. Shanahan and R. Southwick. *Search, Inference and Dependencies in Artificial Intelligence*. Ellis Horwood, New York, Chichester,Brisbane, Toronto, 1989.

[Shanahan, 1987] M. Shanahan. *Solving the Frame Problem: A Mathematical Investigation of the Common Sense Law of Inertia*. MIT Press, 1987.

[Shanahan, 1989] M. Shanahan. Prediction is Deduction but Explanation is Abduction. In *Proceedings of the International Joint Conference on Artificial Intelligence (IJCAI)*, page 1055, 1989.

[Shanahan, 1990] M. Shanahan. Representing Continuous Change in the Event Calculus. In *Proceedings of the European Conference on Artificial Intelligence (ECAI)*, page 598, 1990.

[Shanahan, 1999] M. P. Shanahan. The Event Calculus Explained. In M. J. Wooldridge and M. Veloso, editors, *Artificial Intelligence Today*, volume 1600 of *Lecture Notes in Artificial Intelligence*, pages 409–430. Springer, 1999.

[Sherman *et al.*, 1995] E.H. Sherman, G. Hripcsak, J. Starren, R.A. Jender, and P. Clayton. Using Intermediate States to Improve the Ability of the Arden Syntax to Implement Care Plans and Reuse Knowledge. In R. M. Gardner, editor, *Proceedings of the Annual Symposium on Computer Applications in Medical Care (SCAMC)*, pages 238–242, New Orleans, USA, 1995. Hanley & Belfus.

[Shiffman *et al.*, 2000] R. Shiffman, B. Karras, A. Agrawal, R. Chen, L. Marenco, and S. Nath. GEM: A Proposal for a More Comprehensive Guideline Document Model using XML. *Journal of the American Medical Informatics Association*, 7(5):488–498, 2000.

[Shoham and McDermott, 1988] Y. Shoham and D. McDermott. Problems in Formal Temporal Reasoning. *Artificial Intelligence*, 36(1):49–61, August 1988.

[Shoham, 1987] Y. Shoham. Temporal Logics in AI: Semantical and Ontological Considerations. *Artificial Intelligence*, 33:89–104, 1987.

[Shoham, 1988] Y. Shoham. *Reasoning about Change: Time and Causation from the Standpoint of Artificial Intelligence*. MIT Press, 1988.

[Shoham, 1993] Y. Shoham. Agent-Oriented Programming. *Artificial Intelligence*, 60(1):51–92, 1993.

[Shostak, 1981] R. Shostak. Deciding Linear Inequalities by Computing Loop Residues. *Journal of the ACM*, 28(4):769–779, 1981.

[Shults and Kuipers, 1997] B. Shults and B. Kuipers. Proving Properties of Continuous Systems: Qualitative Simulation and Temporal Logic. *Artificial Intelligence*, 92:91–129, 1997.

[Singh, 1994] M. P. Singh. *Multiagent Systems: A Theoretical Framework for Intentions, Know-How, and Communications*, volume 799 of *Lecture Notes in Artificial Intelligence*. Springer-Verlag, 1994.

[Sistla and Clarke, 1985] A. Sistla and E. Clarke. Complexity of Propositional Linear Temporal Logics. *Journal of the ACM*, 32:733–749, 1985.

[Sistla *et al.*, 1987] A. Sistla, M. Vardi, and P. Wolper. The Complementation Problem for Buchi Automata with Applications to Temporal Logic. *Theoretical Computer Science*, 49:217–237, 1987.

[Sistla *et al.*, 1997] A. P. Sistla, O. Wolfson, S. Chamberlain, and S. Dao. Modeling and Querying Moving Objects. In *Proceedings of IEEE International Conference on Data Engineering*, pages 422–432, 1997.

[Skiadopoulos, 2002] Spiros Skiadopoulos. *Query Evaluation in Spatial Constraint Databases*. PhD thesis, Dept. of Electrical and Computer Engineering, National Technical University of Athens, 2002.

[Skyt *et al.*, 2003] J. Skyt, C. S. Jensen, and L. Mark. A Foundation for Vacuuming Temporal Databases . *Data and Knowledge Engineering*, 44(1):1–29, 2003.

[Smith and Weld, 1999] D. E. Smith and D. S. Weld. Temporal Planning with Mutual Exclusion Reasoning. In *Proceedings of the Internationional Joint Conference on Artificial Intelligence (IJCAI)*, pages 326–337, 1999.

[Smith, 1980] R. G. Smith. *A Framework for Distributed Problem Solving*. UMI Research Press, 1980.

[Smullyan, 1968] R. Smullyan. *First-order Logic*. Springer, 1968.

[Smyth *et al.*, 1997] P. Smyth, D. Heckerman, and M.I. Jordan. Probabilistic Independence Networks for Hidden Markov Models. *Neural Computation*, 9:227–269, 1997.

[Snodgrass and Ahn, 1986] R. Snodgrass and I. Ahn. Temporal Databases. *IEEE Computer*, 19(9):35–42, 1986.

[Snodgrass *et al.*, 1994] R. T. Snodgrass, I. Ahn, G. Ariav, D. Batory, J. Clifford, C. E. Dyreson, R. Elmasri, F. Grandi, C. S. Jensen, W. Kafer, N. Kline, K. Kulkarni, T. Y. C. Leung, N. Lorentzos, J. F. Roddick, A. Segev, M. D. Soo, and S. A. Sripada. TSQL2 Language Specification. *SIGMOD Record*, 23(1):65–86, March 1994.

[Snodgrass *et al.*, 1995] R. T. Snodgrass, C. S. Jensen, and M. H. Böhlen. Evaluating and Enhancing the Completeness of TSQL2. Technical Report TR 95-5, Computer Science Department, University of Arizona, USA, 1995.

[Snodgrass *et al.*, 1996] R. T. Snodgrass, M. H. Böhlen, C. S. Jensen, and A. Steiner. Adding Valid Time to SQL/Temporal. ISO/IEC JTC1/SC21/WG3 DBL MAD-146r2 21/11/96, (change proposal), International Organization for Standardization, 1996.

[Snodgrass, 1987] R. T. Snodgrass. The Temporal Query Language TQuel. *ACM Transactions on Database Systems*, 12(2):247–298, June 1987.

[Snodgrass, 1990] R. T. Snodgrass. Temporal Databases: Status and Research Direction. *SIGMOD RECORD*, 19:83–89, 1990.

[Snodgrass, 1993] R. T. Snodgrass. An Overview of TQuel. In *Temporal Databases: Theory, Design, and Implementation*, chapter 6, pages 141–182. Benjamin/Cummings, 1993.

[Snodgrass, 1995] R. T. Snodgrass, editor. *The TSQL2 Temporal Query Language*. Kluwer Academic Publishers, 1995.

[Snodgrass, 1999] R. T. Snodgrass. *Developing Time-Oriented Database Applications in SQL*. Morgan Kaufmann, 1999.

[Son *et al.*, 2001] T. Son, C. Baral, and S. McIlraith. Extending Answer Set Planning with Sequence, Conditionals, Loops, Non-Deterministic Choice and Procedural Constructs. In *Proceedings of the AAAI Spring symposium on Answer Set Programming*, 2001.

[Song and Cohen, 1988] F. Song and R. Cohen. The Interpretation of Temporal Relations in a Narrative. In *Proceedings of the Seventh National Conference of the American Association for Artificial Intelligence (AAAI)*, pages 745–750. Morgan Kaufmann, 1988.

[Song and Cohen, 1991] F. Song and R. Cohen. Tense Interpretation in the Context of Narrative. In *Proceedings of the Nineth National Conference of the American Association for Artificial Intelligence*, pages 131–136. MIT Press, 12–19 July 1991.

[Song and Cohen, 1996] F. Song and R. Cohen. A Strengthened Algorithm for Temporal Reasoning about Plans. *Computational Intelligence*, 12(2):331–356, 1996.

[Sontag, 1985] E. Sontag. Real Addition and the Polynomial Time Hierarchy. *Information Processing Letters*, 20:115–120, 1985.

[Sripada *et al.*, 1994] S. Sripada, B. Rosser, J. Bedford, and R. Kowalski. Temporal Database Technology for Air Traffic Flow Management. In *Proceedings of First International Conference on Applications of Databases (ADB)*, volume 819 of *Lecture Notes in Computer Science*. Springer-Verlag, 1994.

[Staab, 1998] S. Staab. On Non-Binary Temporal Relations. In *Proceedings of the European Conference on Artificial Intelligence (ECAI)*, pages 567–571, 1998.

[Stillman *et al.*, 1993] J. Stillman, R. Arthur, and A. Deitsch. Tachyon: A Constraint-Based Temporal Reasoning Model and its Implementation. *SIGART Bulletin*, 4(3), 1993.

[Stirling, 1992] C. Stirling. Modal and Temporal Logics. In D.M. Gabbay, S. Abramsky, and T.S.E Maibaum, editors, *Handbook of Logic in Computer Science*, volume 2, pages 477–563. Clarendon Press, Oxford, 1992.

[Stockmeyer, 1977] L.J. Stockmeyer. The Polynomial-Time Hierarchy. *Theoretical Computer Science*, 3:1–22, 1977.

[Street, 1982] R. Street. Propositional Dynamic Logic of Looping and Converse. *Information and Control*, 54:121–141, 1982.

[Streett and Emerson, 1984] R.S. Streett and E.A. Emerson. The Propositional mu-Calculus is Elementary. In J. Paredaens, editor, *Proceedings of the Eleventh International Colloquium on Automata, Languages, and Programming (ICALP)*, volume 172, pages 465–472. Springer-Verlag, Antwerp, Belgium, July 1984.

[Stroetman, 1993] K. Stroetman. A Completeness Result for SLDNF-Resolution. *Journal of Logic Programming*, 15:337–355, 1993.

[Sturm and Wolter, 2000] H. Sturm and F. Wolter. A Tableau Calculus for Temporal Description Logic: The Expanding Domain Case. *Journal of Logic and Computation*, 2000.

[Subrahmanian and Zaniolo, 1995] V. Subrahmanian and C. Zaniolo. Relating Stable Models and AI Planning Domains. In L. Sterling, editor, *Proceedings of the International Conference on Logic Programming (ICLP)*, pages 233–247. MIT Press, 1995.

[Sussman, 1990] G. J. Sussman. The Virtuous Nature of Bugs. In J. Allen, J. Hendler, and A. Tate, editors, *Readings in Planning*, chapter 3, pages 111–117. Morgan Kaufmann Publishers, Inc., 1990.

[Swartout and Nebel, 1992] B. Swartout and B. Nebel, editors. *Proceedings of the Third International Conference on Principles of Knowledge Representation and Reasoning (KR)*, Cambridge, MA, USA, October 1992. Morgan Kaufmann.

[Szalas, 1987] A. Szalas. A Complete Axiomatic Characterization of First-Order Temporal Logic of Linear Time. *Theoretical Computer Science*, 54:199–214, 1987.

[Tang and Young, 2000] P. Tang and C. Young. ActiveGuidelines: Integrating Web-Based Guidelines with Computer-Based Patient Records. In M.J Overhage, editor, *Proceedings of the AMIA Annual Symposium*, Los Angeles, USA, 2000. Hanley & Belfus.

[Tansel *et al.*, 1993] A. Tansel, J. Clifford, S. Gadia, S. Jajodia, A. Segev, and R. T. Snodgrass, editors. *Temporal Databases: Theory, Design, and Implementation*. Benjamin/Cummings, 1993.

[Tansel, 1993] A. Tansel. A Generalized Relational Framework for Modelling Temporal Data. In Tansel et al. [1993], pages 183–201.

[Tarjan, 1972] R. Tarjan. Depth First Search and Linear Graph Algorithms. *SIAM Journal of Computing*, 1(2):215–225, 1972.

[Tarski, 1941] A. Tarski. On the Calculus of Relations. *Journal of Symbolic Logic*, 6:73–89, 1941.

[Tate, 1977] A. Tate. Generating project networks. In *Proceedings of IJCAI-77*, 1977.

[ter Meulen and Smessaert, 2004] A. ter Meulen and H. Smessaert. Dynamic Temporal Reasoning with Aspectual Adverbs. To appear in *Linguistics and Philosophy*, 2004.

[ter Meulen, 1990] A. ter Meulen. English Aspectual Verbs as Generalized Quantifiers. In J. Carter et al., editor, *NELS 20*, pages 378–390. GLSA, Department of Linguistics, University of Massachusetts, USA, 1990.

[ter Meulen, 1995] A. ter Meulen. *Representing Time in Natural Language – The dynamic interpretation of tense and aspect.* Bradford Books, MIT Press, Cambridge (Mass.), 1995.

[ter Meulen, 2000] A. ter Meulen. Chronoscopes: Dynamic Tools for Temporal Reasoning. In J. Higginbotham and F. Pianesi, editors, *Speaking of Events*, pages 151–168. Oxford University Press, Oxford, 2000.

[ter Meulen, 2003] A. ter Meulen. Situated Reasoning in Time about Time. In B. Löwe et al., editor, *Foundations of the Formal Sciences II, Applications of Mathematical Logic in Philosophy and Linguistics*, volume 17 of *Trends in Logic*. Kluwer Academic Press, Dordrecht, 2003.

[Terenziani, 1996] P. Terenziani. Toward an Ontology Dealing with Periodic Events. In W Wahlster, editor, *Proceedings of the Fifteenth European Conference on Artificial Intelligence (ECAI)*, pages 43–47. John Wiley & Sons, 1996.

[Thatcher and Wright, 1968] J. Thatcher and J. Wright. Generalized Finite Automata Theory with an Application to a Decision Problem of Second-Order Logic. *Mathematical Systems Theory*, 2(1):57–81, 1968.

[The STREAM Group, 2003] The STREAM Group. STREAM: The Stanford Stream Data Manager (short overview paper). *IEEE Data Engineering Bulletin*, 26(1), 2003.

[Thiébaux *et al.*, 1996] S. Thiébaux, M.-O. Cordier, O. Jehl, and J.-P. Krivine. Supply restoration in Power Distribution Systems – A Case Study in Integrating Model-Based Diagnosis and Repair Planning. In *Proceedings of the Twelfth Conference on Uncertainty in Artificial Intelligence (UAI)*. Morgan Kaufmann, 1996.

[Thielscher, 1997] M. Thielscher. Ramification and Causality. *Artificial Intelligence*, 89(1-2):317–364, 1997.

[Thomas, 1990] W. Thomas. Automata on Infinite Objects. In J. van Leeuwen, editor, *Handbook of Theoretical Computer Science*, volume B. Elsevier, Amsterdam, 1990.

[Thornton *et al.*, 2002] J. Thornton, M. Beaumount, A. Sattar, and M. Maher. Applying Local Search to Temporal Reasoning. In *Proceedings of the Ninth International Symposium on Temporal Representation and Reasoning (TIME)*, Manchester, UK, 2002. IEEE Computer Society.

[Thorthon *et al.*, 2004] J. Thorthon, M. Beaumont, A. Sattar, and M. Maher. A Local Search Approach to Modelling and Solving Interval Algebra Problems. *Journal of Logic and Computation*, 14(1):93–112, 2004.

[Tobies, 2000] S. Tobies. The Complexity of Reasoning with Cardinality Restrictions and Nominals in Expressive Description Logics. *Journal of Artificial Intelligence Research*, 12:199–217, 2000.

[Toman and Chomicki, 1998] D. Toman and J. Chomicki. Datalog with Integer Periodicity Constraints. *Journal of Logic Programming*, 35(3):263–306, 1998.

[Toman and Niwinski, 1996] D. Toman and D. Niwinski. First-Order Queries over Temporal Databases Inexpressible in Temporal Logic. In *International Conference on Extending Database Technology (EDBT)*, Avignon, France, 1996.

[Toman, 1996] D. Toman. Point vs. Interval-based Query Languages for Temporal Databases. In *Proceedings of the ACM Symposium on Principles of Database Systems (PODS)*, Montréal, Canada, June 1996.

[Toman, 1997] D. Toman. Point-based Temporal Extensions of SQL. In *International Conference on Deductive and Object-Oriented Databases*, 1997.

[Toman, 2001] D. Toman. Expiration of Historical Databases. In *Proceedings of International Symposium on Temporal Representation and Reasoning (TIME)*, pages 128–135. IEEE Press, 2001.

[Toman, 2003a] D. Toman. Logical Data Expiration. In Chomicki et al. [2003b], chapter 7, pages 203–238.

[Toman, 2003b] D. Toman. Logical Data Expiration for Fixpoint Extensions of Temporal Logics. In *International Symposium on Advances in Spatial and Temporal Databases (SSTD)*, pages 380–393, 2003.

[Toman, 2003c] D. Toman. On Incompleteness of Multi-dimensional First-order Temporal Logics. In *Proceedings of International Symposium on Temporal Representation and Reasoning and International Conference on Temporal Logic (TIME-ICTL)*, pages 99–106, 2003.

[Topaloglou, 1996] T. Topaloglou. *On the Representation of Partial Spatial Information in Knowledge Bases*. PhD thesis, University of Toronto, Toronto, USA, 1996.

[Trinquart and Ghallab, 2001] R. Trinquart and M. Ghallab. An Extended Functional Representation in Temporal Planning: Towards Continuous Change. In *Proceedings of European Conference on Planning (ECP)*, 2001.

[Tsamardinos and Pollack, 2003] I. Tsamardinos and M.E. Pollack. Efficient Solution Techniques for Disjunctive Temporal Reasoning Problems. *Artificial Intelligence*, 151(1-2):43–90, 2003.

[Tsang, 1986] E. P. K. Tsang. Plan Generation in a Temporal Frame. In *Proceedings of the Seventh European Conference on Artificial Intelligence (ECAI)*, pages 479–493, 1986.

[Tsang, 1987a] E. P. K. Tsang. Time Structures for AI. In *Proceedings of the International Joint Conference on Artificial Intelligence (IJCAI)*, pages 456–461. Morgan Kaufmann, 1987.

[Tsang, 1987b] E. P. K. Tsang. TLP- A Temporal Planner. In J. Hallam and C. Mellish, editors, *Advances in Artificial Intelligence*, pages 63–78. John Wiley&sons, 1987.

[Tu *et al.*, 1989] S.W. Tu, M.G. Kahn, M.A. Musen, J.C. Ferguson, E.H. Shortliffe, , and L. M. Fagan. Episodic Skeletal-Plan Refinement on Temporal Data. *Communications of the ACM*, 32:1439–1455, 1989.

[Tu *et al.*, 1995] S.W. Tu, H. Eriksson, J.H. Gennari, and M.A. Shahar, Y.and Musen. Ontology-Based Configuration of Problem-Solving Methods and Generation of Knowledge-Acquisition Tools: Application of PROTÉGÉ-II to Protocol-Based Decision Support. *Artificial Intelligence in Medicine*, 7(3):257–289, 1995.

[Turner, 1994] H. Turner. Signed Logic Programs. In *Proceedings of the International Symposium on Logic Programming (ILPS)*, pages 61–75, 1994.

[Turner, 1997] H. Turner. Representing Actions in Logic Programs and Default Theories. *Journal of Logic Programming*, 31(1-3):245–298, 1997.

[Tuzhilin and Clifford, 1990] A. Tuzhilin and J. Clifford. A Temporal Relational Algebra as a Basis for Temporal Relational Completeness. In *International Conference on Very Large Data Bases (VLDB)*, 1990.

[Ullman, 1989] J.D. Ullman. *Principles of Database and Knowledge-Base Systems*, volume 2. Computer Science Press, 1989.

[Valdes *et al.*, 1982] J. Valdes, R.E. Tarjan, and E.L. Lawler. The Recognition of Series Parallel Digraphs. *SIAM Journal of Computing*, 11(2):298–313, 1982.

[van Beek and Cohen, 1990] P. van Beek and R. Cohen. Exact and Approximate Reasoning about Temporal Relations. *Computational Intelligence*, 6(3):132–144, 1990.

[van Beek and Manchak, 1996] P. van Beek and D.W. Manchak. The Design and Experimental Analysis of Algorithms for Temporal Reasoning. *Journal of Artificial Intelligence Research*, 4:1–18, 1996.

[van Beek, 1990] P. van Beek. Reasoning about Qualitative Temporal Information. In *Proceedings of the Eighth National Conference of the American Association for Artificial Intelligence (AAAI)*, pages 728–734, Boston, MA, 1990.

[van Beek, 1991] P. van Beek. Temporal Query Processing with Indefinite Information. *Artificial Intelligence in Medicine*, 3:325–339, 1991.

[van Beek, 1992] P. van Beek. Reasoning about Qualitative Temporal Information. *Artificial Intelligence*, 58(1-3):297–321, 1992.

[Van Belleghem *et al.*, 1994] K. Van Belleghem, M. Denecker, and D. De Schreye. The Abductive Event Calculus as a General Framework for Temporal Databases. In *Proceedings of the First International Conference on Temporal Logic (ICTL)*, pages 301–316, 1994.

[Van Belleghem *et al.*, 1995] K. Van Belleghem, M. Denecker, and D. De Schreye. Combining Situation Calculus and Event Calculus. In *Proceedings of the Twelfth International Conference on Logic Programming (ICLP)*, pages 83–97, 1995.

[Van Bemmel, 1996] J.H. Van Bemmel. Medical Informatics, Art or Science? *Methods of Information in Medicine*, 35:157–117, 1996.

[van Benthem, 1983] J.F.A.K. van Benthem. *The Logic of time*. D. Reidel Publishing Company, Dordrecht, 1983.

[van Benthem, 1991] J.F.A.K. van Benthem. *The Logic of Time: A Model-Theoretic Investigation into the Varieties of Temporal Ontology and Temporal Discourse (second edition).* (Synthese Library, Vol 156) Kluwer Academic Publishers, Dordrecht, 1991.

[van der Meyden, 1992] R. van der Meyden. The Complexity of Querying Indefinite Data About Linearly Ordered Domains (Preliminary Version). In *Proceedings of the Eleventh ACM SIGACT-SIGMOD-SIGART Symposium on Principles of Database Systems (PODS)*, pages 331–345, 1992.

[van Gelder *et al.*, 1991] A. van Gelder, K. Ross, and J. Schlipf. The Well-Founded Semantics for General Logic Programs. *Journal of the ACM*, 38(3):620–650, 1991.

[van Linder *et al.*, 1996] B. van Linder, W. van der Hoek, and J. J. Ch. Meyer. How to Motivate Your Agents. In M. Wooldridge, J. P. Müller, and M. Tambe, editors, *Intelligent Agents II*, volume 1037 of *Lecture Notes in Artificial Intelligence*, pages 17–32. Springer-Verlag, 1996.

[Vardi and Stockmeyer, 1985] M. Vardi and L. Stockmeyer. Improved Upper and Lower Bounds for Modal Logics of Programs. In *Proceedings of the Seventeenth ACM Symposium on the Theory of Computing (STOC)*, pages 240–251. ACM Press, 1985.

[Vardi and Wolper, 1986] M.Y. Vardi and P. Wolper. An Automata-Theoretic Approach to Automatic Program Verification (Preliminary Report). In *Proceedings of the First IEEE Symposium on Logic in Computer Science (LICS)*, pages 332–344. IEEE Computer Society Press, Cambridge, USA, 1986.

[Vardi and Wolper, 1994] M. Vardi and P. Wolper. Reasoning about Infinite Computations. *Information and Computation*, 115:1–37, 1994.

[Vardi, 1982] M. Vardi. The Complexity of Relational Query Languages. In *Proceedings of the Fourteenth ACM Symposium on Theory of Computing (STOC)*, pages 137–145, 1982.

[Vardi, 1988] M. Y. Vardi. A Temporal Fixpoint Calculus. In *Proceedings of the Fifteenth Annual ACM Symposium on Principles of Programming Languages (POPL)*, pages 250–259, San Diego, USA, 1988.

[Vardi, 1994] M. Vardi. Nontraditional Applications of Automata Theory. In *Proceedings of International Symposium on the Theoretical Aspects of Computer Software (STACS)*, volume 789 of *LNCS*, pages 575–597. Springer-Verlag, 1994.

[Vardi, 1996] M. Vardi. An Automata-Theoretic Approach to Linear Temporal Logic. In F. Moller and G. Birtwistle, editors, *Logics for Concurrency*, pages 238–266. Springer Verlag, 1996.

[Vazirgiannis and Wolfson, 2001] M. Vazirgiannis and O. Wolfson. A Spatiotemporal Model and Language for Moving Objects on Road Networks. In *Proceedings of the International Symposium on Advances in Spatial and Temporal Databases (SSTD)*, pages 20–35, 2001.

[Veloso *et al.*, 1990] M. Veloso, A. Pérez, and J. Carbonell. Non-Linear Planning with Parallel Resource Allocation. In *Proceedings of the DARPA Workshop on Innovative Approaches to Planning, Scheduling and Control*, pages 207–212, 1990.

[Veloso *et al.*, 1995] M. Veloso, J. Carbonell, A. Pérez, D. Borrajo, E. Fink, and J. Blythe. Integrated Planning and Learning: the PRODIGY Architecture. *Journal of Experimental and Theoretical AI*, 7(1), 1995.

[Vendler, 1967] Z. Vendler. *Linguistics and Philosophy*. Cornell University Press, Ithaca, USA, 1967.

[Venema, 1991a] Y. Venema. A Modal Logic for Chopping Intervals. *Journal of Logic and Computation*, 1(4):453–476, 1991.

[Venema, 1991b] Y. Venema. Completeness via Completeness. In M. de Rijke, editor, *Colloquium on Modal Logic, 1991*. ITLI-Network Publication, Instit. for Lang., Logic and Information, University of Amsterdam, Netherlands, 1991.

[Venkatesh, 1986] G. Venkatesh. A Decision Method for Temporal Logic based on Resolution. *Lecture Notes in Computer Science*, 206:272–289, 1986.

[Vere, 1983] S. Vere. Planning in time: Windows and durations for activities and goals. *IEEE Trans. on Pattern Analysis and Machine Intelligence*, 5, 1983.

[Vidal and Ghallab, 1996] T. Vidal and M. Ghallab. Constraint-Based Temporal Management in Planning: the IxTeT way. In *Proceedings of the Twelfth European Conference on Artificial Intelligence (ECAI)*, 1996.

[Vila and Reichgelt, 1996] L. Vila and H. Reichgelt. The Token Reification Approach to Temporal Reasoning. *Artificial Intelligence*, 83(1):59–74, May 1996.

[Vila and Schwalb, 1996] L. Vila and E. Schwalb. A Theory of Time and Temporal Incidence based on Instants and Periods. In *Proceedings of the International Workshop on Temporal Representation and Reasoning (TIME)*, pages 21–28. IEEE Computer Society Press, 1996.

[Vila and Yoshino, 1996] L. Vila and H. Yoshino. Time in Automated Legal Reasoning (the long report). Technical Report 96-57, UC Irvine, California, USA, 1996.

[Vila, 1994] L. Vila. *IP*: An Instant-Period–based Theory of Time. In R. Rodriguez, editor, *Proceedings of the ECAI'94 Workshop on Spatial and Temporal Reasoning*, 1994.

[Vilain and Kautz, 1986] M. Vilain and H. Kautz. Constraint Propagation Algorithms for Temporal Reasoning. In *Proceedings of the Fifth (US) National Conference on Artificial Intelligence (AAAI)*, pages 377–382, 1986.

[Vilain *et al.*, 1990] M. Vilain, H.A. Kautz, and P. van Beek. Constraint Propagation Algorithms for Temporal Reasoning: A Revised Report. In D. S Weld and J. de Kleer, editors, *Readings in Qualitative Reasoning about Physical Systems*, pages 373–381, San Mateo, USA, 1990. Morgan Kaufmann.

[Vilain, 1982] M. Vilain. A System for Reasoning About Time. In *Proceedings of the 2nd (US) National Conference on Artificial Intelligence (AAAI '82)*, pages 197–201, Pittsburgh, PA, USA, August 1982. American Association for Artificial Intelligence.

[Visser *et al.*, 2000] W. Visser, K. Havelund, G. Brat, and S. Park. Model Checking Programs. In *Proceedings of International Conference on Automated Software Engineering (ASE)*, September 2000.

[von Wright, 1965] G. H. von Wright. And Next. *Acta Philosophica Fennica*, 18:293–304, 1965.

[Wainer and de Melo Rezende, 1997] J. Wainer and A. de Melo Rezende. A Temporal Extension to the Parsimonious Covering Theory. *Artificial Intelligence in Medicine*, 10:235–255, 1997.

[Wainer and Sandri, 1999] J. Wainer and S. Sandri. Fuzzy Temporal/Categorical Information in Diagnosis. *Journal of Intelligent Information Systems*, 13:9–26, 1999.

[Walker, 1948] A.G. Walker. Durées et Instants. *Revue Scientifique*, 85:131–134, 1948.

[Walther, 1987] C. Walther. *A Many Sorted Calculus Based on Resolution and Paramodulation*. Pitman, 1987.

[Wang *et al.*, 1995] X. S. Wang, S. Jajodia, and V. Subrahmanian. Temporal Modules: An Approach Toward Federated Temporal Databases. *Information sciences*, 82:103–128, 1995.

[Wang *et al.*, 1997] X. S. Wang, C. Bettini, A. Brodsky, and S. Jajodia. Logical Design for Temporal Databases with Multiple Granularities. *ACM Transactions on Database Systems*, 22(2):115–170, 1997.

[Webber, 1995] A. B. Webber. Proof of the Interval Satisfiability Conjecture. *Annals of Mathematics and Artificial Intelligence*, 15, 1995.

[Weida and Litman, 1992] R. Weida and D. Litman. Terminological Reasoning with Constraint Networks and an Application to Plan Recognition. In B. Nebel, W. Swartout, and C. Rich, editors, *Proceedings of the Third International Conference on Principles of Knowledge Representation and Reasoning (KR)*, pages 282–293. Morgan Kaufmann, 1992.

[Weld *et al.*, 1998] D. S. Weld, C. R. Anderson, and D. E. Smith. Extending Graphplan to Handle Uncertainty and Sensing Actions. In *Proceedings of AAAI*, pages 897–904, 1998.

[Weld, 1994] D. S. Weld. An Introduction to Least Commitment Planning. *AI Magazine*, 15(61):27–61, Winter 1994.

[Wetprasit and Sattar, 1998] R. Wetprasit and A. Sattar. Temporal Reasoning with Qualitative and Quantitative Information About Points and Durations. In *Proceedings of the Fifteenth National Conference on Artificial Intelligence (AAAI)*, pages 656–663, Madison, USA, July 1998.

[Wetprasit *et al.*, 1996] R. Wetprasit, A. Sattar, and L. Khatib. Reasoning with Sequences of Events (an extended abstract). In *Proceedings of the International Workshop on Temporal Representation and Reasoning (TIME)*, pages 36–38. IEEE Computer Society Press, 1996.

[Whitehead, 1919] A.N. Whitehead. *An Enquiry Concerning the Principles of Natural Knowledge*. Cambridge, 1919.

[Widom and Ceri, 1996] J. Widom and S. Ceri, editors. *Active Database Systems: Triggers and Rules for Advanced Database Processing*. Morgan Kaufmann, 1996.

[Wiederhold and Genesereth, 1997] G. Wiederhold and M. Genesereth. The Conceptual Basis of Mediation Services. *IEEE Expert*, 12(5):38–47, 1997.

[Wiederhold, 1992] G. Wiederhold. Mediators in the Architecture of Future Information Systems. *IEEE Computer*, 25(3):38–50, 1992.

[Wijsen, 1998] J. Wijsen. Reasoning about Qualitative Trends in Databases. *Information Systems*, 23(7):463–487, 1998.

[Wijsen, 1999] J. Wijsen. Temporal FDs on Complex Objects. *ACM Transactions on Database Systems*, 24(1):127–176, 1999.

[Wijsen, 2000] J. Wijsen. A String-based Model for Infinite Granularities. In C. Bettini and A. Montanari, editors, *Proceedings of the AAAI Workshop on Spatial and Temporal Granularities*, pages 9–16. AAAI Press, 2000.

[Wilkins, 1988] D.E. Wilkins. *Practical Planning: Extending the Classical AI Planning Paradigm*. Morgan Kaufmann Publishers Inc., San Francisco, CA, 1988.

[Williams, 1986] B. C. Williams. Doing Time: Putting Qualitative Reasoning on Firmer Ground. In *Proceedings of AAAI*, pages 105–112. AAAI press, 1986.

[Wolper, 1983] P. Wolper. Temporal Logic can be More Expressive. *Information and Computation*, 56(1–2):72–99, 1983.

[Wolper, 1985] P. Wolper. The Tableau Method for Temporal Logic: An Overview. *Logique et Analyse*, June–Sept 1985.

[Wolper, 1989] P. Wolper. On the Relation of Programs and Computations to Models of Temporal Logic. In B. Banieqbal, B. Barringer, and A. Pnueli, editors, *Temporal Logic in Specification*, pages 75–123. Springer-Verlag, LNCS 398, 1989.

[Wolter and Zakharyaschev, 1998a] F. Wolter and M. Zakharyaschev. Satisfiability Problem in Description Logics with Modal Operators. In A. G. Cohn, L. Schubert, and S. C. Shapiro, editors, *Proceedings of International Conference on Principles of Knowledge Representation and Reasoning (KR)*, pages 512–523. Morgan Kaufmann, San Francisco, California, 1998.

[Wolter and Zakharyaschev, 1998b] F. Wolter and M. Zakharyaschev. Temporalizing Description Logics. See `citeseer.ist.psu.edu/wolter98temporalizing.html`, 1998.

[Wolter and Zakharyaschev, 1999] F. Wolter and M. Zakharyaschev. Modal Description Logics: Modalizing Roles. *Fundamenta Informaticae*, 39(4):411–438, 1999.

[Wolter, 2000] F. Wolter. The Product of Converse PDL and Polymodal K. *Journal of Logic and Computation*, 10(2):223–251, 2000.

[Wooldridge and Jennings, 1995] M. Wooldridge and N. R. Jennings. Intelligent Agents: Theory and Practice. *The Knowledge Engineering Review*, 10(2):115–152, 1995.

[Wooldridge *et al.*, 2002] M. Wooldridge, M. Fisher, M.-P. Huget, and S. Parsons. Model checking multiagent systems with MABLE. In *Proceedings of the First International Joint Conference on Autonomous Agents and Multiagent Systems (AAMAS)*, pages 952–959, Bologna, Italy, 2002.

[Wooldridge., 1992] M. J. Wooldridge. *The Logical Modelling of Computational Multi-Agent Systems*. PhD thesis, Department of Computation, UMIST, Manchester, UK, 1992.

[Wooldridge, 1996] M. J. Wooldridge. A Knowledge-Theoretic Semantics for Concurrent MetateM. In J. P. Müller, M. J. Wooldridge, and N. R. Jennings, editors, *Intelligent Agents III — Proceedings of the Third International Workshop on Agent Theories, Architectures, and Languages (ATAL)*, Lecture Notes in Artificial Intelligence. Springer-Verlag, Heidelberg, 1996.

[Wooldridge, 2000] M. Wooldridge. *Reasoning about Rational Agents*. MIT Press, 2000.

[Wooldridge, 2002] M. Wooldridge. *An Introduction to Multiagent Systems*. John Wiley & Sons, 2002.

[Yampratoom and Allen, 1993] E. Yampratoom and J. Allen. Performance of Temporal Reasoning Systems. *SIGART Bulletin*, 4(3):26–29, 1993.

[Yang *et al.*, 2000] J. Yang, H. C. Ying, and J. Widom. TIP: A Temporal Extension to Informix. In *Proceedings of the ACM SIGMOD International Conference on Management of Data*, page 596, 2000.

[Yang, 1997] Q. Yang. *Intelligent Planning*. Springer-Verlag, Berlin, Heidelberg, New York, 1997.

[Yi *et al.*, 1997] W. Yi, K.G. Larsen, and P. Pettersson. Uppaal in a Nutshell. *International Journal of Software Tools for Technology Transfer*, 1(1), 1997.

[Yoshino, 1994a] H. Yoshino. Representation of Legal Knowledge by Compound Predicate Formula. In D. Tiscornia C. Biagioli, G. Sartor, editor, *Proceedings of the ICLP Workshop on Legal Application of Logic Programming*, pages 128–137. MIT press, 1994.

[Yoshino, 1994b] H. Yoshino. Representation of Legal Knowledge by Legal Flowchart and Compound Predicate Formula. Technical Report TM-1298, ICOT, 1994.

[Younes and Simmons, 2003] H.L.S. Younes and R.G. Simmons. VHPOP: Versatile Heuristic Partial Order Planner. *Journal of AI Research*, (Special issue on 3rd International Planning Competition), 2003.

[Zeman, 1973] J. Zeman. *Modal logic: The Lewis Modal Systems*. Oxford University Press, 1973.

[Zhang *et al.*, 2002] D. Zhang, V. J. Tsotras, and B. Seeger. Efficient Temporal Join Processing using Indices. In *Proceedings of IEEE International Conference on Data Engineering*, pages 103–114, 2002.

[Zilberstein, 1996] S. Zilberstein. Using anytime algorithms in intelligent systems. *AI magazine*, 17(3):73–83, 1996.

Index